25.00/30/AD

2 vol. set

FAULKNER

A Biography

Books by Joseph Blotner

The Political Novel
The Fiction of J. D. Salinger (with Frederick L. Gwynn)
Faulkner in the University (with Frederick L. Gwynn)
William Faulkner's Library: A Catalogue
The Modern American Political Novel: 1900–1960
Faulkner: A Biography

FAULKNER

A BIOGRAPHY

by Joseph Blotner

VOLUME ONE

Random House
New York

Published in the United States by Random House, Inc., New York, and simultaneously in Canada by Random House of Canada Limited, Toronto.

Grateful acknowledgment is made to the following for permission to reprint material from previously published works:

International Famous Agency: For excerpts from "Interview with William Faulkner" by Cynthia Grenier, published in *Accent*, Vol. 16, Summer 1956. Copyright © 1956 by *Accent*.
Little, Brown & Company: For excerpts from *Letters of Sherwood Anderson*, selected and edited by Howard M. Jones. Copyright 1953 by Eleanor Anderson.
Liveright Publishing Corporation: For excerpts from *Soldiers' Pay* by William Faulkner. Copyright renewed 1953 by William Faulkner. For excerpts from *Mosquitoes* by William Faulkner. Copyright 1954 by William Faulkner.
Purdue Research Foundation: For excerpts from "Conversation with William Faulkner," Vol. V, Number 4, *Modern Fiction Studies*, Winter 1959–1960. Copyright © 1960 by Purdue Research Foundation, Lafayette, Indiana.
Random House, Inc.: For selections from the copyrighted works of William Faulkner, published by Random House, Inc.
Saturday Review: For excerpts from "William Faulkner: That Writin' Man of Oxford" by Anthony Buttitta, *Saturday Review of Literature*, May 21, 1938.
Trident Press, a division of Simon and Schuster, Inc.: For excerpts from *My Brother Bill* by John Faulkner. Copyright © 1963 by Lucille Ramey Faulkner.
The Viking Press, Inc.: For excerpts from *The Faulkner-Cowley File: Letters and Memories, 1944–1962* by Malcolm Cowley. Copyright © 1966 by Malcolm Cowley, copyright © 1966 by the Estate of William Faulkner. All rights reserved. For an excerpt from *Writers at Work: The Paris Review Interviews* edited by Malcolm Cowley. Copyright © 1957, 1958 by The Paris Review, Inc.

Since this page cannot legibly accommodate all of the acknowledgments for these two volumes, they are continued in the Notes sections of Volumes One and Two and in the Acknowledgments section at the end of Volume Two.

Library of Congress Cataloging in Publication Data

Blotner, Joseph Leo, 1923–
Faulkner; a biography.

1. Faulkner, William, 1897–1962.
PS3511.A86Z63 813'.5'2[B] 72-11370
ISBN 0-395-47452-X

Manufactured in the United States of America
First Edition

To Yvonne, Tracy, Pam, and Nancy

Foreword

This is meant to be a biography of William Faulkner's works as well as of their creator; since each element of them was in some sense a product of his total life experience, I have tried to present the life as fully as possible. Because he drew more extensively on family and regional lorc than any other major American writer, I have treated these backgrounds in detail. (Here I think one can learn not only from what he used but also from what he discarded.) I have also used other sources and experiences as fully as the material would permit.

A few smaller elements require brief comment. The epigraphs are meant to underline the way in which elements of the life got into the writing, not necessarily that the events of a particular chapter were transmuted into those particular passages (though this was sometimes the case). The notes identifying conversations with William Faulkner and remarks I heard him make are undated; this is because I did not keep such a record, though I later wished at times that I had. The spelling of the family name varies from person to person and time to time. This is not the result of vagary or error but of the highly individualistic nature of the members of this clan.

Though I hope this study will provide some critical insights as well as biographical ones, its main business is not primarily critical in the restricted sense. There are several excellent studies devoted exclusively to criticism. In treating the works I have tried to use a developmental approach: insofar as possible to show authorial intent as each work grew, together with the themes and techniques linking it to other elements in both the canon and the life. The process of composition was often exceedingly complex. I have tried to record the stages as faithfully as possible with the evidence now available. (Specialized technical material has generally been consolidated in the notes.)

FOREWORD

I have tried not to interject unduly personal appraisal into an account meant to be sympathetic yet comprehensive and objective, yet perhaps I can here permit myself to say not just that William Faulkner was a great writer, but that to me he seems America's greatest writer of prose fiction. The narrative will perhaps reveal more clearly how he seemed to me as a man. I cannot hope to look upon his like again.

Contents

CONTENTS

CONTENTS

Illustrations

ILLUSTRATIONS

ILLUSTRATIONS

BOOK ONE
The Ancestors

To 1897

Left, Colonel William Clark Falkner.
Bottom left, John Wesley Thompson Falkner.
Right, Sallie Murry Falkner.

1

The Beginnings

> . . . the Compson domain . . . now it was fit to breed princes, statesmen and generals and bishops, to avenge the dispossessed Compsons from Culloden and Carolina and Kentucky. . . .
>
> —*The Sound and the Fury* (408)

"My ancestors came from Inverness, Scotland," William Cuthbert Faulkner once declared—a region, he added, which produced woolen textiles and whiskey. Inverness-shire is one of Scotland's largest counties, and the "royal and large burgh" of Inverness, a seaport and distributing center, has long been known as the "capital of the Highlands." Faulkner used to say that the principal family lines were Falconer, Murray, McAlpine, and Cameron. Falconer was the only Lowland name among the four and Cameron the only one which does not occur in existing family documents or recollections. In America, he said, Falconer had been corrupted to Falkner. Reminded that the mother of Scottish philosopher David Hume was a Catherine Falconer whose kinsmen were among Scotland's greatest judges, he replied, "We're the same family. The name is just spelled differently." He told a friend, "My great-grandfather Murry had his grandfather's claymore which he had carried at the battle of Culloden. My aunt has it now." (It was Great-grandfather Murry who changed the spelling from Murray.) He wrote another friend that his part of Mississippi was inhabited by descendants of Highland and Lowland Scots, people who had made their way across the mountains from North Carolina. His great-grandfather Murry spoke Gaelic and lived to be a hundred. "When his old wife berated him he used to go up to his room, dress in his kilt, buckle on his claymore, and come down and sulk in the chimney corner." Another time Faulkner recalled how the old man would repair to his room upstairs when his wife nagged him, shortly to return draped in his tartan, whereupon he would stalk to the chimney corner and sit there silent but knitting furiously—a skill quite common and accepted among men of the Highlands.

Actually, there were more versions of the Falkner origins than the number of families Faulkner himself settled on. Alexander L. Bondurant, a student of the career of Colonel William Clark Falkner—great-grandfather of the novelist and founder of this branch—wrote that his family "was of Welsh descent. . . ." Bondurant said he was indebted for valuable information to the Colonel's children, John Wesley Thompson Falkner and Willie Medora Falkner. John Wesley Thompson Falkner's granddaughter recalls a letter many years ago from a New York firm informing him that the name had come from Falconer, and that one of their ancestors had been Keeper of the Falcons to the British Crown. They were also said to have come from an island with something like the same name. The firm offered to provide a family crest. She remembered that Grandfather Falkner didn't buy it. John Wesley Thompson Falkner had two sons: Murry Cuthbert Falkner (William Faulkner's father) and John Wesley Thompson Falkner, Jr. Murry always said the family came from Ulster; John Jr. said they were French Huguenots who fled France and spent one generation in England before coming to America. If Colonel Falkner had made some pronouncement, there would be more to go on. And one might have been expected from this novelist, versifier, and controversialist who was soldier, lawyer, planter, and railroad builder as well. He had a perfect opportunity to allude to the family lineage when he took his daughter Effie on an extended European tour in June of 1883. Soon he began sending travel letters back to the hometown paper, the Ripley *Advertiser.* They visited the ruins of Kenilworth Castle, and the Colonel wrote one of his letters from the hotel where Sir Walter Scott had stayed while he was writing *Kenilworth.* He described a picture of Mary Queen of Scots at Windsor Castle and noted that James I had been imprisoned there. But none of these sights evoked a comment on any ancestral line—Scottish, English, Welsh, Irish, or otherwise.

The situation is different with the Murrys and McAlpines. William Faulkner's grandmother, the wife of John Wesley Thompson Falkner, was born Sallie Murry. Family consensus has it that her father, Dr. John Young Murry, came by McAlpine blood on his mother's side (from him came a

McAlpine plaid, kept in the family for many years until it was lost in a fire.) Thus the Scottish antecedents begin to appear clearly in the generation following that of the Colonel. To see how they affected the imagination and the work of the Colonel's great-grandson, one should glance back to the Highlands again.

In Inverness-shire the clan system had grown from the 1300's onwards, and it was in that county that the system finally reached its fullest power. The Camerons and about ten others formed the strongest clans of the shire. Their involvement in the political and religious struggles of the late seventeenth and early eighteenth centuries culminated in their rising against the English in 1745 under the leadership of Prince Charles Edward Stuart. But this Jacobite rebellion fared no better than the first one had thirty years before. It was disastrously crushed in 1746 on the bloody field of Culloden, from which "Bonnie Prince Charlie" fled to exile in France. The defeated chieftains who stayed behind fared worse. The Highland dress was forbidden, land was confiscated, and estates were sold. Impoverished Scotsmen began to leave the glens as early as 1747 for new homes in North America. Some of the ships which carried them made port in Charleston, South Carolina.

This is the route—Culloden to Carolina—of the progenitor of one of Faulkner's best-known fictional families: Quentin MacLachan Compson, great-great-great-great-grandfather of Quentin, Caddy, Jason, and Benjy Compson of *The Sound and the Fury.* This first Quentin, who had named his son Charles Stuart, was the son, Faulkner wrote, "of a Glasgow printer, orphaned and raised by his mother's people in the Perth highlands" (404), which adjoin Inverness-shire at its southern border.

The other fictional family which suggests real, and less conjectural, counterparts, is the Sartoris family of the novels *Sartoris* and *The Unvanquished.* Colonel John Sartoris is modeled substantially upon Colonel William Clark Falkner. In a passage cut from an early novel called *Flags in the Dust* (rewritten to become *Sartoris*), Faulkner sketched in the "glamorous violence" of Sartoris' ancestors, the Bayard and John Sartoris who served Charles I, and the "earlier John Sartoris who had followed his young prince to France and there led such a career of penniless and glamorous violence that even Charles Stuart was glad when he died. . . ." (2) Heedless and violent like him had been Colonel Sartoris' brother, the "Carolina Bayard," who had died at Manassas. His namesake, an earlier Bayard Sartoris, had "recovered from Braddock's expedition," then "wooed and won a Charleston lady for his wife. . . ." In another deleted passage Bayard Sartoris recalls the words of his father, Colonel John Sartoris, about family history: "In the nineteenth century anywhere chortling over genealogy is poppycock, but it is particularly so in America, where we all have a common ancestry and the only house from which we can claim descent with any assurance is the Old Bailey. Yet the man who professes to care nothing about his forefathers is only a little less vain than he who bases all his actions on blood precedent. And a Sartoris is entitled to a little vanity and poppycock, if he so chooses."

On occasion, William Faulkner showed interest, if not vanity, in the subject of genealogy. On July 13, 1859, his great-great-great-uncle, John Wesley Thompson, had paid one hundred dollars as a shareholder in the Book and Tract Society of the Memphis Conference of the Methodist Church, South. One of the perquisites was a massive "genealogical family Bible and case." In 1862 he inscribed and presented the Bible to his wife, with the stipulation that at his death it should go to his adopted son, John Wesley Thompson Falkner (actually, the Colonel's son by his first marriage). He also provided that the Bible should go always to the oldest son of the following generation. William Faulkner inherited the leather-bound, illustrated tome when his father died on August 7, 1932. Sometime thereafter he made new entries in a few of the genealogical tables—literally hundreds of pages bound into the Bible between the Old and New Testaments. At about the same time, presumably, he traced the family tree as far back as he could.

Tantalizing speculation is about all one can engage in at this point where genealogy and fiction appear to cross, for the Falkner lineage prior to the settling in America finally eludes research. Thus far no ancestral documents of the Falkners have come to light. Few if any may have existed, for many eighteenth-century emigrants, especially from the Highlands, possessed only oral records of their descent and family history. And Faulkner himself was no more a reliable witness than most imaginative, creative, and sometimes playful artists are likely to be. He often told romantic stories that apparently pleased him but appear to have had little basis in fact. Nor was he particularly reassuring when he spoke of himself as a recorder of facts. "I don't have much patience with facts," he smilingly told one group, "and any writer is a congenital liar to begin with or he wouldn't take up writing. And so I couldn't tell the truth even about history. That's why I'll never write a biography. I couldn't tell the truth about Faulkner, I'm sure." On another occasion, though he was willing to talk about the idea of a biography, he envisioned the same results: "I'd rather write my own because I know, being a convincing liar, I never could tell the truth about myself."

But no matter what he said to classes of students, he was convincing when he spoke in conversation. He knew which of his fellow townsmen in Oxford, Mississippi, thinking themselves Irish, were actually descended from Scots who had lived on the Island of Soay (south of Skye) before it was evacuated in the eighteenth century. One of Faulkner's friends, himself of Highland ancestry, was "surprised by his really quite profound knowledge of the Highlands and its history." To him there was no question of Faulkner's lineage: "He was a Highlander and fiercely proud of it." There were certainly elements of Scots culture in his immediate family. It was in the home of his grandfather Falkner that the young ladies of the Methodist Church presented "An Evening with the Scotch," meant to appeal "to those who love the songs and tales of that bonny land of Scotia." With his wife he had sometimes served as chaperone for outings of the Caledonia Club. And on Maud Butler's marriage to Murry Falkner on November 7, 1896, one of the books she brought with her was *The Poetical Works of Robert Burns.*

All that can be said with certainty is that most of Faulkner's people came from the British Isles and that many of his ancestors—perhaps most of them—were Scots. (Perhaps when a man asserts an ancestry as strongly as William Faulkner did the Scottish, this is as important, if in a slightly different way, as would be a sheaf of parchment documents from any heralds' college.) The point at which family lore begins to be supported by recorded fact comes when the Falconers or Falkners made their way to the New World sometime in the eighteenth century, the first step in a migration that would proceed halfway across the continent.

2

1700's-1839

Quentin MacLachan [Compson]. . . . Fled to Carolina from Culloden Moor with a claymore and the tartan he wore by day and slept under by night, and little else.

—*The Sound and the Fury* (404)

That Carolina Bayard had been rather a handful even for Sartorises. Not so much a black sheep as a nuisance, all of whose qualities were positive and unpredictable.

—*Sartoris* (9)

Calvin Burden. . . . The youngest of ten children, he ran away from home at the age of twelve. . . . Ten years later he reached Missouri from the west. Three weeks after he arrived he was married, to the daughter of a family of Huguenot stock which had emigrated from Carolina by way of Kentucky.

—*Light in August* (228)

One of the characteristics of the fictional Sartoris family is the recurrence of pairs of brothers, usually named Bayard and John, in most of its generations. There was something like this in William Faulkner's own family, where two brothers appeared in four of the five American generations preceding his own. Family tradition has it that the first pair set foot on American soil in Charleston, South Carolina, sometime before the Revolutionary War. When the conflict broke out, the older of the young immigrants fought under the new flag in the battles of Cowpens and Kings Mountain. While the younger of the brothers is said to have remained in

South Carolina, the older brother, either just before or just after joining the colors, moved to Haywood County, North Carolina. He apparently settled in that remote northwestern county on the Tennessee border. There near the Great Smoky Mountains he married and raised a family. Like his father, he had two sons, Joseph and John. Joseph Falkner took as his bride a young Carolina girl named Caroline Word. She was probably from Surry County, 150 miles to the east on the Virginia border and just north of the Yadkin River, where Daniel Boone had lived in the years before he set out for Kentucky. The date of their marriage is unknown, as is the date when Joseph Falkner, like his father before him, decided to move west.

Falkner family lore has it that the move came in the late spring of 1825 and that its destination was Ste. Genevieve, Missouri, on the banks of the Mississippi River. Joseph Falkner was apparently undeterred by the fact that Caroline was far gone in pregnancy and that they would have to cross the Great Smokies before they descended over into Tennessee. They made it through one county before she went into labor. Then, on July 6 in Knox County, perhaps in Knoxville, she was delivered of her first child. (The distance between the seats of Haywood County and Knox County was scarcely more than sixty-five miles as the crow flies, but the rugged terrain made it a much longer journey.) The baby was a boy, and they named him William Clark Falkner. They stayed in Tennessee for an undetermined period after his birth. When they resumed their journey they traveled through Tennessee, crossed the Mississippi, and finally arrived in Ste. Genevieve to settle down.

The new home of the Falkners was vastly different from Haywood County. It had been a busy stopping point from which immigrants from Canada to Louisiana made their way across the river and west. By 1836, however, the river trade had declined, the fur trade had moved west, and the population had dwindled to a mere 800 souls.

No one knows how Joseph Falkner supported his family, later enlarged by the birth of another son, James, and a daughter, Frances. One of the few facts that is known about these Missouri years is that his son William left Ste. Genevieve before he was out of his early teens. About 1840 William Clark Falkner set out on foot to make his way south to Tennessee and then into Mississippi. There are two versions of his motives for the journey. One describes the Cain-like flight of a dangerous young man; the other, the courageous setting out of a boy straight from the pages of works such as *Ragged Dick* or *Pluck and Luck.*

The second interpretation, feelingly offered by Professor Alexander Bondurant in 1900, begins with the death of Joseph Falkner. "The lad was now cast upon his own resources," Bondurant wrote, "and, further, felt the responsibility of providing for his widowed mother and orphaned brothers and sisters. The future seemed to hold little promise for him in Missouri, and so he decided to seek fortune elsewhere. Mississippi was, at this time, a virgin land, and thither he determined to go; a bold undertaking for a lad of seventeen with no money, and no friends along the road." In later life William C. Falkner showed a side consistent with this action—he was courageous, generous, and public-spirited. But there was also another, better-known side, one which was violent and impulsive and which fitted the other version of his departure from Missouri. This one, with only the authority of tradition behind it, was described by Robert Coughlan. In 1839 the fourteen-year-old boy quarreled with his brother James, "bloodied his head with a hoe, and was so severely whipped by his father that he ran away from home. . . ." In a variant account there was no parental whipping: he thought he had killed his brother and fled immediately.

There are several versions of what happened next. It is usually agreed that he made his way to Tennessee—probably to Middleton, about five miles from the Mississippi line—and from there trudged the remaining twenty-odd miles to Ripley, the seat of Tippah County. According to the most dramatic version, he was seeking his aunt, Justiania Dickinson Word, and her husband, John Wesley Thompson, only to find that the latter was in Pontotoc, forty miles south, in jail on a charge of murder. Thompson had been teaching school in Plentitude, where he had become "involved in a personal difficulty" and killed the other man. When the boy arrived in Pontotoc, dirty and tired, he had a brief and unsatisfactory interview with his imprisoned uncle. Then, alone in this strange town, he sat down on the steps of Benjamin Anderson's tavern. Folding his arms over his knees, he hid his face and wept in discouragement and weariness. A small girl asked if she could help, and he told her that he would like a glass of water. When her mother returned with her to see the "little old tramp-boy," he told them his story. Being a friend of the Thompsons, Mrs. Vance took him home, cleaned him up, and fed him. The next morning she and her husband put him on the stagecoach back to Ripley. As he left, it was the little girl who wept. "Don't you cry, Lizzie," he said. "When I grow up I'll come back here and marry you."

In the sequel, John Wesley Thompson was acquitted, having eloquently pleaded his own case after studying law during his imprisonment.

Returning to Ripley, he embarked on a distinguished legal career. There his nephew would prosper, too, before his return years later as a widower to marry Lizzie Vance. This account, in its main outline, was very likely one which William Faulkner heard as a child. In reality, however, very little of it is accurate if the Colonel had the facts straight when he recalled them nearly fifty years later.

When Mississippi had been admitted to the Union in 1817, only the southern third of the state had been settled by white men. The rest belonged to the Choctaw and Chickasaw Indians, but they were not to keep it for long. In 1830 the half-white Choctaw chief, Greenwood Leflore, reluctantly advised his people to accept the new white man's treaty, since it was the best they were likely to get. It was called the Treaty of Dancing Rabbit Creek, under which they ceded to the United States (for money and land in Oklahoma) a large part of north Mississippi running eastward from the middle Delta. Two years later, on October 22, 1832, King Ishtehotopah signed the Treaty of Pontotoc on behalf of the Chickasaw Indians. Another signatory of this document, which ceded six million acres in the northernmost part of the state, was Chief Tishomingo, a noble old warrior one hundred years of age. It was 1835 before the Chickasaws began their migration to Oklahoma, and it continued for the next four years. The results of this new exploitation of the Indian were greeted with wild enthusiasm by those who wanted what the virgin land offered. At a dinner held in 1830 for Andrew Jackson—who was regarded as the architect of this policy—one politician excitedly proclaimed, "Already the feet of thousands press upon the borders of this new purchase . . . to pitch their tents in the wilderness . . . . Kentucky's coming, Tennessee's coming, Alabama's coming, and they're all coming to join the joyous crowd of Mississippians. . . ."

By 1836 the migration of the Chickasaws was well under way. As they left, the white men came in. One of them was a brother of Caroline and Justiania Word. Like his sisters, Thomas A. Word had left North Carolina to seek his fortune in the new lands. He had made his way to Pontotoc, Mississippi, and for some time thereafter he practiced law. Thus he had been in this newly settled land a year or more when his nephew fled to the south seeking either haven or help. In Pontotoc on railroad business in mid-May of 1886, Colonel Falkner recalled his arrival for the Pontotoc *True Democrat*:

> He came from Memphis on foot, to meet his uncle here. He was a poor, sick, ragged, barefoot, penniless boy. His cup of sorrow

> was filled to the brim when he learned that his uncle (Mr. Word) had left for Aberdeen the day previous. He sat down on the hotel steps and wept bitterly, as though his heart would break. A little girl came along and inquired the cause of his distress. Having learned the facts from the Colonel she promptly went and obtained the money to pay his hotel bill and gave it to him. The Colonel never forgot the little Samaritan, but married her in Pontotoc years afterwards. When alluding to this episode in his eventful history, Col. Falkner became so affected that utterance failed him, and he had to pause until his emotions had subsided.

Other evidence seems to support this account.

By June of 1845 William Clark Falkner was identified in local records as a resident of Ripley. Though he may have stayed for some time with Thomas Word in Pontotoc, it was in Ripley that his rise began. The governing code there was an uncomplicated one: "A man ought to fear God and mind his own business," recorded one commentator. "He should be respectful and courteous to all women; he should love his friends and hate his enemies. He should eat when he was hungry, drink when he was thirsty, dance when he was merry, vote for the candidate he liked best, and knock down any man who questioned his right to these privileges." It appears that John Wesley Thompson, the husband of Caroline Word Falkner's sister, Justiania, adhered to this code, and it was he who adopted the boy in these years when he was to receive some schooling. Thompson was a man of unusual talent and energy who apparently had a strong effect upon his nephew. William Cuthbert Faulkner must have known something about his great-grandfather's guardian. If John Wesley Thompson was not "fated" or "doomed" like the Sartorises, he was a strong and sometimes violent man, a fitting father-surrogate for the model for Colonel John Sartoris.

His early years seem to have been unexceptional. Born in Haywood County on April 28, 1809, the eleventh of twelve children, he received enough education to become a schoolteacher. At the age of twenty-four he fell in love with seventeen-year-old Justiania Dickinson Word.

Then his troubles began. Her family moved to Clarkesville, Georgia, and for the better part of a year his courtship encountered difficulties which he lamented in passionate verse. These were finally overcome when the two were married on July 24, 1834. But exactly three weeks after he stood up to take his vows, the bridegroom was in jail. The Habersham County grand jury found a true bill against John Wesley Thompson and bound him over for the October term of court in Clarkesville on the charge of stabbing one Calvin J. Hanks to death. Despite the bill of indictment's minute particulars, little can be inferred about the crime beyond the fact that it was one of frontier violence.

The letters of the accused and his wife make clearer the anxious days of that hot rainy summer of 1834 and the fall that followed. In his large bold hand Thompson at first encouraged his bride in Miltonic flourishes, but by October he was rhetorically preparing to bid her and the world farewell. He nonetheless went into the courtroom with his plea of Not Guilty, and at the trial's end the jury brought in a verdict of acquittal.

There is no indication how soon after his acquittal he shook the red clay of Georgia from his feet. If he left for Mississippi about the same time as did his brother-in-law, Thomas Word, it would have been 1836. His route from Habersham County would have been a rough arc only a little more southerly than those of Word and his other brother-in-law, Joseph Falkner. If William Clark Falkner was able to find him in Tippah County in 1839 or 1840, that would have given Thompson just enough time to electioneer for office. That he did so successfully is attested by the ornate commission as district attorney of the 6th Judicial District, made out to John Wesley Thompson and signed at Jackson by Governor Alexander Gallatin McNull on November 13, 1841. The penniless boy had chosen better than he knew. He had come to the place where he would not only outstrip his foster father but literally gain fame and fortune.

3

1839-1859

> . . . he sat . . . with that spurious forensic air of lawyers and the intolerant eyes which in the last two years had acquired that transparent film which the eyes of carnivorous animals have and from behind which they look at a world which no ruminant ever sees, perhaps dares to see, which I have seen before on the eyes of men who have killed so much that never again as long as they live will they ever be alone.
>
> —*The Unvanquished* (265–266)

Once settled in Ripley, William Clark Falkner began to show the energy and enterprise that marked him all his life. According to one source, he began work at the Ripley jail at the age of fourteen. During the four years he worked there he was also busy acquiring what education he could in the rural county seat. An avid reader, he received direction from schoolmaster James Kernan, an ambitious Irish immigrant. Falkner augmented his jailhouse salary with a little teaching in the elementary grades and supposedly sent some of his earnings to his mother in Missouri. Looking beyond these makeshifts, he determined that he would practice law. When John Wesley Thompson refused to allow him to read law in his office on the grounds of inadequate preparation, Falkner turned again to the enterprising Kernan, now set up as a lawyer in chambers housed in a log cabin. Falkner was now nearing twenty.

Not long after he embarked on his study of the law, he became involved in a series of events combining elements that would recur in his career: violence and bloodshed, newspaper publicity, and successful commercial publication. On the night of Sunday, June 8, 1845, Dr. Adcock and the four members of his family were murdered shortly after they had left Pontotoc County with their goods and slaves to move north. Suspicion of the grisly ax murder fell on a shady character named Andrew J. McCannon, and two days later a posse led by the Tippah County sheriff captured him just north of the Tennessee line. With the posse was Falkner. He almost saw a lynching when an angry crowd demanded the prisoner on their return. In a brilliant and desperate stroke, McCannon promised that if they would give him the time, he would reveal the story of his life, including the actual details of the Adcock murders.

McCannon was illiterate, and for amanuensis he chose William Clark Falkner, who would do his best both for the subject and for himself. Suddenly time became crucial once more. When McCannon was tried and sentenced to hang, Falkner set off on the seventy-mile ride to Memphis, waited there while the printer worked at top speed, and then rode through the night to carry the pamphlets back to Ripley. He arrived just in time to hawk them at the actual moment of their subject's execution. Apparently, he pocketed a tidy profit. Moreover, a newspaper controversy arose when an Alabama editor denounced Falkner for disparaging assertions he had attributed to McCannon, and the editor of the Ripley *Advertiser* undertook a spirited defense of Falkner. Three months later the pamphlet was still selling as far away as Memphis. The footsore wanderer of seven years before had achieved a considerable status for himself.

Before long he had a taste of another of his secondary careers. On September 19, 1846, Colonel Jefferson Davis' 1st Mississippi Volunteer Regiment arrived in Monterrey just in time to fight in that crucial battle of the Mexican War. By mid-January, 1847, First Lieutenant William C. Falkner was mustered with the 2nd Mississippi Volunteer Regiment at Vicksburg, and three weeks later they were encamped near Monterrey. There, on April 14, he defied a general order and rode off on some private errand. After he failed to return, a search party found him lying a mile and a half away, his left foot shattered by one ball and the first joints of three fingers of his left hand blown away by another. Later two enemies in a blood feud would claim that Falkner had been ambushed while on an errand of private pleasure, and lines from an autobiographical poem, *The Siege of Monterey*, which Falkner would publish in 1851, suggest that there was something to their charges:

Full well I know the feeling of lead—
I have never fought, but freely bled,
Mexican soil hath drank my gore,
But I disgrace, instead of glory, bore.

Whatever their cause, Falkner's wounds gained him a convalescent leave beginning April 19. Testifying to his recuperative powers was his wedding, on July 9, in Knoxville, Tennessee, to Holland Pearce. He returned to Mexico but soon submitted his resignation on the grounds of disabling wounds. Discharged on October 31, he set out for home with two souvenirs of the inglorious campaign: one was an elegant carved walking stick with silver on both ends and a hollow space where it could be loaded with lead; the other was a machete with a blade inscribed DON'T CHOP STUMPS.

Back home once more he prospered—at first. John Wesley Thompson took him into his office and Falkner passed the bar examination and began to practice. His wife had brought a dowry which included slaves, and now Falkner began buying parcels of land and set up as a planter. On September 2, 1848, Holland Pearce presented him with a son, whom they dutifully named John Wesley Thompson Falkner.

Trouble came the next spring in the form of Robert Hindman, who had been a private in Falkner's company. The Hindmans were a brave, vigorous, and able family also known to be high-strung, reckless, and aggressive. Now Robert wanted badly to belong to another organization in which Falkner had some influence, the Knights of Temperance. Falkner spoke on behalf of Hindman's admission, but someone told Hindman just the opposite, and he swore he would kill Falkner. The young lawyer went out to the Hindman place, and when he denied the blackballing, Hindman angrily replied, "You're a damned liar," and pulled out a revolver. While they struggled it misfired twice. As it clicked a third time, Falkner drove home a knife and Hindman fell dead. It was clear that Falkner had acted in self-defense and when the case eventually came to trial he was acquitted. The verdict made no difference to the Hindmans, however, who according to legend had Robert's tombstone inscribed

Murdered at Ripley, Miss.
by Wm. C. Falkner.

Though they were prevailed upon, it was said, to change "murdered" to "killed," their hatred apparently did not cool.

As Falkner's public life grew more dangerous he was dealt a crushing blow at home. Three weeks after Hindman's attempt on his life, Holland Pearce succumbed to consumption. On top of this, the baby was not thriving, and so the distracted husband took the child to his Aunt Justiania.

"Take him," he said to her, "and do something for him before he dies." Justiania took the baby and gave him a piece of fatback to suck. The father turned to John Wesley Thompson.

"Will you keep the baby?" he asked.

"Yes," his uncle answered, "on one condition—that you won't take him back if you remarry." Falkner agreed, and the childless Thompsons had a son.

Falkner turned back to his law practice and the growing Falkner Farms, but he was harassed by the Hindmans and felt himself in constant danger. The only event which could have given him much joy during these dark days of his life supposedly took place early in 1851. The Tippah County veterans of the Mexican War held a reunion, and it fell to Falkner as ranking officer to lead the grand march. He did not recognize his pretty young partner when she laid her hand on his arm as the band struck up the opening strains. But he soon found that this visitor from Pontotoc was Elizabeth Houston Vance, the same girl who had helped him a dozen years before as he sat on the tavern steps, a despairing stranger in Mississippi. He was immediately taken with her. Apparently he courted her in the days after the reunion, and soon Elizabeth Vance found that she was in love with the young war veteran. Her parents opposed the match, but Falkner kept up his courtship, now determined to marry again.

Before he could press his suit further, another crisis erupted. On February 28 Falkner was discussing the rental of a house with a strong partisan of the Hindmans named Erasmus W. Morris. The two men began to argue. The dispute grew more violent until suddenly Falkner drew a pistol and fired. Blood on his face, Morris fell dead. Falkner was jailed and then released on bail. Indicted for murder again, the twenty-five-year-old defendant walked into the courtroom on March 12 to face, as prosecutor, Thomas C. Hindman, Jr., the brother of the man he had stabbed to death three years before. By the end of the day, the jury had acquitted him, and he headed for the Ripley Hotel to enjoy his dinner. As he entered the dining room, Thomas C. Hindman, Sr., drew and aimed his pistol but somehow dropped it. It discharged with a rcar and the bullet sprayed plaster from the ceiling over Falkner's head. Falkner drew his own pistol but contented himself with ordering Hindman to leave his weapon where it had fallen. The remainder of the day proved uneventful.

The trial had inflamed old animosities, and now feeling more and more threatened and conspired against than ever, Falkner began to make an increasing number of business trips away from Ripley. One of them proved an opportunity which launched him on still another secondary career. In a Cincinnati hotel room he tried the art of narrative verse. The result, *The Siege of Monterey,* was published as a three-by-five-inch book of 131 pages. The frontispiece was a woodcut of a young woman in soldier's uniform on a field of battle. The verse was painfully amateurish but it showed the kind of energy that characterized its author and revealed a good deal about his past life and current concerns. As he told the love story he alluded freely though vaguely to his discreditable misfortunes in the war and to the killings which had been forced on him. Elsewhere the poet celebrated his love for Lizzie Vance and also the benefits of the married state:

It supplies the world with population
Without which we would be awful;
It does all this, besides it makes copulation
A virtue, when under circumstances lawful.

Before the year was out, he tried his hand at another genre. Returning to Cincinnati, he paid Isaac Hart to print a 500-copy edition of a novel called *The Spanish Heroine.* Like her predecessor, the heroine donned a uniform and saved her lover (this time an American) during the battle of Monterrey. Wildly improbable coincidences and amateurish wrenching of situations to meet the demands of a mechanical plot made this second effort decidedly less accomplished than the first. No sales figures have survived for either volume.

He was able to chalk up one triumph, though, before the year's end. Lizzie Vance's parents had even considered leaving Pontotoc to keep their daughter from marrying the young lawyer-planter-author, but Falkner anticipated them, and on October 12, 1851, he was secretly married to "my angelic Lizzie." He began a new domestic life which, in the decade that followed, brought him as much tranquillity as he was ever to know.

It was not long before his responsibilities began to increase. Lizzie Falkner gave birth to William Henry on August 1, 1853, and Willie Medora not quite three years later on July 17, 1856. James Word Falkner moved to Ripley and later William sent his younger brother to the University of

Mississippi as a member of the class of 1860. At least one of Joseph Falkner's children would receive a proper education.

Falkner's relations with his other family were not so harmonious. John Wesley Thompson Falkner was apparently thriving with the Thompsons, but they felt that his father was not making sufficient financial provision for his future. Moreover, Falkner, who had been a staunch Whig, began contributing articles to a Know-Nothing party paper and ran against his uncle for the state legislature. On November 15, 1855, the Ripley *Advertiser* reported his uncle had defeated him. A year later, however, Falkner cast one of the 174 Democratic electoral votes that made James Buchanan president.

The following year the blood feud flared up again. One of Falkner's friends attempted to shoot Thomas Hindman, Sr. Though Falkner wrenched the pistol away, the infuriated Hindman was not appeased and challenged Falkner to a duel not long afterwards. The secret preparations began. At six o'clock one spring morning—possibly April 1—the two principals were to meet across the river from Memphis on the Arkansas shore with only Matthew C. Galloway, editor of the Memphis *Appeal*, as witness. The duelists would face each other at fifty yards, then advance and fire at will. More than two decades later, Falkner's law partner would say Falkner had told him he did not intend to advance on Hindman and would not fire unless his adversary came within twenty paces. Galloway may also have heard Falkner declare his intention. In any event, he succeeded somehow in settling the difficulties between the two men before the duel could take place. At last Falkner was clear of the clouds of suspicion, the smears of obloquy, and the threat of violent death—or so it seemed.

He and his uncle both continued to prosper—practicing law, farming, investing in land, occasionally buying and selling slaves. In 1859 Thompson resigned as district attorney to become circuit judge. In the same year Lizzie Vance gave birth to Thomas Vance Falkner. Her husband, now worth nearly $50,000, had time for politics as well as family and business. His convictions as Whig, Know-Nothing, and Democrat had carried him into vigorous political action; his convictions as a member of the secessionist party would soon carry him into battle.

4

1858-April, 1862

Mississippi and Yoknapatawpha County not last in this, Mississippi among the first of the eleven to ratify secession, the regiment of infantry which John Sartoris raised and organised with Jefferson for its headquarters, going to Virginia numbered Two in the roster of Mississippi regiments . . . not even a regiment yet but merely a voluntary association of untried men who knew they were ignorant and hoped they were brave, the four sides of the Square lined with their fathers or grandfathers and their mothers and wives and sisters and sweethearts. . . .

—*Requiem for a Nun* (230)

"Who ain't heard about him in this country? Get the Yankees to tell you about him sometime. By Godfrey, he raised the first damn regiment in Mississippi out of his own pocket, and took 'em to Ferginny and whipped the Yankees right and left with 'em before he found out that what he had bought and paid for wasn't a regiment of soldiers but a congress of politicians and fools. . . ."

—*The Unvanquished* (58)

Despite the Mexican debacle, Falkner had not lost his taste for martial glory. In the intervening years he had played military politics with some success, for in 1858 he had gotten himself appointed brigadier general of militia. It may have been only a paper commission contingent on plans for reorganizing volunteer units, for by the time Mississippi seceded on January

9, 1861, his rank had evaporated. He stayed in the running for eight ballots when four brigadier generals were elected to command the state militia, but finally he had to settle for a captaincy in a company he helped to raise, called "The Magnolia Rifles." In late April he led their enlistment in the Confederate service. He embraced Lizzie (now five months pregnant), kissed the three children, rode up to the head of the waiting column, and led it onto the northeast road out of Ripley. At Corinth in early May they were merged with other units to form the 2nd Mississippi Infantry Regiment, whose men elected him their colonel. Two and a half weeks later they joined Brigadier General Joseph E. Johnston's Army of the Shenandoah at Harpers Ferry.

Colonel Falkner soon made himself conspicuous. In less than a month he had turned his raw sloppy regiment into a smartly drilled unit, and not long afterwards he was promoted to brigadier general in command of four regiments. Two days later, however, "on finding that the appointment would separate him from his regiment, he promptly and positively declined." Appointed in his place was General Barnard E. Bee, a handsome, six-foot South Carolinian of West Point's class of 1845. Ironically, Falkner would spend much of the remainder of his service vainly politicking for the general's stars he so impulsively renounced that summer day in northern Virginia.

By mid-July the Northern cry "On to Richmond" had been translated into troop movements, and on the eighteenth, units of Brigadier General Irvin McDowell's 35,000-man force met elements of Brigadier General Pierre G. T. Beauregard's 22,000-man army concentrated at Manassas Junction. By the twentieth, Johnston had brought 10,000 men up in support, with Colonel J. E. B. Stuart's First Virginia Cavalry screening him from Federal reconnaissance and Brigadier General Thomas Jonathan Jackson's First Brigade leading his infantry. Beauregard had disposed his men over a winding eight-mile stretch of a thirty-foot stream called Bull Run. By six-thirty on the morning of the twenty-first, McDowell had begun a diversionary attack at a stone bridge where the Confederate left was anchored and sent his main assault group to encircle Beauregard's left and smash at the Confederate rear.

Throughout the morning elements of Bee's brigade absorbed much of the Federal attack. (Falkner's 2nd Mississippi had been moved in to the center.) The battle was moving towards Henry Hill, a mile and a quarter from the stone bridge, where Jackson had disposed his six regiments to support artillery Captain John D. Imboden. From off to the right came a rider who pulled up his mount alongside Jackson. It was black-eyed Barnard Bee, still a dashing figure after the morning's bitter fighting.

"General, they are beating us back," he said. They would breast the hill at any moment.

"Then, sir," replied Jackson, "we will give them the bayonet!"

Bee whirled and galloped back to the remnants of his command. Weary and grimy, they appeared ready to continue their retreat. "Look!" Bee shouted, pointing to the hill. "There is Jackson standing like a stone wall!" Then he issued his order. "Rally behind the Virginians!"

As the hour moved past noon the battle neared its climax. When McDowell paused to reorganize his forces, Beauregard and Bee disposed five more regiments along the line Jackson had formed. Later four more came up and one of them, Falkner's 2nd Mississippi, took its position perhaps half a mile on the left from Jackson's center.

Now McDowell sent forward artillery supported by infantry. From the endangered left flank Stuart attacked. "Just after the cavalry charge," he later reported, "our reinforcements arrived upon the field and formed rapidly in line. The first was Colonel Falkner's regiment (Mississippians), whose gallantry came under my own observation." For two hours the fighting surged back and forth across the slope of the hill and into the nearby pine woods. Jackson had already been down. He had limped up, his coat pierced by the same blast that had killed his mount. Later he had been wounded in the hand. Falkner lost two horses from under him. A special dispatch to the Memphis *Appeal* reported that "The Colonel, who was ever in the van of battle, received a slight wound in the face. . . . When the second horse fell under him, he was thrown violently against a stump, and for some moments lay senseless." When his head cleared he seized another mount and rode back to the front of his regiment. According to one correspondent, "General Beauregard, who had been observing his gallant conduct, shouted to him as he went, 'Go ahead, you hero with the black plume; *history shall never forget you*!' "

McDowell now threw in more men to push this tenacious force off the hill and turn the flank he had been assaulting since morning, but Beauregard committed his last reserves and sent the whole line forward to repulse the Federal attack. By three o'clock Henry Hill was cleared and secured. Barnard Bee had been carried dying to the rear, and Falkner was briefly in command of the brigade. As the long day waned Colonel Jubal Early's brigade went far and deep through the woods to the left, emerged at the tip of the Federal line and outflanked McDowell's army. His right wing began to melt away and his center followed. Then, as darkness fell, terror turned defeat into rout.

The dispatches sent south were triumphant. One that went to Mississippi exulted, "The victory is ours. Colonel Falkner of 2nd Mississippi Regiment charged and took four pieces of [Col. William Tecumseh] Sherman's battery." A Mississippi historian enthusiastically acclaimed it "the most brilliant and decisive feat of arms in the battle." But it had been costly. According to the dispatch, the regiment had lost a hundred in killed and wounded. Four of its captains were among the dead and two more wounded. Lieutenant Colonel B. B. Boone was missing and Major Blair was badly wounded. But they had fought bravely.

According to one of Falkner's men, General Johnston had named Falkner "as one of the thirteen Colonels whose conduct in the battle he considered outstanding." Falkner's courage and leadership had been noted by others among his superiors. Beauregard's comment had earned him the title "The Knight of the Black Plume." Falkner's old friend Colonel Matthew C. Galloway would later say that Beauregard had also added, "Men, you may follow where he leads." Stuart and Johnston had praised him, and according to another source, so had the redoubtable Jackson. So, eleven weeks after he had left home, Colonel William C. Falkner was a hero. The rest of his military career would trail off in anger and resentment, but despite the ensuing bitter frustration, he may have chosen better than he knew when he rejected the general's stars. Falkner might well have left the field as Bee had that hot July day near Manassas if he had been charged with Bee's responsibilities.

Hostilities slowed to sporadic skirmishes during the rest of the summer while commanders went forward with the business of whipping their troops into shape for the campaigns ahead. Falkner busied himself with drill, which was much to his taste.

At home, Lizzie had given birth to a daughter on September 5. Falkner sent word that she was to be called Lizzie Menassah. That fall, when the 2nd and the 11th Mississippi settled into winter camp close to Dumfries, Virginia, near Harpers Ferry, Falkner sent for his family and arranged for their room and board at a nearby farmhouse. A crib was moved in for the baby. But when Falkner's adjutant, Captain J. J. Guyton, returned, he brought with him only Lizzie, William Henry, and Willie Medora. Thomas Vance and Lizzie Menassah had both succumbed to illness and now lay together in the family plot. Apparently Falkner's grief remained keen, and he was said to have described the loss later in a work entitled "The Empty Cradle."

His family stayed on there boarding at the farmhouse. As winter came on, the Colonel was looking ahead to the end of the regiment's one-year enlistment period. In February he went home on a thirty-day recruiting leave, probably taking Lizzie and the children back with him.

When Falkner rejoined the regiment, it was quartered at Yorktown, Virginia. There were new men in the ranks, some of them draftees. Many wanted another election. It began on the evening of April 21, nine months to the day that the regiment had been blooded. It was soon clear that disaffection was widespread, for some said the Colonel "was a martinet and greatly disliked by his men because of his harsh and ruthless disciplinary methods. Others resented his conduct at Manassas, which they considered to be recklessness rather than courage." When the speeches and balloting ended on the morning of the twenty-second, the new colonel of the 2nd Mississippi Volunteer Infantry Regiment was John M. Stone, by a margin of thirteen votes.

Characteristically, Falkner promptly took counteraction. The next day he apparently went to his brigade commander, Brigadier General W. H. H. Whiting, and to the army commander, Johnston. Both wrote to J. W. Randolph, the new secretary of war. Johnston commended Falkner for his handling of the regiment and for his courage at Manassas. Whiting went even further, declaring "he has been defeated by demagogues and affords another illustration of the crying evils that the election system in our army has wrought, and is producing." The results of the election were published in a special order. Whiting then read to all his regiments a commendation of Falkner for his gallantry in the present war and the Mexican War as well. Meanwhile, the letters of recommendation accumulated somewhere in Jefferson Davis' files. He took no action. The subject of the letters returned home—in effect, at liberty.

5

April, 1862–May, 1865

John Sartoris himself, deposed from his colonelcy by a regimental election after Second Manassas, came home and oversaw the making and harvesting of a crop on his plantation before he got bored and gathered up a small gang of irregular cavalry and carried it up into Tennessee to join Forrest. . . .

—*Requiem for a Nun* (231)

Then we listened. We heard: the names—Forrest and Morgan and Barksdale and Van Dorn; the words like Gap and Run which we didn't have in Mississippi even though we did own Barksdale, and Van Dorn until somebody's husband killed him, and one day General Forrest rode down South Street in Oxford where there watched him through a window pane a young girl who scratched her name on it with a diamond ring: Celia Cook.

—*The Unvanquished* (17)

In February, 1863, nine months after his return, Colonel Falkner recalled in a letter the steps he had taken when he got back to Mississippi: "I immediately reported to Beauregard for duty at Corinth, and asked for employment. He placed me in command of the 7th Miss. Regt. til I received authority from the Secretary of War to organize a Regt. of Partisan Rangers. . . ."

His appeals to the governor and to Jefferson Davis for a generalcy went unheeded, and he disdained a majority when it was offered. Once again, if he was to have a permanent command he would have to provide it for himself. He turned his prodigious energies to the task, employing his gifts as a speaker in Tippah, Pontotoc, and Lafayette counties. By the end of July he had six hundred men under arms. His own version of the achievement was not without a touch of bravado: "in fifteen days I had a regiment of one thousand men. I armed and equipped the Regt. by captures from the enemy. Captured my transportation also. Captured nearly as many Yankees as I had men." Despite harassment by elements of Brigadier General Philip H. Sheridan's command, Falkner got his men mustered into service by August 1.

He intended to act as cavalry, not as a guerrilla force, and he wasted no time getting into action. In early August he made away with fifty-five horses from the Federals near Dyersburg, Tennessee, but lost thirty-one dead in the engagement. Two weeks later he returned to Tennessee and burned a bridge just over the line at Chewallah. On the twenty-sixth, Falkner decided on a particularly risky gamble. Stationed twenty miles away at Rienzi were three veteran regiments under the redoubtable Philip H. Sheridan. One report had it that the camp was deserted and could be destroyed quickly and easily. Falkner led his seven or eight hundred men in a thundering charge down Rienzi's main street. Sheridan was taken by surprise but quickly mustered four battalions and sent the attackers fleeing. He later reported that the debris of the rout extended for five miles. He added, "Colonel Falkner, commanding this rebel force, was so hard pushed that he separated from his command on one of the little by-paths and made his escape. He left us his hat, however, as did nearly the whole of his command. . . ."

Through the latter part of August and into early September the regiment moved about on the Tennessee line and in the northeasternmost tip of Mississippi, skirmishing twice with Federal forces and destroying railroad track to cover Major General Earl Van Dorn's retreat. The regiment's last reported combat engagement of the year 1862 came on October 26 when they drove a Federal detachment back toward Corinth. But before the month was out a crushing blow fell from another quarter.

On October 29 the secretary of war ordered the disbanding of all Partisan Ranger units. By mid-November the conscription officers were after most of Falkner's men, who fled them as well as the Federal troops also intent on keeping Falkner from reorganizing his command.

It was a bleak autumn. In early December Ulysses S. Grant took an army south into Lafayette County. He stopped in Oxford, while at the same time William Tecumseh Sherman encamped his 30,000 men at College Hill, just four miles north of Oxford. Before their departure later that month, they had left desolation behind them. Cotton gins and gristmills were burned. In College Hill some homes went up in flames. Food and livestock were confiscated; personal property was stolen and destroyed. To the pious Presbyterians of College Hill this was not just the concept of total war Sherman would later perfect in Georgia. It was cause for them to "acknowledge the hand of a sovereign God in these sore afflictions and submissively kiss the chastening rod. . . ."

By January, 1863, Congressman J. W. Clapp obtained permission for Falkner to reorganize his regiment—so long as he did not take men who had joined regular army units. At the same time Falkner began another letter-writing campaign for promotion. When General Johnston replied warmly, Falkner included a copy of Johnston's letter in an appeal to Richmond. Near the end of the appeal Falkner wrote, "All of my property has been taken by the enemy, and my family driven from home." He mentioned all of this to show, he said, "how unjustly I have been treated by my government." The conviction that he was the victim of ingratitude, injustice, even persecution, grew stronger.

He set up brigade headquarters at Coldwater, thirty-five miles due south of Memphis. When the Federals ordered a detachment out to reconnoiter on April 8, Falkner sent a battalion to meet them. Characteristically, he was unable to stay in Coldwater and wait. Before the day was over he took his regiment, the 1st Mississippi Partisan Rangers, and the rest of the brigade and rode out to join the battalion. Together they drove the outnumbered Federals to within five miles of Memphis before the action was broken off. But suddenly, after this modest triumph, Falkner and the regiment were swamped by the wash of larger events.

On the morning of April 18, Union Colonel B. H. Grierson led 1,700 troopers south out of their base camp at LaGrange, forty-five miles east of Memphis. His mission was a daring long-distance cavalry raid that would take him through Ripley, New Albany, and Pontotoc, and on south through Mississippi to Baton Rouge. Colonel George E. Bryant took his 12th Wisconsin Cavalry out to screen Grierson's movements and create a diversion in his favor. South of Hernando, about twenty-five miles due south of Memphis, Bryant's troopers met the 1st Mississippi Partisan Rangers, killing forty-two of them and capturing seventy-two more. Two companies were practically wiped out in the short fight and all their supplies lost. It is likely that Falkner was not in direct command of the regiment, but it was the beginning of the end for him all the same.

After Hernando, the regiment was splintered into small separate units, but like a stunned boxer who continues to jab out of habit, Falkner continued to urge friends to write letters on his behalf. He led one successful skirmish in late April, but he had probably ceased to lead the regiment by mid-May, and at the end of the month Brigadier General James R. Chalmers replaced him with another officer.

His troubles multiplied as he began to suffer from ill health, but his ambition still seemed unabated. In July he wrote Chalmers from Pontotoc asking that his regiment be detached from the brigade and sent to him. Chalmers did not comply. He sent orders to Falkner in August, but there is no evidence that Falkner received or executed them. Late that month he sent Chalmers his resignation but then withdrew it after receiving a petition from his officers. By September, however, this devotion to the commander was not sufficient to prevent an obvious loosening of regimental discipline and morale. Before the end of the month, it appears, Colonel Falkner had turned from the profession of arms to that of politics. There were reports that he had taken to the stump as a candidate for Congress. He was unsuccessful. On October 25 he submitted his official and this time unequivocal resignation. It would take effect, ironically enough, on the seventeenth anniversary of his resignation of his commission in the Mexican War. He was resigning, he declared, for reasons of health. The specific complaints certified in the accompanying surgeon's report were "indigestion and internal hemorrhoids." The military career of William C. Falkner was over.

Legend has it that Colonel Falkner rode with Major General Nathan Bedford Forrest. Its source may have been the exploits of a Colonel W. W. Faulkner who arrived in north Mississippi just about the time Colonel W. C. Falkner began to drift into the curious obscurity that cloaked him until the end of the war. But even though W. C. Falkner was no longer a soldier, events in those last years of the war would profoundly affect his fortunes and those of his descendants. And Falkner's name could not have been linked with a more legendary one in north Mississippi than that of Nathan Bedford Forrest. A large, towering man, Forrest was a scourge in the field and probably more feared than any Confederate save Lee himself. He might have been "underbred," as Colonel Falkner's great-grandson would call the protagonist of one of his major novels, but Forrest had the same near-mythic attributes.

Outnumbered and undersupplied, Forrest was still trying in late 1863 to do the impossible on both defense and attack as Grant and Sherman increased their pressure. Ordered to prepare an invasion of Tennessee, he slipped into that state to bolster his forces. One of the units he brought back early in the new year was Falkner's old regiment.

Forrest continued to work prodigies as spring came and melted into the grim summer of 1864. Outmaneuvering and outfighting superior forces, he provisioned and armed his often hungry and sometimes barefoot men with captured stores. One of his engagements would have unforeseen consequences. In March he moved on Fort Pillow, a small work on a high clay bluff overlooking the Mississippi River forty miles north of Memphis. Nearly half of its defenders were Negro soldiers. Forrest's men attacked and quickly won commanding positions. When the commander refused to surrender, Forrest ordered a final assault. Before the confused carnage ended, two fifths of the defenders were dead, one fifth were wounded, and most of the rest were captured. A Congressional investigation followed the disaster, and in some Northern publications Fort Pillow became "*the* 'atrocity' of the war." No reprisals were subsequently ordered, but torches that flamed in north Mississippi four months later may have been ignited on the bluffs above the river.

In June, Sherman sent out a third expedition to destroy Forrest and once again the route lay through Ripley. "At Ripley, going out," Federal Colonel DeWitt C. Thomas later testified, "a lady whom I took to be a very intelligent person, Mrs. Faulkner [*sic*], wife of Colonel Faulkner, of the rebel service, informed me, in a laughing manner, in answer to my question as to where Forrest was, that Forrest had gone away from there with two divisions to reinforce Johnston, but had returned again and that we would have plenty to do in a few days." She said Forrest had some 28,000, but the truth was that he had less than 5,000 when he battered the Federal force on the morning of June 10 at Brice's Cross Roads, twenty-odd miles southeast of Ripley. His men "were to fight for almost a year longer, but never again . . . were they to meet in open, pitched battle and to send back in complete, reeling defeat an army . . . [of] overpowering equipment, armament and numbers." Mrs. Falkner had breakfast ready when Colonel Thomas passed through Ripley on his way back. "She wanted to know if I did not find her words very nearly correct." Other Union officers later declared that Forrest had hit them with 28,000 men.

The implacable Sherman immediately ordered an investigation and a new expedition to kill Forrest and destroy his command. On June 22 Major General Andrew J. Smith set out after him with 12,000 infantry, cavalry, and artillery also ordered to devastate "the land over which he has passed or may pass. . . ."

Smith followed Sherman's directive in Ripley. All day long on July 8 troops streamed through the town, and before darkness fell they had "burned the Courthouse, the Female Academy, all the business houses, and the Methodist Church—the Church apparently because it contained a large amount of hay. They did not deliberately fire any residences, but a high wind was blowing at the time and was responsible for the loss of the Cumberland Presbyterian Church and three homes. One of the homes destroyed was that of Colonel Falkner."

Smith pushed the Confederates before him through New Albany and Pontotoc to Harrisburg, where on July 14 he bloodily repulsed them when Forrest's superior ordered an attack on what Forrest called "overwhelming numbers in an impregnable position." After the victory the cautious Smith withdrew and returned to Memphis.

On July 28 Sherman sent him out again with an army of 18,000. By August 10 he had crossed the Tallahatchie and pushed Chalmers' thin line across Hurricane Creek and six miles beyond into the town of Oxford. Smith moved in when Chalmers moved out, but when a Confederate column approached from the east he too withdrew and bivouacked to the north near the Tallahatchie. Oxford citizens who had seen the Courthouse Square filled with blue-clad troops at dark looked in disbelief at dawn to see it filled now with the horses and butternut-clad men of Forrest's division. While Smith waited for supplies, Forrest audaciously set out in a driving rain to raid Smith's base in Memphis, seventy miles to the northeast.

According to family legend, Colonel Falkner inadvertently helped to precipitate Forrest's entry into the city. Supposedly traveling with Falkner was his body servant, Nate, riding a mule laden with pots and pans. When they stopped to rest in the woods Nate dozed on the mule. A Federal patrol appeared and the mule bolted, only to snag himself and his rider in trying to jump a high barbed wire fence. The Federals caught Nate but unaccountably released him when he refused to identify himself. Then they returned quickly to Memphis believing a rebel force to be near. When Forrest learned of the encounter he "decided that he must hasten his proposed attack on Memphis even though he was not yet fully prepared."

In any event, it was not yet four o'clock in the morning when Forrest's whooping scouts galloped into the city and rode through the doors of the Gayoso Hotel into the elegant lobby in quest of two Yankee generals quartered there. Both were sleeping elsewhere that night, but one fled in his nightgown, leaving behind his uniform, which Forrest later returned to him with all due courtesy. Forrest lost 35 men before he withdrew five hours later. By then he had killed and captured a total of 400 defenders and taken 300 horses and mules. Meanwhile, the 7th Mississippi Cavalry was taking losses at Abbeville in one of the "demonstrations" Chalmers was making to keep Smith occupied. By the morning of the twenty-second, on Smith's way back to the Tallahatchie, he moved into Oxford as Chalmers moved out. By eleven, Smith had the news from Memphis. He moved out of the town that same afternoon, but first he left its citizens a reminder of the dangers of supporting Forrest. He burned the center of town and several large homes.

There was more to this than Sherman's directive and the memory of Fort Pillow. Oxford was the home of Jacob Thompson. A congressman and later Buchanan's secretary of the interior, Thompson had seceded with his home state. Supplying funds and orders from Canada for the escape of Confederate prisoners, resistance to the Federal draft, and rebellion by Copperheads and disaffected Democrats, he became something of a symbol. Whatever the causes, where "once stood a handsome little country town," wrote a correspondent of the Chicago *Times*, "now only remained the blackened skeletons of the houses, and smouldering ruins. . . ."

The agony of the war went on until the following May, but Sherman never received a dispatch telling him Forrest was dead. On May 9, 1865, "Old Bedford" made his farewell, telling his men, "You are the last of all the troops of the Confederate States Army east of the Mississippi to lay down your arms." The long retreat was over.

An intriguing question remains. What had Colonel Falkner been doing in the interval between his resignation on October 25, 1863, and the end of the war? Although Mrs. Falkner was back home in August of 1864, there would have been little opportunity there for her husband to recoup his losses through his peacetime means—even if it had been safe for him to be seen in Ripley. He could not practice law and there was no income from writing. Normal planting would scarcely have yielded more than subsistence, and certainly there was no lucrative market in slave trading or local finance. Yet in a comparatively short time after the end of the war the Falkner Farms were reestablished and their owner was making impressive benefactions to his community and region.

Family lore offers an explanation: he was running the blockade that ringed captive Memphis, that center of Union troops, munitions, offices, and hospitals. By 1864 Memphis was booming, with glittering stage entertainment and delightful varieties of imported cigars, wine, coffee, and cognac advertised in the newspapers. The need and the opportunity for contraband traffic were both present, though the dangers might be greater in the case of a former colonel of both infantry and cavalry. But there were comrades to share them, and it was generally understood in Tippah County that Falkner's one-time adjutant, J. J. Guyton, was among those who participated in these ventures. Salt and other staples made this traffic profitable, and it was thought that "they were astute and resourceful enough to make a great deal of money at it." And in the later years of the war, running the blockade was not what it had once been. In fact, in one view, "they were probably public benefactors, for quinine—without which the deaths from malaria mounted to appalling numbers—had been declared contraband of war and was one of the necessities regularly supplied by the blockade runners."

It is probable, then, that if Nate was briefly taken by a Federal patrol on that night before Forrest's dash into Memphis, he was following his master on a commercial rather than a military expedition. In any event, when the war finally dragged to an end, William Clark Falkner was apparently in better financial condition than one might have expected—in good enough shape, at any rate, to respond quickly and characteristically to postwar conditions, to proceed in a new direction and begin the climb which would take him to a modest position as one of the entrepreneurs of the Gilded Age.

6

May, 1865–December, 1885

> . . . by New Year's of '66, the gutted walls (the rain of two winters had washed them clean of the smoke and soot) of the Square had been temporarily roofed and were stores and shops and offices again, and they had begun to restore the courthouse . . . Colonel Sartoris was home now, and . . . Redmond, the town's domesticated carpetbagger, symbol of a blind rapacity almost like a biological instinct, destined to cover the South like a migration of locusts . . . and by New Year's of '76, this same Redmond with his money and Colonel Sartoris and General Compson had built a railroad from Jefferson north into Tennessee to connect with the one from Memphis to the Atlantic Ocean. . . .
>
> —*Requiem for a Nun* (237–238)

> "Stood in the do' of that sto' the day them two cyarpetbaggers brung them niggers in to vote 'em that day in '72. Stood thar in his Prince Albert coat and beaver hat, with his arms folded, when ever'body else had left . . . stood right in the middle of the do' while them two cyarpetbaggers begun backin' off with their hands in their pockets. . . ."
>
> —*Sartoris* (235)

More than a third of Mississippi's Confederate soldiers did not survive the war. Those who did came home to a devastated land. Communication and transportation systems were virtually defunct. Most of the prewar labor force roamed the country in impoverished freedom. Most families struggled with the problem of subsistence. For a fortunate few, however, progress was rapid.

With his family settled in a temporary home, Colonel William C. Falkner turned to public benefaction. He deeded a block of land to the Ripley Female Academy—one of the casualties of General A. J. Smith's visit—and probably contributed to the fund which permitted it to reopen in 1867 as Stonewall College. To celebrate the occasion he set to work on a play. According to one source, he usually did his writing at night in his office, "with his faithful body servant Nathan to whisk the flies and supply him with the bourbon whisky which he consumed in large amounts." Sometimes he would work until past midnight, "and then, to relax his mind and body for sleep, frequently bowled for half an hour or so on the alley he had set up in his front yard, with Nathan as pin boy."

He called the eight-scene work *The Lost Diamond* and helped in its staging. Starved for entertainment and proud of efforts toward recovery, the people of Ripley praised the drama extravagantly. It had a number of elements common to its sub-genre and to some of Falkner's subsequent work: worthy orphans, theft, false arrest, a duel, pairs of lovers at odds, courtroom scenes, and comic relief. No known copy of the play remains, but it is clear that its spectacles, tangled plot, comedy, and clichés all pleased the grateful audience.

There was little in the county of Tippah or the state of Mississippi as a whole that echoed the happy ending of *The Lost Diamond.* The cotton crop of 1867 had come close to total failure. It was much better the next year, but in March of 1869 Brevet Major General Adelbert Ames became commander of the 4th Military District. His administration soon included almost all the abuses most white citizens feared and also raised the dread specter of Negro insurrection. Ames dismissed any official he doubted, and appointed sheriffs, election officials, and others he considered loyal to himself. To such a Democrat as W. C. Falkner the condition of his state was appalling. There were the carpetbaggers—Northern soldiers who had come with the armies or speculators who had followed in their wake, veterans who had tried farming and, it was said, failed at that and turned to politics. There were the scalawags—Southerners who turned opportunistically on their compatriots, or Republicans and Union sympathizers who had opposed secession all along. There were the Freedmen, one of whom became the first Negro to serve in the United States Senate, occupying the seat and filling the unexpired term of Jefferson Davis.

Countermeasures were taken by force or stealth. In April of 1867 a group of young ex-Confederates met in Nashville to turn a secret but hitherto chiefly social group into a political instrument. They adopted a "Prescript" which formalized the Ku Klux Klan, elected as Grand Wizard Nathan Bedford Forrest, and gave him virtually absolute power. Uncounted warnings, intimidations, floggings, and murders were carried out by the white-hooded nightriders of the Invisible Empire before the Grand Wizard suppressed the Klan in the summer or fall of 1869.

Colonel Falkner was as prodigious a worker as ever, keeping long hours in his law office, but according to a grandson he took part in the struggle too. Determined to keep a crowd of drunken Negroes from voting, he seized the opportunity when the first to arrive passed out in front of the polling place. He quickly dashed ketchup on the supine form and was standing there, one foot on the fallen man's chest, when his companions appeared. "This is the first nigger who come to vote," the Colonel said. "Now who's going to be next?" There is no evidence to support this tale, and a gift for inventive storytelling runs in the Falkner family, but this particular deception is not inconsistent with the fertile imagination which would later produce all the deceptions and confusions of *The White Rose of Memphis.*

At this same time vigorous efforts were being made to restore the railroad networks. Reconstruction was surprisingly rapid in most cases, but the legislature of 1871 moved to speed the process further. The state would pay $4,000 per mile to any company building at least twenty-five miles of operating railroad within the state by September 1, 1872, and it would lease convicts to corporations to supply labor. It was now May, and Falkner was one of those quick to see the new opportunities.

Nine days after the law was passed, a charter for the Ripley Railroad Company was issued to W. C. Falkner, R. J. Thurmond, and thirty-four others. Ripley's citizens were enthusiastic at the prospect of their own railroad connecting the town to the Memphis & Charleston at Middleton, five miles due north beyond the Tennessee line. The right of way was apparently donated, as well as the crossties, the use of tools, and much of the labor. Falkner was one of the prime movers, and before the year was out he was elected president of the railroad.

By January, 1872, the legislature had authorized a grandiose name change: the Ripley Railroad Company had become the Ship Island, Ripley & Kentucky Railroad Company, envisioning one terminus in the southernmost part of the state and another two states away to the north—a sweep from the lower tip of Illinois to an ocean port on the Gulf of Mexico. Work was going forward as rapidly as possible. It might be a near thing, but it appeared that the road would be operational by the legislature's deadline.

The first train did steam triumphantly into Ripley, whistle shrieking, with four days to spare. "The engines were narrow-gauged, funnel-stacked wood burners," one Mississippian remembers from childhood. In Tippah County, the Ripley Railroad was soon known as "the Doodlebug line." When it came time to try to collect the state's bounty money, however, this matter of size turned out to be far from comic. The state would pay only for standard, not narrow-gauge track. With no state bounty, the $250,000 worth of bonds went into default, and the New York company which had bought them became trustee of the road.

It was fortunate for W. C. Falkner that he had other sources of income. By now his son William Henry was nineteen. He had turned into "a handsome, likeable, rather wild fellow," with expensive tastes in gambling and dangerous tastes in women. He had all his father's appetite for adventure but none of his talent for constructive achievement. Willie Medora was now sixteen. After the war Lizzie had begun bearing a second set of children whom she recorded in the big Bible her husband had given her in 1852. Like the first set, there would be four of them, and only two would survive: Effie Dun, born January 17, 1863, and Alabama Leroy, born May 7, 1874. Alabama's adoring father called her "Baby Roy," and to the servants there was no doubt that she was his favorite, "The Colonel's Baby."

W. C. Falkner's son by Holland Pearce had apparently inherited a good deal of his father's intelligence and drive, if little of his flamboyance and artistic talent. John Wesley Thompson Falkner had graduated from the University of Mississippi and had been admitted to the Mississippi bar in 1869. In September of that same year he had married Sallie Murry, a sprightly young woman one month shy of nineteen, the daughter of one of Tippah County's leading citizens, Dr. John Young Murry. J. W. T. Falkner entered the law firm of John Wesley Thompson and quickly began to build a reputation for himself as an astute counselor. Their family was not long in coming: a boy whom they named Murry Cuthbert, on August 17, 1870, and a girl, called Mary Holland, two years later on December 16, 1872.

As the firm prospered, taking in J. W. Lowery, J. W. Thompson continued to accumulate land and money. Then, on June 21, 1873, he died. J. W. T. Falkner was suddenly busier than ever, with the estate and other details to be attended to. Before too long, he would be even more so, as he once more came within the orbit of W. C. Falkner, who was about to reenter the railroad business.

By mid-1877 the resourceful R. J. Thurmond was preparing to pull off a startling coup. Before the end of the year he accomplished it: the purchase of the $250,000 worth of defaulted bonds owned by the Southern Security Company. Shortly thereafter Thurmond's controlling two thirds was reduced to one third as he sold half his holdings to W. C. Falkner. For the present they managed to get along, even though it was necessary to hire an arbitrator to come in when the two major and two minor stockholders lined up against each other.

The Colonel was not the only member of his family who needed an arbitrator. According to family legend, the Colonel sent Henry to the University of Virginia, where he preferred gambling and horseplay to studying. His career in Charlottesville ended suddenly when a student with whom he was wrestling on a balcony toppled over the railing to his death.

Back home again, Henry whiled away his time with the attractive young wife of a crippled jeweler. Up to a point the affair resembled a fabliau out of Chaucer or Boccaccio. Then the jeweler appealed to the Colonel, who obligingly again sent Henry away to school, this time in Texas. But he never enrolled. Losing his tuition money in a game, he returned to Ripley and his young sweetheart. But the lame husband had had enough. Unlike most fabliau cuckolds, he shot the seducer. Faithful to protocol, he called upon Falkner. "Colonel," he said, "I hate to have to tell you this, but I had to kill Henry." The Colonel received this news in silence, and then, according to the story, told his visitor, "That's all right. I'm afraid I would have had to do it myself anyway."

Meanwhile, the railroad was doing well, no matter what occasional disharmony grated on its executives. They were not the only railroad men, and men of the old regiment, who seemed to be prospering. John Marshall Stone had become governor. Perhaps it rankled Falkner that the man who had supplanted him as leader of his own regiment had now won the state's highest office. At the same time another former rival, General James R. Chalmers, was making his way towards a seat in Congress. Falkner may have consoled himself that no matter what their prominence in politics, neither was a novelist. His own greatest success in this role lay just ahead.

When Dick Ford lost the Ripley *Advertiser* by fire in early 1880, his friend W. C. Falkner came quickly to his aid. He lent him money and then, to help rebuild circulation, contributed serial installments of a new novel. The title came from the steamboat on which much of the action took place, *The White Rose of Memphis*, and the combination of action, suspense, romance, and mystery soon earned the paper a growing circulation. The author was a much better read and educated man than the one who had produced *The Spanish Heroine* nearly thirty years before.

Falkner used the familiar device of the frame story. Passengers attending the masquerade ball inaugurating the ship's run to New Orleans decide to remain in costume and tell stories to while away the voyage. Mary Queen of Scots presides over a court including Ingomar, Ivanhoe, Napoleon, Henry of Navarre, George III, Don Quixote, the Queen of Sheba, a young woman called Scottie, and an unidentified girl in a black domino. Falkner began with Ingomar and, abandoning the idea of multiple storytellers, allowed him to spin out his tale until the end of the book. This provided the background for the novel's other level, that of the events during the maiden voyage.

In a brief and general plot summary the 542-page novel sounds like unrewarding melodrama. Much of it certainly is, but in 1947 Van Wyck Brooks would add the historian's assent to the reviewers'. He saw the combination of courtly masquerade and violent reality behind it as a kind of paradigm of Southern society. But the book is interesting for more than its view of aspects of the times; the style tells the reader much about the Colonel's abilities and limitations, and the content reveals the borrowing from his own life which went into the novel.

The novel was, finally, a strange and fascinating combination of inner and outer worlds. The scenes of courtroom injustice, the plight of the poor, the shootings and stabbings, the pickpockets, detectives, and gambling hells —all these might seem heightened if not overdrawn, but they had their bases in a reality which Falkner knew well. At the same time, his work had an overwrought, at times hallucinatory quality that could not be ascribed just to the genre. It was as if Falkner's imagination and pen worked only at one setting, only at the highest intensity whether the situation was one of danger or repose, whether the emotion was pain, fear, rage, or love. But almost every chapter displayed the man's catholicity of interest: a concern with the practice of medicine, with homicide by poison, with psychosomatic ailments such as brain fever and heartbreak, and with supernatural phenomena.

The first installment had appeared in the *Advertiser* in August of 1880.

The local reaction and the popularity it gained in Memphis must have convinced Falkner that it would be worthwhile to gamble on a wider circulation. He arranged with a New York publisher to bring out the novel in book form. It went on sale in June, 1881, and inside a month the 8,000-copy printing was gone. In December the *Advertiser* informed its readers that total sales had now reached 10,000 copies. The Colonel's gamble had paid off, as it would continue to do.

While the serial ran there had been good reason for the author to turn his thoughts periodically from his steamboat to the railroad. One day in early 1881 Captain W. H. Hardy traced a line on the map of Mississippi before him. He was in a place he later named Hattiesburg, sixty miles north of the Gulf Coast, and he was envisioning a line which would stretch his New Orleans & North Eastern Railroad (he was vice-president) north through the center of the state. There it could link up with the Ship Island, Ripley & Kentucky. Hardy broached the idea and Falkner fell in with it. In February, 1882, they obtained from the legislature a new charter for the old Gulf & Ship Island Railroad. As president and vice-president, respectively, they were ready to work toward their dream.

Falkner had no sooner put aside his pen than he took it up again to begin another novel. It was published in July under the title *The Little Brick Church.* Though it never enjoyed its predecessor's success, it employed many of the same elements. Part of the action took place on a Hudson River excursion boat, the first narrator gave way to a second, and there were two time-levels, that of the present—1850—and that of the period of the Revolutionary War. There were bouts of brain fever, involuntary confinement, warfare, and fatal misunderstanding before the heroine drowned and the hero died of a broken heart. The two lovers were then buried in a single coffin in the Little Brick Church. This novel suffered from many of the faults of *The White Rose of Memphis*, without that work's compensating vitality and ingenuity.

As he moved into his late fifties, the Colonel found his life busier than ever. That summer he had greeted a new grandchild. On July 29, 1882, the Ripley *Sentinel* reported that J. W. T. Falkner, Jr., "arrived in town Tuesday night, a fine bouncing, handsome fellow weighing 10½ pounds. His father says he can beat any boy in town playing 'bawl' and will make a most excellent 'catch.' " Delegating responsibility and gradually doing less of the work of the law firm, the Colonel had formed a partnership in the lumber business: Falkner, Thurmond & Co. He was also secretary of the Democratic Executive Committee of Tippah County. He had taken a law partner, C. J. Frederick, and that fall they would take the stump against General Chalmers (running for Congress as a Republican) and another opponent contemptuously referred to as "his man Wimberly."

Early in 1883 Falkner began planning a European trip for himself and Effie, his fourteen-year-old daughter whom everyone called "Steffie." The columns of *The Southern Sentinel* covered their preparations, and when Falkner sent back from New York the comments he had recorded in a notebook—he had seen castles and palaces, mountains and volcanoes—the editor published them. Characteristically, the Colonel had no intention that this should be the end of his travel sketches. In late March of 1884 he left for Philadelphia to spend two weeks seeing the book through the press. On May 10 the *Sentinel* reported that he was there again. When J. B. Lippincott brought the book out under the title *Rapid Ramblings in Europe*, Falkner even worked on marketing it locally. The book must have appealed to many readers in Tippah and other counties like it, bringing into the rural environment of north Mississippi the exotic and the faraway. By now he had developed a prose style that was usually clear and often forceful, more

Colonel William C. Falkner's residence, Ripley, Mississippi.

accomplished at dialogue and dialect as well as exposition and narration.

He continued active in politics. Though the suggestion that he run for Congress against Chalmers bore no fruit, he was sent to the Democratic National Convention in Chicago in July as a delegate for the 2nd District. Falkner knew that none of these activities was wasted effort. Political contacts rarely encumbered a businessman, and one who had to deal periodically with the legislature could use all he could get.

The Colonel had been fascinated with European architecture in cathedrals and in larger private homes. He waited and thought, and then he acted. Half a dozen of Ripley's carpenters and decorators swarmed over his clapboard house with their Negro helpers. As the town watched, it swelled, bulged, and proliferated into a three-story structure, Italianate yet hybrid, spacious inside and grotesque outside. In early May the *Advertiser* proudly reprinted a letter to the editor of the Jackson *Clarion* which set forth the progress the writer had seen in Ripley. He noted that Colonel Falkner "has built a residence that is quite palatial in style and proportions. Bel Haven excepted, there is no residence at the state capital that can compare with it." He added, almost as an afterthought, that Captain R. J. Thurmond had also "greatly improved his residence and grounds."

One development of late 1885 cannot have pleased Falkner greatly. In early December J. W. T. Falkner and Sallie Murry, with their three children, moved permanently to Oxford, forty miles to the southeast in Lafayette County. Roads were still abominable, and a journey of that length could be an exhausting one. But his own Steffie and Baby Roy were still at home, and families visited each other a great deal. The Colonel's grandchildren would surely be back to Ripley often to see him. And with the law practice and lumber company, and gristmill and farms and real estate, he did not lack for activity to fill his days. Besides, there was still the railroad. Soon would begin his final efforts to push his dream through to realization.

7

January, 1886–February, 1890

"I have not needed you in my affairs so far, but from now on I shall. I have accomplished the active portion of my aims in which you could not have helped me; I acted as the land and the time demanded and you were too young for that, I wished to shield you. But now the land and the time too are changing; what will follow will be a matter of consolidation, of pettifogging and doubtless chicanery in which I would be a babe in arms but in which you, trained in the law, can hold your own—our own. Yes, I have accomplished my aim, and now I shall do a little moral housecleaning. I am tired of killing men, no matter what the necessity nor the end. Tomorrow, when I go to town and meet Ben Redmond, I shall be unarmed."

—*The Unvanquished* (266)

With the beginning of the year 1886 Falkner turned all his energies to the task of extending his end of the Gulf & Ship Island Railroad toward Hardy's end of the line in south Mississippi. One problem was acquiring land; another was acquiring control of the company. Falkner moved directly toward both objectives.

On April 3, 1886, the Ripley *Advertiser* reported that Colonel W. C. Falkner had bought Captain R. J. Thurmond's interest in the Ship Island, Ripley & Kentucky Railroad, and now owned two-thirds control of the company. The belief in Ripley was that they had drawn lots, with the loser to set a price on his $83,000 worth of first mortgage bonds. Thurmond lost and set a price of $19,000—in gold. Legend has it that Colonel Falkner immediately left for Memphis to raise what he could there. Meanwhile, J. W. T. Falkner scoured the county, appealing to the Colonel's old comrades of the 2nd Mississippi and the Partisan Rangers, and finally amassing—from bank vaults and mattresses and socks and chimney bricks—the rest of the money. Whatever the methods actually were, they obtained the money and the Colonel bought out the partner who by now hated him.

At last it was an actuality. The narrow-gauge northern division of the Gulf & Ship Island Railroad was stretching southward from Ripley toward Pontotoc, thirty-seven miles away. The surveyors had marked the way south, and enough money had been raised to start grading the land, laying the ties, and spiking down the rails. Colonel Falkner was able to lease all the convict labor he could afford. The charge was fifty dollars per man per year plus the expense of feeding, housing, and clothing him. There was, of course, an additional expense: guards, for the state stipulated that "the company was obligated to return the men dead or alive. . . ."

By May, track was being laid, and Falkner was busy negotiating portions of the route. By October, the line had gone five miles beyond Blue Mountain to Cotton Plant, though there would be a considerable delay when it hit the Tallahatchie River ten miles further south at New Albany. But river water would be only one of the troubles that Falkner would have to face in getting the railroad through to Pontotoc. When the Colonel visited J. W. T. Falkner in Oxford in May of 1887, the *Eagle* commented that he was "as active and vigorous as his son, and this is saying a great deal." He was traveling extensively. In June, on his way back from New York, he stopped to see Grover Cleveland in Washington, the *Advertiser* reported, where he "had the honor of being introduced to the President and of giving him a handshaking."

A very different item appeared in the same newspaper three weeks later. On July 23, an article was printed citing "the disclosures of outrages committed upon convicts in Georgia and Mississippi, and the horrible barbarities practiced under this system. . . ." Two weeks later Captain Hardy replied, but his rebuttal scarcely tallied with an account of an incident at Grace's Crossing, a few miles north of New Albany. One of the leased convicts was a Frenchman, supposedly unable to defend himself through lack of English and unjustly convicted and imprisoned. Learning one day that his wife was desperately ill at home, he tried to escape, only to be shot and killed by a guard. He was buried a few feet from the railroad track. His grave, fenced in by white pickets and tended by railroad men, was for years a reminder of the system of leasing men like animals. If Falkner was a benefactor, he was also a railroad builder who was accused of coercing towns into contributions so he would not by-pass them and of helping to perpetuate slavery long after the Emancipation Proclamation.

Tracks were laid into the Pontotoc depot before the end of 1887, but early in the new year the railroad was in financial trouble. Falkner's solution was to bring suit—as an unpaid bondholder—and throw it into bankruptcy. Then, when the railroad was put up for auction he would buy it back. Now he had a further plan—to merge it with another line and expand both into a new company, the Gulf & Chicago Railroad.

By early May of 1888 a passenger could board the train in Middleton, Tennessee, at 7:45 A.M. and arrive in New Albany, nearly forty-five miles away, at 11:10 A.M. By early July Pontotoc was humming with preparations for the great event to be celebrated on Independence Day. That morning at ten o'clock the waiting crowd heard the first blasts of the distant whistle and then broke into cheers as the bunting-draped locomotive chugged into sight, pulling cars carrying hundreds of waving excursionists. Soon Colonel Falkner mounted the speaker's platform and delivered one of his much-enjoyed eloquent addresses, which was followed by congratulatory speeches. Then Miss Effie Falkner drove in the ceremonial silver spike, "after which the procession, headed by the band, marched to the grove under the soul-stirring tune of 'Dixie' where a sumptuous repast was waiting." The Colonel had built his railroad.

It must have pleased him to hear the conductor sing out, "All aboard for Walnut, Tiplersville, Falkner, Ripley, Blue Mountain, Guyton, Cotton Plant, New Albany, Ingomar, Cherry Creek, and Pontotoc!" And some of the names—Falkner, Guyton, Ingomar—must have sounded particularly sweet to him. "The people could call the towns whatever they wanted," his great-grandson remarked fifty years later, "but, by God, he would name the depots." Now a passenger could get on his railroad and make the sixty-three-mile journey from Middleton to Pontotoc in five hours and five minutes—not bad for the Doodlebug line.

By fall the line was doing "an immense business" which warranted the running of two trains daily. One of the engines was named *The General M. P. Lowrey,* the other, *The Colonel W. C. Falkner.* That September, Baby Roy had taken the train to Pontotoc to attend the Chickasaw Female College there. Willie Medora had married Nathaniel G. Carter, a Ripley doctor, and on November 22 Steffie was married in her parents' "Italian villa" to Ed Campbell, a solid young man in the furniture business in Memphis. All the Colonel's chicks had left the nest. Lizzie was often ailing now. The Colonel spent even more of his time on the railroad—and politics.

Since the Mississippi Democrats had wrested control from the Radical Republicans in 1876, two related struggles had been taking place. Within the Democratic party, the "black" or Delta counties on the river—politically dominated by the big planters and their allies—strove to retain control against other sections such as the predominantly white hill counties to the east. Cutting across party lines, the farmers were trying to mobilize against the corporations, including the banks and the "middlemen" but especially the railroads.

On April 4, 1889, Pink Smith had published an editorial in *The Southern Sentinel* announcing that "Col. Falkner asks the Democracy of the county to endorse him as their representative in the next Legislature." Smith endorsed the candidate who had "done more for the poor of Tippah County than, perhaps, any other man within its borders." This candidacy was apparently greeted with some skepticism, for two weeks later Falkner sent the paper a letter declaring, "Persons unfriendly to me have circulated a report that my object in running for the Legislature is to enable me to secure favorable legislation for the railroad. This is unjust, false and slanderous." He pledged himself to look after the farmers' interests, but if the Farmers' Alliance distrusted him, they need only unite behind another candidate and Falkner would leave the field and give him his support.

The Alliance either decided to trust Falkner or could not agree on another candidate, and in May he went to New York. There he persuaded a powerful investor, Christopher C. Baldwin, to back him in his purchase of the two railroads and the formation of the new Gulf & Chicago Line. Writing a letter home to the *Sentinel*, he asked that his name be withdrawn because the press of business would prevent him from making a proper campaign. But friends begged the editor to delay its publication. When he returned during the first week in June, their strong urging prompted another public letter: "I have resolved to continue in the field as a candidate," he declared.

In July and August he was too busy buying railroads to campaign. At foreclosure sales he acquired the Ship Island, Ripley & Kentucky and then the Gulf & Ship Island. He went back to New York in August to push on with the merger of the newly purchased railroads. One of his bitter opponents at home was Richard J. Thurmond, who, characteristically, did not seek the limelight by running for office, but threw his influence against Falkner. It accomplished little. Still in New York when the polls opened on primary day, Colonel W. C. Falkner overwhelmingly won the nomination to the Mississippi legislature, polling four hundred votes more than the total cast for his three opponents.

On one of his trips to New York, possibly this last one, Falkner walked down to the Mora studio on lower Broadway to sit for a striking photographic portrait. If some kind of memorial impulse did not lie behind this portrait, it did behind a commission the Colonel had given for an eight-foot statue of himself carved from Carrara marble. By the time it reached Ripley it had cost $2,022, but it was ready for whatever purpose Colonel Falkner had in mind.

On Friday, October 25, Falkner went to see his friend, neighbor, and attorney, Captain Thomas Spight. Falkner said that he knew Dick Thurmond was planning to kill him. What he wanted now was to be sure that his affairs were in order. Spight told Falkner that he should carry a pistol. No, Falkner said, he wouldn't do that. He had killed enough men already, and he was not going to shed any more blood. Spight turned to the desk, pulled out the long sheets of legal paper, and began to draw up the Last Will and Testament of Colonel William Clark Falkner.

Richard Jackson Thurmond and William Clark Falkner were superficially alike and fundamentally opposite. Both men prospered and both fathered sons who became lawyers. But whereas Falkner was open, flamboyant, and inclined to arrogance, Thurmond was silent and remote. Falkner had been a public benefactor in Tippah County, a role he loved. One relative called Dick Thurmond "a dignified and peace-loving gentleman," but to another he was "hard as flint and entirely selfish. . . ."

It seems that there had been open clashes between the two. One Rippleyan claimed that more than words were exchanged. Falkner walked up to Thurmond in the Courthouse, he said, planted himself before him, stuck his thumbs into his vest, and announced, "Here I am, Dick, what do you want of me?" Thurmond's reply was to knock him down, and though the bystanders intervened as Falkner charged back up at him, Falkner continued to berate Thurmond for cheating him in deals they had engaged in.

Peacemaking was tried without effect by Thurmond's son Charles and Dr. John Y. Murry, who was brother-in-law to Thurmond and father-in-law to J. W. T. Falkner. By the afternoon of November 5, when it was probably clear that Falkner had won his seat in the legislature by an overwhelming majority, it must also have been clear to Thurmond that if Falkner had heretofore made life in Ripley difficult for him, he would now make it impossible.

A little after four o'clock Falkner left his office and strolled on down toward the Square. He crossed Spring Street and stopped just opposite the west door of the Courthouse to talk with a friend, Thomas Rucker. They were standing before the building that housed Thurmond's office. By now it was four-thirty. Suddenly Thurmond was there beside them, and Falkner turned to see a .44 pistol pointed at his head. "Dick, what are you doing?" he said. "Don't shoot!" But the pistol roared and Falkner fell, his pipe clattering on the pavement. He looked up at Thurmond. "Why did you do it, Dick?" he asked. Then he lost consciousness. Willie Medora and Nat Carter were among the first to reach him. Dr. Carter wiped the blood from Falkner's face and swiftly gave orders. The injured man was placed on a wire mattress and carried three blocks back up Main Street to Carter's house. Behind them in the Square, the sheriff swiftly bundled Thurmond off to jail.

Nat Carter wiped off the blood again and began a thorough examination. He found that the bullet had hit the Colonel in the mouth. It had knocked out teeth and broken his jawbone as it passed beside his tongue and embedded itself in the right side of his neck under the ear. His head had also been badly bruised when he fell. Dr. Carter made his father-in-law as comfortable as he could and sent for the family. Lizzie Falkner and Steffie and Ed Campbell were to bring a specialist from Memphis, Dr. W. B. Rogers, while J. W. T. Falkner was to come from Oxford and Baby Roy from Pontotoc. Meanwhile knots of people gathered: friends standing outside the Carter house, gossipers on the Square, and hired guards outside the jail where Thurmond was being held without bond.

As dark fell, and Willie Medora sat anxiously by her father's bedside, his railroad was being used by his enemies. Two of Thurmond's men, Joe Brown and Jim Harris, found a handcar and pumped the twenty miles to New Albany. It was two o'clock in the morning when they pounded on the door of Judge Zacharias M. Stephens, one of the most respected men in north Mississippi. Stephens listened sleepily to their excited recital, agreed to defend Thurmond, and went back to bed. It was a decision he would regret for the rest of his life.

Falkner had regained consciousness by the time Dr. Rogers arrived on the first train Wednesday morning. The doctor told the anxious family that the wound was not necessarily fatal, but Falkner had suffered a hemorrhage and another one would kill him. There was swelling, but Rogers made no mention of an operation to extract the bullet. The wound was too deep for a probe to recover it and he must have been reluctant to go in from outside the neck for fear of striking the carotid artery.

That afternoon the Colonel seemed to be resting somewhat more easily, but Dr. Rogers must have known that he probably could not recover. The artery had already been gashed apparently, with the bullet acting as a partial plug against the blood seeping into the tissues of the neck. If the seepage continued, nothing could save him from suffocation.

J. W. T. Falkner did not arrive in Ripley until nearly nine o'clock that night. When he reached the bedside he found that his father was conscious and wanted to talk. He had made his son his executor, and he instructed him about the estate and his will. By now they were almost all there: Baby Roy and her mother, Steffie and her husband, Willie Medora and the doctor. The Colonel remained conscious but he began to struggle for breath and his color began to change. At 10:40 that night he died.

On Friday morning Reverend W. D. Heath led the services at the Ripley Presbyterian Church "before the largest audience ever assembled there on any previous occasion." Then, under a cold November rain, the horses drew the hearse out to the cemetery. There young Willie Lowrey, the president of Blue Mountain College, led the local Masonic Lodge in burying this high-degree brother. There the metallic case was buried in the center of the Falkner plot on a gentle slope rising above the twin tracks of the railroad. Tributes to his memory followed in verse and prose, in the newspapers and in the legislature.

It was almost mid-February of the next year before the grand jury brought in an indictment, surprisingly enough, for manslaughter, rather than murder, and Thurmond was released on $10,000 bail. There followed a series of postponements, but the lawyers were anything but idle. One account of defense preparations included a card file on every citizen eligible for jury duty, so that they would know whom to challenge and whom to allow to sit. Another account has it that the defense sent men out into the county selling oil-lamp chimneys. Often invited to meals, they would turn the conversation to the forthcoming trial, and if pro-Falkner sentiments were voiced, they would remember so that they could challenge the speaker if he should be proposed as a juryman. Numerous notes which Thurmond held, it was said, were canceled.

Colonel William C. Falkner's monument, Ripley, Mississippi.

When the case went to trial on Wednesday morning, February 19, 1890, the district attorney was Thomas Spight, assisted by three others, including J. W. T. Falkner. It continued until Friday night. At noon on Saturday the jury came in with a verdict of acquittal for Thurmond. One of the few public comments, made in the Grenada *Sentinel*, labeled the trial "a mockery of justice" and implied that money had corrupted the whole process. According to one account the dead man's son intended to take vengeance himself until he was persuaded to allow the feud to end there.

By the time the monument had been put up they had all gone back home. Nat and Willie Medora were there, of course, to see it erected on the iron-fenced plot. The pediment was six feet square and about fourteen feet high—with the single word FALKNER on all four sides of it—and the eight-foot statue rising above it. The figure was relaxed yet commanding—the right arm extended forward from the elbow, and the left-hand fingers, maimed in the Mexican War, inserted into a pocket of the waistcoat spanned by a heavy watch chain. Behind the figure, merging into the long coat, was a stack of books. The Colonel's great-grandson would write of Colonel Sartoris' effigy:

> He stood on a stone pedestal, in his frock coat and bareheaded, one leg slightly advanced and one hand resting lightly on the stone pylon beside him. His head was lifted a little in that gesture of haughty pride which repeated itself generation after generation with a fateful fidelity, his back to the world and his carven eyes gazing out across the valley where his railroad ran, and the blue changeless hills beyond, and beyond that, the ramparts of infinity itself.

8

February, 1890-Early 1897

"Maybe you're right, maybe there has been enough killing in your family. . . ."

—*The Unvanquished* (289)

. . . the long pull was over now; only the aging unvanquished women were unreconciled, irreconcilable, reversed and irrevocably reverted against the whole moving unanimity of panorama until, old unordered vacant pilings above a tide's flood, they themselves had an illusion of motion, facing irreconcilably backward toward the old lost battles, the old aborted cause, the old four ruined years whose very physical scars ten and twenty and twenty-five changes of season had annealed back into the earth; twenty-five and then thirty-five years; not only a century and an age, but a way of thinking died. . . .

—*Requiem for a Nun* (239)

It was a time of change. John Wesley Thompson Falkner had returned to Oxford after being talked out of shooting the acquitted Dick Thurmond, although his friends had not been able to prevent him from assaulting Joe Brown—one of those who had pumped the handcar to New Albany that night to secure Judge Stephens' services. Now the only Falkner left in Ripley was Willie Medora, for many years now a Carter.

J. W. T. Falkner had prospered in Oxford from the beginning. Then in 1886 he had been appointed Deputy United States District Attorney for the Northern District of Mississippi and in that same year he had gone into a law partnership with District Attorney Charles Bowen Howry, an eminent lawyer, former Confederate officer, and protégé of L. Q. C. Lamar.

Things were busy at home as well as at the office. There was frequent visiting—the Murrys coming from Ripley and then the Falkners returning the visit. Sallie Murry Falkner was a strong W.C.T.U. member, attending their meetings and White Ribbon receptions with the same fidelity that her husband gave to the Democratic party.

J. W. T. Falkner's staff of employees grew, both at the office and at home. "Uncle Ned" Barnett came to Oxford after the death of the Colonel, whom he always referred to as "Old Master." The Emancipation Proclamation had made no difference to Uncle Ned, who insisted that it "never took effect as far as he was concerned . . . that he never was freed because he just refused to be freed." A tall, solidly built, dark-brown man with high cheekbones and a dignified manner, he had brought with him to Oxford a trunk of clothes he had acquired from Old Master—frock coats, broadcloth suits, high-crowned hats. He would don them on Saturdays when he strolled down to the Square to socialize with his friends and on Sundays when it was time for church. He had a sense of sartorial propriety as well

The Courthouse, Oxford, Mississippi, in the 1870's.

as splendor, wearing a tie even when he milked the cow. Now he would give to "the Young Colonel"—as people were beginning to call J. W. T. Falkner—the same loyalty he had given to the Old Colonel.

Having to devote as much of his time to the railroad as he did, J. W. T. Falkner was not averse to using it for family purposes. One of the Murrys was working as mail agent in the depot at Pontotoc, a town of 535 souls. In September of 1890 Murry Falkner also was transferred there. The university had not been for him. As one of his sons put it, "the railroad was his first and lasting love. . . . They would send him to Ole Miss and the next thing they would know he would be back on the railroad. After two years of trying to keep him in classes they gave up." Beginning in 1888 he had shoveled coal as a fireman, worked his way up to the peaked cap and gauntlets of an engineer, and now was conductor of one of the trains.

The newspaper item which recorded his new job also remarked that he was a handsome young man. Like his father he was well set up, just an inch or two under six feet and close to 180 pounds. He had blue eyes, wavy light-brown hair, and a pleasant face. He was large-nosed and strong-jawed, though his features were somehow attenuated from those of his father and grandfather. But he was no weakling, and he had some of the Falkner propensity for violence.

By 1891 Murry Falkner had settled into his daily run on the Gulf & Chicago, enjoying his work and such social life as Pontotoc offered. Some evenings he would take Miss Pat Fontaine riding in his smart gig. She was a doctor's daughter, and one of her father's patients, a seamstress named Mollie Walker, had paid her bill by making some clothes for Pat. When Pat said she didn't like them, the two women quarreled.

Soon Murry Falkner was drawn into it. Pat did not want to speak to the seamstress again and asked Murry if he could help stop her malicious talk. The next afternoon, after he had finished his run from Middleton, he walked up the Square to the grocery store kept by Mollie's brother, Elias, who was better known as a professional gambler than as a grocer. Gruff by nature, Murry Falkner spoke straight out. "Tell your sister to stop making remarks about Miss Fontaine," he said. When Walker growled an unsatisfactory reply Falkner knocked him down. He came up fighting, but Falkner knocked him to the floor again and walked out of the store. He had behaved something like the heroes of the Western stories that were his favorite reading.

But the dispute did not end there. By the time Falkner returned from his run at five-thirty the next afternoon, Elias Walker had put in a full day's drinking. Falkner walked up Marion Street to the Square and turned into Thomas Herron's drugstore on the northeast corner. Just then a few children returning home late from school saw another man coming up the hill. He was carrying a shotgun.

Falkner had a headache and felt as though he might be coming down with a cold, so he asked Tom Herron to mix him a powder. A moment later the door swung open and Herron dropped to the floor. Falkner turned his head to find himself looking at the barrel of 'Lias Walker's twelve-gauge shotgun. The blast hit him in the back and knocked him off the stool. In two quick strides Walker was standing over him, a pistol in his hand.

"Don't shoot me any more," Falkner groaned, "you've already killed me."

"I want to be damned sure," Walker said, and pulled the trigger. The slug hit Falkner in the mouth, knocking out teeth, damaging his jaw, and lodging against bone near the roof of his mouth.

The wide-eyed schoolboys watched as the men carried Falkner, unconscious and bleeding, up the street to his room in Nelson's Boarding House. Though the blast had missed the spinal cord, it had gouged a hole in the small of Falkner's back the size of half a grapefruit. The pistol bullet had lodged so deep that the doctor was unable to extract it. If it were not removed, he might die choking in his own blood.

When the telegram reached J. W. T. Falkner, the last train for Pontotoc had gone, but someone found a handcar and two men pumped the thirty miles from Oxford. J. W. T. Falkner had wanted to kill Dick Thurmond for murdering his father, and now he wanted to kill 'Lias Walker for trying to murder his son. As his anger mounted he began to drink. He went looking for Walker and finally found him hiding in back of a hardware store. Falkner jammed a big Navy revolver against him but it failed to fire. When Falkner tried again it misfired six times. By now Walker had managed to pull his own pistol and shot Falkner in the hand. Then he fled, leaving Falkner there nursing his bleeding hand. "If it had hit me in the stomach it wouldn't have hurt so much," he said later.

The doctors had told Sallie Murry Falkner that they despaired of saving her son. "Can I try something?" she asked. Producing a container of asafedita she poured the brown, lumpy, liquid gum resin into his mouth. He gagged and began to vomit. Suddenly there was a clink in the basin. It was the bullet, and no hemorrhage followed.

Shortly thereafter Sallie Falkner took her angry, convalescent husband back to Oxford. A few weeks later her convalescent son was well enough to make the journey too, leaving Nelson's Boarding House for good. They returned to testify at 'Lias Walker's trial, but he was acquitted, and not long afterward Pat Fontaine moved to Texas. Murry Falkner was a strong young man with a hardy constitution, and he recovered quickly from his wounds. Soon he was back at work, his hand on the cord, running a train again for the Gulf & Chicago.

By now J. W. T. Falkner's reputation as a politician and criminal lawyer was growing. "If you want to kill somebody," Courthouse regulars said, "kill him Saturday night, call Johnnie on Sunday, and he'll get you off." He seems to have loved his legal practice, but like his father he found time to invest widely and manage numerous business affairs. Unlike him, he did not place the railroad at the center of his world. He ran it well, but as time went on he began to chafe at the increasing demands it made on him.

And there was politics. By April of 1891 J. W. T. Falkner was being mentioned as a likely candidate for the legislature. He consented to stand, and in the July primary ran first in a field of five candidates, polling 1,068 votes to the 604 of his nearest rival. In June, 1893, President Cleveland offered Howry the position of Assistant Attorney General of the United States. He accepted, and by August he was on his way to Washington. Howry kept in close touch with his former partner, helping him when he could and taking pride in his promising career. He was appointed to several offices in 1894. Then, on November 15, 1895, Governor Stone signed the certificate attesting J. W. T. Falkner's election as state senator for Lafayette County. Two months later Governor Anselm J. McLaurin appointed him a trustee of the University of Mississippi.

But Falkner had time in his life for more than business, and the whole family was active. There was an intensive round of church activities in this Methodist household, varied in summer at the Oxford Camp Ground, a few miles out of town, where religion and vacation were combined. On platforms built a few feet above the ground to discourage snakes and other unwelcome visitors, the families would erect their tents. In some cases these were more like cottages. As chairman of the committee for beautifying the Camp Ground, J. W. T. Falkner took his responsibilities seriously, exhorting others to help with the work and trying to set an example himself.

When the Camp Meeting season was over, the men would take to the woods again, as when the *Eagle* noted that J. W. T. Falkner, his son Murry, three companions, and a cook "left yesterday morning for the mouth of Tippah to give the squirrels, turkeys and fish trouble." On other occasions the men would go west to the Delta for an extended stay to hunt deer, bear, and other game. Besides the game there was the fellowship of the camp and hunt, enhanced by good whiskey. Although Oxford was not as much of a temperance town as Ripley, there was no social drinking in mixed company, and any drinking a husband did with his cronies would have to be tempered in the light of its reception at home, particularly if his spouse were an ardent temperance worker like Sallie Murry Falkner. There were times when the Young Colonel's drinking became more than social and required extreme measures.

Sallie Murry Falkner may have read Dr. Leslie E. Keeley's major work, *The Non-Heredity of Inebriety*, published in 1896, which held that drinking was a disease rather than a vice. Whether she did or not, it seems likely that she was the main force behind J. W. T. Falkner's trips to the Keeley Institute located in Memphis when he went on one of his periodic, near-legendary drinking bouts. The sufferer would be injected with the solution of double chloride of gold which, according to Dr. Keeley, produced "the sudden disrelish of the patient for his whisky." Skeptics asserted

Murry Cuthbert Falkner.

Maud Butler (l.) and Holland Falkner Wilkins, about 1888.

that relapses were frequent, though Dr. Keeley claimed that the rate was only about five percent. It was an indisputable fact that J. W. T. Falkner was among that five (or more) percent. But that did not deter his wife (or later his daughter-in-law) from seeing to it that he returned to the institute whenever he had fallen again.

The children had their own diversions. Murry Falkner sometimes visited friends in Memphis. His sister Mary Holland gave dances, and on one occasion a "Mother Hubbard Masquerade." A frequent guest of Holland's was her girlhood friend Maud Butler, the daughter of Charles Butler and Lelia Swift Butler, who was an Arkansas girl. For a time Charlie Butler was sheriff of Lafayette County, but it was said that he was one of those unfortunate men who were ruined by the war. He had tried to stay solvent, but by 1888 there were attachments and finally his estate was sold to satisfy outstanding claims. It was not too long after that that Charlie Butler disappeared, leaving his wife penniless. Another departure, it seemed, coincided with his—that of Mrs. Jacob Thompson's companion, a beautiful octoroon woman. His son, Sherwood, was old enough to be on his own, but his daughter Maud and his wife Lelia had to try to take care of each other.

Mrs. Butler had won a scholarship to study sculpture in Rome in 1890 but had declined because, she said, she had to take care of her daughter. She was always active—spending hours at her easel, fashioning dolls, sewing doll clothes. Out of kitchen soap she might carve a little boy fishing. A neighbor preparing for a party or fancy luncheon would send over a tub of butter and Lelia Butler would send it back formed into roses, swans, and lions. It was said that she was a difficult woman (and some felt some sympathy for Charlie Butler), but she was unquestionably a gifted woman, too.

Maud Butler inherited much of her mother's artistic talent, drawing and painting with charm and skill. She was a petite girl, standing just five feet tall, with small, even features and striking eyes. The fold of skin beneath the eyebrow which covered the upper lid and slanted down at the outer corner seemed somehow to emphasize the brightness of her eyes, "so dark a brown that they appeared black at times." She had a good sense of humor and a talent for making phrases. A year younger than Murry Falkner and almost a foot shorter, she called him "Buddy," as did Holland. They saw a good deal of each other—apparently more than most people knew.

Mrs. Butler shuttled about, from one relative to another, with her daughter—a graduate of the Women's College in Columbus—supporting them both. For a time they went to Texarkana, where Maud had a job as a secretary. In the late spring of 1896 they returned to Mississippi, where Maud had been invited to spend some time with Holland Falkner and her family. During part of that summer Murry Falkner was handling business for his father, who was off settling Indian depredation claims. But there was still time for him to see his sister's guest often. When summer ended she stayed on in Oxford.

That fall Murry was promoted in the family business. On September 28 he left Oxford for New Albany to take up his duties there as general passenger agent of the Gulf & Chicago. It was a full month before he could get away for a visit at home. He stretched out the visit for better than a week, seeing as much of Maud Butler as he could. "One Sunday afternoon," recalls a relative, "she and Murry took a walk (or a ride) and returned to announce they were married—to the delight of all the Falkners." It was November 7. They had slipped off to the parsonage of Reverend J. W. Dorman, the Methodist minister.

The newlyweds left for New Albany the next morning. It was a busy time for them but they managed to visit relatives at Ripley and Oxford. Then, early in 1897, Maud Falkner was able to tell her relatives that by late summer or early fall there would be three Falkners in New Albany.

BOOK TWO
Childhood and Youth

1897-1918

William Cuthbert Falkner. Top, aged three months and eleven days. Center, aged eleven months. Bottom, aged three years.

9

Summer, 1897–September, 1902

> So there were railroads in the land now; now couples who had used to go overland by carriage to the River landings and the steamboats for the traditional New Orleans honeymoon, could take the train from almost anywhere. And presently pullmans too, all the way from Chicago and the Northern cities where the cash, the money was, so that the rich Northerners could come down in comfort and open the land indeed. . . .
>
> —"Mississippi" (20)

Although some Oxonians were condescending toward New Albany—in 1890 Oxford could boast a population of 1,546 to New Albany's 548—the newer town was also a county seat with its own courthouse where the official business of twenty-year-old Union County was transacted. New Albany was the midpoint of the Gulf & Chicago's southern half, lying almost equidistant from Ripley to the north and Pontotoc at the southern terminus. The tracks of the railroad intersected Main Street and ran north and south through the town. Murry Falkner rented a house a quarter of a mile northeast of the center of town. It was located three blocks east of his railroad and one block north of Nathan Bedford Forrest's St. Louis–San Francisco Railroad, which ran east-west through the town.

It was a plain but roomy house, a one-story clapboard structure with a large attic set on a spacious lot occupying the southwest corner at the intersection of Cleveland and Jefferson streets. There was an ample porch running halfway across the front of the house, and there were large wide windows looking out over the lawn and shrubbery to the unpaved, tree-lined streets.

Like most women in her circumstances, Maud Falkner certainly had help—a cook, surely, and perhaps another servant for chores of various kinds. And Lelia Butler must have spent much of that first year in her daughter's new home, particularly as the summer wore on and her pregnancy advanced. It was apparently an uneventful pregnancy, so much so that Murry Falkner felt free—especially since his mother-in-law was there at home—to spend a few days in Oxford with his parents in early September. He was back in New Albany well before his wife went into labor on September 25. It is unlikely that he was able to transact much business for the Gulf & Chicago that Saturday, knowing that his first child would probably arrive before the day was over. But it was eleven o'clock that night before the doctor emerged from Maud Falkner's room to tell her waiting husband that he was the father of a boy.

Sallie Murry and J. W. T. Falkner lost no time in coming to New Albany to see their first grandchild. He was small and already inclined to be colicky, a baby who would keep his mother up nearly every night for the first year of his life. He was very fair, and as the color of his eyes began to change, they could see that they were not the Falkner light blue but the dark brown-black of the Butlers. They talked of the baby's christening, and with his wife's consent, Murry asked his father to name him. J. W. T. Falkner thought he should be called William. "I'd like to name him for Father," he told his son, "but Father hated 'Clark.' " He thought a minute, then he said, "We'll make it William C., but Cuthbert, for you." And so the Methodist minister baptized Maud and Murry Falkner's first child with the name William Cuthbert Falkner.

In spite of the colic, Billy Falkner thrived. When he was three months and eleven days old his mother had his photograph taken. It showed him dressed in layers of elaborate white hand-stitched baby clothes—a small child with very little hair, gazing at the camera lens with a wide-eyed solemn look. Seven and a half months later there was another set of pictures. Although the little-boy features now gave promise of the generous Falkner nose, the rest seemed to be all Maud Butler. The hair was still wispy but very blond. The mouth was small and thin and the eyes were bright and hooded like his mother's. He wore a white pleated gown which buttoned tight at the neck and stopped just below the knees to reveal black stockings and high-button patent leather shoes. In one of the pictures he was posed on the arm of a rattan chair, balancing himself casually and smiling an elfin smile.

In April, 1898, Murry Falkner had managed a visit to Oxford and in June and July he returned again, taking Maud with him. There was much to get caught up on. Sallie Murry had been involved with the Women's Book Club, which she entertained frequently, as well as her church and temperance activities. Murry's brother, John, had entered the law school at the university and had won a prize for his first year's work. Holland Falkner, Maud's girl friend, had married a local boy named James Porter Wilkins and gone off on a trip to San Francisco—a wedding present from the Falkners. James Wilkins was intent on studying medicine. When he found that the medical school in Oakland stayed in session for the whole year, he and his bride settled down for a year of study—another gift from J. W. T. Falkner. Mr. Bem Price, a family friend, cashier of the Bank of Oxford and wealthy investor and trader, had bought fifty-acre "Edgecomb" on North Street at a cost of $30,000. The *Eagle* had noted that when extensive landscaping and planting were completed it would be "the pride of north Mississippi." There were other reasons for civic pride, among them a possible contract for electric lights on the city's streets. There were threatening reports, however, of the rising toll from the annual summer terror, yellow fever, and before July was over Murry and Maud Falkner returned to New Albany. A month later Sallie Murry and J. W. T. Falkner joined them there, as Oxford was evacuated by its white residents. The *Eagle* suspended publication for more than two months. By the time it reappeared, twelve persons in the town had died of yellow fever.

Murry was gradually moving beyond his job as passenger agent at Ripley into different phases of operations as his father spent more and more time on his other pursuits. For one thing, his duties at Jackson in the legislature occupied him a good deal. They had also brought him some public notice. One of his speeches in particular had been noted in the papers: "a strong and eloquent speech in the Senate . . . in favor of employing convicts on the levees in cases of emergencies."

In a directive signed by J. W. T. Falkner, as president of the Gulf & Chicago, at Ripley on November 7, Murry C. Falkner was appointed auditor and treasurer of the road and would "also have charge of the Traffic and Freight Claim Departments of the Road effective this date." It was mid-December before the *Eagle* got around to reporting Murry Falkner's promotion, but when it did, it was with the notation that he would "move in a short time from New Albany to Ripley." After a lapse of nine years, there would once again be a male Falkner in Ripley.

When Maud Falkner moved from New Albany to her new home two doors from the John Y. Murrys on Quality Ridge in Ripley, she knew that in six months or so she would have another child. In early May, 1899, Lelia Butler, whom Billy called "Damuddy," arrived in Ripley to be with her daughter. In the hot early summer the baby came—"a sprightly, black-haired, black-eyed boy." It was June 26. He was called Murry C. Falkner, Jr., even though his name was not identical with his father's. Cuthbert had already been used as the middle name for his older brother; the middle initial in Murry's name stood for Charles, after his mother's brother, Dr. Charlie Murry. A photograph made on the porch of their new home in Ripley that fall showed the baby held by his mother and dressed in the same kind of voluminous swaddling clothes his brother had worn for his photograph at about the same age. Murry—soon to be called Jack—had the brown Butler eyes and the same fair coloring as his brother. But his face favored the Falkners. Standing beside his mother's rocking chair and looking at his new brother was Billy, wearing an outfit that looked identical with the one in his own photograph at age eleven months.

Jack's infancy proved no easier for Maud Falkner than Billy's had. He didn't have colic, but he was a puny baby who had to be coaxed to eat. It was a trait which lasted even past infancy. As his younger brother remembered it, as much as five years later Jack "simply wouldn't eat. The only things he would stomach were buttered biscuits and sausage and fried eggs. Any time he would eat, feeding him became the first order of business. Damuddy took Jack on as her problem. She called him Little Brother."

Once more Sallie Murry and J. W. T. Falkner made the trip to see a new grandchild. They had greeted another baby of this new generation two weeks earlier in Oxford when Holland Wilkins had given birth on June 14 to a little girl, with the clear blue Falkner eyes, whom they named Sallie Murry. The fourth week in October, however, they were back in Ripley, called there "by the illness of their little grandson, Willie Falkner." What sort of illness the two-year-old boy suffered from was not specified, but there was no further mention of it, and his fond grandparents were free to return to Oxford, where J. W. T. Falkner was engaged in further activities and projects.

He had accepted appointment as county attorney for Lafayette County and had also agreed to stand for reelection to the state senate. At the same time he was vitally interested in city affairs, and thus functioned on three levels. (An urgent concern was the sewage system, finally under construction after having been voted down two years previously, along with electric lights.) And perhaps he was thinking of his position in life as his father had done some years before in Ripley. He had bought the Smither homestead and a full block of land on South Street (running like North Street into the Square to form the town's major axis) and planned to "have the old building removed and a handsome residence erected." He must have felt the appropriateness of this step even more when on November 20 Governor Anselm J. McLaurin signed the large, beribboned document signifying that John Wesley Thompson Falkner would again be senator for the 32nd Senatorial District of the State of Mississippi. Six weeks later, on New Year's Day, 1900, they moved into "The Big Place," as their children and grandchildren would call it. Living with them were their six-month-old granddaughter, Sallie Murry Wilkins, and her mother and father, the latter now a doctor after a year's study in Memphis financed by his father-in-law.

In the first year of the new century, life apparently went on much in the usual manner for the Falkners in Ripley and Oxford. Murry was busy with the railroad and Maud was occupied with her two children. In February her mother spent some time in Ripley, and in mid-March Maud and her husband "and two bright little sons, Willie and Murry, Jr.," went to stay with the elder Falkners in the fine new home on South Street. Murry Falkner was not doing badly himself. In addition to the railroad he had several other interests. He had bought into the Ripley Drug Company and he owned a farm west of town on which he was cutting wood and spoke timber. He was also raising bird dogs. Like horses, they were one of his passions. Even railroads affairs were put aside in late January of 1901 when he traveled to Grand Junction, Tennessee, to attend the field trials which would determine the national bird dog champion. For Murry Falkner this was sheer pleasure.

The pattern of family visits from Ripley to Oxford continued with some regularity. Early that year, however, Maud Falkner found that she was pregnant again, and with spring she began to limit her traveling. She was having a somewhat more difficult time than she had had before. In June she was ill, and Lelia Butler arrived a bit earlier than she had with the coming of the other two children. This did not mean that Maud's oldest boy could not still visit his relatives. He remembered one occasion, at about age three, when he went to spend the night with his aunt Willie Medora and her daughters, Vance and Natalie, in Ripley. But the visit was cut short. "I was suddenly taken with one of those spells of loneliness and nameless sorrow that children suffer, for what or because of what they do not know. And Vannye and Natalie brought me home, with a kerosene lamp. I remember how Vannye's hair looked in the light—like honey. Vannye was impersonal; quite aloof: she was holding the lamp. Natalie was quick and dark. She was touching me. She must have carried me."

On September 24, 1901, one day before Willie Falkner's fourth birthday, his brother John Wesley Thompson Falkner, III, was born. Sallie Murry and J. W. T. Falkner were there for the arrival of this baby, who would prove as an infant to be the most robust of all Maud Falkner's children. But this did not mean that she was to have an easy time, for there were unlooked-for troubles. The grandparents had returned home on Saturday, September 28, but Sallie Murry had scarcely unpacked before she was on her way back to Ripley the following Monday after receiving the news, said the *Eagle*, of "the serious illness of her little grandson, Willie Falkner, of scarlet fever." Before the crisis had come and passed they nearly lost him and his brother Murry as well. It was two weeks before the little four-year-old had recovered sufficiently for Sallie Murry to return home once more. "M. C. Falkner's children are much better," the editor of the *Sentinel* assured his readers. "He has hired a trained nurse to care for them." A month later Willie's grandfather gave him a present to celebrate his recovery: the best-looking Shetland pony he could find. Down by the depot in his saddlery shop, Mr. Cheek worked to finish a handmade saddle. Finally it arrived, with a hand-carved tree and shining leather stitched with special thread. By December everyone was well enough to pay a visit to Grandmother and Grandfather at The Big Place on South Street.

If J. W. T. Falkner talked business with his son during that visit, it is doubtful that the younger man liked what he heard. The demands of the law practice were still heavy, and besides this, the father was exploring other investments which in the next year would lead to the purchase of four buildings and his founding of a new telephone company. There had been reports just before Colonel Falkner's death that he had planned to sell the railroad. Nothing had come of it, but it seems clear that his son must now have been contemplating such a step after serving for a dozen years as a conscientious head of the company. He had scrupulously followed the policies of the Old Colonel. Debts were incurred only for periods of thirty days or less, and no bonds were floated. The line claimed two distinctions, a later historian said: "First, it had no bonded debt and no mortgage on the company; second, it was the only inter-state railroad to have a record of being sued in the courts for personal damages sustained to a passenger from a head-on collision between two hand cars." In spite of this litigation public relations were said to be good, for, the historian added, "the friendship of the people along the line . . . was considered the road's biggest asset, and everything was done to be worthy of that friendship."

During the spring and summer of 1902 the frequency of family calls increased—Sallie Murry Falkner visiting her son and bringing "Master Willie Falkner" back with her, Holland and Sallie Murry Wilkins staying at the Falkners' in Ripley, Lelia Butler arriving to be with her daughter. Sallie Murry Falkner had periodically been in poor health, and in the increased frequency of her visits there may have been a kind of urgency as she perhaps felt the oncoming of what would at first be diagnosed as "stomach catarrh." In the second week of September Murry Falkner went home alone for a visit, which the *Eagle* duly noted, together with the comment that his mother had "been quite sick the past week but we are glad to learn she is improving." On this visit J. W. T. Falkner most likely talked with his son about his future. It seems clear that he had one prospect definitely in mind for him: that he should move his family to Oxford and start over in some new business.

This must have been a heartbreaking prospect for Murry Falkner. He had suffered through two years of college before he was allowed to go to work full time on the railroad. He had advanced from one job to another until he had reached a responsible position. He was thirty-two years old, with a wife and three small children to support, and now his job was being taken away from him, for apparently it was understood that the new owners would be putting in their own supervisory personnel. He was an inarticulate man who was not very adept in personal relationships. None of his virtues —courage, hard work at his chosen profession, honesty, punctuality— could serve him in this crisis. He was apparently a dutiful son, perhaps too dutiful to attempt revolt, and certainly too proud to implore.

After the visit to Oxford, Maud and Murry Falkner must have discussed their future—what alternative, if any, they had to the offer J. W. T. Falkner had probably made to back his son in any business he chose to enter in Oxford. But the silent, austere, hard-drinking, cigar-smoking railroad man seemingly had no more taste than talent for serving the public, unless it should be in a blue serge suit with a ticket punch in his hand. It is probable that this was one of the times when Murry Falkner seriously considered a career that had appealed to him since boyhood. His books showed how strong the taste was: Cooper's *The Pioneers* and *The Pathfinder*, J. B. Jones's *The Warpath*, Peter B. Kyne's *The Pride of Palomar*. It was a taste he had shown years before in the costume he had chosen to wear at the New Year's Eve party in 1888. He had always wanted to be a cowboy, but with a wife and three children he obviously could not work as a ranch hand. Somehow he would have to raise the money to finance a ranch where he could raise cattle himself. But at this point Maud Falkner put her small foot down, firmly. She would not allow him to take her and their three small children out west. Perhaps her time in Texarkana had something to do with it. Whatever it was, she was adamant. Murry Falkner never forgave her for denying him the chance to follow a career which had always fascinated him when the one he loved was taken away from him.

The final documents in the purchase of the Gulf & Chicago Railroad Company by the Mobile, Jackson & Kansas City Railroad Company were not signed until July 1, 1903. But the deal was firmly set by June 24, 1902, when the estate received $75,000 as a "cash payment for the G. & C. R. R." Murry Falkner was still auditor and treasurer of the road. It is not difficult to imagine his reaction to that payment for a railroad which by November would produce for the estate in annual earnings the sum of $34,668.75. But there was nothing he could do about it now, and very shortly new personnel were being installed at various points along the line.

On September 22, the Falkners left Ripley. Ten days later a newspaper item made the change public knowledge. It was brief: "Mr. Murry Falkner and wife and their interesting family have removed from Ripley to Oxford and occupy the residence formerly occupied by Colonel J. W. T. Falkner."

10

September, 1902-August, 1905

> There is a ridge; you drive on beyond Seminary Hill and in time you come upon it: a mild unhurried farm road presently mounting to cross the ridge and on to join the main highway leading from Jefferson to the world. And now, looking back and down, you see all Yoknapatawpha . . . . the rich alluvial river-bottom land of old Issetibbeha, the wild Chickasaw king, with his Negro slaves and his sister's son called Doom who murdered his way to the throne . . . the same fat black rich plantation earth still synonymous of the proud fading white plantation names . . . . Then the roadless, almost pathless perpendicular hill-country of McCallum and Gowrie and Frazier and Muir translated intact with their pot stills and speaking only the old Gaelic and not much of that, from Culloden to Carolina, then from Carolina to Yoknapatawpha still intact . . . and last on to where Frenchman's Bend lay beyond the Southeastern horizon, cradle of Varners and ant-heap for the northwest crawl of Snopes.
>
> —*The Town* (315–317)

"We arrived at Oxford after dark," Jack Falkner recalled later. Sallie Murry and J. W. T. Falkner were there to embrace Maud Falkner and her three little boys as the servants picked up the luggage they had carried with them on their two-day railroad trip. They were hot and cinder-stained from the journey they had made on three separate railroads while Murry was hauling their other possessions overland by wagon. Now they had reached their new home, in the center of north central Mississippi. Jack was stunned.

"We descended from the coach, and Bill and I were speechless with wonder; never had we seen so many people, so many horses and carriages, and so much movement everywhere. And the lights—arc lights! The first we had ever seen. As we drove to Grandfather's house by way of the town square we noticed the fine board sidewalks which extended the whole way. More than that, people were walking along them and it was already past nine o'clock at night. We could hardly wait to see these wonderful sights by daylight." It was September 24, the first birthday of John Wesley Thompson Falkner, III. The Falkner boys did not know what sort of sight they had missed in not arriving by daylight, nor could they have known that the city was still crowded with those who had not missed it. In early January two men had been convicted of the murder of a federal officer sent to arrest them on charges of illegal distilling. At the time the *Eagle* reported that "Upon hearing his sentence to be hung on Friday, February 14, Will Mathis requested Judge P. H. Lowrey to fix the time for his hanging at a different hour from that of the Negro, Orlando Lester, his partner in crime. Mathis stated that his reason for making this request was that he did not believe in social equality with Negroes." Judge Lowrey refused to grant the request. "But as the affair on February 14 is not to be a social function, Mr. Mathis will doubtless be excusable for temporary equality with the Negro. Since his reputation is not unblemished, this slight smear upon his social status will hardly be noticed." An appeal produced a stay of execution, but the *Eagle* for September 25 succinctly noted that the sentence had been executed: "The trap was sprung at 12:50 o'clock yesterday afternoon and the men died game for the Montgomery murder. Fully 7,000 people witnessed the public execution."

In Thursday morning's daylight the boys explored their new town. This was a much bigger place than Ripley. With just over 1,800 people it was three times as populous, and it was actually called a city. A walk of just three blocks along South Street took them up to the Square, dominated by the symmetrical brick building where the county's business was transacted. It was set in an octagonal lawn bordered by an iron picket fence. Inside stood posts with chains to which teams could be hitched. Facing the Courthouse were the rebuilt stores with balconied second-floor offices that still bore an occasional token of A. J. Smith's visit in 1864. Interspersed among them were the new buildings, such as the one which housed their

Mule auction, Courthouse Square, Oxford, Mississippi, about 1901. Center, prize jack, named Silver Streak.

grandfather's law offices at the northeast corner of the Square. The Bank of Oxford stood at the north end of the Square, the red brick post office to the east, flanked by one-story, iron-awninged Neilson's department store. Among the other business establishments there were drugstores on the south side and a hardware store to the west. There were other stores on North Street and South Street, and above them all soared the almost-new water tank. Bulbous and shining, it stood on thin guy-wired girders, capable of holding 60,000 gallons of water 140 feet in the air. Here and there oaks and elms shaded the loungers who talked or played checkers outside the Courthouse. The board walk made it possible for shoppers to complete their rounds with unmuddied shoes when it rained. In some of the occasional summer dry spells the trim buggies and slow, loaded wagons would raise clouds of dust as they circled through the unpaved Square. The four-faced Courthouse clock looked out from the Square to North Street and South Street, to the large, comfortable white clapboard houses, some of them twisted into the most fashionable Victorian shapes, with cupolas, and jig-saw trim and lightning rods. Others were simple and straight, and for this part of the country, quite old. The Isom place had been built in 1835 with slave and Indian labor for Dr. T. D. Isom (dead now only four months), one of the earliest settlers. The Wendel House on Depot Street, just off the Square, had been built by Thomas Wendel in 1848 on land which had belonged, a dozen years earlier, to Ho-Kah, a Chickasaw who held her patent from the U.S. government. Three quarters of a mile southwest of the Square, Jacob Thompson had built himself a home again on the site of the twenty-room mansion that A. J. Smith's men had burned. Across the road from his land, to the west, was the Bailey place, shady and wooded, a haven for small animals that also attracted picnickers and game-playing children. The sturdy and symmetrical two-story plantation-style home was ennobled by a Greek portico and four wooden columns with a second-story balcony set between them. Built in 1844 by an English architect for Robert B. Shegog, it was similar to three or four others in the city and county. Only a few houses rose to the three-storied eminence of the home J. W. T. Falkner had built for Sallie Murry.

A little over a half-mile west of the Square the trains of the Illinois Central would signal their stops at the depot with distinctive whistles. Just across the railroad tracks, a mile west of the Courthouse, lay the campus of the University of Mississippi, with its scattering of Greek Revival and Georgian buildings, set among magnolias, dogwoods, and redbud, as well as the tall shade trees on a square mile of elevated rolling land. Beyond Oxford and the university was the county proper.

The Falkner boys' new county was almost square, roughly twenty-five miles square, with the right-hand half looking as if it had been pushed south about two miles and then reunited with the left-hand half. In the middle of that space but slightly off center to the west was the city, the railroad running between it and the university and angling off a bit to the southwest, as though it had started to bisect the county in a perfectly straight line but then had veered off a bit to its right. Meandering across the county's northern border—and forming most of it save for a few miles at the northwest tip—was the dark, slow-moving Tallahatchie River, with its black bottom land and stands of trees, its thickets and swamps. Flowing into the river in the northwest corner of the county was Toby Tubby Creek, named for the old Chickasaw chief who was a wealthy slave owner when Ishtehotopah signed the Treaty of Pontotoc. (At his death, people said, the remaining tribesmen chose a slave to be buried with him, but the white men heard of it and prevented it. They said too that sometime after Toby Tubby was buried his daughter returned to his burial mound, one of several such mounds dotted here and there in the county. But this was a special mound, not just because it was a chief's but because it might possibly contain, along with Toby Tubby's bones, some of the money the government had paid Toby Tubby under the Treaty of Pontotoc. She hired men to dig in the mound. When night came she sent them home. When they returned the next morning, the hole was deeper and she was gone.) The Tallahatchie River formed the northernmost of three irregular, roughly parallel bands running through the county. The center one was the road linking Oxford with Pontotoc on the east and Batesville in Panola County on the west. The southernmost band, about six miles south of Oxford, was the Yocona River (pronounced Yock-nee), much smaller than the Tallahatchie and bearing, on old maps, the longer name Yocanapatafa.

There were a few small settlements out in the county—College Hill, four miles northwest of Oxford; Taylor, seven miles to the southwest; and Lafayette Springs, a small modest spa near the middle of the county's eastern boundary line—but mostly the houses were scattered, some lining the gravel or clay roads, others back beyond the pastures and cotton fields, still others in the hills where only a pale plume of smoke above the pines would give evidence of life. Some were sturdy farmhouses but many were the plain, raw, unpainted cottages or dilapidated shacks of the subsistence farmers, white and black. A tall roof would shelter the single story with its tiny front porch, allowing the passer-by to look down the hall that bisected the house from front to back, with the small rooms opening off it on either side.

In Tippah the Falkner boys had lived in a county that was less than one-third Negro. In Lafayette, nearly 10,000 of the county's 22,000 inhabitants were Negroes. Directly or indirectly the livings of all of them depended upon cotton. Here the fields did not stretch away, vast and flat to the horizon, as they did in the Delta. There would be some good-sized plantations but there would also be small patches, slanting down to a ravine or stuck precariously on the side of a hill. Cotton was a crop that taxed the land, and here the thin soil—yielding far less than the rich black Delta earth, replenished annually by the overflowings of the Mississippi—was depleted further each year by this single, unrotated crop which took its minerals and nitrogen without any replacement for them. In addition, there was erosion. The gulches and bare hills the cavalry troopers had noted were still everywhere to be seen. Some of the ravines were fifty feet deep, and it would be twenty years before a reforestation program would be instituted to help this "treeless country," as one writer called it. Yet the cotton grew, and enough of it escaped the boll weevil to keep busy the big gin in town and the small ones at the crossroads which strewed the earth with cottonseed and cotton waste. For years farm experts had joined the editors of journals and newspapers in decrying abuses and suggesting remedies. "Unfortunately," wrote one, "the prospector in passing through North Mississippi on the railroad sees the worst portion and is apt to form an idea of all the lands from this uninviting view. The valleys are very fertile, and where any attempt is made to care for the uplands by preventing washing, and an occasional fertilization, they yield abundant crops. The farmers who have pursued the profitless regime of raising cotton to the neglect of all else, as yet knows [*sic*] nothing of the wonderful capabilities of Lafayette and contiguous counties. . . . but it has been left to the progressive farmer to learn what the so-called worn-out land hills can do when assisted by intelligence in the production of as fine stock and the necessary pasturage as the famous blue-grass sections of Kentucky and Tennessee." The writer went on to add, entreatingly, "Lafayette County, with its good, moral citizenship, its superior schools and farming inducements, welcomes all who are willing to help us repair the waste places and add to the material advancement. There is room for all who will come."

For the fortunate there would be occasional trips to Memphis. Unless the traveler took the train, he was in for "hard driving over treacherous gravel, dust, and sand," according to one Oxford resident. "Heavy fogs and stray cattle increase the perils of the trip, not to mention looping the loop over bridges of rough-hewn timber which cover dry creeks and sluggish streams filled with pale green algae, through which lazy turtles snap at insects, and into which Negroes place many lines attached to cane poles in the hope of enticing a sunfish for dinner. The road leads also past gum trees and undergrowth or brier and past sorghum mills which, in the autumn emit the sweet savor of the new-crushed stalk; in winter, the withered sedge and overcast skies collude to depress." Then, after the shopping or pleasure-seeking in Memphis, the traveler would return to the not unwelcome routine of Oxford.

More often than not that was where the money from the cotton crop would be spent—in Oxford. There on the Square the merchants in their stores would wait for the Saturday crowds. Outside, drawn up in a great ring around the Courthouse fence would be wagons from the country, piled high with watermelons, tomatoes, corn, or whatever happened to be in season. After shopping at the dry-goods store a woman might pay a visit to one of the drugstores or confectionaries. Her husband, meanwhile, might poke around at the hardware store, talk to some of his cronies leaning against the Courthouse, and then idle away more time in conversation while he waited his turn in the crowded barbershop on the northwest corner of the Square. If he wanted a drink, he would need to step into a secluded spot with a friend who could provide one. He might even seek out a "blind tiger" where he could get a powerful shot of colorless whiskey made from local corn. A Negro farmhand or sawmill worker might head for Freedman Town, a section comprising about seven blocks adjoining the railroad tracks northwest of the center of town. There he could find convivial companionship, food and drink, and sometimes not unanticipated violence that would require the attention, finally, of the sheriff.

By the Saturday after their arrival, the Falkners had begun to settle into their new house. People still called it "the old Johnny Brown place," after the man who had sold it to J. W. T. Falkner. It was located one block west and three blocks south of his new house on South Street. The Brown house, on Second South Street, was set on a lot that occupied its whole block. It was 400 feet wide and stretched from the street back 1,000 feet to where a wood began which extended a half-mile to the railroad. The back half of the lot was divided from the front by the same kind of crisscross panel fence which enclosed the whole property. The back half provided pasture and a barn for the stock. On the front half of the lot, set well back from the street, was the house, a big one, with a fireplace in every room but the kitchen. A plank walk ran from the street to a small brick patio where the broad front steps led to the wide porch, or gallery, which stretched across the front of the house. It looked rather ornate, with the latticework at the bottom of the porch, slim wooden supports rising to the porch roof, and the elaborate wooden trim covering the tops of the supports where they met the roof. The front door and windows were extra large, and the latter were flanked by tall shutters. The house had been painted in dark hues, which added to the impression of heaviness and solidity.

The Falkners needed the added room, for Lelia Butler had moved in to stay. Her piety continued unabated, and it may in part have been her influence which caused her son-in-law not only to abjure swearing on Sunday but to refuse also to touch a playing card on that day, even to build a card house for the children. She had brought her easel and she spent much of her time at it, but she did try to help with the children and continued to regard Jack as her special charge, preparing eggs and sausage and biscuits for him whenever he showed any inclination to eat. Damuddy found time to do things for the other children, too. She carved a nine-inch-high doll, making the feet separately and attaching them, and dressed it in a blue policeman's suit she had sewn, complete with brass buttons. She topped off the costume with a felt replica of a policeman's hat and then gave the finished product to Willie Falkner, who named him Patrick O'Leary and saved him for play in the roomy attic on rainy days.

Even though Lelia Butler could give her some assistance, Maud Falkner still needed help in taking care of her three active sons. One problem was simply keeping track of them. It was made sharply evident as one afternoon wore on toward suppertime and Willie Falkner was nowhere to be found. They looked in the back pasture, in the barn, and on the neighboring blocks with no success. Then they learned that William Hines, a playmate of the same age, had also failed to show up for his supper. By this time both mothers were nearly distraught. The fathers and friends organized a searching party which began a systematic hunt for the two little boys. Before long they found them both, asleep together in an old culvert. Maud Butler wanted help to forestall this kind of problem—and the ordinary mischief her boys were prone to—as well as to assist her and Mary, the cook, with the logistics of running a family of six, plus servants, in the year 1902. Before long she had that help.

It came in a form as diminutive as her own. Caroline Barr arrived and moved into a cabin in the backyard. Though she still called herself by the name Barr—taken from the Colonel Barr who had owned her—she had also borne the names of four different husbands. She was a neat, thin, black woman, weighing less than a hundred pounds, who had been born in slavery in the western part of the county sometime between 1840 and 1849. She did not know precisely how old she was, though she thought she had been freed at sixteen. She could not read or write, but she had a vast fund of stories about old times in the county before the War and about the lives of the county's people, black and white. She would tell, too, about the days after the War, about frightening riders in the white of the Ku Klux Klan who claimed they were dead Confederates burning in hell but riding at night for brief periods. Though she had raised children of her own who were now living in her home section, she was the kind of woman whose maternal feelings and needs never died out, and she immediately became a second mother to Bill, Jack, and Johncy Falkner. She became second only to "Mis' Maud," in domestic authority over them. The children were taught respect for her, which increased over the years. They instinctively liked her, and she had the knack for pulling them closer to her. "Mammy felt a kinship for every living thing . . . she saw day in and day out and could reckon with," Jack Falkner remembers, "humans and small animals such as dogs, cats, squirrels, and rabbits. These she knew and they were the subjects of many delightful stories that poured from her bright and active imagination."

Always neat, with her starched dress, smoothly ironed apron, and immaculate white headcloth, Callie Barr settled in quickly, often assuming daylong charge of the boys. She adjusted quickly to the personalities and relationships of the adults of the family. The head of the house she addressed as "Mist' Murry." His parents were "Mis' Sallie" and "de Kunnel." She called young William Falkner "Mimmie," adopting Johncy's approximation of his brother's name. To her charges, she was "Mammy Callie," and to some of her friends, who knew one of her particular tastes, she was "Callie Watermelon." She had a wide circle of friends and acquaintances of both races in Oxford. She might appear on the Square in animated conversation with a next-door cook, or exchanging pleasantries with a member of the town's legal fraternity. All of this radiated out from her position in the home. "Mammy was not considered a servant by the family

Caroline Barr ("Mammy Callie").

or by herself," Jack Falkner recalled. "Her small, old-fashioned rocking chair was for her alone and always beside the fireplace. There she would sit in the evenings, as much a member of the family as any of the rest of us, high-button shoes (how small they were) polished and glistening in the dancing glow of the flames in the open grate, her box of snuff in place on the mantel just above her head, a good layer of it tucked beneath her lower lip and her 'snuff stick' held firmly in her mouth."

For the children the firmament of adult authority included—now more than ever—their grandfather and grandmother. As J. W. T. Falkner aged he grew more commanding and more the figure of the Southern Gentleman. He wore a large Panama hat during the hot season and sometimes dressed all in white. He would draw large cigars from the vest adorned with a heavy gold watch chain, and he swung a sturdy, gold-headed stick as he walked. Sallie Murry had not been in really good health for years, but there was nothing of the pallid invalid about her. Like her independent brother, Dr. Will Murry, she was "outspoken, utterly frank, scorning all pretense and making very plain her likes and dislikes. If you heard anything unfavorable the old lady was reported to have said of you all you had to do in order to get the truth was to ask her. You got the truth all right and if she had really said it then the truth as given to you about yourself was usually far more quiveringly naked than the report you had received. Withal, she was a very sweet and kindly and generous old lady with her bark far worse than her bite." She presided over The Big Place with grace and charm, entertaining often for her church groups, the book club, and the United Daughters of the Confederacy.

The Falkner boys saw much now of their aunt Holland, a trim woman, five feet two inches tall. "Huldy" was an accomplished rider and one of the first women in Oxford to wear a divided skirt. She was completely outspoken, completely fearless, and still the best friend of the honest, humorous, harried Maud Butler Falkner. To her oldest nephew, Willie, struggling with a formal term, she became "Auntee." Her whole family returned the fierce loyalty she gave to them, seeing in her "the one whose steadfast devotion never wavered, whose everlasting love never lessened, and whose pride of family was so intense that she sustained and supported the other members no matter what misfortunes they brought upon themselves. . . ." Her husband, Dr. James Porter Wilkins, was well established. He had practiced with Dr. T. D. Isom until the death of that early settler and oldest citizen. For more than a year now James Wilkins had been county health officer, knowing, however, that he was not himself a well man, and suffering increasingly from what would soon be obvious as consumption. Their daughter, Sallie Murry Wilkins, was not only cousin to the Falkner boys, she was one of their best friends. Her standing was equally high with their parents. "Huldy," Murry Falkner would say to his sister, "I'll give you any two of my boys for your girl." She was with them as much as if she had been a member of that branch of the family.

Murry Falkner was settling down to his new life and career slowly and with difficulty. Like his father, he appreciated the solace of good whiskey, and he availed himself of it in this period following his uprooting from Ripley and the railroad. Sometimes he would be unable to contain himself. He would think about the beckoning West, about prairies and cattle, and he would storm and shout. Maud Falkner would jump, but she would remain silent until her husband had stalked out or the storm had blown over. In her character she combined courage and stoicism, born in part, perhaps, of the years when she tried to support herself and her deserted mother. These qualities came through in a cardboard sign which she lettered carefully in red and hung above the stove: DON'T COMPLAIN—DON'T EXPLAIN. But it must have been comforting all the same, on those occasions when Murry Falkner would rage about the lost railroad or the unattainable ranch, to turn for the solace if not commiseration of her sister-in-law.

He was doing his best, though, to do what was expected of him and to provide for his family as a Falkner should. After the loss of the railroad his main interests seemed to be focused on horses and dogs. Fortunately, the new business in which his father set him up provided opportunity for keeping both. There had been a kind of false start when he first arrived in Oxford and the *Eagle* reported that he was "superintending the grading of North Street, making one of the most beautiful drives in town." A month later, though, in mid-November, he was able to sign his name, as manager, to an advertisement signaling a new firm in town: "The Falkner Transfer Company respectfully asks to be remembered when you have hauling to do and guarantees to please you." A week after that the public was informed that Murry Falkner had bought Mr. O. I. Grady's Livery Stable on University Street. He was back in the transportation business, hauling both passengers and goods once more.

Though this was not the career Murry Falkner would have chosen for himself, it had its pleasant side. And it was not excessively demanding. He went each day to his office at the stable, where there were "a gang of

Negroes to attend to the horses, two white men to drive the hacks, and always two to ten cronies to sit about the comfortable stove in his office and tell tall tales about animals, hunting, and fishing, applying themselves to the ever-present crock of good drinking whiskey as the mood and thirst struck them individually and collectively." It was congenial company made lively by the skill at storytelling so common in small Southern towns, and by quickness of wit in repartee.

From time to time, however, the dark side of Murry Falkner's nature broke through and erupted into violence. One such outbreak added to Oxford legend. The constable for Beat One in the county since 1895 had been a mustachioed, dark-haired man named Dick Oliver. In February of the year Murry and Maud had come to Oxford, Oliver had made the pages of the *Eagle* through some involuntary gunplay. "His pistol dropped from his pocket," the account read, "and inflicted a painful flesh wound in his thigh." One day he and Murry Falkner met in the business section of town. Words were exchanged, and Oliver used his fists. Falkner closed with him. The crowd which quickly gathered did not attempt to separate them. Both men were strong, and the struggle became a grueling fight as they forced each other back and forth. It ended suddenly with a shattering crash as Falkner knocked Oliver through the plate-glass window of John's Grocery. But there was a curious aftermath. Not only did the two men become friends, but Murry Falkner assumed a kind of responsibility for Dick Oliver, helping him from time to time for the rest of his life.

Murry Falkner could not have been blamed if he felt that each time he settled into a routine his father eventually changed it. In April of 1903 J. W. T. Falkner was one of more than half a dozen incorporators of the Oxford Oil Mill Company. Construction of the cottonseed processing plant was begun, and though the name of the manager had not yet been announced, it very probably had been understood that the manager would be Murry C. Falkner. His brother John—called "John, honey" by his family—married since December to the former Nina Sue Harkins, had given up the law and was now a partner in a fancy grocery business, his share almost certainly having been put up by his father. J. W. T. Falkner must have felt that he was helping his sons to prosper in the world. It appears that he may have thought of this help in another way, too. It had been noted early in 1903 that the past year would "go down in history as the most prosperous ever known in Mississippi. The crops have been excellent, manufactories and business enterprises have sprung up in nearly every community, and money circulates freely." He was investing the profits from the prosperous law firm—now Falkner and Shands—and from other interests. He was expanding his local holdings in several directions, and his sons would, presumably, help to safeguard his investments. Newspaper accounts reported that he had bought a local transfer line and, by October, the Opera House. It was announced that it would be managed by the Falkner Transfer Company and that "a number of attractive theatricals, operas, etc. have been secured for the coming season."

As if he were not occupied enough with his law practice, his other varied interests, and his duties as city alderman and trustee of the university, he had decided "in compliance with repeated requests from different parts of the county that he should make the race, to offer himself as a candidate again for the State Senate." It may have been in anticipation of this that the firm had taken in a young lawyer trained at the university law school. He was a twenty-seven-year-old native of the county named Lee Maurice Russell. His homeplace was Dallas, a hamlet in the red clay hills of the county's southeastern corner. Lee Russell had been raised as one of a large family in the weathered, tin-roofed house that was all his father, a poor farmer, could provide. It was the fierce ambition and sacrifice of his mother that had pushed him along the rutted gravel roads to the shabby rural schoolhouses, to Toccapola College, and finally to the university at Oxford. There he met some students like himself but many more from the prosperous homes of the professional class or the affluent plantations of the Delta, where the inheritors of power spoke contemptuously of "the rise of the rednecks" even as they were beginning to fear its political consequences. He was put up for membership in a fraternity at the university only to be blackballed. They had crowned the rejection with physical insult. One day, as the tall young man walked past the fraternity, he was doused with a panful of water thrown from a third-floor window. He took his chagrin directly to the board of trustees. On January 4, 1902, he and another student appeared before J. W. T. Falkner and the other members of the board and advocated the abolition of fraternities. Sigma Alpha Epsilon member Falkner and his colleagues were so impressed that they adopted a resolution to abolish all secret societies at the next session of the university. In June this resolution was supplanted by another which outlawed further organizations and rigorously regulated existing ones. But Lee Russell did not abandon his convictions or his aims, as he would demonstrate decisively before ten years had passed. Meanwhile, he worked on his cases in his office on the Square. But he also spent as much time as he could out in the county, where he was gaining a following among the hard-pressed and inarticulate farmers who saw in him one of their own, one who had risen from their class against their handicaps, and one who might give voice and power to their needs and aspirations.

The earliest candidate to announce for state senator had been a man named G. R. Hightower, whose strength lay mainly with the farmers out in the county, especially those who were members of the Grange or the Farmers' Alliance. They constituted one of several embodiments of the agrarian revolt which had been growing in the South during the 1890's. But unlike others, they did not launch a third party as the Populists had done and as the Progressives were to do later. Instead, they chose to work within the framework of the Democratic party, mustering what power they could against the executive committees and rigidly organized nominating conventions, beginning to be able to employ their strength advantageously only when they could compete in a direct primary election, where their numerical strength would tell. In April the Oxford *Eagle* unsurprisingly endorsed the candidacy of J. W. T. Falkner. The campaign went on into the summer, and when the voters went to the polls on August 6, 1903, they could choose among three candidates for the state senate. The result was something of a shock and an embarrassment. Former State Senator J. W. T. Falkner had run third in the field of three. He had been just a little behind candidate Kims, but with 722 votes G. R. Hightower was a good 80 ahead of Falkner. It was the last time he ever ran for anything more than a local office. He would continue to serve the university and to lead all sorts of committees in civil and social projects, but he would never again offer himself to his constituents as a candidate for a county or state position. Unlike the Old Colonel, J. W. T. Falkner had his politics relatively early in his career. Like him, however, he would gradually turn from the law to his multifarious other concerns.

His grandsons were pursuing boyish interests. They would ride through the woods to the plant, Billy on his pony, Jack on his (named Angel Face), and John on a horse ridden by Durwur, the son of Mary, their cook. They loved those woods, and often Mammy Callie would take them for a walk there, teaching them to recognize different birds. Later in the spring of the year she would allow them to climb trees—"bird nesting"—to find eggs to add to their growing collection at home. Walking the children uptown was a different matter. Jack and John presented no problem but without trees and birds' nests to demand his attention, Billy found little entertainment in the simple business of just walking in a straight line with his brothers. As a result, Mammy could never keep him on the plank walks with the other two. Thus she would keep to the walks with John and Jack while their independent older brother would scuff along in the dust of the road. The leisurely summer passed.

The fall of 1903, for Mississippians who knew their history, put the final period to an epoch. "The once great tribe of Choctaw Indians that lived in our state," reported the *Eagle*, "have gone with their pastor and missionary . . . to the faraway reservation to occupy the land that has been allotted them. . . . There is no further work for Home Mission to do among them. Let the prayers of all follow them." Now the migration begun in 1830 was finally ended, and any Indian features to be seen in a Mississippi face would henceforth be mixed with those of the white or Negro race.

The population of Oxford increased slowly during these years as farming families came in from the county and members of the professional class moved from other parts of the state. There was a new girl on the Falkners' block that fall. Her name was Lida Estelle Oldham. That April her father, Lemuel Earl Oldham, had been appointed Clerk of the United States Circuit Court. Since the court met most often in Oxford, he had moved there with his wife Lida Allen, Estelle, and her younger sister, Victoria. The Oldhams were different from most of their new neighbors, not because they had come from Kosciusko, ninety miles due south in the center of the state, but because they were Republicans. Moreover, Lem Oldham's father-in-law was one of the most influential Republicans in the state, as his father had been to an even greater extent before him. Although Radical Republican rule had ended in Mississippi with the impeachment and resignation of Adelbert Ames in 1876, memories were long, and now, nearly thirty years later, there were few Republicans who would be spared the hostility of most of their fellow Mississippians, particularly if their forebears had served in Congress during Reconstruction, no matter how Southern or how noteworthy their other attributes.

Few people in Oxford could boast more distinguished connections than the Oldhams. Mrs. Oldham was related through her mother, Victoria C. Allen, to Brigadier General Felix Zollicoffer, Congressman, founder of the Nashville *Banner*, and one of the first generals of the Confederacy to fall in battle. On her father's side Lida Oldham was related to the legendary Sam Houston. After the death of her first husband, Victoria Allen had married widower Henry C. Niles. Her new husband's father, Judge Jason Niles, had been born into a large and distinguished Vermont family. Jason Niles's father was an Episcopal bishop who had wanted his son to take holy orders. The boy had refused. He followed the law instead and then migrated to Kosciusko in 1848. He had served in the Mississippi Constitutional Convention of 1868 and thereafter in the legislature. For three years he represented Mississippi in Congress. He continued in politics and with his son Henry was one of the principal supporters of W. C. Falkner's old commander and rival, General James R. Chalmers, when Chalmers bolted the Democratic party in 1880 and ran for Congress as a Republican. With the intensity and rancor of Mississippi politics, inflamed by the policies of the Reconstruction Era and the ever-present race issue, Chalmers and those who supported him were the targets of bitter hate and scorn. Among the printable epithets hurled at them were "degenerates," "moral lepers," and "traitors to their race." But according to one Negro leader who fought them for control of the Republican party in Mississippi, they were "typical representatives of the best blood and the finest manhood of the South." He went even further to call them "the better element of native whites." Jason Niles served later as Circuit Judge of the Northern District, and was celebrated not only as a jurist but as a literary scholar who owned, according to one source, the largest private library in the state.

By 1891 the same judgeship had fallen vacant again, and Henry C. Niles was appointed to fill it, to the general pleasure—according to newspaper accounts—not only of Kosciusko but of most of northern Mississippi as well. He was a large, imposing man, who obviously enjoyed his life. Courtroom audiences of his place and time generally enjoyed a flair for words and also some of the intricacies of the law. Judge Niles's charges to juries and instructions on points of law were celebrated in northern Mississippi and relished by the spectators in his courtroom. He dressed well, wearing a black string tie and always showing a wide expanse of white-bosomed shirt, which would often be stained after ample dinners when he concluded the numerous courses by dipping English walnuts in port. His second marriage was a happy one—and fruitful, too, for he had become the father of twin sons, whom they named Jason and Swanson. And he and his wife were apparently pleased with his stepdaughter's choice of a husband. Lem Oldham had attended the University of Mississippi, where he had known Murry Falkner, also a member of the S.A.E. fraternity. He had gone on to earn an LL.B. and then moved to Texas to practice law. There, in Bonham, his first daughter had been born and had lived the first four years of her life. The family had returned to Kosciusko in 1900 on the death of Lem Oldham's father. After seeing to the estate, Oldham settled down to practice law in Kosciusko. Then, partly through the interest of Judge Niles, the appointment as Federal Court Clerk had come through. Apparently the Oldham family was pleasantly received in Oxford. And if anyone had taunted Estelle Oldham about her Republican forebears, she had other credentials to offer which were as good, and sad, as those of any other child in town—her grandfather Oldham had died at Shiloh and her grandfather Allen had died in an Ohio prison camp.

The Oldhams moved into a spacious house on South Street a few blocks from the home of J. W. T. Falkner. A federal court clerk's salary was handsome by Oxford standards, and they lived well. Lem Oldham was a proud, handsome man who dressed smartly and displayed impeccable manners. His attractive wife had the services of Cynthia, their cook, besides those of a maid and a nurse for the children. This freed her for the things she really liked to do: entertaining, supervising the running of her home, playing the piano—she had studied at the Cincinnati Conservatory of Music—and seeing that the grounds were as well arranged and cared for as the house. One of those whom Lida Oldham depended on was Magnolia, the big woman who was the children's nurse. Among Magnolia's tasks was that of curling Estelle's long hair. Often she would use a broom handle. One day, she sat in the front parlor with her young charge and began the ritual. To get Estelle to hold her head still, she told her to look out the window and see what was going on in the street. They were still new in town and she knew few of her neighbors. So she did not know the name of the family strolling down from the direction of the Square. The father and mother walked together, and ahead of them two small boys, the whole procession led by a third boy—the largest—on a Shetland pony. Estelle Oldham raised her hand and pointed to him.

" 'Nolia," she said, "see that little boy? I'm going to marry him when I grow up."

'Nolia kept on twirling the soft hair around the broom handle. "Hush yo mouf, chile," she said. "Folks what say they goin' to get married while they little is sho to grow up to be ol' maids."

Estelle silently watched the Falkners as they walked past her view, on their way back home to Second South Street after a trip to visit Sallie Murry and J. W. T. Falkner.

As 'Nolia took Estelle's appearance for her province, so Judge Niles set out to form her mind. Papa Niles (as Lida's children called him) kept her busy with a wide range of books from the library he had inherited from his father. He wanted her to be grounded in the classics. Often he gave her books that were too old for her, but he took care to explain what she didn't understand. He started her too early on Dickens and Thackeray, with the result that she never cared for either novelist afterwards, but she would move with ease into the Oxford Graded School. He continued to work with her through her early years there, always keeping her somewhat ahead of herself, as when he started her on Voltaire a few years later when she was twelve.

None of the Falkner boys went to school until the age of eight, so that all three of them were still in their time of freedom from regular education. Their grandfather took an interest in their reading and to a certain extent encouraged it, as Judge Niles was doing with his grandchildren. But this training was irregular, and the three boys explored as much as they could of the wide, varied, and fascinating world around them. There were always the woods, the ponies, and sometimes Murry Falkner's dogs to follow. If there was occasional punishment for deviltry, there were seemingly endless sources of pleasure. For someone who liked to dress up, as Billy Falkner

William, Murry, and John Falkner, in front of their home on Second South Street, about 1905.

did, even clothes could be enjoyable. There was a Buster Brown collar worn with a tweed suit that he particularly liked. And there were his brothers to tease. When Johncy turned three on September 24, 1904, Billy perplexed him with the question, "How can I be older than you when your birthday is the day before mine?" That birthday brought Fancy, Johncy's first pony. At the start Fancy was led by Joby Strother, a young Negro boy who helped around the Falkner house and Murry Falkner's stable and also doubled occasionally as a playmate for the boys, especially Billy. Joby had sometimes led Jack's pony, too, for though Jack liked Angel Face, he found sitting her difficult. Each time he tumbled off, Murry Falkner immediately put him back on, and then Joby would be leading not one pony but two.

For rainy days there were other pleasures. Sometimes the three Falkner boys would go to The Big Place to play with their cousin, Sallie Murry, whom they liked just as much as their father did. She and Auntee had moved into the big house on South Street after the end of James Wilkins' long struggle with tuberculosis. By now Auntee had begun gradually to take over the running of the place from her ailing mother. It was a massive white clapboard house—two stories of living space plus a full basement and a full attic. The screened-in porch spanned the front and continued around one side. The large front hall showed off its hand-carved oak stairway. All the woodwork was quarter-sawed oak. The parlor was furnished in mahogany, with the library and the bedrooms done in walnut. It was a perfect house for grandchildren playing hide-and-seek, with its front stairs and back stairs, its main dining room and servants' dining room, its two pantries and back porch. Besides this the house had a parlor with sliding doors and a linen closet with shelved walls, a big kitchen, and walk-in closets in all the bedrooms. On rainy days, when the Falkner boys came to play, Auntee might send all four children upstairs to the attic. It was fully floored, and if they felt like it they could roller-skate. Sometimes they relied principally on pleasures of the imagination. The linen closet on the second floor contained a huge cedar chest which they would use to play ship, with Billy as the Captain, Sallie Murry as the Wife, Jack as the Sailor, and Johncy—the smallest and youngest, with his role assigned—as the Baby, with a bottle full of water. Sometimes Sallie Murry and her friend Estelle would play together. Estelle liked to play paper dolls, or to play lady. But sometimes Sallie Murry's single companion would be Billy, she playing with her dolls and he with Patrick O'Leary.

Other marvelous pleasures of the imagination came at the Opera House where, once Grandfather owned it, the children were always sure of a good seat for every performance. The variety was wide. Each year Ford's Minstrels played Oxford before a capacity house with their advertised complement of forty stars. It was the traditional minstrel troupe, with blackface, gloves, and tambourines. The end men, flanking the interlocutor at either end of the row of performers, would tell the familiar jokes. The performers would present favorite musical numbers varied with a few new ones each season. Sometimes the pleasure at the theater would be mixed with edification, as when an advertisement announced, "Every man, woman and child should take an object lesson given by Willard's revised 'Ten Nights in a Barroom' tonight at the Opera House." The delightful mixture of moral uplift and fascinating horror was subtly called to the prospective theatergoer's attention: "You will see snakes, dragons, and many hideous objects caused by liquor in Joe Morgan's delirium tremens. . . ." John Falkner, Jr., and Lee Russell worked together to book attractions such as "the musical comedy hit, 'Buster Brown.' " Later, when Russell's other duties took him temporarily out of the entertainment business, John Falkner (no longer in the fancy grocery business) was able to bring to his audience the popular *Peck's Bad Boy.* That season he was also able to announce, "At the Opera House tonight, 'East Lynne,' starring the ever-pleasing emotional actress, Miss Addrene LaPorte in the title role with her superb robes of beauty and elegance and her brilliant and charming style." Fifty years later William remembered seeing *East Lynne.* A month earlier the family had made the long trip to Memphis when *Ben Hur* played at the Lyceum. He recalled that spectacle, he said, "because it had live horses in it and a camel and I'd never seen a camel before."

There were other diversions, particularly for those who did not leave town for a time in the summer to vacation at Lafayette Springs, or down on the Gulf, or even as far north as Michigan, as J. W. T. Falkner sometimes did. One was the hunting camp, and the other was the Camp Meeting. Although Maud Falkner had been raised a Baptist, she had had her own children baptized in the Methodist Church, out of respect, no doubt, for the fact that her husband's people (except for the Old Colonel) had been Methodists back to the generation of John Wesley Thompson and beyond. They were sent faithfully to Sunday School during the church year, and it was felt that there was added strength to be derived from the summer Camp Meeting. (Apparently their father felt he could be spared this opportunity.) As many as half a dozen ministers, from Water Valley, Holly Springs, and even as far away as Memphis, would be there. Cottages and tents were erected around the tabernacle. The physical demands created by the services, which went on for several days, were not left unmet by the wives and mothers of Oxford. The meetings "were occasions for monstrous consumption of food, the ladies vying with each other in the production of delicacies. So plentiful was the food . . . that one could not help but wonder how the good ladies found time to devote themselves to the services, though it could certainly be said that those who did were embarking upon salvation on full stomachs." That such embarkations did take place was duly recorded. It came as no surprise, certainly, that "a large number of conversions have been experienced. Many earnest soul-stirring sermons were preached, and much good in the future will probably result from the efforts of these earnest soul-winners." There were concrete results to show. When the annual meeting was concluded in mid-August of 1905, it was possible to announce that there had been "35 conversions, 28 of whom united with the church before the close of the meeting." It must have been this kind of zeal that lay behind the announcement of the results of a religious census of the whole community made just two years later. It revealed that "there were only 180 unconverted persons in the community, 2/3 of this number being under the age of 12 years."

Murry Falkner clearly preferred the hunting camp atmosphere of the Tallahatchie "Club House" to the religious aura of the Camp Meeting cottage. The Club House was a big, two-room cabin, built on poles ten or twelve feet above the ground to discourage snakes. It was located a dozen miles northeast of town at the mouth of the Tippah River where it flowed into the Tallahatchie from the northeast. At this point the converging rivers were as broad as a small lake, and they afforded plenty of opportunity for the fisherman. For the hunter, there were rabbits and squirrels, and, less often, foxes. Although it did not teem with game like the Delta, thirty miles to the west, there were still deer there and an occasional bear.

The Club House was a cooperative venture. Sometimes Lex Ramey or T. W. Yates and their families would go with the Falkners. On other occasions, the men would slip off by themselves—perhaps Yates, Ramey, Murry, and John Falkner, Jr. At still other times, it would be strictly a family affair. Grandfather and Granny (as her grandchildren called Sallie Murry Falkner) would come, bringing with them Auntee and her daughter Sallie Murry. Great-grandmother Murry might come down from Ripley to join Murry and Maud and the boys. Mammy Callie would come with the rest of the family. She would tell wild tales about encounters with wolves and other fearsome beasts in the wilds of the Tallahatchie bottom, and at night, as the boys settled down for sleep, they would whisper to each other, hearing the howls of wolves borne on the dark air from distant tangled shores.

By the fall of 1905 Murry Falkner must have felt especially entitled to whatever time he could manage at the Club House. The Transfer Company remained busy, having added a new service—a daily hack running between Oxford and the university. It had also been formally announced that he was manager of the Oxford Oil Mill Company, now in operation for two years. (One of the employees was Dick Oliver's son, Leslie.) J. W. T. Falkner had joined three friends in organizing the Oxford Brick and Tile Company, but fortunately Murry was not involved in that. Here at the Club House, as in the woods near their home in Oxford, he seems to have been at his best. Normally inarticulate, he would open up and tell the boys stories of hunts he had been on, of the time he had seen a wolf in the Tallahatchie bottom, or the panther he had shot in Tippah County, or the eagle he had killed to oblige the farmer who feared for his flocks and herds. Looking back, Jack Falkner realized "how little I actually came to know him, and perhaps, even less to understand him. He was not an easy man to know." But it was here in the woods that he came closest to his children, and they knew what he was unable to say. "His capacity for affection was limited," Jack remembered, "but I'm sure that to such extent as it allowed he loved us all."

Murry Falkner was a force in his household, but it was Maud Falkner who assumed the fundamental responsibility for disciplining the children, inculcating Christian conduct in them, and encouraging them in school when that time came. She was the steady force that exerted itself in all weathers. In spite of his temper, Murry Falkner tended to be an easy-going man most of the time. When he drank, of course, it was a different matter. In her anxiety about her husband, Maud sometimes overdid it. She seemed uneasy about what he might do when she was not at his side. This was one reason why she went to the Club House on occasions when Murry Falkner could have gone there with his boys, an outing for males only. What a shame, Faulkner would later say, that Mr. Murry and the boys couldn't have gone there to hunt by themselves.

The summer of 1905 was a particularly good one to be out of town, for those who could, for there was another yellow fever scare. In the spring Grandfather had taken Granny to Biloxi in another pursuit of comfort for her. Auntee and Sallie Murry had gone along. In early August, when the four left for Alma, Michigan, the town of Oxford was under strict quarantine. The scare had originated in New Orleans, where by now 616 cases had been reported with 112 deaths. There were no cases in Mississippi yet, and Dr. A. A. Young, who served as the local health officer, was watching the situation closely. Everyone was requested to stay in the county "as conditions may change any day, and you may not be allowed to enter, and a shot gun quarantine established on the borders, but we trust this may not be necessary." On August 8, the Quarantine Order had been published and, by the twenty-fourth, the railroad had discontinued two passenger trains of the six scheduled daily runs. "There is no cause for alarm," the *Eagle* remarked, "but we do think there is too much travelling, especially to Oxford." A few years earlier the paper had commented, "The man-eating mosquito has come to town and makes the night hideous with his song." Now the editor printed excerpts from a circular of the Surgeon General's Office which gave twenty rules for dealing with mosquitoes. By the end of the month the situation appeared critical. Citizens of Oxford were used to the normal perils of the dog days—a flare-up in the number of malaria cases, the need to keep children indoors as the mad dog scares increased—but an epidemic of yellow jack, which had virtually destroyed Memphis as a functioning entity scarcely twenty-five years before, was a different matter. At a special meeting of the mayor and aldermen, the "quarantine regulations of Oxford were made tighter and the limits extended five miles each way from the town. No person can enter Oxford from below Grenada. Any who may wish to enter Oxford can do so only by an application to the authorities with an affidavit signed by the public health officer and notary public seal stating his whereabouts the previous twenty days." But the crisis passed with the coming of cooler September weather.

As the season began to turn, the Falkners and the Oldhams were busy settling and straightening. That spring Lem Oldham had bought the Bryant house on South Street. Besides the finishing touches on arranging the new house and plans for the grounds, Lida Oldham had Estelle's clothes to think about as she prepared her to enter the second grade. Estelle loved laces, bows, and frilly dresses, and her mother enjoyed providing them. The Falkners meanwhile had made two moves. Murry Falkner had bought the Rowsey house on South Street, but it was not ready for occupancy when they wanted it, so they had moved briefly into a small white clapboard house on the same side of South Street as Grandfather's house. Then, when the Rowsey house was ready for them, they moved across the street and up toward the Square, so that they were now diagonally across from the big house where Sallie Murry, her mother, and her grandparents lived.

Maud Falkner also had her preparations for school to make. Her first-born, William Cuthbert Falkner, would enter the schoolroom for the first time that September.

11

September, 1905–September, 1908

> . . . standing at the corner when the dismissal bell rang, standing there while the kindergarten then the first-grade children streamed past . . . then the second grade, standing there while the Lilliputian flow divided. . . . the rules of the school and of respectable decorum . . . the empty room itself smelling of chalk and anguished cerebration and the dry inflexibility of facts. . . .
>
> —*The Town* (144–145)

Maud Falkner had her sons' photograph taken that fall at the studio over Leavell's Plain & Fancy Grocery. She and Mammy Callie had dressed them in their black-velvet best—jackets buttoned tight at the neck with no shirt showing. William sat erect, looking almost plump, turned nearly fullface toward the camera. The Butler cast to his features was clearer now than ever with the snapping black eyes, the thin mouth concealing spiky baby teeth, and the fair hair parted precisely in the middle.

He was a bright and alert-looking student who had a head start on a number of the other first-graders. He skipped the beginners' grade, or chart class, coming as he did from a family where both mother and grandfather had taken a particular interest in his reading. Maud Falkner "had an abiding love for literature," one of her sons remembered, "and that, too, she passed on to all her children. She was really touched by much of what she read. I have many times seen her on the verge of tears over one passage, while another would cause her to chuckle in unabashed delight." She had taught Billy to read and would do the same for his brothers in turn. Graduating from children's books to classic works, magazines, and newspapers, they would be able to read and thoroughly understand the sports page of the Oxford *Eagle* or the Memphis *Commercial Appeal* before they entered school. As he grew up Billy Falkner gradually acquired books that he had first seen in his grandparents' library and books belonging to other members of his family. Precocious reader that he was, he must have known some of them at an early age. His grandmother owned and loved Owen Wister's *The Virginian*, as Murry Falkner apparently did too. *Grimm's Fairy Tales*, *Uncle Remus*, and *Robinson Crusoe* were volumes passed from one child to another in the Falkner household as they grew. His friends remembered that Billy Falkner never forgot a word he read. And though he was not particularly talkative, he had an enormous vocabulary.

It was on his eighth birthday, September 25, 1905, that he made his way three blocks up to the Square and then two blocks west along Jackson Avenue to the two-story brick building that housed Oxford's public school. It provided eleven years of schooling in a well-staffed system that held classes during nine months of the year. The county children were not so fortunate. Those who lived near the railroad could walk the tracks to school in bad weather, but the children from other areas would find the roads impassable. Yet even these students were better off than those in other parts of the state. Only a small proportion of the children "lived in towns comprising separate school districts, and most of the county schools could barely last the four months required by law." But this was not the worst. Two years before Billy Falkner's first year of school the state superintendent had reported that "90 per cent of Mississippi teachers had no professional training and 75 percent had no higher educational opportunities than the rural school afforded." Against these statistics the faculty of the Oxford Graded School must have been conspicuously competent.

The first floor housed the primary or chart class and the seven-grade grammar school. It had its own principal, Mr. R. L. Harris, as did the three-grade high school on the second floor, where Mr. G. G. Hunt was in charge. From the primary through the seventh grades, each grade was taught by one teacher, who covered all the subjects for her charges. In the last three grades the teachers specialized in particular subjects, and the students moved from room to room for their classes. Each day started at about eight in the morning with prayer in the assembly room, which was also called the chapel and which doubled as a study hall. Then the children would disperse to their individual classrooms, each equipped with a wood-burning iron stove. There they would be seated alphabetically, two to a desk, with each desk attached to the seat in front of it. At the head of the room on a small platform before the freshly washed blackboard sat the teacher at her desk. When twelve noon sounded, most of the children who lived in town would troop home for dinner, while the others would file out into the schoolyard in fair weather to open what they had brought from home. Formal work would end at three o'clock.

The first-grade teacher was Miss Annie Chandler. She lived with her family on Pierce Avenue, a few blocks southeast of the Falkner home. The Chandlers were well-connected and said to be related to Jacob Thompson. Annie's father had served as a surgeon during the war and later retired from practice. Her sisters at home were charged with the care of their brother, Edwin, who could be seen playing in fair weather through the high fence that surrounded the Chandler lot. The family had made the tragic discovery during his childhood that Edwin was not normal—a condition that never altered though he lived past the age of thirty. Annie Chandler apparently gave to her pupils the kind of love that her family gave to its own perennial child, for one of them recalled Annie Chandler as, quite simply, "one of the loveliest people who ever lived." Billy Falkner was precocious in drawing and painting as well as in reading, and he put this talent to use for Miss Chandler, presenting her with a watercolor comprising not one but three separate scenes. A book still in the artist's library half a century later may indicate Annie Chandler's reciprocal feeling for her pupil. It was a melodramatic story of Reconstruction days entitled *The Clansman: An Historical Romance of the Ku Klux Klan*, by Thomas Dixon, Jr., and it bore the inscription "Annie J. Chandler 1905."

Apparently Billy Falkner's artwork was not always so deliberate. One Sunday, when Damuddy took him to the Baptist church, she became sufficiently engrossed in the sermon so that she failed to notice him drawing a picture of a train in one of the hymnals. He chose the same subject for his copy of James Baldwin's *School Reading by Grades: First Year*. The engine and tender he drew in great detail at the back of the book: the wheels and connecting rods, cowcatcher and headlight, smokestack and bellpull. He had also sketched abbreviated engines at the front, where he had carefully inscribed the volume

William
Falkner,
Oxford, Miss
1905

The inattention this sketching suggests may be explained by the fact that the book began with sentences such as "This is a ball," and ended with a poem to be memorized whose last verse ran,

Kind hearts are the gardens;
Kind thoughts are the roots;
Kind words are the flowers;
Kind deeds are the fruits.

Some of his teachers would put his artistic talent to use. If they needed something on the board, Billy would be asked to go up and draw it.

The classwork presented no difficulty for him. The *Eagle* printed the year's first honor roll, noting that "The following pupils, by grades of the Oxford graded school, did not fall below 90 in class standing and deportment, were not absent as much as three days, and were not on the tardy roll during the month ending Friday, October 13." William Falkner was one of the three students listed under the first grade. As it turned out, he would be on the honor roll for all but one of the marking periods of the school year. For the next-to-last marking period of the 1905–1906 school year, he was joined on the first-grade honor roll by Victoria Oldham. Victoria's older sister, Estelle, also made her honor roll. Each time Maud Falkner signed her son's "Monthly Report" card, she could see that she had nothing to complain of. The marks used were Perfect, Excellent, High, Good, or a blank—which meant unsatisfactory—and the first letter of each grade was written on the card. In his year's work in reading, spelling, writing, and arithmetic, her son earned twenty E's and sixteen P's, with no lower grades. He even got six P's and three E's in deportment.

Sometimes the advantage in age which made Billy the leader of his group worked to the disadvantage of his followers. On one such occasion Jack had devised a game he could play alone. He was a bucking stallion. He had tied one end of a rope around his chest and the other to a fire hydrant behind him. When he would lunge forward the rope would go taut and pull him back like a restraining rider. Just as he began one of his lunges, his older brother stepped to the hydrant and slipped the rope from its anchor. This time Jack's lunge took him skidding along the dirt of the street on his chest. He rose, looked around, and chased Billy down the street.

Satisfying deception could take other forms. When the Falkner children lost baby teeth they received dimes in exchange. Being only two years apart, Billy and Jack each happened to lose a tooth at the same time. After comparing them, Billy walked over to the outdoor well and held his hand over it for a moment. "I dropped mine in," he said. Jack walked over and tossed his in too. "So did I," he told his brother. Then Billy stretched out his arm and opened his hand to reveal the tooth still in his palm. "I didn't," he said.

Usually, however, the children played together. They would skate in a pack, rollers clattering on the sidewalk, which was against the law, but J. W. T. Falkner had paid for a double-width sidewalk so his grandchildren could skate in front of his home. At about two o'clock on some Sunday afternoons, after the ample Sunday dinner, Murry Falkner would get out the trap and take his family for a ride out in the country. On other days they might go on a picnic at Bailey's Springs, in the woods behind the house built for Robert Shegog sixty years before. They would fish at Waterford or make their way up muddy Davidson's Creek, three miles northwest of the Square, where they would set out trotlines using jugs as floaters. Or, baiting their hooks with crawfish, they would tie the lines to willow trees leaning out over the stream at places where catfish might be tempted. At other times, when Grandfather would take Billy, Jack, Johncy, and Sallie Murry out in the surrey, they might just drive out to another part of the creek, called Davidson's Bottom, where the worst mischance might be a false step or a push that could result in wet and muddy clothes. The group would often be larger, for the big front yard of the Falkners served as a focal point for the neighborhood children. Occasionally Damuddy would play with them, helping to build miniature villages with whatever came to hand. They built stick huts with grass roofs. They hunted for odd or attractively shaped bits of stone or glass. One of that group of children remembered later, "We built walks, streets, churches, and stores. Both William and his grandmother were good at improvising and using materials at hand. . . . William was the leader in these little projects. He had his grandmother's artistic talents for making things, and his imagination was obvious even then."

Amusement and entertainment were of course provided periodically by community activities. The most impressive one of the spring of 1906 had been heralded early in the year with the news that a contract had been let for a monument to the memory of the Confederate soldiers. "It will be a magnificent work of art," the newspaper writer had promised. This was a subject of intense interest to the senior Falkners. J. W. T. Falkner had always been glad to fill out pension forms for ex-soldiers or widows, and he was the organizer and first commander of the Lamar Camp of the Sons of Confederate Veterans. Sallie Murry Falkner was a past president of the Albert Sidney Johnston Chapter of the United Daughters of the Confederacy. Though the war had been over for forty years, nothing was needed to keep its memory green, especially among the women of Sallie Murry Falkner's age and station. The previous year a traveling elocutionist named Henry Watterson had presented a program at the university which featured his recitation of Fred Emerson Brooks's "Pickett's Charge." It was a poem of twelve thundering stanzas meant to stir the blood and grip the throat. Watterson was at his best in stanzas such as the fourth:

'Tis Pickett's charge at Gettysburg
None but tried veterans can know
How fearful 'tis to charge the foe;
But these are soldiers will not quail,
Though Death and Hell stand in their trail!
Flower of the South and Longstreet's pride,
There's valor in their very stride!
Virginian blood runs in their veins,
And each his ardor scarce restrains;
Proud of the part they're chosen for:
The mighty cyclone of the war,
In Pickett's charge at Gettysburg.

The advertisement for the program carried the assertion that Brooks's poem was easily superior to Tennyson's "The Charge of the Light Brigade." It certainly seemed so to many Oxonians in the audience that night, particularly to those whose relatives had fought beside Pickett. And there were many who might have made that claim, for it was the boast of the University of Mississippi, and of Oxford, that the students, "organized as the University Greys, reached the highest point of the Confederacy, forty-seven yards beyond the farthest point reached by Pickett's men at Gettysburg."

But the anticipation of the glorious unveiling, promised for May 10, was soon marred by controversy. The word leaked out that the committee planned to erect the monument not in the Square, but instead on the campus where the University Greys were said to have stacked their books when they mustered and marched away in '61. One of those most angry was Sallie Murry Falkner. Certainly the Greys deserved credit, but they weren't the only soldiers from Lafayette County, and it wasn't just university money that was putting up the monument. But the plans were carried forward, and on the appointed day the First Regimental band struck up a march and led the way from the Square to the campus. They were followed by the ladies of the U.D.C. and "the veterans, some with tottering steps, but inspired at the sight of their comrades in gray and the old banner they followed so closely in the carnage of war." At the monument, the Reverend W. D. Hedleston gave the invocation and the Honorable Charles Scott gave the address. He recalled "the glorious deeds of the men in gray and pointed out that all history had no parallel where men fought such a great fight for the sake of principle alone." The statue was unveiled, "an imposing shaft . . . 22-1/2 feet high surmounted by a figure of a Confederate scout, 6 feet 6 inches high. . . . " It was, the writer pridefully noted, "strictly Southern, being of Southern material, manufactured by Southern men, and designed by a Southern man." The thoroughgoing Southernness of the monument did nothing whatever to assuage the anger and indignation Sallie Murry Falkner felt. So she took the most drastic step she could think of: she left the U.D.C.

It must have been indignation like hers that lay behind the resolution adopted in June by the United Confederate Veterans "to build a monument in the Courthouse Square of Oxford, Miss., in honor of Lafayette County's patriotic dead." But even as she read it, she must have known that she would never live to see the dedication. Her ailment had been called catarrh of the stomach—a diagnosis behind which the family saw the dreaded word, cancer. On their last trip from Alma, Michigan, J. W. T. Falkner had brought back with them a Canadian nurse to care for her. Miss Gibson massaged her daily with cocoa butter and fed her Battle Creek prepared foods—the only thing she could keep down. Holland Wilkins, recently bereaved herself by her husband's death from tuberculosis, did the best she could to look after her father, who was already plagued by growing deafness and now bowed by the growing threat to the person he loved most in the world.

It was not surprising that from time to time Grandfather should take solace from the whiskey he kept in the barn. The trouble was, of course, that often he could not content himself with a few stiff drinks or even a twenty-four-hour release. Instead, the drinking might go on for three or four days. He was by no means alone in this behavior pattern, for "liquor was an accepted way of life as far as many of the menfolk were concerned. Few women would touch it on pain of certain and universal condemnation by the community. This did not mean that men were taught to indulge in it, any more than they were instructed to rise when a lady entered a room, to lie only when it would be of great value to another, or to take pride in their family and their country. These things—the drinking, the code of personal conduct and philosophy of life—were simply passed on from generation to generation by manners and deportment, no succeeding one having sought or found a more agreeable way to live with his fellows."

This transmission had clearly taken place in the case of Murry Falkner, and quite early. During his relatively brief tenure as a university student he had been known for sprees in which he would gallop a fast horse around the campus. Now he continued to drink—and sometimes to ride off the after-effects—but without the dash of his student days. Sometimes normal withdrawal would not work, and he would have to follow in J. W. T. Falkner's footsteps in another way. He would be taken to the Keeley Institute, fifteen miles from Memphis, for the salubrious effects of the Cure. The fastest route was via the Illinois Central Railroad—for which J. W. T. Falkner and G. D. Shands were local attorneys. Although J. W. T. Falkner would not take the train—he would have his bags packed and Ned Barnett would drive him in the carriage—this was the conveyance that Murry Falkner would use.

Maud Falkner detested whiskey. She could not understand what made her husband drink it to excess, and she was terrified of the results. But it was she who had to see that her husband got to the institute when he reached that certain state, and it was she who had to stay—or felt she had to stay—outside Memphis until he was ready to return to Oxford, debilitated, yet dried out and sober. In spite of having Mammy Callie at home, Maud Butler felt better having her children along with her. So, on more than one occasion, Billy, Jack, and Johncy Falkner went along with their diminutive mother when Father was transported to Memphis. Perhaps she hoped that this would be an object lesson for them. Actually, they were much more impressed by the facilities for fun during their stay at the institute. They were allowed to ride by themselves, so long as they promised not to get off, on the four-wheeled, open-vestibule streetcar that traveled from the Cure to Memphis and back. For the first thirty minutes they would travel through the changing rural countryside, but soon, moving along at the rate of eight or nine miles per hour, they would reach "the immense and wonderful city itself. . . . Large, imposing residences lined each street. . . ." But there was even more, for "John it was who, one never-to-be-forgotten day, happened to glance across the aisle and happily announce a sight that held us spellbound. It was a fleeting glimpse of the Mississippi River. We all stood up to get a better view and what we saw almost stunned us with excitement. . . . It was the first time we had ever seen a boat, or water deep enough to support one." Finally, the course of treatment would come to an end and the Falkner family would board the train for Holly Springs, Oxford, and home, leaving the wonders of Memphis behind.

Disrupting though it was, Murry Falkner's fondness for whiskey gave him an insight denied the other members of his immediate family. He displayed it on the occasion of the visit of Aunt Willie Medora from Ripley. She had come by train, shipping her luggage in the coach and carrying only her handbag. When she was in the buggy on her way to the Falkner home, she found that her grips had by mistake gone on to Water Valley. Murry Falkner immediately called the station to wire ahead and have them taken off the train and shipped back to Oxford. She said she didn't mind the inconvenience. The only thing was, she did have her medicine in her luggage and she was supposed to take it faithfully. It was Peruna, she confided to Maud Falkner, a preparation for female ills. When Murry Falkner came home from work that evening, he found that the luggage had not yet arrived and that Aunt Willie was nervous, irritable, and displayed a slight but noticeable tremor. Murry Falkner called his wife into the next room. "For God's sake, Maud," he said in a gruff whisper, "take Aunt Willie upstairs and give her a couple of shots of my whiskey!" Dedicated opponent of the Demon Rum though she was, Maud Falkner took the sufferer upstairs and did as her husband suggested. The symptoms disappeared, and later that evening the luggage arrived.

Murry Falkner may well have felt he was paying for his sins—or encountering a further run of bad luck—when he had to take to the road in periodic efforts to retrieve Mammy Callie. Although she had been married four times, and although she must now have been nearly sixty at the very least, her willingness to try again had not been worn out. Off and on, she would take up with some attractive man and leave—for the Delta, Texas, or Arkansas. Then, when the bloom had faded, sometimes weeks later, she would send word by someone she knew: "Mammy Callie says this is where she is and to come and get her." The appeal would be directed to Murry Falkner rather than his wife, because Caroline Barr knew that her stock would then be low with Maud Butler. Often Murry Falkner would be able to get one of his friends at the stable to do the job for him. The Arkansas trip, however, he had to make himself. Arriving at the small town depot, he was met by the happy, smiling Mammy Callie, whose first question was, "Mist' Murry—when does us git home?"

The summer was a time for reading as well as for play, particularly late in the season when the dog days came and the threat of hydrophobia kept the children indoors. All of the Falkners took to reading naturally. Sallie Murry Falkner entertained the Women's Book Club often, and at one meeting a long poem had been read on the question, What is the best time in a woman's life? The writer answered with a kind of happy variant on the seven ages of man. When the editor of the *Eagle* printed it, he included the initials of the poetess, "S.M.F." Maud Falkner played hostess to the Twentieth Century Book Club, and both women were interested in the local chapter of the Browning Society.

The boys' reading kept pace with their age, and they began to read in Cooper and Dickens as soon as they were able. They enjoyed *The Youth's Companion*, and Billy was particularly fascinated with *The American Boy.* He had a subscription, and when each issue of the large magazine came he pored over it—over the short stories, which might be comic, sentimental, or uplifting; the articles on famous men; departments such as "The Boy Debater" and "The Boy Coin Collector"; ads for moneymakers a boy could sell; or wonderful items for sale, such as a camera or a real Morse telegraph. There was material in the *Eagle* from time to time that could have amused them if they had taken the time to puzzle it out. For years columns written in the tradition of back-country humor had appeared. One typical one, full of phonetic spellings, was "Josiah Slick's Letter to his Old Woman." There was something of the same flavor in the noms de plume of the correspondents from the outlying areas of the county, as when the Live Oak news would be written by "Clod Knocker," the Oak Grove news by "Cucumber Green," and the Pleasant Ridge news by "A Peach Bud." Some of the real given names would have had something of a made-up air about them if it had not been for their Scottish ring, as when a reader might pick up a copy of his paper and note the marriage of a Mr. Balken McGonnigil and Miss Maud Littlejohn.

Often a program at the university might encourage an interest in reading. Earlier in the year the university lyceum course had offered a "grand Shakespearean recital by one of the greatest artists of our time." He was "Thomas C. Trueblood, A.M., Prof. of Elocution and Oratory, University of Michigan." His program was a "monologue recital" of *Hamlet*, concluding with "a selection of the lighter vein." At this point in their careers, however, the Falkner boys preferred the usual run of boys' adventure-story reading, favoring particularly a curious novel by J. A. Mitchell called *Amos Judd*, in which an Indian prince demonstrated his clairvoyance and foreknowledge by predicting his own death. Apparently Maud Falkner would leaven such fare with works by authors such as Rudyard Kipling and Edgar Allan Poe.

If there was romance between the covers of Kipling and, in a different way, of Poe, it was also there to be seen in Lafayette County. It was the romance of local history, myth, and legend, embodied in the stooped frames of the men who made up the thinning lines of the soldiers in gray. In early August, J. W. T. Falkner's committee had begun making plans to entertain the Confederate veterans assembling on September 6 at a reunion for the survivors of General Edward C. Walthall's Mississippi Brigade, who had fought under Forrest and particularly distinguished themselves at the battle of Lookout Mountain. As the day approached, the committee took no chance on running short of anything. They promised "An old fashioned barbecue and Brunswick Stew on the university grounds, served to the heroes of the Lost Cause and their friends and the people of the county by the citizens of Oxford." When all was prepared, the cooks and servants stood ready to ladle out no less than 100 gallons of the savory stew, made of several different kinds of vegetables and meat—including squirrel. As insurance, there was also 2,500 pounds of barbecued meat, not to mention the pies and custards. Fully 3,000 of Walthall's men turned up.

This was not the only unit celebration, however, for periodically J. W. T. Falkner would sponsor a reunion of W. C. Falkner's Partisan Rangers. He put many of them up in his home, lining the upstairs halls with cots and using every available spare bedroom. Sallie Murry Wilkins helped her mother with this sudden extra stress on the household. (Murry Falkner was suddenly hard-pressed too, for he had acquired another enterprise—an ice plant near the oil mill, where Leslie Oliver and the other men would freeze ice in 300-pound blocks which would later be split into cubes of 50 pounds or less. With the increased orders for ice being telephoned to the oil mill, he must have had all he could do to keep up with this one phase of the celebrations.) The three small Falkner boys were fascinated at the chance to see the old veterans assemble and to hear their stories. They had, of course, heard stories about the war for as long as they could remember. There were certainly enough told in their own family. They would sit on Grandfather's big front porch in the gathering twilight and listen to his tales of Mississippi in those far-off days. He would retell stories told to him by "Kunnel Falkner," as he always called his father, about the fighting in Virginia in the first years of the war. Then, the next day, as the boys rode Fancy and Angel Face, they would be Jeb Stuart and W. C. Falkner galloping at the head of gray-clad columns in the Shenandoah Valley.

It was fine to have a grandfather who could tell what it was like to be left at home with mother and the slaves, to be faced at age fourteen with the actual likelihood of a blue-uniformed patrol riding up to the house and demanding all you had—this was fine, but at these celebrations the boys could listen to the men who had actually ridden out to screen Forrest's movements as he started off to raid Memphis, men who had themselves screamed the rebel yell and charged the enemy. "I can remember the old men," Billy Falkner said later, "they would get out the old shabby grey uniforms and get out the old battle flag. . . ." The Old Colonel's son was typically hospitable to these guests, supplementing the big barbecue with food and drink at his own home. Some of the latter may have moved one of the men of the Old Colonel's regiment to rise and recall campaigns they had fought. He spoke at length of the dangers they had encountered and the hardships they had endured. But he maintained with his most forceful oratory that this service and sacrifice was a privilege of the highest order. "Now what air more noble," he asked rhetorically, "than to lie on the field of battle with your car-case filled with canyon balls?" From time to time thereafter Billy would fix Jack with an imperious glance and repeat the orator's question, at which they would both double up with laughter.

When Billy Falkner had brought home his first-grade report card on the last day of school, it bore on its face the note "Promoted to Second Grade," precisely lettered in the copperplate script of Miss Annie Chandler. But with the opening of school again in September, 1906, Mr. R. L. Harris, the principal, telephoned Miss Maud to tell her that Billy was so far ahead of the rest of his class that he was being skipped to third grade. It was taught by another of Oxford's most talented and best-loved teachers, Miss Laura Eades. Billy demonstrated almost immediately that he was going to perform as well for her as he had for Miss Annie Chandler. They began with reading, writing, spelling, and arithmetic, adding drawing in the second month. Once again his grades would be all P's and E's.

He made a few new friends in third grade. One was Myrtle Ramey, the daughter of Lex Ramey, who hunted with Murry Falkner and sometimes placed some of his eggs and other produce on sale at the Transfer Company. Myrtle was a delicate child, always in and out of school, partly from the after-effects of scarlet fever which had settled in her throat. Dr. Culley, her physician, would let her attend school only for part of the morning. Billy Falkner became a particular friend of hers, demonstrating a friendliness and sympathy for those who were ill which he was to display many times later in his life. Myrtle Ramey remembered one of his skills. Miss Eades had asked the class to make cubes out of paper. Her father and her brother had helped her, but she cried over the task out of sheer frustration. When she took hers to school the next morning and placed it on Miss Eades's desk, she could not help comparing it with William Falkner's perfect specimen.

Myrtle Ramey's doctor was one of four long-time physicians in town, the others being Drs. Rowland, Bramlett, and Young. Dr. A. A. Young was an impressive, full-bearded man who had his M.D. from the University of Pennsylvania. His daughter, Julia, studied music, and his son, Stark, was doing well as a teacher and gave signs of becoming a writer. These four doctors had been recently joined by another physician, Dr. F. B. Linder. Dr. Linder was a small, capable widower with three sons and a daughter who settled into Oxford's professional and social life quickly and easily. His two older boys, Felix and Dewey, were enrolled in the Oxford Graded School. Dewey, the younger, was in the third grade and soon became one of William Falkner's friends. (Miss Laura Eades and her colleagues did not use diminutives, and each pupil could expect to be called by his full and proper given name.) They would spend Friday nights at each other's homes. At the Falkners' they would occupy themselves with pigeons in a loft in back of the house. When it was fair they might play baseball in the side lot.

They would walk to school together each day, barefoot while the weather stayed warm, carrying their satchels. By now both were well acquainted with student protocol. Boys with grudges left over from the previous day would settle them on the way to school. They would place their satchels on the plank walk and step into a ditch which separated the walk from the road at the northwest corner of the Square. There they would pummel each other until both were down—the one remaining on top being adjudged the winner. At school there was plenty of room for horseplay on the playground. Serious matters which had to be settled were usually taken to a deep gully behind the school, where the combatants would close with each other under the same rules that obtained on the Square.

Billy Falkner's temperament led him in a different direction. His desk mate, Leo Calloway, recalled Billy's response when Miss Eades would ask the students to rise, one after another, and tell the rest of the class what they wanted to be when they grew up. Billy's statement never changed. "I want to be a writer like my great-granddaddy," he would say. Although this was the time when he liked drawing better than writing, before he had begun to produce the stories and poems which came when he was in the higher grades, his classroom avowal was "in accord with his character and his dreams," his brother later said. In fact, Jack Falkner always felt that his admired elder brother "more or less unconsciously patterned his life after the Old Colonel's."

As the fall months of 1906 went by, Billy Falkner brought home the report card with the E's and P's on it, and made the honor roll. But even through the parental praise these achievements must have brought, he could surely sense the family's strain and grief and the suffering being endured in the upstairs bedroom of The Big Place. For months now Sallie Murry Falkner had been unable to eat even the Battle Creek foods. Desperate to give her some nourishment, Holland Wilkins would steam beefsteak and then dip soda crackers for her into the broth she had made from it. Even then it would not be long before she needed the stomach pump. She remained conscious to the end, and until two days before it she continued to make entries in her diary. On her last page she wrote, "of divine peace and resignation her portion here and an unfading light now in the Land of Life." She died four days before Christmas.

All of the Murrys came from Ripley, including Sallie Murry's aged father, Dr. John Young Murry. Holland Wilkins and Maud Falkner had herded the children to the back of the house, but John Wesley Thompson Falkner asked that they come into the parlor. So Billy and Sallie Murry stood there with Jack and Johncy to hear the minister's funeral service for their grandmother. Then, with the others, they went out into the rain of the bitter cold December day and rode to St. Peter's Cemetery. When the funeral was over and the mourners had dispersed, Holland Wilkins tried to set things back to rights. Maud Falkner helped as best she could, for Holland was herself not a particularly robust woman, outspoken though she might be. There was, some thought, a strain of melancholia and hypochondria in her which could only have been aggravated during this long illness. In the weeks after his wife's death, her father began to retreat further into his deafness, and into his memories. When the warm weather came J.

W. T. Falkner would sit on his front porch, and his daughter, or sometimes his grandchildren, would silently watch him as he traced a name on the air with his finger: "Sallie." Some days he would walk out to the cemetery to the monument that bore the epitaph he had chosen: *The heart of her husband doth safely trust in her. Her children arise and call her blessed. Her husband also, and he praiseth her.*

There was no chance for the family's mood of grief and oppression to lift, for even as Granny's long ordeal ended, Damuddy began to display ominous symptoms. Devout as always, she prayed a great deal, her Bible always near her. To some she appeared harsh, but to her grandsons she seemed quiet, gentle, and long-suffering. Finally Maud Falkner took her to the doctor's for a thorough examination. She was by now making periodic visits to the doctor herself, for in the late summer she would have another child. The doctor's quiet words after his examination of Lelia Butler told her daughter what she must have feared: it appeared to be uterine cancer. Naturally, they tried to keep it from the children.

Maud Falkner's eldest child was doing quite as well in third grade as he had in first. Most months he was on the honor roll, joined sometimes by Myrtle Ramey and Dewey Linder. Curiously enough, he would go the whole year without receiving a single P in drawing or writing; he received an E each time. Jackie Falkner had started to school, and twice his name was listed on the primary grade honor roll.

This certainly would have been reason enough, if a reason were needed, for rewards such as attendance at *Rip Van Winkle, or The Sleep of Twenty Years* when it came to the Opera House. (But Grandfather didn't require reasons. "We saw everything that came along," Sallie Murry Wilkins said.) And there was more exotic fare produced under university auspices. Stark Young's pupils did Sheridan's *The Rivals.* Calvin S. Brown's students enacted Molière's *Le Malade Imaginaire,* a performance hailed as "the first production of a classic play in any foreign language ever given in the South. . . ." If contrast were needed to show the range of experience available in Lafayette County, it was provided by another item a week later. "Quite an excitement prevailed in Potlockney neighborhood Saturday," the report began. "Charley Mize's hounds gave chase to a wolf-like varmint." Shot by Ernest Mize, it measured six and a half feet from tip to tip.

At least one event of that spring of 1907 was dramatic enough to make the Falkner boys (and perhaps the men) forget momentarily the new ordeal being undergone on South Street. The United Confederate Veterans were going ahead with their plans to raise money for a monument to be placed in the Courthouse Square. On April 26 they had held an Old Folks Ball at the Opera House, with an "old time square dance, cotillion and Virginia reel." But the event the boys waited for came the next day: a sham battle on the university grounds. The reporter for the *Eagle* described it: "The battle opened with a cannon shot from the Southern forces, then the sharp shooters were sent out by both sides and they had quite a realistic skirmish, the Southerners being driven back until reinforced. This was followed up by quite a big fight by most of the contending armies in the middle of the field. The roar of the cannon and musketry and the movements of the two armies was real exciting to the spectators." The final result could not have been entirely unexpected. "After a considerable battle in mid-field the Southern line reorganized and then drove the Northern line over the hill into the cover of the woods, and after a considerable struggle the Southern forces came out victorious." It could only have deepened the impression the battle must have made on boys aged nine, seven, and five, to know that "Mr. Paul Ramey's left hand was seriously injured during the sham battle Saturday by the explosion of a giant firecracker."

No matter how much Maud Falkner's men may have been enjoying the spectacle, the boom of cannon and rattle of musketry a mile away can only have been unnerving to her as they drifted through the windows now opened to the warm spring air. She was spending more and more of her time in the upstairs room with Lelia Butler. She would be relieved at times by her brother, Sherwood, whenever he could get away from his job as manager of the telegraph office. Sometimes he would bring his wife, Addie Buffaloe Butler, and their son, Ross. Sherwood Butler was an apt complement to his sister. Charming and outgoing, he possessed the qualities of ease and polish which she lacked. They had taken their mother to Memphis for treatment, but without encouraging results. From time to time her grandsons would go in to see Damuddy, now thin and shrunken, but still anxious to see them even though she had little strength to talk. Her principal medication was morphine, mixed by the doctor himself and measured into small squares of paper that he folded carefully into cylindrical pillboxes. She never let the children see her take any of the morphine, so that they remembered only, as Johncy recalled, "how gentle and kind she always was, and how patient with us even amid what I know now to have been almost unbearable pain."

She died at seven o'clock on the evening of June 1. The next day was

Sunday, and she was buried that afternoon after a funeral service in Maud Butler's front parlor attended by a large number of mourners, including many from the Baptist church Damuddy had faithfully attended over the years. The children most probably did not attend these services. The grim and unsettling effects of the long illness must only have been increased when the three boys were sent to Grandfather's house while their own home was fumigated to expunge any lingering traces of Damuddy's last illness.

But the long summer days brought their customary amusements. The children would wait for the oxcarts bringing lumber from the sawmills into town. The easy-going drivers would let them cling to the tailgates and ride to the lumberyard, where they would play hide-and-seek among the house-high stacks of newly sawed pine. They would roller-skate on the double sidewalk or play baseball in the street of a late afternoon, when Miss Maud would have it watered to keep the dust down. There were fewer trips to the hunting camp in the Tallahatchie bottom now, and none for Miss Maud, who was coming near her time.

It arrived in the heat of midsummer, when her fourth boy was born on August 15, two days before his father's birthday. "He's my birthday present," Murry Falkner said. Faithful to custom, he walked across the street to his father's house and, shouting through his deafness, asked him what he thought they should name the baby. The Colonel thought back to the gay and handsome half-brother, dead now almost forty years. "Let's name him Henry," he said. When Murry Falkner relayed the suggestion to his wife, she thought of Henry and the gambling and the jeweler's wife and promptly vetoed the suggestion. "Over my dead body," she said. The boy was named for Damuddy: Dean Swift Falkner.

Now the children were left more often to their own devices, as their mother was busy with their new brother and Mammy Callie was occupied with helping her mistress. Both women had their hands full, for Dean had been born bald with a milk crust on his scalp that required unguents and silk caps. The boys would spend much of their time at Grandfather's with their cousin. Sometimes Grandfather would take the four of them out in the surrey, to their favorite place in Davidson's Bottom or to his farm in the country north of town. John remembered that Billy would seek out the Negro blacksmith on the place. "Jack and Sallie Murry and I always headed for the apple orchard or the peanut patch but I can remember Bill bearing away from us as soon as we got in the gate if he could hear the hammer ringing in the shed. He would be the last one back when Grandfather

Murry, John, and William Falkner, about 1906–1907.

rounded us up to go home. . . ." They might bring back a sack of apples, potatoes, or peanuts. When they were left to themselves, they might crawl out the back hall window of The Big Place and onto the back porch roof. From there they would climb into a tree and down to the ground. They might climb Grandfather's peach trees or split up, Sallie Murry and Jack against Billy and Johncy, and have fights on the roof of the coal house. Sometimes they would be joined by one of the best-liked members of the band of children who roamed South Street—Victoria Oldham, whom they all called "Tochie." A tomboy, a pretty, devil-may-care little girl who could hold her own in racing or scrimmaging, she was particularly fond of the Falkner boys. They returned the compliment, especially Billy, who admired Tochie's spirit. But he was forming a closer attachment to her older sister, Estelle, who seemed to many of the children even then to be different—beautiful and ladylike.

For all of his leadership in neighborhood exploits, Billy Falkner was basically quiet, showing signs of becoming as much an observer as a doer. He and Estelle Oldham had found they had many things in common. They were both fastidious. They liked clothes. (There was already a touch of the dandy about Billy. He had taken to wearing a "katie," as the men's straw hats were called, keeping it on even when he played croquet.) Another trait they shared was imagination. Some afternoons when they would sit and watch the cloud formations, they would make out designs and shapes in the distant billowy masses. "Do you see that knoll?" one would ask. "Yes," the other would reply, "and do you see that mountain, way over there?"

But there was more to see in the sky than cloud formations that summer of 1907. On August 22 the *Eagle* had asked, "Have you seen the comet? At three o'clock in the morning look north of east and you will see this fiery visitor with its sweeping tail which is growing larger and brighter each night." Estelle had already begun to be interested in astronomy, and Billy shared some of her interest. It was Daniel's Comet, "as dazzling as a star of the second magnitude." It was the brightest object of its kind that had appeared in the heavens for twenty-five years, and the two were allowed to see it. It may have been partly under the spell of such experiences that Billy Falkner and Estelle Oldham came to a decision: they would get married and have a chicken farm. But their accord was short-lived; they quarreled about what kind of chickens they would have.

That fall William Falkner entered fourth grade. Another student remembered him as "a little fellow." He was clearly below average in height; already Jack was edging close to him. "On the school ground he stood around a great deal. . . . more of a listener than a talker, yet everyone liked him and no one ever called him a sissy." He was one of the two brightest boys in his class, and his ability to draw still singled him out from the others. He had always been a reader, and now this interest too was intensified. He would open a book and become absorbed in it, encouraged, as always, by his mother. He might not be ready for the Plato and Aristotle she herself read from time to time, but there were Conrad and Shakespeare and Balzac. These might be difficult for him, but better that they should be too demanding than not demanding enough. There were others, too, that she had ready for him—Hugo, Voltaire, Fielding. Compared with the fare at home, much of that in the Oxford Graded School must have seemed overly simple to him. In the fourth-grade curriculum, grammar and geography were added to the earlier core of the three R's plus spelling and drawing. But suddenly difficulties arose.

The fourth-grade teacher was Miss May McGuire, a somewhat erratic woman and a severe disciplinarian. There had apparently been some thought of skipping Billy again, but nothing came of it, and from the first he did well. It may have seemed to May McGuire that he did too well, for he seemed to do little in the classroom. As one of his friends put it, "he just sat there and behaved." His teacher very probably did not know about the strictly supervised homework periods in the Falkner house every night after supper—regulated by the small, upright woman whose motto was still "Don't Complain—Don't Explain." One day on her way home after school Miss McGuire came to call on Mrs. Falkner. She did not stay long, but when Murry Falkner came home from the stable that night, his wife was still fuming. May McGuire had actually asked her why she didn't stop writing Billy's exercises. Maud Falkner had been unable to convince the woman not only that Billy wrote every one of them himself, but that she didn't even know anything about these particular exercises. Eventually, however, Miss McGuire's doubts must have been assuaged, and her pupil kept on turning in the same quality of work week after week. As a matter of fact, he would never again do so well as he did in her class. When she completed her records in June of 1908, William Falkner had been on the honor roll for every period. His deportment had been excellent, too. The same could not be said at home.

Billy Falkner's run-ins with authority seemed to fall into two classes, temperamental and technological. His experiments might produce chaos, and his practical jokes often produced tears. On one occasion he told Johncy that Santa Claus was coming that night, pointing to the stockings he and his accomplice, Jack, had hung up over the fireplace. Johncy trustingly put his up, too. When Murry Falkner came home from work, he failed to see anything funny in the deception of a seven-year-old child. Later that evening he went down to the Square and induced the owner of the ten-cent store to open up for him briefly. He bought an assortment of small presents. The next morning, when the three Falkner boys awakened and raced into the parlor, Billy and Jack casting covert glances at each other, they found that Johncy's stocking was bulging. The other two were empty. On another occasion Billy persuaded John, Jack, and Sallie Murry to touch an iron hitching rack with their tongues. The weather was below freezing, and he found his expectations confirmed when their tongues stuck.

The American Boy continued to run articles about flying machines which Billy avidly read. Such may have been the genesis of a pair of wings made of corn shucks. Johncy was persuaded to be the first to use them. His flight, from a second-story window, was straight down; as he remembered later, he "like to killed himself." Pursuing a different branch of science, Billy began to dabble in photography. Again John was allowed to assist. Billy emptied the powder from several of his father's shotgun shells into a bowl. Then he positioned it in front of his brother. "I'm going to take your picture, Johncy," he said. "When I tell you, drop a match in there." Billy readied his camera, sighted it, and said, "Now!" There was a roaring flash in which John momentarily seemed to disappear. When they fanned the smoke away, Johncy reappeared—minus his eyebrows and much of his hair. "Well, I'll be damned!" the photographer said. Playing in the woods one Saturday morning they found a Confederate cap-and-ball horse pistol, rusted and earth-clogged, its butt plates and grip eaten away. In a week's time they had cleaned and oiled the weapon to the point where they thought it would work. Their replacement parts included a rubber band from a slingshot for the firing mechanism. Billy searched among his cache of things —he was already one of those people who throw away nothing—for ammunition. He finally hit on the idea of stuffing cap-pistol caps into the percussion tubes. Then he went again to his father's supply of shotgun shells and used their powder to load the six cylinders of the huge ancient pistol. Wet newspaper, buckshot, and wads of chewed paper completed the charges. Then, standing on the back porch steps, his two brothers below him, the young gunsmith grasped the pistol in both hands. He raised it skyward and pulled the trigger. The snap of the first cap was followed by a terrific roar as all the loads began to fire one after another and smoke and flying pieces of burning newspaper filled the yard. Maud Falkner looked out into her backyard in time to see her oldest son disappearing into the smoke cloud. Then, his brother remembered, "she called to Bill and asked him where we were. He could only look at her for a minute before the smoke enfolded him, and stand there with the pistol in his hand. He wasn't so much scared as surprised. None of us expected all those shots to go off at once, least of all Bill. He had invented the rubber mainspring and tested it out. He knew it would work." As with previous pyrotechnical displays, the neighbors were immediately drawn to the Falkner yard. "They had heard the explosion, of course, but what really brought them was all that black smoke. They thought we had set the house on fire at last." Confiscation and punishment naturally followed.

In that fall of 1908 Mammy Callie took her three oldest charges into the woods as usual. Wearing her blue dress, white apron, and black hat, she would take Johncy's hand, and they would go "bird-nesting." They would gather hickory nuts and walnuts as they ripened. Returning to Mammy's cabin in the backyard, they would build a big fire and sit around it, eating the nuts and big peppermint sticks Mammy provided. They would talk and tell stories. Mammy would describe her girlhood on the Barr plantation under "Old Mistis," the frights her family had known when the Klan rode, and eerie experiences involving wolves and other varmints down in the Tallahatchie bottom. At about this time Billy began joining in, and some of his tales seemed to enthrall even Mammy. But early in September a grislier tale than either of them could have told swept through the county, drawing in its wake an aftermath terrible and violent.

About ten o'clock on the morning of September 8, Nelse Patton walked up to the door of a small cottage one mile north of town occupied by Mrs. Mattie McMillan, her seventeen-year-old daughter, and two smaller children. Mrs. McMillan had rented it to be near her husband, who was in the county jail in Oxford. He had sent a message to her by way of Patton, a Negro trusty. Patton walked in and sat down. According to subsequent reports, the trusty was drunk. He apparently thought Mrs. McMillan was alone and made advances. When she ordered him out, he responded angrily. She turned quickly to the bureau drawer but, before she could grasp the pistol lying inside, Patton sprang forward and slashed her throat with a razor, nearly decapitating her. Dying, she rushed screaming from the house. Nearby, her seventeen-year-old daughter heard her and ran to the house only to be seized by Patton. She managed to wrench herself free, however, and fled to neighbors who telephoned the sheriff and Dr. Young, county coroner as well as health officer. Her mother, she knew, was dead.

One of the deputies the sheriff immediately called was Linburn Cullen, the father of Hal Cullen, one of Billy Falkner's classmates. As soon as Linburn Cullen left the house, John Cullen and his brother Jenks disobeyed their father and raced, shotguns in hand, to head off Patton at the point where they thought they could intercept him in his flight to concealment in the wooded Toby Tubby bottom. There, fifteen-year-old John Cullen spotted him in a thicket. When Patton tried to run past them, Cullen called to him to halt. When he kept coming, Cullen fired and hit him with two loads of squirrel shot. Then the two boys stood guard over the murderer until the posse came up. When they searched him they found a nicked and bloody razor in his pocket. The piece broken from it was later found embedded in one of Mrs. McMillan's vertebrae.

The posse took Patton to jail, where guards were then posted. Meanwhile the news spread, and by sundown hundreds had gathered. Judge W. A. Roane and several ministers spoke to the crowd from the porch of the jail, exhorting them to go home and let justice take its course. They were greeted with ominous silence. Immediately afterwards, W. V. Sullivan sprang to the porch and spoke to the crowd, by now close to two thousand. He was a former United States Senator whose nomination for that office had been seconded eight years earlier by J. W. T. Falkner, and who had been serenaded with him by the Citizens' Band of Oxford. He harangued the crowd and by eight o'clock had succeeded in turning it into a mob. As they began to move and shout, Sullivan drew his revolver and handed it to a deputy sheriff. "Shoot Patton," he told him, "and shoot to kill."

The mob surged forward and boosted John Cullen and the sons of some of the other guards through the jail windows. They held their fathers while the doors were flung open and the mob rushed in. The sheriff had hidden the keys to Patton's cell block, and when he refused to tell where they were, the mob took crowbars and pickaxes from hardware stores and blacksmith shops and began to assault the thick old walls of the jail. It was after midnight when they broke through into Patton's darkened cell. He had armed himself with an iron bed railing, and as the first three rushed in he battered them down in succession. He crouched in the dark corner as the voices shouted to him to come out. There was a pause, then a volley of pistol shots. When the body was thrown out of the jail it was quickly castrated and the head mutilated. By means of a rope tied to the neck, it was dragged by car to the Square. Then it was hung, naked, from a tree. The next morning, Linburn Cullen bought a pair of overalls and put them on the body.

The coroner's jury found that "the said Nelse Patton came to his death from gunshot or pistol wounds inflicted by parties to us unknown." Senator Sullivan told the Associated Press, "I led the mob which lynched Nelse Patton and I am proud of it. . . . I wouldn't mind standing the consequences any time for lynching a man who cut a white woman's throat. I will lead a mob in such a case any time." The adult population could look at the body or read the newspapers. This was not necessary for boys in the fifth grade of the Oxford Graded School. They had as an actual classmate the brother of the boy who had first shot Nelse Patton, then had helped bring him in, had leaped through a jail window, watched the mob crash in, and seen the mutilated body suspended from a tree. And one of Hal Cullen's good friends was Billy Falkner. When Miss Kate Kimmons' fifth-grade class was organized that September of 1908, the knots of boys standing around the playground had more to talk about than just the summer past and who was new in the class.

12

October, 1908–December, 1910

Will Varner, the present owner of the Old Frenchman place, was the chief man of the country. He was the largest landholder and beat supervisor in one county and Justice of the Peace in the next and election commissioner in both. . . .

The son, Jody, was about thirty, a prime bulging man . . . who emanated a quality of invincible and inviolable bachelordom. . . . He managed the store of which his father was still titular owner. . . .

. . . Monday morning . . . Flem Snopes came to clerk in Varner's store. . . . a man whose name they had not even heard two months ago, who answered Yes and No to direct questions and who apparently never looked directly or long enough at any face to remember the name which went with it, yet who never made mistakes in any matter pertaining to money.

Now . . . there was something in Jody's eyes that had not been there before. . . . This was the time they referred to later, two and three years later, when they told one another: "That was when he passed Jody," though it was Ratliff who amended it: "You mean, that was when Jody begun to find it out."

—*The Hamlet* (5, 6–7, 51–56, 60)

Seven weeks after the death of Nelse Patton an entertainment came to Oxford which would have made it even easier to rouse the mob to violence. It was Thomas W. Dixon's dramatization of his novel *The Clansman*, which had opened before an enthusiastic New York audience in early 1906 (and six years later would serve as the basis for D. W. Griffith's *The Birth of a Nation*). Advertisements in the newspapers proclaimed that though this production had been adapted for the Opera House stage, it would be performed by forty people and a troop of cavalry horses with "a carload of effects." There was one particularly large ad with pictures of hooded horsemen which no doubt helped to fill the Opera House when the company came to town. This kind of entertainment and promotion could not have come as a surprise to those who had taken seriously an announcement which had appeared one year earlier. "The undersigned has the management of the Opera House for this season," it read. "Heretofore the former managers were so pressed for other business they were unable to properly look after the Opera House work. This will not be the case under the new management." The notice was signed "Respectfully, Lee M. Russell."

If variety was any criterion, Lee Russell soon made good his boast. He reengaged the popular company which had performed *The Beggar Prince* the previous season. Then he brought in *As You Like It.* Even more marvelous was a relatively new thing called a picture show, which cost only five cents. On summer nights films would be shown in an open-air establishment called the Air Drome, but this apparently made no serious dent in Lee Russell's entertainment revenues. As a matter of fact, within six months he would own the Opera House.

Motion pictures and the law had been only two of this enterprising young man's concerns. For a time, he had written a regular column in which he had let the county electorate know where he stood. It was a part of his drive toward a third goal: the governor's chair in Jackson. His poverty was merely another obstacle to be surmounted. Looking with admiration at his ability to survive, William Faulkner later said, "he lived on a pot of peas." He made his bid for the legislature in the fall of 1907, and in January of 1908 he was seated in that body as a representative—at the same time as Senator G. R. Hightower. He had his feet firmly planted on the ladder.

Although he now represented the whole county, Lee Russell did not forget his special power base, as he demonstrated in a petition to the county school board asking for an agricultural high school in the eastern part of the county. Co-signers with him were his brothers, Albert, Lucius, and Cleveland, and together they proposed to deed to such a school "20 acres of good land."

Things were going his way in the law practice, too. There was enough business so that John Falkner, Jr., would soon enter the firm. And two years later, when Colonel Falkner would enter the banking business, the Honorable Lee M. Russell would have an even larger role in the firm's affairs. For the present, the situation of the new representative and his senior partner (once more the city attorney) was made clear in a brief report among the Local Items in mid-October of that year of 1908: "Messrs. Falkner and Russell are having their law offices handsomely fitted up."

Billy Falkner had just made the fifth-grade honor roll with eight of his classmates, but he did not repeat the performance the next month. He was studying the same subjects with Miss Kate Kimmons as those they had covered in Miss May McGuire's class, with one exception: history had been added. It did little to make the class more attractive to him, and it appeared that his interest in schoolwork was going into a steady decline. If the honor roll was any indication, this was certainly true, for his name did not appear on it again for the rest of the year.

The end of school in early June of 1909 must have been even more welcome to Billy Falkner than in previous years. He had to work from time to time, it was true, but he was still free of schoolroom constrictions. Now eleven going on twelve, he was able to spend time at the livery stable. There he seems to have been put to work helping to collect money and assisting in some of the business of the office. One result, he later said, was that he was not subjected to so much female authority as were his younger brothers, at home under the watchful eyes of Miss Maud and Mammy Callie. "I more or less grew up in my father's livery stable," he wrote. "Being the eldest of four boys, I escaped my mother's influence pretty easy, since my father thought it was fine for me to apprentice to the business." An unforeseen result was the purchase of a mount very different from such animals as Angel Face and Fancy.

A wide variety of horseflesh had periodically been available in north Mississippi. In the 1890's Robert Kleberg had an immense corral, constructed of cut-down trees, on the enormous King Ranch in Texas. In it his vaqueros trapped 4,000 wild mustangs. When fifty riders went in to move them, the beasts rampaged their way out of the trap. It took six months before they could be tricked into the corral again. This time the vaqueros "entered the enclosure and began to drive the captured horses around and around, without rest. After ten days of continual driving, the mustangs were so weakened by lack of feed and rest that they were manageable. One whole train load of them was eventually shipped to Mississippi and Tennessee, where Kleberg traded them for a few head of well-bred, gentle horses." Texas continued to be a source of stock for Lafayette County. In the late summer of 1887 the *Eagle* noted that "Dr. F. M. Collins left last Friday morning for the Rio Grande. He will be absent several weeks and expects to bring back a fine lot of mules and ponies." More than twenty years later this interchange was apparently still going on.

Again looking back over fifty years, William Faulkner said, "I bought one of these horses once. They appeared in our country, every summer somebody would come in with another batch of them. They were Western range-bred ponies, pintos—had never had a bridle on them, had never seen shelled corn before, and they'd be brought into our town and auctioned off for prices from three or four dollars up to six or seven. . . . My father, at that time, ran a livery stable, and there was a big man, he was six feet and a half tall, he weighed two hundred pounds, but mentally he was about ten years old, too. And I wanted one of those horses, and my father said, Well, if you and Buster can buy one for what money you've saved, you can have it. And so we went to the auction and we bought one for $4.75. We . . . had a two-wheeled cart . . . and we fooled with that critter—it was a wild animal, it was a wild beast, it wasn't a domestic animal at all. And finally Buster said that it was ready, so we . . . put a croker-sack over the horse's head and backed it into the cart with two Negroes to fasten it in . . . and me and Buster got in the seat and Buster said, All right, boys, let him go, and they snatched the sack off the horse's head. He went across the lot . . . it hung the inside wheel on the gatepost as it turned, we were down on one hub then, and about that time Buster caught me by the back of the neck and threw me just like that and then he jumped out. And the cart was scattered up that lane, and we found the horse a mile away, run into a dead-end street. All he had left on him was just the hames—the harness gone. . . . But we kept that horse and gentled him to where I finally rode him."

There were other diversions that summer and fall. Although Billy Falkner enjoyed the society of Buster Callicoat, he still moved with the group of children that ranged out from South Street. One playmate of those years recalls that Billy "was very active physically and he loved to play baseball, and was by far the best player among the boys who played together those summers. Also he was very much a leader among the boys, and we usually followed his suggestions and guidance in our activities. Particularly

I remember the great mass of honeysuckle that grew in the wasteland back of my grandmother's home. . . . We used to dig in under the massive growth and have secret hiding places to which Bill led us. The honeysuckle was a great place for birds' nests, and Bill was a collector of bird eggs. I remember that he gave a blue egg to me . . . the egg of . . . the China bird. The egg was considered very rare."

By August the Camp Ground Meeting was being prepared again, but it is unlikely that Billy Falkner was much tempted by the idea of the exhortations of the ministers J. C. Park and B. P. Fullilove. It was about this time that his father instead began to take him on fox hunts. The hunters would take their pack of dogs out into the county. Once they had come upon a scent, the pack would take off in pursuit. Meanwhile, the hunters would establish themselves comfortably, building a fire if the night was crisp. Sitting around it, they would listen for the voices of individual hounds. They would tell stories to pass the time, taking refreshment which depended upon the age of the hunters and the length of time they waited before sounding a horn that would bring the hounds back. Murry Falkner had kept his own foxhounds in Ripley, but there were fewer foxes in Lafayette County and he now kept only bird dogs. He depended on the hospitality of friends such as Mr. Ike Roberts, who still kept packs of foxhounds and would invite him to join in on a hunt. Roberts was a lifelong resident of the county who had from early manhood gone to the Delta to hunt deer and bear and who would live out his long life in that pattern: farming his land and faithfully following the hunt in all forms and seasons. Young Bramlett Roberts would follow Mr. Ike and Billy Falkner would follow Mr. Murry, riding when they pursued the hounds and waiting—sitting and listening to the tales being told—when the pack was out on the scent and all listened for the hounds to give tongue.

On Monday, September 20, 1909, school began again, as the new principal, Professor R. W. Philbeck, welcomed 350 pupils. After the freedom of the summer, William Falkner must have found Miss Minnie Porter's sixth-grade classroom painfully confining. The teacher was a nervous woman who found her roomful of sixth-graders taxing and showed it. They knew she could be rough on them in class. "Why, she'll rip you up just for the fun of it," they said. As it turned out, Miss Minnie Porter would last only a few weeks. She was replaced by Laura Eades's sister, Miss Essie, who took a group photograph of her new class. William Falkner's face was one of the most serious of the thirty-five. He stood near the center of the back row, taller than the smallest boy but considerably shorter and slighter than the half-dozen big boys in the row.

William Falkner had a new desk mate. He was Ralph S. Muckenfuss, whose family had moved to Oxford four years earlier when his father had come to assume the chairmanship of the chemistry department at the university. Ralph was a stocky, bright-looking, blue-eyed boy, whose hair was parted precisely in the middle. He was a fifth-grader, one year behind his seat mate but a member of the same Methodist Sunday School. At the summer outing of their Sunday School they had teamed up for one of the events. Billy Falkner was small for his age, but he was well-coordinated, and he and Ralph Muckenfuss had run and jumped their way to victory in the three-legged race.

Now their day would start in the assembly room. Sitting side by side, they would join in the prayer and hymn and then listen to the morning's announcements. They would go from there to their classrooms, returning to the assembly room later for vacant periods and study hall. Ralph Muckenfuss observed his desk mate. The two of them were friendly, and Billy Falkner seemed to be liked by his classmates, but he was intimate with no one in school so far as Ralph could see. In spite of his earlier honor-roll status, he never seemed to do any work in school. The fact was that it was getting harder and harder for Billy Falkner to stay interested in the sixth-grade curriculum, even though a class in physiology had now been added to the staple reading, writing, spelling, arithmetic, grammar, geography, and history. He was still quiet and well-behaved, but in study hall he did not study. Ralph Muckenfuss saw that instead he was drawing pictures. There was one of a cowboy being bucked over a corral fence by his horse. Billy had always been drawing pictures, but this time he was using them to illustrate stories which he was apparently writing for his own amusement. As September turned into October and the business of school lost whatever novelty it might briefly have possessed, Ralph noticed that his desk mate seemed to care for nothing but his writing and drawing.

The tedium of schoolwork was gloriously shattered in the last week of October as Oxford filled up for the Lafayette County Fair. There were all sorts of events and prizes—for the best preserves, the best saddle horse, the most attractively decorated buggy, and literally dozens of other categories. Fully 3,000 people came to the fair during its two days of events and exhibits. There was no question in the minds of the Falkner boys, however, about which event would be the most startling and marvelous. They were actually going to be able to see a man go up in a balloon.

OCTOBER, 1908–DECEMBER, 1910

By Thursday morning, October 21, the Square was jammed with canvas display booths backed against the hitching chain that ran from post to post surrounding the Courthouse grass. In the booths next to the biggest potatoes and ears of corn were the cakes and preserves that the farmers' wives had carefully brought into town. These held no attraction, however, for a young boy who could try, for ten cents, to win a prize by pitching a ring at a peg or fishing in a canvas trough. Other attractions even more exotic fascinated Johncy Falkner. There was "a lady snake charmer, and a wild man from Borneo, that some English explorer had caught in a net. The scene of his capture was always depicted on the front of his tent. We stared at it and believed and paid our dimes to go inside and stare at the wild man, seated in a cane-bottomed chair with one leg chained to the stand on which he sat, and gnawing at the bones scattered about him." Murry Falkner had given them money for the carnival. It did not take Jack and Johncy long to spend theirs. Their older brother tried a few of the sideshows and games, but, characteristically, he saved some of his money and still had it when the fair was over. But now it was the morning of the last day, and the booths and sideshows were deserted as the crowd grew at the corner of the Square.

The surly, dirty balloonist and his tall, thin Negro helper had erected a frame, draped the canvas balloon on it, and started a coal-oil fire beneath it. As the morning wore on the boys watched while the balloonist supplied the fire with coal oil and the Negro supplied the balloonist with whiskey. As the canvas began to take shape, the greasy smoke billowed out into the Square, so that before long such faithful spectators as Billy, Jack, and Johncy Falkner were soot-blackened. Tears streamed from their fascinated eyes. The balloonist himself was a marvel to the boys. How could he stand it, Jack wondered. Billy told him drily, "He's probably spent so much time in that smoke that good fresh air would likely kill him."

At noon they evaded Mammy Callie when she pushed in among the crowd. They had no intention of quitting this scene for anything so prosaic as the midday meal. Gradually the rough and leaky surface of the balloon swelled taut, straining against the ropes pegged to the ground. At last, the balloonist was tumbled, whiskey in hand, into the basket beneath his craft. Leaning out, he shouted to his helper, "Cut, damn it, cut!" The ax severed the ropes, and soon the mephitic balloonist was as high as Grandfather Falkner's law office. A moment later a gentle breeze caught the bulbous shape and began to nudge it southward. Billy caught John's arm. "It's going directly over home!" he shouted. "Let's go!"

They raced from the Square across lots and gullies in advance of the shouting pack of citizens who followed them. With their eyes fixed on the balloon, they sped over well-known paths, tumbling and rising often as they struck unnoticed obstacles. At full speed they scaled Mrs. Powell's fence and dashed through the yard where they had sometimes picked her forbidden green apples. "William Falkner," she called out sharply, "you boys stop right—" Then she saw the balloon and heard its drunken pilot cursing as it drifted, descending, across her yard. "Oh, my Lord," she said. (Billy later said that if they'd had a balloon with them every time they raided Mrs. Powell's yard she never would have caught them taking green apples.) Now they saw with delighted astonishment that the balloon was going to land in their own back lot. Suddenly, the balloonist descended with a crash on the chicken house as the collapsing balloon cascaded over the barn.

Maud Falkner and Mammy Callie had been standing there discussing flowers. An instant later the boys' three ponies stampeded and the air was full of flying feathers and desperate squawks of the terrified chickens. Miss Maud moved toward the balloonist as Mammy Callie grabbed up a long thin piece of lumber. "This man may be hurt," Miss Maud said. Clutching the scantling tightly, Mammy Callie made ready to charge. "Eff'in he ain't hurt, ah garntee he gwine ter be," she muttered. As she raised the weapon over her head, she caught sight of the silent, staring figures of William, Jack, and John Falkner—grimy from their day's work, ragged and skinned from their cross-country dash. She and Miss Maud stood there in simultaneous arrested motion and speechlessness. The balloonist quickly rolled away from the chicken house and tottered reeking out of the lot.

A week after the stalls from the fair had been taken down, Estelle Oldham sent out invitations to a Halloween party. It would not have surprised her if Billy Falkner didn't attend. Along with his quietness there was a growing tendency to withdrawal. Sometimes there would be taffy pulls in the spacious Oldham kitchen; Jack and John would always be there, but Billy would never come. Sometimes neither sociability nor food seemed to hold much attraction for him. This strategy of withdrawal was one he would employ increasingly to avoid certain situations. He was already using it in one: he was playing hooky from school.

"I never did like to go to school," he said much later, "and I stopped going to school as soon as I got big enough to play hooky and not be caught at it. That was about the sixth grade." He was not, of course, able to quit school entirely, and it would be four years before he did, but his pattern of consistent attendance was broken, and as time went on he would spend less and less time in the classroom. "He would do anything to get out of school," Estelle Oldham remembered.

Maud Falkner would have had little sympathy with complaints or evasions on the subject of schoolwork. Murry Falkner might have been sympathetic because of the small attraction the classroom had held for him, but almost certainly he would have decided that if his eldest son did not want to spend his time there, he could certainly spend it in the livery stable —working. But Billy Falkner was already showing a disinclination to work —he would try to dodge some of the chores his father assigned—so it must have been obvious to him that there was no relief to be had from either parent. He would have to go to more distant relatives.

He went to his uncle John, who had returned to the university to study law. He had passed the state bar examination and begun to work in Colonel Falkner's office while he completed the last year at the law school to obtain his degree. "I just browsed through those books of his," Bill Faulkner later said. "I don't know, maybe I learned a bit about the law. I remember I was very interested in Roman law." His actions belied his interest. In a momentary fit of rebellion, or perhaps simple devilment, he filled a water pistol full of "stink water" and stationed himself on the gallery outside the law office where Uncle John was working. From that vantage point he took pot shots at passing pedestrians. As a result the student of Roman law was kept home from the circus.

On other occasions he wound up in Ripley, with his great-grandfather, Dr. John Y. Murry, or one of his sons, Dr. John Y. Murry, Jr., Dr. Will Murry, or Dr. Charlie Murry. "I ran away to a doctor in the family and I browsed through his books," he said. "I learned plenty from them. I was interested in the brain. I learned that it had parts—a section for speech, for touch, and so on." All the children retained vivid memories of Great-grandfather Murry. (He remained active despite advancing years, but he took care of himself. Sallie Murry Wilkins remembered that when he visited them in Oxford he would never fail to take his afternoon nap. Holland Wilkins would assist her grandfather as, clad in his union suit, he would climb into bed and carefully arrange himself, his long beard outside the coverlet.) He had been a standard fixture in their childhood.

The children didn't think of him as particularly pious or stern, Billy recalled. Rather, "he was simply a man of inflexible principles. One of them was, everybody, children on up through all adults present, had to have a verse from the Bible ready and glib at tongue-tip . . . if you didn't have your scripture verse ready, you didn't have any breakfast; you would be excused long enough to leave the room and swot one up (there was a maiden aunt, a kind of sergeant-major for this duty, who retired with the culprit and gave him a brisk breezing which carried him over the jump next time)." But Great-grandfather Murry was not an easy mark. "It had to be an authentic, correct verse. While we were little, it could be the same one, once you had it down good, morning after morning, until you got a little older and bigger, when one morning (by this time you would be pretty glib at it, galloping through without even listening to yourself since you were already among the ham and steak and fried chicken and grits and sweet potatoes and two or three kinds of hot bread) you would suddenly find his eyes on you—very blue, very kind and gentle, and even now not stern so much as inflexible; and next morning you had a new verse. In a way, that was when you discovered that your childhood was over; you had outgrown it and entered the world." As he tried to separate himself from school, Billy Falkner must have had something of this same sense. Yet in a way he was trying to preserve some of the conditions of earlier childhood.

When he could not play hooky without being caught, he would forget school in other ways. On the weekend he might go out into the country to visit Hal Cullen, who with his seven brothers and sisters lived on Old Thompson Lake. There they would wade and swim or hunt bullfrogs or cottonmouth moccasins with the .22 rifle he had received after serving his apprenticeship in weapon-handling with an air rifle. On other occasions he would wander over to see Grandfather Falkner, with whom he still had a special bond. He obviously enjoyed his grandfather's stories of the war. And there was more than stories, for sometimes he would get out the mementos of the Old Colonel—his cane, the machete he brought back from the Mexican War, his books, his silver watch, the pipe he was smoking the day he was shot—and Billy would be allowed to examine them. (If Grandfather needed any added incentive to recall the days of the Civil War, he had received one that spring when he had been named Judge Advocate General for the Mississippi Brigade of Forrest's Cavalry of the United Confederate Veterans.) Sometimes he would recite bits of poems for the children. "Twinkle, twinkle, little star," he would say, "how I wonder what you air." Increasingly hard of hearing, and gruff, he was formidable to many, but not to Billy. "I would sit there with him on the gallery," the grandson remembered. "He would have his feet up on the balustrade and a horse would come and put his head between his feet. He and the horse would look at each other and talk to each other. And a Negro would come and bring Grandpappy drinks." If it happened to be a toddy, sometimes Billy would be allowed to drink the "heeltaps," the last little bit of diluted liquid left in the glass. He would sit and gaze admiringly at the well-turned-out old man. "Grandpappy," he said one day, "I like your fob and that vest." The Colonel looked at him with his intense black eyes. "Well, Billy," he replied, "we'll get you the same thing." A few weeks later the replicas arrived and both Falkners went to church together wearing them. "I was the proudest boy that ever breathed," William Faulkner said. But he had to keep on going to school.

Christmas came, bringing with it an unaccustomed eight inches of snow. The Falkners went to The Big Place for Christmas dinner as they always had. In the year since his wife's death, the Colonel seemed to want more than ever to have his family with him there on Christmas day. The calendar changed, and it was 1910. Oxford was changing too—slowly, perhaps, but changing nonetheless.

The editor of the *Eagle* had already set forth the community's claims in an editorial entitled "Oxford is a Progressive City." He had pointed out a number of advances. "Oxford today is not what it was twenty, even ten, years ago," he wrote. "We have an up to date electric light system, sewer system, well-equipped water plant, and besides this we are now laying down paved walks and streets." Education was keeping pace too, for an eleventh grade had been added to the Oxford public school system. And Oxford was not simply indulging in the narrow enthusiasm of the booster or the go-getter. The report of the Aesthetic Committee of the Civic League made this clear, urging better sanitation practices and proposing watering, grading, terracing and several other methods of "beautification." The arts, too, were being furthered. Dr. Young's son Stark had gone off to Austin to teach drama at the University of Texas, but the Ole Miss dramatic club was still active, scoring a great success at the Opera House with Goldsmith's *She Stoops to Conquer.*

And there was one Oxonian who was moving forward with the times, probably a good deal faster than many of his fellow citizens realized. Young Lee Russell was meeting some of the great and, incidentally, sharpening his powers of oratory whenever he got the chance. He provided himself with a splendid opportunity to do both when he booked into the Opera House no less a figure than William Jennings Bryan, who spoke on the subject "The Prince of Peace." The writer for the *Eagle* noted that the three-time presidential candidate was introduced by Lee Russell. Although Bryan did not have a capacity audience, the reporter declared that "Skepticism was dealt a knockout blow."

Shortly before this Russell had chosen an even more spectacular way to keep himself in public view, not only in Oxford and Lafayette County, but in that whole part of north Mississippi. It was the subject of prideful comment in the local press. "Mr. L. M. Russell, one of our most progressive young men, has purchased an elegant touring car," the account read, "and while this great invention is not new to our people who travel a great deal, [this] is the first owned by a citizen of the town and therefore marks a distinct historical fact in the history of the town. It will only be a matter of time until automobiles will be all over this country, but it takes progressive men to start things. . . . Oxford should feel proud of this new automobile." This was not actually the first automobile which had been seen in town (Colonel Falkner had owned a rubber-tired buggy in which a motor had been installed by Mr. John Buffaloe, a relative by marriage of Maud Falkner's brother, Sherwood), but this was the first manufactured automobile. Lee Russell may have bought it in emulation of his senior partner, and it is not unlikely that the money may have come from a new enterprise in which they were jointly engaged, a general real-estate business including both town lots and farms. Colonel Falkner still favored a smart buggy and often drove about in one. It would have been convenient for appraising properties, and it is highly probable that, from time to time, residents of the

Murry, William, John, and Dean Falkner, about 1910–1911.

city and county may have seen the buggy go past with two seemingly mismatched occupants: the crusty, mustachioed, cigar-smoking old man in the big Panama hat and the shrewd, thin-faced young lawyer-politician from the county's southeastern hills.

Murry Falkner, on the other hand, may have been a little less busy than before. He had given the Ramey Produce Company part of the office space at the livery stable, and for some time now, it appears, he had been out of the oil mill business. When the stockholders had last met they had reelected the same board, which had immediately decided "to put the property in good repair and in good management."

No matter how Murry Falkner may have felt about business, he could be proud of his four sons. A group photograph of them taken about this time shows curly-headed Dean in a romper suit, small and wistful, and his three older brothers in knickers and jackets with firmly knotted ties affixed to high collars. Jack was almost as tall as Billy now, though he was not yet eleven. Large-eyed and dark-haired, he looked more and more like a Murry. In Billy, the Butler features stood out sharply, with the narrow mouth and sharp eyes, and the light brown hair with a good bit of red in it. Johncy seemed a blend of both parental strains, which together would make him one of the best-looking boys in Oxford. As if to be worthy of the appearance in the photograph, Billy had exerted himself in school and made the honor roll for the month ending January 11. It was the last time.

He was finding other uses for his talents. One of his chores in that winter of 1910 was to bring in enough buckets of coal to supply each of the several fireplaces for the evening and next morning. Maud Falkner began to notice that every day after school Billy was bringing home with him a big boy from his class named Fritz McElroy. She did not know that though Fritz was basically good-natured, his hobby was fighting. He had already licked Billy once, and in retaliation Billy had tricked him into diving into a hog wallow outside his own barn into which Fritz thought he would be pushing Jack, John, and the Linders. But now, Maud Falkner noticed, they had become friends. She watched them through her kitchen window as they walked to the coal shed. There Fritz would load the two coal buckets and carry them back to the house. The trips would be repeated until all the fireplaces were supplied. During the whole procedure, Maud Falkner could not see her son raising a finger to help; all she could see was that Billy seemed to be constantly talking. Her curiosity was piqued. Somehow she finally found the explanation. Billy was telling stories to Fritz and breaking them off at a suspenseful point which would bring Fritz back the next day to learn what was going to happen. Some of the stories Billy had read. Others he made up as he went along. Between the two sources of supply, he had enough so that Fritz McElroy carried his coal all that winter. By this time others were noticing his inventive powers. Looking back, Sallie Murry said, "It got so that when Billy told you something, you never knew if it was the truth or just something he'd made up."

For the imaginative, 1910 was a year to watch the skies. In late January the *Eagle* reported that "The fall of a meteor in the east was noted by many of our citizens last Wednesday night about 10:30. The explosion was distinctive, to those who realized the cause really terrifying." But the real attraction would come three months later. After an interval of seventy-five years, it was time again for Halley's Comet to pass between the earth and the sun. Not only would the comet be of extraordinary brightness, but it would also pass over the sun's disk. Its tail was between 20 and 120 million miles long —miles of brilliant and poisonous gases, an idea which terrified more than a few nonscientists because on May 18 the earth would plunge through that tail.

During the weeks as the comet became clearer in the morning sky, increasing numbers of amateur astronomers would rise to glimpse it. Among those in Oxford were some of the Oldham and Falkner children. Lem Oldham would set the alarm and wake Estelle and Tochie when it went off at four A.M. They would dress and then walk to the Falkner pasture for an unobstructed view of the great splash of light that seemed to stretch all the way across the eastern sky. Jack and Billy would be there ahead of them. They would watch it for the better part of an hour, until it faded in the pink shafts of the rising sun. Estelle and Jack were the ones most fascinated with astronomy, and after a while Tochie dropped out. Billy seemed to go just to be along with them rather than out of the same kind of interest they had. Once Murry Falkner took them out to Pea Ridge, a high spot east of town where they had a beautifully clear view.

As the time approached for the earth to pass through the comet's tail, panic began to spread through the Negro community. Some thought that the deadly cyanogen gas mentioned in the newspapers would destroy all human life; others simply thought it would be the end of the world. When May 18 came, many of the servants did not come to work, 'Nolia among them. They had locked themselves in their cabins, preparing to face the end. All that happened, however, was that the next night the comet, having reversed its position, appeared in the western sky head down and tail up. Auntee took the children to the well-equipped campus observatory to see the comet through the telescope. After they had looked, the professor of astronomy told them that the comet would make another transit in seventy-five years. They added it up in their minds—that would be 1985. On their way back home Billy and Jack talked about the return of Halley's Comet. "Will we see it again?" the two small boys wondered.

The terror that had gripped 'Nolia and some of her friends was a reaction as old as humanity based on the belief that such natural phenomena as comets were omens, signs, and portents. A few years earlier a phenomenon had appeared in Mississippi's political skies which proved to be as true a portent as the astronomical one had proved fanciful. Its name was James Kimble Vardaman. A young man of the "small-farmer" class in central Mississippi's hill country, he had added newspaper editorship to law practice with marked success. Preaching many of the doctrines of the agrarian reformers, he hotly attacked Governor Anselm J. McLaurin and his Democratic party machine. Though he failed in two attempts at the governorship, he built a substantial following as he rose to become speaker of the house in the legislature. He ran for governor again in 1903, waging his campaign primarily upon an issue on which he and his bitter rivals were in fundamental agreement. Here his affinity was not so much with Georgia's Populist Tom Watson as with South Carolina's demagogic "Pitchfork Ben" Tillman. In one debate Vardaman declared, "The Negro is necessary in the economy of the world, but he was designed for a burden-bearer. Six thousand years ago the Negro was the same in his native jungles that he is today. . . . Then why squander money on his education when the only effect is to spoil a good field hand and make an insolent cook? God Almighty fixed his position, and it remained for that coon-flavored miscegenist, Teddy Roosevelt, to attempt to improve on the plan."

A number of things seemed to work in Vardaman's favor. Scandals in Jackson hurt the incumbents. Meanwhile, the handsome indefatigable candidate traveled over the state, usually clad all in white, delivering tirades in his flowery, oratorical style. Finally, after a second primary runoff, he won by 7,000 votes. In his inaugural address Governor Vardaman noted the "intestinal conflict" just passed and pleaded for party harmony to bring progress in Mississippi.

Although he continued to urge the abolition of Negro schools and the repeal of the Fourteenth and Fifteenth Amendments, he compiled a distinguished record in other areas. The school system was improved, the prison system was reformed, and laws were passed regulating railroads, insurance companies, banks, utilities, and trusts. He vetoed legislation favoring these interests and urged better social welfare provisions. The prison reforms had reflected something besides Vardaman's humanitarian concerns. For years the small farmers had seen the convict-leasing system as a special advantage for a few big Delta planters. When Vardaman eliminated the last of it, he was working in the interest of the class which had helped make him governor. The "revolt of the rednecks" might be a long way from victory, but it had certainly begun. James K. Vardaman was both a portent and exemplar of these changing facts of Mississippi politics, but his transit through the firmament was not nearly so steady as that of Halley's Comet.

Because he could not succeed himself, Vardaman ran for senator in the summer of 1907. He lost to Delta planter John Sharp Williams, but the next year he found himself in another heated struggle when Anse McLaurin died and a joint caucus of the legislature heard candidates for his unfinished term. The balloting dragged on amidst charges of bribery. Then, after six weeks, State Senator Leroy Percy, another Delta aristocrat, won by a slim margin. Vardaman's deeply embittered supporters soon made plans for the campaign of 1911, when "the White Chief" would challenge Percy again for a full six-year term. This time they would be ready to take on both the McLaurin machine and the Delta politicians.

Some of the organizing had begun even before the results of "the Secret Caucus" (the Percy faction had pushed through the provision for voting by secret ballot) were revealed. In late January, when reports of bribery attempts were circulating but it was still thought Vardaman might win, the *Eagle* carried a brief but significant item. It read, "A Mass meeting was held at the Courthouse Saturday. A Vardaman Club was organized by electing Hon. J. W. T. Falkner President." Six weeks later the object of all this activity was actually in Oxford. On Monday, March 14, 1910, farmers on the far edges of the county, from Harmontown on the northwest to Dallas in the southeast, rose earlier than usual to be sure they would finish the farm chores in time to make the trip over the rutted roads to hear him. By noon 5,000 citizens had assembled at the Courthouse to see "the White Chief," and it was reported that "the enthusiasm that greeted him was phenomenal." The hill counties had supported him in victory, and they seemed only to have closed behind him more solidly in defeat. Young Lee M. Russell mounted the platform to speak at length about the severe difficulties which had beset Governor Vardaman in Jackson. Then, at 1:30 P.M., J. W. T. Falkner rose and stepped to the center of the platform, where he proceeded to introduce James K. Vardaman "in a beautiful and eloquent speech." This kind of occasion, rather than the quick cut and thrust of debate, was what Vardaman liked best. Responding typically to the occasion, "For nearly two hours he charmed the eager crowd of listeners."

James K. Vardaman did not come from J. W. T. Falkner's social stratum any more than Lee M. Russell did. But apparently sectional loyalties were intensely strong, and even though Vardaman advocated federal ownership of the railroads, old railroad-man Falkner must have far preferred Vardaman in a position of power to an unscrupulous "ring politician" of the McLaurin stripe or a rich Delta planter like Leroy Percy. Apparently Vardaman's personal magnetism was very considerable, and even the hostile description of William Alexander Percy, who had helped his father campaign against Vardaman, reveals some of it. Percy saw Vardaman as "a kindly, vain demagogue unable to think, and given to emotions he considered noble. He was a handsome, flamboyant figure of a man, immaculately dressed, wearing his black hair long to the shoulders, and crowned with a wide cowboy's hat. . . . He had made a good governor . . . and he craved public office because the spot-light was his passion and because, eternally in need of money, he abhorred work. . . . For political platform he advertised his love of the common people. . . . He stood for the poor white against the 'nigger'—those were his qualifications as a statesman."

There were men coming along who would follow in the path James Kimble Vardaman had cleared, without, however, possessing his ability, honesty, and commitment to reform. On August 2, 1910, one of them appeared at a barbecue on the Camp Ground. His name was Theodore G. Bilbo, and he came from Pearl River County, in the southern tip of the state. He had burst into sudden notoriety after the secret caucus by declaring that, with the concurrence of Vardaman leaders, he had set out to trap the opposition by allowing them to think they had bribed him and then revealing their names. According to Senator Bilbo, a wealthy planter and Percy adherent named L. C. Dulaney obliged by paying him $645 with a promise of more to switch his vote from Vardaman to Percy for U.S. Senator. These sensational allegations, charges, and countercharges were followed by two trials, one to expel Bilbo from the senate and the other to convict Dulaney of bribery. The resolution to expel Bilbo failed of passage by one vote.

Dulaney was acquitted. The Percy faction hit at both Bilbo and Vardaman, declaring that Bilbo "has destroyed his usefulness to The Ambitious One," and suggesting that the solution to the problem of Theodore G. Bilbo was "to confine the malodorous creature in a small room with a dozen polecats until they stink each other to death." Bilbo's counter-blast was a declaration that "the fight between the classes and the masses, between the corporate influences and the people is on, and it will be a fight to the finish." It proved impossible to determine objectively whether the bribery charges by Bilbo or those of his enemies were true, but it was unquestionable that political lines "were to be drawn more tightly and with more vindictiveness than ever before in the history of the state, and scarcely a man in politics but believes that he owed his success or his defeat to his stand on the question. . . . The malice, ignorance, and thoughtlessness with which the factions carried on their fight convinced many good people that a great wrong had been perpetrated. The result was a great political upheaval and the bringing of the revolution, started by Vardaman in 1903, to complete fruition."

Colonel J. W. T. Falkner was completely committed to support "the White Chief" but not the ambitious Theodore Bilbo. It appeared, however, that Lee M. Russell was prepared to work closely with Bilbo. There was evidence that he was preparing for intensified political campaigning ahead. He had leased out the Opera House. The campaign of 1911 had virtually begun, though it was nearly a year away on the calendar, and now he would not have to worry about what attractions were to be booked into the Opera House or who was running the projector. There were also indications that the young man from Dallas was beginning to acquire further affluence. "The city is to have a new automobile," the *Eagle* reported. "Mr. Lee M. Russell has recently purchased a new 7-passenger 60 horsepower Thomas Flier and will have the same here the latter part of this week. The Thomas Flier is the highest class car built in America."

Spurred, perhaps, by the example of his junior partner, Colonel Falkner had bought another automobile. But this time it was not a homemade device put together by Mr. Buffaloe but an elegant Detroit-manufactured vehicle. "It was a 1909 model Buick touring car," his grandson remembered, "no doors in front, a rubber bulb horn attached to the steering wheel column, brass trimmings all over, right-hand drive, gasoline and spark levers on a quadrant above the steering wheel, completely smooth, no-tread tires, carbide lights, big gear shift, and hand brake levers offset on a heavy rod extending out from the right front floor board." It was driven for Grandfather by Chess Carothers, a freckled, mocha-colored man of considerable ingenuity and imagination. The trips which really tested his mettle were the family excursions all the way to Memphis, with Grandfather up front beside him and Auntee, Sallie Murry Wilkins, and Billy and Jack Falkner in the back seat. It was Chess's responsibility to pack the tool kit with extra fuel, spare parts, chains, a lantern, rope, a hammer, and a hatchet. It was Auntee's responsibility to see that the food basket was amply loaded with lunch and dinner. Another of her duties was restraint of Grandfather, as when a blowout plunged his right elbow into the apple pie: "Grandfather's face took on the reddish hue of pre-explosion anger, his linen tourist cap trembled on his head, and he was just about to blow up like the tire, when Auntee reached over, touched him gently on the arm and said, 'Now Pappy, don't.' " She would have to perform that same office again four miles north of town at College Hill when the auto bogged down in a sand bed and he had to pay three dollars to two men—standing by, virtually, waiting for such a misfortune—to pull the Buick out.

J. W. T. Falkner's growing irascibility was no indication of decreasing vigor. That fall of 1910 he demonstrated again his ability to organize a business and develop it quickly on a paying basis. There were two banks in Oxford, the Merchants and Farmers and the Bank of Oxford. The vice-president of the latter was Lem Oldham and its president was James Stone, a well-to-do lawyer, originally from Panola County. He had succeeded Falkner as local counsel to the Illinois Central Railroad, and some said that a kind of rivalry existed between the two men, although both families were on good terms and Mrs. Stone and Maud Falkner were particular friends. Whether a sense of rivalry entered into the Colonel's motivation or not, it turned out to be a good stroke of business when he opened a new bank chartered October 4, on the west side of North Street where it joined the Square. It was the First National Bank of Oxford: capital stock, $30,000, J. W. T. Falkner, President, and O. B. Boone, Cashier. An enormous cherry desk, five feet wide with a roll top, was moved in for the president. Often, though, he would be seen sitting on the corner, his chair tipped back against the wall of the building. He would retire to his office faithfully every day, however, after the heavy noon meal. There, his privacy guarded by the napping Chess Carothers, he would enjoy a midafternoon rest on an old leather couch.

In six weeks business had increased to such an extent that an assistant cashier was employed to help O. B. Boone. The bank continued to grow, and though it had other stockholders besides himself, Falkner seems always to have considered it *his* bank and no one else's. On one occasion, returning late with several cronies from Jackson, he descended from the train and ushered his guests into the car. All were by now both high-spirited and tipsy. Falkner ordered Chess not to drive to the respective homes but to circle the dark and deserted Square for a while. As they approached the bank on one of their circuits, the Colonel ordered Chess to stop and fetch him the brick he saw lying by the board walk. That done, he ordered Chess to drive slowly by the bank. Steadying himself, he faced the shiny plate-glass window of the First National Bank of Oxford. To the encouragement of his fellow revelers, he drew back his arm, took deliberate aim, and let fly with the brick. The car passed, and there was the resounding smash as the big pane was shivered into splinters. Later that night one of his friends asked him why he had done it. Buoyed up by still more bourbon he replied, "It was my Buick, my brick, and my bank."

Although his father and Lee Russell, and others, might spend their money on contraptions such as automobiles, Murry Falkner was sticking to the tried and true. The new firm of Falkner & Bennett advertised "Several nice buggies. If you are in the market we will be glad to show you what we have." And in 1910 he was right; Lafayette County along with most of the rest of the nation still operated on a horse-and-buggy economy. Observant Billy Falkner must have watched his father as he dealt in both horseflesh and buggies. And he must have absorbed much of the lore of horses and horse-trading. For those who wanted to learn there were always aids to experience. One publisher advertised, "Don't buy a doped horse and don't let yourself be swindled by a crooked horse dealer on any of the score of tricks he has up his sleeve. The 'gyp' is abroad in the land. Every day buyers of horses are shamefully fleeced. Don't be one of the victims. Learn how to protect yourself in buying, selling, or trading. Get this sensational new book, 'Horse Secrets,' by Dr. A.S. Alexander and make yourself horse-wise and crook-proof. Learn how 'bishoping' is done, how a 'heaver' is 'shut,' and a 'roarer' is 'plugged,' how lameness, spavins, and sweeny are temporarily hidden. The 'burglar' dodge. The horsehair trick. Cocaine and gasoline doping. The ginger trick. The loose shoe trick. In short, how to beat all the games of crooked auctioneers and dealers." All his life Billy Falkner would own and ride horses. No one could say that he did not have the background for it.

Though Grandfather might turn to automobiles and Father display continued interest in horse-drawn vehicles, Billy and Jack had interest to spare for Great-grandfather's love: the locomotive. In late February or early

March when the fruit trains began carrying strawberries to the North, Billy, Jack, and Johncy would slip out before daybreak, position themselves on a high bank south of the station, and wait. They would know both the engine and the hand on the whistle when the sound came. There would come the first faint intimations, then as "the train entered the level straightaway track south of town we could plainly hear the quickening of the locomotive's exhaust—at first heavy and dull, then (as the speed increased) light, sharp, precise, and distinct. When it had regained almost full speed on the level track, the wheels hummed on the rails, and the exhaust beats were so rapid that one was barely out of the stack before another exploded upon it—and again the magnificent whistle spilled and spread out its song upon the quiet countryside, at once lonely, lovely, and unforgettable." Then, reluctantly, they would tear themselves away, regretting the locomotives still to the south of Thacker's Mountain, and make their way home to breakfast and thence to school.

But there was another machine that would ultimately have more fascination for all four Falkner boys than any buggy, automobile, or locomotive. It was relatively new, and it was called an aeroplane. That spring, one of the issues of Billy's magazine, *The American Boy,* had carried an article about this new machine complete with structural drawings and instructions for building one. It was perfectly natural, then, that Billy should call Jack, Johncy, and Sallie Murry together in the carriage house to tell them that they were going to build an aeroplane and to explain how they would do it. They set to work in the old barn using Murry Falkner's house tools. For the framework they used the long poles that normally supported Maud Falkner's bean plants. For fabric they pasted on newspapers but later switched to sturdier wrapping paper. One day at suppertime Maud Falkner asked the children what they had been building. An aeroplane, they replied matter-of-factly. After a moment she did a classic double take, then stopped and turned to Billy. "Did you say an aeroplane?" she asked. Jack remembered his answer. "He looked up at her with steady, open affection as I have seen him do a thousand times and replied 'Yes'm.' " Somehow satisfied, Maud Falkner went on with supper.

Finally the monoplane was finished and hauled to the takeoff spot by the assembled Negro crew: Mink and Jessie Hayes, Mallory, and "Right-now-for-Bear" Dooley. At first they couldn't budge it, but finally they were ready. "Let go!" shouted Billy from inside, and the crew gave a powerful heave. Airborne for an instant, the plane pitched as the tail rose. Then it swung through an arc in a half-revolution so that Billy was for a moment suspended upside down. Then pilot and craft thumped down into the bottom of the ditch in a flutter of paper and bean poles. Billy silently picked his way out of the shattered fuselage as his crew looked on, dumb with disappointment. Finally they turned and walked back to the house for supper.

Each day might bring new triumphs (or disasters). If there were no project to be planned, there were always games to be played—like baseball. Billy was usually the pitcher, Johncy played shortstop, and to Jack fell the knuckle-crippling position of catcher. They would have no difficulty organizing teams on South Street, and Billy would usually captain his. The game would become more exciting, complicated, and difficult on some late summer afternoons, however, when some of the adults would manage to get away from their businesses on the Square to join them. Opening the Falkner gate, free of the department store for an hour, Mr. Neilson would shout, "Me and Ed and Jim will take on the Falkner boys!" Then the contest might rage until twenty or thirty runs had been scored, the boys trying desperately to hang on and stay in range of their older opponents.

The summer wore on, the long days waned, and on Monday, September 12, 1910, Billy Falkner returned to the Oxford Graded School, along with 400 other students. Professor E. S. Balthrop, yet another new principal for the Oxford school, noted that "from present indications it will be necessary to enlarge the building at an early date to accommodate the pupils." The seventh-grade curriculum had been enlarged over previous years, and in addition to the staple courses, the students would be exposed to U.S. history and sanitation. The teacher was Miss Ella Wright, a handsome-looking woman with a reputation for excellence and versatility. She was particularly good at mathematics, but she also taught some agriculture to her students and specialized in Misissippi history, with heavy emphasis on the Civil War. This was a subject it would have been difficult to avoid at any time in Oxford, but it was particularly true now.

During the winter and spring of 1910, a dozen issues of the *Eagle* had carried a column entitled "Early Recollections of Oxford," which had set forth some of the history of the town from its earliest times. Then, in June, the editor made another appeal: "All persons that remember incidents of interest that occurred in our country during the war or the reconstruction period are personally invited to contribute to this column." The response had been quick in coming. A series in "The Confederate Column" had been entitled "Secession in Lafayette County." It was prime material for young imaginations. One installment had described the mustering of troops into state service in the Courthouse yard on February 23, 1861. "A few nights afterward," it went on to note, "there was a brilliant reception at the Female College in honor of The Lamar Rifles and The University Greys. . . . The young soldiers with their brilliant uniforms and the young ladies, both of the college and the town, with their lovely costumes and lovely faces made it a scene of beauty and uniqueness long to be remembered."

Miss Ella Wright would teach Billy Falkner and the other seventh-graders about Vicksburg and Shiloh and Brice's Crossroads if they hadn't heard those stories already—perhaps from the mouths of men who had fired muskets or swung sabers there. But she could have told her class better than any veteran at a reunion or maiden aunt recounting history, about such Mississippi history as the development of the Natchez Trace, before Oxford was founded—how this wilderness road not only provided better communication between Washington and the isolated Natchez district but attracted settlers and planters while making it easier and safer for traders and boatmen, returning from New Orleans or Natchez, to make their way home to Tennessee or on to Kentucky or Ohio. The students would learn how mail-route messengers would leave Nashville to ferry across rivers and spend nights out in the canebrakes before changing horses at Chickasaw and Choctaw agencies, pushing on through desolate swamps before Natchez came into view. They would learn too about the infamous Harpes and other cruel and depraved outlaws who preyed on the weak or unwary who used the Trace. By 1830 this route began to decline in importance, just before the great removals of the Choctaws and Chickasaws and before the settlement of Oxford. Those few who did not know about John Chisholm, John J. Craig, and John D. Martin would doubtless learn from tall, commanding Miss Wright how the three had opened a trading post where the dark, moccasined men came with pelts to trade in what was now the Courthouse Square. After them came Robert Shegog and Thomas Dudley Isom, and in time Shegog had his big columned house and Isom had his M.D., and the legislature created Lafayette County, and Ho-kah decided she would sell to Chisholm, Martin, and Craig the virgin land that became Oxford, the county seat. This was June, 1836. It thrived though other towns did not. Wyatt, thirteen miles north on the Tallahatchie, saw more hooting steamboats at her wharves than did Memphis. The Panic ruined Wyatt, but settlers kept coming into this new country. The times and men were violent, though Miss Wright no doubt spared the children the grislier atrocities (not knowing, perhaps, what Hal Cullen could tell them about Nelse Patton). And then, inevitably, they came to the War.

Some of them were raised, of course, by the undefeated aunts who would never surrender. Most of them had lost ancestors, and for those in whom memory was not green, there were celebrations meant to keep it so. (In January when the U.D.C. had met to memorialize Robert E. Lee, a young soprano had rendered "Just Before the Battle, Mother," another young lady had recited "The Sword of Lee," and a male quartet had sung "Tenting Tonight.") Some had no doubt found mementos such as old horse pistols. But there was also less perishable history, right around them. Just across the street from The Big Place stood Henry Tate's house. In one of its windowpanes, faintly scratched there by a diamond ring, was a name: Jane Taylor Cook. She had carved it there, people said, during the dark days of 1863. She was watching through that window one day when she saw the 7th Tennessee Cavalry moving down South Street in retreat before the advancing Yankees. Incensed, she ran out into the street and "cursed the men out" for running from the bluecoats. A captain in the regiment saw her and admired her. "I am going to come back and marry that girl," he said. He was William Montgomery Forrest, old Bedford Forrest's son. He kept his word.

Some romantic tales did not end so happily. There was the legend of beautiful, tragic Judith Shegog. (Estelle Oldham heard it first from Miss Ellen Bailey one day as Miss Ellen handed tea and cookies around to Lida Oldham and the other ladies who had come to her for their ceramics lesson.) When A. J. Smith had brought his army to Oxford in 1864, some of them had bivouacked on Jacob Thompson's place, right across from Robert Shegog's big, gracious house, which Miss Ellen now occupied. Young Judith Shegog had fallen in love with a Yankee lieutenant. When it came time for the troops to leave Oxford, the young lovers decided they would not be separated. Judith would leave with the lieutenant. They knew, of course, that her father would never consent to such a scheme, so they devised a plan. Under cover of darkness, the lieutenant silently made his way across the Thompson place, across the road, and to the shadow of Judith's porch. She was waiting on the small second-story balcony framed by the big pillars on either side of the door. He quickly uncoiled a rope ladder and with one sure cast pitched the end of it over the balcony railing. She made her end of the rope fast while he held tight to the loose end. Carefully, moving slowly because of the voluminous skirts and the bag she carried, Judith swung herself over the balcony railing and began to place her small feet on the uncertain rope rungs, one after another. Suddenly she lost her balance. With a shriek and a swirl of skirts she lost her hold and pitched backwards in the darkness. She struck headfirst on the brick walk with a sickening thud and lay there before the horrified eyes of her lover, her slim neck broken. Now on some nights Miss Ellen could hear the faint steps, and feel, as her skin prickled, the sad ghostly presence of the dead girl.

And everybody knew the other stories, not just about how A. J. Smith had burned the town but about how the university had been turned into a hospital for part of the war, how they had brought them in, shattered and bleeding, from the fields at Shiloh. Nearly two thousand had been cared for in the old buildings, and more than a third of them had never left Oxford, lying now in the quiet cemetery beside the campus. They knew too how Grant had made his headquarters in Oxford that fall after Shiloh, and how he was supposed to have looked down South Street and said he thought it must be one of the prettiest streets in the country.

In spite of Miss Ella Wright's skill, Billy Falkner often sat in her class gazing out the window, thinking of something else. There were numerous distractions. Overcrowding was one. (Miss Annie Chandler and Miss Laura Eades each had seventy-five pupils crammed into her room, and while one of the three high school teachers stayed on duty in the hall, the other two had to teach 117 students between them.) Another distraction, for Billy, came from events in the contemporary world.

In July of 1909 the Frenchman Louis Blériot had won the £1,000 prize offered by *The Daily Mail* for flying the English Channel. He had done it in a 25 h.p. monoplane made from his own design. Now, in the fall of 1910, there were touring aviators staging "aviation meets" in American cities. There was one in Los Angeles, sometimes attended by as many as 50,000 people in one day, at which a Frenchman named Louis Paulhan and an American named Glenn H. Curtiss smashed the old aeroplane speed records one after another. Then, marvelously enough, a group of flying daredevils came to Memphis to stage an aviation meet there. The pages of the Memphis *Commercial Appeal* were full of it. There were pictures of Blériot and the craft he had designed to fly the channel. One of the Frenchmen in the Memphis show was flying a Blériot monoplane, an exotic craft they called "Demoiselle." There were aerobatics, speed tests, and a race between an aeroplane and an automobile. The two daredevils would roar around the track, the driver straining the blunt, ugly car with its great plume of dust, and the pilot, perhaps eight feet above him, canting one wing to within five feet of the dirt as he banked his fragile, awkward craft. Now when Billy Falkner sketched in class he would still draw pictures of guns (he drew a whole set inside the spelling book of Fred Ward Wright, Miss Ella's nephew), but instead of the locomotives and cowboys being bucked off their horses, he carefully filled pages with pictures of goggled men and their fragile, angular machines. In a way this might have seemed like vindication, if any were needed, of the hours of work that came to an end in the pile of sticks and paper at the bottom of the ditch.

But other changes were taking place in Billy's life besides his growing impatience with school and the increasing frequency with which he played hooky. (He had not been to Sunday School for the better part of a year.) For one thing, Maud Falkner's keen eyes had noted a stoop developing in her oldest son's shoulders. The solution was clear; there were pictures of it in the newspaper every week: shoulder braces. So that winter Billy Falkner—and Sallie Murry too—were laced into the corset-like contraption that Sallie Murry found a torture. It was like a canvas vest, with armholes that cut when the laces in back were drawn tight and tied—out of reach of the sufferer's fingers. Sallie Murry got out of hers whenever she could manage it. Billy apparently acquiesced, even though it meant a cessation of baseball and the other activities that required more freedom of movement than the shoulder braces would allow. But in a way he didn't mind as much as Johncy, for instance, would have. Billy would play baseball again, and football and tennis, but there was a strong and growing tendency in his make-up to the sedentary, to conservation of energy and movement, to direction and observation rather than participation. And there were other factors, too.

When Billy Falkner had first become interested in the new girl on South Street, he "tried to attract her attention by being the loudest one, the daringest. But the more he tried the more mussed he got, and sweaty, and dirtier, and Estelle simply wasn't interested." Later, of course, he had discovered that he really liked wearing stylish clothes. Now, he "found he could stay neat all day and didn't necessarily have to get dirty and mussed just to have a good time. He learned to entertain himself in other ways, like reading and painting. He found that Estelle liked him better neat and with her listening Bill found he could talk. From then on he spent more and more time down at her house, being with her and talking to her and listening to her play. She was an accomplished pianist even then, for Miss Lida was a music teacher and taught all her daughters to play, Estelle best of all."

For another thing, Billy and Estelle shared an interest in writing—his writing. For now, at age thirteen, he was producing not only sketches and stories, but bits of poetry too.

13

January, 1911–October, 1915

> . . . that April morning when you woke up and you would think how April was the best, the very best time of all not to have to go to school, until you would think *Except in the fall* with the weather brisk and not-cold at the same time and the trees all yellow and red and you could go hunting all day long; and then you would think *Except in the winter* with the Christmas holidays over and now nothing to look forward to until summer; and you would think how no time is the best time to not have to go to school and so school is a good thing after all because without it there wouldn't be any holidays or vacations.
>
> —*The Town* (301–302)

One of the Falkners' neighbors on Second South Street was a tall, elegant bachelor named Watson Wardlaw. The Falkner boys would hang on the fence to watch him pass, driving a shining buggy pulled by a "spanking bay." On his way to give some young lady a ride, he would be dressed in a neat suit, a handkerchief rakishly displayed in his breast pocket. Wat Wardlaw was the opposite of his partner, Ed Davidson, a rotund, white-haired little man whose flushed complexion gave rise to knowing surmises among his customers. The good business done by Davidson and Wardlaw's was due primarily to Wardlaw, who was pleasant, polite, and got along with everyone. Their place on the the north side of the Square was a combined jewelry shop and bookstore. Wat would stand behind the counter, a Beau Brummell in his frock coat, and would sell a customer a two-dollar book with the same flourish he would employ with a diamond ring. One of the store's chief attractions was a small back room, comfortably furnished with chairs and book shelves where customers were equally free to make a selection or simply sit and read. It was well patronized. There would be townspeople, two or three university students, and, in the afternoon, high school students on their way home. Billy Falkner and Estelle Oldham would see each other there. Often she would be reading fashion magazines and he would be reading poetry. They discovered, though, that the latter was a love they shared, with Estelle's taste usually leading her to the works of the Brownings. From time to time he would lean over and ask, "What are you reading?" On other occasions he would bring a book to her. "Look here," he would say, "I found something you might like."

One day in Davidson and Wardlaw's he handed her a few sheets of paper. They bore verses, rather formal with a good deal of pastoral imagery. Periodically, he would bring her more of his poetry to read. One day he gave her two sheets carefully bound together and covered with lines written in his upright yet flowing hand.

"Which one do you like better?" he asked.

Estelle read them both carefully and then pointed to the right-hand page. "This one," she answered.

"You may not be a poetess," he said, "but you're a darn good literary critic." He smiled. "Those are from 'The Song of Solomon.' The others are mine."

Estelle was pleased. She was also curious. As soon as she reasonably could, she excused herself. Then she hurried home to get out her Bible and read the rest of "The Song of Solomon."

But poetry—his and other people's—was not the only medium Billy Falkner was working in. One day after school Robert Farley walked into Davidson and Wardlaw's. He was a classmate and the son of the dean of the university law school. When he walked up to the counter he saw a tablet lying on it. "That's a story Billy Falkner wrote," Wardlaw told him. "He left it here." Wardlaw thought it was good. "Why don't you read it?" he said. Robert Farley could not recall anything about the story years later, but the tablet, with its precisely written lines, was further evidence that the boy who used to draw pictures, then supply texts to go with them, was now becoming more and more interested in what had started as an adjunct—no matter how much Miss Maud might be pleased if he followed Lelia Butler's bent and became an artist. By now, even though Murry Falkner liked pictures of dogs and horses, he must have found it still harder to understand this son who was quiet, sometimes withdrawn, who would evade his chores or talk someone else into doing them when he could, and who now spent time not only reading poetry but writing it and then copying it out into a tablet.

Murry Falkner's business seemed to be doing well enough. This was due in no small part to his manager and junior partner in the buggy agency, Mr. Charlie D. Bennett, a white-haired aristocratic-looking man. Not only did he see to it that the books of the stable and transfer company were kept in order, and that the ice orders in summer and the coal orders in winter were filled promptly, but he sometimes went out to bring back Mammy Callie after one of her departures. With Charlie Bennett in the office, and Buster Callicoat in the stable to handle the horses and Earl Wortham to shoe them, Murry Falkner could mount and ride off somewhere knowing that he would hardly be missed. His father's enterprises were prospering. The gilt lettering on the law office door read, "Falkner, Russell, and Falkner." "John, honey" had his diploma on the wall now, along with the certificate testifying that he had passed the state bar; so now he was a full, though junior, member of the firm. His help made it easier for J. W. T. Falkner to spend the greater part of his day at the bank, whose capital stock had now increased to $50,000. The bank was attracting investors. By the summer of 1911 one enterprising businessman named T. W. Avent would have a place on the board of directors. Not too much later another investor would come in, a shrewd country man named Joe Parks, who was already making a name for himself in Lafayette County and Oxford.

It must have come as something of a surprise to J. W. T. Falkner to find suddenly that he had something of a social life. William Burns and his sister, Miss Sallie Burns, were Ripley connections of the Falkners who now lived in Oxford. William Burns had become interested in a young Californian named Bess Kennedy, and he had invited her and her mother to visit him and his sister. When they arrived, Holland Wilkins and Sallie Burns gave a reception for them at The Big Place. Bess's mother, Mrs. Mary F. Kennedy, was the widow of a ship's cabinetmaker. She was attractive, and some of the Falkners thought she had come on the trip with her cap already set for a Southern Colonel. J. W. T. Falkner had not stopped grieving for Sallie Murry, but he found Mrs. Kennedy a very attractive woman. He began to see more of her.

Things seemed to be going the Colonel's way politically, too. On May 23 the Central Vardaman Club of Oxford presented its Vardaman Day program, presided over by the club president, John Falkner, Jr. The tempo of the campaign picked up in July when local candidates announced for office. Joe Parks was running for supervisor from Beat Two, Buck Collins (whose sideline was curing warts and wens with a black salve handed down in his family) from Beat One, and J. B. Bundren from Beat Four. Announcing for county attorney was John Falkner, Jr. Vardaman sentiment seemed to be higher than ever. The town of Taylor, eight miles southwest of Oxford, had organized its own Vardaman Club, with Robert X. Williams as president. One of those even more pleased than Colonel Falkner about the way things were going was Lee M. Russell. This time he was running for the office of state senator.

"The Great White Chief" campaigned for the U.S. Senate throughout the state. A tall, commanding figure, Vardaman would orate dramatically from an eight-wheeled lumber cart pulled by matched teams of white oxen. The previous year Leroy Percy had become enraged on one occasion by heckling Vardaman supporters and had denounced them as "cattle" and "rednecks." Vardaman's use of the oxen threw the word back into Percy's teeth, and when Vardaman's supporters wore red ties at his rallies, they were picking up Percy's contemptuous epithet and using it for their own purposes.

Theodore G. Bilbo, now running for lieutenant governor, had been educated as a Baptist minister as well as a lawyer, but he had by now gained a reputation as a master of invective, a speaker who would use the lewd or profane whenever it suited him. During the campaign his insults had already brought quick retaliation. When he had called two men nearly unprintable names, one had caned him and the other had pistol-whipped him into unconsciousness. Charges of all kinds were leveled against him. One was that he kept a young girl in a Jackson assignation house run by a mulatto woman. Tricked into speaking on the same platform with him, Leroy Percy lost his temper again and hearkened back to the senate vote which, with one more yea, would have expelled Bilbo from the chamber. He declared that Bilbo then was "a mark for the scorn and contempt of all honest men, only one figure, a characterless man, a self-confessed liar, a self-confessed bribe-taker; and for his only ally, a poor, broken-down, shameless woman of the streets." Now, Percy predicted, before this campaign was over, Vardaman would rue his choice of this "vile degenerate," and would pray, "Oh God! deliver me from this body of death." But the large crowds continued to turn out for the object of this abuse as well as for his running mate.

Vardaman was bitterly opposed by the interests he habitually attacked, particularly—in an irony which must have outraged J. W. T. Falkner—by the Gulf & Ship Island Railroad Company. But in many Mississippi counties these attacks were a sheer waste. In the northern hill counties, wrote one Vardaman supporter, "You had just as well go to church anywhere in Pontotoc . . . get up in the pulpit and tell the people that Jesus Christ is a bastard as to say anything against . . . Vardaman to the people here."

The vote cast was the heaviest in the state's history. By early August it was established that Vardaman had received 76,000 votes, nearly half again as many as Percy and Alexander (the third candidate) combined. And Bilbo had run almost as strongly. Mississippi voters, observed the New Orleans *Picayune*, were "putting the foot down firmly on all that remains of the old aristocracy . . . and they are choosing their representatives among the new generation." In Lafayette County, Bundren, Lovelady, Carothers, and Joe Parks all won election. So did Lee M. Russell, and six weeks later he sold the Opera House. But J. W. T. Falkner, Jr., was defeated for county attorney by a vote of almost two-to-one. However, he quickly applied for the position of secretary of the state senate. And got it.

It had been a pleasant summer for the children. Tyler's Air Dome was operating again, with two shows each night. Three thousand feet of film and one illustrated song cost ten cents—fifteen if you wanted to sit on a chair. For a lucky few there were vacations away from home: perhaps to Michigan or the Gulf Coast for the really affluent; for others, perhaps just to Lafayette Springs, sixteen miles away at the eastern boundary of the county. Lafayette Springs was a popular summer resort which boasted a hotel and cottages. Its attractions were said to be many: "Beautiful shady grounds for children. Cool and airy sleeping rooms. Picturesque walks and lawns for outdoor exercises are a few of the attractions the place offers to those seeking brief escape from the heat and turmoil of city life and lost health. . . ." The last claim was based upon the "waters of the springs," which were "of seven different kinds" and abounded in "health-giving properties. Very effective in obstructing diseases of the kidney, liver, and bowels."

There had been several guests from Oxford that summer. Holland Wilkins had packed up all the children; then, recalled Johncy, "she took all Grandfather's horses and carriages and buggies and Negroes and took us all for a summer trip to Lafayette Springs and left him to walk home from his bank in the rain, and . . . the townspeople heard him cussing every step of the way and never using the same word twice from the corner of the Square to his own side gate." One of the other children taken along to the Springs was Myrtle Ramey. She enjoyed the old hotel and its grounds and she liked the oldest Falkner boy, who was a leader among the youngsters she knew. They would fish in a green, sun-dappled pond. He rolled her first cigarette for her, making it of rabbit tobacco in paper torn from a Sears, Roebuck catalog. Once as she played in the sluice, Billy Falkner, standing on the bank, called that he was going to dive in. She warned him not to, but he dived in anyway and came up covered with green slime. "You were right," he admitted. Other amusements were more restrained. The two would stretch out in barrel-stave hammocks strung between oak trees. There were cords attached to each hammock so that they could pull each other. They took turns reading *The Arkansas Traveller* aloud, though Billy read more than Myrtle did. He tried that summer to get her interested in *Pilgrim's Progress*, but without any luck. Then it was time to go back home.

At home Billy didn't have much more success directing Jack's reading tastes. He had discovered a wonderful book by Herman Melville called *Moby Dick*. He loved it. "It's one of the best books ever written," he told his brother. Jack tried it, decided he didn't care for it, and put it down. It seems likely that William Falkner's tastes in reading were by now more sophisticated than those represented in the curriculum for the eighth grade, which he entered that fall of 1911.

He was one of 112 students in the high school. (Total enrollment was 400, and the annex was supposed to be completed by mid-October.) He no longer stayed in one room with one teacher, but moved from one classroom to another. There was history from Mr. George G. Hurst, the principal of the high school grades, English from Miss Pearl Hickey, and mathematics from Mr. Robert Good. The study periods had been reduced to two, and parents were urged to "see that they get up their lessons at home. Unless lessons are prepared at home," ran the warning, "they will fail to keep up with their class and they will be put back in the next class." Maud Falkner heeded this injunction. Every evening after supper she faithfully cleared the round table in Billy and Jack's bedroom and then placed at its center a freshly cleaned and filled oil lamp. Billy would provide his pocketknife and Jack would sharpen the pencils, as the three boys tried to forestall for a short while longer the plunge into study by discussing the day's events in school or how Halley, Jack's new pony, was performing. It was another ritual which was not likely to revive a fast-waning taste for classroom education.

The List of Educable Children for Lafayette County included "Willie, 14" along with the names of his three brothers under their father's name, but he was not recorded present at the high school for the prescribed number of class days. Maud Falkner was too intelligent a woman not to know that her oldest son was cutting school, and it must have filled her with anger and frustration. Her husband's indifference to formal education placed the burden squarely with her, and inevitably she took her son to task for his truancy. When she did, he would listen submissively. "He never struck back at her," Johncy remembered. "If he couldn't turn her off with a laugh, he simply stood there and listened."

Though Billy Falkner was spending less time at school, he was seeing as much as ever of his particular friends. That fall he and Dewey Linder would go hunting rabbits together behind two beagle hounds Murry Falkner had bought for his older sons. One day when Dewey walked home with him while he dropped off his books, Billy picked up his shotgun and they set off with the barking hounds for Dewey's house. They began their hunt across the road from his place, the dogs ahead of them, scurrying and sniffing as they tried to flush a rabbit from the brush. Suddenly, one darted zigzag up a slope. As the beagles began to drive it toward a ditch, the two boys made for higher ground where they could get a good shot. The dogs followed the rabbit as he raced out of the ditch and then hopped back into it. By now the two boys were running, too. "Watch for him when he jumps out," Dewey shouted to his companion. Billy stopped and quickly brought up the sights as the elusive rabbit hopped up the bank out of the ditch. But the instant he pulled the trigger, one of the dogs sprang up the bank. The shotgun blast took him in the back of the head. Billy Falkner dropped his gun and ran to the dog. He knelt beside him, then picked up the limp form. Carrying his dog in his arms, he ran home and laid him on the porch. Then he went up to his room. Locking the door, he let the tears come. Dewey had watched his friend as he ran out of sight carrying his burden. On the ground lay the Damascus steel gun, Murry Falkner's own, which he had given to his eldest son. Dewey walked on down to South Street and left it at the house, but Billy Falkner never used it after that, and it was years before he hunted again.

Another friend of these years was John Ralph Markette, whose father was an engineer on the Illinois Central. Listening to the fruit trains on a spring morning or the boxcars rumbling by with the bulging bales of cotton, the Falkner boys would catch a certain inflection of the train whistle, and they would say to one another, "That's Mr. Markette with Number 849." Now, when Mr. Markette was switching cars with his engine on the Oxford sidings, Billy Falkner would be allowed to climb aboard. He was welcome as the son of Markette's old railroad friend, Murry Falkner. Billy and John would follow Mr. Markette as he manipulated the whistle, throttle, and brakes. They watched fascinated as the cars coupled, shunted, and uncoupled. Often Billy would shovel coal into the bright, hot firebox of the engine. Sometimes Mr. Markette would even let them hold the throttle in the yard while they were switching. John would stay for a visit at the Falkner home, and it would be Billy's turn to go to Water Valley, fifteen miles south, to visit John. And he would naturally travel in the cab of Number 849. Then, with a good head of steam up, Mr. Markette might let them hold the open throttle again. In Water Valley the two boys would wander through the shops and sheds, closely following the assembling of an engine or the preparation of a locomotive for a trip. Sometimes Billy was boisterous when John and his friends were, but generally he was quiet and often uncommunicative. "He would roam through the woods with us looking for plums, chestnuts, and blackberries," his friend said. "When we piled up leaves to jump in, or made sand houses, he would stand by and observe."

Billy Falkner's absenteeism must have paled into insignificance (for all the family but Miss Maud) next to what Holland Wilkins, and probably the others, could clearly see happening that fall. If Mary Kennedy had deliberately set her cap for J. W. T. Falkner, she had done it cleverly enough. The family was abruptly informed that they were to be married. The wedding was to take place on January 10, 1912, at the home of the bride in San Jose, California. Only later did the family learn what had happened before the union was solemnized. On the night before, J. W. T. Falkner had realized that he really didn't want to get married again after all. Mrs. Kennedy was understandably annoyed. She informed her fiancé that if he did not take his vows with her on the following day, her lawyer would file suit for breach of promise. The unwilling groom decided to go through with it. He did, but spent his wedding night in the bar of their hotel, consoling himself as best he could. The next day the newlyweds left for Oxford.

Colonel Falkner's new stepdaughter, Miss Bessie Kennedy, went along. The *Eagle*'s social writer described the Oxford reception, with Holland Wilkins and Maud Falkner, "all elegantly gowned." Other members of the family participated: "Little Miss Sallie Murry Wilkins and William C. Falkner presided at the punch bowl and aided in making the afternoon a pleasant one for the friends of the family. Dainty refreshments were served and there was a constant stream of friends greeting and welcoming the wife and daughter and wishing them all the happiness anticipated by them in their new home in the sunny South." It seems unlikely that Holland Wilkins and Maud Falkner would have been able to share any of the fine optimism sounded in the social notes of the *Eagle.*

These difficulties were, of course, kept in the family as much as possible. There were difficulties in J. W. T. Falkner's professional family, however, which could not be kept quiet. Lee Russell was working toward a cherished goal, and he had antagonized many and finally embroiled himself in fierce controversy as a result. He had introduced in the state senate bill Number 227 prohibiting all Greek-letter fraternities and other secret societies at the University of Mississippi. Strict enforcement measures were provided. By mid-February the counterattack had been mounted. Most of the businessmen of Oxford signed a circular branding Russell's allegations about the fraternities and their members as untrue. Twenty-six members of the faculty signed a similar circular. As evidence Russell cited the "Alright Club," whose three requisites for membership, he said, were "that the candidate be first a drunkard, secondly a gambler, and that he indulge in the grossest form of licentiousness." He had had a photograph of the club, he maintained, but the book containing it had been stolen from him.

The faculty countered with the assertion that there was no appreciable difference in morality between fraternity and non-fraternity men. Russell replied through the columns of the *Eagle,* defending himself against charges of libeling fraternity members; but more than this, he said, "I am fighting for the University and manhood and womanhood of Mississippi. Myself and hundreds of men throughout this country are right, and right will win. The House of Representatives of Mississippi will seal the doom of the fraternity system in a few days, and this alone will allow the University to prosper." By February 27 the bill had passed both chambers, by a margin of nearly two to one. By September of 1912, when the students would return to Oxford for the new academic year, it would be law. They would be required to sign pledges that they did not belong to Greek-letter fraternities or sororities and would not join one in their time as students at the university. Lee Russell must have been canny enough to realize that he had not democratized the

University of Mississippi by the passage of a law. The matter of fraternities, in any event, was by no means settled.

By now Lee Russell, J. W. T. Falkner, and Lem Oldham were not the only men in Lafayette County who owned automobiles. As the number grew, Murry Falkner's livery-stable business declined. Casting about for something to replace it, he obtained the Standard Oil agency for the county. It was not lubricating or fuel oil, however, but coal oil for lamps. He rented an office near his storage tanks down by the railroad depot, where the tank cars would bring the oil in. One of the Negroes who worked for Murry Falkner would periodically drive up to the storage tanks in a wagon to fill the 500-gallon tank the wagon carried. Then he would begin his rounds of the county. Alternately, the Falkner boys would be allowed to go along (with an ample packed lunch) for an all-day outing. But again Murry Falkner found himself in a not very propitious enterprise. J. W. T. Falkner had kept an eye on his oldest son ever since he had brought him from Ripley to Oxford ten years before. He could see that again something had to be done. Murry Falkner had come to the same conclusion himself. He would have to buy another business, but there was not a great deal left out of the livery-stable investment, and he lacked any substantial cash reserve. He finally had to use the only substantial thing he had—their home. And when December came, they would indeed move to another house on South Street. Grandfather provided the rest of the money needed, and in early March it was announced that M. C. Falkner had bought the hardware store of Mr. Relbue Price.

The only competition would be the Porter-Sisk Hardware Company, and Murry Falkner dutifully began advertising his new enterprise. He listed the names of the wagons and buggies they carried in addition to the standard line of tools, nails, paint, bits, collars, hames, trace chains, and rope that a hardware store had to carry. He was now three removes from the railroad. There had been a sense of motion about the transfer company and livery stable, but there was something distinctly sedentary about the hardware business. He began the new venture with little enthusiasm. A reason for his inauspicious career in merchandising, one of his sons realized, was "that Father was not a natural-born salesman—of hardware or anything else. In fact, he told us several times that he never heard of a Falkner who could sell a stove to an Eskimo or a camel to an Arab." Actually, the Old Colonel had been a spectacular salesman. He had sold his railroad to Mississippi towns and New York bankers and his novels to readers all over the United States, even handling some of the accounts and mailing of the books himself. Murry Falkner's misfortune was that though he lacked this ability, he had the Old Colonel's temper and imperiousness, attenuated though it may have been. As things settled down, however, Murry Falkner's new way of life was not substantially changed, for the store on the southwest corner of the Square "was less than a block from the old livery stable, the office was bigger, the stove warmer, and there were more chairs to accommodate his ever-present cronies."

For the Falkners' neighbors, the Oldhams, things were prospering. Governor Brewer had appointed Lem Oldham a member of his staff with the rank of major. It would be his duty "to appear in full regimentals on all state occasions to assist in lending dignity to the Governor and the state." In that spring of 1912 Lem Oldham's business affairs looked propitious enough for him to undertake the expense of remodeling the Commercial Hotel, which he had purchased.

Lem Oldham's family was prospering, too. Miss Lida had finally shaped the grounds of their home to her satisfaction. There were symmetrically arranged flower beds along the semicircular walk in front of the house as well as at the sides. In the rear there was another flower garden and a vegetable garden. By now Estelle and Tochie had a sister and a brother: eleven-year-old Dorothy Zollicoffer and four-year-old Edward DeGraffenreid. And there was no doubt about the way this family was structured. "Major Oldham was treated like a prince in his home," one friend said. It

William Falkner, about 1911.

was a busy home of constant goings and comings. Estelle and Tochie often gave parties and now were beginning to make frequent trips, sometimes to Memphis or even to Jackson. For the last weekend in October, Estelle and her friend Katrina Carter had been invited to Jackson for a weekend house party at the home of Senator James Kimble Vardaman. Lem and Lida Oldham had not wanted their daughter to go. "But I fussed until I got permission," Estelle later said, and when she and Katrina returned they told their friends that they had had a fine time.

Another invitation came a month later, and again they went. This time on the train ride back to Oxford they were accompanied by James K. Vardaman, Jr. Estelle was conversing happily when the door of the coach opened and Judge Henry C. Niles came walking down the aisle. He greeted his step-granddaughter and told her he was on his way back from holding court at Biloxi. He waited. Then she introduced her friends and young Vardaman. She caught her breath in shock as, for the first time in her life, she saw Papa Niles be rude to someone. He was red-faced with anger. "Do you mean to tell me your father permits you to associate with such people as the Vardamans!" he roared in a voice the whole car could hear. Estelle broke into tears. She had attended her last house party at the Vardamans' in Jackson.

Estelle Oldham was growing up fast. "She was as pretty as a little partridge," one friend recalls. Slight and graceful, she was a good dancer. And she possessed all of the Southern Belle's traditional conversational skills with a young man. There were many of them ready to pay their addresses to her. Billy Falkner loved his cousin Sallie Murry, and like the rest he was captivated by Tochie—gay, confident, and brave, and with something yet of the tomboy about her. He was still close to Myrtle Ramey, and he continued to include her in a very small circle by showing her, from time to time, some of the stories he had written and pictures he had drawn. But there was no doubt that the feeling which had earlier driven him to boisterous actions to gain Estelle Oldham's attention was still deepening.

He was spending more and more of his time at the Oldhams' rather than at home, and soon Jack would begin to do the same. There was an appreciable contrast between the two houses. Maud Falkner was as busy as ever, so busy that she never had time to play the piano, as she had done in New Albany and Ripley. Murry Falkner had flashes of good nature, and sometimes (though he would be just a bit tipsy then) he would sing a favorite song, "The Glow-worm," in a soft but suprisingly good voice. But he would more often be uncommunicative. One of his rules grew out of this trait. There was to be no talking at the table. He would eat, breathing heavily, and when at last he put down his napkin, conversation might begin, but until then Billy and Jack and Johncy and Dean Falkner ate in silence. At the Oldhams' Miss Lida might be playing for her husband, or they could listen to Tochie, who was already so accomplished that she had been chosen to play a solo at the seventh-grade graduation exercises in May. Billy and Estelle might sit and talk about what they were reading or he might show her what he had just written. Often there would be other callers there. Before long some of the callers would be very much in earnest. There was, of course, already some disparity between the two. Estelle had always been precocious. She had worn long dresses before the others had, and now she was a young lady popular enough to be invited to house parties by prominent people in the state capital, whereas Billy was a ninth-grader, concerned with problems such as how to get out of the shoulder braces his mother had laced onto him so he could play football. And there was something he didn't know—next year Estelle's parents would be sending her away to school.

The summer of 1912 proved to be a good deal pleasanter for J. W. T. Falkner than the earlier part of the year. His wife and stepdaughter were spending it in California. If he had found the two of them a trial, no one could deny that his wife had endured her share of provocation. Some of it came from a familiar cause: whiskey. On one occasion, quickly absorbed into Oxford legend, the Colonel was sitting in a chair propped against the bank when Joe Miller went by driving the wagon, pulled by a goat, which he used to deliver milk in Oxford. A friend no sooner dared Falkner to drive the goat-cart around the Square than he was up and in motion with Miller's inelegant rig. This could hardly have been the kind of behavior Mary Kennedy had bargained for when she married her Southern Colonel. But she retaliated. When he came back from carousing in Jackson with his cronies, she would put ipecac in his first drink or in a cup of coffee. As he retched from the dose he could have thought almost fondly of the Keeley Cure.

After his wife left for California he might spend the day driving to Memphis. Once he took Sherwood Butler and Charlie Sisk (a relative of Murry Falkner's hardware competitor) along with him. Unlike other occasions on which they had gotten stuck in the Hurricane Creek bottom or other trouble spots, it was such a good trip that he wrote a letter to the editor about the method that had been used to repair the roads they had traveled. He worked, too. In May he had helped prevent the removal of the federal court from Oxford to Grenada, calling on his old partner, Judge Howry, for help. In August, he defended an old friend in Ripley. His speech, reported the *Sentinel*, "was one of the best, clearest, and ablest ever heard in Ripley. With Colonel Falkner it was a labor of love. His many friends in this county were glad to see him and to hear his voice ring out in the historical courthouse where in former days he met so many big lawyers and where his illustrious father made a great reputation at the bar." But then, in late October, his wife returned from the coast. Along with her daughter, she brought her son, A. R. Kennedy, and his wife and baby.

Physically there was enough room at The Big Place for these houseguests, but emotionally there was not. This was too much. The visit of Mr. and Mrs. Kennedy and their baby turned out to be a very brief one. Then, scarcely two weeks after her return to Oxford, the second Mrs. J. W. T. Falkner, her husband, and her daughter spent a week in Memphis. Maud Falkner accompanied them. Not long after that, it appears, Mrs. J. W. T. Falkner and her daughter left for California. Later the family learned how Grandfather had done it. He had offered to build Mary Kennedy Falkner a house out there and to remember her in his will. She accepted. He built her a $30,000 house, and he told Holland, Murry, and John to remember that when he died she was taken care of. When they all gathered before the groaning table Holland Wilkins set at The Big Place that Christmas, it was just his family seated around the old man once more. This visit to the familiar house must have been especially welcome to Billy Falkner and his brothers, for early in December Murry Falkner had moved his family to the Beanland house. It was on South Street, too, but they had spent half a dozen years in the other house, and this move put a period, somehow, to one part of their childhood.

The situation at school remained much the same. But now, like his grandfather, Billy Falkner began to be seen sitting looking out across the Square. He would prop an old kitchen chair on its back legs against his father's store and sit there for hours. "He was generally almost inert," his desk mate of the previous year remembered, "the laziest boy I ever saw." In school, "he would do nothing but write and draw—drawings for his stories. He couldn't help it. I don't think he could have kept from writing. It was an obsession." His friends would see him sitting in Davidson and Wardlaw's, reading magazines or sometimes writing. He apparently had no thought of publication. He would write stories to entertain Estelle, but on a deeper level he seemed to be writing because he couldn't help himself.

By now, in early 1913, this group of eighth-, ninth-, and tenth-graders was becoming increasingly more social. A few of the older ones would venture into Chilton's drugstore, which was mainly a hangout for college students. It was run by two brothers, Uncle Bob and Uncle Top. Bob was lean and not particularly trusting, whereas Top—whose name came from his shape—was fat and jolly and gave credit.

Most of the socializing was done at people's houses. The girls had formed the MAN Club, the name being derived from the title *Much Ado About Nothing* with one of the middle letters omitted. Myrtle Ramey remembered one particular dance at the Oldhams' and how welcome the children were there. To Rodney Sisk's horror and mortification, he knocked over a table lamp which crashed into pieces on the floor. As he stammered his apologies Miss Lida said simply, "That's nothing. It shouldn't have been there."

Often, the dancing was done to Gramophone accompaniment. Sometimes, though, the girl who was hostess would sit at the family piano and from the gaudy sheet music play the favorite fox trots, waltzes, and two-steps of the moment. In summer the dances would be held on the wide front porches, and if the occasion was special a fond parent might pay for a band from Memphis. One favorite was an amiable forty-year-old Negro named W. C. Handy, who played a golden trumpet. He would bring his band down for a few dollars a man and expenses. When Myrtle's cousins Marvel and Lucille (whom Johncy was growing to like) gave dances, W. C. Handy would play alone, sitting at the piano and fingering the rich chords and steady rhythms that would bring him fame in compositions such as "Yellow Dog Blues," "Aunt Hagar's Blues," and "Beale Street Blues." Billy Falkner attended those parties, as he did those at the Oldhams'. He was not as good a dancer as Johncy, but he was better than Jack, who had no confidence in his ability to steer a girl around a crowded floor amidst gyrating couples. But if John danced best among the Falkner boys, Billy was the best dressed.

He would dress carefully, neatly knotting rich silk ties beneath high starched white collars. There was a kind of dandyism that came out now, and he had a graceful slim figure that the tight clothes flattered. Jack had

William Falkner, 1914.

passed him in both height and weight, and his predisposition to slightness was augmented by the fact that now, in emulation of Estelle, he took only toast and black coffee for breakfast. His looks were changing, too. Sometimes he would comb his hair in a high, pompadour-like style without a part. His forehead was higher now and his nose was still generous. His mouth still looked narrow and set, and the eyes were somehow even keener, more piercing. The face had lengthened and narrowed. It no longer showed the symmetry and charm of the little-boy face, but it was still a striking one. Sometimes the new clothes would be paid for by Grandfather, who would periodically take the three oldest boys with him and herd them from one store on the Square to another, buying three sets of suits, shoes, or overcoats. It was a welcome assistance to Murry Falkner, who had told his prospective customers in the *Eagle*, "we will do a cash business and will appreciate your patronage. We can save you money on anything in hardware. Small profits for cash is our motto."

Estelle Oldham loved to dance. Light and graceful, she never lacked for a partner. And though she had an understanding of sorts with Billy Falkner, she received and accepted invitations from a number of other boys. Unlike her, he moved in a predominantly male society, and though his tastes in clothes had changed, his tastes in activities had not. He loved the outdoors as much as ever. He roamed the woods with his brothers, and as his increasingly erect posture—an almost ramrod straightness—began to reassure Maud Falkner, he was able to evade the torture of the shoulder braces and play pick-up games of baseball again. Football also was popular, and though he was too small and light to be a lineman, his coordination and quickness gave him some of the requisites of a quarterback. Another outdoor activity he enjoyed was scouting. He had always loved camping, and the woodcraft and Indian lore taught in the patrols must have appealed to him. He was still a quiet boy, but he displayed enough talent for leadership and achieved enough popularity to be nominated for president of the troop. The first ballot was inconclusive, and the scoutmaster announced that there would have to be a runoff election between Billy Falkner and the other high-scoring candidate. Suddenly Jack Falkner felt himself confronted with a crisis of conscience. He was devoted to his brother, who had been his leader as long as he could remember, but he thought to himself, "that other boy hasn't got any brothers to vote for him and that's not fair." He voted for the other boy, and to Jack's distress, he won—by *his* vote, Jack was convinced. When the meeting was over, he and his brother walked home in silence. Jack wanted to explain what had happened, but somehow he couldn't bring himself to do it. Finally he blurted it out: he had voted for the other boy. Billy remained silent—not reproachful, but just silent, asking for no details. Jack went on miserably to tell him why he had felt he had to do it. The brothers walked on wordlessly. Clearly, Jack could do what he wished. Billy would stick to the two precepts Maud Falkner had hung over the stove in the kitchen.

By the time scouting activities were getting into full swing that summer of 1913, a sensation occurred which stirred up old animosities to a new pitch: a group of members of the bar of Oxford started proceedings to disbar Lee Russell from the practice of law. At issue was his defense, in several courts, of a student expelled from the university for carrying brass knuckles and a pistol and committing a number of assaults. The Oxford *Eagle* editorialist was among those who supported him. "A motive usually underlies all actions," he wrote. "The records of the court show that the firm of Falkner, Russell, and Falkner, of which Mr. Russell is now the most active member, handles by far the largest business at this bar as against all the combined lawyers, a dozen or more. Sometimes during a whole term of court there is hardly a case that they are not engaged in. That is the rule. Is this not the main reason why these men seek to destroy him? There are certain suits now pending. In the process of filing some of these men at least are vitally concerned. It is freely talked that this is the chief reason why this young man must be destroyed." Among the seven men who brought the disbarment proceedings was James Stone, lawyer and president of the Bank of Oxford. The other authors of the charges were prestigious men, too. Most of them had gone to the university and belonged to a class quite different from that out of which the senator from Dallas had risen. There was talk that the anti-fraternity law had done nothing to make Stone and his confreres any more charitably inclined toward Russell. There were postponements, and it was December before the case was heard by Judge Niles. As usual, he did not disappoint his auditors—most of them, at any rate. "Judge Niles then in his characteristic way," went the report, "most emphatically exonerated Sen. Russell and dismissed the groundless and maliciously designed charges." Some Republicans and most conservative Democrats might lament the rise of the redneck, but Vardaman was still in the Senate, Theodore Bilbo was still the state's lieutenant governor, and Lee M. Russell, beating off a deadly attack on his home grounds, was looking ahead very carefully.

Visiting his stepdaughter and her husband, Judge Niles could see how they were prospering. So, for that matter, could every citizen of Oxford. It had been declared that "Major Lem E. Oldham has proved he is one of the most progressive and public spirited citizens by donating 50 carloads of gravel for the public square from the famous gravel pits at Iuka." Besides such investments as this one, Lem Oldham had his handsome salary as federal court clerk, an income matched by few in Oxford. He and Miss Lida decided to use some of it to give Estelle and Tochie the benefits of a private school education. For Estelle they chose Mary Baldwin College, a Presbyterian institution located in the Blue Ridge Mountains at Staunton, Virginia. Estelle favored Episcopalian Stuart Hall, a boarding school also in Staunton, but Presbyterian Lem Oldham insisted on Mary Baldwin in spite of Staunton's being the birthplace of Democrat (though Presbyterian) Woodrow Wilson. Estelle was not enthusiastic about being cooped up with a bunch of girls, but Miss Lida agreed that it would probably be a good idea for her to have a year at Mary Baldwin anyway. Tochie, her mother insisted, must go to Immaculata in Washington. It had a very good music faculty and Tochie was a promising musician. As for its being a Catholic school, Lida Oldham felt no strangeness about that. She was an Episcopalian herself, although like her husband she never went to church. It was settled. Both girls would go off to school.

Other Oxonians were leaving, too. James Stone's son Phil, a Mississippi B.A. cum laude to his credit, was off to try for another one at Yale. Estelle's friend Janette Stowers was also going to Mary Baldwin. So the Oldhams loaded their touring car and drove to the depot and waited, valises around them, for the train to come in. In quick succession there was the whistle heard from Thacker's Mountain, the roar of the approaching engine, the loading of bags in the hissing steam, and then the quick last goodbye. Estelle Oldham was setting out for the world beyond Mississippi, beyond Jackson and Memphis, beyond the boundaries of her childhood. Back on Jackson Avenue off the Courthouse Square, Billy Faulkner gritted his teeth, pushed open the door, and entered the tenth grade of the Oxford High School.

There was no livery stable to go to now. Even the building had been torn down to make way for the new Opera House. Billy would still sit in front of the hardware store, but the idea of working inside it was even less appealing than working at the transfer company, even though it appears that his father could have used cut-rate help. In December he tried the expedient of cash prizes. The caption above his ad read, TEN DOLLARS IN GOLD! If the customer could answer ten questions—such as, How many men work in Falkner's Store?—he would win a gold piece. And Murry Falkner had other things on his mind besides business at the store. The family was going to move again, for he had bought the home of Mr. M. P. Bishop at the end of North Street and they would move before Christmas. It was another break with the past. The Big Place would still be there, but now the four Falkner boys would be over half a mile away on the other side of town.

Tenth-grader William Falkner kept on reading. Some of the books were mentioned in school, but more often they were ones Miss Maud suggested or others that took his interest in Grandfather's library: volumes of Shakespeare, Fielding, and Conrad. There were translations of Balzac and Hugo, and he read some of these, too. And he continued with his writing. Ralph Muckenfuss noticed no difference in his behavior. If anything, it must have been more pronounced—the quiet student never rude or boisterous, ready to put something on the board whenever he was called on. He might seem abstracted, gazing out the window, but he was capable of the keenest attention with those piercing brown-black eyes when something or someone caught his interest. He wrote letters to Staunton, sometimes with little drawings enclosed or scrawled in ink on the sheets themselves. Finally it was Christmas vacation.

Estelle and Janette came back together in mid-December. Billy Falkner must have felt relieved when he learned that his sweetheart had not been particularly impressed at her school. (They had been taken to tea at Mr. Wilson's house and she thought it rather dour and the whole occasion a bit lugubrious.) She was anxious to extricate herself as soon as she could.

Christmas passed, and then New Year's, and Estelle and Janette went back to school. Billy was left waiting for the spring. His life went on as before, his connection with school growing more tenuous and with little in the way of external activity to replace it. By now his generally remote and dreamy behavior began to be commonly noted, and though he still pitched in baseball season and quarterbacked pick-up football teams, he was decidedly different from the rest. He wrote and drew, and he read. He was silent and tended to keep to himself. Some of the students at the Oxford High School began to tease him and to call him "quair." He made no response.

Oxford felt a brief furor in mid-January when the Merchants and Farmers Bank failed. James Stone's bank and Colonel Falkner's bank stood firm, however, and by March the creditors and depositors of the Merchants and Farmers Bank were being paid off. There was still money for investment as witnessed by the opening of the new Opera House, which was packed in April for the speakers in the Declamation Contest at the County Field Day Meet. A month later the new Lyric Theatre opened its doors. And now, as the spring came in, there was outdoor amusement. "Auto riding is the favorite pastime these warm days," reported the *Eagle*. A week later so many Oxonians had taken up that pastime that the "Local Items" column carried the notation, "Oxford has the auto fever bad." By then the out-of-town students at Ole Miss were streaming home as Oxford families welcomed their own children who had been away at school. Billy Falkner was extremely fond of Miss Lida, and he had continued to call at the Oldhams' house while Estelle was away in Staunton. Now that she had returned he was there nearly every day. But there was another returning student whom he began to see, one whose friendship and interest would have a decisive influence upon his career and his life.

Phil Stone—born Philip Austin Stone—was four years older than William Falkner. Though the tall, thin, brown-eyed young man knew who the younger boy was, there had never been any occasion for either to cross that gulf made by their ages. James Stone wanted his son to have the benefits of both a Southern and a Northern education. Brilliant and precocious, he did not disappoint his father, returning home that June with another B.A., again cum laude, from Yale. Although he was intended for a career in the law like his father and older brothers, Phil Stone's real delight was literature. He had come back from Yale filled with enthusiasm for new novels and books of verse. "Have you read this?" he would ask excitedly. "You must read that," he would say. "I'll lend you my copy." He was interested to learn from his mother, Rosa Alston Stone, that young Billy Falkner was writing poetry. (The families had been friends for years. "Miss Rosie" Stone and Sallie Murry Falkner "ran" the Methodist Church, people said.) Miss Maud had told Miss Rosie that Billy didn't know what to do with his poems, though, and he didn't know of anyone in Oxford who could tell him. Perhaps they weren't good enough to try to do anything with them. Stone was curious to see what the boy had done, so one Sunday afternoon he went over to the Falkner house and Billy got out the meticulously written verses for him to read. The author sat there silently. Stone found himself reading with growing excitement. The verses were by no means brilliant or finished work, but they were clearly promising. "Anybody could have seen that he had a real talent," Stone said. "It was perfectly obvious." Volatile and enthusiastic, Stone immediately set out to give the younger boy encouragement, advice, models for study, and any other help that occurred to him. It was the beginning of a close and fruitful friendship.

Phil Stone was uniquely fitted to serve as William Falkner's friend and mentor. In appearance they were radically different: Stone, tall and full of movement; Falkner, short, slight, and quiet. But their other differences were complementary. Stone was a compulsive talker, a man who loved to teach and tell stories. He had impulses toward literary creation which, without the drive to carry them through to fruition, could only be satisfied vicariously. Billy Falkner was a good listener, and it was a time in his life when he was particularly ready to learn. He was reading as avidly as ever, but he was ready for a change of direction in his reading. He would continue with the masters he had read at his mother's suggestion, but he was ready for the contemporary masters who were doing things in prose and verse of which he was only vaguely aware. He prized Estelle's warm and flattering interest in his work, but as he had said, she was an intuitive critic. Though it was fine to have this encouragement, Stone offered probing questions, specific criticisms, and new examples. Stone was also a complicated person who must have fascinated his younger friend. A college graduate twice over, he had succeeded in the big world of the Northeast as well as in the small world at home. He was different from anyone the boy—already something of a student of human nature—had ever known. Stone was a complicated person. There were pride and vanity in his make-up along with the humor and friendship. But he was highly intelligent, with a facile, multifaceted, quick-silvery mind. He combined dogmatism and intuition. William Falkner had his intuitive qualities, too, but his mode of thought and apprehension must already have been moving in the direction of the deeply meditative, steady and brooding habit of mind which would become increasingly characteristic of him. There were striking differences between these two Southerners, but they were complementary, and they functioned on a basis of a common culture, attitudes, and feelings.

The Stones had come from Wilkes County, in north Georgia, which, the Stones said, had been set aside by the Georgia legislature at the request of the Virginia House of Burgesses for younger sons who had to seek their fortunes elsewhere because of the new world's version of the law of primogeniture. Like other "New Men" from the Carolinas, Kentucky, and

Tennessee, the Stones came to Mississippi. Rosa Alston's people, by contrast, were an old, established line at the top of the social hierarchy of Panola County, immediately to the west of Lafayette County. It was from these two stocks that Phil Stone had come. Miss Rosa was an introspective woman with a tendency to hypochondria and a morbid fascination with disasters reported in the newspapers. James Stone was a big man with a commanding manner. (His honorary title, "General," came, some said, from this quality; others said it was because he was general counsel to the Illinois Central Railroad.) For years his law practice and banking business prospered so well that he was able to invest in land in different parts of the state, some of it—in the Delta—being used annually for the deer and bear hunts which meant a great deal to his son Philip and, ultimately, to his son's new friend. General Stone was a robust man with tastes that men like J. W. T. Falkner and Murry Falkner shared. He liked hunting and fishing. He drank hard and he gambled, sometimes for high stakes. He was a rugged man who had done well in a demanding time. His oldest son, James, Jr., was much like his father. The next, William E. "Jack" Stone, IV, had been sickly in childhood, but in manhood he too resembled his father. He was extremely masculine and fond of the outdoors. James Stone's youngest, Philip, also sickly as a child, would not resemble General Stone. But Phil was not so radically different from his father as William was from Murry Falkner. In his way, he must have been just as ready for this relationship as was the younger man.

Much abed as a child, Phil had invented games to play and he had read exhaustively, particularly in Southern history and the Civil War. At Ole Miss he had studied Greek and Latin, reading widely in both literatures. He delighted in poetry, fiction, and drama, ranging from the British and American to the French and Russian. At Yale he had been exposed to contemporary currents. He would browse for hours in the Brick Row Book Store in New Haven. He bought scores of books. He read his way voraciously through the Symbolist poets and through Yeats, learning something too of the work of the young artists of the avant-garde such as James Joyce. Coming home in the summer, Phil began to see a good deal of Stark Young, who was still teaching literature at the University of Texas but returning each summer to visit his father. Stone was strongly drawn to the older man—although he was also drawn to a much rougher group than Stark Young knew. "I owe my education," Stone later said, "to Greek and to playing poker. It was Mr. Stark Young who opened my mind when we would come home here in the summers, but Greek taught me to use my mind and poker taught me people." Stone pressed his books on his friends, and now he had another friend on whom he could exercise his gifts as a teacher and tastemaker. And it was all the more pleasing to the volatile, talkative Stone that Bill Falkner was a fledgling artist. Stone found no kindred spirits on the university faculty—instead, only "the usual veneer of thin pedagogical aestheticism which colleges usually bring forth." Discouragingly, he noticed "very little enthusiasm over any literature except that produced by men who were safely dead and whose work had been evalued [*sic*] with comparative assurance of safety. . . . There was no meddling concern with literature which had just been getting born. . . ."

As the summer of 1914 turned to fall, the tempo speeded up in Oxford. Phil Stone joined the entering class in the Ole Miss law school and Billy Falkner went through the motions of entering the eleventh and final grade of the Oxford High School. In October Governor Bilbo appeared to speak at a rally, and in that same month the high school football team (whose first team Billy still couldn't make) had defeated Holly Springs and lost to the alumni. And every week since August, at least half of the front page of the *Eagle* was covered with news of the Great War which was spreading in Europe.

As the year of 1914 began to draw to a close, the distractions from schoolwork were more numerous and powerful than ever for the half-hearted eleventh-grader. Each day he and Jack avidly read the dispatches from the war fronts in the Memphis *Commercial Appeal.* He continued to visit with his old regularity at the Oldhams' house, and he would go to see Phil Stone at General Stone's spacious old home. Recalling that summer, Stone said that Falkner "was painting some then and was faintly interested in writing verse. I gave him books to read—Swinburne, Keats and a number of the then moderns, such as Conrad Aiken and the Imagists in verse and Sherwood Anderson and the others in prose." Apparently Miss Maud still hoped that her son would become a painter, but Stone's own bent was toward poetry, and he encouraged his friend to experiment in that medium. Stone was giving him a kind of college seminar in modern literature. It is not surprising that Billy's attendance at school soon grew sporadic. By the start of Christmas vacation he had probably stopped attending altogether. If he returned at all in the new year, it was only to pitch or play shortstop on the baseball team.

He still saw his high school friends—Dewey Linder, Myrtle Ramey, and a few others. And for a time he joined in one high school activity: the planning of the eleventh-grade yearbook. Naturally enough, he would do the illustrations. He set to work with pen and ink on eight-by-five-inch sheets of plain white paper. He drew several sketches. One showed Miss Ella Wright lecturing on American history. Part of the sketch was a likeness of Abraham Lincoln and below him the tiny forms of a Confederate and a Union soldier fighting. Another sheet was divided in half. Under the caption "We Have Put Away Childish Things," a girl graduate pushed away an assortment of toys. In the adjoining panel the artist had drawn a loaded car identified by a streamer proclaiming the Oxford team as baseball champions. On the other side of the sheet he had lettered "De Faculty." He showed the school principal, Mr. Hurst, teaching history, and with him the teachers who taught English, agriculture, mathematics, and Latin. The drawing was clear and firm, with the individuals easily recognizable. The sketches combined the familiar high school yearbook motifs of idealistic dedication to the future and affectionate satire directed at the faculty. Another of the sheets was divided into two panels. One of them, entitled "How He Looks to Us," showed Mr. Hurst behind his desk on a small raised classroom platform. Mounted on the desk was a large cannon pointed at a shrinking student. (Hurst made a strong impression on all who knew him in spite of the fact that it would be years before he succeeded in earning a bachelor's degree. A big man, he was quick and formidable but also humorous and versatile. In addition to his job as principal of the high school he was also editor of the *Lafayette County Press*.) In the other panel a teacher was using a funnel to pour knowledge into a student's head. Another double-paneled sheet was captioned "Burning Midnight Oil." Half of it depicted a piratical-looking figure moving a hogshead. In the other portion a man sat in a deep armchair, a book in his lap and a lamp glowing on a table beside him. The artist had done the sketches with care and, apparently, pleasure. But when June came, there was no yearbook. The project never got beyond the planning stage, and the sketches were never published.

But this was not the last of William Falkner in high school activities. In the fall of 1915 he returned briefly for what surely would have seemed the wrong reasons to Miss Annie Chandler, Miss Laura Eades, and Mr. G. G. Hurst. If he was still unconcerned about the schoolroom, there was another area in which he was determined. "I hung around school just to play baseball and football," he said, "and then I quit." Since he had skipped school for most of the previous year, he may have returned in September on the pretext of completing his eleventh-grade year and thus finishing high school. Whatever the rationale was, the high school coaches accepted it. He was no taller than he had been the previous year—touching barely five feet five inches—though he probably weighed a few pounds more. He was fast, well-coordinated, and now he had a year's more experience. When Oxford started its season on September 24, 1915, one day before his eighteenth birthday, Billy Falkner was the starting quarterback.

Although he liked to pass, he could count on only his right end, Edward Moore, as a receiver. The left end was a lean, hard country boy named Benjamin McDaniel. His teammates called him "Possum" because they thought he looked like one. He had the longest arms Johncy Falkner had ever seen. He could bring down the ball carrier and his interference too in the grip of his enormous arms, but he was incapable of catching a pass. Even if the ball was thrown to him perfectly, it would bounce off his chest or slither out of his hands. Billy directed his attack with confidence and threw to Ed Moore, who took the ball over the goal line for the first touchdown. Like most of Oxford's opponents, Holly Springs generally avoided running plays toward Possum's side of the line. Now behind Oxford, they began attempting more passes.

As the ball was snapped to the Holly Springs quarterback, he faded back and threw a long pass intended for his left end. He did not see that Possum had diagnosed the play and cut diagonally across to cover the end as Billy came up from his safety position to help. Possum outran the end and, to the amazement of his teammates, intercepted the pass. Tucking the ball under his arm, he sprinted hard for the goal line—his own goal line. He raced down the field, oblivious to the anguished shouts of the Oxford players and fans. Recovering from his shock, Billy realized that he was the only man between Possum and the goal line. Changing his course he launched himself at the hard-running end just as he approached the last white stripe. They collided with a crash as the quarterback brought his own end down. Billy rose with blood on his face. His nose was broken. Rapidly swelling, it already showed a hump he would carry for the rest of his life. But he had kept one of his own men from scoring a touchdown against Oxford. The final score was 20–0. The local sportswriter reported the outcome with militant satisfaction. "Holly Springs had two good coaches with them," the account concluded. "They had been working with them so they were confident of victory but they had not counted on the fighting blood in our men." The next day Billy Falkner celebrated his birthday, feeling the pain from his nose yet the satisfaction of having guided his team to a victory over its traditional rival in his first game as starting quarterback.

The rest of the season did not go quite so well. On October 15 Oxford played Water Valley. This time the left end was not McDaniel but Rodney Fisk, who starred for Oxford. Catching a pass (the quarterback's name was not mentioned), Fisk made a sixty-five-yard gain before he was tackled on the two-foot line. On the next play an unnamed Oxford back plunged into the line. He fumbled and Water Valley recovered, going on to win by a score of 7–3. Nothing if not partisan, the Oxford sportswriter declared, "The local squad played a good game from beginning to finish but were greatly outclassed in weight."

Thus there is no direct evidence that Billy Falkner threw the pass for the sixty-five-yard gain, or even that he played. But one thing is certain: he was now, finally, finished with the Oxford public school system, both academically and athletically. A more intense kind of education and study lay before him.

14

Summer, 1914–April, 1918

From his sorry jacket he drew a battered "Shropshire Lad" and as he handed it to me he quoted the one beginning, "Into my heart an air that kills—" telling us he kind of thought it was the best he had seen.

"Why don't you go home?" I asked him.

"I will, some day. But that ain't why I liked that one. I like it because the man that wrote it felt that way, and didn't care who knew it."

—"Out of Nazareth" (48–49)

At this time the young man's attitude of mind was that of most of the other young men in the world who had been around twenty-one years of age in April, 1917, even though at times he did admit to himself that he was possibly using the fact that he had been nineteen on that day as an excuse to follow the avocation he was coming more and more to know would be forever his true one: to be a tramp, a harmless possessionless vagabond.

—"Mississippi" (21)

From the summer of 1914, when Phil Stone came home from Yale with a B.A., until the fall of 1916, when he returned to New Haven to study for a second LL.B., he and William Falkner spent a great deal of time in each other's company. They would read or talk in General Stone's big, six-columned house that had once been occupied by L. Q. C. Lamar. It contained thousands of books, some of which had once belonged to Lamar, to his father-in-law, Augustus Longstreet, and to Jefferson Davis. For someone with Phil Stone's taste for both literature and history, it was pleasurable to take down a first edition of Algernon Charles Swinburne's *Laus Veneris* and see from the autograph on the flyleaf that it had been a gift from Jefferson Davis to L. Q. C. Lamar. Stone and Falkner would stride off on long, cross-country walks, sometimes covering as much as fifteen miles over the unpaved roads and red-clay hills of Lafayette County. Billy Falkner liked to hear his friend recite Greek poetry. So sometimes, as they walked along University Avenue toward the campus or turned back through the woods toward the Stone home on College Hill Road, Phil Stone would raise his voice in the lines of Oedipus' lament. On occasion they would take freshly ground flour to a neighbor of the Stones who would turn it into dough and put it in the oven. Later they would return for the loaf of hot bread and eat it there, sitting on a side porch.

Some days before he went off to the law school, Stone would load his family's seven-passenger Studebaker touring car with books. Besides a play of Sophocles, there might be works by Socrates and Plato. There might be volumes by Roman philosophers, dramatists, and poets too. Then he would turn the car over to his young friend, who would drive out along a country road until he found a quiet, shady spot. There he would park and spend the day reading. On another day Billy Falkner might work at the process of teaching himself French. Other times he might read in English literature, or German volumes in translation.

But there was more to this mentor-pupil relationship than just reading and talk, as Phil Stone recalled it years later. He drilled the younger man in punctuation, he said, lectured him on goals as well as grammar, encouraged him to write, and then gave close scrutiny and criticism to what he wrote. Stone said he would work on punctuation in his room in the rear of the house. "Listen to this sentence now," he would say. "When you come to the pause, you put in a mark like this." And he would indicate a comma.

Writing about these and other sessions nearly twenty years later, Stone described much more extensive instruction. "There was no one but me with whom William Faulkner could discuss his literary plans and hopes and his technical trials and aspirations," he wrote, "and you may be sure I kept his feet upon the ground. Nay, I stood upon his feet to keep them on the ground. Day after day for years—and his most formative years at that—he had drilled into him the obvious truths that the world owed no man anything; that true greatness was in creating great things and not in pretending them; that the only road to literary success was by sure, patient, hard intelligent work. . . . Most of all was drilled into him through that great weapon ridicule the idea of avoiding the contemporary literary cliques with their febrile, twittering barrenness, the idea of literature growing from its own natural soil, and the dread of the easy but bottomless pit of surface technical cleverness." Phil Stone also taught by example. Not only would he lecture the younger man about writing, but he would take him to see a writer in the flesh, his admired friend, Stark Young. And quiet Billy Falkner would sit and listen to the conversation between the developing writer-teacher and the talkative law student-literary critic.

It was not surprising that some friends of both men should have said, "It was Phil who educated Bill." Neither was it surprising that Jack Falkner, who still shared a room with his brother, if not his literary tastes or aspirations, should note the assertion that "literate friends guided his selection of what he read." But Jack took a less sweeping view. "He had such friends, and I'm certain he would not have disdained any suggestions they might have made, but he was perfectly capable of making his own selections, and I'm certain that, to a large extent, is what he did." There was validity in both points of view.

Billy Falkner had been reading widely for years before he met Phil Stone. He had also apparently begun to imitate certain poets. And though his attendance at school had long been sporadic, an honor-roll student like himself would scarcely have found a comma unrecognizable. He would gladly look at a book recommended to him by a friend—and eagerly consume books which offered him models at this uncertain point in his career—but it was unlikely that anyone could force him to read one he did not like. Also, his habit of silence was becoming clearly evident by this time, so that a man as voluble as Stone could well go on talking at his rapid rate, assuming that material he was presenting was new when, in fact, his hearer might already be acquainted with it.

But if William Falkner was moderately knowledgeable before his acquaintance with Phil Stone that summer of 1914, what he began to receive now was the equivalent of a university seminar or tutorial. And Stone also supplied an unceasing flow of books, avant-garde works as well as classics, which the young writer devoured, and which in the long run would doubtless help him more than any course in grammar and punctuation or exhortation about goals and methods. "I was subject to the usual proselyting of an older person," he later wrote, "but the strings were pulled so casually as scarcely to influence my point of view."

The two men had more in common than just literature. They were both interested in Southern history, particularly the Civil War. But whereas Falkner had obtained most of his knowledge from family stories, local lore, and the instruction of Miss Ella Wright, among others, Stone had given himself an intensive course in Civil War history. All of this lore had been made even more vivid for him, if sadly so, when he was seven and General Stone had sent him and Miss Rosie to Holland, Michigan, to spare him the heat and contagion of summer in Mississippi.

Their hotel was patronized chiefly by vacationing Southerners. One of them, Stone told his wife years later, was James Longstreet, a short, broad-shouldered, heavy old man who had been one of the most prominent and controversial generals in the Confederate army. Tenacious, but slow and hesitant when he distrusted a superior's strategy, Longstreet had delayed for a whole day before obeying Robert E. Lee's order for a charge on Cemetery Ridge at Gettysburg. By the time the Confederate lines finally began their advance, the Union position had been reinforced, and the attack met a bloody and disastrous defeat. To many, however, he was still one of the demigods of the Confederacy. Young Phil Stone had read about him, and to his delight General Longstreet would take him for walks along the lakefront. By the time the visit drew to a close, the child idolized the deaf, taciturn old man. They would sit by the lakefront and Longstreet would draw lines in the sand, explaining to the boy where his position had lain and where Lee had placed his troops, sketching in the course of battles as they developed. One day as they were walking back to the hotel, hand in hand, the white-bearded old soldier sensed that the boy wanted to ask him something. He told him to go ahead.

"General," Phil said, "I don't want to make you mad."

"Go ahead, son," Longstreet said.

The boy hesitated but finally blurted it out. "General," he said, "is it true you disobeyed General Lee's orders to charge until it was too late?"

The General flung away the child's hand and shouted "No!" He stamped off to the hotel and did not speak to him again. Whenever he could, Phil would approach the old man. "I'm so sorry, General," he would say, "I'm so sorry." But the General never replied. Thus when Falkner and Stone talked of the war, Stone brought to their conversation more than fifteen years' emotional involvement as well as constant interest and steady reading.

Stone and Falkner had an eye for current as well as past history. Stone could mark the ongoing process of change by what he saw and heard in the family law office. For that matter, William Falkner had heard his grandfather and his uncle John talk about county and state politics. But with his reading and his particular love of anecdote, Phil Stone must have missed little of "the rise of the rednecks" as it manifested itself in Lafayette County. As Senator Vardaman began to devote most of his energies to national politics, Lieutenant Governor Theodore G. Bilbo began to move into the resulting power vacuum. His principal rival for party power was Governor Earl Brewer. With Brewer coming from the Delta and Bilbo from the coastal piny woods, the two were class symbols as well as rivals. Brewer operated from traditional bases of power and wealth in Mississippi politics, but Bilbo began to show a breadth of support matched only by Vardaman at his peak. The people loved him, said William Alexander Percy, a hostile witness, "because they understood him thoroughly; they said of him proudly, 'He's a slick little bastard.' He was one of them and he had risen from obscurity to the fame of glittering infamy—it was as if they themselves had crashed the headlines."

The deadly antipathy flared up late in 1913 when Bilbo and State Senator G. A. Hobbs were indicted on charges of having solicited a bribe almost two years earlier to help secure the passage of a bill creating a new county in the Delta. At the trial of Hobbs it was revealed that Brewer had hired detectives who had installed "detectaphones" in an effort to record evidence when the parties met to work out the deal. Although Hobbs appeared, Bilbo never did, and he continued to insist that the whole thing was a plot conceived and sprung by the Brewer forces to ruin him. The trial went on almost for the whole month of December. Hobbs was acquitted, but the affair left a stench in the nostrils of many Mississippians.

Bilbo's case came to trial in mid-June of 1914. Again there was much evidence and testimony suggesting corruption on both sides, but again the verdict was Not Guilty. The Oxford *Eagle* was one of many newspapers which approved. It had been the most spectacular case in state history, the editor was sure, and just as surely Brewer had been out to get Bilbo and was deservedly foiled.

The gubernatorial campaign was steadily heating up. Oratory and invective were not the only verbal devices put to partisan uses. Most of one column of the *Eagle* was taken up in the issue of February 25, 1915, with a long poem entitled "We Are Coming, Governor Bilbo, One Hundred Thousand Strong." The fourth stanza ran,

We are coming from the workshop
From the factory and mill,
We're a band of loyal Rednecks
With a mission to fulfill,
To secure relief eternal
From the secret caucus wrong,
We are coming, Governor Bilbo,
One hundred thousand strong.

At the conclusion of the tenth stanza appeared the name "Dave Lowbrow."

By mid-July the candidates were locked in bitter combat, sometimes pairing off for acrimonious debates. When Vardaman had waged his hot campaigns, the rallies held for him in Oxford were gala affairs. A fifty-foot trench would be dug. Then, when the fire in it reached the right temperature, wire would be stretched over it and the barbecue meats would be prepared. Although Bilbo and Russell did not inspire the trust that Vardaman did, they were met by large and enthusiastic crowds, as when they appeared in Oxford for an afternoon rally on July 28. But this was nothing to their jubilation in early August when it was announced that the Democratic primary, which was tantamount to election, had named Theodore G. Bilbo and Lee M. Russell as candidates for governor and lieutenant governor of Mississippi. "A number of Oxford citizens went down Monday to attend the Bilbo-Russell rally at Jackson," noted the reporter for the *Eagle.* "They report a glorious time." Among those who made the trip to the capital were T. W. Avent and John Falkner, Jr.

By the fall of 1915 the rise of the New Man in Mississippi was clearly to be seen in business as well as politics. When the quarterly report of the First National Bank was published, J. W. T. Falkner was not listed as a member of the three-man board of directors. T. W. Avent and J. W. Parks were, however. Phil Stone was a keen observer of this process. As he and Billy Falkner took their walks through Oxford and out into Lafayette County, Stone would talk. He knew the stories of country people who were painfully pulling themselves up by their bootstraps, as Lee Russell had done with his mother's help. For some of these strivers, the two privileged young men had a kind of admiration. Others among the "rednecks" seemed monsters of acquisitiveness and boorishness. For them they felt contempt and a kind of wonder.

Lee Russell's story, of course, was well known to the Falkners—how he had been a "goat" at Ole Miss, receiving no bid to join a fraternity; how, one day as he walked by Gordon Hall, he was doused with a deluge of water by fraternity boys on an upper floor; how, when he began to read law in the Young Colonel's office, he had told him, "When I graduate, I'm going to run for the legislature, and when I'm elected the first thing I'll do will be to introduce a bill to abolish fraternities and sororities." That bill had been on the books for three years now, and suddenly its sponsor was readying himself to occupy the lieutenant governor's chair. He must have felt that his new status changed a good many things. One Sunday afternoon the lieutenant governor-elect walked up the front porch steps of The Big Place and knocked on the screen door. The rapping finally penetrated old J. W. T. Falkner's deafness, and he answered the door himself. Opening it, he saw Lee Russell standing there. Falkner asked him what he wanted.

"To pay a visit," his caller said.

The irascible old man drew himself up sternly. "Sir," he said, "our relations are business and political, not social." And with that he slammed the door.

There were, inevitably, other changes. Dr. John Young Murry found it harder to travel and most of the visiting that summer was done by his Oxford relatives. Sally Murry Wilkins remembered going to see her great-grandfather in Ripley. He died that July, having survived one wife, his beloved daughter Sallie Murry, and numerous other relatives, including the Old Colonel. The hardy old man was buried with all the rites of the Methodist Church and the Masonic Order (Scottish Rite) as all of the Falkners but the Young Colonel stood among the mourners.

The children's social activities increased that fall. Sallie Murry would give dances at The Big Place as would Estelle and Dorothy Oldham at their home and Myrtle Ramey at hers. Some were unplanned. A group would meet at the drugstore after the picture show, and when they had finished their sodas Sallie Murry would invite them home with her. Chess Carothers would be pressed into service, if the Young Colonel did not need him, to pump the player piano in the big entrance hall. There would be dancing on the downstairs porch that ran all around the front of the house. At Estelle's home, too, they would dance on the porch, and sometimes the music might be furnished by Lucius Pegues' three-piece band. By now Estelle was going to a good many dances, a number of them at the university.

During the summer when Estelle thought about Mary Baldwin she realized she couldn't stand being shut in with all those girls in that oppressive, heavily Presbyterian atmosphere. So she was delighted when she succeeded in persuading Major Oldham and Miss Lida to allow her to stay home as a special student at the university instead. She registered for courses in English, philosophy, and psychology. It was the beginning of one of the happiest periods of her life.

She was immediately popular. An attractive girl—petite, blue-eyed, and brown-haired—she was a charming companion, and she loved to dance. Extremely feminine, she dressed with her own kind of chic. "She was," recalled one friend, "the essence of 'it.' The college boys were crazy about her." She had invitations to all of the dances at the university. By custom a girl's escort would call for her in a hansom cab. When they departed for the dance, her mother would enter it too and sit opposite the young couple. "We were violently chaperoned," Estelle Oldham remembered. Although Miss Lida might be incapacitated at other times, she never missed a dance, and she would always be one of the chaperones who sat watching the young people whirl and dip in the enormous ballroom in Gordon Hall. There would be elaborate decorations—flowers, potted palms, bunting—supplied by sponsoring organizations such as the Red and Blue Club. W. C. Handy's band would come down from Memphis, or Bynum's band would play. First would come the Grand March, and then the general dancing would begin. There were no tangos yet; instead there were fox trots and one-steps of the day interspersed among the jazz numbers. A year before, Handy had composed a popular piece which he had called "The St. Louis Blues." Late in the evening he might launch into its melancholy, syncopated strains or those of another one he had called "The Memphis Blues." The boys would go to the refreshment table to get coffee or cake for the girls. And although there was a university rule against drinking, here and there one could see hip flasks bulging under the tuxedos.

Billy Falkner would go, too, though not as Estelle's escort. By now he seemed not to care much for dancing. Occasionally he would ask Estelle to dance or cut in on her partner of the moment. The two of them had an understanding, however, and from time to time she would sit out a dance with him. The rest of the time he would spend on the sidelines looking on. He would watch, standing there, while the musicians played on until the early hours of the morning. Then Miss Lida would invite twelve, fourteen, or sixteen people back to the house for breakfast. Discriminating and extremely proper in her way, she got along very well with Billy Falkner. Very proper himself and very much the fashion plate, he would sometimes accept her invitation and go home with the rest. Other times he would wander away by himself. He seemed to be content with the understanding which he and Estelle had that a special relationship existed between them. She accepted fraternity pins from her other beaux. In the same light-hearted way she had accepted a proposal of marriage from a small, handsome young man with dark hair and dark eyes, who had tried to woo her during her spring vacation from Mary Baldwin, thinking that it meant no more to him than it did to her. His name was Cornell Franklin. Seven years older, he had since graduated from the law school and gone out to Hawaii to begin his career. To her, his proposal had been just like another fraternity pin and she gave it no further thought.

William Falkner went his own way, seeing Phil Stone, going on walks with him, reading, and writing poetry. It must have been about this time, perhaps the fall of 1915, that he resumed another activity. He began to hunt again, but now the game was deer and bear. Stone had told Falkner about some of his hunting experiences as a boy at his father's camp located about thirty miles west of Oxford just below Batesville in the rich bottom land of the Tallahatchie River. By the time he was ten, General Stone's sickly son had persuaded his father to let him go with the others to deer camp in the fall. He took his place on the stand that year and the next. Then, when he was twelve, he experienced one of his great moments as a bear materialized before him in the gloom of the autumn woods. He fired two blasts. Opening his eyes, he saw the bear's bulk on the ground before him. His father rode up, and then some of the other men of the hunt. "They smeared my face with blood," he said, "as they always do with your first bear. I never wanted to wash it off any more." By the time he was sixteen, however, he had turned against the hunt. He had seen death in the eyes of a buck one day and later concluded, "I couldn't give an animal life and I couldn't take it away." But Billy Falkner had heard so much about the hunts that Phil made arrangements, and together they joined the hunters when they made their yearly journey westward.

Billy Falkner must have absorbed a good deal of Stone family lore even before he rode into that Delta hunting camp on the mule-drawn wagon. Major Philip Alston, after serving under Bedford Forrest, had moved to Memphis and married a girl who was a Potts. One of her relations was a Methodist circuit rider reputed to have owned ten miles up and down the Tallahatchie River. His twin sons, Theophilus and Amodeus Potts, were the great-uncles of Phil Stone. The Stones had settled some rich bottom land years before in a place close to the land that the twins—called Uncle Buck and Uncle Buddy—had settled. The Illinois Central Railroad ran a line in that area and, as an accommodation, put in Stone Stop. There General Stone ran his camp. And each November the tents would have to be set up and the barbecue pits dug before the hunters followed the equipment wagons in.

They would cut wide intersecting paths or hacks through the cane so the hunters could take their assigned stands and wait for the dogs to drive the deer past them. The bear, on the other hand, might make his way through the thickest canebrake. There was one bear in particular, called Old Reel Foot, an immense and crafty old bear, who could be identified by his track: he had lost two toes from his front left paw. Now when he fled into the tangled vine-and-thicket jungle that was his lair, he was both secure and deadly. Once, reputedly, a pack of twenty-seven dogs had raced, barking and baying after him, into the thicket. Only two of them, it was said, emerged alive. Some of the men in the camp were memorable like Old Reel Foot: Uncle Ad Bush, the old Negro cook who would wake them for scalding coffee at four and flip hot flapjacks high with his smoking skillet; Buster Callicoat, whose brute strength was even more useful in General Stone's camp than it was in Murry Falkner's hardware store, but who was scarcely less a problem here. Once Bill Falkner was assigned the task of accompanying Buster to Memphis for whiskey to replenish the camp's depleted supply. When they returned Buster had the whiskey and also "the partially wrapped corset he had bought as a present for his wife trailing under his arm." Bill Falkner found all his old enthusiasm for hunting rekindled. For some years he would go whenever he could. He enjoyed the camaraderie in his quiet, withdrawn way, as in the evening the men would sit about the campfire, smoking pipes and cigars, passing the whiskey, and telling tales of other hunts and days. He smoked his pipe and drank with the rest.

Back in Oxford he saw his friends as before. One Sunday afternoon he drew up in front of Bob Farley's house in Murry Falkner's new Model T Ford. Bradford Haynes and Rodney Sisk were in the car with him. Bob got in and they went for a ride, around the Square and then on out South Street and into the country. On their way back they began to overtake another Model T. Soon they could make out the driver. It was Will Mize, one of Oxford's best-known residents. He was a wholesale grocer and something of a Dickensian character. Although he shaved regularly, his beard was so heavy that his cheeks were usually blue-hued. He had a broken nose and habitually wore a high, standing-wing collar. A self-made man, he had been born in Tula, in the same southeastern section of the county that produced

Lee Russell. He had lifted himself by hard work and determination. Some of that determination showed now as Billy Falkner drew up on him and prepared to pass. Mr. Mize's whole outfit matched the high collar; he was in his Sunday best and he did not propose to absorb the dust that would be thrown up by another Model T passing him on the dry cinder road. So he speeded up. Billy responded with a kind of recklessness Bob had noticed before. In spite of the danger of encountering horses and buggies on the narrow road, he opened his throttle. Soon both machines were running wide open. Gradually Billy gained on Mr. Mize and slowly pulled away, leaving his adversary furious in a choking cloud of dust.

Mr. Mize told Murry Falkner. When Billy told his friends of this development, Bob suggested that he and Rodney and Bradford should go to Mr. Falkner and tell him what had happened. But Billy refused to let them do it. He and his father had clearly had words about the incident. Thereafter, whenever the boys asked each other, "Who can get a car?" Billy always had to say that he couldn't. As far as Bob Farley knew, his friend never drove his father's car again, and he may not even have ridden in it again. Farley had the feeling that Mr. Murry was always hard on his oldest son, more so than on the others, perhaps because he simply did not understand him.

By now the older boys sensed that they were living pretty much on their own. In some way a protracted summer illness of Miss Maud's may have contributed to this new phase of the family relationships. It was not for anyone else, they felt, to make decisions for them. Murry Falkner must have found it increasingly hard to understand this oldest son of his, so completely different from himself. He had shown no enthusiasm for school, little for the livery stable and transfer company, and even less for the hardware store. There is no evidence that the son went anything like halfway to meet his father. His attitude was always respectful, but his "sir" had distance as well as courtesy in it. He apparently felt that his father was a dull man, as he once confided to Phil Stone. There was an occasion, however, when Murry Falkner did make a gesture toward his son. It was evening. The boy was sitting on the front gallery when his father sat down in the rocker beside him.

"I understand you smoke now," he said.

"Yes, sir," Billy answered.

"Here," his father said, reaching into his vest pocket. "Try a good smoke." He handed the boy a cigar.

"Thank you, sir," he said. With that he reached into his pocket and pulled out his pipe. He broke the cigar in half, put one half in his pocket, stuffed the other into his pipe, and lit up. His father watched him. Bill Falkner would remember the incident to the end of his life. "He never gave me another cigar," he said.

Christmas came, and New Year's, and then it was 1916. And Billy Falkner showed no sign that his father or grandfather could see—or that they could understand—that he was doing anything with his life. Murry Falkner went up to The Big Place to talk about the problem. The Young Colonel may very well have felt that he had been there before, that he was repeating with his grandson an experience he had undergone with his son. Apparently, he resolved to deal with it in the same way. He would find something for him to do and put him to work at it. He no longer had a railroad to provide jobs for needy and unpromising relatives, but he did have a bank. Billy Falkner went to work as a bookkeeper in the First National Bank of Oxford.

Now he was again confined indoors for a certain portion of each day, as he had been when he attended school. Jack never saw him at work there on the Square and didn't know what he did. But once, thinking about his brother at the job, he laughed and said, "I bet he didn't do much." Estelle never saw him at his banking labors, either. But she imagined him sitting in a back room with his feet on a table, reading. And no one would bother him, she was sure, for after all, he was the founder's grandson. But it was not an easy situation. He would not have taken a menial job, and he did not have the training or desire to be a teller or bookkeeper, although there was a draftsman-like neatness about the figures and columns he drew. He let Estelle know how he felt about working in the bank. He hated it. Money, he told her, was a contemptible thing to work for. Later he recalled that job in a jocose way. "Quit school and went to work in Grandfather's bank," he said. "Learned the medicinal value of his liquor. Grandfather thought it was the janitor. Hard on the janitor." He had known the taste of liquor since the time when Grandfather had let him drink the "heeltaps" in his glass that remained of his toddies. Now on the hunts the boy sometimes drank the powerful corn potion made by stills concealed in the hills and pine barrens. With Grandfather's private store he had a chance to drink very good whiskey indeed. And he drank it for more than just the taste and feeling of well-being. He found himself in a situation he detested yet from which he could not escape. Liquor apparently made it easier to bear. He did not confine himself to secretive nips at the bank, however.

At eighteen, Bill Falkner began to be seen with well-known drinking companions. One was "the town drunk," a harmless, amiable man named Charlie Crouch. The association gave rise to situations that amused Jack and Johncy Falkner, though they could scarcely have given any pleasure to Maud Falkner or her husband. On one occasion Bill had met Charlie and begun to drink with him. They warmed up to the task, and Bill did not come home that night. "The next morning when Jack and I were on our way to school," wrote Johncy, "we met him coming home. He was in a foul humor and had on Charlie's hat. They had swapped during the night." Bill's hat was narrow-brimmed, selected especially to go with a highly prized suit of the latest mode. "Charlie always wore a sort of a cowboy hat, a black one with the crown creased fore and aft and a big wide brim. Bill sure looked funny in that suit and Charlie's cowboy hat. Jack and I stepped off the walk and bowed as he passed. Without looking at us he said, 'God damn it!' "

The suit Billy Falkner wore gave a good indication of his dandyism. It was one of those he bought after opening a charge account at Phil A. Halle's men's store in Memphis. (Most of his bookkeeper's salary apparently went on his back, and he had elegant, twelve-dollar Johnston & Murphy shoes to go with the suit.) As usual, he asked his mother to alter the seventeen-dollar suit for him, especially to make the legs tighter. By the time Miss Maud had taken them in enough so that the image in the mirror suited her son, they were close to skintight. But there was a more striking demonstration of his sartorial splendor. Many students were content to rent dress clothes at Ed Beanland's tailor shop. Not Billy Falkner. He went to Phil Halle's and bought a twenty-five-dollar "Styleplus" dress suit, the first boy of his age in town to own such an outfit. These clothes, when they were actually seen, would be worn at university functions. But full-dress suits would also be seen in illustrations of romantic magazine stories and in films, where they might adorn the elegant forms of self-satisfied members of the nobility. And by this time Billy's carriage resembled that of his grandfather who, with ramrod-straight back and elevated jaw, would stare ahead of him as he walked slowly down the street. With this appearance and these clothes, it was not surprising that William Falkner won from some town wit the sobriquet "the Count."

The newspapers were providing a very different vision of human life from that suggested by the dances in Gordon Hall. "When war broke out in Europe in 1914," Jack Falkner remembered, "Bill and John and I would get together in our bedroom at night, spread out some maps of that continent, get the morning newspaper, and figure out the lines of battle. This was especially true during the battle of Verdun from February to September, 1916." For day-to-day news they could turn to the Memphis paper. But even the *Eagle*, when it appeared each Thursday, gave its account. "Verdun Battle Is Terrible," proclaimed one large line of type. "Throbbing thunder and heavy guns mark World's mightiest struggle." The boys read everything they could get their hands on, and they discussed the fighting avidly yet with wonder—bemused at how those folks were killing each other and what they could possibly expect to get out of it.

But it was not the grinding trench warfare that seized their imaginations. Instead, they thought of combat in the clouds. "This was 1915 and '16," Bill Faulkner later recalled. "I had seen an aeroplane and my mind was filled with names: Ball, and Immelman and Boelcke, and Guynemer and Bishop, and I was waiting, biding, until I would be old enough or free enough or anyway could get to France and become glorious and beribboned too." By summer hostilities seemed even closer, though in a different theater. WAR IS INEVITABLE ran the banner headline, while immediately below was a photograph of American cavalrymen on the Mexican border. It was a time when Billy Falkner, like many young men, must have felt conflicting emotions, being imaginative and pulled by romantic yearnings in two different directions. On the one hand there was the girl he loved, and now, though he despised it, his job made the idea of marriage less preposterous than it had been a short while before. But there was also the war, couched in the dramatic and simplistic terms of the magazines: the gallant French and Britons, outnumbered, facing their implacable, spike-helmeted enemies. Like many another eighteen-year-old, he must have found it easy to imagine himself, white squadron leader's scarf streaming out behind him, adjusting his goggles as he climbed toward the red sun on the dawn patrol.

Yet they were far removed from the struggle. The same issue of the paper that reported troubles on the Mexican border devoted almost equal space to "the boll weevil menace." Local drama, if there was any, was likely to come from the familiar sort of shooting affray or that fascinating menace, the motorcar. It had, of course, met opposition. "Town Board Says Autos Must Not Run in Oxford," read one column head. The ordinance forbade them the public streets of Oxford, but it was a frail barrier against the tide. In September of 1916 an "Overland Parade" of autos was held in Oxford, and in October came the word, "Oxford to be Great Highway Center." Already under construction from Memphis to Oxford and on southward was the Jefferson Davis Highway. It was a national highway, built in part with federal funds. To the editor of the *Eagle*, it was nothing less than "the great Highway of all Highways," and the successful strategy by which it was routed through Oxford and Lafayette County was "the greatest victory for the hill section of the state ever won by citizens of Mississippi." Still another highway was proposed, this one to be named for Colonel William C. Falkner. It would go through Ripley, and these same Oxonians wanted to be sure it would go through Oxford too. But others besides the councilmen who had passed the ineffectual anti-motorcar ordinance could see that the arrival of the Automotive Age was not an unmixed blessing.

One month later Sheriff Sneed, his deputy, the town jailor, and Tax Assessor Buck Collins went out for a spin in the sheriff's new Ford. Just as they reached the end of North Street, reported the *Eagle*, Sneed was distracted by something, "and as he turned his head to look back the car ran off the bluff in front of Murry Falkner's and turned turtle." Bruised, shaken, and frightened, the men crawled out from under the car. "It was a narrow escape to say the least and the men were fortunate to get out with their lives." Since the accident occurred about six P.M., it is not impossible that the spectators looking down at this harbinger of the new age may have included Dean, John, and Jack Falkner, if not their brother William.

Late that summer Stone and Falkner had gone on their rambles together whenever they could before Stone went back to New Haven to match his Mississippi law degree with another from Yale. Things were happening in the county as well as in the city. There was reforestation under way to counteract the forest depletion and erosion. There was the flood control program which created the Yoknapatawpha Drainage District in Beat 5, near the southern boundary of the county, to control overflow from the Yocona River, Toccopola Creek, and Potlockney Creek. As the fall began, Billy Falkner would occasionally hunt those bottoms, but he also began to spend more time on the campus. He made a few new friendships there, and in one of them he took on a new role. Instead of being the protégé, he was the mentor.

One of the freshmen entering the university in the fall of 1916 was a short, blue-eyed, fair-haired sixteen-year-old from Greenville named Ben Wasson. "He looked like a seraph when he came to Ole Miss," another student recalled. He had the kind of male beauty which made some call him pretty. "He was a sweet kid," the former student said, "and he was taken up by upper classmen. His classmates were jealous." One day at the start of the semester Ben Wasson was making his way across the small campus with a new friend from the senior class. "Coming towards us, under the just beginning to be scarlet and yellow trees," he remembered, "was a small, slight fellow. He was wearing a pair of baggy, gray flannel trousers, a rather shabby tweed jacket and heavy brown brogans [with] the like of which I was unfamiliar." The senior made the introduction. "This is Bill Falkner," he said.

Falkner nodded, and as he and the senior began to talk, Ben studied him. His eyes, he observed, "were very brown and somewhat almond-shaped and very penetrating. His nose was quite aquiline. . . ." He had a thin, straight mouth, Ben noticed. As Falkner went on with his conversation in his soft-spoken way, he dazzled Ben with his discussion of a book he was reading by A. E. Housman. "I had never known anyone who loved poetry enough to be so bold as to quote it." When the two concluded their conversation Ben Wasson told his new acquaintance in an excessively polite and somewhat flowery way how glad he was to have met him. Falkner turned to him with a look of amusement.

"Ah," he said, "we seem to have a young Sir Galahad on a rocking horse come to our college campus."

Later Falkner looked Wasson up. Eager to write, Wasson was grateful for this attention from the older, pipe-smoking youth. Falkner talked with him about poetry, fiction, and philosophy, and he would take Wasson to the Stone home, where he was a frequent and welcome visitor. Selecting a record from the collection of his absent friend, he would place it on the Victrola turntable. Then, after he had cranked up the machine and placed the needle in the groove, he would extinguish the lights and seat himself to listen. "Even light can be too much distraction when music is being played," he told his profoundly impressed friend. Bill Falkner's favorite choices were the symphonies of Beethoven. Occasionally, moved by their harmonies and power, he might make a brief comment. "Listen to those horns of triumph and joy," he remarked once, "crying their golden sounds in a great twilight of sorrow." The younger boy may not have realized that his friend was employing a device—trying out on a receptive audience phrases which he had honed with the care he gave to his lines of verse. As Wasson looked back later, the things he recalled most were his friend's "innate kindness and gentleness and a rare ability to dramatize himself interestingly."

Bill Falkner had not only been reading and quoting the poetry of A. E. Housman—he had been imitating it. In the future he would date some published poems from "the time when you write poetry just for the pleasure of writing poetry and you don't think of printing it until later." Still later he would push this formative period back a year earlier when, he said, he discovered Swinburne. "Or rather," he wrote, "Swinburne discovered me, springing from some tortured undergrowth of my adolescence, like a highwayman, making me his slave." He read Keats and Shelley then too, but they did not move him. Swinburne "completely satisfied me and filled my inner life." When Swinburne palled, there was Housman to round out this early phase. "It was 'The [*sic*] Shropshire Lad' which closed the period," he recalled. "I found a paperbound copy in a bookshop and when I opened it I discovered there the secret after which the moderns course howling like curs on a cold trail in a dark wood, giving off, it is true, an occasional note clear with beauty, but curs just the same. Here was reason for being born into a fantastic world: discovering the splendor of fortitude, the beauty of being of the soil like a tree about which fools might howl and which winds of disillusion and death and despair might strip, leaving it bleak, without bitterness; beautiful in sadness." From there, he said, he went on to Shakespeare, Spenser, and the Elizabethans, taking particular joy in Shakespeare's "Music to Hear," and in Keats's "Ode to a Nightingale" and "Ode on a Grecian Urn." But it seems doubtful that any body of poetry ever again struck him with the force of Housman's verse.

Much of the verse he was writing in 1916 in his often large, very flowing, and sometimes almost flowery hand, bore the unmistakable imprint of Swinburne and Housman in diction, tone, and form. He apparently found the most famous of Swinburne's choruses from "Atalanta in Calydon" memorable, particularly the striking diction and imagery of the concluding stanzas:

And Pan by noon and Bacchus by night,
Fleeter of foot than the fleet-foot kid,
Follows with dancing and fills with delight
The Maenad and the Bassarid;
And soft as lips that laugh and hide
The laughing leaves of the trees divide,
And screen from seeing and leave in sight
The god pursuing, the maiden hid.

A fragment of one of Billy Falkner's early poems reveals long stanzas, using the couplet form, in which the phrase "maenad and bassarid" appears not once but twice. Falkner's was a poem of stillness rather than action, just as he chose to employ his leisurely iambic pentameter rather than follow the example of Swinburne's galloping anapests and headlong dactyls. But again and again he would use the images of the faun and nymph. His setting would often be the forest or field. The world-weariness of the poet complaining of his unrequited love would frequently be his subject, as might the languid fatal woman who did not return his passion.

Falkner also seems to have followed Swinburne in several of his experiments. Swinburne's "In the Orchard," subtitled "(Provençal Burden)," may have provided the model for a four-stanza poem Falkner called "Aubade," subtitling it "Provence. Sixth Century."

It seems likely that Falkner was interested in Swinburne's imitation of dialect ballads. If he was, it would be a small step to follow after Housman with his ballads in a modified Shropshire dialect rather than Swinburne with the heavy Scots speech he used in poems such as "The Bloody Son" and "The Sea-Swallows." One fragment shows Falkner attempting a narrative ballad about highwaymen, and another fragment suggests their end on the gallows. The image of the hanged felon dominates Housman's "On moonlit heath and lonesome bank":

A careless shepherd once would keep
The flocks by moonlight there,
And high amongst the glimmering sheep
The dead man stood on air.

In one fragment Falkner wrote,

Mankind called him felon
And hanged him stark and high
Where four winds could watch him
Troubled on the sky.

One of Housman's best-known themes, the bitter-sweet passion of love and the fickleness of lovers, moved the young poet to wholehearted imitation in one poem of three quatrains:

I give the world to love you:
Now, cross your heart and say—
By moon and stars above,
You'll be true for aye.

So her sweet fire had filled them
With song of youth to youth
And the solemn moment stilled them
Inarticulate with truth.

But again, when skies were lighted,
'Twas easier to say:
She another Harry plighted
And he another May.

Falkner did a series of poems on this subject.

This was the poetry of youth, but as Phil Stone said, it was enough to show that the writer had talent. He was clearly experimenting, trying his hand with different forms and themes. The melancholy of Swinburne, together with his verbal luxuriance and play of the senses, seems to have appealed genuinely to the boy. So, it appears, did Housman's cynicism about love and general pessimism about the human condition. For all his imitativeness, however, the young poet displayed his own attractions and avoidances. There was nothing of the grotesque and bizarre such as sometimes appeared in Swinburne's verse, nothing of the sadistic or masochistic overtones that sometimes came through the luxuriance of the poetry. And there was in Falkner's verse a frank heterosexual eroticism which contrasted with Housman's often plaintive passion and euphemistic personal pronouns. Falkner could enjoy dark gardens as much as Swinburne. He could also glory, like Housman, in tree and bush and flower. But why, at age seventeen, eighteen, or nineteen, if the mature man's recollection was right, should the boy have embraced a view which seemed so often and so pervasively melancholy? Was it a pose, or simply a late adolescent malaise from which he would soon recover? Or was it just a fairly common literary posture he had assumed?

He could scarcely have been called a deprived young man. He lacked nothing that he really wanted of the material comforts. He had a substantial home and a family around him. He was in love. (Among these fragments of early work was one in the style of "The Song of Solomon," work from that earlier time, perhaps, when he had juxtaposed lines by the Biblical poet with his own.) To some extent, his adoption of this melancholy tone and point of view was probably the age-old device of the poet's creating a persona which may bear little relation to the person he actually happens to be. But in this case it was more than that. Although he could be a good companion and a witty friend, William Falkner already showed a distinct tendency toward silence and withdrawal. And just as it was neither arbitrary choice nor sheer chance that made young Ernest Hemingway imitate Ring Lardner, so it was not unmeaningful that William Falkner's lyrics should so often sound the elegiac note with the pastoral.

Although he enjoyed the beauty of the land and the society of his few friends as much as ever, there could have been little sense of movement or progress in his life—linked as he was to a job he despised yet with no sign of another he could like. Childhood was over, and though the members of the family would remain reasonably close, they were beginning to follow their own paths. Billy no longer rose each morning to a new series of events in which he would be the unquestioned leader of his brothers Jack and John. And even though no real financial disaster threatened the integrity of the family, he was the son of a man rather generally regarded as the unfortunate son of a brilliant and driving father, a prodigious, cyclical drinker shifting from one business to another without success.

There were other, highly personal factors which were forming his psychological attitudes and responses to life. He was five feet five and a half inches tall and he would never be any taller. No smart dress suit or bench-made shoes could conceal the fact that the oldest of the three grown Falkner boys was also the smallest. He was built on the Old Colonel's lines, but his grandfather, his father, and his younger brother Jack were all six-footers. In adolescence his face had somehow lost the balance and symmetry which had combined with his clear, self-possessed gaze to make his countenance the most interesting and arresting among the children. Now, in post-adolescence, his face seemed to drop away, below the cheekbones, to a narrow and immature thinness, and below the long Falkner nose his mouth seemed even smaller and straighter. (Miss Maud once confided that Mr. Murry sometimes would refer to his son in rough teasing as "Snake-Lips.") Although he still had his understanding with Estelle, she had become even more popular. Thus he may have felt sure of a special place in her affections, but he was only one of many boys she dated and one, at that, who refrained from dancing—something she enjoyed and did superbly well. And though their relationship could continue on its present basis for a while yet, he was acute enough to see that it could not do so indefinitely. So, if anyone had taxed him with the melancholy in his verse—along with the joy in nature and love of beauty—he might well have answered, with Housman,

Therefore, since the world has still
Much good, but much less good than ill,
And while the sun and moon endure
Luck's a chance, but trouble's sure,
I'd face it as a wise man would,
And train for ill and not for good.

As the fall wore on, Bill Falkner continued to see Ben Wasson. Ben lived in the Lyceum Building, one of the Greek-revival style buildings which dotted the campus. Inside, its space was curiously divided. On the main floor were some of the university administrative offices. On the second floor there was a suite of three bedrooms and a big sitting room. The boys were congenial—Russell Pigford and Lowry Simmons, Spot Petty and Dutch Rainold. Falkner would see them when he came to visit Ben. He also began to know students involved in the intellectual life of the campus, people such as R. H. Shackleford, the editor of *Ole Miss*, the yearbook, and J. E. Fontaine, his assistant editor. Now, at an age when Falkner would have been a freshman or a sophomore if he had shown any inclination for higher education, he was slowly being drawn into some of the peripheral aspects of university life.

He was spending less and less time at his job in the bank as winter came on. Thanksgiving was over and the Christmas season approached. Christmas was a doubly special day in the Oldham household, for it was also the birthday of Edward DeGraffenreid Oldham. They would decorate the house and hang gifts on the tree for the invited guests. There would be the traditional feasting and sometimes even an old-fashioned Virginia reel. This year Ned would be nine. One late November afternoon he came home from a possum hunt with Dean Falkner. He was feverish and complained of pain, so Miss Lida called Dr. Culley, who diagnosed the illness as a touch of malaria. By the time a Memphis specialist recognized it as an acute attack of rheumatic fever, it was too late. He grew worse, and then, suddenly, he was gone. Billy Falkner grieved for the Oldhams and for "Little Major," with whom he had often played. The Oldhams were glad when that Christmas of 1916 was past.

January of 1917 roared into north Mississippi with snow and freezing cold. By the middle of the month horse-drawn sleighs pulled laughing students out onto country roads, and ice skates flashed on frozen ponds. On these frigid mornings the front pages were full of the increasing U-boat menace, and by now many readers of the Memphis *Commercial Appeal* and the Oxford *Eagle* could feel the irresistible pull toward war. Then on Saturday, February 3, an extra edition of the *Eagle* appeared on the streets with the banner headline U.S. BREAKS WITH GERMANY TODAY. Three weeks later American merchant ships were armed. In early March there was the news of the intercepted Zimmermann telegram, in which the German foreign secretary suggested to the German minister in Mexico that he urge the government to make war on the United States to recover the U.S. Southwest. Then, on April 6, war was declared.

By early May the draft bill was adopted, specifying compulsory military service for physically able men between twenty-one and twenty-seven. This was superfluous legislation to the Falkner boys. "We all wanted to enter military service," Jack recalled, "and each understood that the other was going to do so if possible." Fifteen-year-old Johncy succeeded in convincing the recruiting officer in Jackson that he was eighteen before Murry Falkner retrieved him by means of a telephone call to the adjutant general of Mississippi, who just happened to be a friend of his. John was determined to enlist again, but for the present, he reluctantly decided, it would be fruitless to try. Bill kept his own counsel.

The week that war was declared, the *Eagle* reported a local conflagration. Early on the morning of April 3 fire had broken out in R. H. McElroy's dry goods and clothing store, a two-story landmark which had remained standing when A. J. Smith's men burned the Square. Valued at about $5,000 but uninsured, it was a total loss to owner J. W. T. Falkner. A more spectacular fire blazed six weeks later, however, one which a sensitive man might well remember all his life.

The headless body of a sixteen-year-old white girl had been found outside Memphis in a wooded area near the Wolf River bottom on the Macon Road. Two weeks later, on Tuesday morning, May 22, a mob gathered near the same spot, bringing with them the killer, a Negro named Eell C. Persons, for "an execution probably without parallel in the history of the South." "The approximate hour and place of the lynching were advertised widely," reported the *Eagle*, "but the organized forces of the law and order operating at the meeting of the court dared not say nay to the outraged community in which Antoinette Rappel lived." As Persons was led out chained to a log, the mother of the victim implored the crowd to make him suffer ten times as much as he had made his victim suffer. The crowd roared its willingness. The pyre was doused with gasoline and then "some 5,000 men, women, and children cheered gloatingly as the match was applied and a moment later the flames and smoke rose high in the air . . . the frenzied men cheered as their victim writhed in agony and then was stilled in death." The account went on with post-mortem details. "When the body had burned sufficiently to satisfy the lust of the executioners, one man in the crowd cut out the Negro's heart, two others cut off his ears, while another hacked off his head." The poet of nymphs and fauns could scarcely have remained unaware of these frenzied rites—of both dreadful deaths—in a woodland near a familiar city.

That spring the poet was also at work as artist. Putting together the university yearbook, Shackleford and Fontaine asked Bill Falkner for a drawing. When *Ole Miss* for 1916–1917 was published, page 163 displayed a drawing introducing the "Social Activities" section which was signed "William Falkner." He had done a dancing couple, highly stylized. The girl wore a white bouffant dress, and her short hair, confined somewhat by the thin band running from her forehead across her temples to the back of her head, emphasized a kind of Grecian cast to her features. Her partner was lean, angular, and somewhat grotesque. He wore a stylish full-dress suit and spats, but his gloved hands seemed somewhat skeletal, and his bald-headed noseless face with pencil mustache and slit eyes gave an appearance that was sinister rather than romantic. But it was the best artwork in the book. He had a good sense of design and a satiric eye, and the lines he drew were fine, clear, and in their own way graceful.

Spring activities looking toward commencement filled the calendar. Estelle Oldham was invited to many of them. She also heard from other friends, such as Cornell Franklin, who was doing very well as a lawyer in Hawaii. When Billy Falkner went to a dance, he was still an observer rather than a participant. Sometimes he and Ben Wasson would go together. When the Red and Blue Club gave a dance which was only for upperclassmen, they stood outside and looked through the windows at the orchestra and the dancing couples.

Then, in the long slow days of summer after the students had gone, Bill and the others would sometimes walk down North Street through the Square and on down South Street to The Big Place. There, on the tennis court Grandfather had built for Sallie Murry, Bill and Jack would play John and Dean. In mid-July Phil Stone came back from New Haven, and the two

Drawing by William Falkner
for "Social Activities" section of *Ole Miss*,
1916–1917.

friends resumed their walks. Falkner would show Stone new poems and rewritten versions of verses he had sent to him in New Haven. Sometimes he would go along when Stone visited his brother, William Evans Stone, IV. Fourteen years older than Phil, Jack Stone ran a branch of the family law firm in Charleston, Mississippi, forty-five miles southeast of Oxford in Tallahatchie County. Jack was a hunter, an outdoorsman, and Falkner liked him. Jack in turn made his brother's young friend welcome. There was a fine golf course in Charleston—better, at any rate, than the rudimentary nine-hole course at Ole Miss which Billy Falkner had learned thoroughly caddying for players such as Peter Whitman Rowland, one-time dean of the school of medicine. Now he was developing into a sound, accurate player himself, and sometimes he would take advantage of these visits to play the Charleston course.

At home, there was little recreation for Murry Falkner. "The Falkner hardware store," noted the *Eagle*, "has been removed to the old McElroy stand next to the *Eagle* building." Now he had to relocate all his stock and attend to the other hundreds of details that moving a business involved. The location would not be any better than the old one, but his father owned the building.

When Bill Falkner was not visiting or walking through the countryside or writing, he was likely to be reading. He and Stone both liked Balzac, whom Stone considered a great psychologist and student of human nature. It was probably about that time that Falkner wrote his name in his copy of the volume combining *Les Chouans* and *A Passion in the Desert*, doing the same with Jane Porter's historical romance, *Thaddeus of Warsaw.* A far different kind of novel which vastly amused him and Jack was one entitled *The Military Wildcat.* The title character was a Negro who had been drafted into the army. Mr. Murry didn't care for the book, but the three oldest boys and Miss Maud read the story dog-eared. Bill and Jack marveled at it. The author was from San Francisco, and they wondered how he could possibly know as much as he seemed to about Negro psychology.

The war was considerably grimmer now. Long lists of draft numbers began to appear. There were newspaper French lessons for the boys who would soon be embarking for France. In mid-October Governor Theodore Bilbo startled several thousand of his fellow citizens with a speech in Meridian which gave them a new view of the war. "Did you know that Mississippi today is covered with German spies?" he asked. "Did you know that in the last thirty days a dozen or more have been arrested in the state, and that one man had in his grip blueprints of every saw mill in Mississippi?"

The Falkner boys thought of the war in other terms as fall turned to winter and 1917 became 1918. Jack was already leaning toward the Marine Corps. But there was much to remind the eligible young man of opportunities in the emerging air services. The *Eagle* was running a series entitled "The Training of an Air Man." "Picture the thrill of the first flight with the instructor," it read, "then the feeling of power that gradually begins to come as the control of the machine is more and more taken over; the exasperation and then the joys, the all-difficult work of landing is conquered; finally the exaltation of the first soaring aloft, alone. Bit by bit the air man stretches out his wings, flying a little further, a little longer, a little higher each day, until he feels himself master of the air." Maud Falkner thought all her boys were too young to go. This dampened Jack's ardor not a bit. But Bill was quiet as always. His direction would be determined by an aspect of his personal life which would soon reach a crisis.

Estelle Oldham was wearing Billy Falkner's gold ring with the gothic *F* carved on it, but she continued to accept invitations from other young men. She even had a few dates with Jack. She enjoyed herself, although Jack remained rather silent and she had to do most of the talking. A charming university boy from the Delta proposed to her and she accepted him in the same way she had accepted Cornell Franklin's proposal more than three years before. Her father was furious with her. "You can't marry him," he said, and Estelle was very willing that that should be the end of it.

Cornell Franklin was doing well. After his career as a prominent Ole Miss undergraduate and then a law student, he had accepted his uncle Malcolm's advice and settled in Hawaii. Malcolm Franklin was collector of the port of Honolulu, and he was in a good position to introduce his nephew to his many friends as an enterprising young lawyer. Cornell was a gregarious man with a particular passion for gambling, but he was able and industrious, and he had built up a rather lucrative practice in a relatively short time. Moreover, he had been appointed assistant district attorney in Honolulu. Cornell Franklin had military as well as social standing now, for he had enlisted in the National Guard of Hawaii in August of 1917, and in December of that year he had been commissioned a major and judge advocate general of the Hawaiian Territorial Forces. Estelle would hear from him from time to time. Now, as winter ended, she heard from him again, indirectly and directly. If what seemed to be shaping up was a courtship, it was equally tending toward a family-arranged marriage. Both Cornell's mother, Mrs. Hairston, who lived in Columbus, Mississippi, and Mrs. Oldham thought it would be wonderful if Cornell and Estelle were to marry. Both apparently began to do all in their power to encourage the young people. At what she judged the propitious moment, Mrs. Hairston sent Estelle a double diamond ring. It was her engagement ring, Cornell wrote her from Honolulu. He was coming home in April, he said, and they could be married then.

The reaction of Estelle's parents was very different from the explosion which the proposal from her Delta beau had produced. Lem and Lida Oldham were delighted. Mrs. Oldham thought the ring was beautiful and urged her daughter to wear it. Estelle found that she didn't want to. She couldn't find it, she told her mother. This precipitated frantic searching, which turned up the ring at the bottom of a dresser drawer. The lines suddenly began to be rather tightly drawn.

Estelle talked the situation over with Billy.

"I suppose I *am* engaged to Cornell now," she said, "but I'm ready to elope with you."

He reacted as she thought he would. "No," he answered, "we'll have to get your father's consent."

She knew him as a great one for protocol, so she was not really surprised when he decided that he would have to inform both Major Oldham and Murry Falkner. Both fathers hit the ceiling.

In the heated family councils that followed, both sets of parents took the same position. To begin with, they considered their children under age. And even though Billy had said he would go back to work in the bank to support Estelle, this did not seem to offer much of a future. He had no prospects, when they came right down to it, nothing the elder Oldhams and Falkners could see that offered a successful basis for marriage. The Oldhams were extremely fond of Billy Falkner, as he had always been of them. But they did not see him as a husband for their eldest daughter.

The two principals considered their situation. Meeting at The Big Place, they would sit in the large parlor or in the grape arbor behind the house, trying to find a way out of their dilemma. It was clear that both families were unalterably opposed to their marrying. If they were to do it, they would have to elope. They decided they would not marry if they had to run away. At some future time they would be able to do it properly. Now all they could do was fight a holding action, and the burden of it would fall on Estelle.

She soon found it was becoming an uneven contest. Tochie was already spoken for. Young Lieutenant Pete Allen, a former Ole Miss baseball star, had put the question to Major Oldham. If he came back from France, could he have Tochie's hand? Major Oldham had not wanted to give his consent, but he had said yes. It would certainly be nice, her parents thought, if her older sister were to be married this spring, and to such a promising young man. Cornell's mother was just as enthusiastic. Estelle had visited their home in Columbus several years before, when she was fourteen. Cornell Franklin, seven years her senior, she had then thought of as a distinctly older man. She had been allowed to go out with a boy her own age and had paid Cornell little heed. His mother she had loved. She was a beautiful and charming woman, and now, as Estelle talked with her again, she thought her even more so. Estelle and Billy found themselves blocked at every turn. Cornell wrote again, looking ahead to the wedding, to their honeymoon, and to married life in Hawaii. Family pressure increased, and by late March the date had been set. Lida Estelle Oldham would become the bride of Cornell Sidney Franklin on the evening of April 18, 1918.

Billy brought her verses still. One set he had lettered beautifully on a single white sheet folded into four parts. On the back, in pen and ink, he had done a sketchily dressed nymph raptly listening to a satyr who crouched near her feet playing on his pipe. In the upper left-hand corner, as though looking down on the scene, was a devil's head adorned with horns, eye-mask, and Mephistophelian mustache and beard. Inside, on the second page, was an eight-line poem entitled "Dawn," while facing it was one of five lines called "An Orchid." The first poem focused on sleeping lovers in the early light. The second saw the flower as born of the caress and kiss of light and air. On the front section of the folded sheet the poet had printed the title, "A Song." In an idiosyncrasy he would later repeat, he had reversed all the letter *s*'s. There were two stanzas:

It is all in vain to implore me,
To let not her image beguile,
For her face is ever before me—
And her smile.

Even though she choose to ignore me,
And all love of me to deny,
There is nought then behind or before me—
I can die.

This was a reworking of an earlier version. In that previous draft the second stanza had taken a different turn:

It is vain to implore me
I have given my treasures of art
Even though she choose to ignore me
And my heart.

The two young people continued to meet, but gradually Billy began to realize that the wedding was really going to take place. It was a deeply traumatic experience for him. As his brother later put it, "his world went to pieces." Mixed with his feeling of loss was a reaction of bitterness toward Estelle. Somehow, he felt, she could have refused to bow to parental pressure; she had betrayed him by taking Cornell Franklin as her husband, no matter how many people told her that she should. She had tried to make it clear to him that it was not that, and that she certainly did not prefer another man to him. She was still unsure what she should do or what she *could* do. But she was unable to reach him. He withdrew further into his silence and pain. He began to consider now what he would do.

He had started spending days away from Oxford, in Memphis, or in Charleston or Clarksdale, where he had gone with Phil Stone. His friend Arthur A. Halle, Phil Halle's son, had opened a store at Second and Madison in Memphis. The clothing section was in the basement, and there Halle had arranged a number of comfortable chairs. Sometimes Falkner would stay there all day, writing or simply observing the people who came and went. Sometimes he would walk up the back stairway to Halle's room, and Halle would come home to find him there, sleeping on the bed. He had been turning the alternatives over in his mind. There were not many. But to be there in Oxford to see his sweetheart married to another man, this was one he could not accept. He resolved to enlist for military service as soon as possible. He would try for the goals romantically described in the *Eagle* by the author of "The Training of an Air Man." He would experience for himself, if he could, "the conquest of the air, a commission in the air service, and a place in the battle skies of France."

Before he could embark upon that career of glamorous fatality, however, he had to be accepted for training. And he knew that to be accepted for pilot training by the Aviation Section of the United States Army's Signal Corps he had to weigh more than he did. There was no time for an extended course of body building, with barbells and roadwork, even if he had been willing to indulge in one. He had heard about a desperate expedient for situations such as his and he tried it. He stuffed himself with all the bananas he could hold and drank all the water he could swallow, he said, and presented himself at the recruiting station. He was rejected as under regulation weight and height. This was another blow. In spite of his sensitivity about his short stature, he talked about it in Clarksdale to Eula Dorothy Wilcox, a girl he had met there at a house party.

"Dot," he said, "do you know anything that would make me grow tall?"

"What do you want to get into that mess for?" she said.

"I think it would be a pretty good life for a while," he answered.

It was now late March. In New Haven Phil Stone learned of his friend's unsuccessful attempt to enlist. As he thought about the total situation he began to fear that now, blocked in this attempt, Billy might turn to the desperate gambit he had rejected earlier. If he and Estelle ran off, Stone thought, the marriage would spell the end of Falkner as a writer. Stone decided to act. He called Maud Falkner from New Haven and told her that Billy had tried to enlist because Estelle was going to marry Cornell Franklin. For all Stone knew he might now turn elsewhere and try to enlist again.

Miss Maud was furious. Following her first impulse, she called Estelle and bawled her out for her part in what she considered Billy's foolhardy action. Miss Maud talked to her silent son and to his father. She told Mr. Murry about something else Phil Stone had said. He had suggested that Billy come up to New Haven and stay there with him for a while. He could get away from Oxford, get a job or not as he chose, and have an opportunity to think things through. This would be better than his going off and doing something impulsive that he might later regret. As for military service, his parents knew that, like Jack and John, he would want to go, but that would come soon enough in any event. In September he would be twenty-one and then he would be drafted. Meanwhile, he could visit his friend. He could see another part of the country, he could see Yale University. He agreed to go.

They drove to Memphis, Jack at the wheel with Bill beside him, Miss Maud in the back with Johncy. There at the station he kissed his mother, shook his brothers' hands and swung himself aboard the train that would take him to New Haven. The Oldhams and Falkners were relieved. Back in Oxford, Estelle awaited the arrival of her fiancé as the preparations began for her wedding. Her sweetheart traveled north, beyond Mississippi, beyond Tennessee, into a new phase of his life.

BOOK THREE

Soldier, Student, and Public Servant

1918-1925

William Faulkner, December, 1918.

15

April-December, 1918

> I quit moving around and went to the window and drew the curtains aside and watched them running for chapel, the same ones fighting the same heaving coat-sleeves, the same books and flapping collars flushing past like debris on a flood. . . .
>
> . . . I began to listen for the chimes . . . the bitten shadows of the elms flowing upon my hand. And then as I turned into the quad the chimes did begin and I went on while the notes came up like ripples on a pool and passed me and went on, saying, Quarter to what?
>
> —*The Sound and the Fury* (96, 212)

> He was a strange mixture of fear and pride as he opened the throttle wide and pushed the stick forward—fear that he would wreck the machine landing, and pride that he was on his own at last. He was no physical coward, his fear was that he would show himself up before his less fortunate friends to whom he had talked largely of spins and side slips and gliding angles.
>
> —"Landing in Luck" (43–44)

In October of 1916 Yale University had celebrated its two-hundredth anniversary at New Haven. It was, for America, a venerable institution, combining pride in its idea of democracy with considerable social snobbishness, and a strongly Calvinist background with a tradition of service in politics and law; an institution whose sons were exhorted to greater effort "for God, for Country, and for Yale!" Its popular image was created out of photographs of the Yale Bowl jammed on a late fall afternoon for "The Game" with Harvard, of college battlements rising up among leafy elms in old brick quadrangles. For those a little more knowledgeable, the idea of this university might bring to mind robed processions of junior fraternity men calling for newly elected sophomores, of sophomore-freshman conflict in the annual "Fence Rush," of solemn elections to the handful of senior societies such as the prestigious Skull and Bones. For many readers of boys' books the name of Yale University would have evoked the exploits of Frank Merriwell or the long process, related in Owen Johnson's *Stover at Yale*, by which that beau ideal, Dink Stover, scaled the heights at New Haven.

Phil Stone had, of course, given his friend the benefit of his observations. So Billy Falkner had a fairly good idea of what he would see as he stepped down from the train in the dingy New Haven station. The city itself was a manufacturing center with a population of more than 160,000, though it struck most visitors as being considerably smaller. Now, however, it was in many ways a different city and a different university from the one which had greeted that fictional visitor, Dink Stover, on his arrival nearly ten years before. The chimneys of the Winchester Repeating Arms Company spewed smoke as the factories turned out munitions for the Allies, and the university seemed almost as much a seat of military training as of humane and scientific learning. The German offensives of that spring and summer had once again thrown the Allied forces into crisis. To defeat this dangerous and convulsive effort they strained to mobilize every resource. In America a bill was introduced which would lower the draft age to eighteen and raise it to forty-five. Students' Army Training Corps units were set up in colleges and universities across the country.

At Yale an artillery unit was staffed by a retired U.S. army captain assisted by a French captain from the French military mission to Harvard and two more captains who were disabled veterans of the Canadian field artillery. A battery of four French 75's supplied the ordnance. Still, the departures of students from the campus continued. Some volunteered at home and a few waited to be drafted. Others succumbed to the glamor of high-mortality units such as the British Royal Flying Corps, volunteering for training in Canada. By the fall of 1917, the enrollment had dropped from 3,262 to 2,122. Of these nearly half were enrolled in the R.O.T.C. or the Yale Naval Training Unit. By April, 1918, R.O.T.C. men were being called to training camps. When the university convened again in the following fall, there would be only two hundred students at Yale in civilian clothes.

That April of 1918, Phil Stone was living in a college rooming house owned by two old-maid sisters. When Billy Falkner moved in with him, Stone reported the fact by letter to Oxford. He had arrived Thursday, he said. He was a good roommate, never getting in the way, never failing to be considerate. "He is a fine, intelligent little fellow," he wrote, as if to reassure both the Stones and the Falkners, "and I am sure he will amount to something." Before long Stone would find that his guest had some disconcerting habits: he would polish his boots and put them on the table, and sometimes he would leave his trousers on the floor. But apparently these were his only objectionable traits, and the two friends got on as well being roommates as they had before.

The gregarious, talkative Stone had a number of friends and acquaintances, and he introduced Falkner to several of them. While he went to class or studied, Falkner read or wrote, going on walks sometimes through the campus, the city, and even out into the countryside beyond. He would go with Stone for meals, eating at his table in the Commons or accompanying him to a bar that served good Irish stew. They would talk aesthetics and poetry. Both had fallen under the sway of William Butler Yeats, and sometimes in their room Stone would read him aloud. One favorite was "The Hosting of the Sidhe," in which the beautiful Niamh calls seductively to mortals. " 'Away, come away,' " Stone would chant, imitating Yeats's own reading. Falkner's favorite lines from Yeats came at the beginning of "He Remembers Forgotten Beauty":

When my arms wrap you round I press
My heart upon the loveliness
That has long faded from the world. . . .

Another favorite he might recite was Shakespeare's eighth sonnet:

Music to hear, why hear'st thou music sadly?
Sweets with sweets war not, joy delights in joy. . . .

Stone would finish his work for the LL.B. in the summer. Falkner planned to stay until then, perhaps even until September if the bill for lowering the draft age to eighteen had not gone through. When he was eligible for the draft he would enter military service at home. Meanwhile, he would do something to earn a little money. There wasn't much in his background apart from his clerkship in his grandfather's bank that qualified him for gainful employment, but fortunately industry needed workers to fill the booming war orders. Through some friends Stone got Falkner a job as a ledger clerk for the Winchester Repeating Arms Company. On Wednesday, April 10, the poet was back at a high desk before ruled ledgers, his pen at the service of profit and loss rather than the promptings of the muse. On April 12, a thousand miles away, Cornell Franklin would be arriving to claim his bride.

Later that summer Maud Falkner would send her son newspapers from home. She was probably loath to send them at this time because of the social columns. The campus newspaper described the forthcoming Franklin-Oldham marriage, noting that "Many of the members of the younger set in Oxford will participate in the wedding." There was a bridge party, a breakfast party, and then a bridal party the day before the wedding. That night Estelle stayed with a great-aunt. Instead of sleeping, she wept. The sympathetic older woman sat with her, and they talked all night. In the morning Estelle's aunt dressed and prepared to leave the house.

"I'm going to go to your father and make him call this wedding off," she said.

"No, you mustn't do that," said the wan bride-to-be, "Daddy will be furious. It's too late."

Cornell knew she did not love him, but he was willing to marry her anyway.

A little after seven o'clock that Thursday evening, April 18, the Oldham car, a Cole Eight, pulled up in front of the house. It was driven by Johncy Falkner. Walking carefully in her satin brocade gown, Estelle Oldham came down the porch steps and, holding her court train, stepped into the car. Johncy closed the door, seated himself behind the wheel, and set off for the First Presbyterian Church.

Entering the vestibule with Tochie, who was her maid of honor, and her mother-in law Mrs. Hairston, her matron of honor, Estelle stood and waited for the organ peal, a shower of orchids and valley lilies in her hand and a coronet of orange blossoms on her veiled hair. The organ notes sounded, filling the church with the strains of "Here Comes the Bride." Mrs. Hairston's and Lida Oldham's hopes were about to be fulfilled. Pale and hesitant, Estelle turned and murmured a few words to Katrina Carter, one of her bridesmaids. "I don't know whether I love Cornell," she said, "or if I want to marry him." But the organ notes swelled, and suddenly time had run out on her. Her hand on Lem Oldham's arm, she advanced toward the rose-decorated altar and the waiting groom, resplendent in white full-dress uniform with gold braid and saber. The minister intoned the words of the Episcopal wedding service, and they were man and wife.

Johncy drove them back to the Oldham house, where sixty guests watched Estelle Franklin cut her wedding cake. Shortly afterwards, Estelle tossed her bouquet to the clamoring bridesmaids and then vanished up the stairs. When she and Cornell reappeared, Johncy drove them to the station. He said his goodbyes with the others and then watched the receding lights of the nine-forty as it carried the newlyweds toward Memphis.

The couple visited Washington and then returned to visit both sets of parents once more in Oxford and Columbus before leaving to set sail for the Orient. In Oxford, two weeks after her own wedding, Estelle Franklin was matron of honor for Tochie, as overseas veteran Lieutenant Pete Allen claimed his bride in the flower-decked Oldham house. By June 1, Major and Mrs. Cornell Franklin were at home in Honolulu.

In New Haven, Billy Falkner continued his temporary career as a ledger clerk. In the evenings and on weekends he would see a number of Stone's friends. One whom he came to know was a tall, thin, bespectacled nineteen-year-old named Stephen Vincent Benét, a member of the class of 1919 at Yale. At seventeen Steve Benét had published six dramatic monologues in verse entitled *Five Men and Pompey.* Now he was busy with *Young Adventure,* a second book of poems which the Yale University Press would bring out late that year. The critics would call it derivative—finding there the monologue of Robert Browning, the "diablerie" of Amy Lowell, and the lyricism of Alfred Noyes—but they would also find it vivid and colorful, an astonishing achievement for an undergraduate. It was an example that might well have encouraged the aspiring poet from Mississippi. Billy also met the poet Robert Hillyer and was fascinated by his war experiences.

To a boy who had read avidly about such heroes as Ball, Guynemer, and Bishop, three of Stone's other friends were particularly fascinating. Two, like the Canadian officers at the R.O.T.C. unit, had been wounded in action. Another was a subadar, the ranking Indian officer under the British Imperial officers who led his unit of Indian troops. Still another companion on some of these walks was a German who would sometimes break into German drinking songs in spite of the atmosphere at Yale—then so super-patriotic that instruction in German had virtually stopped. Falkner must have made clear his admiration for the British forces and particularly for the celebrated Royal Flying Corps, since April 1 the Royal Air Force. When Stone's officer friends learned of his intention to return home for the draft, they urged him to try for the RAF. For over a year now the Royal Air Force had been working to equip twenty squadrons in Canada with the American "Flying Jenny" to train pilots for the Western Front. Stone decided he might like to try for the British service, probably in the artillery. Falkner decided to follow these urgings. He was determined not to repeat his earlier failure at a recruiting station. Now, with Stone, he entered upon an intensive preenlistment training program.

They assumed that they would have to pass themselves off as Englishmen, or at the very least as "territorials." (In fact, however, though RAF acceptance of American citizens was irregular, qualified volunteers were not turned away.) The two Mississippians decided that they would first of all have to learn to sound like Englishmen. This would not be easy but they were offered expert instruction. One of the men at Stone's table at the Commons was an Englishman, and he began drilling them at mealtime in English pronunciation, diction, and usage. Falkner apparently began to make good progress. But their instructor despaired of one point: neither man could roll his *r*'s properly. No matter how familiar they might become with English speech patterns, with those *r*'s they could never convince a true Englishman that they were fellow countrymen. Their instructor suggested that they pose as Canadians. Stone decided that he was probably right, but Falkner doggedly went ahead asking for the salt and discussing the weather in the best English he could muster. He had an unusually acute ear for speech rhythms and accents, and strangers would later be surprised to learn that he was not an Englishman. By mid-June he was ready to put his new persona to the test. On June 14 he went to New York, determined to pass himself off to Lord Wellesley's staff as a Briton abroad and enlist in the RAF.

As William Falkner walked toward the RAF recruiting office on Fifth Avenue, he must have taken some comfort from the fact that all his hopes would not ride on his sedulously practiced English accent. He had in his pocket letters of reference from the British officers in New Haven. According to a story Phil Stone would later tell, they also had forged papers to show they were Englishmen. Their tutor from the Commons had abetted them in further forgeries. He had given them his sister's name and address in London, and she had consented to act as a "mail drop" for them. They invented a vicar, Stone said, whom they called the Reverend Mr. Edward Twimberly-Thorndyke. Then they wrote letters of reference in which Reverend Twimberly-Thorndyke called them "god-fearing young Christian gentlemen." They mailed the letters to the tutor's sister in London and she in turn posted them to the recruiting office in New York. These precautions may have been dictated by instructions issued to recruiting officers the year before. RFC recruits must "bear the ear-marks of a gentleman," read the order. Also, they had to be between eighteen and thirty, and parental permission was required for volunteers under twenty-one. It appears that the RAF in 1918 did not follow this latter scruple of the RFC in 1917. And whether or not the "ear-marks of a gentleman" were now among the requisites for pilot training, a height of more than five feet, five-and-a-half inches was not—in an army in which whole regiments of English foot soldiers might boast only a few men of that height.

William Falkner was accepted and enlisted as an applicant for pilot training in the RAF–Canada. It might no longer be the romantic RFC of the earlier years of the war, but it was still an elite combat force. He was ordered to report to the RAF Recruits' Depot in Toronto in three and a half weeks, on Tuesday, July 9.

He took the train back to New Haven, where he gave the good news to Stone, his accent tutor, and his other British sponsors. The next day he went for the last time to the Winchester Repeating Arms Company. There he resigned his position as ledger clerk and walked out, once more free of inkpot and pen and the workaday schedule. He packed his clothes, said goodbye to his friends, and took the train for Mississippi. His time as clerical worker, Connecticut resident, and observer of life at Yale was over.

Oxford must have seemed a town of missing faces to Billy Falkner when he returned that June. Estelle was gone. Tochie was gone. Jack was at Quantico, Virginia, undergoing rigorous training to turn him into a combat-ready marine. John was working as a time-checker in a power plant at Muscle Shoals near Sheffield, Alabama. The only one of the Falkner boys now at home was eleven-year-old Dean.

Whether or not Billy Falkner looked any different to his fellow townsmen, some of them must recently have seen evidence that there was talent behind that deceptive manner of his. When the university yearbook, *Ole Miss*, had come out that spring, it had contained two of the drawings which J. E. Fontaine, now the editor of the art department, had asked him to do. One of them depicted a couple under the legend "Red and Blue," a senior dancing club. The other drawing introduced a section entitled "Social Activities" and was much more elaborate. The girl at left center wore an

Drawing by William Falkner for "Social Activities" section of *Ole Miss*, 1917–1918.

extremely low-cut gown. Standing with her were two elongated male figures in white full-dress suits, the trouser bottoms distended. Both had little waxed mustaches. One sported a topper and monocle, and the other wore an expression that suggested the Mephistopheles figure on the cover of *The Smart Set* magazine, which Falkner must have found attractive. The drawings may not have been original, but they were by far the best pieces in the book and they showed a facility which was already professional. Both carried the printed signature "William Falkner."

In the three weeks of his leave he did the usual things—read, visited Stone and his other friends, and sometimes went on outings. Oxford had a swimming pool now, one of the largest in the state according to its owners' boast, and on occasion Falkner swam there. He read a book Jack had bought the month he left, Harry Leon Wilson's *Ruggles of Red Gap*, and he enjoyed it as much as Jack had. Another book which he enjoyed was James Branch Cabell's *The Rivet in Grandfather's Neck*. Like Jack, he enjoyed Kipling's "The Man Who Would Be King." He had been home less than two weeks when the *Eagle* took notice of his presence, erroneously placing him in New York for the previous months and then noting that he "had joined the English Royal Flying Corps and leaves on the 8th of July for Toronto, Canada, where he will train." Before that time came, the family drove to Sheffield, Alabama. Johncy Falkner looked up from his work to see a friend and co-worker leading his brother through the plant toward him. "Bill grinned when he saw me. We went out to the car where Mother and Dad and Dean were waiting, and visited for a while. Then I told Bill goodbye." Not long after this leave-taking, Maud Falkner had to say goodbye to her first-born in the Memphis station. Ahead of him waited training in flimsy and dangerous machines which were to lead toward combat in the skies of France.

As the train rolled north Billy Falkner must have thought about the seven to nine months' work that would begin following the final physical examination in Toronto. As the war had worn on, the magazines had documented the expanding aerial warfare. Billy clearly knew that it was one of the most dangerous branches of the service. The mortality rate of airmen, especially single-seater pilots, was thought to exceed that of all others save infantry second lieutenants. And the duration of peril was greater for the airman. He began risking his neck from the day he first soared aloft in the fragile canvas, wood, and wire "kites" powered by rasping engines and fueled with highly flammable gas and oil. Although Falkner had, in effect, taken his time in his efforts to become an airman, seeming more anxious to become a husband than a pilot, his present course was the logical result of flying homemade airplanes in the back pasture and following the exploits of aces on the Western Front.

He shared too the kind of glamorous idea of combat which persisted even in spite of the ghastly slaughter in battles such as Verdun. An ideal for him and Phil Stone was the legendary Chevalier de Bayard, "*chevalier sans peur et sans reproche.*" Their imagination, like that of Southerners before them, was captured by the image of this early sixteenth-century French knight who had fought gallantly for his king in Italy, falling finally before overwhelming numbers. By this time the idea of military heroism had become inextricably linked with death. With it was also associated the idea of living as intensely as one could in a short time. Death had come to have a kind of fascination for many of the young men who so eagerly boarded the troop trains and transports. As one veteran put it, "In those years death itself exerted a curious magnetism on young men . . . and death became a romantic dream for the new generation of American writers." As young

John Dos Passos waited to go overseas, the executors of his father's estate tried to interest him in various plans. "But what use," he asked, "was an income to a man who expected to get killed within the year?" Poets like Alan Seeger wrote poems such as "I Have a Rendezvous with Death." Seeger kept his rendezvous on July 4, 1916, just a few months after a young Southerner named James McConnell had begun flying as a combat pilot in an American escadrille in the French air force. McConnell wrote about the experience. "Know what I want?" a comrade had said to him. "Just six months of freedom to go where and do what I want. In that time I'd get everything I wanted out of life, and be perfectly willing to come back and get killed." Still alive in March of 1917, the young University of Virginia graduate wrote about one of the members of the escadrille who had "gone west": "I do not think Prince minded going. He wanted to do his part before being killed, and he had more than done it." Before the month was out, McConnell was dead too, shot down over Verdun. Even if he did not share the passionate certainty of Seeger's poem, this whole complex of emotion could not have been wholly uncongenial to a young man who responded to Yeats's early poems and felt he had been betrayed in love.

There was still another appeal of the RAF that the young Mississippian must have felt. Before he had gone to New Haven he had told Jack that in New York he hoped "he might be able to find some means of getting into military service other than by enlisting as a private." He wanted to be an officer—not surprising in a boy who had invariably directed the activities of two brothers and one cousin. In this war a pursuit pilot had much more freedom, usually, than men of the same rank in other services. And for a man used to servants, the services of two mechanics and a batman would not be unwelcome. Airmen generally fared better than others, eating in better messes, living in towns, and sometimes even being billeted in châteaux. "We had come to believe," McConnell had written, "that we would wage only a *de luxe* war." And for one with a taste for smart, trim clothes, what could be more attractive than the slim boots, shining leather harness, peaked cap, and light blue of the RAF?

When William Cuthbert Falkner arrived, suitcase in hand, at the Jesse Ketchum School, loaned to the RAF by the Toronto Board of Education to serve as a recruits' depot, he continued his impersonation. The entries the clerk made on his Royal Air Force Certificate of Service gave some indication of his imaginativeness. He had changed the facts in no less than half a dozen instances. To begin with, he had changed the spelling of his name: he was now William Faulkner. His birthplace, he had declared, was Finchley, in the county of Middlesex, England. He had been born on May 25, 1898, into the Church of England. His occupation in civil life was that of a student. His mother resided in Oxford, Mississippi, but her name too was now spelled Faulkner. (Presumably he had been staying with her prior to his arrival in Canada; his large suitcase was clearly labeled "Wm. Faulkner, Oxford, Mississippi.")

The physical details were more authentic. He was five feet, five-and-a-half inches tall, with a chest measurement of thirty-three inches. His eyes were hazel, and his hair dark brown. His complexion was put down as "dark." Identifying scars were to be found on the back of his neck and the inside of his left knee. Though the certificate did not record it, he had the beginnings of a mustache. He had passed himself off as an Englishman, without doubt, and one exactly eight months younger than William Falkner of Oxford. Had he hoped that this shaving of his age would mitigate the facts of his height and weight? A boy not yet twenty-one might conceivably still grow, and there was, after all, a considerable period of time involved in the process of becoming a pilot, if the student could survive the canvas crates he would train in.

Entering upon active service on July 10, 1918, William Faulkner was given Canadian serial number 173799. His "trade in Royal Air Force" was marked "Cadet for Pilot," and his rank was "Private II." He had signed up to take the king's shilling, or $1.10 (Canadian) per day.

For two and a half weeks he was stationed there with the other recruits of his class. They were issued rough wool uniforms, including the large greatcoats and the white-banded overseas caps that identified them as cadets. Cadet Faulkner was not inconspicuous. "Naturally we all knew Faulkner," wrote J. M. Hinchley. Helping to make him stand out on the first day at the Recruits' Depot were his "diminutive physique, his feeble moustache, his rich Southern drawl, which Monson thought was English. . . ."

The cadets' training began with basics: lectures on military discipline and personal hygiene. Out on the field they would be instructed in elements of military drill. Cadet Faulkner began to learn the erect British marching posture with the exaggerated arm swing. He practiced the British maneuvers for Left Face, Right Face, and About Face, with the pivoting foot, the high raising of the knee, and the loud stamp of the descending foot. But he must have welcomed RAF Brigade Orders No. 103 when they came through, posting him from the Recruits' Depot to Cadet Wing effective July 26.

Cadet Wing was located at Long Branch, just west of Toronto on the shore of Lake Ontario. It was a small city of "bell" tents which housed an oil stove and four cots, each of whose occupants would receive five blankets as the cold weather came on. Here, infantry battalion style, the four squadrons of cadets with their headquarters company, comprising in all more than 1,600 men, plunged into the full range of basic training. The parade ground drill continued, along with physical training, but now there were subjects directly related to Faulkner's RAF "trade": wireless telegraphy, topography, and air force law. Beyond this, there was the task of inculcating military discipline and building esprit. One of the instructors was a particularly impressive flight sergeant. Formerly a cavalry drill sergeant, Flight Sergeant Tabernacle was described in *The Cadet Wing Review* for November, 1918, as "a disciplinarian." The writer also noted, "His business is soldiering; his hobby, parades; and his amusement, 'orders.' " Under his supervision, Sergeant Basket put Squadron A through rigorous close order drill. John Falkner remembered that Bill wrote him from Canada about one sergeant "who was forever giving them a hard time. So one night they slipped in on him while he was asleep, wrapped him in his blanket and before he could wake up threw him in the lake." Cadet Faulkner was substituting the wish for the deed. A group in Squadron A had certainly thought of it, J. M. Hinchley said. They had even crawled through the darkness to his tent and let down the guy ropes. But suddenly, before they could creep into it, let alone overpower him and carry him a quarter of a mile to the lake, he had emerged and blown an ear-splitting blast on his whistle to summon the guard. The dunking party hastily fled.

Some of the officers were impressive in different ways. Most of them had seen combat; many had been wounded. One of the squadron officers was probably typical. William M. Chester was a twenty-four-year-old lieutenant who had been born in London, Ontario. After enlisting in the Canadian Expeditionary Force in 1915 he had gone overseas, where he had been wounded the next year. Then he had transferred to the Royal Flying Corps and served as an observer until he was wounded again in late 1916. In 1917 he had been transferred to the training command and posted home to Canada where he became adjutant of the Cadet Wing at Long Branch. A muscular young man who was an ardent rower, he wore a mustache and, with his calm, cold-eyed gaze, gave the effect of a studied yet nonchalant arrogance. By the time Cadet Faulkner arrived at Long Branch, Lieutenant Chester had been made one of the squadron commanders. Writing home to his mother in the month after his posting to Cadet Wing, Faulkner told her, "I am trying to learn to walk and salute nasty, like a British officer."

Even though there was book work in this basic training, there was plenty of the physical, some of it predictably inelegant. One day Faulkner and Hinchley shared squadron latrine duty, cleaning mirrors, washbowls, toilets, and floors. This was not what Faulkner had in mind when he enlisted. "Before the day was over," said Hinchley, "I understood quite clearly that in his country there was a special race of people to perform such work." Their next joint assignment was only a little more elevated: standing guard duty at the Special Hospital, where the patients were all being treated for various forms of venereal disease.

In August Faulkner was writing home that he was gaining proficiency at taking Morse code. Earphones clamped over their heads, the cadets would translate the crackling dots and dashes into printed letters and numbers. He reported with satisfaction that he had passed a test which many of the other cadets had failed. If they failed another such test in October, they would be held back to repeat that part of the course.

The physical training outside the classroom was rigorous. There were long route marches to harden the cadets. And the weather had changed. On September 6, writing home on stationery topped by the RAF wings-wreath-and-crown symbol, he told his mother, "I am wearing all my sweaters and my shirts. I have to wear them all under my shirt, so I look like this." In the left-hand corner of the sheet he drew a picture of himself—smoking a pipe, hands in pockets—wearing shorts above bare knees and puttees. His tightly buttoned shirt bulged like that of a man padded to play Santa Claus. He thanked Miss Maud for sending the *Commercial Appeal*, the bath towel, the cigarettes, and the socks. The training might be rugged, but "Some one remarked today that this life certainly agreed with me. . . ." He had gained so much weight, he said, that his uniforms were tight even without the added clothing worn underneath.

To his brother John he wrote about the events of air force life. "He told me how they washed their greatcoats, putting them on under a shower and scrubbed each other with soap and brushes. Bill said it got the coats clean all right but it took them two or three weeks to dry. He sent me a picture of himself in cadet uniform." Much as he must have fancied himself in the uniform, it was one of the least flattering photographs he had ever had taken. His lower face had not yet begun to fill out, and the mustache was just a suggestion above the small mouth. He wore the tilted overseas cap with the white cadet band. John wrote him back that he would like to have one of the bands, and Bill sent one to him.

In the letter to his mother he had mentioned an acquaintance, a Lieutenant Todd who had gone on to the School of Aeronautics; being an officer he did not have to go to ground school. Faulkner hoped to follow him there in two weeks. He might well have felt that it was taking him inordinately long even to get into the vicinity of an airplane. In one of her front windows Maud Falkner had hung a two-foot cloth with a red silk border. On the white ground of the cloth were two blue service stars. After his enlistment in May, Jack Falkner had gone to Parris Island, South Carolina, for the rugged training of wartime marine boot camp. Then, after advanced training at Quantico, he had shipped out of New York. The convoy put in to Brest in August. Now he was with the 5th Marine Regiment, among the hardened survivors of the ferocious fighting at Belleau Wood and Soissons. Well might the older brother wait impatiently for the end of the eight weeks' training on the shores of Lake Ontario.

On September 20, exactly two weeks after he had written Johncy, RAF Brigade Orders No. 37 posted Cadet Faulkner and most of the men of Squadron A to No. 4 School of Military Aeronautics in Toronto. By 1918 the University of Toronto had provided nearly a dozen buildings for the School of Aeronautics—dormitories, classroom buildings, dining halls, and for a time even an indoor machine-gun range. With four other cadets who had joined the RAF on the same day, Faulkner was assigned to the university's Wycliffe College, where their second-floor room in the Neo-Gothic building looked out over Hoskin Avenue. There was another American in the room, Edward Delaney, from Mount Vernon, New York. Justin Hubert Dyer and Albert Monson were both Canadians. The fifth cadet was Durla Bushell, a muscular, good-looking young man who had come from India. Dyer would later recall Faulkner as being quiet and intellectually inclined. Well-mannered and sedate-appearing, he reminded Dyer very little of "the gushy type of American. . . ." Monson, too, thought of him as quiet, neat, and businesslike. Well up in his work, he never got into trouble and was unfazed by officers. He spoke little and confided in no one. But when he did talk, it seemed to Monson that his speech was British without affectation—even the first thing upon arising in the morning. Though no one was intimate with him, Monson seems to have been closer than most—close enough, at any rate, to borrow a pair of very smart Hannam shoes which Faulkner owned. Faulkner seemed to him "meek and mild," yet at the same time alert, quick, and generally "just an outstanding little fellow." He read little beyond course texts. Sometimes he would break out of the pattern of reticence and silence by singing or reciting limericks. He particularly enjoyed "The Ballad of Captain Kidd," singing in his light, pleasant tenor:

Now to the gallows you must go,
To the gallows you must go.
And your friends all down below,
They will say, I told you so—
Damn your eyes.

Hinchley remembered Faulkner as having "a wealth of unprintable Limericks which he recited frequently in his delightful Southern accent." He also liked to drink, and the noise which came from Faulkner's room on some occasions when Hinchley wanted to sleep did not seem to him so amusing.

Despite the uncertain mustache, Cadet Faulkner of Wycliffe College was still recognizable as William Falkner of Oxford. At the same time, however, he gave signs of constructing a persona that apparently pleased him a good deal better than his own identity five months before. "I always had the idea that he had been a student at Yale," Hinchley recalled, though he was not sure how or when he had received that impression. The amiable Monson felt sometimes that Faulkner might be assuming an air of confidence he did not actually feel, that he might be overcompensating for his shortness or his generally unimpressive appearance. On one occasion, after using his monthly check from home to provide drinks for himself and his roommates, he was seen out on Hoskin Avenue, conducting a one-man drill on the sidewalk, calling out commands loudly and then executing them smartly. He seemed to be in the process of building a new exterior for himself. There were few clues beyond the occasional letters home to what was going on in the interior. There were a few indications, however, in a place one might have expected: the small notebook that he used for class notes and also for the drawings and the occasional snatch of verse that he penned on his own time.

The notes in Cadet Faulkner's loose-leaf notebook were impeccable. Lettered neatly on the first sheet of lined paper was the legend:

173799 William Faulkner
Royal Air Force
Course 42, School of Aeronautics.
University of Toronto
Canada

The lecture notes were taken for the most part in pen, generally with categories written at the tops of the unnumbered pages and subdivisions in the left-hand margins opposite the neat blocks of text. Although the handwriting showed the familiar long vertical strokes, they were not as long as they had been in the manuscripts of early poems, and the flowing calligraphy was giving way to a script that was not far from slightly joined printed letters. It was quite legible. The first seven pages dealt with aircraft rigging. They were followed by two pages on the theory of flight, ten on aerial navigation, and nine on motors. Then came one page on "Bomb Raiding," two on signaling, and two on artillery observation. There were also passages on reconnaissance and photography. They were all full yet concise, seemingly the work of an attentive and interested student.

The cadets' actual flying training (after the School of Aeronautics and then Armament School in Hamilton) would be taken in the Curtiss JN-4 two-seater biplane. Better known as the Curtiss "Jenny," this American trainer was also built in Canada under license. Most of the notes on rigging pertained to this aircraft. All of the components that made up its wood and fabric frame—which came to just over twenty-seven feet in length and forty-three feet in upper wingspread—were described in precise detail: fuselage, longerons, empennage, ailerons, and the rest. There were long paragraphs on the structural wiring and on the process of "truing a fuselage" so that none of the components of the frame would be out of line. There was a page on covering the frame: "Fabrics, Dopes and Doping." The most impressive part of this section's notes was a full-page, side-view sketch of the JN-4. From propeller to tail surfaces everything was carefully and precisely drawn—wheels, wings, cockpit, guy wires, and tail skid, with the major dimensions neatly lettered in the manner of an architect's drawing. Then, at the end of that section, was a list of sixteen Allied military aircraft. There Cadet Faulkner had listed the famous Nieuport fighter plane among the less well-known machines. Fifteenth on the list was the most glamorous and fatal of the lot: "Sopwith Camel. tractor biplane. 130 HP Clerget. Span 28, Length 18–9 chord and gap 4–6, 104 1/2 mph at 10,000. climbs 10,000 11 minutes." What student, writing those specifications, could not imagine himself at the controls of that stubby, spin-prone, rasping wasp of a warplane?

The notes on motors and aerial navigation, on tactics and weapons, were detailed. The accompanying freehand sketches were almost as precise as manufacturers' schematic drawings. In the whole notebook there were only four minor corrections in the orange pencil of the instructor.

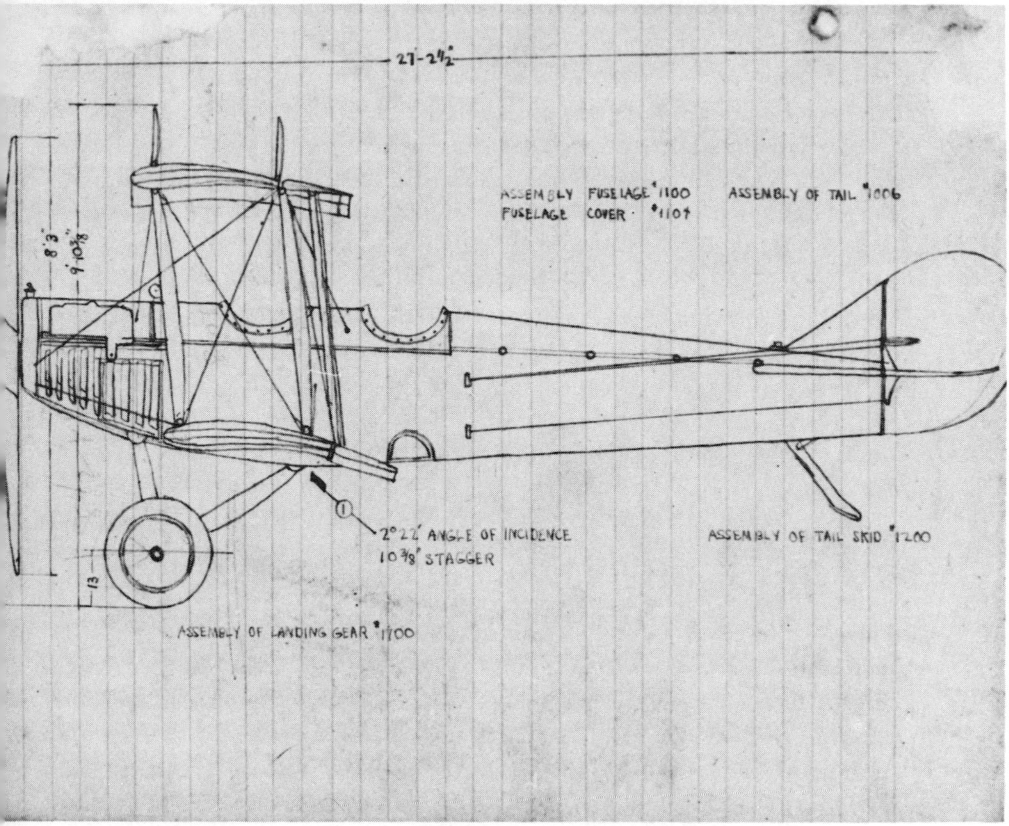

Drawing of the Curtiss JN-4 in the notebook of Cadet Faulkner, RAF.

Although the notes on the arts of war were quite professional, occasionally the impulses of the illustrator for *Ole Miss* would break through. On one sheet Faulkner wrote two dozen aircraft identification numbers. Later he crossed out a group of them, turned the page upside down, and began to sketch in the same blue ink he had used for the numbers. One drawing showed a girl in the extremely brief chemise-like garment he had often used before. Another showed the stylish sort of couple he liked to sketch. But the man was not in evening dress. He wore the full-skirted uniform of a mustached, cane-carrying RAF officer. The smallest drawing on the page was that of a male head. The thick-necked, pug-eared, pushed-in face was surmounted by a low brow and small skull. Perched atop it and

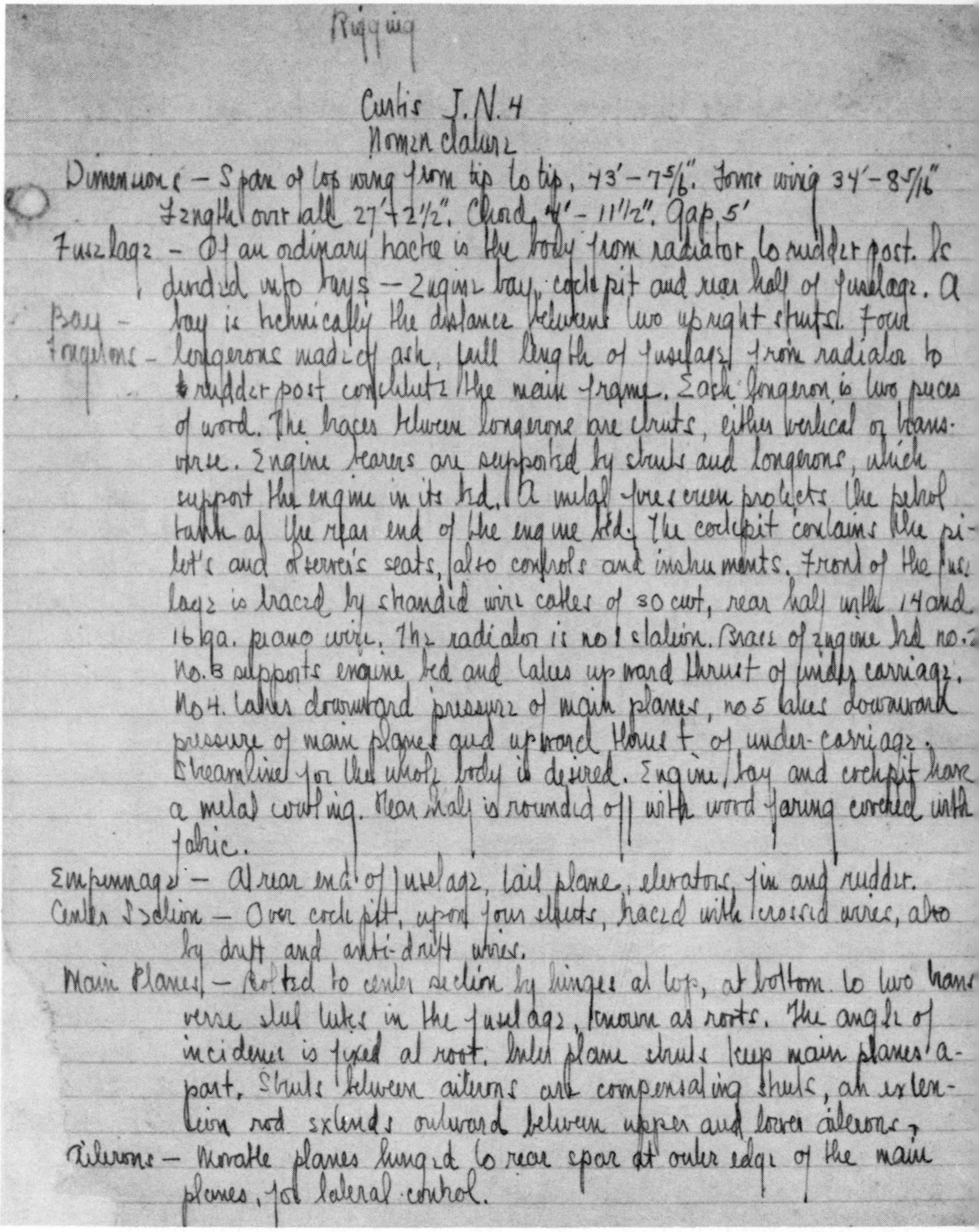

Rigging

Curtis J.N.4
Nomenclature

Dimensions — Span of top wing from tip to tip, 43'-7 5/16". Lower wing 34'-8 5/16"
Length over all 27'-2 1/2". Chord 4'-11 1/2". Gap 5'

Fuselage — Of an ordinary machine is the body from radiator to rudder post. Is divided into bays — engine bay, cockpit and rear half of fuselage. A
Bay — bay is technically the distance between two upright struts. Four
Longerons — longerons made of ash, full length of fuselage from radiator to rudder post constitute the main frame. Each longeron is two pieces of wood. The braces between longerons are struts, either vertical or transverse. Engine bearers are supported by struts and longerons, which support the engine in its bed. A metal fire screen protects the petrol tank at the rear end of the engine bed. The cockpit contains the pilot's and observer's seats, also controls and instruments. Front of the fuselage is braced by stranded wire cables of 30 cwt, rear half with 14 and 16 ga. piano wire. The radiator is no 1 station. Brace of engine bed no. 2 No. 3 supports engine bed and takes upward thrust of under carriage. No 4. takes downward pressure of main planes, no 5 takes downward pressure of main planes and upward thrust of under-carriage. Streamline for the whole body is desired. Engine bay and cockpit have a metal cowling. Rear half is rounded off with wood fairing covered with fabric.

Empennage — At rear end of fuselage, tail plane, elevators, fin and rudder.

Center Section — Over cockpit, upon four struts, braced with crossed wires, also by drift and anti-drift wires.

Main Planes — Bolted to center section by hinges at top, at bottom to two transverse steel tubes in the fuselage, known as roots. The angle of incidence is fixed at root. Inter plane struts keep main planes apart. Struts between ailerons are compensating struts, an extension rod extends outward between upper and lower ailerons,

Ailerons — Movable planes hinged to rear spar at outer edge of the main planes, for lateral control.

Description of the rigging of the Curtiss JN-4 by Cadet Faulkner.

low down over the right eye, RAF style, was an overseas cap. Like the other sketches it bore no identifying legend. But in the not unlikely event that the first sketch owed something to Lieutenant Chester, perhaps this one bore some relation to Sergeant Tabernacle. On the other side was a single drawing: a mustached lieutenant in a campaign hat, tight-fitting tunic, and leather leggings that looked very much like an American uniform. In addition to the loose-leaf notebook Faulkner had at least two smaller notebooks about the size of the ordinary stenographer's note pad. Each contained lined paper, one coarse and the other fine. In these Faulkner attempted much more careful compositions, but none of them appeared in the glossy *Cadet Wing Review*. They were apparently for himself.

Albert Monson recalled that whenever Faulkner had the chance, he "would take his notebook out and quickly sketch the officers or N.C.O.'s who were taking the parade or giving the lecture." He did one such sketch on the light, lined paper measuring eight by five inches. At the bottom he supplied the legend, "C.O.'s Parade 4. S. of A. RAF." Before a background of university buildings and trees were drawn up three squadrons of cadets in parade formation, the cadet officers positioned before each formation. In the foreground, dominating the sketch, were six RAF officers. Stick under his arm, one was saluting the commanding officer, whose adjutant stood at his side. All were similarly dressed, with Sam Browne-type belts over full-skirted jackets and tapering whipcord breeches. The garrison caps and shiny boots which the C.O. and his adjutant wore, like the sticks which they held, imparted a distinct air of military elegance and *élan*.

Faulkner did other drawings which must have had imaginary or photographic models. One showed an American infantryman wearing a campaign hat and carrying his pack on his back, his bayonet sheathed at his belt and his Springfield rifle on his shoulder. There were three more sketched with the same rather blunt blue crayon. Standing fullface, another infantryman held his grounded rifle, straps crossing his chest from the equipment on his back. He wore a large mustache and had a rather sinister aspect. Here again the artist had supplied a title: "The 'un." A kilted officer strode briskly in another sketch, stell-helmeted and carrying a cane in one hand and a pistol in the other. In the fourth sketch of this set, a Negro trooper stood, arms akimbo, wearing a rakish campaign hat and tight cloth leggings. Not nearly so stylized as the pen-and-ink drawings, these sketches showed the artist to be as much at home with straightforward, accurate proportions as he was with the distortion he employed so often in the other sketches.

One of the thin, lined sheets he had used not for a picture but for a poem. He had not completed it, and the neat lettering of the first stanza, with the characteristically long verticals, gave way to strike-outs in the second and accent marks in the unfinished third. The fragment was entitled "The Ace":

The silent earth looms liquid in the dawning
Black as poured ink beneath the grey
Mist's spectral clutching fingers

The sun light
Paints him as he stalks, huge through the morning
In his fleece and leather, gilds his bright
Hair and his cigarette.

Makes gòld his flèece and leàther, ańd his bríght
Hair.
Then, líke a shòoting stár,

He stopped there, perhaps as the squadron fell out for close order drill, or as the notes of "Last Post" sounded through the northern darkness. Or perhaps he found himself dissatisfied with what he had written, unable yet to catch the sights and emotions he wanted to express. Whatever had happened, the lines were evidence that the soldier and artist had not completely squeezed out the poet.

The imagery of "The Ace" raises a question which is underlined by one more sketch. It is a side-view of a single-seater biplane. The pilot sits waiting in the cockpit while one crewman holds on to the leading edge of the lower wing and another grasps a propeller blade. Was this—and the scene painted in "The Ace"—a product of direct observation, as was "C.O.'s Parade," or was it, like "The 'un," something imagined or seen in a magazine or Sunday rotogravure? Faulkner had drawn the preflight scene in blue crayon on half of a legal-sized sheet of Hammermill bond. The aircraft was not the Curtiss Jenny. It was shorter and stubbier, with a thick body and a heavy, cylindrical engine housing, the top wing fixed so close to it as to give the pilot little more than the minimum visibility required in that sector. It looked like, if any aircraft, the Sopwith Camel.

There were no Sopwith Camels in the RAF Canadian training command. If there had been any, they certainly would not have been based at the fields to which the cadets would go for flying instruction. What experience by now *had* William Faulkner had with real aircraft? When the cadets studied motors they would spend a certain amount of time at the Leaside airfield, in north Toronto. There they observed different types of motors set up in special sheds. Cadets Dyer and Faulkner learned the procedure for starting aircraft motors. "Switch off," they called. Then, "Switch on," and then "Contact!" They swung the propeller down through half an arc and leaped back as it caught and roared. But this was as close to flight as their course took them—spinning the propeller of a bolted-down motor inside a tin shed. The envied cadets were the ones who managed at odd times to go aloft as unauthorized passengers on brief local flights. They could not really count on flying until they finished the course at the School of Aeronautics and went on to Camp Borden, which was 50 miles northwest of Toronto, or to Camp Rathbun or Camp Mohawk, both at Deseronto and located about 130 miles east of Toronto. And there was no telling, at this point in the war, how long it would take them to get out of the School of Aeronautics and on to flight training. Earlier in the program some fortunate cadets had spent as little as six weeks at the university, but now September turned to October and they were still there, studying and seemingly no nearer to a cockpit than they had been the week before. Bill had by now passed another Morse test. But again, it was a vastly different activity from the kind Jack was engaged in. Bill might study scale maps of sectors of the French front; Jack was fighting over them.

In mid-September Jack had advanced with his comrades over stone walls, dodging machine-gun fire and shooting at gray-clad figures glimpsed through the haze of smoke. Then, in the days immediately after Saint-Mihiel, he helped escort prisoners to the rear, sometimes in batches of five or six hundred. After a short time at the rear his unit started for the front again. By September 27 they were on their way to the Champagne sector. There Jack was badly gassed, but somehow he managed to stay with his unit. Before long they were fighting at Épinal, advancing through the battlefields of 1914 and 1915, French and German bones beneath them. Rusted helmets lay scattered about, and here and there fragments of cloth fluttered in the limbs of the blasted trees. By October 10 they had gone to the rear again for rest and replacements. When they went back into the line it was the night of October 31, on the edge of the Argonne Forest. German star shells signaled for the artillery in the dark hours of the morning of November 1, and one of the men in the trenches where the barrage came crashing and clanging down was Jack Falkner. At the instant when his platoon sergeant shouted to his men to crouch down in the trench, the "whiz-bang" from a German .77 exploded with a roar. His right knee laid open by a piece of shrapnel, a shell fragment lodged against his skull, Jack was out of the war. His letters stopped coming. Soon Maud and Murry Falkner were beside themselves with anxiety and worry. John and Dean felt it too. "Dad sort of went to pieces," the older boy later said, "but Mother kept telling him, 'Hush, Buddy. He'll be back.' "

Bill Faulkner was a lot farther from the front than many noncombatants. But it was by no means a protected existence. The cadets were exposed to one of the risks that was taking a heavy toll of the noncombatants, particularly pregnant women as well as the old and infirm. It was the great Spanish influenza epidemic of the autumn of 1918. More than a quarter of the officers and men at Long Branch came down with the flu. The School of Aeronautics was placed under quarantine, and another series of long marches was scheduled to keep the men's resistance up. This apparently worked with Cadet Faulkner, who not only did not fall ill but even gained a total of nineteen pounds before his training was through. Death came to the second-floor room, however, and in a curious way. Good-looking, well-built Durla Bushell liked to play rugby. On Friday, November 1, the day Jack lay flat in the muck of a muddy trench in the Argonne, Durla Bushell lay flat on the rugby field after falling in the scrum or being hit in the hard-running pack. He was taken to the hospital with a fractured skull, and by Monday evening he was dead.

The epidemic had interrupted the training program at the School of Aeronautics. And now, as the incidence of flu cases began to decline somewhat, the Allied drive of early November began to push ahead, rolling back the German lines. Then, on November 11, the war suddenly was over. Cadets who had accepted the combat flier's assumption that they were already, in effect, dead men, had to adjust to a completely different idea. For those who had waited eagerly to learn to fly, there was a depressing prospect: after the months of drill and ground school, they might not get into the air at all.

The members of Course 42 were still at the School of Aeronautics. On November 18 their picture was taken. There, amid the massed faces of the four-foot-long photograph, was William Faulkner's. The overseas cap was cocked rakishly on the right side of his head, the white cadet band so low that it concealed one eyebrow and the tip of an ear. The mustache was now quite dark, and the expression seemed dour. The prospects of Cadet Faulk-

Course 42, No. 4 School of Aeronautics, Royal Air Force, Toronto, November 18, 1918.

ner's getting any flying time now were very dim. This possibility was shortly confirmed. J. M. Hinchley remembered that "orders came through to discontinue all flying in Canada and from that date we simply marked time while awaiting demobilization." On November 22 a Toronto newspaper reported that the "RAF situation is very indefinite at the present time. Flying is optional for cadets in training . . . and cadets who have finished their entire course are sent home on indefinite leave. . . ." One officer reported that the cadets were not encouraged to continue: "we had enough in training to carry on for the next twenty months." For those who had not yet begun flight training, being posted to one of the three camps for instruction appeared to be out of the question.

The letters Maud Falkner received during that month gave a quite different impression. Her son wrote that he had gone on a "joy ride" in a plane in August. After that time he had gotten rides with other friends. And the armistice did not end his flying, according to his letters. He had finished ground school on November 13, he wrote, and had begun to fly at more frequent intervals. On November 22 he went aloft, a day when he was "so cold he had to be helped out of the cockpit." Two days later he made another flight, and by November 30, he told

Miss Maud, he had four hours of solo time to his credit. He was glad, he said, that the war had lasted long enough for him to get flying training. This sanguinary view must have been a difficult one for Murry Falkner to accept. On November 17 he had written to marine authorities asking where the 66th Company of the 5th Regiment was now located. On November 23 they wrote that it was with the 2nd Division, which two weeks before had been in action on the Meuse near Mouzon. He was to write to the Casualty Office for further information. So now he knew that his son had been wounded in action, but he knew neither how badly he had been wounded nor where he was.

As Miss Maud read Billy's letters in Mississippi, reports in Toronto newspapers indicated that such good luck as her son described must be extraordinary indeed. On November 23 the Toronto *Star* reported that in a few days the demobilization of Toronto RAF personnel would get under way. On the twenty-eighth the same newspaper reported that "Flying except for a very little photographic work, has entirely stopped." By December 2 the *Star* was able to inform its readers that in the interval since the November 26 "Over two thousand Cadets of the RAF have been demobilized. . . ." It had been announced at the start of the demobilization that the first cadets to be processed would be those at Cadet Wing, the School of Aeronautics and the School of Armament at Hamilton. Course 42 was never posted from the School of Aeronautics to Camps Borden, Rathbun, or Mohawk. Monson and Dyer did not fly. Nor did Hinchley. "That Faulkner," he wrote, "could have been doing solo flying at that time when all activities were at a halt is hardly credible." But according to stories he would tell after his return home, he was doing even more spectacular things than simply flying an aircraft solo.

"The war quit on us before we could do anything about it," he told Jack the following spring. "The same day they lined up the whole class, thanked us warmly for whatever it was they figured we had done to deserve it, and announced that we would be discharged the next day, which meant that we had the afternoon to celebrate the armistice and some airplanes to use in doing it. I took up a rotary-motored Spad with a crock of bourbon in the cockpit, gave diligent attention to both, and executed some reasonably adroit chandelles, an Immelman or two, and part of what could easily have turned out to be a nearly perfect loop."

"What do you mean—part of a loop?" his brother asked.

Cadet Faulkner.

Bill laughed. "That's what it was; a hangar got in the way and I flew through the roof and ended up hanging on the rafters." He had to climb down on one of the hangar support poles, he said.

John Falkner's recollection was that his brother "had flown his Camel halfway through the top of a hangar. The tail of his ship was still outside and they got Bill down from inside the hangar with a ladder." When he got home to Oxford, John recalled, he still had a limp as a souvenir of the accident. A long time later Bill Faulkner would tell his stepson, Malcolm Franklin, that he got his broken nose "honestly by landing upside down. . . ." To Phil Stone he gave a happier version. He had taken a companion up with him, and after the crash they felt well enough to apply themselves to the bottle again. "Funniest thing you ever saw," a bystander was reported to have said, "the two of them hanging there trying to drink from a bottle upside down." Nearly a dozen years after the event, Faulkner would produce a written and amplified account:

War came. Liked British uniform. Got commission R.F.C., pilot.
Crashed. Cost British gov't 2000 pounds. Was still pilot.
Crashed. Cost British gov't 2000 pounds.
Quit. Cost British gov't $84.30. King said, "Well done."

These stories of a gradually mushrooming catastrophe call into question the credibility of some of the accounts Cadet Faulkner had written home to his loving mother. One was the possibility that he could be graduated from ground school two days after such a spectacular disaster. Another was that he should ever be allowed near another military aircraft in the wake of such damage to government equipment, installations, and personnel. Another unlikelihood was that it should have escaped the notice of his fellow cadets, the inscribers of official records, and the newspapers. There was never any awareness of such an event in any of these quarters. The crash Faulkner described would have been a dramatic though ludicrous close to a brief and finally disappointing military career. The creative imagination had apparently made up the deficiencies of reality. It seems clear, then, that Cadet Faulkner did not crash. Did he ever fly?

Since he was never posted from the School of Aeronautics to one of the fields where the cadets received flying instruction, any flying would have had to be on a commuting basis. But Camp Borden was fifty miles away and Rathbun and Mohawk were nearly three times further. That would leave Leaside airfield, in north Toronto. If he could catch a ride there, the other places would be likely landing fields before making the return trip. But how could he get away from the School of Aeronautics to go flying even after—as Hinchley remembered it—they were simply "marking time" after the armistice?

He did have a folded piece of pasteboard a little larger than a book of matches. Stamped in the blue leather of the outside surface were the RAF wings and the words "No. 4 School of Aeronautics, Royal Air Force, Permanent Pass, Cadet." Opened up, the pass revealed the owner's name, printed in his draftman's hand at the top and signed in his distinctive calligraphy at the bottom. He had permission to be absent from his quarters from "after duty to 12.00 m.n., while at No. 4 S. of A. Toronto." The days on which this applied (again printed in the cadet's hand) were "Wed. Sat. Sun." It was dated September 21, 1918, and the last printed line specified, "This Pass must be carried by the Owner at all hours." Of the flight dates he had specified to his mother in the letters, November 22 had fallen on a

Friday, but the twentieth-fourth was a Sunday and the thirtieth was a Saturday. He should have had no difficulty getting from Wycliffe College to Leaside and back between the end of duty on those days and midnight.

What would a cadet as reticent and unprepossessing as this one do even if he had somehow made his way to the ready room or the flight line at Leaside on a Wednesday, Saturday, or Sunday? He would be unlikely to ask a stranger—a pilot and an officer—for a ride. Probably he would follow his natural inclinations. An inveterate watcher and listener, he would be likely to study the pilots as they stood about discussing their machines or missions. (If some Saturday or Sunday morning he had no duty at all, he might even have arrived at Leaside in time to see an early pilot, and later to take out his pen and write, "The sun light/paints him as he stalks, huge through the morning/In his fleece and leather, gilds his bright/Hair and his cigarette." Or he might have used his blue crayon to capture the motions of the uniformed airman as he turned the propeller for the waiting pilot in the heavy training machine that looked like the deadly Camel.) What had happened to Lieutenant Todd—the one who was also an aspiring pilot but did not have to go to ground school? Todd would by now have been well into flying instruction. If this were so, being an officer already, he might not have found it difficult to arrange a flight for Faulkner or to take him up himself. If Todd had been far enough along, he might even have passed on to the cadet some of the instruction he had himself been receiving. He might even have let him handle the controls. If the lieutenant had been sufficiently bold and the cadet sufficiently adept, he might have been allowed to try some maneuvers, and perhaps even to shoot a few landings or try a takeoff. But to provide a chance for solo flight, let alone four hours of it, would have been enormously difficult even for a lieutenant. Without the rather conjectural Lieutenant Todd or someone like him, such activities could hardly have been possible at all.

Faulkner was given his Medical Boards examination under the authority of the demobilization order on December 5. The results of the examination placed him in "Category A." Under the system which had been devised, each man was first given a temporary discharge. Then, after further paper work, the final entries on the certificate would be completed, and it would be stamped in blue: DEMOBILIZED, DATE______. The clerk would fill in the date of final and official demobilization in pen, after which the certificate could be mailed to the cadet. For Faulkner that date was January 4, 1919. Page 3 of the four-page form was headed "Character and Trade

Proficiency." In the place for the former, there was another blue stamp: ASSESSMENT OF CHARACTER DISCONTINUED. Under the legend "Degree of Proficiency," following the trade classification "Cadet for Pilot," the clerk had on January 4 written, "Groundwork 70%." The meticulous notes and precise drawings had somehow in the end merited no more than this. (Perhaps Cadet Faulkner had not been so meticulous and precise on examinations.) On page 4, the "Special Qualifications and Courses of Instruction" column listed only Cadet Wing and School of Aeronautics. "Time Forfeited" was blue-stamped —NIL— and under "Casualties, Wounds, Campaigns, Medals, Clasps, Decorations, Mentions, Etc." appeared again only that dead and empty word: —NIL—. Also on page 3 the clerk had stamped a kind of summary paragraph and Captain J. R. Reilly had signed it "For G.O.C. Royal Air Force, Canada." The paragraph read, "Discharged in consequence of being Surplus to R.A.F. requirements. (Not having suffered impairment since entry into the Service.) para. 392 (XXVa), (b), K.R.)"

There in the cold phrases of the King's Regulations was the death of the hopes that, jacketed and goggled, he might walk out to the flight line for the dawn patrol or lounge on leave in the smart blue uniform. These hopes were reflected in six lines he penciled, probably very early in his training, on the front flyleaf of a small black Modern Library copy of *Poems* by Algernon Charles Swinburne. A projection of his hoped-for career, they read:

W. Faulkner
Royal Air Force
Cadet Wing
S of A
Borden
Australies [?] Wing

But even though the final expectation had been frustrated, there had been some benefits and advantages. He *had* been an RAF man. He had enjoyed the chance to absorb some few aspects of the British culture which he admired. He might have been a noncombatant, but like most of the cadets he kept up on the exploits of the great British aces—Mannock, and McCudden, and the Canadian, Billy Bishop. By late June of 1918 Bishop had been posted from France to Canada to help with the organization of the RAF–Canada. In November Faulkner had written home of his delight at observing a real hero of the air war. The training was based on the lessons of combat as well as traditional methods and materials. Much of this sense of combat and death his extraordinary imagination absorbed. Some of it in a way became transmuted into his own experience. This was true of the comic as well as the grim. Faulkner would tell, years later, of an ambitious commanding officer who loved to exercise even the least combat-ready of his men. One day the C.O. ordered out all of his cooks and bakers. Equipping them with whatever could be found from tin can covers to butcher knives, he sent them skirmishing back and forth across the apron in front of a row of aircraft hangars. In the midst of this, Faulkner would say, laughing, a plane landed. In the observer's seat sat a general from Wing, come to make an inspection.

Erroneous reports of aerial combat would get into biographical notes on William Faulkner, for he gave the impression that he had seen actual fighting. Later he would talk about the dangers of simply flying in those days, the strain they produced, and the way a man would wonder if he would be able to walk away from the next day's flight. The dangers, particularly in aircraft such as the Sopwith Camel, had been amply reported. This sense too Faulkner absorbed, so that when he spoke of it his hearer could not doubt that it was something he had known firsthand, and in his vitals.

His time in the RAF had lasted not quite five months—179 days, the clerk had written on his Certificate of Service. But the products of the experience, observation, and imagination they had brought would last a lifetime. Now there were more immediate benefits.

When his twenty-eight days' furlough pay and ration allowance, his "allowance for plain clothes," and war gratuity were added up, he was due the sum of $89.83. From this was deducted $16.14—in part, advances already made to him by his unit. Some of the money would be sent to him later; now, as he went through the process of temporary discharge, he was presented with a draft for $31.11. He had a use for it—paying for an order he had obviously placed some time before. A document handed out along with the draft and other papers was a notice informing airmen and cadets "that they are only entitled to wear their uniform up to the time they receive their permanent discharge . . . ." Faulkner must have been but little concerned about the relatively coarse cadet uniform. Some time before this he had ordered a complete officer's uniform. As usual, where clothes were involved, he had ordered the best—a garrison cap made by William Scully, Ltd., Montreal, the smart, blue-gray belted tunic, trousers, and a trench coat complete with the flaps and equipment rings that made it combat-worthy as well as smart. He would make the trip home in style.

He had a few mementos which he could carry in one pocket. There was a shoulder patch lettered "Royal Flying Corps," which, when fastened to the tunic of a former artilleryman, infantryman, or cavalryman, gave notice that he had joined that elite band superseded by the RAF. There was a 1901 Canadian sixpence, a lucky piece or talisman of the kind carried even by the great ones such as Mannock and Bishop. There were pieces of blue piping and a wallet-sized, nearly transparent Union Jack of the kind that appear on dining tables at the captain's dinner on the last night at sea.

Older and heavier, William Faulkner boarded the train in Toronto and set out for Lafayette County, Oxford, and home.

16

December, 1918–September, 1919

. . . they had stopped the war on him.

So he sat in a smoldering of disgusted sorrow, not even enjoying his Pullman prerogatives, spinning on his thumb his hat with its accursed white band. . . .

. . . New York swam flatly past; Buffalo was imminent, and sunset.

. . . He saw a belt and wings, he rose and met a young face with a dreadful scar across his brow. My God he thought, turning sick. He saluted and the other peered at him with strained distraction.

. . . Had I been old enough or lucky enough, this might have been me, he thought jealously.

—*Soldiers' Pay* (7, 13, 25)

Outside the windows the landscape changed as the train rattled south over the border and into the United States. Besides the young men in RAF garb, there were other soldiers on the train—American officers and enlisted men, some of them forgoing the scenery for toasts to the end of the war. William Faulkner talked and drank with a few of them. Toronto had vanished and then Buffalo, to give way in turn to Cincinnati and, finally, Memphis. When No. 23 from Holly Springs pulled into the depot in Oxford about eleven o'clock on a morning early in December, the Falkner Model T was waiting. His mother and father, Johncy and Dean, and Mammy Callie were there to meet him. It was a vivid moment for seventeen-year-old John Falkner: "Bill got off the train in his British officer's uniform—slacks, a Sam Browne belt, and wings on his tunic. He had on what we called an overseas cap, a monkey cap that was only issued to our men if they had served overseas. A part of the British uniform was a swagger stick and Bill had one, and across his arm a trench coat." Before the eyes of his proud family he took the salutes of American veterans who had noted the cap and belt. "To them it meant he had been overseas and they saluted an overseas man. They turned up their noses at our own officers who had not been over and refused to acknowledge them in any way." Johncy also noticed that his brother was limping. When he asked what had happened, Bill told him about the crash into the hangar roof. He explained that after the armistice the cadets had been allowed to take flight instruction if they wished. So was his account of his RAF experience fixed, and so would it stay.

The family's joy was diluted by their fears for Jack, who had still not been heard from. Desperately concerned for her son's safety, Miss Maud nonetheless went on with preparations for Christmas, hanging his stocking on the mantel with the others. At last a letter arrived for Murry Falkner from Jack the week before Christmas. He had been in a French hospital recovering. It was a cheerful letter, omitting mention of his gassing and minimizing the shrapnel wounds. He had much to tell them when he got home, which would probably be "some time this winter or early spring."

The returned airman was obviously enjoying himself. The regulation restricting the wearing of the uniform to military occasions bothered him not a whit. He wore his military garb at home, around town, and also to dances in neighboring towns. He posed for photographs in half a dozen different combinations. In one he wore the overseas cap, Sam Browne belt, whipcord breeches, and tightly wrapped puttees. For another he donned trousers, doffed the Sam Browne belt, and nonchalantly wore a garrison cap —grommet-less, "hot-pilot" style. The airman's "badge" with the RFC wings glittered on the left breast of the tunic. Smiling, he leaned lightly on the rattan cane, a cigarette between his lips. Two other touches helped make him the embodiment of the smart-looking sort of officer Lieutenant Chester must have been: a linen handkerchief tucked up into his sleeve and a pair of leather gloves—carried, not worn—in the same hand that held the slim cane. But he had not yet received all of his accoutrements. Phil Stone was with him on Christmas Eve when the mail brought his second lieutenant's pips. (It would be fifteen months before he would be gazetted an honorary second lieutenant and longer before the commission itself would actually arrive.) His friend Robert Farley remembered how he walked into Mr.

Tomlinson's jewelry store that evening with Faulkner, who opened the box and showed the pips to Farley and the jeweler. One friend recalled seeing him on the Square "wearing his British uniform with all the regalia. He cut quite a swanky figure. . . . He gave the impression that he did not have a care or worry in this world, or give a damn about anything or anybody." An object of admiration to some, he was a source of curiosity to others. One day when he accompanied the family to Memphis, he caught the attention of some country people. One finally walked up and asked him what kind of uniform he was wearing. "A Rooshian general's," he replied, eyes bright and face serious. Johncy liked it, and on several occasions his brother let him wear it.

Periodically, Bill Faulkner would don the uniform later in life. But now he had to revert to civilian clothes. His brother John remembered one garment in particular, bought at Halle's in Memphis, one of the first sports coats he had ever seen. "It was a heather tweed, sort of smoky-looking, with raglan shoulders and pleats behind each arm, and leather buttons. Bill wore it for everything." He had developed one persona as far as he could; now he would begin to build up another that was very different. On December 31 the RAF Records and Recruiting Office sent him his Certificate of Service. Two weeks later the Paymaster's Office dispatched a money order for the $42.58 due him on his discharge. The brief era was at a final end.

It did not take him long to become reacclimated to Oxford. There had been changes, of course, but nothing like those in the recent past when the automobile had begun its rapid conquest. Judge Niles had gone to his reward, full of years and honors. Many Oxonians had fallen ill when the flu epidemic had struck the town in October, and now it was about to lay siege to Oxford once again. By mid-January Dr. Young would order the closing of schools and churches, and it would be two weeks before the ban was rescinded. The health of the body politic was still on the feverish side, too, as Lee M. Russell had begun his campaign for the governor's chair, using the traditional tools of oratory and patronage. Some of the latter was dispensed close to home.

J. W. T. Falkner must have decided that he had lost all the money a father could be expected to lose in setting up a middle-aged son in a series of businesses, with each one failing a bit more decisively than the last. The University of Mississippi was growing, and J. C. Eskridge was both secretary and proctor. Undoubtedly with the approval of Lee M. Russell, the post of assistant secretary was filled on December 1, 1918, by Murry C. Falkner. The salary was adequate, and a house was provided on the campus.

This perquisite was not immediately available, however, and it would be about a year before they could actually move in. Mr. Murry now went to his office on the campus each day. Students would pay their tuition to him, and gradually he began to assume additional duties. His job-shifting was over.

Bill Faulkner did not spend nearly as much time at home now as he once had. His father had given up trying to understand this boy, who now even spelled his name differently from his own. And he had no business in which his son could conceivably work. The young man's grandfather must have known that the experiment in the bank had not been successful. To try it again would probably have resulted only in irritating bookkeeper Ruby McCoy and J. E. Avent, cashier and kinsman of bank director T. W. Avent. Murry Falkner would nonetheless give his eldest son food and shelter. There was real affection between the father and Jack, who would start his letters home with a warm "Dear Pardner." Johncy and Dean both excelled at sports, becoming fierce competitors whom their father would cheer on first high school and then college fields. Murry Falkner would go into the woods to hunt with Dean in a companionship that seemed closer than any he had enjoyed with the others. Between him and his oldest son there now seemed only distance. Although Murry Falkner may have felt baffled by his son, the reverse apparently was not true. It seems likely that twenty-one-year-old William Faulkner may have taken the same sort of view that other Oxonians—perhaps even Grandfather—took of Murry Falkner, even though he shared certain traits with him. He certainly did not measure up, in terms of this world's standards, to such men as Colonel Falkner, General Stone, and Major Oldham. And even if none of them ever served as a father-surrogate for Bill Faulkner, it is not surprising that he got on with them a great deal better, for the most part, than he did with his own father.

He saw much of the Stones—not only Phil, but his brother Jack and his wife Myrtle, with whom Phil lived in Charleston, where the two brothers handled that branch of the firm while the General and Jim, Jr., took care of the Oxford business. In a different way, Bill Faulkner had as much of an affinity for Jack Stone as he did for his younger brother. In Jack's sickly infancy, wrote one member of the family later, "his adoring grandparents cared for him on their farm in Panola County. It was the Indians thereabouts who got Jack well enough to go hunting before he was old enough to hold on from behind a saddle. 'Feed him bear gravy,' they told his grandmother." Faulkner was fascinated with Indian lore, and he liked this rich, densely forested Delta land, flat though it was compared with his native hill country to the northeast. When he visited Phil, Myrtle and Jack Stone would invite him to stay as their guest. He enjoyed this, playing golf from time to time on the good course nearby. Sometimes he would leave to be gone for days, walking over miles of Tallahatchie County, roaming, looking, and listening to the country people talk.

Before the 1918 holiday season was over, Bill Faulkner had begun to spend considerable time in the northwest corner of the Delta and to make new friends. He drank more there than when he was at home, and he was also somewhat more approachable and affable. In Clarksdale, at a house party given by their mutual friend Curry Ellis, he had met Eula Dorothy Wilcox. Born in McAlester, Oklahoma, and orphaned at twelve, Dot's heritage included one-quarter Cherokee blood and some property. At sixteen, she took a course as a beauty operator. Then she sold some of her property and moved to Clarksdale, where she supported herself as a beautician. By the time she met Faulkner and Stone—whom she remembered as inseparable—she had her own beauty parlor and her own home. Stone and Faulkner would visit her there.

Faulkner liked her friends, too. One was a dark-haired, dark-eyed gambler of French descent named Reno DeVaux. Proprietor of Reno's Place in Clarksdale, he was a popular man who contributed generously to charitable causes. Rolling and smoking his own cigarettes, he would tell jokes and laugh infectiously, his dark eyes crinkling at the corners. He would talk about his childhood in Mobile, where his mother had singled him out from among his brothers for the priesthood. "Mrs. DeVaux," the parish priest had told her, "you have had a great many troubles, but I believe that your old age is going to be very happy. You have a jewel in Reno."

By the age of seventeen, Reno was an acolyte serving at High Mass, a boy who would surely go on to the seminary. One day, however, his crowd introduced him to a game called craps which was played for money. The effect of the dice in his hand was electric.

"I told the father that I could never become a priest," Reno said. "He said for me to pray for help and not worry. Instead that night I climbed the fence and was gone."

During the day, as the waiters changed tablecloths and prepared for the evening's business, Reno would sit with his friends and talk about the games he had played in and the nightclubs he had run since that night in Mobile when he had put both his childhood and the priesthood behind him. He liked Phil Stone and offered him a job playing cards for the house. Stone was flattered, but he said he thought he'd stick to the law and play poker for fun and the valuable lessons it provided in human nature. Occasionally he would receive a letter in Charleston from Reno. "Come back soon," Reno wrote in one, "and bring The Poet with you." And so he would return to Clarksdale periodically, taking Bill Faulkner with him. Even after adopting the new persona of a bohemian poet, Faulkner still retained some British mannerisms. One took the form of his always addressing his friend as "Stone," never as "Phil."

Sometimes Faulkner would drift over to Clarksdale by himself. Once he arrived when Dot and Reno, Willie Mays and his wife, and a group of other friends were going to New Orleans. They asked him if he wanted to go along.

"Yes," he said, "but I've only got fifty cents in my pocket."

"That's all right," Reno said. "Come on along. I'll take care of it." The party went by train, drinking and enjoying themselves on the way. They would stay at the Roosevelt in New Orleans, Reno decided, and have dinner in the hotel's stylish Blue Room.

After they checked in, Faulkner said he was going to see a friend. It had begun to rain, and when he returned, some time later, what had been an unprepossessing set of garments now appeared completely disreputable. Reno looked at him.

"Come on with me," he said. "You can't go to the Blue Room looking like that."

When they returned to the hotel a little later, the old clothes were in a box under Faulkner's arm. Reno had bought him a new outfit. Faulkner opened the box to hang up his traveling ensemble, but Dot intervened before he could begin.

"Here," she said, "you don't want those old clothes any more." With that she threw them out one of the windows. Still in high spirits, they were preparing to go down to dinner when they were stopped by a knock at the door. Two policemen had come to investigate the shower of old clothes onto Baronne Street.

Reno, who was an expert at mollifying policemen, tried to explain that it was just a harmless joke. As he talked, the officers began to check the room, opening drawers and closets. One of the party was an agreeable and sizable young man from Pocahontas, Mississippi, named Walter Lee Bates. He was still legally a member of the United States Army and had ridden the train in his private's uniform. He felt, however, that he could not lower the tone of the group during the evening and had brought along a tuxedo, which he now wore. One of the policemen found in the closet the drab khaki tunic, breeches, and puttees which Walter Lee should have been wearing. He turned to the merrymakers.

"Who owns this uniform?" he asked.

For the moment Reno found himself without an answer. Walter Lee stood there, immobile in his satin-lapeled dinner jacket. Bill Faulkner spoke.

"I do," he told the policemen. Neither Reno nor Dot was prepared for this sudden volunteering of information. Faulkner's afternoon had been a convivial one. His own momentum matched that of the party, and now he had apparently decided in a spirit of camaraderie to offer himself as some sort of sacrifice for his friend. The police could arrest him for giving them misinformation, but at least Walter Lee would have a chance of avoiding trouble with the M.P.'s and the army. But there was one immediate problem. Walter Lee weighed a good 170 pounds, and notorious though army quartermasters were, one could not conceivably have issued a uniform of this size to the slight man who had just claimed ownership of it. There were more annoyed questions from the police followed by a good deal of conversation. Reno recovered his aplomb, and after more protestations of innocence and good will, he persuaded the police to join him and the others in a drink and forget the whole business. When they had finished their drink they were seen to the elevator, in courtly fashion, by William Faulkner. There was now no impediment to the celebration in the Blue Room and the rest of their brief stay in New Orleans.

Walter Lee Bates remembered Bill Faulkner's effort to help him. Not long afterwards he was discharged from the army, and they would see each other from time to time in Clarksdale, sometimes at Dot's home. He was now making a comfortable living transporting and supplying liquor without benefit of the blessing of state and federal agencies. (He would make an even better living a year hence when national prohibition went into effect.) He was a lively companion but not, his friends insisted, ever rowdy. Occasionally, he liked to try his hand at the manufacture, as well as the transportation and sale, of hard liquor. Dot Wilcox's backyard, enclosed by a seven-foot board fence, struck him as a perfect place to carry out one of these efforts. He found a ready assistant in Bill Faulkner.

Together they suspended a five-gallon jug up in a tree. It was full of spirits which needed further processing. Through a hole in the stoppered neck of the jug, they ran a strand of wool yarn down to a five-gallon crock on a platform close to the ground. In the crock was a quantity of charcoal which was meant to purify the liquor after it had made its way out of the jug and down the yarn. Walter Lee and Bill kept checking frequently to see how the run was coming, dipping samples out of the crock to test the quality. From time to time Dot would come out with snacks. Deviled eggs were one of Bill's favorites. On one of her trips out to check on her two guests he said to her, "Put some devil in those eggs, Dot." Eventually, she found Bill Faulkner asleep on the floor of her quiet, latticed back porch, a pillow under his head.

It was a foot-loose life—Charleston, Clarksdale, New Orleans, Memphis—with the only limits imposed by what he could afford. He did not want for much. The trench coat he had brought home from Canada was more than enough protection against Mississippi weather, and the pockets were capacious enough for a bottle of whiskey, a book or two, and whatever other items he wanted to carry. There were friends who would entertain him and put him up if he wanted to stay. He still saw a good deal of the Oldhams and he would often drop in on a Sunday night. Rob, the houseboy, would be off, and he and Dot Oldham would go to the kitchen and make roast beef sandwiches with chili. They would take them on trays up to the Oldhams' bedroom and have supper by the fire. They would talk easily about local happenings, and about Honolulu and Estelle. Bill would drift back into the Oxford routine as if he had never left it. And when the spirit moved him, he would don the RAF blue again. It moved him that February. The Kodak Brownie clicked, and there was another photograph of the elegant, nonchalant airman, as—Jekyll-like—he momentarily displaced the vagrant bohemian poet. On the back of the photograph someone—perhaps Miss Maud—wrote, "Lt. Bill. 2/11/19."

There were eddies of news in Oxford as the winter of 1919 wore on. Lee Russell was an avowed candidate for governor. Lem Oldham, after sixteen years as Clerk of the U.S. Circuit and District Courts and U.S. Commissioner for the Northern Judicial District, had resigned to open a law practice. A month later he would be appointed general counsel of the Kosciusko & Southeastern Railroad Company. The influenza epidemic began to recede and more soldiers kept trickling home from camps in the United States and posts in Germany and France. For Bill Faulkner there were two items that dwarfed all the rest. A day before the new RAF photo had been taken, the Oldhams had received a cablegram from Honolulu. On February 8 a baby had been born to Major and Mrs. Cornell S. Franklin. They named her Melvina Victoria DeGraffenreid Franklin. "The Major wears his new dignity of Grandpa very becomingly," the *Eagle* commented. It could not have been easy for Faulkner to offer his congratulations to the Oldhams. A year ago Estelle had been his sweetheart; now she was a wife and mother. His bitterness remained, but this could not change the fact that he still loved her.

The other item had been long awaited, a telegram from Jack saying he had landed on March 11 at Hampton Roads, Virginia, and was now in the U.S. Naval Hospital at Norfolk. He had been convalescing in the hospital at Hyères on the Riviera, just thirty-five miles from St. Tropez, where, he said later, "I spent two months enjoying the sun outside and shooting craps inside." In two weeks he would be home once more. Maud Faulkner got the good word to her eldest son, who had apparently taken off again. Two days after Jack landed he had a wire from his brother, who told him how proud he was of him. HAPPY YOU'RE HOME, the wire went on. SEE YOU IN OXFORD. CHEERIO. BILL. During the next week the family waited in eager anticipation, enduring a cyclonic storm which brought the heaviest rain in living memory. "It was," remarked the *Eagle* with something like awe, "a trash-mover and a bridge-floater." A week later they had their reunion. His brothers and his parents watched, smiling and wet-eyed, as he took from the stocking on the mantel the presents Miss Maud had put there almost three months before.

Now that his boy was back, Murry Falkner started thinking about his future. For one thing, he wanted to keep him home. Direct as usual, he wrote on April 15 to the "Commandant, U.S. Marines," and requested an immediate discharge for Jack. He explained that "the Chancellor of the Mississippi State University has offered to returned soldiers who have seen overseas service the privilege of entering the university without the necessary high school units and as my boy quit the high school before finishing his last year in order to volunteer in the Marines, this offer means the saving of one year's time to him." Jack returned to Norfolk and two days later his discharge papers were ready for him. He was back home permanently before April was out. He could do as he liked until it was time for him to go to the university in the fall. The same course of action was open to his brother. Billy Faulkner may not have served overseas, but he too was a returning serviceman. If that were not enough, Murry Faulkner was assistant secretary of the university and Chancellor Joseph Neely Powers had apparently taken a liking to him. At this point, however, it looked like the university held no more attraction for Billy than had the bank. Besides, he was busy writing poetry.

He seems to have been working in two different areas that spring. A number of poems and fragments which apparently date from that time were much like the verses he had composed before he left for Canada, verses which often echoed Swinburne, Housman, and others, and which showed him tentatively moving in several directions as he experimented. Another mass of verse was much more homogeneous. During April, May, and June, according to his own later dating, he worked on a cycle of pastoral poems.

It is as though he had set himself both a model and a problem in the writing of these poems. In subject, style, and idiom, they were in the oldest formal poetic tradition. They were pastoral eclogues, linked together by observations on the seasons of the year. They were pervaded by a melancholy arising out of meditations on youth, beauty, love, nature, and mutability voiced by the marble faun himself, who asks, in the last lines of a poem which was to serve as prologue to the published volume:

Why am I sad? I?
Why am I not content? The sky
Warms me and yet I cannot break
My marble bonds. That quick keen snake
Is free to come and go, while I
Am prisoner to dream and sigh
For things I know, yet cannot know,
'Twixt sky above and earth below.
The spreading earth calls to my feet
Of orchards bright with fruits to eat,
Of hills and streams on either hand;
Of sleep at night on moon-blanched sand:
The whole world breathes and calls to me
Who marble-bound must ever be.

The poems were peopled by other fauns and their nymphs, by shepherds and shepherdesses. They pined or dreamed in "quietude" by "ivied walls" in the "leafy shade" or the "westering sun." In some lines he struck the tones of a pensive Keats, in others, those of a melancholy Yeats. He had chosen a mode, wrote another poet later, whose virtues were "restraint, formality, and power in disguise, not dramatized. . . . Faulkner's concept of the use of poetry was a lofty one, and in a sense, an inhibiting one for the poet." Working within these self-imposed limitations, Faulkner stretched the boundaries somewhat by invoking myths such as that of Narcissus. There were also lines which echoed writers more contemporary than Theocritus, Bion, or Moschus. Philomel chanted her sad song, and the sea beside the bower where it was heard felt a breeze which had slipped "across the dappled lea." From there it would sweep on

To comb the wave-ponies' manes back
Where the water shivers black. . . .

Nine years earlier, in "The Love Song of J. Alfred Prufrock," T. S. Eliot had written of his mermaids,

I have seen them riding seaward on the waves
Combing the white hair of the waves blown back
When the wind blows the water white and black.

There were other lines, though, which foreshadowed more individualistic utterances. In one poem the faun ran before a wind

Like a fox before hounds
Across the mellow sun-shot downs
That smell like crispened warm fresh bread. . . .

In the fertile spring he rolled in the grass. Later he was silent under the stars to

lie and hear
The voices of the fecund year. . . .

All in all, it was an extremely ambitious exercise. He used a twelve- or fourteen-line stanza as his basic unit, but he experimented with a total of fourteen different lengths, ranging from six lines to twenty-six. He varied both rhythm and rhyme, here and there employing half-lines and run-on lines, relying principally on masculine end rhymes but introducing feminine rhymes from time to time. The formal poetic diction and predominantly static quality of the poems resulted in their seeming limited and highly imitative. If nothing else, however, these poems showed enough dedication for the writing and rewriting of hundreds of lines of poetry in completing the task he had set for himself.

Other lines, very likely written in that spring or early summer of 1919, showed that the poet was experimenting with sense imagery, and—making music visual—with synesthesia, the device that interested not only the imagist and symbolist poets but also such experimental prose writers as James Joyce. He struck the melancholy note, but the ring was now more lyric than elegiac. His lines were still written rather than printed, and they were still quite legible for all their stylized quality, but the letters were becoming more vertical and more angular. He took a sheet of linen stationery and wrote at the top in black ink, "Music dying languidly in darkness." Then he set down four lines:

The darkness shakes its hair
Stiffened with music, vagrant formless gleams
Like dreams to haunt our dreams, a threading of violins
And horns draw sensuously in darkness.

The poet was working in more than one key, and the results would soon be displayed more prominently than even he must have imagined.

He was writing for pleasure, of course, but there was ambition, too. On one of the long walks out into the country, Stone said he thought "the main trouble with Amy Lowell and her gang of drum-beaters was their eternal damned self-consciousness, that they always had one eye on the ball and the other on the grandstand." Faulkner smiled, and said that his "personal trouble as a poet, seemed to be that he had one eye on the ball and the other eye on Babe Ruth." He was swinging, he might have said, for the fence.

Some of the melancholy in his lines that spring was more than just poetic convention. There was the still unassuaged loss of his love. There was also real grief to infuse his lines on the death of youth and beauty. Wed like her sister in April, Tochie also became pregnant in the first year of her marriage. Her husband was fearful for her because of the known susceptibility of pregnant women to Spanish influenza. Her resistance held up through the January epidemic, but then, as it seemed to be on the ebb, Tochie Allen began to show fever and the other dreaded symptoms. It turned to pneumonia, and her young husband and her parents stood powerless and watched her die. It must have seemed incredible to all of them, to her family and friends like Billy Faulkner, that anyone as gay and brave and young could suddenly be gone. In May, Estelle Franklin wrote to her grieving parents that she was coming home to be with them for a while.

She arrived in Oxford during the first week in June, bringing with her Tochie's four-month-old namesake, Victoria Franklin. Bill Faulkner was often there to visit. Obviously, his feelings had not changed. His old fondness for children had, if anything, increased, and he liked to sit and watch little Victoria, who was called "Cho-Cho" (which means butterfly) by her Chinese amah. There was a series of houseguests to see the returned traveler. She settled in for a good long visit.

One of the pleasures of that spring and summer was golf. The university course consisted of nine holes with identical greens of sand, and fencing here and there to keep the cows off. A ridge of dirt surrounded the greens to prevent rain from washing them away. Mr. Friedman, a Russian-educated storekeeper of refinement and culture, called the course "the golfing pasture." This amused Bill Faulkner. He and his brothers loved the game, and on a good afternoon he would say, "Let's go out to the golfing pasture." Sometimes the brothers would play alone and other times there might be eight or nine in the group. Because of Faulkner's stature and frame, power was not his forte, but he was an accurate and consistent golfer. He would smile and shake his head at his larger brother. "Jack, you're the only man I've ever seen," he said on one occasion, "who can slice every time —right-handed, left-handed, or cross-handed." In his own way, however, Bill was as unusual a golfer as his brother. His costume comprised his expensive sports jacket, his RAF breeches, and the heavy green wool stockings Miss Maud had knitted for him. His game was out of the ordinary too, due partly to his persistence. "Bill figured out that the main thing in a good golf shot was to keep the left elbow stiff," Johncy remembered. "So he rigged up a piece of tin stovepipe with a strap on it to hold it over his elbow. He practiced with that till he cut a hole in the sleeve of his jacket." But by this time he could take a pail of practice balls and stroke each one of them through an open space between tree limbs.

One of the principal pleasures of the county-at-large as they moved into the heat of the summer was a perennial one: politics. By mid-July Lee Russell was running full-page newspaper ads in his bid to win the Democratic primary against former governor Longino and two other opponents. In the state-at-large the voters reacted with lethargy. Many had been soured on politics by the scandals of the Bilbo administration and others were devoting their energies to combating the boll weevil. Some observers called it the dullest campaign in the history of the state. This was not true in some northern hill counties. John Falkner, Jr., put aside his other interests to manage Russell's campaign in Lafayette County. Those interests were multiplying—he had moved into new offices on the Square, he was one of the directors of his father's bank, he was in charge of the Falkner Hardware Company—but he was Russell's partner and he meant to do all he could for him. Also, it was quite clear that, as far as politics was concerned, he had attached himself to Russell's kite. His father might think a Russell was below a Falkner, but there was no doubt that John Falkner, Jr., was Lee Russell's man. Falkner canvassed the four corners of Lafayette County for his candidate.

Russell polled 48,000 of the 150,000 votes cast, but there had to be a runoff between him and Oscar Johnston, who was 9,000 behind. In mid-July Russell won it by a majority of 8,000 votes. Not everyone in Oxford shared John Falkner's satisfaction. Miss Minnie Carter, the mother of Estelle's friend Katrina, was a sharp-tongued woman who was well known for the way her sympathies shifted and wavered. One afternoon the three elder Falkner boys walked past the Carter yard as Miss Minnie worked with a trowel setting out flowering plants. She stood up and they greeted her courteously.

"Well," she responded acidly, "I reckon you Falkners are hurrying to get on the bandwagon now that Mr. Russell has been elected governor."

"No, ma'am," Bill replied quickly. "We're jumping down so you folks who didn't vote for him can climb up on quick!" With that they strolled on as Miss Minnie, speechless, glared after them.

On the evening of September 3, Lee Russell returned to Oxford in triumph. He and Mrs. Russell were met at the depot by hundreds of friends and a brass band. In a torchlight procession they were escorted from Depot Street up to University Avenue. The lights dancing in the blue summer evening, the procession turned into South Street and then, swelled to two thousand, filled the Courthouse yard and most of the Square. There toastmaster John Falkner, Jr., conducted the rest of the program in honor of the returning hero. The "redneck" from the southeast corner of Lafayette County, the "goat" who had been doused by men of the fraternity he aspired to, was now governor-elect. This successor of Vardaman and Bilbo would take office with the new year. There were others in the Magnolia State besides the Delta planters who now needed to be on their guard.

The only literary hero who came anywhere near the stature of Oxford's political hero was Stark Young, now a professor at Amherst College and the author of a book of verse and ten published plays. Three weeks after Russell's triumph, the first conspicuous sign appeared that the town might have another citizen of Young's sort. When Bill Faulkner had put aside the linked pastoral poems, he turned to a poem much longer and more ambitious than any in that cycle. The idea may have come to him a good deal earlier, perhaps while he was in Canada. On the back of an early version of the poem depicting the pilot in his flying clothes at dawn, he had written:

I have a sudden wish to go
Far from this silent midnight now
Where lovely streams whisper and flow
And sigh as sands touched by the moon.

These four lines were now incorporated into the middle portion of a new poem. The basic situation was familiar: the lover, immobilized like the marble faun, can only lament as the wild, nymph-like beloved flees from him, perhaps toward a fatal union with another. Hair flying and eyes flashing, she has sped through the trees. The lover is left, her kisses lingering, as he mourns:

For ere she sleep
The dusk will take her by some stream
In silent meadows dim and deep—
In dreams of stars and dreaming dream.

In the last lines the lover sees dancers whirling past as the worn moon peeps through the silent trees. Then suddenly, though the dance goes on, "lorn and cold," comes the sound of "some great deep bell stroke," which the lover recognizes:

It was the earth's great heart that broke,
For springs before the world grew old.

There were in the first section of the poem half a dozen cross-outs of whole lines and false starts on new ones. He wrote out a shorter draft and worked on a segment which changed the meaning:

Now hand in hand with her I go
Where night stands in the silver west
Of vague stars, pale row on row
Like ghostly hands. . . .

He made other minor changes in punctuation and diction. Then he added a title: "L'Apres-Midi d'un Faune." In 1876 Stéphane Mallarmé, French poet and leader of the Symbolists, had published a poem under the same title, and in 1892 it had inspired Claude Debussy to compose an orchestral prelude which used the poem's title. Mallarmé's poem was more than three times as long as Faulkner's, and his Sicilian faun roused from sleep to muse erotically on an encounter with two nymphs, a vision of naiads, and a dream of love with Venus herself. The young aesthete who had advised Ben Wasson to listen to Beethoven in darkness may have found Debussy's dreamy strains to his liking, too. He had obviously made use of the poem which had inspired the composer.

He read the new work to Phil Stone, who had been taking Faulkner's poems to his office, where he would have them typed and then send them out to various magazines. All had thus far been returned promptly. Stone gave this poem to his secretary, who typed it on the back of a sheet of stationery marked "The First National Bank of Oxford, Oxford, Miss., J. W. T. Falkner, Pres." Stone and Faulkner decided to send a subsequent copy to *The New Republic*, which sent back an acceptance and a check for fifteen dollars. The poem was scheduled to appear August 6. When the poet received his copy he very carefully wrote his name across the front page in a flowing hand and put the magazine away.

Stone quickly put other poems of Faulkner's in the mail, but the manuscripts kept coming back as they had before "L'Apres-Midi d'un Faune." Finally they decided that no more Faulkner poems were likely to be accepted. That being the case, they might just as well have some fun with these supreme arbiters who decided who would get published and who would not. Stone later recalled their strategy: "without title and without Mr. Faulkner signing the poem, we copied John Clare's poem about the asylum in which he was then confined ['Lines from a Northampton Asylum']." They sent it to *The New Republic* asking for payment "at your usual rates." If the magazine accepted it, they were going to remain silent until publication and then "secretly notify *The New York Times* of the fact and let the dull *Times* rib the smarty *New Republic.*" But the poem was returned, with no covering letter, so that they never knew whether the poem had been recognized or whether the poetry editor simply did not care for it, no matter whose name it followed. Stone thought of one more shot to fire. They copied out Coleridge's "Kubla Khan" and sent it to *The New Republic.* Again their offering was rejected, but this time the editor had appended a note. "We like your poem, Mr. Coleridge," he wrote, "but we don't think it gets anywhere much." That was the last bogus effort they sent out.

The failure to place other poems did not lessen the thrill of the appearance of his work in a New York magazine. And that minor success gave some of his jocular remarks a ring which had a little more than just levity in them. In late August he visited a friend, Estelle Lake, and her aunt, in Memphis. Back home again in Oxford, he sent her a thank-you note. "Dear Miss Lake," he wrote. "May I thank you again for the trouble you went to for me and my eccentricities? I am sending you a drawing which, when I have become famous, will doubtless be quite valuable." He signed it, as he did his poems, "W. Faulkner."

Faulkner was apparently working on another poem that summer which may have dated from the time of "L'Apres-Midi d'un Faune." He did a draft on a sheet from an early version of the latter poem and entitled it "A Dead Dancer." Again the young poet was probably performing a literary exercise, trying the kind of thing Eliot was doing with his long, languid, low-keyed conversational lines, attempting to convey an emotion of exquisite sadness at the death of beauty, of youth, and of love. But here again there was private emotion. Estelle Franklin was there at home for the moment, but soon she would leave once more for the other side of the world.

He did not give her a copy of this poem. Instead he gave her the small, black-covered copy of the poems of Swinburne which he had brought back from Toronto with him. When she opened it she saw there his name and the RAF wings, the places where he had trained and the posts he had never reached. Below he had inscribed the book to her, but the inscription was so passionate that she felt she had to tear off the bottom half of the flyleaf which contained it before she could take the volume of poems with her when she and Cho-Cho left Oxford for Hawaii on September 29.

This leave-taking must have reawakened something of his anguish eighteen months before, though there had been time to absorb the bitter facts. But Faulkner was looking ahead. In late September he had received a thick envelope from Toronto soliciting his subscription to *Air Force Album: A Pictorial History of the Royal Air Force Canada.* The covering letter, which saluted him as "Dear Faulkner," noted that the album would include photographs and brief histories of former officers and cadets. "A book of this kind [which would cost ten dollars] will be looked at in years to be by your children's children when the question comes up as to where was your Daddy when the great war was on." Faulkner put the letter, personal data form, and order form away in a drawer and left them there.

Besides his writing and travel to Charleston and elsewhere, there was something else to occupy him in that September of 1919. The student who had left school as soon as it suited him, whose temperament ran counter to the classroom atmosphere, had agreed to go back to school. He had enrolled in the University of Mississippi, not as a degree candidate but as a special student, a returned veteran for whom the ordinary admission requirements had been waived. Perhaps he did it to placate his mother and father, or as a gesture toward orthodoxy, toward momentarily conforming to some recognizable pattern for a young man his age. Whatever it was, William Faulkner was entering—very tentatively—into the life of a student once more.

17

September, 1919-June, 1920

. . . a snatched coat under her arm and her long legs blonde with running, in speeding silhouette against the lighted windows of the Coop, as the women's dormitory was known, vanishing into the shadow beside the library wall. . . .

This was on week nights. On alternate Saturday evenings, at the Letter Club dances, or on the occasion of the three formal yearly balls, the town boys . . . watched her enter the gymnasium upon black collegiate arms and vanish in a swirling glitter upon a glittering swirl of music. . . .

—*Sanctuary* (28–29)

All our eyes and hearts look up to thee,
For here all our voiceless dreams are spun
Between thy walls, quiet in dignity
Lent by the spirits of them whose lives begun
Within thy portals. . . .

—"Alma Mater"

. . . Exams are near
And my thoughts uncontrollably
Wander, and I cannot hear
The voice telling me that work I must,
For everything will be the same when I am dead
A thousand years. . . .

—"Study"

In the fall of 1919, 592 students were enrolled in the various divisions of the University of Mississippi. They comprised the schools of liberal arts, English, law, engineering, education, medicine, pharmacy, and commerce and business administration. The mile-square campus was modest but attractive, with its cluster of Georgian revival buildings and its parklike expanse of tall trees and flowering shrubs. Its people were proud of its natural beauty and such particular features as the arched Memorial Gateway and the Old Observatory, modeled after one in Russia and designed to accommodate the world's largest telescope. If the instrument it now housed could not claim quite that preeminence, it was still one of the major telescopes of the United States. The faculty of close to forty members was for the most part hardworking, earning modest salaries and almost no fringe benefits. There were no pensions, but a professor could go on teaching as long as he was able to meet his classes.

In the small faculty the strengths and foibles of individual teachers stood out, and the most prominent members formed a kind of inner circle. Dr. Muckenfuss, the father of Bill's former desk mate Ralph, was chairman of the chemistry department. Actually, Dr. Muckenfuss *was* the chemistry department, managing the entire curriculum with the help of one assistant. Dr. A. L. Bondurant, professor of Latin, was noted for his elaborate courtesy as well as his interest in the Civil War. Dr. Calvin S. Brown was a versatile professor who taught German, French, Italian, and archaeology. A stout, clean-shaven, pleasant-looking man, he collected petrified wood and was regarded as a great lover of nature. He would often show slides to his students and talk to them of his love for music, leaving them impressed with a certain soulful quality. General Hemingway, of the law school, was a big, hearty, Taft-like man whose courses varied in difficulty according to the athletic prowess of each particular student. Dr. D. H. Bishop was head of the English department. In his academic robes he wore a dour expression which was faintly reminiscent of the later Woodrow Wilson. To some he was a rather tiresome old man, though very learned. One of the courses he taught was an elective for juniors and seniors which treated the major plays of Shakespeare. This was one of the three courses for which William Faulkner was registered.

Unlike Jack Falkner, who had two years of liberal arts and two years of law ahead of him, Bill Faulkner could take what he liked. He was registered as a special student on September 19 when he signed up for courses in English, French, and Spanish. Apparently, he began earnestly.

Miss Maud said he had the greatest powers of concentration she ever saw. He would stand at the mantel in the living room and study while John and Dean would be making noise virtually at his feet. (People outside the family were also noticing these powers of concentration—of thought or imagination which removed him completely from his immediate surroundings—though they would usually attribute his behavior to something else. An acquaintance would meet him strolling in the Square; he would speak, and Faulkner would pass him in silence, looking straight ahead. To the other it would more often than not seem a demonstration of arrogance, rudeness, or addled absent-mindedness.) No matter how well he might know the assignment, Faulkner apparently never volunteered a comment or an answer in class. Louis Cochran, a fellow student, remembered that the others "thought him queer. He spoke to no one unless directly addressed. He mingled not at all with his classmates." Another student later recalled a comment forced out of him. During a session devoted to *Othello*, Dr. Bishop read a passage aloud. Then he looked at Faulkner.

"Mr. Faulkner, what did Shakespeare have in mind when he put those words in the mouth of Othello?"

"How should I know?" Faulkner replied. "That was nearly four hundred years ago, and I was not there."

Faulkner was apparently something of a trial to some members of the faculty. Although he was a special student, they seemed to assume he had some plan of study in mind and would urge him to take certain courses leading to a degree. He told them that all he wanted to study was languages and English. He cared very little for formalities in the subjects he did study. Usually he skipped quizzes and examinations. On one occasion, however, according to his uncle John, he received a grade of 99 in English. Through some error it was credited not to him but to Jack. Mr. Murry learned of it and suggested that he have the record put right. His son didn't want to. "Dad," he said, "I don't care what the mark is. I've got everything from that class up here," he added, tapping his temple with his index finger. "Let them leave it the way it is. Maybe it will please Jack."

All his fellow students knew was that he stayed away from the examinations they took. "The story was that he never bothered to take examinations, and would have been dropped except for the fact that his father (whom everybody liked) was an administrative officer and that the Falkners were an old-time Mississippi family and among the leading lights in that part of the state." This could scarcely have endeared him to classmates to whom he did not speak and who knew that he had been nicknamed "the Count" for what seemed to be put-on airs.

If his course work was less than absorbing, there were other activities that he apparently enjoyed very much. Louis Cochran had been appointed editor of the yearbook, *Ole Miss*, for 1920. Knowing that Faulkner had a reputation as an artist, he asked him to do five drawings. Faulkner agreed and presented the drawings punctually to Cochran, who was much pleased with them. Later he would ask Faulkner for written work, too. These meetings were businesslike but pleasant. This same kind of relationship existed between Faulkner and other students, except for a few he had known in boyhood. If someone spoke to him on campus, Cochran said, Faulkner "would stop, discuss the matter at hand briefly and pleasantly, and to the point, and continue on his way." As to his misinterpreted mannerisms, the cause was quite the reverse of what many thought: "during that period of his life Faulkner was almost painfully shy; he felt that many of the other students did not like him, and he retaliated by affecting a total indifference he did not totally feel."

There was a good deal of literary activity on the campus, with three literary societies, Phi Sigma, the Hermean, and the Scribblers of Sigma Upsilon, organizing meetings, readings, and social events. Faulkner was still deeply involved in his own poetry. *The New Republic* had seemingly closed its pages to him but he found another outlet: the student newspaper, called *The Mississippian.* It was nothing like a prestigious magazine, but people who knew him would be more likely to see his work there than in *The New Republic.* Some of his friends had already appeared there. Ben Wasson had published two short stories in October and another, heavily loaded with dialect, in November. Faulkner followed suit, publishing one poem October 29—a revision of "L'Apres-Midi d'un Faune."

Two weeks later, on November 12, *The Mississippian* printed a new Faulkner poem entitled "Cathay." The nine lines of the first stanza suggested something of Shelley's "Ozymandias," with its commentary on the vanity of an ancient tyrant and the transience of his power and memory:

> . . . *Where once thy splendors rose,*
> *And cast their banners bright against the sky,*
> *Now go the empty years infinitely*
> *Rich with thy ghosts. So is it: who sows*
> *The seed of Fame, makes the grain for Death to reap.*

The eleven lines of the second stanza considered sharp-faced, faithless wanderers in the desert who

> *. . . know thee* [*Cathay*] *not, nor will*
> *To see thy magic empire when the Hand*
> *Thrusts back the curtain of the shifting sand,*
> *On singing stars and lifting golden hill.*

This imagery, with its slightly Yeatsian cast, was shaped into a rather elaborate rhyme scheme, though the lines themselves were here and there rather rough and uneven metrically. Like several of Faulkner's other publications in *The Mississippian,* "Cathay" was printed in the next issue of the Oxford *Eagle,* too, appearing there on November 13. His readership, by local standards, must now have been considerable.

Two weeks later, on November 26, *The Mississippian* presented William Faulkner's first published prose fiction, a 2,500-word short story entitled "Landing in Luck." Pleasant and amusing, it was the story of a cadet's first solo flight. Faulkner had obviously drawn upon the triad he would often cite later in life as the artist's sources: observation, imagination, and experience. The scene was an aerodrome near "Borden." The protagonist was a young man named Cadet Thompson, who growls about his RAF instructor, Mr. Bessing, a "blasted Englishman." Still inept after more than seven hours' instruction, Thompson is finally pushed into the air alone. He loses a wheel on a bad takeoff, then freezes in terror as he comes in for a landing. Miraculously escaping injury, he is credited by Bessing with a skill he does not possess. The story ends after Thompson, a "barracks ace," has lorded it over his fellow cadets. Striding by them, arm in arm with his instructor, he murmurs an airy and patronizing "Hello, you chaps." The story was economically done and both the Cockney and cultivated English accents were convincingly handled. The author shifted from ground to air with ease in his narration. The story did not suffer by comparison with much of the light fiction appearing in popular magazines.

In a display of virtuosity, Faulkner was represented in the same issue of *The Mississippian* by a poem as well. Few readers could know that "Sapphics" was a condensation, in most lines word for word, of Swinburne's twenty-stanza poem of the same name. Again Faulkner seemed to luxuriate in rich imagery and a not unpleasant despair. The sleepless, lovelorn speaker relates a vision of Aphrodite, but it is a vision of the goddess of love in her cruel aspect. In stanzas which must have seemed strange to some members of both faculty and student body, the speaker concluded his vision of the goddess:

She sees not the Lesbians kissing mouth
To mouth across lute strings, drunken with singing,
Nor the white feet of the Oceanides
Shining and unsandalled.

Before her go cryings and lamentations
Of barren women, a thunder of wings,
While ghosts of outcast Lethean women, lamenting,
Stiffen the twilight.

Two weeks later still another poem appeared in *The Mississippian* over the name "W. Faulkner." "After Fifty Years" was more formal than "Sapphics." It was much like a Petrarchan sonnet, but the tone was familiar: a lover enthralled by a *belle dame sans merci.* This constituted his last appearance in *The Mississippian* for 1919, but with the other three poems and the short story, it was an auspicious beginning.

In that fall of 1919, all of the buildings which had once been fraternity houses were occupied by families or university departments. But this did not mean that the fraternity spirit was dead, and Lee Russell knew it. On November 6 "one of the largest gatherings of students ever assembled at the University of Mississippi listened with rapt interest to a forceful address by Governor-elect Lee M. Russell. . . ." He told the student body of the charge that fraternities were still running at the university in defiance of the law. He deplored this report if it were true and warned that a student who belonged to a fraternity would be dismissed if it were discovered. Russell declared that "this was too high-toned a body of students for any such conduct" but promised an investigation of the charges. In fact, there were three fraternities operating sub rosa at the University of Mississippi even as Russell spoke, though they had no houses. They were Kappa Alpha, Sigma Chi, and Sigma Alpha Epsilon. All of the Falkners—as well as Lem Oldham, Jim Stone, and other family friends—had been S.A.E.'s. Murry Falkner might be a university employee and his brother John might be a member of the State Board which controlled the university, but some of the active members of Sigma Alpha Epsilon expected Bill and Jack to join. So did their father and uncle and grandfather, state law or no.

The only problem that fraternity meetings posed was assembling without being noticed. On a Saturday or Sunday evening the twenty-odd members would drift away from their dormitories by twos and threes. They would make their way into town through the wooded area that bordered the campus. Sometimes they would walk the mile and a half out to Jim Stone's house. At other times they would meet at the Oldham home, or up the street at The Big Place. At an early meeting during that fall the question of pledging new members had arisen. The name of William Faulkner was one of those mentioned.

As it happened, he knew several S.A.E.'s and would often see them when he visited Ben Wasson on the second floor of the Lyceum Building over the administrative offices of Chancellor Joseph Neely Powers. Ben still found Faulkner impressive. Now "he sported a small neatly trimmed moustache which struck me as quite worldly and daring." From time to time he would extract a handkerchief from his coat sleeve. Faulkner noticed Wasson watching him, and said, "The British wear their handkerchiefs in their jacket sleeves. I prefer the sartorial usage also." He had, it appears, rather pronounced and expensive views regarding sartorial usage. At one point his bill at Halle's men's store in Memphis mounted so high that something had to be done about it. Finally Miss Maud gave Sallie Murry her diamond ring, and Sallie Murry was able to sell it to a girl working with her at the Colonel's bank. Miss Maud paid the bill at Halle's. When Murry Falkner learned of the transaction he was furious at all three of them, but there was nothing he could do about it.

Well-dressed William Faulkner would sometimes talk about his war experiences to Ben Wasson and the other S.A.E.'s who lived in the Lyceum Building: Russell Pigford, Dutch Rainold, and Lowry Simmons, whose father had been a friend of Murry Falkner's since the latter's days as a conductor on the railroad. Murry Falkner took an interest in his friend's son, and the two boys were on good terms in spite of the way Bill seemed to Lowry to combine shyness and reticence with not giving a damn. Some of the other S.A.E.'s were well known on the campus, like Jeff Hamm, who had been the first boy from Ole Miss to see action in France, and Rufus Creekmore, who was captain of the football team. Not all of the actives were particularly fond of Faulkner, and Lowry Simmons sensed some outright opposition to him, but he and Russell Pigford and a few others went ahead anyway. One problem was establishing whether or not he actually wanted to receive a bid. One day, as part of a prearranged plan, Jeff Hamm walked him down to the Square and up to John Falkner's office. Faulkner listened as his keen-eyed uncle extolled the fraternity's virtues and reminded him that all his kinsmen had been S.A.E.'s. John Falkner finished, looked at his nephew, and waited for him to speak. When he did, he surprised his hearers.

"Yes," he said without hesitation, "I'd like to join."

Faulkner's partisans were successful, and a bid was issued which Faulkner accepted. Jack Falkner accepted, too. David Callahan was among those who also received a bid. Callahan was glad to share this honor with Faulkner, two years his senior but "a little bitty fellow." He and his friends admired Faulkner in his RAF jacket because they had only been in the Students' Army Training Corps. With nine other pledges, they prepared for their solemn initiation, which would take place on December 10. A few of the brothers talked about the preliminaries to the awful and solemn rites ahead. Phil Stone, though not an S.A.E. himself, joined in the hazing. He looked at his friend. "I don't believe this boy will ever stand this initiation," he said. "Dave might pass it, but I don't think Bill ever will."

On the appointed night the brothers slipped away from the dormitories in their twos and threes, soberly dressed for the occasion. They made their way through the woods to Jim Stone's house, and the solemn ritual began.

Mississippi Gamma Chapter of Sigma Alpha Epsilon, University of Mississippi, fall of 1919. William Faulkner, back row, extreme right.

It was conducted by William C. Levere, Eminent Supreme Recorder of the fraternity. Billy Levere was a big man who had, thought Callahan, the largest head ever known around Oxford. He led the brothers and the pledges through the candle-lit Masonic-style ceremony. Afterwards the solemn atmosphere gave way to celebration as the new members were welcomed into the Mississippi Gamma Chapter of Sigma Alpha Epsilon.

They could not, of course, wear fraternity pins for fear of instant suspension or dismissal from the university, but in due course they were given their membership scrolls. The next fall a group photograph was taken with almost all of the brothers present. Standing on the extreme right in the back row was William Faulkner. His picture resembled the early RAF photo made in Canada, where he seemed a boy trying to look like a man.

There is no indication that he was ever a very active member. He had joined S.A.E. only because of the family tradition. "It wasn't a breath-taking experience for him," his brother said. But he had good friends in the fraternity, and occasionally there may have been an element in the business of scrolls, secrets, and rituals that pleased him. His college experience, like his wartime experience, was not really broad, but it was enough to draw on later for whatever needs might arise in his fiction.

As William Faulkner went through this further transition in status, so did his immediate family. Since Murry Falkner's job at the university carried the perquisite of housing, they decided to offer their home on North Street for sale. They would not have the responsibilities of landlords and they could use the money. There was no difficulty in making the sale. Joe Parks had sold his plantation near Etta and bought Maud and Murry Falkner's house. By early January, he had moved his family in from the country to occupy it. For a brief time the Falkners stayed at The Big Place with the Colonel, Auntee, and Sallie Murry. But independent Maud Falkner predictably did not care for that arrangement, and she had her eye on a house they could rent on Van Buren Street, southwest of the Square and just four blocks from the house they had first occupied when they had moved to Oxford nearly sixteen years before. It was a rectangular house painted a bright yellow, and Miss Maud called it The Birdcage. Soon they were able to move in and set up housekeeping while they waited for the university quarters to become available.

In late December an announcement had appeared in the *Eagle* which foreshadowed a change in the Colonel's status. It appeared over his name. "Notice is hereby given," it read, "that the regular annual meeting of the stockholders of the First National Bank of Oxford will be held on Tuesday the 13th day of January, 1920, for the election of the Board of Directors to serve the ensuing year and the transaction of such other business as may be properly considered." Under his name was that of J. E. Avent, Cashier.

The Colonel had continued doing business in the same way over the ten years since he had founded the bank. Others had invested in it, but he was the majority stockholder and he felt it was really his bank. He would sit in his office at the rear before the big, cluttered, roll-top cherry desk. If a customer wanted a loan, the Colonel would naturally ask what he wanted it for, what kind of security he could offer for it, and how long it would take him to pay it back. Because of the Colonel's deafness, the prospective borrower had to raise his voice. Sometimes the Colonel would sit at a desk in the front and would not hesitate to carry out such an interrogation there. Some people understandably preferred to negotiate loans without broadcasting their financial condition. And the documents drawn up might be less than completely satisfactory. Some time earlier, most likely before he became one of the stockholders, Joe Parks had come to the Colonel for a loan. The Colonel agreed to it, reached for a blank note form, and filled in the particulars with rapid strokes of the pen. He handed it to Parks for his signature. Parks studied it silently and handed it back without signing it. Falkner looked at him.

"I can't read it, Colonel," Parks said.

Falkner held it at arm's length and peered at it intently. "Be damned if I can either," he said and tore it up. This time the big large-veined hand lettered in the blanks legibly.

By now Joe Parks was one of the most prosperous men in the community, and his figure, with its bow tie, was a familiar one. Like a number of other relatively latecomers to Oxford from the county such as the Avents, he had worked hard for his present affluence. Now, as a stockholder, he must have been disturbed at the way the bank was lagging behind its competitors. It must have been particularly unsettling to see the Colonel almost intent on turning business away. After his hearty noon meal he would either nap at The Big Place or return to the bank and stretch out on the huge leather couch. As he settled himself Chess Carothers would pull one of the big matching chairs into the doorway and seat himself there to prevent customers from disturbing his employer's rest. There Chess would catnap, managing somehow to awaken a few minutes before the Colonel roused himself for the short balance of the banking day.

The Colonel may not have been aware of it, but a number of his fellow stockholders had had enough of this style of commerce. Times were changing whether he knew it or not. Just two days before the scheduled meeting the *Eagle* had trumpeted the news of great things ahead. OXFORD WILL BE MIGHTY CITY, proclaimed a banner headline. "Oil Fields are to be Developed," ran the subhead. Prime movers in forming the North Mississippi Oil and Development Company were Joe Parks and J. E. Avent. Two Texas oilmen had arrived and soon many knew that they were going to carry out prospecting operations to see if the oil-bearing sands of Pennsylvania extended into Lafayette County. Excitement gave way to visions of splendor. "The eyes of the world are now being turned towards Oxford and Lafayette County," the story ran. "Hotels and boarding houses will be filled to an overflow with hundreds of people rushing into Oxford to get on the ground floor." Obviously, to serve the community properly and profitably in the golden days ahead the First National Bank of Oxford would have to change. By the time stockholders gathered for their annual meeting on the evening of January 13, 1920, Joe Parks and several others had carefully worked out a way to change it.

Excerpts from the annual report were read to the stockholders. Then, when the meeting was open for discussion of new business, they broke it to him. They wanted him to resign as president of the bank. The old man apparently reacted with shock and then outrage, but finally he must have seen that he had little support. Evidently, he decided that for the good of the bank he would resign—but on his terms. He was the majority stockholder, and if Parks and the others wanted this change, they would have to pay for it by getting up the money to buy a large block of his stock. This they agreed to do, and Joe Parks was elected president of John Wesley Thompson Falkner's bank.

When he had cooled down somewhat, the outgoing president did what he could to put the best possible face on things. He wrote a public letter addressed to his friends and patrons of the bank. "On account of my age and impaired health," it read, "I have retired from the Presidency and active control of the bank." Then, in words he must have written with gritted teeth, he said, "Mr. J. A. Parks . . . will assume control of the affairs of the bank backed by ten conservative business men as directors. . . . Mr. Parks has served the people in positions of honor. He is honest capable and faithful." He asked continued support of the bank and noted that John Falkner, Jr., had charge of the legal department of the bank. It was not clear whether his son was staying on for career reasons, because he and his father both thought it would be a good idea still to have at least one Falkner on the inside of the bank's affairs, or whether this ambitious son was sympathetic to the concern felt by the other stockholders. The *Eagle* news story in the same issue with Falkner's letter included a statement from J. E. Avent, who was continuing as cashier. "We are going to reach out and get the business," he said. A half-page advertisement testified to that intention.

In spite of the public letter, the Colonel could not keep his resentment wholly in check. He must have brooded about his virtual eviction. One of his friends was Daniel Edward Fielder Webster, who had bought the Colonial Hotel and now lived in it. It had been Webster who had lost ten dollars betting the Colonel that he would not go out and take Joe Miller's goat cart and drive it around the Square. They would often sit together, their two cane-bottom chairs tilted against the bank wall. As they sat there one day soon afterwards, Colonel Falkner suddenly told Webster in his loud deaf-man's voice to go to Relbue Price's hardware store and get him some tin buckets.

"Who do you think you're telling what to do?" Webster answered resentfully, and someone else went to Price's store. Then, buckets in hand, the Colonel strode into the bank and withdrew all the cash in his accounts plus the papers and notes he kept there. His resentment of Parks greater than his rivalry with Stone, he marched across the Square and opened an account at the Bank of Oxford. He might retain some of his stock, which would eventually go to his children, but he would not deal with the bank which had repudiated him, public letter or no.

The old man no longer sat in front of the bank. And in the course of running it he had pretty much turned the law practice over to his son and his colleagues. Thus there was suddenly little to occupy him. Again his family would see him tracing the name Sallie Murry in the air. "He was, I think, the loneliest man I've ever known," thought one of his grandsons. The forces which took him out of the forefront of town life were signs of the times. Old families like the Stones might well have pondered what was happening.

If the Colonel found little to occupy him as 1920 began, his grandson Bill must have found himself busier than he had been in some time. He still went to the dances, where the couples glided to the popular strains of "Alice Blue Gown" or fox-trotted to the rhythm of "Dardanella." He was more in evidence than he had been during much of the preceding year. Even though he shunned examinations, he did go to a number of his classes. And he would shortly publish more verse in the pages of *The Mississippian.* He had been at work upon one long poem in particular, first writing tentative lines on leftover sheets of Murry Falkner's hardware store stationery. From the first the tone was one of death in life:

One should not die like this
His voice has dropped and the wind is mouthing his words
While the lilacs nod their heads on slender stalks
Agreeing while he talks
And cares not if he is heard or is not heard.

He had chosen a figure he would use again: the maimed soldier. It was as though he had thought back to the image of the pilot in the dawn. But this time, instead of being immense and impressive in his flying gear, he was a casualty who looked back at his brief and fatal glory. On another sheet he had tried a flashback:

It was a morning in late May.

Then, with false starts and cross-outs, he had gone on to try another stanza, in which a compatriot echoed the speaker. In still another, he sketched in details of the combat:

We had been
Raiding over Mannheim, you've seen
The place? Then you know
How one hangs just beneath the stars, and seems
To see the incandescent entrails of the Hun.

He went on with the poem, doing a version in pencil, then revising and rewriting in ink. Finally he had twelve verse paragraphs, ranging in length from one line to eighteen—in all, ninety-eight lines. He had given it a title, "The Lilacs." Now it began:

We sit, drinking tea
Beneath the lilacs of a summer afternoon
Comfortably, at our ease
With fresh linen napkins on our knees
We are in Blighty
And we sit, we three
In diffident contentedness.

The speaker's mind wanders and his vision is apparently impaired, but he appreciates the solicitude of his English hostess, and he is aware of

Smooth-shouldered creatures in sheer scarves, that pass
And eye us strangely as they pass.

His hearing is keen enough for him to catch the whispered questions and answers:

—Who?——Shot down?
Poor chap—Yes, his mind
The Doctor says—hoping rest will bring.

He tells his story, perhaps to one of the other two who sit with him "in silent amity." On a late May morning he had gone out in his aeroplane to pursue the nymph-like dawn. But at the instant he found her, the enemy found him:

The bullet struck me here, I think
In the left breast
And killed my little pointed eared machine. I watched it fall
The last wine in a cup. . . .

Then, at the poem's end, the sun is gone, leaving the speaker cold and unable to see the pale lilacs against the evening sky. But he hears the lilacs as they bend to him:

Old man—they say—where did you die?. . . .
I—I am not dead
I hear their voices as from a great distance—not dead
He's not dead, poor chap; he isn't dead—
We sit, drinking tea.

When he had completed the poem, he hand-lettered it himself and bound it as a booklet, something he would often do in the next several years for special friends. Before giving this particular gift to one of them, he dated it January 1, 1920, and signed it "W. Faulkner."

On January 28, Faulkner published the first of the nine poems which would appear beneath his name in *The Mississippian* during the course of the second semester. (This time his name appeared as "W. Falkner.") He had called his poem "Une Ballade des Femmes Perdues." As if to point up the relationship to François Villon's "Ballade des dames du temps jadis," Faulkner had used Villon's famous refrain, "Mais où sont les neiges d'antan," as his epigraph. Both the personality and the work of the fifteenth-century student-poet-rascal had fascinated other poets, too. Dante Gabriel Rossetti had tried his hand at a translation of this particular poem. Faulkner's admired Swinburne had published translations of ten of the Frenchman's poems—which may have been the original source of Faulkner's interest in him rather than the course in French which he was now taking at the university. The title and epigraph were the closest resemblances between the two poems, however. Whereas Villon pondered the whereabouts of fabled beauties such as Thaïs and Héloïse, Faulkner wrote instead of "Gay little ghosts of loves in silver sandals," of women who "brush my lips with little ghostly kisses" before stealing away. Then, in a voice like that of the marble faun, his speaker concluded:

I am old, and alone
And the star dust from their wings
Has dimmed my eyes
I sing in the green dusk
Of lost ladies—Si vraiment charmant, charmant.

A week later, on February 4, *The Mississippian* published another Faulkner poem. Unlike its predecessor, "Naiads' Song" drew upon classical mythology. In it these nymphs of lakes, fountains, and streams sang like the Lorelei, or like Yeats's immortals to his mortals, enticing them to easeful death. Each of the four stanzas of couplets began with the same line, the siren song sung clearly from the first:

Come ye sorrowful and keep
Tryst with us here in wedded sleep,
The silent noon lies over us
And shaken ripples over us,
Our arms are soft as is the stream.

Unlike the somewhat exotic "Une Ballade des Femmes Perdues," this poem was reprinted the following day in the Oxford *Eagle.*

This was the sixth poem William Faulkner had published in the student newspaper, and he had a right to assume that his work would by now have come to the attention of members of the three literary societies on campus. The monthly meeting of the Scribblers of Sigma Upsilon was reported on the front page of the issue of *The Mississippian* which printed "Une Ballade." One paper was read at the meeting by Professor Erwin, whose class produced *The Mississippian*'s short stories. Another was presented by a very active undergraduate named Louis Jiggitts. Erwin's paper dealt with Lord Dunsany, and that of Jiggitts treated a recent dream. "The object of his dream," reported the paper, "was 'a flirt' and he certainly gave his readers [*sic*] an excellent description of that peculiar creation of the female of the species." Louis Cochran had put Faulkner up for membership in the society, but he was blackballed. "That was a shame," Cochran wrote later, "though I think it should be said in extenuation that it was partly Faulkner's fault. . . . he had rather needlessly offended many of the students by what they thought his 'arrogance'; the way he was believed 'to put on airs.' That was the period when he earned the nickname 'Count No 'Count.' " If Faulkner was hurt (and Cochran thought he was), he kept it to himself. He was acute enough to realize that a membership which could relish a dream about "A Flirt" would be unlikely to favor a poem about lost ladies. Few knew for certain who had kept Faulkner out, but most had their suspicions, which centered on two or three student members. The animus behind the blackball did not remain behind the doors of the meeting. It came out in print in *The Mississippian.*

A squib entitled "Dedicated to Will Faulkner" appeared there on February 11 and in the *Eagle* the next day. "Yielding to the requests (?) of thousands," the anonymous author began, "I have written a parody to W. Falkner's great poem, entitled 'Une Ballad Hedes [*sic*] Femmes Perdues.' If you will find this poem in *The Mississippian* of January 29, 1920, you will get the significance. If my parody does not have clearness, please remember that I am modelling it after the Count's both in substances [*sic*] as well as form. Thank the author." There had been no issue of the paper on January 29, 1920; the paper had come out the day before, and the parody would not appear until May 12. But the announcement was the first shot in a volley, even though it was a blank.

When the course grades were posted for the first semester's work, they revealed that William Faulkner had received A in French, B in Spanish, and D in English. A non-degree student still, he acted pragmatically, continuing the French and Spanish and dropping the English. He had probably been most interested in the French course anyway. And there was one writer in particular who appealed to him. Undeterred by either the blackball from the Scribblers or the threat of parody, Faulkner gave the editors another poem, which they printed in the issue for February 25. It was entitled "Fantoches," with the subtitle "à Paul Verlaine." It was the first of four translations of poems by Verlaine which Faulkner would publish there during the next seven weeks. Some years later the poet Paul Valéry, himself much influenced by the Symbolist movement, would write a study entitled *Villon and Verlaine.* Faulkner may have felt the affinity Valéry felt, or his taste for the work of Oscar Wilde and Aubrey Beardsley may have led him to one of the French "Decadents," to Charles Baudelaire or Arthur Rimbaud, or perhaps to Rimbaud's sometime companion, Paul Verlaine.

Faulkner might well have come to read Verlaine through Phil Stone. Without any of these paths, the young poet, trying his French, might simply have been struck by this unique voice. Verlaine sometimes treated subjects which particularly interested Faulkner. One of his best-known poems was "Le Faune," in which the inanimate subject was made of terra cotta rather than marble. In other poems, such as "Pantomime" and "Columbine," he had used Harlequin, Pierrot, and other traditional pantomime figures who interested Faulkner as subjects for drawing and verse.

In his "Fantoches," which had appeared in his *Fêtes Galantes* of 1869, Verlaine had used two traditional figures from the Italian commedia dell'arte: Scaramouche, a braggart soldier, and Pulcinella, a roguish wit. Together they plot in the moonlight as "the doctor from Bologna" picks medicinal herbs while his passionate daughter slips out to the arbor to meet her ardent and dashing Spanish pirate. In his translation, Faulkner kept the French word as the title, instead of using "puppets" or "marionettes." He also kept Verlaine's rhyme scheme, but he changed the sex of Pulcinella, presenting her and Scaramouche as lovers embracing against the mellow night sky. The other characters were the same, but Faulkner's last line departed materially from the original, in which the love-pain of the pirate is like the song of the nightingale. In the last line he reverted to French: "La lune ne garde aucune rancune [The moon takes no notice]." In *The Mississippian* "Fantoches" became "Fantouches," while Scaramouche gained a final *s* and the doctor's city was Bogona rather than Bologna. But there were probably few to note these variants from Verlaine's original in a translation that took numerous liberties. And it was certainly much more elegant and exotic fare than that usually provided by poetry in *The Mississippian.*

Verse in *The Mississippian* tended toward humor which often employed rural dialects. There were also romance, uplift and inspiration, and occasionally a rather rigid imitation of a classical model. In the column next to "Fantouches" was a specimen of the more familiar kind of verse:

A Pastoral Poem

Ah, fair one, with those dreamy eyes,
That have the raven robbed
Of all his darkened, mystic lustre,
Heed now my sobs and sighs,
Consider my plight
This dreary night
'Neath lowring and blackning skies.

Why must I brave this threatning storm
That rumbling far away
Comes closer to the near-at-hand,
Forebiding grief and harm.
Consider my plight
This dreary night
And leave me to my fireside warm.
She chews her cud with dainty jaw,
As now I milk her, "saw cow, saw."

It was signed "—*Jiggitts & Lester* Inc." These were familiar names to many of the students. W. H. Drane Lester and Louis M. Jiggitts were both Mississippians who had come to the university determined not only to excel there, but to point toward a Rhodes scholarship as well. They were congenial and roomed together. Inducted into the Scribblers of Sigma Upsilon, they told Louis Cochran that they wanted to write for the newspaper too. He was glad to oblige, and as staff members they conducted a feature called "Hayseed Letters," in which an Ole Miss student named Hiram Hayseed wrote letters to his father on the farm. In broad and labored phonetic spelling he would describe his problems, faux pas, and pleasures on the campus. The father, Si Hayseed, would then reply, recounting happenings on the farm. It was in a tradition stretching from James Russell Lowell to Chic Sale, and Jiggitts and Lester were undoubtedly right if they thought that their prose as well as their verse was more appealing to their fellow students than any translation of a poem by a decadent Frenchman or a story about a cocky cadet in Canada. There were some who thought that Jiggitts and Lester (and perhaps another Rhodes scholarship aspirant named Bryan England) were responsible for the Scribblers' blackball. Whoever had administered it, that had been an attack in secret. Now, the public attacks would be resumed.

Another Faulkner translation appeared in *The Mississippian* for March 3. Again he retained the French title, "Clair de Lune," and added "From PAUL VERLAINE." The original, comprising four rhyming quatrains, has been called Verlaine's first purely Symbolist poem. The subject is the soul of the poet's beloved, which he likens to a pastoral landscape. In his translation Faulkner stayed close to Verlaine's words and tone, supplying smooth rhymes broken only by *The Mississippian*'s typesetter. He ended with the sound of the shepherds' song:

In the calm moonlight, so lovely fair
That makes the birds dream in the slender trees,
While fountains dream among the statues there;
Slim fountains sob in silver ecstasies.

It was a very professional job.

In the same column, however, two inches below, was another poem which was clearly not a professional job. It was entitled "Whotouches," with the explanatory line, "Just a parody on Count's 'Fantouches' by Count, Jr." The commedia dell'arte figures were replaced by a servant who brought in fish, wurst, and "the sausage of Bologna," all served, in the last stanza, to

A big mouth from the Spanish main,
Whose jaws crush it with a strain—
How long the old aucune raccoon!

Below this, "Count, Jr." was identified as "J."

The next time Faulkner submitted poetry he also sent a letter counterattacking the parodist. It was published on the editorial page under the title "The Ivory Tower." In something under four hundred words he noted that the first poem submitted by his "unknown 'affinity' " was stupid, "for my own poem was stupid." With a flick of the wrist he added, "One sees at a glance then, the utter valuelessness of an imitation of an imitation." He deplored the vulgar ostentation of the writer's Latin phrases mingled with the English of the poem. The parodist's second effort, he said, was beneath notice, "closely resembling the first in being a vulgarly stupid agglomeration of words." It also served to prove of the writer, he said, that "while he continues to commute between the library and Helicon on his two cylinder unicorn, he has also provided himself with the Improved Graphometer Attachment for Tired Typewriters." But if the parodist had somehow achieved his intended humorous effect, "the answer is, of course, simply de gustibus."

The letter was accompanied by not one poem but two. "A Poplar" was short and slight, focusing on the image of the tree shivering in the sunlight and reaching for the clouds as covering. It was a translation, again, from Verlaine, and was signed "W. Falkner."

Faulkner kept Verlaine's title, "Streets," in the second poem, as well as the refrain "Dance the Jig!" In the first three stanzas he followed Verlaine as the speaker described the attractiveness of a former love and congratulated himself that his heart was now impervious. But he changed the last stanza. Whereas Verlaine's speaker closed by recalling fondly "hours intimate and trivial," Faulkner's last stanza read:

Her face will ever be
In my mind's infinity
She broke the coin and gave it half to me.

By now both Drane Lester and Louis Jiggitts were listed on the newspaper's masthead. Lester was an editor and Jiggitts wrote a column, "The Cynic's Ban." Their positions may have had something to do with the fact that in the lower right-hand corner of page 3, symmetrically opposite "Streets" on page 2, appeared another poem entitled "Meats." It was subtitled "A dainty little parody on Count's 'Streets,' by Count, Jr., Duke of Takerchance," and bore the attribution *"From Pall Vaserline."* Composed of three stanzas rather than four, its refrain was "Hold the Pig!" and its burden was an apostrophe to "that ham what am." Someone had given the parodist a copy of the new poem in good time.

Apparently there had not been time to write a reply to Faulkner's "The Ivory Tower" for the issue of March 17. This omission was remedied the following week, in the issue of March 24. In a letter dated March 20 and entitled "The 'Mushroom' Poet," J. combined heavy-handed irony and personal attack on "a peculiar person who calls himself William Falkner. . . ." J. declared that he had written the parodies to give the Count's poems a meaning. Then he suddenly switched his attack. "Mr. Editor," he wrote, "wouldn't this be a fine University if all of us were to wear sailor collars, monkey hats, and brilliant pantaloons; if we would 'mose' along the street by the aid of a walking prop; and, ye gods forbid, if we should while away our time singing of lascivious knees, smiling lute strings, and voluptuous toes? Wouldn't that be just too grand?" J. closed with an epithet he took from Byron: "He brays, the Laureate of the long-eared kind."

This was not the only attack in that issue of *The Mississippian* on the slight young man who dared to carry a cane and imitate the French Symbolists. There was a poem entitled "Eheu! Poetae Miselli." The first quatrain was typical:

You laugh at our simple rhyme,
You make it a sneering jest;
Sed,—
Hoc opus, hic labor est.

The final stanza was followed by the initials L.M.J. and a P.S.: "With apologies to Count for the vulgar Latin phrases." It appeared that Louis M. Jiggitts—fullback, debater, crack pistol shot, columnist, track captain and cornet soloist—had almost, if not quite, come out in the open in his struggle to defeat by ridicule the embodiment of affectation and foreign decadence on the Ole Miss campus.

The following week, however, in the issue for April 7, another parody appeared. It was entitled "Cane De Looney," with the attribution "From Peruney Prune." Dispensing with rhyme and often with sense, the three stanzas ended with an entranced female voice murmuring, " 'Who is the beau-u-tiful man with cane?' coyly!" The note at the end, "Apologies to Count and Count, Jr.," suggested that some new poetaster had joined in the game. On the same page, however, there was a paragraph in "The Cynic's Ban" (presumably Jiggitts' work) asking that the paper's readers bear with the efforts of amateur poets. It was not without a barb at the end: "Just remember all our poetry is 'homemade' and that always lends a charm that 'bought' or borrowed goods can never have."

The same issue contained a riposte to L.M.J. from Faulkner and, surprisingly, a long letter in support of him. Faulkner was brief, supercilious, almost bored. "An anonymous squib in the last issue of your paper was brought to my notice as having a personal bearing," he wrote the editor. "I could, with your forbearance, fill some space in endeavoring to bite the author with his own dog; but I shall content myself by asking him, through the columns of your paper, where did he learn English construction?" The letter defending Faulkner was entitled "The 'Mushroom Muse' and The 'Hayseed Hoodlum,' " thus further identifying Faulkner's scourge as Jiggitts. In nearly six hundred words, the writer—identified only as "F."—

jocosely attacked J. ("his customary habitat is in the Chinatown section of Canton, Mississippi"), and good-humoredly praised Faulkner, who, as a poet, was among all nature's creatures "the least able to protect himself in such a dilemma." Actually, the tone was different from that of both Jiggitts and Faulkner. There was no acrimony, and the barbs aimed at Jiggitts were rather conventional and nonvenomous. It was as if one fraternity brother were engaging another in a kind of good-natured ritual jousting. His Latin was "corrugated" and his verse was "paranoiac" rather than "parodic." "Poets don't sprout in every garden of learning," F. went on, "and how can they grow and bloom into a genius when they are continually surrounded by bitterweeds." He ended with a toast to the "Mushroom" poet.

As though in reply, another Faulkner translation from Verlaine appeared a week later on April 14. Like "Fantoches" and "Clair de Lune," "A Clymene" had also appeared in the volume *Fêtes Galantes.* For three of the five quatrains Faulkner kept close to Verlaine. Then he allowed himself more liberty:

Because all of my being
In my breathing and seeing
Is a lingering like flowers
Of your hours.

One week later, apparently still undaunted at the prospect of further parody, Faulkner published "Study." (The *Eagle* picked it up the next day.) In this four-stanza poem he treated a familiar situation, the distraction of beauty, nature, and daydreams in the face of the necessity to study.

Then, after a two-week interval, Jiggitts published a reply to F. Under the title "Chimes" in *The Mississippian* for May 5, J. wrote to the editor that he had not responded to F.'s letter because he assumed that he had "been shipped to Jackson for treatment." But it turned out that he was not at the state asylum, and he urged the editor to help see that appropriate action was taken. In a P.S.—still playing the letters-to-the editor game—Jiggitts went part of the way toward unmasking F.: "He is from Meridian. His name starts with H. and ends with N. He is a blonde [*sic*]." No more letters on this subject appeared, either from F., from J., or from Faulkner. But there were still a few more salvos to come before this battle of the poems was ended.

Faulkner's last poem in *The Mississippian* for that year appeared the next week in the issue for May 12. Surprisingly, it treated a much more conventional subject for collegiate verse than even "Study." It was a Shakespearean sonnet entitled "Alma Mater." The sentiments were familiar: gazing through the college portals the speaker and his comrades see

Upon the mountain top the shining sun
Success, drawing us infinitely
Upwardly, until Life and Task are one.

If there was something besides the general facility to differentiate this poem from the usual effusion of its kind, it was the quality of dreamy languor. Also, the female personification was a little more sensuous than she usually seemed, as though the fostering mother had somehow taken on something of the Symbolist mistress.

Another anonymous poet appeared in the same issue, and by oversight or intent, the editor had placed his work in the column next to "Alma Mater." He signed himself "Lordgreyson" and entitled his poem "Une Ballade d'une Vache Perdue." The three eight-line stanzas described the heifer, Betsy, lost and wandering far from home. The poet had enjoyed himself describing the pastoral scene, and her "rounded curves" and "waving tresses" as "she stood there nude. . . ." In spite of the one-word refrain "Ahem!" to each stanza, it was a tour de force which must have amused others besides himself. Not the least of these, apparently, was the author of "Une Ballade des Femmes Perdues" himself.

Faulkner's last poem for the academic year 1919–1920 appeared when the yearbook *Ole Miss* came out. This was another sonnet, called "To a Co-ed." The poet compared his subject to the dawn. After that classical allusion he praised her in the Symbolist manner, for the beauty of her "twilit" eyes and her throat, "a slender bridge," where all dreams hovered. Then, perhaps recalling Villon in his "Ballade des dames du temps jadis," he compared her to fabled fair women—Venus, Helen, Beatrice, and Thaïs:

For down Time's arras, faint and fair and far,
Your face still beckons like a lonely star.

Faulkner was more liberally represented in the yearbook in another medium. He had supplied all the drawings Louis Cochran had asked. The four which bore his name (spelled with a *u*, unlike his signature beneath "To a Co-ed") were far and away the most professional artwork in the book. His drawings—all pen-and-ink, it seemed—introduced various sections of the annual. For "Organizations" he had done a full-page spring scene. A young man and woman faced each other, a budding bush between them.

Drawings by William Faulkner for *Ole Miss*, 1919–1920.

As the girl restrained her billowing skirt with one hand, she reached for her flying hat with the other. The illustration for the A.E.F. Club had been much reduced in the printing, but it had the same sharp lines, stylized figures, and symmetrical composition. An elegantly gowned and hatted woman looked out of the sketch as a blasé American lieutenant spoke to her. The minute lines below the picture were lettered in Faulkner's precise printing. "Le grand Americaine [*sic*]" asked, "Parlez-vous Anglais, mam'-zelle?" In response "La petite Francaise" answered, "Mais oui, m'sieur, un peu; Do you lofe me? Kees me queek! Damn! 'ell!"

His most ambitious and interesting drawing occupied a full page introducing "Social Activities." To symbolize the dances, music, and dramatics at Ole Miss, he had taken characters from the same sources Verlaine had often used: the commedia dell' arte and the pantomime. Before two seven-branched candelabra, stark against a black background, he had posed three figures. At the right was Harlequin, an elegant frock coat covering most of his familiar domino costume, his hands grasping those of Pierrette. She bent back from him, her pointed clown's hat angled back toward a half-kneeling

Mezzetino, his lute slung round his neck. The checkerboard parquet floor picked up the domino motif and relieved the black of the backdrop. It was a highly sophisticated drawing. It might also be interpreted as a highly ironic comment on social activities at the university which few of the participants would have recognized.

For "Red and Blue," the senior dancing club, he produced a drawing—again much reduced in size—which could stand as counterpoint to the other. Her back to the viewer, a girl in a low-backed gown was doing a dance suggesting the Charleston with a black-clad partner whose head was obscured by her own. The couple's outflung legs and arms formed a geometric pattern which somehow froze the furious dance, fusing the two figures so that they vaguely resembled a many-limbed Hindu deity. Each of these drawings bore the highly stylized signature "W. Faulkner," the verticals longer than the body of the letters, and the *r* enormously enlarged.

There was other evidence of Faulkner in the yearbook besides the poem and the drawings. One of the six art editors listed was W. Falkner. On the facing page, one of the twenty-five ovals showed the artist in RAF uniform, eyes squinting against the smoke from the dangling cigarette, a quizzical expression on the thin face. Under "Special Students" was the listing "Faulkner, William." On the facing page, in the roll of the "Freshman Literary Class," some waggish member of the *Ole Miss* staff had entered the name "Falkner, Count William."

In mid-May, Lida and Dot Oldham left for San Francisco to sail for Honolulu, where they would be the guests of Estelle Franklin. Lem Oldham closed up the house and went to stay at the hotel. He stood it for one day, then sent for the cook and reopened the house. He invited Bill Faulkner to come and stay with him for the week before he went to Chicago for the Republican National Convention. The invitation was accepted, and Faulkner went to spend some time there with the man he had once hoped would be his father-in-law.

The Major's legal affairs kept him in his office a good part of the day. With only the end-of-term Spanish and French classes to attend, Faulkner must have spent a good deal of time alone in the silent house where he had come to see Estelle, where he had listened to her play the piano and watched the dancing figures of the young crowd which often gathered there. Lem Oldham had told Billy Faulkner how much he liked Cape jasmine, and the boy had gotten him some. The scent on the soft spring air could have done little to purge his poetry of its melancholy visions of lost nymphs.

If he took any time to assess the results of his academic year, Faulkner could scarcely have found the balance very favorable. Although he received grades (and good ones, of course, in the French and Spanish), this must have been in large part through the sufferance of teachers who could see that he was talented though heterodox, and who knew his father. There was little in the literary study which had opened his eyes, apart perhaps from whatever new material he had discovered in reading and translating French poets. He had found an outlet in which his work could appear. If it excited admiration among a few readers, it also elicited mockery and personal attack. The appearance of the drawings may have pleased him on that score. Reactions to poetry were highly subjective and beauty really tended to be in the eye of the beholder. But let a bungler try to draw a sketch and all the world could see he was a bungler. Faulkner and anyone else who cared to look could see that his drawings were good. They might in some ways be imitative and immature, but they showed talent. It is likely that he was thinking now of fusing the two media, the visual and the verbal, in some new work.

At the very end of the year came an accolade. To encourage young writers Professor Calvin S. Brown had set up an annual prize carrying the substantial sum of ten dollars. A committee would help him in making the selection and then he would make the award himself. In his Excelsior diary for Tuesday, June 1, 1920, Professor Brown wrote, "Commencement Exercises." Then he wrote, "The little prize which I offered for the best poem went to William Faulkner." He did not note which poem had won, but the poet was indubitably ten dollars richer for his labors. Once again the Muse had brought him something other than work and brickbats.

The experiment of attending college must have been wearing thin by now. Summer vacation had arrived, and for the most part he could loaf or roam as he liked. But what then—back to school in the fall? His underlying discontent would soon flare up again. And before he would emerge from it, he and his friends would go through a briefly dramatic series of events.

18

May, 1920-November, 1920

"I learned in spite of the instructors we had. They were a bunch of brokendown preachers: head full of dogma and intolerance and a belly full of big meaningless words. English literature course whittled Shakespeare down because he wrote about whores without pointing a moral, and one instructor always insisted that the head devil in *Paradise Lost* was an inspired prophetic portrait of Darwin, and they wouldn't touch Byron with a ten foot pole, and Swinburne was reduced to his mother and his old standby, the ocean. . . . But in spite of it, I kind of got interested in learning things."

—*Mosquitoes* (116)

Life in Oxford had been going its variegated way. The eyes of the world were apparently no longer focused on the town, for the *Eagle* had sourly concluded that the oil boom was "a dead issue." What's more, there had been no possibility of success from the outset. "In our opinion it was a bunco game," the commentary read, "and the leases are not worth the paper they are written on." Citizens who had hoped for affluence had to content themselves with cultural uplift instead, as the annual Chautauqua Week brought the Red Grenadiers Band and Male Chorus together with the usual inspirational lecturers.

There was also tragedy that spring. Chess Carothers had long since mastered the operation and repair of the Colonel's Buick. One Wednesday afternoon in late May he was driving down College Hill Street with a friend when the machine coughed and sputtered to a stop. Chess coasted to the side of the street, got out of the car, and bent down to scan its underside. He saw the trouble right away: there was a leak in the gasoline line. Chess pushed himself under the car. It was hard to see what he was doing, but he thought he would try to repair the trouble there. His friend bent down and lit a match so that he could see better. With a flash the vapor from the line exploded. As fuel that had dripped onto Chess's clothes ignited, he scrambled out and ran blazing to the nearest house. A man rushed out with a quilt and smothered the flames, but not before Chess was burned over most of his body. He lingered until Sunday morning. There were others who would drive the deaf old man from The Big Place wherever he wanted to go, but with the passing of Chess Carothers, another link with the past was gone.

By now Murry Falkner and his family had, technically, moved out of Oxford onto the campus—University, Mississippi, a legal and geographical entity separate from the town, with a post office of its own. The Falkners moved into the old Delta Psi house, near the center of the campus and almost a mile west of the Square. Standing on a slight hill just across from the home of Dr. and Mrs. Calvin S. Brown, the three-story structure was so solid and imposing that it reminded some of the old, ornate Geology Building. Three large, semicircular steps led up to the open marble terrace-like porch. An enormous arch set into the brick framed the double front door opening onto a large foyer. To the right was a huge many-paned set of three windows whose arched shape repeated that of the front entry. Five arched second-floor windows looked out on the front of the elm-shaded lawn, and set into the third floor below the peaked roof were three more windows. The most notable feature was a round tower attached to the front at the right. Rising to the top of the second story, it ended in a pointed conical roof which made it look like the donjon of a medieval castle. Murry and Maud Falkner had a downstairs bedroom. An old-fashioned circular stairway led to the second floor where the boys had their rooms. For a time Billy had a back bedroom upstairs; then he exchanged it for the small room in the tower. Besides his bed and dresser there was a table where he worked at his manuscripts. The room also accommodated the supply of liquor he laid in whenever he could afford it. It was a spacious and comfortable house. Out to the rear was the stretch that Mr. Friedman, the merchant, always called the Golfing Pasture. Murry Falkner was apparently content to settle in there, as, unquestionably, was the Colonel to see him there.

As the Colonel retreated further from the public eye, his other son was growing more prominent. A resignation had given Governor Russell the opportunity to make an appointment, and John Falkner, Jr., was now Judge of the 3rd Judicial District of Mississippi. The *Eagle* endorsed the governor's sagacity in making the appointment and printed the new judge's photograph. It was a Falkner visage that stared out at the reader: large-nosed and broad-browed—an imposing man.

The Judge's nephew was following a very different course. He was very much a private citizen who did only what he wanted to. If he did perform any act resembling a public service, it was because he derived personal pleasure from doing it. That summer he played. Occasionally he might do something for pocket money. His father would now and then get him a job such as painting the roof of the observatory. But Faulkner preferred leisure. There was one activity that often lured him from both pen and paintbrush that summer.

In mid-November of 1916 a new minister had come to the Presbyterian church. He was the Reverend Mr. J. Allan Christian, a tall, thin man with dark curly hair. He and his short, plump wife took a great interest in young people, from the smallest boy scouts up to university students. Faulkner was interested in scouting too, and he and Mr. Christian became friends. The Falkner boys had played tennis from time to time on courts in town and at the university. Bob Farley had built courts with two or three other boys, but often they would clear a space and mark it off for a court only to have the owner of the property start building in the space they had cleared. They decided to build a court where no one would show up with stakes, and when they got it done Mr. Christian could give them some coaching. Two more of Christian's friends, Hubert Lipscomb and Harry Bryan, joined the work crew, and before long they had a very serviceable clay court in the yard of the old Delta Psi house. With the same kind of concentration he had displayed when he took up golf, Faulkner addressed himself to learning the art of winning at tennis. He had some natural advantages. He was fast when he cared to exert himself, and he had quick hands; besides that, he had considerable power for his size and he was a persevering retriever. He also developed some new tactics. Usually, if a player missed with his first serve, he would let up on the second one in an effort to avoid a double fault. Faulkner was the first one of the group to risk hitting his second serve as hard as the first. "With him it was all or nothing," Bob Farley remembered. He did not have a powerful smash, but he could drop the ball just over the net or place it in the back court. "He was the kind of a player who would bedevil you to death," Jack Falkner said. But he played with style, almost as though he were a weekend guest at an English manor house playing a set or two in white flannels and an ascot. "When he scored a point," recalled Hubert Lipscomb, "he would always apologize." Some days they would play all afternoon long, and by midsummer their enthusiasm had reached its apex. They held a Fourth of July tournament and played all day. Faulkner won his matches from his brothers and from most of his other opponents as well.

He no longer played baseball with the frequency and fervor he had displayed earlier, though John played and Dean was showing the kind of skill that would make him the best of the brothers. But Bill still liked to watch the game, even when it included the church league teams. One day he sat looking on, bemused at the vociferous intensity of members of the Baptist team. "I don't know what church God belongs to," he murmured to a friend, "but I know he isn't a Baptist because he permits the other sects to exist."

He still played golf. Now that Dean was big enough to play the nine-hole course, the brothers would make a foursome. They all played a crisp, fast-moving game, and sometimes they would have to stop for more leisurely players, often senior professors, who were also taking advantage of the absence of the students.

He often saw their neighbors that summer. Calvin Brown was interested as always in his writing. His wife was a lively woman who had long known the boy's family. Ida Maud Brown had, as a matter of fact, received her middle name as a result of her mother's friendship with Maud Butler Falkner. An Ole Miss M.A., Mrs. Brown was not only a publishing historian but one of the best raconteurs in an area that abounded in talented storytellers. Although she welcomed Bill to her house, it was actually her sons, Calvin, Jr., and Robert, that he came to see. They would turn eleven and thirteen, respectively, later that summer. On Sunday afternoons Bill and Dean, who was now nearly thirteen, too, would walk across the street to the Brown home. The fifth one who was usually there was Rip Van Santen, who lived with his uncle, A. L. Bondurant. In spite of the dozen years' age difference between the leader and the other four, they made a close-knit group. "I have never known a man less capable of sham," Calvin Brown remembered later. "Billy never pretended to be 'one of us'—the difference in ages was too great to be overlooked. He accepted the leadership and authority that naturally fell to him, but he exercised them with a wisdom which was deeper than mere tact." His natural temperament stabilized the relationship "because he was never effusive or demonstrative; he was always somewhat aloof, even with close friends of his own age. Billy's attitude toward us boys was simply that of a close friend who keeps his distance because of a basic respect for the individual." He had not entered into this relationship in order to serve as a friendly guide to youth: "we were simply four quite different persons that met with him to do things that all five of us enjoyed."

They did a number of things together, the most sedentary of which was roasting hot dogs and marshmallows. Their passion was games of skill, endurance, and woodcraft. They might play stalking games that pitted one camp against another or one player against the rest, like running-through, in which one took the football and tried to run around, through, or over the rest to the imaginary goal line. But hare and hounds—or paper-chase, as they usually called it—was their favorite. They would draw straws to choose the two hares, who would then set off to a starting point with a sack full of small bits of newspaper. Five minutes later the hounds would set out in pursuit. There at the starting point they would pick up the paper trail. They would try to outthink the hares, to cut by a loop and thrust on ahead to where they might even get a glimpse of the quarry. When the pieces of paper were exhausted, the hares would drop the sack and sprint for the agreed-upon goal. After the hounds had picked up the bag— to show that they had followed the trail—they would cap their three-mile jog trot with a breakneck half-mile steeplechase. Billy Faulkner had never been systematic about exercise, but he asked no quarter from these iron-lunged teenagers, and he still held his own. Once he enticed Phil Stone into one of their Sunday afternoon hunts. It was Stone's first and last time running over courses such as Davidson's Bottom and Bailey's Woods. "It nearly killed him," said Calvin Brown.

The other stalking games were slower and craftier. The group might split into two camps a few hundred yards apart, each one marked by a flag of sorts tied to a stick or a tree. Each camp would try to steal the other's flag while protecting its own. Or one man might be stationed on a small hill or rise and others had to creep up Indian-fashion, taking advantage of whatever cover there was, to seize him before he could spot them. If he called out their name and position, they were out of it; if he called the wrong name, they had won, just as if they had crept up and grabbed his ankle. Calvin Brown managed this last feat one moonlit night in the pasture of the chancellor of the university. He crawled to within thirty feet of Billy, and then, silently cutting a bush, soundlessly pushed it ahead of him at long intervals. "It was a glorious moment when I finally seized him by the ankle," he remembered.

Calvin Brown wondered if he hadn't been helped in his stratagem by Billy's tendency to withdrawal, the process that was responsible for his passing friends on the Square without so much as a flicker of recognition. "This ability to lose himself in his own private world was one of the unheeded signs of things to come," Brown thought. Another quality which marked Billy Faulkner in those days was his ability to improvise fascinating ghost and horror tales by a campfire. "I can't recall any of the plots, but the general impression is clear enough. The tone was one of supernatural horror, but always relieved by enough humor, fantasy, or irony to give the tale some aesthetic distance. . . . Billy set out to amuse us by terrifying us, and . . . he never failed to pull it off." Obviously, he enjoyed all this as much as the boys did, and if this was a part of their boyhood that would later profit them as men, it was—in a curious way—a part of his apprenticeship that would later profit him as an artist. The motif of the hunt, in which the quarry was not animal but human, would appear often in his work. Surely it owed something to those Sunday afternoons which would find him with the hounds pursuing the quarry past the Hathorn Farm, or, one of two fleeing hares, slipping swiftly through the woods near the old Shegog place with the pack in full cry less than five minutes behind him.

Later, when Calvin Brown looked back on the night of his signal triumph, he knew that Billy would never have just allowed him to win; that would have been a violation of their unspoken code. It is very likely that he had simply begun working as he sat there, and external reality faded and was gone. To compose a work as much as possible in his head before he set it down on paper was apparently a technique he developed early, and he may well have been working that moonlit night on a poem like the one Phil Stone's secretary typed for him in July, 1920—a three-stanza, free-verse poem about the beauty of the beloved, against a background of silence, darkness, and dreams, which ended,

Lift your hand and touch your hair
Parted simply backward from your face
Like wearied wings. Let the silence smooth your brow
And wreath our dreams like lilacs in your hair.

There was not a great deal of news for the men to talk about that summer as they sat propped against storefronts around the Square or watched the checker players on the benches in the Courthouse yard. Joe Parks announced that the First National Bank had bought the Colonial Hotel and would presently have it refurbished. The governor issued a proclamation declaring that because the population of Oxford had dropped below 2,000, and with the citizens being dissatisfied with the commission form of government, he was changing the classification from city to town and appointing the mayor and others to serve on the governing body of the municipality. To many this was another affront from Lee Russell, and there was murmuring that when the new census count was tabulated that fall they would see whether Oxford was a city or not.

The tempo of events began to pick up as August turned into September. John Falkner, Jr., announced that he was a candidate in the election recently called by the governor for the office of circuit judge, which Falkner had been filling on a temporary basis. Two weeks later Lida Oldham and her daughter Dorothy returned from their summer in Honolulu, just in time for the beginning of the school year of 1920–1921.

It had been a marvelous trip. One of its highlights had been an informal visit by the touring Prince of Wales. When he had stopped at Honolulu in mid-April, the American governor had given a formal reception for the prince, to the delight of his two plain and aging daughters. The prince had preferred to dance with Estelle Franklin and one or two other young matrons. He later presented her with a souvenir: an autographed photograph of the H.M.S. *Renown*. Going back to school seemed a very dull business to Dorothy Oldham.

One of the reentering students that fall was Bill Faulkner. On September 21 he was welcomed in *The Mississippian* by Louis Jiggitts in his epistolary guise of Hiram Hayseed. "Me and Blind Jim [a Negro who for years had been adopted affectionately by students as a kind of mascot], T. J. Tubb and Hannibal, Bill Falkner and Paul Rogers is all here now so school can comminct whenever it wants to." Faulkner was still far from enthusiastic about school and even less certain now of what he wanted to study. He had talked with Professor Brown about it. "Billy seemed to be faltering and groping his way," Maud Brown recalled later. "He told my husband that he felt his thinking was fuzzy and wondered whether studying mathematics would help him. My husband said he certainly thought it would." Billy took Professor Brown's advice and enrolled in one of the lower-level mathematics courses. For a few weeks he seemed interested, but then began to cut classes and finally stopped going. "He seemed to be the same way in most of the subjects he took. He was a gentle, nice boy, quite shy and sensitive, and always courteous." Maud Brown thought he was wonderful with children, and she could see how much her boys thought of him. "This was an outstanding characteristic I remember from those times, and the other was his intellectual groping." At times, his friend Lowry Simmons remembered, no one knew where he was. He would simply leave Oxford.

He was not alone in feeling there was not enough stimulation. So did Ben Wasson and Lucy Somerville, a lively and attractive girl from Ben's hometown of Greenville. She was also an ardent theatergoer, and when Ben asked if she was interested in forming a dramatic club, she quickly agreed. On one of the first days of the new semester Lucy and Ben sat in the shade of a tall campus oak and scanned Ben's list of prospective members. "Bill was planning to write a play," Lucy Somerville recalled; "he was reading plays and he was interested in the drama as an art form and in all phases of the theatre." As a matter of fact, he had already tried his hand at a one-act play in which an emancipated young woman rejected a worldly suitor in favor of another whom she considered dominating though he was actually subservient. Faulkner talked about plots of plays he knew, about characterization, about actors and the theater. He especially liked George Bernard Shaw's *Candida*.

They were successful in their recruitment. Lucy interested a relative of hers, Ella Somerville. Daughter of a former dean of the law school, she was a young woman of intelligence and taste. She offered to help with directing or anything else that needed doing. Katrina Carter was good at sewing and designing, and said she would help with costumes. Jane Foote and Sis Hopkins were interested in acting, although Sis's six-foot stature limited the number of roles she could play. Ben's sister, Mary Helen, joined too. There was Ben—who was handsome enough to play any lead but was a bit shorter than Faulkner—and Phil Davidson, a preacher's son from Greenville who also played end on the football team. Looking with quizzical amusement at the newly gathered group, Bill Faulkner called them a collection of he-women and she-men. Ben was elected president. They now had everything but a name, and when Ben suggested "the Marionettes," the members quickly agreed to it. Enthusiastic and anxious to begin, they chose Norman Lee Swartout's three-act farce, *The Arrival of Kitty*.

The Marionettes were a lively group whose interests extended to other areas besides drama. Lucy Somerville was an avid reader. Shortly after they had organized the club, she had seen a review of Helen Haiman Joseph's *A Book of Marionettes*. She had promptly ordered it and circulated it among the club members. It was a clear and comprehensive history of the development of the marionette art form from its beginning in ancient Greek and Oriental cultures up through the work of such contemporary artists as Tony Sarg. She gave it to Bill, but she never knew whether he read it or not. If, however, he had not already been well acquainted with Harlequin, Scaramouche, Pantalone, Columbine, and Pierrot, this volume would have given him enough for the references which would appear in his poems. Whether from that inspiration or some other, he had decided he would do a new play which, conceivably, the club might stage. It wouldn't bring him—or any of them—any money, but it would "mean recognition and this was important to him"—no matter what self-styled satirist might refer to him as Count No 'Count.

Lucy was starved for current books. There was no bookstore in town, and the university library did not spend any of its appropriation on contemporary writing. She had seen Ben reading books which Bill—still to some extent his guide—had lent to him, books supplied him in turn by Phil Stone. Every year Stone ordered dozens of books on approval from the Brick Row Bookshop, one of his favorite New Haven haunts, and he kept most of them. After he read them he would press them on friends such as Ella Somerville and Bill Faulkner. Some books he would order with Faulkner specifically in mind. Now, through Ben, Lucy was included in the privileged circle. She decided to pass the benefits on to others. It was suggested that she edit a book review column. Drane Lester liked the idea, and "Books and Things" became a regular feature of *The Mississippian*. One of the first contributions she asked for was from Bill. Ben had a copy of William Alexander Percy's new collection of poems, *In April Once*, and Bill agreed to read it and write a review. Before it would appear, however, the reviewer would be among those involved in a series of incidents which would rock the Ole Miss campus and send shock waves spreading into the state.

When the Honorable Lee M. Russell had moved into the governorship in January of 1920, one of the things uppermost in his mind was his plan for the University of Mississippi. He was still obsessed with the idea of fraternities. Clannish organizations like the one that had humiliated him were still operating, in defiance of a state law placed on the books principally as a result of his own work. Russell appointed a committee to investigate conditions at state institutions of higher learning. The committee chairman found nothing startling, but in his report in late June he had assured his fellow citizens that "these institutions will be thoroughly democratized and every Mississippian will feel and know that these in deed and truth are the schools of the people." The university would no longer be a place where cotton-rich planters' sons came to play, lording it over red-necked boys whose fathers scrabbled out a marginal living on hill farms.

By the fall of 1920 Lee Russell was ready to carry out his plan. Every month he would visit each of the institutions in his capacity as president of the university board of trustees. The faculty was divided. Russell had told the student body at Ole Miss that it was too high-toned to engage in conduct that would bring discredit upon the school. And now, zealous as a Roundhead stamping out Cavalier excesses, he meant to see that this was true. The Puritanical aura was conspicuous already in some state schools. In January the faculty of Mississippi State College had banned smoking by the student body anywhere except in private, but there were other things going on at Ole Miss besides tobacco smoking. There were dances and parties and long weekends which saw drinking and a lot more.

In late October the board made public a series of resolutions. The heads of the university and the colleges were to remind their students that state law forbade "the organization of secret societies and the making of secret pledges" in such state institutions, and they were to punish violations with dismissal or expulsion. This was not new, but the resolutions which followed were. The big dances at the university, resolved the board, were too costly and too long. Therefore, they would be shortened and strictly regulated. Moreover, there were to be no more than three such major dances at an institution during the year. The board had rolled back the clock.

Many of the students were angry at these edicts, none more so than the members of the Red and Blue Club, the dancing club of twenty seniors who sponsored two dances each year. During the course of their year they might elect as many as fifteen honorary members. This year two S.A.E.'s were members: Russell Pigford, who was a premedical student, and Rufus Creekmore, the football captain, who was preparing for law school.

Resentment boiled over on the night of Wednesday, October 27. A group of students threw a rope over a limb of one of the campus oaks and hauled a rag-stuffed effigy into the air. Then they set it afire. Before the figure was consumed, the spectators could make out the pinned-on legend very clearly. It read, "Lee M. Russell." The Jackson *Daily News* played up the account on its front page, and by Thursday morning there were rumors that the governor and an investigating commission would soon be on the campus. The S.A.E.'s held an emergency meeting at Jim Stone's house and decided to go to see Chancellor Joseph Neely Powers. He was the governor's man, but perhaps they could reach some sort of understanding. They were particularly anxious to protect their seniors and to avoid jeopardizing any chance the fraternities might have for future reinstatement. Sitting in Powers' office, they told him they had indeed been running sub rosa. They surrendered the fraternity's charter and asked for his protection. When they left his office, they felt that he had promised it. It was now known that the governor and four members of the board would be in Oxford on Monday, November 1.

The board convened at the Lyceum Building in the chancellor's office, immediately beneath the suite that so many S.A.E.'s had occupied. Seated at the long table with the governor were J. R. Tipton from Hernando, J. S. Howerton from Guntown, A. A. Cohn of Brookhaven, and John Falkner, Jr., of Oxford. Under the governor's direction, the inquiry immediately turned to the question of illegal fraternity activities. A stream of students was interrogated without revealing any incriminating information.

By the next day the atmosphere in the chancellor's office was taut with hostility. One of the committee members removed his boots and propped his stockinged feet on the table directly in front of the witness chair. They called in Lowry Simmons, a thin-faced, intense young man who played end on the football team. He was ostensibly just a representative of the Red and Blue Club, but he was an S.A.E. as well, as Chancellor Powers knew. Simmons answered the committee members' questions with a combination of nervousness and anger. Finally Governor Russell leaned forward. "Mr. Simmons," he said, his jaw outthrust, "if I were a student here at Ole Miss, would I be invited to join the Red and Blue Club?"

Now angry and defiant, Simmons answered quickly. "I imagine it would be just as it was when you were here, Governor, you wouldn't get in."

By Wednesday the committee members knew what they wanted to do. For burning the effigy of the governor, they dismissed four students and suspended another for thirty days. By "high noon," one week later on November 10, all students were to file their names and addresses together with the names of organizations to which they belonged and any information they possessed about fraternity activities. Anyone supplying false information or failing to file a declaration would be "shipped" from the university.

Suddenly the chancellor's promise of protection seemed a very thin shield. Hiram Creekmore came up from Water Valley to talk with his sons and their fraternity brothers. Lowry Simmons' father joined him. "Resign before you get shipped," Simmons told them. "Get your credits."

The "high noon" deadline on Wednesday, the tenth, was approaching. The brothers apparently decided that they would take advantage of what time they had left. Perhaps some loophole could be found. If not, they could withdraw from the university just before the deadline.

There was one exception. On Friday, November 5, 1920, William Faulkner withdrew from the University of Mississippi. As far as the university records were concerned, this must have made little difference, for although his grades had been duly recorded for the courses he had taken the previous year, there was no notation of any courses at all for the first semester of 1920–1921. So the last item of information on his sketchy transcript was simply the phrase "Withdrawn from the University Nov 5/1920." He must have seen clearly what the result of the "high noon" ultimatum would be, and he simply withdrew without waiting, as almost all the rest would do. He was probably glad of an opportunity to withdraw under circumstances to which his family could not object. (Jack seems to have withdrawn on the same day.) But he had endured more than enough of the classroom experience, and now the university was beginning to institute new procedures such as compulsory medical examinations, measures which might well have seemed to him to be intrusions on his privacy. The things he wanted to do at the university—drop in on Marionettes rehearsals or meetings occasionally, contribute a poem or review to *The Mississippian* now and then—he could do just as well as a non-student. His emotions must have been totally different from those of his brother and the fourteen other members of the fraternity who resigned on Wednesday, the tenth, just before the deadline for handing in the completed questionnaires. Finally all but a handful of S.A.E.'s were gone. They scattered—Simmons to Alabama, Pigford to Tulane, the Creekmores and Callahan to Mississippi State. Bill Faulkner stayed where he was, and kept on doing what he wanted to do.

The denouement took about three weeks. Late in November the board of trustees ordered the disbanding of the Red and Blue Club and three other social clubs at the university. Perhaps thirty students had left; nearly six hundred remained. The governor apparently had decided that the board had gone far enough, perhaps too far. Nine months later they would permit all students who withdrew during the first semester of 1920–1921 to reenter the university. Ole Miss had apparently weathered the acute phase of Lee M. Russell's plan to democratize it. It would later seem like a trifling threat compared with the one which his mentor would mount against it.

One of Bill Faulkner's last acts while he was still technically a student was to give Lucy Somerville the review he had promised. By coincidence it appeared in *The Mississippian* for November 10, the same issue which announced the thirty departures. A few readers may have noted how even a volume of poetry could call up violent political associations in Mississippi. William Alexander Percy, the author of *In April Once*, was not only a poet; he was also the son of former Senator Leroy Percy. He had accompanied his father through the violent campaign in which the self-appointed champion of the rednecks soundly defeated the Delta aristocrat. Will Percy would later write one of the most vitriolic descriptions of Theodore G. Bilbo ever put on paper. Now, however, he was writing lyric and dramatic poetry.

The volume took its title from the forty-page play with which it opened. In blank verse Percy set forth the drama of a young man, Guido, who sacrificed his life in Renaissance Florence for a leper and a jailer. The first section was completed by seven short poems chiefly on Greek and Roman subjects. The lyrical pieces of the book's middle section ranged from plaintive nature poems such as one entitled "Sanctuary" to imitations of ballads and thirteenth-century songs. The last third of the 134-page book was called "From a Soldier's Notebook." It concluded with "An Epistle from Corinth," in which Paul of Tarsus meditated in blank verse on the effect of Christ upon his life. The major reviews were fair.

Faulkner's 500-word review was a curious mixture, combining occasional high praise with what was really sweeping dismissal. Percy had unfortunately been born out of his time, Faulkner said, "like alas! how many of us—." He should have lived in Victorian England or the Italy of Swinburne, some of whose tastes he shared. He reminded the reviewer of a Latin muse, displaying "poignant ecstasies of lyrical extravagance and a short lived artificial strength achieved at the cost of true strength in beauty." Although he found that "As a whole, the book sustains its level of lyrical beauty," the war poems would tend to help it "oblivionward." He mixed daggers and bouquets in the last paragraph. Percy was "a violinist with an inferior instrument," but in spite of this "the gold outweighs the dross."

Time would prove he was right in dismissing the book, but the review itself was vulnerable to the charge that can be made against the majority of student reviews: the writer seemed as much interested in his own phrase-making as in a just assessment. Four years later Faulkner would write in an essay on the sins of the American literary critic, "He takes the piece under examination for an instrument upon which to run difficult arpeggios of cleverness."

The following week he received in the mail a foot-and-a-half-long tube from London. It contained a large parchment scroll and a covering letter. The Air Ministry informed him that on 9 March 1920 he had been gazetted Honorary 2nd Lieutenant with effect from the date of his demobilization. The granting of the commission involved no training obligation, and, the Director of Personnel added firmly, "It is to be distinctly understood that the grant of this commission carries no claim to increased pay, gratuity, etc." Permission to wear the uniform could be granted only for military business "or on special occasion when attending ceremonials and entertainments of a military nature." The commission, twelve by sixteen inches, was an impressive document. It was "Given at Our Court at Saint James's the First day of January 1920." The grantor, his name large in flourishes of scrollwork, was "George, by the Grace of God, of the United Kingdom of Great Britain and Ireland and of the British Dominions beyond the seas, King, Defender of the Faith, Emperor of India, &c." To his trusty and well-beloved William Faulkner (in script) his majesty gave Greeting. And, reposing trust and confidence in his Loyalty and good Conduct, did Constitute and Appoint him to the Honorary Rank of Second Lieutenant in His Royal Air Force. William Faulkner had his commission framed. After that it hung on the wall of his room in the old Delta Psi house.

He was now twenty-three. Boyhood grew daily more remote, and family bonds weakened as his own life became progressively more internalized. Each year severed ties with the past. Great-grandfather Murry had lived out his long life, and now Faulkner's remaining grandfather dwelt more than ever in the past and became increasingly dependent on Auntee and Sallie Murry Wilkins. There was nothing to hold Faulkner in Oxford except finances. But somehow he usually had a little money. And there were still friends who would put him up when he unexpectedly arrived. Now the absences from the campus which Lowry Simmons had noted would increase, and for the next year the pattern began to appear that would grow even more marked: an alternation between home and away. He would indulge his taste for roaming and then return to his base. For despite his seeming lassitude and the often vague and preoccupied air which had helped earn the "Count No 'Count" nickname, he was engaged in the most intense kind of work as he struggled to master poetic forms, to experiment with drama, and to explore again his potential in another genre: prose fiction.

19

Autumn, 1920-Autumn, 1921

> In any case, he was quite ripe to make the acquaintance, which began with that of the lumber company which at the moment was taking a leisurely bankruptcy in a town where lived a lawyer who had been appointed the referee in the bankruptcy: a family friend of the young man's family and older than he, yet who had taken a liking to the young man and so invited him to come along for the ride too.
>
> —"Mississippi" (21–22)

In Charleston, Jack Stone had been appointed receiver in the bankruptcy of the Lamb-Fish Lumber Company. Lem Oldham and other Oxonians had lost money in the firm. It had carried out one of the biggest operations in the state, buying up tracts of land and methodically cutting flat all the usable timber, destroying them as game-producing areas in the process. General Stone had built his hunting camp near Charleston and had also owned a four-hundred-acre tract there called the Porter farm. The tract he let go in default of drainage taxes. Lamb-Fish bought it and cut the timber, so that in 1916 there had been "lumber in stacks high as a man could make them." Then, the wilderness gone, they sold the land to farmers.

The process of collecting debts which were owed the defunct company and liquidating its assets involved considerable traveling. Phil Stone assisted his brother in some of the work. Faulkner would travel with both of them, to relatively close places such as Clarksdale or to more distant destinations such as Memphis. This suited Faulkner's roaming, foot-loose mood and taste for new and varied experience, stimulated, no doubt, by those months in the foreign environment of Canada. Phil Stone took him on other trips which had little relation to business. By Oxford standards Stone was a sophisticate, a man of the world. He was also an expert poker player. And, being a trial lawyer, he had some experience of people living on the fringes of the law or, indeed, outside it.

Phil had yet to accept Reno DeVaux's invitation to play poker for him, but he still dropped in to see him occasionally. Faulkner would go with him, and sometimes he would see Walter Lee Bates again. If people like the campus wits saw Faulkner as an object of satire, some of his friends had feelings of concern. Dot Wilcox would see him with mismatched shoes, with the elbows out of his coat. Sometimes, she thought, he looked pathetic—trampy and raggedy-looking. (Katrina Carter saw him waiting to change trains at Holly Springs barefooted—the same young man Myrtle Ramey had seen strolling down to the Square adorned with pocket handkerchief, cane, and spats.) And he drank a good deal. He carried his whiskey well, so one could hardly tell that he was feeling it except that he would get just a little thick-tongued.

"Bill," Dot would say, "why do you want to go around looking like that? Don't you want to make something out of yourself?"

"All I want to do is write," he would reply quietly. He was amused at her concern about his appearance. "Who knows, someday you may see a headline in the newspapers, 'Tramp Becomes Famous.' "

At times, however, he would surprise her. One day he telephoned. "Put on your best bib and tucker," he said. "I'm going to take you up to the Moon Lake Club. We'll crash the party." She was ready when he arrived that evening, waiting for him in a white evening dress beaded with gold, wearing her gold evening slippers. They had no trouble getting into the party, and they had a good time, though Faulkner was quiet as usual and danced little. It was nearly three o'clock in the morning by the time they left. Their return along the dark roads was uneventful until suddenly one of the wheels spun off the axle. The car swerved but Faulkner fought it to a stop in a cotton patch. He descended and walked through the mud to the nearest cabin. There he roused a Negro who fetched his team and dragged the car through the mud of the cotton patch and back onto the road. They put the wheel back on and finally Faulkner delivered Dot to the door of her home, safe but wearing golden slippers covered with mud.

Dot was an attractive girl with self-reliance and forthrightness that

Faulkner must have admired. If he wanted to write, that was fine; but it didn't amuse her or overawe her—then or later.

"Dot," he would say, "I could write a book about your life."

"Yes," she would answer, "and nobody would read it." And she would smile and go on to something else.

At home in Oxford Faulkner often appeared to be devoting himself to nothing more strenuous than reflection and recreation. He would join Florrie Friedman, the merchant's daughter, and a few others at the home of Miss Nan Hooper, a music teacher who lived on South Street. They would play five hundred, and it seemed to Florrie that Bill enjoyed the big box of candy Miss Hooper always offered to her guests as much as he did the cards. Occasionally, Florrie would join him and Katrina Carter in a popular group pursuit: a combination possum hunt and picnic.

Sometimes Faulkner would simply go along with the rest. At other times he would be the organizer. First they would engage a Negro who had a good pack of hounds. They would plan to go by moonlight, but if the moon was not bright enough, they would carry lanterns. The hounds would pick up a scent, give tongue, and take off after their quarry. They would eventually tree the possum, after which he would wind up in a sack the Negro carried, later to appear on his table. About ten o'clock, or sooner if the hunting had been particularly good, they would stop and build a bonfire. Chaperon Mae Carter's description of one of these hunts was savored by a student at Natchez High School, where Bob Farley was principal. Farley had particularly enjoyed the hunt, she said. They had gone through country traversed by gullies twenty or thirty feet deep. As the hunt went on, she said, Bob Farley began drinking. Then he had wandered off and walked right into one of the gullies. No one heard him fall, and the impact had knocked the wind out of him so that he couldn't call for help. When he got his breath, he found that the sides were too steep to climb. He decided to make the best of the situation. He got out his miraculously unbroken bottle and waited for rescue. Not at all disturbed, he reasoned that they had to find him before they went home. This account finally got to Farley. It was a good story in a way, but there were two things wrong with it. The victim of the mishap was not he but Bill Faulkner. Farley hadn't even gone on that hunt, but the story nearly ruined him in the eyes of the student.

There was no question about Bill Faulkner's fondness for liquor. He could not afford the brand he found in the Colonel's stock when he worked in the bank, so now he took what he could get, including the powerful "white mule" made by county moonshiners. When he couldn't afford that, there were other sources. An enterprising young man from the county named Edison Avent, another kinsman of T. W. Avent, had moved into town to improve his position in the world. He was a quiet youth with large eyes, a wide, thin mouth, and a nose that looked like the beak of some predatory bird. "He started out with nothing," one observer remarked, "and got rich by being the sharpest horse trader for miles around." At this time he was working as a pharmacist in Dr. Bramlett's drugstore. "He tried to promote some dances to make him some money," Faulkner recalled later. "He asked me to help him. . . . So I'd go by the drugstore in the afternoon and drink Edison's or Dr. Bramlett's prescription alcohol, and talk about the dance. After a week or so of that, then I wouldn't help Edison with his dance." He had of course come by his taste and his capacity naturally. But there were obviously other factors at work besides heredity and conditioning. In his verse he had often imitated Verlaine and Swinburne, neither noted for abstemiousness. And Swinburne—like Verlaine and Rimbaud—had been influenced by the gifted and rather sinister Charles Baudelaire, the poet whose work, in books such as *Les Fleurs du Mal*, had created what Victor Hugo called "a new shudder." Baudelaire courted the muse in any way he could. Toward the end of his life his addiction to both liquor and drugs was notorious. Faulkner was playing the bohemian poet as he experimented with verse forms and images. It is not unlikely that he was interested in experimenting with the preverbal portion of the creative process, too. And for a man who liked liquor anyway, it would provide a pleasant form of experimentation.

Murry Falkner could certainly understand a man's drinking, and probably the impulse toward vagabondage and the avoidance of work, too. But when you put it all together—the drinking, the roaming, the often seedy appearance, plus the assertion that he was going to be a poet—it didn't add up to much for a man already twenty-three years old. Murry Falkner was working hard at his job, and he expected his sons to do the same. And it was difficult for him to credit some of the things Billy's friend Phil Stone would tell him.

"Mr. Murry," he said, "I'm not a writer, I never will be a writer, but I know one when I see one."

The truth was that Murry Faulkner thought this unconventional young lawyer was a bad influence on his son, so he was doubly skeptical of what he might say, particularly when he talked in terms of the distant future.

"He may not make a lot of money for you in your time," Stone said, "but he's got the stuff." Stone would shake his head at the disbelief he met. "I'm a male Cassandra," he would say.

There was, of course, one person who agreed wholeheartedly with Stone's view that Billy Faulkner would become a great man. Maud Faulkner thought he was a genius. This child had gotten his genes from her, not from her big, gruff, sincere, lumbering husband, and she said that if Billy wanted it—this career of a poet—why, so did she. She made Mr. Murry give Billy room and board, some said. But Phil Stone declared that Mr. Murry, too, deserved some credit, for he was, after all, an ordinary man.

Bill Faulkner was doing more work than anyone except a few of the Marionettes realized. He had already finished the one-act play he had told Lucy Somerville about, and the members were free to perform it if they liked. He gave it to Ben, who read it with growing unease. The play was so British it was embarrassing. He couldn't imagine the Marionettes staging it—for Faulkner's sake as well as theirs. But how could he tell this to his shy, diffident friend whose connection with the club was nebulous enough as it was? Apparently Ben handled it tactfully. He simply kept it, and it remained unproduced and unpublished. Faulkner may well have been unconcerned about its reception, for he was working on a very different sort of play which must have absorbed him for a considerable time. Near the end of 1920 Ben received a copy of it.

It was called *Marionettes*, and it was a work as much of visual art as dramatic art. The slim fifty-five-page booklet was one of six copies, and he had made the whole thing himself. The black lettering was fine and sharp, with the characteristic reversed *s*'s. And there were ten drawings: black, exquisitely thin-line pen-and-ink work. The pages were a kind of parchment bound with two staples between cardboard covers with paper pasted over them. The front was black with a white label on which he had lettered:

Marionettes
A Play in One Act
by W. Faulkner

On the verso of the title page within, he had printed, "First Edition 1920." Ben promptly inscribed his name on the flyleaf of the book.

If the text of *Marionettes* displayed some of the themes and conventions of the commedia dell'arte and the pantomime as adapted by Verlaine and others, the illustrations showed a "decadent" influence. This decadence was not unusual. As one writer put it, "Youthful writers trying to look like

Marionettes.

'prematurely decayed poets' read Swinburne, Walter Pater, Ernest Dowson, and Oscar Wilde, and studied the art of Aubrey Beardsley." Faulkner signed his name in his copy of Oscar Wilde's *Salome: A Tragedy in One Act*, illustrated by Beardsley. Though it is impossible to tell when he came into possession of the book, it was an edition published in 1912. In any case, *Marionettes* left no doubt that the author and artist was probably quite as familiar with the work of this English "decadent" as he was with that of his French colleagues. It was scarcely a conventional taste to which Beardsley appealed, with "his playful whimsy, his extravagant grotesqueness, his teasing suggestiveness—often erotic, often hinting at perversity, but always suave, always self-contained." As one writer said, "A Beardsley drawing seems to hide, just beyond the observer's awareness, a sinister and abominable fascinating story. His strange cast of characters includes dwarfs, living human fetuses, Pierrots, Harlequins, satyrs, fauns, hermaphrodites, wan, beautiful and all-knowing women and ugly fat ones, all in ingeniously invented costumes and betraying in their facial expressions, their postures and their gestures a complacent and mildly pleased ennui, a smoldering eroticism, a thoroughly refined and passive licentiousness. The libidinous content of the Beardsleyan tableaux is rendered with an uncompromising and chaste artistic control."

Facing the title page of *Marionettes* was a drawing in which two hugely elongated figures stood on either side of a garden, while in the middle Pierrot—his head bowed, one knee to the ground—held to his face the hand of a slim young girl. Above them, in the upper portion of the drawing, was the legend "Persons." There were six: Pierrot, Marietta, Shade of Pierrot, A Grey Figure, A Lilac Figure, and Spirit of Autumn. Facing page 1 was a night scene: two black, curved poplars framing the full moon which looked down at the highly stylized, thin-line figure of Pierrot asleep. He slumped, his head and arm on a table on which stood a bottle and an overturned wineglass; a high-heeled slipper lay on the ground before the table. The stage directions set the scene in a garden with a pool and foun-

Pierrot.

tain. Pierrot would not stir from his drunken sleep during the entire play. The action would presumably be a wish-fulfilling dream in which the drunken Pierrot's desires were satisfied through the Shade of Pierrot.

A connoisseur of Beardsley might have been reminded of several Beardsley drawings in reading through *Marionettes*. For *Salome* he had done one called "The Woman in the Moon." As the tailpiece for that play he had drawn a satyr and a black-clad figure in a half-mask about to deposit the nude figure of a beautiful nymph in a casket. One of his calendar designs was dominated by a tall, long-gowned figure called "Autumn." He had often used formal gardens in his drawings, sometimes with fountains, and one of his *Yellow Book* covers he had called "The Mysterious Rose Garden."

But if Faulkner had learned something from Beardsley, the finished work was clearly his own—the thin, fine lines quite unlike the often thick bold ones of the Englishman. The figures were chaste and often austere, very different from Beardsley's combination of the sinister and beautiful. And if he had borrowed from the pantomime, the commedia dell'arte, and Verlaine for elements of character and setting, the mood and the lyrics were quite distinctly his own. There was the same melancholy that ran through the cycle of poems about the marble faun. And though the languishing sufferer this time was the girl rather than her suitor, the emotions were the same. Faulkner had combined elements of modes he had worked with before to produce a new resultant. Neither strictly pastoral nor elegiac, neither decadent nor Symbolist, not pantomime and not commedia dell'arte, it was his own attempt at a private vision of beauty. As the cold moon shone down, love lived a little while, then languished and died to the faint strains of music before the tall shadows of the peacocks.

The Arrival of Kitty, which the Marionettes put into production after the Christmas holiday of 1920, was as different from *Marionettes* as could be imagined. It was a broad farce, the action fast and the stage directions full of bits of business. Pretty Jane Foote played Jane, the marriageable niece, and Sis Hopkins played her old-maid aunt. Ben was Bobbie Baxter, the young man who finally got Jane, but not before he had impersonated a Broadway actress named Kitty Benders. To confound the confusion, Kitty Benders of course arrived at Halcyon House, the Catskill hotel setting, during the course of the action. That role was assigned to young Willeen Tull. Lucy and Ella Somerville directed and Bill Faulkner sometimes offered advice on how to portray character. Phil Davidson was gradually becoming very interested in Jane Foote, so he attended the rehearsals even though he was not in this cast. He remembered Faulkner's wandering around in the back of the auditorium, smoking his pipe and giving directions from time to time during rehearsals. His main contribution, though, was in the staging. "The great excitement then in staging," Lucy Somerville remembered, "was to give depth to a set and to avoid absolute dependency on proscenium lights. With an assortment of borrowed lamps and electric wires in everyone's way we managed a fairly natural living room scene." Then, after only a week's rehearsal, "in spite of a doubtful feeling and a fear of bombardment admitted by certain of the members," the curtain of Bob Williams' Lyric Theatre rose for *The Arrival of Kitty* on Friday night, January 7, 1921.

Even the gallery was packed. Each actor seemed to have a following from among the student body, and enough local and topical jokes were slipped in to delight the hometown spectators. The audience "showed its appreciation of the splendid acting and evidence of preparation in almost ceaseless applause." The production was, according to *The Mississippian*'s critic, "a huge success." His praise for the cast was lavish, and he added, "We must commend the Misses Somerville and Mr. Falkner on their fine work in directing and staging the attraction." Pleased with their success, the Marionettes decided to present *Green Stockings*, a romantic play, in two months.

The work with the Marionettes must have been pleasant relief for Faulkner from his intensive reading and poetry writing. He was reading widely in prose. At Christmas one of his gifts had been Sofja Rygier-Nalkowska's *Women: A Novel of Polish Life*. And he read in Hardy and Tolstoy as well as Balzac and other favorites. On his birthday he had received *A Miscellany of American Poetry: 1920*, and on January 5, 1921, Ben had made him a present of William Stanley Braithwaite's *Anthology of Magazine Verse for 1920 and Year Book of American Poetry*. Braithwaite's short introduction was called "Tap-Root or Melting-Pot?" Recent American poetry was more brightly colored and diverse than British but not "so solid or so downright." England might not have so many-faceted a poet as Amy Lowell or one with so resounding a clang of cymbals (both iron and gold) as Vachel Lindsay, but neither did America have "a poet of the deep integrity of Thomas Hardy, a poet so rooted in ancient soil, ancient manners, ancient dialect." It had taken centuries to fuse the myths, legends, and histories which the British poets had at their disposal, and the Americans must await a similar process. "We must convert our necessities into virtues," he wrote; "lacking the deep soil of memory, which is also prejudice and tradition, cultivate the thinner soil which may also be reason and cheerfulness. Our hope lies in diversity, in variety, in colors yet untried, in forms yet unsuspected." Braithwaite was willing to grant that Lindsay had lately been using African materials for poetic purposes, and that less well-known poets were now turning to Indian materials. But "Indian and negro materials . . . are in our poetry still hardly better than aspects of the exotic. No one who matters actually thinks that a national literature can be founded on such alien bases." Making one of his extremely rare marginal comments, William Faulkner drew an arrow pointing to this passage. Above it, in large letters, he wrote, "Good God."

Though Braithwaite might look to the future for real poetic achievement in America, Faulkner saw it already in the work of a man Braithwaite hadn't even mentioned, a poet beside whom "the British nightingales, Mr. Vachel Lindsay with his tin pan and iron spoon, Mr. Kreymborg with his lithographic water coloring, and Mr. Carl Sandburg with his sentimental Chicago propaganda are so many puppets fumbling in windy darkness." The poet was Conrad Aiken, a South Carolinian who had graduated from Harvard in 1911. In an essay on Aiken's *Turns and Movies* (1916), which appeared in *The Mississippian* for February 16, 1921, Faulkner set forth in his emphatic critical style the reasons for Aiken's preeminence. "He, alone of the entire yelping pack," he wrote, "seems to have a definite goal in mind." Faulkner had liked Aiken's *The Jig of Forslin*, of 1917, a kind of novel in verse which bodied forth Forslin's dreams patterned after musical theory. Faulkner had admired his facile and melodious but difficult and often vague tone poems in *The House of Dust*, of 1920. The younger poet was fascinated by what he saw there as "an abstract three dimensional verse patterned on polyphonic music form . . . for as yet no one has made a successful attempt to synthesize musical reactions with abstract documentary reactions." *Turns and Movies* consisted of fifteen short sketches of stage life followed by four longer poems. One reviewer had called the work "bloodshot," and others had been shocked by its "naturalism" or "raw realism." Unlike the other two books this one was much more concerned with narrative and with concrete, familiar human situations. Faulkner apparently liked this as well as the technical facility, and he quoted three quatrains from "Discordants," one of the longer poems. Thirty-five years later he would remember some of the lines he quoted:

Music I heard with you was more than music,
And bread I broke with you was more than bread. . . .

Amy Lowell had tried polyphonic prose which was to him "merely a literary flatulency." But Aiken had developed steadily, absorbing many influences while shaping his own style, so that at times "it seems that he is completing a cycle back to the Greeks, again there seem to be faint traces of the French symbolists. . . ." His work was "one rift of heaven sent blue" in the fog "generated by the mental puberty of contemporary American versifiers. . . ." In perhaps fifteen years he might emerge as "our first great poet. . . ."

As for prose fiction, there was no doubt in Faulkner's mind, or Phil Stone's, about who was the greatest artist in the field. It was Balzac. Faulkner would later say that he and the Young Colonel would read through Dumas every year, but now he could not compare with Balzac. He and Stone would read Balzac in a set Stone owned that was full of annotations. They admired him particularly for his handling of motivation, of human psychology. "By God, Balzac was right and we were wrong," Stone said, recalling the way they would analyze character as they read. "He always kept doing just what we didn't expect." Sometimes, in the evening or on weekends, the two men would go riding in Stone's convertible, nicknamed "Drusilla." When they went to Memphis, the places and scenes they would see there would have much more in common with the harsh realities of Balzac than the musicalized visions of Aiken.

Memphis had no monopoly on violence. Indeed, the *Eagle* regularly ran new accounts of officers seeking stills and moonshiners greeting them with gunfire. Often the officers would "capture" the stills and arrest the manufacturers of the "white mule." Violence was endemic. In March a Water Valley Negro was sought for attacking a sixty-year-old woman on a lonely road in the woods. Bloodhounds tracked him down and he was jailed. Shortly afterwards, however, a mob broke in and seized the prisoner. Then, four miles outside of town, they riddled his body with bullets. Two weeks later, in April, there was a double murder: two prohibition agents killed in a gun battle near Jackson. But Memphis was a special area. Historical forces had combined to make it so.

Before the bluff on which the city stood a panorama had passed: "the French, the Spaniards, the Chickasaws, the Indian factors, the land speculators, the flatboatmen, the slave-traders, the Whig merchants, the Federal soldiers, the carpetbaggers, the doctors and priests who had died fighting the yellowjack—but like the buffalo and the wild pigeon they were forgotten. In their places were a new people who knew not their fathers. . . ." It was the yellow jack that hit the city in 1878 as neither the war nor anything else had ever done, evoking heroism as well as baseness. "Vance Avenue Alma," one of the most celebrated madams in Memphis, turned her house into a hospital and nursed the stricken until she succumbed herself. The disease spread as far upriver as St. Louis before it subsided. In Memphis, most of the Germans had moved out, while the Irish and others had stayed and died. The people who replaced them were for the most part white and Negro country people from Arkansas, Mississippi, Alabama, and Tennessee. Memphis became a city of Anglo-Saxons and Baptists. It was also a city of transients. As much as forty years after the epidemic, only two percent of its inhabitants had been born there. It had been a riverboat town, a town "of frontier commerce, tough, unkempt, and sin-ridden." With the influx of Negroes after the Civil War, Beale Street began to open up; and in that burgeoning district there were not only the whores and pimps of an earlier day, but flashy gamblers and bad men, killers with names such as "Totelow" and "Joe Baby." By the time Bill Faulkner and Phil Stone became frequent visitors, Memphis had become notorious as "the murder capital of the United States."

New factors compounded those which had made Memphis so violence-prone in the past. The white people moving into the city brought with them certain agrarian values which their champions might link to concepts such as honor and duty, but a major tenet was white supremacy, and a corollary to it was the "sub-human position of the Negro. . . ." By 1906 the *Commercial Appeal*'s editorial writer was moved to protest. "This thing of killing negroes without cause," he wrote, was being "overdone. . . ." What some people apparently did not realize was that "white men who kill negroes as a pastime . . . usually end up by killing white men." There were other kinds of license. The unwritten law was invoked by pistol-wielding husbands, and personal grievances were often settled under a vulgarized code duello. Two years after the turn of the century, it was estimated, one man in every six in Memphis carried a pistol. The statistics were staggering: 18 known houses of prostitution in 1878 in a trade employing more than 1,500 women; more than twice as many saloons as Birmingham and Atlanta together in 1903; 181 preachers and 163 saloon keepers in 1900. By 1916 there were 89.9 murders per 100,000 population in Memphis. The next highest city in the United States was Atlanta, with a figure of 31. The picture could be summed up simply: "Used to plenty of room in the open spaces, its citizens were addicted to violence, carried guns, and believed in the right of private vengeance. In general their views about health and sanitation were almost aboriginal." A reform movement had made Ed Crump (originally from Holly Springs, Mississippi) mayor of the city in 1909. He was beaten six years later and would not regain the office until the 1920's. By 1921 Memphis' preeminence was unchallenged. It was unquestionably "the toughest town on the river."

Memphis' notoriety came from more than just its boisterous history plus a recent overlay of certain "agrarian" values. It was as much due to the organized vice which flourished during both reform and "regular" administrations. Individual entrepreneurs might here and there own houses of prostitution. But given the necessity of buying protection from politicians, police, and others, practiced professional criminals with underworld connections were more often the owners and chief profiteers. Even before the turn of the century Memphis' sporting life boasted "some of the plushest brothels along the Mississippi." They were located on Gayoso Street, a lively thoroughfare named after Manuel de Gayoso, the Spanish governor when Spain's flag flew over Natchez near the end of the eighteenth century. Some were celebrated, like the Stanley Club at 121 Gayoso. Mrs. Grace Stanley, a Negro, ran the establishment with a kind of elegance, until she was stabbed to death by one of her girls. Twenty years later, in 1921, Gayoso was still the heart of the Tenderloin District, which lay closer to the major downtown shopping area than any counterpart in a major American city. Gayoso started at Riverside Drive, overlooking the Wolf River and the Mississippi into which it flowed two blocks further south. The street ran east, crossing Front Street, Main Street, and then Second Street. From there for more than three solid blocks—across Third Street, Hernando, and South Fourth to Wellington—it was lined solidly with two-story brownstone houses. And between Second and Third on Gayoso, the rear ends of several of these raffish establishments presented themselves to the back premises of the stately Hotel Peabody, facing the other way and looking down on Main Street. To the west, off Gayoso and parallel to the river, was Mulberry Street. There stood the lesser houses staffed with white girls and then, contiguous with them, the Negro houses. By 1921 Memphis had a population of over 162,000, and a not inconsiderable fraction of it depended on or did business with those variously sad, rowdy, sedate houses of pleasure on the far west side of the old river town.

Phil Stone would go to Memphis from time to time for business—for local clients or perhaps Lamb-Fish bankruptcy affairs—and pleasure. He knew friends of Reno DeVaux there (Stone spelled his name Deveau), and he doubtless enjoyed pitting his skill against professionals at the green baize-covered tables. Being a man of the world, Stone would sometimes visit in Gayoso Street or Mulberry Street. And he would take Bill Faulkner along with him, just as he had asked the younger man along to similar, if more modest, places in Clarksdale. Faulkner apparently enjoyed these trips and this brief immersion in such an alien atmosphere. For one so much a spectator and increasingly fascinated by human behavior, it was an admirable opportunity to watch, and to speculate. He had always been interested in strange, out-of-the-ordinary people, and there were plenty of them here. For another thing, there was a greater variety of whiskey in Memphis. So it was a pleasant change for him to visit one of the brownstones on Mulberry or Gayoso with his friend, whether he went upstairs or just sat downstairs in the parlor, listening quietly and putting in an amiable word now and then.

Faulkner rarely gambled, but he was not impervious to temptation. On one occasion, he seems to have embraced it almost fatalistically. He returned one noontime to the room he and Jack were sharing at the Peabody and asked Jack if he had any money left. Jack knew that when his brother had gone out earlier he had close to one hundred dollars with him. He also knew that since then Bill had been drinking. Jack told him he had about twenty dollars. Bill said he would like to borrow it. When Jack gave it to him, he walked to the door and then stopped and turned. As though he felt Jack was entitled to some sort of explanation, he told him he had lost his money in a crap game—in about fifteen minutes, as a matter of fact. When he admitted that he was going back to the same game, Jack asked him if he thought this twenty would go the way of the others.

"It probably will," he said. "But I've got to go back."

To Jack's surprise, Bill asked him if he wanted to go along. As they walked under the hot midday sun, Jack tried to point out the folly of throwing good money after bad. Bill paid no attention as they made their way up North Main Street. Finally he climbed the steps of a shabby, rundown brownstone and knocked on the door.

The door was opened by a "seedy looking character" who silently admitted them. Closing the door, he picked up a jug of clear corn liquor, lifted it, and drank. Jack watched him, shuddering inwardly. Then the man wiped his forehead, staring straight ahead at the cracking plaster of the wall. "Aah-aah," he said. "Eeyie!"

Bill took the jug from the man's seemingly nerveless grasp and passed it to Jack. Lifting it, Jack wondered "as I always did how a man could bring himself to partake of something so murderous to the taste and so repellent to the smell." Next Bill helped himself. Then he looked at the owner of the jug, who simply pointed to the room above.

"Follow me," Bill said, and preceded Jack up two rickety flights of stairs. They entered a large bare room in which only one window was raised against the oppressive heat. The silent players stood about a large table covered with a white sheet. As one grasped the dice, Bill stepped into the circle. When the perspiring shooter put down a ten-dollar bill, Bill covered it with his twenty and said that there was ten more against the shooter. Jack watched another gambler immediately cover what had been his twenty-dollar bill. Drops of sweat splattered on the sheet as the man threw the dice. Jack saw his brother turn from the table even before one voice spoke: "A natural eleven, baby, a natural eleven!"

Bill was silent walking back to the Peabody. Wondering what had drawn him to that ill-omened place and what had caused him, moreover, to return to it, Jack thought that "perhaps he felt that the only way he could disassociate himself completely from something undesirable was to buy himself out just as he had bought himself in." Jack couldn't resist one question, though. How, he asked, had he come upon such a dump? "It wasn't hard to do," Bill said. As far as Jack knew, this was Bill's last experience with the dice. But it was by no means his last visit to the purlieus of the Memphis netherworld.

In Oxford the Marionettes were going ahead with rehearsals of *Green Stockings.* Bill Faulkner "worked like a beaver," according to president Wasson, on sets and props, taking particular pleasure in finding out-of-the-ordinary props called for in the script. (He would be listed a "Property Manager" in *Ole Miss* for 1921.) Ella Somerville directed. The play was staged at the Lyric on March 4 to enthusiastic applause. On the twelfth the Marionettes had a meeting with refreshments at which they could look back on their second triumph in as many tries. All the members were present but three—one of them Bill Faulkner, who, according to the *Mississippian* item, "was at the time at Memphis. . . ."

There were other conspicuous successes in Oxford that spring. In early April it was reported that Lemuel E. Oldham would probably be appointed United States Attorney for the Northern District in Mississippi. By mid-June he had been confirmed in the U.S. Senate and sworn in at the county courthouse. In other fields of endeavor, Johncy and Jack Falkner had made the town baseball team. Murry Faulkner had been advanced from assistant secretary to secretary of the University of Mississippi. In May, Ben Wasson was granted a license to practice law. Dewey Linder was home visiting his sister. He now had a D.D.S. after his name. Billy Faulkner was still writing poems and drawing pictures.

He was doing a series of drawings for the volume of *Ole Miss* which would appear that spring. On May 5 he published his last poem in *The Mississippian*, something very different from the thirteen which had preceded it there. "Co-Education at Ole Miss" was light and satiric, its eleven lines of monologue combining diction both slangy and archaic. It was the proposal of Ernest to Ernestine, which ended,

An lov'st thou me
As I love thee,
Let's off to Gretna Green—O.

Like almost all its predecessors, it was signed "W. Falkner." He was currently engaged in something very different: the longest series of poems he had hitherto assembled. Some were new and some had been composed the previous summer or earlier. Estelle Franklin was coming home that month. Bill and Jack never mentioned the thwarted love affair, but it was scarcely out of mind. "I don't think Bill ever stopped thinking of her during the years she was gone," Jack later reflected, "or ever had an idea of someday marrying anyone else." The poems were for her.

Commencement came and went. Bill Faulkner watched part of the ceremonies. "I remember only too well meeting Bill at the Flagpole during Commencement," Russell Pigford said, "how he spoke to me, 'Hello, Piggy,' pinching the word Piggy, and how he with apparent timidity handed me one of his six copies of *Marionettes.*" It was apparently his last copy, given to a friend and brother S.A.E. After he had given Ben his copy he had made the other five and asked Ben, "Will you sell them for me at five dollars apiece?" Ben had sold four, and this was the last one.

It was a busy season for Estelle. She and Katrina Carter went to Memphis to spend a week. She and Cho-Cho paid their usual visit to Mrs. Hairston, her beloved mother-in-law, in Columbus. But Bill Faulkner was often at the Oldham home, sitting, talking with Estelle, listening to her at the piano, or playing with Cho-Cho. His time was not completely free, however. His father had gotten him work at the university, and faculty members would see him in unlikely places. His brother John recalled one:

"They were painting the law building, which had a steeple. No one else would paint the steeple so Bill did. He tied himself to it with ropes and painted it from top to bottom. After that Mother told Dad not to get Bill any more jobs without talking it over with her first." He worked painting the inside and outside woodwork on the Lyceum Building, and one day Vice-chancellor Alfred Hume stood and watched him neatly letter the numbers over doors.

But he managed to find time that summer to complete the book of poems, now grown to eighty-eight pages, and present it to Estelle. It was another carefully crafted gift volume. He had covered the thin 5 1/2-by-8-inch boards with a brownish-green mottled paper. On a small square of white linen paper in the upper right-hand corner in India ink he had lettered the title, *Vision in Spring*, and his name. He had pasted a strip of white parchment or vellum over the spine. The white pages within were stapled together. The table of contents showed fourteen sections—ten titled, and all identified with Roman numerals. This time he (or perhaps Stone's secretary) had typed the poems neatly, using a purple ribbon and making few overstrikes or erasures.

The six-page title poem, which in typescript had been characteristically worked and reworked, showed signs that it was linked to both "L'Apres-Midi d'un Faune" and the cycle of poems about the faun. The speaker's voice is like the faun's. He looks back, "old and weary and lonely," to a vanished love. The pain he feels (as at the end of "L'Apres-Midi d'un Faune") "Was my heart, my ancient heart that broke. . . ."

The four-page "Interlude" which followed consisted of eight six-line stanzas which often used couplets but were actually irregular in meter and rhyme. Though the scene was an empty darkened street, the lone speaker heard reeds and pipes, envisioning dancing feet. The recurrence of music and dreamy imagery suggested both Verlaine and Aiken, but some of the lines suggested another poet.

The horned gates swing to, and clang,

says the speaker, in a figure reminiscent of T. S. Eliot's "Sweeney Among the Nightingales."

The twenty-page, eight-part poem which followed drew on a familiar source of imagery and characters. It was entitled "The World and Pierrot. A Nocturne." Again there were echoes of Eliot's "The Love Song of J. Alfred Prufrock" and "Preludes":

Now that the city grows black and chill and empty,—
Who am I, thinks Pierrot, who am I
To stretch my soul out rigid across the sky?
Who am I to chip the silence with footsteps,
Then see the silence fill my steps again?

Surprisingly, there was an echo of Kipling's "Recessional" in lines like

Now that the tumult and shouting has died away,

and

The shouting dies, the kings depart. . . .

But this poem was another tone poem, free verse made of long lines that occasionally rhymed. It was actually much like *Marionettes*, with Pierrot alone under the starlit night, before a tree-fringed wall, dreaming, hearing music, and seeing imaginary dancers.

"After the Concert" was much less self-consciously poetic in its idiom. Its lines were still uneven—though the first portion used irregular rhyming, somewhat in the manner of some of Yeats's later conversational poems—and halfway through it resolved itself into quatrains. The lover's description was quite realistic. After a concert, "Arm in arm in intimate talk" they stroll

In a spring of certainties whitely shattered about us,
To a troubling music oft refrained,
Into the darkness that some day will enfold us,—
When that is gained, then all is gained.

"Portrait," the three-page poem which followed, was similar. In its six quatrains the lover spoke softly, as they strolled after "tonight's movie." The first quatrain suggested Yeats in a poem such as "After Long Silence":

Lift your hand between us, dimly raise your face,
And draw the opaque curtains from your eyes.
Let us walk here, softly checked with shadow
And talk of careful trivialities.

Section VI was untitled. Again lovers walked together hearing music where lilacs grew against a wall. The three-and-a-half-page poem used an easy Yeatsian rhyme scheme, but two thirds of the way through, the voice of Eliot broke in again:

Let us go, then; you and I, while evening grows
And a delicate violet thins the rose
That stains the sky;
We will go alone there, you and I,
And watch the trees step naked from the shadow
Like women shrugging upward from their gowns.

Estelle Franklin lettered in the title "A Symphony" at the top of the six-page poem which came next in the book. Made up of irregular stanzas of couplets, the poem was also divided, roughly, into three movements, like a musical composition. As day changed to night, Faulkner described the dark, the moon, silence, and the stars, in terms of half a dozen instruments. Again there was the pervasive melancholy, as the specter of man's mortality mocked his pleasures as finally transitory.

Neither the author nor the reader supplied a title for poem VIII. In it a sleeper on a darkening beach is waked by rain. He listens to the sea and a tolling bell, then meditates on change and death before sleeping again as darkness falls and the rising sea laps at "his limbs and back and thighs."

In the 118-line "Love Song" which followed, Faulkner had seemingly set himself the task of paraphrasing Eliot's 131-line poem of four years before. Though it was an imitation, it revealed states of mind which might lie behind Faulkner's behavior. Prufrock's sense of boredom and unease was one Faulkner knew well. He began,

Shall I walk, then, through a corridor of profundities
Carefully erect (I am taller than I look)
To a certain door—and shall I dare
To open it? I smooth my mental hair
With an oft changed phrase that I revise again
Until I have forgotten what it was at first;
Settle my tie with: I have brought a book,
Then seat myself with: We have passed the worst.

The speaker hears the party chatter and tries to join in. He observes a disquietingly attractive woman, then goes to receive his cup and napkin. He thinks of walking the street outside, while passing time "ticks" his "thinning hair," and laments to himself, "I grow old, I grow old." Like Prufrock, the speaker feels he should have had another identity:

I should have been a priest in floorless halls
Whose hand, worn thin by turning endless pages,
Lifts, and strokes his face, and falls. . . .
While darkness lays soft fingers on his eyes
And strokes the lamplight from his brow,
to wake him, and he dies.

So it ends, even closer to Eliot's poem than the beginning.

Section X of the book was a two-page poem called "The Dancer." The cruel dancer was "Youth," and she carried on a dialogue with her lover. Section XI, an untitled nine-page poem, was very different and clearly the best of the book's longer works. In one typed version Faulkner had called the poem "Marriage." It was couched in a modern idiom, and it seemed the most clearly personal of all the poems. Here was no faun mourning for vanished nymph, but instead a man sitting by firelight, watching a lovely woman, hearing her at the piano, wanting her, and striving desperately to control his precarious emotional balance. The poet immediately established a tension between the melancholy yet sensual external environment and the almost hysterical turmoil in the man's mind:

Laxly reclining, he sees her sitting there
With firelight like a hand laid on her hair,
With firelight like a hand upon the keys
Playing a music of lustrous silent gold. . . .
The firelight steadily hums, steadily wheeling
Until his brain, stretched and tautened, suddenly cracks.

In the next section—Faulkner may well have thought of it as a movement of a piano sonata or tone poem—he moved into the mind of the woman at the keyboard:

Could she but stay here forever, where slow rain slants
above them,
With starlight soft as rain upon her breast;
Could she but dream forever on this river
Through springs and springs, back to a certain spring
That blossomed in shattering slow fixations, cruel in beauty
Of nights and days. . . .

Finally the music ceases. She turns and rises. He watches her as she mounts the stair, seeing, as he hungers for her, "That nervous strength that was ever his surprise." Then suddenly, in the poem's last line, a dramatic reversal occurs:

At the turn she stops, and shivers there,
And hates him as he steadily mounts the stair.

The next poem, entitled "Orpheus," had been reworked extensively before Faulkner included it in *Vision in Spring.* Faulkner had rearranged the order of some of the original six stanzas and had made one very effective addition. The original poem had shown Orpheus singing in the desolate dusk. Then he spoke, recalling his beloved, after which the poem ended in a stanza almost identical with the opening one. Now Faulkner introduced Eurydice, though without name, speaking of her love and longing, before he closed the revision with a stanza identical with the first stanza of the earlier version:

Here he stands, while eternal evening falls
And it is like a dream between grey walls
Dimly falling, dimly falling
Between two walls of shrunken topless stone,
Between two walls with silence on them grown.
Here he stands, in a litter of leaves upon the floor,
In a solemn silver of scattered springs;
Among the smooth green buds before the door
He stands and sings.

"Philosophy" was a poem which might have been written by a member of the English "graveyard school" of poetry in the eighteenth century. The shadowed gloom of the cemetery frightened "the pulsing thrush" to silence, there where "headstone glimmers dimly in the gloom."

The book ended with a softer poem. The four stanzas of "April" adhered to an unusually elaborate rhyme scheme, but the imagery was familiar. Somewhere a slim girl went at sunset "To meet her shepherd" before the night descended. The poem closed to a nightingale's song by starlight:

. . . In dim-lit ways
A sighing wind shakes in its grasp
A straight resilient poplar in the mist,

Until its reaching hands unclasp,
And then the wind and sky bend down and kiss
Its simple, cool whitely breathless face.

Vision in Spring was a personal gift, which Estelle would take back to the Far East with her. At the bottom of the simple title page was the typed phrase "Manuscript Edition. 1921." But the poet meant some of his poems to be read by others, too. Phil Stone's secretary kept sending manuscripts out, and they kept coming back, gradually filling a filing cabinet. It had been nearly two years since the acceptance from *The New Republic.* Some of *Vision in Spring* did appear that summer, but in a local publication: *Ole Miss* for 1920–1921. Faulkner took Section II of the poem—which concentrated on Columbine—and used it alone under the title "Nocturne" with a few small changes. He printed the poem, as always, with the *s*'s reversed, dividing it into two boxes on the left- and right-hand pages. Against a black background, broken only by stars and moon, he drew Pierrot and Columbine rising out of the tops of tall candle flames.

Faulkner was also represented by four other drawings in *Ole Miss* that year. One, entitled "Fish, Flesh, Fowl," showed three junior officers of the Navy, Army, and Air Corps. Below were listed the members of the university's American Legion post. His drawing for the A.E.F. Club showed a bearded sergeant leaning against a lamppost on the Boulevard des Italiens. An illustrated border for the Marionettes' section bore the clear marks of his style: elongated figures in meticulous fine-line strokes. He signed a third drawing—an illustration for that club of recent memory, the Red and Blue. It showed a seven-piece Negro jazz band and two graceful dancers. The musicians were apparently drawn for comic effect, some of them in violent motion, others in frozen stylized postures. It was a craftsman's work, and it seems possible that he might still have been thinking of some sort of profession in art.

From time to time he would put on his house-painting clothes. Like the Falkners, Dr. Brown and his family lived in a university house, and he did some painting for them. One of his jobs was the main staircase. He would apply the brush, slowly and meticulously, and fifteen-year-old Edith Brown would sit on the stairs and engage him in long conversations.

He got out on the golf course that summer, with his brothers and with another foursome, comprising J. D. Thames, an end on the football team named Frank Leftwich, and Sonny Bell, the son of James Warsaw Bell, who was dean of the school of commerce and business administration and a camping friend of Murry Falkner. The boys would flip a coin for partners and tee off. If they were rich, Jack Falkner said, they might play for a nickel a hole. Faulkner had by now given up the RAF breeches for plus fours so baggy that they seemed to reach nearly to his ankles. He was an unorthodox player, using an open stance and sometimes cocking the club over his shoulder, but he was accurate. He might not drive far, but he always stayed on the fairway. To men such as Thames and Leftwich, Faulkner had something almost birdlike about him, with his short stature and sharp features. He was amiable but unpredictable. After raking the sand of a green and playing it, they might go up to the next tee only to find that it was Faulkner's turn and he hadn't even teed his ball up. Instead he would be off to one side, writing something down on an envelope. "Come on, Bill," they would say, "you're costing us money." Sometimes they felt that he was not just one but two or three people. And as the summer wore on he appeared more moody, more eccentric.

In one respect it had been an eventful summer. The former dean of the school of education had publicly charged the chancellor with gross immorality. Chancellor Joseph Neely Powers was guilty, said former dean Roswell W. Rogers, of having illicit relations with women. He also charged that Powers, an appointee of the Bilbo-Russell faction, "Lacks the educational equipment essential . . . does not hold a degree from any reputable institution of learning . . . is lacking in executive ability and does not possess the backbone essential to proper performance of the duties of his office." At the trustees' hearing, James Warsaw Bell and Vice-chancellor Alfred Hume—men deeply loyal to the university—testified to the chancellor's good character. Rogers, said Powers, was an unstable man and actually Powers had cautioned Rogers about an affair that he had been carrying on. The trustees exonerated the chancellor.

Oxford could scarcely have looked any different to Professor Stark Young when he returned on September 21 to visit his father after traveling in Italy for a year. There was news, of course, some of it from his friend Phil Stone. At the age of twenty-eight he had been appointed Assistant United States District Attorney for the Northern District of Mississippi. Attorney General Daugherty had appointed him on the recommendation of United States Attorney Oldham. Stone had made a brilliant record, the *Eagle* reported, which everyone knew. In the family it was said that when he finished at the Yale Law School, former President Taft, a faculty member there, had asked him to come into his own firm. But Stone declined. Mississippi was the only place for him. Now his career had justified his choice. Not only would he assist Lem Oldham in the federal work, he would be a partner in private practice, for a merger had been announced. The new firm of James Stone, Oldham, Stone & Stone would operate in both Oxford and Charleston. Stone told Young all about this, and also about the efforts of his friend Billy Faulkner, the aspiring writer.

They were an oddly assorted trio of Oxonians—a forty-year-old writer and Amherst English teacher, a twenty-eight-year-old lawyer, and a twenty-three-year-old aspiring poet. Young and Stone were both above middle height and bald, Stone so sensitive that he wore a hat whenever he was not alone or in court. They both loved literature passionately, with a special feeling for the classic languages. But beyond this there were more differences than similarities. Phil Stone always said that when he was an Ole Miss undergraduate, Mr. Stark Young had opened his mind with the talks they had during Young's summer visits to his father. But Stone's tastes had grown more catholic, and some of Young's enthusiasms he could not share.

Young liked to keep working while he was vacationing so he rented a room over a store in the northwest corner of the Square. Sometimes on a hot summer day Stone and Faulkner would climb the stairs to Young's workroom. (Other Oxonians had left to escape the heat—John Falkner and his family and Sallie Murry, for instance, were guests of Lee Russell at Biloxi on the Gulf Coast.) On one of these visits the variance in taste became embarrassing. Young was still full of Italy. He had embraced all things Italian, even speaking sympathetically of Mussolini and the Fascists. He was enthusiastic about the swashbuckling poet-aviator-lover Gabriele D'Annunzio. Young immediately sensed that Stone and Faulkner felt there was something a bit ridiculous about D'Annunzio. Young's long face stiffened. "He still has quite a following, you know," he said coldly. Stone and Faulkner burst out laughing. Young sat there, silent and furious.

But both men admired Young. If they were rare birds in the eyes of the average citizen of Oxford, Young was a true exotic. Even his own father, old Dr. Young, hadn't the vaguest idea of what writing was all about. He couldn't understand the imaginative process by which a man made something up that had never existed before. Young wryly remarked that local people who had read his stories would tell him they didn't understand how he could remember so much. Faulkner sympathized. He knew how people could fail to understand that fiction could be written so truly that it would be what people would do or had done in specific situations the writer never heard of. And Young returned this sympathy and understanding—generously, as it would turn out.

Some thought that Young had helped Faulkner before. When he had decided to enter the university, Maud Brown said, Young had "presented a letter to the administration stating that William had gifts that would prove to be of value to the university and asked, as a personal favor, that he be allowed to enter and take such courses as he desired," He had first met the boy in the summer of 1914 when Faulkner had accompanied Stone on one of his visits to Young. Since then Young had watched his progress in the poems he wrote. Faulkner, Young recalled, "would bring me a notebook of them. I can still see it lying in the parlor table drawer." He had no doubt seen the pastoral poems and most of those that went into *Vision in Spring.* He remembered, he said, that "they strove for great intensity of feeling." During these summer visits Faulkner would sometimes open up a bit and tell Young something of his life in Oxford. "It seemed more and more futile," Young said, "that anyone so remarkable as he was should be thus bruised and wasted. . . ." Young wanted to help. "I suggested that he come to New York and sleep on my sofa till Miss Prall, a friend of mine, manager of the bookshop in Lord and Taylor's corner, could find him a place there and he could find a room." She "would be able to give him a job there that would tide him over till he found something better suited to his needs . . . ." Now Faulkner had an escape if he wanted it. He could get away, go north again if he liked, as he had done three years before.

Young went back to New York, and school began again at the university. Soon Cornell Franklin would arrive to join his wife and daughter. He had become a federal judge, trying cases and transferring his court periodically from one of the Hawaiian Islands to another. Now he was moving, however, and when the visits to the Oldhams and the Franklins had been concluded, he and Estelle and Victoria would return to Honolulu briefly before traveling further east to settle in Shanghai. Stone was busy with his new federal job as well as his private practice. Many students Faulkner had known were now graduated and gone or immersed in graduate school. As his general sense of dissatisfaction gnawed at him, his moodiness deepened. Stone urged him to do something to change his circumstances. In New York he could at least try to meet some editors and critics and attempt to interest them in his work. He could also spend some time in studying art. He had done very well up to now as a self-taught artist, but if he were to go any farther, he would profit from some professional instruction. He considered going to Cuba, he later said, to do some interpreting in connection with the Lamb-Fish bankruptcy proceedings, even though he felt that his year of college Spanish did not qualify him for the job. Instead, he decided to take Young up on his offer, and Stone wrote Young that Faulkner was coming.

"I had one hundred dollars," Faulkner later said. "I had been painting, you know. So with sixty dollars of my stake spent for railroad fare I went to New York." Once more he left the Memphis station in the home-and-away pattern of alternation that would increasingly mark his life.

20

Autumn, 1921

So we taken the train in Memphis that night and the next day we was in Virginia—Bristol then Roanoke and Lynchburg and turned northeast alongside the blue mountains. . . .

. . . New York wasn't made for no climate known to man but at least some weather was jest made for New York. In which case this was sholy some of it: one of them soft blue drowsy days in the early fall when the sky itself seems like it was resting on the earth like a soft blue mist, with the tall buildings rushing up into it and then stopping, the sharp edges fading like the sunshine wasn't jest shining on them but kind of humming, like wires singing.

—*The Mansion* (165, 166)

"Greenwich Village. . . . a place with a few unimportant boundaries but no limitations where young people of any age go to seek dreams."

—*The Town* (350)

"Young wasn't at home," Faulkner later said. "He wasn't at home for a week. Lived on my forty dollars till he got to town. Then I moved in on Young. He had just one bedroom so I slept on an antique Italian sofa in his front room. It was too short. I didn't learn until three years later that Young lived in mortal terror that I would push the arm off that antique sofa while I slept." Young, too, would recall the visit, but not with the same particulars. "How . . . different that homely denim sofa, bought at a sale, was from that of the interviews: an antique I so preciously feared would be ruined by the wild young genius!"

Early in Faulkner's stay, perhaps while he waited for Young to return, he took on some odd jobs, he said. One was washing dishes in a Greek restaurant. Finally, Young was able to get him the job he had promised. Young had met Elizabeth Prall, manager of the Doubleday bookstore at the corner of 38th Street and Fifth Avenue, through her brother, David. When he and David returned from their European trips, she had first chance at the new books they had collected. The bookstore was, in effect, a subsidiary of Lord & Taylor's department store, and as a convenience to customers, books could be charged on Lord & Taylor accounts. It was a good spot, with both transient trade and steady customers from a nearby club next to the Farmers' and Loan Bank. One day Stark Young had broached the subject to Elizabeth Prall, a tiny, cultured woman who had once taught Greek. "Don't you want a nice young man from the South?" he asked. She was glad to take Faulkner on Young's recommendation. Thanksgiving was coming and they usually had to put on more help for the Christmas rush, anyway. He began work, and she immediately found that she had made a good choice.

Bill Faulkner was a good book clerk—polite, interested, and one of the best salesmen in the store. He got along well with his boss, always addressing her as "Miss Elizabeth" in his soft-spoken way. She would have him wait on old ladies, who loved him. He would suggest things for them to read. "All the customers fell for him like a ton of bricks," Miss Prall said. "He sold armfuls of books." Soon they were sending the tough customers to him. "They looked at him and were charmed."

Every day Elizabeth Prall found herself busy until six, so she did not see much of her nice young man from the South. But she did get some sense of what he was like. He had lots of ideas, she remembered, and he gave the impression that "he thought he could do lots of things." What he did on his own time was of course his own business, but Miss Prall sometimes got the impression that he did quite a lot of drinking. As a matter of fact, Stark Young was shocked at how much this short, slim twenty-four-year-old could consume. It may have been one of the reasons why Young did not insist that he remain with him. Also, he had the somewhat annoying habit of cleaning his shoes on the table and simply leaving them there when he had finished. Faulkner moved out and found himself a room near Elizabeth Prall. It cost him $2.50 of his $11-a-week salary, he later said. It was a dreadful room, Elizabeth remembered, but the would-be poet was now residing in that American substitute for the Left Bank, Greenwich Village.

Eighty-five years earlier a center of rural aristocracy far north of Manhattan's noisy center of trade and commerce, Greenwich Village had long since been surrounded and by-passed as the city pushed north to the Harlem River and beyond. Beginning at 12th Street and ranging from Washington Square west to the Hudson River, it extended southward until it came up against crowded stretches of Washington Market and the modest skyscrapers above Battery Park. But to some it was not so much a place as a state of mind. Young men and women from all parts of the country came there to be freer of restraints, to embrace the cult of the new—whether in surrealist art or radical manifestoes—to try free expression and perhaps free love, but also to try to paint, sculpt, write, or compose. There were many Village residents who followed the most ordinary and mundane of pursuits, but the special cachet the Village had acquired came from those who were different—who, at their best, were lively, creative, and colorful. There were many who were colorful.

"The people who call themselves Villagers are generally consecrated to some artistic pursuit," wrote one observer. "As the Quartier Latin is to Paris, so is Greenwich Village to New York. It is, indeed, from the Quartier Latin that the women have borrowed the smocks, the sandals, the bobbed hair and the tam o'shanters. . . . If you are a male Greenwich Villager you often don corduroys or a flannel shirt or a flowing tie. You are likely to go without your hat, as does one widely known poet down this way. And if you wear a woolly white overcoat in mid-winter you are subject to no unfavorable comment." It was a sympathetic environment for experimental magazines and small theaters, as well as experimental dress. It was the relatively inexpensive habitat of the young artist who had not yet established himself or scored any conspicuous successes. And as for success, many of them scorned it. Faulkner lived near the heart of the Village, and no matter how dreadful the room by Elizabeth Prall's standards, he at least had a base to operate from as he tried at close range to sell his work to New York magazines.

One poem remains which seems likely to have been written at this time. He called it "Two Puppets in a Fifth Avenue Window." It was written in eight-line free-verse stanzas which kept threatening to turn into blank verse. Imagistically he played with the forms of the clothing dummies, their postures defying gravity and mimicking emotion. In the third stanza of the poem he addressed the passers-by, telling them that they too were puppets at the mercy of forces which controlled them.

Another poem may date from this time. It would have been natural for a young man who was intensely interested in the graphic arts to spend some time in New York's great museums. One undated typescript bore a short poem entitled "On Seeing the Winged Victory for the First Time." A full-size plaster cast of the great Nike of Samothrace had stood in Hall 38 of the Metropolitan Museum for eleven years by the time Faulkner arrived in New York. The dramatic statue of the goddess on the prow of a ship, commissioned by victorious King Demetrios of Macedonia, was one of the favorite exhibits at the museum. Faulkner's impressionistic poem began emotionally:

O Atthis

For a moment an aeon I pause plunging
Above the narrow precipice of thy breast.

In the last three lines of the nine-line poem he tried to capture the sense of motion the statue conveyed:

Wind on hill tops blond with the wings of the morning
What wind O Atthis sweeping the April to Lesbos
Whitening the seas

It seems likely that Faulkner was working on prose as well as poetry at about this time. In a few months he would publish his first prose work, other than reviews, since "Landing in Luck" two years before. He had done a good deal of talking—or listening—to Stone on the theory of fiction. There was one book that had captivated Stone, Willard Huntington Wright's *The Creative Will: Studies in the Philosophy and the Syntax of Aesthetics.* Stone would later declare emphatically that "the aesthetic theories set forth in that book, strained through my own mind, constitutes [*sic*] one of the most important influences in Bill's whole literary career." He went further: "If people who read him would simply read Wright's book they would see what he is driving at from a literary standpoint."

Wright was best known as S. S. Van Dine, the author of the popular Philo Vance detective stories, and he had also edited *The Smart Set* before World War I, but he was passionately concerned with serious literature. A pyrotechnical nonstop talker, he would sometimes lard his conversation with obscenities purposely to shock his hearers. There were no obscenities in *The Creative Will*, but it read as though he had composed it of these verbal essays. They were divided into four categories: "Art and Life," "The Artist," "The Individual," and "Problems of Aesthetics." The artist could not go to the science of aesthetics to learn how to produce art, Wright wrote, but beauty in art could be "corroborated and analytically explained by the science of aesthetics. . . ." In Faulkner's review of Aiken's *Turns and Movies*, it was as though Faulkner had accepted Wright's position and then gone further. "Many [poets] have realized that aesthetics is as much a science as chemistry," he wrote, "that there are certain definite scientific rules which, when properly applied, will produce great art as surely as certain chemical elements, combined in the proper proportions, will produce certain reactions. . . ."

Faulkner could well have found a number of Wright's observations congenial. Wright spoke contemptuously of the realistic novel. For him, the real artist "takes the *essence* of his special world, color or document, and creates a new world of them." He should produce work of "emotional intensity," which was the hallmark of great masters such as Beethoven, Michelangelo, Balzac, and Flaubert. There were many reasons why Balzac was superior to Zola; for instance: "Balzac creates first a terrain with an environmental climate; and the creatures which spring from this soil, and which are a part of it, create certain unescapable conditions, social, economic, and intellectual. Furthermore, the generations of characters that follow are, in turn, the inevitable offsprings [*sic*] of this later soil, fashioned by all that preceded them." Wright was all for "progressive innovations," however, such as *vers libre*, which was "the result of an impulse toward profounder effects and richer achievements." Conscious imitation of those who had perfected new forms was right and necessary: "Every man of genius has at some early period played the plagiarist to more than one master." But though the artist might imitate, he should in other ways be completely independent. Wright detested "quarters" where groups gathered. "The great creative artist could not exist in such a *milieu*," he declared. "His nature is necessarily solitary. . . ." He rejected the separation between genres. "The ability to write great poetry is an excellent preparation for the writing of great prose," he said. "Indeed, fundamentally, they should be synonymous." Often, however, recognition of greatness would be delayed because of "hostile criticism and indifference." But even so, there were compensations during his lifetime. "In all great and profound aesthetic creation the artist is an omnipotent god who moulds and fashions the destiny of a new world, and leads it to an inevitable completion where it can stand alone, self-moving, independent. . . . In the fabrication of this cosmos the creator finds his exaltation. . . ." Most critics would not understand his work. "The man who fills the critic's chair rarely possesses sufficient initiative to have commandeered his position unassisted." In spite of the chaotic state of literary criticism, certain qualities could be named which ordinarily determine literary greatness: "philosophic import, character analysis, the portrayal of realistic segments of life, cosmopolitanism of outlook, spiritual exaltation, dissection of manners and customs, the solution of social and sexual problems, moral and ethical determinism, psychological research, and fanciful creativeness." It was an inspiring if demanding gospel to preach to a young artist, and apparently Faulkner tried to heed it.

It is possible that it was during this year that Faulkner wrote a sixteen-page short story called "Moonlight." The narrative follows Robert Binford and his friend George on a hot Saturday night. They hector the drugstore clerk who serves their Coca-Colas, and they size up two "flusies" whom they agree to try to "make" at eleven that night after George has kept a date with Cecily, his girl. They are superficially hard and cynical, fancying themselves men of the world. In the dark shade of the courthouse trees they drink corn whiskey and smoke cigarettes. With Robert's help, Cecily slips out to meet George. He tries to entice her to an empty house but she resists. When he reproaches her with not really loving him, she suddenly and passionately relents. Her consent gained, George changes his mind. As the story ends and they walk back downtown, she promises a tryst in the house for the next night. The setting, the hard, clipped dialogue, and a certain frenetic quality in Cecily marked this story.

Another story Faulkner may have worked on at this time was very different. "Love" was quite clearly apprentice work and very complicated. Set in 1921, it involved two plots linked by a girl named Beth Gorham. In one she courted her father's houseguest, Hugh, a major who had led a French Nieuport squadron composed chiefly of Americans. He had saved from death a young Indochinese soldier called Das, who had become the Major's devoted valet, addressing him reverently as "Tuan." His main task now is to protect the Major from the passionate Italian maid who puts a love potion in the brandy sent up for the Major each night. Das expects her ultimately to substitute poison out of jealousy. Central to the other plot is

Bob Jeyfus, Beth's one-time fiancé, now suspected of lying about his war service. Tricked into flying a plane or backing down, he chooses the latter, murmuring only "nerve's gone." The two plots are joined again when the Major verifies Jeyfus' story. Shot down and placed among the dead, Jeyfus was subsequently unable to fly; he then served out the rest of the war in disgrace as a cook. Beth marries him, "to save my self respect," then sends him away. Throughout, the Major remains a godlike silver-haired figure, sipping tea, standing about immaculate at the Country Club, looking much like the man in Cadillac limousine advertisements. This is in part due to Das, who not only cares for his impeccable clothes, but insists on sampling his brandy. When it finally contains the poison, he staggers toward the antidote he has prepared. At this point the forty-nine-page typed manuscript breaks off.

Faulkner had combined different materials. The elaborate and melodramatic romantic triangle was quite common both in motion pictures and magazine fiction. Though the Major may have been American, his elegant appearance and clipped speech suggested a certain British stereotype. The batman-valet and the house-party situation both reinforced this effect. The relationship between Tuan and Das suggested another kind of writing which Faulkner had apparently studied, that of Rudyard Kipling. (There may also have been echoes of Conrad.) Still another kind of writing described the Italian maid and the butler, Ernie. His realistic-sounding speech was close to the colloquial dialogue in "Moonlight" and the argot of gangsters who would appear in later fiction. "Love" was serious apprentice work in which Faulkner would learn from his mistakes.

When he was not working for Elizabeth Prall, Faulkner had plenty of opportunity to indulge his taste for solitude. Occasionally a fellow Mississippian would seek him out, as when William Alexander Percy took him to the New York City Library and introduced him to a friend who worked there. He was almost completely unknown in New York, but there were a few people who provided hospitality. One was a man named John K. Joice, who had been in the lumber business in the South. Faulkner apparently knew a number of his friends and acquaintances through the Lamb-Fish Lumber Company. Joice lived with his French-born wife and their two-year-old daughter at the Belmont Hotel on Pershing Square around the corner from Grand Central Station. One evening John Joice told his wife that he had invited Faulkner to join them for dinner. She could converse with him in French, he said. When Faulkner arrived, he made a vivid impression on her. "He was just back from the war and, in fact, he had a cane and walked with a limp. He was dressed in a light beige mackintosh, a dusty dark brown hat and a pipe. He was generally nice looking with dark brown eyes and hair."

Taking her husband at his word, Mrs. Joice immediately began speaking French. Had he been wounded, she asked. He replied that "he had just been released from the hospital and had a metal disc close to his hip." It was only a good deal later that Mrs. Joice learned that Faulkner had done his RAF service in Canada. As she recalled that evening, however, she remembered that "he did nothing to dispel my illusion that he was a wounded hero returning from France." Conversation and drinks continued after dinner, as Faulkner seemed to know the names of all the lumbermen Joice mentioned. The sequel, recorded much later by Mrs. Joice, had a bizarre quality.

It seemed to her that from then on he appeared every evening at dinner time, when the pattern would be repeated. But never, she said, did he take off his hat or his mackintosh. One evening when Joice found himself unable to attend a play, he asked Faulkner to escort Mrs. Joice in his place. It was in the theater, she said, that she first saw him without his hat and coat. He wore a drab gray suit which gave off an odor she took to be a combination of alcohol and perspiration. He did not speak or turn toward her. All she could see was his profile, "and I could only tell from a fleeting smile if he was enjoying the play." In spite of all this, he was "so mystique" that she was intrigued by him. When she asked her husband about him later, Joice told her that Faulkner was "a struggling young writer" and had told him that he and his wife lived at a hotel patronized by artists.

Mrs. Joice's interest cooled, however, when her husband told her that Faulkner had asked him for a loan until he received some money from home, which was "a Southern plantation." She was also growing very tired of the nightly sessions after dinner. Finally, Joice decided that he could not continue at his present pace and still do justice to his business. So they found an apartment and left the hotel. One day, however, Mrs. Joice answered the doorbell to find Faulkner standing there, apparently angry and asking for "J.K." Mrs. Joice responded abruptly. "I told him he was not home and slammed the door in his face and never saw him again."

The persona of the wounded pilot had made another appearance, as it would sometimes do when Faulkner found himself in a new environment. He had created an impression partly through his fictitious story and partly through the assumptions he allowed his hearers to make; "he did nothing to dispel my illusion," as Mrs. Joice put it. Actually, he had this time combined the elements of more than one persona: the wounded hero, the struggling artist, and the Southerner from the plantation.

At home Miss Maud worried about him. Phil Stone was concerned in other ways. Faulkner obviously wasn't doing any better in New York than he had in Oxford. Stone feared that he might slide into some sort of bohemian existence. He might lose his drive toward becoming a writer; he would also find himself cut off from one of his fundamental sources of strength: the land and the people of Mississippi. Completely committed to Faulkner's success, he believed in him enough to spend a great deal of time and energy as well as some money. His involvement had a strong vicarious element, for though Stone loved literature passionately, he knew he would never write it. Thus, if he could not be a poet, he would help to create one. Now this possibility might be slipping away in the maze of midtown Manhattan and the tearooms of Greenwich Village. He went to work.

District Attorney Lemuel E. Oldham got in touch with M. J. Mulvehill in Vicksburg, the dispenser of federal patronage in Mississippi. D. R. Johnson was quitting as postmaster at the university office to open a law office in Batesville. Mulvehill granted Oldham's request: Faulkner could be appointed temporary postmaster. After he passed the civil service examination, his name would be sent to Congress for confirmation along with those of hundreds of other political nominees. Stone wired Faulkner to come back home; they had a job for him. Stone waited for a reply. When it came it said, NO THANKS.

In New York Faulkner must have faced a set of unattractive alternatives. He would have liked to stay in New York but he was tiring of the bookstore job. Elizabeth Prall knew that a job at home was hanging over him and that he had no qualifications for another job in New York. If he didn't stay on at the bookstore he would probably have to go home. But being shut up in a post office would be worse than the schoolroom and the bank. He stayed, he later said, "until I got fired. Think I was a little careless about making change or something." Elizabeth Prall remembered nothing like this, only that he finally drifted away. He had remained a valued salesman—English-looking, reserved, "with his chin tucked down toward his collar." His assurance (or, perhaps, impatience) had, if anything, grown.

When customers picked up books he thought worthless he would be abrupt, almost rude. "Don't read that trash," he would say, pressing other books on them, "read this." People bought piles of books from him. Though it was true that he would fail to keep his accounts in order, the bookstore had a good accounts secretary to take care of that. But by now he had had enough of the selling end of the book trade.

Stone had wired a reply to Faulkner's refusal. It was time he got to hell back, he told him. If he stayed in New York he'd be around people who would talk the Great American Novel, not write it. Again Faulkner replied, NO THANKS. Stone refused to give up. The job was all set. Faulkner could just as well earn a living and write on his own time in Oxford as in New York. There would be fewer distractions and pitfalls. By now Maud Falkner must have let her son know how she felt, even if she did not put it in so many words. Stone composed his last wire. He had this job for him now, he said. Now was the time for him to accept responsibility and a job of some kind. This time Faulkner capitulated. Looking back later, Stone said, "I forced Bill to take the job over his own inclination and refusal. He made the damndest postmaster the world has ever seen."

21

December, 1921-September, 1924

look, cynthia,
how abelard evaporates
the brow of time, and paris
tastes his bitter thumbs—

the worms grow fat, eviscerate,
but not on love, o cynthia.
—XXXII, *A Green Bough*

On Friday, December 2, 1921, word had been received, according to one account, that William C. Faulkner had been named acting postmaster for the University of Mississippi post office; he had been in business in New York City for the past year and would arrive to take charge on Saturday or Sunday. *The Mississippian* noted eight days later that the temporary postmaster had been in New York City for some time studying art.

Faulkner was one of three candidates when the formal examination for the position was held on Saturday, December 10. Presumably the other two candidates, Messrs. W. B. Potts and Evern Jones, did not know that both the examination and the ratification of its results in the United States Senate three months later would be only formalities. Faulkner had faithfully completed the paper work of application-filing. Testimonials to his fitness had been given by Jeff K. Hamm, now a university employee, by Phil Stone, and by the applicant's one-time English teacher, Dr. D. H. Bishop. He was ready to begin work.

The station was a fourth-class post office. (Faulkner would later say he had served "as a 4th class postmaster.") The centrally located University

United States Post Office, University, Mississippi.

Store Building was a brick structure with two large plate-glass windows. According to a later post office employee, it was "the only thing that could be called a student activities building in those days. There was a book store in the back, and a general, typical eating place with a soda fountain in front. Then, there was the post office in the other side of the front with the boxes making one side of the hall which led back to the book store and to a barber shop immediately behind the post office. . . . Above the boxes a sort of heavy cage material furnished the wall on to the ceiling. This gave the postal workers inside seats to all of the outside gossip, which might have been passed in the belief that it was confidential." Walking up a half-dozen steps to the small roofed-in porch in front, the student would go through the double doors and into a small lobby. Sometimes Faulkner would close the door that led from the lobby to the barbershop, an act which did little to endear him to proprietor Slim Billingsley. With the help of his friends and his brother he set about running the office and learning how to be a postmaster.

Faulkner might be tied during the week to Oxford, with its population of a little over two thousand, but he and Stone traveled together as before. From time to time he would turn south to New Orleans. After Greenwich Village—about which Faulkner and Stone talked while Edith Brown and her friends listened carefully—New Orleans' French Quarter must have seemed particularly congenial. Exciting things were happening there. Young artists in revolt and champions of the arts had responded enthusiastically to H. L. Mencken's kind of icon-smashing, as in his attacks on the staid, the mediocre, and the stodgy. When he represented the South as a cultural wasteland in his famous essay "The Sahara of the Bozart," many bright young Southerners were forced to agree with him. It affected some others differently. In the summer of 1920 two Orleanians, boyhood friends named Julius Weis Friend and Albert Goldstein, had talked with newspapermen about starting a magazine. At first it was not to be literary but instead a shocker like *The Mascot*, which had profitably retailed New Orleans scandal forty years before. But then they had a change of heart. That would be "kid stuff." They wanted to show that what Mencken had charged was true need not necessarily remain so. Their part of the country, far from being a desert, could support a magazine like *The Smart Set*, edited by Mencken and George Jean Nathan in New York. All the prospective founders were in business, but Basil Thompson and John McClure had written prose and poetry. (McClure had published both in *The Smart Set.*) Friend and Thompson were listed as editors, Goldstein and McClure as associate editors. Friend would be concerned with financial as well as editorial matters, and Paul Godchaux would serve as business manager.

They named their magazine *The Double Dealer* after the play by William Congreve, in which he wrote: "I can deceive them both by speaking the truth." This line appeared on the masthead when the first issue came out in January of 1921. As Julius Friend put it, they were "scornful of politics," but in art they "shared the enthusiasm of the revolt" set off by the work of Joyce, Lawrence, Pound, and others. "We had [no] patience with the slick fiction which was catering to America's current image of herself." As to Southern writing, "we were sick to death of colonial mansions and ante-bellum nostalgia." In their editorial statement they seemed to be saying that they wanted to shake everyone up: "We mean to deal double, to show the other side, to throw open the back windows stuck in their sills from disuse, smutted over long since against even a dim beam's penetration." The first issue, like the next eighteen, bore on its cover a drawing whose black background and antic, ornate figures immediately suggested the work of Aubrey Beardsley. The poetry of men such as Hart Crane, Donald Davidson, John Crowe Ransom, Allen Tate, and Robert Penn Warren would appear in the magazine, with prose by such writers as Thornton Wilder, Arthur Symons, and Sherwood Anderson. They had begun with a gesture toward *The Smart Set*, using the subtitle "A Magazine for the Discriminating." The editors soon changed it to read, "A National Magazine from the South." As they approached their first anniversary they could take pride in the distance they had traveled between wish and fact.

One Saturday afternoon during that winter of 1921, James K. Feibleman, a seventeen-year-old would-be poet, decided the time had come. He dressed carefully and then, his poems under his arm, set out for the offices of *The Double Dealer.* These were located in an old, nearly deserted building owned by Julius Friend's uncle, Sam Weis, in New Orleans' business district but near to the French Quarter. Feibleman climbed the three flights of stairs leading to the rent-free loft which sheltered the editors and their stream of guests. He was admitted to the large room and sat down quietly to listen. About fifteen men—mostly writers, he thought—were drinking whiskey and talking. He noticed another man as quiet as himself, who was sitting on the floor in one corner in spite of an empty chair quite near him. He was "a little man with a well-shaped head, a small moustache and a slightly receding chin." He had a bottle of whiskey, "which he held near his head and tipped into his mouth from time to time." Watching this process, Feibleman "had the impression more of nursing than of drinking." Finally the conversation turned to Shakespeare and to *Hamlet.* It was only then that the little man in the corner spoke.

"I could write a play like *Hamlet* if I wanted to," he said, and then lapsed back into silence. Later Feibleman found out his name from one of the others. Mulling the experience over, Feibleman decided that though he could not tell which of the aspirants would become a great writer, he could be sure which one wouldn't. Without question it was William Faulkner, the small, silent man who sat drinking whiskey in the corner of the large, bare room.

Faulkner was writing literary criticism again. He gave Lucy Somerville an essay-review which was published in "Books and Things" in *The Mississippian* for January 13, 1922. The subject was *Aria da Capo,* a thirty-one-page experimental play by Edna St. Vincent Millay. The play had been produced by the Provincetown Players on MacDougal Street in Greenwich Village, just a few blocks from where Faulkner had lived. It had been the most successful offering of the Players' 1919–1920 season. An expressionistic work richly praised by Alexander Woollcott and others, it would be one of the high points of Miss Millay's career. On a stage set for a harlequinade, Pierrot and Columbine sit, traditionally dressed but speaking in a modern idiom. Miss Millay describes Pierrot as one who "sees clearly into existing evils and is rendered gaily cynical by them; he is both too indolent and too indifferent to do anything about it." He is convinced "that all beauty and romance are fled from the world." Their brittle chatter is interrupted as Cothurnus, the Masque of Tragedy, brings on two young shepherds, Corydon and Thyrsis, to play their pastoral tragedy. As in Chaucer's "Pardoner's Tale," cupidity leads to death. Corydon strangles Thyrsis and then dies from water poisoned by his victim. When Pierrot and Columbine ask Cothurnus at least to drag the bodies offstage before they go on with their scene, Cothurnus refuses. He tells them merely to pull the tablecloth down to conceal them, for "The audience will forget." Harold Lewis Cook called *Aria da Capo* "a telling comment on human treachery and self-betrayal, which often nurture war because they ignore human need and human love." A year later Frank Shay wrote that *Aria da Capo* and Eugene O'Neill's *The Emperor Jones* represented "the high accomplishments of the art theatre in America. . . ."

Faulkner's 400-word review, signed simply "W.F.," was compounded of contempt for the sort of poets he had chastised in the Aiken review and high praise for Miss Millay's play along with rather vague comments about it. Miss Millay's brevity showed "heaven sent genius. . . ." The gods had given her "a strong wrist," and the idea here was so good that it would live "even though Miss Amy Lowell intricately festoons it with broken glass, or Mr. Sandburg sets it in the stock yards, to be acted, of a Saturday afternoon, by the Beef Butchers' Union." Lapsing into French construction, he found the idea so beautifully simple "that it does give to wonder why under heaven no one has thought of it before."

A very different article by "W.F." appeared in "Books and Things" three weeks later on February 3. He had really put his heart into this one. The 900-word essay was entitled "American Drama: Eugene O'Neill." He began by exploring a thesis first stated, he thought, by a Frenchman, that "art is preeminently provincial: i.e., it comes directly from a certain age and a certain locality." He ticked off great examples: *Hamlet*, for instance, could have been written only in England during Elizabeth's reign. (He also cited Flaubert, Balzac, and others—Hauptmann, Moeller, and Synge—but Shakespeare was the nonpareil; he left "behind him a drama which the hand does not hold blood that can cap. . . .") There were, however, two exceptions to the general rule: Joseph Conrad and Eugene O'Neill. And the latter "might go to astounding lengths in a land possessing traditions." The problem, he wrote, echoing Braithwaite's preface to his anthology, was that "America has no drama or literature worthy of the name, and hence no tradition." O'Neill was remarkable for his range and variety, and one of his great strengths, as with Synge, was his language. "The Emperor Jones' 'who dat dare whistle in de Emperor's palace' goes back to the 'Playboy's' 'the likes of which would make the mitred bishops themselves strain at the bars of paradise for to see the lady Helen walking in her golden shawl.' " (He was quoting Synge from memory.) Language was the greatest source "of natural dramatic material" in America. "Nowhere today," he concluded, "saving in parts of Ireland, is the English language spoken with the same earthy strength as it is in the United States; though we are, as a nation, still inarticulate." It is not surprising that his next published work did not suggest the pastoral, the commedia dell'arte, or the Symbolists. It could very easily have been set in Lafayette County of 1922.

"The Hill," which appeared over the initials "W.F." in *The Mississippian* on March 10, was an 800-word sketch without a plot. It began with suggestions of *Marionettes.* The hill crest "was clearly laid on the sky." The nameless, roughly dressed figure who climbed toward it moved in a kind of stasis, "as though his body had been mesmerized by a whimsical God to a futile puppet-like activity upon one spot. . . ." Breasting the hill, he saw the "hamlet" in the valley now revealed. Three poplars moved "to the quiet resistless compulsion of April in their branches, then were still. . . ." Most of this was lost on the itinerant laborer, whose "featureless mediocrity" indicated "a mind heretofore untroubled by moral quibbles and principles. . . ." But now his features twisted to "the terrific groping of his mind shaken at last by the faint resistless force of spring in a valley at sunset." The "tieless casual" stood there until darkness broke the spell. Familiar imagery flooded in with the last lines: "Here, in the dusk, nymphs and fauns might riot to a shrilling of thin pipes, to a shivering and hissing of cymbals in a sharp volcanic abasement beneath a tall icy star."

This sketch formed an important transition between the poetry behind and the fiction ahead. Faulkner was sketching familiar country with a combination of realistic description and symbolist imagery. It demonstrated in an early and elementary form the central fact about his style as a fiction writer: he thought and wrote in poetic terms within a realistic framework which provided sufficient room for symbolist techniques.

A week after "The Hill," Faulkner appeared again in "Books and Things" over the familiar initials, "W.F." In a little over a thousand words, he addressed himself to the problem, "American Drama: Inhibitions." Again he wrote about an indigenous national literature and weighed assets and liabilities: "Our wealth of language and our inarticulateness. . . ." The American dramatist faced crushing problems. "Writing people are all so pathetically torn between a desire to make a figure in the world and a morbid interest in their personal egos—the deadly fruit of the grafting of Sigmund Freud upon the dynamic chaos of a hodge-podge of nationalities. And, with characteristic national restlessness, those with imagination and some talent find it unbearable." O'Neill, writing of the sea, not of America, was one. Others were Marsden Hartley, Alfred Kreymborg, and Ezra Pound, who "furiously toys with spurious bronze in London."

As to assets, America had "an inexhaustible fund of dramatic material. . . ." Two obvious ones were "the old Mississippi River days and the romantic growth of railroads." But only one writer, conspicuously, had used the former. He was Mark Twain, "a hack writer who would not have been considered fourth rate in Europe. . . ." In a statement Willard Huntington Wright would have endorsed, Faulkner declared, "a man with real ability finds sufficient what he has to hand." At the same time, however, those artists "who are doing worth while things really labor infinitely more than the results achieved would show, for the reason that they must over come all this self torture, must first slay the dragons which they, themselves, have raised." He gave one example which had been related to him, he said, by a drama critic for a New York magazine (most probably Stark Young). Robert Edmond Jones, a stage designer, began having difficulty with his work, even with sleeping and eating. A friend advised him to see "a certain practitioner of the new therapeutic psycho-analysis." He followed the advice and was "siked," Faulkner wrote, after which he returned to normal. This was the kind of thing that writers who are exposed to the prevailing literary tendencies in America must combat; "and, so long as socialism, psycho-analysis and the aesthetic attitude are profitable as well as popular, so long will such conditions obtain." But again, language as spoken in America was the one "rainbow we have on our dramatic horizon. . . ." Beside it, British English was like melodious but ineffectual birdsong.

It may have been at about this time that Faulkner wrote a short story in the vein he had begun to explore in "The Hill." Moreover, he was obviously trying to exploit in it the linguistic resources and the "provincial" quality he had extolled. "Adolescence" centered on a child named Juliet Bunden. Unable to get along with her stepmother, she is sent to live with her grandmother in an isolated hill cabin. At thirteen she finds a playmate, Lee Hollowell. The two develop a comradeship with erotic overtones, as when they swim nude and then doze wrapped in a blanket. The next summer, Juliet's grandmother surprises them together and sees her "layin'-up" with a no-good Hollowell as evidence of bad blood coming out. In another year the old woman has grown feeble, but with her awkward and somewhat self-conscious dialect she seems as villainous as the witch in "Hansel and Gretel." A plan to marry Juliet off is halted only by the death of her father. Lee has left the country, and Juliet's eleven-year-old brother, Bud, comes to her before he too leaves. She gives him her meager savings and watches his small figure vanish, knowing she will stay with her dying grandmother. Going back to the pool where she and Lee swam, she lies face down in despair under the October sky.

This story, with Faulkner's name and the page number typed at the bottom of each sheet, must have been one of those sent out to magazines only to return to Stone's filing cabinets. Though it remained unpublished, it provided an important transition between "Landing in Luck," with its alien setting; "The Hill," which was native but undramatic; and coming fiction which would set dramatic events in this authentic milieu.

Post office patrons must have concluded that articles by "W.F." in *The Mississippian* might have been written on the job. One remembered that "he would sit in a rocking chair with a writing arm attached, in the back of the post office, and was continuously writing. Patrons would come to the window at the front of the post office to get their mail or purchase stamps. Faulkner would pay no attention to them but [would] continue with his writing. They would rap on the counter with a coin to attract his attention, and finally he would begrudgingly get up to serve them." One part of the job which he apparently enjoyed was handling some of the magazines. He and his friends would read those which suited their taste before they put them in the subscribers' boxes. There were newspapers too, of course, and some of the stories in the early months of Faulkner's stewardship made fascinating reading.

Governor Lee M. Russell was being sued by his former secretary for $100,000 on the grounds of seduction and breach of promise. With avowals of love, charged Miss Frances Birkhead, and promises of marriage "after he could get a divorce from his wife," the governor had persuaded her "to yield to his will." When she became pregnant, she underwent a criminal operation "at the instigation of Governor Russell which totally ruined and wrecked her health causing her to suffer untold anguish and pain, that she is now an invalid and must remain so for the rest of her life." Governor Russell denounced the suit as "the most infamous conspiracy ever concocted." Oxonians could now look forward to the most sensational events in the Courthouse Square since A. J. Smith burned the town in '62.

Lee Russell would come to trial without one of his most generous sponsors. "Col. Falkner Dies Sudden," proclaimed the front-page left-hand column of the Oxford *Eagle.* In the two years since he had been forced out of the bank he seemed not to have changed greatly. His movements were as forceful and abrupt as ever. But the deafness increased, and sometimes he would even hold the end of his ear trumpet to his teeth to try to catch some of the sound vibrations. But his idleness had increased his isolation from the life around him. March had come in raw and cold, and on the morning of the third it was sleeting, so he decided to go back to bed and read for a while after breakfast. There, while Auntee and the cook moved about quietly downstairs, his seventy-three-year-old heart failed from a sudden attack. They laid his body in the front parlor of The Big Place, where his kinsmen took up the vigil. The Falkner boys sat up in their turn. They wanted to smoke but couldn't, John remembered. One of them passed some chewing tobacco to the others. But they had forgotten one thing; if smoke and ashes were unseemly, so was tobacco juice. By the time they left the parlor, they were all sick.

The next morning Reverend Lipscomb of the Methodist church led the mourners in prayer. Conspicuous in the cortege that made its way out to St. Peter's Cemetery was the tall, thin figure of the old man's one-time partner, Lee Maurice Russell. In the tree-shaded old section of the cemetery the Colonel's lodge brothers said the final words over this Mason of high degree. Then they formed a line, and the first prepared to throw a ritual shovelful of earth on the coffin of his departed brother. Jack Falkner stood watching. Then, "Bill turned to me and in a low voice told me to note the third and fourth men in the line. I recognized them as two individuals for whom the Colonel had as little admiration while alive as he probably now had in his grave. I nodded and Bill said, 'When the Colonel was alive he wouldn't speak to them. Now that he's dead, they throw dirt in his face.' "

They read the will which the old man had drawn up almost exactly ten years before. He and Bem Price, an influential businessman with varied holdings, had jokingly agreed that they would both have the same kind of monument, but that the survivor could build his six inches higher. But the

Colonel would not, like his father, plan a grandiose monument to himself. He did specify, however, that he wanted "a medallion of myself on my monument in St. Peter's cemetery." It was a short and simple document which emphasized that Mary Kennedy "has a separate estate of her own and does not need a share in mine. The sole purpose I have is that my three children shall have equal benefit of my property." He had done the best he could, and his instructions were followed. But he could neither foresee nor control the fact that the end result would be dissension and bitterness.

Now the last of the grandparents was gone. General Stone had resigned as president of the Bank of Oxford. Soon that whole generation would be gone. Signs of the active new generation were abundantly to be seen, particularly at General Stone's office. Rob, the General's horse, was still tethered there, but Drusilla would be parked in front on the days when Phil was home from Charleston, ready for the group of young people that gathered there every Sunday afternoon. Phil would serve "the Bunch" watermelon in the summer and something hot in the winter. In one room there was a miniature roulette wheel—which Bill Faulkner never played.

They might live in a small town, but they had a lively social life. Katrina Carter, in whom Phil was romantically interested, might be on her way to a house party at the Cotton Plant estate of Captain Paul J. Rainey, a New York millionaire who had built up the largest game preserve in the state and redone the plantation residence to accommodate his guests. Edith Brown was going to be a bridesmaid at a wedding in the Delta, and the Bunch was avidly discussing the event. Phil and Bill worked out an elaborate plan, involving phone calls, flowers, and other devices to dazzle the Delta boys with Edith's popularity. The two loved stratagems and hoaxes, and they delightedly worked out their scheme. One of the boys in the office demurred.

"Sister Edith don't need all that help," he said sourly.

"Everybody needs all the help he can get," replied Bill Faulkner.

Stone would load Drusilla up with boys and girls to go for a drive in the country, talking, joking, laughing, voluble as ever. Faulkner would sometimes fall into a brief storytelling mood, but more often he listened with the others to Stone's stream of comment and anecdote. Sometimes they would hear Stone haranguing Faulkner. As one of the Bunch remembered, "To say that Phil 'encouraged' Bill . . . is gross understatement. He cajoled, browbeat, and swore at him; he threatened and pleaded; encouragement came later." Stone was always recommending the books he had discovered.

"Bill," he would say, speaking surprisingly fast in his Deep South accent, "have you seen this book?" He would tell him to read other books that he himself didn't have time for. "Bill, if you want to be somebody," he would say, "you've got to do it yourself. There isn't any reason you can't do it."

The Bunch responded to the warmth of these two older men, expressed in such different ways. Both were eccentric. Stone, supersensitive to his baldness, wore a hat even to play tennis; Faulkner, lapsing into the bohemianism Dot Wilcox had seen, wore very old clothes and sometimes walked around barefoot. None questioned their right to these idiosyncrasies, and "we reacted with fury to criticism from 'outsiders' of Phil and Bill's right to do as they pleased."

There was plenty to do in Oxford. They would dance to phonograph records of that spring's favorites—Fanny Brice singing "Second-Hand Rose," or such lively tunes as "Stumbling" and "Kitten on the Keys." Bill Faulkner would sometimes carefully lead a pretty dancing partner around the floor. In town the boys and girls kept on pairing up permanently. Bob Williams now possessed an LL.B. as well as the Lyric Theatre, and on April 20 he and Sallie Murry Wilkins were married at The Big Place. But Stone and Faulkner, the senior bachelors, had enough to keep them busy without matrimony.

When *Ole Miss* came out that spring at the end of the academic year 1921–1922, it gave an indication of some of Faulkner's activities. A drawing for the French club showed a modishly dressed man and woman at the rail of the *Richelieu.* Though unsigned, it was clearly his, the skill now quite professional. It would be his last drawing for *Ole Miss.* This year he was also the subject of an illustration. A small drawing showed three men selling stamps and handling mail. Under the legend "Postgraduate Club" appeared the motto "Never put the mail up on time." The hours were listed as "11:20 to 12:20 every Wednesday." "Diversion" was reported as "Read all the mail." Among the eight names that followed were those of Bill Falkner as Supervisor, Jack Falkner as Carrier, and Sonny Bell as Chief Assorter.

Something which doubtless pleased Faulkner considerably more than either of these items came at about the same time. A poem called "Portrait" appeared in *The Double Dealer* for June, 1922. It was poem V of *Vision in Spring,* with only a few words changed in each stanza. He would later tell an aspiring writer, "It takes you 200 rejections before you get up to zero." Perhaps he could now feel that he was past zero, no matter how many rejections had been recorded on the suit box which bore the names of the stories, the dates they were sent out, and the dates they came back.

Faulkner was fortunate that the handling of his stories did not rest exclusively with postmasters like himself. "It never ceased to amaze us all," said Jack, "here was a man so little attracted to mail that he never read his own being solemnly appointed as, one might say, the custodian of that belonging to others. It was also amazing that under his trusteeship any mail ever actually got delivered." Bondy Webb, who picked up the mail at the train station and delivered it to the post office, often observed the postmaster walking alone, stopping to watch a squirrel or bird or standing before a tree he passed every day "as though studying each leaf." When Webb arrived, Faulkner would engage him in a brief conversation before getting on with the business of sorting the mail and putting it up. Ten or fifteen minutes would elapse. Boisterous and impatient students in the gathering crowd would sometimes complain noisily about "that slow poke postmaster," and on one occasion impatient patrons threw pebbles and pieces of clay through the grating above the mailboxes. Once the distribution began, however, Faulkner finished it rapidly. Sometimes he would handle other items. "I do remember Bill putting notes in my post office box from the girl friend," recalled an acquaintance named Ashby Woodson, "his way of trying to help along a college romance."

But his demeanor rarely seemed cordial or efficient. He appeared always to be sitting down, at work with pencil and paper. One young aspiring writer screwed up his courage one morning. When he went up to the stamp window he saw that Faulkner was sitting reading the current issue of *Liberty* magazine. The student waited, then gently tapped at the window with a quarter. Faulkner came to the window, still holding the magazine. He listened, expressionless, to the polite request. Then he produced the stamps, slid the quarter into the change drawer, and sat down to resume his reading. Frustrated in his twenty-five-cent venture, the student was emboldened to speak.

"Mr. Faulkner," he said politely, "I hear that you have contributed some very interesting stories to national magazines."

Faulkner looked up and replied, with no coloring whatever in his tone. "I haven't met you yet," he said.

The student retreated, but without resentment. He had been told Faulkner wouldn't speak with students he didn't know.

To acquaintances, he was polite but scarcely more accommodating. Requests for college catalogs went to the office of Chancellor Powers, where

Mary Betsy Maltby would promptly answer each request. That spring the chancellor began to receive complaints from people to whom Miss Maltby had quite distinctly sent catalogs. Mr. Powers went down to the post office to investigate. Faulkner explained what had happened.

"Well," he said, "I . . . the way I do: I put [them] in the cart that we take down the hill to the railroad station and when it gets full we take it down, and then I start on a new batch."

"Bill," Powers said, "we want the catalogs to go out every day."

To his friends, however, the postmaster was a comfortable if not a genial host. To Jack, now an LL.B., and Sonny Bell, whom he had appointed part-time clerks working three two-hour shifts a week, he was the most lenient of bosses. There were bridge games in the afternoon and a mah-jongg table for those who favored a different sort of divertissement. Jack remembered "the cheerful afternoons when, following our earnest efforts on the golf course, the restful and comforting tea hour at the post office attended to our social needs." Tea was served in the rear of the office, where the accommodations consisted of a desk, a swivel chair, and two plain chairs. They called this area "the Reading Room," for there, on the desk, as on a coffee table, lay the latest magazines: *Scribner's*, *Harper's*, *The Saturday Evening Post*, *The Atlantic Monthly*. They put these reading materials to good use, Bob Farley remembered. The postmaster saw to it that they were placed in their proper boxes after a few days or so.

When Faulkner talked, he seemed to prefer real talk rather than trivial conversation. He and Farley had fallen into the habit of going for a Sunday afternoon stroll, when a friend named Walter Campbell sometimes accompanied them. As they walked Faulkner would lead discussions that touched on religion, politics, and current events. He might even philosophize a bit. Sometimes Farley would walk the nine-hole golf course with Faulkner. Occasionally that spring Lucy Somerville would see him there, dressed in his plus fours. His game seemed lackadaisical to her, and he himself beset by a "brooding melancholy." She knew how much he already detested the job Phil Stone had urged on him, and she said nothing. As the summer began he and his brothers engaged in another sport, playing baseball for the Methodists in "the Church League." Bill still pitched and Jack still caught. John played shortstop and Dean, a versatile athlete and fierce competitor, was an outfielder. Murry Falkner would proudly come to watch his boys play. Bill helped Reverend Christian from time to time with his troop of boy scouts, going along on hikes or campouts at the Club House on the

Tallahatchie River. When he could get away for the weekend, he might go to Charleston to visit the Stones. This was easier now, for out of his $1,500 yearly salary, he was making payments on a car.

For $300, borrowed from the First National Bank of Oxford, he now owned what was almost a custom-made motorcar. He had bought a Model T Ford chassis, built a racer body on it, and then painted it yellow. On a Friday, in the long summer afternoon, he would pack his suitcase and golf clubs and drive the forty-five miles to Charleston. There he could walk the fairways, enjoy the hospitality of Jack and Myrtle Stone, and listen to the conversation of his mentor, gadfly, and admirer, Phil Stone. It was exactly the kind of change from the post office routine that he needed. Later that summer he would send "Miss Myrt" a proper and affectionate thank-you note: "I want you to be sure and know how much I appreciate your's and Mr. Jack's kindness to me during my vacation. It's been so nice, being able to pick up and go to Charleston at any time, as I have done."

It was another summer of politics in Mississippi. There were divisions now among the Vardaman-Bilbo-Russell faction. Having lost his senate seat six years before to a handsome and impressive young Congressman named Pat Harrison, Vardaman was running for the seat to be vacated by Senator John Sharp Williams. It would not be an easy campaign, for his old enemies from the Delta were still mobilized against him. Still hanging over Russell was Miss Birkhead's suit, which could end his political career. The wily Bilbo was a key figure. He took the stump for Vardaman, but he said little about the Russell-Birkhead case. There were rumors, however, that a rift had developed between him and Lee Russell. Meanwhile, of course, the governor carried on as before with his duties. One executive action that July was his appointment of Judge John Falkner of Oxford as Judge of the 3rd District Court, Mississippi, to fill the vacancy created by the death of Judge W. A. Roane. It would give him some advantage, presumably, in the August primary election when he stood as a candidate for that judgeship. He assumed his new duties as Jack Falkner looked after the law office for him.

In late July, Vardaman spoke at a large rally in Oxford, and by mid-August he was reported to be leading his chief opponent, Hubert D. Stephens. But then he began to miss rallies and meetings. On one occasion when he did appear, he spoke for only twenty minutes in a voice so feeble that it hardly carried. Then he stopped abruptly and sat down. Soon the word began to leak out. He was mentally ill. Indeed, he was so sick as to be virtually incapacitated. As an emergency measure, Theodore Bilbo began a speaking campaign in his behalf, a move repugnant to many Vardamanites. But they need not have worried about Bilbo's gaining control of the senator. Vardaman lost to Stephens in the second primary held in early September.

John Falkner had conducted a vigorous campaign for the judgeship. He had bought a Model T Ford so that he could cover the whole circuit, and his nephew William usually served as his chauffeur. On one trip into Calhoun County they made an overnight stop at Pittsboro, thirty-five miles south of Oxford. It was an ordinary stop and the candidate gave his standard speech. A series of incidents took place there, however, which another of his nephews recounted forty years later. "Bill was sitting on the front porch of the boardinghouse late that evening when some men brought in a string of calico ponies wired together with barbed wire. They put them in a lot just across the road from the boardinghouse and the next morning auctioned them off, at prices ranging from about five dollars apiece on up." When the new owners went into the lot to claim their purchases, John Faulkner wrote, the ponies bolted through the open gate to freedom. "Bill sat there on the porch of the boardinghouse and saw it all. One of them ran the length of the porch and he had to dive back into the hallway to get out of its path. He and Uncle John told us about it the next day, when they got home."

Nothing in the rest of the campaign was so spectacular. Falkner had many friends in the judicial district. He was what people called "a strong pleader" in court, but he had the Falkner trait of outspokenness, and he made enemies. He was constitutionally incapable of taking the advice that served a younger colleague well in politics: make as many friends as you can and when you have to speak, "be as vague as hell about everything." His assiduous campaign finally did him no more good than Bilbo's help did Vardaman. He lost again.

Judge Falkner's nephews had been active, too. On September 2, just three weeks before his twenty-first birthday, Johncy married his long-time sweetheart, Lucille "Dolly" Ramey. He had dropped out of the university, but now he and his new wife decided that he should try it again. They moved into an upstairs room in the old Delta Psi house and John enrolled in the engineering school. This time he was determined to see that it "took." Four days later Jack married another local girl, Cecile Hargis, though they would keep it a secret until the following spring. It must have been partially because of his new marital status that Jack gave up his arduous duties at the post office. He had talked about other jobs briefly with Bill.

"I don't think I'm ever going to get over my love for locomotives," he said.

"Well, why don't you do something about it?" his brother asked. "They run down here every day." He smiled as Jack wryly remarked that he had certainly left himself wide open for that one.

Very soon he did go to the offices of the railroad his grandfather had helped build. By now he looked a lot like Murry Falkner, and at this point he apparently felt that his vocation might be the same one his father had wanted, LL.B. or no. They gave him a job as a fireman on the run between Water Valley and Jackson, Tennessee. The experienced fireman who rode along helped him occasionally. "Those old wide-door 800's were killers," he remembered. "No automatic foot pedals in those days to let that door close between shovelfuls. You swung that fire door open with a chain, latched it, and put in a big fire in all that heat. What we got [to Water Valley] that boy had blisters on his hands and arms and was pretty well cooked." Jack stayed on the job for about two weeks before he decided that he would see what he could do with a law degree.

If Lee M. Russell was worried as his case came to trial he did not show it. Oxford was "electrified" when it was announced that the proceedings would begin. "The lobby of the Colonial Hotel is crowded day and night with men who have come from every section of the state to be present when the excitement starts," reported the *Eagle*. Testimony began before a courtroom jammed with spectators, the beautiful Mrs. Russell among them. Handkerchief to her eyes, Miss Birkhead testified as the packed courtroom strained to listen. She had wanted to have the child because she thought her lover wanted one eagerly. To her shock, he gave her medicine to produce an abortion. Then he handed her an instrument she was to use if the medicine failed. The final result was that she went to Memphis, where a doctor "finished the job."

Russell's attorney attacked Miss Birkhead's character and her testimony. Her attorneys had subpoenaed Theodore G. Bilbo, but the days passed and he did not appear. After a week the case went to the jury. It took them less than ten minutes to find in favor of Governor Lee M. Russell. A citation was issued for Theodore G. Bilbo for his failure to appear. He had connived with this woman to ruin Russell, said the governor's supporters, in revenge for Russell's refusal to issue a pardon Bilbo had asked. They quoted Russell on the stand under oath: "If Miss Birkhead was seduced by anyone in the Governor's office, she was not seduced by Lee M. Russell."

Now, wrote the Memphis *Commercial Appeal*, "Bilbo still has his eyes on the governorship. It is claimed he would welcome a jail sentence for contempt of court, his enemies state, because he could then conduct a theatrical campaign from behind prison bars." There was more drama ahead for Oxford, but little for Lee Russell. He had won the case, but it had "left a nauseating stench in the nostrils of many Mississippians." To one editor, recent Mississippi governors suggested Nero, Claudius, and Caligula. Lee Russell still had a year left in the governorship, but politically he had come to the end of the line.

A week after the trial an article in *The Mississippian* for December 15 alluded to a "strange case of sex crucifixion turned backward upon itself. . . ." This was not a partisan journalist referring to the Birkhead case. It was a reference by "W.F." to what he called "a deliberate pandering to the emotions" in the work of Joseph Hergesheimer. (Faulkner and Lucy Somerville had shared a taste for Hergesheimer's prose as they had for Aiken's poetry.) Again Faulkner had been drawn to the work of a master of words, but he was impatient with him as he had been with William Alexander Percy: "He is subjective enough to bear life with fair equanimity, but he is afraid of living, of man in his sorry clay braving chance and circumstance."

Faulkner dealt with three of Hergesheimer's novels. *Cytherea*, of 1919, was an anti-sentimental novel whose heroine died in the squalor and filth of a Cuban village hotel. To Faulkner it was a "palpable and bootless attempt to ape the literary colors of the day." *The Bright Shawl*, 1922, was better. He found this story, about a romantic young American fighting for Cuban freedom, beautifully written. But Hergesheimer had been corrupted by Sinclair Lewis and *The New York Times*, and the result was a "sublimated dime novel." He liked best *Linda Condon*, also published in 1922. It was the story of a lovely woman whose irregular upbringing had helped to make her emotionally withdrawn, detached and speculative, suffering at the same time that she evoked love. Faulkner declared that it was not really a novel but "more like a lovely Byzantine frieze: a few unforgettable figures in silent arrested motion, forever beyond the reach of time and troubling the heart like music." The essay then took a curious turn, as though Faulkner might be repudiating the kind of thing he had done in *Marionettes* and the dreamy poems of unrequited love. Hergesheimer's people did not respond to compulsions from within, he wrote. Instead, "They are like puppets assuming graceful but meaningless postures in answer to the author's compulsions. . . ." The book had a dreamlike quality: "La figlia della sua mente, l'amorosa l'idea." Hergesheimer should describe only inanimate objects, he concluded. "As it is, he is like an emasculate priest surrounded by the puppets he has carved and clothed and painted—a terrific world without motion or meaning." This last piece of writing Faulkner would do for a University of Mississippi publication displayed some familiar characteristics. He was a critic of extremes, praising highly and damning completely, and his essay was a showcase for spectacular metaphors. He deplored prevailing taste and the tendency of artists to pander to it. As for his own stance, it combined an almost tremulous sensitivity with an arrogant assurance of his own taste.

The professional reviewer he had probably been alluding to in "American Drama: Inhibitions" was home again that February of 1923. Stark Young continued as Oxford's most eminent man of letters, just back from a speaking tour of the Northwest and author of a book of drama reviews to be brought out by Scribner's. Still a loyal son, he would give *The Mississippian* a piece called "The Flower in Drama" to publish in "Books and Things." Though Faulkner would publish nothing at all there or elsewhere

Self-portrait by William Faulkner, with Lottie Vernon White, spring, 1923.

that year, he was still writing. "It was 1923," he later recalled, "and I wrote a book and discovered that my doom, fate, was to keep on writing books; not for any exterior or ulterior purpose; just writing the books for the sake of writing the books. . . ." The completion of what would be his first published book was still more than two years away. But he had completed *Vision in Spring*, in "manuscript edition," and he had composed the poems he would send off in less than half a year to a real publisher.

He polished the verses that spring, changing a word or a line here and there, arranging the poems in different orders. Jack would hear him tapping away at the typewriter in his room in the tower. But he did have some social life. There were dances, and occasionally he would lead Lottie Vernon White, a pretty Oxford girl, through the steps of a popular waltz such as "A Kiss in the Dark," or something faster like "Toot, Toot, Tootsie, Good-Bye." After one such dance that year he did a pencil sketch on white linen stationery. To the right was the standard Victrola of the period. Though the two figures were among the most realistic he had ever drawn, they were slightly elongated and the features had a stylized quality which suggested caricature. Faulkner leaned backwards in a neat herringbone-tweed suit with wide-bottomed trousers. Lottie dipped forward, her slim right leg extended, the spike heel pointing straight back. She looked seriously past her partner. His thin face, with the narrow eyes and small mustache, was intent on the steps of the dance. His curling hair was shaped as carefully as her sculpted bob. As Bill Faulkner liked books just for writing's sake, so he apparently liked drawing in the same way. He sent the sketch to Lottie. This was a personal drawing for a friend whom it might please or amuse, yet he took more time on it, very probably, than most of the sketches that had appeared over his name in *Ole Miss*.

That spring Jack and Cecile announced that they had been married since September. Murry and Maud Falkner could scarcely object. Elopements seemed to run in the Falkner family, and Jack, after all, had finished school and had his law degree. And though he could presumably remain in Uncle John's law office, he was beginning to look around for something that would pay better. John and Dolly were living in comfortable domesticity across the hall from Bill. Now he and fifteen-year-old Dean were the only unmarried Falkners. He became interested in an attractive coed from Natchez named Elise Huntington. He would take her for drives in the Ford and sketch her, but that ended in early April when she married a boy in the medical school. He wrote letters to Mary Victoria Mills, Lida Oldham's niece, a student at the University of Oklahoma. He might write as often as once a week, mentioning local happenings. Sometimes he would include a page of something he had written, or a sketch—perhaps of himself in his RAF uniform, or of Mary Vic with the line "I suppose you look like this now." The girls in the sorority house would wait for the letters. "Read us some more from that cute man in your hometown," they would say. Mary Vic thought he wrote because he was lonely.

It was a lively March that year. At five o'clock on Thursday, March 8, just as the afternoon show was letting out at the Lyric Theatre, someone saw smoke issuing from the three-story building. Quickly the alarm was sounded as Bob and Sallie Murry Williams struggled to save their things from the apartment in the rear of the building. Soon a crowd had gathered to watch the firemen's unavailing efforts. "Due to the tallness of the building and the low water pressure," explained the *Eagle*, "the fire boys were unable to cope with the situation." Billowing black smoke poured from the tar-paper roof while the volunteers tried to arch their feeble streams of water high enough to reach the flames. Bill Faulkner was among the crowd watching the ten-year-old building—worth more than $25,000 but insured for $4,000—go up in smoke. As he stood and saw his cousin's home and livelihood destroyed, the curious kind of black humor he sometimes displayed flickered out from him. Eyes on the fire, face straight, Faulkner spoke to young Calvin Brown standing next to him: "This is the only good show they've ever had in that place, and there are a lot of damned fools out there trying to ruin it."

There was a different kind of commotion one month later as they prepared to put the former governor of Mississippi in the Lafayette County jail. Responding to District Attorney L. E. Oldham's query, Theodore G. Bilbo pleaded guilty to contempt of court in failing to respond to the subpoena of Miss Birkhead's attorneys. He made a long statement of contrition and defense for not taking part in "the nauseating affair." Fined $100 and sentenced to thirty days, he was conducted to the jail by the U.S. Marshal. Mr. Patterson, the jailor, and his wife went to great pains to make Bilbo comfortable in the parlor of their living quarters in the jail. (His statement had so affected the judge that the sentence had been reduced to ten days.) There Bilbo entertained visitors and dictated letters opening his campaign for the governorship of the sovereign state of Mississippi. Mrs. Patterson prepared chicken dinners for the prisoner, and Chancellor Joseph Neely Powers had trays of hot food sent over from the university cafeteria. Swinging on the porch swing, "The Man Bilbo" held court. From the parlor he sent forth a public letter reflecting his indomitable spirit. "Stone walls do not a prison make," he wrote, "Nor iron bars a cage. . . ." On the last day of his sentence, he breakfasted with the chancellor and his wife at the university. On Saturday afternoon in Oxford he delivered a slashing address to 900 cheering citizens. Then, smiling and waving, he drove out of town on his way to stump the state.

At that same time Faulkner too was aiming for a definite goal. He had reworked most of the poems in *Vision of Spring*. Now he wanted to go beyond his "manuscript edition" for Estelle. On June 20, 1923, he wrote a letter to The Four Seas Company of Boston. They had published several books of verse, and Phil Stone had bought one of them, William Carlos Williams' *Sour Grapes*, the previous year. Faulkner's letter was short. "I am sending you today under separate cover a manuscript entitled 'Orpheus, and Other Poems,' " he wrote. "Enclosed find postage for its return if the manuscript be not accepted." He signed himself "Respectfully, William Faulkner," and waited.

Although he found the post office job to be growing progressively more onerous, it did make possible such luxuries as a car. In fact, he was moving up the scale in transportation. Murry Falkner had his eye on a new red Buick convertible. By now he was business manager as well as secretary of the university, and he could afford it. His son got him to agree to a trade. He would swap his present car for Billy's Ford and trade that in on the new Buick. His son became the new owner of the dark green, four-cylinder roadster, which he immediately painted white. And he had other uses for the car besides visits to Charleston and rides with coeds.

In a few months Reverend Christian would resign to take over the First Presbyterian Church of Tupelo. The Synod would provide a new pastor in Oxford, but he had to find someone to replace him as scoutmaster. He liked the way Bill Faulkner had helped him. "He was especially good with Nature Study and the boys ate it up," he recalled. "He was good and helpful, a gentleman always and a fine influence upon the boys. I appreciated then, and still do, his volunteer service."

As assistant scoutmaster Bill had once taken the troop by train to a summer camp at Waterford, twenty miles north of Oxford. There they had hiked three miles into the woods, where they put up tents, made camp, and stayed a week. Bill Faulkner played baseball with his scouts. He also wrote a story while he was there, they said. Often he would transport the scouts in his Ford, jamming in as many as he could and making several trips. Sometimes Mr. Murry would help, too. Now the minister asked him to become scoutmaster of the troop, and Faulkner agreed. He would hold meetings once or twice a month in their scout room on the second floor of Ira "Shine" Morgan's appliance store overlooking the Square. At other times they would meet at the Presbyterian church. J. B. Roach had stayed on after he passed the age for scouting and served as Faulkner's assistant scoutmaster. He found his chief very plain-spoken, direct, and devoted to what he was doing. Together they made plans for the summer's activities.

Again Faulkner took the troop on the train north to Warren Lakes, near Holly Springs. One of the scouts was young Dean Falkner. Another was his friend Eugene Bramlett, who, with most of the rest, looked forward to a standard after-dinner feature: Faulkner's stories around the campfire. Like Calvin Brown in the past, they would listen with horrified delight. Calvin Brown was not there now, for "with the cocksure intolerance of the adolescent, I shared the general contempt for the ineffectual Count Faulkner. He must have known this, but with his own invincible independence of public opinion, he was probably neither surprised nor hurt." Eugene Bramlett knew Faulkner as a shy man, but the shyness vanished when he began one of his tales. Others noticed these two different sides to the scoutmaster. One was a ten-year-old country boy named C. C. Hathorn. With his brother he had been invited to camp as a scouting prospect for next year. When he would walk through the university grounds on his way to school he would often see Faulkner, who sometimes would speak and other times act as though the boy were simply not there at all. But here in scout camp he was another person—outgoing, straightforward, and authoritative. But that did not mean that Hathorn liked scout camp. After two days he was homesick. And besides, coming from a farm, he was used to solid fare. Here breakfast consisted one morning of pork and beans and apple jelly. He and his brother went home.

Some of the scouts had a less reverent attitude toward their scoutmaster. Once, at a lake on Dr. Hedleston's property at College Hill, they had decided to see how impervious his quiet calm really was. His camping tastes were not spartan, and he had brought along a bedroll which the boys considered fancy. One night a few of them caught a grass snake and slipped it into the bedroll. At about ten o'clock they all went to bed. They listened, hopefully expectant. Suddenly their scoutmaster squirmed, then leaped up with a string of expletives. He recovered as they struggled to contain their laughter. "I'm sorry, boys," he apologized. "That snake must have wanted to find a warm place out of the cold."

It was the end of that same year that Ole Miss athlete Sollie Crane was asked by the Holly Springs P.T.A. to form a scout troop. In preparation for this job, Crane would go to the post office, where Faulkner would admit him to the back. There Faulkner would tell him at some length about how he handled scout work in Oxford. Sometimes, for instance, he would bring in guests, such as his friend Phil Stone, to address the scouts on some topic. He liked to see his boys advance from one grade to the next. He was a good instructor himself, naming flowers for them on hikes with the skill and knowledge of a botanist. Faulkner and Crane would study handbooks together and exchange ideas. When there was going to be a hike, Faulkner would come to work in his scoutmaster's uniform, including campaign hat, rather than the usual tweed suit, collar, and tie. He seemed a model troop leader. It was only later that Crane learned with surprise that he was also a writer.

With the fall came tryouts for the Marionettes. Social events, such as the possum hunts given by premedical students, were beginning. Faulkner presumably still joined in them from time to time. He kept on writing and reading. There had been no word from The Four Seas Company about *Orpheus, and Other Poems*. One of the books published that year which found its way into his library was entitled *Horses and Men: Tales Long and Short, from Our American Life*, by Sherwood Anderson.

Faulkner almost never did research as such for his work, but he may have been doing some now. Another possum hunt enthusiast was his boyhood friend and fellow railroad enthusiast, John Ralph Markette. Beginning his senior year at Ole Miss that fall of 1923, Markette would sometimes see Faulkner at the post office. "Often when I opened my box he would be looking through at me," Markette remembered. "We would talk to one another and reminisce about past events. He seemed to be interested in my studies and questioned me about my professors." The answers to those questions may have gotten into some material that would appear in a few months, attributed in part to Faulkner.

In November Faulkner decided to write The Four Seas Company. On November 13 they replied that they had written him about the manuscript on June 26. They enclosed a copy of that letter. The company's editor (identified only by the typed initials RES) had enjoyed reading the manuscript very much. It had some fine work in it, and though he heard echoes of Housman "and one or two other poets perhaps," they were no more than echoes. "You certainly have a flexible poetic method of your own," he wrote. It was the kind of book they would like to accept without question, but they had already "invested a good deal in poetry, which you probably know, and we can afford only two or three new books more a year entirely at our expense." So, there was only one thing they could suggest: "if you are in a position to stand solely the manufacturing cost of the first edition we might be willing to co-operate with you in trying to bring out this book, paying you a royalty on each copy sold sufficient to bring back the return of your original investment out of the sale of the first edition." If it were a success, they would issue future editions at their expense, paying him the standard royalty. "This, however, is only a suggestion." He replied on November 23. "As I have no money," he wrote, "I cannot very well guarantee the initial cost of publishing this mss.; besides, on re-reading some of the things, I see that they aren't particularly significant. And one may obtain no end of poor verse at a dollar and twenty-five cents per volume."

Six months earlier Faulkner had offered to read some of his poetry to J. D. Thames, an Ole Miss student, and a few others. They thought it was beautifully written. Now, seeing Faulkner in the post office again, Thames asked, "What happened to your book?"

"The publisher sent it back to me. It's beautiful but it's not what they're reading," Faulkner said. His face flushed. "Dammit, I'll write a book they'll read. If they want a book to remember, by God I'll write it."

He had turned twenty-six in September. This was not the only birthday to make him feel older. In mid-July John and Dolly had made him an uncle with the arrival of James Murry Falkner. Now the Oldhams received word that on December 3, in Shanghai, Estelle had given birth to a son, Malcolm Argyle Franklin. Faulkner might have felt like William Butler Yeats, who, in his poem "Pardon, old fathers," apologized for having reached the age of forty-nine with no children and "nothing but a book" to show for his life so far. He had been writing for years, and apart from things in student publications, all he had to show was the one poem in *The New Republic* and the other in *The Double Dealer*.

At the university post office, the Christmas rush came and went. The students departed for vacation, and then it was 1924. When *The Mississippian* appeared on Friday, January 11, half of page 7 was occupied by an advertisement. Most of it was set in the largest and boldest type the printer could find. It was an offer from "The Blue Bird Insurance Co." to insure students "Against Professors and Other Failures." The coed could take out insurance against a clumsy dancer's trampling her feet. A male student could insure against his girl's being wooed away by a campus "Sheik."

Insurance was offered against failing courses. Next week the premium rates would be published, scaled to the known proclivities of each professor. At the bottom of the ad were listed the company's officers: Louis Jiggitts, President; James Bell, President; William Falkner, President.

The second advertisement appeared as promised on January 18. The formula for the Examination Failure Rates was elaborate: "The professor's knowledge and experience plus the size of his class divided by the ignorance of his students. For example, where the ignorance of the class is predominant, the rate is low, as in the pharmacy department. On the other hand, the knowledge of the professor may off-set the ignorance, as in the freshman English classes, where the rate is very high."

In the next week's issue of *The Mississippian* there was another advertisement, even larger. The faculty had counterattacked. It was signed "A. P. Hudson, L. Wallace, B. England, D. H. Bishop, Salesmen." It had been written by Hudson, a lively man who liked younger people and welcomed this chance to see if he could reply to his friend Faulkner in his own terms. In blocks of type as large and black as those in the Blue Bird ad, the Midnight Oil Co. made its appeal. As recently as the summer before last there had been another questionable scheme briefly reviving hopes that Lafayette County might possess rich deposits of oil. The other kind of oil, the midnight oil burned by a student studying his work, would in most cases make unnecessary any kind of hedge against failing—insurance or any other protection. The first of three bogus endorsements was from "L. M. Jiggitts (late Oxoniensis), alias Viscount de Swank." The second was from "Count Wilhelm von Faulkner, Marquis de Lafayette (County), Postmaster-General (Retired)." In the last endorsement, "J. W. Bell, Jr., Retired Newspaper Man," described his discovery of Midnight Oil, which permitted him "to RETIRE into the postal service and GOLF with my good friend the Marquis de Lafayette." Hudson had not only used one of the devices of the Blue Bird advertisement, he had also reflected the campus images of the three men. And William Faulkner's image had come through clearly: a rather idle dreamer who enjoyed giving himself the airs of two rather different personae, the literary bohemian and the elegant foreigner.

He was probably still working on his poems at this time, sketching out new ones and revising those rejected in the *Orpheus* book. He still could not subsidize a book of his poems, but next time that might not be asked of him. And if he needed an incentive, there was always Stark Young to provide it. A versatile man, he had directed one play for the Theatre Guild on

Broadway and now he was going to "stage" a new play by Eugene O'Neill called *Welded* for the producers of the Provincetown Playhouse. And soon his new book, *The Three Fountains, or Italian Sketches*, would appear.

There was at least one other friend at home besides Phil Stone with whom he could talk literature. He was Eric Dawson, who taught French at the university and who had staged several French plays there. He had done more to put the university on the map, declared one writer in *The Mississippian*, than any of its organizations had. He had also published a book, *Henry Becque: Sa Vie et Son Théâtre*, and he had inscribed his name in a copy and given it to William Faulkner. In an unusual gesture, the recipient had added his own name and the same date just below.

Faulkner was reading widely that year. Phil Stone had passed one book on to him with the words, "This fellow is trying something new. This is something you should know about." It was a copy of the fourth printing of James Joyce's *Ulysses*, dated January, 1924. Faulkner took it and wrote his name and the year in it. When his Uncle John had seen how much Jack liked *Candide*, he had given him and Bill a set of Voltaire's works. Both brothers read extensively in the set. Another writer, vastly different from the great Frenchman, may also have been engaging Faulkner's attention about this time particularly through the pages of the magazines that came into the post office. This was Thomas Beer, whom Faulkner would later say he read as a young man and who "influenced me a lot." In the years 1918–1925 Beer published many short stories, with widely varying styles, in *The Saturday Evening Post* and a number in *Harper's* and *The Century*. Sometimes there was the toughness one would associate with writers such as Dashiell Hammett and Raymond Chandler or the satire of Sinclair Lewis. At other times he would use extravagant masses of the most romantic imagery. One interesting aspect of his technique, however, was his use of a community and a connected set of characters which reappeared in his fiction. A rather dominant woman named Mrs. Egg appeared in many of the stories, and the recurring locale was the town of Zerbetta, Ohio. "I got quite a lot from him," Faulkner would assert. He provided "a good tool, a good method, a good usage of words, approach to incident."

At this same time he was continuing his explorations in other areas of life. Reno DeVaux's place in Clarksdale had been closed down some time before. Now he was well-established just south of Memphis—as well-established as the Volstead Act, the vigilance of the law, and sharp competition would allow. In the spring of 1924 he was running a supper club in a big old-fashioned house just south of the suburb of Whitehaven. This was just a bit north of the Mississippi line, and when Bill Faulkner went to Memphis, he would sometimes call on Dot Wilcox, and together they might drive out to Reno's place. It was called the Belvedere Club, but the newspapers referred to it as Reno's Roadhouse. As time went on, Reno appeared more frequently in the papers.

Ostensibly, the club was an ordinary eating place. But one could get a drink there, in spite of prohibition. A customer could also play poker if Reno admitted him to one of the special rooms, or he could take a place at a crap table. If Reno admitted him to the attic, he could put some chips on a roulette number. Reno was doing his best to run a high-class club. He would wear a dinner jacket, and his guests had to wear dinner clothes, too. But Faulkner was an exception, and the doorman had standing orders to admit "the poet" no matter how he looked. Reno had an eye for detail. He thought that having dishes of peanuts around cheapened the appearance of the club and made it look like a bar. To tease him, Dot and Bill would sneak them into the club and then offer some to him. "Dot," he would say, "you're ruining this place." Sometimes Dot and Bill would stay for the whole evening and close up the club with Reno the next morning.

Faulkner never gambled there, though his friends did. Phil Stone still liked poker and sometimes he would shoot craps. Dot might try her luck at the same table. She had invested her money wisely, and now she owned five houses, so that when she wanted to play, she had the money to do it. One night Bill watched her lose nine hundred dollars. He made only one comment. "Dot," he said, "you shouldn't gamble."

But Reno ran honest games, and sometimes the house would lose. One afternoon Bill suggested to Dot that they go out to the club for supper. He knew that Reno had been suffering a run of bad luck all that week. On the way out to the club Bill had an idea.

"Dot," he said, "I'm going to have some fun with Reno. I'll tell him it's his magnolia tree that's causing it and I'll bet you a hundred dollars he'll cut it down."

When they got there Reno was in the front yard with his chauffeur. "Reno," Bill said, "that's the worst luck a person can have."

"What is?" Reno asked.

Bill gestured with his head. "To have a magnolia tree in your yard. Didn't you know that?"

"No," he answered, "I never knew that before." They talked for a while longer, then had dinner and left. The next time they went back, the magnolia tree was gone.

Reno's luck continued to run against him. On the night of April 20, 1924, Sheriff Will Knight received a message that liquor was being served at Reno's Roadhouse. As he drove up the road, a car with drunken passengers went by. When the doorman opened to Knight's knock, the sheriff put him under arrest. He found twelve couples in the dining room, he reported, several of them "prominent Memphians." Reno, his brother, and two employees were taken to the county jail and lodged there, charged with violating the liquor law and a threatened breach of the peace. For quite a while Reno would not have to worry about how his luck ran at the tables.

At home in Oxford a few weeks earlier, it had seemed that charges of financial irregularity might be lodged by the state legislature against such unlikely parties as Chancellor J. N. Powers and Secretary M. C. Falkner. The attorney general's department was looking into the alleged payment by Powers of federal funds to the board of trustees by way of the legislature. Both men denied the charges. By May 1 the investigating committee had issued no report, but they apparently did not feel that Powers had done anything discreditable or illegal. (This would be of no particular help to him the following July when the board would replace him with Alfred H. Hume and he would have to return to Jackson to sell real estate.) Murry Falkner, as gruff and busy as ever, kept on running the business end of the university.

The eldest son of the secretary and business manager was by now back on the golf course in the bright May sunshine. He won his first match in the annual spring tournament of the Ole Miss Golf Club and advanced at least as far as the semifinal round, where he met Robert Torrey, professor of mathematics, whom the Blue Bird Insurance Co. had rated exactly in the middle of the premium scale, equidistant from General Hemingway and Professor Hudson. The results seem not to have been recorded.

He and Jack went around the course together occasionally. One day as they began, Jack said, "I'd better win today. This course has cost me enough, what with the time I've spent." Jack had written a golf course story and sent it to *The Saturday Evening Post*, which rejected it. "Let me see it," Faulkner said. A week later he gave it back, partly rewritten. "There," he said, "it's better now, isn't it?" Jack thought so, but he did not submit it to the *Post* again.

One day A. P. Hudson called for Faulkner at the Delta Psi house and they went out to the course together. Hudson knew him to be a serious and accurate golfer, but he could never tell what his manner would be. On some days he might display a rapid-fire talkativeness between shots, and on others he might go the whole round barely answering the questions put to him. Now he seemed "more than usually withdrawn. . . . Several times I saw him on the tee, waiting for the golfers ahead to negotiate the rocks, stumps, gullies, etc., in the fairway, thoughtfully plunking on the seat with his putter, as if he were a blacksmith beating out something." When they played again a few days later, Faulkner asked Hudson home for a drink. They walked up the staircase and entered the room at the top of the small tower. Hudson saw manuscript material scattered on a worktable. The subject of Faulkner's writing had never been broached between them before. In the mood of the moment, Hudson ventured a question.

"What are you working on now?" he asked.

"This," Faulkner replied, picking up two sheets of his small printed script.

"Would you mind reading it?" Hudson asked.

As Hudson listened, glass in hand, Faulkner read the poem "in his shy, almost singing voice":

Once upon an adolescent hill
There lay a lad who watched amid the piled
And silver shapes of aircarved cumulae
A lone uncleaving eagle, and the still
Serenely blue dissolving of desire.

In the next two stanzas, imagination took the boy up where the now-vanished eagle had soared. He sailed over the vast lake of the sky, past the huge headlands of the clouds,

And saw the fleeing canyons of the sky
Tilt to banshee wire and slanted aileron,
And his own lonely shape on scudding walls
Where harp the ceaseless thunders of the sun.

Now, at twenty-six, he was using the remembered dreams of Billy Falkner at ages fifteen and twenty-one.

At the time he read to Hudson he must have had a good many other poems on his mind. Phil Stone had written The Four Seas Company on May 13, 1924, informing them that he had a manuscript by a young man of great talent. He knew that Four Seas had been especially good to young poets.

Would they publish this work by an unknown poet if he personally advanced the cost of publication? And would they quote a price? Four Seas replied by return mail. They were interested and would probably do it. In less than a week Stone set off a manuscript entitled *The Marble Faun,* consisting of the pastoral poems Faulkner had written five years before, now reworked into a tighter cycle. Enthusiastically throwing himself into the role of literary agent, Stone told Four Seas they they would profit financially as well as artistically. A young writer had a special debt to his first publisher, Stone wrote, and this author already had in preparation some work much better than *The Marble Faun.*

In three weeks the reply arrived from Boston. The editor (who signed himself "EID") had found the manuscript excellent; many of the couplets were striking and beautiful. They would be glad to bring out an edition of a thousand copies for about $400. They would set a royalty rate that would pay the money back on the first edition, and subsequent printings would be made at their own expense. The cost apparently dampened the pleasure of the agent and the author somewhat, but it did not really daunt them. Neither of them, Stone wrote back, could put up $400 right now. But he thought they could soon, so they could send the contracts on. They were mailed on June 30, and they specified a retail price of $1.50 with an author's royalty of 30 percent on this first edition of 1,000 copies. The agent and author could now study at length and in detail the terms on which William Faulkner (and Phil Stone, vicariously) could make his entry into the world of genuine authorship.

This must have made Faulkner's duties a little more bearable as he sold stamps and sorted mail. Now, of course, just after graduation, these duties were at a minimum. As a subsequent postmaster put it, "there was very little to do except read magazines and cards. . . . the postmaster could take a seat somewhere in the vicinity of the service window and go uninterrupted for hours during this summer period." Walking home at four after one such day, Faulkner heard his name called from a parked car. It was Bob Farley. After serving simultaneously as student body president and mayor of Oxford, he was preparing to practice law in Oxford. With him was a Tennessean named Ridley Wills, who wrote a column called "Rambling with Ridley" for the Memphis *Commercial Appeal.* He had already done a column on Farley. Returning to Oxford, he had asked Farley if he could introduce him to Faulkner. Farley said he would try, but he couldn't make any promises—Faulkner talked only to those he liked. "He might just leave you," Farley said.

When he introduced them he found to his relief it was one of Faulkner's "good days." Farley asked if he wanted to go for a ride and he immediately accepted. Miss Maud was entertaining her bridge club and he wanted to get out of the house.

"Wait for me," he told them, "I have to go in the house for a minute." He emerged soon, his shirt front bulging, and got into the back seat of Farley's car. As they drove away Faulkner produced from under his shirt a bottle of "white lightning" and a single glass. This came as no surprise to Farley. If Faulkner didn't enter into conversations at the post office, said a friend, he didn't miss a word—or a drink. "There is no such thing as bad whiskey," Faulkner declared, "some are just better than others." So now, as Murry Falkner began to drink less—substituting pleasures such as racing one of the daily trains to the bridge in his red Buick—his son began to drink more.

It was a hot July day. Faulkner, Farley, and Wills began to drink, turn and turn about, working their way through the bottle of corn liquor which "burnt going down and kicked like a mule." The tenor of the conversation changed and deepened as Faulkner began to discuss philosophies of religion. Asked about his beliefs, Wills said he was not much of a Christian.

"If you could be anything you want to," he asked Faulkner, "what would you rather be?"

"A lay reader in the Episcopal Church," Faulkner answered.

"Oh," Wills said. "You're a real Christian. You want to go to heaven."

"Certainly," Faulkner said solemnly.

"You want to be an angel. What would you do until you got to be a full-fledged angel?"

"I'd manicure the wings of the other angels, do what I could."

"That's no goal!" Wills said derisively.

Faulkner clapped him on the back. "My boy," he told him, "you don't have the true Rotary spirit."

As the afternoon drifted away they began to feel dehydrated. Farley drove to the golf course, where they went to the stand Ned Beanland kept. Nearby stood Oliver Abbott Shaw, dean of the school of education, ready to tee off. Suddenly Wills ran out, seized the driver from the astonished man, and hit the teed-up ball. Then he ran down the fairway, retrieved the ball, and returned to hand both the ball and club to Shaw. Farley just stood there. Shaw's partner, Judge Thomas Charles Kimbrough, dean of the law school, came over.

"Who is that fellow?" he asked Farley.

"I don't know, Judge," the young lawyer about to go into practice answered, "just some fellow who came over here with Bill Faulkner."

When they managed to return to the car, Farley declared he had had enough. He wanted to go home, but Faulkner and Wills demurred. They wanted to finish the bottle. Finally Farley let them out at the Colonial Hotel, where Wills was staying. Wills would be stuck with Faulkner all night, he thought to himself. This was usually what happened now that the drinking had become such a serious pastime with Faulkner. Farley drove home. The next morning Wills returned to Memphis and Faulkner reported for another day at the post office.

By July 19 Faulkner had entered the correspondence with Four Seas. "I believe I shall be able to supply the guarantee of $400," he wrote, but first he wanted some information. Clause 10 specified that if the company decided against reprinting the book, the author might buy the plates for "the manufacturing cost of such plates." Could this be changed to "the actual value of the melted plates"? And could they include in the contract a definite publication date? Four Seas answered affirmatively by return mail. He could change Clause 10 as he suggested, and if the contracts were signed now and returned he could write in the publication date as "not later than November 1, 1924." This Faulkner did. And, with a frugality Great-grandfather Murry himself might have admired, he made a few more changes. The author might buy the plates, he wrote in, by paying the "value of the plates as old metal at current prices." The handwriting had completed the metamorphosis begun with the early poems in a flowing hand. The printing was now small and tight, and neat, but just this side of legible. It would change little during the rest of his life.

On August 4 Four Seas added the proviso that the author would advance $200 with the contract and $200 "with complete proofs." President Edmund R. Brown of Four Seas signed the contract, and it was sent off to Oxford. It was duly returned, presumably with a check for $200. The acknowledging letter thanked Faulkner and assured him that the dedication would be included. It was, simply, "To My Mother."

By August 20 Stone had resumed the Oxford end of the correspondence. Faulkner had received Four Seas' letter of August 6, but "Mr. Falkner is not so very keen at attending to business and I shall probably have to handle most of the business matters connected with his part of the publication of this check." (He had actually dictated—or his secretary had typed—"check" for "book." Was it an insignificant error, or some sort of slip?) Stone said he would supply a short preface which would include the biographical sketch they wanted, a list for review copies, another for advertising circulars, and a paragraph describing the book. Four Seas had also asked for a half-dozen glossy prints. "Mr. Falkner is not keen on photography and flatly refuses to put out any money on photographs," Stone wrote. "However, I am sure that I can handle this part of it all right and can have these photographs in your hands not later than September 15th." Things seemed to be moving along.

One reason Faulkner could not attend to *The Marble Faun* was that this was the scouts' camping season. He took the dozen and a half members of the troop on an overnight outing near Thacker's mountain, where the fruit train engineers used to sound the whistles on those far-off mornings of his childhood. Wayne Sneed and some other scouts, on their first outdoor trip, took note of Faulkner's "apparent familiarity with outdoor life. He had already impressed us with his sincerity, interest in our welfare and dedication to his job as scoutmaster." Scout W. H. Hutchinson of the Eagle Patrol felt the same way. Faulkner "was patient, also caustic when needed, and by our inept standards he was wonderfully competent in the woods, especially on overnight hikes." Besides this, he understood very well "the childish savage's mental and psychological processes. . . ." Much from those outings remained vivid, particularly "the manner in which we made the days and nights reasonably hideous by emulating the eagle's scream of SK-REEEEEEE! with a rising inflection at the end."

On Monday, August 18, Faulkner had taken his scouts to Hedleston Lake. He had saved his two weeks' vacation for this encampment. A week later he was joined by assistant scoutmaster R. M. Guess. Johncy came for the second week and spelled his brother at telling campfire ghost stories. The climax of the formal program came on the evening of the twenty-sixth when the Oxford Rotary Club motored out to the lake for supper, the presentation of awards to the scouts, and a demonstration. Scout Dean Falkner won a piece of jewelry for hitting the most home runs in the fourteen-and-up group. And after some comic skits by the troop members, he put on a life-saving exhibit with another scout. "The Rotarians were impressed with the life of the camp and intend to cooperate more fully next summer in this work," reported the *Eagle*. Faulkner had worked hard in organizing and running the camp, and obviously he had enjoyed leading the Peckerwood baseball team over R. M. Guess's Bullfrogs and captaining the Catfish baseball team even when they lost to Guess's Mud Turtles. He liked

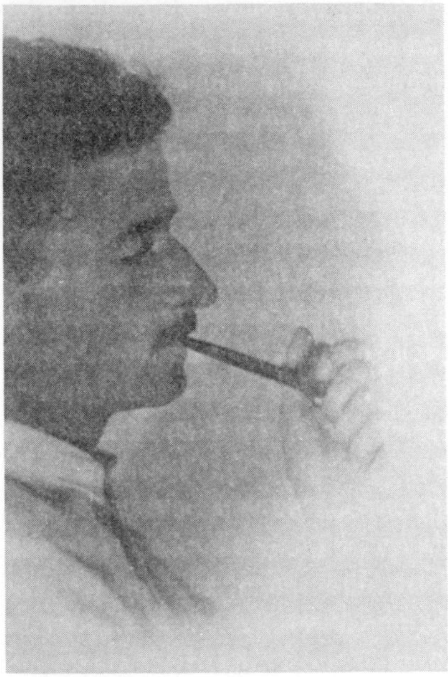

Publicity photographs of William Faulkner, late summer, 1924, for promotion of *The Marble Faun.*

camp life—the outdoor food, the early rising, and perhaps even a bit of cold lake water. Breaking camp to return to the post office could hardly have been pleasant.

Faulkner's attention to duty in that brick building had been lately growing even less rigorous than usual. The Reverend W. I. Hargis had failed to receive a letter from the bank, and then his *Baptist Record* stopped coming. He wrote to the publisher and learned that the *Record* had been sent out on time. Going to the post office, he found several copies in the garbage can at the rear of the building. Another boxholder argued with Faulkner about the nondelivery of a magazine. When he left, Faulkner told Jack he didn't see why anyone should get upset over mail. "Why couldn't he wait?" he said. "He probably would enjoy it more if he waited for it." The simmering discontent of some of the patrons was suddenly close to boiling. Phil Stone called Senator Pat Harrison, a family friend, and asked for help.

"What in hell am I going to do, Phil?" the senator answered. "Why don't you let us go on and fire him?" To Stone it was not that simple. The job represented income, and there were the costs of *The Marble Faun* to meet and the need to lay up something for the future. "He needs the money, Mr. Pat," he said. "He's going to quit pretty soon anyway." There the matter rested for the moment. Stone turned again to *The Marble Faun* and managed to get the author to help with "the business end of its production."

Stone had to deliver the photograph he had promised to Four Seas. "We went up to Memphis to have it made," he said later. The photographer posed the poet almost in profile. His white shirt was tieless and his dark hair slightly tousled. His face seemed to have filled out a bit, almost to have lengthened. The eyes and nose still dominated, but the mustache was full and the jaw was strong and firm. Nothing indicated his slight stature, and the pictures were those of a man who looked appraising, both wary and intense. "See there where Bill's collar is open?" Stone would say. "We wanted him to look like a romantic poet—you know, like Byron with his thrown-back head and flowing tie. Except we couldn't put on him a tie like that."

On September 9 Faulkner wrote Four Seas to say that he was sending two photos and a short biographical sketch. He had typed the sketch himself. It read, "Born in Mississippi in 1897. Great-grandson of Col. W. C. Faulkner, C.S.A., author of 'The White Rose of Memphis,' 'Rapid Ramblings in Europe,' etc. Boyhood and youth were spent in Mississippi, since then has been (1) undergraduate (2) house painter (3) tramp, day laborer, dishwasher in various New England cities (4) Clerk in Lord and Taylor's book shop in New York City (5) bank- and postal clerk. Served during the war in the British Royal Air Force. A member of Sigma Alpha Epsilon Fraternity. Present temporary address, Oxford, Miss. 'The Marble Faun' was written in the spring of 1919."

It was a sketch containing—for a creative writer—really very little elaboration upon the truth. And there were two particularly interesting touches. He had changed the spelling of the Old Colonel's name to accord with his own, and he had given Oxford as his "Present temporary address. . . ." Was he going to Charleston again for an extended visit? Did he mean to try New York once more? Some of his friends certainly traveled. Stark Young had been in town in mid-July to visit his father after having spent two months in Italy. In early June, Eric Dawson had sailed for Paris, where he would be a guest of honor at the National Theatre for a gala performance of Henry Becque's play before returning in September.

Faulkner had been at the post office job for the better part of three years now, and he must have felt ready to move. If he had not thought recently about such a change himself, he had a few days earlier received a letter that would immediately have suggested the idea.

It had been sent from the office of the postal inspector in Corinth on September 2, 1924. And it was not just a letter. The information at the top revealed that it was "Case No. 133733-C." The heading "Subject" was followed by a brief statement: "*University, Mississippi*: Charges vs the postmaster: neglects official duties; indifferent to interests of patrons; mistreatment of mail, etc." In considerable detail the nearly three-page letter set forth seven different categories of charges. And though Inspector Mark Webster signed himself "Respectfully yours," he ended on rather an ominous-sounding note: "You will please advise me in writing, within five days from this date, stating whether the charges are true, in part or wholly so, and show cause, if any, why you should not be removed. Failure to receive a reply in this prescribed time will be deemed as evidence that you have no defense to offer, and action will be taken accordingly." It was now the postmaster's turn to worry about the mail.

22

September, 1924-January, 1925

—to look out at the outdoors—the funerals, the passing, the people, the freedom, the sunlight, the free air—

—*Requiem for a Nun* (198)

It was as though he had not seen a railroad in thirty-eight years. . . . But now it would be different. He could watch them, himself in freedom, as they fled past in freedom, the two of them mutual, in a way even interdependent: it to do the fleeing in smoke and noise and motion, he to do the watching. . . .

—*The Mansion* (405)

The trouble was, of course, that the charges were true. There was little he could say in rebuttal of Paragraph 1, which charged "That you are neglectful of your duties, in that you are a habitual reader of books and magazines, and seem reluctant to cease reading long enough to wait on the patrons; that you have a book being printed at the present time, the greater part of which was written while on duty at the post-office; that some of the patrons will not trust you to forward their mail, because of your past carelessness and these patrons have their neighbors forward same for them while away on their vacations. . . ." The names of six such patrons, including Reverend W. I. Hargis and General Hemingway, were listed. It also appeared that paid-for mailboxes had been closed, paid-for C.O.D.'s had been sent back, and claimed parcels had been returned marked "unclaimed."

Each of the succeeding six paragraphs seemed equally damaging. One patron had been obliged to get a note from Murry Falkner before the postmaster would deliver a letter to him. Another also needed Murry Falkner's help before he could obtain a package. Other charges were sweeping: "That you are indifferent to interest of patrons, unsocial, and rarely ever speak to patrons of the office unless absolutely necessary; that you do not give the office the proper attention, opening and closing same at your convenience; that you can be found playing golf during office hours." Some of the attention he had paid to business had been irregular at the very least: "That you mistreat mail of all classes, including registered mail; that you have thrown mail with return postage guaranteed and all other classes in the garbage can by the side entrance, near the rear door. . . ." Twenty-six addresses were listed, both individuals and institutions, whose mail had been handled thus. As a matter of fact, "this has gotten to be such a common occurrence that some patrons have gone to this garbage can to get their magazines, should they not be in their boxes when they looked for them." His treatment of return receipts and postage-due mail was equally negligent. A final charge, almost like an afterthought, alleged "That you have permitted the following unauthorized persons to have access to the workroom of the office: Dick Bell, D. B. Holmes, Jimmy Jones, M. A. Pigford and others, and have permitted card playing in the office." The crisis had come as no surprise to members of the family. Uncle John put it succinctly: "He just *wouldn't* work."

There is no indication that Faulkner replied to Inspector Webster's letter. Stone may have advised him to try to get the office in order, sit tight, and wait. Perhaps Faulkner was now able to recall patches of pleasure that had relieved the annoyance of the job. He had organized a society based at the post office called the M.O.A.K.S. The first two letters stood for "The Mystical Order of," but no one besides Faulkner knew what the rest stood for. The others suspected it was something bawdy. Faulkner, Sonny Bell, Holden Van ("Skeet") Kincannon, Branham Hume (the new chancellor's son), and the eleven other original members all carried one-dollar canes on club occasions. They had appeared together with canes and derbies at a football game and other events. When a new member was tapped for M.O.A.K.S., one of the old members sold him his cane for fifteen dollars. There were no other bylaws that he had to learn.

Musicales had also been held, when Johncy strummed his mandolin and Branham Hume plunked his ukulele. There had been hours on the golf course, when Jack had minded the office for him and Sonny Bell or closed it and come along. Then there was teatime after golf. It was, apparently, too late in the day to change now. Faulkner was playing out a rubber of bridge one day with George Healy, Skeet Kincannon and Sonny Bell when they were disturbed by an insistent knocking at the General Delivery window. Faulkner turned to see a stranger standing there. When he walked to the window the man wordlessly held out a card bearing his credentials. He was Inspector Webster from Corinth.

Faulkner admitted him and then returned to the bridge table. "Well, we've got to go," he said. They all rose and left the building.

As they crossed the street, Skeet Kincannon broke the silence. "Bill, don't you feel strange leaving this place for the last time this way?" he asked. "Next time we come here it'll be like everybody else. We'll have to treat the post office like a post office and not like a club."

Faulkner was silent as they walked for the better part of a minute. Finally he spoke: "I reckon I'll be at the beck and call of folks with money all my life, but thank God I won't ever again have to be at the beck and call of every son of a bitch who's got two cents to buy a stamp."

But the break was not to be that quick or easy. There was still the matter of complaints and charges, the mail to be found, and accounts to be rendered. Clues to the missing mail were supplied by the signed complaint forms Inspector Webster brought with him. Jack Falkner returned to the post office with his brother to watch. "I remember the postal inspector as a conscientious, hard-working public servant," he wrote. Webster found a number of the undelivered items. Later, recalling the inquiry into his handling of mail coming into the post office, Faulkner said, "I'm glad they didn't check the outgoing mail."

It seemed to Jack that Webster was confronted by a unique and frustrating dilemma with no rules to guide him. "He could not accuse us of having misdirected mail which we had never touched, or of concealing that which we had never seen." Jack now had to depart to take up his job with the Treasury Department, but there was no mistaking the upshot of the investigation. "Bill wasn't postmaster much longer."

Jack had been right in his assessment of Mark Webster. The inspector had lectured them, telling them that the mail was a public trust and that they had made a complete mess of operations in this little fourth-class post office. But he was understanding too, and in the conferences he had had with Faulkner while the post office affairs were being unscrambled, a kind of friendship had sprung up between the two. Faulkner told the older man he was glad that the postal authorities had sent someone to conduct the investigation who had a sense of humor and who also realized what "a hell of a job" he had.

Finally Webster had located all the missing mail he could and sifted his way through the office records. Faulkner could relax. He certainly could not continue as postmaster, but neither did he have to worry about prosecution. He was allowed to hand in his resignation, and on October 31 he turned over his keys and the office's $1,300 in cash and stock to the new postmaster. The incumbent—strangely enough the same Sonny Bell who had served as clerk—duly made out a receipt to "W. C. Falkner." Faulkner signed other forms and was finished, once and for all, with the post office.

It was an enormous relief. No longer would he pay any attention to the demands of the clock or allow himself to be restricted by the routine of an employee's day. He was free now, he said, to be outdoors, once again the observer he had for so long been. People had called him a dreamer. Well, now he could smoke and dream on his own time. And he could write.

The post office job was not the only thing Faulkner had lost recently. It was well-known that he, like his father and grandfather in their times, drank heavily. This was particularly repugnant to one of the local ministers, not only on general principles, but also because he was entrusted with the care of the young: the leadership of a more or less church-affiliated scout troop. Faulkner was removed as unfit for the job.

Faulkner had kept in touch with Ben Wasson, now practicing law in Greenville. His letters to Ben were frank and sometimes amusing. In one he told him that he knew he was a genius (as he had matter-of-factly informed Dorothy Oldham on the golf course one day). In another he wrote of his admiration for Sherwood Anderson's short story "I'm a Fool." In still another he related to Wasson some of his difficulties at the post office. He apparently thought rather well of his reply to Skeet Kincannon's question about his feelings on leaving. But he rather primly used dashes rather than spelling out "son of a bitch."

Occasionally he had visited Ben at his home, where he was a welcome guest. Ben's little sister, Ruth, would sometimes come in when he and her brother were talking. She would often be carrying gold slippers which belonged to her sister, Lady Ree. A ritual evolved between Ruth and Faulkner. She would bring the slippers and he would make up stories about them. Listening and watching, Ben had the feeling that Faulkner somehow yearned for a sister of his own.

On some of these visits to Greenville, Faulkner and Ben would walk along the oak-shaded streets down to the high massive levee that held back the Mississippi. Sometimes they would sit down there and stretch their legs, looking out over the wide muddy river at the small boats and the large barges on their way down to New Orleans. On one of these occasions Faulkner brought along Sherwood Anderson's *Horses and Men.* As they sat there, Faulkner read one of Anderson's stories to Ben.

By this time Anderson's reputation was extremely high. He was warmly admired by sophisticated readers in America, and in England he was attracting almost as much attention as Sinclair Lewis. His work appeared often in the *Dial,* and that influential magazine had presented him with its first annual $2,000 award. By early 1922 Anderson had settled briefly in New Orleans. He liked it immediately. He worked well there, enjoying the atmosphere, the good company, and the good food. His open warmth attracted friendship, and his work earned him the worship of young literary aspirants. He liked the place so much that he did an article for *The Double Dealer* entitled "New Orleans, *The Double Dealer* and the Modern Movement in America."

Anderson described the great change wrought by "the speeding up and the standardization of life and thought. . . ." A magazine such as *The Double Dealer* fortunately worked against the standardization and falsification of the big-circulation periodicals. In a way, New Orleans too represented the same saving individualism. He wanted other writers to know about the Vieux Carré, where he had a room. "I want to tell them of long quiet walks to be taken on the levee in back-of-town, where old ships, retired from service, thrust their masts up into the evening sky. On the streets here the crowds have a more leisurely stride, the negro life issues a perpetual challenge to the artists, sailors from many lands come up from the water's edge and idle on the street corners, in the evening soft voices, speaking strange tongues, come drifting up to you out of the street." He said that he was writing about New Orleans from his own "angle." And the city might not thank him. "Perhaps if I can bring more artists here they will turn out a ragtag enough crew." In any event, it seemed a genuine invitation.

Anderson had been back in New Orleans since the summer. He had brought his new wife with him, the former Elizabeth Prall. Faulkner had kept in touch with his one-time employer by way of Stark Young. Ben thought it would be a fine idea for Faulkner to renew his acquaintance with Miss Elizabeth and get to know her husband. "Why don't you go to New Orleans and meet him?" he suggested. Faulkner had doubtless been thinking of the same possibility himself, but his reticence had increased rather than diminished in the three years since he had seen Miss Prall. He might take advantage of such a trip, though, to drop in at the offices of *The Double Dealer* to talk to Julius Weis Friend or John McClure, perhaps, to see if they would take another of his poems.

Though he did not propose to join any literary group, he did feel a certain pull, he later said—the pull any young writer feels "to be with people that have the same problems and the same interests as him, that won't laugh at what he's trying to do, won't laugh at what he says no matter how foolish it might sound to the Philistine. . . ." In the end, probably on a subsequent visit, he took the train south to New Orleans.

The Andersons had taken an apartment in the Pontalba Buildings in the heart of the Vieux Carré on the south side of Jackson Square. They had been erected in 1849, it was said, by James Gallier, Sr., for the Baroness Pontalba, who had become interested in beautifying the Place d'Armes, as the Square was known under French rule. These two buildings flanking the Square had become increasingly popular as interest in the Vieux Carré had grown. A number of artists had moved into them, but few could afford to refurbish and redecorate as attractively as Elizabeth Anderson was doing. It was probably there that she greeted her former clerk and introduced him to her husband.

"I happened to be in New Orleans and I had gone to call on her," Faulkner later said, "because I wasn't going to bust in on Mr. Anderson without an invitation from him. I didn't think that I would see him at all, that he would probably be in his study working, but it happened that he was in the room at the time, and we talked and we liked one another from the start, and it was just the chance that I had gone to call on Miss Prall that I had known who had been kind to me when I was a clerk in a book store that I came to meet him."

The man Faulkner met embodied a set of physical contradictions: his face combined oversensitivity and strength, his dress blended bohemia and the race track, and his figure was bulky yet somehow undersized. Two years before, at the New York apartment of Scott and Zelda Fitzgerald, he had struck John Dos Passos as "an appealing sort of man with curly graying hair and strangely soft wrinkles in his face." He had "large shadowed eyes and prominent eyebrows and a self-indulgent mouth." He looked swarthy, sometimes florid. "His features were broad," wrote one friend, "crude-cut like the not quite finished work of a genial wood-carver, yet exaggeratedly, almost femininely tender, and his eyes had both an animal distance and a depth of human subtlety and candor." He favored corduroy shirts and tweed jackets, loud socks and velour hats. Faulkner would later recall from one of his costumes a "bright blue racetrack shirt and vermilion-mottled Bohemian Windsor tie. . . ." But there was no doubt what was most striking about him: his deep-set, sometimes merry, and often brooding eyes, "black and impenetrable and receiving—receiving you, receiving all and mingling us all with those dreams that came back changed into imperishable stuff. . . ." Faulkner was surprised, though, that he was such a short man; "when he was sitting behind a table . . . he looked like a big man, but when he stood up he wasn't. And I think that he maybe would like to have been more imposing-looking. . . ." It seems clear enough, however, that Faulkner was impressed with the author of *Winesburg, Ohio* and *Horses and Men*, and set out to create an impression which would not be lost on him.

Hamilton Basso, an aspiring writer then enrolled at Tulane University, recalled an occasion such as Faulkner's first meeting with Anderson must have been. "Almost every Saturday night he and his wife . . . had some of us to dinner. It was on one of these occasions that Faulkner and I were introduced to each other. He was then twenty-seven. . . . I recall that we talked about the South—Faulkner's South: the world of Oxford, Mississippi . . . but what I best recollect are his beautiful manners, his soft speech, his controlled intensity, and his astonishing capacity for hard drink." Apparently Faulkner demonstrated other propensities, too. One was his love for —or need of—role-playing. This time it was not the role of the bohemian artist he had essayed from time to time in Oxford, but the one Mrs. Joice remembered from New York in 1921. The limp that Johncy had noticed when his brother descended from the train had apparently returned, and it was much worse. Nor was it the extent of his injuries. Most of the new friends he made in New Orleans remained convinced for years that his airplane accident had left him with a silver plate in his head. They could see that he drank heavily. Soon the impression was general that this alleviated the pain from these wounds. Outgoing and sympathetic, Anderson at once took to this young guest who was only a little more than half his age.

Anderson had knocked about a good deal both as boy and man, and he had developed something of a taste for the low life and raffish company. He had visited bordellos and—like Faulkner with Stone in Memphis and Clarksdale—sometimes enjoyed talking to the worldly-wise but often sentimental women who ran them. He had not lost this taste. The January–February 1925 issue of *The Double Dealer* would contain a poem by him entitled "One Puzzled Concerning Himself." The first of the six stanzas accurately signaled the contents of the others:

I had been at the flesh pots, all
night—sitting beside them, walking
back and forth in the moonlight. I
had gourged [sic] *myself. My body was distended.*

There lived at this time in New Orleans a woman named Aunt Rose Arnold who owned three or four houses in the city. She lived in one on Chartres Street next to Le Petit Théâtre du Vieux Carré, one block west of St. Louis Cathedral and half a block north of Jackson Square, which it faced. Aunt Rose stood over six feet tall. She was not particularly attractive, but her tightly corseted big-bosomed figure exuded a motherly quality. Well before the turn of the century she had worked as a telegrapher in Chicago, and her hair was still as red in 1924 as when she had tapped the key for the Inter-Ocean News Service. But she did not earn her living from telegraphy after she moved to New Orleans.

In the years before 1917, when New Orleans was a wide-open city, one of the most striking evidences of its flamboyant vices was "the Blue Book," a directory of New Orleans prostitutes including photographs of the prettiest ones. There, flanked by advertisements for distillers, cigar-makers, and taxis, would be printed testimonials for such stars of the Tenderloin as May Spencer, Gipsy Shaffer, and "Countess" Willie Piazza and her girls, who plied their trade amid a décor of gilded mirrors, green plush chairs, and a white grand piano. Although Aunt Rose and her charges never worked in the midst of such elegance, the names and addresses were there for the discriminating reader in the pages of "the Blue Book." She had prospered, and though she had not married, she gratified her maternal instinct by adopting a two-year-old waif whom she raised with great propriety. When the war came her adopted son joined a Scots regiment. After his death on the Western Front his effects were sent back. Sometimes she would show a close friend some of her mementos, including his regimental kilt. At the insistence of American military authorities, Storyville, the red-light district just northwest of the Vieux Carré, had been closed down in 1917. But Aunt Rose's place continued to flourish; rooms were rented to individual girls and to couples seeking safe assignations. Downstairs in a large room was a green, baize-covered table. She did not run the game played there, but the house took its percentage from each pot. Her motto, framed behind glass, hung on the wall. It read, 'DON'T BE A GOOD FELLOW.'—JOHN D. ROCKEFELLER. She also ran a candy shop.

Aunt Rose had remained vigorous despite her years, and she enjoyed entertaining. She was said to be very generous, helping itinerant writers and looking after sailors off ships. Stories had grown up about her. She had a sheet-copper bathtub which had been made to order for her, it was said. She was helped into its steaming water, then bathed and finally massaged by her German butler, who had supposedly been rendered impotent by an excess of saltpeter consumed during long years in the army. She would often be heard shouting for him. But now he was gone, and she lived alone, her only company a parrot.

Apparently one day Sherwood Anderson and Faulkner went out for a stroll together, Anderson walking slowly as Faulkner limped along beside him. Both, it seems, were feeling their liquor. Finally Anderson made his way along Chartres Street to Aunt Rose's house with its little patio at the rear where a banana tree grew. This must have been one of the times when Faulkner felt like talking, as he had when Basso listened to him. It seems that he talked about his home, among other things. At this time Anderson was deeply absorbed in the writing of his novel *Dark Laughter.* Behind the frustration and seeking of his main characters, he meant to have "the mysterious, detached laughter of the blacks." Providing a counterpoint to the neurotic rush of modern life would be the "dark, earthy laughter—the Negro, the earth, and the river—that suggests the title." Anderson was a Midwesterner—a man of Ohio, of Chicago—and when Faulkner spoke of home in that soft Mississippi drawl, Anderson listened intently.

They kept on drinking, and eventually, it appears, Faulkner simply went to sleep. But by that time he had talked even more about his home and his family, his wartime experiences, and the wounds which caused this kind of search for sleep. What Anderson did not know was that Faulkner cared as little for "facts" as he did. If he had known him as Phil Stone had, or Estelle Franklin, he would have been aware that "after a few drinks, he would tell people anything." But his invention had done no one any harm, and he and Anderson had enjoyed it. Besides, Anderson had a story. It was entitled "A Meeting South." The protagonist was "a little Southern man" named David, who was befriended by a retired madam called Aunt Sally. David was modeled after Faulkner, and Aunt Sally after Aunt Rose Arnold.

The manuscript was in New York by November 12. Faulkner, of course, had been back in Oxford for some time, but his experience of New Orleans had encouraged him to return. And apparently Miss Elizabeth had told him that he was welcome to stay with her and Sherwood whenever he did.

At home Faulkner still had the golf course, and his occupational troubles had not hurt his game. Knowing the course intimately, he was able to play in very fast company. William Eidt, the golf pro at the Tuckaway Country Club in Milwaukee, wintered each year in Natchez, George Healy's hometown. He had written George that he would pass through Oxford on his way this fall and suggested a match. He would bring along another pro named Byrd, from Muncie, Indiana, and they could play an exhibition match. Healy lined up two other professionals and sold close to 500 gallery badges at fifty cents apiece. A half-hour before the match, one of the pros sent word that he couldn't come. Healy telephoned Faulkner and explained his predicament.

"Will you play?" he asked him.

"I planned to watch it anyway," Faulkner said. "I guess I might just as well watch it while I'm playing. I don't mind losing my amateur standing."

When the foursome had twice covered the nine holes, Faulkner had the low ball for the match.

Page proofs of *The Marble Faun* had arrived in late September. Four Seas had sent them on the twenty-third, informing Faulkner that Stone's preface had never been received. Stone sent it on the twenty-fourth, and five days later he sent back the proofs corrected by both the author and himself. Four Seas had done a good job, but he suggested some design changes and told them that the author preferred pale green boards for the binding with straw-colored labels for the front and spine. Stone also informed Four Seas that Mr. Faulkner would send the additional $200 "today or tomorrow." On October 5 Stone sent a list of people and publications for the promotion of the book. He and the author had worked on Sunday morning to get it in the mail, Stone said, and they would supplement the list daily. The next day Four Seas wrote Faulkner that his check had been received that day. Because of the number of revisions, they were sending another set of proofs. Inside a week Stone had corrected them, and Faulkner was supposed to do the same and put them in the mail by October 13. Stone sent another list of people to be circularized about the new book. It included William Alexander Percy and his father, Joe Parks, Edison Avent, and just about everyone else Stone knew in Oxford and eleven other Mississippi communities.

Phil Stone was still writing letters indefatigably on October 15. Earlier he had written Four Seas suggesting that they should appeal to state pride in their advertising circulars by emphasizing the fact that the poems had been done by a Mississippian and that he, a Mississippian too, had written the preface. But he was not going to risk all on the potential Mississippi market. He wrote to the Yale *Alumni Weekly* informing them about the book. It had the imperfections that first books had, but one day this writer would do some excellent work. Before noting that the book would be published about November 1, Stone added, "This poet is my personal property and I urge all my friends and class-mates to buy his book." Doubtless he meant to strike a jocular note, but the words suggested a very real and deep proprietary feeling.

By October 16 the corrected proofs were safely back in Boston. There would be no problem in binding them for the author as he had requested. Three days later Stone sent them a form letter he had composed which was to be reproduced and sent out to friends. He had spent about fifty dollars of his own money, he said, as well as a lot of time in the interests of this Mississippian. Another purpose, he wrote, was to put the state on the map artistically. He also enclosed some new poems Faulkner had written, offering a choice of them for use with the promotional material, so long as Faulkner was free to include any chosen in his next book of poems.

One poem, cleanly typed and dated October 17, 1924, was entitled "Mississippi Hills: My Epitaph." (It was only slightly changed from a version done the day before on October 16.) The four stanzas also adhered strictly to a rhyme scheme; in this case, *abba.* It was much the most powerful poem of the set. The poet looked at the "Far blue hills, where I pleasured me," and then contemplated his death, thinking how he would lie in this earth and then wake from his sleep with the spring. Much later he would discard the first and fourth stanzas, reworking the second and third:

Let this soft mouth, shapèd to the rain,
Be but golden grief for grieving's sake,
And these green woods be dreaming here to wake
Within my heart when I return again.

Return I will! Where is there the death
While in these blue hills slumbrous overhead

I'm rooted like a tree? Though I be dead
This soil that holds me fast will find me breath.

Four Seas thought the poems were good and would probably use "My Epitaph" in the promotional circular they were preparing.

In mid-October Stone had to make a business trip to St. Louis and Chicago. On this trip—or a subsequent trip to Chicago—he took Harriet Monroe to dinner. In 1912 Miss Monroe had founded the influential *Poetry: A Magazine of Verse.* Stone, like Faulkner, was not particularly fond of Carl Sandburg and the so-called Chicago school of poetry. The real flowering of modern American poetry, he told Miss Monroe, would come in the South. And he did not neglect the opportunity to mention the name of William Faulkner.

By late October and early November, anticipating the publication of the book any day, Phil Stone was caught up in a paroxysm of letter-writing and promotional activity—so much so that it is difficult to imagine how he could have devoted much time to his law practice. On November 5 he sent to Four Seas a mailing list seven and a half pages long. They covered fifty Mississippi communities and other locations as widely separated as Denver, Colorado, and Halifax, Nova Scotia. Stone had included Mrs. Cornell Franklin, Mr. and Mrs. Sherwood Anderson (care of *The Double Dealer*), William Lyon Phelps, Governor and Mrs. Lee M. Russell, Stark Young, and William Howard Taft. He also included a two-page covering letter. With it were copies of letters to Stark Young and *The New Republic*, and copies of two articles which he and Faulkner had submitted to the magazine. Faulkner was soon going to go to Europe, Stone wrote, and he proposed to support himself by supplying articles each week to local papers. (He may have known that Ernest Hemingway had done the same for an extended period.) They planned subsequently to collect the articles in a book. But now, because Faulkner needed money for a stay of two or three years at least, they proposed to sell the rights to the book, waiving the author's royalty, for the sum of $250. Because they had published *The Marble Faun*, Four Seas was getting the first chance. Faulkner planned to leave the country by about December 1, so Four Seas would have to act by November 15 if they wanted to accept the offer. Meanwhile, Stone asked that they please hurry with the copies of the book, because he didn't want the enthusiasm they had aroused to die down before they could satisfy it. He was very confident they would sell out the first edition.

The reply of November 10 was doubly disappointing. Although Four Seas would like to see the articles when they were completed, they could not contract for them now. And because of the delay in receiving the preface and the extra time correcting a second set of proofs, *The Marble Faun* would not appear until December 1. Faulkner and Stone waited with growing impatience. On November 13 the *Eagle* reported Faulkner's resignation and his replacement by Bell. "Reports are current," the account went on, "that Mr. Falkner will go abroad in the near future." Stone and Faulkner knew that it had been in England, not America, that Robert Frost had first made his reputation. It was in Europe that Ernest Hemingway was doing the work that would lead to fame. And certainly there were no immediate prospects to keep Faulkner on this side of the water. For another thing, he wanted to visit the European battlefields about which he had read and heard so much. They began to make further preparations. Faulkner executed a power of attorney so Stone could handle his literary affairs while he was in Europe.

Stone wrote to *The Atlantic Monthly* on November 13 enclosing "An Armistice Day Poem." The first of the four quatrains painted the day's desolation in an almost Hardyesque fashion. In the next two the poet reflected that there was no need for the earth to break its wintry sleep because there would be so few hearts to beat with it when spring did return. The last stanza was more explicit:

The hushed plaint of wind in stricken trees
Shivers the grass in path and lane
And Grief and Time are tideless golden seas—
Hush, hush! He's home again.

Stone advised the editor not to let the seeming simplicity of the poem fool him. This young poet had been through the new verse movement, he said, and "has come out on the other side," having learned from its practitioners on the way.

Another poem typed in Stone's office about this time bore the date 10 November 1924, and was entitled "Pregnancy." The images suggested the betrayed maiden in works such as *Marionettes*:

As to an ancient music's hidden fall
Her seed in the huddled dark was warm and wet
And three cold stars were riven in the wall:
Rain and fire and death above her door were set.

The last stanza played on the idea of waking or quickening in three ways: the girl waking within a cave, the seed quickening within her body, and in the world outside the coming of spring.

On the seventeenth, Stone wrote to Four Seas again, in what had by now become a familiar refrain. Would they please speed things up as much as they could? Faulkner had hoped to leave for Europe by November 20 and was waiting only for the book. Inside a few weeks, however, two things would happen which would alter the tone of the past months' events.

In the early days of December Estelle Oldham Franklin arrived in Oxford after the long boat trip from Shanghai and train ride from San Francisco. On December 3 Malcolm Argyle Franklin turned one, and his sister Victoria was now almost five. Estelle had fortunately had the help on this journey of Nyt Sung, the children's amah. She was a petite and lively woman. It was she who had given Victoria her nickname, "Cho-Cho." Except for the presence of her three charges, she was in a totally alien land, where the only other Chinese was Hum Wo, who ran the Oxford laundry. He was of a distinctly different social station and spoke Cantonese anyway. For Estelle, of course, the reverse was true. It was a return from an alien land, one where she and her husband lived the active life of the international set's upper echelon. In Shanghai there were the dances, the parties, the games of mah-jongg for high stakes, but it could be a lonely life. Cornell Franklin was able and attractive, and his calendar was always full. He liked a drink and he liked to gamble. At home there was a full staff to carry out his wife's wishes. As the months passed, his activities began to take more of his time, and his household saw him less. For Estelle, being back in Oxford was a welcome change, with her family to lavish love, to talk to her, to shop with her, and to help with Cho-Cho and Malcolm when she wanted to go out. And there was Billy.

She still loved him. In that way nothing had changed, just as his own feelings—love and regret and a sense of betrayal—remained constant. But she was still Mrs. Cornell Franklin, and now she had two little children instead of one. The time was 1924 and the place was Oxford, Mississippi, where Billy had just lost the only job he had ever held for any length of time. And he still had dreams that would have to be fulfilled soon if they were not to thin out and vanish. So her feelings were mixed at the idea of his departure, perhaps only a few days after her return. The times they spent together on these visits bridged some of the gaps to the past. Now she would be in Oxford amid the familiar sights and sounds and fragrances while he would be the absent one. But he wanted to go, and she could understand that he had to.

By now even Hiram Hayseed had heard something. "It is rumored," he wrote in *The Mississippian* on December 5, "that Bill discouraged by the failure of the Blue Beard Insurance Company will retire to some tropic iland, lay in the sweet smelling locust leaves and gourd vines and indite sonnits to the pore helpless world, what no one can diagnose." The book of poems he had already indited had still not arrived from Four Seas, so four days later on December 9 Phil Stone sent off another wire. The delay was hurting sales, he said. The author was anxious to leave for Europe, but he couldn't until the arrival date of his author's copies was known. Stone was delighted when the Western Union boy delivered a telegram to his office on the same day. The book was ready, they could ship it now.

Phil Stone's secretary had been busy. On December 5 she had done a clean copy of a four-quatrain poem entitled "To Elise," which began as if the poet were once more echoing Villon:

Where has flown the spring we knew together?
Barren are the boughs of yesteryear. . . .

She had been spring to him, even in the depth of winter. Now that her love was gone like the spring, he was left with desolation and "A bare and bitter year within my heart."

Another poem typed afresh was entitled "Cleopatra." At the bottom Faulkner had written in pen, "9 December 1924." It was an irregular Petrarchan sonnet whose octave considered her fatal beauty, seemingly rendered harmless by entombment, but still powerful. The sestet began by affirming her death but then, in the last two lines, repeated the same reversal performed in the octave:

Ay, Cleopatra's dead, and she is wombed,
And breaks his vine, and slowly eats the fruit.

A few days later he penciled in the date 13 December 1924 below the best sonnet he had written. It was entitled "Spring" and it was neither Petrarchan nor Shakespearean. The violent wind, symbol of the spring, is a magnificent stallion. He leans on the skies, browses in the fields, and then

within the trees that he had reft and raped
his fierce embrace by riven boughs is shaped,
while on the shaggy hills he stamps and neighs.

In this poem Faulkner had treated a favorite subject—the beauty of the earth—with more striking images, with a richer and more vigorous diction than he had usually been able to command.

The poet's trip would not interfere with other poems in progress. According to a New Orleans *Times-Picayune* account datelined "University, Miss., Dec. 16," "William Falkner is preparing to leave the University of Mississippi campus for England and Italy, where he will spend the winter months in study." This information had probably been provided by a local correspondent such as George Healy. "Young Falkner is expecting also to complete a number of poems started in this country," the item added.

By December 16 the books still had not arrived. This time the author sent a telegram: IF YOU HAVE NOT SHIPPED MY TEN FREE COPIES MARBLE FAUN AND IF CAN BE SHIPPED FOR GODS SAKE SHIP THEM AT ONCE AS THIS IS HOLDING UP MY SAILING EVERY DAY. WILLIAM FAULKNER. The next day Four Seas wrote that his copies had been shipped. The actual publication date was December 15. They had also shipped twenty-five copies to Stone and twelve to Davidson and Wardlaw. Now a book by Bill Faulkner would stand on the shelves where he and Estelle had browsed. On December 19 he held a copy of the slim green volume in his hands. There were copies for Estelle, Miss Maud, and a few others. On that day one went "To Major and Mrs. L. E. Oldham, with gratitude for many kindnesses, and a long and charming friendship. William Faulkner."

Jack knew that his brother was doing other kinds of writing. He was sending manuscripts to Eastern magazines which regularly sent them back. One day his mother handed him one which had just been returned. Taking it, he told her, "This one is back from *The Saturday Evening Post*, but the day will come when they'll be glad to buy anything I write, and these too, without changing a word."

Stone's 500-word preface began Faulkner's 51-page book. It was a curious mixture of somewhat patronizing praise and deprecation. "These are primarily the poems of youth and a simple heart," Stone began. They had the defects of youth: impatience, unsophistication, and immaturity. At the same time they had "an unusual feeling for words and the music of words, a love of short vowels, an instinct for color and rhythm," and promise of accurate observation and firm statement to come. The writer had certain Southern traits, and above all, "rigid self-honesty." Parts of the essay read like a pastiche of things Stone and Faulkner had read and said. Stone ended his first paragraph with the statement that Faulkner had "roots in this soil as surely and inevitably as has a tree"—a paraphrase of two lines from "Mississippi Hills: My Epitaph." Faulkner had "a hint of coming muscularity of wrist and eye"—a compliment much like the one Faulkner had paid to Miss Millay's wrist in his review of *Aria da Capo.* Stone's citation of George Moore's dictum that "all universal art became great by first being provincial" was the one Faulkner had used—and misattributed in his "American Drama: Eugene O'Neill." In his concluding paragraph Stone mentioned his remark that Amy Lowell "and her gang of drum-beaters" always had one eye on the ball and the other on the grandstand. Then he related Faulkner's rejoinder about *his* other eye being on Babe Ruth. Perhaps in his rush to supply the overdue preface, Stone had sent in the first set of coherent remarks he could get down. Or perhaps, as he would later say of some of Faulkner's fiction, the two had talked so much together that it was hard to tell who had said what. He closed with the modest prediction that "there must be possibilities inherent in a mind so shrewdly and humorously honest."

Early responses to the book in Oxford were mixed. The title troubled some readers. After Faulkner had given Bob Farley his copy, Farley discussed the book with Major Oldham. The Major was aghast at this use of the title of Nathaniel Hawthorne's novel. He had asked Bill about it. Faulkner's only answer was, "Who's Hawthorne? The title is original with me." Major Oldham walked away from the conversation convinced of Faulkner's innocence of the New England writer and his work. J. D. Thames expressed his concern to Faulkner and Stone. "When somebody goes into a bookstore and asks for *The Marble Faun*, they'll get Hawthorne, not you." The two told Thames they had simply forgotten about the Hawthorne title. As to the poems themselves, one Oxonian recalls that people thought they didn't make any sense. In spite of this, Stone was able to inform Four Seas on December 29 that he had sold fifty copies very easily. He enclosed a check for fifty dollars for the last fifty copies. He may have been operating through the Variety Store, buying copies at a bookseller's price and selling them at the regular list price. This meant, presumably, that the return on the printing costs advanced before publication would include not only the author's royalties but the retailer's markup as well. Stone added that they could probably sell 500 more copies in Mississippi by April 1. But he had put on no big sales campaign yet because of the holidays and probably wouldn't until after Faulkner sailed for Europe the next week.

As December drew to a close, Faulkner was busy with last-minute details. He sent a copy of *The Marble Faun* to Corinth. It was inscribed on the flyleaf "To Mr. Mark Webster, to whose friendship I owe extrication from a very unpleasant situation. William Faulkner." On the title page he had carefully written, "William Faulkner/26 December 1924."

The day before New Year's Eve, Phil Stone asked Myrtle Ramey to his office for tea. "Getting very British, aren't we?" she said. When she got there, Faulkner was there, too. As they sat drinking tea he presented her an inscribed copy of *The Marble Faun.* She had always been interested in his work, and before she left Stone's office that afternoon she had another testimonial of friendship. It was a sheaf of onionskin sheets, autographed for her, bearing carbon copies of twelve poems. At the top of each page Stone had written in pen, "Publication rights reserved. Not to be published without the written consent of the author or that of Phil Stone." For some time Faulkner had apparently been going through his stock of poems, selecting a group and then experimenting with an order for them. Then he might go through the process again with new additions or perhaps a completely different set of poems. This was apparently the body of one such sequence with other poems grafted on to the end of it. When *The Mississippian* would reprint on January 9 part of Stone's preface to *The Marble Faun* as a notice of the book's publication, the article would conclude with the comment, "The author's friends will await with much interest a second book from his hand." The comment may have sprung simply from politeness. The writer may have known something about the book of articles Faulkner planned to do. Or, Faulkner may at that time have been planning a second book of verse made up of a longer sequence of poems such as that which he gave to Myrtle Ramey.

The first seven poems bore Roman numerals, some with titles and some without. The remaining five poems had titles but no numbers. The last four were dated, each having been written within the last two months. Seven of the twelve were signed. The first poem of the sequence was the one beginning, "Shall I recall this tree." Dated October 18, it was probably one of those Stone had sent to Four Seas in October. The second poem, which began, "Moon of death, moon of bright despair," ran to four stanzas and played a variation on the theme of the first poem. The third poem, a sonnet entitled "Indian Summer," used the idea of death a different way:

The courtesan is dead, for all her subtle ways,
Her bonds are loosed in brittle and bitter leaves. . . .

From there the poet moved to winter, sweeping out the room she had occupied. The sestet of the roughly Petrarchan sonnet provided the expected reversal:

Spring will come! rejoice! But still is there
An old sorrow sharp as woodsmoke on the air.

The fourth poem was called "Wild Geese." Flying south against the November moon, they send out their cries, waking the poet's blood to unease, as he asks himself if he was once free like them. He ends by admiring their wild and lonely flight as, crying, they "cross the rim of the world again."

In the untitled eight-quatrain poem which followed, he had successfully fused his praise of natural beauty, his pastoral verses, and the vocabulary of pieces such as "The Hill." His subject was a farmer, who "furrows the brown earth. . . ." He turns to the blackbird whistling "Against the shimmering azure of the wood," and then from him to another creature as

Rabbit bursts, its flashing scut
Muscled in erratic lines
Of fright from furrow to rut.

The poet looks at sheeplike clouds against green hills, then closes with the farmer, who could

Furrow the brown earth, doubly sweet
With his own sweat, since here a man
May bread him with his hands and feet.

Faulkner was moving toward a kind of indigenous pastoral.

Poem VI was entitled "The Poet Goes Blind" and dated 29 October 1924. Like "Moon of death," it was steeped in melodramatic despair. Poem VII, the last of the numbered poems, bore the typed title "My Epitaph." Penciled in before it were the additional words "Mississippi Hills."

The eighth poem, "March," was closest to a Shakespearean sonnet; it pictured Eve, contorted with temptation, the Serpent's coils glittering around her body. The next four lines switched to Eve's children. In the sestet "the Snake" was "throned and crowned," his the golden apple of temptation, a prize which will not slake,

> *But ever feeds man's crumb of fire, when plover*
> *And swallow and shrill northing birds whip over*
> *Nazarene and Roman and Virginian.*

Faulkner saw the New Year in at home in Oxford but his tasks there were about finished. On Saturday, January 3, Stone wrote again to Four Seas. He had easily sold seventy-five copies of *The Marble Faun* in Oxford and was ordering fifty more. In a few days he was going to start selling hard, but first there was a trip he had to make. William Faulkner was departing for New Orleans the next day, Stone wrote, and he was going along to see him off to Europe.

BOOK FOUR
The Vagabond

1925

William Faulkner in Paris, 1925.

23

January-June, 1925

Outside the window New Orleans, the vieux carré, brooded in a faintly tarnished languor like an aging yet still beautiful courtesan in a smokefilled room, avid yet weary too of ardent ways.

Above banana and palm the cathedral spires soared without perspective on the hot sky. Looking through the tall pickets into Jackson square was like looking into an aquarium—a moist and motionless absinthe-cloudy green of all shades from ink black to a thin and rigid feathering of silver on pomegranate and mimosa. . . .

—*Mosquitoes* (10, 48–49)

To starboard the island stretched on, bastioned and sombre, without sign of any life at all. Across the Sound a low smudge of mainland lay like a violet cloud. From beyond the island we could hear the boom and hiss of surf, but inside here the water was like a mill-pond, with sunlight slanting into it in green corridors. . . .

—"Once Aboard the Lugger"

New Orleans in 1925 was still, many of its citizens would claim, America's unique city, the only one with so varied a history, so rich and diverse a culture, and so charming and easy a way of life. The legacies from the days of French and Spanish rule made it the most European of American cities. There were not only the public buildings of vanished empires and the streets named for long dead explorer-soldiers, but the sense and sound of a Latin culture blended with the successive waves of the Anglo-Saxon. Here were the Mardi gras each February and a Catholic tradition far different from that of austere dioceses such as Boston and New York whose prelates took their models from the stern Catholicism of Ireland.

If some writers liked to describe New Orleans as being pervaded by a certain languor, the history of this part of the New World suggested very different qualities. The sixteenth-century explorations of the Spanish, under De Soto and others, brought the rapine and murder of Spanish incursions farther south. After Marquette and Joliet traced the Mississippi's course as far as the mouth of the Arkansas, Robert Cavelier, Sieur de La Salle, pushed to the mouth of the great river itself and claimed the whole territory for "Louis the Great, King of France and Ruler of Navarre" in April of 1682. By the turn of the century, other Canadian Frenchmen were striving both to explore and to colonize. Heading the list were two brothers: Pierre Le Moyne, Sieur d'Iberville, and Jean Baptiste Le Moyne, Sieur de Bienville. In 1718, de Bienville stood with his engineers, Le Blond de la Tour and Adrien de Pauger, on the north bank of the Mississippi at a bend where a man could see up and down the river for miles. They surveyed it, then cleared and leveled the Place d'Armes for a parade ground. Staking out the sites for government buildings, they named the settlement after the Regent of France, the Duc d'Orléans. By 1793 it had become the new capital of the territory. A century later this settlement would be known as the Vieux Carré, the hundred-odd square blocks stretching from Canal Street on the south to Esplanade on the north, and from North Rampart Street to the river.

Consignments of brides came from France to wed the Canadian *coureurs de bois.* The issue of these marriages formed the Creole stock which helped to make New Orleans a little Versailles under the Marquis de Vaudreuil. By the time he left the governorship in 1753 a tone had been set: the elegance of empire softened by the charm of Creole life, and, beneath both, the lustiness of a river town. After the partition of Louisiana it took three years for the Spanish authorities to arrive and three more until they returned in 1769 with enough troops to enforce the transfer. The Place d'Armes remained the Plaza de Armas for over thirty years, and the Vieux Carré gradually assumed the characteristics that would make "the French Quarter" almost as much Spanish as French. The wide carriage doorways and discreet archways in the irregular plaster and stucco-covered houses followed the Spanish style. Brick walls enclosing paved courtyards and gardens full of flowering shrubs and trees suggested Castile rather than Orléans. The airy balconies with their wrought-iron filigree shaded tall shuttered windows, combining beauty and sense to cope with the sultry climate. One kind of New Orleans heat was induced, however. Garlic and spices made savory stews and gumbos that added a Spanish touch to Creole cookery.

New Orleans had scarcely been handed back to France on November 30, 1803, when, twenty days later, its 10,000 subjects found themselves soon to be American citizens. There were more than 24,000 of them when Louisiana was admitted to the Union in 1812. Fifty years later, the stars and stripes replaced the stars and bars above the Place d'Armes when the hated Ben Butler entered the city on May Day to enforce harsh Yankee rule until the end of the war. The violence, lawlessness, and corruption of ten years of reconstruction left a legacy of debt and ring-politics which would continue beyond the turn of the century. These burdens, together with the enormous city debts and the yellow fever epidemic of 1878, nearly completed the depredations begun by the war.

By 1925, however, the city had nearly 425,000 inhabitants. Not only was it continuing its forward surge as one of the leading banking and shipping centers of the "new South," it was becoming the nation's second busiest port. In the essentials, its business district was little different from those in other parts of the country. In the rush of "progress" many old structures were torn down to make way for new building. So it was with the French Quarter. At about the turn of the century, however, a philanthropist began to restore some of the Quarter's most valuable buildings, while writers and artists began to find it a cheap and congenial place to work. Before the postwar price rise, $2,500 would buy a two-story house there with ironwork balcony, courtyard, galleries, and slave quarters. Many of these houses, of course, were demolished for tenement shacks to accommodate in-flooding European immigrants, and now the accents heard in the Vieux Carré would more often be those of Sicily or Naples than France or Quebec.

But as Greenwich Village had been "discovered" in New York, so the Vieux Carré was discovered in New Orleans. Old legends about plots, ghosts, and haunted houses would be revived. Indignation about neglect would become indignation over exploitation for the tourist trade. Though it would at first be only a moderate influx, prices would rise and something more of the old, easy-going air would vanish. But St. Louis Cathedral still stood facing the Place d'Armes (renamed Jackson Square), the Presbytery its neighbor to the north, and the Cabildo, where the Spanish governors convened, to the south. Enclosing the other two sides of the square were the upper and lower Pontalba Buildings, with their great balconies and spiral staircases. In 1916 the Drawing Room Players had founded the Little Theatre, and when the group had outgrown its Pontalba apartment, they moved to 616 St. Peter Street, where 500 people could sit in Le Petit Théâtre du Vieux Carré to watch a one-act play by someone as noted as Eugene O'Neill or by one of their own, such as the lively and imaginative young Flo Field. For those who could afford them, there were the great restaurants such as Antoine's and Galatoire's. Cafés such as the Absinthe House catered to other purses and tastes. For the artist hoarding his money while he tried to learn his craft, the Quarter had good, cheap restaurants. And though prohibition might in theory be the law of the land, few laws could be more inimical to the spirit and traditions of the Vieux Carré. And so the artist needed to fear the absence of something to drink no more than the lack of a good meal at least once a day. This was the New Orleans to which William Faulkner came, at twenty-seven, in the first days of the new year of 1925.

Bill Faulkner and Phil Stone arrived there on Sunday, January 4, if they kept to the schedule Stone had mentioned in his last letter to Four Seas. Faulkner still thought about working his passage to Europe, but he had not yet been able to arrange it. Riding south, they talked about Faulkner's plans and their visit. Sherwood Anderson's living in New Orleans added to the city's luster. Faulkner said he ranked Anderson's "I'm a Fool" with Conrad's *Heart of Darkness* as the two finest stories that he had ever read.

They checked in at the Lafayette Hotel two days before the Ball of the Twelfth Night Revelers would signal the Mardi gras festivities to come. They met George Healy and went out together. Later the two young men went to call at the Andersons' attractive apartment at 540 B St. Peter Street in the lower Pontalba Building. Although Sherwood Anderson had already left to begin a speaking tour that day in Cleveland, Miss Elizabeth was still in town.

She welcomed them and then they asked her to go out with them. Bill was his usual quiet, courtly self. Phil was very gallant and commanding. The two men had planned some sightseeing, and Phil insisted that Miss Elizabeth must go with them. So they took her around with them and for three days they saw much of each other. It was very gay, and to Elizabeth

Anderson it later seemed as though they had laughed for days. Phil Stone finally had to return to Oxford. Faulkner still needed a place to stay, though, if he wanted to wait for a ship that would exchange work for passage. The Lafayette would be expensive, so Elizabeth Anderson invited him to stay in the apartment. They had a spare room, and Sherwood would be away for two months anyway. It might not be as fine a place as some, but it was pleasant enough. The Andersons had had the floors sanded and the ironwork refurbished, and by comparison with most they lived in elegance. The other artists' quarters in the building tended to be rather sketchy, with dangling electric wires and bare light bulbs.

Bill Faulkner found there was now no need for haste. His lodging was free, and his considerate hostess would offer him morning coffee and invite him to share a meal now and then. The rest of the time he could eat cheaply and well in the aromatic restaurants of the Quarter. He was free to wander by the wharves and to stand looking at the pictures in the numerous art shops, the odds and ends in the secondhand stores, the greenery of the park by the cathedral. And he began to spend part of each day on new writing.

At home in Oxford, Phil Stone continued promoting *The Marble Faun*, hectoring Four Seas about review copies in a letter of January 13. They complied promptly, and on January 19 Stone acknowledged with thanks. Faulkner was still in New Orleans, he said, and he would send the letter on to him for suggestions. Stone would write them when he heard from him. Faulkner was apparently too busy with new work to concern himself with old, for it was nearly two months before Stone wrote to them again.

The Double Dealer was still being run from the loft of the building at 204 Baronne Street owned by Sam Weis, uncle of editor Julius Weis Friend. It had been nearly three years, though, since contributors had been paid for their work. Julius Friend's sister, Lillian Friend Marcus, had recruited a group of "guarantors" whose monthly contributions of ten dollars were meant to keep the magazine solvent. But Julius Friend still had to dip into his own pocket to see that all the bills were paid. Though the magazine's circulation was never large, it reached as far as India, Tasmania, and the Gold Coast. Besides publishing unknown writers such as Hemingway, Faulkner, Robert Penn Warren, Thornton Wilder, and Hamilton Basso, they had been hospitable to other new names such as Hart Crane, Edmund Wilson, Jr., Allen Tate, Donald Davidson, and John Crowe Ransom. And some of the well-known—Sherwood Anderson, Ezra Pound, Lord Dunsany, H. D., Elinor Wylie, Amy Lowell, Arthur Symons—had given poems or essays to the magazine. *The Double Dealer* had drawn praise from Mencken and attention from the Manchester *Guardian*, even if it was not entirely favorable. But the death of handsome, magnetic Basil Thompson had shaken the veteran collaborators on the staff. And as if that loss was symptomatic, the magazine had for some time been appearing at less frequent intervals. Yet Friend continued to meet with John McClure—poet, journalist, and critic—and Albert Goldstein, his colleague on the *Times-Picayune*, to keep the magazine going. They would still gather in the loft's main room, furnished with a table, borrowed typewriter, huge couch, and one good chair. The adjoining room was used from time to time for fund-raising parties and other social events.

When the staff composed the "Notes on Contributors" for the January–February issue, the first and longest was on William Faulkner. "Although in his twenties," it read, "he has served in a wide variety of capacities. He has worked in turn as clerk in a book-store, postmaster and dishwasher. During the war he was with the British Air Force and made a brilliant record. He was severely wounded. To date his literary interest has been chiefly in poetry." With a minimum of punctuation, the account concluded, "He has lately published 'The Marble Faun' a book of poems and is about to publish another 'The Greening Bough.' "

Faulkner had no less than three contributions in the number. The first was a 900-word essay entitled "On Criticism." The critics, he wrote, did little to follow Walt Whitman's adjuration that there had to be great audiences in order to have great poets. "All that is necessary for admission to the ranks of criticism," he said, "is a typewriter." The American critic generally was a showman displaying his own virtuosity. The few good ones were ignored by the influential magazines. British criticism, on the other hand, could instruct the artist as well as the reader. In brief, the "English review criticises the book, the American the author." Finally, it came down to the fact that the critic was competing with the artist, which was ludicrous, for "Surely, if there are two professions in which there should be no professional jealousy, they are prostitution and literature."

A five-quatrain poem followed the essay. "Dying Gladiator" departed radically from the cutting and coldly contemptuous tone of the previous piece. The lover adjured his beloved not to grieve. Faulkner had used some of his favorite imagery—the shepherd, the starlit hill, the beautiful maiden—together with the characteristic sadness and awareness of the presence of death. The first stanza set the tone:

What sorrow, love, that the wind and the raining wake?
Man's life is but an April without a morrow
Between a snow and a season of snow. What sorrow
That winter again about his head must break?

Two pages beyond Sherwood Anderson's poem, "One Puzzled Concerning Himself," was Faulkner's most imaginative and promising contribution. It was a 3,000-word piece entitled "New Orleans," comprising eleven sketches. "Wealthy Jew" was the monologue of an old man who loved three things: "gold; marble and purple; splendor, solidity, color," and who asserted the victory of his race through the Nativity, and through endurance. "The Priest" was an impressionistic sketch. As in the poetry of Gerard Manley Hopkins, the beauty of the day led the watcher to the adoration of heavenly beauty, expressed finally in the litany, "Ave, Maria; deam gratiam . . . tower of ivory, rose of Lebanon. . . ." In the next, "Frankie and Johnny," the lover sounded like a thug constantly on the verge of lapsing into poetic imagery. The short monologue entitled "The Sailor," with its poetic brogue, suggested that Faulkner might be drawing on some of Eugene O'Neill's one-act plays. In "The Cobbler" an old man lamented a long-lost Tuscan love in a voice suggesting soliloquies from *Marionettes.* "The Longshoreman" and "The Cop" were, like the others, exercises in quick characterization, by turns poetic and realistic; and though they were brief, they were obviously meant, like James Joyce's epiphanies, to illuminate the essence of the character's life or personality. "The Longshoreman" was experimental in another way, shifting back and forth from dialect to poetic speech meant to express the inarticulate impulses of the heaving, laboring man.

This technique in "The Beggar," which followed, produced an extremely reflective policeman whose diction wavered between Dickens and Twain. "The Artist" described "a dream and a fire which I cannot control." Though it was a burden and a labor, the artist exulted at the end: "But to create! Which among ye who have not this fire, can know this joy, let it be ever so fleet?" In "Magdalen" two opposing tones were joined again: first were the waking thoughts of the prostitute, then her recollections of the wants and lures that had betrayed her, "all the bright chimaerae of the brain!"

The last sketch, entitled "The Tourist," gave an impressionistic picture of New Orleans: "A courtesan, not old and yet no longer young," she is a seductress to whom all return "when she smiles across her languid fan. . . ." One indication of the fact that Faulkner had by no means forsaken poetry was a surprisingly regular Petrarchan sonnet entitled "New Orleans," in which the last lines of the sestet were almost completely identical with the last lines of the sketch. A three-line verse fragment entitled "The Priest" suggested a similar correspondence.

But his prose was more promising than his verse, and his fiction was more promising than his nonfiction. It was probably at about this time that he composed a one-page essay entitled "Literature and War"—intended, perhaps, for *The Double Dealer.* In five paragraphs totaling a little less than 300 words, he assessed the use of war material by two poets and two novelists. He wrote that Siegfried Sassoon "moves one who has himself slogged up to Arras or its corresponding objective. . . ." Henri Barbusse (who had received the 1917 Prix Goncourt for his novel *Le Feu*) had authentically portrayed the horrors of trench warfare. One could be moved by Rupert Brooke if he had not known either such experience and "if war be to him the Guards division eternally paraded. . . ." It remained for R. H. Mottram (whose novel *The Spanish Farm* dealt with British troops in France) "to use the late war to a successful literary end." Faulkner summed up in his familiar tone of irony and world-weariness. "Business as usual. What a grand slogan. Who has accused the Anglo-Saxon of being forever sentimental over war? Mankind's emotional gamut is like his auricular gamut: there are some things which he cannot feel, as there are sounds he cannot hear. And war, taken as a whole, is one of these things." Though "Literature and War" remained unpublished, it gave some indication of the extent of Faulkner's reading about the war. For one who had seen no combat, work such as that of Barbusse and Mottram would constitute a valuable source of realistic detail.

In spite of his habitual taciturnity—shyness or simple disinclination to talk as it might be variously construed—Faulkner soon met the city's best-known literary figures. Most of them lived in the Quarter or gravitated there. Stone had doubtless introduced Faulkner to John McClure when he went to the *Times-Picayune* office to see if McClure's review copy of *The Marble Faun* had arrived. In the view of one friend, "he ran the best literary review page in any southern newspaper." He also worked on the newspaper's copy desk, but he liked best his literary page and the editing and criticism he did for *The Double Dealer.* A number of his poems appeared there, and in *Dark Laughter* Sherwood Anderson referred to him as the "ballad-maker." He was now thirty-two. One volume of his poems had been published by Knopf in 1918, but Knopf had rejected a second. After that he submitted no more book manuscripts in spite of the urging of admirers such as H. L. Mencken. He was the acknowledged leader of the group which had welcomed Sherwood Anderson and made him what Hamilton Basso called "our Royal Personage." Short and slight, with curly hair above regular features, McClure was a sympathetic man who endeared himself to others. He knew how to listen and he was receptive to others' ideas. Moreover, he could gracefully accommodate himself to the moods of the temperamental people in that group. He became one of Faulkner's friends and an admirer of his work.

McClure was a discriminating admirer, as his review of *The Marble Faun* showed when it appeared in the *Times-Picayune* on January 29 in "Literature—and Less." He began with the proposition that there were probably fewer than a dozen really successful long poems in English. This meant that a young poet was predestined to failure in this form. "The most he can hope for, even if his name be Keats, is to fail with honor. Mr. William Faulkner, a Southern poet from whom we shall hear a great deal in future, has failed, it seems to this reviewer, but with real honor." McClure offered succinct and sympathetic analysis. "The excellences of *The Marble Faun* are sporadic charming couplets or passages sandwiched between stretches of creditable but not remarkable verse. The general effect of the poem is vague. It is a prophetic book rather than a chronicle of past performance. Mr. Faulkner possesses to an exceptional degree imagination, emotion, a creative impulse in diction and a keen sense of rhythm and form—all attributes demanded of a fine poet. The deficiencies of *The Marble Faun* are deficiencies of youth—diffuseness and overexuberance, impatient simile and metaphor which sometimes miss the mark and a general galloping technique which runs away with the author every now and then. Immaturity is almost the only indictment which can be brought against the work." McClure's prophecy for Faulkner was favorable: "Those who wish to keep in touch with the development of Southern poetry will do well to acquire *The Marble Faun* and the new book when it appears. One day they may be glad to have recognized a fine poet at his first appearance."

Often Faulkner and McClure would sit at a corner table in a café on Franklin Street near Canal to drink and listen to the clarinet of "Georgia Boy," a Negro whose talent Faulkner particularly admired. Sometimes they would go to a café whose proprietor apparently had a profitable interest in some of the Quarter's less legitimate enterprises. They might be joined by Roark Bradford when his schedule coincided with theirs. Bradford worked on the "nightside" city desk of the *Times-Picayune*, and ordinarily he would stay until early morning. Then friends would begin dropping in at his place. By three o'clock it would be lively with good talk as they sat and drank, discussing work they were doing, arguing and laughing. Less than a year older than Faulkner, the Tennessee-born Bradford was a big-faced, balding man with a thickening waistline who still had something of the country boy about him. He was also an expert mimic, particularly adept at Negro dialect. Bradford was like Anderson in that he loved to tell stories. Both would tell them in the first person sometimes, and after a while the line between truth and fancy would become blurred if not eradicated. He was full of vitality, both physical and mental, and he would often rage against the arbiters of propriety who were the enemies of magazines such as *The Double Dealer.* He loved to sing, too, especially cowboy songs and Negro songs. Finally, his friends would remember that this was the end of a long day for him. It would be dawn when he got to bed, and they all knew that during the day no one must ring his doorbell.

Another genial host was Lyle Saxon, a tall, plump, blue-eyed man. He worked as a reporter and feature writer on the *Times-Picayune*, but he had been raised on a large Baton Rouge plantation, and from there, apparently, came the means to buy a balconied three-story house at 612 Royal Street. It was so "typical of the aristocratic houses of the Rue Royale" that it had appeared in *The Mentor* in March along with the home prepared for Napoleon I, the Cabildo, and St. Louis Cathedral. There Saxon had entertained Sherwood Anderson, Lord Dunsany, and other, less well-off guests. Gentle and urbane, Saxon loved to stand, glass in hand, talking with writers, whose company he enjoyed most. Like Bradford, he was drawing heavily on his native region in his writing. He, too, took to the silent, seemingly aloof young writer six years his junior, and he was pleased when Faulkner was given the chance to earn a few dollars writing for the *Times-Picayune.*

Faulkner, quiet as usual, would sometimes accompany the others to the newspaper offices. He would talk in the company of a few friends such as McClure and Bradford, but he was close-mouthed in larger groups, particularly when they were enlivened by the company of someone as well-known and voluble as that self-appointed terror of "the booboisie," H. L. Mencken. Faulkner had been introduced to Colonel James Edmonds, the managing editor of the paper, and he had made a good impression on him. Then, with Bradford's help, he became a free-lance contributor. The first series of sketches that he brought in was accepted. Before the end of January he wrote and sold four more for a total of twenty dollars. At this rate, he thought, he might earn as much as ten dollars a week while he was in Europe.

"Mirrors of Chartres Street" appeared in the *Times-Picayune* on February 8, 1925. The subject of the thousand-word story was a loud one-legged beggar who spends the narrator's quarter for a movie rather than food. When last seen he is being driven away in the patrol wagon for drunkenness and possession of liquor, but the narrator admires his exploited-but-undaunted stance. As in the "New Orleans" sketches, Faulkner was mixing realistic and nonrealistic styles, dialect and poetry. One passage praising the beggar's spirit echoed earlier poems: "his the same heaven-sent attribute for finding life good which enabled the Jews to give young Jesus of Nazareth with two stars in His eyes, sucking His mother's breast, and a fairy tale that has conquered the whole Western earth. . . ." In flamboyant imagery the iron filigree work was "Mendelssohn impervious in iron. . . ." His metaphors came from art as well as music: "The moon had crawled up the sky like a fat spider and planes of light and shadow were despair for the Vorticist schools."

A week later, on February 15, "Damon and Pythias Unlimited" appeared. It was twice as long. In it the first-person narrator allows himself to be taken to the track by a tout named Morovitz, who has a "broad Semitic face" and a demotic accent. His accomplice, supposedly a knowledgeable jockey, is a consumptive boy named McNamara with "foreknowledge of certain death in his eyes." As the story ends they struggle for the narrator's five dollars. Faulkner began with an impressionistic description of the Cabildo and satiric observations about Midwestern tourists and "progress" of the kind Anderson had come to New Orleans to avoid. Then he shifted completely to the colloquial. The Jewish dialect was insistent, but the sketch moved and the two characters were convincing.

"Home," which appeared on February 22, was more experimental, ambitious, and imitative. It began with a Provençal air played with a bow on a carpenter's saw. The 1,500-word story's single character was a dissatisfied immigrant. If his name, Jean-Baptiste, suggested characters of Joseph Conrad, his inner turmoil suggested Eliot's Prufrock: "His decision he could still revoke, though, there was yet time. . . ." The author's ruminations suggested Housman: "Thinking, indeed, lays lads underground." In a few places the author borrowed imagery from his own poems, as when Jean-Baptiste watched "the stars like cast roses arrested above an open coffin." Jean-Baptiste's dilemma is whether or not to fulfill his promise and help Pete, the General, and Tony the Wop rob a bank. He hears the music, "half string and half pipe," that began the story, and with the dawn comes an epiphany: he must find fulfillment in the land of his birth. Faulkner had set himself an interesting exercise. He had to maintain suspense about the robbery while revealing enough of the protagonist's background and mental processes to make the dramatic change believable. Although he began with straight third-person narrative, he shifted midway into a 200-word passage of interior monologue.

If Faulkner had drawn upon imagination for Jean-Baptiste, it is likely that the three robbers, or at least their names, may have been suggested by Italians in the Quarter. He may well have used such models—or at least certain temperamental qualities of Italians in popular fiction—in "Jealousy," which came out a week later on March 1. At least one of his characters was Sicilian, like many of the market vendors. The setting was an Italian family restaurant such as one Faulkner and his friends patronized. The 2,000-word story was the melodramatic tale of the tublike restaurant owner's baseless, obsessive jealousy of his innocent wife and his handsome, equally guiltless young waiter. Here Faulkner essayed the surprise ending. After the waiter announces that he will leave, the husband suddenly shoots him. Again there were echoes of Housman in the husband's melancholy meditations and a strong suggestion of Conrad in the treatment of the husband-wife relationship. The attempts at foreign idiom sometimes went awry, and there was considerable melodrama, but it was an interesting effort to combine realism with psychopathology.

In late February Elizabeth Anderson was preparing to meet her husband in Chicago at the end of his two-month lecture tour, and Faulkner decided to return home briefly. The time in New Orleans had been extremely fruitful for Faulkner and he would return soon. He had met people like McClure, Bradford, and Saxon. He had heard a great deal of talk—about art, about Freud—some of it silly, no doubt, but more provocative for a burgeoning artist than the conversation at home. He had worked hard, but he had also relaxed, drinking, sitting with friends, and reading in Sherwood Anderson's library. One book he read had been almost as influential, in its way, as some of the writings of Freud: Sir James G. Frazer's great anthropological-mythological study, *The Golden Bough.*

Faulkner had begun to publish again—for money—and he was beginning to spend much of his energy on prose. He had by no means abandoned poetry, however, nor the subject matter and mood so often predominant in his verse. One untitled four-stanza poem bore at the bottom the typed legend "William Faulkner/New Orleans/10 February 1925." The last stanza suggested something of Hardy and Housman as well as Faulkner:

Where I am dead the aimless wind that strays
The greening corridors where spent springs dwell:
"How are you? are you faint? or sad?" it says.
And where I'm dead I answer: "O, I'm well."

Another poem apparently was inspired by a contemporary event. On January 30 Floyd Collins had been trapped in Sand Cave, ten miles from the famous Mammoth Cave in central Kentucky. Discoverer of Crystal Cave, the explorer and guide had been seeking a new and more beautiful cave when a falling rock pinioned his foot. For seventeen days rescue parties tried to reach him while radio reports focused national attention on his plight, but he died just before help arrived. Faulkner entitled his ninety-two lines simply "Floyd Collins," his only allusion to the Kentucky tragedy. The richly impressionistic blank verse described the caves and the protagonist's phantasmagoria before the death implied in the last lines. There was the familiar figure of the *belle dame sans merci*, as well as others such as the

Kings and mitred bishops tired of sin
Who dreamed themselves of heaven wearied,
And now may sleep, hear rain, and snore again.

But there was no question that Faulkner was writing more fiction now than before, and it was longer fiction. He apparently became so caught up in what he was doing and his new pattern of life that he virtually stopped corresponding. Stone later said Faulkner would write to him even when his family had not heard from him. But now even Stone heard nothing from him. Finally he sent Faulkner a wire. WHATS THE MATTER? it read. DO YOU HAVE A MISTRESS? Faulkner wired his reply: YES. AND SHES 30,000 WORDS LONG. He had begun a novel and he had given it the working title "Mayday." By the time "Jealousy" appeared he was back home.

The work he did on his return to Oxford was a change after the intensive labor in Anderson's Pontalba apartment. The previous fall George Healy, Raymond Beltzchasser (nicknamed "Bullshazzer") Zeller and half a dozen others had made plans to publish *The Scream*, a satiric humor magazine. One night in Healy's room Faulkner had offered to write something for them, but Healy asked for drawings instead. He knew Faulkner's poetry from *The Mississippian* and was afraid it would not appeal to the audience he wanted to attract. Faulkner agreed to supply some cartoons and drawings.

Apparently he did some work with other members of the staff in planning for future issues, being listed subsequently as one of the art editors for 1925. It was probably then that he supplied three drawings which were to appear in the May issue of the magazine. One covered the lower half of a page. It showed a girl boarding a streetcar, her taut skirt exposing a frilled bloomer. Two other girls waited to follow her, while two men watched them. In the caption, "Lit" asked "Law" if he wasn't going to the show, and received the answer, "Na-ah, what I wanta spend good money on a show for?" The drawing was still stylized but somehow less cluttered than his previous ones, the lines stronger and more precise. Three pages further on was a quarter-page drawing of two men, one holding up another in a state of drunken near-collapse. They stood before the statue of a nude. The caption read, "Poo' girl, poo' li'l girl; shree mile' f'm town, no clo', ca' even walk!" The male figures were familiar shapes, but the lines were thicker and the whole drawing much darker and bolder, the statue a mere outline against the unbroken background of black trees and shrubs. The next page bore another Faulkner drawing (without a caption) in this same style. A pipe-smoking man in an open roadster talked with a cigarette-smoking man standing with a foot on the running board.

Publicity was not neglected. A March 9 dispatch reported that the new magazine was recruiting "the most versatile and most complete contributing staff in the United States." Several "literary lights" among the alumni had promised to contribute. Mentioned first was Bill Faulkner, who was "preparing a sketch." Stark Young would also help, as would Phil Stone, "whose preface to 'The Marble Faun' created nationwide comment."

Faulkner found time during this brief trip to Oxford for writing as well as drawing. He dated one long poem February 26. It began,

The Raven bleak and Philomel
Amid the bleeding trees were fixed.
His hoarse cry and hers were mixed.
And through the dark their droppings fell. . . .

T. S. Eliot had used the myth of Tereus, Philomela, and Procne as one of the "creative borrowings" of "The Waste Land." The image mixing bird droppings and death had closed his short poem "Sweeney Among the Nightingales." Faulkner was still under the spell of much of Eliot's verse, as he would be for some time to come.

This may have been another poem meant for *The Greening Bough*, a projected work intended to follow *The Marble Faun.* By now, if he was running true to form, Phil Stone was probably involved in the project, reading the poems, having them typed, and trying to help find the most effective order for them.

By mid-February Estelle had returned with Cho-Cho and Malcolm after a visit to her inlaws at Columbus. Cho-Cho had just celebrated her sixth birthday, and Faulkner had a gift for her. On a sheet of white letter-size paper he had sketched part of a house in blue ink. In the roof section he had written in pencil, ". . . . . for children." Against the wall below was a cat with large whiskers who appeared to be spread-eagled in the air. Behind a window with curtains and flower box stood an elderly woman in a ruffled shirtwaist with a high collar. She wore glasses and her hair was done up in a bun. Her hands were raised in astonishment and her mouth was a round *O* of shock. Below the simple line drawing was the poem, titled "If Cats Could Fly":

If cats could fly
Then I would say
(Behind her back) a
Hungry sound
And when he flew
Across the way
From off his ledge
(If cats could fly)
And through my window,
Wouldn't I
Bangitshut
And wouldn't she
Look surprised a-
Cross at me
When she turned
Around

Though Estelle's visit would extend into the summer, this was only a brief return for Faulkner. On March 1 he and Stone made the drive to Memphis. With them was Ross Brown, another Oxford boy, on his way back to school at Washington and Lee. It is possible that this was the occasion on which Faulkner earned the persevering enmity of Miss Monte Cooper, according to Stone the self-styled "literary arbiter of Memphis." Faulkner had accepted her invitation to what was probably a literary lunch. But when the time came, he did not appear, being then engaged in the business of "getting drunk with his friend Reneau De Vaux [*sic*], well-known Memphis gambler and road-house proprietor. . . ." Miss Cooper, Stone said, never forgave him.

Faulkner had plenty of company. He and Ross Brown stayed together overnight at the Gayoso Hotel. That night Reno and some other friends showed up for a party in the room. It was in the nature of a send-off, really, for Faulkner told Brown that he was headed for New Orleans to find a ship and work his way across to Europe.

Faulkner was back in New Orleans on Tuesday, March 3. On the day before, Sherwood Anderson had returned with his wife, making a leisurely trip home by way of Natchez. This time, Faulkner later said, he did not mean to see Anderson. He intended to catch a freighter and sail for Europe, just as he had told Brown. But by the time he showed up at the familiar Pontalba apartment, according to Anderson's later account, he had changed his mind again and decided to stay awhile, just as he had done two months before.

Faulkner "had on a big overcoat, it being winter, and it bulged strangely," Anderson wrote, "so much, that, at first glance, I thought he must be in some queer way deformed." The big coat so swallowed him that it reminded Anderson of Abraham Lincoln's remark about Confederate Vice-president Alexander Stephens: "Did you ever see so much shuck for so little nubbin?" Faulkner's response was more positive. "I liked him," he would remember later, "and we . . . got along fine together." As Elizabeth Anderson recalled it, Faulkner asked, "Can I stay on?" But her husband was tired after the tour and she was determined to shield him. Elizabeth Anderson told Faulkner she was sorry, but there really wasn't enough room for him to stay. Faulkner then told Anderson that he intended to stay in New Orleans for some time and asked if he could leave some of his things there while he was looking for a place. "His 'things' consisted of some six or eight half gallon jars of moon liquor he had brought with him from the country and that were stowed in the pockets of the big coat," Anderson

William Spratling's drawing of himself and Faulkner in New Orleans' Vieux Carré.

wrote. Faulkner had also brought along a gift for Elizabeth Anderson: a box of narcissus from Miss Rosie Stone's garden. Anderson had an idea. "Look," he said, "our friend, Bill Spratling, has an extra room there in Pirates' Alley. Why don't you just move over there with him?" Faulkner walked the two blocks north to investigate.

When he went around to what old Orleanians called Orleans Alley, he found that Spratling's address, 624, overlooked the green and pleasant expanse of St. Anthony's Garden, which lay behind and to the northwest of the cathedral. Spratling himself proved to be a dark twenty-four-year-old inclined to thinness with a dour look about him. He had dark skin and eyes, a long strong nose and jaw, and a neatly clipped dark brown mustache above a rather sensitive mouth. In a place and time where flair sometimes passed for talent, Bill Spratling had both and a touch of genius besides. Born in New York State and orphaned at ten, he had spent an unhappy adolescence with relatives in Atlanta. He attended Alabama Polytechnic Institute and then switched to Auburn University, where he became a teaching assistant in his sophomore year. Four years later he was an instructor on the staff, though he had not accumulated all the credits necessary for his degree. Soon he had both the degree and membership in the American Institute of Architects. In 1921 he went to Tulane to teach. Besides his own painting and drawing, he also did detail drawings for local architects, sometimes as many as seven at once. A man of enormous energy, he would later run his own night art school before striking out on a completely different career at the age of twenty-eight. Spratling's dour expression was deceiving. He was a raconteur who loved parties, and his apartment, like Roark Bradford's, was one of the main gathering places for the bright young spirits who were making the Quarter a lively place to live. Yes, Spratling did have an extra room, though the apartment was by no means spacious. The room was on the first floor, across a little areaway from the bathroom. Faulkner could move into it.

Faulkner contined to see Anderson, for he admired the older man and enjoyed his company. "We would meet in the afternoons," Faulkner later said, "we'd walk and he'd talk and I'd listen, we'd meet in the evenings and we'd go to a drinking place and we'd sit around till one or two o'clock drinking, and still me listening to him talking." Next to writing, this seems to have been Anderson's most striking talent. He would tell stories, another fascinated listener recalled, "of his youth, of chance encounters with strangers in bars, of adventures which in the frequent retelling became his adventures," and as they listened, Anderson's hearers shared his "magical ability to illuminate the commonplace and endow it with significance." It was not just the stories themselves that created this effect. "He had a deep and ringing voice which he used with humor and slow effects. Ordinary things shone and secret universal meanings were disclosed in ordinary events as Anderson told about them in his hushed voice, as though he were recounting ghost stories."

There was, of course, considerable variety in Anderson's tales as in his tastes. He had been raised in a very ordinary environment and though his sensibilities were keen, they were not always delicate. He liked off-color songs and ribald fantasy. He had spent part of his childhood in his father's harness shop, just as Billy Falkner had hung about his father's livery stable. Neither man was interested much in facts. These intersections of taste and experience led the two writers into brief collaboration.

Once Faulkner found Anderson sitting on a bench in Jackson Square, laughing about a dream in which he had been walking country roads trying to swap a horse for a night's sleep. (It was no dream, Faulkner guessed, but rather a story symbolic of the dream of America which Anderson offered in his work.) Then, on one of those afternoons or evenings of talking and drinking together, "he, with a little help from me, invented other fantastic characters like the sleepless man with the horse. One of them was supposed to be a descendant of Andrew Jackson, left in that Louisiana swamp after the Battle of Chalmette, no longer half-horse half-alligator but by now half-man half-sheep and presently half-shark. . . ." They enjoyed their creation so much, and it became so "unwieldy," that they decided to write it in the form of letters. Faulkner tried one which was an awkward combination, written in the first person about "my father and his four sons" yet supplied with ludicrous footnotes. It may have been then that they shifted to the idea of letters "such as two temporarily separated members of an exploring-zoological expedition might." Faulkner brought his new letter to Anderson and waited while he read it.

"Does it satisfy you?" Anderson asked him.

"Sir?"

"Are you satisfied with it?"

"Why not?" Faulkner answered. "I'll put whatever I left out into the next one."

As soon as he had spoken Faulkner realized that Anderson now was not only displeased but almost angry. "Either throw it away, and we'll quit, or take it back and do it over," Anderson said, fixing him with those deep-set black eyes.

When Faulkner brought the revised letter to him, Anderson asked, "Are you satisfied now?"

"No, sir," Faulkner replied. "But it's the best I know how to do."

"Then we'll pass it," Anderson said, his voice warm as he pocketed the letter.

Faulkner's double-spaced letter covered three sheets of legal-size paper. Following the usage he had long before adopted with Phil Stone, Faulkner had used the salutation "Dear Anderson." During a boating party on Lake Pontchartrain over the weekend, he said, he had seen the Jackson place, the one-time home of descendants of "Old Hickory." The pilot had told Faulkner about the sole survivor, Al Jackson, and his family. His mother's intensely religious childhood was described with hyperbole Mencken might have used upon Deep South evangelism. Her husband, equally religious, had proposed when she was twelve, having been "ravished by her prowess on the melodeon." Later Jackson began to raise sheep, hoping his swamp would make the fleece more luxuriant. Soon the sheep began to take to the water so much that "When shearing time came, he had to borrow a motor boat to run them down with." Before long, however, their legs had atrophied and disappeared, scales had begun to appear, and their tails had flattened like beavers'. Fearing that they would all turn into alligators, Jackson agreed when his son Claude, "the wild one that was always after women," offered to catch them in return for half of those he retrieved. But as he worked in the water for longer and longer periods of time, his own arms and legs began to atrophy, "and the last time any of the family saw him his eyes had moved around to the side of his head and there was a fish's tail sticking out of the corner of his mouth." A year later reports described a lone shark bothering fat, blond lady bathers. " 'That's Claude,' said old man Jackson, 'he was always hell on blondes.' "

Anderson's lengthy reply, which began, "Dear Bill," must have been written before mid-April. He had been on the Jackson family's trail for a year now. "You know, I am a professional writer," he explained, "and if I could ever get this Al Jackson's story straight, get a firsthand interview with him with pictures and all, I'd have a gold mine." He had first heard about Al Jackson from a former fishherd named Flu Balsam, "a nervous, erratic kind of a man with a tin ear got from the kick of a horse, and if he had web feet, like they say so many of the fishherds get, I couldn't notice. He had on congress shoes." Balsam was troubled with insomnia, Anderson wrote, "and so he traded his horse to an easygoing, restful kind of a Texan, and an expert sleeper, for a night's sleep." But the Texan was very late and Balsam lost both horse and sleep. After that he joined Al Jackson. You could always tell a fishherd, Anderson had learned, by the congress shoes, which were especially good for concealing webbed feet. Before he closed, Anderson warned Faulkner against the Jacksons. They were not related to "the Stonewalls or the Andrews," instead their people were "straight slave-running folks."

Faulkner's reply was as long as his first letter. Anderson had said that he preferred to hear no gossip about Al Jackson or his sister Elenor. Faulkner wrote that Elenor's story was scandalous: "She slid down a drain pipe and eloped with a tin peddler one night." Like Anderson, Faulkner wanted to meet Al Jackson, who was "the finest [type] of American manhood, a pure Nordic. During the war he took correspondence course after course to cure his shyness and develop will power in order to help the boys over there by making four minute Liberty loan speeches, and he is said to be the one who first thought of re-writing Goethe and Wagner and calling them Pershing and Wilson. Al Jackson likes the arts, you know." Faulkner then went on to dispute Anderson's genealogy of the Jacksons. Not only was Al related to them, but General Jackson himself had webbed feet, otherwise how could he have won against an army that outnumbered him? "The detachment which saved the day was composed of two battalions of fish-herds from Jackson's Florida swamps, half horse and half alligator they were." And if Anderson would examine the statue in Jackson Park, he would see that the General wore congress shoes. He described other Jacksons, such as Herman, who with Al's help invented a way to make pearl buttons from fish scales but died as a result of convulsions after reading Sir Walter Scott's complete works in twelve and one half days.

Faulkner did not keep the fun of this joint project to himself. He told Phil Stone, but by the time Stone relayed the information, it had changed substantially. When he wrote Four Seas on March 31 to thank them for copies of their spring catalog, he told them that Faulkner was in New Orleans and was "writing some very good stuff in verse." Faulkner was also writing a novel, he said, and "He and Sherwood Anderson are writing a novel together." On April 18 he informed Four Seas that Faulkner was still in New Orleans and had "postponed for some months his departure for Europe because of the fact that Sherwood Anderson has been kind enough to write a novel in collaboration with him." It would be published, Stone thought, sometime in the fall. The only collaborative work Anderson and Faulkner appear ever to have done was the Al Jackson letters. How had Stone come to represent this as a novel? Perhaps at first Faulkner and Anderson had actually intended to do a sort of *jeu d'esprit* together. Or perhaps it was only Faulkner who thought so. It is possible that Faulkner was pulling Stone's leg, though this does not seem in character, given their relationship then, and Stone's tone to Four Seas seemed perfectly serious. The report must certainly have been a welcome one to Stone. Collaboration with Anderson would ensure the end of what Stone and Faulkner had called the long "drought." At the moment, however, it had not broken, for James Feibleman remembered seeing a drawer full of rejections Faulkner had received from *Collier's* and *The Saturday Evening Post*.

No matter what brought the Al Jackson letters to an end, Anderson showed continuing interest and concern. Faulkner later wrote that Anderson once told him, "You've got too much talent. You can do it too easy, in too many different ways. If you're not careful, you'll never write anything." Anderson may have been thinking of the essays, poems, and sketches that were appearing in the *Times-Picayune* and *The Double Dealer*, fearing that Faulkner would dissipate his energies by doing too many things. As for actual work time, Anderson knew he was no sluggard. "I used to hear his typewriter rattling away as I went through the passageway," he later recalled. "I heard it in the morning, in the afternoon and often late at night. He was always at it, pounding away." Bill Spratling could certainly confirm Anderson's recollection. "By the time I would be up, say at seven, Bill would already be out on the little balcony over the garden tapping away on his portable, an invariable glass of alcohol-and-water at hand."

From the outset he had known where *Mayday* was going. He had sketched out the novel in four paragraphs of notes on half of a sheet of legal-size onionskin. "Cecily," he began, "with her luck in dramatizing herself, engaged to an aviator reported as dead." At the end of this line, and the three other lines that made up the first paragraph, were check marks, as though he had checked off the elements of his outline as he wrote them into his manuscript. The second paragraph broke Parts Two, Three, and Four of the novel into numbered segments listing the principal characters involved. The last of these read simply, "Part 4. Death of Mahon. Rector's story. Rector and Gilligan." The third paragraph characterized Januarius Jones and included one of his epigrams which compared Napoleon, Joseph Conrad, and John Brown. The last paragraph of notes listed principal characteristics ("Jones—Boldness") and foreshadowed the book's last lines: "Wind wafting Feed thy sheep, O Jesus into the moonless world of space, beyond despair." On another similar sheet he had written a twenty-line synopsis of the action concluding Part Three of the novel. A note at the bottom of the first of the two sheets showed that he had been planning more than plot. It read, "Scribners/597 5th Ave."

If he was following what would be for years his standard practice, he was composing the manuscript in pen, adding and cutting as he reread it, and then typing out a copy for further revision. He wrote initially by hand, he later said, because the words didn't feel right coming out on a typewriter. But he had to transcribe quickly because, as he said someone had put it, a sheet of his manuscript looked as though a caterpillar had fallen into the inkpot and then walked across the page. When he had wired Phil Stone that his mistress was 30,000 words long, he probably had something like a hundred typed pages, each of the first dozen bearing his name at the bottom and none of them numbered. By the time he had typed out a whole draft, he had 238 pages. He may actually have done still another typescript before he began the final one, and even if it was not a whole typescript, most of the material had been typed more than once, the body of it on white legal-size bond and onionskin paper. Following another practice he would habitually employ, he shifted whole sections and chapters from one spot to another, seeking the most effective place to use them. Now, as he finished

Notes for *Mayday*, later *Soldiers' Pay*.

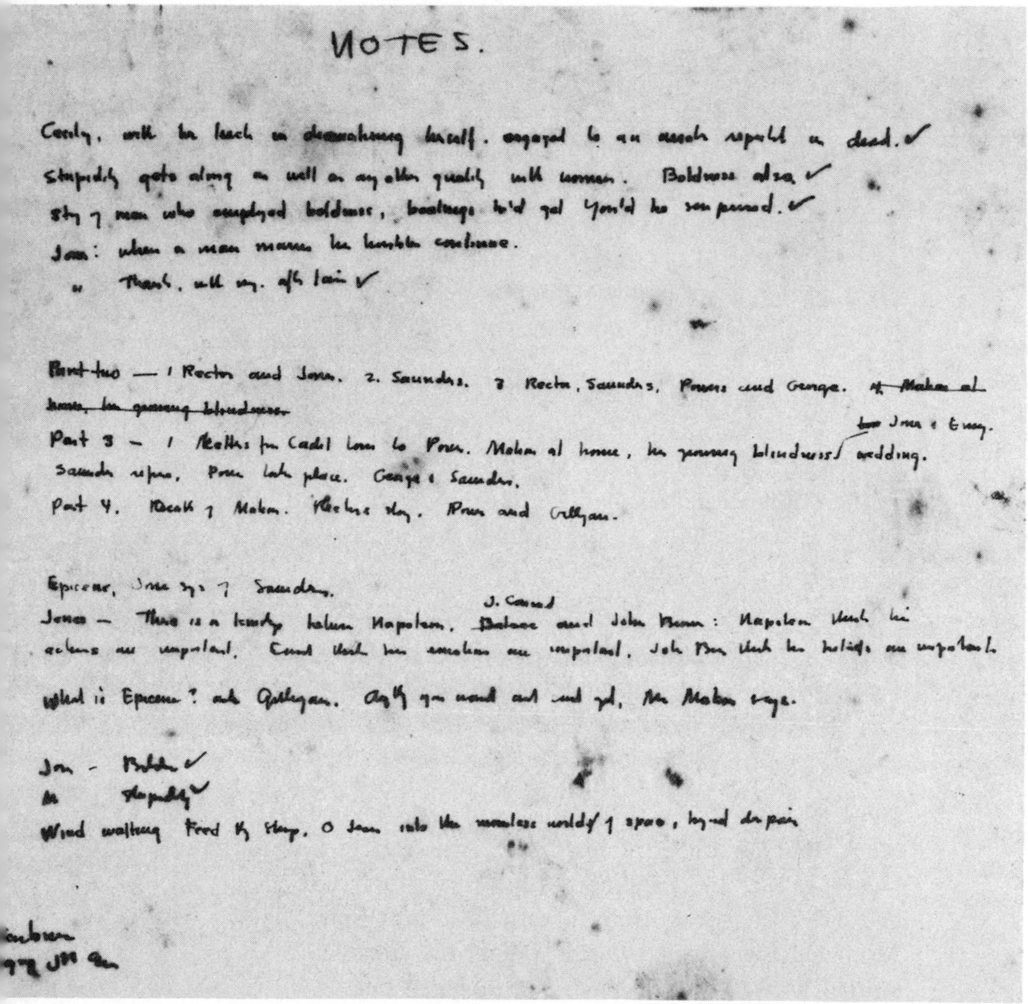
NOTES.

Cecily, with her knack in dramatizing herself, engaged to an aviator reported as dead. ✓
Stupidity gets along as well as any other quality with women. Boldness also. ✓
Story of man who employed boldness, boasting he'd get. You'd be surprised. ✓
Jones: when a man marries he [illegible] continues.
" Thank, with my. after learn ✓

~~Part two~~ — 1 Rector and Jones. 2. Saunders. 3 Rector, Saunders, Powers and George. ~~4 Mahon at home, his growing blindness.~~
Part 3 — 1 [illegible] from Cadet [illegible] to Powers. Mahon at home, his growing blindness / two Jones & Emmy. wedding.
Saunders refuses, Powers takes place. George & Saunders.
Part 4. Death of Mahon. Rector's story. Powers and Gilligan.

Epicene, Jones says of Saunders.
Jones — There is a trinity between Napoleon, ~~Balzac~~ J. Conrad and John Brown: Napoleon thinks his actions are important, Conrad thinks his emotions are important, John Brown thinks his beliefs are important.

What is Epicene? asks Gilligan. Anything you would eat and not get, Mrs Mahon says.

Jones - Boldness ✓
" Stupidity ✓
Wind walking [illegible]. O Jones into the [illegible] world of space, beyond despair

407

his expanded final copy of *Mayday*, using a purple ribbon and inexpensive white letter-size typing paper, he would count up the number of words in each section and then neatly inscribe the total in the lower right-hand corner of the last page of each section. On the last page of each chapter, he would write—in pen, now—the total number of words in the chapter. Chapter One of his revised typescript was, according to his count, 13,626 words long. Chapter Two ran to 11,021 words, and Chapter Three to 13,478. So he must have been well into Chapter Three by the time Spratling would see him on the balcony overlooking the garden, typing in the warm New Orleans morning. He was frugal as always. He had started a poem on one sheet but then abandoned it. So the back of page 93 of his typescript bore the single line in black ink: "O fair my sweet, and sweet my most sweet fair."

Another resident of the same building was Joyce Stagg, who would later become the wife of John McClure. Faulkner spoke so rarely and behaved so quietly that they hardly noticed him, she said. And much of the time he was in his room, working. When he had quit for the day he might go for a stroll down toward the docks or sit in Jackson Park, gazing at the cathedral, watching the people, or staring off into the distance.

From Faulkner's first chapter Anderson must have seen that the facility of the sketches and the imagery of the poems had carried over into the fiction. He probably did not recognize a habitual trait: economy of means. Faulkner did not hesitate to cannibalize, adapt, or repeat material he had used elsewhere. As the epigraph for the book he would use the last quatrain of "An Armistice Day Poem," which Stone had sent to *The Atlantic Monthly* the previous November:

The hushèd plaint of wind in stricken trees
Shivers the grass in path and lane
And Grief and Times are tideless golden seas—
Hush, hush! He's home again.

Nineteen-year-old Flying Cadet Julian Lowe, "known as 'One Wing' by the other embryonic aces of his flight," was clearly Cadet Thompson, the "barracks ace" of "Landing in Luck" with forty-seven hours' flying time and only two weeks to go to earn his wings when the war had ended. Moribund Lieutenant Donald Mahon, the amnesiac RAF pilot, with his scarred brow, withered hand, and incipient blindness, was the dim-eyed convalescent of "The Lilacs," who sat, nearly oblivious, watched by solicitous women, and remembered:

The bullet struck me here, I think
In the left breast
And killed my little pointed-eared machine. . . .

Faulkner was using his life, of course, as well as his works. As epigraphs for sections of the first chapter he employed army jokes about government-issue razor blades and lines used for the cadence count of marching formations:

Who sprang to be his land's defense
And has been sorry ever since?
Cadet!

(Here he crossed two bawdy lines out of his typescript.) His own chagrin at the white cadet cap band and the inability to prove himself in combat was projected onto Cadet Lowe. His own trip home from Canada at the war's end gave him the setting and most of the action of this first chapter, and he apparently based "Yaphank," Private Joe Gilligan, on a man he met on the train. Spratling said that Faulkner had used some of his traits for Gilligan—his authoritative way, for instance, of taking care of people. The train conductor's reference to his marine son, not heard from for six months, suggests Jack Falkner during the time after his wounding in France. Donald Mahon had been thought dead, and his sad homecoming may well have owed something to Faulkner's speculations about his briefly missing brother. Even Margaret Powers, a war widow who joins with Gilligan to see Mahon home, had a familiar aspect. In her and in Cecily Saunders—Mahon's pretty, vain, and heartless fiancée—Estelle Franklin would see a partial portrait of herself, drawn by Faulkner as he remembered their blighted romance.

Margaret Powers prompted an early revelation of one of the author's tastes. "Had Gilligan and Lowe ever seen an Aubrey Beardsley," he wrote, "they would have known that Beardsley would have sickened for her: he had drawn her so often dressed in peacock hues, white and slim and depraved among meretricious trees and impossible marble fountains." (31) In succeeding chapters there would be Beardsleyesque gardens and forest scenes, with appropriate characters and actions. The typescript Anderson probably saw was quite neat for the work of an amateur typist, and the revisions were few—here and there a line crossed out. There was much of that facility Anderson had warned against—facility a lesser man would have envied. Anderson probably noticed something else, too, the familiar susceptibility of a young writer to other writers' matter and manner. He may have thought, for instance, of Scott Fitzgerald's story about returned soldiers entitled "Mayday," about Fitzgerald's practice of interpolating lines from songs into his stories in which characters drank quite as heavily as did Faulkner's. Anderson had a strict directive for Faulkner during the writing of the rest of the book: Don't read the work of anyone else.

Anderson could scarcely have blamed Faulkner if he disobeyed this edict in one instance. Phil Stone, in his March 31 letter to Four Seas, had mentioned a forthcoming work by Anderson. "Mr. Faulkner is the original," he wrote, "of the story by Anderson in the *Dial* for April. The title of the story is 'A Meeting South.' " It seems unlikely that Stone would have learned this from Anderson. What does seem likely is that Anderson told Faulkner something about the use he had made of their evening together and perhaps even showed him the story. It would have been difficult for an aspiring writer to resist reading it in print.

It had the familiar Anderson magic, vividly presenting unusual characters whose inner personalities he tried to penetrate in the seemingly simple evocative prose. The story also included a passage which described New Orleans' charm and attempted to explain why Anderson loved it. Another passage described a businessman-writer for national magazines, pandering to the tastes Anderson had criticized in his *Double Dealer* essay of 1922. For a number of the Quarter's residents there would be recognizable elements in "A Meeting South" besides Anderson's style and Aunt Rose Arnold, transformed into "Aunt Sally." Faulkner had told several people that he had been shot down and bore a silver plate in his head as a consequence. He drank, he would add, to relieve the pain. To some his speech was not a Mississippi drawl but clipped, upper-class English. At other times, however, he would elaborate upon his Southern background. He would go back to Oxford, he might say, to see his illegitimate children. He told Anita Loos that one of the Negroes on their place had said to him, "Don't get married and have a family because we can't take care of any more of you." His favorite persona, however, was still the RAF officer. In his assumption of this role he was, in effect, performing a fusion of two of his characters. Like Lieutenant Donald Mahon, former RAF pilot, he had sustained serious combat injuries to his head and to one of his limbs. But like former RAF Cadet Julian Lowe, he was young and had life still ahead of him.

Actually, Faulkner might well have been known by now to some Orleanians living beyond the Quarter. One of the *Marble Faun* publicity photographs had appeared in the *Times-Picayune* under the legend "Southern Poet in Orleans." The caption identified him as the author of *The Marble Faun*, "who is visiting Sherwood Anderson here." His photograph was shown again in the lower left-hand corner of the front page of the New Orleans *Item-Tribune* on Saturday, April 4. He was almost fullface to the camera, thick hair *en brosse*, deep-eyed and fine-featured, almost handsome and very youthful. He had won $10 by answering in 250 words or less the question "What Is the Matter with Marriage?" Before presenting his answer, the writer told the reader that Mr. Faulkner had been in New Orleans "for some time writing books of poetry. . . . He has a thorough understanding of life and its complexities, and is therefore qualified to speak." There was a caption under his photograph: "Poet, philosopher, student of life, WILLIAM FAULKNER says that passion is a fire which quickly burns itself out. Love is enduring, he believes, a fuel that feeds a never-dying fire." There was nothing wrong with marriage, said the young philosopher, it was the people who entered into it without being prepared to give and to understand.

Apparently Faulkner spent some time as Anderson's guest in spite of his having been sent to Spratling's to live. Young Anita Loos was there in New Orleans visiting the Andersons with her husband, John Emerson, the actor-director, who had been Anderson's boyhood friend in Clyde, Ohio. Faulkner would straggle down to breakfast, she remembered, carrying in his hand a glass of what she was sure was corn liquor. He would drink it before breakfast. Quiet, easy, gentle, and never opinionated, she saw him living the life of a war hero. "You can't expect much of Bill," she heard others say, "because he has that plate in his head and he isn't very smart." She did remember his participating in one activity, however. Together they would mount the stone steps of the cathedral tower and climb to the belfry. There, she said, they would order their liquor from a young priest, who was later unfrocked. But Anita Loos did not have much time herself for such pursuits. She too was busy writing. She was at work on a book about a young gold-digger who was firmly convinced that diamonds were a girl's best friend.

During this time Faulkner still managed somehow to write for the *Times-Picayune*. He would buy yellow copy paper over on Canal Street, one friend remembered, bringing back ten cents' worth each time. He would often type his material at night, to the annoyance of some of the other tenants, and then take his copy over to the *Times-Picayune* office. During the month of April, 1925, he contributed three more short stories. "Cheest," of Sunday, April 5, showed quite clearly how he had been impressed by Anderson's use of native materials and a conversational, colloquial style. In fact, it read almost as though Faulkner were doing his own 1,500-word version of Anderson's "I'm a Fool." Faulkner's narrator was a jockey who spoke of "swipes" and "skates" and "janes"—terms foreign to Faulkner's vocabulary. The tough, wisecracking argot of jockey Jack Potter was not unlike that of some of Ring Lardner's characters. The race-track environment was one Anderson had known most of his life and used profitably for his fiction. A measure of the difference in the maturity of the two artists was the end result of each tale. In "I'm a Fool," failure humanized the rough young man who told the story and made him a poignant figure. In "Cheest," Jack Potter met two girls watching a racing film and gained not only the regard of one but her garter as well, which served as a good-luck piece when his horse won. If it was nothing more, "Cheest" was a lively story and a sincere gesture of admiration.

A story which Faulkner may have begun at this time—featuring another wanderer and also suggesting Sherwood Anderson—displayed autobiographical borrowing. Entitled "And Now What's To Do," the 1,200-word fragment started with the family background of the young protagonist: "His great grandfather came into the county afoot from the Tennessee mountains, where he had killed a man, worked and saved and bought a little land, won a little more at cards and dice, and died at the point of a pistol while trying to legislate himself into a little more; his grandfather was a deaf upright man in white linen, who wasted his inherited substance in politics. He had a law practice still, but he sat most of the day in the courthouse yard, a brooding, thwarted old man too deaf to take part in conversation and whom the veriest child could beat at checkers. His father loved horses better than books or learning; he owned a livery stable, and here the boy grew up, impregnated with the violent ammoniac odor of horses." Faulkner went on to describe the onset of the boy's adolescence, troubled by sexual longings and feelings of social inferiority because of his father's occupation. Developing a fondness for liquor and an expertise with dice, he got a girl in trouble and left town, traveling northward through Kentucky and Ohio. "In an Ohio town one night, in a saloon, he got to know a man who was traveling from county seat to county seat with a pacing horse, making the county fairs. The man was cunning in a cravatless collar, [delivering] a lachrymose panegyric [upon] the passing of the horse; and together they drifted south again, and again his garments became impregnated with ammonia." Here the story broke off. It was full of canceled lines and rewritten passages, rambling and unfocused, but it contained elements that would reappear: not just the image of geese flying south, their cries "lonely and sad and wild" in the "season of sin and death," but also the young man whose wanderlust betrays impulses radically different from those of his forebears.

"Out of Nazareth," which appeared in the *Times-Picayune* on April 12, showed Faulkner using a contemporary setting. He was with Spratling, "whose hand has been shaped to the brush as mine (alas!) has not," and he had remarked to him "how no one since Cezanne had really dipped his brush in light." Like Anderson, Faulkner was still interested in painting. He would try pen, pencil, or paint from time to time, but as he wrote here, he knew that "words are my meat and bread and drink. . . ." The subject of the 2,000-word story was a seventeen-year-old vagabond with a face so beautiful that Spratling offered him pay to pose. They bought him lunch and Faulkner gave him a dollar as advance payment. Unwilling, the boy told them he might be on the road once more by tomorrow and gave them something in return in case he should not appear. It was an account of experiences on the road—"blundering and childish and 'arty,' " Faulkner said, just as he had received it. It was filled with love of nature and of people, sounding strangely as would some of the proletarian novels in the next decade singing the love of fellows. More interesting was Faulkner's use, once again, of a man climbing a hill. But this was different from "The Hill" of three years before. This time he did not suggest the exploited figure of "The Man with the Hoe" of Jean Millet and Edwin Markham. The boy had the same strength and closeness to the soil, but he also had poetic sensibility and inspiring faith. And there was something here of the compulsion to create which Faulkner had sketched in that part of "New Orleans" subtitled "The Artist." Again he had drawn upon himself as he would nearly thirty years later, describing "the avocation he was coming more and more to know would be forever his true one: to be a tramp, a harmless passionless vagabond."

The following week's 1,600-word story was entitled "The Kingdom of God." Its central character was not, like the vagabond, by implication Christlike. He was one of the little children who, according to Christ, made up the Kingdom of God. But he was a child in mind only, an idiot with eyes as "clear and blue as cornflowers, and utterly vacant of thought . . . ." He is kept quiet, as his brother delivers bootleg liquor, by the narcissus he holds. The hoodlum unloading the cases distractedly strikes the idiot when he cannot respond to his command to help. When the normal brother retaliates, the fracas brings the police. Faulkner was using the New Orleans underworld milieu and again sketching characters who would reappear later.

Another character in a work which probably dates from this time stood midway between the idiot of "The Kingdom of God" and the vagabond would-be poet in "Out of Nazareth." The nameless protagonist of an eight-page typescript entitled "Nympholepsy" was, in fact, the solitary rural laborer of "The Hill" given greater awareness and an adventure only hinted at in the earlier sketch. Near the end of the short time-span covered in "The Hill," Faulkner wrote, "Here, in the dusk, nymphs and fauns might riot to a shrilling of thin pipes, to a shivering and hissing of cymbals in a sharp volcanic abasement beneath a tall icy star." In "Nympholepsy" the farm laborer again climbed a hill at sunset. But now, in place of catching sight of a church spire, he saw Ionic columns: "From here the Court-house was a dream dreamed by Thucydides. . . ." Having glimpsed a girl in the failing light, he played faun to her nymph. Giving chase unsuccessfully, he narrowly escaped drowning in a stream and finally walked in the moonlight toward the lights of the town and the Court-house clock, thinking that tomorrow after work he might see again "a girl like defunctive music." Echoes of "The Hill" sounded in the last paragraph: "Behind him labor, before him labor; about all the old despairs of time and breath. The stars were like shattered flowers floating on dark water, sucking down the west; and with dust clinging to his yet damp feet, he slowly descended the hill." The sketch was another attempt to render a private vision, but it failed to fuse successfully the pastoral and the realistic elements.

Anderson and Faulkner continued to meet in the spring afternoons after work, in gatherings at the Andersons' or other favorite places in the Quarter. They would go occasionally to Aunt Rose Arnold's house on Chartres Street and sit with her in the little patio where the banana tree grew. By now Aunt Rose had become still fonder of Bill Faulkner. One day she even asked him to put on the kilt of her adopted son who had been killed on the Western Front, but he declined. Later she asked him again, but he would never don the Scots regimental dress. The evenings with Anderson were memorable: "now he would really talk; the world in minuscule would be there in whatever shadowy courtyard where glass and bottle clinked and palms hissed like dry sand in whatever moving air." As Faulkner later remembered their meetings, Anderson was always the mentor. "You're a country boy," he said; "all you know is that little patch up there in Mississippi where you started from. But that's all right too. It's America too; pull it out, as little and unknown as it is, and the whole thing will collapse, like when you prize a brick out of a wall." Anderson might well have thought to himself that Faulkner could do worse than to follow *Winesburg, Ohio*, where he had used the people of one small town, examining their lives to portray common fears and hopes, making this microcosm emblematic of the whole big world beyond its confines. Faulkner would try other strategies before he adopted that one, as Anderson knew when he read the typed pages of *Mayday*. America, Anderson told him, should be their subject, to interpret and explain it. "That's why ignorant unschooled fellows like you and me not only have a chance to write, they must write." And you had to keep trying. It may have come as something of a shock to Anderson to read one of the next efforts of the young man he was trying to instruct in these principles of writing.

Faulkner found time for some literary criticism that month. John H. McGinnis, the first book editor of the Dallas *Morning News*, liked what he had read of Faulkner's. Then running a series on contemporary American writers, McGinnis asked Faulkner to do an essay on Sherwood Anderson. In 2,000 words, Faulkner assessed seven of Anderson's major works. Faulkner had learned a lot from him, he had said, and the essay showed fairly extensive reading, including some criticism. He thought it was foolish to say that Anderson derived from the Russians, or the French. "I prefer to think of Mr. Anderson," he wrote, "as a lusty corn field in his native Ohio." After the brief preamble he turned to the books.

He liked the simplicity of the title *Winesburg, Ohio*. "His very inexperience," his urgency, Faulkner thought, "taught him one of the first attributes of genius." And there was sympathy. It would have been "mawkish" had the form been that of a full-length novel, but "Again the gods looked out for him." The characters were beautiful, and behind all was the force of nature and the seasons. Anderson's first two novels, he thought, displayed "a fundamental lack of humor." *Poor White*, his third, was good, but his fourth, *Many Marriages*, showed a bad ear. There were other serious faults, for "he gets away from the land. When he does this he is lost. And again humor is completely lacking." *Horses and Men* made you want to reread *Winesburg*, "Which makes one wonder if after all the short story is not Mr. Anderson's medium." The story "I'm a Fool" was, to his thinking, "the best short story in America. . . ." Faulkner liked the first half of *A Story Teller's Story,* with its brilliant characterization of Anderson's father, but the second half suffered from a familiar fault: "an elephantine kind of humor about himself. . . ." In closing, Faulkner recounted Anderson's dream of selling his horse for a night's sleep. He scoffed again at the idea of foreign antecedents for Anderson. One friend had called him "the Phallic Chekhov." Actually, he was unquestionably American and Middle Western, "as typical of Ohio in his way as Harding was in his."

Faulkner probably had not concluded by then, as he later would, that "the great tragedy" of Anderson's character was that he "expected people to make fun of, ridicule him. He expected people nowhere near his equal in stature or accomplishment or wit or anything else, to be capable of making him appear ridiculous." He was a sentimentalist about people, Faulkner would decide. Believing in them in theory, he actually "expected the worst from them, even while each time he was prepared again to be disappointed or even hurt, as if it had never happened before, as though the only people he could really trust . . . were the ones of his own invention, the figments and symbols of his own fumbling dream." He must not have realized that his essay, if Anderson read it, could only be shocking and hurtful, in spite of the compliments here and there. It would not be just Faulkner's coupling Anderson with Harding, head of what had been called the most corrupt administration in the history of the United States. It would be as though a skating instructor should suddenly see his erstwhile pupil skating around him in flashing circles—executing spins, turns, jumps, and pirouettes—with all the while a condescending smile on his face. Even if Faulkner had not yet made the judgment of Anderson's personality he would later describe, the essay showed that he had arrived at the aesthetic judgment he would subsequently render: Anderson was "only a one- or two-book man. He had to believe that, if only he kept that style pure, then what the style contained would be pure too, the best." In 1925, with *Dark Laughter,* "he had reached the point where he should have stopped writing. . . ."

Faulkner retold the story of Anderson's dream in the Dallas *Morning News* article, but changed the locale. Anderson had told him about the dream not on a bench in Jackson Park but instead on a river boat, where they were spending a weekend, as they watched the sun rise over the Mississippi. Their rapport at that time was apparently still intact. They were both students of the Civil War. They both enjoyed dabbling at painting.

And no matter what reservations Faulkner might have about the limitations of Anderson's art, he talked about things that could only have fascinated the younger man. Anderson had found in Gertrude Stein's theory and practice of prose-writing an instrument that helped him to free and develop his own style. He had visited her in Paris, that literary center toward which Faulkner had been aiming. Anderson had also learned from the work of James Joyce. *Ulysses*, he wrote, had given him "a starting point for the prose rhythms" of *Dark Laughter*. But that boat trip, or another like it at about this time, was to provide Faulkner with more than just an opportunity to hear his friend talk.

Bill Spratling remembered Anderson's storytelling on boating expeditions. He wanted to be the center of attention, Spratling felt, and he would sulk if he were not. He kept up a stream of conversation and anecdote for most of one day-trip to Grand Isle, forty-one miles east of the City Yacht Harbor. One of the passengers very soon had had enough of the monologue, as Spratling remembered it, and spent the rest of the day on the prow of the boat by himself.

Another time more than a dozen friends from the Quarter contributed ten dollars apiece to hire the yacht *Josephine* for a day's outing to Mandeville, twenty-three miles due north across Lake Pontchartrain. Sherwood and Elizabeth Anderson formed the nucleus. Besides Faulkner, there was Sam Gilmore, whose tall, languid form was pictured in a fresco above the fireplace in the *Double Dealer* office. Many of his short, imagistic poems had appeared in the magazine along with a number of one-act plays, some of which had been produced at Le Petit Théâtre du Vieux Carré. There was Hamilton Basso, still a Tulane student but now beginning to write for local newspapers. He was a short young man whom Spratling recalled sitting at the feet of Sherwood Anderson. Tulane anthropologist Franz Blom joined the group. Another from Tulane was Richard Kirk, a bespectacled and mustached young English teacher who had contributed to *The Double Dealer*. Sharp-featured, black-haired Lillian Marcus, who was largely responsible for keeping the magazine afloat, was there too. Blond Virginia Parker Nagle, a slim and pretty painter, also came aboard. So did Lucille and Marc Antony, who owned the building that Faulkner and Spratling lived in and ran one of the many art shops and galleries in the Quarter. It was by no means an ordinary group, but if there was a true exotic among them that day, it was apparently Colonel Charles Glenn Collins, a Scot with a career of varied adventure and misadventure behind him, and an amusing way of telling tales from it. Faulkner, the Antonys remembered, always carried with him a bottle wrapped in a newspaper. He, like the rest, must have looked forward to a pleasant, relaxing day on the waters of Lake Pontchartrain.

With Anderson along, there would be no lack of entertainment, but there were other good talkers aboard if they could obtain a hearing. Faulkner and Basso might talk about wharves they had walked or books they had read, though Basso was just beginning with Conrad and Melville whereas Faulkner "had got past Verlaine, Eliot, Pound, and Joyce. . . ." Collins' talk was more lively if less literary. He was alleged to have not too long ago successfully fought off extradition to India for failing to pay for jewels worth $50,000. His charm and influence had made it possible, it was said, for him to leave his New Orleans jail cell from time to time to go on just such cruises as the present one. His diverting company on the lake and on its beaches was prized by Faulkner and the others. Faulkner might have talked poetry with Sam Gilmore, but if he had, it would hardly have been about *The Marble Faun*, even if it was still mentioned occasionally in newspaper reviews here and there. "He was boiling with ideas all the time," Spratling remembered, and he had the impression that Faulkner's horizon was broadening so rapidly that he was glad to forget *The Marble Faun*. This may, as a matter of fact, have been what happened to *The Greening Bough*, and perhaps the Al Jackson letters, too.

This particular trip, however, would not be as pleasant as others they had made. The day darkened and a drizzle began to fall. Then, as a storm rumbled in the distance, the engine started to smoke and miss, steadily losing power. Although they were now virtually stranded, the shore was close enough for the mosquitoes to find them. The passengers took refuge in the main cabin, but the smoke from the engine hung in the air and soon they were coughing as they scratched their bites. No one wanted to try for Mandeville, whose amusement area Spratling thought of as "a sort of poor man's paradise." But then Bill Faulkner and Virginia Parker Nagle decided to brave the mosquitoes. They got off and "went skirmishing around at Mandeville," as Sam Gilmore remembered it. (David, in "A Meeting South," told Anderson's narrator that he would sleep in the fields at home in spite of the mosquitoes, whose bites didn't bother him much because he got drunk enough not to mind.) It was dark when they got back to New Orleans. Some had mosquito bites. Others, doubtless, would have hangovers. Faulkner had considerable literary material.

Hamilton Basso introduced Faulkner to another diversion. From time to time Basso would do an assignment for the *Times-Picayune.* One day the city editor asked him for a feature story on an organization called "The Gates Flying Circus." They would take passengers up in their decrepit two-seater Wright Whirlwind airplanes and show them New Orleans from the air or execute a few spins, stalls, or loops if the passenger wanted them. Basso found it a frightening experience, but he liked these barnstorming aviators well enough to return, taking Faulkner with him. The Flying Circus stayed in town long enough for Basso to have half a dozen more Whirlwind rides, and for Faulkner, "who was a bit hipped on the subject of flying anyway, to become an almost constant companion." This created a bond between the two men far stronger than literary tastes could ever provide, for "Nobody *else* in our crowd had gone looping-the-loop in a bucket seat and open cockpit over the Mississippi River."

Faulkner knew a few other junior reporters on the *Times-Picayune.* One was a quiet twenty-three-year-old from Pascagoula named Josh Baird. He had been an asthmatic child, overshadowed by two brilliant older brothers, but now he was making a successful career as a sportswriter. Sometimes he would appear at Lyle Saxon's or Spratling's when everyone would seem to be talking at once in a crowded room, smoking and dipping their drinks from a large bowl of absinthe or pernod poured over a big piece of ice. Spratling liked Josh's twenty-one-year-old sister Helen, an artist and sculptress who struck people as elfin or spritelike. Barely five feet tall, she had light blue eyes, a wide mouth, and dark hair and skin. To some she looked as dark as a gypsy. The night Faulkner met her at one of Spratling's parties, she was in white, and she wore what Spratling called her don't-give-a-damn look. She was quick, volatile, and amusing, with a straightforward manner. The Antonys thought of her as a warm and happy girl, and Faulkner may have, too. Bill Spratling good-naturedly said that he had been interested in her first and Faulkner had taken her away from him. The truth was that Helen Baird liked people who did not care about convention, who had talent and something of her own devil-may-care manner.

There was no lack of attractive young women in the Quarter. Another was twenty-four-year-old Margery Kalom Gumbel. Three years before, she had come to New Orleans with her husband, Irving Gumbel, a securities broker who had contributed a review to *The Double Dealer,* where he had been described as a businessman "whose leisure moments are devoted to study in the arts." She was taller than Helen Baird, but she seemed fragile, her large eyes dominating her heart-shaped, fine-featured face under a mass of pale gold hair. She had grown up an only child whose parents were often in Europe. Now she was ill and unhappy, and she did not like New Orleans. She first met Faulkner at Sherwood Anderson's and would see him too at the home of painter Ronald Hargrave. Faulkner was drawn to her, and she felt that he, too, was unhappy. At parties he seemed to dislike the blaring jazz from the phonograph. He would walk out into the soft night air and stand gazing at the dark trees of Jackson Square below the iron tracery of the shadowed balconies.

At their first meeting his speech seemed to her very British and he carried a cane. He mentioned the plate in his head. At other times, though, he talked about the plate in his face. She thought he was young and had to mature, but she liked him very much. Sometimes a group would cross Lake Pontchartrain and drive fifteen miles north to Covington, beyond Mandeville, in what was called the Ozone Belt around New Orleans. There were clear streams under the pines, and on a hot sultry day some of the more vigorous would throw off their clothes and go swimming in their underwear. On other days they might make the short drive from the Quarter to the south shore of Lake Pontchartrain. They would walk out onto the long, catwalk-like wharves and drink tepid home brew. It was so shallow that a swimmer could go out the length of a city block and still be only waist-deep in the warm waters of the lake. Sometimes Faulkner would be there in his swimming trunks with the rest. As Margery looked on from the wharf, he would come up and join her. He stood there beside her once, watching the swimmers, hearing their shouts. He looked at her. "Margery," he said in his soft voice, without preamble, "we believe in God, don't we?"

He had other friends with connections in both art and commerce. Harold Levy's family had done well in business, numbering among their enterprises a curio shop in the Quarter. Levy lived in the Quarter, his apartment, with its large double parlor and chandelier-lit grand piano, one of the best-furnished in the Pontalba. He had studied conducting in Paris and now worked with the New Orleans Little Symphony. Sometimes he and Faulkner would eat together at Madame Gaye's on Royal Street or Madame Petrie's on Chartres Street. They could enjoy an excellent lunch for thirty-five cents, a succulent dinner for half a dollar. Madame Gaye was the cashier and her husband the waiter. Levy and Faulkner would speak French with Madame Petrie, whose two sons, Dave and Eddie, waited on tables. Madame Petrie was another excellent businesswoman whose activities were not limited to the restaurant business. At other times the two men would sit in Joe Joseph's bar at Orleans and Bourbon streets. Faulkner seemed to Levy to be still all tied up in the war. He talked in his British accent about flying and about his wound. He looked gaunt, and Levy got the impression that he had a pension coming. In his way Faulkner liked stories as much as Anderson did, though he would tell them to a companion or to an audience of only a few. And he liked tall tales, as did Anderson and others in the Quarter, where they constituted part of an evening's entertainment. Levy was writing verse then, too, and sometimes they would talk about poetry. Faulkner seemed to him somehow insecure, but he was clearly "not just another rhymester."

One night as Levy sat in his living room there was a knock on the door. He opened it to admit Faulkner and a friend. He mixed drinks, and soon they were talking poetry and music. Faulkner told Levy that he had written the first lines of a sonnet but that he was having trouble even getting through the octave. He recited the three lines he had composed. It interested Levy and he suggested a phrase. Faulkner began to work at the poem, trying new lines and ideas. Levy made other suggestions, and finally Faulkner finished it. After he had typed it out, he inscribed it to Harold Levy, "to whom credit is due for the above sonnet after my own inspiration had failed."

Dedicated "To H.L.," the poem appeared in the April issue of *The Double Dealer* under the title "The Faun." It was a blending of the Petrarchan and Shakespearean forms. March was a stamping faun vainly pursuing the dryad May, "yet unwombed of the moist flanks of spring. . . ." He looked ahead to the time when May would incite him

To strip the musiced leaves upon her breast
And from a cup unlipped, undreamt, unguessed,
Sip that wine sweet-sunned for Jove's delight.

The same issue of the magazine printed more of his literary criticism. The early ardor had been replaced by an almost world-weary tone. In some passages the piece sounded like one that would appear in the next issue, Frank Harris' "How I Gave Up Writing Poetry." Faulkner's 2,000-word essay was entitled "Verse Old and Nascent: A Pilgrimage." He described a pilgrimage that had taken him from Swinburne to "the moderns," of whom he could now read only Robinson, Frost, Aldington, and Aiken in his "minor music." He did not mention T. S. Eliot. In Housman he had then found what he thought the moderns had been fruitlessly seeking. From there, he said, he went on to Shakespeare, Spenser, the Elizabethans, then Shelley and Keats. In the last four years modern verse had interested him only in its tendency "to revert to formal rhymes and conventional forms again." Keats touched him most deeply and apparently represented his ideal. "Is there nowhere among us a Keats in embryo?" he wondered. "Is not there among us someone who can write something beautiful and passionate and sad instead of saddening?" It was, of course, what he himself was at that moment trying to do, but the medium was prose fiction rather than poetry.

As interesting as the tastes he enumerated was the persona he described. A "youthful morbidity" had prevented him from appreciating Shelley and Keats the first time. He had first written verse to advance "various philanderings" and "to complete a youthful gesture . . . of being 'different' in a small town." But by now he was cynical: "Ah, women, with their hungry snatching little souls!" Though they appeared interested in art, what they really wanted was the artist. As he looked back at Swinburne's verse he saw no sex in it, but rather an eroticism which was related to the normal play of the senses. There was nothing there like "that tortured sex in—say—D. H. Lawrence." (Though Anderson thought Lawrence "a pretentious fool" in his *Studies in Classic American Literature*, he later called him a "kingly man" and declared *Lady Chatterley's Lover* the book *he* had wanted to write.) Faulkner described his present situation in Henleyesque words that suggested Stone's introduction to *The Marble Faun*: "I have this for which to thank whatever gods may be: that having fixed my roots in this soil all contact, saving by the printed word, with contemporary poets is impossible." In fine, this cynical idealist knew where he had been and where he was going.

The essay functioned in a way Faulkner probably had not anticipated. Miss Monte Cooper used it, together with his "On Criticism," when she reviewed *The Marble Faun* on her book page in the *Commercial Appeal* on April 5. From "Verse Old and Nascent" she concluded that his work must be measured against that of Swinburne. When she made the test, Swinburne unsurprisingly won. Though Faulkner's "delicate rhyming couplets" rang with a "a silvery daintiness" that evoked "The image of a kitten stepping fastidiously through wet leaves," the final result was that "Fifty pages of monotonous, if silvery, intoning, must prove to be soporific. . . ." Miss Cooper found other defects, too: mixed metaphors, disregard for meaning, descents into the commonplace, and what she took to be unforgivable localisms in pronunciation. Moreover, the "disarming simplicity" of *The Marble Faun* was "dimmed" by his dogmatism in both essays. Besides, they contained "a sneering quality, especially in regard to women, that is half-baked and raw, and in one or two places faintly evil smelling." One turned from them, she wrote, to the poems, where "an undeniably sensitive nature, so evidently now abraded" expressed itself in clichés and outdated images, displaying occasionally "real delicacy and a pensive charm. . . ." It was a review which was unlikely to convince him that he had been wrong in "On Criticism."

By mid-April Sherwood Anderson was reading more of Faulkner's novel in progress and still reacting favorably. It was now substantially different from what Faulkner had given him before. One hundred and thirty-one pages into his typescript, he had gone off in a new direction. He had dropped Cadet Lowe, though he would avoid total abruptness by introducing at intervals his letters to Margaret Powers. With him had gone the army sayings and cadet phrases. The scene shifted to Charlestown, Georgia, as Margaret Powers and Private Joe Gilligan brought the dying Donald Mahon home to his father, Episcopal Rector Dr. Joseph Mahon. There too were Donald's reluctant fiancée, flapper Cecily Saunders, and his one-time mistress, Emmy, the rectory housemaid and cook. Faulkner was now interested in personal relationships, and he would examine them closely as they developed and changed during Donald Mahon's decline and death. Faulkner constructed a series of triangular and quadrangular relationships: Mahon and Margaret, Cecily, and Emmy; Cecily and Mahon, her town boyfriend George Farr, and goatlike Latin teacher Januarius Jones. Margaret was still involved in varying degrees with Lowe, Mahon, and Gilligan; Jones was alternately pursuing Cecily and Emmy. At the same time Faulkner was keeping these relationships integral to the plot: would Cecily go back on her engagement to Mahon, yield to Jones, or run off with Farr? What effect would this have on the clearly failing Mahon? How could Margaret influence the course of these events, aided by Gilligan, who now loved her?

Faulkner was still displaying economy of means and familiar influences. Mahon had been faunlike as a boy and Jones was certainly satyrlike now. The settings were classic, Beardsleyan, and poetic: "Beyond the oaks, against a wall of poplars in a restless formal row were columns of a Greek temple, yet the poplars themselves in slim, vague green were poised and vain as girls in a frieze. Against a privet hedge would soon be lilies like nuns in a cloister and blue hyacinths swung soundless bells, dreaming of Lesbos." His images of beauty were characteristically drawn from antiquity: "Who was the old pagan who kept his Byzantine goblet at his bedside and slowly wore away the rim kissing it?" (61) He alluded to Atalanta and to *A Shropshire Lad*, and, revealing a taste he and his brother had shared, to Cabell's *Jurgen*. But he was also drawing on the early short-story materials with native settings. Cecily's developing affair with George Farr was much like that in the version of "Moonlight" which described the near seduction of a girl named Cecily by her sweetheart, George. And Emmy's early relationship to Mahon, tearfully confided to sympathetic Margaret Powers, was very close to that of Juliet Bunden and Lee Hollowell in "Adolescence," even down to the companionable nude swimming and bundling. At the same time, Faulkner was briefly sketching life in the small town of Charlestown. One passage would have amused Sonny Bell, Skeet Kincannon, and perhaps even Mark Webster: "There was a general movement into the post office. The mail was in and the window had opened and even those who expected no mail, who had received no mail in months must needs answer one of the most enduring compulsions of the American nation." (111)

At this same time he was turning out fiction set in New Orleans, and in the mirrors of Chartres Street which his *Times-Picayune* sketches offered, the characters came from the world of Joe Gilligan rather than that of Donald Mahon. On each of the five Sundays in May the paper carried one of his sketches. Two were surprise-ending formula stories and one was a romantic retrospective tale expanded from earlier work. The two others were genuinely ambitious, one placed in a gangster milieu and the other principally in a rural setting.

"The Rosary," of May 3, was a 1,300-word story of enmity between Mr. Harris, who hates the title song, and Juan Venturia, who goads him by whistling it and finally even buys a saxophone so he can play it where Harris might hear it on his deathbed. "The Cobbler" of the following Sunday was an expansion of the section of the same name in "New Orleans." It was a sentimental tale of lost love in which the Italian dialect was labored, and only the imagery, with its occasional synesthesia, sounded like Faulkner: "That night, amid the hills where I walked, the great stars were loud as bells in the black sky, loud as great golden-belled sheep cropping the hill of heaven. . . ."

Another tale of an unsuccessful lover, this one unpublished, depended heavily on satire and irony. By the time Faulkner typed it a second time, he had adopted the title "Don Giovanni." The eight-page story employed both fictional and factual models. The protagonist was a department store buyer of women's clothing named Herbie, a man insecure about his appearance and attractiveness to women yet determined to keep on trying despite repeated failure. Though he was more substantial and energetic than T. S. Eliot's J. Alfred Prufrock, his fears were of much the same kind. Needing counsel, he sought out a friend in the French Quarter who tried unsuccessfully to avoid him. Though Faulkner did not describe the friend, Morrison, at length, he was a writer who vaguely suggested Sherwood Anderson. Herbie outlined to him his new strategy to seduce a Miss Steinbauer and then departed, only to return two hours later to describe another ignominious failure. His ludicrous recital, involving an attempt to bribe a taxi driver and the loss of the girl to a stronger man at a dance, moved Morrison to annoyance rather than sympathy. Apparently feeling that Herbie's ineptitude produced the kind of sequence of events an artist might envy, Morrison told him to go and pick up a girl if he must, but not to bother him any more. "I am trying to write a novel," he said, "and you have damaged my vanity beyond repair." Herbie went home to soak his feet in water and chew "a digestive tablet." Then, still hopeful, he telephoned Morrison, waking him to describe a newly devised stratagem to achieve romantic mastery. When Morrison hung up abruptly, Herbie heard over the buzzing line the operator's derisive advice: "You tell 'em big boy. Treat 'em rough." Essentially a satiric character study hung on a slight incident, "Don Giovanni" gave an effect at once static and undeveloped. Faulkner put it with the other pieces that also bore the Orleans Alley address. Refusal in this summer of 1925 did not mean it could not be used profitably later, in some other form. The newspaper did take, however, another story with a protagonist of a much lower social station than Herbie's.

"Chance," of May 17, was a 1,400-word account of a bum's brief affluence. Only the title of the story suggested Conrad. Faulkner may have been thinking of Anderson's stories, but he was certainly trying to learn how to write commercial fiction which he could produce and sell quickly. Yet some of these stories, such as the last two in May, appear to have caught his imagination. With the others he was probably thinking principally of the money and regretting the time lost on the novel.

The title of the next story was "Sunset." Twenty-five hundred words long, it prefigured later stories. Faulkner began with an item from "the *Clarion-Eagle*" (which might well have appeared in the Oxford *Eagle*), telling of a nameless Negro who had terrorized a locality for two days, killing three men. "No reason has been ascertained for the black's running amuck," the account went on, "though it is believed he was insane." In the story that followed, Faulkner used a strategy that Conrad had often employed. He was interested not so much in what had happened as why it had happened, and therefore he gave away suspense to achieve psychological penetration. The protagonist was a country Negro who wanted to go to Africa, where their people had come from, his preacher had said. He does not know where Africa is, nor what state he himself lives in, but he believes he will have to take a boat to get there. The frightened man is ridiculed, robbed, and exploited. The steamboat captain who has robbed him puts him ashore one day out of New Orleans, telling him "Africa is about a mile across them fields yonder." Terrified after shooting what he does not know is a farm animal, and after killing two men and sustaining a wound himself, he takes refuge in a copse. Faulkner enlivened the terrible with the humorous, as he would do again. "I'll jes' rest here twell dark," the Negro decides, "and den I'm gwine back to Mist' Bob. Af'ica sho' ain't no place fer civilized folks—steppin' on lions, and bein' shot, and havin' to shoot folks yo'self. But I guess dese Af'icans is used to it." Waking from dreams in delirium, he kills still another man before the National Guard machine gunners find him. "His black, kind, dull, once-cheerful face was turned up to the sky and the cold, cold stars. Africa or Louisiana: what care they?" In this story Faulkner was clearly at home with his materials. He presented the Negro and his troubles realistically and sympathetically. He handled the dialect well, spelling phonetically when he could and avoiding the overscrupulous use of apostrophes that often make dialect speech a puzzle for the average reader. "Sunset" was a powerful and adroit sketch which showed how far he had come since the first things he had published in New Orleans.

"The Kid Learns" appeared in the *Times-Picayune* on the last day of May, 1925. It was an expansion of the "Frankie and Johnny" segment of "New Orleans." In the course of the expansion he developed images he would employ again. The protagonist of the 1,700-word story was a young hoodlum who had already shown promise by hijacking a bootleg shipment. For Johnny's inevitable death scene, Faulkner did not use the blatant gunplay which the material seemed to call for. Instead, he mixed fantasy, symbol, and allusion. When a girl steps from a doorway, "with her young body all shining and her hair that wasn't brown and wasn't gold and her eyes the color of sleep," Johnny thinks it is the sweetheart he has just left. When he calls her name tentatively, she replies, "Little sister Death," and takes his hand. Replete with derbies, belted coats, hijacking, slugging, and murder—and narrated rapidly with stilted gangster dialogue—the story was almost redeemed by the sudden shift from the realistic to the symbolic in the poetic ending.

Faulkner enjoyed giving the impression that his experience with bootleggers was considerable. Evidence of the brisk liquor trade abounded in the Quarter, in spite of prohibition. Joe Cassio's grocery store, at the corner of St. Peter and Royal streets, rang up many of its sales on Scotch, bourbon, and gin. The same was true in the grocery of Manuel and Teresa, directly across the street. The customer could not always be sure, however, that the bottles' contents corresponded exactly with the labels. It was commonly supposed that Cuban alcohol served as a base; it was readily available. "You would go fishing and come back with a five-gallon can," Keith Temple remembered. "A speedboat would have brought the alcohol to the marshes, and all you would have to do would be to rent a skiff from a fisherman to get to the marshes. You would pay him for the skiff and the alcohol." Then it would be processed, with the addition of iodine for bourbon, creosote for Scotch, and juniper-berry juice for gin. Faulkner doubtless knew as much as his friends did about this traffic, and it appealed to his imagination. Some of his amusement may have come from the idea of his working as a rumrunner while his brother served as one of J. Edgar Hoover's G-men. Soon he began to use it as an adjunct to an early persona—that of the writer who had bummed around doing a little of everything, partly because he needed to earn a little money and partly because he enjoyed seeing the variety of life. Until the end of his life he would talk about rumrunning with considerable amusement. "I ran a launch," he would say, "from New Orleans across Pontchartrain down the Industrial Canal out into the Gulf where the schooner from Cuba would bring the raw alcohol and bury it on a sand-spit and we'd dig it up and bring it back to the bootlegger and his mother—she was an Italian, she was a nice little old lady, and she was the expert, she would turn it into Scotch with a little creosote, and bourbon. We had the labels, the bottles, everything—it was quite a business."

Twenty years later Faulkner would talk of being hijacked, of seeing a crewman murdered. One of his friends would hear that he had also flown whiskey into the United States from Canada. Faulkner told his brother Jack that he had made one trip with some bootleggers who went from New

Orleans to a place on the Mississippi coast to pick up a shipment. Bill Spratling said his friend had no more run alcohol for bootleggers than he had delivered liquor to a writer who gave him one-dollar tips, as he had once declared. But the illicit liquor trade was no secret. One of the best-known suppliers in the Quarter was a man called Slim, who apparently used his own boats. He knew newspaper reporters as well as barkeepers, and would act as a banker for some of the less frugal on the *Times-Picayune* staff. Faulkner certainly knew of him, and the fact that he was said to have studied for the priesthood would have reminded him of Reno DeVaux. It is possible that Faulkner went out into Lake Pontchartrain with him under cover of darkness for the contraband. Whatever his actual experience, it was the business of the bohemian and the war hero all over again. He wanted to create for himself the image of a man, adventurous and brave, who lived a rather exciting life.

In spite of this taste, Faulkner spent some of his leisure in very comfortable circumstances, as when he visited Harold Levy or Mrs. Kalom, Margery Gumbel's mother. Mrs. Kalom served hearty meals, and sometimes afterward, as they would sit sipping coffee in the living room, Mrs. Kalom would see Faulkner begin to nod. But when she would move to take the cup from him, he would not relinquish it. (This pattern of dozing was one which would become stronger as he grew older, for he still rose at dawn, and he had by now begun to experience periodic insomnia.) Faulkner liked Margery's mother and spoke freely to her. Margery remembered one remark she thought she must have heard half a dozen times. "Mrs. K," he would say, "I'm a genius." He let them read some of the manuscript, and Margery was shocked at the two bawdy lines in one of the cadet songs. It may have been in deference to her reaction that he deleted the two lines.

He was still counting the words, section by section and chapter by chapter. The first and third chapters had run to over 13,000, the second to 11,000, and the fourth had dropped to 7,000. The fifth chapter was nearly 11,000 words long; the sixth, 9,000. On typescript page 412 he carefully noted the word count for Chapter Seven in ink as usual: 9,650. But then the word counts ceased. He was approaching the novel's end, and he either had tired or was too caught up in the thrust of his narrative to stop and count.

He was still drawing on life as he went. ("The reason why Bill's characters are so real," his friend Bob Farley would say, "is because they were real.") Reverend Mahon, big-boned and bulky, was a good deal like Murry Falkner. The night fighting and gas attack undergone by Margaret

Powers' husband was like Jack Falkner's experience in the Argonne. And Mammy Cal'line Nelson showed the same solicitude for her returned "baby," Lieutenant Mahon, that Mammy Callie Barr did for Private Falkner. The same literary tastes reappeared as Faulkner borrowed from Swinburne and Housman. Januarius Jones garbled a line from "Fantoches" as he grappled with Emmy, and whispered the first three lines of "On Seeing the Winged Victory" as he embraced Cecily. Margaret Powers paraphrased the same two lines from Swinburne that the priest had intoned in "New Orleans."

As Faulkner finished the middle chapters, the experimentation increased. He continued to interpolate songs ("I Wish That I Could Shimmy like My Sister Kate") as Fitzgerald did to suggest time and tone. He employed interior monologue and associated devices in a way that suggested James Joyce. He set up the thoughts of the characters in the form of a play script and called one of them "The Town," much as Joyce had done in the "Circe" chapter of *Ulysses.* After a comment by Reverend Mahon about Mrs. Powers, he gave Jones's responding thoughts in parentheses, using phraseology which suggested similar ruminations of Leopold Bloom on female anatomy and wiles. One section of Chapter Seven consisted only of sequential summary statements by characters, some drawn from "The Town." Joyce had used discrete statements in this way for the "overture" to "The Sirens" chapter of *Ulysses.* Tricks of phonetic spelling suggested Joyce's rendering of characters' perceptions of sounds in the "Circe" chapter. As if to show he was not entirely unaware of new currents in other fields, Faulkner gave Jones a single line in which he spoke of both "libido" and "complex." But he cut several long, poetic passages titled simply "He" and "She" in which the two voices meditated on time, death, and nature—passages which suggested *Marionettes.*

In "Verse Old and Nascent" Faulkner had called for "something beautiful and passionate and sad. . . ." As he drew his novel to a close, this seemed more and more what he was trying to achieve. After Cecily had run off with George Farr, Margaret Powers had offered herself to Donald Mahon. Her blind bridegroom dreamed away his life: "Day became afternoon, became dusk and imminent evening: evening like a ship, with twilight-colored sails, dreamed down the world darkly toward darkness." (292) Then, after a terrifying memory of the fatal aerial duel, Mahon was suddenly gone. "God is circumstance," Reverend Mahon said to Gilligan. "God is in this life. . . . We make our own heaven or hell in this world. Who knows: perhaps when we die we may not be required to go anywhere nor do anything at all. That would be heaven." Margaret and the lovelorn Gilligan were separated by a mischance, and in the earlier typescript the novel had ended with Reverend Mahon and Gilligan gripping each other's hands, weeping, as they spoke inwardly and poetically to the lost Donald Mahon and the lost Margaret. But now Faulkner cut this odd tableau, ending instead with the soft sounds in the night of Negro choir voices singing "Feed Thy Sheep, O Jesus." (317) By May 25 he had finished. On page 473 he typed two last lines: "New Orleans/May 1925." Except for minor revisions to come, he had completed his first novel.

Sherwood Anderson never saw the last page. As a matter of fact, it appears that after the early encouragement he did not read much more of the novel. Anderson was caught up in the writing of *Tar: A Midwestern Childhood*, and from mid-April on he had even stopped answering his mail. In later years Faulkner would tell with obvious enjoyment a version of what had happened. Elizabeth Anderson had relayed her husband's words to the young writer: "He said that he will make a trade with you. If he don't have to read it, he will tell his publisher to take it."

"I said, 'Done,' " Faulkner would add. "And so that was how . . . my first book got published."

Elizabeth Anderson recalled that she had relayed that message from her husband. And Anderson did, as a matter of fact, write to Liveright urging him to publish Faulkner's book. But Faulkner told Estelle Franklin about the message in a bit more detail. It sounded as though it had come from a very harassed man to another whom he had earlier promised a favor. "I'll do anything for him," was the message, "so long as I don't have to read his damn manuscript." Coming from someone who had admired the early chapters and encouraged him to go on with the rest, it stung. "Bill remembered those words," Estelle said.

Though Faulkner may have been hurt, he was not going to be foolish. He would send the manuscript to Boni & Liveright. Horace Liveright had always been highly unpredictable. At the start of his career he had married the daughter of a paper magnate who had made him president of a toilet paper company. Admiring the tactics of Commodore Vanderbilt and other early American tycoons, Liveright set out, some later said, to corner the toilet paper market. His competitors simply produced more toilet paper and his father-in-law fired him. Moving to New York to promote new inventions, he met newspaperman Albert Boni. In 1917, with $25,000 from Liveright's father-in-law, they founded The Modern Library. Whatever Liveright's deficiencies might have been, he had style. He also bore clear resemblance to John Barrymore and, using a long cigarette holder, would conduct conversations in profile as much as possible. He gambled for high stakes at the Hotel Algonquin with Heywood Broun, Franklin P. Adams, and others in that literary crowd. He had a love of publicity, both for himself and for the books he was putting out. As he began to spread himself in the world of New York publishing, his enemies called him a drunkard, a rake, and a pathological liar. But he prospered, and the firm became a training ground for publishing executives: Julian Messner, Richard Simon, Donald Friede, Ted Weeks, and a number of others got their training there. Editor Manuel Komroff increased the Modern Library list from thirty-eight titles to about a hundred. Meanwhile, the Boni & Liveright trade list grew. They published Pound and O'Neill, Eliot and Freud, and were soon to bring out Hemingway's *In Our Time* and Dreiser's *An American Tragedy.*

Someone—probably Phil Stone, though it could have been Aunt 'Bama —had even prematurely relayed news of acceptance to the Memphis *Commercial Appeal.* "Since the publication of his book 'The Marble Faun,' " the item read, "William Faulkner has been living in New Orleans. He is writing a novel that will be published in the fall by Boni and Liveright." Faulkner would finish the editing of his typescript and then it would have to be retyped. Since he knew he could count on Phil Stone, the logical thing was to send it to Oxford to be typed. He decided, apparently, to take it there himself.

He would go home. He was entitled to loaf after the concentrated effort of the productive months behind him. He might even go down to Pascagoula, where Jack Stone had a place. Helen Baird would be there and a few others from the New Orleans crowd. He could think about Europe again and the next steps along the path that appeared now to be opening for him. He and Anderson had been together a good deal for the past three months. In June, leaving the city, Faulkner would not see him at all.

24

June-July, 1925

> The man remembered that from his youth too: one summer spent being blown innocently over in catboats since, born and bred for generations in the north Mississippi hinterland, he did not recognize the edge of a squall until he already had one.
>
> —"Mississippi" (29)

> . . . the young man . . . in a pair of disreputable khaki slacks and a sleeveless jersey undershirt and no hat in a region where even young people believed the summer sun to be fatal, seen usually walking barefoot along the beach at tide edge. . . .
>
> —*The Wild Palms* (5)

When Faulkner would enter Stone's office, he could hear the secretary's typewriter going. At any given time the work in the machine might just as well have been a Faulkner poem or story as a brief or deed. Grace Hudson, working for Phil that summer while Arthur Palmer Hudson was off at the University of Chicago getting his M.A., remembered that the Faulkner material kept coming in. Besides the poems and stories, and now the manuscript of the novel, there were letters in Faulkner's behalf. Several went to Harriet Monroe, with poems or stories enclosed. Publication of the novel must surely help, as should the appearances in *The Double Dealer*. But both men still felt, apparently, that it might be in Europe that he would make his breakthrough, as Frost and Hemingway had made theirs.

After the variety of New Orleans, Oxford must have seemed more quiet than usual that summer. Jack was away. Dean was enjoying the leisure of the vacation before the beginning of his last year of high school. Johncy and Dolly were still living with Murry and Maud Falkner. Their small son Jimmy was enjoying attention as the only child in the house. Now he had even more with the return of his uncle. He was a sturdy child, blue-eyed, with the strong Falkner nose and the features of his father in miniature. Billy enjoyed playing with him.

Estelle Franklin was still in Oxford with Cho-Cho and Malcolm. Her periods of separation from Cornell Franklin had grown longer over recent years as he had become increasingly caught up in his activities in Shanghai. He had a familiar circle of men friends who enjoyed gambling for high stakes as he did. And as he grew more influential he remained handsome and dapper, a man who was very attractive to women. He had worked out what was in effect a separate life from that of his wife and children.

Bill Faulkner may have decided on his return to Oxford in that late spring of 1925 that he did not want to spend the summer there. Phil Stone may have felt that it was time for his friend to get away again from the possibility of what Stone would consider an entangling alliance. If his career were now to open up, he should be ready to grasp whatever opportunity offered. If the "drought" were to continue, even if not in so severe a form, he had to be able to sustain himself and wait it out. Stone asked his sister-in-law, Myrtle Lewis Stone, to invite Bill Faulkner down to Pascagoula to the summer place she and Jack Stone had there, and he accepted.

Pascagoula lies in the low terraces of the Gulf coastal plain. "Pascagoula" once meant "bread eaters"; unlike most other tribes, the Pascagoula raised corn, ground it, and made bread. Eight flags would fly over this summer tribal camping ground, but the indolent, good-natured Pascagoula would see few of them. They were outnumbered by the warlike Biloxi, and when a Biloxi princess ran off with a Pascagoula chieftain, the Biloxi chieftain to whom she was betrothed led his men against the Pascagoula. Faced with subjection or death, the Pascagoula joined hands and waded out into the Pascagoula River to drown in its muddy waters. Their death chant could still be heard, it was said, rising from the Singing River, as the Pascagoula came to be called. Disbelievers said the sound came from fish, from sand grating on the hard shale bottom, or from natural gas escaping from the sand beds. Still, in the quiet of early summer evenings, a sound as of a great swarm of bees would begin. When it grew until it seemed to come up out of the very earth, believers said it was the mournful sound of the dying tribe heard over the slow dark waters.

A barrier of pine ridges and marshy swamps shut the settlement off from most of the world outside. A few big men touched on its life—Zachary Taylor built housing there and David Farragut (a local boy) captured it—but it remained a quiet backwater of the coast. One hundred miles east of New Orleans and forty miles west of Mobile, it went at its own pace. It was incorporated as a village until 1892, and a dozen years would pass before it achieved city status.

Industry had come in the 1870's. Masses of yellow pine logs floated down the river. It developed that Pascagoula was the best loading point on the coast. Boats had always been built there to put off into the blue waters of the Gulf, and after a time Pascagoula luggers were as distinctive in these waters as Gloucester fishing boats were at the other side of the continent. As railroad shipping increased, the luggers would come in heavily laden with deep-sea snappers to be sent north. Smaller vessels would bring in loads of shrimp and oysters. Then in 1900 a new industry came with large-scale growing of paper-shell pecans. The First World War brought the International Shipbuilding Yards to Pascagoula. New money came from other yards up and down the river, and the cacophony of whistles and hammers and bells signaled a feverish boom. It all but ceased, even more quickly than it had begun, when the armistice was signed. The hulls of half-finished schooners, like skeletons picked bare by scavengers, marked the death of the boom. Pascagoula resumed its old pace, and a clangor would rise from one of the ways only when someone finally had to purchase a new schooner or a Pascagoula lugger.

Bill Faulkner came to this pleasant, leisurely city of something over 4,000 in June of 1925. It was moist there, and the temperature, averaging near seventy degrees the year round, might go up to one hundred on a hot summer day, but the prevailing winds were southerly. The sun would ride high in the blue skies, but the heat would not pour down with the intensity that drove people from the Delta and the pine hills to the north. At night the heavens were indigo. The stars seemed very close, and the heavy fragrance of the flowering jasmine and the purple-blossomed wisteria would float in soft waves on the evening air. There were huge old live oak trees, draped with mistletoe and Spanish moss like great clouds of green gauze. Out toward the marshes were the scrub forests.

There were a number of old homes. Myrtle Stone's parents, the

Lewises, had one, belonging as they did to one of the pioneer families in Pascagoula. Frank and Gertrude Lewis lived on the west beach, in the center house in a row of three between Pascagoula Street and Market Street. West of them lived druggist Tom Kell and his wife Lola. To the east was "The Camp," the summer home of their daughter Myrtle, Jack Stone, and their children—little Myrtle, Allie Jean, Jack, Jr., and Rosebud. Myrtle and the children would travel from Charleston to Pascagoula when the warm weather came, and Jack would join them for weekends. The accommodations were simple: four rooms partitioned off by screening, plus a side porch and front porch. There were awning shades in each room which could be lowered for privacy. The children saw nothing unusual in a magnolia and a live oak being built into the structure, running up through the board flooring and out through the roof. The pale sand ran right up to the door, one hundred feet from the lapping waters of the bay. As with Lake Pontchartrain, the swimmer could go out the equivalent of two or sometimes three city blocks before the water's level reached above his head. Back from the beaches among the scrub pine and oak were palmetto trees and small wild palms that grew right up out of the ground with no trunk. If a plant survived, some sort of trunk eventually would evolve. When the southerly wind blew, it would whisper drily through the palms. In the wind before a storm they would clash and rattle as the dry fronds rasped against each other.

The Stones were sitting out in front of the house one evening when Bill Faulkner came walking around the corner, carrying his typewriter and little else. He had come by train from Oxford and then ridden the streetcar to the dead-end street where The Camp was located. Myrtle Stone showed him the side porch, where he would sleep. He put down his typewriter and the few other possessions he had brought and then followed her as she went to get him something to eat after his 300-mile trip.

Faulkner settled quietly and easily into the camp routine. He came and went like a member of the family. No one asked him about his writing and he never talked about it. He found a favorite work place on a sort of bluff where a board seat encircled a big oak. He would pull up a wooden bench to support his small typewriter and become absorbed in his slow, steady, two-finger tapping. Jack Stone might be a few yards away on another tree seat, reading a newspaper. Sometimes Faulkner would go for a swim with the children. He was a good companion, and they adored him. Myrtle Stone knew he was careful; besides, there were no waves to speak of, and a shallow level could be found for the smallest ones, such as Rosebud. When it was nap time for Rosebud and her four-year-old brother Jack, Faulkner would return to his typewriter. When he and his sister awoke, Jack would recall, Faulkner "would take them on long walks along the tidal flats looking for soft-shell crabs and telling them stories of pirate treasure. There was a cabin or storage shed at the rear of our house and Bill painted the head of a pirate on the door, complete with eye patch, and told us this had once been a pirates' den and that the ghosts of the pirates were abroad at nighttime." In the evenings after supper Myrtle and Jack would walk next door to sit on the screened-in porch, rocking and talking with Frank and Gertrude Lewis while the children went for another walk with Billy. He would tell them more stories. One was Washington Irving's "The Legend of Sleepy Hollow," and the Headless Horseman virtually materialized there before their eyes, pounding down the beach and away to the horizon in the dusk. It chilled them, and they never tired of it.

Faulkner was polite but quiet and withdrawn when friends of the Stones would drop in. One of Myrtle's friends was Ann Farnsworth, whose people were also old settlers in Pascagoula. At first she hardly ever heard him speak. She would see him sitting on the beach, just looking. The water was full of mullet, and at the right time of day the surface would erupt in a constant shower of small splashes. Fish from three inches to half a foot long would leap as high as two feet into the air, shooting up through the water as though squeezed out of a powerful fist. He would sit and watch.

He came to know a few people in Pascagoula. He liked Tom Kell, an easy-going, companionable, and generous man. He would see Mr. Ebb Ford, a Rhodes scholar and lawyer. Ford was an exemplar of a Southern type: a lawyer of great intelligence, erudition, and skill living out his life in a small Southern town. Faulkner would spend time lounging on the piers and in the bars where the Pascagoula fishermen congregated. It would have been very unlike him if he missed the chance to tell these acquaintances something of the legend of Al Jackson.

After a while Ann Farnsworth got to know him a little better. For some time she had wanted to go to one of the prize fights held in Pascagoula, but ladies rarely attended them, much less unescorted ladies. Fortunately, Josh Baird had come over from New Orleans to spend a few days at the beach. He was covering the fight for the *Times-Picayune*, so he took Ann with him. He also brought Bill Faulkner, who sat there beside Ann in the noisy, smoky arena, looking bored. The shouting and the thudding punches of the sweating fighters had little effect on him that she could see. But now he knew her better, and when there was something doing that he really enjoyed, she sometimes went along. Fishing parties would be made up at night, and they would go out with spears and lines, torches flickering over the quiet water, and Ann Farnsworth would hold one of the flaring torches for him.

There would be boating parties that sailed to Round Island, three miles out in the Gulf. A cousin of the Stones from Mobile, Alfred L. Staples, had made a fortune in real estate, and now each summer he would sail his fifty-foot yacht from Mobile to Pascagoula, where he would take his relatives and their friends out on excursions. *The Flying Cloud* was thirty years old but still serviceable, with a two-masted yawl rig, gas screw, and spacious deck with a large canvas canopy. Faulkner went along on several trips, but rather than shelter himself from the sun under the canopy and mingle with the others, he would go forward, and as little Jack Stone watched admiringly, he would nimbly make his way onto the ten-foot bowsprit. There he would stretch out full-length, gazing into the waters of the Gulf forward of the wake curling from the bow. They would anchor within the sound of the surf, where the waves rolled onto the islands that shielded the placid inshore waters. Those who liked could fish or swim. There would be food as well as bottles of beer and stronger drinks. Someone might bring a ukulele or guitar. It was a good way to spend summer days and nights.

There was other sailing that summer. Sam Gilmore was staying at Pass Christian, forty miles west of Pascagoula. He decided one day to come over and visit Josh Baird. Josh was not there, but he found Bill Faulkner. They talked and then decided to go for a sail. Sam was much more at home in the offices of *The Double Dealer* than in the cockpit of a small sailboat, and though Faulkner had been out in one, he was not yet adept. They had trouble getting under way, and when they did get out from shore all they could do was to sail in circles. They gave it up and managed to steer their way back to the dock.

Faulkner had always enjoyed going barefoot, and the beach was the perfect place for it. He might walk into town the same way and simply sit there looking, as he did in his own Courthouse Square at the other end of the state. That was the way he would drive the Stone four-door Lincoln automobile—barefoot. Riding along a Pascagoula street he might salute a young lady he knew by sticking a foot out the window and wiggling his toes at her. He usually wore a white shirt and white duck trousers with a rope tied at the waist. His shock of dark brown hair with its red glint was usually uncombed. He had a good meerschaum pipe that summer, which contrasted oddly with the beachcomber effect of his simple dress and unkempt appearance. The mustache was full but neat, and though he shaved the rest of his face, he would sometimes skip a day or two or wait until evening, so that often there would be a dark stubble on the thin cheeks.

Helen Baird's mother was little impressed with this young man. "How can you stand going around with someone who looks like that wild man?" Mary Lou Baird would ask her daughter. But Helen Baird's appearance showed that she set no great store by clothes—for herself, at any rate. As often as not she would be wearing a paint-smeared smock. She did not hesitate to put on a bathing suit or evening dress even though they revealed the scars of a terrible accident. "I was burned," she would say offhandedly in her direct, abrupt way, her voice just this side of harshness. Brusque but darkly attractive and vivacious, she was good company though she said she couldn't stand people for more than an hour. She enjoyed them for a while, but then they could go on, as far as she was concerned. She liked out-of-the-ordinary people, as Bill Faulkner did. One of Helen Baird's beaux, a New Orleans lawyer named Guy Lyman, accused her of collecting "screwballs." She would use the term herself, if a little wryly. As for Bill Faulkner, she would later say, "He was one of my screwballs." With his short stature and that shock of hair, she said, "he reminded me of a fuzzy little animal."

Bill Faulkner's feelings for Helen Baird seemed to be moving in a very different direction. He was usually attracted to petite women, and there was something childlike about young Helen Baird in her directness and brusque honesty. And as he always found himself attracted to children and sympathetic to the ill or unhappy, so he could not fail to respond to the way this young girl accepted her maiming with the courage of disregard. And she was creative. As an artist he respected that. In the kind of reverse psychology which often operates in human relationships, her disinterest in books —so different from the questions about his work at New Orleans parties which would produce only silence—may well have acted to make him open to her. Of course it was summer, too, and he was a man to respond to women, as his love poetry, much of it frankly erotic, clearly showed. And she was there.

Sometimes they might swim together. Often they would go out on one of the piers over on the east beach. As they lay there in the sun he would make up stories to tell her. In "Verse Old and Nascent" he had presented himself as a cynical poet who used his work to further "various philanderings." The June number of *The Double Dealer* printed his long poem "The Lilacs" with the subscripts "TO A . . . . . AND H . . . . ., ROYAL AIR FORCE/ *August 1925.*" He had a copy of the poem with him in Pascagoula. After making a few corrections, he presented it to Helen. And there were other gifts. With the novel finished he had gone back to poetry, returning to the sonnet form. He lettered a sequence in his thin, fine presentation script, bound it, and gave it to her.

As June began to draw to an end, Myrtle Stone made preparations to welcome a new set of guests—her sister-in-law, Jim Stone's wife, and her three daughters. Helen Baird and Ann Farnsworth left with their mothers to travel in France and Italy. Back in Oxford, Grace Hudson had worked long and carefully on the typescript of the novel. In Pascagoula, the author packed his few things, thanked the Stones, made his brief goodbyes, and rode the train into the early summer heat of north Mississippi.

Not only Stone but some of the Bunch were allowed to read the novel. "My chief reaction at the time," Edith Brown remembered, "was to be shocked at how badly it was punctuated. I offered to repunctuate it, and Bill said he didn't care, so I did. As I remember it, Bill didn't seem to care a bit about that novel. . . ." If Faulkner didn't care, Stone most certainly did. He took the typescript to Ella Somerville, who read it that evening in her bedroom. The June breeze blew through the tall open windows, scattering the pages over the floor. She painstakingly put them back in order and went on until she had finished the novel. She knew she could not be enthusiastic about it when she gave it back to Phil the next day. When she entered his office he immediately asked her what she thought of it. She answered him truthfully, but her reservations did not affect his enthusiasm. "I think it's a damn fine book," he said.

Faulkner was pleased enough with it to bring it, in a black and orange "Allen-A" underwear box, for the post office gang to read. Some of their reactions must have been like Ella Somerville's. Baxter Elliott typed up an anecdote, either about Faulkner or about the work, and circulated it. Faulkner never gave them another typescript to read.

He saw Estelle and the children and friends who had remained in town. In the first days of July, Grace Hudson acted as chaperon for her sister Margaret and her date, Hugh Worley, on a drive to the big new Water Valley swimming pool. Bill Faulkner went along, taking Bessie Storer. They stayed into the evening when the arc lights flickered on. Then it began to rain. Twenty miles of unpaved, ungraveled road lay between them and home, so they started back. As the rain increased, so did the mudholes. Periodically, Worley's Model T Ford would flounder to a stop, the wheels spinning vainly. Grace, Bessie, and Bill would pull off their shoes and stockings and heave at the fenders until the car slithered up out of the mud. They did not get back to Oxford until two in the morning, but in all of this, Grace Hudson remembered, "Bill was the readiest and jolliest of the lot." The expedition ended with a snack at the Hudsons' home.

Even though the recopying of the novel had been completed, the literary typing in Phil Stone's office was by no means at a halt. There were still the ordinary submissions of stories and poems. Stone had begun to feel that his friend would do better if he devoted himself to novels rather than verse, a view Faulkner not only did not share but seemed to resent. Faulkner still apparently considered himself a poet who occasionally wrote prose. Stone was now dictating letters like those he had written earlier to Harriet Monroe. With the trip to Europe on again, Stone was writing letters of introduction to T. S. Eliot, Arnold Bennett, Ezra Pound, James Joyce, and others.

Faulkner had the typescript of the novel packaged and wrapped and sent it off to Boni & Liveright in New York. Now he was free to go. He packed his few traveling things and said another round of goodbyes. He arrived in Memphis with just time for a few visits before taking another train south to New Orleans. This was the third time he found himself heading for New Orleans as a stopover on the route to Europe. This time he meant to go all the way.

Of course, the money situation was no better, as Arthur Halle could see when his friend visited him at his store.

"Arthur," he said, "I'm going to Italy."

Halle knew something of his friend's circumstances. "What are you going on, Bill?" he asked.

"I have fifty dollars for expenses going over."

Halle looked doubtful. "How can you go on so little to a strange country?"

"I'm going to write for the *Commercial Appeal*," Faulkner told him.

"How? You don't have a signed contract, do you?"

Faulkner did not reply directly to the question. "You'll see," was all he said.

He visited Aunt 'Bama. She was as deeply and proudly interested in his career as ever, but she was known for her frugality. She did not believe in helping people too much, for she thought they ought to work out their problems themselves. It would bring out the best in their character. Her help lay mainly in encouragement and interest. She set high standards for people she loved and then expected them to live up to them. One did not complain around Aunt 'Bama. She was distinguished by what Faulkner once called her "charming grand-duchess air" and a proclivity for "penetrating stage asides." She was drawn to Billy not only by her pride in his work and accomplishments (sometimes they would correspond in French), but by his admiration for the Old Colonel, her adored father. She saw in her grandnephew another Southern literary artist like the author of *The White Rose of Memphis.* She had certainly not helped with subsidizing *The Marble Faun,* but now she may have thought for a moment of her father's trip to Europe over forty years before—the trip which had produced *Rapid Ramblings in Europe.* She may have reflected on the contrasting circumstances of the affluent Colonel and his down-at-the heels great-grandson. Aunt 'Bama broke a rule. She gave him twenty dollars.

He told Dot Wilcox about the unexpected windfall. He had sewn it into his trench coat, he told her, where he couldn't lose it or even spend it very easily, and it would be there to meet any emergency that might arise when he was far from home and friends. Dot still didn't think much of his appearance, particularly for someone going to Europe. He was wearing old work shoes, and his plaid jacket hung on him with one elbow out. But, of course, he knew she was viewing him with the eyes of a woman. Why should he look like someone in the rotogravure? He was not going to travel first-class. And besides, when he got to Europe, he would not need much. Since the time of François Villon, poets had been able to make do with a good deal less than the bourgeois's minimum. And he was a poet.

In New Orleans, Bill Spratling was busier than ever. He, too, was preparing for a trip. The *Architectural Forum* had asked him to do some articles on northern Italy and illustrate them. He had arranged passage on the *West Ivis,* a 3,600-ton steamer of the United Gulf Steamship Company, which had made a run from Galveston to Houston to Mobile and was now being loaded for the voyage to Savannah. Thereafter, she would sail for Genoa and Naples. Faulkner may well have tried again to find a vessel he could ship on as an ordinary seaman in order to conserve his resources. They would be augmented in three weeks when the *Times-Picayune* would publish another of his stories and then another, shorter sketch, three weeks after that, but he meant to stretch them as much as he could.

By Sunday, July 5, Faulkner had apparently decided he had better give up the idea of trying to work his way across. He would go with Spratling if there was room for him. When they went down to the shipping office on Monday morning they found that there was room. On Tuesday, July 7, 1925, they sailed aboard the *West Ivis* for Europe.

25

July-October, 1925

There was really very little time to be lonely at sea . . . . twenty days on a freighter pushing one empty horizon before and drawing another one behind, empty too save for a green carpet of wake unrolling across that blue monotone. . . .

And in Milan, they . . . sat drinking beer within the shadow of the cathedral, gazing upward among its mute and musical flanks from which long-bodied doglike gargoyles strained yapping in a soundless gleeful derision, where niched were mitred cardinals like Assyrian kings and lean martyrs pierced dying in eternal ectasy and young unhelmetted knights staring into space. . . .

—*Elmer*

It had been a gray day, a gray summer, a gray year. On the street old men wore overcoats, and in the Luxembourg Gardens . . . the women sat knitting in shawls and even the men playing croquet played in coats and capes, and in the sad gloom of the chestnut trees the dry click of balls, the random shouts of children, had that quality of autumn, gallant and evanescent and forlorn. From beyond the circle with its spurious Greek balustrade, clotted with movement, filled with a gray light of the same color and texture as the water which the fountain played into the pool, came a steady crash of music.

—*Sanctuary* (308)

Compared with the voyage he had planned, this trip was luxurious travel. Bill Faulkner and Bill Spratling had neat, compact staterooms meant for officers in charge of cargo or for the occasional traveler who did not mind a slow passage. The two men ate their meals with Captain E. C. McLain and his officers. Faulkner began collecting from the start. He clipped the "River and Marine List of Vessels in Port" and circled the line "*West Ivis* (Am.). . . . Italy." Another tiny clipping gave the name of the vessel, her captain, route, and owner.

"When we were some two days out in the calm waters of the gulf stream," Spratling later wrote, "one morning Faulkner appeared on deck with a mass of MS about four inches thick. This he laid on the deck and proceeded to dispose of by tearing in batches and dropping overboard." Faulkner confirmed this. He said that one of his duties (he had none; he was inventing again) was throwing the garbage overboard. He threw some sonnets overboard with it. "It made me feel clean," he said. These were probably juvenilia and poems that had not borne the periodic scrutiny as he reviewed them to make up new selections. He did not reject all of the effects of his Swinburne and Housman phases, however, and the jettisoning of the sonnets may have been the cynical poet deprecating romantic verse. It may also have been the choice of a man who—though he may not have realized it clearly—had changed his medium from poetry to prose, even though he would continue to write poetry for some time.

Faulkner was completely free now to do some of the things he enjoyed best: to look at nature and to watch men at their trades. He could dream or read or write all day if he liked. He had brought books with him. If he packed some light reading, it may have been mystery stories, which everyone, it seemed, had been reading in Pascagoula. His writing would suggest that among the serious books was Elie Faure's *History of Art.* He had Hamilton Basso's copy of Ludwig Lewisohn's *A Modern Book of Criticism*, published by Boni & Liveright in their Modern Library series. He was saving it for Europe.

On July 11 the *West Ivis* tied up at Savannah. Faulkner had plenty of time for walks along the docks and in the city before she sailed on July 14. He may have used some of this time on work for the *Times-Picayune.* A little over two weeks later the paper would print a Faulkner story which he could have mailed from Savannah. It was called "The Liar." Nearly 4,000 words long, it was notable, like "Sunset," for its rural characters and scenes. Again he was dealing with homicide, though here he withheld that fact until the end, in the manner of the mystery story genre rather than Conradian psychological exploration. The locale was Will Gibson's country store. The taleteller was Ek, who gave an account of a love-murder in the hills seen from a distance. It was only when one of his hearers shot him and fled on a passing freight that Ek realized that he had revealed himself as the only eyewitness to the murderer himself. "If you were lying," Will told him, "you ought to be shot for telling one so prob'le that it reely happened somewhere; and if you were telling the truth, you ought to be shot for having no better sense than to blab it out in front of the man that done the killing."

Faulkner clearly was writing a commercial story which fitted a standard formula for short detective fiction. He apparently felt some distance from his characters, striking a note both superior and Rousseauistic: "Though like all peoples who live close to the soil, they were by nature veracious, they condoned [Ek's] unlimited imagination for the sake of the humor he achieved and which they understood." These people amused him and he liked them, though they seemed as different from his fauns and dryads as Balzac's peasants from the *Fantoches* of Verlaine. He was dealing with something he knew very well—from his walks with Stone, his rambles alone, and everything he had absorbed about the hill regions of Lafayette County and north Mississippi. He had begun to find his métier. And he had discovered something which Hemingway would seek in the bullring: an arena in which basic issues would be presented dramatically and often resolved in death. The story also employed an increasingly useful technique: the representation of country speech which would be faithful to accent, diction, and syntax yet easily intelligible to the reader.

It is possible that Faulkner may have also worked on another sketch in Savannah. "Episode" was a 1,000-word piece which would appear in the *Times-Picayune* for August 16. He put Spratling in it, and once again Faulkner's character study paralleled Spratling's sketch. Faulkner used the currently popular surprise ending. Spratling's sketch revealed the unidentifiable quality Faulkner had seen in the face of the old woman who was the subject: "brown, and timeless and merry as a gnome's and toothless. . . ." It was exactly the expression on the face of the "Mona Lisa." Spratling remembered that both of them had drawn from life, and that Faulkner had loved the picture of the old woman.

Another sketch which probably dates from this summer might almost have been a companion piece to "Episode," but it never appeared. It too was told by the "I" narrator who observed while Spratling drew. Spratling's subject this time was the door of a Negro brothel, and Faulkner's title, "Peter," referred to a small mulatto boy, the son of an inmate of the house called Mable. The story combined diverse elements such as the ribald dialogue from inside the house and the child's naïve description of his mother's various relationships. Faulkner's sketch was at times personal, like "Episode," as when he wrote, "(if I slept and waked, I think I could know afternoon from morning by the color of the sunlight)." It was also more experimental, as when he shifted briefly to a dramatic format, assigning lines to "Peter," "Spratling," "A Voice," and "I." The gaminess of both the subject and dialogue was clearly enough to have discouraged any of the *Times-Picayune*'s editors if it was offered to them. This was not, however, the predominant impression the sketch left. As Spratling finished his work, he talked about returning later when Peter would have learned to spin the top given him by one of his mother's customers. It was the pathetic element, not the risqué one, which Faulkner clearly meant to remain uppermost in the reader's mind.

By July 14 all of the *West Ivis*'s new cargo of rosin and short-fibered cotton leavings had been stowed. Piloted down the long estuary to the ocean, Captain McLain set his course for the Atlantic crossing. Again there was the leisure of the shipboard routine which would stretch out for nearly three more weeks. Passing finally through the Straits of Gibraltar, the *West Ivis* steamed slowly by the Balearic Islands of the west Mediterranean. Faulkner was composing sonnets again as if to replace some of those he had thrown into the waters of the Gulf. Some he had dated at sea. Others he now dated off Majorca and Minorca. Nearing the French coast, the *West Ivis* passed Hyères, where Jack Falkner had spent time recuperating from his wound and the gas. Then the Ligurian coast rose out of the north, and Captain McLain entered the ancient port of Genoa. It was Sunday, August 2, 1925.

Spratling and Faulkner left the ship at Genoa instead of continuing on to the final destination of Naples. There were no currency exchanges open, but the first mate and chief engineer said they knew where they could exchange dollars for lire and have some fun, too. Spratling and Faulkner went with them, following a red carpet down a flight of steps to a cabaret where they were soon seated at a large table. Very shortly they were joined by several companionable girls. Rounds of beer were ordered, and despite the linguistic barrier, they began to enjoy themselves, talking somehow, laughing, and dancing.

After several dances Spratling's partner drew him away from the group to talk with her "business manager" at another table. By now Spratling had reached "that stage where everything seemed irresistibly amusing," and it occurred to him "to see what they would do if I dropped some coins under the table." The girl and her manager scrambled for the coins. Finding they were only copper, they were furious. Suddenly the *carabinieri* materialized at the table. Grim in their patent-leather "airplane" hats, they seized Spratling and bore him protesting away before Faulkner and the others knew he was gone. He spent the night in Genoa's vermin-infested Palazzo Ducale jail.

Managing somehow to smuggle a note to the American consul, that afternoon he was brought before a municipal official. Seated beside him were the *West Ivis*'s purser and Bill Faulkner. The official informed Spratling of the gravity of his offense: a crime against the Italian royal family. The coins he had thrown on the cabaret floor—and he had stamped on them—bore a likeness of the king's face. It was so serious a crime that there was only one solution—to expunge it from the record. As Spratling walked blinking out into the bright sunlight, Faulkner said nothing.

Finally he spoke. "You no longer look so vulgarly healthy," he said.

Expecting sympathy rather than comments on his appearance, Spratling told Faulkner that he sounded sore.

"What the hell," Faulkner said. "Why shouldn't I be? Missing an experience like that." When Faulkner wrote Ben Wasson about the incident he said it had happened to him.

Spratling and Faulkner may have spent a day or so together before they separated for a time. Spratling was sketching some romanesque structures for the *Architectural Forum* series. Faulkner went with him, meditating, sometimes rambling aloud as he worked. Spratling recalled his companion's saying that for him there were "only two basic compulsions on earth, i.e., love and death." He found these meditations distracting, but one he remembered very clearly. The subject was borrowing from life for art. "I don't take whole people," Faulkner told him, "I do this." And he placed both palms together, fingers outstretched, then rotated his hands, intertwining his fingers.

The two went off now in different directions. Spratling took the train for Rome and Faulkner traveled twenty miles east along the coast to see what Yeats called "Rapallo's thin line of broken mother-of-pearl." This small town on the Tyrrhenian Sea was no ordinary coastal village. Max Beerbohm had lived there for some time, and thirteen months earlier Ezra and Dorothy Pound had come there from Sicily to settle. In Rapallo, Pound could bask in the adoration of the townspeople. He could look back on his successful efforts to help advance the careers of Robert Frost, James Joyce, T. S. Eliot, and Ernest Hemingway, and to help William Butler Yeats explore new ground and strengthen his style. Faulkner admired the poetry of Yeats, Joyce, and Eliot, and apparently learned from the prose of Joyce. He shared the opinion, said Phil Stone, that "Ernest Hemingway is so far the greatest American fictionist." Pound was a champion of the new—both the art and the artist. In Rapallo he was reading Jefferson and John Adams and working on *The Cantos.* Clearly, when Phil Stone wrote to Pound he must have hoped that Pound would interest himself in another young American. There appears to be no evidence, however, that Faulkner ever tried to see Pound in Rapallo, though Spratling said later that they both wanted to visit him.

On August 5 he sent a post card to his two-year-old nephew Jimmy. He was starting out from Rapallo the next day, he wrote, to walk to Paris. "I have a knapsack—le sport baggage, they call it." He signed it "Brother Will." On the sixth he wrote his mother that he had begun the journey by train, leaving Genoa for Milan, but then "I looked out and saw Pavia." Glimpsing the cathedral, the bridges, and the tile roofs, he left the train. At noon he found a wineshop where the boatmen ate. He liked the way they took their time and enjoyed themselves, just as he liked the relative lack of automobiles. "People in Italy all think I am English," he added. "Which is good, because Americans are charged two prices for everything." He was staying at a fifteenth-century inn called the Pesce-d'Oro, which was staffed by a single family. For dinner, he wrote, "You are conducted with honor to a vine-covered court, all around are old, old walls and gates through which mailed knights once rode, and where men-at-arms scurried over cobble stones." Beyond the narrow streets and the city walls, he wrote Aunt 'Bama, you saw "an old red-tiled bridge crossing a stream in quiet meadows where cows ruminate in a mild wonder at the world, and sunset like organ music dying away." Tomorrow he was off to Milan, he said, and from there to a town called Spezia, in the Italian lake country.

The next day he sent his mother a post card from Milan showing the Piazza del Duomo. "This Cathedral!" he wrote. "Can you imagine stone lace? or frozen music? All covered with gargoyles like dogs, and mitred cardinals and mailed knights and saints pierced with arrows and beautiful naked Greek figures that have no religious significance whatever." He added that he was going to Stresa that night, and signed it "Billy."

In Stresa he met Spratling and they went to see Anita Loos, only to find that she was away. The weather was cold and depressing, and the town was full of American tourists. Faulkner did not stay long. "I took my pack and typewriter and lit out for the mountains above Lake Maggiore," he told his mother in a letter he later wrote from Paris. On a post card mailed the eleventh he told her, "I have been 2 days at a grand village on an Alp above Stresa." Its name was Sommariva, and like Pavia it was beautiful. He later wrote Aunt 'Bama that he "lived with the peasants, going out with them in the morning to cut grass, eating bread and cheese and drinking wine from a leather bottle at noon beneath a faded shrine with a poor little bunch of flowers in it, and then coming down the mountain at sunset, hearing the bells on the mule jingle and seeing half the world turning lilac with evening. Then to eat supper outdoors at a wooden table worn smooth by generations of elbows, to get mildly drunk and talk to those kind quiet happy people by signs." He had even gotten some work done—"a sort of amusing travelogue."

In the post card to his mother he said he was leaving that day for Mattarone, Switzerland. From there he would go on to France, arriving in Paris, he thought, by August 25. It did not take nearly that long. "Switzerland is a big country club with a membership principally American," he wrote Aunt 'Bama. "And I am quite disgusted with my own nationality in Europe. Imagine a stranger coming into your home, spitting on your floor and flinging you a dollar. That's the way they act. I dont blame these people for charging them for the privilege." Apparently he turned around and returned to Stresa. There he met Spratling again and together they took the train for Montreux.

It was all "tunnels, and rushing rivers, and chalets hanging on the mountains someway," he wrote his mother from Paris. "And bells everywhere. In churches, on cattle and sheep—all you hear is bells." Before the train raced into the Simplon tunnel, they had seen the snow-capped St. Gotthard peak in the distance. By the time they emerged from the tunnel, it was too dark to see the Jungfrau, but in the morning at Montreux, there was the great snowy mass of Mont Blanc. When they got off the train it was cold. "Montreux is on Lake Geneva," he wrote Miss Maud, "where the castle of Chillon (you remember The Prisoner of Chillon?) is, not far from Lausanne, where the peace conference was." He gave an account of unusual sightseeing. "We climbed an Alp and called on a Russian princess, daughter-in-law to a member of the Czar's family, and herself a daughter of the last Doge of Venice." Arriving in Geneva, he sent his suitcase on to American Express in Paris, putting all his clothes in it except a spare shirt and a change of socks and underwear. But Switzerland was expensive, and the next day, August 13, they took a train for Paris.

The country they crossed reminded him of a big Woodson's Ridge, "all dotted over with rows of poplars, straight as soldiers, and villages with red tile roofs among rolling fields of grain, and hills covered with vineyards. Burgundy, famous for wine. Then straight still canals bordered with trees, and stone houses about—a lovely country in the sunset." They went through Dijon, "a grand old gray city in a level plain," and from there on to Paris. It was eleven o'clock by the time they arrived, and with the city full of American tourists, it took them two hours to find a hotel. They finally moved into a nice one in Montparnasse, on "the left bank of the Seine, where the painters live. It is not far away from the Luxembourg Gardens and the Louvre, and from the bridge across the Seine you can see both Notre Dame and the Eiffel Tower." Room and board would cost them only thirty francs—a dollar and a half—a day. He was going to have his typewriter fixed and settle in for some time, he thought. "I am waiting to hear from my novel, as well as to write some travel things I have started."

He would not have long to wait. At about the time he was writing his mother, Horace Liveright was writing Sherwood Anderson in New Orleans, and Anderson relayed the word to Phil Stone. Liveright said that two of his readers had been enthusiastic about the novel but the third had not. So Liveright was going to read it himself and decide. "I have a hunch he will take it," Anderson wrote. He was not sure that the novel either wanted or needed the introduction by him that Stone had apparently suggested. But if Liveright wanted a jacket blurb, "I'll be glad to do it, as I certainly admire Bill's talent. The jacket serves the purpose wanted without being a part of the book itself."

The boy from Lafayette County had seen New York and New Orleans, and now he would experience Paris—the Paris that the artists of his generation had known: Hemingway, Dos Passos, Fitzgerald, and the others. It was this consideration, as well as economy, that took him to the Latin Quarter. He was eagerly taking it all in. "I've had a grand time today," he wrote Miss

Maud on Sunday, August 16. He had taken a *paquebot* down the river past Auteuil and Meudon to Suresnes. Crossing the river, he had walked through the Bois de Boulogne, then up the avenue to the Place de l'Étoile and the Arc de Triomphe. He sat there awhile "watching the expensive foreign cars full of American movie actresses whizzing past," and then he walked down the Champs Élysées to the Place de la Concorde and had lunch. As in Italy, he chose a workingman's restaurant, one patronized by cabmen and janitors. After lunch he took the *métro* to the Père Lachaise Cemetery. "Alfred de Musset is buried there, and all the French notables and royalty, as well as many foreigners. I went particularly to see Oscar Wilde's tomb, with a bas-relief by Jacob Epstein." Then he crossed to the corner café opposite the cemetery. He drank a glass of beer and smoked his pipe. He planned another article—two were already finished, he said—and watched the people. On his way home he stopped in the Luxembourg Gardens to observe the children sailing boats on the pool. He liked the way grown people sailed them, too, with crowds composed of wives and children cheering the miniature regatta. The Notre Dame Cathedral was grand. It was like the one at Milan. (He used almost the identical phrases to describe it.)

He had met a few people, "a photographer, and a real painter. He is going to have an exhibition in New York in the fall, and he sure can paint." But he was dissatisfied with the pension where he was staying. "It's full of dull middle class very polite conventional people. Too much like being at a continual reception. Country folks are my sort, anyway. So I am going to move next week." He thought he could live on less than a dollar and a half a day, anyway. There were two positive things to report. His French was improving, "only I find after about 5 minutes that my opponent has been talking English to me." He ended his letter with another bit of information: "And—dont faint—I am growing a beard."

He had lost little time acquiring a few characteristics of Latin Quarter artists: some knowledge of Paris, a bit of French, and a beard. He may have known already that his stay would not be lengthy. The idea that he planned to spend two or three years, said Spratling, was "humbug." His current role-playing was more legitimate, however, than that of the maimed war hero. But if he looked the part, he also acted it, for he was apparently working intensively. The two articles he had mentioned to his mother could have been the kind of thing he had told Arthur Halle he was going to do for the *Commercial Appeal.* He had also begun work on another novel. His working title was *Mosquito.*

The photographer he had met was William C. Odiorne, from New Orleans—a quiet man with a broad forehead and a small mustache, known to his friends as "Cicero." Now forty-four years old, he had visited Paris during the previous year and decided to stay. He had a ground-floor apartment on a little street, the Rue Léopold Robert, a block from the Dôme in Montparnasse. He was now doing a little portrait work in his sitting room, and friends such as Spratling often dropped in to see him. Odiorne and Faulkner had friends in common and they got along. Occasionally they would walk along the quays together, strolling along the Left Bank by the bookstalls above the river. Sometimes they would sit in a café, drinking and talking.

Often Spratling would be with them. Though he was busy with his own pursuits, he and Faulkner would still go out together. They liked the St. Germain-des-Prés district and frequented the Deux Magots, sitting at one of the famous café's sidewalk tables and watching the life of the Left Bank stream by. They visited Shakespeare & Company but never saw Sylvia Beach, the proprietor of the well-known bookstore. They did not see Ernest Hemingway, who frequented it, or another American celebrity of Paris, Gertrude Stein. Once they saw Ezra Pound, Spratling thought. Faulkner talked a good deal about him, he remembered, and admired him tremendously. They saw another celebrity, Odiorne recalled, in a café near the Place de l'Odéon. It was James Joyce. Remembering, thirty years later, Faulkner would say, "I knew of Joyce, and I would go to some effort to go to the café that he inhabited to look at him. But that was the only literary man that I remember seeing in Europe in those days."

When he wrote his mother again two days later on August 18, it was moving day. "I have a nice room just around the corner from the Luxembourg gardens," he told her, "where I can sit and write and watch the children. Everything in the gardens is for children—its beautiful the way the French love their babies." He liked his new location at 26 Rue Servandoni, in one of the typical narrow-fronted buildings whose four or five stories accommodated rooms for rent, flats, or modest pensions. He did not mind being on the top floor. The tile roofs and chimney pots had been a part of the poetic imagery of Paris long before such poets as E. E. Cummings had used them. The Rue Servandoni ran from the church of St. Sulpice to the Luxembourg Gardens. Not only was it in the Quarter, but the immediate neighborhood was rich in resource and association. Nearby were the Luxembourg galleries, with their Post-Impressionist paintings.

There were also many small galleries in the Quarter, some of them showing the work of artists rejected by the Salon. There was a wide range of exhibitions to see, from the cubist paintings of someone like André Lhote to the strong nudes of Jules Pascin. Nearby too was the Rue Guynemer, named for the French ace whose combat exploits had inflamed Faulkner's youthful imagination ten years before. To the southwest rose Montparnasse, and four blocks to the north was St. Germain-des-Prés, the heart of the Quarter. But he was growing tired of cities again, and he thought he would be off in about a week to Touraine, "where all the grand chateaux are," and to Brittany. He was also thinking about a few weeks in England in September.

Meanwhile, he was still seeing all he could. "I spent yesterday in the Louvre, to see the Winged Victory and the Venus de Milo, the real ones, and the Mona Lisa etc. It was fine, especially the paintings of the more-or-less moderns, like Degas and Manet and Chavannes. Also went to a very very modern exhibition the other day—futurist and vorticist. I was talking to a painter, a real one. He wont go to the exhibitions at all. He says its all right to paint the damn things, but as far as looking at them, he'd rather go to the Luxembourg gardens and watch the children sail their boats. And I agree with him."

His next letter, five days later, began with the usual affectionate "Dear Moms." But it was unusual in that he began to talk immediately about his writing. "I am in the middle of another novel, a grand one. This is new altogether. I just thought of it day before yesterday. I have put the 'Mosquito' one aside: I dont think I am quite old enough to write it as it should be written—dont know quite enough about people." Then he shifted to the weather. "It has rained for 3 days now, but I dont mind, so long as I can sit in my room and write. I will have this one finished by November, I think."

He had a big room on a court. It cost him eleven francs a day, but his total expenses were still less than twenty francs a day. "A franc is 5¢," he noted. There was one aspect of his domestic economy, however, which was not functioning quite properly. The suitcase had not yet arrived from Geneva and he was still making do with only one change. He hoped it would arrive the next day.

A poem which he dated "27 Aug 1925" suggested a possible reaction to all he had been seeing and doing, a combination perhaps of fatigue and saturation. The first quatrain began with the question "What'll I do today?"

and the second with "And where'll I go today?" The last segment suggested E. E. Cummings in both form and imagery:

Or what'll I be today?
The swallows have tinkled all their marbles
and now are wrapped around themselves in
somebody's pocket, and somebody
has stood the brooms in a corner of the sky and flowers
yawn their red and yellow mouths at you
you've
got
to be
something besides
asleep

However much of this he had actually addressed to himself, he had not been idle.

The day before he had written that he was hard at work on the novel. "I think right now its awfully good—so clear in my mind that I can hardly write fast enough." He did not elaborate. Instead, he gave some of the details of his day. He had gotten into "a dreadful habit of sleeping late." He always woke at eight o'clock now, and sometimes later. He would take a book and go to a sidewalk café for a breakfast of chocolate and bread. He would buy a roll and a half-litre of wine for his lunch and then "walk back home through the Luxembourg garden, to watch the lads laughing and playing and the just-grown people sitting and reading books and papers, while the old men who at home would sit in the court-house yard and sleep, play croquet." He would write until two, eat his bread, and then go back to the Luxembourg or take a walk. "When it rains—as it has for a week almost,—I go to picture galleries." By seven o'clock he would be ready for dinner at one of the sidewalk tables, at a cost of seven francs. "Then to one of the popular cafés for coffee while the people walk back and forth. I usually write from 9 to 12 at night. I am anxious to get this novel down on paper."

The only thing he found expensive in Paris was good tobacco. He had to buy English tobacco, but "Luckily, I'm so busy writing I dont smoke much. So a can lasts almost 10 days." He had written her every Sunday and Wednesday since August 4. She was not to worry if the mail was irregular, "just remember when Sunday and Wednesday come, that I am allright, feeling fine, and sitting down at the table writing you a letter."

The novel he was now working on so intensely did not present the problem *Mosquito* did—of his not yet knowing quite enough about people to write it. He knew so much about Elmer Hodge that his attitude toward him was often superior and ironical. At some point he had begun a short story called "Growing Pains," in which Elmer, a fourth-grader, was taunted and abused by older boys, chiefly by one whose cruel beauty he admired. Faulkner tried five times, breaking off each time before he had completed a page. The story moved more easily when he recast it as a novel entitled *Elmer.* He began with Elmer, an aspiring artist, twenty days at sea on a freighter and now almost within sight of Sicily. He used Elmer's paints for transition into a long flashback. Red reminded Elmer of fire, which had struck his family of transients when he was five. Faulkner sketched the tenor of their life, moving from Mississippi to Tennessee and to Arkansas—the lazy father, the gaunt and haggard mother, the loutish brothers and Elmer's adored sister, Jo-Addie, whose bed he shares. When he is eleven and she is sixteen their relationship suggests that of Juliet and Lafe in "Adolescence." Elmer watches his sister undress, her body straight and flat as a boy's. She sleeps nude, and slipping into bed she sometimes lets him briefly touch her skin for reassurance, still faintly traumatized as he is by the fire. The first chapter ended as she ran away from home, like her brothers before her. As with *Mayday,* Faulkner kept a word count. But this time he simply estimated that he was writing 25 twelve-word lines to the page. He multiplied 300 by his 19 pages and then twice underlined the figure, 5,700.

Chapter Two also began on the freighter but quickly slipped into flashback: Elmer's "bastard son" in Houston and his love for Myrtle Monson, whom he had met there in 1921. Still limping from his wound in the war, Elmer had asked Myrtle to marry him, but she had simply sailed for Europe with her snobbish mother. Once grown, Elmer received none of the sympathy Faulkner lavished on Donald Mahon. Instead, the treatment resembled that of Julian Lowe, as though Faulkner might have been drawing again upon Huxleyan satire. His entry at the end of Chapter Two recorded 3,600 words.

As summer drew to a close, Faulkner was still savoring French life: the rare bright days, the games of croquet, and the old men sailing their boats in the great circular Luxembourg pool. "Think of a country where an old man, if he wants to, can spend his whole time with toy ships, and no one to call him crazy or make fun of him! In America they laugh at him if he drives a car even, if he does anything except play checkers and sleep in the courthouse yard." He still deplored the boorishness of rich American tourists and praised the simple courtesy and love of children he saw in the French. He described the formality one encountered in buying toothpaste, supplying (in English) eleven lines of dialogue between customer and clerk to show how the formulas were politely used.

His travel notes for his mother sometimes suggested the Old Colonel in *Rapid Ramblings in Europe.* "I went out to Meudon this week," he wrote, "where Madame de Pompadour had a castle, where folks fought duels all over the place. And I have seen the chapel where James I of England was buried after both the French and English threw him out. Those poor Stewarts had an awful time." There in the country, and in the city too, the weather was changing. It was quite cool, and a trench coat felt comfortable at night. "Summer is almost gone. Lots of the trees are dying here, the elms about the Place d'Etoile and some of the old chestnut trees in the Luxembourg." But he had not lost his inclination to travel. "Tomorrow I am going to Versailles—Marie Antoinette's hang-out—and Fontainebleau."

Early September found him working even harder on *Elmer.* On Wednesday, the second, he put in his usual morning and afternoon stint. He resumed at eight-thirty in the evening and continued until almost one o'clock. Then he dutifully wrote his Wednesday letter to Miss Maud. "I am working steadily on my novel," he told her, "besides a book of poems for children I am writing, and a few articles on the side, you might say. So much writing that I feel fairly 'wrote out.' " It was not surprising that he was not keeping the diary they had talked about. "I'll write it all someday though," he said.

He continued to intersperse work with sightseeing. "I went to the French National Exhibition today. Like a big county fair, only it was planned (houses, bridges, etc) by real sculptors and painters, I went with a sculptor, Jean Couvray, who did some of it. It was sort of nice—like reading a gorgeous fairy tale. Nothing especially good though. Too colorful and French."

He did not describe the articles he had mentioned, but one story for the *Times-Picayune* may have been in the mail by now and perhaps a second as well. They appeared on September 20 and September 27. Both were successful "commercial" stories which showed how he was working at short-story craftsmanship while borrowing from other writers.

"Country Mice," like F. Scott Fitzgerald's *The Great Gatsby,* was narrated in the first person by a man of some cultivation who had become the confidant of a bootlegger who drove an ostentatious motorcar. In this story, however, the voice of the bootlegger gradually assumed all of the burden of the narration. Faulkner was very likely following the method of a master common to both himself and Fitzgerald—Joseph Conrad. It was as though Captain Charles Marlow set the scene, introduced the main character, and then stood by only to relay his narration to the reader. The bootlegger told a complicated story of running "a bunch of hooch into New Haven, a town up the road from New York, where they was going to have a big football game. . . . New Haven is where one of them big colleges is, I forget the name of it. . . ." While escaping hijackers, the driver had been overtaken by a country policeman, and the shipment had subsequently been impounded by a justice of the peace. Bribing a deputy and hiring a pilot had only compounded the disaster. The deputy and pilot were revealed as twin sons of the justice of the peace. The story explained the bootlegger's wariness of country constables: "when you fool with one of them birds, get up early in the morning to do it, see?" The 3,700-word story showed a distinctly Faulknerian trait: pleasure in a complicated plot with elements of mystery-story technique. All the facts were given, but only at the end was their causal relationship explicitly revealed.

"Yo Ho and Two Bottles of Rum" may have been conceived and perhaps even started aboard the *West Ivis.* This last work of Faulkner's to appear in the *Times-Picayune* was a tribute, in effect, to Joseph Conrad. The setting was Conradian and the narrative voice Marlovian. The third paragraph of the 3,300-word story was pure Conrad. The *Diana* plied "Eastern waters from Canton to the Straits, anywhere the ingenuity of man might send a cargo. She might be seen anywhere; tied rolling heavily to a wharf in Singapore, weathering a typhoon in an anchorage known only to admiralty charts, next year in Bangkok or the Dutch Indies. Strangely enough her personnel did not change much. It was as though every soul aboard had been caught hopelessly in an inescapable dream." The nameless narrator remarked the East's enervating effect on some white men. He noted their attitudes of superiority and the Orientals' inscrutability. "There is something eternal in the East," he mused, "something resilient and yet rocklike, against which the Westerner's brief thunder, his passionate, efficient methods, are as wind." The effects took various forms. "The American or the Latin 'goes bad' and drops out of sight, assimilates himself with people and conditions among which his destiny casts him, becomes (sentimentally perhaps) non-committal regarding his nationality. But the Britisher is still British, the lower he goes the more blatantly British he becomes." There were landscapes as well as seascapes: "The sun was red and implacable as a furnace mouth; once the beach was behind and they were among great impenetrable trees the heat became terrific."

What was not Conradian, however, was the callous flippancy at the heart of the story. Used to beating the bosun with a short heavy stick, the mate had mistakenly struck instead the messboy, whom he had named "Yo Ho." His defense to the acquiescent captain was indignant: "ain't I a white man? Can't I kill a native if I want to?" The decomposition of the body makes Yo Ho's presence nearly as oppressive as that of James Wait in *The Nigger of the Narcissus.* Accompanying the body and the coolies ashore for the land burial they demand, the mate and the other officers discover the two bottles of whiskey placed with the body as propitiatory offerings. The officers drink the whiskey and then decide they can obtain more by the simple expedient of killing another Chinese. Quarry and pursuers are reunited the next morning and return to the ship.

Faulkner had put together a story which might interest and amuse the readers of the *Sunday Times-Picayune.* Most of them could scarcely have been expected to appreciate Conradian subtleties. Conversely, the sensibilities of most of them might not have been outraged at the homicide. And the events of the story followed Faulkner's version of the line from the pirate chantey. Later he would borrow again from Conrad. But the borrowings would usually be in technique—the handling of chronology and point of view—rather than in the external specifics of setting, character type, and incident.

Near the end of the first week in September, Faulkner had done something very different from this last *Times-Picayune* story. It was personal, poetic, and passionate. "I have just written such a beautiful thing that I am about to bust—2000 words about the Luxembourg gardens and death," he wrote Miss Maud. "It has a thin thread of plot, about a young woman, and it is poetry though written in prose form. I have worked on it for two whole days and every word is perfect. I havent slept hardly for two nights, thinking about it, comparing words, accepting and rejecting them, then changing again. But now it is perfect—a jewel. I am going to put it away for a week, then show it to someone for an opinion. So tomorrow I will wake up feeling rotten, I expect. Reaction. But its worth it, to have done a thing like this." The now-vanished composition was clearly another step in Faulkner's transition from poet to fiction writer. And his letter gave the clue for the understanding of much of his later work: "it is poetry though written in prose form." Faulkner's pursuit of the *mot juste* clearly followed that of Gustave Flaubert. Much later he explained his admiration: "in *Bovary* I saw, or thought I saw, a man who wasted nothing, who was—whose approach toward his language was almost the lapidary's, that he was . . . a man who elected to do one book perfectly. . . ." His own manner would eventually come closer to that of Balzac, "a man who was so busy writing about people that he didn't have much time to bother about style. . . ." Faulkner could never be too busy to bother about style, but he would not later be the Flaubertian or Joycean lapidary he was now. Though the 2,000-word piece seems not to have survived, the emotion and care and sleeplessness he lavished on it would not be entirely lost.

He had other progress to report. "I have over 20,000 words on my novel," he wrote, "and I have written a poem so modern that I dont know myself what it means." Out of this European stay would come at least one poem using European materials in the manner of E. E. Cummings—without capitals or punctuation, with the position of lines arranged for aesthetic effect rather than by convention, and with words and abbreviations all run together. This one he mentioned to his mother might have been done in that manner.

Chapter Three of *Elmer* presented Elmer's fourth-grade year in flashback. In Chapter Four, Faulkner emphasized Elmer's liking for the shape and feel of his tubes of paint as an outgrowth of his early fascination with cigar butts, which he collected. Other objects also attracted him: "long tapering whips fixed pliant and slenderly recovering in their sockets on the dashboards of buggies; and he would stand in a dull trance staring at a factory smokestack." Faulkner conveyed other aspects of Elmer's psychosexuality. He had seen something of his mother in his beloved sister, whose "Dianalike" beauty was transfigured into his ideal. The fleshly women he later knew tended, curiously, to see him as a brotherly figure, no matter how intimate their relationship. The end of this chapter brought Faulkner's total to 15,300 words.

The words continued to pile up, first in the minuscule characters in blue ink, then in the slowly typed pages. Elmer's sweetheart, Ethel, became pregnant. He went off to the war, was wounded, and was shipped home in 1917 to recover. Finally through with most of the long expository flashbacks, Faulkner brought Elmer up to date: "here was Paris: the Louvre, Cluny, the Salon; all that he had wanted for so long. . . . that homely informal garden where the ghost of George Moore's dead life wanders politely in a pale eroticism. . . . that merry childish sophisticated cold-blooded dying city to which Cezanne was dragged by his friends like a reluctant cow, where Degas and Monet fought obscure points of color and life and love, cursing Bougereau and his curved pink female flesh, where Matisse and Picasso yet painted——." At the end of this chapter Faulkner returned to the novel's opening scene. Myrtle had been three years in Europe and Elmer's vessel was about to make port in Venice. At this point, he noted, his novel was 19,800 words long.

He was quite on his own in Paris now. Spratling had to think of the fall semester at Tulane, and he had left for New York. Faulkner had gone to the station with him at six-thirty on September 6 to see him off. He found Paris lovely in the morning, with the streets washed, the Seine still as a pond, and little traffic but for the wagons bearing vegetables or masses of violets, dahlias, and big chrysanthemums. But it was unseasonably cool, and if the rainy season came before he finished the novel he would probably go back to Italy. For the present he was enjoying the brisk cool weather. He would don his trench coat and sit "in the garden. I have come to think of the Luxembourg as my garden now. I sit and write there, and walk around to watch the children, and the croquet games. I always carry a piece of bread to feed to the sparrows."

He was still going to galleries. There was one marble he liked especially at the Exposition gallery: a little boy trying to pick up his ball. "He is so fat and bundled up that he can hardly bend over, or straighten up again: you want to go and help him." He was also finding new ways to spend his leisure. "I have a new vice," he wrote, "bus rides." He had gone up on Montmartre "to see the lights of Paris come on in the dusk. Lovely." He noticed the omnipresent pictures of Sainte Geneviève, patron saint of Paris. There was a beautiful one in the Panthéon, "where the unknown soldier's grave is." On a wall panel there he had seen a wreath to Guynemer. He was struck by the inscriptions to dead soldiers, and by the living dead, too: "so many young men on the streets, bitter and gray-faced, on crutches or with empty sleeves and scarred faces. And now they must still fight, with a million young men already dead between Dunkirk and the Vosges mountains, in Morocco. Poor France, so beautiful and unhappy and so damn cheerful. We dont know how lucky we are in America."

He reported another kind of progress: his beard was coming along fine—"Makes me look sort of distinguished, like someone you'd care to know." At the end of the letter was a pen-and-ink sketch, fullface, an inch high and half an inch wide, of himself with beard. It was pointed and quite full. The mustache drooped a bit, and above the sharp ears was a full and tangled head of hair. It was like a sketch of the young Bernard Shaw—not so elongated and not so Mephistophelean, but instead rather faunlike.

When he wrote his Wednesday letter he reported with satisfaction, "The novel is going elegantly well—about 27,500 words now. Perhaps more." He began Chapter One of Book Three with a description of Venice and then appropriated Bill Spratling's misadventure in Genoa. As Elmer succumbed to drunkenness Faulkner depicted his stream of consciousness and rendered his reactions impressionistically. The result suggested a blend of *Marionettes* and the "Circe" episode of Joyce's *Ulysses.* Faulkner then closely followed Spratling's incarceration and release.

In the next two chapters Faulkner began to move his characters with more purpose. In one, Elmer and Angelo (his emissary from prison) rode a train for Paris. In the other, Myrtle and Mrs. Monson voyaged expensively from the United States to Europe. He was now setting the stage for a confrontation.

It was still quite chilly and gray in Paris with "just enough light in the sky to turn these lovely faded green and gray and red roofs into a beautiful faint lavender at sunset. After dark a glow in the sky over Paris itself—Montparnasse, where I live, is quite a distance from downtown, like Place de l'Opera and les grands boulevards." He liked his quarter and its denizens.

Pen-and-ink self-portrait in a letter home from Paris.

"They are grand people, the working classes, among whom I live myself." He told his mother he had gotten to be a "croquet fiend," wasting half the day watching the play in the gardens. He used to return to his room and be at work by nine-thirty; now he never seemed to get back before noon. "But," he admitted, "its so nice to dawdle around in the gardens, helping the lads sail their boats, etc." He was still exploring, having walked out to the Bois de Meudon on Sunday and enjoyed the feeling of dirt under his feet again. His living expenses were now down to a dollar a day. He had discovered a fine restaurant, the Three Musketeers, where he dined for five francs. His energetic young landlady saw to it that his shoes were kept shined. He also managed other savings. "I dont know what laundry costs," he wrote, "not having had any done yet."

He conscientiously reported his sightseeing, having gone that day to the Hôtel des Invalides and observed the war relics: "crashed aeroplanes and guns and tanks and alarm klaxons." He had seen the great marble cenotaph bearing the single word "Napoleon." He gave his mother his reaction: "Quite impressive." And there was one other report: "Beard's long enough to hold water now."

On September 9 or 10 he had received a letter from Aunt 'Bama. The same day he wrote her an affectionate reply, describing some of his travels in Italy. His unfavorable impression of Switzerland and his own countrymen abroad remained unchanged while his feeling for the current country of his choice had deepened: "France, poor beautiful unhappy France. So innately kind, despite their racial lack of natural courtesy, so palpably keeping a stiff upper lip, with long long lists of names in all the churches no matter how small, and having to fight again in Maroc." He described the Quarter and the things he enjoyed doing. "When I am old enough to no longer have to make excuses for not working," he told his great-aunt, "I shall have a weathered derby hat . . . and spend my days sailing a toy boat in the Luxembourg Gardens."

He told her about the "amusing travelogue" he had written in Sommariva and said he had done another in Paris. He mentioned the poem so modern he didn't know himself what it meant, and that now he was engaged in writing the book of verse for children and the novel. The reaction of depression over the story of the girl in the Luxembourg Gardens had not developed. He still felt the same exultation: "I have just finished the most beautiful short story in the world. So beautiful that when I finished it I went to look at myself in a mirror. And I thought, Did that ugly ratty-looking face, that mixture of childishness and unreliability and sublime vanity, imagine that? But I did. And the hand doesn't hold blood to improve on it." Boni & Liveright had a novel of his, he said, which should appear in the fall. "And that's my history." It is not clear whether he had actually heard from the publisher or Stone, or whether he had something like the hunch Anderson had. He told Aunt 'Bama about his beard and penned a sketch at the bottom of her letter like the one he had done for his mother.

Aunt 'Bama's letter had informed him that relatives from Ripley would be coming to Paris. In his letter to his mother on Sunday, September 13, he described his meeting with them. He had remembered his honey-haired Aunt Vannye—Mrs. Vance Carter Witt—from the visit to Ripley when he was three. She was the daughter of Willie Medora Carter, the Old Colonel's oldest surviving child by Lizzie Vance, his second wife. When she arrived in Paris with her daughter, Willie, Faulkner sent a note to her hotel. The answer was an invitation to lunch on Saturday. He presented himself for the engagement and found Vannye looking quite young and Willie sweet if unprepossessing. "They are very nice," he confided to his mother, "of the purest Babbitt ray serene. They carry their guidebooks like you would a handkerchief." They were not discourteous like the other American tourists he had observed, but "Europe has made no impression on them whatever other than to give them a smug feeling of satisfaction for having 'done it.' "

There were other Americans, though, whose company he enjoyed. "I have fallen in with a gang of Chicago art students here," he wrote, "a girl and 3 young men. I like them—kind of loud and young and jolly, saying Paris cant compare with Chicago." It appears that one of them was William M. Slavin. He introduced Faulkner to another American artist, a non-Chicagoan named Bill Hoffmann, who was in his company quite often thereafter. Hoffmann remembered Faulkner's enjoying himself at a party given by another Chicago artist, Paul Berdanier, in his Montparnasse studio. There Faulkner recited a risqué poem which began, "Let's see, I'll say, between two full balloons of skirts." The other Chicagoan might have been Sol Kogan, Bill Hoffmann thought, and the girl, Martina Steere, a Chaloner Prize winner and later Mrs. William Hoffmann.

Faulkner and Hoffmann would stroll along the quais, stopping occasionally at the open-air bookstands. For one book Faulkner expressed great admiration: Margaret Kennedy's *The Constant Nymph*, a first novel. (Some found it a mixture of pathos and satire which treated sordid relationships with outspoken vulgarity. To others it was not a novel at all but a lyric about young girls and love and music in a pagan world.) Although Faulkner was now the bohemian artist, he preserved something of the New Orleans persona. "He talked occasionally about his experience in the RAF," Hoffmann remembered, "and gave a humorous demonstration showing how each of the fliers walked to his plane carrying an iron stove lid under his arm upon which he sat in the plane to protect him from bullets from below." He also described bringing in liquor from Caribbean islands and flying a plane for New Orleans bootleggers—an exploit which might have reminded a *Times-Picayune* reader of "Country Mice."

Faulkner was not limiting himself to Americans. He wrote his mother that he had met an old priest in the gardens. "I see him occasionally and he lets me practice my french on him." There was no literary progress to report this time, however; it was just the reverse. "I have put the novel away," he wrote without explanation, "and am about to start another one—a sort of fairy tale that has been buzzing in my head." The projected work aroused a temperate and somehow curiously diluted enthusiasm. "This one is going to be the book of my youth, I am going to take 2 years on it, finish it by my 30th birthday." But for the immediate present he had become tired of Paris. The rainy season with its cold weather would begin any day, and he was ready to be off. "I think I'll go down into Burgundy again, and see the peasants make wine, and tramp from there down to the Mediterranean." It would be another full week, however, before he got away from the attractions of Paris and its environs, no matter how tired of the city he thought he was.

A post card which Billy sent to his mother in fun on September 15 may have caused some slight disturbance to her Methodist sensibilities. It showed the church of Saint Sulpice. He told his mother that he lived nearby and went there on Sundays. "Be a good catholic soon," he wrote. But he would not be there this Sunday. "I am off to the country again today. Tired of cities." Vannye would be sailing for New York next week. In the meantime, he was going to visit Belgium and Holland.

He had been to Vincennes, the first royal habitation, which was quite small: "a chateau the size of the campus in a park 3 miles across." The king had moved to the Tuileries, which was located on the Seine, included the Louvre, and was "smaller than the town of Oxford." Since this was also too small, the king had moved to Versailles "and built himself a regular city." Now the kings were dead, and the government charged you two francs to look at their "ruined splendor." It would be grand, though, to know that there was a king in the Tuileries, to go to the Place de la Concorde "and see him drive out in his carriage with footmen in scarlet and gold and powdered hair."

In the interval he saw Vannye again several times. Though his beard was getting along quite well, Vannye had laughed at it "because she could see right through it the little boy I used to be." Twice she took him to lunch, astounding the restaurant staff by asking for all the dishes she wanted at once—the food all fried—avoiding wine and demanding coffee *with* the meal. He wrote out for his mother, in a literal, unidiomatic translation meant to amuse, the dialogue between himself and the waitress as he conveyed Aunt Vannye's heretical order to her. But his opinion had softened to amused tolerance by the time she left for home. He had told her he was soon off on a trip, and at their last luncheon she had handed him an envelope—for his birthday, she had said. He opened it to find a thousand-franc note. "So I taken part of it and bought her some hand-made handkerchiefs," he wrote.

Another diversion was somewhat different from lunch with a great-aunt. The previous evening (probably September 20), he had gone to the Moulin Rouge—most likely with some of Vannye's francs. "Anyone in America will tell you it is the last word in sin and iniquity," he informed his mother. Actually, "It is a music hall, a vaudeville, where ladies come out clothed principally in lip stick. Lots of bare beef, but that is only secondary. Their songs and dances are set to real music—there was one with not a rag on except a coat of gold paint who danced a ballet of Rimsky-Korsakoff's, a Persian thing; and two others, a man stained brown like a faun and a lady who had on at least 20 beads, I'll bet money, performed a short tone poem of the Scandinavian composer Sibelius. It was beautiful." Some plays, staged here by the French but never patronized by French audiences, were nastily suggestive and meant to appeal especially to Americans, who would stand in line for hours for tickets. "After having observed Americans in Europe I believe more than ever that sex with us has become a national disease. The way we get it into our politics and religion, where it does not belong anymore than digestion belongs there. All our paintings, our novels, our music, is concerned with it, sort of leering and winking and rubbing hands on it. But Latin people keep it where it belongs, in a secondary place. Their painting and music and literature has nothing to do with sex. Far more healthy than our way."

He was still delighting his eye in the museums. "I have spent afternoon after afternoon in the Louvre," he wrote. He visited the Luxembourg, seeing Rodin's museum and two private collections of Matisse and Picasso, "as well as numberless young and struggling moderns." Another Frenchman's work excited him: "And Cezanne! That man dipped his brush in light like

Tobe Caruthers would dip his in red lead to paint a lamp-post." He had stayed over one more day to please another of his senses. "The Belgian Military Orchestra . . . is in Paris and there is to be a musical combat between them and the French trombone battlers this afternoon. . . . The bandstand is outdoors, in a grove of chestnut trees in the Luxembourg Gardens. It is lovely, the way the music sounds. And these people really love good music. The bands play Massanet [*sic*] and Chopin and Berlioz and Wagner, and the kids are quiet, listening, and taxi-drivers stop their cars to hear it, and even day laborers are there rubbing elbows with members of the Senate and tourists and beggars and murderers and descendants of the house of Orleans."

In this letter he inadvertently combined a report on his beard and his writing. He had done a three-by-three-inch pen-and-ink self-portrait much more painstaking and representational than the first one. It was almost full profile, the face in shadow, the beard heavy and obscuring the lips, the hair thick and curly. His landlady had lent him a mirror, and it was not until later that he noticed he had been drawing on a used sheet which was part of *Elmer.* "I have him half done," he told his mother, "and I have put him away temporarily to begin a new one. Elmer is quite a boy. He is tall and almost handsome and he wants to paint pictures. He gets everything a man could want—money, a European title, marries the girl he wants—and she gives away his paint box. So Elmer never gets to paint at all."

But Elmer was not now in the forefront of his mind. Today (probably the twenty-first) he was off on his trip right after the military concert. "I'm glad to be getting away again. So much more fun not knowing where you'll be when night comes." He was off, he expected, for Belgium and Holland. At home in Oxford *The Mississippian* had just caught up with him a few days earlier. "Mr. William Falkner," noted the writer of "Social Observations," "former postmaster of the University office, is in Paris now."

He bought a two-dollar ticket to Rennes, 180 miles west-southwest of Paris on the Paris–Brest line. Located at the center of a basin between two rivers, the Ille and the Vilaine, it was the ancient seat of the dukes of Brittany and had once been the capital of that province. It was now a road and railroad junction, a trading center for an agricultural region and a city with industries, but the signs of the past lay all around in such structures as the fine cathedral begun in the fifteenth century. On the train and during his brief stay in Rennes he apparently found time for some reading as well as sightseeing.

When he had packed his "sport baggage," he had included Ham Basso's copy of Ludwig Lewisohn's anthology *A Modern Book of Criticism.* He had by now added his own name on a flyleaf in pencil. As he read in it, he did something that was relatively rare for him: he underlined and wrote comments in the margins and on blank pages. In his introduction, Lewisohn made it clear that the book was meant as ammunition for America's young liberal critics in opposition to those Lewisohn considered repressive and arrogant—the so-called American Humanists, chiefly Paul Elmer More, Irving Babbitt, and Stuart P. Sherman. The excerpts and essays were presented in four groups: French, German, English and Irish, and American. Although Faulkner, as an artist, might have been presumed to sympathize with Lewisohn, most of the six comments he made were critical. And some were tinged with indignation and disgust. He would continue to read and comment as he traveled.

Late the next day, September 22, he took the train from Rennes for Rouen, 150 miles to the northeast. It may have been on the train that he started a letter which began, "Dear Stone—I've had a look at Brittany" and then broke off. He had repeated the error he had made with the pen-and-ink self-portrait for his mother, using the back side of a typed page of *Elmer.* Either he had brought some of the manuscript with him by mistake, or the story was still very much in his mind despite his comment that he had put it aside.

He arrived in Rouen that evening. One of the first things he must have done was to write a post card that went out that night at 10:10. On the other side of a picture of the former abbey church of Saint-Ouen, he told Miss Maud he was "On a walking tour. I have a good second-hand bicycle promised me next week in Paris, then I'm off for a good long trip, all about. This time I'm on my way to Amiens, and Soisson [*sic*] and perhaps Belgium." The capital of Normandy, Rouen was called "the Museum City." It seems unlikely that Faulkner visited any of its museums, though he must have gazed at the great medieval Notre Dame Cathedral with its carillon and lofty central tower, the tallest in France. Now an active trading and manufacturing center, Rouen had greeted figures such as Julius Caesar and England's Henry V. Characteristically, however, Faulkner headed away from it toward the small town of Bois Guillaume. But now the weather had turned against him. And suddenly the weather was not the only source of unpleasantness: "The French are polite, but not really courteous," he wrote his mother later; "they are not kind-hearted (Monsieur le Compte de Boisguilliaume [*sic*] turned me out of his chateau in the rain one day in Normandy). . . ." In spite of the rain and the discourtesy, he derived benefit from the expedition. He wrote a sonnet, entitled "Cathedral in the Rain." It was a verbal landscape—dominated by a "sad and silver music," by "this soundless sorrowing of trees"—which had been seen and heard, according to the last line, "above Rouen, in the rain." There may have been still another result besides the poem. "I developed a cold," he told Miss Maud in the same letter, "and bought a throat spray for $1.00. . . ."

On Thursday, the twenty-fourth, he headed northeast, covering nineteen miles before spending the night in the town of Buchy. He arrived in Amiens from Buchy on Friday, his twenty-eighth birthday, probably having covered the forty-three miles by train. His post card showing the great Notre Dame Cathedral told his mother where he had been and that he was "Off again walking tomorrow, in the general direction of Soissons, then to Paris. Be in Paris again about Tuesday, where I have engaged to buy a bicycle. Then I think I'll go south again. But I dunno." As unconcerned about time as he was about his itinerary, he wrote at the bottom of the card, "either the 24, 25, or 26 of Sept." (The postmark told Miss Maud that her son's card had been stamped at midnight, September 25.) He was now in the presence of modern history. Amiens had fallen to the Prussians in November of 1870. German troops had occupied it again briefly in their attempted grand envelopment at the start of the Great War. On August 30, 1914, they had taken it but then had withdrawn. It showed few signs of the contest which raged for it. Walking southeast on the morning of the twenty-sixth, Faulkner began to see the signs in ghastly abundance.

"I passed Cantigny, where American troops first entered the war," he wrote later. Now scenes began to take on a personal meaning: "I think that was where Madden Tate was wounded." Madden Tate had stood at the end of Billy Falkner's row, a smiling boy no bigger than himself, in Miss Essie Eades's picture of their sixth-grade class. Faulkner was about twenty miles southeast of Amiens now. He walked two miles east to the larger town of Montdidier. The next day he would proceed twenty miles further to Compiègne. On March 21, 1918, the German high command had ushered in the spring with a last desperate drive toward Amiens. Seventy-one German divisions pushed the twenty-nine British divisions, which fought and fell back before them. Five days later the French were able to send reinforcements, and by April 5 the assault had ended in bloody exhaustion, still ten miles from Amiens. The British had lost 163,000 men, the French, 77,000, and the Germans, a quarter of a million. The land and the people still showed effects of the vast carnage. "Compiegne and Montdidier were 8 miles behind the front for 3 years," he wrote, "so they are not damaged much. But beyond that eight miles it looks as if a cyclone had passed over the whole world at about 6 feet from the ground. Stubs of trees, and along the main roads are piles of shell cases and unexploded shells and wire and bones that the farmers dig up."

His sympathies were now totally engaged, and so was his indignation. "Poor France! And now America is going to hold their noses to the grindstone. If some of those Senators would just come over here, see what France has done to repair that country in which every single house was burned, see farmers plowing and expecting every minute to strike an unexploded shell and be blown to kingdom come, see children up to 10 and 12 crippled, jerking with ricketts from lack of food—when I get home I think I'll make a speech before the senate, if they'll let me. Certainly a country rich enough to afford Prohibition can help them a little." The French were polite but not kindhearted, he said, recalling his treatment at the hands of the man he described as Monsieur le Compte de Boisguilliaume; but the French "are heroic. In England, in America, there would have been a revolution, as there was in Russia."

He sent his mother a post card from Compiègne on the morning of September 28. It showed a crossroads at Rethondes, just east of Compiègne, where the beginning of the armistice was commemorated. He sketched in a few of the sights he would later elaborate for her. "Walking through the war-zone," he wrote. "Trenches are gone, but still rolls of wire and shell cases and 'duds' piled along the hedge-rows, and an occasional tank rusting in a farm yard. Trees all with tops blown out of them, and cemetaries everywhere. British, mostly." Marshal Foch had signed the armistice in his personal railway coach in the Forest of Compiègne six miles to the northeast. But the great stands of oaks and beeches had witnessed more lugubrious events. Formerly considered part of the defenses of Paris, the forest had seen the penetration of the German armies in 1870, and the city of Compiègne had been used by the Prussians as their headquarters. Joan of Arc had languished there in the chains of the Burgundians. It was here too that Napoleon I had restored the magnificent palace built for King Louis XV.

In the sight of splendor, Faulkner was living frugally. He had spent one dollar for "brandy to keep me warm when I was sleeping in haystacks and things," he wrote Miss Maud later, but most of his money went "for eating, as I was pretty hungry with walking, averaging 25 miles a day." In the evenings, as he sat in a restaurant or café, there would be time to read. He may have finished with Lewisohn's anthology before the end of his trip. Twenty pages beyond Wilhelm Dilthey's essay, he unscrewed his pen again and wrote a long comment at the end of Hugo von Hofmannsthal's "The Poet and His Hearer." It revealed not so much a literary or aesthetic position as a violent antipathy to things German. His RAF indoctrination and his reaction to the war's desolation got into his response to the essay. After the clear chiseled prose of Anatole France, Lemaître, and Remy de Gourmont, it was difficult to determine what Von Hofmannsthal was saying apart from his insistence that the poet's work was an integral part of life and could be for some a religious experience. The breathless hyperbolic enthusiasm tossed up clouds of words at times so mystical and romantic as to defy understanding. Moreover, the translation was painfully awkward. Faulkner appended a nine-line comment: "I'll be goddamned if I ever read such a bulging mess of sweetness and light in my life. Imagine a fattish man with a blond well-nourished moustache carrying a flash light, and you've got the picture. What is the matter with these Huns? They composed music once, once some of them painted pictures; but now they cant even seem to win bicycle races with dignity. But I retract: Mr Ludwig Lewisohn must have translated this stuff." Faulkner had apparently skipped Lewisohn's note at the beginning—that he had done all the German translations but this one, the work of a lady from Cleveland.

Richard Mueller-Freienfels' "Creative Art in Life" was very different in style if not substance. Mixing pedantry and dogmatism, he treated several themes in five long, numbered paragraphs. It was no longer possible to see literature as removed from reality, concerned as it was with "the enrichment of life." Using a vocabulary from the natural sciences in the tone of a drillmaster, the author marched through his disquisition, concluding, "the more closely one analyses the different tendencies of art, the more their fundamental differences seem to disappear or to become merely differences of degree, so that even in naturalism and romanticism one finds certain idealising elements which have simply not reached the point of conscious and clear unfoldment." Faulkner contented himself with one sentence: "As the young fish, staring up through the ice at the lady skaters, said: 'For Christ's sake.' "

Alfred Kerr's "The Critic as Creator" comprised eighteen furious but numbered paragraphs. The symbolical elements of the critic were the sling and the harp; he should hate or love. Not only was criticism as creative as poetry—the critic as much an artist as the poet—but he was set above the ruck of wretches struggling with their muses: "The critic contemplates poets as the poet contemplates men." When in paragraph 12 Kerr delivered himself of the aphorism "Imagination is memory," Faulkner drew a line to the inner margin and wrote, "Like hell." At the end of the essay he first wrote the line he had used to comment on the Mueller-Freienfels essay. Then he crossed it out and appended four short paragraphs, taking enough care in two places to cross out his first thought and rewrite it:

> You damn right. It takes a good short-stop to report a baseball game.
>
> Mencken on a hobby-horse; Billy Sunday having a nightmare in the Browning society.
>
> His idea seems to be to take the toy train someone else has made, and make a toy aeroplane of it.
>
> When a man lets the sheer physical pleasure of a galloping pen get him he should by all means confine himself to vagueness, else some dull soul may prove facts on him afterward.

Lewisohn's own essay, "Literature and Life," drew Faulkner's silent approbation. He marked one short passage with blue crayon. There Lewisohn said of the American reader, "He is an absolutist in morals, rather tolerant of defections that are not found out, and a pragmatist in business and politics. Since his methods in the latter seem to have paid, he stamps them as truth and is thus fortified as by triple steel against any literary or philosophical assault."

In spite of his reaction of anger, Faulkner kept the book. There is no evidence that he ever opened it again, but he may have derived more from it than he realized. Later in life when people would ask him about the sources of the artist's work, he would invariably respond, "imagination, observation, and experience." Something of the ars poetica he evolved for himself may have come from his brief angry involvement with this small book in 1925. It must also have left him with something else: a deepening of the sentiments he had expressed in "On Criticism." He had distrusted and denigrated most critics then. Now most of them might well have seemed the artist's natural enemies.

On September 28 Faulkner struck off toward the southwest. After the sad sights of the war zone, the deep forest was a welcome change. Compiègne, he wrote his mother, "was once a royal city, when the king went to hunt wild boars and deer in the Forest of Compeigne [*sic*]. I walked through the forest, following the old hunting paths, and every so often I'd sit down and imagine I could hear horns, and dogs, and see huntsmen in green jackets galloping past, and then the king and his cavalcade in gold and purple and scarlet." He was now taking his time. "Spent a whole day walking 10 miles from Compeigne to Pont Sainte Maxence, and another day from there to Senlis. Senlis is an older town than Paris, even. Once Paris had no Bishop of its own, but the Bishop of Senlis would ride over occasionally to run things for them." A little over five miles south of Pont Sainte-Maxence, Senlis bespoke the past even more than Compiègne did. A royal residence from the time of Clovis, fifth-century Frankish king and first of the Merovingian line, the inner city showed medieval buildings circled by the remains of Gallo-Roman walls.

He continued southwest and by nightfall of the twenty-ninth must have been in Chantilly. This resort, frequented by Parisians, was vastly different from such towns as Cantigny. Though Chantilly had been occupied in 1870 and 1871, the visitor scarcely thought of hobnailed troops. There at the château, near the park, were the stables built in the early eighteenth century to house 240 horses. Now the sweep of greensward was broken by the tan oval track before a Dufy grandstand and sky where the French Jockey Club held its elegant races each year. In Chantilly the traveler wrote a post card to his father. It showed a pack of hounds in the forest. Two handlers managed them as three pink-coated huntsmen looked on, great brass horns slung round their chests. "A sporting place peopled principally by English," he wrote Murry Falkner. "Race course, private deer and foxes, and the best-looking horses you ever saw. Every bar is full of bow-legged cockney grooms and jockeyes [*sic*], and swell-looking Lords and dukes spinning along in carts behind trotting horses. They go out hunting in red coats, and ride right over you if you dont dodge." He signed it "Billy" and wrote, "Chantilly, 29 Sept."

He waited to mail it until the next day, however, when he was back in Paris. It went out that afternoon at 2:45, stamped with the legend Rue de Vaugirard, the place where he often posted his mail on the way from the Luxembourg Gardens to the Rue Servandoni. He put a card to his brother Dean in the same mail. It showed a deer lying in the forest where the hunt had brought him down. "What do you think of a country like this?" he asked his sportsman brother. "But you cant kill a deer like this here unless you got a red swallow-tail coat."

On October 2 three letters from Miss Maud arrived at once. Her son answered them with a running account of his trip, though he said he saw so much that he would not try to write it; he would save it to tell when he got home. "My expenses will amaze you," he wrote. Even though he had spent two dollars to get to Rennes, two dollars for other railroad fares, one dollar for the throat spray and another for the brandy, "altogether I spent $15.00 for nine days." But there was an unexpected after-effect. "I have got sort of restless in France, in Paris, that is. When I came back from my walking trip I felt fine and peaceful, but now after only four days I am a little bit discontented." But the idea of the bicycle and a trip south no longer appealed to him. "So I am going to England to walk a bit before the bad weather sets in, in November."

The English lords, dukes, grooms, and jockeys Faulkner had seen in the streets and bars of Chantilly may have piqued his imagination. He told his mother that he thought he would be in England about a month and reassured her about his finances. "I will even be able to buy some clothes in London, to which town I am going tomorrow." She was to continue to address her letters to Paris, however. "There is a man here who admires me very much, who kind of looks after me." He (probably Odiorne) would forward them. "I will tell George V howdy for you, and that you was just too busy to write."

Billy Faulkner had another piece of news for his mother in the long letter. The same mail that had brought three from her had brought one from Bill Spratling. He had been in New York about September 10 but apparently had waited until he returned to New Orleans to write: "he has seen Liveright and my novel is to be published."

26

October-December, 1925

London, that gray and timeless one: Saint Paul's brooding alone above the City and across houses to the river bridged and invisible; the strand blooming like an odorless and colorless flower already tarnished and old ere birth; Nelson fatuous and dim and somehow beautiful with sheer height above the tamed somnolence of his stone lions; beggars with waxed moustaches and frayed trousers in Piccadilly, importunate and bitter with matches or shoelaces, or resigned and skillful with colored chalk on the dirty pavement; sentries in scarlet tunics measuring the pavement before Buckingham palace and autobusses in dreadful and endless laden ellipses and the endless and aimless moiling of mankind . . . .

—*Elmer*

It is afternoon: a gray afternoon, across the boulevard Montparnasse, the boulevard Raspail, the opposite building is potted with smug tile against a sky as gray as the long gray surge and heave of the Atlantic itself. . . . autumn mounting Montparnasse permeated the traffic of Montparnasse and Raspail teasing the breasts and thighs of young girls clothed excitingly and movingly musical in the lavender glittering-dusk between old walls. . . .

—"Portrait of Elmer Hodge"

As usual, it took a bit longer to get started than he had thought it would. He boarded the train from Paris at eight-thirty on the evening of October 6. It reached Dieppe "under the crispest sky and the most elegant moon you ever saw. Clear and chill, but the boat was waiting, so I popped aboard. It was an English boat and I heard my native tongue (or something kind of resembling it) on all sides for the first time in quite a while." While most of the others went in to the laden dining room sideboard, he watched the deckhands cast off the lines. Soon they were under way at a speed that threw up a white wave before the bow. Four hours later they were docking at Newhaven. The other passengers took a very early train to London, but Faulkner got a blanket from the steward and slept until seven o'clock. He rode a local train to Brighton, where he caught an express which arrived in London at eleven o'clock. "I thought Italian and French trains were funny, but English trains not only never bother to turn the engine around, but sometimes it is in front, sometimes behind, and this morning in our train the engine was in the middle, pulling some of it and pushing the rest. Funny."

He had no sooner arrived in London than he decided he would leave the next day. It was dirty and "awful expensive." A hotel cost seven shillings—$1.75—and dinner cost four more. In Paris both would have come to no more than ninety cents. He had spent the whole day looking for a hotel—walking and riding buses in the morning fog that was greasy and full of coal smoke, "worse than Pittsburgh about spoiling clothes." He was appalled at the high cost of living he saw everywhere, "and the streets full of beggars, mostly young, able-bodied men who simply cannot get work—just no work to be had. They sell boxes of penny matches, play musical instruments, draw pictures on the pavement in colored chalk, steal—anything for a few coppers. And France moaning and groaning over her rising mortality rate! I've seen a lot: Buckingham Palace (the King never came out, though) with sentries in scarlet tunics and steel breast-plates on white horses, Westminister, the Tower, all those old coffee houses where Ben Jonson and Addison and Marlowe sat and talked, and Dickens' Bloomsbury, and Hounslow Heath where they robbed the mail coaches, and Piccadilly and St Paul's, and Trafalgar and Mayfair—everything, almost, despite the fog. The sun has looked like a half-spent orange all-day sucker." He had had more than enough of London. He was going south to Kent and west to Devon and Cornwall. "But if I dont find things cheaper there, I'm going back to Paris until time to start home." Apparently Spratling was right; the two or three years Stone had said Faulkner contemplated had dwindled into a few months. But the green counties of England—home of the RAF whose wings he had so coveted—lay before him.

Two days later he was in Kent, thirty miles southeast of London, at Tunbridge Wells. He was fascinated by cultural differences and stunned at the English. "These people!" he wrote. "The French live to make money and love, and the English live to eat. Five times a day they do it, and nothing under heaven is allowed to interfere with it." He described an average day's collations to his mother. And, of course, there was the ever-present tea. "They even roll tea wagons up and down the railroad platforms with tea and muffins: I have seen the engineer in the cab with a cup." But when it came to stronger drinks they were more temperate than he had been led to believe. Not so their cousins: "The Scots, of course. Whenever you hear anyone ask for whiskey in a bar you can count on looking up and seeing a face that looks like it had been left out doors for about 5 years."

He faithfully described to Miss Maud much of what he was seeing. "I am tramping again—en promenade, as us french fellers says. This is a funny place I have got to now. It is a watering place where the water tastes like hell and where earls and dukes that had too much fun while they were young, and old women of both sexes whose families are tired of looking at them, come to drink the water. They all have those nasty fuzzy white dogs that look like worms. The dogs are so old and blind and there are so many of them that you cant stop to look in a shop window without one of them doddering up and feebly wetting your leg and ankle." But the Kentish countryside was beautiful, with its sheep-filled meadows of deep green grass and its quiet lanes bordered by trees turning red and yellow. "Quietest most restful country under the sun," he thought. "No wonder Joseph Conrad could write such fine books here."

But the prices were no better. It was costing him $3.50 a day to live. And he had allowed himself a sizable expenditure. "I've got the best looking sport-jacket you ever saw. It is of hand-woven Harris tweed and has every possible color in it. The general tone is bluish-grayish-green; it is a shooting coat with natural-color leather buttons; fits me like a balloon and was cut by the swellest West-End tailor—one of those places 'By Appointment to H.M. the King, H.M. the King of Sweden, H. R. H. the Prince of Wales.' It does look like it needs a shave though. Whiz [Dean] will curl up and die when he sees it." He would be moving on, walking west into Sussex the next day. But soon he would return to France, he thought, because of the prices. And there was another reason: "Sort of feel that I'll get to work on my novel again."

By the time Maud Falkner heard from her son again, nearly a week had passed. He was back in France but he had not yet returned to Paris.

His memories of England, expensive though it had been, were good ones. "I walked some," he wrote, "saw quite a bit of the loveliest, quietest country under the sun. . . ." He was writing from Dieppe, where he had been for two days, apparently working on a Breton fishing boat which, like the *Diana* of "Yo Ho and Two Bottles of Rum," rocked and rolled in a calm sea. "We made a good haul," he wrote. It had included two small sharks which they killed with boat hooks. The cook was marvelous and the crew ate anything. So, he said—in an observation that must have made Maud Falkner purse her lips—he didn't doubt but what he had "eaten shark without knowing it and liked it, too." He liked sailing with Dieppe fishermen, different though it was from traveling the waters of Lake Pontchartrain and the Gulf. "It was cold, cold! Hands raw all the time. Weather was good, though a high sea running. Fall has come here sure enough. Cold and crisp as our January almost."

He planned to return to Paris the next day, October 16. The experience with the Breton crew, like the trip with the rumrunner, was now stored in memory, as real as the cold out on the water. And William Faulkner was never one to seek out and endure discomfort for any longer than necessary. Besides, his work was again making its demands on him. Before his trip he had written most days for long periods. Then he had needed to get away. Perhaps like Ernest Hemingway, who had pushed himself too hard and written too much in the first draft of *The Sun Also Rises*, Faulkner had learned through this experience something about pacing himself. He may even have been disturbed about having to put the novel aside. "I have got started writing on my novel again, glory be," he told his mother, "and I've written a queer short story, about a case of reincarnation." The latter was, it appears, one tangible result of his visit to England.

He was anxious to get back to Paris, perhaps to see if he could finish the novel by November, as he had so confidently written to his mother nearly eight weeks before. And there was something else. "I am expecting to hear from Liveright when I reach Paris. I waked up yesterday with such a grand feeling that something out of the ordinary has happened to me that I am firmly expecting news of some sort—either very good or very bad."

Faulkner's hunch was right. Boni & Liveright had accepted his novel, and editor-in-chief T. R. Smith would now put it into production. A Falstaffian man with a huge capacity for drink, Smith regularly made the rounds of the principal Manhattan speak-easies. He was equally welcome in the houses of the city's outstanding madams, where he was friend and confidant to the girls. He was a talented editor of nearly impeccable taste. Working for Horace Liveright he had helped to publish Dreiser, Anderson, O'Neill, Hemingway, Jeffers, and others. It is likely that he had already applied his craftsmanship to the manuscript from the house's new novelist from Mississippi. *Mayday* had a new title. Someone in the office had suggested "Soldiers' Pay," and Faulkner liked it.

Years later Faulkner said that there was a letter waiting for him from Liveright in Paris which contained a $200 advance. But then, as he told it, he encountered totally unexpected difficulties. "Nobody would cash the check for him," a friend later said. "The American consul told him to send it back to Liveright and ask for a draft. But he went to the British consul, showed him his British army dogtag, and the consul gave him the $200."

In spite of the expense, the trip to England had been profitable. It had given him material, plus a sense of place which he would use in future stories. And he would publish the story about reincarnation nine years later under the title "The Leg." It began with a flashback to 1914. The narrator, a twenty-one-year-old American at Oxford University named Davy, quickly sketched in his English friend, George, and Everbe Corinthia, the girl both love. "We were twenty-one then . . . tramping about that peaceful land where in green petrification the old splendid bloody deeds, the spirits of the blundering courageous men, slumbered in every stone and tree." In the summer of 1915, Davy loses his leg in France. When George comes to his bed, Davy pleads with him to find his leg and be sure it is dead. "It jeers at me," he tells him. "It's not dead." But it becomes clear that Davy has been speaking with a ghost. George has been killed at Givenchy, where Davy was wounded. Fitted with an artificial leg, Davy now walks with a limp—like Elmer Hodge, like David in "A Meeting South," and like Faulkner's persona in New Orleans. He also becomes a flier, for an aerial observer does not need two legs.

The story grew even more complicated, almost in the manner of Henry James and Rudyard Kipling in the ghost-story genre. The malevolent force in the severed leg—manifested to Davy as an "It" combining a sense of horror and the reek of sulphur—reappears in a body identical with Davy's; before the story ends, the girl and her father and brother as well follow George in death. The supernaturalism of the story clearly suggested the fantasy of *Marionettes* and the supernatural conventions and creatures on which Faulkner had drawn in his poems. The haunted English towpaths were not vastly different from the sinister Beardsleyan gardens. But he was obviously becoming absorbed with forms of prose fiction and working diligently to master them.

When Faulkner resumed his work on *Elmer,* it began to sound as English as "The Leg." Arriving in Europe, Mrs. Monson decides to join the Church of Rome in order to get on faster socially. She has been advised by George Blyeth, a stupid and loutish Cambridge graduate. His father is Lord Wysbroke, in whom "is vested a barren earldom, three spent baronies, and a Spanish marquisate," and who recognizes in Mrs. Monson "a moral piracy matching his own." Myrtle Monson would be a perfect heiress for Blyeth or his elder brother, Lord Wohleden, who has lost so many teeth that he can hardly clench a pipe and is nearly as impecunious as his father, who must borrow a cycle to get to the train station. As plans are laid for Wohleden to sue for Myrtle's hand, Faulkner switched to the Monsons.

Now he called into play other European sights and impressions. He did a short set piece on the sea at Rapallo and sketched dessicated aristocrats, "all emanating something as intangible as an odor: a heritage of an old and splendid thing worn out with time, tarnished by sheer passing from one hand to another hand that changed perforce to keep pace with the changing times through a world in which there was no longer any place for it, soiled with handling, useless." Myrtle makes observations about Switzerland, where it was "like living at a country club where they only had dances once a week. . . ." She herself had begun to anticipate sensual Faulkner heroines to come, as her "desirable heavy young flesh even when she stood erect, seemed yet to sprawl in a rich abundant abandon. . . ." Another confrontation had now been anticipated: Myrtle and Wohleden rather than Myrtle and Elmer. But with more than 31,000 words written, Faulkner again put the novel aside.

When he was asked years later why he had left *Elmer* unfinished, he answered that it was "funny, but not funny enough." The English characters might have offered possibilities for more sustained comedy, but there was little about Elmer that was very funny. Faulkner seemed ambivalent —sympathetic toward him as a psychologically stunted migrant child, yet superior and satirical toward him as a bumbling adult. Another difficulty lay in the fact that there were so many subplots and places which did not fuse into a coherent narrative: not simply in the case of his childhood and adulthood, but also in his relationships with Ethel, with his son, with Angelo, and finally with Myrtle. The novel had no scene nor set of characters to hold it together as *Soldiers' Pay* had. But it was far from a profitless project, as future uses would show.

In one long poem which he may well have begun and perhaps completed in Europe, Faulkner combined tourism, the poignant beauty of the spring, antimilitarism, and a lament for the war dead. In his style, with no punctuation save parentheses and no capitalization, he seemed strongly indebted to E. E. Cummings. Lines and fragments of lines were arranged in an irregular pattern. Words were joined to form compounds, and flat colloquial language was juxtaposed to romantic lyricism. There were references to "russel square," "the ymca," "the american express," and "thos cook" as spring came "in the year mille neufcentvingtsomethingorother. . . ." As the voice of the guide intones tired phrases ("on our left we see"), the poet thinks of the struggle that once raged, but

the general himself
is now on tour somewhere in the states
telling about the war
and here
battalioned crosses in a pale parade. . . .

Above the earth in which these dead lie, the beauty of the new season springs forth:

o spring
above unsapped convolvulae of hills april
a bee sipping perplexed with pleasure o spring
o wanton o cruel. . . .

The poet thinks once more of the quiet dead as the voices of tourism close the poem:

8 rue diena we take care of that yes
in amiens youll find 3 good hotels.

The poem might be clearly imitative, but it was one of his most successful efforts.

Not all of his writing was serious. At one point during his stay in Paris he sent a bogus letter to H. L. Mencken. Signed by one "Ernest V. Simms," it urged the publication of an enclosed poem by William Faulkner, who "wants to get a start at poetry." The two-page poem was entitled "Ode to the Louver [*sic*]." Faulkner sent carbons of both the letter and the poem to Phil Stone. There is no evidence that either Simms or Faulkner ever received an acknowledgment. Faulkner did get letters from Stone, who had been faithfully looking after his interests at home. In August he had written to Four Seas to ask about royalties from *The Marble Faun.* He had headed his letter with the somewhat ominous phrase "In Re William Faulkner." It appeared that perhaps as much as $81 might be owed to the author, but the August 1 royalty statement was delayed and by November 1 he still had not received any money from the publisher. On November 6 Stone wrote to complain, telling Four Seas that Faulkner had been writing him for this money. This inquiry may well have been prompted by a letter from Miss Maud or Mr. Murry. The General Accounting Office of the Post Office had discovered in October that William C. Faulkner, Former Postmaster, still owed the Department $21.85. His father had replied for him, asking "if it will be agreeable to hold up this matter until my son Wm. C. Falkner returns from abroad which will be about the middle of November next." He would, of course, take care of it if they could not wait. In early November the Comptroller General of the United States acknowledged Murry Falkner's letter and informed him that his son now owed the Department not $21.85 but $38.25. The statement "should be presented to the former postmaster immediately upon his return from abroad. It will be appreciated if you personally see that the amount is forwarded to the postmaster at Vicksburg, Miss."

So the matter must have stood, in abeyance, as the still delinquent postmaster began to contemplate his departure for home. Once again the actual date would be later than the estimate, for he stayed the month of November. He must have fallen into his routine once more, writing, spending time in the Luxembourg, occasionally seeing Odiorne and Bill Hoffmann and his friends. Odiorne was now doing some portrait work in the sitting room of his fifth-floor cold-water walk-up. He had already done pictures of Paris so striking that Harold Levy would urge him to send them to New York for an exhibition. It was arranged that Odiorne would do some portraits of Faulkner, for what Odiorne remembered as a modest price.

He did a series—a formal portrait study and several made outdoors. The portrait was done in deep shadow. Faulkner held a pipe, the strong, shapely hand highlighted more than the thin, bearded face. It was a meditative picture, the aura one of dreamy silence in the dusk. In one of the outdoor photographs the subject was standing, puffing his pipe, wearing hat and trench coat, near what appeared to be a church. In others—wearing the

Faulkner in Paris.

same pepper-and-salt suit and vest—he sat on a bench. In these more light fell on the thin face and ample beard, now grown to the fullness of a Vandyke. Now the eyes were narrowed, the expression speculative. At the lower right-hand corner was the India-ink signature, "Odiorne——Paris." The European experience was now memorialized just as the one in Toronto had been. Faulkner sent one of the Odiorne portraits to Estelle, who by late November had sailed for Shanghai with Cornell and the children. She did not care for the beard any more than Miss Maud did. But Faulkner liked it and apparently had no intention of shaving it off.

He packed his few belongings—his typewriter and manuscripts, the new jacket from London, and a few souvenirs. Among them were post cards: Notre Dame, Les Invalides, the Place de la Concorde, and "The King Leading the Horse Guards Parade at the Head of the Guards." The European experience was almost over. It was probably the morning of December 9 when he boarded the boat train for Cherbourg.

Faulkner's return was different from his departure. He traveled third-class on the S.S. *Republic* of the United States Lines. This probably meant sharing a small cabin with three other men on C deck or one of the other lower levels of the *Republic.* She had sailed from Bremen on December 8. A day after leaving Cherbourg on the ninth, she docked at Queenstown, then set her course for New York on the same day, December 10. A winter crossing on the north Atlantic is rarely calm: this one was evidently extraordinary. A photograph from the *Commercial Appeal,* probably clipped by Miss Maud, showed white water towering over the *Republic*'s stern. Faulkner was apparently sailor enough to attend the "Dîner d'Adieu," however, on Thursday, December 17, and to take his choice of the haddock, pheasant, prime ribs, or chicken offered on the menu which he kept. The caption of the photograph reported that upon "the arrival of the steamship Republic at New York, tales of the sea's wild fury were told. . . ." Faulkner must have been glad to walk down the gangplank when the *Republic* tied up at the Second Street pier in Hoboken, New Jersey, on December 19. He was back home again after nearly half a *Wanderjahr* in Europe. He would draw on it in his fiction for some time to come.

BOOK FIVE
The Novelist

1925-1929

William Faulkner in New Orleans.

27

December, 1925–June, 1926

> They drove on and mounted the shady gradual hill toward the square, and Horace looked about happily on familiar scenes. Sidings with freight cars; the platform which in the fall would be laden with cotton bales in serried rotund ranks; the town power plant, a brick building from which there came a steady, unbroken humming and about which in the spring gnarled heaven-trees swung ragged lilac bloom against the harsh ocher and Indian red of a clay cut-bank. Then a street of lesser residences, mostly new.
>
> —*Sartoris* (165)

He had to take the ferry, of course, to get to Manhattan to catch a train for home. But it seems that he decided first to drop around at the offices of Boni & Liveright. The firm was located in a brownstone house on Forty-eighth Street between Fifth and Sixth avenues, next door to an almost identical brownstone housing a speak-easy named Toni's. If Faulkner did not see the tall, silver-haired senior partner, he might see Tom Smith, a small round man who looked like a Buddha and worked hard at publishing but seemed more at home with John McGraw and his New York Giants, not to mention girls of Manhattan's demimonde. One never knew which writers might be passing through. Dreiser and Jeffers were Boni & Liveright authors as well as Gertrude Atherton, Edgar Lee Masters, E. E. Cummings, Ben Hecht, and Gene Fowler. And the Europeans on the list included Emil Ludwig, Roger Martin du Gard, George Moore, Hendrik van Loon, Bertrand Russell, Sigmund Freud, and Wilhelm Stekel. None of them appeared to be passing through that day, however. Manuel Komroff greeted Faulkner cordially and ushered the thin, bearded young man into his office.

They talked briefly about *Soldiers' Pay*, which Komroff had voted for only on the strength of Sherwood Anderson's recommendation. Faulkner said something about another manuscript. "It's not my department," Komroff said, "but I'll see it gets a good reading." Of the conversation that followed, Komroff remembered only Faulkner's telling him about an accident in which he had fallen out of an airplane and cracked his skull. Then he left, presumably to return home, having actually seen something of the firm which was going to publish his first book.

When he stepped off the train, Miss Maud and Mammy Callie were waiting to meet him with the family's new four-cylinder Cole touring car. John and Dean were there with Jack, who had come down from his FBI office in Jonesboro, Arkansas. After his mother kissed him, she took a good look at him. The dark brown beard reached down to the knot of his necktie. "Billy," she said, with the old joke about the Smith Brothers obviously in mind, "what do you do with that thing at night, wear it inside the sheets or out?" Later there was another reminder that he was home once more. He had been six months without benefit of dry cleaning and with a minimum of laundering. "For heaven's sake, Billy," said Miss Maud to her twenty-eight-year-old author, "take a bath."

He moved into a room in the Delta Psi house across the hall from Johncy and Dolly, and gradually he caught up with events of the last six months. That summer John Markette had died, shot to death in the cab of his own locomotive by a member of the crew as they sat in the station at Coffeeville. Dr. A. A. Young had succumbed in his eightieth year and was buried with Confederate honors. Of course, not all the news he received was so somber. There were the details of Dean's triumphs as an Oxford High School football star. Other news combined the funerary and the sartorial. Mrs. McMahon, the widow of one of Oxford's first generation of physicians, had engaged in a new enterprise during Faulkner's absence. She began sewing burial shrouds, and finally staged a fashion show. Her handiwork was strikingly displayed by a young female instructor in physical education, with an extremely attractive figure, who modeled the shrouds in a reclining position.

When Faulkner would stroll down to the Square, loungers would watch the bearded figure entering the Gathright drugstore where he would browse through the current magazines. In a sudden period of good weather shortly after his return, Ella Somerville went out to the golf course. Coming up on one tee she was startled to see a bearded man emerge from a hollow nearby. He spoke to her. "What's the matter, Ella?" he asked. "Did you think I was Jesus Christ?" It was William Faulkner strolling about the familiar "golfing pasture."

There was plenty of time to do whatever he wanted. He read Miss Maud's new copy of *Suspense*, Joseph Conrad's unfinished, posthumously published novel. Phil Stone was giving him books again, as usual. As a change of diet from poetry, perhaps, he lent his friend James B. Gillett's *Six Years with the Texas Rangers.* On January 10 Faulkner put his name in a book Manuel Komroff had probably sent along to him, *The Le Gallienne Book of American Verse.* Cecile and Jack gave him a book in a different vein, Frances Newman's *The Hard-Boiled Virgin.* And he himself did some bookmaking, rebinding Estelle's copy of *Vision in Spring.* On a blank page at the end, he neatly lettered a fine line in India ink: "Rebound 25 January 1926. Oxford, Mississippi."

Early in the new year of 1926 he began to grow restless. It may have been the same kind of restlessness that had seized him on his return to Paris after the walking trip. He began to fall into his pattern of disappearances again, though sometimes he was not very far away. He would drift over to the university and spend time with Bob Terry, the son of a prosperous mule trader and now a senior law student. Terry had been a star basketball player, and his roommate, "Bat" Mustin, was an athlete too, as were most of their friends. One young student, C. M. Smith, remembered meeting Faulkner there. As a freshman, "Tad" Smith had to perform services for upper classmen. His specific assignment was Terry and Mustin. Tad would serve as bartender, mixing drinks from a can of New Orleans alcohol, sugar, and water, and pouring them into glasses borrowed from the dining room in Gordon Hall. As the boys drank, they would often put a foot upon a pull-out dresser drawer as though it were a brass rail. They liked to hear Bill Faulkner tell stories and would try to get him going about his trip. Occasionally he would speak French to them, Tad recalled. "My last job before hurrying to class was to give Bill a little drink with sugar and water. He'd lie down and sleep until Bob and Bat got back from class, and then they'd start him all over again." Faulkner was a familiar visitor there, sometimes staying in the dormitory for two or three days. Some mornings as Tad went to class, Murry Falkner would come out of his office and call to him. "Tad," he would say, "have you seen Bill?" Tad would say no and go on to class.

Faulkner continued to write. "During the next year or so," recalled John Falkner, "Bill wrote mostly short stories." Two other stories besides "The Leg" clearly reflected the European experience, and Faulkner may well have worked on them soon after his return home.

"Divorce in Naples" was interesting not only for itself but for what it conceivably said about *Elmer.* It too made use of the Spratling incident in Genoa, suggesting that Faulkner may have been cannibalizing *Elmer,* having decided to abandon it. The story dealt with two crew members on the thirty-four-day ocean crossing: George, a large dark Greek, and his beloved Carl, a small, blond, eighteen-year-old Philadelphian of Scandinavian descent. (The cargo of the ship was the same as that of the *West Ivis*: "Texas cotton and Georgia resin.") When Carl had slipped out of the harbor café with a prostitute, George had gotten drunk and thrown his money about. Arrested for stamping on the king's likeness, he had been released after a fellow prisoner had gotten a note to the consul. Their reconciliation was shadowed by an indication of future heterosexual betrayals by Carl.

"Mistral" began with two young Americans—Don, aged twenty-three, and the narrator, twenty-two—drinking "the last of the Milanese brandy." Walking north into the mountains they encounter not only the cold, dry, maddening wind which gave the story its name, but also a case of murder in an Alpine village. Romantic suspicion and intrigue suggested stories such as "The Cobbler" and "Jealousy," but a number of the details recalled phrases in Faulkner's letters home. Packs on their backs, Don and the narrator are traveling "en promenade." Interspersed through the story are the sound of goat bells and glimpses of roadside shrines with small bunches of faded wildflowers. There is also a jacket which Don and the narrator share, "a shooting coat of Harris tweed; we paid eleven guineas for it, wearing it day about while the other wore the sweater." This story showed growing assurance in a developing technique which would become a hallmark: withholding information and working by implication rather than statement. He did this here in writing about the passion of an anguished priest for his seductive ward, the murder of her fiancé, and the relationship between the girl and her guilty lover.

It was not the last time that Faulkner would recount an adventure this narrator shared with Don. In another story, called "Snow," the two would still be in their early twenties, and as they moved from the Italian Alps to the Swiss, they would encounter still another case of love and death in an

Alpine village. In a third story, called "Evangeline," Faulkner would give back to Don's companion the role of "I" narrator. Here the setting would be Mississippi rather than the Alps, and the mystery which the narrator and Don would try to unravel would be more complex, involving as it did the efforts of a man named Colonel Sutpen to found a house and family and the way in which the Civil War and the tangled lives of his children eventually doomed his design.

Very different was a story which Faulkner remembered having begun after his return from Europe. He called it "The Devil Beats His Wife." It was actually a series of fragments rather than a completed story. One of the three handwritten pages seemed to represent a stage Faulkner often bypassed: notes for the story, beginning with a few lines of dialogue in the fashion of a play script. On the half-page of notes, Faulkner sketched in Doris' taunting of her young husband, Harry, and his sudden blow which produces a breach between them. As their maid, Della, produces a reconciliation, she watches sunshine break through the rainy sky, murmuring to herself, "Hey, hey . . . devil beatin' his wife." Faulkner then tried a new version, sketching in a flirtatious conversation between Doris and another man on the remaining two sheets, with Della again solving the problem. Although Faulkner worked out the last few pages of the story in some detail, he did not complete it. It apparently would have been a commercial story, written with an eye to one of the big magazines and featuring a stock character, the loving illiterate servant who is really wiser than those she serves.

He appears to have been writing verse at this time, drawing on the European experience. One fragment may have been a kind of Italian counterpart to "Cathedral in the Rain." In the first stanza (of three couplets) the poet hears the worshipers at prayer and murmurs:

Ah, lay your mouth against the ear
Of the perplexed God, and he will hear.

In the second stanza of ten lines he sorrowfully listens to a sheepdog baying in the valley as darkness falls.

His poems were no longer carried in the Oxford *Eagle* (although that January a local poetess of note, Mrs. Lemuella Almond, published "To Our Soldiers Asleep in the Heart of Ole Miss Woods"). He did appear on one sports page, however, in the *Commercial Appeal.* The university golf club was holding its annual late winter tournament. On February 11 the paper carried an item reporting that "Bill Faulkner, novelist and sportsman who recently returned from Europe, is acting as chairman of the tournament committee." He was assisted by Frank Leftwich and Sonny Bell, only recently resigned from the postmaster's job. He continued to polish his game as winter faded and spring came in. Teeing off one day on a 132-foot hole, he hit a straight drive which dropped just short of the green but kept on rolling up and over the ridge. When he and the others walked onto the green, his ball was nowhere in sight. They finally found it in the cup. Besides the congratulations, he eventually received a dozen new golf balls and a pipe bearing the inlaid lettering "Hole in One."

He had doubtless spent some time by now in Memphis, where there was news to catch up on. In the spring federal officers had raided Reno's place near Whitehaven. Reno was arrested and freed on bail. When his case had come up in November he had pleaded guilty and paid a $500 fine. Still philosophical, still smiling, he was concentrating on getting back into business. Dot Wilcox was glad as always to see Bill Faulkner and to hear his account of his travels in Europe. She remembered his saying that his shoes began to wear out with all his walking, and that he would sometimes take them off, sling them over his shoulder, and trudge along barefoot. He forgot the twenty dollars sewn into his coat, he said, didn't even know he had it until he returned home and was asked about it.

It could have been about this time that an incident took place which might then have seemed only bizarre but which would later have the most important consequences. One evening as he sat with a companion in a night club, another young woman walked over to their table and joined them. She talked freely with them, and soon her conversation took on an intimate tone as she told them something of her life. She had been born in a village called Cobbtown. When she moved to the city, she became associated with a rising young gangster. (He was probably one Neal Kerens Pumphrey, nicknamed "Popeye." Only twenty-three, he had already been arrested for liquor-law violations, housebreaking, assault with intent to kill, and several other charges.) In spite of his seeming masculinity, the gangster was said to be impotent. He still persisted in having relations with women, however, using a variety of objects to compensate for his own psychosexual deficiency. He had raped one of these women with a particularly bizarre object and kept her in a brothel for a time. After a half-hour the girl left, but Faulkner brooded about the horrifying events she had described. To any one of his friends on the *Times-Picayune* this story might have seemed unusual though not extraordinarily shocking, but Faulkner was still in many ways a romantic, still the young man who had written feelingly about nymphs and fauns. And he was anything but a libertine. "Do you know what the trouble is with me?" he had once said to Dot Oldham. "I'm a puritan." He would continue to dwell on the girl's story and its possibilities for fiction.

Faulkner made use of a character named Popeye in a story called "The Big Shot." He may well have written it not long after the incident in the night club. Not wholly successful in itself, the story employed material which could later be reshaped. The frame was elaborate. In three lines a nameless first-person narrator introduced a newspaper reporter who told the story. (The first-person narrator would reappear to close out the story in four lines.) This Conradian device encountered Conradian difficulties, such as the reporter's precisely describing events taking place in a room in which only one character is present. The basic plot was simple: a political boss protects a gangster against prosecution for traffic violations. He does it again when the offense is hit-and-run driving, not knowing that the victim is his own daughter. Ironically, he has just spent $50,000 bribing a socialite (who later kills himself in shame) to put the daughter's name on the list for the city's premier debutante ball. It was a surprise-ending, formula story, but its base was social criticism and the object was gangsterism in the South. Southern cities have been aping Chicago and New York, says the reporter, but "there is still a kind of hearty clumsiness to our corruption, a kind of chaotic and exasperating innocence. . . ." It was not so much this theme as the three principal characters, however, that would prove useful later.

The reporter describes Popeye as "a slight man with a dead face and dead black hair and eyes and a delicate hooked little nose and no chin, crouching snarling behind the neat blue automatic. . . . a little, dead-looking bird in a tight black suit. . . ." But he is attractive to the prostitutes of DeSoto Street and considerate of his "aged mother," whom he visits each summer in Pensacola, "telling her that he was a hotel clerk." He is a bootlegger who hates liquor and a dope fiend who takes "snow." He is a murderer who can lie in his cell all day without bothering to deny the crime or obtain a lawyer. Popeye seemed a caricature rather than a character.

His protector is Dal Martin, "this Volstead Napoleon, this little corporal of polling booths. . . ." Martin is the son of a Mississippi tenant farmer. Physically he is a "peasant," large, stolid, and slow-moving. Rich enough to have built a mansion on political graft, he still dips the cheapest snuff and characteristically sits "motionless save for the slow thrust of his lower lip." The crucial experience of his life occurred when his tenant-farmer father sent him to the big house with a message. Standing there at the front door, a small boy, he heard the owner say, "Dont you ever come to my front door again. When you come here, you go around to the kitchen door and tell one of the niggers what you want." This is the stimulus on which he builds his whole career, aping the man who has humiliated him before the grinning Negro servant, so that he may ultimately be the one to tell others where to go and come. His blindness will finally cost the lives of his wife and daughter.

Martin's daughter, Wrennie, is "a thin creature, a little overdressed" in whose "little vivid shallow face" the eyes move "like darting mice." Her father does not know what goes on behind "her little painted mask" of a face or who is really taking her to "the Chinese Gardens, the Gold Slippers, the Night Boats. . . ." (During his career Reno DeVaux operated places called the Showboat and the Crystal Gardens; another entrepreneur ran one called the Silver Slipper.) He does not care who her escorts are "just so they were not bums, the Popeyes and Monks and Reds that he used. . . ." Faulkner would return to these characters, this locale, and these themes.

By the time *Soldiers' Pay* was published on February 25 in an edition of 2,500 copies, Faulkner was back in New Orleans. It was just as well. He had inscribed presentation copies for his mother, Estelle, Myrtle Ramey, and a few others. Miss Maud soon found that it differed from *The Marble Faun* in more ways than just its genre. Her standards—religious, moral, and aesthetic—were all of a piece, and they were rigorous. (The first words Jimmy Falkner, Johncy's boy, remembered hearing were "Nanny's": "You've got a back like the Old Colonel's," she said, "but you've got to be a better man than he was.") She could no doubt adjust to Donald Mahon's maiming, but the sexual by-play involving Januarius Jones, Emmy, Cecily Saunders, and George Farr must have come as a shock. She wrote to her son in New Orleans and told him that leaving the country was about the best thing he could do. "You know, Holland," she confided to Auntee, "there wasn't anything else for Billy to do after that came out—he couldn't stay here." Murry Falkner had been told that the book wasn't fit to read. So he refused to open his son's first novel and went on with his Zane Grey. Phil Stone tried to give a gift copy to the University of Mississippi library, which declined to buy one. The university also declined to accept the gift copy and would continue to do so for some time. Before long Miss Maud would change her mind, gradually becoming convinced that her son would be a great man. But this was scarcely an auspicious debut as far as Oxford was concerned.

On his return to New Orleans, Faulkner had moved in with Spratling in a new place on the other side of the old block. Marc and Lucille Antony had taken a long-term lease on a building at 632 St. Peter Street, almost at the corner of Cabildo Alley and just diagonally across the street from Le Petit Salon. Their gallery and shop were on the first floor and their apartment was on the third. They rented out the second floor, and Bill Spratling was their attic tenant. The accommodations were roomier than Faulkner's former ones. The main room was large, the brick walls surmounted by a sharply sloping roof supported by thick beams, so that the effect was much like that of an A-frame house. At the far end were a kitchen and bathroom. One visitor remembered the light filtering through the dusty windowpanes to illuminate "a large room, littered with odds and ends of painting paraphernalia, a palette, uncleaned from the day before, an empty easel, empty bottles on the floor, a low bed cut off from the rest of the room by drapery of indistinct design, carelessly thrown over a wire that stretched from one wall to the other." With Faulkner's help, Spratling made some additions and alterations. Opening a dormer window, a guest would see a bare wooden platform built on the sharply sloping rear roof. At one party Spratling called Faulkner out of the shadows to meet an attractive girl named Flo Field. She had written some one-act plays but made her living by organizing the first guide service in the French Quarter. To her, Faulkner looked like a shy man who found meeting people actually distasteful. He discovered that he liked her, however, and after a while invited her to crawl through the window and out onto the platform with him. She looked out, she said, saw pure death in the runways of the alleys below, and declined.

At other parties Faulkner must have felt even more like escaping. On one occasion Spratling borrowed from the Antonys a set of a dozen glasses, in an expensive pattern with red diamonds on a white base. One of the guests that night was Oliver La Farge—a young writer who talked a lot about the Southwest. Sometimes he wore a beaded Indian headband to emphasize his dark good looks and would do "the Eagle dance," climbing up onto a table and leaping off for verisimilitude. He would later create something of a scandal in giving vent to his anger at his dinner partner by biting her arm and drawing blood. This night he was less vociferous. He merely started dropping the Antonys' glasses out the dormer window, one by one, to hear them crashing on the pavement of the alley below. Ham

Basso remembered a more spectacular diversion in which Faulkner actually joined: "a fine game of tag one night across the steeply angled roofs of a narrow block of the Quarter. . . ." Not all of the contestants could have passed a sobriety test. Often, neither could Faulkner, but his heavy drinking seems to have been little noted. "*Everybody* was a heavy drinker then," Louis Andrews Fischer said, looking back at those days in the Quarter.

Faulkner continued to see friends he had made in New Orleans—but not all of them. A coolness had developed between him and members of *The Double Dealer* group who had never particularly taken to him after his comment that he could write a play like *Hamlet* if he wanted to. (Neither had they been charmed by his attributing his not listening to them to defective hearing.) The publication of his first novel had done nothing to lessen his self-assurance or their resentment. But often George Healy, now a member of the *Times-Picayune* staff, would see him visiting the newsroom "to talk with Bradford, Lyle Saxon, and others on the staff who, like himself, were turning out books."

He kept track of other friends through their work. Anita Loos had scored a great success the previous year when Boni & Liveright had published *Gentlemen Prefer Blondes: The Illuminating Diary of a Professional Lady.* In it Lorelei Lee charmingly and pseudo-naïvely related the story of relationships with several gentleman friends and with her similarly inclined friend, Dorothy. Faulkner wrote Miss Loos from New Orleans in a letter which he dated "Something Febry 1926." He had just read Spratling's copy of the book, "So I galloped out and got myself one." He sent her his "envious congratulations" on Dorothy, on the way she had portrayed her through the diarist, "through the intelligence of that elegant moron of a cornflower." But Anita had played a rotten trick on her admiring public, he said. "How many of them, do you think, will ever know that Dorothy really has something, that the dancing man, le gigolo, was really somebody? My God, its charming—best hoax since Witter Binner's [*sic*] Spectral School in verse—most of them will be completely unmoved—even your rather clumsy gags wont get them—and the others will only find it slight and humorous. The Andersons even mentioned Ring Lardner in talking to me about it. But perhaps that was what you were after, and you have builded better than you knew: I am still rather Victorian in my prejudices regarding the intelligence of women, despite Elinor Wylie and Willa Cather and all the balance of them. But I wish I had thought of Dorothy first."

On New Year's Eve, Sherwood Anderson had written to Alfred Stieglitz that they were off for California on January 2, 1926, but would return to New Orleans about February 15 to stay there until May when they would go to their farm in Virginia. On February 22 he was back in New Orleans. "Both I and Elizabeth, my wife," he wrote his brother, "are pretty sick of people." He did not elaborate. Faulkner had seen the Andersons in February according to his letter to Anita Loos, and he had not indicated that any of their displeasure with people had been directed toward him. Soon, however, he must have felt it, and to such an extent that he forgot or blocked out the memory of the meeting he mentioned to Anita Loos. Writing to Manuel Komroff, Faulkner mentioned getting to know Anderson in New Orleans in 1925. "When I next saw him in New Orleans," he continued, "he had taken umbrage at me in the meantime; I never did know why, and he wouldn't even speak." Anderson made the "umbrage" a matter of record about two months later when he wrote Horace Liveright on April 29. The context was generous: he had seen a good review of *Soldiers' Pay* in *The New York Times* and he hoped that the sales would be encouraging both to Faulkner and Liveright. He hoped Liveright would encourage Faulkner to keep at work. Liveright was free to repeat some of the good things Anderson was saying about Faulkner but Anderson himself could not say them. "I do not like the man personally very much," he said. "He was so nasty to me personally that I don't want to write him myself. . . ."

The breach was now real enough. Faulkner felt it and Anderson said it. What had caused it? The relationship had started well enough, if in a somewhat one-sided way, with Elizabeth Prall and Sherwood Anderson in turn being benefactress and benefactor to young Bill Faulkner. Yet there had been rough spots. Once during his previous stay in New Orleans, the Andersons had invited Faulkner to meet a close friend, Ferdinand Schevill, when he came to New Orleans to visit them. After Schevill had departed Elizabeth Anderson told Faulkner she thought he had been rude to him, and Faulkner "denied that he had been rude at all." She may not have been surprised at this response. Faulkner thought what he thought, and it was hard if not impossible for anyone to change his mind. He had a superiority complex, she said, and he let it show. Moreover, he was a complicated man with expensive tastes that he could not satisfy. This left scars on him, and perhaps increased what was already a supersensitivity.

Any resentment or coolness Anderson's wife felt would inevitably have had some effect on the two men. Another family matter might have had an even more direct consequence. In August of 1924 Anderson's eldest boy, seventeen-year-old Bob, had come to New Orleans to visit him. Spratling and Faulkner came to know Bob sometime during that visit or a subsequent one. Neither found him particularly appealing now. Faulkner told Spratling they ought to send Bob Anderson to college where he would learn how to buy clothes and ties. Spratling said they found him "uppity," and their response was direct. "Bill and I took his clothes," said Spratling, "and set him loose in the street naked." There is no indication of Sherwood Anderson's knowing about this or reacting against either Spratling or Faulkner because of it. But it was the kind of thing which could come to mind later to intensify a resentment once it had taken root from some other immediate cause.

Anderson and Faulkner had been cross-grained of each other more than once despite their playful collaboration and pleasure in each other's company. For one thing, there was the matter of background. Anderson and Faulkner were alike in many of their impulses and attitudes toward their art. But apart from that area they were very different. As Faulkner had said in his Dallas *Morning News* essay, he thought Anderson as Middle Western as a field of corn. And though Anderson loved New Orleans and enjoyed Mobile, and though he had bought a Virginia farm for a permanent home, he would criticize the South to Faulkner, from the wealthy class to the slave class. Faulkner could not but have resented some of the criticism, on behalf of the Old Colonel if not for himself. Moreover, Anderson thought that Faulkner himself was poisoned with pernicious Southern attitudes. He wrote later about a kind of insanity in the South from "those decayed families making claim to aristocracy, often living very isolated lives in lonely run-down Southern towns, surrounded by Negroes." There was cruelty toward the Negroes, Anderson said, which often took the form of sexual aggression by white men. On the plantations and in the small towns there were no books. "Faulkner has got hold of the queer sort of insanity that results. He understands and draws clearly the little white businessman, the small white farmers; still at the same time, there is in him also a lot of the same old bunk about the South. I remember, when I first met him, when he had first come from his own little Southern town, sitting with him one evening before the cathedral in New Orleans while he contended with entire seriousness that the cross between the white man and the Negro woman always resulted, after the first crossing, in sterility. He spoke of the cross between the jack and the mare that produced the mule and said that, as between the white man and the Negro woman, it was just the same." It is not impossible that Faulkner, at twenty-seven, may have believed this, but it seems highly unlikely. Evidence to the contrary had been around him all his life. It seems likely that Faulkner was engaging in another form of tall-tale telling, but doing it so convincingly that Anderson bit again, as he had in "A Meeting South." Yet Faulkner surely must have sensed something of Anderson's anti-Southern attitudes which in some way spilled over to include Faulkner himself. And Faulkner was keenly aware not only of regional differences but also of social ones—even to the extent of exaggerating them. Anderson's mother, he wrote years later, "had been a bound girl, his father a day laborer. . . ." This was hardly true. Anderson's mother had been sent by her widowed mother to live and work for another family at the age of eight, and Anderson's father had been both a dealer and manufacturer of fine harnesses before he began to fail. But to Faulkner—the aristocrat in lineage despite the bohemian role—Anderson's lineage was thus metaphorically of the peasantry. And that was how Faulkner always thought of him, though with affection. He once remembered aloud, smiling, how Anderson had looked at a reception: "like an old carriage horse all dressed up in Sunday finery."

If Faulkner was sensitive enough to feel some of Anderson's unspoken attitudes about him, the same must certainly have been true of Anderson—a man who, according to Faulkner, "expected people to make fun of, ridicule him." Apparently he felt that one of the ways in which Faulkner did this was to make him look ridiculous in print. Anderson may not have read the Dallas *Morning News* essay when it came out, but he did learn of it. If he read it, he could scarcely have missed the implied reservations along with the qualified praise, a praise that might seem even patronizing. Moreover, Anderson felt that Faulkner had made him look ridiculous through his *own* writing. Anderson had accepted as true the things Faulkner had told him about himself early in their acquaintance. He put many of them into the character of David in "A Meeting South." And everyone who knew the two men knew who David was. But afterwards Anderson had learned that Faulkner had not suffered a leg injury in the war. (How much he continued to believe is questionable, though even Phil Stone apparently accepted Faulkner's claim of having a silver plate in his skull—unless he was abetting Faulkner in his pretense.) Much later, when Ben Wasson raised the subject of the breach in their friendship, Anderson told him it had stemmed from that—Faulkner had lied to him about the injury to his leg. He had also mentioned it to Jimmy Feibleman. The story may have cut both ways. Stone was pleased that his friend should be a subject for the pen of the much-admired Sherwood Anderson. Faulkner may have felt some similar reaction, but it may have been accompanied by a distinctly negative one, too. He recognized himself in the story, he said, but "I think that when a writer reaches the point when he's got to write about people he knows, his friends, then he has reached the tragic point."

Of course, the fundamental causes lay deeper—deeper than Faulkner's resentment at Anderson's saying he would recommend Faulkner's "damn manuscript" if he didn't have to read it, deeper than Anderson's chagrin at being taken in by one of Faulkner's stories about himself. Neither man used Hemingway's metaphors about "getting in the ring" with another artist, or winning or defending a "title." But they were both keenly aware of other men's achievements—Anderson perhaps the more generously so of the two. In his way Faulkner was as competitive as Hemingway, though he did not show it as much. Of the writer's goals he would later say, "he don't want to be as good as his coevals, or even as good as Shakespeare, he wants to be better than Shakespeare. He knows that he can't. But that's what he works for." Anderson had once stood in relation to Theodore Dreiser almost as Faulkner had stood in relation to himself. Dreiser's books "filled me with admiration and courage," Anderson wrote. "Here was a man doing something that I also wanted to do." Dreiser was a great writer, Anderson said, but "No more awkward writer ever lived. He can write sentences that fairly jar the teeth out of your head." And then he had ended with a tribute that would cut Dreiser to the heart: "He will remain a significant figure to other American men working in the arts long after men have quit reading his books." Faulkner spoke of Dreiser as Anderson's older brother. Faulkner called Anderson "a giant," the "father of all of my generation." But he made only "two or perhaps three gestures commensurate with gianthood." His prose style was characterized by a "fumbling for exactitude, the exact word and phrase within the limited scope of a vocabulary controlled and even repressed by what was in him almost a fetish of simplicity," and, besides this, his work—his whole output, finally—was that of "only a one- or two-book man."

Anderson would sometimes put his deepest thoughts into acecdote or story form, as with the "dream" of his trying to swap a horse for a night's sleep. He did this later in giving another reason for the estrangement. It reminded him, he said, of a politician's remark about a man who was fighting him. "What is the matter with Bill?" he asked. "Why is he so against me? I can't understand his hatred of me. I never did anything to help him." Elizabeth Anderson had another answer. "Sherwood and Bill were too much alike," she said. "This probably caused the eventual coolness between them." They were both taletellers, both driven to study and to understand people, and to create through their art a reality more satisfying than the one they lived in. They were both supersensitive. Both were geniuses. They were two artists, one declining from the summit of his career, the other beginning the ascent to his zenith. And both probably knew it. The master-disciple relationship is usually doomed from the moment the disciple shows signs of outstripping the master. Before Anderson's death the two men would manage to get on friendly terms again, but the old camaraderie was gone for good.

Anderson had used Faulkner for the purposes of fiction when their friendship was warm and firm. One aspect of Anderson's experience may have gotten into a story which Faulkner could have written during this year when, according to his brother John, he was writing mostly stories. While Faulkner had been in Europe, Anderson had spent part of the summer writing near Marion in isolated southwest Virginia. By the time Faulkner saw him again in February, 1926, Anderson had bought Ripshin Farm, near the one-time lumber town of Troutdale, close to Marion. There was a tiny house on the place and Anderson was planning to have a cabin built there. Troutdale itself had suffered from the failure of its only factory, and people were leaving the ruggedly beautiful country, but Anderson loved it there. In a story called "Black Music," Faulkner used the Virginia mountains for his setting, "the quiet mountains where never many lived." In the action, a New York couple moved there and began to disrupt the ancient order of things.

"Black Music" combined elements which had appeared in earlier stories: a narrator, intellectually superior to the protagonist, who relates the story to him in a port called Rincon; the supernatural as an operative force; and a faun with a supporting cast. The self-exiled protagonist described a vision of Pan which transformed him for one day into a "farn." In this guise he frightened away the *nouveau riche* who had offended the spirits of the mountain with imitation coliseums and amateur theatricals. Now a contented, impoverished old man, he sleeps every night in a roll of tar paper on the roof of the cantina. This is at the suffrance of Mrs. Widrington, wife of the local manager of the Universal Oil Company, which dominates the town.

Another story, radically different in type but possibly written about the same time, made use of similar elements. The title, "Carcassonne," suggested the ancient French city southeast of Toulouse where tourists could see the finest remains of medieval fortifications in Europe. But the setting was again Rincon, and the third-person narration described a protagonist who slept "beneath an unrolled strip of tarred roofing made of paper." It was a short, almost surrealist story of the poet whose skeleton groans and speaks to him and across whose consciousness a wild horse gallops. The poet thinks of Tancred and Godfrey of Bouillon, great leaders of the First Crusade, whom one might imaginatively link with a city such as Carcassonne. But what the protagonist wants most is "to perform something bold and tragical and austere," and he envisions himself "on a buckskin pony with eyes like blue electricity and a mane like tangled fire, galloping up the hill and right off into the high heaven of the world." In the manuscript Faulkner had called the protagonist David, the name Anderson had used in "A Meeting South" and he himself had used in "The Leg." Mrs. Widrington (in the manuscript, "Mrs. Maurier") appeared in this story, too, again the wife of the company manager (this time Standard Oil) by whose sufferance he sleeps under his tar paper in a garret. (It was "slanted in a ruined pitch to the low eaves," and thus not entirely dissimilar from the room Faulkner was sharing with Spratling.) Years later Faulkner called the story fantasy and said, "That's a piece that I've always liked because there was the poet again." It may have been like the poem he wrote in Paris which was so modern he said he didn't know what it meant himself. If so, he had come another step further on the road from poetry to prose, still trying to adapt the devices of one medium to the other.

Another of his efforts at this time may have been a work that proved less recalcitrant than *Elmer* but ultimately no more successful. One version, which apparently started as a story entitled "Once Aboard the Lugger," was begun more than once. At one point Faulkner used the subtitle "The Prohibition Industry in Southern Waters." Less than a dozen manuscript pages and less than four dozen typed pages would survive, but one typed segment which brought the action to a close was numbered sequentially in pen from page 252 to page 268. The first-person narrator was the engineer aboard the lugger, a former pilot adrift after the war had ended on him. But Faulkner drew little on the war and much on what he had gathered of the gangster milieu of New Orleans and the rumrunning trade. The other major characters were the Captain, two brothers from New Orleans named Pete and Joe—the latter running the operation—and the cook, referred to simply as "the nigger." Another segment described an expedition to an island in the Gulf where the crew braved wild cattle and vicious mosquitoes to dig up illicit alcohol intended for conversion into bootleg liquor. The story ended with both Pete and the cook shot by hijackers. In the last lines the latter fled at the approach of a Coast Guard cutter while the narrator dragged the bodies to the galley. Faulkner had finally made fictional use of the rumrunning activities he had often alluded to, and Pete and Joe were apparently drawn from a family he often referred to in later years. He would also remark later that he had destroyed two novels because they just weren't good enough. This apparently was one of them. He would, however, be able to salvage some of its elements for further use.

At this time Faulkner's stories and poems would often go to Phil Stone's office where Sallie Simpson would type them. The Lamb-Fish receivership was still dragging on, and if it had not been for that, there would have been little work in the office. So there was plenty of time for her to type and for Stone to correct and punctuate. Then the stories would go out to the magazines and, just as regularly, come back again. But though Faulkner's name was not appearing in the *Post* or in *Scribner's*, it was appearing elsewhere. It was printed, with his picture, in *The Record* of Sigma Alpha Epsilon, for March, 1926. Ben Wasson had sent them the picture and a few lines about *The Marble Faun*. *The Record* now singled out Faulkner and several other brothers throughout the United States for recent achievements. The brief caption noted that his "book of poetry, 'The Marble Faun,' is attracting wide attention in the South." He continued to attract attention from another source, too. On March 3 the Comptroller General of the United States wrote again, this time not to Murry Falkner but to the former postmaster himself. Where was the $38.25 due to the United States? "Unless this matter is adjusted without further delay," wrote Mr. McCarl, "it will be necessary to make the collection from your bondsmen."

Faulkner turned the letter over to Stone, who wrote their Congressman, B. G. Lowrey, on March 9, asking him to check into the matter to see if the auditors had not made a mistake. Lowrey replied on the nineteenth that the errors arose out of Faulkner's arithmetic in money-order accounts. There was no error in the department's figures. "The auditor did not seem to think that there was anything unusual or reprehensible in a matter of this sort," the old man added reassuringly. "It evidently arose simply through an error in totalling a long column of figures without an adding machine." Having now used all of his political contacts on Faulkner's behalf in his struggle with the United States Postal Department, Stone must have counseled capitulation. There is no evidence that the matter ever came up again.

There were other reasons for Faulkner to travel from New Orleans back to Oxford that spring. On May 24 young Dean Falkner graduated from Oxford High School, and there were other diversions and occasions. *The Phantom of the Opera* came to the Lyric Theatre, and some weeks later ex-Governor Bilbo addressed a public meeting at the Courthouse. With his gaunt, lined cheeks, high forehead, staring eyes, thin mouth, and jutting teeth, he might have been a stand-in for Lon Chaney's Phantom. The master of ceremonies introducing Bilbo was the Honorable John Falkner. In mid-March, Estelle and the children had come home again. Her family teased her about her shuttling back and forth from the Far East, calling her a commuter. The teasing was doubtless meant in part to cover a nagging worry of the Oldhams. Estelle had found conditions unchanged in Shanghai. Hers had been an arranged and enforced marriage, but she had tried to make it work, the more so after the children had been born. Now she could see that the dissolution of the bonds between herself and her husband was continuing, and time and distance, which she had first thought might reverse the process, had only made it more inexorable.

When the warm weather came, there was the Oxford golf course. The freshman greenskeeper, Thomas D. Clark, met Faulkner then, "a short little man dressed in baggy, worn golfknickers . . . his hair was graying and he had a funny moustache." The nine-hole course, broken by clumps of trees, was in the same shape as ever. "It was hard to tell at times where fairways ended and roughs began—it was all rough." There was a good deal to do: cutting and raking grass, adding new sand to the "greens" and then pouring used motor oil on it to keep it in place. Sometimes Clark would be aided by two volunteers: Faulkner and a small Negro boy named Willie. One of the perquisites of the job was fishing balls out of the three water holes, "and Bill was not averse to picking up a few stray balls to replenish his own slender stock." In a rare talkative mood Faulkner might fall in beside Clark and stroll with him past the cemetery, which held both Confederate dead and cadavers no longer substantial enough for the dissection room of the medical school. At other times, when Faulkner had retreated into his interior world of imagination or dream, it was "truly marvelous to see him play by us as though we were complete strangers."

But when he concentrated on his game, as he might in a friendly twosome with Phil Stone or foursome with Ella Somerville and Dot Oldham, he was again the hole-in-one golfer, for he knew "every gully, stump hole, and clump of weeds on the course." He had more than usual to mull over as he strolled the course that spring. Reviews of *Soldiers' Pay* had been appearing since early April.

One of them was the review in the *Times* which Anderson had mentioned in his letter to Liveright. The anonymous reviewer said that the novel treated a theme as old as the *Odyssey.* It was a book that ranked among great conceptions of war and man such as Laurence Stallings' *What Price Glory?.* In form, it displayed "the episodic and elliptical pattern of experimental fiction." Written with "hard intelligence as well as consummate pity," the novel showed "a sensuous regard for the feeling of life that is quite Hellenic." And it rang true. Anderson had written Liveright, "I have a hunch on that he is a man who will write the kind of novels that will sell. He is modern enough and not too modern; also he is smart. If I were you I would encourage him to keep at work. . . . He may be a little bit like a thoroughbred colt who needs a race or two before he can do his best."

In the same month E. C. Beckwith wrote in *The Literary Review* that *Soldiers' Pay* stood alone among novels of disillusioned veterans, and though Thomas Boyd disliked the "honest but slap-dash" impressionistic manner, he liked the book's "fervor and strength." In unsigned reviews, the Springfield *Republican* deplored the soldierly language and the *Independent* acclaimed "an extraordinary performance." In June, Larry Barretto regretted in the *Herald Tribune* Faulkner's lack of restraint and discipline, for it was "almost a great book." L. S. Morris in *The New Republic* disliked the self-consciousness and straining for effect, but saw beneath them "a nervous, swift talent." In July, Louis Kronenberger would also deplore in *The International Book Review* what he called a lack of control in the novel's method while granting that "it very often achieves a vividness, a fervor, an immediacy which ordered procedure would not project." Later, however, in *The Literary Digest,* he would remark on the book's "rich compound of imagination, observation, and experience." It was a world of Faulkner's own creation in which shadows with the reality of men groped "through a maze complex enough to be at once pitiful and comic, passionate, tormenting and strange." Nearer home the reviews were even better. In his widely read *Times-Picayune* column, John McClure called *Soldiers' Pay* the "most noteworthy first novel of the year." The novel moved him so much that he could think of "none of the younger novelists, and few of the older, who write as well as Mr. Faulkner." Donald Davidson, writing in the Nashville *Tennessean*, could think of three whose writing Faulkner's excelled: Theodore Dreiser, Sinclair Lewis, and John Dos Passos; though there were mannered phrases and attempts at smartness in the prose, the novel displayed a judicious use of techniques developed by Joyce and others, and it combined sensitivity and power. All in all, it was an encouraging reception for a first novel. As Boni & Liveright sent the author copies of the reviews, he would give them to his mother. Doubtless they helped to alter her original judgment of the book. Years later Miss Maud would tell one of her daughters-in-law that she loved the book, that it was the Faulkner novel she should read first.

Full spring came to Oxford with blooming roses and magnolias and burgeoning trees. In June, Myrtle Ramey would be married to a Harvard boy named Fred Demarest. Dolly would be matron of honor and Johncy one of the ushers. The Oldham house was busy with business as well as social concerns. Major and Mrs. Oldham and Dorothy (now an M.A. in history from the university) were preparing to go into business that summer, incorporating the Oxford Beverage Company to market beverages and confections. Later Estelle and the children would go to Monteagle, Tennessee, to spend the summer. It was time for Bill Faulkner to leave Oxford again, too.

Five-year-old William Evans Stone V was always glad to see his uncle Phil's Model T Ford pull up in front of his home in Charleston. He liked his uncle's friend, who was "Bill" to him. Uncle Phil had already told him about the flying accident in Canada that had left Bill with a silver plate in his head. "On these visits," Billy Stone remembered, "my uncle and my father, law partners, would discuss the business of the firm while Bill would entertain my sisters and me by telling us stories; or he would play golf on the local links." And he was apparently still as welcome among the adults as he was among the children. So it was natural that, when the Stones prepared to spend the summer in Pascagoula, they should invite him to spend some time with them again.

He was glad to accept the invitation. He liked the Stones and he liked the place. Helen Baird would probably be there, too. Pascagoula would provide a wonderful retreat from the heat of north Mississippi, and the working conditions would be ideal: time to write in the morning and afternoon, and diversion when he wanted it. These conditions would be especially welcome now. He would begin another novel. The subject was ready to his hand, and much of the material was ripe for treatment now that he had some distance from it. Other material, though, had an immediacy which would give the intensity a novel ought to have. There were plenty of people for him to draw on: Lillian Marcus, Julius Friend, Sam Gilmore, Bill Spratling, Josh Baird, Helen Baird, Sherwood Anderson. He would put them all in it.

28

June, 1926–June, 1927

The next summer he returned because he found that he liked that much water . . . the pre-dawn, to be broken presently by the violent near-subtropical yellow-and-crimson day almost like an audible explosion, but still dark for a little while yet, the dark ship creeping onto the shrimp grounds in a soundless sternward swirl of phosphorus like a drowning tumble of fireflies, the youth lying face down on the peak staring into the dark water watching the disturbed shrimp burst outward-shooting in fiery and fading fans like the trails of tiny rockets.

—"Mississippi" (29–30)

"He was a white man, except he was awful sunburned and kind of shabby dressed—no necktie and hat. . . . He said he was a liar by profession, and he made good money at it, enough to own a Ford as soon as he got it paid out. I think he was crazy. Not dangerous: just crazy."
"What was his name? Did he tell you?"
"Yes. It was. . . . Wait. . . . Oh, yes, I remember—Faulkner, that was it."

"A book is the writer's secret life, the dark twin of a man: you can't reconcile them."

—*Mosquitoes* (145, 251)

That summer of 1926 the accommodations were considerably better than they had been at The Camp the previous year. Frank Lewis, Myrtle Stone's father, had taken the Baird house with a view to buying it eventually. Mrs.

James H. Baird had come down from Nashville on a visit one summer and bought the house for $12,000 because she liked the roofline. It was set back 100 feet on a lot 110 feet wide and 500 feet deep. The front yard was shaded by live oaks and oleanders, and the back 300 feet was thick with tall grass. There the Bairds would make home movies, dressing the servants as natives and themselves as explorers. On the broad expanse in front of the house they would sometimes hold tea parties, dressed in costumes of the 1890's.

The Bairds were a Scotch-Irish family who had settled in east Tennessee and prospered there. Dan W. Baird was a successful lumberman who, with his nephew, A. E. Baird, had founded *The Southern Lumberman*, in which he was among the first to advocate conservation and reforestation. In 1890 one of his two sons, James H. Baird, took over his interest and married autocratic Mary Lou Freeman. She gave him four children: Louis Foster ("Lefty"), Kenneth, Peter ("Josh"), and Helen. Lefty had been born in 1898, and the others had followed at two-year intervals. Their father did well enough to build a mansion in Nashville with a wine cellar, a ballroom, and forty-four other rooms.

Lefty and Kenneth were ingenious and mischievous boys who made life difficult for both men and animals. The two younger children could only watch and admire them. Josh was asthmatic and Helen had been badly burned with gasoline from her waist to her upper arms. Longing to join in the older boys' hoaxes and devilment, she sat instead in her father's four-wall library and read voraciously. When she was little, Josh had read to her. As she grew he would sometimes play Noah's Ark and other children's games with her. She was her father's only daughter—one girl among three boys—and her mother's favorite.

In 1915 Dan Baird died and James lost his life in an accident. Mary Lou Baird and her children divided their time between Nashville and Pascagoula. Helen still read and listened quietly to her lively brothers. At mealtime their conversation would range from religion and history to tall tales. She was close only to Josh. But they were all talented people, well-read, quick with ideas, retentive in memory—and very emotional.

The only formal education Helen had received was at Miss Hare's School for Girls in Evanston, Illinois. It was essentially a finishing school, where she had plenty of opportunity to continue her reading and to work in several media. She had early shown a talent for sculpture. Sometimes she would take wire and shape it into a frame. Then she would wrap it in strips of crepe paper, using LePage's white paste as a binding agent, and the wire form would gradually assume the shape of a horse, a man, or a woman.

Sometimes she would use other materials—clay or papier-mâché. She was back home again before long to enter the swirl of the Nashville debutante's world, where she became one of the pacesetters. She liked the crowd and the life, and she thought rather well of herself, too.

The summers in Pascagoula were as lively as the winters in Nashville. Such friends as Guy Lyman would come to visit. Guy was a bright and attractive young man who moved in influential circles in New Orleans and would later make a career there in insurance. The only book he admitted reading was *Black Beauty*, but his friends said he could sell ice to Eskimos. The group would swim, sail, and fish. With Lefty and Kenneth urging him on, Guy would harpoon a manta ray from a thirty-five-foot boat, then put a skiff in the water and hold fast as the ray dragged him along. He would try to maneuver the beast into shallow water or up on the beach. Seizing an ax, he would leap onto the ray's back and try to sink the blade into its brain before the wings could crush him.

By this summer Josh was established as a sportswriter for the *Times-Picayune*. Lefty, the imaginative, high-strung boy who could do anything, was now a naval architect. Kenneth was gone, too, living now in Hammond, Louisiana. Still brilliant, still charming, they were well-off, traveling with people like themselves, talking a good deal and drinking a good deal. The family had begun to drift over to New Orleans, where Helen had been living when she had first met Bill Faulkner. Mary Lou Baird had moved to North Carolina, but Helen spent a good deal of time in Pascagoula at the home of her aunt, Mrs. E. B. Martin, next to their old home. And Josh would come over from New Orleans whenever he could. Bill Faulkner was ready to take up his relationship with Helen Baird where he had left off the previous year, and to improve it if he could.

That was the summer the seawall was built, for more homes were going up and Pascagoula was changing. But Bill Faulkner found that nothing seemed to have changed between Helen and himself. They would go sailing, together and in groups. Sometimes Josh might join them, quiet, whittling on a special kind of pipe he had designed himself. They would lie on the jetties, and he would tell her stories. They would sit at night on the swings of porches screened in against the mosquitoes.

One night as they sat there she gazed up at the indigo heavens. "Look," she said, "the moon looks like a fingernail in the sky."

"May I use that?" Faulkner asked.

Bill gave Helen gifts, as he had earlier. He made a little book for her, a forty-eight-page allegorical novelette which may have grown from stories told on those sunny afternoons. He gave it the title he had meant for his first novel: "Mayday." The protagonist was another of his wounded-soldier heroes: Sir Galwyn of Arthgyl. Like a quester-knight he had journeyed on, flanked by companions called Hunger and Pain. He conversed with a figure called Time and was vouchsafed a vision of St. Francis of Assisi. He finally freed himself of his troublesome companions as, joining a maiden called Little Sister Death, he drowned himself in a river at the end of his quest. Faulkner had used her image in "The Kid Learns," but setting, idiom, and treatment were different here. Bound in with the story were colored drawings he had made.

Helen Baird was no longer an avid reader, and apparently she did not set any great store by these homemade books. She had not even known, the previous year, that Faulkner was a writer until he had told her. The truth was that she appeared only to tolerate him. This was the feeling her friends had. She would lecture him about his drinking; "I know," he would say. To someone like Helen, who had enjoyed the company of the Nashville boys in dress suits and patent-leather slippers, this small man was different and strange. Barefoot, wearing an open shirt and white duck pants tied with a length of rope, he looked unkempt if not downright disreputable. His thick shock of now slightly graying hair was often uncombed. He did not shave every day, and when he did, he might wait until evening. Mary Lou Baird found the shoelessness and the strong pipe a particular strain on her sensibilities. Young Betty Black, from New Orleans, dared to defend him to Mrs. Baird.

"He has great talent," she said.

"He smells," the older woman replied.

Moreover, this young man persisted in associating with shrimp fishermen and other Pascagoulans whom people like the Bairds would not normally meet. He showed a particular fondness for a man called Bill Lolo, or Lollo. People thought him a kind of bogeyman who was not very bright and spent his time wandering around the bayous. He didn't work, and he would emerge from the woods from time to time with a horse and cart. He had no shoes, and he had been without them so long, people said, that his big toes stood so straight that he couldn't possibly get a pair of shoes on his feet if he wanted to. He seemed a harmless wild man. This was the kind of person Bill Faulkner chose to associate with. Mary Lou Baird would have been unalterably opposed to anything other than a casual relationship between him and her daughter. "How can you stand going around with someone who looks like that wild man?" she would ask. But it was no real source of worry, for Helen appeared not to think about any such thing herself. As the languorous days of the summer unfolded, this was not true of Bill Faulkner.

He thought a good deal about this short, stocky, vivacious girl with the dark hair and gypsy-like look. He also put up with a good deal from her. Once she stood him up on a date. Returning home, she found he had been sitting there for four hours. When she apologized he said, "That's all right, I've been working." That didn't surprise her, for by now it seemed to her that writing was what he lived for. It might have been love that he felt, or passion, compounded with admiration for a girl who was talented, forthright, and belonged to a physical type which appealed to him. She had been badly injured, as the scars testified, and suffering always affected him. Moreover, that childlike directness, the determination to have relationships on her own impatient terms or not at all, appealed to him. He loved children as much as ever—especially their honesty and lack of pretense—and these qualities in a grown woman could be particularly disarming.

If she was not especially impressed by the poems or by *Mayday*, he would write something else. He began a novel which he called *Mosquitoes* —a title close to the one he had used in Europe before he put the work aside for *Elmer*. One of the major characters—himself a novelist—in these new pages would say, "I believe that every word a writing man writes is put down with the ultimate intention of impressing some woman that probably don't care anything at all for literature, as is the nature of women." (250) Another character (who meticulously carried a stick and wore a hat) thought how "it was unbearable to believe that he had never had the power to stir women. . . ." (346) Elsewhere the fictional novelist would remark, "you don't commit suicide when you are disappointed in love. You write a book." (228) Later, speaking about creation, he would mention the "voraciousness" that made the artist "stand beside himself with a notebook in his hand always, putting down all the charming things that ever happen to him, killing them for the sake of some problematical something he might or he might not ever use. . . . love, youth, sorrow and hope and despair—they were nothing at all to me until I found later some need of a particular reaction to put in the mouth of some character of whom I wasn't at that time certain. . . ." (320)

As in the summer before, the living and working conditions were good.

His room in the big two-story house was furnished with the essentials: a day bed, a chair, and a table for his typewriter. Myrtle Stone still made her own bread and served plenty of ice cream. Wooden benches had been built encircling the bases of the big live oak trees on the front lawn. Faulkner would carry pen, paper, and a camp stool out with him. Bending over the wooden bench, he would begin to cover the sheets of plain white paper with the tiny letters printed in black ink. For a change he might shift to the tree seat and pull up a wooden bench to serve as a desk. Rising early as he did, he could get in some work before the children got up. Then at swimming time he might take them out into the shallow water. He would tell them stories as before. One photograph showed him with Rosebud on his lap. As he leaned on one arm his pose was relaxed, yet it was close and protective. He could always work in the afternoon, too, when they were napping. Occasionally he would have the benefit of their comments and questions. Did he get any money for writing, Jack Stone once asked him. "Sometimes I get a nickel and sometimes a dime," he answered. Jack was impressed. When a section of a chapter was completed, Faulkner would transcribe it on his portable typewriter, stiff now in its action and clearly in need of adjustment. One thing which he had done when he was typing *Soldiers' Pay* and *Elmer,* he did not do now. He no longer counted the number of words in each section and chapter. On page 125 he wrote the small figure 28,000 in pencil in the lower right-hand corner. But after that he did not bother.

Faulkner with Rosebud Stone, Pascagoula, Mississippi, summer, 1926.

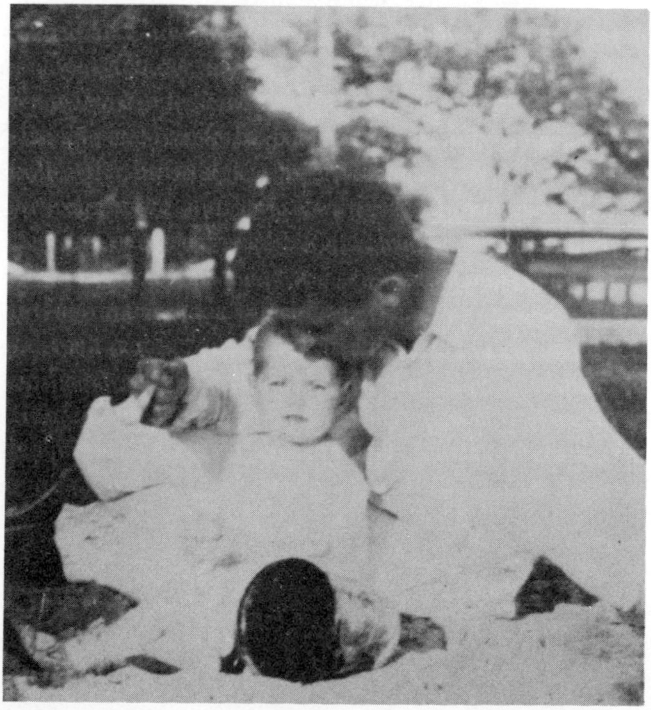

While the pages piled up, he drew on both Pascagoula and New Orleans, primarily the latter. As in earlier fiction, he was also using his own previous work, published and unpublished. At the same time he was sketching in situations, character types, and relationships which he would develop in later work. He seemed to be writing quite consciously in a well-known vein: the novel of ideas with just a touch of the *Künstlerroman.* It was a work about artists and hangers-on, the sort many were doing. Aldous Huxley was probably best-known among them, although D. H. Lawrence had treated some of the same concerns, if in a much different manner, in *Women in Love.* Also, if it was a novel which would chastise dilettantes and poseurs, it would also shock the bourgeois. In its pages the author would mention, and in one instance describe, masturbation, conception, constipation, evacuation, lesbianism, syphilis, and perversion. Characters would use words like "bastard" and "whore." It was a very different book indeed from *Soldiers' Pay,* not to mention *Mayday.*

If the subject and manner of the novel suggested Huxley, the protagonist suggested Eliot. Widower Ernest Talliaferro, a wholesale buyer of women's clothing, was cut from the same pattern as Prufrock. Aging, worried about his attire and thinning hair, he was excited by women but unsuccessful despite a self-regenerating faith in the ultimate success of stratagems of seduction which were mainly verbal. The prose was full of echoes of Eliot, not just from "The Love Song of J. Alfred Prufrock" but from other poems such as "The Waste Land" as in the scene-setting in the Vieux Carré, where Faulkner wrote, "Spring and the cruelest months were gone. . . ." (10) But through the course of the novel he would borrow more from himself than from anyone else, as he demonstrated in the same passage. New Orleans was like "an aging yet still beautiful courtesan" (10), the operating simile he had used in the sketch "New Orleans," which had appeared in *The Double Dealer,* and in the companion poem. Other descriptions of Jackson Square closely resembled those in the *Times-Picayune* stories.

The most obvious borrowing, though few could know it, was from "Don Giovanni," the unpublished story which he had written in the summer of 1925 and probably intended for the *Times-Picayune.* As Herbie had been transformed into Ernest Talliaferro, so Morrison would become the writer, Dawson Fairchild. Even Miss Steinbauer, the object of Herbie's designs, would reappear, this time provided with a first name, Genevieve, and with still another suitor whom she preferred to the women's clothing buyer. Faulkner was using the early story as a frame for his new novel, a strategy he would continue at the end.

Though Talliaferro's general configuration resembled Prufrock's, he also suggested Januarius Jones of *Soldiers' Pay* and in some specific details seemed quite close to Elmer Hodge. Though he was no satyr, Talliaferro seemed to think about seduction as much as Jones did, and his advances to a lush young woman named Jenny strongly resembled Jones's pursuit of Emmy. Like Elmer, Talliaferro (born Tarver) was climbing from a most undistinguished background. (Three of his brothers achieved careers identical with those of Juliet Bunden's brothers in "Adolescence.") Like Elmer, he had one serious relationship with a woman which was followed by a fruitless questing after another. (Jenny closely resembled Myrtle Monson, unsuccessfully pursued by Elmer.) But he was even more of an anti-hero than Elmer was. For whereas Elmer aspired to art, Talliaferro was a hanger-on, tolerated by artists and used by a gushing patroness of artists. He was a little like the annoying mosquitoes which reappeared throughout the novel as a leitmotif, or recurring image.

On the August evening when the novel opens, Talliaferro is visiting a sculptor named Gordon, inviting him on a yachting party on behalf of the patroness, Mrs. Maurier—who is fascinated by artists as was her namesake (later changed to Mrs. Widdrington) in "Carcassonne." Gordon's attic studio, with its high windows and curtained-off bed, its "unevenly boarded floor . . . rough stained walls" and "crouching lintels cutting the immaculate ruined pitch of walls" (11) suggested Bill Spratling's apartment of St. Peter Street quite as much as Gordon suggested Spratling himself. The sculptor had blue eyes, curly hair, and a red beard, and was often inarticulate. But his manner and talent, his power and his "intolerant hawk's face" (318), suggested the dark-haired mustachioed artist who taught sculpture as well as architecture at Tulane. And as Faulkner had envied Spratling's talent, so Talliaferro returns to Gordon's dirty studio "under that spell put on us by those we admire doing things we ourselves cannot do. . . ." (10)

Mrs. Maurier was a Helen Hokinson cartoon of a woman, but rather loud, affected, over-genteel, and self-congratulatory, priding herself on her devotion to the arts and the duties of her station. To some Orleanians she would suggest wealthy Elizabeth Werlein, of the music store family, who was thought to have a penchant for artists and intellectuals and appeared very soignée. But Mrs. Maurier had no more rapport with Gordon than did Talliaferro. Through the course of the novel it would become clear that

Gordon—awkward, arrogant, withdrawn, and unhappy—was more truly the archetypal artist than any of the group Mrs. Maurier would gather together.

Her niece, eighteen-year-old Patricia Robyn, was drawn to a marble by Gordon which was much like herself. Faulkner had exalted the type before and would continue to regard it as the highest kind of female beauty: "you got again untarnished and high and clean that sense of swiftness, of space encompassed; but on looking again it was as before: motionless and passionately eternal—the virginal breastless torso of a girl, headless, armless, legless, in marble temporarily caught and hushed yet passionate still for escape, passionate and simple and eternal in the equivocal derisive darkness of the world." (11) The statue was Faulkner's own Winged Victory of Samothrace, the archetype to which Jo-Addie belonged as would later Faulkner heroines. As he got further into the novel he would make Pat Robyn less and less feminine despite her swiftness and grace. She was brusque and mannerless. There was "something masculine" (23) about her jaw. Running, she showed "her taut simple body, almost breastless and with the fleeting hips of a boy. . . ." (82) Called "Gus" by her brother, she ducks men and outswims them. She is direct and simple as a child. ("I love bread, don't you?" she asks. [170]) Because of her, Gordon agrees to join the party. Before the trip is over she will obsess not only Gordon but also steward David West. Her appeal to them is enormous despite her reluctance at emotional involvement with any man but her brother and despite her real plainness, as manifested in the careless bangs of her short, dark, coarse hair. Many of her attributes in both appearance and manner would remind other Orleanians of Helen Baird.

As if to show that there were types even more antagonistic to art than the dilettantes, Faulkner introduced a Rotarian as unsubtle as some of Sinclair Lewis' broadest characters. He may have been suggested by the Northern commercial magazine writer whom Sherwood Anderson had mentioned in *The Double Dealer.* There was no doubt that novelist Dawson Fairchild, the host at the luncheon table, was Sherwood Anderson. Though he was unmarried and came from Indiana rather than Ohio, his burly physical appearence was Anderson's. His locutions and garrulousness were Anderson's, and so were his literary strengths and weaknesses. (He had even appeared in the *Dial.*) Genial, gentle, and speculative, he was warmly drawn, the center of any group in which he appeared. He had a "blobby benign face." (245) Born "an American of a provincial midwestern lower middle class family" (241), he stands in awe of education. "His writing seems fumbling, not because life is unclear to him, but because of his innate humorless belief that, though it bewilder him at times, life at bottom is sound and admirable and fine. . . ." (242) But if he can get "himself and his own bewilderment and inhibitions out of the way by describing . . . American life as American life is, it will become eternal and timeless despite him." (243) Sometimes Faulkner gave Fairchild Anderson's very words as well. They included not only the Al Jackson stories—Faulkner would expand the ones he and Anderson had made up—but characteristic remarks and turns of speech, too.

Also seated at Fairchild's table at Broussard's were a poet and critic. The poet, Mark Frost, was "a tall, ghostly young man with a thin evaporation of fair hair and a pale prehensile mouth" (34) who produced "an occasional cerebral and obscure poem in four or seven lines reminding one somehow of the function of evacuation excruciatingly and incompletely performed" (54). Now and again throughout the voyage, Frost would utter a ghostly apothegm or lay claim to being the best poet in New Orleans. Noting his appearance, his propensity for stretching out flat whenever possible, and the brevity ascribed to his poems, some residents of the Quarter thought of Samuel Louis Gilmore, long-standing contributor to *The Double Dealer* and author of one-act plays produced at Le Petit Théâtre.

The other man at Fairchild's table was at first designated only as "the Semitic man." Later his first name was revealed as Julius. Brother of another member of the yachting party, Mrs. Eva Wiseman, he was also the grandson of an entrepreneur named Julius Kauffman. Short, bald, and fortyish like Fairchild, he spoke with intelligence and discrimination in a tone somewhere between world-weariness and cynicism. Later he would say, "I love three things: gold, marble, and purple—" (340), a borrowing from the section of "New Orleans" Faulkner had entitled "Wealthy Jew" in *The Double Dealer.* The man in the Vieux Carré–*Double Dealer* crowd who seemed closest to this character was Julius Weis Friend, who had helped organize *The Double Dealer* and then enlisted the aid of his sister, Lillian Friend Marcus, to keep it going.

Before putting the party aboard the yacht, Faulkner introduced Patricia's brother, Theodore Robyn, whom she called "Josh." She spends all her time, he complains, following him around and seriously intends to accompany him to New Haven when he enters Yale in September. She follows him into his bedroom at night and pleads to be allowed to stay, finally departing after administering a ritualistic nip on his ear. As her jaw is masculine, so his seems feminine, and he later pets with Jenny, a voluptuous shopgirl, in what seems a perfunctory manner. Pat bridles, however, and warns Jenny away from him. Josh is clearly the master, giving her a minimum of attention and information, as when he grudgingly tells her about the pipe he is making. But as Gordon's devotion and David's are doglike toward her, so hers is toward Josh. At times it seems almost the mindless imitativeness and devotion of a younger brother for an older one. Their relationship looked backward to the seemingly sexless, passionate relationship between Jo-Addie and Elmer and forward to much more complicated sibling relationships in fiction to come. Just as Pat Robyn immediately suggested Helen Baird, so Theodore "Josh" Robyn, pipe and all, suggested Peter "Josh" Baird.

Finished with his "Prologue" section, Faulkner began "The First Day" as Pat boarded Mrs. Maurier's *Nausikaa* with two uninvited guests. Genevieve Steinbauer was, in a way, a foil to Pat. Fleshy rather than slim, untidy rather than clean, she was overpoweringly female. But there was a kind of ambivalence in her description, which made clear her sensual appeal yet remarked her soiled green dress, dirty fingernails, and "little soft wormlike fingers. . . ." (202) It may have related to a more general hostility toward women of the sort expressed by Dawson Fairchild when he calls them, after all, "merely articulated genital organs with a kind of aptitude for spending whatever money you have. . . ." (241) The fictional predecessor she most resembled was Myrtle Monson. The other uninvited guest was Jenny's boyfriend, Pete Ginotta. Familiar with the New Orleans underworld, he suggested the milieu of "The Kid Learns," and that mosquito-ridden tale, "Once Aboard the Lugger."

When Faulkner had the party aboard the *Nausikaa*, he introduced three remaining subordinate characters. One was a florid, tweed-clad Englishman with false teeth. Major Ayers had been at Sandhurst, served in the war, and for some shadowy reason had since then found several places forbidden to him. Declaring all Americans constipated, he proposed to make a fortune by packing salts in "a tweaky phial. . . ." (64) For a model, the knowledgeable reader would not have to look beyond that exotic visitor to New Orleans, Colonel Charles Glenn Collins.

Mrs. Eva Wiseman, the Semitic man's sister, was a poetess. And Faulkner paid her the compliment of assigning to her some of his own poems. She was also an estimable woman beyond her poetry: wise, tough-minded, compassionate, and humane. She shared some of the characteristics sometimes attributed to Lillian Friend Marcus, a brilliant, original, and determined woman. Mrs. Marcus might rub many the wrong way, but to her friends she had a marvelous personality, a woman with no humbug. Not even bothered by mosquitoes, she impressed William Faulkner. A foil for Eva Wiseman was Dorothy Jameson, a painter with "a bold, humorless style" (101) who does still lifes though she prefers portraits.

Once Faulkner got his characters out on Lake Pontchartrain there was little action except on the part of the mosquitoes. This was, in fact, part of the plot. Josh takes a rod from the steering mechanism in order to heat it and bore apertures in his pipe. The *Nausikaa* goes harmlessly aground, and as they wait for a tugboat from New Orleans, Pat runs off briefly with the adoring young steward, David West. Like Faulkner, David had lain above Lake Maggiore, gazing at the "Alps Mountains, and little white boats on it no bigger than water beetles." (124) His feeling for Pat would in the end be as unrequited as that of Bill Faulkner for Helen Baird. Tortured by mosquitoes and thirst, they return ignominiously to the yacht. With its return to New Orleans, Faulkner had only to write the epilogue to complete his book.

It was August now, the month in which the book's action was set. In the evening the mosquitoes hummed and sang outside the thin protection of the porch screens. One evening Bill Faulkner took a sheet of his plain white paper and wrote to Helen Baird in North Carolina. Some of the lines trailed off into illegibility, but most of them were clear. The message certainly was. "Helen," he wrote, "your name is like a little golden bell hung in my heart. . . ." He told her about visiting her aunt, who was preparing to leave, about telling stories to the children, and about his work. "Your book is pretty near done. Just a few more things. They are nice people [:] Jenny as ineffable as an ice cream soda, and Pete will have queer golden eyes, and Mr. Talliaferro." He remembered writing chapters in her front yard. "I have made you another book," he wrote. "It's sonnets I made you, all bound. . . . you must come back. . . ." But he never mailed the letter. It was written on the back of page 269 of the typescript of *Mosquitoes.* It may have been a preliminary draft, or he may have picked up a page of his work by mistake, as he had done in Europe, and later decided that it was not worth the work of retyping the page or typing the letter. Each of the small lines in black ink was crossed out. Or, perhaps he simply decided the next day that he would not send the letter and frugally used it in his typescript. In either case he got back to work on the book.

Faulkner shaped the "Epilogue" so its symmetry would match that of the "Prologue." The yachting party dispersed, leaving Gordon, Mrs. Maurier, Fairchild, and Talliaferro, and then finally Talliaferro alone. Faulkner had saved one fillip for the end. With the artist's powers of divination, Gordon had done a clay head of Mrs. Maurier which revealed essentials of her character. Using a technique he would employ increasingly, Faulkner briefly interpolated the story of her life, reaching back to the Civil War. She was a Northerner, said the Semitic man, who had been married off to a plantation overseer who had disappeared in '63 and when the war was over had "turned up again riding a horse with a Union Army cavalry saddle and a hundred thousand dollars in uncut Federal notes for a saddle blanket." (323) After dubious land deals with Julius Kauffman, the Semitic man's grandfather, Maurier had added respectability to wealth by taking a bride, the two of them issuing from the church, "her beautiful secret face beside that cold, violent man. . . ." There had been no children and no love, and Mrs. Maurier's lavish attentions to artists bespoke "something thwarted back of it all, something stifled, yet which won't quite die." (326)

What Faulkner had done in these pages was to begin mining a new vein, not in some imagined Georgia town or the Vieux Carré, but in his home country. He had used a local tale for the seed of the interpolation: people in Oxford said that it was Katrina Carter's grandfather on the Wohlleben side who had taken the Yankee banknotes and very carefully, at each Thanksgiving time thereafter, peeled off a layer and spent them. Faulkner had used other indigenous material. The malarial man whom Pat and David had hired to take them back to the yacht was sly, obscene, and avaricious. He was hardly distinguishable from others Faulkner would use in fiction set not in Louisiana but in Mississippi. He might still be dealing here with artists and poets of various degrees, with dilettantes and bohemians, but he was coming closer to types and classes which would be more fruitful for his art.

Faulkner closed the novel with another flourish of frugal versatility. The next-to-last section followed Gordon, Fairchild, and the Semitic man into the red-light district. Italicized paragraphs of impressionistic prose rendered something of the *Walpurgisnacht* effect Faulkner seemed to be seeking—another parallel to the "Circe" chapter of Joyce's *Ulysses.* These passages were taken from Elmer's debauch with the mate and the Genovese prostitute. The Semitic man now resembled Leopold Bloom, giving Gordon money to visit a prostitute and caring for Dawson Fairchild (an aging Stephen Dedalus), drunk and vomiting beside him. Faulkner ended the last section of *Mosquitoes* as he had begun, with Talliaferro and his concerns —"His hair was getting thin, there was no question about that. . . ." (347)

There were borrowings and allusions throughout. Characters talked of Cyrano and Byron, Shelley and Swinburne, Ibsen and Sassoon. There were even more lavish musical references: Chopin, Grieg, Debussy, Berlioz, Gershwin, and Sibelius (the latter a memory, perhaps, from the Moulin Rouge). As to technique, Faulkner had used again some of the devices of *Soldiers' Pay*: the structuring of chapters by subdivisions captioned with the hour of the day, and by setting dialogue as in a play script. He had employed several "running gags": Talliaferro's soiling his immaculate clothes in Gordon's studio, his sessions of amorous strategy with Fairchild, the surfeit of grapefruit on the voyage, Pete's concern for his hat, the drinking on the dogwatch. There were also repeated poetic phrases. Consistent as the motif of the mosquitoes, however, was that of the endless talk (droning, perhaps, like the mosquitoes). "Talk, talk, talk: the utter and heartbreaking stupidity of words," thought Gordon. (186) Faulkner might have talked poetry, literature, and aesthetics with Phil Stone, Ben Wasson, and Sherwood Anderson, but more and more, as he grew older, he would agree with Gordon. And coupled with a distaste for excessive talk, there was already growing a contempt for those who were talkers rather than doers. "You begin to substitute words for things and deeds," as Fairchild put it. (210)

In this novel of apprenticeship Faulkner had made gestures of homage to a master other than Joyce and Eliot. One passage might have described Captain Marlow's steamboat plodding up the Congo rather than Mrs. Maurier's yacht sailing up the Tchufuncta: "at halfspeed [she] forged slowly into a sluggish river mouth, broaching a timeless violet twilight between solemn bearded cypresses motionless as bronze. . . . The world was becoming dimensionless, the tall bearded cypresses drew nearer one to another across the wallowing river with the soulless implacability of pagan gods, gazing down upon this mahogany-and-brass intruder with inscrutable unalarm." (82–83) If "Yo Ho and Two Bottles of Rum" paid tribute to *Typhoon* and other Conrad works, *Mosquitoes* glanced directly at *Heart of Darkness.*

There were far more private references, however, that only a few would recognize or understand. Major Ayers referred to the "beastly" (73) American expeditionary forces during the war. But even they, he said, were better than the Canadians—a reference which might have amused men of Course 42 in Toronto. Fairchild remarked that "ninety out of a hundred Yale and Harvard turn out are reasonably bearable to live with, if they ain't anything else" (115), a remark that might have struck Phil Stone as friendly raillery. Anyone who knew Faulkner could tell from Jenny's description that the man she was describing was indeed the author. But few would know that one of the names she tried for him—"Foster"—belonged to Helen Baird's oldest brother. If Helen did indeed receive Faulkner's love letter, she would have been unlikely to miss a twice-used phrase in Gordon's stream of consciousness: *"your name is like a little golden bell hung in my heart."* (267–268)

But again, Faulkner borrowed most from himself. Gordon's stream of consciousness echoed that of the poet in "Carcassonne" with his "the agony of wood" (118) and "autogethsemane" (48). David West's likening the coming of love to the coming of dawn was almost identical with that in "Frankie and Johnny." There were three poems of his own Faulkner gave Mrs. Wiseman. Throughout there were other echoes—of pipes, for instance, together with the recognition that, in the light of the moon, Gordon's face was *"a silver faun's face. . . ."* (152) The last line was borrowed word-for-word from the ending of "Don Giovanni," as Talliaferro heard the telephone operator's jibe: "You tell 'em, big boy; treat 'em rough." (349)

If *Mosquitoes* was an apprenticeship novel, it gave signs of mastery to come. If it was imitative, it intimated where Faulkner's strength really lay. Dawson Fairchild spoke of his own early infatuation with words, now gone. "So I can't write poetry any more. It takes me too long to say things, now." (249) Speaking of Fairchild, the Semitic man said, "Life everywhere is the same, you know. Manners of living it may be different—are they not different between adjoining villages? family names, profits on a single field or orchard, work influences—but man's old compulsions, duty and inclination: the axis and the circumference of his squirrel cage, they do not change." (243) Willard Huntington Wright had written about the universal and the regional, and Phil Stone had preached arriving at one through the other. Balzac, thought Stone, had demonstrated it. And Sherwood Anderson had told Faulkner, "You're a country boy; all you know is that little patch up there in Mississippi where you started from. But that's all right too." Faulkner would continue to write poetry, but prose was his medium. He would return in his fiction to New Orleans, but north Mississippi was his country.

On page 464 he finally typed the word "End." Then he wrote in ink in the lower left-hand corner, "Pascagoula, Miss/1 Sept 1926." That was a Wednesday. The same week Miss Maud and Dean had visited him at Pascagoula. Their return was reported, with the information that Faulkner had been "spending the summer there getting his forthcoming novel in shape for publication." They had no doubt brought him news of home, some of which was spectacular. Oxford had suffered its worst fire, losing a planing mill, a gas refining and distributing station, and the Oxford Ice Plant, just purchased by Major Oldham. Soon enough Faulkner could see for himself if he wanted to. The Stones would shortly be returning to Charleston. He would stay on for a while longer in the house by himself to finish any corrections or rewriting the typescript needed. Then he would return to Oxford.

He did a good deal to the typescript. While here and there he made one- or two-line deletions, there were more than a dozen additions, ranging from a few sentences to a paragraph—all added in minuscule pen strokes. He kept on pondering some of his character names. In the late section describing Joe's family and occupation, he had typed in the surname Minelli. Later he reconsidered and substituted Maccini. This he replaced with Mancini, which he used for the remainder of the sequence. On rereading, however, he crossed out Mancini in pen and substituted a new name: Maccocelli. On a subsequent reading he thought of another—Ginotta. Then he went through the section, crossing out Maccocelli and substituting Ginotta. He left it at that, apparently satisfied on the fifth try.

He returned to Oxford. Barefoot, in his white trousers, he looked to some of his friends like a beachcomber. Ben Wasson was in town and Faulkner gave him the manuscript, which he read at the Delta Psi house. Faulkner was amused, Ben saw, at the way he had put himself in the book. He called on Phil Stone and Sallie Simpson for typing assistance. Stone would still correct and punctuate, and Sallie would do her best to follow the handwritten material Faulkner sometimes gave her, as well as Stone's corrections. She did not assign particular importance to her literary duties, but "she did a lot of work for Bill," one of the office habitués remembered, "taking infinite pains with typing and proofreading and making sensitive suggestions." Faulkner added the last touches and sent the manuscript off to New York.

Estelle was not in Oxford. Things had come to a head after her return from Monteagle in the summer. Cornell was ready to consider a divorce. Estelle and Miss Lida went to see Bob Farley, who also knew Cornell and was on good terms with him. After consultation with Cornell it was agreed that Estelle should go back to Shanghai. She would stay there briefly, then go to Honolulu for a "probationary" period, as she thought of it. After that, if she still felt the same way, the final papers could be filed and the long legal process set in motion.

Before the last weekend in September Faulkner was back in New Orleans, where he was now good for an interview in the *Item.* He had returned to the Vieux Carré on Sunday, the account ran, in order to plan his work for the winter. He was bronzed from working on a Pascagoula fishing schooner. During the interview he smoked his pipe as he looked out at the rain falling on the roofs of the quarter. (He had won the inscribed pipe with his hole-in-one that spring at Oxford, where he had been a golf pro, according to the interviewer.) He had "announced the publication of *Mosquitoes,*" and had told of "a summer spent working in a lumber mill, until a finger was injured, and then on the fishing boats of the Mississippi coast. At nights, after working hours, he wrote his new book." If the Stones or the Lewises saw the report, Faulkner's commercial fishing must have come as something of a surprise. George Lewis thought he might have gone out once and stayed for two or three days, until they got a load of shrimp, but he doubted that he made any more trips at that time or did any work on the one he had made. The new persona of the bohemian knockabout artist was growing, a layer at a time. Faulkner was going back to Oxford for a brief visit, the interviewer continued. At the end of September he would return to New Orleans for the winter.

He moved back into the attic apartment with Bill Spratling. Little had changed apart from the fact that Sherwood Anderson—now at his farm in Virginia and soon to leave for Europe—no longer occupied the same place in their lives. The Quarter was as lively as ever, with parties four or five nights a week, often at Spratling's or Lyle Saxon's, with everyone talking, smoking, and dipping drinks out of whatever liquid filled the big bowl on the table. A Swiss living in the Quarter made pernod. He would bottle it, affix his own labels, and then sell it for six dollars. They would pour it into a pitcher of crushed ice and add a little water. For other parties Spratling and Faulkner would make their own gin, using gallon cans of alcohol. They would put it in a barrel and, to aerate it, would roll it across the floor until the tenants below complained. On Sundays they might enjoy the hospitality of a well-known figure of the Quarter, a man called Baron Hanno von Schucking, who had enjoyed a romantic relationship, it was said, with a wealthy and generous woman. They would go to the Baron's apartment for Sunday breakfast preparatory to setting out for a picnic. After breakfast they would have a drink and drift into lunch. Then, after another drink, they would forget about the picnic.

For rainy days there was a diversion which did not even require leaving the attic apartment. They would take down a Daisy air rifle from the wall and open one of the windows that overlooked St. Peter Street. Unseen, they would aim at passers-by, the buttocks their usual target. A point list on the wall was graded for various targets. An ordinary citizen counted for little, but a nun from the nearby convent was worth several points, and a Negro nun several more. There were other prime targets. One day as a wealthy resident of St. Peter Street disengaged her portly figure from her limousine, Spratling pulled the trigger. Years later he remembered with pleasure the look of incredulous outrage on the dowager's face.

Faulkner still rose early each morning and often went to a coffee stand in the French Market down near the river. It was fashionable to end a night's gaiety with the strong black coffee, and mornings after gala Mardi gras balls men and women in evening dress would sit before the high mirrors drinking the steaming, chicory-flavored brew. It was said that duelists met there, which gave rise to the saying "pistols for two, coffee for one." Flo Field remembered Faulkner's coming back with three doughnuts powdered with sugar. He consumed them, she said, with a tumbler of whiskey.

There were, of course, more substantial repasts. Marc and Lucille Antony had met him on St. Peter Street shortly after his return and suggested that they go and eat. Faulkner agreed and accompanied them to the St. Regis, an inexpensive place on Royal Street. As they were about to enter, the headwaiter stopped them. The gentleman would have to wear a coat, he said; he could use the manager's coat, hanging there on the rack. Faulkner was furious, but he accepted it. When they were finally seated he told Marc and Lucille about working for months on a shrimp boat out in the Gulf. He had gone barefoot, he said, for long stretches on the schooner. Now his feet hurt, so he thought he would just take off his shoes while they were eating. He was amusing during dinner, telling them about a woman in Oxford he was going to marry with the agreement that she would adopt all his illegitimate children. After dinner, at the door, he returned the borrowed coat to the headwaiter. Then, he turned, walked back, and retrieved his shoes from under the table.

By now, it seems, he had received a response from New York about *Mosquitoes.* A young woman named Lillian Hellman had gone to work for Liveright as soon as she had left school. Although everyone did a little bit of everything there, she had been hired primarily as a reader and *Mosquitoes* had been assigned to her. She had read it and written an enthusiastic recommendation. The firm accepted the novel for publication and sent Faulkner a check for an advance against royalties. He used part of it to invite a party to dinner at Galatoire's, famed for its *haute cuisine* and its rich air of tradition. When his guests—Margery and Irving Gumbel, Lillian Friend Marcus, and Julius and Elise Friend—called for him, he was not dressed for the occasion. But this time there was no incident. His friends obtained a coat and tie and forced them on him before they left. As usual, Faulkner was a gracious host, entertaining a party including two who had served as models for characters in the novel which was going to pay the check.

His relationship with Margery Gumbel had remained close, and he saw her again at a party given by Lillian Friend Marcus. "I want to talk to you," he said, and she walked with him out onto a screened porch. There he told her that he had fallen in love with a girl in Pascagoula named Helen. He described the way they had sat on the beach together. He talked on and on about her before they finally drifted back to the party inside. It was the last time Margery Gumbel saw him.

Now that *Mosquitoes* was presumably being put through the editorial process that would culminate in publication the next spring, he could turn his energies to new work he had been planning. There was not just one project but two and, though they were radically different, they were related. One began in town but then, in a vast flashback, dealt with Mississippi hill people, with the yeoman stock which had first populated that part of the country, and with the new breed of unscrupulous, acquisitive tenant farmers who had appeared in the decades after the war. The other was set principally in town and focused on the established class, but as the novel developed, elements of both the county yeomanry and the unscrupulous hill people would also be introduced. Both locales had the same county seat, the town of Jefferson. The further Faulkner got into both works, writing at them alternately it seems, the more he found himself in a process of discovery as well as invention. Long afterward he said, "I discovered that my own little postage stamp of native soil was worth writing about and that I would never live long enough to exhaust it, and that by sublimating the actual into

Charcoal portrait of Margery Gumbel by William Spratling.

the apocryphal I would have complete liberty to use whatever talent I might have to its absolute top. It opened up a gold mine of other people. . . ." Sherwood Anderson had been right.

Shortly before meeting Faulkner, Anderson had been working on a biography of Abraham Lincoln under the title *Father Abraham.* It seems likely that he would have mentioned the work to Faulkner. If Faulkner did appropriate Anderson's title, this could have been the only resemblance between the two works. Not only were Faulkner's title and intention ironic, but he was thinking not of Lincoln but of his namesake, the patriarch who migrated from Ur of the Chaldees, leading his people into the Land of Canaan, where they prospered greatly. Flem Snopes was the local Abraham, and the clan he led displayed his traits: cunning, rapacity, and utter amorality, plus the seething vigor of a swarm of vermin. The story began with Flem Snopes gazing, Buddha-like, from behind a plate-glass window in the Jefferson bank, the presidency of which marked the pinnacle of his success. It was a career which spanned forty-five years, and Faulkner quickly flashed back to its beginnings.

Flem Snopes—with his unblinking eyes the color of stagnant water, his slit of a mouth like a patent opening on a tobacco pouch, his steady ruminant tobacco-chewing jaw—was the apotheosis of the rise of the redneck. (In several ways he resembled political boss Dal Martin in "The Big Shot.") In heavily ironic rhetoric, Faulkner called him "a living example of the astonishing byblows of man's utopian dreams actually functioning; in this case the dream is democracy." Phil Stone had been a close student of the poor whites who had flocked to Vardaman, Bilbo, and Russell, and had put them in power. Faulkner would soon be caught up in the story itself, but at the start he was dealing as much with types as individuals—types which his grandfather and his uncle had known well.

He set the story southeast of Jefferson "in the hill cradled cane and cypress jungles of Yocona River. . . ." The settlement of Frenchman's Bend stood in about the same relation to Jefferson as did the hamlets of Yocona and Tula to Oxford, ten and twelve miles away, respectively. Situated close to the Yocona River, both lay a few miles northeast of Dallas, birthplace of Lee M. Russell. The ruined grandeur of the Frenchman's mansion contrasts with the undistinguished affluence of Uncle Billy Varner—headman of the settlement and rich from monopoly, moneylending, and politics—and the obsessive drive toward wealth of monomaniacal Flem Snopes. It is on the old Scots-Irish families of Frenchman's Bend—the Turpins, Haleys, Whittingtons, MacCallums, Murrays, Leonards, and Littlejohns—that Flem battens, bringing in one after another of his kinsmen. He has risen from Varner's store clerk to his son-in-law by marrying his pregnant daughter. Eula is the figure toward which Emmy, Myrtle, and Jenny had been tending, rich and rife, "a softly ample girl with eyes like cloudy hothouse grapes and a mouth always slightly open. . . ."

Returning from residence in Texas, Eula brings back a precocious-seeming baby and Flem brings back a gaudy herd of varicolored ponies, beasts so wild and fractious that the Texan named Buck who herds them has secured them to the wagon by a barbed-wire hackamore. Alternating richly comic hyperbole and droll understatement, Faulkner described the way the men of Frenchman's Bend, bargain-prone and gullible, bought these mustangs wilder than any ever shipped by the vaqueros of the King Ranch. He was now using and embellishing whatever he and his uncle John had seen from that boardinghouse veranda in Calhoun County four years before.

Faulkner showed unlovely aspects of human nature beyond the avarice and deceit of Flem and Buck. There was the cold cruelty of mad Henry Armstid, buying one of the ponies with money his gaunt wife had earned for their children's shoes. As though adhering to the Unities, Faulkner set the central part of the story on one day. Preparations for the auction began at dawn, and the night was loud with the thunder of hooves, the cries of men trying to head the newly bought horses, and the groans of the injured. Under the minute strokes of his pen the Snopeses began to proliferate, with merry predators such as I. O. Snopes, and even an anomaly: a good Snopes —the blacksmith Eckrum, father of the small, tow-haired Admiral Dewey Snopes.

Faulkner now had over 14,000 words written in ink on legal-size paper. He began Section III of *Father Abraham* with a favorite and recurrent image: twilight. Henry Armstid and Vernon Turpin convalesced from their injuries as Turpin prepared to sue Flem. Faulkner could now work out the legal intricacies which would further demonstrate Flem's diabolical cleverness and provide more satiric comedy as well. He was still introducing new characters, however. One was V. K. Suratt, whom he first called a "patent medicine drummer" but changed to a sewing machine agent. Shrewd, affable, and voluble, he seemed the only man in Frenchman's Bend, apart from Uncle Billy Varner, who might conceivably fathom some of Flem's designs.

On page 25 of the manuscript Faulkner began crossing out more lines than usual. Halfway down the page he started his third paragraph but stopped in the middle of the third line and scratched the paragraph out. He wrote two more lines, describing Suratt in his buckboard. Then he crossed them out, stopping in mid-sentence. The lower half of the page remained blank. Thereafter he would work only sporadically on *Father Abraham.*

It had, however, been an extremely fruitful project, even though he may not then have realized it. He had begun to explore an indigenous vein which would prove enormously rich and just as rewarding stylistically. The material demanded realistic treatment, yet he could build on this base with hyperbole and, finally, even myth. And as for the texture of the prose, as he wrote about dawn-wet grass and moon-blanched dust, he was drawing on the pastoral lyricism which was so natural and compelling for him, using it now where it would function to counterpoint and enrich the realism, dialect, and humor.

A drawing on the back of page 8 was highly emblematic. The fine, light pencil lines sketched a scene such as he might have drawn to amuse Cho-

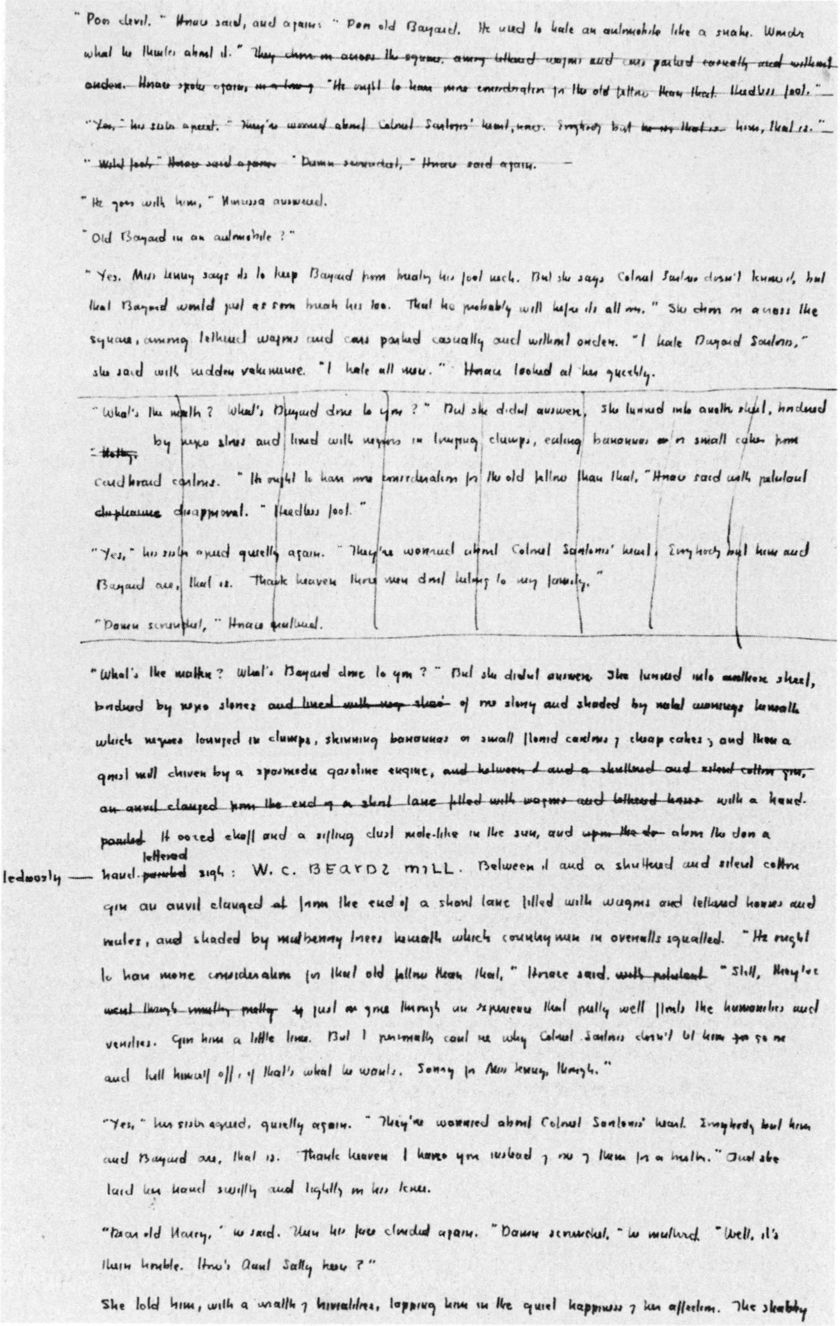

"Poor devil." Horace said, and again: "Poor old Bayard. He used to hate an automobile like a snake. Wonder what he thinks about it." [illegible] "He ought to have more consideration for the old fellow than that. Heedless fool."

"Yes," his sister agreed. "They're worried about Colonel Sartoris' heart, now. Everybody but [illegible] him, that is."

"[illegible]" "Damn scoundrel," Horace said again.

"He goes with him," Narcissa answered.

"Old Bayard in an automobile?"

"Yes. Miss Jenny says it's to keep Bayard from breaking his fool neck. But she says Colonel Sartoris doesn't know it, but that Bayard would just as soon break his too. That he probably will before it's all over." She drove on across the square, among tethered wagons and cars parked casually and without order. "I hate Bayard Sartoris," she said with sudden vehemence. "I hate all men." Horace looked at her quickly.

"What's the matter? What's Bayard done to you?" But she didn't answer. She turned into another street, bordered by negro stores and lined with negroes in lounging clumps, eating bananas or small cakes from cardboard cartons. "He ought to have more consideration for the old fellow than that," Horace said with petulant ~~displeasure~~ disapproval. "Heedless fool."

"Yes," his sister agreed quietly again. "They're worried about Colonel Sartoris' heart. Everybody but him and Bayard are, that is. Thank heaven there are dust belongs to my family."

"Damn scoundrel," Horace muttered.

"What's the matter? What's Bayard done to you?" But she didn't answer. She turned into another street, bordered by negro stores ~~and lined with~~ of one story and shaded by metal awnings beneath which negroes lounged in clumps, skinning bananas or small florid cartons of cheap cakes, and then a grist mill driven by a spasmodic gasoline engine, ~~and between it and a shuttered and silent cotton gin, an anvil clanged from the end of a short lane filled with wagons and tethered horses~~ with a hand-painted. It oozed chaff and a sifting dust mole-like in the sun, and ~~upon the~~ along the door a

ledmostly — hand-~~painted~~ lettered sign: W. C. BEARDS MILL. Between it and a shuttered and silent cotton gin an anvil clanged ~~at~~ from the end of a short lane filled with wagons and tethered horses and mules, and shaded by mulberry trees beneath which countrymen in overalls squatted. "He ought to have more consideration for that old fellow than that," Horace said. ~~with petulant~~ "Still, they're ~~[illegible]~~ just as [illegible] through an experience that pretty well flouts the humanities and verities. Give him a little time. But I personally can't see why Colonel Sartoris doesn't let him go some and kill himself off, if that's what he wants. Sorry for Miss Jenny, though."

"Yes," his sister agreed, quietly again. "They're worried about Colonel Sartoris' heart. Everybody but him and Bayard are, that is. Thank heaven I have you instead of one of them for a brother." And she laid her hand swiftly and lightly on his knee.

"Dear old Narcy," he said. Then his face clouded again. "Damn scoundrel," he muttered. "Well, it's their trouble. How's Aunt Sally now?"

She told him, with a wealth of trivialities, lapping him in the quiet happiness of her affection. The shabby

Part of page 87 of the manuscript of *Flags in the Dust.*

Cho or Malcolm. On a sloping hillside were two toys, half lamb and half rocking-horse. Gamboling near them were two real lambs, however, and piping the music to which they danced was a seated faun, his back against a tree. At his side were two rabbits, and above them a flight of swallows sped against the clouds of the sylvan scene. The faun's profile was quite distinctly like William Faulkner's. He had pictured a scene which might have illustrated a portion of *The Marble Faun.* In the prose he employed the new kind of pastoral which would henceforth distinguish much of his work.

It may have been late 1926 or early 1927 when he put aside page 25 of that manuscript. The decision to do so was probably related to the progress he was making with the other manuscript he was working on at the same time. He would call it *Flags in the Dust*, and in it he was giving rein to his romantic imagination while he used the lore both of the South and of his own family, employing the second, in a way, as emblematic of the first. One event of the summer would have been enough, had he needed outside stimulus, to send his mind ranging back over the stories Grandfather had told. It was an article from *The Southern Sentinel* republished in the *Eagle.* The Old Colonel's railroad had now become part of still another larger system, the Gulf, Mobile & Northern. The story was captioned "Dreams of Col. Falkner are Real," and the text explained that "Last Sunday the first train in the history of the Road went through to Chicago and points north of here." Thirty pages into his manuscript Faulkner wrote, "But now the railway belonged to a syndicate and there were more than two trains on it that ran from Lake Michigan to the Gulf of Mexico, completing his dream, while John Sartoris slept among martial cherubim. . . ."

Two years later, in a highly rhetorical and sometimes illegible sheet and a half of manuscript, he set down something about the genesis of the work. As he was "speculating idly upon time and death" the thought occurred to him that the day would come when he would no longer "react to the simple bread-and-salt of the world" as he had done during his growing years, and so he began casting about. "All that I really desired was a touchstone simply; a simple word or gesture, but having been these 2 years previously under the curse of words, having known twice before the agony of ink, nothing served but that I try by main strength to recreate between the covers of a book the world as I was already preparing to lose and regret, feeling, with the morbidity of the young, that I was not only on the verge of decrepitude, but that growing old was to be an experience peculiar to myself alone out of all the teeming world, and desiring, if not the capture of that world and the feeling of it as you'd preserve a kernel or a leaf to indicate the lost forest, at least to keep the evocative skeleton of the dessicated [*sic*] leaf.

"So I began to write, without much purpose, until I realised that to make it truly evocative it must be personal, in order to not only preserve my own interest in the writing, but to preserve my belief in the savor of the bread-and-salt. . . . So I got some people, some I invented, others I created out of tales I learned of nigger cooks and stable boys of all ages between one-armed Joby, 18, who taught me to write my name in red ink on the linen duster he wore for some reason we have both forgotten, to old Louvinia who remarked when the stars "fell" and who called my grandfather and my father by their Christian names until she died, in the long drowsy afternoons. Created, I say, because they are composed partly from what they were in actual life and partly from what they should have been and were not: thus I improved on God who, dramatic though He be, has no sense, no feeling for, theatre."

If this account accurately reflected his feelings, it was not surprising that he chose for a time to forgo capturing the world of the Snopeses to try to present forever a world he felt himself about to lose.

Although this novel too was set in Jefferson, its action traveled far beyond the borders of what Faulkner called Yocona County. He began the manuscript with old Bayard Sartoris musing in the attic over relics untouched for twenty years—the family Bible, a Toledo blade, Mechlin lace, two pipes, a cavalry saber. His train of recollection would provide background for the present action, set just after the Great War. The old man meditated on the family's hereditary affinity for lost causes and fatal violence. The genealogy was a long one, as testified by the Toledo blade. In the time of Charles I a Sartoris had brought it with him to Virginia "and little else save the romantic fatality of his name and the jeweled poniard which Aylmer Sartoris, having followed Henry Plantagenet to Rouen and there met and married the Provençal lady who had borne him the first Bayard Sartoris, had slung about the young hips of that first Bayard Sartoris who carried it to Agincourt. . . ."

As early as the second page of his manuscript Faulkner had introduced another generation of Sartorises, also named Bayard and John, in whom the old strain ran strong. Bayard had remained in Carolina while John had emigrated to Tennessee, fought in the Mexican War, and then moved to north Mississippi where he gradually acquired land and slaves. "His dream was a railway, an outlet to the world and its markets, but 1861 occurred first, whereupon he organized a regiment of infantry, elected himself its Colonel and took it to Virginia, where it conducted itself worthily. But the Army of Northern Virginia was also an army of factional politics, and presently an election of officers came around and Colonel Sartoris was deposed by his senior Major and returned to Mississippi in a high dudgeon to work off his spleen at the well-nigh hopeless task of making another crop. But comparative inactivity soon palled on him, and then Grant came into the country on his way to Vicksburg, and so he raised a body of guerrilla horse, commissioned himself Colonel anew as Napoleon dubbed himself emperor and . . . presently become a byword among Federal picquets, he proceeded to annoy Grant after the dashing and glamorously impractical fashion of his race. In the midst of this he learned of his brother Bayard's death at Manassas, still in the family tradition: leading a doomed charge." Twelve pages further in the manuscript the story of "that Carolina Bayard" was told with loving embellishment by Aunt Jenny. (Virginia Du Pre, sister to Bayard and to John Sartoris, had been widowed in the war and had come to live at Sartoris in 1869.) A wild, gallant cavalryman and aide to Jeb Stuart, he had ridden into Virginia with black-plumed "Beauty" Stuart. There, with his general and eighteen other men, he had raided General Pope's headquarters for coffee. Riding back into the bee swarm of men and bullets minutes later to capture some anchovies, he had been killed by a derringer fired by a cook from under a table. Over the years Aunt Jenny added touches until "what had been a prank of two heedless and reckless boys wild with their own youth, was become a gallant and finely tragical focal-point to which the history of the race had been raised from the old miasmic swamps of slow decay by two angels valiantly and glamorously fallen and strayed. . . ."

After that war, the widowed John Sartoris had married a girl who had ridden with his partisan troop. He had restored the land and built the railroad, killed carpetbaggers and disfranchised Negroes. Then, elected to the legislature over his erstwhile partner and bitter rival, he accepted the idea of death: "Redlaw'll kill me tomorrow, for I shall be unarmed. I'm tired of killing men. . . . Pass the wine, Bayard." Faulkner was now nineteen letter-size pages into his manuscript. As omniscient narrator, he had related all of this through old Bayard's memories. He had mentioned his son John, dead twenty years of "yellow fever and an old Spanish bullet-wound," and he had come up to the present generation, his grandsons: Bayard and Evelyn John Sartoris.

It may have been at this point that Faulkner went back to the beginning of his manuscript and added seven pages to precede his original page 1, describing Bayard and Evelyn (he would soon switch to John) as pursuit pilots in France. He sketched in their education and training and then Bayard's marriage to Caroline White. He described Bayard's unsuccessful efforts to dissuade John from the fatal recklessness of flying his Camel alone into a dangerous airspace behind German lines. Like other new characters he had been working with, Bayard and John had antecedents—young Donald Mahon and Josh Robyn, brash, self-centered, and ruthless, yet somehow fascinating to their creator. With these twenty-six pages—not quite as much as he had done on *Father Abraham*—Faulkner had worked out in some detail the background of another saga antithetical to that of the Snopeses. He had set up the two poles of the fictional county which he now called Yocona.

Before he went home for Christmas he became involved in another project. It was a collection of sketches Spratling had done of people in the Quarter. The Mexican artist Miguel Covarrubias had published a book called *The Prince of Wales and Other Famous Americans.* Spratling and Faulkner decided to call this book *Sherwood Anderson & Other Famous Creoles.* Faulkner would do whatever text they needed. For epigraph they chose the phrase "Ave et Cave per Ars ad Artist" and dedicated the book "To All the Artful and Crafty Ones of the French Quarter." There were forty-one drawings in all. The frontispiece was a view from St. Peter Street of Cabildo Alley, which ended at the east wall of the cathedral in the background. Leaning out of a small fourth-floor window was a figure who looked like Faulkner. An arrow connected the figure with the word "Writer." Crawling out of a skylight, pad in hand, was a figure resembling Spratling and labeled "Artist." Spratling's initials at the bottom were done in broad strokes, whereas the labeling in the picture was fine and precise. The caption read, "The Locale, Which Includes Mrs. Flo Field." Near the bottom was a small figure labeled "Our Flo." She appeared nowhere else in the book in spite of her charter status in the group.

Spratling had given sittings to each of those to be in the book, but Flo had not liked his drawing of her. When Spratling did another, she liked it less than the first and asked for a third sitting.

"Flo," Spratling said, "you're out of the book!"

"Oh, no, Bill," she cried, "I can't be!" But she was.

The 500-word "Foreword" signed "W.F." was a subtle and unmistakable parody of the style and some of the views of Sherwood Anderson. "First, let me tell you something about our Quarter, the Vieux Carré," it began. "Do you know our quarter, with its narrow streets, its old wrought-iron balconies and its southern European atmosphere? An atmosphere of richness and soft laughter, you know." The writer was not a native, he said, but he felt a kinship with the artists he had seen at work there. He described his meeting with Spratling and his wish to "talk my thought out to him," for he felt a fellowship between them. But at their next encounter, wrote W.F., in sentences that may have had a certain ring for Anderson, "I had a kind of vision. I saw myself being let in for something. I saw myself incurring an obligation which I should later regret. . . ." He agreed, however, to serve as "a wheelhorse." On the facing page was a sketch of a large-headed, small-bodied man in garish clothes. Beside his chair was a book entitled *Tar* and below the caricature was the legend "Mister Sherwood Anderson."

The other pictures showed Spratling's versatile command of charcoal, pen-and-ink, engraving, and other media. A sketch of a bespectacled figure as languid and elongated as Lytton Strachey's had been entitled by Faulkner "Oliver La Farge of Harvard, A Kind of School Near Boston." Another showed Odiorne on the sidewalk at the Café du Dôme, near him a ribald drawing of a familiar Paris street convenience. A drawing of two men at work at a news desk was captioned "Roark Bradford/Story-Teller" and "John McClure/Ballad-Maker." A few pages further Lillian Marcus smiled from the cover of *The Double Dealer.* An elegantly clad Lyle Saxon read a copy of Strachey's *Eminent Victorians.* Beneath his name was the subtitle "The Mauve Decade in Saint Peter Street." Near the end of the book was a sketch of a reclining Sam Gilmore, a blossom curling from between his feet, and the caption "Le Repos de Florizel." The last sketch was of Spratling and Faulkner. On the wall hung the air rifle and the legend "Viva Art." Below Faulkner's chair were three jugs.

By December they had the book ready for publication. Spratling was well pleased with the results. The foreword, he thought, was "a more subtle and sweeter parody on Anderson's writing style than was *The Torrents of Spring*, where Hemingway permitted himself to sneer at Sherwood, a friend who had helped him to find a publisher. Faulkner's analysis was warm and delicate, as was his nature." (They had both rather resented Hemingway's parody of Anderson.) They took the material to old Mr. Pfaff at the Robert H. True Company and paid him for 400 copies. In a week they were all sold at a dollar and a half each. But their pleasure was short-lived. Anderson was much more vulnerable, seven months after Hemingway's destructively intended parody, than Spratling realized. When Spratling saw Anderson, "Sherwood said he didn't think it was very funny. . . ." Spratling had not found him angry, but he was hurt, Faulkner thought, and he later referred to his collaboration with Spratling as "the unhappy caricature affair." Neither he nor Hemingway "could have touched, ridiculed, his work itself," Faulkner said, "but we had made his style look ridiculous; and by that time . . . he too must have known in his heart that there was nothing else left." For those in the Quarter who were "hipped" on Freud, there could scarcely have been a more graphic example of the son asserting his freedom by slaying the father. In January the Pelican Press did a second printing of 150 more copies.

Jack Falkner was now attached to the Atlanta office of the FBI, but he and his wife managed to get back to Oxford for Christmas. His brother was glad, in his undemonstrative way, to see him again. They fell back easily into some of their old habits, going out at night and identifying planets. They would also have a drink together. Under this influence, and perhaps the holiday spirit, Bill might begin to sing his favorite song, "Yes, Sir, That's My Baby."

John Falkner was doing well. He had taken his degree at Ole Miss and was now the city engineer. Toward young Dean Falkner, the oldest brother felt protective as well as loving and, like his parents, a bit apprehensive. Dean was quick and well-coordinated, a natural athlete. But he was also a combative competitor who weighed only 130 pounds. He had hoped to star at quarterback for Ole Miss as he had done in high school. In his second year, however, the coach had come to Murry Falkner. "Mr. Murry," he said, "I got to find some way to get Dean to quit football. He's gonna get himself killed." They finally arrived at a solution: Dean would quit football and concentrate on baseball. When he did, he became a crack outfielder. But he also had time for golf and hunting. He could play the entire course with a number two iron, his family said, and still come in at par. When he went squirrel-hunting, he would not shoot the squirrel; instead he would "bark" it, shooting off the limb on which it crouched so it would be stunned by the fall. He went all out at whatever he did. Like the other active boys of his age, he liked a good time, but his idea of a good time did not always coincide with that of his parents, and they feared the Falkner wildness in him. Bill made a proposal probably intended to divert his energy into safer and more productive channels. Dean could do sketches for his books. Perhaps with this incentive, Dean continued to work at his drawing and painting, but there was no significant lessening in the other activities.

It would not have been surprising if Dean's intensity had reminded his brother of two other boys: John and Bayard Sartoris. His work was surely not out of his mind over the holidays, particularly when he was with Phil Stone. Stone was fascinated with the material about the Snopes family, feeling that it was he who had first suggested this theme—the rise of the rednecks—to Faulkner. This kind of material would be just as rich for Faulkner, he thought, as it had been for Balzac. "You can never practice law in Lafayette County until after you've read *Père Goriot*," he would tell a younger partner. There was an historical perspective which interested Stone. There was, he thought, a curse on the land which could be expiated only over a long period of time. But he was entranced with the turns and twists of human behavior which his legal practice daily showed him. Faulkner knew much of this lore, too, as most long-time residents of Oxford had a common fund of shared experience and anecdote. There in Stone's law office the two men would talk about the actual doings of people like the Snopeses. And when the fancy struck them, they would make up wild, outrageous stories of things which no Snopes-counterpart may have done, but things of which they thought them perfectly capable.

They were amused, too, at material in *Flags in the Dust*—at the wild, outrageous behavior such as that which cost the Carolina Bayard his life. And it was no accident that this foolhardy apotheosis of Southern chivalry fed on the romanticism of Sir Walter Scott should also bear the name of the legendary "Chevalier sans peur et sans reproche." Just as the two men talked about the new class and its incursions, so they talked about the established class, its performance during the war and its steadily fading influence since then. "I invented more of *Sartoris* than I did of any of the other books," Stone would later say, but models abounded in Oxford. Young Dr. Alford, who advised excising a wen on old Bayard's cheek, would remind some readers of young Dr. Ashford Little. Dr. Lucius Quintus Peabody, who advised against it and who "had practiced medicine in the county when a doctor's equipment consisted of a saw and a gallon of whisky and a satchel of calomel" (98), would remind others of Dr. A. A. Young, Stark Young's father. Ninety-three-year-old Will Falls, one-time trooper of the Old Colonel and friend of Bayard, seemed to owe something to both Mr. Charlie Bennett and Mr. Buck Collins, both Lafayette County residents.

In the family they would later say that there was no mistaking Grandfather as the model for old Bayard and Auntee as the model for Aunt Jenny. The deaf old man, shouting in his bank president's office, could have been John Wesley Thompson Falkner quite as well as Bayard Sartoris. It was natural for Faulkner to turn to his family for models. Character came out of family, he told Stone. Environment was important, too, he granted, but it was mostly a matter of genetics. "You do the best that you can," he said. And he did not stop with blood kin. Simon, old Bayard's coachman, owed something to Ned Barnett, a retainer for generations. Simon's son Caspey, "uppity" since his return from a labor battalion in France, also seemed drawn from life. The name they both bore, Strother, was that of the other family of Falkner servants, to which Joby had belonged. There might be this indebtedness to models, but the characters lived in their own right. Stone was enthusiastic about the manuscript, hoping that Faulkner would have the big critical and commercial success which had eluded them with the first two books. Stone quickly and easily again slipped into the role of press agent.

In the early months, most probably, of 1927, Stone composed a release meant for the Oxford *Eagle.* Boni & Liveright had just announced "the approaching publication" of *Mosquitoes,* he wrote. In a rather truncated account of his friend's activities he noted that "Since his return from Europe Faulkner has been here at home playing golf and writing two new novels which are already under contract. Both are Southern in setting. One is something of a saga of an extensive family connection of typical 'poor white trash' and is said by those who have seen that part of the manuscript completed to be the funniest book anybody ever wrote. The other is a tale of the aristocratic, chivalrous and ill-fated Sartoris family, one of whom was even too reckless for the daring Confederate cavalry leader, Jeb Stuart." He went on to praise Faulkner's golf as well as his writing, asserting that he consistently scored under forty strokes for nine holes. "He is planning to enter the State Golf Tournament in June," Stone added, "and some think he has a good chance for the State championship."

Stone erroneously asserted that *Soldiers' Pay* had gone into a fifth edition already, and he was probably mistaken in writing that both new books were under contract. Faulkner was obligated to offer his next manuscript first to Boni & Liveright, but they were not obligated to publish it. To Stone, however, the assertion must have seemed like good press agentry. And it must have been deeply satisfying to write those lines as he looked back over the local response to the past work of "the Count" and his own predictions.

Faulkner wrote occasionally to some of his friends in New Orleans. In the first letter he sent to Margery Gumbel he told her he had a good job for a writer: painting a house. But liquor was costing more than he made, he said, so he quit. One phrase she treasured from the second letter. He wrote, "I was just thinking about what your hair looks like: it looks like Chablis in a glass." Later there was a third letter, but after that she did not hear from him again.

Estelle had returned to Oxford in January. She and the children had docked in San Francisco, without maid or amah this time because they would not be going back to Shanghai or Honolulu. She telegraphed her father for help, and the Major quickly sent it. She had waited out her probationary period without any change of heart or mind, greeting its expiration with relief. She had embarked for home just as soon as she could after the depositions were taken and the papers filed. If all went without delay or hindrance, the divorce would be granted in two years. Now she and Bill Faulkner knew better where they stood, though the proprieties of both the law and a small town would impose limits on their association scarcely less rigorous than those which had bound them during the previous eight years.

Faulkner had been attending to his business correspondence. On January 11, 1927, he wrote from Oxford to thank Horace Liveright for sending him "the Napoleon." It was physically a beautiful book, and he had read a hundred pages before he could put it down. He was also enclosing a dedication for *Mosquitoes.* "I made the promise some time ago," he wrote, "and you can lie to women, you know, but you cant break promises you make 'em. That infringes on their own province. And besides, you dont dare." He was grateful too, he said, for the Le Gallienne anthology he had received earlier. It had given him a good start on the library he hoped to own someday. "I possess no books at all, you see," he concluded.

His next letter to Liveright, written a week later from Oxford on February 18, struck a different note. "I'm sorry my letter about 'Mosquitoes' sounded querulous: I was not trying to complain at all. I understood why the deletions were made, and I was merely pointing out one result of it that, after all, is not very important." Faulkner had apparently received the galley proofs of the novel and found that four good-sized passages had been deleted. Ben Wasson would later say that the book had been badly cut. The first deletion consisted of two pages of Fairchild's conversation in which the Semitic man told him that writing was a kind of perversion. The second excision was another two-page passage which also smacked of perversion. In the darkness of the cabin, Pat lies in the same bunk with Jenny who is sleeping nude. As Pat caresses Jenny's flank, Jenny sighs in her sleep, turns, kisses Pat on the mouth, and seems softly to envelop her. But then Pat jerks her mouth away and sprawls across Jenny to spit.

" 'Ugh!' She made a harsh shuddering sound. 'Good Lord, who ever taught you to kiss that way? Ugh!' she exclaimed, spitting again."

After an argument about who "started it," Pat tells Jenny that only "common people" kiss that way. Jenny whimpers but then after a while she asks Pat to show her how "nice people" kiss. Just as Pat leans forward in the darkness, Mrs. Wiseman enters the cabin and stands there "staring at them with a dark intent speculation." In the third two-page passage Pete complained that the voyage and its people "Damn near refined me out of my girl." The last excision came after Fairchild's remark that the population would decline if a man had to watch himself making love. The editorial pencil had descended when Mrs. Wiseman asked about women and Fairchild replied that there would not be much of them in sight and, besides, it is the backside that is ridiculous. Then, to Mrs. Maurier's horror, Fairchild, the Semitic man, and Mrs. Wiseman worked variations on the theme of "a mechanical contrivance to do the work." The excised passage ended with Fairchild's demurrer: "I'll always vote for the old orthodox way: what was good enough for my fathers is good enough for me."

In his letter Faulkner also accepted criticism on another score: "Regarding the punctuation: that was due to my typewriter, a Corona, vintage of 1910. I have a better one, now. . . . Thank you for the enclosed memoranda showing why, etc." He would not be so tractable with future editorial changes.

He had apparently asked about money, too. "I didn't know when the advance would be due, being practically a vestal in the field of professional lit., but I am damned tired of our H-99° winters of this sunny south." Liveright was about to go to Europe. "I envy you England," Faulkner told him, adding "England is 'ome to me, in a way."

As for his work, he was now busy with two things, a novel and "a collection of short stories of my townspeople." He told Liveright that he had also dug up something else for him, "a mss. by one who has no literary yearnings whatever and who did this just to pass the time. Some one is to see it, and it might as well be you, so I have persuaded the author to give you first shot at it. I think it is pretty fair." While Estelle was in Shanghai she had written a novel which she called *White Beeches*, and when she had shown it to Bill, he had encouraged her.

Faulkner closed his letter with a one-line postscript: "Just received a blank form from 'Who's Who in America.' So I guess maybe I am." He had filled in the form economically, describing his wartime experience with the modest notation "Served with British Royal Air Force." But the entry under which his name was listed showed a kind of curious reversal. "FALKNER, William," it read, "(surname originally Faulkner)."

There was one work which Faulkner had not mentioned to Liveright. It was already published in the fashion in which he had "published" *Vision in Spring.* It was called *The Wishing-Tree.* He had typed and bound it himself in varicolored paper. On the flyleaf were the words

single mss. impression
oxford-mississippi-
5-february-1927.

Four days later, on February 9, he had brought it to the Oldhams' house inscribed

For his dear friend
Victoria
on her eighth birthday
Bill he made
this Book

His storytelling was one of the chief attractions at the birthday party. He told fairy tales, Arthur Guyton remembered, but "sometimes laden with mild degrees of horror and always couched in plenty of fantasy. The important feature of these stories, however, was their absolute reality to those of us who were his listeners. His telling of the stories was always with an element of complete sincerity, an absolute belief in them himself, so much so that he could capture the mind of anyone and carry it along with him however preposterous the nature of the tale." Cho-Cho's first memories of Billy were bound up with his storytelling. He would buy a five-cent box of vanilla wafers and they would go for a walk in the woods together. As they politely and scrupulously shared the wafers, he would tell her about fairies and other creatures who lived there. Out of this had come the gift he had carried for her to the party that day.

The forty-seven-page book was an account of the birthday of a little girl named Dulcie, who waked to see a strange red-headed boy named Maurice standing by her bed. He quickly organizes an expedition for Dulcie, her brother Dicky, their maid Alice, and George, the little boy who lives across the street. Seeking The Wishing-Tree, they find a castle and observe Maurice's magic at work. Like Lewis Carroll's famous Alice, they are all in peril for a short time when they shrink in size. Finally arriving at The Wishing-Tree, they find it "a tall old man with a long shining beard like silver," and the leaves are "birds of all colors and kinds." The omniscient narrator calls him "the good Saint Francis." The mellomax tree they had discovered earlier was really The Wishing-Tree. If they will give him the leaves they plucked, he will replace them and give them each a bird instead. They step through, rather than over, a river, and Dulcie wakes to find herself in her bed, a caged bluebird her first present of the day.

It was the kind of tale they loved to hear Billy tell. And it had ended with a suitable moral: "the good Saint Francis had said that if you are kind to helpless things, you don't need a Wishing-Tree to make things come true." The tale was another demonstration of Faulkner's economy. Saint Francis had of course appeared at the end of *Mayday*, and though there was here no Little Sister Death, there was the curious stream which "stood up on its edge, like a gray wall . . . and the water smelled like wistaria." It was, at the very least, a river dividing sleep and waking. Maurice's eyes had "queer golden flecks" like Pete's eyes in *Mosquitoes.* Producing magic ponies, Maurice reassured the children that "They're gentle ponies"—a phrase almost identical with Buck's deceptive assurance, "Them's good gentle ponies," in *Father Abraham.* And Alice, speaking about the circus she wants to see, thinks of "Spotted Hawses, and folks spanglin' through the air. . . ." Her one-time husband, Exodus, describes his wartime experiences in hyperbole much like that of Caspey in *Sartoris. The Wishing-Tree* was a magical, amusing tale for an eight-year-old girl, but its fabric of dreams came from the same source as works very different from it. Cho-Cho proudly took it to school to be read aloud to the other children.

Just as Faulkner had here and there written into *Mosquitoes* a word or phrase which only a special reader would recognize, he had apparently included one private reference in *The Wishing-Tree.* Cho-Cho was obviously meant to associate Dulcie with herself. One page from the end, the narrator wrote, "Dulcie's mother was beautiful, so slim and tall, with her grave unhappy eyes changeable as seawater and her slender hands that came so softly about you when you were sick." Most of these details might have been expected in a description of the loving mother in such a book. But there was one detail that was totally incongruous here and did not fit with anything else in the story: the mother's "grave unhappy eyes."

Faulkner had been thinking about some of his early work in these first months of 1927. William Stanley Braithwaite had included "The Lilacs" in his *Anthology of Magazine Verse for 1925*. Now Faulkner wrote him for advice about *The Marble Faun*. "I paid the manufacturing costs and I have a contract signed by Mr Brown as president, by which I am to be paid my royalties in the usual manner. In the fall of 1925 I received a statement from them to the effect that they owed me $81.00." But he had received neither the money nor even a reply to his registered letter. Did Braithwaite know anything about the people at Four Seas? Was it possible to collect without litigation, which he could not afford, "having no income beyond that derived from more or less casual manual labor?" He apologized for bothering him, "but I dont know exactly whom to ask about such a situation. It never occurred to me that anyone would rob a poet. It's like robbing a whore or a child."

Braithwaite wrote him a reassuring letter, and Faulkner sent his thanks on February 25. He was still nettled, however, that no one at Four Seas had even replied. "Of course, if it is just a matter of temporary financial embarrassment, I shall rest easy: I have been without money too damned often myself, to annoy anyone who is himself unable to meet an obligation." He congratulated Braithwaite on the new anthology. "The last two of them," he added, "have revealed a very healthy thing in America, I think: the number of people more or less unknown, who are writing verse. I think I counted more than three hundred in the one for 1925."

Stone sometimes helped him with a loan, and often he would provide transportation. Together they would drive to Memphis occasionally. One day when they went to Dot Wilcox's home for dinner, Faulkner brought along a copy of *The Marble Faun*. In the flyleaf he wrote down the year, 1927, and the inscription "To Dorothy, in memory of many pleasant occasions, Bill Faulkner." Below those lines, Phil Stone wished Dot good luck and signed his name too.

"Dot," Stone said, "you keep this book. Someday this tramp will be famous."

"Yes," Faulkner added, "it will come out in the paper in headlines, 'The Tramp Who Became Famous.' " The three of them laughed and went on with their dinner.

But though he could enjoy himself with friends like these, his dominant emotional state was often one of melancholy. He was too old now to write verse in which he followed models he did not feel. For one sonnet, which he dated "14 March 1927," he used the title "Admonishes His Heart." He began with the words "Be still, my heart, be still," as the poet grieved for a lost love but tried to remember the time before it. He concluded with the sestet

Once there was lightless time: I had not birth
—Be still, my heart, be still: you break in vain:
A shattered urn in wild and bitter earth—
There was beauty then, grief and pain
But I lay close and dark and richly dearth.
Why did I wake? When shall I sleep again?

Consciously or unconsciously, Faulkner was borrowing again from *A Shropshire Lad*, from poem XLVIII, one of Housman's darkest. Though this was one of Faulkner's favorite poems, his own sonnet—typed out in these last days of winter during a brief break from his novel—must have been something more than just an admiring gesture or a literary exercise.

Composing a section in longhand, typing it, then returning to longhand, Faulkner was going ahead with *Flags in the Dust*, elaborating the plot and thickening the texture through contrast between generations and classes. As Colonel John Sartoris represented a vanished order, so his son, old Bayard, symbolized a vanishing one. Contrasted with his wild grandson, young Bayard, racing over the countryside in his dangerous and symbolic roadster, old Bayard was as archaic as the buggy driven by old Simon. That the line shall not die out is one of the overriding concerns of Aunt Jenny. To this end she subtly encourages twenty-six-year-old Narcissa Benbow to think of young Bayard. At this point Faulkner reached back into what he would later call his "lumber-room" for additional characters. One was Byron Snopes, the bookkeeper at old Bayard's bank and author of obscene anonymous letters to Narcissa.

The theme of contrast between the generations, and between old ways and new, was reinforced by Dr. Alford's insistence that old Bayard's wen be excised and Dr. Peabody's advice that it be left alone. Aunt Jenny's concern for old Bayard was counterpointed by the anxiety they both felt for Bayard. Faulkner showed Bayard acting out his death-wish not only with the automobile but with a stallion just as dangerous as Flem Snopes's ponies yet much more powerful. Bayard grapples with him as Buck does with one of the ponies, and as he mounts, "The beast burst like bronze unfolding wings. . . ." (133) In the wild ride two little children miraculously escape trampling, like Admiral Dewey Snopes before the rush of the spotted horses. And when Bayard is taken home from Doc Peabody's office, it is V. K. Suratt who drives him in his sewing-machine demonstration truck.

Faulkner had models all around him as he shaped his characters. One in particular, a man named Hugh Miller Suratt, might have helped with V. K. Suratt. Originally a country boy, he was a natural-born salesman, his friends said, and he made a good local agent for "Home Comfort Ranges." He was an able storyteller and an affable man who liked a taste of "white mule" now and then but did not drink to excess. Other characters, such as old Will Falls, suggested fused traits of several Oxford residents. If Falls's appearance suggested Mr. Charlie Bennett, his attainments were not unlike those of J. L. Shinault, an eighty-one-year-old veteran of the war. The salve which Falls used to cure old Bayard's wen was like one passed down to Mr. Buck Collins. As to young Bayard's reckless driving, Murry Falkner used to race the train in from Harrykin Creek in his red Buick until one day he hit the bridge on the home stretch and Miss Maud made him stop.

Faulkner did make a deliberate attempt, however, to avoid the direct equation of the two milieus. Jefferson, he wrote, was twenty-five miles from Oxford. Jefferson certainly had more in common with Oxford than any other Mississippi county seat, but some would see in this mythical town scenes from New Albany and Ripley as well. Just as he was trying to capture a whole generation or type with characters such as Colonel Sartoris and his son rather than simply to recount family history under the guise of fiction, so he wanted to give a concrete sense of place without specifying one particular spot in space and time. When he wrote that Belle Mitchell's house was located on "the most beautiful lot in Oxford," he immediately crossed out "Oxford" and substituted "Jefferson."

He continued to build his narrative, introducing Rafe MacCallum, one of six brothers with whom John and Bayard had hunted foxes in the hills in the years before the Great War. They lived there on their own place, like John Cullen and his brothers, members of a "yeoman" class. The society which Faulkner was creating now extended from the Negro laborers and white sharecroppers through the dirt farmers, merchants, and professional people up to the Sartorises and Benbows.

After some uncertainty about where to use him, he introduced another character who would serve as a foil for young Bayard and pick up a theme he had used before. Young Bayard embodied the wildness that had cropped out in the Old Colonel, who had killed two men; in his son Henry, who had killed a fellow student and later been shot by an irate husband; in the Young Colonel, who had wanted to shoot his father's assailant and finally tried to shoot his son's; in Murry Falkner, who had beaten at least two men with his fists, one badly enough to provoke gunplay; and in young Dean Falkner, who feared no man and thought he could do anything. William Faulkner had not shown these tendencies, probably because of his Butler genes. Now the character of Horace Benbow embodied traits very different, some probably closer to his own. He was called "a poet," and he was a devotee of Keats. A Y.M.C.A. worker, Benbow returned from the war with a glass-blowing set. After four failures he had produced "one almost perfect vase of clear amber, larger, more richly and chastely serene, which he kept always on his night table and called by his sister's name in the intervals of apostrophizing both of them impartially in his moments of rhapsody over the realization of the meaning of peace and the unblemished attainment of it, as 'Thou still unravished bride of quietness.' " (182) He was glad that his sister, like the figure on Keats's Grecian urn, had consummated no marriage, and their relationship suggested the vaguely incestuous intimations between Jo-Addie and Elmer and Pat and Josh.

Both would turn outward toward others, however. For Horace, there was Belle Mitchell, described with a simile Faulkner had used for Eula Varner: her "eyes were like hothouse grapes and her mouth was redly mobile, rich with discontent." (183) Horace is trapped. He is a lawyer who is a talker rather than a doer. Displaying a "taut and delicate futility" (171), he looks "a little mad, passionate and fine and austere" (203). Two close friends of Faulkner's were lawyers. If Phil Stone seemed an articulate and volatile talker rather than a doer, Ben Wasson also little resembled the average small-town lawyer. He was still noted for his beauty, and some would later say that Benbow was a pun on "Ben-beau." Similar to Benbow in family, diction, and devotion to justice, Ben would later be asked, "Are you the original of Horace Benbow?" and he would answer, "I'm afraid so."

Faulkner wrote on into the spring. It seemed a promising one for him. His last manuscript was due to be published in late April or early May and the present one was accreting in page after page of the tiny script. He did odd jobs occasionally to make a few dollars, and when he felt like it he went out to the golf course. An enigmatic-seeming figure, he would play his steady, accurate, thoughtful game. "Bill Faulkner was a man who had certain qualities about him which did not seem present in any of my other customers," recalled greenskeeper Tom Clark. "He had a certain kind of sophistication about him which belied the general regard with which most people seemed to hold him. I thought it was all due to the careless, irresponsible existence which he seemed to lead. He might come out to the golf course early in the morning and play all morning long by himself, or he might come along in the late afternoon. Time seemed not to mean anything to him. He appeared to live independent of the tyranny of the clock."

There was a tyranny more oppressive that many of his countrymen would feel that spring of 1927. It began to loom in early April as the waters started to rise after the heavy spring rains. The Mississippi had always overflowed its banks—levees were built, of course, and there was periodic agitation for federal flood control, as when Calhoun, Lincoln, and others had declared something must be done—but the river still rose and sent its waters out over the fields of the Delta. The flood of 1912 had destroyed forty million dollars' worth of property. Five years later the first Federal Flood Control Act became law. In 1922 flooding began in the Mississippi Valley in March and continued into June. Now, in 1927, by April 15 masses of water were sweeping down the river from Cairo to the sea. In four days' time twelve were dead and 25,000 were homeless. Thousands of men struggled to shore up the levees at New Orleans against the sweep of the pounding brown waves. A week later the flood had spread over 9,000 square miles and typhoid serum was being rushed in to stem an epidemic. It looked as though they would have to blow up the levee at Poydras to save New Orleans, and people were already fleeing the land that would be inundated. On April 30, at a cost of two million dollars, mud and water shot skyward with a tremendous roar as they dynamited the levee. (On the same day, in New York, William Faulkner's second novel, *Mosquitoes*, was published.)

By May 2 five more levees had broken and the main levee system was now endangered. Boats, aircraft, and federal troops were desperately conducting relief and rescue operations. Three million acres were now underwater, and in other areas not completely inundated looters were at work. The French Red Cross was sending vaccines. Expressions of sympathy came in from Norway, the king of Rumania, and French schoolchildren. At the beginning of the second week in May, the heavens opened again and flung tornadoes upon the stricken land as earthquakes erupted beneath it.

Anthrax had broken out among the cattle. Now the "Sugar Bowl" of southern Louisiana faced the same disaster that had scourged the cotton lands. By May 18 the Bayou des Glaises levee had broken in eighteen places, and thousands fled before waters rising in the Atchafalaya Basin. The Tchefuncta looked like the Amazon. Towns simply vanished as dikes broke before thirty-foot-high avalanches of water. The lucky ones were evacuated to the refugee camps, but some of the Acadians preferred plunging into wilderness areas rather than going to the camps and being herded in with thousands of people they had never seen before. By May 23 authorities were saying the crest had passed, but three days later emergency warnings were still going out to people about to be inundated or marooned. On the last day of the month, finally, the flood waters were falling everywhere but in the Sugar Bowl. At the end of the first week of June there were new floods in Arkansas, but by mid-June refugees were beginning to stream out of the camps and back to see what home looked like as the waters eddied away and revealed the mud, silt, and wreckage to the light of day. The damage would amount to two hundred and thirty-six million dollars. But there was some optimism here and there. In late June spokesmen in Ben Wasson's hometown of Greenville, contemplating their battered levees and debris-strewn streets, said they expected tourists and quick crops to cut down their losses. "The Old Man" had exacted his tribute.

In mid-June the reviews of *Mosquitoes* had begun to come in. There was a nice reciprocal quality about the first major one. It was written by Conrad Aiken, the poet whose work Faulkner had considered "a rift of heaven sent blue" in the fog generated by most American poets. The novel had humor and style, wrote Aiken in the New York *Evening Post.* He liked the characterization and dialogue, so much so that he thought the work might almost better have been cast in play form; in any case, the setting was amusing and original. The next major review was not so encouraging. Ruth Suckow wrote in the New York *World* that some of the characterization was clever but obvious. The dialogue was amusing here and there and the writing was occasionally good "when it isn't Joyce." It was all familiar, though—"the all too recognizable mixture of suavity, brilliance, cynicism, tragedy, philosophy, obscenity, pure nature and thoughts on art. . . ." This was what happened to "the English attitude" when south winds blew upon it; but, wrote Iowa-born Miss Suckow, "it does not manage to acclimate itself to the climate of New Orleans." New Orleans-born Lillian Hellman took a different view. The novel had humor and style, she wrote a week later in the New York *Herald Tribune*, and "a brilliance that you can rightfully expect only in the writings of a few men."

The July returns would be somewhat less encouraging. The Boston *Transcript*'s reviewer tired of the novel's irony and "broad humors," but he could see promise when the author "settles his manner and gets his stride." Like Ruth Suckow, Donald Davidson saw the influence of Joyce, but he found it happily assimilated by Faulkner. His review in the Nashville *Tennessean* saw the novel as an example of the Grotesque. The final result was to leave the reader "full of admiration for the skill of his performance, but conscious of some discomfort before the performer." Faulkner could have derived little satisfaction from John McClure's review in the *Times-Picayune.* The new book was a disappointment after "his extraordinary first novel." *Mosquitoes* was playful but cruel, brilliant but shallow. Faulkner really did not seem serious about the novel.

The book had gone out into the world bearing the dedication "To Helen." Somewhere the epithet which originally followed the name—"Beautiful and Wise"—had been deleted. The author had inscribed her copy, but by that time she was no longer Helen Baird. On May 4 she had married Guy Lyman in her aunt Martha's home in New Orleans. Bill Faulkner had not been invited. Helen still had a few of his letters, and the poems and stories, though she did not read them much. Later she would sell them to a collector.

When Ann Farnsworth read that *Mosquitoes* had been published, she told Helen, "I see Bill Faulkner has a new book out."

"Don't read it," Helen replied. "It's no good."

Those lines he had written nearly ten years before might have crossed his mind:

It is vain to implore me
  I have given my treasures of art
Even though she choose to ignore me
  And my heart.

But now he had a world to make, in which he could interpret and transform the reality he knew—the world of the Sartorises.

29

June, 1927–September, 1928

> . . . seeing the land for that moment before mule and plow altered it right up to the water's receding edge, then back into the River again before the trawlers and cruisers and cutters became marooned . . . back onto the Old Man, shrunken once more into his normal banks, drowsing and even innocent-looking, as if it were something else beside he who had changed, for a little time anyway, the whole face of the adjacent earth.
>
> —"Mississippi" (28)

> The streets are paved now, and the telephone and electric companies are cutting down more and more of the shade trees—the water oaks, the maples and locusts and elms—to make room for iron poles bearing clusters of bloated and ghostly and bloodless grapes . . .
>
> —"That Evening Sun" (289)

The Mississippi summer transformed the fields as he went on with *Flags in the Dust*, taking time occasionally for familiar pursuits such as golfing or visiting Memphis, and unfamiliar ones such as reading fan mail. He even answered one of the queries from strangers, a thing he would do less often as the flow of mail grew heavier. It came from Miss Fanny Butcher, who was running a series called "Confessions" in her column in the Chicago *Tribune.* What book would he most like to have written? *Moby Dick*, he wrote back; "The Greek-like simplicity of it: a man of forceful character driven by his sombre nature and his bleak heritage, bent on his own destruction and dragging his immediate world down with him with a despotic and utter disregard of them as individuals. . . ." This was an understandable preference for a man now writing a novel about people only a little less dangerous to their fellows than Captain Ahab. But he mentioned others too. The creator of Eula Varner remembered "Moll Flanders and all her teeming and rich fecundity." Having just written about Dulcie and Dicky and Maurice, he thought about Christopher Robin and Pooh-Bear and Eeyore: "when I recall *When We Were Very Young*, I can wish without any effort at all that I had thought of that before Mr. Milne did."

In the novel, he was continuing to move his several plot lines forward: bringing Horace and Belle closer together, moving Narcissa from seeming hatred for Bayard toward something like reluctant love, and following the destructive growth of Byron Snopes's furtive lust for her. He also moved back and forth between Will Falls's treatment of old Bayard's wen and his grandson's oscillation between his bent toward destruction and the palliative of work upon the land. As his story set in present time went ahead, Faulkner was constantly buttressing it with flashbacks and retrospective scenes—the Old Colonel capturing Yankees and killing carpetbaggers, young Bayard growing up merry and wild with his twin, John.

Oxonians were now leaving for summer vacations. Estelle and Cho-Cho and Malcolm were going to Columbus to visit Mrs. Hairston. Others, like city engineer John Falkner, could see a hot and busy summer ahead. Johncy would be working with gravel and steaming tar as the streets were paved. No longer would citizens have to walk through inches of muck left in the Square by fall or spring rains. Merchants and shoppers were pleased, but a few like Bill Faulkner saw the breaking of another link with the past. There were more autos and fewer horses around the Courthouse these days, and the macadam encroachments would spread swiftly. Sidewalks went in as streets were laid down. At the same time big lots with sweeping lawns were being chopped up. Twenty-five new houses, reported the *Eagle*, were now under construction or shortly would be.

Faulkner left town periodically—sometimes with Stone, sometimes alone. One letter to Horace Liveright in mid-July briefly mentioned both his literary and nonliterary activities. "Lost some money last week-end gambling," he wrote, "and I have drawn a draft on you." It was for $200 and they could turn it down if they wanted to. If they decided to honor it, the money could be charged against his next advance. He was halfway through the manuscript against which it would be charged, he said, and he hoped to send the whole thing to New York by September 1.

Liveright wrote back on July 23 asking him to let them know in advance next time. Faulkner offered an explanation with his letter of thanks. "Its quite a yarn," he said. "I had just purchased twenty-five gallons of whisky, brought it home and buried it in the garden. Two days later I went to Memphis, lost over three hundred dollars on a wheel, and gave a check for it. I had about one-fifty in bank, and I knew I could dispose of my whisky and raise the balance with only the minor risk of being had by the law for peddling it. So I came home in about three days, found that one of our niggers had smelled the whisky out, dug it up, sold a little and had been caught and told where the rest of it was. So I lost all of it." He would not have turned to Liveright, he added, but for the fact that "what with the flood last spring, southern people have no cash money for gambling debts."

If Faulkner had lost money on a roulette wheel, it had probably been in a club such as the one Reno DeVaux ran. It is not unlikely that he also visited some other familiar places in Memphis, for it appears to have been during these years of the late 1920's that he knew a businesswoman in Memphis named Bella Rivers or Mary Ware. She had come from Alabama as a girl to work in the Memphis Tenderloin, but she had felt herself superior to the other girls for she had pretty much stuck to one man on her own time. Now she ran her own house, which she tried to make a model of decorum. Out of Faulkner's observation of it probably came the offer of a job he described: "to become a landlord in a brothel. In my opinion it's the perfect milieu for an artist to work in. It gives him perfect economic freedom; he's free of fear and hunger; he has a roof over his head and nothing whatever to do except keep a few simple accounts and to go once every month and pay off the local police. The place is quiet during the morning hours which is the best time of the day to work. There's enough social life in the evening, if he wishes to participate, to keep him from being bored; it gives him a certain standing in his society; he has nothing to do because the madam keeps the books; all the inmates of the house are females and would defer to him and call him 'Sir.' All the bootleggers in the neighborhood would call him 'Sir.' And he could call the police by their first names." This account was probably no more true, literally, than that of the silver plate in his skull. But just as that tale was related to a reality out of which came such figures as Donald Mahon and Bayard Sartoris, so this description bespoke another kind of acquaintance which would be just as rich for the purposes of fiction. Faulkner did nothing to counteract the impression that he was well-acquainted with the Memphis demimonde. One story, which sounded as though it might bear the mark of the author himself, suggested the way he used this milieu for purposes of humor as well as squalor. According to this account, Faulkner was approached, as he sat quietly enjoying the sociability of the parlor, by one of the inmates of the house. She asked if he wouldn't like to go upstairs with her, only to be stopped by his reply. "Please leave me alone," he said. "Can't you understand I'm on my vacation?"

In the letter relating the loss of the whiskey, Faulkner included a progress report and two queries. The new novel was coming fine, he said. "It is much better than that other stuff. I believe that at last I have learned to control the stuff and fix it on something like rational truth." He might refer thus offhandedly to his first two novels, but it was partly bluff. "How are the reviews of Mosquitoes?" he asked. "I have seen one or two. Are they satisfactory, do you think? As a whole, I mean." In his last paragraph he told Liveright that he had enough verse in manuscript for a book. "Would you care to look at it? Rather, could you be prevailed to look at a book of poetry?"

He was well past the point he had described in Paris, when he told his mother he was putting aside his novel because he didn't know enough about people. Now nearing thirty, he felt that he could determine "rational truth." He had known he possessed the technical equipment; now he felt he was using it with greater assurance. His last question was a significant one. He still esteemed his poetry, but this was a by-the-way query from a man who was a professional fiction writer.

Liveright replied promptly, addressing him as "Dear Faulkner" and calling him "old boy." He had been amused by Faulkner's letter, but would he please remember not to draw any unpremeditated drafts again. As for the reviews, "They aren't anything to sing halleluiahs about, but on the other hand, they weren't particularly bad either." Liveright was hardly more encouraging about the poems. "Shoot them along," he wrote, "and although they won't sell, if they're awfully good we may want to lose a little money on them." He ended on a cautionary note. "We don't publish much poetry as you know, so yours must be outstanding or there will be little sense in our doing it."

He pushed ahead with *Flags in the Dust*, from time to time echoing earlier work. As Narcissa watched the sleeping Bayard, convalescing from a car wreck, he woke from a terrifying nightmare of aerial combat. Her words were precisely those of Jenny to Mr. Talliaferro: "You scared me so bad." (251) Bayard Sartoris has taken bullets in his cockpit just as Donald Mahon had, and Byron Snopes, falling into a flower pit after stealing into Narcissa's room, is put to flight no less certainly than Januarius Jones by Joe Gilligan.

In spite of Bayard's clear death-wish, Narcissa's incestuous feelings, and her professed hatred for men in general, she was drawing closer to Bayard. At the same time, Faulkner brought the Snopes subplot to an end as Byron Snopes—constantly blackmailed by young Virgil Beard—left town in the dead of night. Now Faulkner could move toward the final action. At the top of page 159, he carefully printed the numeral IV.

He was still rising at first light and writing often until noon, so that he usually had much of the day for other activities. Dot Oldham would see him at the golf course where he had taken to earning a little money at a refreshment shack. When Nehi was delivered from the bottling company that Dot and Major Oldham ran, Faulkner would put the bottles in a big barrel he had lined with sawdust, filled with ice, and covered with tow sacks. Presiding over the shack in white duck pants, he would dispense nickel and dime commodities to hungry and thirsty golfers. There one day he explained his general behavior to Dot as he had to Margery Gumbel's mother. "Dot," he said, "I'm a genius." But soon he had had enough of the golf course and—as the sun rose higher in the cloudless skies—enough of Oxford too.

Returning to Pascagoula in that summer of 1927, Faulkner planned to finish his new novel there as he had his previous one. It appears that this time he stayed on after the Stone family left. At one point, living by himself, he very properly invited the two children of Helen Baird's Aunt Martha to have dinner at his cottage. Aunt Martha had no idea what the strange young man would give Peggy and Jean Martin. When they returned home, she found that there had been only the three of them. The host had served bacon and scrambled eggs, and the children had enjoyed the occasion very much.

Tom Kell remembered Faulkner staying at the Turnbull place and coming to his house for meals. He would see him on the beach from time to time, sitting there, "not missing a trick," or simply strolling, barefoot. To some Pascagoulans he was "the wanderer." Sometimes, with Kell and a friend, he would go on the three-mile sail to Round Island in Kell's sixteen-foot skiff. As they sailed, or strolled on the island, Faulkner would talk with admiration about his grandfather and his uncle John, each man a proto-Sartoris, and thus especially in his mind now.

On occasion, Faulkner apparently ventured further out than Round Island. He wanted to go out on a shrimp boat again for one of their average trips, which might take from three days to a week. He went on one or two of them, Kell remembered, but one of the captains was not used to having a man on board who might just sit motionless for hours without speaking or lie up forward looking down into the waters dividing before the bow. "I don't want that damn fool on my boat," he said to Kell after tying up at the dock.

A friend who first moved to the Vieux Carré in 1927 remembered Faulkner's appearing there in white ducks. He had "bummed" his way from Pascagoula to New Orleans on a schooner, he said. He looked up some of his friends, among them Lyle Saxon. It turned out that Saxon was addressing a meeting of the Alliance Française, made up mostly of old ladies, at Le Petit Salon. Faulkner waited for him for a considerable time. When he finally walked in he asked Saxon, to the shock of those members nearby, "Lyle, you old son of a bitch, what's been keeping you?"

At a certain point that summer, Kell began to sense that Faulkner was "crowded," running low on both money and liquor. Faulkner finally told him about a debt of several hundred dollars.

"Phil Stone lent me that money," he said, "but I'm not gonna be obligated to him. I'm gonna pay that money back." Then he added, "Nobody dictates to me what I can write and what I can't write."

"Well, Bill," Kell said, "you don't have to pay for your liquor here." Then Kell had another thought—why didn't Faulkner come and stay with him at his house in town?

Faulkner accepted. One day after he had moved in, he said to Kell, "Tom, I need some whiskey."

"Do you know where you can get it?" Kell asked.

"Yes," Faulkner answered.

Kell gave him five dollars. Faulkner left, returning a few hours later with two gallons of moonshine procured in the Pascagoula swamps.

Kell noticed that Faulkner sometimes drank when he was working. He did it for inspiration, he decided. The two men would drink together, and Kell would be surprised at his guest's capacity and capabilities. Once when Kell declared he had had too much, Faulkner said, "Tom, my dear boy, I will recite the conversation." This he proceeded to do, going back a considerable time and repeating it in detail.

"Tom," Faulkner once said to him, "you know, what makes me act kind of peculiar sometimes is I've got a silver plate in my head and I drink on account of it."

"No," Tom retorted, "you're just mean," and they both laughed.

By late September Faulkner was in the final stages of the manuscript. Three pages into Part IV, Bayard and Narcissa were married and she was pregnant, expecting a child whom Aunt Jenny unquestioningly thought of not only as a boy but as another John Sartoris. There were passages of comic relief, but soon the doom, staved off for a time, began to descend. Feeling guilt for the car wreck which brings on old Bayard's final heart attack, young Bayard goes to his friends the MacCallums, in the hills. He then makes his way to a railway depot and waits for the first train out. As he had done before, Faulkner might at this point have been projecting elements of himself into his protagonist. Bayard's appearance suggested the author's on some past occasions: "Unshaven, in his scarred boots and stained khaki pants, and his shabby, smoke-colored tweed jacket and his disreputable felt hat, he found a vacant seat and stowed the jug away beneath his legs." (350)

The other catastrophes followed: Horace's marriage to Belle, Simon's murder by a rival in his mistress's cabin, and Bayard's fatal test flight of an experimental airplane. Holding her child, born the day of his father's death, Narcissa realizes "as she never had before the blind tragedy of human events." (356) The last passages of the novel held echoes of Faulkner's verse. He mused on "the Player, and the game He plays . . . He must have a name for His pawns, though. But perhaps Sartoris is the game itself—a game outmoded and played with pawns shaped too late and to an old dead pattern, and of which the Player Himself is a little wearied. For there is death in the sound of it, and a glamorous fatality, like silver pennons downrushing at sunset, or a dying fall of horns along the road to Roncevaux." Aunt Jenny snorts at the thought that Narcissa's naming the boy Benbow rather than John will have any effect on his life, but Narcissa smiles dreamily in the twilight as she softly fingers the piano keys, while "beyond the window evening was a windless lilac dream, foster dam of quietude and peace." (380)

Faulkner had apparently continued his usual practice of typing his manuscript in sections. This time when he went through the typed material, he apparently did more changing and rearranging than he had done with either of the two preceding novels. There were not as many individual changes of lines and insertions of passages, but five lengthy sequences underwent relocation. And there were deletions. The description of John and Bayard in wartime England was cut then or later, as was that of Caroline, Bayard's first wife. Deleted too was old Bayard's recapitulation of the long Sartoris genealogy from the time of the Plantagenets through that of the Stuarts. The novel would now open in present time, with Will Falls telling old Bayard about his father's escape from the Yankees.

Finally, on page 583, he was finished. There he put down the date in pen: "29 September 1927." He had finished this book of his "growing years" four days after his thirtieth birthday. It may have been then, as ordinary concerns began to intrude once more, that he wrote an undated letter to Aunt 'Bama in Memphis: "Grandest weathers. I finished the book today. Will get it off tomorrow, and next time I come up, I'll try [to bring] it to you. I don't know when that'll be, as I have a job of work I'll be doing this month. Painting signs."

On a Sunday, probably October 16, Faulkner wrote Liveright from Oxford. He was in a confident, slightly euphoric mood. "At last and certainly, as El Orens' sheik said," he told his publisher, "I have written THE book, of which those other things were but foals. I believe it is the damdest best book you'll look at this year, and any other publisher." With another flourish he said, "I dont think that even the bird who named 'Soldiers' Pay' can improve on my title." He was looking ahead with some apprehension, however, to the book's production. He had enclosed a few suggestions for the printer which he hoped Liveright would look over and, "if possible, smooth the printer's fur, cajole him, some way. He's been punctuating my stuff to death; giving me gratis quotation marks and premiums of commas that I dont need."

There was nothing about the poetry, though he did return to another subject of his earlier letter. "As usual, I am broke, and as usual, I want some money." He was "going on an expedition with a lady friend for purposes of biological research" and would appreciate any advance Liveright could let him have. In a postscript he switched back to the book: "I also have an idea for a jacket. I will paint it soon and send it up for your approval soon." The book itself would be in the mail on Monday.

On October 20 Liveright promised Faulkner that he would read the book as soon as it came in, "and if I get as het up about the book as you have stimulated me by your letter, you will get the rest of the advance post-haste." He was passing on to the manufacturing department Faulkner's suggestions for the printer. As to the title, Liveright couldn't say that he was crazy about "Flags in the Dust," but that didn't mean anything until he had read the book. Faulkner waited.

Oxford had by now resumed its normal mien after the furor of the summer's gubernatorial campaign. Many were enraged by Theodore Bilbo, even though Lafayette County was generally considered Bilbo territory. An advertisement in the *Eagle* gave a breakdown of the pardons he had signed: thirteen for rape, four for attempted rape, four for incest, and two for seduction. Yet he had "the brazen affrontery," wrote the signatories, "to ask the home-loving and law-abiding men and women to re-elect him to the office which he disgraced." Bilbo carried the county by 350 votes more than his nearest rival and went on to win the runoff in late August. No one could then know how fateful for Oxford that election would prove to be.

The boom in other parts of the country continued in a somewhat attenuated way in Oxford. New houses—small bungalows, many of them—were still going up. "The Shack," advertised as "Oxford's most beautiful soda parlor and sandwich shop" was now open for business, its lunch counter run by former high school football player Rusty Patterson, sometime house painter and occasional drinking companion of Bill Faulkner. There was also a private dining room where patrons could listen to the newest hit records (also sold at The Shack), such as "Ain't She Sweet?" and "My Blue Heaven."

The Falkners were busy, too. Jack was preparing for a transfer from the Atlanta FBI office to Salt Lake City. Uncle John was occupied in a different way. As executor of John Wesley Thompson Falkner's estate, he pondered what to do with The Big Place. For a time he rented it to his father-in-law, Mr. Bob Harkins, who made it a boardinghouse. But soon it was vacant again, and the rent from occasional tenants was not enough to keep it from eating itself up. From time to time Murry and Auntee made suggestions but John did not consider them feasible. Finally he agreed to buy their interest in the house, which was valued at ten thousand dollars. Murry was willing to take a note for his share, but he insisted that his brother pay cash to their widowed sister. When John replied that he did not then have the money to do it, Murry lent it to him. There was no note between the brothers, just John's word. As part of the transaction Murry received a building lot carved from the southern portion of the property.

John began a development of the property which would exploit it in several ways. He had the old house moved back from the corner to the west, so that, turned ninety degrees, it now faced onto University Avenue. Then he sold the corner lot thus formed to the Standard Oil Company for ten thousand dollars. They would dig up the grass, excavate, pour concrete, and install gas pumps to create a modern service station. Then he had the house renovated, so that before the year was out he would be able to advertise for tenants for "The University Apartments . . . the first complete apartment house in the city. . . ." In its metamorphosis The Big Place had been altered —big rooms cut up, partitions installed, new entrances cut in—to provide two apartments on the first floor and one on the second. Electric lights and paving had changed Oxford, but for Bill Faulkner this change must have been just as sweeping.

There was still no word from Liveright about *Flags in the Dust.* During this fall Faulkner probably took part in what would become for him a regular custom: the annual deer hunt at General Stone's lodge below Batesville on the edge of the Delta. It was thirty miles from Oxford on the map, but because of the unpaved highways and the rugged terrain of the bottom lands, it took more than a hundred miles and two changes of trains to get there. Dean asked his older brother what rifle he would take to hunt for bear. Bill told him that he did not intend to take a rifle with him at all: if he met a bear he did not want to have to take the time to throw a rifle away before he could start running. Actually, Faulkner was a good hunter. "Because he was a writer," his brother Johncy remembered, "the town had already begun to look on him as a little queer, and at first the other hunters didn't know whether they'd get along with him or not." On the first trip he proved himself, however, for he "asked no favors, just to be allowed to hunt with them and be one of them. They assigned him the most remote and least likely stand of all because, as a novice, that was all he rated. He took it without a word and stood fast till they came for him each evening." He gained quick acceptance as well as valuable material for his fiction.

If he went to camp that year and returned at the usual time, he found a letter waiting for him at home on about the last day of November. It was from Horace Liveright. Rather than beginning with the usual comradely "Dear Faulkner," it was quite formal. The first four words told everything. "It is with sorrow in my heart that I write to tell you that three of us have read Flags in the Dust and don't believe that Boni and Liveright should publish it." The second sentence was even worse: "Furthermore, as a firm deeply interested in your work, we don't believe that you should offer it for publication."

On occasion, particularly as he grew older, Faulkner would ask for criticism and welcome it. At the same time, however, he was quickly resentful when it was unsolicited, particularly if he thought it missed the point of what he was trying to do. The rest of Liveright's letter must have been particularly painful in its rough handling of the book Faulkner had so euphorically described six weeks earlier, the book that Faulkner and Stone counted on for popular as well as critical success. Liveright paid him a compliment and then began to cut the ground out from under him. "Soldier's Pay was a very fine book and should have done better. Then Mosquitoes wasn't quite as good, showed little development in your spiritual growth and I think none in your art of writing. Now comes Flags in the Dust and we're frankly very much disappointed by it. It is diffuse and non-integral with neither very much plot development nor character development. We think it lacks plot, dimension and projection. The story really doesn't get anywhere and has a thousand loose ends. If the book had plot and structure, we might suggest shortening and revisions but it is so diffuse that I don't think this would be any use. My chief objection is that you don't seem to have any story to tell and I contend that a novel should tell a story and tell it well."

Two years later Faulkner still remembered his reaction vividly: "I was shocked: my first emotion was blind protest, then I became objective for an instant, like a parent who is told that its child is a thief or an idiot or a leper; for a dreadful moment I contemplated it with consternation and despair, then like the parent I hid my own eyes in the fury of denial. I clung stubbornly to my illusion. . . ." He wrote a short reply to Liveright and apparently sent it off quickly, perhaps even by return mail, since he dated it November 30. "It's too bad you dont like Flags in the Dust," he wrote coolly. Unless they were holding the manuscript against the two hundred dollars they had advanced to him, "I'd like for you to fire it on back to me, as I shall try it on someone else. I still believe it is the book which will make my name for me as a writer." He apparently thought that Liveright might actually hold the book as a hostage against the money he owed, for he mentioned it again in his second paragraph. He would see that they got another manuscript in its place: "I am working spasmodically on a book which will take three or four years to do; also I have started another which I shall finish by spring, I believe." The first book was probably *Father Abraham*, and the second may have been the book of short stories about fellow townspeople he had mentioned to Liveright earlier. But, whatever he did with those books, he would feel better if *Flags in the Dust* were out being looked at by other houses.

Liveright checked with Arthur Pell, the firm's secretary, to find out if there were any other charges against the book. Then he wrote Faulkner on December 10 that they were returning the manuscript that day. He did this with the understanding "that you may place it elsewhere, but that you are to give us the refusal of your next book." They would charge the advance against it, and hopefully it would be the book he thought he would have ready in the spring.

He was having no better luck with his short stories. Johncy had enjoyed *Flags in the Dust* just as he had the short stories about flying. Whenever Faulkner finished a new one, he would give it to Johncy to read and then sit there smoking his pipe, awaiting his brother's reaction. One story was about a Scotsman named MacWyrglinchbeath who flew airplanes in combat not for patriotism or glory but out of avarice and frugality. Faulkner entitled it "Thrift." Once when he called Johncy into his room, Johncy saw him making an entry on "a piece of typewriter paper tacked up on the back of the closet door. On it were ruled columns, with lines drawn across them like the pages of a ledger. In a wide column to the left were the names of various stories. The rest of the page was double columns. At the top of each double column was the name of a magazine—the *Post, Collier's, Atlantic Monthly, Scribner's,* etc. When he would send a story to the *Post* he would mark the date down in the first half of the column; then, when they'd return it, he would mark down that date alongside. He said he kept a record like that so he wouldn't send the same story to the same magazine twice." He had yet to record an acceptance.

That Christmas Jack was back home after a bankruptcy case, in which he had counted assets in the form of sheep on wind-swept plains in Idaho. Almost any new working conditions in his line would have to be better, so when a chance came to join a national credit association, he quickly took it and resigned from the Bureau. Estelle, of course, was home too. But it was not a particularly joyful holiday for Bill Faulkner. Liveright's decision had shaken him more than he had let his publisher know, and he was finding it difficult to get on with the book he had promised for the spring. His mood must have been much like that which his friend Bill Harmon saw one day when Faulkner met him on the Square and invited him to go and have a drink. Afterwards, they decided to go for a ride. In a borrowed car they headed south on Highway 7. Bill was singing a song that Harmon remembered as being very morbid. About seven miles south of town where the woods began, they topped a rise which overlooked an expanse of country.

"There," he said to Harmon, "is a beautiful spot. I'd like to be buried in a spot like that—right there. You know, after all, they put you in a pine box and in a few days the worms have you. Someone might cry for a day or two and after that they've forgotten all about you." And as for any kind of final display, he didn't want it. He would rather be hauled to the cemetery on a wagon by mules than taken in a Cadillac limousine.

When Liveright returned *Flags in the Dust,* Faulkner did not send it out again immediately, as he had said he wanted to do. He may have spent some time rereading to see if Liveright's criticisms had any merit and, if so, perhaps revising to meet them. Or he may not have been able to look at it again for a while. Two and a half months later he still had it, so that when he was ready to try again, he felt compelled to write to be sure they were both clear about it. Would Liveright agree to his submitting it to another publisher with the understanding that Faulkner would pay the advance back or submit the next manuscript to him first? He had put aside the novel he had in mind in order to do some short stories. He had sent them to an agent, and perhaps he could get something from them to pay what he owed. "Otherwise I dont know what we'll do about it," he wrote Liveright, "as I have a belly full of writing, now, since you folks in the publishing business claim that a book like the last one I sent you is blah. I think now that I'll sell my typewriter and go to work——though God knows, it's sacriledge to waste that talent for idleness which I possess." He closed with best regards to the people at Boni & Liveright and to Liveright himself, whom he apparently rather liked. In a postscript he added that he knew that a New Yorker couldn't conceive of anyone's being able "to live day in and day out without ever having as much as a hundred dollars or ten dollars, but it is not only possible in the provincial South; damn near 90% of the population does it." If he could sell the book and pay the debt, "at least I'll have incentive to light in and bang you out a book to suit you.——though it'll never be one as youngly glamorous as 'Soldiers' Pay' nor as trashily smart as 'Mosquitoes.' "

He had apparently determined to do some revision on *Flags in the Dust* before he sent it out again, but it was proving no easy job. "I've been thinking that I'd get to Memphis again soon, and also I have been trying to get the mss. in some sort of intelligible shape to send you," he wrote Aunt 'Bama. "But neither has come to pass, so I am sending the press clippings, and when I do get the script in order, I'll send it too. Every day or so I burn some of it up and rewrite it, and at present it is almost incoherent. So much so that I've got a little weary of it and I think I shall put it away for a while and forget about it."

He wanted her to see the reviews of *Mosquitoes*, it seemed, but that was not all. "I told the family that you had almost promised to drive down and see us. We all wish you would. I have something—someone, I mean—to show you, if you only would. Of course it's a woman. I would like to see you taken with her utter charm, and intrigued by her utter shallowness. Like a lovely vase. It isn't even empty, but is filled with something—well, a yeast cake in water is the nearest simile that occurs to me. She gets the days past for me, though. Thank God I've no money, or I'd marry her. So you see, even Poverty looks after its own." But nowhere in the letter did he mention the lady's name.

On February 27 Liveright formally gave Faulkner permission to sell the novel to another publisher but cautioned him to "make no arrangement with him to give him an option on any forthcoming novels." They would apply the advance they had paid him last July to the next novel. In Faulkner's undated reply, he said he would take advantage of Liveright's permission immediately. It was a much livelier letter than his previous one. "I have got going on a novel," he wrote, "which, if I continue as I am going now, I will finish within eight weeks. Maybe it'll please you."

His mood had obviously lightened now that he had three things working for him: the chance to sell *Flags in the Dust*, the stories the agent was marketing for him, and the new novel which might be done by May. The agent was Ben Wasson, who had tired of practicing law in Greenville and gone to work for Leland Hayward in New York at the American Play Company. This was a major literary agency which handled many prominent novelists as well as playwrights. In addition to his work there, Wasson was also free-lancing for advertising firms and reading manuscripts for motion-picture companies. He would certainly have enough contacts to give the stories a better chance than they had ever had under Faulkner's own system of laboriously sending them out repeatedly with only a brief covering letter to speak for them.

Faulkner was not the only one in Oxford who had been having a difficult time in the early months of 1928. Late in 1927 Governor-elect Bilbo had resumed a campaign initiated eight years before. He was trying to move the university from Oxford to Jackson. It might be more accessible there, but it would also be much more susceptible to political pressure and patronage. Chancellor Hume earned the new governor's bitter enmity when he campaigned vigorously to keep the university where it was. Judge John Falkner must have had to walk a tightrope. In 1920 he had worked to defeat the proposal; now he was one of the guests at Bilbo's inaugural ceremonies.

In mid-February the legislature went on record as overwhelmingly opposing any such transfer. But Governor Bilbo was by no means done with the university.

As spring came in Faulkner worked at his new novel, taking a break from it occasionally with a brief trip. He might go to watch his youngest brother, "Speedy" Falkner, star as an Ole Miss outfielder. Often he was with Estelle. "Cornell had his lovers in Shanghai," she would later say. "Mine was in Oxford." From time to time when Estelle would go to Columbus to visit Mrs. Hairston, he might go down and see her during her stay there. Her mother-in-law was an open-hearted, indomitably hospitable woman. Moreover, she said she loved this young man who was so obviously interested in her daughter-in-law, and he was equally welcome in the eyes of her brother-in-law, Malcolm Franklin. Uncle Malcolm admired Bill Faulkner's writing and had begun collecting it with the *Times-Picayune* stories. He had saved copies for Estelle when she was away, and now he had added Faulkner's three published books to his collection. He lived in a hotel in Columbus, a popular, sociable man who would go as far as Oxford to attend a dance he particularly fancied. Faulkner returned Uncle Malcolm's admiration, and when he sketched him in a semifictional work a quarter-century later, the colors were bright and clear: "an invincible and incorrigible bachelor, a leader of cotillions and an inveterate diner-out since any time an extra single man was needed, any hostess thought of him first . . . a young man's man, who played poker and matched glasses with the town's young bachelors . . . who walked not only in spats and a stick and yellow gloves and a Homburg hat, but an air of sardonic and inviolable atheism too, until at last he was forced to the final desperate resort of prayer. . . ." Rushing down a mountain in a frail Model T with two young blades, one of them driving with the benefit of an appreciable amount of the moonshine they had gone to procure, he prayed into the darkness: "Lord, You know I haven't worried You in over forty years, and if You'll just get me back to Columbus I promise never to bother You again."

Faulkner's life in Oxford went along much the same as ever. He still took the occasional odd job. Applying clear lacquer with a brush, he gave Hugh Clayton's brass horn such a finish that bandsmen from Mississippi State would cross the field in the fall to examine his "gold" instrument. This job earned Faulkner five dollars. He needed only a little money, he later said, "thanks to my father's unfailing kindness which supplied me with bread at need despite the outrage to his principles at having been of a bum progenitive." To those like the Browns, who understood him better, he was basically the same Billy Falkner. He might seem abstracted and distant, but at times he still entered into their lives. Margaret Brown, sister of his friends Edith and Calvin and youngest in the family, had always suffered from a birth defect. Now there was something else. She had developed cancer of the throat, and early in the new year the family had begun to fear that it was irreversible. From time to time Faulkner had stopped at the Browns' and occasionally told stories that Margaret seemed to enjoy. One morning a parcel for Margaret lay inside the front screen door. When they opened it they found it was a typescript of *The Wishing-Tree.* Often during these last six months of her life the family read it to her.

The new novel had grown in a way Faulkner had not anticipated. It had not begun as a novel at all, he would always say afterwards, but as a short story. It seems likely that he had started it as he had some of those he had mentioned to Liveright. One early short story which might have been in this group was first entitled "Never Done No Weeping When You Wanted to Laugh." The eight manuscript pages centered around Nancy, a Negro laundress and occasional cook for the Compson family. Quentin, the narrator, looked back from adulthood as he recounted it. He and his sister Candace and, to a lesser extent, their small brother Jason, realize that Nancy is in trouble. Her conversation with their father makes it clear that she is terrified of her lover (or common-law husband) Jesus, whom she feels lurking in the darkness near the lane to her cabin. She has prostituted herself for white men, and now that she carries the child of one, Jesus waits with a razor.

The Compsons' main response is impatience, and Mr. Compson callously remarks, "I think she's coming to feel about it almost like I do; wish that he'd come on and have it over with." The story ends as they escort her back to her own cabin and to the death which will follow—the unspoken but clear implication. A series of contrasts and ironies is set up, not the least of which is the fear Jason felt in the lane at Halloween and the fear Nancy now feels at the propinquity of death. In a longer version (called "That Evening Sun Go Down" and offered for sale two years later), Faulkner would nearly double the length of the story, inserting more initial background material on Nancy, more description, and more dialogue. In the third version, the drama and hopelessness of Nancy's dilemma were still emphasized, but Faulkner was at considerable pains to play off the adult consciousness against that of the children—specifically the degree of awareness of Caddy, and more particularly of Quentin, of the desperate and tragic situation they were witnessing.

As the elder Falkners could provide models for the Sartorises, so the younger ones could sit for the Compsons. The shared experiences of childhood were there in vivid memory: Billy, Johncy, Jack, and Sallie Murry riding in the Colonel's carriage and then splashing or trying to catch fish in Davidson's Bottom or Burney Branch. There were grim memories, like those of Damuddy's lingering illness, and lively ones such as climbing out a window of The Big Place and down a tree. And there was Oxford lore absorbed in childhood. In "That Evening Sun Go Down," wrote John Cullen, Faulkner was writing about something that actually happened. A Negro named Dave Bowdry cut his wife's throat and threw her behind their bed. "There is a ditch like the one Nancy had to cross behind the place where the Falkners used to live," Cullen noted. "Dave committed the murder a short distance from the Falkner home."

For the story "A Justice," Faulkner apparently drew on another set of memories just as real. Grandfather, Quentin, Caddy, and Jason drove out to Grandfather's farm, where Quentin spent the whole visit listening to the Negro-Indian blacksmith, Sam Fathers, tell the story which Quentin relayed to the reader. The same thing used to happen, Johncy Faulkner recalled, when Grandfather would take them to his farm about three miles north of town. There Billy would slip away to listen to the stories of John Henry, the Negro blacksmith on the place. Faulkner here used the children's activities, as in "That Evening Sun Go Down," as a frame for the other story to which they would react. This was a different sort of story from that of Nancy and Jesus. It was the account of how Sam, fathered by an Indian on a Negro slave, got his name. Again Quentin reacted more than the other children, and again his reaction related to the increasing knowledge of death. Looking back on childhood from a later perspective, in the last paragraphs he recalled his feelings. Faulkner here chose to use an image he had employed before, one of the most persistent in his imagination. "We went on," Quentin said of the ride home, "in that strange, faintly sinister suspension of twilight. . . ." Grandfather had asked him what he and Sam Fathers had been talking about. Quentin realized he did not know; "I was just twelve then, and I would have to wait until I had passed on and through and beyond the suspension of twilight."

At some point in the late winter or early spring of 1928 he started another short story to which he gave the working title "Twilight." "I thought it could be done in ten pages," he remembered. There was a factual analogue just as there had been for "That Evening Sun Go Down" and "A Justice." His mind went back to Sunday, June 2, 1907, to the funeral of Damuddy—Lelia Swift Butler. It was at first "a story without a plot," he said much later, "of some children being sent away from the house" because they were "too young to be told what was going on and they saw things only incidentally to the childish games they were playing, which was the lugubrious matter of removing the corpse from the house, etc. . . ."

He would later write, "I did not realise then that I was trying to manufacture the sister which I did not have and the daughter which I was to lose, though the former might have been apparent from the fact that Caddy had three brothers almost before I wrote her name on paper. I just began to write about a brother and a sister splashing one another in the brook and the sister fell and wet her clothing and the smallest brother cried, thinking that the sister was conquered or perhaps hurt. Or perhaps he knew that he was the baby and that she would quit whatever water battles to comfort him. When she did so, when she quit the water fight and stooped in her wet garments above him, the entire story, which is all told by that same little brother in the first section, seemed to explode on the paper before me."

In this story, as in the others, Quentin, Caddy, and Jason would presumably be ready to his hand. But then, he recalled, "the idea struck me to see how much more I could have got out of the idea of the blind, self-centeredness of innocence, typified by children, if one of those children had been truly innocent, that is, an idiot." The tragedy of birth defects was as well-known in north Mississippi as elsewhere—better, perhaps, in the small inbred settlements near Oxford. In one town a few miles away there was one such affliction in almost every family, Oxonians said. Just a few blocks away was the boy—now a man—Faulkner had seen behind his iron fence since childhood. And now, whenever he visited the Browns, he could see there in a particularly heart-breaking way the innocent and afflicted. Just as he had drawn from memory for the title of the story, so he could for a study of the "truly innocent" child. It was in "The Kingdom of God," published in the *Times-Picayune* nearly four years before. There in the first paragraph was the idiot as an adult, sitting in a car, tightly gripping a narcissus. His face "was vague and dull and loose-lipped, and his eyes were clear and blue as cornflowers, and utterly vacant of thought. . . . always in his slobbering, vacuous face were his two eyes of a heart-shaking blue. . . ." But then, Faulkner said, he became involved in more than just the idiot's reaction to the funeral: "I became interested in the relationship of the idiot to the world . . . and just where he could get the tenderness, the help, to shield him in his innocence. . . . And so the character of his sister began to emerge. . . ." As it did, the whole shape and meaning of the story started to change.

"I saw that [the] peaceful glinting of that branch was to become the dark, harsh flowing of time sweeping her to where she could not return to comfort him, but that just separation, division, would not be enough, not far enough. It must sweep her into dishonor and shame too. And that Benjy must never grow beyond this moment; that for him all knowing must begin and end with that fierce, panting, paused and stooping wet figure which smelled like trees. That he must never grow up to where the grief of bereavement could be leavened with understanding and hence the alleviation of rage as in the case of Jason, and of oblivion as in the case of Quentin.

"I saw that they had been sent to the pasture to spend the afternoon to get them away from the house during the grandmother's funeral in order that the three brothers and the nigger children could look up at the muddy seat of Caddy's drawers as she climbed the tree to look in the window at the funeral, without then realising the symbology of the soiled drawers, for here again hers was the courage which was to face later with honor the shame which she was to engender, which Quentin and Jason could not face: the one taking refuge in suicide, the other in vindictive rage which drove him to rob his bastard niece of the meager sums which Caddy could send her. For I had already gone on to night and the bedroom and Dilsey with the mudstained drawers scrubbing the naked backside of the doomed little girl—trying to cleanse with the sorry byblow of its soiling that body, flesh, whose shame they symbolised and prophesied, as though she already saw the dark future and the part she was to play in it trying to hold that crumbling household together."

There had been no lack of little girls to admire in his life. Sallie Murry had been almost as close as a sister—a plucky good sport of a girl, brought up without a father in the sad home where her mother kept house for her own widowed father. And just one house away had been Estelle Oldham —the oldest of the children in a family every bit as proud of its status and lineage as the Compsons. The images began to fuse in a powerful and unexpected way: the funeral, the children's ignorance, and Caddy. Faulkner later said that he experienced a kind of ecstasy when he began to write. Years later he would call this fused image "the only thing in literature which would ever move me very much: Caddy climbing the pear tree to look in the window at her grandmother's funeral while Quentin and Jason and

Benjy and the negroes looked up at the muddy seat of her drawers." The emotion was so strong that his conception of the vehicle had to be altered. "I loved her so much I couldn't decide to give her life just for the duration of a short story. She deserved more than that. So my novel was created, almost in spite of myself." He could describe the incident in the tree in the length of a short story (though that image did not appear until page 18 of the surviving manuscript), but he could not explore the relationship between Caddy and Benjy—and the others which it brought into focus—in anything short of novella length. And he would discover, as further problems arose from the work's mode of growth, that he could not do it in novella length, either.

On page 1 of his manuscript Faulkner wrote "Twilight." He underlined it twice and then wrote "April 7, 1928." He began with Benjy. Tended by T.P., one of the Negroes a year younger than himself, he watched the golfers play on what had once been the pasture he loved. From the beginning Faulkner limited Benjy's narration to a set of capabilities defining his idiocy. He could not reason; cause and effect were beyond him, as was sequential thinking. One time-plane would replace another through a certain stimulus which would produce a shifting stream of consciousness like the association of ideas in a normal mind in reverie or nearing sleep, as with Stephen Dedalus and Molly Bloom in *Ulysses.* Benjy could record, like a camera eye, and he could remember enough to make analogies, but he could not name or interpret. The men were not playing golf; they were "hitting." And they hit not from the tee but from the "table." For Benjy there was no causal relationship between the movement of his body and the movement of his shadow. When his clothing catches on a nail in the fence and T.P. moves to free him, present time is replaced by past time as Caddy, his sister, performs the same function for him more than twenty years before. As Caddy tells him to keep his hands in his pockets because of the cold, the scene is instantly replaced by another, earlier on the same day, before he was allowed to go outdoors. On the first page Faulkner had introduced two time-planes or levels, without any device of punctuation or typography to distinguish them.

He continued to introduce time-levels brought to Benjy's consciousness by different sensory stimuli. Some of these time-levels would encapsulate incidents which, had they been expanded, probably would have been shaped into stories like "That Evening Sun Go Down." In one, occurring in November, 1890, Benjy's name is changed from Maury. His handicap now obvious, his mother feels he should no longer retain the name of her brother, his namesake. This time-level, that of the present—April 7, 1928—and that of Damuddy's funeral in the early fall of 1898, would be the three principal ones. Ten others would be set in 1904, 1905, 1906, 1908, 1909, 1910, and 1912. On these levels past events would supplant the present in Benjy's mind: Caddy and her lovers, Caddy's wedding, the day of Quentin's death, Mr. Compson's death. Thus Faulkner moved forward in time, so that the episode of the children during Damuddy's funeral had evolved into a study of the whole family over a thirty-year time span.

When Faulkner wrote about the novel's composition five years later, he presented it as a reaction, in part, against the rejection of *Flags in the Dust.* (And by the time "Twilight" changed into a novel, *Flags in the Dust* could have been rejected again.) "When I began it I had no plan at all," he said. "I wasn't even writing a book. I was thinking of books, publication, only in the reverse, in saying to myself, I wont have to worry about publishers liking or not liking this at all." He was tired of submitting his work to the judgment of others. He had shown *Flags in the Dust* "to a number of friends who told me the same general thing—that the book lacked any form whatever. . . ." By now it had undergone so much revision that he had typed it over. Finally he sent it to Ben Wasson. "Will you please try to sell this for me?" he asked. "I can't afford all the postage it's costing me." Ben was able to do little better. It would go to twelve different publishers, he recalled, before it was finally accepted. It was not surprising that Faulkner's attitude toward what he had thought of as his profession underwent a change. "One day I seemed to shut a door," he remembered, "between me and all publishers' addresses and book lists. I said to myself, Now I can write. Now I can make myself a vase like that which the old Roman kept at his bedside and wore the rim slowly away with kissing it. So I, who never had a sister and was fated to lose my daughter in infancy, set out to make myself a beautiful and tragic little girl."

If Faulkner's recollection of these circumstances was neither erroneous nor fictional, it throws some light on his wry comment to Liveright about the new novel he was writing: "Maybe it'll please you." It apparently mattered little to Faulkner whether it did or not; he was writing it for himself. When he could, he would pay back the advance out of proceeds from short stories. Meanwhile, he was experiencing something new each morning as he sat down before the accumulating pages—"that emotion definite and physical and yet nebulous to describe: that ecstasy, that eager and joyous faith and anticipation of surprise which the yet unmarred sheet beneath my hand held inviolate and unfailing, waiting for release." It was, however, a time of emotional ambivalence, if Faulkner's recollection nine years later was correct. There must have been a drastic contrast between inner and outer worlds. He wrote the novel, he later told his French translator, at a time when he was struggling with difficulties of an intimate nature —"Ecrit alors que l'auteur se debattait dans des difficultes d'ordre intime." He did not reveal what they were.

He was constantly expanding and elaborating, as shown by the first dozen letter-size pages of manuscript. On page 33 he came to the end of the Benjy section. "Then the story was complete, finished," he later wrote. "There was Dilsey to be the future, to stand above the fallen ruins of the family like a ruined chimney, gaunt, patient and indomitable; and Benjy to be the past. He had to be an idiot so that, like Dilsey, he could be impervious to the future, though unlike her by refusing to accept it at all. Without thought or comprehension; shapeless, neuter, like something eyeless and voiceless which might have lived, existed merely because of its ability to suffer, in the beginning of life; half fluid, groping: a pallid and helpless mass of the mindless agony under [the] sun, in time yet not of it save that he could nightly carry with him that fierce, courageous being who was to him but a touch and a sound that may be heard on any golf links and a smell like trees, into the slow bright shapes of sleep." Faulkner had treated many major events in the lives of this Jefferson family, but as he looked at his manuscript, and particularly at parts of it—page 20, for example, where almost all of the two-inch left-hand margin was filled with additions—he saw that it would not do. It was, he said, "incomprehensible, even I could not have told what was going on then, so I had to write another chapter. Then I decided to let Quentin tell his version of that same day, or that same occasion, so he told it."

Although there were links between Quentin and Benjy, Faulkner could scarcely have picked two seemingly more dissimilar narrators. In contrast to the mind of the idiot, that of his psychotic older brother was filled with allusions to the Bible, to Shakespeare, to other works of literature, and to family lore. This narrator would provide more latitude and complexity, but also proportional risks. It may have been at this point, as he was about to begin Part Two, and commit himself definitely to a novel-length work, that Faulkner made a third of a page of jottings.

At the top he wrote "Twilight—Notes." On the same line, to the right, was the word "Dates." Below was an attempt to establish or codify some of the information that he had been able to leave inferred, free-floating, or unknown in Benjy's stream of consciousness:

Quentin born 1890
Caddy 1892
Jason 1894
Maury 1897
Damuddy dies 1900
~~Roskus dies~~
Caddy marries 1910—age 18
Quentin dies 1910—age 20
Father dies 1912
born
Quentin ~~arrives~~ ~~1913~~ 1911
~~Quentin~~
Roskus dies 1915
Quentin runs off 1928—age 17
Benjy's nurses.
Versh-- --5
T. P. 5 --------------------18
Luster 18 ------------------------------

Near the top of the page at the left he had written:

> Show resemblances between Jason and Uncle Maury.
> Father said because of the fine sound of it. 40 acres of land little enough to pay for a fine sound.

Notes for *Twilight,* later *The Sound and the Fury.*

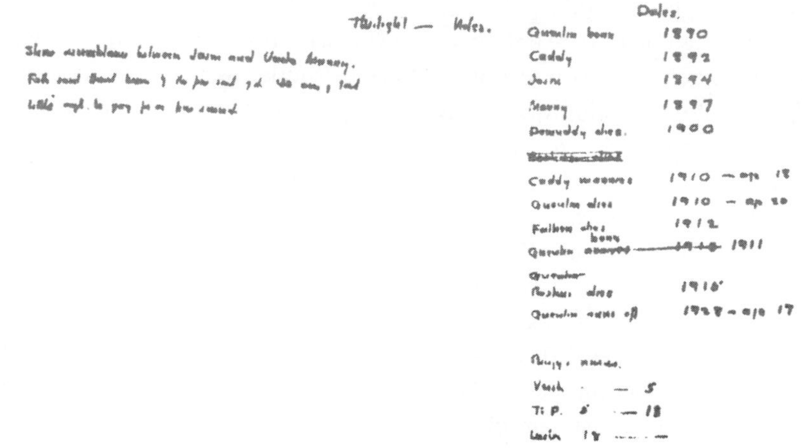
Twilight — Notes.
Dates.
Quentin born 1890
Caddy 1892
Jason 1894
Maury 1897
Damuddy dies. 1900
Caddy marries 1910 — age 18
Quentin dies 1910 — age 20
Father dies 1912
born
Quentin ~~arrives~~ ~~1913~~ 1911
~~Quentin~~
Roskus dies 1915
Quentin runs off 1928 — age 17
Benjy's nurses.
Versh — 5
T. P. 5 — 18
Luster 18 ———

As he had done with Benjy, he would fill in Quentin's characteristics as he went along. Later he would say that he occasionally used such notes in writing the novel—usually throwing them away, however.

On page 34 of his manuscript, headed "June 2, 1910," Faulkner began with Quentin's memory of seeing Benjy cry and paw at Caddy's dress, signifying his recognition of her fall from virtue which will eventually help prompt Quentin's suicide. Most of the sequence that followed was concerned with Quentin's proposal of a suicide pact to Caddy and his attempts to prevent her rendezvous with her lover, Dalton Ames. But when he reached page 40, Faulkner put the seven-page sequence aside and started Part Two over again, this time on letter-size onionskin paper. He began with the appearance of the shadow of the sash on the curtains of Quentin's dormitory room at Harvard, telling him as he awoke that he was "back in time again" on this last day of his life. When Faulkner reached page 43, he inserted the old pages 34–40, renumbering them so that they became 43–49. But they were not fixed yet. Twice more he would insert additional passages, so that the seven pages became 44–50 and finally 70–76 before they came to rest.

In this space Faulkner had further thickened the texture of the narrative, presenting the central events from the perspective of this other principal participant—as Joseph Conrad had done, though not so directly, in novels such as *Victory*. Early in the section Quentin thought of a characteristic reflection of his father's: how "down the long and lonely light-rays you might see Jesus walking, like. And the good Saint Francis that said Little Sister Death, that never had a sister." (94) Thus Faulkner set the tone for the whole section and began pointing toward the suicide that would end it. He also reused an image almost as persistent as that of twilight: Little Sister Death and Saint Francis, one or both of whom had appeared in "The Kid Learns," *Mayday*, and *The Wishing-Tree*. Through Quentin's stream of consciousness he began to elaborate the relationship between Quentin and Caddy. Quentin's dependence upon her is as great and obsessive as is Benjy's. The Compson children have grown up deprived of love in a home poisoned by a cold, hypochondriacal mother and a weak, nihilistic, alcoholic father. (Like his creator, Mr. Compson read Housman.) Rather than face the fact of Caddy's growth to maturity and her taking of lovers, Quentin wishes to abolish her promiscuity by asserting to their father that her transgression was incest. Though he does not seem to want her body, his love for her is super-fraternal. So is hers for him. "I got pretty jealous," her fiancé tells Quentin, "because . . . it never occurred to me it was her brother she kept talking about she couldnt have talked about you any more if you'd been the only man in the world husband wouldnt have been in it. . . ." (133) Faulkner was thus reworking, with a greater intensity and for different purposes, the subject he had treated earlier through Jo-Addie and Elmer, Pat and Josh Robyn, and Narcissa and Horace Benbow. In spite of the unhealthiness of the relationship between Quentin and Caddy, the reader would feel little sympathy for Herbert Head, her fiancé. A cheater and a boor, he was as full of slogans and hypocrisy as the most unbearable of Sinclair Lewis' villains. But Faulkner did not overdo this character. He had not only read Lewis, he had introduced Ben Wasson to Lewis' work. "He's very good," he had told Ben, "but very tiresome."

Now the first seven pages of Quentin's section, supported by forty more, had filled in the facts—as seen by Quentin from his special vantage point. They had grown up with little parental guidance or sustaining love. Quentin thinks, "*My little sister had no. if i could say Mother. Mother.*" (117) The invitation to Caddy's wedding had simply made more unbearable for Quentin the destruction of his world—begun through lovers such as Dalton Ames and continued through other lovers, by one of whom she is now pregnant. Throughout these pages the images of honeysuckle and twilight were wafted in and out, now symbolizing to Quentin his sister's promiscuity and his own approaching death.

As the manuscript grew, Faulkner employed a device he had used in earlier novels: keeping track of its length as he wrote. From page 60 through page 67 a series of numbers appeared giving line totals: 39, 30, 24, 38. His small script gave as many as twenty words to a full line; thus forty lines would be the equivalent of almost two printed pages. There were also other marks on some of these manuscript pages. The bond sheet on which he began what was now page 70 bore (like page 47) several dots of paint—cream-colored house paint, it appeared. It could have gotten onto the manuscript in any number of different ways and places, but it does not seem too unlikely that the man who would write in as many different places as Faulkner had done would not hesitate to write a few lines on work in progress during, perhaps, a noon-hour break on a painting job—one of his staple money-earners. Half a dozen other pages in the fourth and last section of the manuscript would show similar evidence on their margins.

Moving toward the end of Quentin's section Faulkner brought present events to the foreground. Ironically, Quentin is accused of molesting a little

Italian girl who attaches herself to him as he wanders in a little town outside Cambridge. He calls her "sister," thinking both of his own sister—violated with her own complicity—and of Little Sister Death. Vouched for by friends, he attempts to attack one who suddenly reminds him of Dalton Ames. Sympathy and understanding seem to come only from his roommate, Shreve MacKenzie, whom Faulkner made a Canadian, thus preserving his record of introducing into each of his novels the country where he had trained for the Great War.

As in the Benjy section, where sensory cues were enormously important, Faulkner employed here one of his favorite devices: synesthesia. Quentin's nose could "see" gasoline, and his hands can "see" the door. (215) Faulkner reached back to that privately important short story "Carcassonne" for a line as Quentin slipped further into madness. Drifting toward death by water, Quentin thinks how, beneath that surface, he can "knock my bones together and together." (216) The idea of twilight comes to dominate his mind, as it had at the end of "A Justice," and soon it occurs no fewer than five times on one page. To him the "draft in the door smelled of water, a damp steady breath. Sometimes I could put myself to sleep saying that over and over until after the honeysuckle got all mixed up in it the whole thing came to symbolise night and unrest I seemed to be lying neither asleep nor awake looking down a long corridor of grey halflight where all stable things had become shadowy paradoxical all I had done shadows all I had felt suffered taking visible form antic and perverse mocking without relevance inherent themselves with the denial of the significance they should have affirmed thinking I was I was not who was not was not who." (210–211)

Quite early Faulkner had begun to develop his own conventions of punctuation. Even in correspondence he omitted the period in "Mr." or "Dr.," in the British fashion. He also dispensed with apostrophes where it was clear that the word was a contraction, as in "dont" and "arent." As he moved through the Benjy section and the Quentin section, he retained these conventions and added others. Sometimes, following Joyce's lead, he would omit all punctuation to denote the flowing stream of consciousness. He would switch from roman type to italics and back to indicate a shift from one time-level to another. In the Quentin section he would put present-time dialogue in quotations, whereas he would usually omit the quotations for dialogue on past-time levels. In interchanges which Quentin remembers with strong emotion no initial lines would be capitalized. As his disintegration accelerates it is paralleled by the syntax and punctuation on the page. At the end of the segment he thinks about the progenitors of his tragedy, his weeping mother and his cynical father, who "was teaching us that all men are just accumulations dolls stuffed with sawdust swept up from the trash heaps where all previous dolls had been thrown away the sawdust flowing from what wound in what side that not for me died not." (218)

Quentin had given his version of the day Damuddy was buried. "Then there had to be the counterpoint," said the author later, "which was the other brother, Jason." He took another sheet of onionskin, marked it as page 87, and wrote at the top, "April Sixth, 1928." A few of the pages near the end of the Quentin section had been changed about, moved back as other material had occurred to him and he had inserted it. Now, however, he apparently moved along quite rapidly. Pages 87–124 formed an unbroken sequence and, as with the Quentin section, the Jason section had not quite the copybook quality of much of the Benjy section, as though it had been written at a faster speed. Jason Compson might be a monster of cruelty and hypocrisy, but his mind worked with a self-consistent logic. Once Faulkner started him talking he moved rapidly, flashing back to the past like his brothers but spending much less time reflecting on it and very little, actually, on the day of Damuddy's funeral when Caddy had climbed the tree. Traumatized by his loss of a promised bank job when Herbert Head divorced his illicitly pregnant bride, Jason is embittered by the past, but his mind is shallower than Quentin's and far closer to objective reality than that of either of his brothers. Thus the stream of present-time events stands in the forefront, with relevant prior information provided where necessary from Jason's sardonic and sometimes humorous ruminations.

Jason supplied information about events since Quentin's suicide which Benjy could not know or understand, sense some of them though he might. It is Jason who makes clear the death of Mr. Compson, Caddy's divorce, and her surreptitious visits to Jefferson to glimpse her daughter, Quentin, being raised beyond the mention of her mother's name. The reader infers, in large part, his years of embezzlement of money sent by Caddy for young Quentin. Jason fumes about Quentin's promiscuity. He likens it to her mother's, without accepting any responsibility for making the house she lives in even more loveless than it was in her mother's time. The reader follows Jason as he pursues Quentin and her current lover into the country outside Jefferson. He follows him as he goes to his room in "the decaying house" (355) and counts the money he has saved and embezzled. He is about to retire on Good Friday evening, unaware that the Resurrection day of the Christian calendar will be for him a day of unmitigated disaster.

"So I wrote Quentin's and Jason's sections," Faulkner later said, "trying to clarify Benjy's. But I saw that I was merely temporising; that I should have to get completely out of the book. I realised that there would be compensations, that in a sense I could then give a final turn to the screw and extract some ultimate distillation. Yet it took me better than a month to take pen and write *The day dawned bleak and chill* before I did so." Putting it another way, he said that he had realised that "by that time it was completely confusing. I knew that it was not anywhere near finished and then I had to write another section from the outside with an outsider, which was the writer, to tell what had happened on that particular day." Now, however, "that particular day" was not the day of Damuddy's funeral, but the day on which a long chain of events finally came to an end in the Compson house and family. At the top of page 125, Faulkner wrote, "April Eighth, 1928." Now it was Easter Sunday, following Benjy's Holy Saturday and Jason's Good Friday. As Faulkner worked his way through the novel, and particularly as he revised it in the typing, these days would take on symbolic significance so that certain parallels were suggested—a number of them ironic—between Christ's passion and death and the agonies of the Compsons. Faulkner had probably envisaged some such symbolic counterpoint from the beginning, even when "Twilight" had not yet shown signs of expanding beyond short-story length. From Faulkner's reply to Horace Liveright's letter of February 27, it appears that he had begun what he was even then calling a novel, close to the beginning of the Lenten season. He had written through Lent and through Easter. In chronological time he must now have been writing in Oxford's hot summer. But like his characters he was operating on several time-planes, and now he moved to this special Easter Sunday.

Midway through the first section had come the image of Caddy climbing up one tree. Near its end had come the commotion—though Benjy did not realize its cause—of her daughter Quentin's climb down another. In the fourth section of the novel Faulkner would explore some of the effects of the retributory act Quentin had performed. Breaking a window and slipping into Jason's room, she had taken money he had saved from his salary and appropriated from the maintenance checks Caddy had sent for Quentin. She had stolen almost seven thousand dollars, Faulkner would later write, four thousand of it rightfully hers. Pursuing her and the money, Jason would be frustrated in both attempts, and he would return with a violent headache from gasoline fumes, having nearly sustained a split skull at the hands of a little old man he had attacked in his furious search for his twin objects.

Faulkner was still reaching back into his lumber-room. Just as he had found Benjy in earlier fiction of his own, so he apparently found there a prototype for Dilsey Gibson, the Compsons' cook. In his notes for "The Devil Beats His Wife," he had tried out several names for the man and wife, but the name Della remained constant for the Negro maid who worked to keep this small family together and dominated what action he had sketched out. Physically she resembled Dilsey, too. Something of Dilsey's love and devotion doubtless derived from Mammy Callie, though Dilsey was nothing like her physically. But something of Mammy Callie was there, like the faint echoes of other works of fiction.

The pear tree Quentin climbed bloomed in this section as had the one in *Father Abraham.* There was no pathetic fallacy here: nature in her prodigal springtime beauty provided no sympathetic background for the anguish of men. While Jason Compson provided the section's dramatic action, Dilsey Gibson provided its moral center. In her ministering to the helpless Benjy, the sadistic Jason, and their brittle niece and neurasthenic mother, she embodied the Christian virtues—above all the ability to give love as well as labor. Returning from the Easter service at her church with Benjy in tow, she weeps for broken lives. She had been there in the family when the boy Quentin had been born; she had been there when his namesake had left: "I've seed de first en de last." (371) Entering the gate, "all of them looked up the drive at the square, paintless house with its rotting portico." (372) It is as though she knows what the future holds: Mrs. Compson's death, Benjy's commitment to the asylum at Jackson, and Jason's cutting the old home into apartments before selling it as a boardinghouse. At the last, after his bellows of alarm at a wrong turning in a trip to the cemetery, Benjy is quiet and serene. Like the idiot in "The Kingdom of God" he holds a broken narcissus and watches as "cornice and façade flowed smoothly once more from left to right; post and tree, window and doorway, and signboard, each in its ordered place." (401) But it is a static and a sterile order, a foreshadowing of the end to come.

He had, he later said, "written my guts into *The Sound and the Fury* though I was not aware until the book was published that I had done so, because I had done it for pleasure." The familiar words of the title had come one day "out of my unconscious. I adopted them immediately, without considering then that the rest of the Shakespearean quotation was as well suited, and maybe better, to my dark story of madness and hatred." But in one sense this manuscript did not mean what the others had, because "I believed then that I would never be published again. I had stopped thinking of myself in publishing terms." Nonetheless, emerging from the intense concentration of the writing, Faulkner may have felt a little like Lemuel Gulliver returning from one of his voyages. On June 12 Margaret Brown's suffering had ended. Three days later Lida Oldham had been called to Kosciusko by the death of her half-brother, Jason Niles. In the distance had resounded the noise of other events that summer: the presidential conventions and the ensuing contest between Herbert Hoover and Alfred E. Smith. Now that the hardest pull of the work had been completed by, perhaps, September, Faulkner could let up a bit. Even though he may not have thought of the book in terms of publication, if it was to be like the vase which the old Roman would wear away by kissing, he would want to shape it lovingly before he put it on its pedestal.

He was not able to relax on the golf course during the summer months of 1928. One day on the course he had paused for a drink of water, and when he turned back to pick up his clubs they were gone. He and Tom Clark and Willie vainly searched virtually every foot of the course for them. Without the clubs Faulkner could not play; he said he was too poor to buy others and, without saying so, he was too proud to borrow. That fall in Virginia, Clark received a crumpled envelope. It contained an angry letter from Bill Faulkner. He had recognized his clubs in the possession of a geology professor who told him Clark had loaned them to him. Clark wrote angry letters to both Faulkner and the professor. A week and a half later Clark received a letter of apology from Faulkner. He had interrogated the professor again and discovered that the professor "had picked up his clubs while Bill was over getting a drink of water and could never exactly account for the fact that somehow or other he had come by a strange set of golf clubs." This incident could scarcely have made Faulkner feel he had distorted human nature in his portrayal of Jason Compson or the Snopeses.

Faulkner had continued to see Stone as before, but he had not told him what he had been working on. This may have been a part of the resentment Faulkner had voiced to Tom Kell over Stone's real or fancied attempt to dictate what he should write. Whatever the cause, this signaled something of a new phase in their relationship, for Faulkner consistently gave to those close to him fragments of work in progress to read. When Faulkner invited him to his small tower room one night, Stone had no idea what was in the sheaf of pages his friend began to read aloud. It became an experience Stone would cherish, sitting "night after night in Bill's little room," as he listened to the story of the little girl with the muddy drawers who had climbed the tree to see what the grown-ups were doing.

Faulkner had been keeping in touch with Ben Wasson in New York. They would write from time to time about the stories Ben was trying to place, but occasionally Faulkner would send a jocular post card such as the one which read, "Sometimes I think when my linen is clean and my bowels are open this hand holds genius." It must have been in September that Wasson wrote to suggest that he come to New York. Estelle had often urged him to try New York again, particularly now that two of his novels had been published. "You've got to keep yourself in the public eye if you want to get ahead," she had told him. But he had not particularly cared for the city seven years before, and he was not especially anxious to go now. Besides, there was always the problem of money. But Wasson had been faithfully trying to place *Flags in the Dust* as well as the short stories, and it appeared that he might succeed.

Wasson had given the manuscript to his friend Harrison Smith. A nephew of the playwright Winchell Smith, Hal Smith was one of the editors of the eight-year-old house of Harcourt, Brace and Company. The firm had done well and was now expanding, having recently become American agents for the Pegasus Press, in Paris, which specialized in art books. Smith was a man of considerable if sometimes eccentric charm and literary taste combined with a high degree of business acumen. From time to time he would do reviews and articles on the business aspects of publishing, such as the one two years before about how to market and sell books on Abraham Lincoln. Ben dropped the manuscript off at Smith's office and then went upstate to Woodstock to escape the city's late summer heat. A few days later he received a note. Smith wanted to see him.

As soon as Ben returned to the city, he went up to Harcourt, Brace. Smith greeted him warmly. "Hey, fella," he said, "this is a mighty fine book you wrote." With all the handling the manuscript had received, the title page had been lost, and Ben had not yet replaced it.

"I didn't write it," he said, "William Faulkner did."

"He's good," Smith said. "I know his *Soldiers' Pay.*"

Smith told him that he had written a favorable report on *Flags in the Dust* and the decision was now up to Alfred Harcourt. Smith took him in to see Harcourt, who said he was in doubt about publication. He liked the 600-page manuscript, but there was one thing that troubled him: a prolixity in both style and content.

"I don't think he can cut his work," he told Ben. "Will you do it for fifty dollars?"

Ben immediately agreed. Rather diffidently, he inquired about an advance on royalties.

"How about three hundred dollars?" Harcourt asked. Ben accepted.

He sent the money to Faulkner and briefly explained that part of the deal was that the manuscript had to be cut. They had shown it to so many publishers that when a reputable firm like Harcourt agreed to take it, and with such a decent advance, Ben had not wanted to quibble. If Faulkner wanted to take the time from his new work to cut the book, that was fine. If he didn't, Ben would go ahead and do it as he had promised Harcourt. In that case especially, it would be a good idea for Faulkner to be there while Ben was doing it. Why didn't he use the advance to come to New York for a while? He could bring along whatever he was doing and maybe they could place that too while he was there.

The contract arrived. Dated September 20, 1928, it called for delivery by October 7 of a novel of approximately 110,000 words called *Sartoris.* Faulkner signed it and sent it back. He put his few presentable clothes in his suitcase and carefully wrapped the manuscript of his novel and the typed pages he had accumulated so far from rewrite and revision. He may still have thought of it as a private thing he had made, the vase for himself, the cherished shape that moved him and was his alone. Yet Harcourt, Brace liked *Flags in the Dust* well enough to take a chance on it—even though they evidently preferred their substitute title—and now he would be a published author again. The rejections of the novel had hurt enough so that he would later see himself as having totally rejected the publishers who had spurned him. He was proud and sensitive enough to do that. But now, apparently, things were beginning to open up for him as they had once before. He still owed money and the first refusal of his next book to Boni & Liveright. If they didn't like *Flags in the Dust,* he couldn't expect them to like the new book. But maybe Harcourt, Brace would. If *Sartoris* became the critical and popular success he and Stone hoped, how could they not take a chance on the next novel? There must be some way to get free of Boni & Liveright. He must have felt that any debt he owed them had been discharged when they refused his book about the Sartorises, his last look at "the finding years" of his life.

He said his goodbyes and boarded the train for Memphis and New York.

30

September-December, 1928

They seemed to bring with them the smell of the snow falling in Seventh Avenue. Or perhaps the other people who had entered before them had done it, bringing it with them in their lungs and exhaling it, filling the arcade with a stale chill like that which might lie unwinded and spent upon the cold plains of infinity itself. In it the bright and serried shop-windows had a fixed and insomniac glare like the eyes of people drugged with coffee, sitting up with a strange corpse.

Now and then, with a long and fading reverberation, a subway train passed under their feet. Perhaps they thought momentarily of two green eyes tunneling violently through the earth without apparent propulsion or guidance, as though of their own unparalleled violence creating, like spaced beads on a string, lighted niches in whose wan and fleeting glare human figures like corpses set momentarily on end in a violated grave yard leaned in one streaming and rigid direction and flicked away.

—"Pennsylvania Station" (609, 613–614)

William Faulkner stepped from the Pullman car amid the redcaps' shouts and hissing steam of Pennsylvania Station. There on the platform he sighted Ben—small, fair-haired, and handsome. They shook hands and Ben took his bag.

"Bud," said Faulkner, smiling, "I'm glad you met me at the depot."

Ben was living in a Greenwich Village brownstone at 146 MacDougal

Street, just across from the Provincetown Playhouse. His room was so tiny there was barely room for his bed, so he could not put his friend up. This was no problem, however, thanks to what was jocularly called "the Southern Protective Association." A writer such as David Cohn would say to a Southerner on his first trip to the unknown North, "Look up Ben Wasson when you get to New York." By now Ben knew the ropes of the publishing world, and he would show the newcomer around. He could introduce him to an agent and to congenial friends. If he needed a place to stay, he could often arrange that, too. There would be no problem making such arrangements for Bill Faulkner. He was known in New York and had friends there. Living in the city at the time were Stark Young, Lyle Saxon, and Bill Spratling.

Now thirty-seven, Lyle Saxon had scored a success the previous year with *Father Mississippi*, an account of the river's history and legends which incorporated articles based on his three months of rescue work during the great flood. He was working on a book to be called *Fabulous New Orleans*, but what he wanted most, he said, was to do fiction, and Hal Smith had managed a thousand-dollar advance for him on a novel. Saxon was still the same elegant bachelor, still the charmer and raconteur whom Spratling had pictured in *Sherwood Anderson & Other Famous Creoles.* Women were particularly attracted to him. They liked his soft, cultured speech and his accounts of his youth on his family's plantation. Rachel Field and Irita Van Doren were among his special friends. He spent most of his time, said one intimate, lecturing for free and being invited out. Another of his friends had found him a pleasant apartment over a bookstore on Christopher Street, a convenient location near Sixth Avenue and Eighth Street that was close to the Jefferson Street Market. It was a favorite meeting place for members of the Southern Protective Association and their friends. Faulkner could stay there with him for a while.

When Ben broached the subject of cutting *Sartoris*, he received an unexpectedly vehement answer. Faulkner refused to have anything to do with the process. Two years later he remembered arguing with Ben about it: "I said, 'A cabbage has grown, matured. You look at that cabbage; it is not symmetrical; you say, I will trim this cabbage off and make it art; I will make it resemble a peacock or a pagoda or 3 doughnuts. Very good, I say; you do that, then the cabbage will be dead.'

" 'Then we'll make some kraut out of it,' he said. 'The same amount of sour kraut will feed twice as many people as cabbage.' A day or so later he came to me and showed me the mss. 'The trouble is,' he said, 'Is that you had about 6 books in here. You were trying to write them all at once.' He showed me what he meant, what he had done, and I realized for the first time that I had done better than I knew . . . and I contemplated those shady but ingenious shapes by reason of whose labor I might reaffirm the impulses of my own ego in this actual world without stability, with a lot of humbleness, and I speculated on time and death and wondered if I had invented the world to which I should give life or if it had invented me, giving me an illusion of greatness. . . ."

The cutting was extensive. Ben deleted a long passage of Narcissa's reflections about Bayard as a boy and shortened Bayard's balloon ascent. He did the same thing with other passages in which Narcissa conveyed background material. Several scenes involving Byron Snopes, Virgil Beard, and Mrs. Beard were cut from the text. Long passages also went in which he had described Byron Snopes's twin torments: his anonymous lust for Narcissa and Virgil's blackmail. His final flight from Jefferson to Frenchman's Bend disappeared, as did the brief appearances of I. O. Snopes and his son Clarence. Horace's role was reduced: his one-time desire to become an Episcopalian minister, his sense of doom, his affair with Belle, a brief affair with her sister Joan, his prior involvements, his incestuous feelings toward Narcissa—all these were removed or drastically cut.

Finally it was finished. Faulkner added a dedication which, like that of *Mosquitoes*, was a gesture toward the past. It was to Sherwood Anderson, "through whose kindness I was first published, with the belief that this book will give him no reason to regret that fact." The grateful acknowledgment was balanced by the self-confident assertion of independence and talent. They gave the book to Hal Smith, who put it into the works for house editorial checking before production began. Smith did not especially care for that end of publishing himself; his chief pleasure came from working with the authors rather than their books. On October 4 *The Mississippian* reported that " 'Sartoris,' the latest novel written by William Faulkner, local poet and novelist, temporarily in New York, has been accepted and will soon be published by Harcourt, Brace and Company, according to information received here from Mr. Faulkner." Apparently Harcourt, Brace had—like Boni & Liveright—its own Tommy Smith who could supply better titles for new books than their authors. The account noted that while "all of the characters are entirely fictitious, the general theme of the novel is taken from the life of the author's great grandfather, the celebrated Col. W. C. Faulkner [*sic*], whose namesake the author is. . . ." There was also a glimpse of the future: "Faulkner has nearly completed a fourth novel, which will probably be published in the spring."

The reporter's source was very likely Phil Stone, who told a correspondent that it had "none of that flip and youthful smartness of *Soldiers' Pay* and *Mosquitoes*, but is a sad and lonely simple book." Moreover, "It is a far better book than I ever thought Bill would write by now. . . . Bill thinks it will sell. I think it's too good to sell, but I do think that it will make Bill's literary reputation and sell his future books. There's a good deal of humor in it, and it is the humor of people in action, not mere cleverness or wit, and parts of it is beautiful prose."

There was still the worrisome problem of owing Boni & Liveright an advance and first chance at his next book. He had by now seen Spratling, who had an apartment near Saxon's, and told him about his situation. It was not just the money and the contract; at heart Faulkner rather disapproved of his publisher. Liveright had always been a rather spectacular sort of man for the publishing business, with his notorious amours and other nonliterary interests. Now he was heavily involved in Wall Street speculation. At the same time he was growing steadily more fascinated with the idea of becoming a Broadway producer. He had been a pretty fair publisher when he took time off from pursuing one of his flames, Faulkner admitted, but he felt Liveright "should have probably been a stockbroker or something,——anything rather than a purveyor of creative literature." Together, according to Spratling's reconstruction much later, he and Faulkner devised a way out of the predicament.

By now they knew that Hal Smith wanted Faulkner to come over to Harcourt, Brace. "We had a good lunch down on Christopher Street, with cocktails and red wine," Spratling remembered, "and over lunch we contrived our little plan." They probably did not know what a potentially dangerous game they were playing. Bennett Cerf, who had worked for Horace Liveright for two years before buying The Modern Library from the company in 1925, had a sincere respect for some of Liveright's qualities. He could be, said Cerf, "one of the most attractive men. If you approached him openly and honestly he would treat you well. He would treat you as a gentleman. He was the soul of generosity and decency. But if he thought you were trying to cheat him, then he could be terrible."

At about two-thirty that afternoon Faulkner and Spratling dropped in to see Horace Liveright—just for a chat. After some preliminaries, Spratling remembered, Faulkner came to the point.

" 'Look, Horace, it's this way. I just can't seem to get down to writing when I'm all sewed up in a signed contract. It's inhibiting.'

"Horace, doing his best to seem pleasant, was, I am sure, very bored with the interview.

"He said to Bill, '. . . why Bill, if you think you can do a better job without a contract, that's easy. Let's tear it up.'

"The contract went into the waste basket and we said goodby to Horace and pulled out. From there we strolled over to Madison Avenue and fifteen minutes later Faulkner was signed up by Harrison Smith for Harcourt Brace."

A letter which Faulkner wrote to Aunt 'Bama suggests that this account had a good deal in common with some of the fictions which Faulkner had presented as truth and which Spratling had enjoyed.

"Well," he wrote, "I'm going to be published by white folks now. Harcourt Brace & Co bought me from Liveright. Much, much nicer there. Book will be out in Feb. Also another one, the damndest book I ever read. I dont believe anyone will publish it for 10 years. Harcourt swear they will, but I dont believe it." As for himself, he was "Having a rotten time, as usual. I hate this place." Ben Wasson thought Hal Smith "had a great editorial nose," and the assurance that they would publish *The Sound and the Fury* came probably from Smith, rather than Harcourt. Hal Smith had already discussed with Faulkner some of the technical problems raised by the novel. One day, when the two men sat with Ben Wasson in a speak-easy, Faulkner had tried to convince the other two that the use of colored inks would provide information that would help the reader keep some of the time-levels in the Benjy section apart. Now, as Faulkner wrote to his aunt about the book—the damndest he ever read—he was adopting a curious stance he would assume about other works, a kind of distance from it as though, once written, it had a life of its own, so that he might appraise it as if he had not been its creator. The letter suggested that Harcourt, Brace had provided the money to pay what Faulkner owed Boni & Liveright, and there may well have been some added consideration for taking over an author who still owed the old firm first look at a new manuscript. But the account Spratling gave had a kind of symbolic as well as literal truth. Faulkner wanted to be free of the obligation, but Liveright had on the whole been good to him: he had taken a chance on him when he was a virtually unknown author, and now that he had a name and wanted to go to someone else, he let him go.

Maud Falkner took no charitable view, however, of either Horace Liveright or his firm. She was a frugal woman who tended to feel that people were taking advantage of her, particularly in financial matters. About five years later her son would write that *Soldiers' Pay* earned him about five hundred dollars and *Mosquitoes* perhaps a hundred less. At this point, however, Miss Maud was convinced that Boni & Liveright were cheating Billy on his royalties. She wrote and told them so. When Faulkner learned about it he was furious. "Every woman," he said to Ben, "ought to have a big washing every day to keep her out of trouble."

Faulkner went on with his revision of *The Sound and the Fury*, typing away in a small furnished flat he had taken in Greenwich Village. Lyle Saxon had been hospitable as ever, but Faulkner had stayed just for the weekend. Saxon was so hospitable—"Father Superior of the group," one called him—that Faulkner found the atmosphere hectic. A pot of Southern drip coffee was always on the stove and served with ceremony. People knocked on his door day and night, and there was usually a crowd there. Faulkner had to get a place by himself where he could concentrate.

Though he was working steadily he managed to see a number of people, many of whom he had met through Saxon. One was Carl Carmer, who had left his job on the New Orleans *Item* to join *Vanity Fair* in New York. He would sometimes join Saxon and Faulkner for dinner at the Athens Chop House at Sixth Avenue and Ninth Street. Carmer remembered that the food was terrible. He also remembered going back down the stairs and into the restaurant to retrieve the shoes Faulkner had left under the table.

In spite of the size of New York, Faulkner kept unexpectedly seeing familiar faces. One day as he sat looking out the window of a train jolting along on the Third Avenue Elevated, a man got up from his seat and walked over to him. "Good Lord, the Little Confederate," the man said. It was Ham Basso. Faulkner grinned and they shook hands. They sat and talked, riding to the end of the line and then back again the opposite way. Basso was working for an advertising agency and not especially happy with the work. Faulkner, he thought, was in an easy mood. He told Basso something about *Sartoris.* Harcourt, Brace was a good publisher, he said, and besides, Harcourt believed in him. When they reached Faulkner's stop, they shook hands again and parted.

Faulkner made some new friends. Eric James Devine was a slim, blue-eyed, brown-haired Ohioan who had studied at Western Reserve and later transferred to Centenary College, in Shreveport, Louisiana. He had worked on campus literary organs and sung in the glee club. After graduation he went to New York, where he worked at Doubleday, Doran for a time. He did free-lance writing when he could and began work on an M.A. in journalism at Columbia. By the fall of 1928 two friends from Centenary, Robert Walton and Leon Scales, had moved in to share his second-story walk-up apartment on Amsterdam Avenue at 111th Street. Walton was studying pharmacology at Columbia, and Scales, a Louisianan, was doing graduate work in philosophy there, attending an eight A.M. seminar given by John Dewey to which he would sometimes take Jim Devine. One of Jim's friends was Joe Titzell, the editor of *Publishers Weekly,* who had an apartment in Greenwich Village. Through him he had met Lyle Saxon and been invited to visit him. There Devine and Titzell had met Faulkner. He had a beautiful Harris tweed overcoat with raglan sleeves, Devine remembered. Because of the coat's flared skirt the pockets would easily conceal two square bottles of bootleg gin. They knew that he was supposed to be working on a book but he remained quiet and said nothing whatever about it. By now Devine had concluded that it took liquor to warm him up.

Scales was fascinated. Faulkner, he thought, "had strange, almost hypnotic eyes, and yet his speech was as picturesque as that of anyone with whom I had ever talked. He usually spoke with a slow Southern drawl, but when he got excited, he would speak with a rapid staccato-like speech interspersed with profanity. I got the impression that here was a very earthy, but keenly intelligent man." Devine remembered such an evening with several of them sitting on the floor around a fifth of gin. The label proclaimed it Gordon's Dry Gin and it looked authentic, though it was actually bathtub gin bought at a nearby delicatessen for one dollar. Faulkner sat there with his shoes off. He began to talk, telling them a story about a man who brought a herd of wild ponies into a Mississippi town and sold them to the unsuspecting natives. He was apparently trying out *Father Abraham* on a new audience.

During this time there would be periods when convivial new friends such as Devine, and old ones like Spratling, would not see Faulkner for several days. He would later say that, of all his books, *The Sound and the Fury* required the most rewriting. He was doing extensive revisions, striving especially to link the first, third, and fourth sections closer together. Early in Benjy's section, Luster, Benjy's current nurse, now revealed that today, April 7, 1928, was Benjy's thirty-third birthday and that there would be a small cake (bought by Dilsey) to celebrate it. Thus he opened out for himself further possibilities in the use of Christian symbolism for ironic commentary on the Compsons and for echoes in the reader's mind which might resonate with the kind of practical Christianity Dilsey embodied. There were a number of other consistent, linked revisions.

Eleven new passages in the typescript supplied the information that Luster was trying to find a golf ball to sell, having lost the quarter given him to buy a ticket to the carnival. This pointed forward to the events linked with the presence of the carnival people. Jason's refusal to replace Luster's lost quarter and his anger at the money the carnival would take out of the county would add impact to his loss of seven thousand dollars when Quentin ran off. These new paragraphs necessitated few changes in existing material, but Faulkner would often alter or reshape a phrase as he went.

He further refined Benjy's characterization, adding two more synesthetic passages in which Benjy could smell "the bright cold." He also made the speech of the Negro characters less heavily colloquial and dialectal than it was in the other sections. Benjy could record a variety of sensory stimuli accurately, but there were some fine discriminations he would be unlikely to make. Faulkner was still concerned with conveying this complex of experience with as little unnecessary confusion as possible. In the typing he virtually doubled the number of italicized passages and continued to insert new material into passages already typed, finally finishing the Benjy section on page 84.

He increased considerably the number of italicized passages in the second section as he had done in the first. In nearly thirty places he broke down long passages into shorter ones—as many as eleven in one instance. He compressed dialogue into interior monologue. He also deleted several descriptive passages. For one which likened the peace of the New England countryside to that of "broken machinery heaped in orderly discrimination and healed over with tentative greenery," he had obviously drawn on his time as an employee of the Winchester Arms Company. There were a total of eight new "A" pages inserted into the regularly numbered sequence of this section. The way he kept working as he typed was shown clearly on page 200. After he took the page out of his typewriter he made six corrections in pen, all in the last eight lines. Then, still dissatisfied, he crossed the passage out and expanded and retyped it at the top of page 201. Years later when he was queried about a reference in the Quentin section, he would say, "I worked so hard at that book that I doubt if there's anything in it that didn't belong there." In revising and typing this section he had shaped it even further in the mode of the stream-of-consciousness technique than he had done originally. But at the same time he was trying to signal, where possible, specific switches in time-levels and to sensitize the reader to what he was doing.

One major change made in revision was all for clarity and explicitness. A marginal addition in the manuscript had emphasized the death-by-water imagery: "in darkness in silence the bridge arching into silence darkness sleep the water peaceful and swift not goodbye." (214) In the typescript Faulkner italicized these lines and the seven preceding them. More than that, he inserted a short passage earlier in which Quentin purchased two six-pound flatirons. Another passage half a dozen pages later made it clear that he would use them to weight his body for its descent into the river. In another, briefly calling attention to them again, he told Shreve that the package contained a pair of shoes he had had half-soled. Finally, Faulkner rounded off the whole section with a 200-word passage in which Quentin brushed his teeth and then his hat before heading for the river. Calmly and serenely mad, he was emotionally at rest, like Benjy after his outburst near the end of his section. The prose—well-punctuated now and comprising chiefly simple and compound sentences—mirrored this state faithfully.

The first two sections of the typescript contained by far the bulk of the revisions. He began the Jason section on page 213 and finished it on 321. There were no corrections in pen, and only here and there had he divided paragraphs into new ones. The same was true of the Dilsey section, which he completed on page 392. Unscrewing his fountain pen, he wrote in the lower right-hand corner in blue ink: "New York, N.Y./October 1928." He had finished the typing in Ben's room on MacDougal Street. He flung the manuscript on the bed and said, "Read this, Bud. It's a real son-of-a-bitch."

One Saturday night—it may well have been about this time, after Faulkner had given the book to Wasson, who would in turn pass it on to Harcourt—Jim Devine and Leon Scales decided to make the subway trip from 111th Street down to the Village to see Faulkner. "It was fairly late and we were uninvited, but this was the way that New York City dwellers lived in those days. Saturday night was always the night to prowl around looking for a drink perhaps, or just a visit with someone you happened to know." They knocked and turned the front doorknob to go in but found the door locked. They waited, but there was no sound. This seemed strange because they could see that the lights were on inside. When Scales lifted Devine up to the transom, he saw Faulkner stretched out on the floor, near him some of the familiar square bottles, empty. Devine thought they ought to see if he was all right, so they forced the door. When they roused him they found that he had not eaten for a couple of days. He needed nourishment and nursing, and the only place they could think of to take him was their apartment. He was too debilitated to be of much help as they slipped an overcoat around his shoulders, but with Devine on one side and Scales on the other, they got him out of the apartment. It was about midnight as they made their way slowly to the 14th Street subway entrance. There they paused to rest before descending. Faulkner sat on the curb, his head in his hands. He was ill and he looked, thought Scales, very sad. But he roused himself for a moment.

"Don't make me go up to your place," he said, "I have never been upstate on the subway."

Devine and Scales couldn't help laughing. Carefully negotiating the grimy steps they made their way down, passed the turnstiles, and caught the next uptown express.

If this sequence of events did in fact occur after Faulkner gave the book to Wasson, it foreshadowed many repetitions. Ernest Hemingway would later speak of the irresponsibility that comes after the awful responsibility of writing. There were the other after-effects: a feeling of exhaustion, of being spent, and an accompanying depression and lassitude. Liquor was an anodyne that would drown it all out. It was one to which Faulkner would resort with some frequency, and almost always he would seek it when he had finished the creative labor of a book.

He enjoyed himself upstate at 111th Street. Breakfasts were particularly pleasant. With Devine and Scales he would go to some small restaurant on Broadway or Amsterdam Avenue, where he would order toast and coffee. When breakfast arrived he would draw from one of the tweed overcoat's capacious pockets a large crockery jar of Crosse & Blackwell's marmalade. He would apply the marmalade to the toast and then, at the end of the meal, he would carefully wipe off the jar, snap the metal retainer in place on the lid, and return it to his overcoat pocket. He soon felt well enough to work again, and during the day, while Devine, Scales, and Bob Walton were out, he could write. They thought he was working on a book, but they did not ask him.

There were modest parties during his few weeks' stay in the apartment. They were informal, and after the few pieces of furniture were occupied, newcomers would sit on the floor. That was the place Faulkner seemed to prefer. He would drink with the rest, returning to moderation—for him—after his period of concentrated drinking. He would take off his shoes and begin to tell stories which would make him the center of attention. The stories purported to be autobiographical—about his youth in Mississippi or his service in Canada where, he said, he cracked up two airplanes before they discovered he didn't know how to fly and washed him out. He told about the woman in New Orleans and the two children she had had by him. Someday, he said, he was going to go back and marry her. Scales had the impression that Faulkner was making up the stories as he went along and that he could go on as long as he chose. Later, when Scales read some of his fiction, he had the feeling that he had heard the story before.

Lyle Saxon's apartment remained the chief meeting place. Another young Southerner often there was an attractive, even-featured young man from Shreveport named Owen Crump. He had come to New York in 1922 to study at the Art Students' League. After two years he had quit but stayed on trying to earn a living as an artist. He was no poorer than most of his friends, and when one of them sold something they all celebrated. It was, as Flo Field had said about the Vieux Carré, very much "la vie bohème." Crump had met Faulkner at Lyle Saxon's. It must now have been late October or early November. One evening during a discussion at Saxon's, the question arose about where Faulkner should stay. He was well enough to leave Jim Devine's rather crowded quarters, and he did not, apparently, want to return to the furnished apartment he had so briefly occupied. Crump had a studio on the fourth floor of a small building at the corner of MacDougal Street and Sixth Avenue, just a short way up from the Provincetown Playhouse. The studio had a skylight, fireplace, and bed, for which Crump paid $7.50 a week. It was determined that Faulkner would move in with him.

Once more he was living in an attic studio in the artists' quarter. The rocketing trains of the El roared by outside the window, shaking the whole building, but after a while you got used to it. You never even heard it, Crump assured Faulkner. The routine here was as easy as it had been in New Orleans. For breakfast they would have eggs and coffee in the studio or go out to MacDougal Street or Third Avenue for a breakfast roll. Crump had his easel set up to catch the morning light. As he began to mix his paints, Faulkner would remove his shoes and seat himself in the middle of the bed. Still properly dressed in tweed suit and tie, he would begin to write.

He would open one of the small notebooks, Crump said, which he bought at a nearby Woolworth's five-and-ten on Eighth Street. (When he laid in a supply he would also buy a big ten-cent bag of tasty and filling roasted peanuts.) Faulkner would number a notebook and then start writing. When he reached the back he would write his way through to the front on the backs of the pages. Then he would drop the notebook into something on the floor that looked like a doctor's valise. Also there by the bed would be a bottle of gin procured from the neighborhood bootlegger on the fourth floor of a tenement just a block away in an Italian district. Occasionally Faulkner would sip at the gin as he wrote. When enough of the small notebooks had accumulated in the valise, he would take them up to Ben Wasson's office, where one of the secretaries would type them.

Lunch and dinner did not normally offer much variety. Crump had a hot plate and liked to cook. They would buy bags of rice on Avenue A, six blocks up from Greenwich Village. At nine or ten o'clock in the evening, when the pushcart vendors were ready to close up, they could buy whatever fruits and vegetables were left for next to nothing, laying in a plentiful supply for the succulent stews Crump would prepare on the hot plate with spices from home. There would always be a pot of stew to be heated up, as well as the strong, black, chicory-flavored Luzianne coffee which Crump would receive from Shreveport.

After lunch both men would go back to their work until four or four-thirty in the afternoon. "We really worked," Crump remembered. At that time Crump was using a pallet knife to do rough-textured impressionistic painting. If Faulkner finished first, he might sit and watch Crump quietly. Sometimes he would mix paints for him. Crump did not know what Faulkner was working on; all he knew was that he hoped to sell it while he was there in New York. They discussed one joint project they might undertake. Talking about the graffiti they saw in subway lavatories and similar places, Faulkner had said to Crump, "Let's do a book." They would take tracings from the walls and run these illustrations off the side of the page to avoid troubles with the censor. Then they would supply straight-faced, profound-sounding commentaries. The more they talked about it the more hilarious it got. Faulkner had a long involved title for it, but somehow it never got beyond the planning stage.

Their ordinary routine might be varied by having dinner in the Italian section just a block away from their part of the Village. Normally they avoided this area, for they did not feel particularly welcome there. There was one place, however, where they were made to feel at home. It was a restaurant and speak-easy called The Black Rabbit. Prices were particularly good, because The Black Rabbit was not so much a self-sustaining enterprise as a front for a warehouse run by gangsters as a bootleg liquor distribution center. When the two men would come in for the big seventy-five-cent dinner they would be greeted warmly. There might even be a free drink. "For you artists," the proprietor would say, "it's on the house." They could take their choice of two drinks that normally sold for a quarter apiece: a Black Rabbit Special, made of dark rum in hot water with spices and lemon rind, or a White Rabbit Special made with light rum. Then would come the food: platters of steaming spaghetti and ravioli, baskets of hot crusty Italian bread, and brisk Chianti. It was not just good, Crump recalled, it was a feast.

On Sunday afternoons there might be a very different kind of fare. Lyle might invite them out to eat. Or, this being the era of literary teas, they might be asked to one of the salons. The invitation would arrive impressively in the hands of a Western Union messenger—the only telephone was a communal one in a hallway and could not be depended on to reach the Parnassian height of Crump's studio. They would dress with some care for these affairs where there would be mounds of sandwiches and a variety of drinks made with good liquor. Crump could see that Faulkner had become a kind of celebrity. He already had two novels and a book of poems, and some of the guests knew that another novel would be out before long while still another was being read at the publisher's. At some of these parties, as at their own, Faulkner might sit on the floor and begin to tell some of his stories. He would sit cross-legged, his shoes beside him. Crump thought that he was rather vain of his small, shapely feet. At other parties he would seem an intellectual, a dapper figure, and when his silent mood was on him, almost a kind of mystery man. He was always, Crump remembered, an object of curiosity, and so he had developed strategies for bores. If silence or brusque answers failed to daunt them, he would use another device. When they asked about what he was doing, he would begin by telling a long and involved story. Sometimes a person named E. V. Trueblood would figure in it. The story would purposely have no point and get nowhere, but it would be full of directions about how to get places, going through meadows and across creeks. Sometimes the tale would vary. It might involve a baseball game in a cow pasture in which a runner slid into third base. Faulkner and Crump would covertly watch to see how long the hearer could stand it before he made a lame excuse and moved away.

But these literary occasions were the exceptional ones. Both artists were small-town boys in an overwhelmingly big city. "We were lonely," Crump said later. They would take walks around lower Manhattan to Battery Park and other places where there was a little space to provide relief from the concrete and the looming buildings. They would go on walking excursions to places where famous people had lived. The most exciting kind of entertainment was free. Crump knew a girl at the Civic Repertory Theatre on 14th Street, where Eva Le Gallienne produced and sometimes starred in a wide variety of dramas. The appeal they all felt was "part of an intellectual thing we were all going through," Crump said. "We haunted that place." He had seen Ibsen's *Hedda Gabler* there in March. Now, together, they saw Chekhov's *The Cherry Orchard* and Barrie's *Peter Pan* —both starring Miss Le Gallienne.

Faulkner had a number of contacts, Crump knew, and he would often go off by himself. By now, with Ben Wasson's help, he had met several magazine editors to whom he was trying to sell short stories. It seems likely that he still had in mind the idea he had described to Liveright: putting together a volume of short stories. That way he could get two prices for his work, a magazine appearance first and then a book. And he hoped too for an advance on *The Sound and the Fury.* What he wanted was to go home with money to live on until *Sartoris* brought financial success. Among his new contacts was Alfred Dashiell, one of the editors of *Scribner's* magazine. Faulkner had previously mailed "Moonlight" in to him. It had, of course, been rejected, but in late October he had gone to see Dashiell, taking three stories with him.

Like "Moonlight," two of them were not new. "The Leg" and "Mistral" dated from his time in Europe. The third, which he called "Bench for Two," was set in New York. It might have dated from his first stay in the city seven years before. It might also have been one of the stories written in the Woolworth notebooks and typed at the American Play Company. Both characters and setting represented a new departure: two vagrants, one old and one young, sheltered from a New York winter night in Pennsylvania Station. Using a device he had employed before, Faulkner began as omniscient narrator and then used the older man to tell the story, spurred on by the sometimes brusque and often cynical younger man's questions. Dealing with a hoodlum son and a long-suffering mother, the story was an exercise in understatement in the portrayal of filial treachery and the capacity for human misery and stoic suffering.

In his letter to Faulkner on November 3, probably sent care of Ben

Wasson, Dashiell said he remembered having seen "Moonlight" before. He thought it an effective story, but he was unable to get much from "Bench for Two." The other two were far too long for the magazine. But he had read the stories with a great deal of interest and would hold them for Faulkner.

Faulkner apparently returned to Dashiell's office, perhaps as soon as he had heard from him. He retrieved the stories and left two others. The material of both was more congenial to Faulkner's talents than "Bench for Two." One was entitled "Once Aboard the Lugger"; the other he had called "As I Lay Dying." The first recounted the expedition for bootleg alcohol from the longer, earlier work of the same title. Here the nameless first-person narrator sailed out into the Gulf with the captain of the lugger, a Negro hand, and Pete—Jenny's escort on the *Nausikaa*. Now Pete had a new quality of viciousness. Reluctantly going on this run for his older brother, Joe, he spent his time alternately being seasick and cursing the others. Once on the sand-spit, the party evaded a rush of wild cattle (who seemed almost as mad as the spotted horses) and dug up the alcohol. There the short tale ended as they slept briefly before making the run back to New Orleans. It was a strangely static story, with little real conflict between characters, and little danger, apparently, that the "rum chaser" which passed would arrest them. But the texture of the prose was rich and smooth, and the last paragraph contained a tribute to Conrad. The narrator, watching the "rum chaser," thought of "Conrad's centaur, the half man, half tugboat, charging up and down river in the same higheared, myopic haste, purposeful but without destination, oblivious to all save what was immediately in its path, and to that a dire and violent menace."

In "As I Lay Dying" Faulkner had condensed the principal events of *Father Abraham* into twenty-one typed pages. The story was no longer related by an omniscient narrator; instead, it was told by a man driving a team for his uncle (who is addressed as "Judge") during "our quadriennial vote-garnering itinerary." Faulkner had excluded all the initial material of *Father Abraham* about the rise and subsequent career of Flem Snopes. He was obviously thinking now strictly in short-story terms, focusing on incident to reveal character. This version lacked the drama of the longer one, however, because the principal events—the arrival of Buck and Flem with the spotted horses, the auction, the purchasers' attempts to catch them, and the aftermath, including Henry Armstid's injuries—were related in retrospect. Suratt and others, sitting on the porch of Varner's store, recounted the action as they discussed it, Suratt trying to gain an admission of ownership of the horses from Flem, and Flem remaining silent. (This was not the only time Faulkner reworded part of *Father Abraham* under the title "As I Lay Dying." Another version—early work replete with phonetic spellings —was exclusively dialogue without any quotation marks. Its title page listed the author in care of Ben Wasson at 146 MacDougal Street, New York. Curiously enough, the typed pages were numbered from 204 to 221, as though Faulkner had extracted them from a collection including other stories.)

Dashiell rejected both stories. The first, he wrote Faulkner on November 23, was "a nice piece of atmosphere." The second was "amusing dialogue" and sounded very real. Then he took the trouble to write a paragraph of criticism and advice. In the work Faulkner had shown him there seemed to be too much atmosphere and not enough story. He felt that Faulkner was skirting around the drama that should be at the core of a story: "It would seem that in the attempt to avoid the obvious you have manufactured the vague." He suggested straightforward narration. Once he had this, the background and atmosphere would "make your work distinctive." He would hold the manuscripts for Faulkner to pick them up. Both stories would eventually appear, the first probably in much the same form as this one Dashiell had seen, the second under a different title after several more revisions.

This rejection may well have exhausted the supply of stories Faulkner had with him in New York. It was late November and he must by now have been anxious to return home. He must also have been hoping for some word on *The Sound and the Fury* from Harcourt, Brace. It seems likely too that he would have submitted some of his stories to editors at other magazines such as *Harper's*, *The Saturday Evening Post*, *Forum*, and *Cosmopolitan*. It appears that he must have given himself until the end of the first week in December to wait for results before returning home.

At the end of that last week, about December 8, Faulkner came back to the studio with something over two hundred dollars. He told Crump that it was an advance. The next day, he said, he was going to go back home and finish the book he was working on. He would stretch his money by taking a job as a janitor. "I'm gonna live and sleep in the basement where it's warm and finish the book."

It did not take him long to pack his work and his few possessions. "Now, Owen," he said, "we're gonna go out and have some fun." They began making the rounds of the speak-easies in the Village, meeting friends and buying them drinks. They moved from smoky downstairs taprooms to equally crowded walk-ups. Once they were asked to leave because their rendition of "I Can't Give You Anything but Love, Baby" was too loud. One place began to merge into another, and it was late when they finally made it back up the suddenly steep stairs to the studio.

They did not wake until ten o'clock the next morning. When Faulkner remembered that his train left Pennsylvania Station at noon, they both arose in a rush. Faulkner said he wanted to go first to the bootlegger's to lay in a supply for the train trip. When he pulled on his trousers, he found that his money was gone; his pocket had been picked. Crump had only five or six dollars. In spite of this disaster, Faulkner was still determined to go home that day, and on the same train, so they went down and hailed a taxi. As Crump remembered it, they went pounding on doors borrowing money. They appealed to Rachel Field, who had a big flat on St. Mark's Place, and then to Lyle Saxon. Hal Smith helped, too. Finally they had enough for the ticket, with twenty dollars extra for food and perhaps a berth. At last they were on their way uptown to Penn Station.

"Wait a minute," Faulkner suddenly said, "I've got to get a couple of bottles—that's more important than food or a berth." He asked the driver to detour by way of the bootlegger's. They made a hurried climb up and down the tenement stairs and then raced through the light Sunday traffic to the terminal. When they made their encumbered way across the cavernous grand concourse of the echoing station, Faulkner's train had already been called. The two men bolted through the gate and down the stairs to the platform where the train was moving out. Crump handed over the suitcase, and without breaking stride Faulkner jumped aboard.

He was on his way home again with no definite word about *The Sound and the Fury*. And he had not sold any of his short stories. But *Sartoris* would be out in six weeks, perhaps. And the next mail might bring him a contract for the new book or a check for a story. He would wait for success on his home grounds.

31

December, 1928-June, 1929

He walked to town and crossed the deserted square. He thought of the other morning when he had crossed it. It was as though there had not been any elapsed time between: the same gesture of the lighted clockface, the same vulture-like shadows in the doorways; it might be the same morning and he had merely crossed the square, about-faced and was returning. . . .

—*Sanctuary* (214)

There had been considerable activity in Oxford while he was away, including a particular distinction. A "Clean-up and Paint-up" campaign had been sponsored by the state Federated Clubs, and in late November Miss Dorothy Oldham, secretary of the local unit, had been informed by Ralph Waldo Emerson, executive secretary of the national campaign bureau in New York, that Oxford had been awarded a trophy as "Cleanest Town" in Mississippi.

Just as he returned home, six new dormitories were named at the university. They included Longstreet Hall, Vardaman Hall, and Falkner Hall—the latter in memory of the Young Colonel. More construction was ahead, too. A man from the state would soon be there to select a site on which twenty convict carpenters would erect a stockade to house the fifty convicts who would do the grading on the $1,600,000 project.

And politics was in the news. Lem Oldham was being mentioned as a possible candidate for a proposed additional federal judgeship for the Northern District of Mississippi. John Falkner was going to offer himself to the electorate again. Wall Doxey had resigned as district attorney to run for Congress and John Falkner would stand for the office. His nephew would help him campaign again, but first there were some things he wanted to do.

In what must have been mid-December he mailed two more stories to Alfred Dashiell at *Scribner's.* One bore the title "Once Aboard the Lugger," but it was not the same one Dashiell had seen. He was using the same title for the remainder of the episode which Dashiell had already read under that title. He hoped this would suit him better. Presumably, he had taken existing material and reshaped it with Dashiell's strictures in mind about more story and less atmosphere. The other story, entitled "Miss Zilphia Gant," had been there before. He told Dashiell that it might "be too diffuse, still; I dont know." He added another appraising comment: "I am quite sure that I have no feeling for short stories; that I shall never be able to write them, yet for some strange reason I continue to do so, and to try them on Scribners' with unflagging optimism."

Faulkner had written "Miss Zilphia Gant" in blue ink on nine sheets of legal-size onionskin and he had done considerable revision before the eighteen-page typescript was finished. The story was set near Jefferson, seventy-five miles south of Memphis, but it bore a resemblance to work of both Sherwood Anderson and James Joyce. Faulkner began with a crude stock trader named Jim Gant. When he deserts his wife and three-year-old daughter, Zilphia, for a female tavern-keeper, the wife goes off after the two with a pistol. Then she moves to Jefferson where she sets up as a dressmaker and guards Zilphia rigidly, becoming increasingly masculine as she ages. At this point Faulkner introduced a situation which he had used twice before. Like Jo-Addie Bunden in "Adolescence" and Emmy in *Soldiers' Pay,* Zilphia—now thirteen—watches a beautiful young man swimming nude and then joins him in his blanket. Like Jo-Addie, Zilphia is caught. After her mother's death Zilphia keeps track of the boy. She disappears when she reads of the birth of his child and a motor fatality almost directly in front of the hospital, returning four years later with a wedding ring and a child. At the story's end—working as a seamstress, overprotecting "Little Zilphia"—Miss Zilphia Gant has become a copy of her mother.

This exploration of inarticulate country people groping for communication and love, this attempt to penetrate blasted lives, suggested the kind of thing Anderson had done with less of the macabre and more tenderness in *Winesburg, Ohio.* The turning point—a young girl's rejecting a departing sweetheart to care for a parent—suggested Joyce's beautifully economical

"Eveline" in *Dubliners.* Faulkner's story had a grim power unlike these possible models. It relied substantially (in spite of Dashiell's advice) on inference and indirection. There was also an exploration of sexual pathology, involving dreams and hysteria, which did not occur in the Joyce story and was less explicit in comparable stories by Anderson.

At the end of his covering letter Faulkner asked Dashiell to return the stories to him in Mississippi if he reached a decision before January 15. After that, he could hold them for him, because "I shall return to New York about Feb. 1, as Harcourt is publishing a novel of mine at that time." He did not have to wait nearly that long, for Dashiell returned both stories on December 22. "Miss Zilphia Gant," he wrote, was "by far the most coherent thing of yours I have seen." But it was not quite what they wanted. "I think perhaps you may be right in that you are like a distance runner trying short sprints." Faulkner would continue, however, to enter both sprints and distance events. That December he sent Dashiell another story.

The new year of 1929 came in with no less violence than the old. There had been nine lynchings in 1928, three of them in Mississippi. In the first days of the new year a Negro convict at the Parchman Prison Farm had murdered a guard and forced the dead man's daughter on a thirty-hour march. Later a mob tied him to a pile of logs, saturated his clothing with gasoline, and set him afire. In Oxford, two white boys robbed a Negro porter. Due to the diligence of Sheriff Ike Roberts, they were quickly apprehended. Then, from mid-January on, political news began to push other items off the front page.

The race for district attorney of the 3rd District was heating up. On January 10 the Jackson *Clarion-Ledger* endorsed Fred M. Belk and denounced John Falkner. "Falkner is a red-hot Bilbo man," wrote the editorialist. "He practically led the fight for Bilbo in Lafayette county last summer. To him as much as any other man, probably, is due the credit for Bilbo's overwhelming majority in Lafayette county." In a full-page ad in the *Eagle* Falkner was endorsed by General Stone, Phil Stone, Lem Oldham, Bob Williams, Bob Farley, and Taylor McElroy, all members of the bar and public officeholders. Then the candidate took the stump.

He asked the help of Mac Reed—slight, blue-eyed, and soft-spoken, and by now universally well-liked in Oxford as he had been in Chickasaw, his home county. Falkner asked him to take a day off from his work at the Gathright drugstore and accompany him to Chickasaw to introduce him and help distribute campaign literature. Bill Faulkner was going along to do the driving. "I came to know William Faulkner that day as a splendid driver over wretched roads," Reed remembered, and "as a most attentive listener. . . . I came to realize that he was asking the questions and that I was doing most of the talking. He was never prying, just interested apparently." The two had been on good terms since they had first met in the drugstore, but this was the beginning of a lifelong friendship.

There was rain on February 19. This meant that many rural voters would forgo the long cold ride to the polls on a wet wagon pulled by steaming mules. Belk won by 700 of the more than 5,000 votes cast as Falkner took only three of the seven counties in the district. It looked as though what they said was true: John Falkner was the best campaign manager in north Mississippi, but he couldn't get himself elected.

In the last days of the campaign William Faulkner had been doing work of his own as well as for his uncle. For one thing, he wrote Alfred Harcourt about *The Sound and the Fury.* The answer Harcourt sent him on February 15 must have been disappointing and perhaps infuriating. Harcourt thought there had been some confusion about the manuscript: when it came in to Harrison Smith it had gotten into the firm's manuscript safe. "A couple of us have read it," Harcourt told the author, "with mingled admiration and doubts as to whether its unusual qualities could find a profitable market." But the matter had been cleared up that very morning when Hal Smith had dropped in "and explained to us that you brought it in for his personal opinion and not with the idea of regularly submitting it to Harcourt, Brace and Company. Relying on his statement to this effect, we delivered the manuscript to him. . . ." Smith had taken the manuscript to his new office at 139 East 46th Street and Faulkner would be hearing directly from him.

That was all right about the manuscript, Faulkner replied three days later. "I did not believe that anyone would publish it; I had no definite plan to submit it to anyone. I told Hal about it once and he dared me to bring it to him. And so it really was to him that I submitted it, more as a curiosity than aught else. I am sorry it did not go over with you all, but I will not say I did not expect that result."

What had actually happened had been simplified in the telling. Hal Smith had obviously been thinking for some time about going into publishing for himself, and his negotiations with Jonathan Cape, the English publisher, must have been well advanced. Ben Wasson was very much an interested party, for he was to join the new firm as an editor. So now he and Smith were both thinking ahead. One day Ben walked into the office of the Harcourt editor who was nominally in charge of *The Sound and the Fury.* "Are you going to do this book or not?" he asked. The editor could not give him a definite answer, and Ben remembered Alfred Harcourt's misgivings about whether or not Faulkner would be able to cut *Flags in the Dust. The Sound and the Fury* in time went back into the manuscript safe.

When Hal Smith found out he went to Alfred Harcourt. "You're never going to publish that manuscript," he told him. "Why don't you let me have it?"

"All right," Harcourt replied. "You're the only damn fool in New York who would publish it."

Jim Devine thought that when Hal Smith finally left Harcourt, Brace and Company, William Faulkner was a going-away present.

Alfred Harcourt had been right in his prediction that Faulkner would hear directly from Hal Smith. On February 18, 1929, the new firm of Jonathan Cape and Harrison Smith executed copies of the contract for the publication of *The Sound and the Fury* and sent them to William Faulkner. It was a standard printed, eighteen-paragraph "Memorandum of Agreement." Typed in was paragraph 5a, which specified that the author would receive a $200 advance on royalties on signing the agreement. The royalties would be 10 percent for the first 5,000 copies and 15 percent thereafter. Paragraph 17 specified that "the Publishers shall have the first opportunity to consider for publication the next two books by the same Author. . . ." This was the same kind of agreement he had signed with Boni & Liveright. It was a small advance and not a particularly generous provision for escalating royalties. But there was nothing in the sales history of the author's previous books to argue for a bigger advance or suggest that sales would go very much over 5,000 copies. This was Faulkner's fourth publisher in a little over four years. He may have felt he was fortunate to have one. He had moved from subsidized publication to a house that published some of the best contemporary writers. Then he had moved to a newer firm, and now he had signed with one that had been formed barely two months before. However, Jonathan Cape published an impressive list in England including H. G. Wells, T. E. Lawrence, Liam O'Flaherty, Rebecca West, Sinclair Lewis, Sherwood Anderson, Eugene O'Neill, H. L. Mencken, and Fannie Hurst. Hal Smith was determined to build up the new firm's list of titles and authors in America. And it would be a select list rather than the common "mass market" approach of most of the old houses. Moreover,

Smith really cared about him and had confidence in his work. If *Sartoris* sold as he hoped it would, Alfred Harcourt might be sorry he had so casually let him go.

A few days later another letter arrived, from Alfred Dashiell, which seemed to supply added evidence that Faulkner was a miler rather than a sprinter. It was a rejection of the story which had been lost in the mail in December and replaced by the carbon copy in February. Dashiell wrote that they had read with interest the story "Selvage" done by him and E. Oldham, but they found it was "too febrile." "Selvage" was the product of a sequential rather than a simultaneous collaboration. Estelle had thought of an idea for a story and written it up only to find it thin and unsatisfactory. When she showed it to Bill he suggested that they rewrite it together. She decided she didn't want to, but she'd be happy for him to try it if he liked. In the six manuscript pages that he composed, the plot line remained much the same, but the texture thickened and darkened. It was the story of a Jefferson girl named Corinthia Bowman. Like Zilphia Gant and Jo-Addie, she was juxtaposed to a harsh and tyrannical parent-figure, in this case her grandmother. Engaged to a dull and proper young banker, she chooses to seduce a handsome young Louisianan in the hope that he will marry her. Her horrified grandmother tells her that he has Negro blood. When he refuses marriage, she wrecks the car in which the three of them are riding. At the story's end she gazes, bleeding, at the wreck where the two bodies lie. There were numerous cross-outs and a few large marginal additions on the manuscript sheets, but the fourteen-page typescript followed them very closely, as though Faulkner felt little additional revision necessary as he went from the one stage to the other. Now the story went back into the files. He would send it out again, but for the present he was busy with something else.

Sometime in late January or early February, when he had sent Dashiell the second copy of "Selvage," he had still intended to return to New York. This was no longer true, apparently, when he thanked Alfred Harcourt for his copies of *Sartoris.* "I have got involved in another novel," he wrote. He called the new work *Sanctuary* when he began the manuscript. On the legal-size manila folder in which he kept the onionskin sheets as they accumulated, he noted the starting date as "January, 1929." For the crucial incident, however, he had gone back to the ghastly story he had heard in the night club a few years before about the girl who had been raped by the impotent gangster using a bizarre object. This novel would, in the long run, exact as much labor from him as any but the longest of his books, and it would give rise to questions of motivation and intent which would be put to him every year of his life.

He would be asked so often about the book's conception and birth that he would develop formulaic answers for the inevitable questions: "Well, that book was basely conceived. I had written and had never made much money, and I—when I was footloose I could do things to make money—I could run a bootlegging boat, I was a commercial airplane pilot—things like that—then I got married and I couldn't do things like that anymore, and so I thought of the most horrific idea I could think of and wrote it." Or, exhausted after the composition of *The Sound and the Fury*, "I believed then that I would never be published again. I had stopped thinking of myself in publishing terms. . . . But when the third mss., *Sartoris*, was taken by a publisher . . . I began to think of myself again as a printed object. I began to think of books in terms of possible money. I decided I might just as well make some of it myself. I took a little time out, and speculated what a person in Mississippi would believe to be current trends, chose what I thought was the right answer and invented the most horrific tale I could imagine and wrote it in about three weeks. . . ." These answers, which Faulkner would give in essentially unchanged form for thirty years, were to do the novel itself a great disservice, emphasizing, for the uncritical reader, its shocking aspect and distracting attention from its artistry and moral force. A complicated psychological process evidently lay behind the early formulation and consistent repetition of these answers. For the knowledgeable, the inaccuracies in these assertions might have made them suspect: he was not married then and he had done little if any bootlegging or commercial flying; he had not invented the most horrific part of the tale, and the writing took a minimum of four months rather than three weeks. What kind of truth, then, even if it was symbolic rather than literal, resided in those curiously persistent and self-condemnatory answers?

Those summers in Pascagoula it had seemed that all of them were mystery-story fans. Dr. Albert B. Dinwiddie, the president of Tulane, had given Ann Farnsworth a number of mystery novels and she had passed them on to Helen Baird. Between the Lewises and the Bairds there must have been hundreds of them around, Ann thought. Later, Bill Faulkner and other members of his family would regularly exchange mystery and detective stories. He had already used the gangster milieu in short stories, and he knew something of it at first hand through roadhouses, gamblers, and the Memphis Tenderloin. He had worked hard at his chosen craft and it would not have been unreasonable for him to want some of its rewards. Though he was not yet married, he knew that Estelle's final decree would be issued in the spring, and he would have immediate uses for any money he could earn. What he set about writing now was a book in which he could test his skill, full length, at a sub-genre he enjoyed. If he made it spectacular enough, he could earn some money, too. This was not to say that these two factors would exclude a third: that it should be a satisfying work of art. But for a man who still thought of himself as a poet *manqué*, just a little contamination of motives could later loom larger than he might now imagine.

It seems likely that there was still another element present which had also been given expression in *Father Abraham*: an awareness of the depths to which human beings could sink. Like Suratt—aghast at Flem Snopes's importing wild Texas ponies to fleece his neighbors—Faulkner contemplated the darker sides of human nature. And it was not simply the atavistic capabilities Conrad had revealed in *Heart of Darkness.* It was the kind of thing manifested in society at large. "Billy looks around him," his mother would later say, "and he is heartsick at what he sees." If what he saw made him a misanthrope, he could not be charged with lack of cause. Wherever one looked, there appeared the taint of corruption. The reek of the suit against Governor Lee Russell—with its allegations of seduction, abortion, bribery, and perjury—still lingered. It was not for nothing that Theodore Bilbo had been called a polecat. And if Leroy Percy was a Bourbon who had entered politics and left it with an unsullied character, he was about the only one. The national scene hardly presented a brighter vista. The administration of Warren Gamaliel Harding, which had ended five years earlier, had set a new record for corruption in high places.

At this juncture Faulkner may have considered something like a three-horse parlay: a spectacular mystery-detective-gangster story, a commercially successful novel, and a work of art which would mirror the corruption of society at large in the lives of a small number of people from different levels of society. (There had been something of this in that novel Faulkner so much admired, Flaubert's *Madame Bovary.*) He would disclose not only the expected horrors of the criminal class but also the hypocrisy and self-righteousness of the "good people," particularly the Southern Christian ladies nominally the pillars of their communities. From what Faulkner had seen, there was more virtue in dumb, suffering country people and honest, compassionate madams than in most of the "respectable" folk.

In *Sartoris* he had found he could handle not only disparate generations, but also disparate strata of society: Sartorises, MacCallums, and Snopeses. He would do the same thing in this new novel, plus another kind of virtuoso act. He now had the ground of Jefferson (and Yoknapatawpha County) firmly beneath his feet. He would set part of the action there. He would set another part in the Memphis Tenderloin and outlying nightspots. Then he would bridge these locales and actions with a few central characters. He had fallen into the custom of setting new technical challenges for himself in successive novels, and this would be another one.

The city of Memphis provided a rich source for the novel of crime and violence. It was perhaps the best such setting in America—undisputed claimant, as it now was, to the title "Murder Capital of the U.S.A." Though without such names as Al Capone or Legs Diamond, the Memphis underworld was nonetheless rich in the bizarre and bloody. One celebrated case involved the man Memphis police called the "slickest and most daring" criminal in the city's history. He was a "second-story man" with a penchant for diamonds and no compunctions about murder. "One-thumb" John Revinsky, "the Russian Fox," combined business and pleasure in frequenting the house of Mae Goodwin, queen of the Memphis underworld. A brothel madam who posed dreamily for a portrait photo in a riding habit with a crop in her gauntleted hands, she was also a receiver of stolen goods. Her house at 3rd and Vance was just across from Union Station. Elegantly furnished, it displayed rows of leather-bound volumes including sets of Balzac, Thackeray, Baudelaire, and other masters. There she entertained, richly gowned and decked in diamonds. On the night of October 9, 1916, she was shot to death by someone who had hidden himself when the doors were locked at the close of business. The murderer was identified by a terrified Negro maid, one of Mae Goodwin's girls, and a bloody handprint in a bathtub, the thumb missing. Revinsky had killed her in a dispute over stolen diamonds, said the police. At his trial he testified that this was not the reason at all: it was revenge for Mae Goodwin's having lured his sister into a life of sin. He was sentenced to ten to twenty years' imprisonment, but he served only a few years, escaping from three different prisons. It was 1928 before he was brought back to Tennessee to serve out the remainder of his time.

Popeye Pumphrey was not quite as spectacular as John Revinsky, but he was somewhat more elusive. Once arrested (he claimed) thirty-one times for vagrancy in two months, he had beaten every charge lodged against him, charges which by now included safecracking, bank robbery, gambling, and hijacking, as well as bootlegging. He remained a paradoxical figure: a handsome man never seen with girls, a temperate bootlegger, the grandson of an Arkansas attorney general yet one who "has just been different from other children," beginning a long criminal record in early youth. He was not, of course, a solitary bandit. Behind him was the shadow of the mob.

Pumphrey's mob was not the only one in Memphis, and now others came in from outside the state. Before 1929 was out Reno DeVaux's New Crystal Gardens would be burned, as would the Showboat. DeVaux stoically insisted that the blaze was caused by an overheated flue in the men's room, but the newspapers reported that "one local whisky faction backed by Al Capone's gang at Chicago and another faction backed by a New Orleans–St. Louis outfit are struggling for control here." DeVaux, supported by local men, had been the most successful night club operator in the area. Now he was out of business. He denied having received threats that he would be killed if he kept on operating his place.

During these same years, Lafayette and surrounding counties were far from tranquil. Lynchings and burnings occurred every year. Federal officers periodically "captured" or destroyed "white mule machines," some officers occasionally dying in the process. As the decade of the twenties advanced, its frenetic excesses seemed to be reflected in rural crime as well as urban. A father, mother, and their sixteen-year-old son were jailed in Jackson for cooperatively murdering a neighbor with an ax and butcher knife. Inside a one-month period, Jim and Estin McGonagil were among those arrested for running a one-hundred-gallon still fifteen miles southeast of Oxford, and a minister was taken into custody, also near Oxford, after a knife fight. The city marshal of Blue Mountain was charged with murdering a county constable. And in April, while Faulkner was engaged in writing *Sanctuary*, a drunken man in Washington County tried to shoot his two small children. When his own father picked up the children to save them, the son shot him in the leg and then pursued him around the house, where he placed the gun at his back and finally dispatched him. If William Faulkner possessed a strain of misanthropy, there was much on the local, regional, and national scenes to feed it.

Each spring the Ole Miss baseball team would play its arch-rival, Mississippi A&M, at Starkville, seventy-five miles to the southeast. The rivalry was intense, and the fans who made the trip to see the game expected a wild time. Because the roads were still so bad, Ole Miss students and alumni would charter a train, where many of the spectators would take an anticipatory drink or two. There would be plenty more when they got to Starkville, where, despite prohibition, demijohns of corn whiskey would circulate in the crowd. This did nothing to reduce the number of fights. The whole weekend would be festive as well as raucous, with a dance on the night of the game. Sometimes the injuries would be more than superficial bruises and cuts. People in Oxford talked covertly about one of these more serious incidents at Starkville. Whatever it was, it happened to an Ole Miss co-ed, an extremely popular girl who somehow left the train and suffered some sort of sexual molestation. She had lived on University Avenue across from the Kirkwood house, just two blocks north of where the Falkners had lived as boys. If William Faulkner needed a bridge between Popeye's alleged Memphis outrage and the milieu of Yoknapatawpha and the university, this would have provided it.

Faulkner apparently started with much of the novel already thought out—at least the trial in which his heroine, Temple Drake, would be forced to testify. But there were two false starts. In one, he wrote down "Sanctuary," underlined it, wrote in "Chapter One," and then began a description of Judge Drake entering court to take his daughter off the stand and away with him. In another he described Temple Drake as she might be seen running to hop into a car driven by her escort. He abandoned both of these after about a dozen lines. His third opening came between these two events in the novel's final chronology. It began with a description of the Yoknapatawpha County jail, which housed moonshiner Lee Goodwin as he awaited trial for murder. His lawyer, Horace Benbow, talked with him. Faulkner was still working after the fact—unlike most detective-story writers. Throughout the intensive rearranging to come, his tendency would be toward greater suspense and stricter chronology, further from Joseph Conrad and closer to Sir Arthur Conan Doyle. There was one familiar touch about the new beginning. Though he used no names, it seemed clear that he was drawing on events forecast in "That Evening Sun Go Down," namely, the murder of Nancy by her wronged common-law husband, Jesus: "At first there had been a negro murderer there, who had killed his wife; slashed her throat with a razor so that, her whole head tossing further and further backward from the bloody regurgitation of her bubbling throat, she ran out the cabin door and six or seven steps up the quiet moonlit lane." This was only the first of seven violent deaths to come.

The first five pages apparently went smoothly as Faulkner introduced

Goodwin's common-law wife and seemingly moribund child, then switched to Horace as he explained the case to Aunt Jenny and his sister Narcissa. Through dialogue he made it clear that Goodwin feared a gunman named Popeye and that Horace had walked out on his wife, the former Belle Mitchell. In Chapter II, however, he apparently wrote the material several times, saving some of it for later portions of the book. The signs of exhaustive experimentation with various sequences of events would appear throughout the growing manuscript. For example, before page 11 was finally permanently fixed in that sequence, it had borne seventeen other page numbers. The completed manuscript comprised 139 pages, only 34 of which bore just one page number. Ninety-three pages showed interpolations in the two-inch left-hand margin which might run from a brief phrase to well over 100 words. Forty-four of the pages bore careful paste-ons from discarded manuscript pages. Sixteen of the novel's twenty-seven chapters were tried in other places before achieving their final placement. By the time Faulkner reached page 80, however, there were fewer paste-ins and shifts of pages. He had, though, done so much experimenting that it would be almost impossible to trace with any precision the growth of the manuscript. The first stage at which it would be possible to see the overall shape he had given the narrative would be at his final typing. And even that typescript would later be drastically rearranged.

Some of this changing about was probably due to the mystery-story mode, to an effort to heighten suspense and emphasize action. It seems likely that other changes were to contrast people and places, often for purposes of irony. One of the eventual results would be certain disturbing loose ends of fact and motivation.

By mid-April Faulkner had hopes of finishing the novel in the summer. *Sartoris* had been published on January 31 with an initial printing of 1,998 copies. In February he had told Alfred Harcourt how much he liked the book's appearance. (When Harcourt replied, he was under the impression, curiously enough, that they would get a look at the new novel.) On April 8, Harcourt inquired if he would like to see reviews, and he replied quickly that he would like that very much, for he had seen only one. "I live in a complete dearth of print save in its most innocent form," he explained. "The magazine store here carries nothing that has not either a woman in her underclothes or someone shooting someone else with a pistol on the cover; that includes newspapers, too." They had asked if he had any ideas for selling the novel, but he had none. There was a local druggist who handled books, "but anything without pictures, selling for more than 50 cents is indeed a drug here; the man handles them mostly out of friendship for me." So Faulkner hoped they would make as easy an arrangement as they could. "Mr. Reed is a good fellow. If you could permit him a consignment basis, he will sell a copy now and then for three or four years, as people here learn that I am a 'book-author.' I'd not like to deprive them of their Tanlac and Pinkham's Compound by tying Mr. Reed's capital up in books, you know."

The review Faulkner had seen might have been that of Dana Trasker in *Outlook* or of Mississippian Herschel Brickell in the *Herald Tribune*'s book section. Both appeared in February. The first tended to vindicate Alfred Harcourt's criticism. The canvas was too big, Trasker said, and the Byron Snopes–Narcissa plot seemed superfluous. But the novel was "quite a good piece of workmanship, well organized and well told." Brickell disliked the novel's slow start and complex style, but the work disclosed "a novelist of real imaginative power, who is more than half a poet." Two weeks later, however, an anonymous reviewer for *The New York Times* found the work uneven and loose, as well as inconsistent in theme and character.

In April and May the reviews continued to be mixed. The one nearest to home was the influential Donald Davidson's, whose Nashville *Tennessean* column was reprinted in the Knoxville *Journal* and the Memphis *Commercial Appeal*. The Southern writers, he began, were "doing about as well as anybody." Evidence was to be found in Faulkner's novel and Ben Wasson's newly published *The Devil Beats His Wife*. As to the former, he made his judgment firmly: "as a stylist and as an acute observer of human behavior, I think that Mr. Faulkner is the equal of any except three or four American novelists who stand at the very top." The main difficulty was that he had not yet found a theme or character that would fully exploit his gifts. Ben Wasson's novel elicited Davidson's approval too as "a really promising first performance." This was the peak of the reviews. Taken as a whole, they were not likely to make author, publisher, or agent particularly happy.

The author was going ahead with his new fiction. A strange figure to many, he was often absorbed in that inner world where much of the work was done. A distant relative from Ripley named James Herman Adams had entered the university the previous fall and found that Bill Faulkner was well-known in Oxford. Adams would see him at the depot, barefooted. By now Faulkner had accessories that Adams thought were a kind of trademark: a bandanna and a crooked stick. He carried these no matter what the rest of his attire—floppy hat, English tweed coat, worn khakis, or dusty shoes. Adams understood when Faulkner failed to recognize him. "He adored Cousin Holland," but sometimes "he would pass without seeing *her.*" On one spring evening Phil Stone had gone to see Faulkner and had listened, sitting in the small tower room, while he read from his work in progress. He was aware that Faulkner had been turning this material over in his mind for a considerable time. He knew the subject matter well, and he also felt absolutely sure that Faulkner was intent on shaping it into a serious work of art rather than a sensational potboiler. But he was not convinced that this novel would do any more for Faulkner than *Sartoris* had. He spoke frankly. "Bill," he said, "this won't sell. The day of the shocker is past."

When Stone rose to leave, Faulkner accompanied him down the narrow staircase and out the front walk. As they stood talking for a moment, Faulkner admitted his discouragement. Stone had tried to help him shape *Sartoris* into a popular book, but Harcourt hadn't particularly cared for it and now the public seemed to share his feeling.

"Bill," said Stone, "forget about trying to please them. Just go on and write what you damn please." On the basis of results to date, it appeared that he might just as well.

"I think I not only won't ever make any money out of what I write," Faulkner said; "I won't ever get any recognition either."

Stone did not say so, but he shared the same fear. "We had done everything we knew to do and we had got nowhere," he later recalled. "I knew he had the stuff all right enough. I never had any doubt about that. But I didn't think we were ever going to convince anybody in the publishing world. . . ." Even if there had been some sort of campaign they could have put on, the demands of Stone's legal business were greater than they had been five years earlier. And though he was doubtless ready to offer clerical help again, Faulkner was by now typing almost all of his own work. The two men were still close—their views on many subjects were almost identical, and they enjoyed laughing together about the Snopeses, those of Lafayette County and Yoknapatawpha County—but it was not the way it had been before. Whereas Stone had gone over poems line by line and punctuated pages of prose, he apparently had not even known about *The Sound and the Fury*—the book Faulkner called his favorite—until it was completed.

Faulkner had let Ben Wasson know what his new work was about.

Apart from Ben's interest in what he was doing, the information would be useful to him, perhaps, in arranging a contract with Hal Smith. "I am now writing a book," he said bluntly, "about a girl who gets raped with a corn cob." But then he went on to refer to another level of meaning. The thing that he was really interested in was "how all this evil flowed off of her like water off a duck's back." And he was ready to generalize from this. "Women are completely impervious to evil," he wrote.

Besides his visits with Stone, Faulkner found relief from his intensive work on *Sanctuary* in time spent with Estelle. He was frequently at the Oldham house, and some days he would appear in the schoolyard at recess to see Malcolm and Cho-Cho, often bringing candy. To the children he was a glamorous figure—a pilot and a man untrammeled by office, store, or farm. He would occasionally take other children along with Cho-Cho and Malcolm on walks in the woods. He would tell them about flying, about his experiences in the RAF. They loved these stories and, even more, those about fairies or goblins. Sometimes, flushed and sweaty from running, they would gather about him in the dusk on the semicircular steps of the columned Oldham home. Estelle would alternate with him at telling ghost stories. He seemed totally relaxed, free of the stiff posture he took with most adults, who often bored him. Malcolm was fascinated by the modulations of his voice, its softness as he held the children's attention. He and his sister looked forward to Billy's visits. There were more now, as the long courtship wore on. Then, on April 29, Estelle's final divorce decree was issued.

During April and May the tempo of events quickened in Oxford. The Lyric Theatre showed *The Jazz Singer*, featuring Al Jolson and sound. The city and county jointly acquired thirty acres for an airport. Governor Bilbo, now in control of the board administering the university, increased the pressure for the ouster of Chancellor Hume. It is likely that most of the time Faulkner was only vaguely aware of such external events, immersed as he was in the final revisions and typing of his manuscript. If he had mentally taxed Horace Liveright and Alfred Harcourt with lack of faith in his talent, he could hardly do the same with Hal Smith. On May 6 Smith filled in the contract forms between Cape & Smith and William Faulkner, signed them for the firm, and sent them off. The advance on royalties was, like that for *The Sound and the Fury*, only $200, and the escalated royalty clause was again the same, but Smith did not even know the title of the new work he was contracting for. In the blank where the title was supposed to appear was just the phrase "A Novel." Faulkner signed the copies and returned them.

Typing slowly and methodically with his two index fingers, he worked as frugally as ever. Among the onionskin sheets he used for the carbon copy were a dozen he had salvaged from false starts during the writing. He would trim the sheets from legal- to letter-size, so that the tiny blue pen strokes would appear, faint and reversed, at the top of occasional pages in the carbon copy. When he had finished the job, he wrote on the title page in blue ink, "Oxford, Miss./January–May, 1929." On page 358, the last page, he wrote the place again and a more precise date: "25 May 1929." The last step for this copy, which he kept as he had the carbon copies of his other novels, was to bind it with a craftsman's care.

The typescript of *Sanctuary* revealed that Faulkner had finally employed a double strategy. He had used the shocking Pumphrey material, grafting it onto now-expanded elements which had first appeared in *Flags in the Dust.* He had apparently come to accept Wasson's view—as he would later write—that he had put into that book the material for several novels. What had been most liberally cut from *Flags in the Dust* had been material about Horace Benbow—as foil to Bayard Sartoris—and Horace's relationship with his sister and Belle's sister. Now Horace stood in the forefront of the new novel and many of its events would, in a Jamesian fashion, be as important for the way they impinged upon his sensibilities as for their intrinsic function in the plot. The cuts from *Flags in the Dust* had reduced the incestuous component of Horace's relationship with Narcissa. Chapter II of *Sanctuary* made it clear that one of the reasons Horace had married Belle Mitchell was that Narcissa had refused to cancel her imminent wedding to Bayard. Horace had proposed that they abandon fiancé and mistress and cleave to each other: " 'Narcy,' he said, 'dont do it, Narcy. We both wont. I'll—Listen: we both wont. You haven't gone too far that you cant, and when I think what we . . . with this house, and all it—Dont you see we cant?' " Belle had even taunted him: " 'You're in love with your sister. What do the books call it? What sort of complex?' " This book would be a shocker, all right, with rape at one extremity and something like incest at the other.

Married to corrupt Belle Mitchell for ten years, Benbow is now a distinctly Prufrockian figure, seeing himself in a mirror as "a thin man in shabby mismatched clothes, with high evaporating temples beneath an untidy mist of fine, thin, unruly hair." He thinks of Kinston, in the Delta, where they had moved to suit Belle, "because of that land, the black, rich, foul, unchaste soil which seemed to engender money out of the very embrace of the air which lay flat upon it. . . ." He had learned about evil not only from his sultry discontented wife, but also from her daughter, Little Belle, whose voice in the late spring twilight (a word which would recur often) "would seem to be the murmur of the wild and waxing grape itself." As she sat with boys in the hammock (like Caddy and then Quentin with their boys in the swing), Horace would hear her dress "whispering to the delicate and urgent mammalian rifeness of that curious small flesh which he did not beget."

The first chapter placed Horace in the jail talking with his client, whiskey-maker Lee Goodwin, in the presence of his common-law wife, former Memphis prostitute Ruby Lamar. It also revealed that he had finally left Belle, meeting Goodwin on his walk from Kinston to Jefferson. Stopping for a drink at a spring, he had been detained by Popeye, the Memphis bootlegger, who was preparing to run a truckload of Lee's moonshine up to Memphis. As Horace related these events to Aunt Jenny and his sister, often in a confused way, it became clear that a scale of good and evil had been set up, as embodied in the women in his life. As Belle and Little Belle suggested repugnant sexuality and promiscuity, so Aunt Jenny suggested a kind of nobility and honor, tempered by pragmatism and the wisdom of the aged. As the novel developed, Narcissa would show herself quite as capable of evil as Belle. The same thing would be horrifyingly true of the wronged Temple Drake when she appeared. By paradoxical contrast, the other "good" woman was Ruby Lamar, who would prostitute herself for Goodwin, bear his child, and live with him in a remote wreck of a house. As Horace stayed two days at the Sartoris home with his sister and Aunt Jenny, Faulkner indulged himself in writing of the kind he had done in *Sartoris*: romantic reminiscences of the past, of Aunt Jenny's life and her people. Horace described events at the Old Frenchman place in long talks with Aunt Jenny. Temple, raped several days before, would not appear until Chapter VI in a flashback to a time preceding her ordeal and the murder of the half-wit, Tommy, with which Goodwin had been charged. Thus Horace Benbow remained in the forefront of the novel's first five chapters despite abrupt time-shifts which showed that not all of Faulkner's repositioning of manuscript pages had worked out successfully.

Now Faulkner switched to omniscient narration, describing the movements of Temple Drake and her escort, Gowen Stevens, whose drunkenness stranded them at the Old Frenchman place. First Ruby and then the omniscient author narrated the succeeding events culminating in Temple's undescribed rape. Faulkner shifted the narrative to Ruby and then to the omniscient narrator again as Popeye installed Temple in Miss Reba's Memphis brothel, presumably to keep her under cover against the need for a respectable alibi for Tommy's murder. At this point Faulkner again turned to material first exploited in *Flags in the Dust*: the Snopeses. Horace was forced to deal with Senator Clarence Snopes to locate Temple, who could testify that the murderer was Popeye. Virgil and Fonzo Snopes provided comic relief: country boys come to Memphis to barber college, they were amazed that their landlady, Miss Reba, had so many daughters. The murder of Red—brought by Popeye to Temple as a surrogate lover—was related by the omniscient narrator; so too was the trial, at which Temple's callous perjury permitted the conviction of Goodwin.

Chapter XXV, the novel's third from last, took the form of a letter from Horace to Narcissa. (Faulkner surely remembered Conrad's frequent use of such devices—occurring, some have said, when his energy flagged near a novel's end.) It was a letter bearing here and there the tones of madness, as Horace confessed to flight after the jury's verdict. He had returned to Belle and abandoned the case, but he wanted Ruby to know he would obtain the best lawyer he could find for Goodwin's appeal. Chapter XXVI was Narcissa's seventeen-line reply: she had cut his message to Ruby out of the letter and mailed it to the jail. Goodwin had been moved, for the town (convinced he had raped Temple unnaturally as well as killed Tommy) had been preparing to lynch him.

The last chapter briefly recounted Popeye's conviction for a crime he had not committed and his strange passiveness even up to the scaffold. The narrative suddenly shifted to Temple and Judge Drake in the Luxembourg Gardens at twilight. She listened to the band playing "Massenet and Scriabine, and Berlioz like a thin coating of tortured Tchaikovsky on a slice of stale bread. . . ." She gazed idly at her discontented face, then closed her compact, "and from beneath her smart new hat she seemed to follow with her eyes the waves of music, to dissolve into the dying brasses, across the pool and the opposite semicircle of trees where at sombre intervals the dead tranquil queens in stained marble mused, and on into the sky lying prone and vanquished in the embrace of the season of rain and death." But then, deliberately, Faulkner undercut this sonorous and evocative passage. In the preceding sequence Popeye had whispered harshly through the minister's prayers, asking the sheriff to smooth his slicked-down hair. The novel's last line gave the reply: "*Sure, the sheriff said, I'll fix it for you; springing the trap.*" The simile Faulkner had used to describe the sound of the Berlioz was closer to some of the flip, arty passages of *Mosquitoes* than to the more controlled writing he had done since then. Actually, the original of the passage had probably been written nearly four years before. Now less than 250 words long, it had probably first taken shape in the work he had described to his mother in his Paris letter of September 5 or 6, 1925: "I have just written such a beautiful thing that I am about to bust—2000 words about the Luxembourg Gardens and death. It has a thin thread of plot, about a young woman, and it is poetry though written in prose form."

Temple thus dominated the last sustained passages, but the major figure, overall, remained Horace Benbow, even though he had drifted out of the novel two chapters earlier. He remained the Prufrockian figure: a lawyer, he had attempted to fight evil and failed; a husband, he had left his mocking concupiscent wife only to return abject. Benbow had been de-emphasized in *Sartoris*, but he had not suffered the same fate in *Sanctuary*.

After making last revisions and corrections, Faulkner sent the typescript off to New York and gave Estelle the carbon copy to read. When she finished she was furious.

"It's horrible," she said.

"It's meant to be," he answered. Then he added, "It will sell."

In spite of Hal Smith's ability to spot promising manuscripts, he apparently read few of them. When *Sanctuary* arrived, three other members of the new firm read it carefully. Like the others at Cape & Smith, Louise Bonino, Evelyn Harter, and Lenore Marshall all helped with reading manuscripts in addition to other specialties, Louise Bonino working on publicity and Evelyn Harter on production and manufacturing. Lenore Marshall had tried for a job at Cape & Smith on the recommendation of Joseph Wood Krutch, and she had landed one as an editor. All three had been impressed with *The Sound and the Fury*, though each felt that it was confusing and ought to be clarified where possible. Lenore Marshall had an impression of sheer power in reading it, and on two pages of yellow lined paper she wrote an enthusiastic report which she gave to Smith. "It's a great book," she had written. Now she and her two co-workers were given *Sanctuary* to read.

One of Lenore Marshall's friends who had fallen ill and then gone to Ft. Lauderdale, Florida, had asked her to come down. When she had asked Hal Smith if she could go, he had replied, "Yes, and take this manuscript with you." He had handed her *Sanctuary*. She read it on the sleeper between New York and Florida. Like *The Sound and the Fury*, it made a strong impression on her. But though she was struck with its power, she didn't care for it.

Evelyn Harter read it and then brought the manuscript to Louise Bonino.

"I don't think we can publish this," she said.

"Why?" Louise asked.

"It's just very shocking," Evelyn told her.

Louise took the book home. Later she remembered that she found it very violent, vivid and very disturbing. She agreed with Evelyn and went to Hal Smith. "Do you realize what you have here?" she asked him.

When Smith wrote to Faulkner his response was more than definite: "Good God, I can't publish this. We'd both be in jail." Faulkner later recalled that he told himself, "You're damned. You'll have to work now and then for the rest of your life." It is likely that his response, however internalized, was a good deal more bitter and less laconic than that. (He may at first have been stunned; he apparently did not even ask Smith to return the manuscript.) When *Sartoris* was accepted for publication he had begun thinking of himself "again as a printed object." Now his new manuscript had received a flatter debarment than ever *Sartoris* had. Once again he had hoped to make some money out of his intensive and laborious work. Though the returns from *Sartoris* had been disappointing, there had at least been some royalties. Now Smith was telling him that not only would there be none from *Sanctuary*, the very government would prosecute them if they tried.

It must by now have been early or mid-June. Though he might engage himself for spells of work from time to time, he would not do so immediately, for something else would preempt his attention. One day before he finished *Sanctuary* he had met Jack, now working in Memphis, at the airport there. Jack had asked him how the work was going. "Slowly," his brother replied. Then he looked at him and added, "I'm going to marry Estelle." Jack knew what the financial situation was and suggested a postponement. "I got what I deserved," he later recalled, "no reply at all."

Faulkner had not told his brother how he hoped *Sanctuary* would solve his financial problems. Now he may have been inclined to think that Jack was right. But with Estelle's divorce now final, there was no longer any legal obstacle. And there were other considerations. It seemed to some Oxonians that Bill Faulkner was always at the Oldhams', seeing Estelle, eating meals with the family, and sometimes baby-sitting. After a certain point, this could become an embarrassing situation. But Lem Oldham was not now much more inclined to welcome Bill Faulkner as a son-in-law than he had been eleven years before. He still had no steady income and he could not in honesty say that his prospects were encouraging. One late spring day, however, the situation boiled over into a family argument at the Oldhams', with the upshot of Dot's calling Bill Faulkner and telling him it was time he married Estelle. As for money, he could get a job at the university if he had to, as he had told Owen Crump he would. And for immediate expenses, he knew that he could count on help from Bob and Sallie Murry Williams. On Wednesday, June 19, 1929, they decided they would go ahead. The next day Faulkner went to the Courthouse and obtained a wedding license.

Estelle dressed carefully in the wedding gown made in Louisville and waited with Dot, who was to be her attendant. Faulkner arrived in Miss Maud's little Chevrolet coupé and the three of them squeezed themselves in. Estelle settled back nervously for the ride to the church, but Faulkner turned instead toward the Square. When she asked why, he said he was going to her father's office. It was a point of honor that they tell him first before doing it. He had already told his mother and father, who were far from happy at the news. Phil Stone had seemed even more unhappy. Like the parents, he was reacting as he had done eleven years before. He still felt it would be ruinous to Faulkner's career for him to marry Estelle. How could he go on working for real recognition, which was proving so hard to achieve, if he were saddled with the responsibilities of a family? Where would they live? He had no steady income—how could he pay the bills? Faulkner doubtless responded to his strictures as he had to Jack's that day at the airport in Memphis. And the breach now opening in the once intimate friendship grew wider.

Faulkner swung the little Chevy into the Square. He pulled into one of the diagonal parking places, got out, and closed the door after him. As Estelle sat there she suddenly realized she was trembling. She and Dot waited as his slow measured stride took him up the stairs to the second-floor gallery where Lem Oldham's law office overlooked the southeast corner of the Square.

It was a brief interview. "Mr. Lem," Faulkner said, his back straight, " 'Stelle and I are going to be married."

"Billy," said Major Oldham, "I've always been fond of you as a friend, but I don't want you marrying my daughter." Oldham was still inclined to be imperious, yet he held his temper. "But if you're determined," he said,

"I won't stand in your way." Bill and Estelle were mature adults. Oldham could not consider applying sanctions to prevent the marriage, and even if he had, it would not have done any good. Provision by Cornell Franklin for Malcolm and Cho-Cho had been part of the divorce settlement, so there was no likelihood of actual hardship for the children, nor actually for their mother or stepfather-to-be. Now there was silence in the room. The obligations of honor had been satisfied and there was nothing more to be said. Faulkner bade his future father-in-law goodbye and returned to the car. They left the Square and headed west on North Depot Street for the College Hill road.

BOOK SIX

Husband and Father

1929-1932

William Faulkner, early 1930's.

32

June, 1929-March, 1930

> . . . the days themselves were unchanged—the same stationary recapitulation of golden interval between dawn and sunset, the long quiet identical days, the immaculate monotonous hierarchy of noons filled with the sun's hot honey. . . .
>
> —*The Wild Palms* (110–111)

They could not be married in Estelle's church. Old Reverend William McCready said he was sorry, the laws of the Episcopal Church on divorce just didn't permit it. But they would be welcome to come back and attend services after they had undergone a year's "probation." They had turned then to one of the best-liked ministers in the county, and now they drove to College Hill to his church.

The Reverend Winn David Hedleston, D.D., professor of philosophy and ethics at the University of Mississippi, pastor of the College Hill Presbyterian Church, was a small man with close-cut hair which emphasized his hairbrush mustache and prominent ears. His forehead was deeply lined and he wore a keen-eyed, quizzical look. When the wedding party arrived he welcomed them and said they could get Mrs. Hedleston to act as the witness. They found her in the kitchen of the manse, both ample arms black with berry juice. She was making blackberry preserves, she told them. (Estelle felt sure it was really blackberry wine.) She'd be right with them, she said, moving to the sink to wash off the stains.

They walked to the stately tree-shaded church nearby. It had been built in 1837, one of the oldest structures in the county, with white Corinthian columns that gave it strength and dignity. Careful workmanship of the same kind distinguished the bright white interior, with the old slave gallery in the back and the main floor lined with private pews, each with its own door on the aisle. Dr. Hedleston's words sounded clearly in the near-empty church, and soon the simple ceremony drew to a close as he pronounced the couple man and wife. Afterwards he signed the marriage certificate in his shaky, old-man's hand. The newlyweds accepted the Hedlestons' congratulations and drove away.

Once back in town, Dot helped Estelle finish her packing while Bill drove to the campus to exchange Miss Maud's car for Mr. Murry's. With a loan from Bob Williams, they were now ready to leave on their honeymoon. Malcolm Franklin received the news of the wedding with absolute delight. "Mama and Mr. Bill got married," he joyfully informed neighbors on South Lamar. Now they put him in the car and set off for Columbus, eighty-five miles to the southeast.

When they finally pulled up in the driveway of Mrs. Hairston's house, Cho-Cho raced out to greet them. Mrs. Hairston welcomed them in, and they stayed for supper. That evening they traveled back twenty-five miles in the direction of Oxford to spend their wedding night in Aberdeen. The next day they picked up Malcolm and prepared to set out for Pascagoula, but Mrs. Hairston insisted that they could not go on their honeymoon without help; they must at least take Emma, her white-haired servant of many years. They must also take some of her silver. Finally they agreed. It was arranged that Mrs. Hairston and Cho-Cho would join them at Pascagoula in three weeks.

It took them most of June 21 to cover the 190 miles through the hills, the brief strip of prairie, and the long stretch of piny woods before the flat green coastal meadows came into view. At last they turned down onto the beachfront road in Pascagoula where the flat sheen of the Gulf stretched out to the boat-dotted horizon. The only bodies of water Emma had ever seen were creeks, plus an occasional river and lake. She gazed out silently over the calmness of the Gulf curving away to east and west. Finally she spoke. "My God," she said, "all that water—what am I gonna do?" It was also the first time five-year-old Malcolm had seen that much water. He decided that he would do a lot of swimming.

They spent their honeymoon in the Turnbull place, a two-story house Frank Lewis had rented to them. It was located on the east beach, just three homes away from the bayou. The Turnbull place was by now considerably run down. Estelle, however, dressed with the same style she had displayed in Honolulu and Shanghai, and was consequently an object of considerable interest to the neighbors. Mrs. Hermes Gautier gave an afternoon party to welcome Mrs. William Faulkner to Pascagoula, which was a rather casual place. A heavy rain was falling at the time, but Estelle arrived at the party wearing a black velvet dress and a big black hat to match. Her clothes, the other ladies agreed as they saw more of them during that first week, were gorgeous. One neighbor thought that both the bride and her husband dressed every night for dinner. They drank quite openly. Some evenings Pascagoula would see them going for walks along the beachfront. They would probably have had more privacy at home in Oxford, where, on June 27, the *Eagle* took official notice of their new status and offered congratulations. "Mr. Faulkner is a writer of note," the social editor added, "being the author of several important books. Mrs. Franklin is the daughter of former United States District Attorney Judge Lemuel E. Oldham."

Mrs. Faulkner was learning more about her new husband. She had taken a chance in marrying him, she reflected, because geniuses weren't like other people. Some of his habits were curious. Undressing, he would put his clothes on a chair and his shoes on the dresser for polishing. His movements were as slow as ever. He was always punctual, because this was a courtesy one owed others, a part of politeness, but his view of time, of the need to rush, was very different from that of most people. "I have all eternity ahead, why worry hurrying to get things done today?" he said. "Time is a man-made convention." They began to establish their own conventions and unspoken agreements. One was that they would not discuss politics. He knew that she was a Republican born and bred. She knew that he was a Democrat in the Southern tradition. Neither was likely to sway the other in argument.

Malcolm found Mr. Bill the same as ever. There was just more time now to do things with him. Faulkner would go in the shallow water every morning with Malcolm, and the Stone children too if they happened to be there. They would amuse themselves fishing and crabbing on one of the long wharves stretching out into the brown water. He began to tan quickly and before long began to look the way he had when he lived in Pascagoula before. He would go without shaving for days at a time. Sometimes he would stroll along wearing moccasins; other times he would be barefoot. Their neighbors, Mr. and Mrs. Martin Shepherd, would see them often. Sometimes Faulkner would ask to use their telephone to order groceries. He would speak French with Shepherd, a New York-educated architect. On one of these visits Mrs. Shepherd ventured a question.

"Why does a man of your education dress that way?" she asked.

"I prefer to dress like this," Faulkner answered shortly.

Normally, however, he was gallant, his manners beautiful. He was, recalled Mrs. Shepherd, "a regular Chesterfield."

He was seeing his friends from those earlier days, too—Bill Lolo, now living at Bayou Casatt, and Tom Kell. His relationship with Kell was still warm and easy and sometimes he would open up. Once when Kell commented on his new marital status, Faulkner said, "Tom, they don't think we're gonna stick, but it is gonna stick." Kell would come to see them often. Occasionally his wife Lola would join him. Now Faulkner began to work again, and when Kell thought time was hanging heavy on Estelle's hands he would invite her to go for a ride in his car. Sometimes at night they would get torches and go fishing for flounder in the shallow water. Kell kept up his easy badinage with Faulkner. If he thought he saw his friend showing signs of strain, he would say, "Bill, you're getting irritable and cross. Let's you and me and Lola go floundering." And Faulkner might join them.

The proofs of *The Sound and the Fury* were sent to him, it appears, in early July. Though his initial reaction must have been one of anger, it had simmered down by the time he wrote a two-page letter to Ben Wasson. In copy-editing the manuscript, Wasson had deleted all of the italics he had indicated in the Benjy section. Instead, he had introduced more space between the various passages to indicate time-shifts. The italic-roman system could differentiate only between two time-levels, he felt, whereas Faulkner had used at least four. Faulkner rejected Wasson's revision, laboriously restoring the italicized passages, and italicizing additional passages to help clarify the time-shift. Of the editing he wrote, "It seemed pretty tough to me, so I corrected it as written. . . ." Actually, he told Wasson, there were more than four dates involved in the actions Benjy remembered. He listed eight events at different times by way of example.

He also rejected Wasson's proposed system of spacing principally on aesthetic grounds, because "a break indicates an objective change in tempo, while the objective picture here should be a continuous whole, since the thought transference is subjective; i.e., in Ben's mind and not in the reader's eye. I think italics are necessary to establish for the reader Benjy's confusion; that unbroken-surfaced confusion of an idiot which is outwardly a dynamic and logical coherence. To gain this, by using breaks it will be necessary to write an induction for each transference. I wish publishing was advanced enough to use colored ink for such, as I argued with you and Hal in the speak-easy that day." Now more of his annoyance began to show through. He would have to save the idea about the inks until publishing grew up to it. In the meantime, the italics were to be restored, and the passages would have to be repunctuated. "You'd better see to that, since you're all for coherence. And dont make any more additions to the script, bud. I know you mean well, but so do I. I effaced the 2 or 3 you made." There was only one conversational note in the whole letter: "We have a very pleasant place on the beach here. I swim and fish and row a little. Estelle sends love."

After Wasson replied, he received at least two more letters. In the first Faulkner instructed him to see that two more passages were set in italics —one to signify the speech of one person within that of another, and the other to indicate another "transference." He was feeling penitent now about the tone he had taken. "Excuse recent letter," he wrote. "Didn't mean to be stubborn and inconsiderate. Believe I am right, tho. And I was not blaming you with it. I just went to you with it because I think you are more interested in the book than anyone there, and I know that [we] both think alike about it, as we already argued this very point last fall. Excuse it anyway. Estelle sends regards. Love to all. Bill."

Wasson had sent the manuscript to Evelyn Scott, another Cape & Smith author who had also been with Boni & Liveright and Harcourt, Brace. Born in Tennessee and educated at Newcomb College and the Newcomb School of Art in New Orleans, Evelyn Scott had early found herself in revolt against the Southern ante-bellum tradition. She was passionately absorbed in Russian and French literature and had espoused such radical causes as racial equality. Now, at age thirty-six, she was the author of five impressive novels. She had just published *The Wave*, a huge experimental novel of the Civil War which had been enthusiastically praised and criticized. Wasson could hardly have chosen a more intelligently sympathetic reader. On May 10 she typed out a one-page, single-spaced letter to him. It was, she thought, "a novel with the qualities of greatness." The method of using the four sections to tell the story was, as far as she knew, unique. The best was the first section; Benjy was "a better idiot than Dostoyevsky's because his simplicity is more convincingly united with the basic animal simplicity of creatures untried by the standards of a conscious and calculating humanity. It is as if Blake's Tiger had indeed been framed before us by the same hand that made the Lamb and, in contradiction of Blake, with the same soul. Innocence is terrible as well as pathetic; and Benjy is terrible—

sometimes also terrifying. He is a Christ symbol, yet not, in the way of even the old orthodoxies, Christly. . . . Benjy is like Adam, with all he remembers in the garden and one foot in hell on earth." There was one phrase in particular which would please an admirer of Joyce: "The author is very often able to see here as one of the gods, remote, and at the same time immanent in all the emotions so inevitable to his creatures." Although she spent almost the whole of the letter talking about the Benjy section, she mentioned the other sections before she closed: "Dilsey is beautiful. Luster is perfect. Mrs. Compson is good. Jason is a devil that, as you are compelled to the vision of the gods, you must compassionate."

Delighted, Wasson took the letter to Hal Smith. "Let's make a pamphlet out of this," Smith said. Evelyn Scott agreed and expanded the letter into a six-page essay, calling the novel a tragedy with "all the spacious proportions of Greek art," a work which was "an important contribution to the permanent literature of fiction."

Ben wrote Bill and asked for names to which the pamphlet should be sent. The response was not that of a man particularly concerned about sales. "You know all the people in Oxford whom I know," he wrote, "and how many of them would buy a book." He finally listed ten in Oxford and half a dozen others. He suggested that they send Mac Reed a handful and a few to himself. "I'll mail them out as I recall names," he said. Meanwhile production of the book was going forward. Arthur Hawkins worked one day a week at Cape & Smith interviewing artists and assigning the jacket work for new books. He took this one himself (as he did most of the others) and did a dramatic illustration for the front cover: a shadowy scene in which two nude male figures, one white and one black, wrestled, locked struggling together.

Perhaps Evelyn Scott's response took some of the sting out of another *Scribner's* rejection by Dashiell, written in New York on July 2 and probably forwarded to Pascagoula. Dashiell thought the story, entitled "Through the Window," was "nearer to being publishable than most of your short pieces." He still found it difficult, however, to get into a Faulkner story and find out just what the story actually was. "The background is interesting but comes up and overwhelms the early part of the story." This one was actually fairly straightforward. The mainspring of its plot went back to *Flags in the Dust.* The obscene letters Byron Snopes had written to Narcissa and then stolen back had been obtained by the FBI agent investigating Byron's robbery of the Sartoris bank. As ransom for the letters, Narcissa had slept with the agent, and this knowledge had killed Aunt Jenny. The background that Dashiell objected to was supplied by the servant, Elnora. Early in the story she told her son Aunt Jenny's history. Faulkner had done it lovingly and in detail, as fascinated again with the elaboration of the Sartoris saga as he had been in *Flags in the Dust.* A novel could accommodate such material, but it pulled the short story all out of shape in showing how Narcissa's conduct would be just enough to snap the thread of life in a gallant ninety-year-old woman who had seen more than her share of disaster. Faulkner would revise the story and retitle it "An Empress Passed," but it would not sell under that name, either. He probably did not spend much time thinking about it, however. It seems likely that he was still working at *Father Abraham*, reshaping the events in other versions and styles titled variously *Abraham's Children* and "As I Lay Dying."

Three weeks after the honeymooners arrived at Pascagoula, Mrs. Hairston came for a visit bringing Cho-Cho with her. Cho-Cho enjoyed the crabbing and flounder-spearing at night by torchlight with Billy and Malcolm, and she and Rosebud Stone played ladies in some of Estelle's dresses. Mrs. Hairston was an easy guest who made herself at home, enlivening things for Estelle by organizing a bridge party. Yet the routine was still the same. Breakfast was a leisurely meal for which Bill might appear dressed in shirt and bathing trunks. By this time he had bought a touring car with wire wheels—perhaps, after all, in anticipation of some royalties from *The Sound and the Fury.* Some evenings he and Estelle, the children, Mrs. Hairston, and Emma would climb into the car and drive forty miles along the silvery beach. They would pass Biloxi with its old homes and moss-hung trees, then stop in Gulfport for dinner. After a week Mrs. Hairston took the children back to Columbus. Dot Oldham came down for a visit, and then Bill and Estelle took a brief trip themselves.

They went to New Orleans, putting up at the elegant old Monteleone. Estelle met newspaper friends of her husband such as John McClure, Roark Bradford, and Hermann Deutsch. Horace Houghland was there, whom Estelle had known at Ole Miss. Weeks Hall—one of those Spratling had caricatured—was very attentive and sent her flowers. Lillian Marcus, Julius Friend, and Sam Gilmore came to see them at the Monteleone. These friends whom Faulkner had shanghaied aboard the *Nausikaa* could not know how far he had gone since *Mosquitoes.* Sam Gilmore remembered, though, that Faulkner had just finished what must have been the proofs of *The Sound and the Fury* and thought it would be a great success—or at least told them so. By the time they returned to Pascagoula it must have been getting on toward late summer.

In spite of the summer's diversions, there had been strains and emotional crises. One of them had frightened the Faulkners' next-door neighbor, Mrs. Shepherd, who had watched Estelle in her imported silks and satins. One night, she later recalled, Estelle had walked down to the beach in one of those gorgeous silk dresses after an evening of heavy drinking. The next thing Mrs. Shepherd knew, Bill had called out to Martin Shepherd sitting there on his porch. "She's going to drown herself!" he shouted. Shepherd ran down and into the shallow water. He waded and stumbled more than the length of a block before he reached her almost at the point where the shelf of the beach dropped away at the channel. He said she fought him off before he was finally able to bring her in to shore. They immediately called Dr. Kell, who administered an injection and ordered her to bed. In a few days she was better.

Now with the summer waning it was time finally to pack and leave Pascagoula. When they returned to Oxford, they rented the downstairs floor of Miss Elma Meek's home at 803 University Avenue. Miss Elma, a small woman with a large mouth, lived upstairs. Her glasses rested on the bridge of a rather sharp nose, and her gray hair was pulled straight back to a bun at her neck. But she had a surprisingly sweet smile and a keen sense of humor. Lasting fame of a kind had come to her when she had won a contest to choose a familiar name for the university. "Ole Miss" had been her selection—the name by which the mistress of the plantation was known in ante-bellum days. Her white house was large and imposing, with a porch and balcony running from the front door to the right-hand side of the house. On the first floor a drawing room, two bedrooms, dining room, bath, and kitchen gave off the enormous twelve-foot-wide front hall which ran almost the full length of the house. Estelle's furniture had been shipped from Honolulu, and it filled the ample apartment with its twelve-foot ceilings.

Now it was time for Faulkner to look to the new obligations he had incurred. He knew he could count on his father and Uncle John in finding a job. The question was, what job? For some time he had been on a friendly basis with two brothers named Furr. One was usually seen carrying a force pump with which he attacked plumbing stoppages. The other, Tom Clark remembered, "was a big, harried-looking man who constituted almost the entire technical staff of the buildings and grounds department. He actually had more degrees than many members of the faculty." Faulkner had apparently frequented the university power plant from time to time. He had mentioned some such place to Owen Crump in New York, and it was logical for him to think of it again. It was there, probably sometime in the early fall, that Faulkner would accept his first steady job since his resignation from the United States Postal Service nearly five years before.

The children started school and Estelle assumed her housekeeping duties. She had a girl to do housework, and Cornell Franklin's child-support payments provided a nurse for the children. Estelle did the cooking. Her husband was fond of the exotic Eastern dishes she loved to prepare, especially the hot curries seasoned with imported spices.

They fell into new routines. Every day Faulkner would walk to the old Delta Psi house to visit Miss Maud and have coffee with her. It was the kind of filial duty that would increasingly typify Faulkner's relations with his family. To Phil Stone it would be further evidence for a view he would later express often—that all the Falkner boys were tied to their mother and resented it. This was probably partly responsible, Stone thought, for an animosity toward women that he saw in Bill. Stone's possessive feelings had abated little; as his proprietary status, such as it was, declined further, his feelings of injury and hostility would increase.

Occasionally Estelle would join her husband in one of his visits to her new mother-in-law, sometimes bringing a small gift. She noticed, though, that Miss Maud would shortly fall silent. She felt sure that this did not happen when Billy went by himself. The truth was that Miss Maud was not reconciled to her son's marriage. Instead, she had nagging worries about it. One was very specific. Far from being an implacable enemy of alcohol like herself, Estelle drank. When Billy drank too much, Miss Maud was likely to feel not only that Estelle didn't try to put a check on him but also that she encouraged him—if he needed any encouragement—by her example. Over the long run, Estelle would see more of Maud Falkner than her other three daughters-in-law. But it would be no easy relationship at best.

Miss Maud had given her eldest son a frail spindle-legged writing table. John Falkner thought it was so frail that it "belonged in some lady's parlor." Bill placed it sideways at one of the parlor windows where the light would come in from his left. One story he probably worked on at that table was entitled "A Rose for Emily." His boyhood friend, John Cullen, thought Faulkner took much of this one from life: from the courtship of Miss Mary Louise Neilson by Captain Jack Barron, a Yankee who had come into Oxford with the W. G. Lassiter Paving Company when the streets had been paved two years before. The couple had married in spite of the Neilsons' objections. What Faulkner wrote about, Cullen thought, was "events that were expected but never actually happened."

When Faulkner began the story in the familiar blue ink on the white legal-size sheets, he called his protagonist Miss Emily Wyatt. On five pages he told the story of a young woman spurned, and he made few changes when he typed it out. He had skillfully built up an oppressive air of dread. The inferences from Homer Barron's jilting of Emily and her purchase of arsenic were clear, but there was still a quality of mystery and suspense. Five pages from the end, however, Miss Emily, on her deathbed, spoke openly to her only servant, an old Negro man, of the body of her betrayer and victim lying upstairs. After this two-page digression gave away what had been established more effectively by inference, Faulkner went on to the Poe-esque ending. The ruined room was decorated as for bridal rites—much like the decaying room of Miss Haversham in *Great Expectations*, by one of Faulkner's favorites, Charles Dickens. In this story Faulkner had returned to a technique he had practiced in the *Times-Picayune*: the surprise ending. A strand of gray hair on the pillow next to the corpse showed that this was a drama not only of fornication and murder, but of a kind of necrophilia as well. In September the story went to Alfred Dashiell at *Scribner's.* The next month Dashiell wrote that in spite of good characterization and an "unusual situation," it unfortunately did not "fall within our fiction needs." The letter was dated October 7, 1929, the publication day of *The Sound and the Fury.*

The reviews were not long in coming. On October 9 Harry Hansen, literary editor of the New York *World*, gave qualified endorsement. The best review appeared four days later in the book section of the New York *Herald Tribune*. It was written by Lyle Saxon, who may very well have requested it of his friend Irita Van Doren, the editor. "I believe simply and sincerely that this is a great book," Saxon wrote. It was a merciless novel which would evoke strong reactions, but if Faulkner seemed obsessed with futility and insanity, so did Dostoevsky. If Faulkner even appeared mad, so did Joyce. Later in the month the Boston *Evening Transcript*'s reviewer saw the book as Greek tragedy in north Mississippi. It was a novel "worthy of the attention of a Euripides," wrote the anonymous reviewer. "Would we dare give higher praise?" The reviews would keep coming in during the fall and early winter. The *New York Times* reviewer thought the author's use of four styles unusual, yet they were welded together in perfect unity.

Basil Davenport, writing in *The Saturday Review of Literature*, praised Faulkner's power and tenderness, adding "This is a man to watch."

The enthusiastic reviews would not be translated into commensurate sales. A little more than two weeks after the book appeared the downward trend of the inflated stock market turned to panic, and on October 29 the market crashed. Book sales held up surprisingly well during the holiday season and into the new year, but by early March articles began appearing in book trade journals with ominous-sounding titles such as "75% of All Bankruptcies Are Needless." The total printing of *The Sound and the Fury* was 1,789. It would be enough to satisfy all demand for the book for nearly a year and a half.

In Oxford the novelist in all likelihood was working on his short stories, writing new ones and resubmitting old ones. It was probably when the letters of rejection continued unabated that he bowed to necessity and went to work at the university powerhouse. But the job was not a demanding one, and the newlyweds were able to entertain. Aunt 'Bama promised to come down with her husband, Walter B. McLean. "Let me know when to expect you," her great-nephew wrote. "I work all night now in a powerhouse, and my wife is quarantined with a scarlet fever patient at her father's home, so our apartment will be at your disposal and you can stay as long as you like. I am free all day, however, and it'll be fine. . . . If you will let me know when and what hour, I will be awake." Other visitors that fall included Cornell Franklin and Dallas, his new wife. Faulkner was polite and hospitable to his guests, but he did not remain at home for the whole of their visit. He went to Memphis and returned after they had left.

In years to come, when he was going to write away from his home workroom, he would roll up the segment he had begun together with an ample supply of blank sheets, secure the roll with a sturdy elastic band, and put it in his pocket. This may have been the way he set out for the powerhouse each evening with a packet of his favorite Fidelity Onion Skin, legal-size. On October 25, 1929, the day after panic had broken out on Wall Street, he took one of these sheets, unscrewed the cap from his fountain pen, and wrote at the top in blue ink, "As I Lay Dying." Then he underlined it twice and wrote the date in the upper right-hand corner.

Faulkner would later speak of "passing coal in a powerhouse," a phrase to conjure up a grimy fireman heaving huge shovelfuls into red furnace maws. It was a twelve-hour shift, he said, beginning at six P.M. "I shoveled coal from the bunker into a wheelbarrow and wheeled it and dumped it where the fireman could put it into the boiler. About 11 o'clock the people would be going to bed, and so it did not take much steam. And so we could rest, the fireman and I. He would sit in a chair and doze. I had invented a table out of a wheelbarrow in the coal bunker, just beyond a wall from where a dynamo ran. It made a deep, constant humming noise. There was no more work to do until about 4 A.M., when we would have to clean the fires and get up steam again." This gave him enough time each night, he later said, so that he "could write another chapter by about 4 A.M." The creative imagination had been at work again—as when he recalled crashing airplanes and swabbing decks. Not only was the job at the powerhouse a supervisory one, with two Negroes to do the labor he later arrogated to himself, but it apparently involved principally his just being there. His wife recalled that he would go to work after dinner, immaculate, and return before breakfast, still immaculate. After breakfast he would sleep for about two hours and then arise, piecing out his rest with brief naps later in the day. He would show her what he had written during the night on his shift.

His mood as he began the new work was very different from that with *The Sound and the Fury.* In writing *Sanctuary*, he would later say, he had discovered that there was something missing. The kind of rapture he had felt with *The Sound and the Fury* was not there. "When I began As I Lay Dying," he wrote, "I had discovered what it was and knew that it would be also missing in this case because this would be a deliberate book. I set out deliberately to write a tour-de-force. Before I ever put pen to paper and set down the first word I knew what the last word would be and almost where the last period would fall. Before I began I said, I am going to write a book by which, at a pinch, I can stand or fall if I never touch ink again. . . . that other quality which The Sound and The Fury had given me was absent: that emotion definite and physical and yet nebulous to describe: that ecstasy, that eager and joyous faith and anticipation of surprise which the yet unmarred sheet beneath my hand held inviolate and unfailing, waiting for release. It was not there in As I Lay Dying. I said, It is because I knew too much about this book before I began to write it. I said, More than likely I shall never again have to know this much about a book before I begin to write it. . . ."

He had already used the title twice before on versions of the spotted horses episode from *Father Abraham*. It was a curious title but the source was impeccable: the Eleventh Book of *The Odyssey.* When asked, Faulkner would quote the speech of ghostly Agamemnon to Odysseus: "As I lay dying the woman with the dog's eyes would not close my eyelids for me as I descended into Hades."

What Faulkner did night after night as he wrote to the hum of the powerhouse dynamo was to structure the novel about a family which had not appeared in *Father Abraham.* (It was also set twenty-five years later.) But their traits were not entirely new. Anse Bundren was as shiftless as Henry Armstid, and whereas Mrs. Armstid was so overworked she looked moribund, Addie Bundren actually was dying. A one-time schoolteacher, she had been as crudely courted by her husband-to-be as had the schoolteacher courted by shiftless Joe Bunden in the early unpublished story "Adolescence." The Bundrens had a family of five children, of whom the youngest two—a girl and small boy—slept together, as did Jo-Addie and Elmer Hodge in *Elmer.* The idea from which the whole book grew, as Allen Tate remembered Faulkner saying, would be embodied in Anse Bundren's reflections that his troubles had come with the building of the road, that once it was built it was easy for bad luck to find him.

A number of people from *Father Abraham* and its offshoots would appear in *As I Lay Dying*: Vernon Turpin, the Bundrens' closest neighbor; Henry Armstid, not nearly so mad as before; Will Varner, using his veterinarian's instruments to set Cash Bundren's leg as he had that of Henry Armstid. There would be a male Littlejohn, rather than a female. There would be one spotted horse—actually ridden as a saddle horse by Jewel Bundren. Young Vardaman Bundren might have been not too different from young Admiral Dewey Snopes had it not been for the traumatic loss of his mother. Faulkner had drawn nubile and sultry country girls before; in Dewey Dell Bundren he would outdo himself. One brother, Darl, at first glance might seem unfamiliar: mad, poetic, and utterly different from the other Bundrens. Actually, however, he was another representative of a type which had always fascinated Faulkner, the sort of madman with poetic gifts who was the sole character in that story which had so much private meaning for him, "Carcassonne."

In *Father Abraham* Faulkner had used the horses to subject a community to catastrophe. In *As I Lay Dying*, he employed a variant of this strategy. As he later said, "I took this family and subjected them to the two greatest catastrophes which man can suffer—flood and fire, that's all. That was simple *tour de force.* That was written in six weeks without changing a word because I knew from the first where that was going." In the first story, the disaster had sprung from the greed of Flem Snopes, the complicity of Buck, the Texan, and the foolish susceptibility of Frenchman's Bend's males. Now, because of shiftless Anse's desire for false teeth and a new wife, Addie's children and her own putrefying body would be subjected to the twin catastrophes. Faulkner was still dealing with some of the same constants: the evil and folly of men, creating a spectacle mitigated only by humor, compassion, and indignation.

His title was now much more closely linked to the story. It was true that whereas in *Father Abraham* it had been a man, Armstid, who had been stretched out supine as in death, it was now a woman, Addie Bundren. But as Clytemnestra had betrayed her husband Agamemnon with Aegisthus, so Addie had betrayed Anse with the Reverend Whitfield, the father of her son, Jewel. The major aspect, though, in which the reader would see her was that of victim rather than victimizer—lying on a corn-shuck mattress dying while her husband looked toward her burial.

The manuscript pages accumulating under the minuscule strokes of his pen made it clear that Faulkner knew exactly where he was going. They contradicted the claim, however, that he never changed a word. Unlike the manuscript sheets of the other novels—full of canceled lines and paragraphs, marginal inserts, and lengthy paste-ins from previous versions—these pages were often almost completely clean. Over half of them had no marginal inserts at all, and there were very few paste-ins. There were only four pages which bore crossed-out numbers that testified to their having occupied other places in the manuscript. He did make changes as he went, however. On the very first page he changed Turpin's name to Tull. His use of dialect was not nearly so oppressively heavy as it had been in the seventeen pages entitled "As I Lay Dying," but his care for levels of usage was still acute. In Darl's first soliloquy he began with the subject "Father and I," but returned and substituted "Pa and Vernon Tull."

The novel resembled the seventeen-page version in one aspect, however: its experimental style. He was using the stream-of-consciousness technique sparingly, and even when he used it with a madman, Darl, it was never as hard to follow as it had been with Benjy and Quentin. But he had employed again the device of shifting points of view—not just four, as in *The Sound and the Fury*, but a total of fifteen whose interior monologues might vary in length from one line to several pages. And as the narrators in *The Sound and the Fury* had turned for the most part toward a central female figure, Caddy, who had no segment of her own, so more than one of these characters was preoccupied with another female figure, Addie, who was given only one narrative segment—after her death. The fourth section of *The Sound and the Fury* gave the omniscient author a chance to describe and interpret events of the story. The mode of presentation here was not as starkly unadorned as the seventeen-page version had been, but there was not one whit more authorial intrusion.

Another familiar motif would appear in this novel: an abnormal bond between a sister and brother, though it would not be incestuous. It actually appeared as early as page 11 of the manuscript, in two paragraphs which Faulkner crossed out. Dewey Dell anticipates her mother's death: "Darl and me have known all along that she is going to die. He was the one told me, not with words at all. He just told me. And I believed it." Dewey Dell is pregnant by her lover, Lafe, and hopes to abort the pregnancy when they take her mother's body to Jefferson for the burial Anse says he promised her. Darl has known about the pregnancy, too. The second canceled paragraph described this knowledge with curious fetal imagery and commented subtly on their special relationship: "Because there is something between Darl and me. It was outside of me at first, and Darl was outside of it. But now it is inside of me and I am inside of Darl. Like I was inside a wall made of little rocks, the little rocks Darl's eyes, not looking at me any more now the wall is sealed up, the gap in it sealed. And the thing inside of me and Darl's eyes looking through me at it. And so that's where I want it to be, hid from seeing with sight. And so I can never be mad again at Darl because." Darl's clairvoyance was made clear in subsequent scenes, but instead of the mutual empathy expressed here, Dewey Dell's feeling would change to destructive hostility.

Though Faulkner was creating new characters and fleshing out others not fully treated before, he could, when he chose, reach back into his lumber-room for an inhabitant of Jefferson, for instance, who could play a useful part in the present story. Not only would this be economical, it would also serve to link this work to those already created. "I found out," he later said, "that not only each book had to have a design, but the whole output or sum of an artist's work had to have a design." One such linking character here was Doc Peabody, who had appeared in *Sartoris.* Seventy years old, weighing over two hundred pounds, he sees himself "hauled up and down a damn mountain on a rope" (42) to see a patient already dying—a patient whose death will send her family out to meet the twin disasters in store for them. Once again, as he had done in *Sartoris*, Faulkner would demonstrate the wisdom bought with age and experience. He would take character names from stories written as long ago as "The Liar"—Starnes and Mitchell—only to replace them with more recent names more clearly a part of the Yoknapatawpha Saga: Armstid and MacCallum. Others such as Suratt and Littlejohn would be mentioned but would not appear.

To give a sense of immediacy, of present action, he couched many of the interior monologues heavily in the present tense. To avoid monotony, however, he also used the past tense. In some cases, he would go down a page and change all the past tenses to present tense. In a few instances he seemingly left the tenses as they were but changed them when he typed the manuscript.

He was striving for a wide range of effects in these interior monologues. In some, such as those of Cora and Vernon Tull, the voices were so authentic and believable as to win the reader's immediate acceptance and delight. In others he immediately imposed a convention upon the reader: a kind of poetic license whereby a character's thoughts would be rendered with syntax, diction, and figures of speech far beyond his literal capabilities. This was true of Darl, who spoke like a mad poet. It was also true of Vardaman, who could say of Jewel's horse, "I see him dissolve—legs, a rolling eye, a gaudy splotching like cold flames—and float upon the dark in fading solution. . . ." (55) Just a few lines before, however, Faulkner would be at such pains to depict dialectal speech faithfully that he would change "Then it wasn't" to "Then hit want." As in *The Sound and the Fury*, he was attempting to render his unique vision without undue concessions to the reader.

When he started page 54, he had reached the halfway point in what would be the final manuscript. The work was now apparently going smoothly and rapidly. The evidence was there on the long onionskin pages: from 54 through 67 there was not one passage added in the wide left-hand margin—for him an extraordinarily long stretch without additional thoughts. And there were few canceled lines. When he did cross one out, it was usually because he had thought of something more that he wanted to say, and the canceled line would reappear at the end of the paragraph. He knew this material well. Either he had written it out before, perhaps somewhere among those lost 203 pages that preceded the surviving episode he had called "As I Lay Dying," or he had used what he would later call his favorite method of composition: to get it as right as he could in his head before he put it down on paper.

The outer life was going on routinely as the novel grew. There were still the daily visits to Miss Maud and to the post office in the hope of a check from Ben Wasson, Alfred Dashiell, or some other editor. From time to time he and Estelle would make the long drive to Memphis. Johncy's six-year-old son Jimmy would sometimes ride along. His parents would wake him at three-thirty so he would be ready in time to complete the seventy-mile journey by noon. The late autumn mornings were chill, and they would take along hot bricks to keep their feet warm as they drove north in the pale light before dawn.

In one way, however, things were beginning to change. An unsolicited ten-page essay arrived in the mail at Cape & Smith. It was from a Faulkner fan who wanted to give others the experience he had enjoyed in discovering Faulkner's work. He thought him the Deep South's first major novelist. The talent displayed in his first three books was as unmistakable as that in Joseph Conrad's first three, and someday his work would be more highly valued than that of Sinclair Lewis or Sherwood Anderson. His new book, *The Sound and the Fury,* was as powerful and terrible as any ever written by an American. Faulkner's mail at home was now heavier. In the aftermath of the new novel there were days when as many as two dozen letters would arrive from readers who had undergone the same experience as the essayist. Faulkner would ask Estelle to attend to the letters for him.

There was public as well as private praise. The autumn number of *The Southwest Review* carried an article entitled "Oxford, Mississippi." In it Medford Evans wrote about town and university, past and present. He devoted most of a paragraph to Stark Young and his work. "But Oxford's most immediate claim to the notice of the literati," he wrote, "is that it is the home of William Faulkner." Evans described the author's family and enumerated his books. In another paragraph he praised the work sympathetically and judiciously. He also sketched the man in terms that would soon be echoed in other articles in more prominent journals: "His fellow-townsmen make no pretense of being able to understand him. He is one of the most talked-about and most seldom talked-to persons in the community. He walks a great deal by himself, carries a cane, and wears a moustache. . . . He is said to be temperamental even with his friends, being at times a ready talker and again incommunicative." Only after devoting more than a page to Faulkner did Evans turn to the "most portentous man in Oxford," Chancellor Alfred Hume, at the time in danger of losing his job because of his sturdy opposition to Governor Bilbo.

It was not fame, but it was more than notice. The beginnings of a Faulkner cult were appearing. But he still had not benefited much financially. If he ever did make any money, he wrote Ben Wasson, he would have a dynamo put in his workroom because he liked the hum it made. Night after night, with that hum in the background, he continued to plot the journey of the Bundrens—each with his own secret wish—as circling buzzards followed the pathetic and grotesque cortege.

Addie had died at that Faulknerian time of day: twilight. But it had been three days before the Bundren wagon, repaired at last, had returned for her body, putrefying in the July heat. Encased in the coffin Cash had made, it began the forty-mile journey toward her family burying ground in Jefferson. Later, one of the monologues would relay to the reader Anse's partial summary of the trip: "he told a long tale about how they had to wait for the wagon to come back and how the bridge was washed away and how they went eight miles to another bridge and it was gone too so they came back and swum the ford and the mules got drowned and how they got another team and found that the road was washed out and they had to come clean around by Mottson. . . ." (194) Like most of the women in the novel, Cora Tull is incensed at these outrages visited on Addie's body, feeling them symbolic of the hard lot of a hill farmer's wife. When her husband tells her that it was a log which upset the wagon in the river, Cora replies that it was the hand of God—presumably showing His displeasure too. It may have been with this line in mind that Faulkner added a marginal insert to the preceding passage describing the actual event. He wrote of the log: "It surged up out of the water and stood for an instant upright upon that surging and heaving desolation like Christ." (141) It is impossible to tell when this marginal insert was added. It suggests, however, the revisions of the Benjy section of *The Sound and the Fury*—a deliberate afterthought adding overt Christian symbolism to the narrative.

Another change, however, worked in the opposite direction. Just before the catastrophe of fire was to be visited upon the Bundrens, Faulkner deleted from page 87 of his manuscript a passage heavy with Christian references. It was a portion of Darl's interior monologue in which he decided to set fire to Gillespie's barn to dispose of his mother's body: "Once when I was dead I heard the sad horns. I heard the sad suspirant they call Christ when the earth turned in slumber and slept again. . . . Once I was a little Child and I set up in dying. My father set me up in dying. It was a good business but I just wasn't the man for it. I hadn't the aptitude for it. For not all men are born carpenters, good carpenters, like Christ. He made His mother a boat to ride in, but His Father upset it in the stream.

So he said Well I'll try her by fire next because you dont ravel beyond fire. And that will be nice. It's because he thinks he cannot bear it, O gods. Darl thinks he cannot bear it. You understand. It's because he can bear a buzzard but not a cat. . . ." The deletion served to make the outbreak of the fire more dramatic than it would have been, thus prefigured, and provided suspense about the origin of the fire. It also worked as others had: to reduce the irrational content in the interior monologues of the Bundren family.

After the catastrophe of the flood, Faulkner had given to this novel's central female figure something he had thought inappropriate for Caddy Compson: a chance to speak for herself. Placed between monologues of the garrulous, obtuse, and self-righteous Cora Tull and the sanctimonious Reverend Whitfield, Addie's words revealed her sense of isolation, alienation, and bitterness. They also revealed a causative factor in this tragedy which provided a link with that of the Compsons: a father whose voice was full of barrenness and defeat. Quentin Compson's father had told him, "no battle is ever won. . . . They are not even fought. The field only reveals to man his own folly and despair, and victory is an illusion of philosophers and fools." (93) Addie Bundren's father had told her that "the reason for living is getting ready to stay dead." (67)

The Bundrens' trip had taken them even beyond the boundaries of Yoknapatawpha County before they dug Addie Bundren's grave (with borrowed spades) and buried her among her kinsmen. It had been costly for all of them: Cash's flayed and broken leg has made him a cripple for life; Darl has been taken off to the insane asylum at Jackson; Jewel has lost his horse; Dewey Dell has failed to obtain an abortion; Vardaman's emotional trauma has been deepened. But they have endured the catastrophes. Jewel has saved Addie from flood and fire as she had predicted. Not only has Anse kept his promise, but he has gained his ulterior objects: false teeth and a wife to replace Addie.

Faulkner completed the final five pages of the manuscript without any marginal inserts, pasting onto the last page two passages from an earlier sheet. Then he wrote at the bottom of page 107, "Oxford, Miss./11 December, 1929." Forty-seven days had elapsed since he had started.

When he began typing the manuscript he did less revision than he had with his previous books. Repeated changes consisted mostly of increasing the use of present tense and eliminating some of the phonetic dialect spellings. A few passages were lengthened, particularly that of Jewel's near-fight with a man who, he thinks, has made a remark about the odor of the corpse.

Other passages were shortened, as with drugstore clerk Skeet MacGowan's comments as he prepares to give Dewey Dell the "treatment." Though there were dozens of corrections on the original copy and the carbon copy which Faulkner kept, the changes were minor and their number was small compared to the earlier books. On page 265, the last page, he wrote in ink, "Oxford, Missippi [*sic*]/January 12, 1930." He sent off the original to Hal Smith, to whom the book would be dedicated. By this book, he wrote Smith, he would stand or fall. Then he bound the carbon copy—using mottled paper with a design that looked like blue, green, and cream nebulae—and put the book on his shelf.

During the time that Faulkner had been typing the manuscript of *As I Lay Dying*, his name had been brought to the attention of English readers by an influential if not unqualifiedly enthusiastic advocate. Arnold Bennett, prestigious and successful through grimly realistic novels such as *Clayhanger* and *The Old Wives' Tale*, wrote in the *Evening Standard* on December 19 that he had heard from an Englishman of the promise of William Faulkner and had sent to New York for his books. He had been able to obtain only *The Sound and the Fury.* His reaction alternated praise and blame. He evidently had "great and original talent," but, influenced by Joyce, he was "exasperatingly, unimaginably difficult to read." Bennett was infuriated by the book but would not have missed it. If Faulkner emerged from "this youthful stage of eccentricity," he wrote, he would find "wide appreciation."

The man from whom Bennett had learned of Faulkner was the Welsh dramatist and novelist Richard Hughes, whose own novel of that year, *A High Wind in Jamaica*, also dealt with the reactions of a group of children to death and facets of adult life. In New York Hughes had asked Ben Wasson who the best young author was in the United States. Wasson had told him it was Bill Faulkner and had given him a copy of *Soldiers' Pay.* Later Hughes went sailing with Hal Smith. When Smith's yacht was fogbound off Nantucket, Smith gave him another copy of *Soldiers' Pay,* plus *Mosquitoes* and a set of galleys of *The Sound and the Fury.* Hughes read them all with excitement. When he returned to England he persuaded his own publishers, Chatto & Windus, to bring out these Faulkner titles in England and offered to do the introductions himself. Faulkner would now be published abroad as well as at home.

His fan mail was becoming more diversified. He would later recall that he received "two very intelligent, sensible letters in the '30s from Osbert

Sitwell after I had written *The Sound and the Fury*. . . . He did not say that this or that writer was terrible, but he spoke of what we in the writing world should believe in and what we ought to do." Faulkner left these letters unanswered like the others. "I would have answered them, but I didn't understand. I was uneducated and had never been in touch with anything literary."

With the manuscript of *As I Lay Dying* in New York, he could concentrate on short stories for immediate income. He began to keep a record of submissions to various magazines, using homemade ledger sheets of the kind Johncy had seen tacked on his closet door at the Delta Psi house. Unlike those sheets, however, these would survive to provide a record of the stories he sent out over nearly a two-year period beginning on January 23, 1930. On that day and from then on he wrote down the date when the story went out. He wrote at the top border the names *Forum*, *The American Mercury*, *The Saturday Evening Post*, *Scribner's*, *Miscellany*, *Liberty*, *College Humor*, *American Caravan*, *Cosmopolitan*, *The Southwest Review*, *Blues*, and *Woman's Home Companion*. He also wrote down the names Hal Smith and Ben Wasson and then drew lines to form columns. At the top of six of the fourteen columns were titles without dates which indicated, presumably, stories sent out before those with the progressive series of dates below them. (Later, when stories were accepted, he would circle the titles.) Three stories had gone to H. L. Mencken's *American Mercury* sometime prior to January 23. The first was "The Big Shot," which had also been refused by *Forum*, *Liberty*, and *Miscellany*. Next was "Miss Zilphia Gant," which *The American Mercury* had, like *Scribner's*, rejected.

The third title was a new one. Faulkner had entitled the story "Idyll in the Desert." Like "Selvage," it had begun with an idea Estelle had explored but then abandoned. Her husband had become interested in it and reworked it in a four-page manuscript. He employed the technique he had used in such early stories as "Country Mice," the Conradian device whereby a nameless narrator questioned another who told the story which he himself had observed as a minor participant. Faulkner had treated the theme before: the woman who sacrifices herself for her lover, only to be deserted. The setting was very different, however—somewhere west of Phoenix where Easterners arrived periodically, "lungers" seeking health though in the last stages of tuberculosis. The narrator-on-the-spot was "Lucas Crump, Mail Rider," who described the twenty-five-year-old New Yorker whom he drove to a lonely Western mountain camp where he would engage in a two-year struggle with acute tuberculosis. He described the woman, ten years older, who abandoned her two children and well-to-do husband to nurse him. The story took an ironic turn with the flight of the recovered patient, not knowing that the woman he had left behind had contracted his disease. Dying, she would see him once more—now married to a beautiful and wealthy girl and failing even to recognize her. In the narration Faulkner tried to balance—perhaps heighten—the tragic story of the abandoned woman with the often humorous by-play between the quizzical narrator and Crump, who often fell into the tone of the Western spinner of tall tales. He had something of V. K. Suratt's easy garrulousness, without his heavy dialect. As in the revisions of *Father Abraham*, Faulkner had sacrificed immediacy in this after-the-fact narration, presumably to achieve greater depth or a thicker texture with heavier irony. He would use elements of this situation later. "Idyll in the Desert" was rejected by *Liberty* as well as by *The American Mercury.*

At about this time—perhaps in late January, certainly before February 5—Faulkner submitted a story to *The Saturday Evening Post* entitled "Smoke." This was another effort in the detective-story genre, running to twelve manuscript pages. The story was set in Jefferson, and like "A Rose for Emily" it was told by a nameless narrator. Always using "we" rather than "I," he spoke for the town—its knowledge of the circumstances, its guesses about facts and causes, its reactions to mystery unraveled. It was an ingenious story which revealed the murderer of a misanthrope to be a cringing nephew who had tried to cast the blame upon the victim's disowned son. The story was interesting for other reasons. It introduced a character Faulkner would later use extensively: County Attorney Gavin Stevens, who cleverly led the murderer into revealing himself. Stevens was "a Harvard graduate: a loose-jointed man with a mop of untidy iron-gray hair, who could discuss Einstein with college professors and who spent whole afternoons among the squatting men against the walls of country stores, talking to them in their idiom. He called these his vacations." Building a distinguished career after a sickly youth, bachelor Stevens seemed markedly to resemble Phil Stone, though there might also have been something of Faulkner's uncle John in the portrait. Later, when Stevens reappeared in other stories, some readers would say that every county seat had at least one lawyer like him—brilliant, loquacious, foreign-educated yet wed forever to his own provincial place. To these readers he would appear both as an individual and as a distinctive Southern type. Like Faulkner's other stories of this period, "Smoke" looked backwards as well as forwards, for the desperate murderer had hired a grotesque Memphis thug who resembled no one so much as Popeye. The *Post* refused the story. Again, Faulkner would use elements of it later.

During this same period he was sending out another story which was equally ambitious technically, though in a different way. The eleven manuscript pages of "A Fox-Hunt" gave evidence of extensive revision. Like "Idyll in the Desert," it was set outside Yoknapatawpha County. The action was actually brief. Harrison Blair has pursued one vixen mercilessly for three years on his Carolina preserve. Symbolically the fox suggests Blair's slim wife, whose red hair gleams like a fox's brush. By the end of the few hours covered by the story he tramples the vixen to death with his boot-heels. His wife, whom he systematically persecutes, has given herself to a lover in the woods during the hunt, but the gesture is futile. She is a lost woman; in her husband "there walked the tragic and inescapable shape of her ruin."

Point of view was unusual in that the action was seen through three different perspectives. The omniscient narrator described the preparations for the hunt through the comments of the three Negro stableboys. Then he switched to the perspective of two "clay-eaters," gaunt hill men who follow the hunt at a distance. The third perspective was that of Blair's valet. The first point of view expressed only pleasurable interest. The second was strongly ironic: the older of the two hill men wondered "how a man rich as folks says he is is got time to hate one little old fox bitch like that"; the younger man empathized with her, "projecting, trying to project himself, after the way of the young, toward that remote and inaccessible she. . . ." The valet's air, as he provided background for the chauffeur and comic relief for the reader, was one of seeming detachment mixed with cynicism.

The girl's being forced into marriage by a strong grandmother served to link this story with others such as "Selvage." For the circumstances if not the character of Harrison Blair, Faulkner probably drew upon the legendary Paul Rainey, whom Murry Falkner had advised about his stables and who had stocked his eleven thousand acres with foxes and pheasants and then brought in guests (thought not red-coated) to hunt them. Faulkner used a few technical phrases indicating that his interest in fox-hunting was more than cursory—an interest which would increase over the years. "A Fox-Hunt" (retitled "Fox Hunt") was not a wholly successful story, but it showed that he was trying to achieve two effects rather than one: the richness that could be obtained by filtering events through the comments and attitudes of observers such as the valet and the hill men plus the immediacy of events described in progress, which he had sacrificed in the short revisions of *Father Abraham*, in "The Big Shot," and in "Idyll in the Desert."

One of the last of his undated submissions was "A Rose for Emily," which had gone off to *Forum.* It seems likely that he had now deleted the deathbed scene of Miss Emily which undercut the final one, making the story tighter and more effective. (By now, probably, he had changed her name from Wyatt to Grierson.) It may have been about this time that he received word that *Forum* had taken "A Rose for Emily." It would be in the April number and would represent his first appearance in a national publication, apart from *The Double Dealer*, in eleven years. During that long interval he had published five books but had achieved no success in the magazine market. Perhaps encouraged by this acceptance, he sent out eight stories during the month of February. (On January 23, the earliest date on this new sending schedule, he had sent off to *The American Mercury* a story called "Fire and Clock.")

Four of the stories were apparently new ones. Two of them—"Per Ardua" and "A Dangerous Man"—would remain, like "Fire and Clock," unpublished. "A Dangerous Man," which went out on February 6, one day after "Per Ardua," was another story which had apparently begun with Estelle. Called "A Letter" and then "A Letter to Grandmamma," it had been at least partially typed with Estelle's name on the title page. It was about a woman with a difficult past: a hard father and a cruel husband who was perhaps a murderer. The couple lived on money sent by his mother, and when he left his wife he concealed the fact for fear his mother would stop the money. The wife was befriended by a railroad agent, but here the surviving manuscript and typescript fragments broke off. Faulkner apparently renamed the story "A Dangerous Man." His narrator (who alluded to Balzac's *La Maison Nucingen*) filled in the character of Mr. Bowan, the freight agent (himself the killer of a holdup man), and described his courtship of the deserted wife. The surviving typescript, which stopped at this point, gave no indication that either of Faulkner's two versions had finally jelled any more satisfactorily than Estelle's.

On February 8 he sent to *The American Mercury* a story called "Drouth." The unnumbered eight-page manuscript was divided into sections by five roman numerals. The first introduced Miss Minnie Cooper, once popular, now a neurotic spinster. In Section II the story moved to a barbershop buzzing with the rumor that she had been raped by a Negro named Will Mayes. As a sadistic veteran organized a mob, a compassionate barber named Hawkshaw tried to prevent a lynching for a crime that even Plunkett, the veteran, apparently doubted. The section that followed described the mindless homicidal response to the idea of the rape. The fourth section showed hysterical Minnie Cooper, once again the center of all eyes, comforted by doubtful yet prying women friends. Section V showed Plunkett returning, even more hostile toward his wife than was Harrison Blair toward his, another trapped woman, in "Fox Hunt." The *Mercury* rejected the story.

On February 14 Faulkner sent out a story Johncy had read a few years before, perhaps revised now after rejection. The RAF motto was "Per Ardua ad Astra," and it seems likely that "Per Ardua" made use of RAF materials. "Thrift" unquestionably did, but it was more comic than dramatic, more unrealistic than realistic. The protagonist was a Highland peasant named Wully MacWyrglinchbeath. Apart from the dialects—Scots, Cockney, and upper-class English—the comedy was meant to derive from the character of MacWyrglinchbeath, whose appearance suggested Possum McDaniel, the maladroit Oxford end responsible for the hump in Bill Faulkner's nose. Actually, MacWyrglinchbeath was a monster of avarice and miserliness whose twin goals were to survive the war and make as much money in the process as possible. These goals had led him to self-maiming to aid in gaining a transfer from infantry to air corps, in going A.W.O.L. to join a combat squadron, and in an unauthorized solo to achieve flying status. (The latter sequence suggested the central episode of "Landing in Luck," with a less happy ending.)

Faulkner was writing of an imagined Scotland and a wartime France which he knew only from books read and from tales heard. He probably would have maintained, however, that he was dealing with very familiar subject matter: the kind of people who populated Yoknapatawpha County's Beat Four. This was the remote region inhabited, he would later write, by "people named Gowrie and McCallum and Fraser and Ingrum that used to be Ingraham and Workitt that used to be Urquhart," living on hills that seemed to hang suspended above the plateau as "the Scottish highlands did except for this sharpness and color. . . ." MacWyrglinchbeath's quiet parsimony, his taciturnity in the face of both hardship and good fortune, the closeness with which he computed the variables in money matters—these characteristics were precisely those one would see in Frenchman's Bend. There was nothing technically unusual about "Thrift," for Faulkner used an omniscient narrator who told the story as he had heard it in military messes. Faulkner had probably enjoyed writing it. Though it lacked the power of "A Rose for Emily" or "Drouth," it was a well-plotted, well-made story combining a kind of rural comedy with wartime adventure. *The Saturday Evening Post,* Faulkner's first choice, accepted it for publication in September. From that time on Faulkner thought consistently of the *Post,* with its premium prices, as a market for much of his short fiction. As for immediate effects, this sale must have made the power plant job much less a necessity than it had been, if, indeed, Faulkner still sat there every night, reading or writing to the dynamo's hum.

In the next month Faulkner made eight more submissions to magazines. John McGinnis had written asking him for a story for *The Southwest Review.* Faulkner sent him "Miss Zilphia Gant." He was paid for it, but the story was too long for the magazine; it would not appear for over two years, and then under a different aegis. Three of the other stories Faulkner submitted were seemingly new. On March 7 he sent one called "Ad Astra" to *The American Mercury*. In it he had gathered together several characters who had first appeared elsewhere. Like "Thrift" it used RAF materials, but the tone was tragic. It seems likely that he drew here on such magazine articles as the series in *Liberty* which Ben Gray Lumpkin remembered seeing Faulkner reading in the post office. This was probably *War Birds: The Diary of an Unknown Aviator*, which was serialized in *Liberty* and then published by George H. Doran Company in 1926. Like many others, it emphasized the high casualty rate among combat airmen, the frenetic life they led on the ground, and the way the war had left the survivors maimed, psychologically if not physically. This was the point of "Ad Astra," set immediately after the armistice yet told in the year 1930. The nameless narrator was one of six RAF fliers. He and three others were Americans: Bayard Sartoris out of *Sartoris*, Gerald Bland out of *The Sound and the Fury*, and Monaghan, self-proclaimed shanty Irishman, Yale graduate, and son of a millionaire sewer magnate. The other two were a huge belligerent Irishman named Comyn and a philosophical Indian called the subadar, the latter based perhaps on a model Faulkner had met in Stone's company at New Haven. The story's action developed out of Monaghan's insistence on bringing into a French café a German he had shot down that day. The end, after the ensuing riot, found them in the cold empty plaza preparing to go to a brothel, while from a distance came the sound—as in *Sanctuary*—of a band, "brassy, thudding, like the voices, forlornly gay, hysteric, but most of all forlorn." (This was an afterthought for the most part. In the manuscript the band was mentioned once; in later revision Faulkner elaborated on it for contrast and irony.) The German and the subadar were foils for the violent Anglo-Saxons. The former was a petty Prussian baron who loved music and rejected his violent heritage. The latter, a prince who had made an almost identical rejection, put into words the meaning of the public and private violence leading up to that moment: "All this generation which fought in the war are dead tonight. But we do not yet know it."

This story constituted a return to the subject matter of *Soldiers' Pay*, and Faulkner would treat war and its effects many times again. "Ad Astra," like several of his other stories, was ironically titled. It was also grim and powerful—too much so, perhaps, in the opinion of the editors of *The American Mercury*, who rejected it. On March 25 it went out again to the editors of *American Caravan IV*, who took it.

"Point of Honor" was another apparently new story which Faulkner had mailed on March 7 to *The Saturday Evening Post*; the *Post* rejected it. On the twenty-fifth Faulkner sent to *Scribner's* a story entitled "Honor." The similarity between the titles and the dating suggests that he had revised, or at least retitled, the rejected story and sent it out again. What he did in "Honor" was to employ the familiar strategy of following subsequent events in the life of a character treated earlier—this time into a kind of flying career that exercised an increasing fascination for Faulkner. The character was Monaghan, now barnstorming with an aerial circus. Faulkner's interest in the Gates Flying Circus in New Orleans in 1925 had probably been revived by his occasional visits to the Memphis airport. The living such men made was precarious and, as he would say later, "ephemeral" enough to provide vivid proof of the subadar's words about the future of the lost generation. Monaghan was somewhat more resilient than most, however, though by 1922 he was a drifter, an unemployed automobile salesman. In a passage Faulkner might have spoken, he recalled the "campuses full of British and French uniforms, and us all scared to death it would be over before we could get in and swank a pair of pilot's wings ourselves." Monaghan went so far as to quote the subadar, whose words he could now understand, and to recall in one paragraph the events of "Ad Astra." What the bulk of "Honor" actually treated, however, was an illicit love affair which confirmed Monaghan as a drifter. Here Faulkner was using a character who had appeared in his work before and would figure in a novel later: the self-sacrificing husband who cares only about the welfare of the wife who has betrayed him. There was a kind of neat ending to the story which suggested that Faulkner might be tailoring it to the requirements of popular fiction: Monaghan was the godfather of the boy born to the reconciled parents. *Scribner's* rejected it.

On March 20 he tried *The American Mercury* with another story which further explored the life of a character treated earlier. "Hair" took up the barber, Hawkshaw, after the events of "Drouth." It was as though Faulkner had become intrigued with characters he had created and was impelled to discover what would happen to them in later life. The story was told by a drummer, a much more humane one than Plunkett's accessory in the murder of Will Mayes. The drummer spoke directly to the reader in a highly conversational tone such as Sherwood Anderson's narrators often used, describing Hawkshaw's fidelity to a dead fiancée and to her parents. Hawkshaw—prone "to tilt at windmills"—displayed characteristics of a Faulkner type who would become more familiar: the good, decent, frugal, self-effacing man who is almost a victim but who is finally rewarded. The *Mercury* quite promptly sent "Hair" back.

One concrete form which Hawkshaw's fidelity to his dead fiancée took was to pay off the mortgage on her widowed mother's home. In one passage Faulkner's narrator quoted from a record Hawkshaw kept of the payments which finally canceled the mortgage. This passage may have represented something more than just the needs of the story. Faulkner was by now thinking about mortgage payments of his own. He and Estelle were very seriously considering buying the old Shegog place out on the Old Taylor Road where they both had played as children.

33

April, 1930–January, 1931

So it was finished then, down to the last plank and brick and wooden pin which they could make themselves. Unpainted and unfurnished, without a pane of glass or a doorknob or hinge in it . . . it stood for three years more surrounded by its formal gardens and promenades, its slave quarters and stables and smokehouses; wild turkey ranged within a mile of the house and deer came light and colored like smoke and left delicate prints in the formal beds. . . .

—*Absalom, Absalom!* (39)

"Colonel" Robert B. Shegog was an Irishman who left the County Down during the first third of the nineteenth century to sail to America. He prospered in Tennessee, and by the time he moved to Mississippi he was a wealthy man. In 1844 he purchased a tract in Lafayette County that had been sold eight years earlier by a Chickasaw named E-Ah-Nah-Yea, who had received the land as a grant from the U.S. government. Shegog hired William Turner, an English architect, to build a two-story colonial-style home. They picked an elevated site, the land sloping off around it to bluffs and ravines. The house would face south. There, seven tenths of a mile from the Courthouse, the land was cleared and the kiln was built in which slaves would bake brick for the foundation.

The L-shaped house rose slowly. It was sturdy and roomy, appearing symmetrical from the front with parlors on both sides of the wide entrance hall and a dining room and kitchen extending back from the one on the right. Upstairs were three bedrooms. The portico comprised four tall wooden columns supporting the Grecian roof. Above the Georgian front doors was a balcony. On either side of the portico, above the wide, open gallery, were two large shuttered windows upstairs and downstairs. The work was completed when a professional gardener landscaped the grounds, curving a long, cedar-lined drive to approach the house. Near the front a magnolia tree would grow, encircled by flower beds traversed by brick walks. Shegog was proud of the house—there were only a few others like it in the region—and improved it whenever the opportunity arose. A lightning-rod and rain-gutter salesman came through Oxford in 1848 and Shegog gave him an order for the whole house.

In 1872 Mrs. Julia Bailey bought the house and much of the land from Colonel Shegog. As the years passed few builders were attracted to the rugged terrain, but often a party of picnickers would follow the paths to the springs in Bailey's Woods. For the boys of Oxford it was a special hunting and swimming preserve, perfect too for games such as hare-and-hounds. In 1923 Miss Ellen Bailey died there in the house and Mrs. Sallie Bailey Bryant inherited the property. She lived with her husband, Will Bryant, on his large plantation in Coffeeville, thirty miles southwest of Oxford. Though the house was falling into disrepair, it was certainly best from all points of view to keep it occupied; after a series of tenants, however, it fell vacant. Then, in late May, 1928, the Bryants rented the house to Mr. and Mrs. Claude Anderson of College Hill. Carrie Anderson had lived in Oxford before and was happy to move in in spite of the weeds and bushes growing up to the front door. Her husband solved that problem by plowing up the weeds, bushes, and what was left of the lawn for corn. He was going to run a dairy and chicken farm, and the luxury of cultivating formal gardens did not figure in his plans. For nearly two years now the Andersons had been selling their eggs, milk, butter, and produce to residents of Oxford. The house had continued to run down. Beams were rotting and sagging. The roof leaked, and mice and squirrels scurried in the attic. Stained and faded paper covered cracking plaster on the once-bright walls.

The Bryants hated to see the old place deteriorate, but they did not want to sell to the few people who offered to buy. One prospective purchaser told her that he wanted to turn it into a mule farm. When Mrs. Bryant learned that William Faulkner not only was interested in the house but talked about restoring it, she was determined that he should have it. With the Depression, money was tight, but Mr. Will Bryant began trying to work something out. A friend of Lem Oldham's, he was a thin old man whose weather-beaten appearance belied his aristocratic background. He had taken to Bill Faulkner and would talk to him about old times in north

Mississippi, about families dead and gone, about others whose descendants seemed little like their upright, hardy forebears. He finally made a proposal. Faulkner could buy the house and four acres of land for six thousand dollars, and he could add adjoining lands when he could afford them. There would be no down payment. Mrs. Bryant would give him possession and he would begin monthly payments of seventy-five dollars on June 1, paying an interest rate of six percent. On April 12, 1930, Bill Faulkner signed the papers drawn up by Jack Stone for Mrs. Bryant. The house was his on a deed of trust.

He could not move in, however, because the Andersons refused to vacate. Apparently they felt that their old arrangement with Mrs. Bryant gave them the option of renewing the lease. The Bryants did not agree and neither did Faulkner's uncle John, who served notice on the Andersons to vacate by June 1. Even though it would be seven weeks before they could move in, William Faulkner was now a property owner. They would move out of Miss Elma Meek's apartment onto their own four acres, into one of the oldest homes in the county.

A week after Faulkner signed the deed, *The Mississippian* reprinted a column noting attention being devoted in England to new Southern writers. Chatto & Windus had added William Faulkner to its list, Herschel Brickell observed, and though Faulkner "has not done his big book yet and his work after the first novel has been spotty and uncertain . . . there are moments in such books as 'Sartoris' and 'The Sound and the Fury' that are fairly breath-taking. . . ." At the time, however, Faulkner was still at work primarily as a short-story writer rather than as a novelist, trying to sell to the *Post* and other magazines which would not only take care of the seventy-five-dollar mortgage payments but also permit him to begin the long process of repair and refurbishing.

During the month of April he sent out a total of six stories. On April 21 "Drouth" went out to *Scribner's*. Faulkner had made several changes which gave him a much more powerful and ominous opening. In *As I Lay Dying* Doc Peabody had contemplated the approaching storm: "That's the one trouble with this country: everything, weather, all, hangs on too long. Like our rivers, our land; opaque, slow, violent; shaping and creating the life of man in its implacable and brooding image." Now, at the beginning of "Drouth," Faulkner struck the same note: "Through the bloody September twilight, aftermath of sixty-two rainless days, it had gone like fire in dry grass—the rumor, the story, whatever it was." The harsh, intense weather helped to trigger the violence lying just under the surface of mentalities like those of Plunkett—whose name was changed to McLendon—and the equally bloodthirsty Butch. Throughout the story Faulkner used the weather for a kind of symbolic reinforcement of the emotional climate which bred the storm of violence. In another revision Faulkner made the previously nameless town into Jefferson. Apparently he was even integrating his short stories, where he could, into the design that he had perceived as necessary to a whole body of fiction as well as to individual novels. The death of the accused Negro, Will Mayes—with only one man of good will courageous enough to dare McLendon for him—was another crucifixion of the innocent, the kind of act symbolically represented in Benjy's castration and institutionalization. "Drouth" was now superior to anything Faulkner had hitherto done in the short-story form. His apprenticeship in this genre had been longer than in the novel, but he had finally reached a point, at his best, of mastery here too.

Faulkner must have been disconcerted to receive "Drouth" back again within a few days. The explanation came on April 28 in an apologetic letter from assistant editor Kyle S. Crichton. It had accidentally been put with manuscripts being returned and had not been read. He hoped that Faulkner would return it to them because they were always glad to see his work. Though these assurances may by now have carried a somewhat hollow ring, Faulkner did return the story. On May 1, *Scribner's* took it, for two hundred dollars. Under a new title, "Dry September," it would appear early in 1931.

On April 22 he had sent to the *Post* a story entitled "Beyond the Gate." The central character was a judge and a widower like Judge Dunkinfield in "Smoke." "I am a Federal judge," he said. "My wife's father was a Republican, even though I do hail from a Democratic stronghold." In this story, set in the Hereafter, the newly arrived judge looked for his son somewhere among the hosts of the departed. The judge was in part a composite of Lem Oldham and Papa Niles. Oldham had lost his son at age nine; the judge in the story, at age ten. Niles was a federal judge and a vehement agnostic. Some touches suggested "Mistral" and other early stories: there was a cathedral nearby and "the sound of sheep bells in the twilight." Faulkner juxtaposed the judge to other souls: an Alpine guide, a friend from Jefferson who remains an atheist and anarchist, and another who is identified as Robert Ingersoll. Speaking to the famous agnostic, the judge sounds like Quentin Compson: "what I have been, I am; what I am,

I will be until that moment comes when I am not. And then I shall never have been at all. How does it go? *Non fui. Sum. Fui. Non sum.*" Even when the judge finally meets his son, his skepticism still shows in his voice. "Beyond the Gate" was not a particularly successful story. Divided into seven sections, it produced a disjointed, episodic effect. Characters faded in and out and finally the story trailed off in an uncomfortable, unresolved way. When Faulkner had dealt with the supernatural in "The Leg," he had written more in the tradition of the English horror story. Here his concern was religious-philosophical. There was no horror, but neither was there drama or force. When the *Post* returned it, Faulkner filed it away, not to touch it again for three years.

On the day he sent "Beyond the Gate" to the *Post*, he also sent "Honor" to *The American Mercury*, which accepted it for publication in July. Ben Wasson may have figured in the sale of this story. In an undated letter to his friend, Faulkner wrote, "It's fine about the good price for the story. You can just send the check on to me here, as I am not likely to move for a month, anyway. And get it to me as soon as you can; the first of the month only ten days away now." *The American Mercury* was the only one of the magazines in which Faulkner would publish that year which ran biographical notes and sometimes photographs of contributors together with whatever text the writer supplied. Faulkner told Wasson, "Sorry, I haven't got a picture. I dont intend to have one that I know of, either. About the biography. Dont tell the bastards anything. It cant matter to them. Tell them I was born of an alligator and a nigger slave at the Geneva Conference two years ago. Or whatever you want to tell them."

If he could sell a few more stories from his backlog, he wouldn't have to worry about mortgage payments for the rest of the year. On May 2 he sent out "Selvage" again and on May 21 a story called "Equinox," which was rejected by *Forum* and apparently does not survive. Six days later he sent to the *Post* a story he entered on his sending schedule simply as "Lizards." Its inception may have been much earlier.

It seems likely that sometime in the late 1920's, perhaps after the completion of *Flags in the Dust*, probably after he stopped work on *Father Abraham*, Faulkner began a manuscript which he called "Omar's Eighteenth Quatrain." The lines he cited were these:

They say the Lion and the Lizard keep
The Courts where Jamshyd gloried and drank deep:

And Bahram, that great Hunter—the Wild Ass
Stamps o'er his Head, and he lies fast asleep.

The eleven manuscript pages which remain of this story began with Suratt emerging from Mrs. Littlejohn's door and driving off in the summer twilight. He calls for Henry Armstid and Vernon Tull. It is dark when the three crawl to where they can watch the Old Frenchman place unobserved. Here Faulkner described the legendary Frenchman and what had happened to his domain. The two paragraphs were almost identical with two others early in *Father Abraham*. Faulkner had perhaps copied them from an earlier manuscript. It is also possible that he knew the material so well that it was almost formulaic with him by now. Certain people, certain incidents in the history of Yoknapatawpha County, apparently came to his mind—in whole paragraphs of description—with only the most minor variations. This would occur in his works with increasing frequency.

The eleven pages very likely represent fragments of not one but two versions of the story. Even so, the generating circumstances of the action were clear. The three men were watching Flem Snopes digging in the garden of the Old Frenchman place. To help them discover what Flem was seeking, Suratt had driven thirty miles to fetch an ancient dowser named Uncle Dick. There the fragment of the story ended.

Characteristically, Faulkner continued to work at the story, trying to get it "to come right," as he would later describe this kind of process. He started another version under the title "In Jamshyd's Courtyard," apparently abandoned it, and began it again as "Lizards in Jamshyd's Courtyard." This time he completed it in eight pages of compressed handwriting. He revised through two incomplete typescripts and finally finished it to his satisfaction in another which ran to twenty-three pages. Now the climax and denouement were clear. By the time the three buyers realized they had been duped with the old "salted-mine" trick, each had signed thousand-dollar notes to Flem in joint purchase of the Old Frenchman place. Suratt had gotten the better of Flem in a minor deal at the beginning of the story. He was beaten now only because greed had overcome his natural decency, stripped him of his habitual caution and skepticism, and left him vulnerable.

"Lizards in Jamshyd's Courtyard" suggested elements of Chaucer's "Pardoner's Tale." Here the three treasure-seekers did not die, but they lost a great deal of money and one—Armstid—was driven mad. By the story's end he was the same vicious man as the Armstid in *Father Abraham* and radically different from the decent Henry Armstid of *As I Lay Dying*. Vernon Tull was described as a "well-to-do bachelor" and Flem Snopes was as yet unmarried—all of which meant that these events took place before Flem and Buck brought the spotted horses into the county. Faulkner must by now have been working out in a more conscious way than he had done before the sequence of the major events in the history of Yoknapatawpha County. The *Post* apparently returned the story to him. But the refusal must have been a qualified one, for he would submit it to them again in less than three months.

When the Faulkners moved into the old Shegog place in June, 1930, Faulkner may have thought ruefully of Suratt surveying the new domain of which he was one-third owner. The Shegog house was in much better condition than the Old Frenchman place, but it had little more in the way of conveniences. There was no electricity and no plumbing, just the telephone which the Andersons had needed for the dairy and produce business. The Faulkners used oil lamps and fetched their water from the vine-covered wellhouse. It was there that they took their baths in tandem: Cho-Cho and her mother soaping themselves and rinsing each other off with buckets of water, then Malcolm and his stepfather doing the same. Not far away was the outhouse in which reposed last year's Sears, Roebuck catalog. But the children loved this new life. Here, even more than at Miss Elma Meek's, they were very much a part of things, whereas in Shanghai they were in the care of amahs and usually found themselves somewhere out of the way when the adults gathered. Here there was work for everyone to do. The house needed a new roof, wiring, plumbing, paper, paint, screens, and foundation beams. The grounds, too, suffered from the years of neglect and misuse.

Faulkner was determined to do as much of the work as he could himself. He was handy with tools and experienced as a house painter and handyman of sorts. Often he would hire a single helper to work with him. The first thing he did was to jack up the house section by section and replace the old beams with new ones. To help with the painting he hired Joe Peacock. (Joe's sister, Dewey Dell Peacock, had been a classmate of Estelle's in grammar school.) Sometimes Rusty Patterson would work with him. A short, dumpy molasses-blond, he was a good-natured man with a loud haw-haw laugh often heard on the Square or at the ticket window of the Lyric Theatre as he stood telling stories and gossiping. He came of a good family but had simply refused to go to the trouble of acquiring an education, just as he now refused to pursue the goals of most other Oxonians of his age. His English was colloquial but grammatical, and some said that Rusty and V. K. Suratt had the same kind of aphoristic style. Rusty and his employer were companionable. They would take a break from their work under a mulberry tree with a pitcher of home brew. When that was finished Rusty would uncork the bottle of corn he brought to work. After that gave out, Bill would get some from the house. When they finished painting, Johncy remembered, they went to work on the beams. After a while they took a break and sat there under the house, having another drink. Later Rusty informed his friend that he was not going to charge him for any of the time they spent under the house putting in beams. "He said he had too much fun, it wasn't like working at all." Faulkner's industry did not flag. Jack remembered him in work clothes attacking the many jobs around the place. He complimented him on what he had accomplished, both in his writing and in other projects such as the house. "Well," his brother answered, "as big as you are, you can march anywhere you want, but when you're little you have to push."

By July he was able to get to the screens to keep out the flies by day and the mosquitoes and moths by night that had fluttered about the oil lamps casting their eccentric shadows on the old walls. He charged over a hundred dollars in materials for that job at W. W. Elliott's lumberyard and one of the hardware stores. In August he charged nearly two hundred more at Elliott's for the roof and paid Evans Smith and W. B. Mayfield a total of eighty-five dollars for labor. His next order would go to Sears, Roebuck for the materials he would need for bath and kitchen plumbing.

Almost every day, it seemed, the Andersons would drive up to the house in their creaking one-horse wagon. Carrie Anderson would tell Estelle that she had remembered something they had left in an upstairs closet. Estelle would tell her to go right on up, feeling perfectly sure that what she really wanted was to see what they were doing now to the old place.

Meanwhile, almost unbidden, the staff was beginning to gather. Uncle Ned Barnett took over as general factotum. As yard man he milked and also cared for Faulkner's and Malcolm's horses. As butler he served at the table. He had brought with him clothing of the Young Colonel's and still other garments handed down by Murry Falkner. A man with a sense of elegance, he loved to dress up. He wore a tie even when he milked or chopped kindling, and on other occasions he would appear in frock coats worn by the Young Colonel when he practiced law. Josie May, the Oldhams' cook, came to take charge of the kitchen. Mammy Callie would help look after Cho-Cho and Malcolm and, when she felt like it, would cream butter and sugar for the cakes Estelle would bake in the big, wood-burning kitchen range. The eggs came from the fawn-colored Buff Orpingtons Faulkner had bought for Estelle. He built an enclosure, but the big birds kept getting out and scratching up her newly arranged flower beds, and so one by one they went into the pot.

Estelle often thought to herself that Mammy Callie was more of a

Ned Barnett ("Uncle Ned").

nuisance than a help in the kitchen, but she would not have thought of refusing to have her there. It was somehow in the natural order of things that, having served Miss Maud, she should serve her daughter-in-law, especially now that Dean Falkner had long been grown. As for Uncle Ned, he was simply taking care of another generation of Falkners. In return they got only their food during those early months, for there was no money for salaries. Faulkner accepted his role. He was responsible for their food, shelter, clothing, medical and dental attention, and pay, when he could afford it. That he should do this was exactly what Mammy Callie and Uncle Ned expected.

There were occasionally moments for pause and reflection during the long days of work. Their first guest had been Miss Ella Somerville. They had sat by candlelight in the summer night on the east gallery, the abandoned sunken garden across the lawn sloping down at its edge to the surrounding woods. They had a long way to go, but they had already done a good deal. There was room now for all of Estelle's furniture. In the parlor was her piano, its strings tautened by travel and exposure. On some of those candle-lit nights, Estelle remembered, they would hear music, notes sounding like a piece a child might play. Cho-Cho and Malcolm shivered in their beds. They knew it was Judith Shegog's music, a tune loved, or perhaps even played, by the beautiful girl who had died trying to elope with her Yankee officer, and whose slight form still returned to her father's house which she could never flee. Judith was a friendly ghost, they were sure, but it was eerie to hear the piano notes drifting up the broad staircase in the still night. Once Faulkner went downstairs, but there was no one there. Later, they heard the sounds again. This time Estelle descended the stairs to peer into the moonlit darkness, but again, there was no one. Once Cho-Cho saw a slim young woman standing in the back bedroom, Judith's room. It was she—frail, disembodied, wistful, and somehow benevolent.

It was not fitting that their new home should still be known just as the old Shegog house, or the Bailey place. Faulkner had been reading in Frazer's *The Golden Bough*. A passage describing the Beltane fires in Scotland mentioned the ancient superstition that witches went abroad on the night of May 2, casting spells on cattle and stealing the cows' milk. "To counter their machinations," wrote Frazer, "pieces of rowan-tree and woodbine, but especially of rowan-tree, were placed over the doors of the cowhouses. . . ." This tree, indigenous to Scotland, is not actually an oak but rather a type of apple or ash with white flowers and red pomes. In various parts of Europe the tree had come to signify peace and security. William Faulkner renamed this portion of E-Ah-Nah-Yea's land "Rowanoak." Later, engraved stationery would bear that name in solid gothic script. In building his home William Faulkner would characteristically neglect little.

During this time when he busied himself with Rowanoak, his name was suddenly current in British book circles. Chatto & Windus' edition of *Soldiers' Pay* had appeared in England on June 20 with a sympathetic introduction by Richard Hughes praising Faulkner's extraordinary achievement in this first novel. Gerald Gould gave the book a very bad review in *The Observer*, but the reception elsewhere was generally favorable. The most prized review was published by Arnold Bennett in the *Evening Standard.* The book would be "an extremely valuable collectors' item in twenty years' time. Faulkner is the coming man. He has inexhaustible invention, powerful imagination, a wondrous gift of characterisation, a finished skill in dialogue; and he writes generally like an angel. None of the arrived American stars can surpass him in style when he is at his best." The novel had the usual defects of a first novel, and *The Sound and the Fury* was much more difficult than it had any right to be, but Faulkner was the most promising American novelist Bennett knew, more promising even than Hemingway, and he had in him "elements of real greatness." Two days later another reviewer for the *Evening Standard* wrote that no first novel in the previous thirty years "had attained such perfection" and ranked the author above D. H. Lawrence as well as Hemingway.

Events were going very differently for Murry Falkner from the way they were going for his eldest son. Alfred Hume had been chancellor of the university for nearly six years, and now he was fighting Governor Bilbo's determined efforts to incorporate the university into his patronage system. Questioned by a reporter about one of Bilbo's allegations, Hume had replied, "The Governor is either grossly misinformed or a deliberate liar." Few had forgotten Bilbo's attempt to move the university to Jackson or Hume's role in repulsing the attack with an eloquent appeal to a commission from the legislature. William Faulkner was one of those who admired his courage and his integrity. Hume, someone said, had "a ramrod down his back." "Yes," Faulkner agreed, "a moral ramrod." But now, in the late spring of 1930, Bilbo was ready to crush his opposition.

On Friday, June 13, the board of trustees of the state university and colleges met. Bilbo finally had a majority, and the board replaced the head of every state institution of higher learning but two. Alfred Hume was through at Ole Miss. So, apparently, were the other principal officers and most heads in all the university's schools and departments. "Feel Fall of the Political Axe," the Oxford *Eagle* reported tersely. Bilbo's favorite, Joseph Neely Powers, was back in as chancellor. Some, like Bob Farley, did not wait for the axe, but resigned. All state employees above a certain grade, it was said, including those at the university, had been directed to send a contribution to the Bilbo organization. Murry Falkner's family believed that the amount he had been assessed was five hundred dollars. His annual salary was three thousand dollars, and he wrote to say that he could not meet the assessment. He faced the inevitable results with a strategy his father had employed before him. It was reported in the *Eagle* for June 26: "Mr. M. C. Falkner, who has been Secretary and Business Manager of the University of Mississippi for the past twelve years, has announced that he will not be an applicant for the position again. His reasons are that there is too much work attached to the position, and also that he is growing too old to keep up with it. No statement has been made about his future plans." Murry Falkner actually had few plans. On July 23 he contracted for the construction of a modest brick home on the same lot on which The Big Place stood on South Lamar. After he had cleaned out his desk and helped his successor get settled, he found he had a lot of time on his hands. He took out one of his old railroad ledgers and from time to time would paste in it pictures of horses and dogs he had cut from magazines.

Chancellor Hume had no difficulty in getting another job. He chose one not far from home, accepting the chair of mathematics at the Southwestern College of the Mississippi Valley in Memphis. At a tea for new faculty members he met an English professor named Robert Penn Warren. Learning that Hume was from Oxford, Warren asked if he knew William Faulkner.

"I love him," said Hume.

Warren told Hume enthusiastically that Faulkner was a great writer.

"Oh, yes," Hume answered. "I've never read any of his books, but he was the best scoutmaster we ever had."

Tom Clark noted a variant of that attitude when he made a brief visit to Oxford during that summer of 1930. Going over a "hogback" near the railroad track on his way to the fourth green, Clark met a well-known foursome of university deans. During a brief conversation, he observed that "our Bill" was becoming famous, his picture appearing in "highbrow publications." One of the deans moved close to Clark, cupped his hand around his mouth, and said, "We don't talk about him around here."

If his story-sending schedule was any indication, Faulkner must have forgone writing for most of July in favor of repair work. It was not until the twenty-fourth that he recorded a submission: a story called "Red Leaves," to *The Saturday Evening Post*. He had moved the small desk Miss Maud had given him into the library. He placed it next to one of the two windows looking out to the west, and there he now wrote. In "Red Leaves" he explored a new stratum of Yoknapatawpha County: the Chickasaws. He chose as the subject one of the oldest tribal customs: the burial of the dead chief with his horse, his dog, and his body servant. On the first of the twelve manuscript pages he referred to him simply as "the old chief." His successor bore only his titular name, "the Man." In a few pages, however, Faulkner supplied names for them: Issetibbeha and Moketubbe. These were not names of actual Chickasaws, but they had an authentic ring to them. The body of the story followed the pursuit of Issetibbeha's Negro servant.

The chase motif was familiar, but Faulkner did several other things, too. Drawing upon his reading, perhaps, or upon the stories of experts such as Lyle Saxon, he gave a capsule history of the relationship of Doom, Issetibbeha's father, with an equivocal French noble said to be an intimate of New Orleans' great ones. Faulkner tried to convey the attitude of the Indians toward change, toward the white man and the Negro slaves. His presentation of the servant was compassionate. Two details of this character's history revealed something of Faulkner's attitudes toward slavery and its causes. During his transportation the servant "had lived ninety days in a three-foot-high 'tween-deck in tropic latitudes, hearing from topside the drunken New England captain intoning aloud from a book which he did not recognize for ten years afterward to be the Bible." The slave trader was "a deacon in the Unitarian church. . . ." This was a view which he would express thirty years later: granted the cruelties practiced upon slaves in the South, the first responsibility had to be borne by the Yankee traders who had brought them there for profit.

Just as characters in this story would reappear later, so motifs in the story—the need to bury a body putrefying because of delayed rituals—had appeared before. As *Father Abraham* was a seminal story prefiguring Snopes lore to come, so "Red Leaves" anticipated other tales of Yoknapatawpha Chickasaws. This title revealed again Faulkner's taste for the impressionistic but it had a literal relevance, too: it referred to the Indians. "It was the deciduation of Nature which no one could stop that had suffocated, smothered, destroyed the Negro," he later said. "The red leaves had nothing against him . . . they probably liked him, but it was normal deciduation which the red leaves, whether they regretted it or not, had nothing more to say in." When the *Post* replied, Faulkner was able to circle the story on his sending schedule. They bought it for $750 and would publish it within three months.

Now they could afford to put in electricity. Estelle ordered an electric stove, for though Josie May could manage the wood stove, she herself could not get used to it. One night after dinner they went into the single room off the hall to the left. Faulkner turned on the bare bulb that dangled from the cord. The harsh light made more garish the murals Miss Ellen Bailey had painted years before: blue and pink flowers among green leaves, and gold peacocks on the black plaster fireplace. He stood there looking for a moment, then went out to the barn. Returning with a pail of whitewash and a large brush, he covered Miss Ellen's handiwork. Shortly thereafter they bricked the fireplace and put cases around two of the walls for the books that lay in piles on the floor.

During August Faulkner sent out four stories. He had an additional incentive to increase his earnings, if he needed one, for Estelle was expecting a baby in March. His love of children was as strong as it had ever been, the story sessions and walks in the woods continuing whenever he could take time from the building and writing. Now he hoped for a little girl of his own. The joy was attenuated by worry, however, for Dr. Culley was uneasy. Estelle had experienced a difficult time with both her babies, and now she weighed less than a hundred pounds. Suffering from anemia, she began taking iron and calcium. She would have to be very careful.

None of the stories Faulkner sent out that month was new: "Lizards in Jamshyd's Courtyard," "Per Ardua," "There Was a Queen" (a revision of "Through the Window," treating Aunt Jenny Du Pre's death), and "The Peasants" (still another reworking of *Father Abraham* under a new title). Except for a newly interpolated section which followed Mrs. Armstid back to the hill cabin, "The Peasants" was more effective than any of the other forms in which Faulkner had cast the story. But it was now close to 15,000 words long, much too long for *Scribner's*, which rejected it. There was an acceptance, however, from among the August submissions. *The Saturday Evening Post* bought "Lizards in Jamshyd's Courtyard." Again they paid $750.

The appearance of "Thrift" in the *Post* for September 6, 1930, occasioned comment among Oxonians. To publish a book or two was one thing, but to appear in a national magazine, a household reading staple like the *Post*, that was real success. The *Eagle* acclaimed its author as one "who is fast gaining national and international recognition. . . ." Two more of his stories had been accepted and would appear soon, the account continued. A much more improbable item had appeared in the newspaper a week earlier. William Faulkner was going to appear in a major role in an amateur theatrical.

In August the Oxford Junior Chamber of Commerce had arranged with the Universal Producing Company to stage *Corporal Eagen*, "that wonderful, side-splitting, three-act comedy drama that has taken the northern and eastern states like wild fire." The proceeds were to go toward the planned city park and playground. The Universal Producing Company provided playbooks, costumes, and a young woman to direct. She arrived in Oxford on Sunday, August 31. Casting and rehearsals would begin on the next day to prepare for the two performances scheduled for September 11 and 12. The production had been planned on the theory that if the cast were large, enough relatives would buy tickets to ensure success.

The play's action centered around "Red Eagen, an Irish doughboy," and "his screamingly funny Jewish buddy, Izzy Goldstein." Besides the ordinary contretemps of stage army life, there was a search for a spy, romantic misunderstandings, and final unitings. Jim Stone was a logical choice for Red Eagen. Connie Love would be one of the nurses who would provide romantic interest and Bill Harmon would be the guard assigned to the spy. Bob Farley and Ike Roberts were selected for the "Awkward Rookie Squad." Connie Love remembered everyone's surprise when Bill Faulkner agreed to play Izzy Goldstein.

Rehearsals went on for the next week and a half. A good dress rehearsal did not prevent the usual flutterings before the curtain rose in the grammar school auditorium on Thursday night, September 11. Adjacent to the auditorium was a dressing room which the whole cast contrived to share. Because the performers totaled 218, both the dressing room and the wings were crowded. Connie Love noticed that there was a surprising amount of traffic in an unusual direction—out one of the two windows of the dressing room. From the first act on, it seemed that one of the men was always disappearing or reappearing through the window. Bill Harmon knew quite well what was going on. Placed against the wall outside the window was a ladder, a short distance from which was the concrete platform leading to the boiler room. There Ernest, the shoeshine boy at the barbershop, had set up a bar stocked with cups, ice, and a gallon jug of corn liquor.

Onstage the action continued interspersed with special numbers and musical selections. Mrs. David Neilson rendered "The Rose of No Man's Land" and the Minstrel Chorus provided lively selections such as "Over There." Outside the boiler room William Faulkner lounged with Rusty Patterson, tonight a member of the Soldiers' and Sailors' chorus. Bill Harmon noticed a tendency toward ad-libbing as the play progressed. At one point, when George Buffaloe was supposed to hide beneath a stovewood pile, the script called for Izzy Goldstein to make a remark about a "nigger in the woodpile." Faulkner looked where he was supposed to and then commented that "there was no woodpile and, in the second place, there was no nigger," which brought a roar of laughter from the audience. "I remember," said Harmon, "that we all commented on how well Bill Faulkner played his part."

Corporal Eagen had a small audience the second night because of a sudden rainstorm. To make up for it, the play was presented again on Monday night. "Many compliments have been heard from every side relative to the show," noted the Oxford *Eagle*. The cast enjoyed the show, too, including Faulkner. "He was very sociable," Connie Love remembered.

The *Eagle* mentioned William Faulkner again the next week, this time on the editorial page. Sherwood Anderson had published an article in *The American Mercury* entitled "They Come Bearing Gifts." Anderson had begun his essay by calling Faulkner and Hemingway the "two most notable young writers who have come on in America since the war." Both had been "terribly injured in the war" and he had known "both men rather intimately" just after it. He had quarreled with both, Hemingway by mail and Faulkner in person as they sat on the cathedral steps one night in New Orleans. Anderson said he had laughed at Faulkner's assertion that there would be no offspring between Negroes and whites after the first crossing, as with mules. Angered, Faulkner "accused me of being a damn Yank, absolutely ignorant and stupid concerning all Southern things. . . . It may be we had both been drinking. We separated, each walking off alone and each turning to swear at the other." This did not make any difference, however, in Anderson's attitude toward Faulkner's fiction. *The Sound and the Fury*, he said, was "a beautiful and sympathetic piece of work. . . ."

The *Eagle*'s editorialist briefly reviewed Faulkner's books and concluded, "this fall late he will have another volume off the press which critics believe will be his most successful." The steps in the publication of *As I Lay Dying* had gone forward fairly smoothly. Faulkner had been punctual in correcting proof, returning segments as he finished them. He had first sent to Edith Greenburg at Cape & Smith the sheets which showed major errors. In his covering letter, however, he said that the "proof was quite clean, I thought; I found few errors that could be called major ones." The production went along so well that the publication date was advanced to early fall. *As I Lay Dying* appeared on October 6, 1930, with an initial printing of 2,522 copies. The first major review of the novel appeared on October 5.

Margaret Cheney Dawson's review in the New York *Herald Tribune* conveyed a strong sense of uneasiness and uncertainty about the novel. Although it was not as difficult as *The Sound and the Fury*, "something of that extraordinary madness hangs like a red mist over it. . . ." There was a good deal of obscurity, and some passages that were clear were "absolutely unhinged from the point of view of the character whose mind they expose. . . ." The Bundrens would seem almost as strange as Martians to some other New York critics, but someone from the Deep South should be at no such disadvantage. As it turned out, the Southern reviews were more sympathetic. Julia K. Wetherill Baker wrote in the *Times-Picayune* that though this was a horrible novel which would "scandalize" the "squeamish," it would delight "those who respect life well interpreted in fine fiction without attempting to dictate what subjects an author shall choose."

The reviews which came in from New York papers and magazines during November were much like the earlier ones. In *The Nation*, Clifton Fadiman called the novel "a psychological jig-saw puzzle," but granted that Faulkner had "a really interesting mind, apparently untouched by the major intellectual platitudes of our day. His cosmos is awry; but it is his own, self-created." In spite of qualifications, other major reviews added to his stature. But once again, the words of praise would not be translated into substantial sales. This was not surprising, though; by the end of the year *Soldiers' Pay* and *Mosquitoes* together would have sold not quite 4,000 copies.

When his author's copies had arrived, he had inscribed the usual few to his family and friends—to Miss Maud, to Phil Stone, and to Myrtle Ramey Demarest, writing in her maiden name as always. The rest of the copies he put with the others in the glassed-in bookcase in the library. He locked it, gave the key to Estelle, and paid no further attention to them. He did show interest, however, in building up a library of other volumes, now that they were settled at Rowanoak. Spelling it variously "Rowanoak" and "Rowan Oak," he wrote his home, name, and the date 1930 in *The Adventures of Robinson Crusoe, The Stories of Boccaccio, Quentin Durward,* and *The Turn of the Screw & The Lesson of the Master.* He also put on his shelves that year Sherwood Anderson's *Dark Laughter.* A book he did not have, according to his friend Mac Reed, was an English dictionary.

One newcomer to Oxford that fall who was enormously impressed with William Faulkner's fiction was a blond, statuesque Georgian in her early twenties. Newly graduated from the Georgia State Teachers' College at Athens, Emily Whitehurst had come to teach in the junior high school. She had discovered *The Sound and the Fury* back home in Georgia and it had electrified her. "This is the stuff," she had told herself, "this is ours." Now, when John Falkner took a group of admirers including another young teacher, George Marion O'Donnell, out to Rowan Oak, Emily Whitehurst eagerly went along. "I was not a bit surprised to see that Faulkner was a person of presence," she said later, "that his eyes, even then when he was young, burned through the flesh and bone of everybody in front of him and saw clearly down into the ultimate emptiness that is in most of us." This was just what she had expected, doubtless hoped for. "He was a writer, wasn't he?" At one point Mrs. Faulkner entered, wearing an exotic Chinese robe. Faulkner talked a little about the house, about how he had put the electricity in it. Emily Whitehurst's shyness soon turned to embarrassment. When O'Donnell and some of the others were asking nonliterary questions, Faulkner apparently gave mostly factual answers. As they switched to personal questions, he slipped into a familiar strategy—fiction and fantasy. During his RAF days he had crashed into a hangar where he hung upside down. He had not been scared, but for an instant when time had stopped, he had died. His listeners stared. Not long afterward they left.

Another Oxonian who profoundly impressed Emily Whitehurst was Phil Stone. With his quickness of mind, wide reading, and verbal facility, he opened new vistas for this girl from the small teachers' college. It seemed to her that he knew virtually everything. And, of course, he was Bill Faulkner's closest friend. He enjoyed talking about books and directing her reading, as he had done with Faulkner. He showed her some of the Faulkner manuscripts he had in his law office. He picked up one of them. "This is grand," he said. "Listen to it." Later she mentioned the passage to Faulkner and told him she thought it was stirring. "It *is* rather fustian, isn't it?" he replied. When she confided that she wanted to write, he gave her little comfort. "You have to get two hundred rejection slips to get up to zero," he said.

He did not tell her that during the first nine months of 1930 he had been asked for one story (by *The Southwest Review*), or that out of the thirty-seven submissions to magazines he had recorded, only six had been accepted. In October, on the day *As I Lay Dying* was published, he had submitted "That Evening Sun Go Down" to *Scribner's*. They rejected it. Two days earlier he had sent the *Post* a story entitled "A Mountain Victory." It was long—fourteen pages in manuscript and forty-two in typescript. The story was straightforward in outline. A Confederate officer and his Negro servant, returning home after the war, were ambushed and killed by a Tennessee mountaineer in whose father's house they had spent the night. Faulkner did a good deal with the story, however, using some of the effects of *Sanctuary* in reverse. There was an aura of violence hanging over the mean house, and during the uneasy night the father warned Major Saucier Weddel that he must leave then with his Negro servant, Jubal, or he could not speak for his safety. Though the setting was east Tennessee, Faulkner introduced Mississippi lore. The one-armed Weddel was the son of François Vidal, Choctaw chief and son of a French general and a Choctaw woman. It was his exotic elegance as well as his Confederate identity that helped to provoke the tragedy. Weddel was like Monaghan: so deadened by the war that he was glad, in a way, to feel fear once more. Faulkner managed to sustain a mood of ominous suspense throughout the story in spite of the obviously growing inevitability of the death of this man who had already seen, suffered, and endured too much. According to Faulkner's sending schedule the *Post* accepted the story, but it would be more than two years before it appeared.

By fall the Faulkners were ready to give a party at Rowan Oak. It came on October 31, when Cho-Cho asked her friends out for Halloween. "Outside and inside they went to a great deal of preparation for the kids," John Reed Holley remembered, "and, of course, it was always dark, winding in the roads. There weren't any streetlights. It was quite an event for all of the kids in town, really, to go down there." The feature of the party that impressed them most was not the dunking for apples or the games, but the moment when their hostess's stepfather gathered the group of eleven- and twelve-year-olds together in the large foyer. He began to tell about beautiful Judith Shegog and her love affair with the Yankee officer which had ended so tragically just steps from where they sat. But now Faulkner added something he and Estelle had not heard from Miss Ellen Bailey in their childhood.

Arthur Guyton remembered it clearly. Judith had been buried at Rowan Oak and so, eventually, had her officer. "In recent years on each anniversary of the death of her lover she made a pilgrimage that always began at the top of the steps . . . went down the steps, out the front door and out across the spacious lawn to the opposite side where, supposedly, her lover was buried. . . . I doubt that there was a single one of the boys and girls who didn't believe almost every word of the story. I can remember to this very day Mr. Bill walking slowly and majestically down the steps with his eyes lifted slightly, completely steady, looking absolutely in the forward direction and his two hands raised enacting the movements of the girl, and all of us seeing her absolutely instead of him."

There were sounds as well as actions, John Reed Holley remembered, the rattling of chains as the forlorn specter made her way down the stairs. Faulkner asked if anyone would like to go out and see the lovers' graves. As John Reed and Arthur followed him into the October darkness they could hear sounds: "the chains rattled and we saw a white sheet out under the magnolia trees to represent a ghost, and it would move." Most of the boys made it to the tomb, Arthur recalled, but only one of the girls braved it out. "This story came so near to disrupting the party that at its very end Mr. Bill simply stopped talking about it entirely and would not answer any more questions but changed the subject to something gayer and soon had the mood of the party back on course."

When *Scribner's* refused "That Evening Sun Go Down," he sent it to *The American Mercury.* On November 7, *Mercury* editor H. L. Mencken wrote Faulkner that it was "a capital story" and he hoped to use it, but was uneasy about two points: Nancy's husband being named Jesus and her pregnancy being discussed in explicit terms. The name "would make most readers believe we were trying to be naughty in a somewhat strained manner" and the pregnancy dialogue was "somewhat loud for a general magazine. . . ." Mencken closed politely but clearly: "I hesitate extremely to make such suggestions to an author of your skill, but such is my best editorial judgment. If you care to carry them out, let me have MS. back at once. It is a fine piece of work, and I'd like very much to print it."

Faulkner thought about other names for Jesus, first Judah, apparently, and then Jubah. He met some of Mencken's conditions but not all. Nancy was carrying a watermelon, Jesus had said, which had come off somebody else's vine. Faulkner gave in there, but not in the other area. On the back of Mencken's letter he drafted an explanatory note: "I did not delete the section, the dialogue about the pregnancy altogether, because it seems to me that it establishes Judah as a potential factor of the tragedy as soon as possible. Otherwise, to me, the story would be a little obscure for too long a time. However, if you think best, it might be taken out completely. I am glad you like the story; I think it's pretty good myself." He concluded, "I did remove the 'vine' business. I reckon that's what would outrage Boston." Mencken made further cuts before he printed the story in March, 1931.

In November Faulkner aimed for the *Post*'s bigger fees with four stories. The first, entitled "Rose of Lebanon," went out on November 7. Nine pages survive from what appears to be an early manuscript. On the first page, under the title, appeared the name "Dr. Blount." Beginning with impressions of Memphis reminiscent in manner of Faulkner's "New Orleans," Blount spoke for two thirds of that page. "Randolph Gordon" then took up the narrative for three pages, to be followed by Blount with two more before Gordon resumed again for three pages. This resembled the method Faulkner had adopted to tell the story of the Bundrens in *As I Lay Dying*. Dr. Gavin Blount was the same man who had appeared earlier in "The Big Shot." Now, through Randolph Gordon, Faulkner began to explain Blount's obsessive devotion to the Chickasaw Guards' Ball and all that lay behind it. The war was made intensely personal for him through his namesake, a great-uncle killed at Chickamauga. A kind of counterpoint was provided by Gordon's story of the death of his father, a regimental commander killed by a shotgun blast at Holly Springs, not in the main raid on Federal stores there but during a raid on a henhouse. After Faulkner sent the story out, he found that there was something about it that was bothering him. Scanning the carbon, he came to the conclusion that "the induction was very clumsy." He made corrections and sent them to the *Post*, with explanatory notes, on November 9. He hoped they would be clear, "so that you can rearrange the mss. yourself, if you wish and if you have not refused it already." If they had not refused it then, they did shortly thereafter, in spite of the revisions.

Faulkner would try at least twice more to sell "Rose of Lebanon"—unsuccessfully. At some point he attacked the material again, telling the story in ten manuscript pages. Revising as he typed, he completed this version in thirty-one pages. A note at the bottom of page 10 showed how radically his conception of the work had altered: "Editor: From here on, mss. is in order, save pages will need to be numbered anew, and next chapter will be No. III instead of II. Old page #8 is now #11." He was now thinking of "Rose of Lebanon" as a novel, it appeared. Though he did not complete it, this had not been wholly profitless work. There were strands here that went back to past work and forward to future work. Charley Gordon's death was very like that of the Carolina Bayard in *Sartoris.* Another such death would obsess a central character in a novel Faulkner would begin in nine months' time. With his characteristic frugality—or perhaps as the natural working out of a process that began when a character became embedded in his imagination—he would rework material from a story that would not jell into one that would.

On November 14 Faulkner sent to the *Post* a story with the unpromising title "Dull Tale." His use of Gavin Blount in "Rose of Lebanon" may have reminded him of an earlier unsuccessful attempt with the same character, for "Dull Tale" was a reworking of "The Big Shot." Again Faulkner recounted politician Dal Martin's successful efforts to obtain from Blount an invitation to the Nonconnah Guards' Ball for his daughter, Laverne. Again Blount committed suicide, but this time Faulkner concluded with two ironic touches. Laverne had an unhappy time at the ball and her father, musing over Blount's death, muttered, "the durn fool. We could have done something with this town, me and him." The story was rejected and did not appear again on the sending schedule. On November 17 he sent out "The Hound," again to the *Post.* Any reader made squeamish by *As I Lay Dying* might have felt the same response to "The Hound." A poor white farmer, Ernest Cotton, shot an arrogant neighbor, Houston, who had wronged him, tried unsuccessfully to conceal the body, and was caught. In this story, unlike "Smoke," Faulkner did what Conrad might have done. He described the murder at the outset and then studied the psychology of the murderer and the course of retribution. Cotton was both a man and a type. He bore with a kind of fatalism his manifold troubles: the baying hound, the buzzards circling the body in the concealing hollow tree, the perversity which permitted him to retrieve the body only to find that one limb had torn off and remained in the tree. The *Post* rejected their third Faulkner story in two weeks.

It must have been about this time, in mid-November of 1930, that Faulkner opened Box 170 at the post office to find there a parcel from Cape & Smith. It contained the galleys of *Sanctuary.* Sometime during the spring

Smith had undergone a change of heart about the book he said could land both of them in jail. In May the linotype operators had gotten as far as galley 4 when they were given the setting copy for *As I Lay Dying.* On November 3 the setting copy for *Sanctuary* went back on the linotyper's rack. Hal Smith believed in Faulkner's talent and, like Horace Liveright, he had a good working instinct about individual books. Besides, the firm was not doing particularly well. Phil Stone might think the day of the shocker was past, but Smith was ready to gamble, particularly when the firm's account books needed a transfusion of black ink no matter what the source.

When Faulkner read the galleys through, it was almost a traumatic experience. In the many times he described it during the years that followed, the language varied very little. "I read it and it was so badly written," he said, "it was cheaply approached. The very impulse that caused me to write the book was so apparent, every word; and then I said I cannot let this go." Faulkner wrote to Hal Smith and suggested that they abandon any plans for publication. Smith replied, according to Faulkner, that he had already invested money in the book and couldn't afford to drop it now. "You can't print it like this," Faulkner declared; "it's just a bad book." But he could see Smith's point of view and turned it over in his mind. He clearly felt chagrin at a reading public which neglected *The Sound and the Fury* and *As I Lay Dying* for the ephemeral best sellers of the day. He still thought his estimate of the reading public's level of taste might be right. "It might sell: maybe 10,000 of them will buy it," he thought contemptuously. They arrived at a solution. Faulkner would agree to publication after extensive rewriting. In the normal course of publication, they would have expected numerous corrections in the galley-proof stage and some in page proof as well. What Faulkner had in mind would clearly be much more extensive than this. Faulkner and the firm would share the cost of corrections above the normal cost of correcting proof. He began his revisions.

"I tore the galleys down and rewrote the book," he said later. He discarded whole galleys from the sheaf of 103 which Smith sent him. Others he cut up and pasted together to form new ones. In some instances, he trimmed letter-size white paper to galley width, typed in new material, and then joined it to passages cut from galleys by pasting both old and new material to trimmed sheets of onionskin. His revisions were being dictated by aesthetic reasons rather than any concern for readers' sensibilities. Human nature seemed no different to him from the way it had appeared when he began the book nearly two years before. As a matter of fact, events in the interim could have served only to reassure him that the corruption in the novel faithfully mirrored corruption in society at large.

His father had lost his job in a "shakedown" of state officials ordered by a governor whose tax commissioner had been tried on impeachment charges. The governor himself had apparently been buying large parcels of land over a short period and paying in cash. Reno DeVaux had emerged from jail and gone ahead with plans to rebuild the New Crystal Gardens, but no culprit had been found and convicted for the burning of the old roadhouse. DeVaux, still prudent, remained quiet about it. Popeye Pumphrey had been shot in Kansas City as one gang evened its scores with another. (He recovered well enough to be arrested subsequently for bank robbery and a gambling fraud, but neither charge stuck.)

From time to time Faulkner would revisit some of the haunts of his bachelor days. When he and Estelle went to Memphis they would stay at the Peabody, but they would go out to country clubs and now and then visit a speak-easy with friends. Some of these places Estelle found abominable. She noticed, however, that on occasion when they returned to the Peabody her husband would scribble on a pad—impressions, notes, things to remember, she thought.

Faulkner must have been cynically amused at the ironic contrast between obvious lawlessness and the posture of the defenders of public morals. Chief among these was a sixty-four-year-old insurance man who had been born not in Memphis but in the village of Duck Hill, Mississippi. A railway mail clerk in his youth, Lloyd T. Binford had built the Columbian Mutual Life Insurance Company into a firm of national stature. He was also a Baptist Sunday School superintendent and a member of the Memphis Board of Censors. (Acting in both capacities in 1928 he had objected to certain passages in *King of Kings*, a film treatment of the life of Christ.) By now he was the single most influential man in determining which motion pictures should be banned as injurious to Memphians' morals.

Though Faulkner would reduce the incestuous element in the Horace–Narcissa relationship, he would leave unrevised the horrors at the Old Frenchman place and Miss Reba's that would surely offend sensibilities like Lloyd T. Binford's. One gesture would emphasize this most pointedly. Miss Reba's deceased lover, her pimp who had come to live in the whorehouse, Faulkner had named Lucius Binford. Binford was memorialized with still further irony. Miss Reba's white, wormlike dogs (modeled after those

Faulkner said he had seen wetting on people's legs in England) were called "Miss Reba" and "Mr. Binford." And it could hardly have been accidental that Ruby, a former prostitute and now the servant of criminals, bore the same surname as that flower of the Confederacy, Lucius Quintus Cincinnatus Lamar.

The major effect of Faulkner's revisions was to make Temple's story central. Horace Benbow still served as actor and chorus but he no longer dominated the book. Faulkner also reduced Miss Jenny's role and eliminated two of her servants, a boy named Sundy and a girl named Saddie. The action began swiftly, with Horace's meeting Popeye at the spring near the Old Frenchman place. Faulkner quickly introduced Lee Goodwin, Ruby, and Tommy (who was still bearded but no longer looked like Christ, as he had on galley 19). In Chapter III Benbow was back in Jefferson. (His troubles with Belle were explored but he no longer dreamed of his mother and wept, as he had on galley 22, or dreamed he saw black matter run from Belle's mouth as it had from the dead Emma Bovary). In Chapter IV Faulkner introduced Temple and then kept his focus on her through the next ten consecutive chapters. Only after Popeye murdered Tommy and raped Temple did the story return to Benbow at the beginning of Chapter XV. For the ensuing twelve chapters Faulkner alternated between two story lines. One was Benbow's investigation as he prepared to defend Lee Goodwin against the charge of murdering Tommy. The other followed Popeye and Temple at Miss Reba's, then her affair ending with Popeye's murder of Red. Both lines merged in Chapter XXIII when Benbow interviewed Temple at Miss Reba's, then fused again in Chapters XXVII through XXIX. In the latter Faulkner increased, rather than reduced, the horror in the book. He wrote a new segment in which Goodwin, falsely convicted, was taken from the jail by a mob and burned to death. The chapter before last showed Benbow unhappily reunited with Belle, and the final one included more new material. It was a sixteen-page capsule history of Popeye's beginnings and his end. Son of a shopgirl and a syphilitic strikebreaker, grandson of a pyromaniac, he was stunted in childhood, impotent and deformed in adulthood. He died on a gallows, ironically, for a murder he did not commit. The final passage Faulkner left untouched, focusing on Temple. Herself ruined, she had killed Goodwin with perjured testimony. The story closed to the resonant brasses crashing in the Luxembourg Gardens.

The revised and corrected galleys apparently reached New York by early December. As the revised version of the novel was set in type, galleys were pulled of the "killed matter," the lines corrected or cut from the original galleys. There were thirty-seven galleys in all. According to Faulkner, it turned out to be an expensive revision. His share of the cost came to $270, "at a time when I didn't have $270.00." He had to get a job, he said, to pay it.

He had done what his craftsman's conscience and pride demanded. The book was more violent than before—nine murders occurred or were alluded to during the course of the action—but it was aesthetically more satisfying. The focus was clearer and the transitions from one locale and consciousness to another were more explicit. Some flaws from the first version still remained, however, such as the absence of a clearly indicated motive for Temple's perjury and Popeye's complete unconcern at his approaching execution. There were other problems that Faulkner had not worked out, such as discrepancies in the dating of the visits which Benbow made to Memphis to prepare his case. But he had done the best he could with it. He had paid "for the privilege of rewriting it, trying to make out of it something which would not shame *The Sound and the Fury* and *As I Lay Dying* too much. . . ." With a note of assurance many readers would fail to perceive, he added, "and I made a fair job. . . ."

Apparently he returned to the business of writing short stories as soon as he could. It would be months before any royalties from *Sanctuary* would come through. Meanwhile, he had to finance current expenses plus more repairs. On November 29 he sent out two stories. The *Post* had refused "The Hound," so he mailed it to *Scribner's.* He offered the *Post* a story he identified on the sending schedule as "Built Fence." The full title was probably "Indians Built a Fence." It seems likely that it was the same story he would revise and send out again as "A Justice."

He mailed four more stories before Christmas. One of them was new. On the eleven-page manuscript he entitled it "A Death Drag." It reflected the visits during the past two years to the airports at home and at Memphis. As a matter of fact, the story's second parapraph might almost have been a description of the Oxford–Lafayette County Airport six miles south of town: "Our field is still in an embryonic state. Our town is built upon hills, and the field, once a cotton field, is composed of forty acres of ridge and gully, upon which, by means of grading and filling, we managed to build an X-shaped runway into the prevailing winds." The narrator used the same "we" from whose point of view "A Rose for Emily" had been told. He spoke

Rowanoak, later spelled Rowan Oak.

for "we groundlings." Faulkner must by now have been flying as a passenger, perhaps even handling the controls a little.

One of the major characters in the story was a familiar projection of himself. The narrator described him as Mr. Warren, an "ex-R.A.F. pilot" who reminisced with one of the barnstorming fliers whom he had not seen "since I left Toronto in '17 to go overseas." (That had been fourteen years before. As he tended to do with his novels, Faulkner was setting the action in present time.) Warren still walked with a limp and used phrases like "Fancy," and "You don't say." Like Gavin Stevens a man of refinement and experience of the world beyond Jefferson, he had chosen to return and live out his life there. He was the only one able to understand the sufferings of the pilot, Jock, who was like Monaghan in "Honor"—a drifter, a casualty of the war.

Faulkner was trying to combine the tragedy inherent in this situation with a kind of Weber and Fields comedy. The death drag was part of the show Jock put on with his partners: Jake and a man named Ginsfarb, who limped and spoke with a German-Jewish accent. Made grotesque by an outsized head, an enormous nose, and a sharklike jaw that nearly touched it, Ginsfarb made a precarious living as "Demon Duncan, Daredevil of the Air." At the story's climax he deliberately dropped through the roof of a barn rather than complete the stunt after having learned that his partners had collected a smaller advance for the stunt than he had specified. It was an exceedingly narrow line Faulkner was walking, mixing the tragic and the farcical. He finished the typing, corrected it, and sent it off to *Scribner's.*

Their year of probation well over by now, he and Estelle had been regularly attending Reverend William McCready's Episcopal church. Bill even had a Book of Common Prayer in which Estelle would see him make an occasional notation. He would conscientiously join in the hymns with the rest of the congregation. They went there for Christmas Eve services, a custom they would follow often in later years. The next day they made much of Christmas in the traditional way with a big tree, pine boughs in the hall, and banister decorated with holly and ivy from their own woods. Members of both the Oldham and Faulkner families came, some to join them for Christmas dinner and some just to visit. It was a full day, and a taxing one for Estelle, now in her sixth month of pregnancy.

In the last days of December, Faulkner sent out "Fox Hunt" and "Per Ardua" again. He had not sold a story now in over a month, and times were getting harder. On the morning of Monday, December 29, 1930, the news spread around the Square that the Bank of Oxford would not open. Not long thereafter General Stone would call a meeting to describe efforts to reopen the bank, but he was unable to stand as he spoke, and his voice hardly carried to the back of the room. He had always been accustomed to large actions. Unlike Joe Parks, General Stone never hesitated to borrow money; now he owed upwards of fifty thousand dollars. Phil Stone would stand behind his father in this extremity, but there was little he could do now, and the road ahead looked long.

Faulkner was feeling the pinch, too. He walked into the Gathright-Reed drugstore one day and handed Mac Reed a small brown velvet bag.

"Mac," he said, "can you let me have ten dollars for this?" Mac opened the string and extracted a ten-dollar gold piece. "Surely, Bill," he answered. He did not have the ten dollars himself, so he went back to the cash register, put the bag in one of the back compartments in the drawer, and brought him a ten-dollar bill. He did not ask when he would redeem the coin, and Faulkner did not know when he could.

As the year drew to a close, there were a few mildly encouraging notes. On December 12, accepting the Nobel Prize for Literature in Stockholm, Sinclair Lewis had named some young Americans "who are doing such passionate and authentic work that it makes me sick to see that I am a little too old to be one of them." He mentioned Ernest Hemingway, Thomas Wolfe, Thornton Wilder, John Dos Passos, Stephen Benét, Michael Gold, and—lastly—William Faulkner, "who has freed the South from hoop-skirts. . . ." Then, right after Christmas, a young bookstore owner in Milwaukee named Paul Romaine wrote asking if he could print a collection of some of the things Faulkner had published in *The Double Dealer.* It was not certain how much Faulkner would receive, but he would pay what he could. Faulkner wrote back agreeing to the idea.

On New Year's Day he sat down to take stock. He wrote the day's date at the top of a sheet of onionskin, and below it, "Money Earned." Then he listed the June date on which *Scribner's* paid him for "Dry September" and the August dates on which the *Post* had paid him for "Red Leaves" and "Lizards in Jamshyd's Courtyard." Though he had circled "A Mountain Victory" on his sending schedule, he had not yet received a check from the *Post*, and the story would not appear until December, 1932. He had made a breakthrough in 1930, publishing four stories in national magazines. His three sales during the last half of 1930 had brought him $1,700, but he could see heavier financial responsibilities ahead.

In the first week of January he received an envelope in the mail from *Scribner's*. They were returning "The Hound" and "Indians Built a Fence." Assistant editor Kyle Crichton wrote in the covering letter that they were "two of the finest stories we have had in months." The trouble was, *Scribner's* readers had been complaining about horror stories, and they had to think about survival. Crichton said they remembered with pleasure "that long story of yours which had to do with the bringing of the horses from Texas and the resultant auction." If Faulkner could cut it to 8,000 words and still retain its flavor, *Scribner's* could take it. They considered him "one of the greatest writers alive."

Meanwhile, in the offices of the brownstone at 139 East 46th Street, advertising copy was being prepared for Cape & Smith's new titles. The ads would feature *Sanctuary*, which showed "further simplification of an amazing style" which had fascinated readers in *The Sound and the Fury* and *As I Lay Dying*. "Like those novels, *Sanctuary* is a mosaic of furious evil, of cold brutality, of human viciousness and human hopelessness. But despite the fact that here are all the elements of melodrama—in unfolding mystery and intricate plot and blackest sin and crime—the story is always . . . real." It was a novel which was "hideously and terrifically—and therefore beautifully—great."

In Oxford William and Estelle Faulkner waited for the book, and the baby.

34

January-October, 1931

. . . then suddenly the corridor became full of sound, the myriad minor voices of human fear and travail which he knew, remembered—the carbolised vacuums of linoleum and rubber soles like wombs into which human beings fled before something of suffering but mostly of terror, to surrender in little monastic cells all the burden of lust and desire and pride, even that of functional independence, to become as embryos for a time yet retaining still a little of the old incorrigible earthy corruption —the light sleeping at all hours, the boredom, the wakeful and fretful ringing of little bells between the hours of midnight and the dead slowing of dawn . . . this for a while, then to be born again, to emerge renewed, to bear the world's weight for another while as long as courage lasted. He could hear them up and down the corridor—the tinkle of the bells, the immediate sibilance of rubber heels and starched skirts, the querulous murmur of voices about nothing.

—*The Wild Palms* (299–300)

When Estelle woke Bill on the bitter-cold night of Saturday, January 10, 1931, he thought she was imagining things. The baby wasn't due for two months, but the pains kept on. Bill called Dr. Culley, who told him he would meet them at the hospital. Then he got the car out and left the motor running while he helped Estelle down the stairs. Halfway to the hospital he realized she was not imagining things.

It was January 11 when Dr. Culley delivered the baby, a little girl two months premature. She was a very tiny child with beautiful features. They had a name already picked out: Alabama, after Aunt 'Bama, "the Colonel's baby." Tuesday morning Faulkner sent his great-aunt a telegram: ALABAMA FAULKNER BORN SUNDAY. BOTH WELL. Estelle was too ill to see the baby, but Faulkner wanted his wife and daughter home as soon as possible. There was no incubator at the hospital, and he felt that they could be cared for as well at Rowan Oak. In a few days they came home, with a trained nurse for Alabama and a practical nurse for Estelle. Dr. Culley called each day, a good-looking, opinionated man whom Faulkner did not care for. But his wife, Nina, was one of Estelle's best friends, and the choice of the doctor had been Estelle's to make.

Cho-Cho and Malcolm were allowed to tiptoe into the middle bedroom upstairs and peer at the small baby in the bassinet. Their mother still had not seen her. Estelle was very weak, and her husband may have thought it best for other reasons, too. At the end of the week Alabama's condition began to show signs of changing. Faulkner and his brother Dean drove to Memphis for an incubator, but it was too late. In the early afternoon of Tuesday, January 20, Auntee sent a wire to Aunt 'Bama in Memphis: WILLIAM'S BABY DIED THIS MORNING.

Miss Maud and Mr. Murry, Auntee and Sallie Murry, the Oldhams and the rest of the Falkners drove in three cars to St. Peter's Cemetery. Alabama's grave was next to those of Uncle John's and Aunt Sue's three infant sons. As the mourners stood there in the cold January morning, Mr. Murry prayed aloud. He was usually abrupt and inarticulate, but it was a beautiful prayer, Sallie Murry remembered.

That afternoon the nurse brought a sedative in to Estelle. "Mr. Faulkner wants to talk to you," she said. He came in and sat down beside the bed. It was bitterly difficult for him to speak but he did. He told her about Alabama and wept—the first time she had ever seen him cry. She told him they would have another child.

"Bill," she said to him, "get you a drink."

"No," he said, "this is one time I'm not going to do it."

Later, Mr. Murry came to see her. He told her that Billy had held the casket on his lap all the way to the cemetery. The baby had looked like Billy, he said.

As he had promised, Faulkner did not drink to assuage the grief. But there was one curious aftermath. It was a persistent rumor in Oxford that Faulkner had shot Dr. Culley in the shoulder. Though Dr. Culley was in no way responsible for Alabama's death, as Estelle knew, Faulkner still harbored resentment. He apparently felt that if preparations could not have been made for such a critical situation, the parents could at least have been warned of the course events were likely to take. The rumor about Faulkner and the doctor did not die down. Some people said Dr. Culley had not been seen outside his house for two weeks after the supposed shooting had occurred. Yet there had been no shooting. Later that year it would become clear where the rumor had started: with Faulkner himself. He once said that he telephoned for the doctor as the baby grew worse. The doctor never came, he said, and the next morning he went to the doctor's office and shot him. Another time he said that the doctor did answer the summons but too late, and when he stood at the door he had shot at him but missed. Faulkner had not shot Dr. Culley, but apparently he had wanted to, and so he did it numerous times in this verbal fiction.

There was another result. Not long after Alabama's death, Faulkner donated an incubator to Dr. Bramlett's hospital.

His grief would remain acute for that whole year, and occasionally images of violence would appear in his correspondence as well as his conversation. Writing Ben Wasson in late spring he commiserated with him about rheumatism and added, "I had it in my right shoulder for a while myself. But last winter I laid my skull bare in a wreck, and after I was patched up I never had rheumatism again. You might try that."

Faulkner had mailed out his last story to a magazine on January 10. His next submission came on the twenty-ninth. He probably had little heart for the business of sending off manuscripts, but now there were medical bills besides the ordinary ones. Dashiell had rejected "A Death-Drag" on January 27. Though done in his "usual fine manner," it was too long, and the character of Ginsfarb seemed too close to caricature. Like Crichton, Dashiell hoped he would reduce "The Peasants" to a length they could use. He immediately set to work on it. Meanwhile, on the twenty-ninth, he sent "A Death-Drag," "Indians Built a Fence," and "The Hound" to *The American Mercury*. A new story, "The Brooch," went to *The Forum*.

He told "The Brooch" in the third person—another tale of a girl harassed into profligacy by circumstances and an inflexible malevolent older woman. Called Amy, the girl was like Corinthia in "Selvage" and Susan Reed in "Hair." Her husband, Howard Boyd, had attended the University of Virginia, like Gowan Stevens in *Sanctuary* and ill-fated Henry Falkner. As Miss Zilphia Gant's pathetic life had been shaped by her unlucky, implacable mother, so Howard's tragedy had been set in motion in his infancy. Unwilling to leave his mother's house, he tried to make life there bearable for his wife, inadvertently making possible escapades which led to her adultery. The wife's misery was intensified by grief for an infant dead at nine months. (The sex was left unspecified.) At the end Howard sat in a torpor of despair as Amy wept for her baby. Faulkner had used the brooch literally and symbolically. Its temporary loss caught Amy in a lie which proved her guilt. Its ugliness symbolized Mrs. Boyd's unremitting hatred and intent. Though the story weakened toward the end, it achieved a powerful evocation of mood and feeling.

Faulkner had rewritten "The Peasants" very quickly in accordance with Alfred Dashiell's suggestion. But instead of sending the story to *Scribner's*, he decided to try it first on *The Saturday Evening Post*. On February 2, under the title "Aria Con Amore," his revised version went off to Philadelphia. It came back in less than two weeks. So, on February 13, he sent it to Dashiell. In his sixteen-page revision Faulkner had adopted still another narrative strategy. He now told the story in the voice of V. K. Suratt, whose tone suggested several recitals in *As I Lay Dying*. Anse Bundren also appeared here as one of the loungers at Varner's store who had been nameless in "The Peasants." Dashiell wrote back in less than a week that they would pay him four hundred dollars for it. The only thing they didn't like was the title; could he think of a better one? "Why not call it simply 'Horses'?" Faulkner asked. If that didn't suit them, he would try to think of some others by the time the galleys arrived.

Faulkner's first appearance in the new year had come with "Dry September" in *Scribner's* for January. Dashiell knew some readers would be shocked at rape and lynching as subject matter, but there were apparently not enough letters to the editor to indicate a major revulsion. This was not the case with *Sanctuary*, which Cape & Smith issued on February 9, 1931.

Reviews in major media began appearing in early February, and it was clear from the first that there would be two major responses to the novel: horror at its subject matter and grudging admiration for its power. The day after publication, Harry Hansen wrote in the New York *World* that the story would appeal to writers "for its technical side," but the reviewer wondered at Faulkner's "preoccupation with the dregs of humankind." Three days later, in a New York *Sun* review entitled "A Chamber of Horrors," Edwin Seaver called it "one of the most terrifying books I have ever read. And it is one of the most extraordinary." Two days later, under the title "Dostoevsky's Shadow in the Deep South," John Chamberlain wrote in *The New York Times Book Review* that the novel left him limp, feeling as one does after "a frightening experience in the dark or a sudden sickening realization that one has just escaped sudden death."

By March 4 *Sanctuary* had sold 3,519 copies—almost as many in three weeks as *The Sound and the Fury* and *As I Lay Dying* had together since publication. The reviews continued with about the same tone during March. Under the heading "Faulkner Writes Another Novel," the Oxford *Eagle* informed its readers on March 26 that scenes in it were set at Ole Miss and in the Memphis underworld, adding, "It is said that in this novel Faulkner looses all the fury of his pen and this is one of the most stirring of the many books written by him." Sales for the first week of March had spurted to nearly 1,500 copies. On April 1 sales to date stood at 6,457.

Reviews kept coming in as the spring wore on, but as early as April they had revealed a new component. Heretofore some reviewers had expressed horror or distaste. Now others would shift from disgust at the material to attack upon the author. In *The Bookman* A. R. Thompson decried aesthetes so fascinated by virtuosity that they could callously outrage feelings such as kindness and sympathy. Clifton Fadiman, however, declared in *The Nation* that by this book alone Faulkner took his place in the first rank of younger American novelists. He was an original, "And yet it is not hard to understand the point of view of the sweetness-and-lighters who are dismayed by his 'sadism' and his morbidity." On May 21 *The Saturday Review of Literature* devoted more space to *Sanctuary* than it had to any three books since the magazine's founding. "I have chosen Mr. Faulkner as a prime example of American sadism," wrote Henry Seidel Canby. In two thousand words he went on to argue his thesis: "In 'Sanctuary' I believe that sadism, if not anti-romance, has reached its American peak."

By early April sales had passed 7,000. There was another indication of how the book was doing. On March 21 ads appeared in *Publishers' Weekly* seeking first editions. For the next ten weeks there were more ads in the magazine for Faulkner first editions than for those of any other author. This remained true for eight of the next eleven weeks following. By early fall, a first edition of *The Marble Faun* would cost twice as much as a first edition of Nathaniel Hawthorne's *The Marble Faun*—the book Billy Faulkner told Lem Oldham he'd never heard of.

With the summer and fall came high praise for both work and author.

Robert E. Sherwood extolled Faulkner's "prodigious genius" and rewrote Arnold Bennett's phrase: Faulkner wrote not like an angel but "rather like a fiend out of hell." *Sanctuary* was a terrible book and "a great novel." Alexander Woollcott used the same adjective in one of his radio broadcasts. It was not only great, it was an "extraordinary" work of "grandeur."

All these were Northern reviews. Nearer home, Julia K. Wetherill Baker had written her usual perceptive assessment for the *Times-Picayune*. This novel was not as good as *The Sound and the Fury* and *As I Lay Dying*, "which put to shame nearly every living American and English novelist," but it was both sensitive and intense. Having earlier likened Faulkner to Joyce, she now looked at *Sanctuary* and saw Faulkner at home in the Greece of Euripides or the London of John Webster. He was treating the same "dark and malevolent impulses in human nature. . . ." But ironically, the readers who applauded these classic authors would be horrified when a contemporary entered the same dark regions. Mrs. Baker thought Faulkner was probably America's best living novelist, but she hazarded the opinion that he was very likely becoming a scandal in his native state. Confirmation of this impression came from the Memphis *Evening Appeal*'s reviewer. He thought *Sanctuary* was probably the most "putrid" story ever written. Shocked by its "repulsiveness" and its "stark hideousness," he declared the novel a "devastating, inhuman monstrosity of a book that leaves one with the impression of having been vomited bodily from the sensual cruelty of its pages." The citizens of Oxford—the few that had read the book—were much more prone to agree with the *Evening Appeal*'s anonymous reviewer than with Mrs. Baker.

Faulkner was far from impervious. One day he asked Estelle, "What do you think of the reviews?" She may have been shocked by the book herself, but the reviews distressed her. "They don't understand," she told her husband. "It's as if they hadn't read it."

Some of Faulkner's most vociferous local critics had not, of course, read his books. But like those who had, they preferred visions of noble gentlewomen and gentlemen living in columned houses served by happy Negroes. These critics, imbued with Southern wrongs, were quick to resent what they considered slurs upon the South. Here, it seemed, was an author presenting the worst possible aspects of the modern South and its people (not to mention gratuitous horrors a gentleman wouldn't discuss) at a time when—commercially, at least—many Southerners seemed to want nothing more than to be as much like the rest of the country as possible. And this "artist" was one of their own. There were words for people like that, no matter how much New York literary critics seemed to think of them. As for Oxford's being the original of Jefferson, this was the last thing to make most Oxonians feel any sense of pride. Even men friends such as Bob Farley found the book repugnant. Sallie Murry was very direct. "I want to ask you a pointed question," she said. "Do you think up that material when you're drunk?" Billy looked her in the eye and answered, "Sallie Murry, I get a lot of it when I'm drunk." Tad Smith had a different question. "You let your mother read that book?" he asked. "I don't think she read it," Billy told him.

It had become a scandal. Mac Reed loyally stocked copies, but a buyer usually wanted it wrapped in brown paper before he took it out of the drugstore. Professor Calvin Brown, bestower of Billy Faulkner's first literary prize, asked in shock, "Now, why would *anybody* write a book like *that*?" In Murry Falkner shock was mingled with outrage. Though it was questionable if he read it (his standard fare was still Zane Grey and James Oliver Curwood), he had no doubts about what it was. Seeing a co-ed he knew carrying the book on the campus one day, he stopped her. "It isn't fit for a nice girl to read," he said. According to Johncy he was so outraged that "he tried to suppress the book and have it withdrawn from the market. He said that if Bill was going to write, he should write Western stories." But Miss Maud supported her son, not her husband. "Let him alone, Buddy," she said. "He writes what he has to."

If most Oxonians were shocked, Phil Stone was delighted. Faulkner had achieved the fame he had always predicted, even if he had not envisioned anything as sensational as this. Faulkner would say afterwards that when *Sanctuary* became a popular success they got the old stories out of the files and sent them out again, "and the folks that rejected them bought them." Stone would reminisce about retyping the stories with a large price in the upper right-hand corner of the title page. Then, Stone used to say, he told Faulkner he was on his own. "I have a living to make," he said.

Faulkner's sending schedule for the balance of the year 1931 belies the story of sweet retribution for unjustified neglect. The only early stories that he sent out in the months after March were "Divorce in Naples," "The Leg," and "Black Music." He had been sending out the first two of these during 1930. By now he was craftsman enough to know that most of the early work was apprentice work. Just as he was anxious that *Sanctuary* should not shame the two novels that preceded it, so he would scarcely have wished to follow "Dry September" and "That Evening Sun Go Down" (which had appeared in the March *American Mercury*) with work done when he was still uncertain in the genre of the short story. There was some wish fulfillment in Stone's comment, too. Faulkner had been "on his own," as far as any literary reliance on Stone went, for some time before the spring of 1931.

As far as acceptances went, in the early spring of 1931 Faulkner had hit another drought, though it would not be as long as the initial one. On March 2 he had sent "Idyll in the Desert" to *Scribner's*, which had returned it exactly ten days later. On March 5 he sent to *The Saturday Evening Post* a story entitled "Doctor Martino." Again he had written of a girl balked by an older woman, though this was more complicated than the situation in "The Brooch." Dr. Jules Martino, a sick man trying to save the girl, was a character pushed by circumstances beyond the normal boundaries of feeling, like Monaghan in "Honor," Weddel in "A Mountain Victory," and Jock in "A Death-Drag." The *Post* returned the story in less than a week. On March 16 Faulkner sent it out again, to *Woman's Home Companion*.

On the same day he wrote a new title on his sending schedule: "Artist at Home." The setting suggested the much earlier "Black Music," and the protagonist also harkened back. Faulkner described him on the first of the thirteen manuscript pages: "Roger Howes was a fattish, mild, nondescript man of forty, who came to New York from the Mississippi Valley somewhere as an advertisement writer and married and turned novelist and sold a book and bought a house in the Valley of Virginia and never went back to New York again, even on a visit." But for a few details, Faulkner might have been describing Sherwood Anderson at Ripshin Farm in Troutdale. Six years after Anderson used Faulkner for the protagonist of "A Meeting South," Faulkner was returning the compliment. If Anderson had romanticized his subject, the same could not be said of Faulkner. Howes was an amiable, generous man with an unflagging desire to help other artists and an unfailing capacity for being betrayed and hurt. The story was rather straightforward—at first. After urging Howes to halt the visits of impoverished and arrogant New York artists, Anne Howes finally fell in love with one of them. She apparently gave herself to John Blair because she represented to him all that he had missed in life. When Howes took her back she learned he had been waiting for each new development to put it in the story he was writing. By that time Blair was dead of tuberculosis aggravated by his waiting lovelorn for Anne in the rain.

Faulkner had given the unnamed first-person narrator near omniscience. He had also given him a tone or rhythm vaguely reminiscent of an Anderson narrator. The poet, who wore a "sky-blue coat," was as little encumbered with extra clothing as Faulkner had been when he was a guest in Anderson's home and when he tramped European roads. (Blair wore his extra shirt and carried spare socks in his pocket.) Faulkner's relationship with Sherwood and Elizabeth Anderson had scarcely been as intimate as that of Blair with Roger and Anne Howes, but it seems likely that Faulkner was once more extrapolating from what had been to what, under certain circumstances, might have been. He sent the story to the *Post*, which rejected it.

He had sold nothing in March. *Sanctuary* might be doing beautifully, but he had spent the two-hundred-dollar advance nearly two years before. And Cape & Smith would repay themselves that sum before they passed on to him the ten-percent royalties. After the first five thousand copies, he would get fifteen cents per copy. But the statement of sales would not be rendered until June 30, and it would be three months more before he would receive the money. Johncy remembered his brother's disposition. "He was quiet then, worried about money, I reckon. He had wood fireplaces in the house and used to saw his own wood. I would come up out of the big sand ditch, just to the rear of his place, and he'd be out in his pasture with a tree down, sawing it up in firewood lengths. I'd take a hand at the saw and then help him split the bolts and tote the wood to the house. He'd always thank me for helping but didn't have much else to say. I guess he had just too many other things on his mind."

One of the things was unpaid bills for supplies that had made Rowan Oak livable. Another was the medical bills. And there was the mortgage. He did not send Mr. Bryant the seventy-five-dollar payment on March 1 but included it with the April 1 payment. At the same time, however, he asked Mr. Bryant if he could defer further payments until September 1, and Mr. Bryant graciously granted the request.

After mailing "A Death-Drag" to *Collier's* on April 5, he sent "Divorce in Naples," "The Hound," and "Fox Hunt" to Ben Wasson in New York. He apparently felt as he had when he sent *Flags in the Dust* to Ben: it was costing him more postage than he wanted to spend, having typescripts shuttling back and forth between Mississippi and New York. On April 23 he sent another story to *Collier's*. It was called "All the Dead Pilots."

The materials of this story seemed to touch Faulkner more deeply than those of "Dr. Martino" or "The Brooch." For one thing, they were materials which had always evoked in him a romantic response: the Sartorises and aerial combat in World War I. Like "Thrift," this story would combine comedy and death, but here the victim would be the protagonist. There would even be some narration (at one remove) by Ffollansbye, who had performed the same function in the earlier story. The narrator himself was a nameless British officer, thinking in 1931 of the photographs made at the war's end and reflecting that all the old pilots were dead. Those who had survived in body were metamorphosed. For the elegiac beginning Faulkner might have drawn on weekends spent partly at the Memphis airfield and partly at places like Reno DeVaux's New Crystal Gardens: "beside the recent shapes of steel and canvas with the new cowlings and engines and slotted wings, they look a little outlandish: the lean young men who once swaggered. They look lost, baffled. In this saxophone age of flying they look as out of place as, a little thick about the waist, in the sober business suits of thirty and thirty-five and perhaps more than that, they would look among the saxophones and miniature brass bowlers of a night club orchestra." In the flashback which followed, Faulkner chose for their wartime apotheosis that one who had never lived to be an anachronism like Monaghan, Jock, and Captain Warren: John Sartoris. He slightly altered the narrator. Though he was still nameless, the alteration made him more familiar: he was the wounded airman with a British accent and a limp.

In the nine manuscript pages following the nostalgic introduction, Faulkner added to the information about Sartoris' death provided in *Flags in the Dust* and *Sartoris.* He was doing with the Sartorises what he was doing with the Snopeses: exploring other aspects of their lives. The chief matter here was Sartoris' rivalry for the favors of Antoinette, a highly available barmaid, with his squadron commander, a stupid Sandhurst graduate. In the end Captain Spoomer was sent home, but Sartoris was transferred to a casualty-ridden night-flying squadron, equipped with Sopwith Camels, tricky aircraft Sartoris could not fly well even by day.

Faulkner closed with an abbreviated account of Sartoris' death and another apostrophe to such men and moments. He was harkening back to the narrator's promised composite to show "the portent and the threat of what the race could bear and become, in an instant between dark and dark." But something had failed to fall into place. Sartoris came through not as a doomed hero but as an even more violent, self-centered ruffian than he had appeared in *Sartoris.* Spoomer was too hateful to be a comic figure as well as villain, and his huge dog remained a kind of comic-strip device. *Collier's* refused the story.

Faulkner had not sold any stories in April. In May he sent out only one, "A Justice," to *Harper's* on the fifth. It seems likely that he was busy with two other projects. One was the complete rewriting of "Aria Con Amore" before it appeared as "Spotted Horses" in the June issue of *Scribner's.* The editors had apparently relented on their strictures about length, for the story now ran close to 8,000 words. Though Suratt (without being named) still told it after the fact, he began where the omniscient narrator of *Father Abraham* had begun, with Flem's appearance, then his rise and marriage in Frenchman's Bend. In mid-May Kyle Crichton sent copies of the story to poet Horace Gregory and reviewer Clifton Fadiman. The latter compared it to Mark Twain, "flecked by Faulkner's own peculiar morbidity." The former thought of Twain, too—Twain "with an edge of bitterness." Gregory also felt that Faulkner's handling of the "hard-boiled manner" had possibilities "far beyond those of Hemingway's." At the moment, he felt, "his possibilities are infinite. . . ."

One of the other projects for March involved a kind of work he had not done for several years. It was a book review for *The New Republic*, a project perhaps suggested by Stark Young, who was still on the staff. The book was Erich Maria Remarque's novel of postwar Germany, *The Road Back*, and the review was revealing. There was, Faulkner wrote, "a victory beyond defeat which the victorious know nothing of." He was obviously drawing the analogy between the defeated Germany and the defeated South. The latter was a subject which would occupy him increasingly in the next few years. Victory was accomplished and commemorated with monuments, but paradoxically it did not do a people as much good as defeat. "It is the defeat which, serving him against his belief and his desire, turns him back upon that alone which can sustain him: his fellows, his racial homogeneity; himself; the earth, the implacable soil, monument and tomb of sweat." Victory needs no explanation. But with defeat comes the need to talk, to explain, which presented problems for a fiction writer. Remarque's book demonstrated this, with characters saying things which were true but which they never would have said. Thinking, perhaps, of his Bundrens, he asserted: "It is a writer's privilege to put into the mouths of his characters better speech than they would have been capable of, but only for the purpose of permitting and helping the character to justify himself or what he believes himself to be, taking down his spiritual pants. But when the character must express moral ideas applicable to a race, a situation, he is better kept in that untimed and unsexed background of the choruses of Greek senators."

The major project which occupied him in that May of 1931, however, was another book. It would be in part the sort of thing Faulkner had proposed to Horace Liveright more than four years before: "A collection of short stories of my townspeople." Faulkner had used the idea of "my" townspeople through the first-person narrator who had conveyed what "we" felt about Miss Emily Grierson or how "we" reacted to Captain Warren's RFC swear words. The title typed into the blank on the printed contract bore this out: "A ROSE FOR EMILY And Other Stories." The contract was dated May 14, 1931. It provided no advance on royalties, but it did specify a royalty rate of fifteen percent on the regular edition. The author bound himself to give the publishers first chance at his next two books.

There were not enough Yoknapatawpha stories to make a whole book, but there were six which would form the middle portion of the volume. The first portion would comprise four war stories; the last three, stories set in various places outside the United States. To supplement "Ad Astra" and "All The Dead Pilots" in the first section, he went back to much earlier work. He took a story which clearly had its genesis during his trip to England. It conveyed the kind of impression he described to his mother: "the streets full of beggars, mostly young, able-bodied men who simply cannot get work—just no work to be had. They sell boxes of penny matches, play musical instruments, draw pictures on the pavement in colored chalk, steal—anything for a few coppers." The two manuscript fragments and the two typescripts which remain suggest that he may have begun the story not long after his return from Europe, perhaps even before. All four bore the same title: "Victory."

Both fragments treated a man arriving in France and going to a small town where the war had raged. He was a working-class Scot named Alexander Gray who had distinguished himself for savagery and heroism and then tried unsuccessfully after the war to live as a demobilized Guards captain. Faulkner rewrote the story completely, shortening it considerably. "Victory" was still ironic, closing with Gray selling matches on a London street corner. One seventeen-page excision from the manuscript described Gray's patrol falling into a chalk cavern entombing Senegalese gassed in 1915. Faulkner deleted Gray's name, changed the tense from past to present, and entitled his new story "Crevasse."

The middle section of the book was by far the strongest, with "Red Leaves," "A Rose for Emily," "A Justice," "Hair," "That Evening Sun," and "Dry September." The third section comprised three early stories which had not sold: "Mistral," "Divorce in Naples," and "Carcassonne." He had again shown two familiar characteristics: frugality and a dogged confidence in his own work. Although *Scribner's* had just rejected "Artist at Home" and "The Leg," Crichton wired Faulkner for copies of the longer stories, hoping to buy some of them for the magazine before the book would be published under the title "These 13."

On June 5 Faulkner had sent three more stories to Ben Wasson in New York: "A Death-Drag," "Dr. Martino," and "Idyll in the Desert." Ben had sold two of the previous consignment to *Harper's* at $400 each; "The Hound" would come out in August and "Fox Hunt" in September. And business was picking up in other markets besides the magazines.

On April 15 Chatto & Windus had published *The Sound and the Fury* in England. Richard Hughes's introduction defended the novel's technique as absolutely necessary and praised Faulkner's "consummate contrapuntal skill. . . ." On March 23 Professor Maurice Coindreau, of Princeton, had written Faulkner telling him he wanted to be his French translator. He had already written an article on his work which would appear in the *Nouvelle Revue Française* for June. On the twenty-third of that month Gaston Gallimard moved to acquire the French Faulkner rights, with Coindreau to begin on *As I Lay Dying.* Inside ten days they would transmit an offer which Cape & Smith would accept.

After Faulkner and Smith had rushed proofs and carbons to *Scribner's* the results were finally disappointing. On July 7 Crichton returned the proofs to Smith with the comments that "All The Dead Pilots" had been there before and the magazine had had enough war material. He wrote that they much preferred "Faulkner's stuff centered around his own state of Missouri [*sic*]." Two days later Crichton wrote Faulkner, "I am still hopeful that you are going to do a little more with that monumental character, Flem Snopes." Faulkner began another story about Flem Snopes before the end of July.

In that same month a reporter named Marshall J. Smith came down from Memphis one Sunday to interview Faulkner for the *Press-Scimitar.* He found him in the kitchen siphoning home brew from a churn and bottling it. They carried iced pitchers out to a willow table under the shady cedars. Drinking and smoking, they talked about Memphis friends and Mississippi politics. Then Smith brought the conversation around to Faulkner's life.

Faulkner was in his jocose mood, apparently, for his flip answers combined fantasy with the kind of truncated sentences Alexander Gray used in "Victory." He employed the gambit he had suggested to Ben a year before about material for *The American Mercury*: "I was born in 1826 of a negro slave and an alligator—both named Gladys Rock. I have two brothers. One is Dr. Walter E. Traprock and the other is Eaglerock—an airplane." Faulkner may have been combining the kind of "hangar-flying" stories he doubtless heard at the Memphis airport with the improvisation he and Anderson had done about Al Jackson. He told Smith about crashing two planes in Canada. He told him about Stark Young and New York, about Anderson and New Orleans, about Spratling and Europe. From time to time he would relight his corncob pipe. The warm afternoon wore on.

Faulkner spoke of writing *Sanctuary* and composing *As I Lay Dying* to the hum of the power-plant dynamo. The latter was his best novel, he said. Momentarily his tone seemed to change. "I haven't written a real novel yet," said the thirty-three-year-old writer, "I'm too young in experience. It hasn't crystallized enough for me to build a book upon one of the few fundamental truths which mankind has learned. Perhaps in five years I can put it over. Perhaps write a *Tom Jones* or a *Clarissa Harlowe.*" Then he extolled the virtues of work. "Let a man fill his days with hard work, then he will fill his nights with sleep. It he does this, he will not have time to outrage moral law. He will lead a pure life in spite of himself." As for his own life, he was loafing in the peace and solitude of Rowan Oak that was so conducive "to doing nothing."

By the time Smith left, he had absorbed an appreciable amount of home brew and material for his article. The piece was published on Friday, July 10, with a good photograph Smith had made of Faulkner smoking his pipe and looking straight ahead. Smith had more photographs and more notes than he had been able to use in the interview, but he would not waste them.

Now that Faulkner had allowed Smith to photograph him, it was difficult to stick to the line he had taken when the *Mercury* had wanted a picture. Photographer J. R. Cofield recalled that a demand had developed after the commotion of *Sanctuary.* Faulkner disliked the idea of a formal sitting but finally consented to come to Cofield's studio, accompanied by Estelle. He had refused, however, to dress up. He wore white seersucker trousers spattered with red paint. His shirt was open at the neck and a red bandanna drooped out of the breast pocket of the tweed coat he wore when he exercised his horses. He had not shaved and his gray-flecked hair was uncombed. Cofield kept the trousers out of the picture and used a shadowed background to minimize the stubble. The three-quarter shot emphasized the large hooked nose and the new firmer jaw. He looked ahead with the expression of a man who had been through a good deal to reach this point and was not particularly happy about the present moment. But Cofield was

William Faulkner, summer, 1931.

pleased at the results. "He was so natural that I never had to pose him for any photograph. Everything just fell into place without any sweating over getting the right angles." He would do a good many more photographs of this subject.

It is not impossible that the visit from Marshall Smith—a writer come from the city to an old house in the country to get a story—may have in the end been profitable to Faulkner in a way he could not foresee. More often than not, he tended to set his stories at approximately the time he was composing them. He may have done so again when he started the story he called "Evangeline." It began, "I had not seen Don in seven years and had not heard from him in six and a half when I got the wire collect: HAVE GHOST FOR YOU CAN YOU COME AND GET IT LEAVING MYSELF THIS WEEK." Faulkner had used this narrator and his friend Don in "Mistral," which he had based on his European travels with Bill Spratling in 1925. Spratling was clearly the model once more: "Don is an architect by vocation and an amateur painter by avocation." The narrator called himself "a writer, a man that writes pieces for the newspapers and such." Once again the tale would involve romantic intrigue and murder, but this time it would be set not in an Alpine village but in "a Mississippi village so small that the name of the town was address sufficient for a person transient enough to leave at the end of the week. . . ."

If Faulkner worked true to form, several efforts must have preceded the fifteen manuscript pages from which he typed forty more that followed them closely. Don figured in only the first two of the story's seven sections. Under the narrator's questioning he told what he had gleaned about Colonel Sutpen, a long-dead early settler who had built a mansion six miles out in the country. The Negroes living near the run-down old house had told Don about Sutpen and his daughter Judith, about the mysterious objections which Judith's brother Henry had made to her courtship by his friend Charles Bon, which had led to an open break between Henry and his father and a barely aborted duel with Bon. After the three men had joined the Confederate army, Henry had grudgingly acquiesced to the marriage. Ultimately, however, Judith was "a widow without having been a wife," for Henry had finally brought Bon back, "killed by the last shot of the war." Judith had buried him and survived the Colonel's death in 1870, living on in the old mansion, working like a field hand with the help of an ancient, rigid-faced, gnomelike mulatto woman called Raby who ruled all the Negroes on the place. But the part of the tale that affected Don most was the account of a young Negro girl who had seen a terrifying face when she had accidentally been locked in the house just before Judith's burial. One of the headstones behind the house bore Judith's name, but Don was sure some of the Negroes thought her ghost still walked in the old house. Not only that, there was a police dog, or the ghost of one, that had patrolled the grounds during all the years since her death. Section II ended with Don's departure and a final suspenseful paragraph: "And so I did what Don said. I went there and I entered that house. And I was right and Don was right. That dog was a flesh-and-blood dog and that ghost was a flesh-and-blood ghost. It had lived in that house for forty years, with the old mulatto woman supplying it with food, and no man the wiser."

In Section III, when the narrator returned that night against Raby's warning, he found her ready to reveal at last the house's secret: no ghost but instead the moribund Henry Sutpen. In the next section she disclosed Henry's objection to Judith's marrying: he had learned that Charles Bon was already married. But there was still something more that Henry knew, which Raby would not reveal. Though she was reticent on this point, she piled one revelation on another. Judith had sent money to Bon's wife, who later had come for a prolonged visit, bringing her son to see his father's grave. When the woman had left, Judith had sent for Henry in anticipation of her own imminent death—presumably from heartbreak, privation, and weariness. Henry had returned after Judith's death, sequestering himself in the old house but for nightly walks and surreptitious trips for new police dogs. When the narrator asked Raby why she had cared for him during all these years, she had replied, "Henry Sutpen is my brother."

In Section V the narrator left the house but only to disobey Raby once more and return to doze on the front steps in the summer night. There followed a page of dialogue from the narrator's dream in which the speakers could be identified only by inferences from their conversation. As narrator and Bon questioned Henry, the vague suggestion emerged that it was Henry who had killed Bon with "the last shot fired in the war."

Faulkner's last two sections ended the story in four pages. The narrator awoke to find the rotting mansion afire, glimpsing Raby at an upstairs window before the house collapsed in the flames. In the rainy dawn one of Raby's children found "a metal case that closed like a book and locked with a key." It had contained Judith's picture when she had given it to Bon, but when Henry had brought his body home Judith had beaten the case shut. Breaking it open, the narrator discovered not the face of blond Judith but instead "the smooth, oval, unblemished face, the mouth rich, full, a little loose, the hot, slumbrous, secretive eyes, the inklike hair with its faint but unmistakable wiriness—all the ineradicable and tragic stamp of negro blood. The inscription was in French: *A mon mari. Toujours. 12 Aout, 1860.* And I looked again quietly at the doomed and passionate face with its thick, surfeitive quality of magnolia petals—the face which had unawares destroyed three lives—and I knew now why Charles Bon's guardian had sent him all the way to North Mississippi to attend school, and what to a Henry Sutpen born, created by long time, with what he was and what he believed and thought, would be worse than the marriage and which compounded the bigamy to where the pistol was not only justified, but inescapable."

The forty-page work was a fusion of opposites. It began as a ghost story and ended as a tragic tale of miscegenation. It was intended to be exciting and dramatic, yet most of its matter was speculative and even retrospective. Meant to be effective by indirection, it was ambiguous at crucial points. Though it was intended to be gripping, its expository segments were heavy with the two young men's persiflage. The characterization was aimed at portentousness, but the effect was often shadowy and thin. The title alluded, of course, to Longfellow's long poem about the dispersal of the Acadians and the resultant tragedy of two separated lovers. Faulkner's "Evangeline" needed more space for its telling, certainly if he were to retain the narrative method he had chosen. He must have labored assiduously at this tale which acquired meaning by accretion as it moved from an almost formulaic, commercial beginning to an ending laden with great emotional impact, at least for him. He sent it off to *The Saturday Evening Post* on July 17, and they declined it immediately. On July 26 he submitted it to *Woman's Home Companion*, and they refused it too.

Faulkner made no record of further submissions, but the story would not stay quiet in his mind any more than the troubled spirit of Henry Sutpen in the old house. At one point the narrator had mused, "maybe nowadays we can no longer understand people of that time. Perhaps that's why to us their written and told doings have a quality fustian though courageous: gallant, yet a little absurd. But that wasn't it either. There was something more than just the relationship between Charles and the woman; something she hadn't told me and had told me she was not going to tell and which I knew she would not tell out of some sense of honor or of pride; and I thought quietly, 'And now I'll never know that. And without it, the whole tale will be pointless, and so I am wasting my time.' " Faulkner would not allow the tale to remain pointless, this story of bigamy and miscegenation, and when he did ponder it, he would continue to probe, examining motive and act, thinking, brooding, moving perhaps toward a further turn of the screw in this account of the dark history of Colonel Sutpen's children.

In New York, on July 23, Kyle Crichton was writing to Faulkner. They had heard he was working now on Flem Snopes stories and they were extremely anxious to have first chance at them. "We have a proprietary interest in Flem and rather feel that he belongs in Scribner's. Since we did urge the cutting of the story in the first place, featured it as the leading piece in the Magazine and did a great deal of promotion of it in various channels, we should feel very bad if we lost the succeeding ones." He was sorry about the stories they had refused, but they were absolutely certain of their feelings about Flem—and about his creator, for that matter. "We want you both and will be bitterly disappointed if anything intervenes to keep us from you."

Faulkner replied that he had to try to do the best he could, and that meant the *Post* first. Crichton wrote back that he understood, but if editor George Horace Lorimer let any of the Snopes stories get by him, they certainly wanted to see them at *Scribner's.* On July 23, five days before Crichton's reply, Faulkner had sent him "Rose of Lebanon." On August 6 Crichton wrote Faulkner in what seemed acute embarrassment to tell him that though he had liked the story, the others hadn't because it wasn't the kind of Faulkner story they preferred. "We have become so hipped on the thought of Flem Snopes that we are confining all our prayers in the hope that George Horace Lorimer will be struck with lightning just at the time those pieces of yours reach him."

It may have been Crichton's persistence; it may have been that Ben Wasson had tried the *Post* for Faulkner and received a quick refusal. Whatever the reason, the first entry for "Centaur in Brass" on Faulkner's sending schedule was *Scribner's*, on August 11. It was the new Flem Snopes story.

The impressionistic title harkened back to the imagery of *The Marble Faun* and other early poems. All the rest was indigenous to Yoknapatawpha County. Set after "Lizards in Jamshyd's Courtyard," the story followed Flem's activities in Jefferson as he expanded from the base provided by the half-interest in the restaurant Suratt had traded to him. Some of the story was narrated by a kind of Suratt-surrogate: Harker, the night engineer at the city power plant. "There was some of Suratt in Harker too," said the nameless first-person narrator, who used the kind of technical terminology about boilers and gauges which Faulkner had doubtless learned at the Oxford power plant.

In "Centaur in Brass" Faulkner laid down some developmental lines that he would use decades later in treating the rise of Flem Snopes. One was his growth from enterprise to enterprise. Another was his poisoning of the town. Still another was his suspected use of his wife, Eula, for professional gain. The other man was Mayor Hoxey (this story's Yale man), who had appointed Flem superintendent of the municipal power plant. Flem's methods now were bolder, as he stole brass parts from the plant and forced the two Negro firemen to help him while setting them at odds. (Oxford residents recalled the theft of brass fittings long after the power plant's steam boilers were replaced by diesels.)

One difference between this story and its two predecessors lay in the fact that it was basically humorous. There was an element of the fabliau in Turl's seduction of old Tom-Tom's young wife. The discovery scene combined farce and the tall tale: Tom-Tom in women's clothes, waving a glinting knife, astride the terrified Turl—"the two of them a strange and furious beast with two heads and a single pair of legs like an inverted centaur speeding phantomlike just ahead of the boardlike streaming of Tom-Tom's shirt-tail and just beneath the silver glint of the lifted knife, through the moony April woods." This triangle of normal sexuality contrasted with Flem's suspected debasement of Eula in their unnatural triangle formed with Hoxey.

Scribner's rejected the story. "Well, we finally got our Flem Snopes," Crichton wrote Faulkner on August 20, "but, damn it, it is the *last* Flem Snopes and we don't feel like killing the grand character off that quickly." Crichton did not say why he thought Flem's defeat meant his death. Still brooding about the story six days later, he wrote Faulkner again: "We are so keen on that character that you may have the idea that we are urging you to turn yourself into a Flem Snopes machine, whether it is good for you artistically or not. In a measure, that is true; we do want the Flem Snopes in which the old boy is the mean, cagy creature of *Wild Horses*. . . . We want him triumphant to the point where everybody in America will hate him in unison. Then it will be time for his downfall." On August 23, Faulkner had sent the story to *Harper's*, which also rejected it.

It must have been about August 10 that Faulkner received Crichton's letter rejecting "Rose of Lebanon." He probably thought about reworking the story. He was apparently taken with the family history he had invented for Dr. Gavin Blount and with Blount's fascination with that history—the way in which romanticizing the past had misshaped his life. Faulkner had, of course, used this kind of material before: Bayard Sartoris' wild, foolish, gallant fatal charge into the Yankee camp for the anchovies; his nephew, old Bayard, opening a trunk in the attic, examining garments and weapons which evoked the past. Gavin Blount's fascination with his father's fatal exploit was much the same kind of thing. In north Mississippi there had been numerous Confederate attempts to capture Yankee supplies. One of them had served as a model for the main engagement which had drawn Charley Gordon to the town where he had met his death. On December 20, 1862, Major General Earl Van Dorn had successfully carried out a daring raid on Grant's stores at Holly Springs, thirty miles north of Oxford. Faulkner would soon employ this action again with familiar overtones but larger purposes.

He may have been meditating a significant change in his use of these materials. He would move the engagement from Holly Springs to Jefferson, and for Gavin Blount he would provide a surrogate named Gail Hightower, a Doctor of Divinity and amateur physician. It was in the Jefferson raid that the grandfather of Hightower would receive his death wound. Faulkner would even describe a charge that, like the one in *Sartoris*, was full of martial romanticism: "They rush past, forwardleaning in the saddles, with brandished arms, beneath whipping ribbons from slanted and eager lances . . . ." Hightower's obsession with this grandfather and his death would draw him back to Jefferson to play out the secondhand drama of his life and, ultimately, to take part in another far more powerful.

On August 17, 1931, Faulkner sat down at his desk and took up a sheet of the white letter-size paper he had been using to compose his short stories. There was one conspicuous difference, however, on this sheet and the others in the box: two thin, black printed lines provided a margin of more than an inch at the top and nearly three inches on the left. In the middle of the sheet he printed "Dark House" and underscored it with three pen strokes. Down to the left he wrote, "Oxford, Mississippi/17 August. 1931."

The impressionistic, symbolic title may have referred to the home of Hightower, the disgraced minister, who would sit in his unlighted window at dusk waiting for the fantasy of the cavalry charge, although Faulkner would later use that phrase for the forbidding-looking house of a major female character. There was apparently at least one false start. Faulkner had canceled many of the lines in this fragment. He was trying to get into the narrative, it appeared, using different ways of doing it.

He was following his usual regimen of rising early, writing for most of the morning, then spending the rest of the day in leisurely work about the place, riding, or whatever suited his fancy. But he kept on turning the story over in his mind. In the late afternoon he and Estelle would sit on the east gallery. There on the small side porch they would have a before-dinner drink. This was, he would say, the best time of the day. As they sat there one day, Estelle looked out across the grass to the bushes, warm in the afternoon sunlight, and to the sunken garden in the deep shade beyond. She was struck by some hard-to-define quality about the scene.

"Bill," she said, "does it ever seem to you that the light in August is different from any other time of the year?"

He rose from his chair. "That's it," he said, and walked into the house. He returned and sat down again without explanation. His wife, knowing her taciturn husband, said nothing either. What he had done was to go to his worktable and draw four pen strokes through the title "Dark House." Above and slightly to the left he printed "Light in August," underscored it twice, and put the sheet back with the other pages. Estelle would not know what his abrupt exit and return meant until he gave her the manuscript to read. He would later hit on a gloss for the title which amused him, one which he used to answer the questions of Hal Smith and others. When a pregnant woman in his part of the South, he said, looked ahead to her delivery, she would say, "I'll be light in August," or whatever the month might be. But over a quarter of a century later he would say of the title, "I used it because in my country in August there's a peculiar quality to light and that's what that title means. It has in a sense nothing to do with the book at all, the story at all." Actually, he would provide his own elucidation within the text when, near the end of the novel, Hightower waited again for the recurrence of his vision of the charge. His thinking is by now like a wheel spinning in sand: "In the lambent suspension of August into which night is about to fully come it seems to engender and surround itself with a faint glow like a halo." Faulkner had merged the quality of light in August with that time which had ever exercised a spell upon his imagination: twilight.

In what seems another false start, Faulkner described Hightower at his study table. The old man paused in his writing and looked out at the shabby sign in his front yard. Faulkner then began the story of Hightower's birth and the history of his parents, but after two and a half pages he abandoned it. It may have been at this point that his imagination, or a deliberate search in his lumber-room, produced another character who not only revitalized the story but brought at least three others with her, giving the narrative an entirely different direction and making Hightower's function one of counterpoint rather than theme.

"I began Light in August," he wrote about a year and a half later, "knowing no more about it than a young woman, pregnant, walking along a strange country road." He hoped to feel again the rapture he remembered from *The Sound and the Fury.* "It did not return. The story was going pretty well: I would sit down to it each morning without reluctance yet still without that anticipation and that joy which alone ever made writing a pleasure to me. The book was almost finished before I acquiesced to the fact that it would not recur, since I was now aware before each word was written down just what the people would do, since now I was deliberately choosing among possibilities and probabilities of behavior and weighing and measuring each choice by the scale of the Jameses and Conrads and Balzacs. I knew that I had read too much, that I had reached that stage which all young writers must pass through, in which he believes that he had learned too much about his trade." Faulkner was very likely suffering from the condition he had described to Ben Wasson in the spring: he was tired, perhaps written out. But his financial obligations did not cease just because he was tired. He went on with his new work.

As there were links here to *Sartoris,* so there appeared to be links to his most recent novel. It was as though he had asked himself what might have happened if Dewey Dell Bundren, her abortion attempt unsuccessful, had gone off to find her seducer. Except for her sweeter, more placid temperament, Lena Grove was a country girl much like Dewey Dell. (And if there was a semantic similarity between the betrayed—Dell and Grove—so there was at least an alliterative one between the betrayers: Lafe and Lucas.) Some of the same people befriended both in their travels, notably Henry and Martha Armstid, as Faulkner ranged across Yoknapatawpha County from Frenchman's Bend to Jefferson and from Jefferson to Mottstown. One character, who came into the novel after Lena Grove, was returning to north Mississippi after a long absence. Faulkner called him Joe Christmas.

Chess Carothers had been light enough to pass for white in some places, and Rob Boles—Oxford shoemaker, property owner, leader of the Negro community—could pass for white almost anywhere. So could Joe

Christmas, but there the resemblance ended. A more apt Oxford counterpart would have been Nelse Patton, razor-slayer of a white woman and victim of a lynch mob. In one four-line fragment—how early it is difficult to say—Faulkner wrote about the capture of Christmas. He was everything that Lena Grove was not: male, hostile, and death-bearing. But like her, like Gail Hightower, he was a product of his past, though he would claim that his life had been shaped by his own choice. Tortured by his conjectural mixed blood in his quest for identity, he would show the terrible effects of the vicious race prejudice and vindictive religiosity visited upon him from earliest childhood. Critics who had seen Dostoevsky in the earlier novels could well see him again in this character—the tortured murderer, the crucified sinner. A product of her past unto the third generation (like Reverend Hightower) was spinster Joanna Burden. The descendant of an abolitionist murdered by Colonel Sartoris, she lived in her dark house outside Jefferson, her life shadowed by the curse her people had abominated: slavery. A philanthropist to Negro institutions and individuals, she would find in the fugitive Christmas a focus for her cold Negrophilism and frenetic eroticism. (She was described in allusions that might have come from the author a decade earlier: "she appointed trysts beneath certain shrubs about the grounds, where he would find her naked, or with her clothing half torn to ribbons upon her, in the wild throes of nymphomania, her body gleaming in the slow shifting from one to another of such formally erotic attitudes and gestures as a Beardsley of the time of Petronius might have drawn.") With one more major character Faulkner had his cast: Byron Bunch, a good man, like Cash Bundren undersized, literal-minded, scrupulously honorable, truthful, generous, compassionate, and limited.

Light in August would be one of Faulkner's longest manuscripts and one of his most heavily reworked. It is difficult to tell where he was in the manuscript as August turned into September. It seems quite clear, however, that he was not exaggerating when he wrote that he was "deliberately choosing . . . measuring each choice by the scale of the Jameses and Conrads and Balzacs."

Early in September Faulkner had mailed "Doctor Martino" and "Smoke" to the *Post.* When these were returned, he sent the latter to *Scribner's*, which already had "Black Music." The stories were refused there, but *Harper's* paid $500 for "Doctor Martino" and scheduled November publication. Their September issue contained "Fox Hunt." But for one story the next January, these were the last submissions he would list on this sending schedule.

Then, on September 21, *These 13* was published, bearing the dedication "To Estelle and Alabama." A week later the major reviews began appearing. An unsigned notice in *The New York Times* recommended unqualifiedly this collection by the "latest star in the American literary firmament." Moreover, it went without saying that Faulkner was a writer "who must be read by anyone making any pretense of maintaining contact with the significant fiction of our day." The same day in the *Tribune*, Granville Hicks took a very different line: the novel, not the short story, was Faulkner's métier, and *These 13* would probably not add much to his reputation. Though subsequent reviews see-sawed, there were apparently a good many readers who liked such fare. The special signed edition of 299 copies went quickly, and so did the regular edition of 1,928. The book went into a second printing before the end of September.

In mid-September a letter was sent to Faulkner care of Cape & Smith, where it had been readdressed to him at Oxford, Massachusetts. The original sender, Professor James Southall Wilson of the University of Virginia, tried him again at Oxford, Mississippi. The inquiry had been set in motion a year before by a suggestion from Ellen Glasgow, Virginia novelist and literary *grande dame*. Writers who lived in New York were handicapped in seeing each other by the bustle of metropolitan life, she told Professor Wilson. And many Southern writers, who did not get to the literary parties of New York, suffered from their isolation. It would be a good idea, she thought, to get twenty or thirty leading writers somewhere quiet and pleasant where they could talk with each other. Wilson had taken the idea to the president of the university, who had immediately endorsed it. They had organized an informal committee comprising Wilson, Miss Glasgow, James Branch Cabell, Archibald Henderson, DuBose Heyward, Thomas Wolfe, Stark Young, and Paul Green. The committee had issued thirty-four invitations. Now Faulkner was receiving his second one.

Professor Wilson hoped Mr. Faulkner could join them on Friday and Saturday, October 23 and 24. Several of those who were coming hoped Faulkner would be there, "and it was suggested to me by Paul Green that it might be well to say to you that the two days will be kept as free from formal programs as the authors themselves wish; as the whole matter will be in their hands after they get here." Besides the members of the committee, Julia Peterkin, Donald Davidson, the Laurence Stallingses, Sherwood

Anderson, and Allen Tate had promised to attend. Wolfe would be there "unless circumstances interfere. . . ."

Faulkner replied that he would like to avail himself of the invitation, "what with your letter's pleasing assurance that loopholes will be supplied to them who have peculiarities about social gambits." He went on to explain. "You have seen a country wagon come into town, with a hound dog under the wagon. It stops on the Square and the folks get out, but that hound never gets very far from that wagon. He might be cajoled or scared out for a short distance, but first thing you know he has scuttled back under the wagon; maybe he growls at you a little. Well, that's me." He would arrive on the twenty-third unless something came up he couldn't control. Wilson expressed his pleasure and asked for more information on Faulkner's arrival plans. "I plan to be in Charlottesville on the 22nd," he told Wilson. "I have engaged to meet a friend, Harrison Smith, from New York, on the 23rd, at the Monticello Hotel." He would confide to one new friend in Charlottesville that Hal Smith provided a round-trip train ticket to New York and one hundred dollars expense money.

The invitation had come at a good time. Faulkner had been thinking about getting away ever since June. Like many Southerners, he had something of a special feeling about "The University," and this would be a good chance to see the place where his great-uncle had almost matriculated and where some of his characters had. Then he and Smith would go up to New York together. Smith very likely had reasons other than literary ones for making the trip to Charlottesville. Faulkner may not have known it, and there may not have been many who did, but the firm of Cape & Smith was headed for trouble. Jonathan Cape had already booked passage on the *Berengaria* which would put him in New York on October 27. If anything should happen to the firm—any change, any reconstituting—William Faulkner would be one of the first authors to hear from rival publishers. *Sanctuary* had justified Smith's faith in Faulkner's commercial potential, just as *The Sound and the Fury* had vindicated his aesthetic judgment. It seems probable that he wanted one of his star authors close to him until the increasingly fluid situation at Cape & Smith was stabilized in some way.

As for Faulkner, he might talk about hound dogs under wagons, but in New York, whether he wished it or not, he would be a lion. Perhaps he could turn that new status to his financial advantage.

35

October-December, 1931

Talk, talk, talk: the utter and heartbreaking stupidity of words. It seemed endless, as though it might go on forever. Ideas, thoughts, became mere sounds to be bandied about until they were dead.

"We get along quite well with our sleeping and eating and procreating, if you artists only let us alone. But you accursed who are not satisfied with the world as it is and so must try to rebuild the very floor you are standing on, you keep on talking and shouting and gesturing at us until you get us all fidgety and alarmed. So I believe that if art served any purpose at all, it would at least keep the artists themselves occupied."

—*Mosquitoes* (186, 319–320)

Preparations were going forward in Charlottesville. There was lively anticipation in this college town within sight of the Blue Ridge Mountains. More than thirty literary celebrities descending on this quiet county seat could produce the kind of excitement—in some quarters—the city had not known since the university's Rotunda had gone up in billows of book-fed flames in 1895. Advance newspaper accounts indicated an intriguing variety among the participants. There were the prestigious Virginia names of Ellen Glasgow and James Branch Cabell, Nashville "agrarians" Allen Tate and Donald Davidson, figures of both long-standing and recent national stature such as Sherwood Anderson and William Faulkner, DuBose and Dorothy Heyward—authors of the Negro folk play *Porgy*—and Alice Hegan Rice, creator of *Mrs. Wiggs of the Cabbage Patch.*

Faulkner's arrival was awaited with particular interest. There was not only the stir caused by *Sanctuary* and the increasingly frequent stories in national magazines, but growing critical attention as well. Granville Hicks had just assessed "The Past and Future of William Faulkner" in *The Bookman.* Faulkner's outstanding characteristics, he wrote, were his unpleasant subjects and his experimental form. Faulkner's facility might be his greatest danger. And as for the content, "The world of William Faulkner echoes with the hideous trampling march of lust and disease, brutality and death." Advancing a thesis that would haunt Faulkner criticism, Hicks suggested that Faulkner might be playing a game with his readers: one could imagine the author writing his stories in straightforward chronology, "then recasting them in some distorted form." Now other writers and even some academicians could get a close look at this strange specimen.

The University of Virginia would provide for him during the conference, and there would be no strain in managing the other expenses. On September 28 Alfred Dashiell had asked for another look at "A Death-Drag." On October 8 he wrote Faulkner that they had sent "Black Music" back to Ben but were buying "A Death-Drag" for $250. Dashiell scheduled it for January publication. On October 5 Faulkner had sent "Centaur in Brass" to Mencken, who accepted it for February publication in *The American Mercury.* Both these acceptances had been desperately welcome. Faulkner had resumed his mortgage payments to Mr. Bryant as agreed after the four-month hiatus on September 1. But he could not manage the full seventy-five-dollar payment and sent forty dollars instead. On October 1 he sent another check, for the same amount.

Faulkner's visit was heralded in Cape & Smith's "Literary Notes": "After a few days in Virginia, he expects to come to New York with his publisher, Harrison Smith, who will join him for the trip north." Then followed several promotional items: "*These 13* is already in its third printing . . . the limited edition of this book has been over subscribed and is now selling at a premium. The French rights of *Sanctuary* and *As I Lay Dying* have also just been sold." Whether or not Faulkner would be regarded as a hot item in Charlottesville, he certainly would be in New York.

It was probably Tuesday, October 20, when he boarded the noon train for Memphis. (Estelle still had not recovered enough from her anemia to make the trip.) There would have been time for a leisurely dinner with friends before the Southern Railway special pulled out of the station that evening at 7:15. The next morning while the train was stopped at Bristol, Virginia, he sent a telegram to Elizabeth Prall Anderson in Marion, Virginia, where she and Anderson had moved four years before when Anderson had bought two weekly newspapers. A year later he had begun to wander again, and in 1929 the two were separated, but Elizabeth Anderson still lived there. As Faulkner rode northward he thought of how he would like to take Cho-Cho with him on this trip, to tell her about the battles Jackson had won in these valleys and mountains. By five P.M., as the descending sun mellowed the bright autumn colors, the train pulled into Charlottesville.

Lewis Mattison had walked around the corner from the *Daily Progress* office to Court Square to inquire at the Monticello Hotel whether William Faulkner had arrived. Mattison had discovered Faulkner's work during his four years at the university. He had graduated the previous June, and now he was one of the *Progress*'s two reporters. He would have tried to meet Faulkner even if it hadn't been in the line of duty. So now, when the desk clerk told him that the guest had not checked in, Mattison decided he would wait and strolled outside.

Just then a taxi drew up and a small man emerged. As he turned from paying the driver, Mattison stepped up. "Are you Mr. Faulkner?" he asked.

The other man looked up at the slender, six-foot reporter. He glanced to the left and the right, then spoke softly in an easy yet conspiratorial air. "Know where I can get a drink?"

Mattison did. He barely got by on his *Progress* salary, so the only club he could afford to patronize was his undergraduate fraternity, the Sigma Alpha Epsilon house on Rugby Road, a mile west of Court Square and just a few blocks from the Rotunda. When Faulkner checked into the hotel he found waiting for him guest cards to the university's Colonnade Club and to the Farmington Country Club, but he decided he would use neither at this point. He told Mattison they were fraternity brothers, bought a bottle of corn whiskey from Mattison's supplier, and repaired to the S.A.E. house. Mattison thought some of the brothers might be impressed at meeting the author of *The Sound and the Fury* and *Sanctuary.* To his chagrin, they had never heard of him, and attempts at conversation dwindled into mutual boredom. But Mattison and Faulkner stayed there for the rest of the evening disposing of the whiskey. The recollection of Faulkner in the S.A.E. house would remain vivid: a slight, graying man with a sharp nose, "head on one side, the soft voice and the courtly manner. . . ." What Mattison did not know was that this was far more agreeable to Faulkner than what Mattison had wanted. He infinitely preferred whiskey and the company of one congenial companion to the questions of a group.

The next morning he wrote to Estelle. "I can see the Blue Ridge from both of my windows. I can see all Charlottesville, and the University too. The fall coloring is splendid here—yellow hickory and red gum and sumach and laurel, with the blue-green pines. It's just grand." He had received no answer to his wire to Elizabeth Anderson. "Maybe she is still mad at me," he wrote. "I'll find out within the next day or so." (Whatever had happened six years before in New Orleans was still there between them. No word would arrive from her.) Today there would be lunch at the university. In the afternoon Hal Smith would arrive, and then on Friday morning, the twenty-third, the conference would begin with "a formal to-do."

Playwright Paul Green had driven up to Charlottesville from Chapel Hill, North Carolina, the previous day. Born a farmer's son, he had been a champion cotton-picker before he entered the A.E.F. Later he had studied and then taught philosophy at the University of North Carolina before going on to write such plays as *In Abraham's Bosom*, which had won him the Pulitzer Prize for 1927. Green was an outgoing man with a thick shock of hair and aquiline features which gave him a Roman profile. He spoke with a soft and indolent sound that seemed totally Southern. He had written Faulkner about the conference and now he drove to the Monticello Hotel. He telephoned him from the desk, and Faulkner agreed to drive to the first meeting with him. When he came down, Green remembered, Faulkner was wearing what Green took to be an aviation cap. He had been in the Canadian Air Force, Faulkner explained as they drove to the university.

Thirty-four writers assembled that morning. Though Thomas Wolfe, Stark Young, Laurence Stallings, and Julia Peterkin had been unable to come, it was still an impressive gathering. Ellen Glasgow addressed what she called the "round table" as they sat informally in the east room of Madison Hall. (Lewis Mattison was there taking notes, and so was thin, homely Emily Clark, the editor of *The Reviewer*, a little magazine based in Richmond.) The fifty-seven-year-old literary doyenne from Richmond had written *Barren Ground*, *They Stooped to Folly*, and a dozen other novels of Virginia life. Sickly as a child, she had become a commanding woman. Admiring her brown eyes and dark bronze hair, friends spoke of her "autumn leaf" coloring. She had grown increasingly deaf in recent years, but her manner was still urbane and sophisticated. Allen Tate thought she was wonderful, "just like a worldly old French woman of the 18th century." Sherwood Anderson thought she had "tremendous vitality."

The organizing committee had suggested the topic "The Southern

Writer and His Public." Effortlessly, "Miss Ellen" began to talk in a rambling, discursive manner punctuated by flashes of wit. Declaring that the South needed no defense and no apologies, she completely discarded the set topic and talked instead about the relation between historical and fictional truth. Faulkner sat on the edge of his chair, his elbows on his knees and his head between his hands. He had apparently fortified himself for the ordeal ahead. After authoritative pronouncements from Miss Glasgow, he would raise his head slightly and softly murmur, "I agree, I agree." Miss Glasgow went on, oblivious of his encouragement.

A general discussion followed. Emily Clark reported that dramatist Paul Green talked about "the loneliness of the Creative life, but his assumption that the Machine Age would do no harm to the creative mind drew fire from that doughty agrarian, Donald Davidson, who, with Allen Tate, had come from Tennessee to take his stand against the wheels and crankshafts. Sherwood Anderson, quite undisturbed about letters at any point of the compass, prowled about claiming to be Southern by virtue of a dash of Italian blood rather than by the choice of Virginia for a home." Anderson felt Miss Glasgow's talk had been a great success, "and then suddenly the meeting got bad—long, tiresome speeches from professors. Everyone began to think it was going to be like a dentists' convention." He looked closely at his fellow participants. Novelist Struthers Burt was a small, alert man who was a bit dry. Anderson was attracted by Allen Tate's wife, novelist Caroline Gordon, "a fine black-haired, black-eyed creature who talked intelligently about farming." Alice Hegan Rice, on the other hand, looked just like Mrs. Wiggs should have looked in her cabbage patch: "a suggestion of the refined washerwoman." James Branch Cabell was for the most part silent, explaining, according to Emily Clark, that "he wrote only because he could not talk." Anderson heard him talk, however, and remembered him as "placid, 55, face like a baby's in some queer way, clever at retort, always with a sting of maliciousness." The conference was shaping up as a very trying affair for someone with hound-dog-and-wagon propensities.

Anderson's fears were really groundless. As a matter of fact, the sponsors were doing their best to make it what Emily Clark called a house party. They succeeded: "an occasion which might easily have been self-conscious was genuinely gay; an occasion which might, with equal facility, have become trivial, was never worse than convivial. It remained always a party, but a party where people both talked and listened well. . . ." The talking went on that afternoon at a tea at Castle Hill, the mansion of novelist Amelie Rives and her husband, Prince Pierre Troubetzkoy. Located in Cobham, just a dozen miles from the university, Castle Hill was one of the great houses of Albemarle County. There, in 1781, Tarleton's troopers had been detained (with mint juleps, it was said) long enough for Thomas Jefferson and the Virginia legislature to escape capture. One of the oldest county houses, it had entertained five presidents. The prince—an artist who often appeared in Cobham or Keswick wearing tennis shoes—walked down the cedar-lined driveway past the famous boxwoods to greet his guests. In his dining room crystal decanters glinted on the polished wood. Sixty-eight-year-old Amelie Rives Troubetzkoy had once been a golden-haired beauty with fresh coloring and a classic profile. By now her hair had darkened and her pale complexion emphasized her deep-set eyes. She was never seen except by firelight or candlelight. Suffering from rheumatic gout, she was often confined to her room. So it was that afternoon, and Anderson watched a stream of guests go into her room to pay their respects.

A few young admirers had by now sought Faulkner out. One of them was Milton J. Abernethy, a short, round-faced senior from the University of North Carolina. With Anthony J. Buttitta he was running the Intimate Bookshop in Chapel Hill and a little magazine called *Contempo*. Another was Lambert Davis, at twenty-six the managing editor of *The Virginia Quarterly Review*. He and Dayton Kohler, a young teacher, had stopped at the Monticello Hotel to take Faulkner out to Castle Hill with them. He had been sitting on the curb waiting for them, tie askew, a mason jar at his side. When Davis opened the car door, Faulkner eyed him for a moment. "Can we get a drink at Castle Hill?" he asked. Davis was sure they could.

Now, at the tea, they discovered suddenly that Faulkner was not with them. He had decided to view the upstairs of historic Castle Hill. When they finally found him, it was time for him to pay his respects to his hostess.

Amelie Troubetzkoy sat at a beautiful table in her room. Faulkner was presented to her. To James Southall Wilson's wife, Julia, Faulkner seemed a little man, with hair like pepper and salt. He stood erectly, his arms at his sides, looking down his long nose at her. Someone had told her where he had been.

"Mr. Faulkner," she said, "I have seen how you have walked through my house and looked through my rooms, but I've forgiven you because you were accompanied by genius."

"Would that some ten thousand people would say them same words to me, ma'am," he answered.

When someone like Abernethy was not with Faulkner, Hal Smith was. Smith went with him to the dinner given that night at the Farmington Country Club, located a few miles west of town with the Blue Ridge Mountains for backdrop. The oldest part of the club had been designed by Thomas Jefferson. Its classic lines—Emily Clark called it "the loveliest club in Virginia"—were bathed in bright moonlight as the guests began to arrive. As Faulkner's powers of resistance waned, he was becoming more and more a center of attention. As he grew silent, Smith became loquacious. Emily Clark chronicled the effect at some length: "William Faulkner attended meetings and parties intermittently, and was, beyond doubt, the focal point of every gaze, since this new and dazzling light of American letters had never before been in Virginia. . . . Harrison Smith, also down for a day, remarked that Mr. Faulkner, who never can be persuaded to regard his metropolitan reviews with a fitting seriousness, was, like all good Southerners, both serious and flattered in his acceptance of an invitation from the University of Virginia. This exponent of horror beyond all imaginable horrors, a gentle, low-voiced, slight young man, on his first evening astonished his admirers and interested spectators by merely murmuring, while conversation and argument raged around him, the placating phrase, 'I dare say,' at infrequent intervals; and by gently crooning 'Carry Me Back to Old Virginia,' in an automobile between Charlottesville and Farmington." Faulkner ate little at the dinner. So did Abernethy, for whom a place was not laid. Miss Glasgow tried to make up for this by giving him morsels from her plate. After dinner a crowd gathered around Miss Glasgow, Anderson, and historian Stringfellow Barr, editor of *The Virginia Quarterly Review*. Anderson enjoyed this, talking at some length before going back to town to Carr's Hill, where he was the house guest of acting-president of the university, John Lloyd Newcomb. By this time Faulkner was feeling the strenuousness of his activities. Green, who was staying at Farmington, took him upstairs where he went to sleep on the bed of Green's roommate, Archibald Henderson. Eventually he returned to town and the Monticello Hotel.

Like Sherwood Anderson, Faulkner skipped the trip the next morning to Monticello, Jefferson's home. Later that Saturday morning, Faulkner heard one speaker whom he had taken a liking to. North Carolina resident James Boyd had written *Drums* and other historical novels and was also an avid fox-hunter. A brown muscular man with dark hair and mustache, he reminded Emily Clark of Owen Wister's Virginian. Boyd talked of the fixity and stability of tradition which he thought one of the South's legacies to its young people. Green disclaimed fixity and stability as assets and called revolt against the Machine Age "nonsense." Faulkner spoke little, Lewis Mattison remembered, and when he did speak, it did not seem to be to the point.

An enterprising reporter managed a few brief interviews. He wrote that Faulkner reminisced about his service in a Canadian regiment in France, his work as a reporter on the New Orleans *Times-Picayune*, and his first novel, which he wrote at night after his day's newspaper work. "Incidentally," the reporter quoted Faulkner as saying, "that novel, fortunately, never saw the light of day." Another reporter also asked for an interview. Faulkner told him he would see him at his hotel—at midnight on Saturday.

That afternoon there was more tea at a reception at the Colonnade Club on the Lawn of the university, the central portion of the "academical village" Jefferson had designed more than a century before. It was sunset, and a tall ash gleamed at the end of the colonnade, its trunk black and its top gold. It was an evocative time and setting. Nearby, on West Range, was the room where Edgar Poe had lived briefly as a student. Beyond, just outside Alderman Library, was the Gutzon Borglum statue of a winged birdman poised for flight in unchanging bronze. It commemorated a young man named James Roger McConnell, who had written articles about aerial combat Billy Falkner may have read—articles published before his death as a member of the Lafayette Escadrille in March, 1917.

By now Faulkner had lost interest in receptions. Anderson was watching him. "Bill Faulkner had arrived and got drunk," he later wrote. "From time to time he appeared, got drunk again immediately, & disappeared. He kept asking everyone for drinks. If they didn't give him any, he drank his own." (Anderson did not add that on the second morning of the conference Faulkner had entered the Farmington Country Club only to become violently ill, to the consternation of admirers who had approached to greet the literary celebrity.) Anderson had some observations on Paul Green, too, who looked to him like a football player. "He drinks pretty hard," Anderson wrote. "I'm sure they don't all drink like that all the time. They couldn't."

The conference was over and some of the departures had begun. On this final Saturday evening Lewis Mattison took Faulkner to the apartment of a former classmate, now a teacher. There they drank and talked. An architecture major, Mattison had done watercolors. So had he, Faulkner told him. He talked about *Sanctuary*, which he said he had written—purely for money—on an upside-down wheelbarrow in the powerhouse. He talked about Hal Smith, how Smith had given him the money and the ticket to come to the conference. He thought it was a total waste of time, but Smith told him he ought to go. He was relaxed and pleasant, casual and sociable —almost like someone his own age, Mattison remembered, but he had the feeling that "the whole visit was meaningless for him." What's more, "He didn't give a damn about Ellen Glasgow or any of them."

As far as most were concerned, the conference had been a great success. There had been pronouncements they could all agree on and occasionally the feeling of solidarity. They deplored the dearth of Southern book columns and the resultant dependence upon New York reviewers—a result, said Stringfellow Barr, of "the complete disinclination of Southerners to buy books. This, I personally believe, is the exact temper of an earlier South, when everyone wanted to talk and no one wanted to listen. So now in that most articulate of regions, everyone wants to write and no one wants to read." Emily Clark felt that this weekend at Mr. Jefferson's university, with its general concord in which lions behaved like lambs, was a foreshadowing: "all signs and portents point to the incredible but indisputable fact that the literary field held by New England in the middle nineteenth century, and by the Middle West only ten short years ago, belongs, by right of the strongest, to the South today."

On Saturday night, precisely on the chime of midnight, Faulkner was wakened from a deep sleep by a continuous knocking on the door of his room on the top floor of the Monticello Hotel. He roused himself, opened the door a crack, and peered out. Standing in the corridor was a young man. He identified himself as the reporter from *College Topics* to whom Faulkner had granted an interview the day before. Faulkner apologized for the "ungodly" hour at which he had been forced to set the interview and invited the young man in. He seated him and reclined on the bed as the reporter began asking his questions. From biography he proceeded to books. Faulkner answered dutifully. His favorites were Conrad's *The Nigger of the Narcissus* and Melville's *Moby Dick.* For travel reading he had brought along a lesser Dumas novel in paperback. He and his grandfather used to read the whole set every year, he said. As to Southern literature, today's writers were only pioneers and nothing "of any real value" was likely to come out of the South for at least twenty-five years—the Southern Writers' Conference notwithstanding, apparently. When the reporter raised the subject of technique, Faulkner talked about Dostoevsky. He could have cut *The Brothers Karamazov* by two thirds if he had let the brothers tell their stories without authorial exposition, he said. Eventually all straight exposition would be replaced by soliloquies in different colored inks. It must have been well past one o'clock when Faulkner—already an incipient if not actual insomniac—closed the door behind the reporter and tried to go back to sleep.

Paul Green had driven up to Charlottesville from Chapel Hill with Milton Abernethy as a passenger. They were going on to New York, where Green had a play running. Green invited Faulkner and Smith to ride up in his old Buick. Smith could see that Faulkner would be easier to handle in a car than on a train and accepted for them. They set out for New York, it appears, on the morning of Sunday, October 25. Faulkner was in a good humor but he was still drinking heavily. He told Green and Abernethy he had been having a good time with people who accused him of being influenced by James Joyce. He said he told them he hadn't read Joyce. Throughout the trip, he recited Joyce from memory, repeating his special favorite, "Watching the Needleboats at San Sabba," from *Pomes Penyeach.*

If Faulkner had found the presence of fellow writers taxing in Charlottesville, he could have no idea of the pressure to come from publishers in New York. No matter how the year 1931 might add up financially, all other indices spelled dramatic change. He had scored critical successes; even those who disliked his content often grudgingly admired his form. *Sanctuary* and *These 13* were still selling very well. He was in English editions and was going into French ones. First editions of all his works were collector's items, with *The Marble Faun* now bringing better than $12.50 a copy. And even though older collectors in New Orleans either had not read him or thought him "a flash in the pan," elsewhere people were paying premium prices for *Sherwood Anderson & Other Famous Creoles.* One dealer had even gone so far as to buy up all the remaining copies of *Anthology of Magazine Verse for 1925* because it contained "The Lilacs"; he was now offering them to the trade and to collectors at $4.50 apiece. Even if Cape & Smith had not been having difficulties, there probably would have been publishers offering him contracts, but rumors of Hal Smith's troubles must have whetted the hopes of other publishers. Several were waiting for Faulkner's arrival in New York. When they applied the pressure, he would respond with what was by now standard strategy in such situations: drinking.

Why did he drink? There were at least half a dozen situations that would produce drinking. And there were different patterns of drinking. There was, as a matter of fact, abstinence, too. Before he was much older he would abstain completely for a year. Most of the time, however, he did drink. For long periods his intake would be moderate, or considerable, but controlled. It would have had to be so, for him to accomplish all the work he had done. At times, as with Charlie Crouch or Rusty Patterson, he spent an evening in heavy drinking, from which it would take a day or so to recover. There were also extended bouts which would end when he finally stopped drinking and recovered from the after-effects. The family could handle some of these; on other occasions hospitalization would be necessary.

There was certainly a predisposition to drinking, in his culture and in his family. As Jack Falkner would later recall, there was no such thing, when Bill Faulkner was growing up, as social drinking in the modern sense, and nothing like the integration of wine and spirits into family life that some Europeans knew. Drinking was for men—or so it was made to appear—and it was not a drawing-room occupation. In "wet" areas a man could drink in a bar or hotel. In dry areas such as Lafayette County, liquor was bought from bootleggers and consumed sub rosa. As a result, the drinking tended to be hard and often to end in drunkenness. In William Faulkner's family drinking was a tradition. His great-grandfather was said to have been a heavy drinker. (One of the reports, it is true, came from an enemy.) His grandfather and father were both habitual drinkers whose bouts might end in hospitalization. Both had been forced to undergo the Keeley Cure without long-term success. The Colonel had continued to drink heavily until his death. Murry Falkner had begun to cut down only recently at about the time he had begun to suffer from stomach trouble.

Miss Maud met this behavior in her son just as she had met it in his father: with determined but largely undiscriminating resistance. She would pour his whiskey down the sink, and in these early years of his marriage she was convinced that Estelle encouraged his drinking. The example of abstemious Grandfather Murry had not been very persuasive. All of Murry Falkner's sons drank, and to excess. Of the four of them, only Jack finally became an abstainer. Excessive drinking can often be a familial condition. It is not transmitted biologically; it is "passed on in the same way that money is inherited, not in the way that, say, eye colour is." In this case the means of transmission was only a technical matter. The inheritance was conveyed. And he was constantly with fellow inheritors, whether in Oxford or in the Vieux Carré, where one, looking back later on the old days, would not recall him as a particularly heavy drinker. "We *all* drank hard," she said.

Like most people who drink, William Faulkner drank because of the way liquor tasted and the way it made him feel. He had liked the flavor from the time when he was allowed to drink the "heeltaps" that remained in his grandfather's toddy glass. He greatly enjoyed the taste of good bourbon, and by the time he reached mature years he was a wine drinker of knowledge and discrimination. He enjoyed drinking for these "positive" reasons. He enjoyed it because it made him feel good—as he relaxed after work or eased the strain from a variety of causes.

He also drank, in a connected yet separate way, out of avoidance as well as out of gustatory and psychological pleasure. He was a shy man who would wryly say he got "claustrophobia" in crowds. He was a private man who generally disliked questions about himself or his work. For many shy people, liquor is an agent which eases the apprehension that may accompany a crowd situation. It probably acted this way for him. He tended to distrust physicians generally. ("He had a curious way of treating a doctor," one said, "courteous, but you had the feeling that he wasn't paying any attention to you and would go on doing what he wanted to.") Liquor was for him an analgesic, an anodyne, an anesthetic, and he would dose himself with whiskey in treating a sore throat or a bad back. When the ailment persisted he would increase the dosage. He would use liquor to ease worry as well as pain—worry over finances, for instance. If he felt deeply unhappy or depressed, he would turn to liquor. Faced with a situation (sometimes of his own making) which presented equally unacceptable alternatives, he would avoid the decision by removing himself from the whole situation through excessive drinking. When faced with an unavoidable obligation suddenly come due, he might make himself incapable of fulfilling it. Unhappily, however, one of the characteristics of alcohol taken in this way is that it tends in the long run to intensify the thing it is meant to treat. The drinker is less able to deal with his depression, for instance. The alcohol reduces his intellectual control over the response he is using the alcohol to inhibit.

Sometimes these drinking bouts were predictable. They would usually come in the reaction that followed the completion of a book. Each novel but *The Sound and the Fury*, he said, was written with an "accompanying feeling of drive or effort," and a "following feeling of exhaustion or relief or distaste." As Sherwood Anderson expressed it, "then the reaction comes. There has been this intense concentration and now you are striving to come out of it. You go to walk. Sometimes I have found that drink helps at such times. You have been in one world and you are trying to return to another. Your nerves are jumpy." These periods of excessive drinking would usually follow a rhythm. In November came the trip to hunting camp. Here there was a complete change of atmosphere, of scene, of company. There was also the release of intensive drinking, which might ease off or go on, finally terminating the hunt for him. These bouts might occur from two to four times a year. They might last for a week, ten days, or a month and a half.

The bouts were usually deliberate. Faulkner would ensure a sufficient supply of liquor. He would plan when he would start, and he would often plan when he would stop. John Falkner thought these sessions were merely faked drunkenness—when Bill was bored, when he wanted to avoid work or to be waited on. On many occasions, however, they were not fakes but rather serious, prolonged, and debilitating illnesses.

The onset might come at any time. "He'd go along for weeks or months at a normal gait," R. N. Linscott, later Faulkner's editor, would write, and "then the craving would come. Most often he'd fight it off. But once in a while something would happen that would 'get me all of a turmoil inside,' and liquor seemed the only escape. It was only when he was caught in a situation he couldn't cope with that he'd give in to what he called the chemistry of craving and go overboard. You would be aware of the symptoms of increasing tension—drumming fingers, evasive looks, monosyllabic replies to questions—then he'd disappear. . . ." To another Faulkner once said, "I feel as though all my nerve ends were exposed. . . ."

The progress and effects of his drinking bouts were very similar to the average ones of the periodic heavy drinker. Shortly after the cycle began, he would lose interest in food. When his own supply of liquor, sometimes ingeniously cached, would run out, he would become dependent on others. Then he might use food to bargain with those who were nursing him. When he was not yet ready to stop or to taper off, he might accept an eggnog in exchange for another drink.

He would retire to his bed, sometimes dispensing with his pajama top, or bottoms, or both. He might leave his room without donning a robe, to the discomfiture—if he happened to be in a hotel—of guests and staff. One thing which had always struck some of his friends as extraordinary was his ability to recall later the conversation during a period of intensive drinking. He retained this faculty together with what seemed an acute awareness of what was happening to him. Sometimes this could produce a somewhat poignant effect, as when a friend nursing him realized that Faulkner knew the effect that seeing him this way might have. But this was a minor consideration. The bout would go on until he was ready to taper off, or until he was hospitalized.

The reactions following prolonged intensive drinking are far more severe than just headache, nausea, and sensitivity to sound. They constitute withdrawal symptoms very like those caused by other addictive agents. Some of the symptoms are caused by the sudden lessening of alcohol concentration in the blood. Others result from retention of body fluids with accompanying cerebral edema. First to appear is usually acute tremulousness and nervousness which may persist for days or even weeks. There will often be insomnia. There may follow hallucinations as the sufferer sees and hears things which are not there. There is also likely to be an accompanying distortion of the time sense. Even worse, of course, is delirium tremens: disordered mental activity, hypersensitivity to random stimuli, and a pervasive terror produced by the flickering yet absolutely convincing hallucinations. There may be instances of alcoholic epilepsy, after the irritation of neuronal tissue from overfluidation, in which the brain produces a discharge of electricity which disorganizes the body's circuitry and muscular control. The victim may fall into convulsive spasms marked by labored breathing, blueness of the skin from lack of oxygen, and involuntary voiding. At one time or another, William Faulkner suffered all of these effects.

Severe and protracted drinking brings in its wake other ills: gastritis, memory blackouts, cirrhosis of the liver. Faulkner was fortunate. Appetite and digestion never failed him upon his return to health. He remained a gourmet. The few blackouts that he would suffer much later in life came from other causes, and there is no indication that he ever developed the liver ailment. He had a strong constitution and he was spared the extremities to which other writers among his contemporaries were reduced. But the drinking did produce the equivalent of one or two serious illnesses a year for thirty years. His own euphemism for such an illness was "a collapse." In a way, it was just that.

The treatment of such illnesses could extend from home remedies to the ministrations of a specialized hospital. And even in hospitals, the regimen and medication would differ from one to another according to philosophy, theory, and practice. The physician may have to treat several complaints at the same time. The patient on arrival is likely to show malnutrition as well as intoxication. He may be suffering from a cold or an infection contracted during the course of the bout. The physician may administer glucose, vitamins, and antibiotics. With the onset of violent withdrawal symptoms, which may come as late as six days after the patient has stopped drinking, the physician will have to increase or change some of the medication. Whereas he may have administered a mild sedative when the patient was admitted, he may now switch to something stronger. In the 1930's and 1940's it would have been paraldehyde. An alcohol substitute, it was a powerful and addictive drug which could be administered in several forms, some of them characterized by an odor many patients found nearly unbearable. But it acted as a deep sedative for the victim suffering from acute tremulousness and nervousness. (In recent years, of course, tranquilizers and other drugs have been substituted increasingly for the older ones.) Gradually the body's balance is restored. Abstaining now, the patient begins to eat normally. In due course the medication is reduced. The patient may remain in the hospital until he has returned completely to normal. Often he may choose to go home sooner—still a bit shaky and debilitated, with the tag end of a cold, and with a bottle of large vitamin capsules in his overnight bag. Faulkner knew this cycle, too.

Now, riding northward toward New York on the two-lane roads of 1931, he was in no such protective environment. He was with one old friend and two new ones who admired him and would do what they could—like others in New York. For a period of nearly seven weeks Faulkner would be away from home—still grieving for his baby, concerned over his wife's health, worried about money, and engulfed periodically in situations involving tension and crowds. He would not drink heavily all of this time, but he would during much of it. And it would be periodically harrowing for him and for others.

He was still apparently enjoying the trip. He recited Joyce, and then, reaching into the canvas bag, extracted the manuscript of *Light in August* and read some of it aloud. He asked Green to stop so he could replenish his supply of liquor. Green did. By the time they reached Washington, Green had to stop again because of trouble with the old Buick. As he pulled into a service station, Green told Faulkner to be sure to keep the liquor hidden. They had been able to drink all they wanted in Charlottesville, but this was Washington, and Green did not know what view the capital's law enforcement officers took of the Volstead Act. As the mechanic peered at the engine, a policeman strolled by and Faulkner genially offered him a drink. The officer smiled, declined with thanks, and walked on. Green, Smith, and Abernethy looked at each other. Smith did not complete the trip to New York with the rest. It may have been at this point that he took a train instead. It would do a publisher no particular good to be jailed in Washington for violating the liquor laws, particularly when he ought to be in New York trying to start a new business.

It must have been Monday, October 26, when they arrived in New York. Green dropped Faulkner and Abernethy off at their hotel, arranging to meet them that evening for dinner. By the time he returned, Faulkner's telephone had been ringing. Alfred A. Knopf was interested in him, as was Harold Guinzburg. Six years earlier Guinzburg had founded The Viking Press with George Oppenheimer. From the start they had aimed for a small list of quality books and had done well. Now they had expanded their activities to include Canada, and they were ready to add more authors to their list. Four months after Guinzburg and Oppenheimer had organized The Viking Press, Bennett Cerf and Donald Klopfer had purchased The Modern Library from the foundering firm of Boni & Liveright. Five years later they had bought The Sun Dial Press, and now, as Random House, their company was working vigorously to stay solvent in the teeth of the Depression. Cerf had been selling books in the Centaur Book Shop in Philadelphia that February when the manager gave him a new book to read. It was *Sanctuary.* "I read it," Cerf said much later, "and flipped." Like his competitors, he was determined to sign up this thirty-four-year-old author if he could. On that same Monday, he pressed his suit in person. As a token of esteem he presented a copy of the handsome Modern Library edition of one of the two books Faulkner had called his favorites: *Moby Dick.* It was inscribed for "Bill Faulkner from——Random House & The Modern Library." The recipient also inscribed his name and the date in the book.

Cerf had a concrete plan in mind. He wanted to publish *Sanctuary* (which had gone into its sixth printing in July) in The Modern Library. And there was another possible deal. Faulkner had sent "Idyll in the Desert" to

Ben Wasson on June 5, but Ben had not placed it. During the time Faulkner was in New York, Wasson would offer it to Cerf as a possible special Random House publication. Faulkner now responded to the stepped-up tempo of activity by drinking harder. Abernethy got in touch with Smith, who had struck him as a rather dynamic man who would know what to do, and told him what was happening.

It was in these years that a certain kind of motion picture enjoyed a special vogue. It mixed romance, music, and athletics. There were co-eds who sang. Cheerleaders in short skirts and white bell-bottomed trousers danced. One of the female cheerleaders usually fell in love with the college's football star. Often, for a climax, the football star would be kidnapped by gamblers or other foresighted or disgruntled persons. This would happen on the eve of The Big Game. At the last possible moment, the star would escape from his captors and swiftly make his way to the stadium to score the winning touchdown just before the final gun sounded. The fade-out would combine the sweetness of lovers reunited with the triumphal frenzy of the victorious football fans. Hal Smith, beleaguered as he felt by Alfred Knopf (about whom he was particularly worried), The Viking Press, and Random House, may have thought of such a strategem at this precarious moment to protect his literary property. He gave Milton Abernethy money for two tickets on a ship plying the waters between New York City and Jacksonville, Florida. He asked him to get William Faulkner aboard it as soon as he could and to keep him in Jacksonville, or some place other than New York, until the pursuit cooled off. Abernethy said he would do it. Faulkner, if he was consulted, made no objection.

The Clyde-Mallory lines advertised service in big, modern liners sailing between New York and Jacksonville and calling at Charleston. Two vessels made the run regularly: the *Henry R. Mallory* and the *Algonquin.* Abernethy was impressed by the size of the *Mallory* as they boarded it at dinner time on Tuesday, the twenty-seventh. Clad in brown tweeds and smoking his pipe, Faulkner had little in the way of baggage. Not until the ship had nosed its way out of the harbor on its southerly course did they learn that there was no liquor aboard. Faulkner's solution was to procure some German beer from the steward together with sugar and yeast. He then "needled" the beer to increase its potency.

The next morning, Abernethy recalled, they arrived in Norfolk. That day's journey was uneventful, but during the night after both men had retired the wind rose and the ship began taking rough waves. The beer bottles rattled and one popped with a report like a pistol shot that brought Faulkner jumping out of his bunk. The rest remained intact, however. By the time they reached Jacksonville, they were all empty. But now there was a new difficulty: Faulkner had an acute case of hiccups.

They checked into a hotel, where Abernethy tried to help his friend. He suggested the usual folk remedies: drinking water, breathing in a paper bag, holding his breath. Faulkner had suffered this complaint before and knew that none of these would work. There was only one thing to do.

"What is it?" Abernethy asked.

"I have to fly in an airplane, upside down," Faulkner said.

Abernethy thought that if that was the only way to stop the hiccups, Faulkner had better do it. He would wait for him at the hotel.

"No," Faulkner said, "I have to do it *with* someone."

The two took a taxi out to the airport where Faulkner hired a pilot and gravely gave him instructions. They took off, reached a safe altitude, and then, as Abernethy recalled it, flew upside down over the Jacksonville marshes, returned to the field, and landed. Faulkner no longer complained of the hiccups.

Abernethy had had enough of both upside-down flying and Jacksonville, so he invited Faulkner to spend a few days with him in Chapel Hill. Faulkner equably agreed and they left Jacksonville on what must have been Friday, October 30. It seems that they reached their intermediate destination no later than October 31.

The Intimate Bookshop and *Contempo* were both located in an office building next to the post office in Chapel Hill. There Abernethy and Anthony Buttitta, co-owners of the bookstore and co-editors of the magazine, put Faulkner up in a small second-floor room where he could sleep. Later Faulkner told Buttitta that his friends Grace and A. P. Hudson were in Chapel Hill. Buttitta telephoned Hudson and told him a little about the writers' conference and Faulkner's sudden departure from New York. There was some talk about his going fox-hunting with James Boyd in Southern Pines, but it appeared that he would not be well enough for a while yet. Buttitta asked the Hudsons over for the next day.

On what was probably Sunday morning, November 1, Grace and A. P. Hudson knocked at the second-floor apartment. Abernethy welcomed them and asked them to sit down. When Faulkner entered, A.P. saw that he was not himself. He seemed unsteady and distraught. But he shook hands —his hand was still tanned, firm, and slender, A.P. noticed—and smiled shyly in greeting. He seemed pleased to see them. There was a silence and then Grace Hudson, remembering how well Bill loved Cho-Cho and Malcolm, asked, "How are the children?"

Faulkner seemed to choke for a moment. "The child died," he said. Abernethy looked on in silence as the Hudsons tried to make conversation. More and more Faulkner seemed a painfully sensitive man, and very lonely.

It had by now occurred to Abernethy and Buttitta that this might be an unparalleled opportunity for *Contempo.* Perhaps they could do a whole Faulkner issue. The manuscript of *Light in August* was still in the canvas bag, and they hoped for a chapter or a scene. "While he had been sleeping," Buttitta recalled, "we tried to decipher the script, but we made no headway. We told him so. He laughed. Bill told us not to worry, he had stacks of rejected manuscripts, stories and poems yellowing in his files down at Oxford." Buttitta said he planned to visit his parents in Louisiana at Christmas. Faulkner invited him to visit at Rowan Oak, go through the files, and take what he wanted. "This was more than we had hoped for," Buttitta remembered, "from the new literary light of our day." Faulkner also agreed to let them put his name on their masthead, where he would join Louis Adamic, Barrett H. Clark, Langston Hughes, Lewis Mumford, and Ezra Pound as a contributing editor.

By then Faulkner seemed to be feeling somewhat better, so Abernethy and Buttitta decided to take him to nearby Durham to see a motion picture. But Abernethy was as innocent of Faulkner's movie tastes as of his susceptibility to hiccups. They were hardly settled in their seats when the author was ready to leave. "Don't want to hear talk," he said to Buttitta. "Would rather talk myself. Let's go out and talk." Once outside he began to tell them about *Light in August.* And again he recited "Watching the Needleboats at San Sabba."

Faulkner was well enough by Sunday to join a gathering at the home of Phillips Russell, who had married Paul Green's sister, Caro Mae, at the end of October. The conversation was easy and friendly, and Faulkner seemed to be enjoying himself. Russell taught a writing class there at the University of North Carolina, and though he had been warned that Faulkner would not talk to classes, he decided to approach him anyway. Faulkner agreed at once and asked Russell the time and place. Mrs. Russell was not at the gathering and so did not meet the visitor, but she heard him later on. At about three o'clock in the morning there was a knocking at the

Russells' door. They did not answer it, so the would-be visitors serenaded the newlyweds briefly and went on their way.

When the class met on Monday, Faulkner was there. Russell recalled that he "made a short, sensible talk which the class, not all of which had heard of him, applauded. His courtesy and absence of pose made a good impression." He had agreed to answer questions, and an elderly tourist Russell had admitted raised her hand. When Faulkner recognized her she rose and read a passage from his work.

"Now, Mr. Faulkner," she said, "what were you thinking of when you wrote that?"

"Money," he replied.

The students burst into laughter. Russell felt they had sensed that Faulkner wanted to avoid weighty literary discussion and was pulling the lady's leg. It was a successful class.

It must have been Tuesday, November 3, when Faulkner and Abernethy boarded the *Henry R. Mallory* at Norfolk for New York. Left behind for a future issue of *Contempo* was a section of the manuscript of *Light in August.* Abernethy must have sent word ahead, for when the boat docked at dawn on Wednesday, reporter Evelyn Seeley of the New York *World-Telegram* was there waiting for him. There had been no needled beer on the trip back, and Faulkner had recovered enough so that Miss Seeley could describe him as a "well-groomed shy little man with bushy brows and brown eyes as bright as a squirrel."

"I'm a stranger in this town," he told a taxi driver. "Can you take me to a hotel that's quiet and inexpensive?" Miss Seeley followed him into the taxi and began asking her questions. "I'm going to get out of here tonight," Faulkner told her with some acerbity. He spoke again about the feelings of the hound dog under the wagon. He was here only to see Harrison Smith, "my one friend in the North, one man I like." As for New York, he liked Central Park and Washington Square and enjoyed watching the ferryboats on the river, but the rest held no appeal. "I don't like literary people," he told her. "I never associate with other writers. I don't know why—I'm just not social. I can't stand 'literary groups.' " The taxi driver's choice for Faulkner's quiet and inexpensive stopping place was the Hotel Century. He let him and Abernethy off there on West 46th Street. Faulkner had hardly checked in before the battle of the publishers was joined again.

In four days *The New York Times Book Review* would announce Harrison Smith's resignation as managing director and vice-president of

Jonathan Cape and Harrison Smith, Inc. The writer would conclude with the restrained comment that "Mr. Smith's plans for the future have not yet been made public, but there is every reason to believe that he will not abandon the publishing field." Mr. Smith's plans were very specific, not only for his new enterprise but for his authors and their work. When he learned of Faulkner's promise to Abernethy and Buttitta for *Contempo*, he urged Faulkner to change his mind. "No," Faulkner said, "a promise is a promise." Abernethy remained in New York for a week—during which Faulkner seemed often to be in conference with Smith—but when the time came for him to leave, Faulkner assured him the promise still stood.

Besides the fact that he had given his word, Faulkner may have felt that he was suddenly doing so well that a few stories or poems from his file of rejects were now of no moment. That he was apparently doing well was clear in a letter he sent from the Hotel Century on November 4. "I have been meeting people and being called on all day," he told his wife. "And I have taken in about 300.00 since I got here. It's just like I was some strange and valuable beast, and I believe that I can make 1000.00 more in a month. So I want to stay a month longer, or until the middle of December." He did not say what the three hundred dollars was for, whether it was payment for a story or an advance from Smith. Unquestionably, however, he was in the money again, if modestly. He had been able to write a check for $440 dated November 3. It was to Mrs. Sallie Bailey Bryant, and it included his current mortgage payment plus the arrears for the previous six months.

There was the prospect of more money ahead. In the same letter he wrote, "I have the assurance of a movie agent that I can go to California, to Hollywood and make 500.00 or 750.00 a week in the movies. I think that the trip would do *you* a lot of good. We could live like counts at least on that, and you could dance and go about." If she liked the idea, he would talk to the agent. "Hal Smith will not want me to do it, but if all that money is out there, I might as well hack a little on the side and put the novel off. We could go out just after Christmas." Meanwhile, he was paying off debts. "I am paying Guyton for Mac's tonsils," he added, "and why not arrange in Memphis to have Cho-Cho's teeth fixed now?" Baxter Elliott remembered that for half a year Faulkner had owed about four or five hundred dollars for building materials. "I got the mail one day and opened everything but a letter with a publishing house name on the envelope. Finally I was cleaning up my desk and decided to open this letter. It was a check from Bill in New York."

The literary skirmishes had not gone unrecorded. On November 5 Harry Hansen reported in the New York *World-Telegram* that "rival publishers fought a merry battle yesterday for the favors of William Faulkner, America's most promising author, who reached New York City by ship from Jacksonville, Florida, and went into seclusion in the Century Hotel. At the end of the day, Harrison Smith was reported to have Mr. Faulkner down in black and white as one of his galaxy for the new Smith publishing house." The account went on to note that "in the meantime half a dozen publishers had stormed Mr. Faulkner's door, offering as high as twenty-five percent and generous advance royalties." Hansen had evidently talked with Abernethy, for he recorded the fact that this was Faulkner's second visit to New York, "having lived in seclusion last week at the Union Square Hotel while literary groups were searching for him." He had then visited Chapel Hill, "where he gave Milton Abernethy, editor of *Contempo*, the first publishing rights to new prose and poetry." This material would appear in the next number of *Contempo*, for which the editors planned a run of 50,000 copies.

Nearly two years later Faulkner would recall these publishers' wooings. They had learned about *Light in August*, and as a result there were "guys waiting with contracts in their hands and the advance and percentage left blank, outside my hotel door when the waiter fetched the morning coffee. Also one reliable reference to $10,000.00." Almost nine years later, in a financial crisis, he would recall this frenzied time when "a publisher intimated to me that I could almost write my own ticket with him."

Some of the money with which he was paying bills may have been from *Sanctuary* royalties. It would have been well if he could have drawn all then due him, but the uncertain state of Cape & Smith's fortunes must have precluded that. Even in prosperous times, Jonathan Cape had never been noted for largesse. As a matter of fact, at the time of his departure for England there were authors who would say that he had taken their royalties with him. At the moment, he was making his presence felt at Cape & Smith. His temperament was in many ways antithetical to Hal Smith's, and now the two had severed relations in what one observer called "a grand orgy of mutual vindictiveness." Faulkner did call at the offices, however, probably to pay his respects to friends on the staff. One of them, Robert O. Ballou, had received a visit from Cape that morning. He had walked into Ballou's office, laid a copy of *As I Lay Dying* on his desk, and pointed to a sentence. "Can you tell me what that sentence means?" he asked.

Ballou read it and shook his head. "I haven't the slightest idea," he said.

"Does no one read proof here?" asked Cape.

"Of course," said Ballou. "Evelyn Harter does."

Cape asked him to call her in. Miss Harter explained the sentence at length, trying to make the literal-minded Englishman understand what she took to be the symbolic meaning of the passage. Cape remained unsatisfied and that afternoon, when Faulkner appeared, showed the sentence to the author.

"What does that mean, Faulkner?" he asked him.

"Damned if I know," Faulkner replied after a moment. "I was readin' that the other day and wonderin'. I remember I was pretty well corned up when I wrote that part."

In spite of the other man's gruffness, Faulkner apparently regarded him as a kind of engaging old rogue. "I remember him," he said, years later, "snapping his false teeth in the girls' garters."

Faulkner continued to ponder the idea of going to California. Ben Wasson took him to see two different studio representatives despite his conviction that Faulkner would not make a contract writer. The first interview was disastrous, but after the second they received some encouragement. According to Faulkner's uncle John, Tallulah Bankhead had been enlisted by her studio to lend her Southern charm to their overtures. In January of 1931 Miss Bankhead had returned from an eight-year stay in England, where she had played such roles as Iris March in *The Green Hat* and Sadie Thompson in *Rain.* She went to work for Paramount Pictures Corporation in their Astoria, Long Island, studios in *Tarnished Lady* and *My Sin.* "I seemed sentenced for life to playing tarts, reformed tarts or novice tarts," she recalled. She supposedly carried out the special assignment for her studio by telling Faulkner that she admired his work and hoped he would come to Hollywood to write a screenplay for her.

"Well, now," he supposedly replied, "I'd like to help a Southern girl who's climbin' to the top. But you're too pretty an' nice a girl to play in anything *I'd* write. I wouldn't want to do that to you."

On Thursday, November 5, Faulkner met one of those chiefly responsible for his growing reputation in France, Maurice Coindreau, whose translations of "A Rose for Emily" and "Dry September" had already appeared. When Coindreau had first come to Princeton University, he had asked English department colleagues what contemporary Americans he should read. They had suggested Willa Cather and Booth Tarkington. Then one of his students with avant-garde literary tastes had told him to read *The Sound and the Fury* and *As I Lay Dying.* Coindreau read them and then *Sanctuary.* Then he had written one of the Gallimard brothers at their Paris publishing house. "Here is a man you must take," he told him.

Smith had tried before, he told Coindreau, to bring him and Faulkner together. Now the slight, olive-skinned, brown-eyed Frenchman would finally meet him. It was a pleasant luncheon at Hal Smith's apartment. Evelyn Harter and Louise Bonino, who had left Cape & Smith with Hal, were there too. When Coindreau left, he carried an inscribed copy of *As I Lay Dying* and authorization to translate it as well as anything from *These 13*.

Faulkner had made plans to have dinner later with Louise and Jim Devine. When he called for her at her apartment in the East Forties he did not seem well. "Miss Louise," he said, "would you mind if I lie down on your sofa for a minute? My head hurts." She had been told about the terrible headaches he suffered from the silver plate in his head, so she told him to rest awhile. He slept for two hours, and when he awoke they went to Greenwich Village where they met Devine. After dinner Jim took them to the West Side apartment of puppeteers Bil and Cora Baird, where all of them, including the author of *Marionettes*, spent a pleasant evening.

This was the beginning of a much more intense round of social activities than Faulkner had ever experienced. Even though he was now apparently signed up with Smith's new firm, Smith may have felt that it would be a good idea, as well as hospitable behavior, not to leave him completely on his own. Twice Smith and his wife Claire invited him out to their place in Farmington, Connecticut. The weekend of November 7–8 might have been the occasion of the first visit. Smith had inherited the estate of his uncle, Winchell Smith, whose plays *Brewster's Millions* and *Lightnin'* had enjoyed enormous success. Along with the estate in Farmington, Smith had also inherited William, the butler, and his wife, who had become accustomed to wealthy guests over the years and had formed their standards accordingly. Smith wondered how William would face the crisis that Faulkner's appearance would present. He carried no bag, just a few articles in the capacious pockets of his worn trench coat. After Faulkner had been shown to his room and had reappeared, Smith excused himself. He crept upstairs and looked into Faulkner's room. William had meticulously laid out all of Faulkner's things on the bed: his pajamas, his razor, and his toothbrush.

The Smiths invited others in during the weekend. Faulkner helped Hal to mix up a punch using everything in the house, it seemed. An old friend of the Smiths, Mrs. Sewell Haggard, remembered him during the ensuing party, standing against the wall for hours, polite, not talking, and drinking little.

The competition was by no means convinced that Smith had Faulkner sewed up. Harold Guinzburg had not given up, and neither had Bennett Cerf. At Guinzburg's behest, George Oppenheimer was doing his best for Viking. Tall, friendly, and urbane, Oppenheimer had been educated at Williams and then gone on to Harvard where he had been a member of George Pierce Baker's celebrated playwriting class, English 47. He had gone on to work for Alfred Knopf until Harold Guinzburg had left Simon & Schuster to form the new firm with him in 1925. Oppenheimer had first been introduced to Faulkner by one of his good friends, Dorothy Parker, described by Alexander Woollcott as an odd blend of Little Nell and Lady Macbeth. A diminutive, bright-eyed brunette, she had already made a unique reputation with her witty, cynical, satiric verse and craftsmanlike short stories. She had by now scored successes with books such as *Sunset Gun* and *Death and Taxes*. She introduced Faulkner and then said to Oppenheimer, "Look after this guy." This was the reaction Faulkner usually evoked in this woman famous for her sharp and often malicious tongue. "He seemed so vulnerable, so helpless," she said. "You just wanted to protect him." After the weekend in Connecticut, Faulkner may well have evoked this reaction in others besides Miss Parker. It would not have been foreign to Estelle or other members of the family. They felt him to be an expert at playing this role, and as it had produced the not unwelcome effect on such others as Elizabeth Anderson (for a time), so it did now on Dorothy Parker and other highly sophisticated New Yorkers. George Oppenheimer would later recall that his new friend seemed to play the country boy at the Algonquin. Mixed with this, however, was an enormous amount of Southern chivalry. "He was one of the friendliest men I ever knew in my life," said Oppenheimer, "yet his personality had a kind of strict integrity. He didn't want to give himself to too many."

He would, however, give his regards. Walking into Miss Parker's apartment, he saw she was inscribing a copy of *Soldiers' Pay* to Oppenheimer. He signed it too. On that Monday, November 9, in Oppenheimer's apartment, he walked over to the bookcase and pulled out Oppenheimer's copy of *These 13*. He turned to page 81, and at the top, over the title "All the Dead Pilots," he wrote, "This is the best one," then signed and dated it.

It may have been through Dorothy Parker that Faulkner found an entree into still another set, the most cosmopolitan he had known. This included some of the wits who often congregated at the "round table" of the Hotel Algonquin. Several wrote for *The New Yorker.* One was a thirty-six-year-old banker with a distinguished career already behind him. Robert Abercrombie Lovett was a Texan who had received his bachelor's degree at Yale just before Faulkner had arrived in New Haven. He had won the Navy Cross flying in France and returned at the war's end to study law before switching to business administration at Harvard. In 1921 he had taken a clerkship at the National Bank of Commerce, and five years later he had been made a partner in the banking firm of Brown Brothers, Harriman & Company. He and his striking blond wife had just moved into a duplex apartment on 83rd Street that overlooked the East River. The rooms were large and handsome, with eighteen-foot ceilings. There they often entertained their friends—Harold Ross, the editor of *The New Yorker*, and some of those who wrote for him, such as Dorothy Parker and Robert Benchley.

Others who moved among this group and often visited at the Lovetts' were playwrights Robert Sherwood and Marc Connelly. A gathering might include Franklin P. Adams, John O'Hara, Joel Sayre, and Alexander Woollcott, though Woollcott would be there less often than the rest because he tended to be difficult. One of Oppenheimer's frequent visitors was Philip Barry, a former classmate in Baker's playwriting course and a courteous, gentle, rather shy man with something of the mystic about him. These people were old and close friends. They were dynamic people, fond of the theater, of literature and music. It took very little to get them started, and they had what they remembered as screamingly funny evenings together. They welcomed Faulkner, at first, doubtless, for his talent, but they grew fond of him for a variety of reasons and would see him often thereafter when he was in New York.

On one such evening the talk turned to celebrated units in World War I. Lovett had been at Dunkirk with the 5th Group of the Royal Naval Air Service, which would range up and down the coast on bombing and reconnaissance missions. To Lovett the most gallant as well as the most decorated units were those which served in the Coastal Motor Boats, twenty-one-foot shells with a trough down the middle for carrying Whitehead torpedoes. They were powered with big Thornycroft engines and armed with one or two machine guns. Each boat held a three-man volunteer crew: a skipper, engineer, and torpedoman. They couldn't have been past their early twenties, Lovett remembered, and they seemed to him hardly weaned. Most had entered the war right out of school, and he would see them with their long preparatory school scarves wrapped around their necks with the ends hanging down to their knees. These small boats operated from Dunkirk past Nieuport to Zeebrugge and Ostend, where the German U-boats would put in for servicing. The Germans had laid heavy minefields in highly sophisticated patterns to protect them and their support vessels. The skipper would take his CMB in over the minefields as fast as he could go, prow high, and make his run straight at the target ship. Lovett often thought of those kids, as they seemed to him, out in their cockleshells, night after night, in all kinds of foul weather with no rescue gear. The rescue gear would of course do no good if a CMB touched one of the protruding spines on a German mine. Death would be instantaneous.

The effects of this constant presence and eventual probability of death were very like those suffered by pursuit pilots in the regularly decimated squadrons at the front. On occasion the men of Lovett's group would come across some of these CMB boys lying drunk in the gutters of Dunkirk, having unwound from one mission perhaps or momentarily staved off the thought of the next. The Navy pilots would take these sailors home with them to the squadron to recover. Sobered up the next day, the CMB seamen would be fascinated with the big, lumbering Handley-Pages. They would watch the pilots in their bulky Sidcotts as they clambered into their ungainly craft to go off on a mission. The day finally came when they were ordered on a joint operation. The CMB's were to raid Zeebrugge while four Handley-Pages would draw fire away from the boats. Robert Lovett was in one of the big bombers which droned in toward the shore guns as the wakes of the CMB's spurted across the deadly minefield below. They sunk a big freighter off the Zeebrugge mole, inflicted other damage, and, motors roaring, safely negotiated their way out through the minefield to sea. They also earned a DSO.

Faulkner was one of the circle of guests that night who listened as Lovett, tall, slim, and strong-featured, reminisced in his slow deep voice. At the end of the evening, Faulkner and Ben Wasson left together. Walking home, Faulkner could not get the story out of his mind. "Great God Almighty, Bud," he said, "think of those boys lying in that gutter—doomed." He kept returning to it. "Those poor fellows," he said, "those poor fellows." When they reached Faulkner's place, he pressed Ben to come in with him, still obviously haunted by the thought, but Ben had to go on. Faulkner would often say, later in life, that a story would worry and worry him until he had to put it down on paper. This process apparently began now, and whether it was catharsis or simply the brooding imagination of the storyteller, the result was the same. It may have been through this process that Faulkner made two more good friends.

Frank Sullivan was a short, plump, worried-looking man whom the *Saturday Review* called the best slapstick satirist then writing. After graduating from Cornell, he had served as an infantry lieutenant in France and then returned to New York to begin a career in newspaper work. He did three wide-ranging columns a week for the New York *World*, some of which had been gathered together in *Innocent Bystanding* (1928) and *Broccoli and Old Lace* (1931). The thirty-nine-year-old Sullivan shared an apartment on East 51st Street, just off Beekman Place, with another writer, Corey Ford, ten years his junior. Ford wrote for a number of magazines, including Ross's *New Yorker* and *The Saturday Evening Post*, but he appeared regularly in *Vanity Fair* as a literary critic under the pseudonym John Riddell. One of his talents was parody, which in 1928 had produced a book called *Meaning No Offense.* Both men were represented by Ben Wasson, and he was often in their apartment.

Sullivan and Ford did not see a great deal of each other, for Ford was an early riser who kept regular hours whereas Sullivan generally stayed up late and might rise at noon. One noontime, as he affixed his pince-nez and entered the large living room, Sullivan found the dining area already occupied. "I was mystified to see a strange, gnome-like figure, his back to me, sitting at the refectory table tapping away at a typewriter. I couldn't make out who it was and went into the kitchen and in a whisper asked our housekeeper about the stranger." Mrs. Annie Moffitt was a businesslike Scotswoman who managed to preserve neatness and cleanliness in this bachelor apartment. She told Sullivan that the guest "was Mr. Faulkner and that Mr. Wasson had brought him to the apartment to use the spare typewriter." Sullivan was interested, but he did not want to disturb the guest. He fortified himself with breakfast and then introduced himself, asking if Faulkner wanted anything. He did not. He was trying to finish a story for the *Post*, and all he needed was the typewriter and the quiet and seclusion of their apartment. After a few words of brief but pleasant conversation Sullivan went out, leaving Faulkner to his work.

Mrs. Moffitt took a rather different view of this break in the normal routine. The visitor worked in his stocking feet, and, besides this, he would from time to time take a piece of paper out of the typewriter and discard it on the floor. As fast as he would do this, Annie Moffitt would disapprovingly pick the sheet up and throw it in the fireplace. "Mrs. Moffitt was probably only Tidying Up," Sullivan thought, but to Ford it seemed an expression of disapproval from the depths of her prim Scottish sense of neatness.

Faulkner saw his temporary hosts again during the New York visit, and another cordial friendship sprang up. One afternoon when he and Sullivan were having a drink, Faulkner saw a copy of *The Sound and the Fury* in their bookcase. He decided to autograph it. Sullivan struggled silently for a moment with the knowledge that the book belonged to Ford. When he told Faulkner whose it was, he still insisted on signing it, writing neatly on the flyleaf, "To my friend Frank Sullivan, this copy of Corey Ford's book is affectionately inscribed, Bill Faulkner." When Ford came home and saw it, he suspected skulduggery of some sort, Sullivan thought. "Sully would never give it back to me, either," Ford said.

It seems probable that the story Faulkner was typing up at 433 East 51st Street was entitled "Turn About." Faulkner had not only taken Lovett's story, he had taken Lovett himself. The constant figure who served as a kind of center of consciousness for the omniscient narrator was an American pilot in the RFC. Captain Bogard (in a familiar Faulknerian gesture) had the look of a Yale man, "Skull and Bones perhaps." He was also twenty-five, a bit older than Lovett when he was in France but, like him, old enough to be struck by the youth of the British torpedo boatmen with their long club scarves about their necks, and compassionate enough to be helpful rather than angry or indifferent when he saw them lying drunk in gutters.

The things Faulkner did with Lovett's story indicated his growing craftsmanship. He kept the two groups: the airmen and the torpedo boatmen. He also kept the element that had struck him most deeply: the fact that these boys were doomed, and probably knew it. They drank themselves unconscious yet behaved with the most superb kind of nonchalance and coltish grace in the constant face of death. They were dead at the story's end, yet in a dextrous strategy Faulkner managed to use the body of the story for adventure and comedy, walking a tightrope in his avoidance of farce, melodrama, and bathos. It was a symmetrical story: Captain Bogard took drunken Midshipman Claude Hope back to his aerodrome to recover; he took him along as nose gunner on a night bombing mission over Germany; Midshipman Hope took Captain Bogard on a torpedo mission into a German-held port; word was published of the loss of Hope's boat, followed by a vengeance-raid by Bogard and his crew in a style Hope would have approved. There were other balances. A bomb failed to release from under Bogard's wing; the torpedo failed to exit at first from Hope's tube. Hope vomited from airsickness, Bogard from seasickness. The contrasts were as strong as the comparisons: the enthusiastic playfulness of the English boys and the hard-bitten cynicism of the older Americans.

Faulkner obviously enjoyed another chance to do English accents. Hope's clipped speech, with its paucity of subjects and articles, might seem burlesque to an Englishman, but Faulkner was using it as a comic device (as in "Landing in Luck") and doubtless doing it as well and as authentically as he could. Once more he could use the lore of aerial combat, as in "The Lilacs" six years before. Now he was treating in prose what he had first treated in verse. His deepest feelings, however, the ones which had prompted the story, were given overt expression as Bogard dived in vengeance to bomb an enemy headquarters: "God! God! If they were all there —all the generals, the admirals, the presidents and the kings—theirs, ours —all of them." It was a sentiment Faulkner would later repeat.

It appears that he did not get the story into satisfactory shape before he left New York. Whatever the reason, it would be nearly two months before he would send "Turn About" to Ben Wasson for marketing. But Robert Lovett would be able to read it in early March of 1932 in *The Saturday Evening Post.* "It was an amazing tour de force," he thought, "and a damn good basic story."

Writing in another medium was now definitely in prospect. It may have been Wednesday, November 11, that Faulkner talked to a representative of Paramount Studios. When he wrote Estelle on Friday, the thirteenth, he was very definite. "I am writing a movie for Tallullah [*sic*] Bankhead. How's that for high? The contract is to be signed today, for about $10,000.00. Like this: yesterday I wrote the outline, the synopsis, for which I am to get $500.00. Next I will elaborate the outline and put the action in, and I get $2500.00. Then I write the dialogue and get the rest of it." Then they would probably go to Hollywood. Meanwhile, the pace in New York was accelerating.

"I have created quite a sensation," he continued. "I have had luncheons in my honor by magazine editors every day for a week now, besides evening parties, or people who want to see what I look like. In fact, I have learned with astonishment that I am now the most important figure in American letters. That is, I have the best future. Even Sinclair Lewis and Dreiser make engagements to see me, and Mencken is coming all the way up from Baltimore Wednesday. I'm glad I'm level-headed, not very vain. But I dont think it has gone to my head. Anyway, I am writing. Working on the novel, and on a short story which I think Cosmopolitan will pay me $1500.00 for. As well as the Bankhead play. That's why these letters are so short—I spend most of the time writing, you see." Cho-Cho would enjoy learning that he had sat next to Jack Oakie in a restaurant and would see Nancy Carroll next week. At a dinner party he had met Pauline Lord, who had starred in such plays as O'Neill's *Anna Christie*. She had given Faulkner a white rose and said, "I'm famous, too." There was further news on a subject he had mentioned in an earlier letter: "The play from Sanctuary is about finished. Rehearsals start next week, I hear." He had even more work in mind. Would she please send him a big envelope from his workroom? It contained some poems, and it was addressed to Harrison Smith. She should send it to him at 320 East 42nd Street.

Estelle found it a disquieting letter. The handwriting was normal but the contents were not. It did not sound like him. It was not just a matter of expressions such as "How's that for high?," which they never used, but the hectic tone and the recounting of all the varied activities. He was an intense worker when he was going at top speed, but to be almost simultaneously at work on a novel, a dramatic adaptation, a screenplay, and a short story, with a volume of poems in the offing—this was too much. It sounded as though he was headed for another collapse. He had forgotten his own hound-dog-and-wagon metaphor, and now he was paying for it. Her concern was growing. She had tried without success to reach him at the Algonquin. The hotel operator had told her that no one by that name was registered there. She did not recognize the street number given in his letter as the address of the Woodstock Towers, one of the complex of residential hotels that formed Tudor City on Manhattan's East Side. Later he would tell her that he had stayed with Stark Young for three or four days. Young lived in this neighborhood, and Faulkner may have moved from there to this new temporary residence—in the unfamiliar environment of a twenty-eighth-floor New York apartment. Estelle was still not really well enough to travel, but she might have to.

On that same day he had submitted to another interview, and a few of his comments were extreme enough to suggest that some of his normal restraints were no longer operating. The interview took place in Ben Wasson's office, where the reporter found him "a pleasant, somewhat embarrassed young man, until he gets interested in something he is saying when he speaks with assurance. He answers questions slowly, almost reluctantly, in a Southern drawl so low that he is a little difficult to understand." He submitted to a photograph, gazing directly into the lens with an annoyed expression that was almost truculent. His hair was full and his mustache neat in the thin, still youthful face.

Some of the questions turned naturally to home and the past. From his new eminence he could now look back on early and continuing hostility to himself and his work. "I was the only man I ever heard of that was black-balled from the literary society down there," he said. No one in Oxford thought he was a great man, and most of them thought he was merely lazy. The literary question elicited *Moby Dick* and *The Nigger of the Narcissus* as his favorite novels and Ernest Hemingway, whom he had never met, as his most admired colleague: "I think he's the best we've got," he said.

Then the reporter asked him about Southern Negroes. They were childlike in many of their reactions, Faulkner thought. Moreover, they would be better off "under the conditions of slavery than they are today . . . because they'd have someone to look after them." It wouldn't be better for the white man, but it would be better for them. This view would have been far from strange to the average Southerner, but it was not a particularly familiar or welcome one in the North. In the increasingly political literary climate of the 1930's, this pronouncement helped give rise to a conception of Faulkner that would be stated in stronger terms in some leftist journals as the decade wore on. As for his politics, "I vote Democratic because I'm a property owner," Faulkner said. "Self-protection."

He continued to see old friends as well as the new ones. Jim Devine was one of the old. On Sunday they might take a bus to New Jersey, or they might ride a ferry over to Hoboken. Devine would often go there with such friends as Chris Morley and Don Marquis—members of the Three Hours for Lunch Club. Hoboken was a favorite spot because the saloons were wide open. Their favorite served its own beer, and the free lunch counter featured an appetizing clam broth. There were a few theaters there, too, and the trip was a novelty. They would walk from the main part of town to the saloon, and after lunch Faulkner and Devine might shoot a game of pool. On one of these excursions Faulkner loaded up his capacious trench coat pockets with bottles of Rhine wine before they embarked again for Manhattan. He left a testimonial to these outings in a copy of *As I Lay Dying*, inscribing it "To Jim Devine/Baron of Hoboken/from his friend Bill Faulkner/Earl of Beerinstein."

The social events continued. At one, on Monday, November 16, Wili Lengel lamented the fact that he had no book of his own to give to Faulkner and inscribed to him instead a copy of *The Brothers Karamazov.* Faulkner inscribed and dated it, too. On Friday of the same week another new friend, Marc Connelly, inscribed to him a copy of his *The Green Pastures,* a successful dramatization of Roark Bradford's *Ol' Man Adam an' His Chillun.* It may have been that week that Faulkner fitted in some theatergoing, too. Paul Green took him to the Martin Beck Theatre to see his play *The House of Connelly.* Faulkner remained silent throughout, but as they emerged he said, "Do you want to see the structure of your play?" When Green replied that he did, Faulkner walked out onto the sidewalk, took a pencil from his pocket, and approached the front wall of the theater. "I was apprehensive," Green said, "for in those days you never could tell what he would do. . . . He drew a queer geometrical figure, saying that was the shape and meaning of it. And that was all."

As they walked Faulkner told Green that he was doing a play himself, a dramatization of *Sanctuary.* "And more than that, when it's produced, I'm going to act in it."

"What part are you going to play?" Green asked.

"The corncob," Faulkner answered, laughing.

"You'll bring down the house," said Green.

Faulkner had another surprise for his companion. "Wait a minute," he said, and turned into a florist's shop. He emerged with a bunch of roses which he handed to the astonished Green, who began to blush. "What's this for, Bill? I'm not a girl," he said.

"I just thought you might like some roses," Faulkner answered, perhaps remembering Pauline Lord.

Faulkner had told George Oppenheimer that he wanted to see *Earl Carroll's Vanities*, for he was particularly anxious to see the show's staging of Ravel's *Bolero.* Oppenheimer got two tickets. Unlike his reaction to *The House of Connelly*, Faulkner's response to the *Vanities* was immediate.

"This is too soft," he said to Oppenheimer in a clearly audible voice.

He repeated the comment periodically, with gradually increasing volume.

"Bill, I'm going home if you don't quiet down," whispered the embarrassed Oppenheimer. When Faulkner continued undeterred, Oppenheimer slipped out of his seat and departed.

The next morning his phone rang. It was Faulkner. "The *Bolero* was too soft," he explained. It seemed like a penitential phone call, a gesture of apology made in Faulkner's usual indirect style.

The longer he stayed in New York, the more writers he met. A number of them he liked. One was Nathanael West, a tall, dark, mustachioed man who was manager of the Hotel Sutton. Deriving some security, perhaps, from the fact that the hotel's owner was a relative, West would let writers stay free if they were in financial difficulties. He would divert himself from the uncongenial work by "snooping around the lives of the other rather strange guests," but what he wanted most was to write. His first book, published in 1931, was a fantastic novel called *The Dream Life of Balso Snell*, which appeared only to vanish almost without a sound. Though a sad and gentle man, West was a fanatical hunter, spending money on guns and hunting gear he could scarcely afford. He loved talking hunting rather than books, a quality which Faulkner must have found agreeable.

Two friends of West whom Faulkner seems to have got on with even better were also writers: Lillian Hellman and Dashiell Hammett, both Southerners. Three years older than Faulkner, Hammett had been born on the Eastern Shore of Maryland. His description of his French ancestors alone might have endeared him to Faulkner: "they fought in every war and never won." He had engaged in more occupations than Faulkner himself had claimed: newsboy, freight clerk, laborer, and stevedore. One other must have interested the writer of "Smoke." Hammett had been for eight years a Pinkerton detective. Turning to fiction, he had done poems for *The Smart Set* and stories for the *Post* before finding his métier in detective novels. With books such as *The Maltese Falcon* (1930) and *The Glass Key* (1931), Hammett was a leader of a school of detective-story writing in which the stories were realistic and the detectives were tough, even brutal. There was violence coupled with psychological character study—something which would appeal to Faulkner as both the author of "The Hound" and the creator of Joe Christmas. Hammett, for his part, wanted most to write plays and "straight" novels rather than detective fiction.

This tall, thin, elegant man with the neat mustache had worked a profound change in the life of New Orleans-born Lillian Hellman. He had encouraged Lily Hellman in her ambition to become a playwright, and she had quickly fallen in love with him. As yet only a few of her short stories had sold, but she was working at others and on a play with Louis Kronenberger. Once she had worked for Horace Liveright. Later she had been a sympathetic reviewer of Faulkner's fiction, and she felt that they understood each other. Their relationship was an easy one, Faulkner usually addressing her as "Miss Lillian." Faulkner and Dash Hammett seemed to have taken an immediate liking to each other. Hammett always stayed at the Elysee Hotel at 54th Street, and Faulkner visited him there on two or three occasions. These were long evenings of drinking and talking, and in the morning Faulkner might still be there asleep on the couch. Hammett was a heavy drinker for whom a five-day bout was not unusual. But there was much conversation on those evenings, and much of it was literary. Faulkner, Lily thought, talked very well about books.

Hammett "read everything and anything," she remembered. "He didn't like writers very much, he didn't like or dislike most people, but he was without envy of good writers and was tender about all writers, probably because he remembered his own early struggles." Faulkner was one of the writers he admired. When Faulkner said that *Sanctuary* was a potboiler written to make money, Hammett replied, "That's not so, a good writer doesn't write for money." They had a polite argument about it. There was one protracted disagreement, though, which found Lily siding with Faulkner and which turned violent and nasty before it ended. It was about *The Magic Mountain.* Speaking out of his long experience in army tuberculosis hospitals, Dash had said the book was not the truth, and besides Mann was long-winded. Lily thought that politics may somehow have gotten into the discussion, for Hammett was a confirmed Marxist and Faulkner very antiradical. Apparently the effects were short-lived, however, for there were stronger affinities. Hammett had "a deep feeling for isolated places where there were animals, birds, bugs, and sounds." He was a woodsman and a hunter, too. These qualities could more than compensate for a literary disagreement. The men continued to enjoy each other's company at the same time that they presented difficulties to others.

One afternoon they were finishing lunch with Bennett Cerf at Jack Kriendler and Charlie Burns's club at 21 West 52nd Street. As Cerf prepared to leave, the two began to bait him.

"Where are you going?" Hammett asked.

"Back to work," Cerf answered.

"What are you going to do after that?"

"I'm going to dinner at the Knopfs'," Cerf told them. "Willa Cather and Serge Koussevitzky are going to be there."

Hammett looked at Faulkner and then back at Cerf. "We want to go too," he said. "I'm a Knopf author."

Both writers were in tweeds. Cerf told them that it was black tie and that he would call Blanche Knopf—her husband was out of town—and come by for them at seven o'clock. "Oh, where should I pick you up?" he asked.

"Right here," one of them answered.

True to his word, Cerf called his competition. Blanche Knopf had not met Faulkner yet, and she was delighted at the chance to extend the celebrated Knopf hospitality to him as well as to one of their own authors. She did not know, of course, that both men had spent the entire afternoon at Jack and Charlie's. When Cerf returned for them, he tried to dissuade them from going. For one thing, he said, they had not changed. They didn't want to arrive at a party in tweeds with all the other men in tuxedos, did they? They did not care, they assured him; in fact, they insisted on going. He saw there was nothing he could do but read them a lecture on behaving themselves.

At the Knopfs' elegant apartment they were introduced to the other guests, among whom was editor H. L. Mencken. They were quiet, almost decorous, giving polite short answers to their neighbors and from time to time taking glasses from trays offered them by the butler. Hammett was the first to alter his position. He slid quietly off the couch onto the floor and passed out. There was a sudden flurry about his six-foot frame. To some observers Faulkner seemed perfectly sober. But now, as he rose to his feet and announced his departure, he too collapsed. As Hammett was lifted from the floor, Faulkner was helped back to his seat on the couch, where he once more appeared to be in control. Hammett was no sooner removed to a place of recuperation than Faulkner once more rose to announce his departure and subsided onto the carpet. Eventually Ben Wasson and others helped him also to make his exit from the social arena.

This mishap did not deter Cerf from planning a similar gathering at his bachelor apartment at the Navarro overlooking Central Park South. Alfred Knopf told Cerf he would love to meet Faulkner. The ruddy, mustachioed publisher arrived after dinner, bringing with him half a dozen Faulkner first editions. Later in the evening he picked them up and brought them to the author.

"Mr. Faulkner," he said, "I had to go all up and down Sixth Avenue this afternoon to get these books. Most of them are out of print, you know. I wonder if you'd inscribe them for me."

Faulkner looked at them consideringly. "You know, Mr. Knopf," he finally said, "people stop me on the street and in elevators and ask me to sign books, but I can't afford to do this because special signed editions are a part of my stock-in-trade. Aside from that, I only sign books for my friends."

Cerf quickly interposed. "Bill," he said, "Mr. Knopf is a very distinguished man and he's a great admirer of your work."

"Well," Faulkner said, after thinking awhile, "Mrs. Knopf has been very kind to me, so if you want to pick out one of them, I'll inscribe it for you."

Ben Wasson had overheard the interchange and felt that the situation showed signs of deteriorating. He told Cerf that Faulkner wanted to see Harlem. Novelist and critic Carl Van Vechten agreed to take him there—now. Van Vechten had written about Harlem and had several friends who lived there. Ben went along on the hastily organized trip and brought with him a girl named Tiah Devitt, whom Faulkner liked, and who was working on a book which would be published the next year under the title *The Aspirin Age.* Van Vechten knew Harlem well and steered his small group to a number of places. The last was called Gladys's. By now a young Negro man who was a special friend of Van Vechten's had joined them. Gladys proved to be an enormous black woman who wore a dinner jacket. She also helped with the entertainment and began one of her specialties, a "blue" version of the song "Sweet Violets." Faulkner listened with disgust and then rose and left. His evening was at an end.

Accounts of both parties spread quickly. Edith Haggard heard about the latter from Hal Smith. The story apparently gave pleasure to some who felt no particular fondness for the milieu in which Faulkner and Hammett were moving. This was the kind of iconoclasm or temperament—some would call it rudeness—which Faulkner would add to the quickly growing body of Faulkner lore.

If his capacity was unusual, so were his recuperative powers. During the mornings at the Woodstock Towers he kept on with *Light in August,* and by November 25 he had completed his introduction for the Modern Library edition of *Sanctuary*—a sardonic 750-word piece in which he repeated the line he had taken with Lily Hellman and Dash Hammett. It was a piece which showed actual contempt for the reader. He repeated his account of the composition of *The Sound and the Fury* and *As I Lay Dying.* He wrote *Sanctuary* to make money, he said, and then rewrote it for aesthetic reasons. Then it occurred to him that "maybe 10,000 of them" would buy it. "I made a fair job," he said of the revision, "and I hope you will buy it and tell your friends and I hope they will buy it too." Faulkner would receive $100 for the introduction. The next day Ben would receive $200 for Faulkner now that both parties had agreed to the terms of Random House's publication of "Idyll in the Desert." On December 8, the tentative publication date, he would receive $200 more.

Returning to intensive work on the novel, he regretted his gesture in leaving a segment of it for *Contempo* in Chapel Hill. He finally wrote to Abernethy and asked for it back. For one thing, it was not finished work; for another, he needed it for reference as he wrote. In his letter he promised that they could have something else to replace it. To his great relief, the pages were returned.

Alone in the apartment, he might work through lunch or go out with a few friends. On occasion he lunched with Hal Smith and Manuel Komroff. They would meet on the steps of the New York Library and then go to a restaurant they liked on 44th Street. Komroff remembered that once Faulkner talked about Alabama and the aftermath of her death, when he fired at the doctor but missed him. The lunch hour ended in a nearby store. Faulkner had lost his hat and Smith had offered to buy him one. When they left, Komroff remembered, Faulkner was wearing a light-colored headpiece that resembled a sombrero.

There was no mention of the hat in an interview which appeared in the "Talk of the Town" section of *The New Yorker* on Saturday, November 28. He was spending most of his days working alone in the Tudor City apartment on *Light in August*, he said, which was about a quarter done. Around the middle of December he expected to return home, where only a few people at all knew he was a writer. His mother read every line he wrote, he said, but his father didn't bother and suspected that his son was wasting his time. Faulkner had recourse again to fiction, borrowing in one instance, it seemed, from Bob Jeyfus in the unpublished "Love." Like him, he had been shot down in France. The crash had left him hanging upside down in the cockpit with two broken legs and enough strength to correct the ambulance men's conclusion that he was dead. He was flying again, however, and though his course might be wobbly, he had earned a pilot's license. When the reporter asked him when he wrote, he gave an answer that would sound to some younger writers like an aphorism or rule of the craft. " 'Ah write when the spirit moves me,' he [said], 'and the spirit moves me every day.' "

The social activities went on, but then Ben did not see his friend and client for two or three days. Neither did anyone else, apparently. After a time the city would always close in on him. He once wrote Phil Stone that he "felt sorry for all these millions of people here because they dont live in Oxford." Jim Devine remembered times when Faulkner would simply get on a commuters' train to Connecticut. At some station which had woods nearby, he would get off and walk there in the cool.

His friends became used to these disappearances, but then one of them lengthened into several days. Louise Bonino was worried. So were Lenore Marshall and Hal Smith. The new firm, Harrison Smith, Inc., had just been announced, but Smith took the time to go out searching. They found Faulkner, according to Lenore, not in Tudor City but at the Hotel Algonquin. She and Smith sat and had a drink with him. He seemed agitated, emotionally upset. By midnight he still showed no signs of retiring, and he did not want to be left alone. He decided that he ought to replenish the whiskey.

"No, don't do that," Lenore said. "Why don't you try to get some sleep."

Faulkner was courteous but adamant, seeing insomnia ahead, or worse. "Lenore, what would *you* do if you woke up at three o'clock in the morning and found that there was no whiskey?"

The three of them took a cab to a speak-easy at West 52nd Street and 9th Avenue. The place was set among sinister-looking tenements and the patrons were frightening, some of them looking to Lenore as though they were carrying guns. When the drinks came they smelled so strong that Smith whispered that they shouldn't touch them and hurriedly paid the bill. At the hatcheck counter the girl protested at Smith's ordinary tip. He fished a dollar out of his pocket and dropped it on the counter so that they could get out quickly without an incident. After a search they managed to procure some whiskey and dropped Faulkner at the Algonquin. Smith got hold of Ben Wasson, who wired Estelle. Could she come to New York, he asked, as soon as possible?

On Monday, November 30, Estelle traveled to Memphis. There, while she waited for the train, she granted an interview Marshall Smith had requested. He described her now as a young woman with reddish-brown hair and friendly eyes. "She is slender; an animated, vivid person," he wrote.

She said she was going to New York to keep people away from her husband. He was busy working on the scenario for Tallulah Bankhead, who had been a student at Mary Baldwin when she was there. They would return to Oxford for Christmas and then perhaps go to California in the spring if the picture material developed. Inevitably, the question of *Sanctuary* came up. Did she understand it, Smith wanted to know. Not the first time, she answered. But when they had been on their honeymoon, Faulkner had given her Joyce's *Ulysses* to read. It didn't make sense to her, and he told her to read it again. Then she reread *Sanctuary*, and with *Ulysses* as a background, she understood it, she said.

At approximately the same time in New York, her husband was writing a letter. In a mood of penitence he was addressing James Southall Wilson at the University of Virginia, five weeks after the fact. He thanked Wilson for the hospitality and asked him to convey his apologies to anyone he might have offended.

When the Memphis Special stopped in Charlottesville, Virginia, Tuesday night, the porter handed Estelle a telegram. It read, RECEPTION COMMITTEE WILL MEET TRAIN TOMORROW MORNING HURRAY. It was signed THE COMMITTEE. This did nothing to allay her anxieties. Upon arriving in New York, she was met by Ben Wasson, Harold Guinzburg, and her husband. One look told her that her fears had been justified. They went directly to the Algonquin. With the effects of the train trip on top of the persistent anemia, she felt like going straight to bed, but Faulkner immediately excused himself. So did Ben, leaving her with Harold Guinzburg, a charming man but a complete stranger. He invited them to lunch, and she thanked him but declined. He invited them for dinner the next night, and she tentatively accepted. Later she learned from her husband that they had a prior invitation from Hal Smith and that his wife Claire was making bouillabaisse for them. This quickly emerged as the pattern of her stay in New York: trying to keep invitations sorted out, declining as many as possible without offending. They were still being wooed. They would go to dinners where it seemed to her the others were hanging on every word Faulkner uttered. There was a considerable amount of fending-off to do. He had had just about as much of this kind of pressure as he could take, Faulkner told his wife.

The celebrity and affection which the Hotel Algonquin had come to enjoy was primarily the work of Frank Case, a large-nosed, deep-eyed, balding man with a small mustache and prominent chin. He had a special feeling for actors, writers, and celebrities in the arts, and he did his best to make them welcome and comfortable at 59 West 44th Street. "I think that gifted people not only should be tolerated but should be encouraged in their strange and temperamental antics," he wrote, "and I have hewed to that line during all my years at the Algonquin." It was not a large hotel or a luxurious one, but it had a great deal of warmth and a charm that made its guests feel at home, made them even feel something like fondness over its inconveniences and eccentricities. "The Algonquin lobby," wrote Case's daughter, "always unpretentious even at the height of its fame, had a small, warm, jewel-like quality—an affair of lamplight and deep colors. Its one passenger elevator generally had four or five people waiting for it, and they were often such a mixed bag as H. L. Mencken, Fanny Brice, Marilyn Miller, and Commander Evangeline Booth of the Salvation Army." The celebrated gatherings at the Round Table had begun in 1918 with the return of Alexander Woollcott from the war. For more than ten years thereafter many witty and talented writers made it their favorite eating place: Heywood Broun, Robert Benchley, Franklin P. Adams, Robert Sherwood, George Kaufman, Marc Connelly, Laurence Stallings, and, sometimes, Dorothy Parker. Yet they had more in common than wit and talent. One quality was a loathing of pretense and hypocrisy coupled with the kind of gadfly impulse about American culture which Mencken demonstrated at his peak. The Round Table had begun when few of them were very well known. Over the years most of them had moved, but they would occasionally return to "the Algonk" after the table no longer regularly met.

Dorothy Parker was living there still. So was Peter Arno, the cartoonist, who asked Estelle up to his room for a drink, to her husband's considerable annoyance. Estelle declined and went shopping with Dorothy Parker. The Faulkners would often see Benchley and Frank Sullivan, both of whom Estelle immediately liked a great deal. There was no telling who might appear for the impromptu parties. John Dos Passos remembered going to the Algonquin with Donald Ogden Stewart. "It was one of those drunken evenings with all sorts of characters popping in and out of bedrooms. Mrs. Faulkner was there, looking very deep Mississippi and thoroughly unperturbed. I remember wondering how she stood all these goings-on." Frank Case was the accommodating host, moving a piano into the Faulkner suite so she could play if she liked. According to Case's daughter, Faulkner's work was not to Case's taste, but he liked the man, and there was no denying his status as a literary celebrity. Random House had announced for Decem-

William and Estelle Faulkner in the front parlor, Rowan Oak.

ber 15 the limited signed edition of "Idyll in the Desert." One of the New York papers reported this announcement with a six-by-four-inch drawing done of Faulkner "from life" by a staff artist. Above the sketch was the legend "A New Centre of Literary Gravity."

Faulkner had to stay in New York to sign the sheets. Meanwhile, Marc Connelly and his wife took the Faulkners out to dinner. They were asked out by Alfred Dashiell and his wife. They were invited to the Lovetts', where Estelle was struck by the gorgeous apartment and the way the shades of blue and crystal set off Mrs. Lovett's blond beauty. Her response to Bob Lovett was just as warm as her husband's. Ben gave a party for them at the Algonquin, and the Faulkners gave a small party for some of the people who had entertained them. The publication of the book was advanced to December 10, and that night Bennett Cerf gave a farewell party for them. Estelle, the only lady present, grew bored with the talk of books and publishing, and went into the next room to read. Soon Cerf, the gallant host, noted her absence. He found her, put a record on the phonograph, and asked her to dance. They danced for a long time before she and her husband returned to the Algonquin. There they finished packing, including two of Faulkner's latest acquisitions—inscribed books from Conrad Aiken and Philip Barry.

They took the train south with considerable relief, although they were not going directly home. Having accepted an invitation from Mencken, they stopped in Baltimore, where the editor came to their hotel. They had dinner together, at which Estelle found that she did not particularly care for him; he seemed crude to her. She retired and the two men went out together for what turned into an evening of hard drinking. Before they left on Saturday, Faulkner saw Mencken again with an eye to future short-story prospects. By Monday, December 14, they were probably back in Oxford. Faulkner had been away from home almost exactly eight weeks.

Some of Faulkner's friends felt that he left home periodically to renew himself. The interval before he traveled again would be shorter than the previous three-year stretch. On Friday, December 18, Leland Hayward received a telegram at the American Play Company offices from Culver City, California. It read, DID YOU MENTION WILLIAM FAULKNER TO ME ON YOUR LAST TRIP HERE. IF SO IS HE AVAILABLE AND HOW MUCH. BEST REGARDS. It was signed by Sam Marx, of Metro-Goldwyn-Mayer Studios.

36

December, 1931-May, 1932

> We crossed the street toward home. And do you know what I thought? I thought *It hasn't even changed.* Because it should have. It should have been altered, even if only a little. I dont mean it should have changed of itself, but that I, bringing back to it what . . . must have changed in me, should have altered it.
>
> —*The Reivers* (299)

After two months' absence Faulkner would have noted little change. No faculty salaries had been paid at the university since the previous July, and it would be nearly a year before payment would be resumed. The liquidating agent for the defunct Guarantee Bank and Trust Company was still unable to pay anything to its depositors and stockholders. Most people were feeling the full effects of the Depression. The Oxford Beverage Company had defaulted on its bank loan, and now Phil Stone was selling the items the Oldhams had offered as security: the defunct company's equipment plus a store and a lot. Nor was that an isolated misfortune. The Tishomingo gravel pits at Iuka had failed, and Lem Oldham was among the several Oxford investors who felt that blow. There were other kinds of losses, some of them signs of the times. Deaths from automobile crashes now seemed to outnumber those from skirmishes at stills and "difficulties" between hot-blooded neighbors.

Faulkner was home only a few days when he resumed his campaign for short-story sales. No matter how interested Sam Marx was in him as a potential scriptwriter, Faulkner had to think of meeting past and current bills now, if he could. "Home again where it is quiet," he wrote Alfred Dashiell in mid-December. "The novel is going fine." What he wanted to know was, did Dashiell have a story of his called "Smoke"? Yes, he did, and they were regretfully returning it to Ben—a bit "too long and leisurely" when they were jammed up with fiction. But "Death-Drag" was in the January number of *Scribner's*, and his name was being kept before the public in other ways, too, for the interviews continued.

Louis Cochran, who had once asked him to draw for *Ole Miss*, now asked him for an interview. He drove up from Jackson on Sunday, December 20, and found him in work clothes doing some carpentry. Faulkner talked about the trip to New York. Cochran gathered "that he had attended some rather fatuous literary parties and that he did not like them; that he had never been so tired of literary people in his life." New York was a place "where everybody talks about what they are going to write and no one writes anything." As they sat on the front steps, Faulkner said Cochran knew him, and whatever he wrote would be all right. He might talk to Stone if he liked. While remaining cordial, Faulkner had in effect avoided another interview. But before Cochran left, Faulkner told him he would write Harrison Smith about the novel Cochran was writing—a promise he kept.

Cochran walked to Stone's office just off the Square and spent an hour there. He talked with others and found that Faulkner had not been forgiven for *Sanctuary*. One young woman said she would never speak to him again. Another sometime friend declared to Cochran, "I would rather have my right arm torn from the stump than have my name signed to that filth." But Cochran had read each of the novels with enthusiasm as they had come out. "When you and I are not remembered by our grandchildren," he replied half in jest, "people will come to study William Faulkner at the University of Mississippi." The other refused to take it in jest. He was furious.

The account Cochran wrote when he returned to Jackson was sympathetic. He warmly described Faulkner's background, career, and even his appearance: "he has the delicate step and waist line of a girl. His eyes are a soft, luminous brown; his hair, darkly of the same tint, is thick and more often tousled than otherwise. A thin face, wide forehead and high cheek bones complete a countenance that is at once remotely aloof and sensitive to every living thing." Whereas Granville Hicks had compared Faulkner to two writers whom Hicks did not particularly admire—Ambrose Bierce and Edgar Allan Poe—Cochran thought of Mark Twain perhaps smiling with foreknowledge at the coming of "a spirit who can fill and broaden the Master's shoes!"

The following Wednesday, Cochran sent his draft of the article to Stone, who replied in five typed pages covering twenty-two specific points. The letter said as much about Stone as it did about Faulkner. It also revealed something of the changing relationship between the two men. They still saw each other and Stone still took an intense interest in Faulkner's career. Genuine affection was still there: "As I told you, he is the most normal, the sanest man I have ever known." There was understanding: the reason for Faulkner's dislike of literary talk was "a natural weariness after writing about 5,000 words every day." Then the pride and possessiveness came through. He had trained Faulkner for years, he said, and he had been a poet not of his own ambition but because "it was my ambition for him to be one." Stone was jocular about any writing of his own: "if I have to write what good is Bill to me?" There was disaffection, too, some of it stemming from the disagreement about subject matter which Faulkner had mentioned to Tom Kell nearly five years before. Stone agreed with Cochran that Faulkner certainly had his roots in the soil. "My present discouragement about him is as to whether or not this part of him will ever be articulate in prose." He suggested that Cochran might analyze some of his one-time protégé's shortcomings: "I think you should also mention the fact that some of the disagreeable things in Bill's published novels are due, at least to my idea, to that strange sensitive blindness which he has in spots and are really for this reason lapses of [literary] taste." As for what he had been writing, "my present discouragement is due to the fact that Bill has not yet come out of this adolescent groove." Cochran revised the piece and sent it out to *The Virginia Quarterly Review*, which rejected it as unscholarly.

Meanwhile, Marshall J. Smith had expanded the notes of his earlier interview into a seven-page piece which appeared in the December number of *The Bookman.* Also included were eight photographs Smith took of Faulkner, his home, and his town. Faulkner might claim he was virtually unknown to most of his fellow Oxonians, but he could certainly not say the same about followers of contemporary fiction.

Just before Christmas, literary concerns intruded in another way when a letter arrived from Anthony Buttitta. He was visiting his family in New Orleans and wondered if he could see Faulkner on his way back to North Carolina. "I told him all right," Faulkner later wrote Ben Wasson. "I thought it would be a good time to give him some stuff. It was the promise to him I was keeping, as I was sure it was Buttitta who got the other stuff from Abernathy [*sic*]." Again Faulkner had gotten himself into a series of predicaments, and now his promissory notes were coming due.

Christmas passed quietly with the usual family celebrations. They had sent more Christmas cards this year—to Frank Sullivan and other new friends in New York—and more presents—a robe to Ben recalling his hospitality there. And there were visitors off and on, friends such as Tom Kell, and Roark and Mary Rose Bradford. If Faulkner did any work, it was probably on a project that was now almost like a hobby, arranging poems for the volume he had once tentatively entitled *The Greening Bough.* He had carefully ordered the poems for a definite effect. "This is a fair sized book now," he wrote Smith, "and the stuff does not seem so bad, on rereading. I wish you would let the blank pages remain in, as they supply some demarcation between separate and distinct moods and methods—provided such terms can be used in respect to 2nd class poetry which this is. But worse has been published. . . . Let me know what you think about it, also a name. I reckon 'Poems' will do." As for the novel, it was coming along well, a thousand to fifteen hundred words every day and three thousand the past Thursday. He closed with a request for the advance on the novel Smith had promised him and with New Year's greetings.

Then, in the rainy days of early January, Anthony Buttitta arrived. "I will warn you," Faulkner had written him, "that I am trying to finish my novel, and so I am going to let you entertain yourself during the forenoons. But in the afternoons and evenings we can get together." Buttitta's misgivings about his reception were soon allayed. "In many more ways than I had expected, Bill turned out to be something of a conventional Southern host. He went out of his way to see that I was comfortable, apologizing for the dilapidated appearance of his big, two-story plantation house which is over a hundred years old. At the time, it needed a fresh coat of paint pretty badly; the plaster was cracked on the walls and ceilings, the wainscoting was streaked and dry with age." When Faulkner admitted Buttitta to his workroom, he found it "in quite a mess." He sat there while Faulkner worked, a tall waterglass of what Buttitta took to be corn whiskey on his writing desk. "A big, half opened wooden box full of bound manuscripts was on the floor in the middle of the room. Looking through it, I discovered original and carbon copies of his earlier novels. On the mantel over the fireplace, I remember seeing copies of his books, from 'The Marble Faun' to his latest, 'Sanctuary,' between two small bookends. Hunting and fishing togs hung on pegs in the right wall, with rifles and rods nearby. Alongside his writing table was a large cardboard file in which over a hundred short stories—many rejected and paperclip-stained—waited to be pulled out, edited, retyped, and mailed to the magazines." On the desk was a small portable phonograph. He had worn out three records of Gershwin's "Rhapsody in Blue," Buttitta remembered his telling him, playing it to help him "set the rhythm and jazzy tone" of *Sanctuary.*

One afternoon, Buttitta said, Faulkner took him out for a walk. As they rounded a bend, Faulkner pointed ahead. It was the road Lena Grove had traveled, "looking for the father of her child." They stopped before an old barn: "That's where Popeye came to life." He indicated a stream: "That's where the folks dropped the coffin in *As I Lay Dying*" Current work was clearly much on his mind. By now he was absorbed in the odyssey of Joe Christmas. He pointed southeast toward Frenchman's Bend. That, he said, "is where Christmas hid for a while from those white folks that were after him." This was apparently another kind of hospitality the host was offering his guest. Popeye had come alive much earlier, and in a Memphis setting, as "The Big Shot" demonstrated. But Faulkner obviously knew how much pleasure such a tour—factually accurate or not—would give the young man who had been one of his hosts in Chapel Hill. Before Buttitta left Rowan Oak, Faulkner told him to take what he wanted from among the rejected manuscripts. He chose one story and ten poems, enough to fill three of the magazine's four tabloid-size pages.

Even before Buttitta had left Oxford, however, there were repercussions from this project and another as well. On January 4, 1932, Bennett Cerf had sent an inquiry to Philip C. Duschnes, a book dealer and noted book expert. Duschnes had sent Cerf a card advertising *Salmagundi*, by William Faulkner, to be published by the Casanova Press of Milwaukee. *Salmagundi*, Duschnes replied, was to be a 500-copy limited edition with a portrait of Faulkner, selling at $2.50 each. He solicited Cerf's order for *Light in August*, which he said was due that spring. Instead, Cerf ordered two copies of *Light in August* from Hal Smith and asked again what *Salmagundi* was. Smith replied that he had first learned about it when he read a piece in the *World-Telegram*, and all he knew about *Salmagundi* was that Casanova was publishing two editions, one signed and one numbered. "I have no idea what this is and am writing Bill about it. I like the idea of your limited edition of his short story but think he must be very cautious not to scatter himself around too much. His admirers should get up a committee to stop it. Thank God he is in Oxford and away from temptation." But before Smith could write to Faulkner, he apparently received a letter from him about the poems and the story *Contempo* now had. Faulkner was probably concerned lest there be any conflict with the book of verse Smith had agreed to bring out. On January 13 Smith replied in a letter designed to reassure Faulkner and bring him up short at the same time.

There was no harm in letting *Contempo* print what they now had. What bothered Smith was Abernethy's recent declaration that he would like to print a limited edition of Faulkner's verse. "That must absolutely be stopped and I have written him telling him so. You really should be more careful about these little odds and ends of limited editions. . . . you will kill the goose that is going to lay some more golden eggs if your good nature gets the better of you with these little concerns." The Random House *Idyll in the Desert* was all right, but Smith was concerned about the publication of *Salmagundi.* "Again this is probably all right if you got enough money for it, but if it was just a careless gift, that ought to be stopped too if possible. This limited edition business is a most interesting racket but it should be handled with great care. What is SALMAGUNDI anyhow, and do you want me to write to the Casanova outfit about it?" If anybody was to do a collection of Faulkner poems and essays, it ought to be Smith's firm, with Harcourt, Brace distribution, or Random House. Smith was regretful. He wished that Ben had been with Faulkner rather than Abernethy. Smith had enlisted Abernethy to keep Faulkner away from Knopf, Guinzburg, and Cerf, and now it appeared that Smith should have lumped Abernethy with them. "But considering everything," he concluded, "and especially that it probably won't happen again, you came out of your New York visit with colors flying. We'll send Abernethy and his partner a bomb, or a ham sandwich filled with arsenic if they get in your way."

Faulkner reacted immediately to Smith's letter. He wired Buttitta to go ahead with the story he had chosen, "Once Aboard the Lugger," but to send the verse back so he could take out what would be included in the book Smith was going to publish. An answer came from Abernethy: Buttitta was in New York, and the Faulkner issue of *Contempo* had already gone to press. Faulkner sent a note off to Smith that was a mixture of contrition and anger. "I'm sorry. I didn't realize at the time what I had got into. Goddam the paper and goddam me for getting mixed up with it and goddam you for sending me off with that pirate in the shape I was in. I dont think it will happen again. But if I should do so, for God's sake find Ben and turn me on to him next time, for your sake and mine too." As an afterthought he added, "He has one bum short story and some verse. I dont know if any of the verse is in the batch you have or not."

A few days later he wrote to Wasson in some agitation, trying to explain now to him how he had gotten himself into this predicament. "You know the state I seem to get into when people come to see me and I begin to visualise a kind of jail corridor of literary talk. I dont know what in hell it is, except I seem to lose all perspective and do things, like a coon in a tree. As long as they dont bother the hand full of leaves in front of his face, they can cut the whole tree down and haul it off." This was why he had given Buttitta the story and his choice of some verse. "Still running, you see. Trying to stay there and run at the same time. When he said he had what he wanted, I was just thinking Thank God that's over, I suppose. I didn't look at what he chose at all. Some of it may be ones which Hal is going to publish. I dont know. I also remember now (still trying to run and still trying to be host) his talking about a complete F. issue of his paper. I was just saying Yes. Yes., not thinking at all. And when he was gone, I was still just breathing free, thinking I was rid of the whole thing at last." But the day before he had received "a howl" from Hal. Now he needed advice from Wasson as both agent and friend.

"Anyway," he wrote, after his recital of the events, "I am all worried about it again. What do you think? Should we try to stop the paper, until I can straighten them out? I want Buttitta to have something of mine, since I promised and he seems to want it. But I didn't intend to have them actually get out what amounts to a de luxe edition of W.F. Can they be held up? Or is Hal just jealous? If it is best to hold them up, and it can be done, go ahead and do it. I'll pay the costs, of course. If you can get in touch with Buttitta in New York . . . he is reasonable. He wont lie, anyway. Or if I had better go to Chapel Hill myself, I'll do that. Anyway, I want to get completely rid of it. I have already wasted ten novel chapters of energy and worry over that godddamn [*sic*] paper. I am writing Hal today." He damned himself and Smith again for the fix they were in. "In a way," he added, "it serves him right."

He didn't know if the situation was as serious as Hal had said. "But anyway, my country innocence has been taken advantage of. Which is no one's fault except mine, of course. I think I am madder at that than I am at the financial part of it. So you do what is best, or possible. And I solemnly swear that after this I'll never promise anyone anything without first asking your permission." He closed on a familiar note in the postscript: "Do you see any money for me soon? I want to take some insurance. Can get a good rate if within next two weeks."

Now he tried to explain to Smith about *Salmagundi.* "For about a year I had been receiving book lists and telegrams and letters of praise from Casanova Book Shop, Milwaukee. Last winter, right after Xmas, I had a letter from the man asking permission to reprint some things which were published in a New Orleans magazine in '24. He may have said in book form. I dont know. I realise now how inexperienced or how careless I was. I even forget the sum he named. I told him, all right. At that time (*Sanctuary* not yet out) I was not selling short stories even." Later Paul Romaine, Casanova's proprietor, had written Faulkner again asking to include two magazine stories. He refused. Then Romaine wrote asking Faulkner to sign some of the copies. Again he refused. Romaine had his permission for the original project, he wrote to Smith, but that was all. Unfortunately, Faulkner had no copies of any of the correspondence. He was penitent. "Carelessness. But never again. I will never make any agreements about my stuff hereafter without letting you know. But at that time, like the Contempo business, I didn't realise that I had a commercial value, since it was stuff which I had been starving to write for several years. But I have learned my lesson now, and these two instances are all my mistakes. I learned a whole lot during my visit in New York. And what Contempo has is pretty poor stuff generally. Though there may be a few of the poems included which are in your lot. They worried me and worried me until I gave Buttitta a batch of verse and told him to take what he wanted. I didn't look at what he chose, having a certain faith in the infallibility of his poetic judgment. i.e., I believed that he would pick the bum ones without my help."

Smith wrote the Casanova Book Shop and Faulkner wrote Buttitta. As things had turned out, though, none of the annoyance, anxiety, or letters had any effect on the content of either *Contempo* or *Salmagundi.* The former had appeared on February 1. It contained the story and nine of the ten poems Buttitta had taken, as well as reviews of *These 13* and *Idyll in the Desert.* In the latter review Buttitta wrote, "Bill Faulkner told us that he had a peculiar attachment for 'That Evening Sun,' 'Hair,' and 'All the Dead Pilots.' Asked about *Idyll in the Desert,* Bill assured us that it was just another story." He was, claimed Buttitta, America's "most creative, most original and most potential writer. . . ." Smith tried to reassure

Faulkner: "Some people like the verse in Contempo enormously, so it did not turn out so badly." When Faulkner received his author's copies he wrote Buttitta a note; he was glad the issue pleased him. Now he could relax for a bit about special editions. *Salmagundi* would not appear for another three months.

He was free once more to channel his energy back into *Light in August.* And Ben had wired that there would be some money. In the same wire Ben had asked for the novel. Smith was eager to have it, too. "The bookstores are biting for the first edition of *Light in August* like fish on a rainy day," he had written. But both men would have to wait. "I cant send you Light in August," Faulkner told Ben, "because none of it is typed yet. I had not intended typing at all until I finished it. It is going too well to break the thread and cast back, unless absolutely necessary. But I may strike a stale spell. Then I will type some." Ben's wire had apparently introduced another distraction: a generous offer from Hollywood. Faulkner thought Estelle would want him to take it, but he was not anxious to. "I will be better off here until this novel is finished. Maybe I can try the movies later on."

He needed money again sooner than he had thought. For one thing, the renovation of Rowan Oak was a continuing expense—there were hand-hammered locks on the doors and soon there would be new draperies. Since he had ruled out Hollywood for the present, there was only one source he could turn to: Hal Smith. How much, Smith asked, could he manage with? "$250.00 will stave me off for the time," Faulkner answered. "Send it on. Sorry to bother you right now, when you are cluttered up yourself with overhead instead of revenue. But its either this, or put the novel aside and go whoring again with short stories. When it's convenient, send me another slug. I have been caught by taxes and insurance and flood and impecunious relatives all at once." He was also thinking about what he had long ago called *The Greening Bough.* "I wont bother you about the 'Poems' contract. Give me the best you can, tho. I am going cold-blooded Yankee now; I am not young enough anymore to hell around and earn money at other things as I could once. I have got to make it by writing or quit writing. If you can give me 15% I'll promise not to bother you about any advance on it. Is it to be a strictly limited edition, or will it be reprinted in case it sells? I have forgotten." Later, when Smith wrote the contract, he apparently stipulated the fifteen-percent royalty. There was a welcome check not long afterwards when Ben Wasson sold "Smoke" to *Harper's* on January 18 for $400, but Faulkner's $360 of it would not go far with the expenses he had.

Before the month was out, Faulkner found himself involved in another special edition. Nearly two years before, John H. McGinnis had taken "Miss Zilphia Gant" for *The Southwest Review.* Later he had decided that it was too long for the magazine and had offered it to Stanley Marcus for the Book Club of Texas. Marcus had taken it for a limited subscription membership edition for the club to appear that June. Henry Nash Smith, of the Southern Methodist University English department, was to write the introduction. Working part-time for the Dallas *Morning News*, Smith had been sent to Jackson, Mississippi, on a story. He decided he would visit Faulkner to talk about the introduction, for "the pretext of a slight matter of business which I might logically discuss with him was too good an opportunity to be lost."

The false spring of two weeks before had faded, and it was a gray day when Smith made his way up the cedar-lined drive to the house. "I found him a small man in a blue shirt and carpet slippers, standing before a coal fire in a front room," Smith later wrote. After some general, easy conversation, they apparently disposed quickly of the matter of the introduction to "Miss Zilphia Gant." Faulkner showed Smith his workroom and his manuscripts. He enjoyed writing, he said, rising early and generally finishing his day's work by ten-thirty or eleven in the morning. He was working at two novels now, he said, "and it may take me two years to finish one of them." If this was the Snopes saga he and Phil Stone had talked of so much—developing over a period of time through "Spotted Horses," "The Hound," and "Lizards in Jamshyd's Courtyard"—he did not say. On some points he was evasive or misleading. He had never read *Ulysses*, he said. When Smith asked about his wartime plane crashes all he would say was, "I just smashed them up." When Smith tried later to return to that subject Faulkner simply remained silent. A new pattern seemed to be emerging. Whereas he had earlier acted the wounded aviator and told interviewers harrowing stories, now he was drawing back from a similar opportunity. It is possible that on that day it simply did not please or amuse him to tell those stories. But he may also have begun now to feel that they were no longer appropriate for a man who had suddenly achieved some prominence and esteem in a career he cared a great deal about. And if someone should somehow check up on these stories, the effect would be embarrassing.

But Smith was a knowledgeable and sympathetic interviewer, and in some ways Faulkner opened up to him. He liked *As I Lay Dying* best, he said. "He is somewhat apologetic about his earlier work; but in general he has a very objective attitude toward his writing, and seems to take them as facts of nature, like the rain, about which one does not feel impelled to pass judgment, good or bad. He has no theory of fiction, but he does feel that he has passed through three stages in his attitude toward people and thus in his attitude toward his own characters. 'There is the first stage,' he said, 'when you believe everything and everybody is good. Then there is the second, cynical stage when you believe that no one is good. Then at last you come to realize that everyone is capable of almost anything—heroism or cowardice, tenderness or cruelty.' I think that is his attitude now."

The impression Smith took away with him was that of "a quiet, courteous man, unobtrusive and not very much impressed with himself, a little amused at the sudden enthusiasm of Eastern cities for books a good deal like his earlier ones, which they did not even bother to read or dismissed without comment." This was much like the conclusion that Louis Cochran had reached and Phil Stone had confirmed: "that Bill is indifferent to the present adulation of his work. . . ." It was doubtless better to be lionized, but it had come too late, though he was not yet thirty-five. After *The Marble Faun*, *Soldiers' Pay*, *Mosquitoes*, and *Sartoris,* he had closed a door, he had said, between himself and all publishers' addresses and book lists. Now that people were hammering at that door, he did not particularly care to open it.

When the contract for *Light in August* arrived, Faulkner wrote Wasson that it was all right. He had checked carefully to see that the clause calling for submission of his next two books was stricken out. But the same clause appeared in the contract he had signed for the book of poems. "Will this hold me to another mss.?" he asked. He had made that mistake with the last two Cape & Smith contracts. "I thought I was just signing for the present one each time, not having read the contract. I think that this accounts for Hal's request for mss. to submit to Cape. He wrote me that he had cleared the poems all right, and that he needed mss. to clear Light in August." If this clause would bind him, he would write back to Hal and ask him to strike it out.

Now that the novel was "about finished," he was thinking about trying to serialize it in a magazine. Should he tell Hal now? There was something more he was not going to tell Hal—at least for the time being. Hard-pressed, he was recalling Harold Guinzburg's generous offers. "About Harold," Faulkner told Ben, "I wont go behind Hal's back. When I get ready to swap horses, I will tell him. So suppose you dont say anything about it to him until I get this other straight and give you the word."

As Faulkner had worked his way further into the novel, Joe Christmas had taken an increasingly powerful hold upon his imagination. Lena Grove was still an important figure, but, unlike Caddy in *The Sound and the Fury*, she had not remained both the generative figure and the central one. She was integrated into the Christmas plot through her relationship with Lucas Burch–Joe Brown, her betrayer and Christmas' cohort, but she served more and more as counterpoint for the obsessed and doomed Christmas. If Lena Grove had brought with her a hint of *As I Lay Dying*, Joe Christmas had brought with him more than a suggestion of *Sanctuary*. There was not only the brothel but the psychopathology of sex, and it permeated his portions of the novel. For Lena the process was simple and normal: love, conception, birth, and—hopefully—a husband. Christmas' sexual attitudes were strongly conditioned by his neurotic fear and hatred of dominant women and disgust at female physiology. He was still reacting against the loveless environment of his childhood. It had left him not only uncertain of his parentage but with twisted attitudes in which food and sex sometimes merged in a curious way.

Faulkner was concerned with several subjects: the individual's integration into communal life, Negro-white relationships, the effects of uncertainty and deprivation, and the impact of harsh Calvinistic religiosity upon the psyche. But he was also concerned with what lay at the heart of *Sanctuary*: the problem of evil, and sometimes women's impermeability to and affinity for it. He wrote that the people of Jefferson felt that Mrs. Hightower, being a good woman, could not be fooled by evil. Driven to profligacy by an obsessed husband, she would die in a Memphis brothel. (Later Faulkner would change it to a Memphis hotel.) Faulkner interpreted the actions of the orphanage dietitian in terms not only of divination and temporary madness, but also of "her natural female infallibility for the spontaneous comprehension of evil." (117) Mrs. Hines, Christmas' grandmother, is a Manichean unaware: "I would think how the devil had conquered God." (356)

An aura like that of Miss Reba's—though without that establishment's sporadic and tarnished *Gemütlichkeit*—emanated from several passages. Christmas' initiation into adult sexuality came from Bobbie Allen, brought down from Memphis with other prostitutes by Max and Mame Confrey. Like Popeye, Christmas worked in the bootlegging business, unlike him hijacking shipments to Memphis rather than running them. Temple Drake, established at Miss Reba's and lying in bed in the twilight, was suggested by Miss Atkins, the dietitian at the orphanage. "She entered her room and locked the door and took off her clothes and got into bed. The shades were drawn and she lay still in the more than halfdark, on her back. . . . her body open to accept sleep as though sleep were a man." (121) Both she and Doc Hines called her superior not "the Matron" but "the madam." (120) There were other links of tone and phrase. Temple, about to be violated by Popeye, began to say, "Something is going to happen to me." (99) As he described Christmas, preparing to enter the house where he would murder Joanna Burden, Faulkner again wrote the phrase, *"Something is going to happen to me."* (110) Later, like Lee Goodwin, Christmas would die violently in Jefferson after acquiescing to a trial with a foregone Guilty verdict.

Because the setting was Yoknapatawpha, there were familiar names and places. In one instance Faulkner used an equivalent character, a Tennessee furniture salesman whose comments on Lena and Byron at the end of the novel suggest Suratt. There were also familiar elements of technique. As in *Sanctuary*, he shifted from Jefferson and the county to Memphis. As in *As I Lay Dying*, he generally kept present action in the present tense, using the past tense for the extensive flashbacks which supported the events during the nine days of present time. As he worked his way through the manuscript he would occasionally change a whole passage from present tense to past, or the reverse. At one point he printed, "FIRST PERSON" and drew an arrow to a long passage.

It appears from much of the manuscript that Faulkner had begun to write more rapidly. By early February or thereabouts he must have been at work on Christmas' death scene. If he had drawn on Nelse Patton's crime for Joanna Burden's death, there was another act of violence ten years later which could have suggested Christmas' end. In September of 1919 a Negro woman's body was found lying on a bed in her house two miles east of Oxford. She had been disemboweled several days before and the bed had been set on fire to hide the crime. Four months later Leonard Burt, her twenty-four-year-old husband, was captured. The trial date was set for March 12. "At 1:30 Wednesday afternoon," reported the Oxford *Eagle*, "while officers Glen Whitehead and T. G. Metz were escorting Leonard Burt, negro, from the county jail to the courthouse. . . . he made a desperate attempt to escape by snatching Whitehead to his knees and dashing off up the alley, running between the jail and the row of store buildings on the north side of the public square." When Burt did not halt at a warning shot, "Officer Metz let four more Smith and Wesson specials loose at the fleeing man who at the sound of the last shot dropped to the earth." Four bullet wounds in his body, he died the next day at Bramlett's hospital. Burt's killer did not then castrate him, as Christmas' did. But no Oxonian could say that Faulkner was being unrealistic, no matter how much he might abhor homicide in the fictional town so many outlanders took to be Oxford.

Faulkner had carefully developed the background of his major characters. (Christmas was the product of a kind of orthodoxy expressed in an earlier newspaper announcement that "a religious census of Oxford . . . last week [showed] only 180 unconverted persons, 2/3 of this number being under the age of 12 years.") But Faulkner had also been careful to preserve ambiguity where it would serve. Christmas most often acted on the premise that he had Negro blood, but as the Negro workman at the orphanage told him contemptuously, "You'll live and you'll die and you wont never know." (363) As Faulkner later put it, "that to me was the tragic, central idea of the story—that he didn't know what he was, and there was no way possible in life for him to find out." In the manuscript Christmas revealed that he knew little about his parents, "Except that one of them was a nigger." When he typed the line, Faulkner would weaken even that momentary seeming certainty: "Except that one of them was part nigger." (240)

Faulkner took particular care with other details. Joe had been found on the orphanage doorstep on Christmas. The thirty-third year of his age was emphasized. Like Benjy Compson he was beaten and castrated. But whereas Faulkner's rewriting strengthened Benjy's Christian analogues, it did the reverse with Christmas. In the manuscript he appeared in Jefferson when "he was 30 years old." His death three years later would have come at Christ's age. But when Faulkner typed this line, he changed Christmas' age on his arrival to thirty-three. He surely did not want to overdo the Christian analogy with a man who committed several of the major sins and crimes in the religious and legal codes. He obviously did want, however, to reinforce Christmas' role as victim by bringing into play reader-attitudes evoked by these Christian elements. Faulkner's anguished sympathy for this victim was clear throughout the novel, particularly in passages where the helpless child is at the mercy of sluttish Miss Atkins, mad Doc Hines, and glacial Mr. McEachern.

Faulkner presented Christmas in his maturity as thinking he acted out of something like free will, though his history made it clear that he had largely been shaped by his environment. When Joanna Burden suggested that he marry her he thought, "No. If I give in now, I will deny all the thirty years that I have lived to make me what I chose to be." (250–251) As the net closed around him, however, Faulkner used a metaphor which not only made clear Christmas' essential lack of freedom but seemed also to say something about Faulkner's own view of the human situation. Percy Grimm followed in his implacable pursuit, "as if the Player who moved him for pawn likewise found him breath." (437) Three times more Faulkner mentioned "the Player" before the siren's crescendo signaled the end of Christmas' pursuit, mutilation, and death.

Faulkner ended with Lena Grove in the fabliau-like episode in which Byron Bunch tried unsuccessfully to climb into her bed in the back of the furniture dealer's truck. Her story, like Hightower's, had been integrated into Christmas' not so much by interaction (Hightower met the other two briefly, Lena and Christmas meeting not at all) as by linking characters such as Lucas Burch and Byron Bunch and by the use of parallelism in their lives and the forces operating upon them. Isolation, the strength of the past, the effects of Calvinism—these were forces which provided parallels. Hostility and warmth, barrenness and fecundity—these provided linking contrasts. And it was on the notes of warmth, comedy, and acceptance—provided by Lena Grove, soon to be Lena Bunch—that the novel ended. In the lower left-hand corner he wrote, "Oxford, Miss./19 Feb. 1932."

The first hundred pages of the typescript apparently went well. There were a few pen corrections here and there, and only two of the pages had been tried first in other places. By the time he reached page 120, however, he apparently began to make cuts, renumbering a five-page sequence twice. Ben wrote to ask for some of the typescript to show to magazines. "I am still making changes," Faulkner replied in an undated letter. "I see that I shall not know until I have typed it all, whether what I have done already will stand as it is. I should finish it in about two weeks more. I will not want to take less than $5000.00 for it, and not a word to be changed. This may sound not only hard, but a little swellheaded. But I can get along somehow if it is not serialised. But I will take five thousand and no editing." Business disposed of, he turned to another subject before he closed.

Under the name John Riddell, Corey Ford had published a series of burlesques, chiefly in *Vanity Fair.* For the March issue he had done one called "Popeye the Pooh" in which J. B. Priestley, Warwick Deeping, and

A. A. Milne visited Bill Faulkner in Mississippi. His residence seemed to be Lee Goodwin's house. Though Lee did not appear, Popeye, Ruby, the baby, Temple, and Tommy did, amidst chaos, mayhem, fire, and clouds of bats. When Popeye met the three British novelists at the spring, his face "had the vicious depthless quality of old dried library paste." When Bill came up to the house from the corncrib, he "stood in the doorway of the kitchen, a little under-size, with dark eyes and a small dark moustache, smoking a corn cob pipe. There were several wisps of hay in his dark hair." As he gave them each copies of *Sanctuary*, the house collapsed in flames. Faulkner wrote Ben, "I liked Corey's takeoff fine. I enjoyed it a lot. I want to write him, but I have been damn busy as I can be getting this thing typed. Explain to him and tell him how much we both liked it. When I get caught up, I think I will write some John Riddell in the style of Faulkner. Love to Sullivan."

By mid-March he was nearing the end of the revision and typing. The last section went smoothly, and on page 527 the typescript came to an end. After final checking he prepared to take it to Mac Reed at the drugstore for wrapping. Most of the strain of completing the work was now behind him, but it may have been this time that he would refer to, years later, when he described a scene with his wife. She was so angry with him, he said, that she threw the manuscript of *Light in August* out of the car, and he had to stop and go back and pick up the scattered pages.

Whatever happened, the parcel went off. "The mss. goes to you today by express," he wrote Ben. "If you can get $5000.00 with no changes, take it. If not, and the movie offer is still open, that should tide me along. If you cant get $5000.00, I reckon I'll just turn it over to Hal. He wrote that he agreed to wait until October to publish it. You might remind him of that when you let him have the mss. I would like to hear from you about it as soon as possible, as I want to have it all cleaned up when I go to California. I hope you will like it. I believe it will stand up. I will depend on you to protect Hal's equity in the matter, and also my own. . . . As you say, I have enough momentum to coast a while now; particularly as the next novel will take about 2 years in the writing." He may have explored the ground of the Snopes novel in his mind, but he was not yet caught up in it. He was enjoying the feeling of work done, and relaxing. "Spring here," he wrote in closing, "beans and peas and dogwood and wistaria next week."

Ben was having no luck in finding an editor who would pay five thousand dollars for the serial rights to *Light in August* and agree not to touch one of the novel's 165,000-odd words. Bennett Cerf had already talked with Hal Smith and Robert Haas, Smith's new partner, about a 300-copy limited edition of *Light in August* to sell for fifteen dollars a copy, but this plan, as far as Faulkner's immediate situation went, dealt strictly with futures. As the spring came in, Faulkner felt even more pressure. "You wrote me some time ago that you intended coming home," he wrote Wasson. "I am today sending to Harper's a mss. with return postage, because I want to hear from the story as soon as I can, in order to try it on someone else, and I dont want to chance having the story lie idle in your office in case you are not there." If Ben was going to be in New York, he could take the letter to *Harper's* and take charge of the story. "It has been only to Scribner's, and I need money. Dont try it on Mencken save as a last resort; he only pays me $150.00 for stories."

On April 30 Paul Romaine received twenty-six advance copies of *Salmagundi.* He sent six to Faulkner and one to Ernest Hemingway, whose four-line poem "Ultimately" had appeared first in *The Double Dealer,* as had all but one of the Faulkner pieces. In his preface to the attractive fifty-three-page book, Romaine declared that "readers and critics have not taken the time to get an intelligent perspective on the man's genius and its first years of pregnancy." *Salmagundi* was meant to make this possible.

What must have been particularly infuriating to Faulkner was the fact that *Sanctuary* had continued to earn money but he got none of it. He received a royalty statement for April showing four thousand dollars due him, he said, but the firm could not pay it. By March 19 it had become Jonathan Cape & Robert Ballou, Inc., and before the month was out it had gone into receivership. The firm was still solvent, its officers declared, but it had no liquid capital.

Leland Hayward, Wasson's boss, investigated screenwriting possibilities and Faulkner waited. Hayward had a working relationship with the Selznick-Joyce Agency. Myron Selznick's brother, David, was a well-known producer, and the agency itself was one of the largest and most powerful in Hollywood. Meanwhile, Faulkner answered his correspondence—some of it. Maurice Coindreau had sent him copies of his translations of "Dry September" and "A Rose for Emily." The former was excellent, but the latter rendered "even that of which a writer perhaps alone feels in his story but never quite gets into the actual words." He wished most of all to thank Coindreau for the critique he had published in *La Nouvelle Revue,* which a friend had sent him from Paris. "I see now that I have a quite decided strain of puritanism (in its proper sense, of course; not our American one) regarding sex. I was not aware of it. But now, on casting back and rereading now and then or here and there of my own work, I can see it plainly. I have found it quite interesting." If his puritanism had been anomalous in terms of his time and place, it would shortly be even more so.

In his review of *Sanctuary*, Edwin Seaver had written, "After reading Faulkner's latest novel . . . one is tempted to say that as a novelist Mr. Faulkner is a superb movie director. . . . his technique is the technique of the cinema." Actually, however, it was not the cinematic but the literary which interested MGM. Samuel Marx, the discriminating head of the scenario department, recalled that "Irving Thalberg, head of MGM, was of the opinion that fine writing was the only way to film superiority, and any great literary figure intrigued him. We all knew that William Faulkner was a question-mark when it came to screen writing. However, at that time, I offered Tom Wolfe a contract without even asking Thalberg, knowing how much he wanted the best creative talent. He would undoubtedly have okayed the Faulkner deal, and probably did."

The contract Hayward sent to Faulkner was for a term of six weeks, commencing May 1, with no options. It provided a lower berth from Oxford to Culver City, California, and return. The salary was $500 a week. For this sum he was to render services "writing original stories and dialogue, adaptations, treatments, etc. and to render such other services as are customarily performed by writers." His services could also be "loaned to others engaged in producing motion pictures." But there was one difficulty; he couldn't be in California on May 1 because he expected his royalty check for the $4,000 which was due on the first of May according to the statement, and he wanted to be in Oxford when it arrived. It may have been through Ben's response to this letter that Faulkner learned it was uncertain when he would receive his royalties, if he received them at all. By early May the firm had been liquidated, with the Irving Trust Company serving as receiver. Later Faulkner could take a philosophical, even moralistic view of the proceedings. "I was to have $6,500," he said, "but the publisher went broke and I didn't get that, which served me exactly right." At the moment, however, it was a bitterly ironic situation. All that was left, apparently, was Hollywood, and now that *Light in August* was finished, there was no legitimate reason for turning away from the prospect. The pressure of debt was increasing. It must have been then that a new contract arrived from Hayward dated April 15, 1932, which called for him to report for work in Culver City on May 7.

Judge John Falkner said later that his nephew came to him, wanting to borrow five dollars. He had spent the last of his funds to wire acceptance of the studio's offer, he said, "provided it would wire him an advance. The bank had notified him that he was five hundred dollars overdrawn." He needed money to cover the overdraft and to leave something for Estelle and the children until he could send them money from his first studio pay check. "Don't go," said his uncle John. "I'll lend you the five hundred dollars." Faulkner thanked him but said he had made up his mind.

When the reply to his wire arrived, however, it stated that the studio would advance the money provided he signed a contract for three months instead of six weeks. The Judge recalled that his nephew backed off at this. The Judge's son, John Wesley Thompson, IV, urged him not to be foolish about this thing, and a series of family discussions ensued. Then the studio relented and returned, apparently, to the original time span. Murry Falkner's reaction was principally one of surprise. "He was confounded that mere scribbling could earn five hundred dollars a week," his son would later recall. "When I showed him the check, he asked if it was legal." Faulkner turned his affairs over to his cousin, a lawyer like his forefathers, and prepared to depart. On Monday, April 25, he was at Arthur A. Halle's in Memphis, presumably outfitting himself for the trip.

He really did not want to go. But the Cape & Smith royalties appeared blocked and there was no immediate prospect of magazine sales. No one had picked up the serial rights to *Light in August*, which would not go on sale for six months. Where else could he make $500 a week? It would be like selling a short story every week for six weeks. He kissed his family goodbye and boarded the train out of Oxford.

BOOK SEVEN

Scenarist and Aviator

1932-1935

William Faulkner with Waco.

37

May-October, 1932

> The sun, strained by the vague high soft almost nebulous California haze, fell upon the terrace with a kind of treacherous unbrightness. The terrace, the sundrenched terra cotta tiles, butted into a rough and savage shear of canyonwall bare yet without dust, on or against which a solid mat of flowers bloomed in fierce lush myriad-colored paradox as though in place of being rooted into and drawing from the soil they lived upon the air alone and had been merely leaned intact against the sustenanceless lavawall by someone who would later return and take them away.
>
> —"Golden Land" (706–707)

In 1932 Metro-Goldwyn-Mayer was the undisputed leader among motion-picture companies, producing forty feature films a year that grossed more than $100 million annually and played before an estimated total world audience of one billion persons. Every week the studio paid its sixty-two writers a total of $40,000. Three other new writers had been signed to contracts in the same week as Faulkner. (There were more writers on the MGM lot, commented one magazine, than it took to produce the King James Version of the Bible.) Eighteen directors reported to six associate producers who were directly under Irving Thalberg, at thirty-three vice-president in charge of production. As May 7 approached there was some anticipation in the scenario department at the fifty-three-acre Culver City studio "on the dusty outskirts of Los Angeles, opposite three gasoline stations and a drug store."

The shortened workday of Saturday, May 7, had nearly passed before William Faulkner arrived. At last he was shown into Sam Marx's office, "short and shy, mild-mannered and soft-spoken, exceedingly thin, with crew-cut iron-grey hair, a wisp of a black moustache, entirely inconspicuous except for one noticeable attention-getter on his person. His head was bleeding from an open cut." Marx and his secretary wanted to call a doctor, but Faulkner dismissed it. He had been hit by a cab, he said. It was not clear whether he had been hit in New Orleans and recently reopened the cut or if he had suffered the injury in Los Angeles. What he did make clear was that he did not like big cities; New Orleans was too big and Los Angeles was even bigger. They went ahead with the business of getting the new employee settled. He was given Office 27 in the Old Publicity Building, a rickety white structure which had once housed studio publicity but had been given to the new writers brought in with the advent of sound.

Faulkner proposed getting right to work. "I've got an idea for Mickey Mouse," he said. Marx looked at him suspiciously, but he seemed completely serious. Marx gently informed him that scripts for Mickey Mouse films were written at the Walt Disney Studios. Besides, he was already assigned to producer Harry Rapf for a picture called *Flesh.* He would begin work on Monday.

Harry Rapf was a short, paunchy, balding man who favored double-breasted suits and bore the nickname "Mayer's sundial" because of his prominent nose. His specialty was the sentimental melancholy of such hits as *The Sin of Madelon Claudet* and *The Champ.* Wallace Beery had played the lovable pug and Jackie Cooper had wept affectingly as the moppet who adored him. It made sense to try the same combination again, so now Beery had been cast as a wrestler, and the child star would fulfill his same function. Told the star's name, Faulkner asked, "Who's he?" Marx arranged to have some film run off in a projection room so that Faulkner could familiarize himself with the nuances of the Beery style. Faulkner resisted.

"How about my writing newsreels?" he inquired. "Newsreels and Mickey Mouse, these are the only pictures I like." Patiently, Marx explained again, and finally Faulkner allowed himself to be led from the office. Scarcely had the head of the story department begun to relax when the projectionist appeared, perturbed and alone. Faulkner had not wanted to watch Wally Beery; he had wanted to talk about dogs. "He said I should be ashamed not to own a dog," the projectionist said, "and so should everybody else who doesn't own a dog." He had barely gotten the film running when Faulkner had asked, "How do you stop this thing?" There was no use looking at it, Faulkner said, because he knew how it would turn out. After that he had asked for the exit and left. The projectionist did not know where he had gone. Marx began searching for him and called Leland Hayward, but they could not find him.

He was still missing on Tuesday, and somehow he had conveyed the information that he was gone for good. Studio executives, directors, and writers had helped Hayward in the search, but the only thing turned up was the vague report that he was on his way home to Mississippi. "William Faulkner desires to entirely dissolve his contract and has left the studio," wrote Marx to Floyd Hendrickson, who was in charge of contracts, "apparently with no intention of returning." The next day letters were sent to appropriate studio offices canceling his contract. The studio was out both his advance and transportation, but Marx was philosophical about it. He had known from the first that they were taking a chance.

On the following Monday Faulkner reappeared in Marx's office. He had been wandering, he said, in Death Valley. How he had gotten there (150 miles due east) he did not say. Marx concluded that he had spent the time partly in "steeling himself to work in the great grey walls of the overpowering studio, in the enormous area of Los Angeles." Now he was contrite; he wanted to do right. "The truth is," he later said, "that I was scared. I was scared by the hullabaloo over my arrival, and when they took me into a projection room to see a picture and kept assuring me it was all going to be very very easy, I got flustered." Marx welcomed him back. Moss Hart had lucklessly drawn the writing assignment on *Flesh* in his place. There would be plenty of other things for Faulkner to work on. Marx sent another interoffice memo to Hendrickson: "Please reinstate William Faulkner's contract as of Monday, May 16."

Faulkner prepared to go to work. He had taken a thirty-dollar-a-month cottage at 4024 Jackson Street, within walking distance of the studio. (If he needed any spur to homesickness, just seven blocks north of him was Lafayette Place.) But now a new difficulty appeared. "Word of his eccentric antics had been magnified to the producers," remembered Marx, "who were wary of him." His contract specified that he might be assigned to work on original stories for the studio, so Marx solved the problem by asking him to do that, so that he would be reporting to Marx rather than to a producer. He went to work in his cell-like cubbyhole on a story that was not original in the sense that Marx probably had in mind. Called *Manservant*, it was actually a reworking of "Love," the story he had tried unsuccessfully to sell to magazines a dozen years before. True to his frugal nature, Faulkner was thus selling it to MGM for $500, two thirds of what *The Saturday Evening Post* would have paid him for one of his mature short stories.

Faulkner began with the line "India, 1921. A remote British Army post." All of the characters were renamed but one: Das, the Major's faithful servant. The plot was unchanged, but Faulkner was trying to teach himself how to write for the camera. He used newspaper dates to show the passage of time, and in the poison sequence, just before the jealous maid thrust the deadly phial into her stocking, a camera close-up was supposed to show it labeled "Poison."

He was learning terminology if nothing else. *Manservant* was now a "property" formally assigned to MGM. A property was anything that might be turned into a motion picture: an idea, a synopsis, an original story, an adaptation of an existing work, a movie-style "treatment" of one of these, or a script with dialogue and directions. *Manservant* was a treatment with an occasional line of dialogue. With the story divided into fifty-eight sequences, its twenty-one mimeographed pages were ready for distribution by May 25, but in the ensuing days it interested no one in the scenario department.

Though he was gainfully employed in learning a profitable craft, he was not enjoying the process. One of the draft sheets of *Manservant* bore on its other side a letter he had begun and then abandoned: "I am not settled good yet. I have not got used to this work. But I am as well as anyone can be in this bedlam."

In addition he had been working on two more originals. A thirteen-page treatment called *The College Widow* was mimeographed by May 26. This too had an earlier form: a three-page synopsis he had typed and given the suggested title "Night Bird." It seems plausible that this was the story written six months earlier in New York for Tallulah Bankhead. The protagonist was an eighteen-year-old professor's daughter. Prevented by her parents from marrying her sweetheart and bored with college boys, she becomes involved with a sinister stranger. Realizing he is insane, she flees. Later, married to the sweetheart and pregnant, she senses one night that the stranger is in their house. What follows suggests Temple Drake's night of terror at the Old Frenchman place. The woman listens in the dark as the stranger seeks her and her husband seeks the stranger. Her husband kills him and she miscarries. After he repudiates her, she returns to the college town and gradually sinks lower, leaving town before she costs her father his job. Returning to the city, she is now a "night bird," a kept woman who sees her former husband out celebrating with his new wife and child as the story ends.

In the extended treatment which turned "Night Bird" into *The College Widow*, Faulkner emphasized more strongly the girl's ambivalence in seeking thrills and fleeing danger. She was now even more like Temple Drake, and it was as though Faulkner had asked himself what might have happened to Temple after *Sanctuary*. Like *Manservant*, this treatment was not approved for the addition of full-scale dialogue. The reaction must have been much like that recorded in the reader's report when the treatment was reread two and a half years later: "This is told very briefly, but Faulkner would obviously develop another *Sanctuary*. It is an evil, slimy thing, absolutely unfit for screen production, in the face of current censorship . . . . . . or at any future time."

By June 1 the mimeographing department had turned out another Faulkner original. Entitled *Absolution*, it too showed signs of indebtedness, this time to "All the Dead Pilots." In the nine-page treatment he did as he had done in *The College Widow*: he first provided a rather lengthy background, carefully avoiding his favorite technique of the flashback. He began his romantic triangle with the principals aged twelve, fighting over a girl unworthy of either of them. He ended after one had shot the other down in France on the Western Front. Faulkner made it quite explicit that the love of the men for each other and the life of one of them had been destroyed by this unworthy woman.

Though he could not derive any satisfaction from his work or its reception, it was good to have the money coming in. Even after the Selznick-Joyce agent's commission was deducted, he still had $450 a week. His first pay check came on Wednesday, May 25, and the second on June 1. The next day he sent home $100 from this second one and kept the rest for bills and his own living expenses. Sam Marx had found a way to get some value for the studio's money. He would pair Faulkner with an experienced partner who knew the mechanics of writing for the camera. Then Faulkner's fertile imagination could provide new material or plot variations to solve problems and his insight could add plausibility in characterization. His expository rhetoric would clog a script, but his vivid and colloquial dialogue would move it.

Writing Estelle, he described his new assignment. "I am writing one for Wallace Beery and Robt. Montgomery," he told her, "in collaboration with an actor-author named Ralph Graves. I am a sort of doctor, to repair the flaws in it." He was glad of her news from home. Two of their servants, Jack Oliver and his sweetheart Josie, had married. "I reckon we'll have to build a house now—[a] cabin." As for himself, "I am homesick as the devil." But there were a few people he could talk to. "I ran into Laurence Stallings, whom I knew before in N.Y. He is a Georgian, author of 'What Price Glory' and he has given me some good advice about keeping my balance with these people."

Looking back, Stallings said, "If I helped Bill, it was in leading him to understand the tremendous pressure many fine people at MGM were subjected to; and that they, show-people, were in a bracket by themselves." Though Faulkner had looked thin to Marx, to Stallings a short time later he seemed "a little stocky man with a perfect civil war face. It is dark, flushed, framed in tightly crisped, grayish hair. His nose is eaglish, his chin curving. Ten years ago D. W. Griffith would unhesitatingly have cast him as a Confederate brigadier." Carless, Faulkner often rode with Stallings. He could not get used to the Los Angeles scene. One day, as they drove along Wilshire Boulevard, a 300-foot tower loomed up out of a congestion of electric signs. "That a filling station," he asked Stallings, "or the segregated district?" Faulkner told him that he thought that the whole of southern California would eventually crumble away. Stallings later tried to render the dialect of Faulkner's vision: "A hundred yeahs from now the archaeologists will go digging around here and find nothin'. It's all too perishable to wait for the archaeologists. The only thing they'll find will be these heah iron stobs the folks from Iowa drive into the ground to pitch hoss shoes at. Funny thing, but these heah little iron pegs are all that will survive the test of time."

Sometimes when Stallings called for Faulkner at the cottage on Jackson Avenue he would see him standing at the stove. He would go out with friends, occasionally to dinner and a movie perhaps with someone like Stallings or Meta Doherty, an attractive script girl who worked for writer-director-producer Howard Hawks. Hubert Starr, who had earned a law degree at Ole Miss considerably before Faulkner's time there, would also invite him out. One congenial man he met at Starr's house was Jacob Zeitlin. Thereafter he would stop to see Zeitlin occasionally at his bookshop on 6th Street in Los Angeles. Another meeting at Starr's home was not so fortunate. After dinner two uninvited guests appeared. One of them, a gushing woman, began to talk immediately.

"Mr. Faulkner," she said, "I understand that an author always puts himself in his books. Which character are you in *Sanctuary?*"

"Madam," Faulkner replied, "I was the corncob."

Faulkner admired Stallings, a crapshooting marine like Jack Falkner. He had made captain by the time shrapnel wounds in Belleau Wood cost him a leg—one of the experiences that helped make the bitter and successful play *What Price Glory?* and the equally successful film *The Big Parade.* It may have been this admiration that caused Faulkner to start telling war stories again—about how he had broken both his legs in a plane crash—and to fancifully explain his absence over a weekend by explaining casually that he had gone downtown to Los Angeles and had his tonsils extracted. He seemed to talk with some freedom to Stallings. He liked "All the Dead Pilots" best of his own stories, he said, but Hemingway's "Fifty Grand" was the best contemporary short story. "He awaits with great eagerness," wrote Stallings, "the interpretations that the soothsayer critics will bring to an explanation of the title [of his new novel]. He has told me his own." (Stallings did not say what it was, but it seems likely that Faulkner was pleased enough with the pregnancy interpretation he had given Hal Smith to use it on Stallings and to look forward to discomfiting reviewers with it.) Stallings presented him as a model of decorum. "Unlike practically everyone else, he has remained cold sober. He bought one book to read over his lonely nights. It was a second-hand twelve-volume . . . Cambridge edition of the Holy Bible."

The two men enjoyed outdoor activities. In late June they went to see some of the riders and mounts preparing for the 1932 Olympics. James Boyd went with them, and their conversation touched on both sports and writing. Boyd was particularly anxious to see the game on the twenty-fifth which would determine the American lacrosse representative. As they watched, Faulkner suddenly began to laugh. He explained to Boyd: "I was just thinking of how the Injuns must have looked playing shinny, with their stony faces." Stallings had asked him if he knew Boyd's novel *Drums.* When Boyd was out of earshot Faulkner told Stallings, "I've read it a dozen times. I'm going to read it ten more." Boyd admired "Spotted Horses," and Faulkner had told him some of the stories that would go into the Snopes book. He was "whittling away at it," he said. The date he had in mind was "about 1934."

Faulkner had begun work on his collaborative effort with Ralph Graves on June 1. *Flying the Mail* was an original which Graves had done with Bernard Fineman. Like *Flesh*, it was apparently written with an eye on an earlier success. In 1930 Wallace Beery and Marie Dressler had starred as two lovable battlers in *Min and Bill.* Besides this relationship in *Flying the Mail* there was also a conflict between Wally and his son—both of them fliers. The mimeographed copies of Faulkner's sixteen-page continuity treatment were ready by June 3. This was another characteristic which set him apart from most studio writers: whereas the average scenarist would feel satisfied with about five pages a day, Faulkner might complete a long treatment in a few days. This did not endear him to some. To others offended by his silence or resentful of his reputation, there was doubtless some pleasure in seeing how little of this volume ever went before the cameras. *Flying the Mail* went unproduced.

His contract was now running out. On June 21 Floyd Hendrickson informed Messrs. Mayer, Thalberg, Rapf, and Marx that it terminated on June 26 and contained no renewal options. Four days later Marx wrote Hendrickson that it would not be extended. Faulkner's last three days' work could scarcely have made him regret this. It was *Turn to the Right*, a treacly thing written, as it happened, by Winchell Smith, the uncle of Faulkner's publisher. It was a bucolic morality play which resisted his efforts.

Selznick-Joyce also were apparently content that his screen work should end. But now Sam Marx had some second thoughts and offered a year's contract at $250 a week. Faulkner declined. A week later Selznick-Joyce wrote him that they had arranged a new contract for him at that figure. Faulkner felt that not only had the agency done nothing about a renewal, they had not even kept track of where he was. He went to their office and told them he would not accept the offer. Apparently that took care of it. There was another reason, probably, why Faulkner was so quick to reject the offer. On June 16, Paramount Publix Corporation had paid the American Play Company $750 for a four-month option on the motion-picture and television rights to *Sanctuary.* If they decided to exercise their option at the end of that time, they would pay nearly $7,000 more. Faulkner could leave California in a much easier frame of mind than the one he had arrived in.

Yet he did not leave. One of the people who read "Turn About" when it appeared in the *Post* on March 5 was William Hawks. When he finished it was about midnight, but in spite of the hour he telephoned his brother. "Howard," he said, "this is the most exciting story for a picture I've read." Howard promised to read it. William had a good idea of what would appeal to his brother's taste and what would not. Howard Hawks was a thirty-six-year-old Indianan who had gone to Phillips Exeter Academy and competed as a professional racing driver before he was out of his teens. After attending Cornell he had become an army pilot, emerging from the war as a second lieutenant. Four years after he entered the film industry in 1922, he was producing pictures. In 1930 he had made *Dawn Patrol,* which became one of the classic films of World War I aerial combat. All Hawks's pictures were action pictures. He liked "Turn About," and Bill Hawks took an option on it for him through Leland Hayward. *Dawn Patrol* had been based on a story by another World War I flier named John Monk Saunders, and Hawks had hired him to do the adaptation, with good results. Since the author of the new property was there at the same studio, Hawks asked him to come and see him.

When the two met in Hawks's office they presented a strong contrast. Hawks was a slim, blond, broad-shouldered man who stood over six feet tall despite a slight stoop. His face was ruddy, and his pale blue eyes had a straight, penetrating look. He introduced himself cordially in his deep resonant voice and they shook hands.

"I've seen your name on a check," Faulkner said. Then he waited. Hawks began to talk about the possibilities he saw in "Turn About." He wanted Faulkner to do a treatment. If it looked good, his brother would buy the rights and then sell them to the studio. This was a safeguard for both Hawks and MGM. A large percentage of all movie scripts remained unproduced, and if the treatment did not look promising, all that would be lost would be the option money—probably no more than $250. Faulkner remained silent, and his silence began to annoy Hawks. After more than a half-hour, Hawks finished and Faulkner rose to go.

"Do you want a drink?" Hawks asked.

"Yes," Faulkner said.

Hawks went over to the bar. He found enjoyment in doing work with his hands, and he had made it himself from a hogshead, fabricating some of the pieces at his own forge. They finished their drinks and Faulkner got up to leave.

"See you in five days," he said.

"It shouldn't take you that long to think about it," Hawks answered shortly.

"I mean to write it," Faulkner said.

Faulkner had already done some work on the project before pay was mentioned; he told Wasson: "I would have made this script for nothing, being interested in the story." But he knew that if the treatment was approved he would probably go back on the MGM payroll to work on the script. When Faulkner brought in his treatment, Hawks read through it quickly. "That's great," he said. He took it to Irving Thalberg, towering more than a foot above the frail, graceful man. Hawks waited as he read it. Finally Thalberg looked up across the huge desk bearing bowls of apples and dates. "I feel as if I'd make tracks all over it if I touched it," he said in his quiet voice. "Shoot it as it is." After Hawks returned, Faulkner went to see Sam Marx, who put him back on the payroll as of July 26 at the $250 figure he had offered.

Hawks was a strong-minded producer who would hire a writer for just one scene. His pictures usually cost several million dollars and were done his way or not at all. Together, Hawks and Faulkner began turning the treatment into a full script with continuity and dialogue. They had common interests such as flying and hunting and found that they got on well together. Both tended to be quiet and unhurried. "Howard Hawks is the most deliberate man on earth," said one writer. "He can't be hurried. It takes him twenty minutes to tell you what time it is." Hawks knew exactly what he wanted and he would try to tell Faulkner as specifically as he could and then leave him alone.

"I like working for Hawks," Faulkner said later. "Writing for pictures is not exactly my racket, but I get along with him. We usually go over a scene and he says, 'This is the way to get the meat out of a scene.' Then I go and write it." Hawks did not always respond to Faulkner's work as he had to the treatment of "Turn About." Faulkner said, "When I show it to him, we may argue a bit until we get it right." Hawks would use a direct approach in criticism. "Bill," he might say, "this is a lousy scene. You can do better." Faulkner would laugh, sometimes, and reply, "Let's talk it over again."

Hawks came to respect Faulkner's talent for solving problems in individual scenes, and in addition he felt that he had "inventiveness, taste, and great ability to characterize the visual imagination, to translate those qualities into the medium of the screen." Hawks probably enjoyed his association with Faulkner for other reasons. Hawks had made a unique place for himself in Hollywood. He was extremely selective about his friends, entertained in grand style, and was followed, some said, by a coterie. He took pleasure in the company of extraordinary people. He had introduced Gary

Cooper to Ernest Hemingway, and Ernest Hemingway to Marlene Dietrich. Howard Hawks knew quite well who William Faulkner was, as did the more knowledgeable writers, directors, and producers, and though he and Faulkner were not intimate, Hawks enjoyed this friendship with still another uniquely talented person. Faulkner's performance at the studio also reflected credit on Hawks's acumen as a producer. "It is said," Stallings reported later in the New York *Sun*, "that his running gags and bits of business are the best seen around this town in MSS."

As the pages of script accumulated, Hawks oversaw the other preparations for the actual shooting. Gary Cooper would be available, along with Franchot Tone and Robert Young. So, unexpectedly, would Joan Crawford. When Faulkner learned from Hawks about Miss Crawford's availability, he remained silent for a moment.

Then he said thoughtfully, "I don't seem to remember a girl in the story."

"That's the picture business, Bill," Hawks told him. "We get the biggest stars we can, and Joan's a nice girl, too."

With apparent equanimity Faulkner began to alter the story line. He took a craftsman's pride in his script work, but his deepest feelings as an artist seemed never to have been engaged. His vanity, his ego, were very little involved. "Turn About" need not be kept faithful to his own vision in its transference to the screen. It was something of his which had been bought and which in its new form could have no effect on his work in his own medium. So he went ahead, and gave Midshipman Lian Claude William Hope a sister, Anne. As with *Absolution*, he began with childhood background material. But this time he had Hawks's experienced guidance, and the results were markedly different.

The scenario was going well enough for Faulkner to take a long weekend off. It was probably Friday, August 5, when he and another writer, Richard Schayer, made the trip to Catalina Island to hunt some of the diverse kinds of game found there. As far as Faulkner knew, things were all right at home. Estelle had not recovered completely, but she was better than she had been. Miss Maud was active as always and there was apparently nothing new to report about his father. There were signs, though, that Murry Falkner had been going downhill for some time. He was far from the vigorous man who would drink hard all night and then jump on a fine saddle horse in the early morning and ride himself sober. The doctor had told him that he would have to stop drinking or it would kill him. There was another problem, too. All his life he had eaten fried foods, and now the doctor forbade them. One day Dorothy Oldham saw Mr. Murry sitting on his porch, holding a head of lettuce as though it were an apple. When she asked him how he was, he complained about his diet. Dot told Bill about their short conversation. "He thinks if he eats a bushel of lettuce," Bill said, "it will help make up for all that fried fatback he's eaten over the years. It won't."

But the son saw deeper into his father's illness. Murry Falkner had eventually made an adjustment of sorts to the loss of the railroad. He had finally given up the dream of being a cowboy. After the failure of the livery stable and transfer, the oil business and the icehouse, he had gone behind the counter of the hardware store. Then he had sat at a desk in the university business office, doing a good job in a difficult position for which he was temperamentally unfitted. By the time he was forced to resign from the university, his boys were out of school and he could no longer go to the ball fields to shout proudly for them and experience vicariously the violent action of the games. The expeditions to the clubhouse on the Tallahatchie became less frequent, and pasting magazine pictures of horses and dogs in an album was no lasting diversion. His wife had her painting—she did portraits and landscapes in oil which would later label her an American "primitive"—and she had her reading. He had no such resources to fall back on, and the two drew no sustenance from each other. He had never understood the writing and the painting that everybody else in his family seemed to do. He reacted with boredom and a brief blaze of desperation. The family would see him walking up and down his front gallery constantly, "almost like a demented person." But then came a change. "He just gave up," his son said, "he got tired of living."

About the time Billy had gone to Culver City, his father had gone to the doctor's again. He had a heart condition now, and the doctor ordered him to bed. In this illness a kind of latent sweetness, so clearly seen in his son Jack, emerged in the old man. The doctor would come to the brick house on South Street to check on him. After one of these visits he was able to report improvement in his patient. Auntee came in after the doctor had left and asked Buddy how he was. "Huldy," he said, "the doctor gave me permission to get up, but he didn't give me the strength to get up with."

The summer heat was hard on him. He retired as usual on Saturday night, August 6. At 2:30 the next morning an attack came, and he was gone, ten days short of his sixty-second birthday. The family wired and telephoned Culver City, but there was no response from the house on Jackson Avenue. Finally they got in touch with Howard Hawks, who reached Faulkner as soon as he could. He wired that he would start home right away. Sam Marx reported to the payroll department that William Faulkner would be out of town beginning Wednesday, August 10. He would continue to work on *Turn About* while he was at home in Mississippi. The funeral service had been conducted at home by the Methodist minister on Monday afternoon, and then Murry Falkner was buried in St. Peter's Cemetery beside his father. The *Eagle*'s account of his death was captioned "M. C. Faulkner Dies of a Heart Attack." For years they had spelled the son's name as they did the father's. Now, in his obituary notice, they spelled the father's name as they did the son's.

"When our father died," Jack Falkner remembered, "Bill considered himself as head of our clan, and so did we. It was a natural role for him, and he assumed it at once, without fanfare but with dignity and purpose." Murry Falkner had written out his own will nearly four years before in language that was nonlegal but unmistakable. Everything went to Miss Maud until her death or remarriage, after which the boys were to divide the property themselves without accounting to any court. He addressed them directly: "Remember at all times that you are Brothers, and deal justly by each other." He declared that he had made "certain advances and payments to the boys as evidenced by signed notes bearing interest as shown therein. In the division each son is to accept his note or notes as payment on his share of the estate." He ended in a Falknerian tone: "My signature is known and no witness is needed." Bill Faulkner saw to the probating of his father's will, the payment of the insurance on his mother's house, and other matters. He had his own business affairs to manage, too. On September 1 he wrote a check for six months' mortgage payments on Rowan Oak. The weekly checks were still arriving from MGM, and he had received $2,250 when the option on "Turn About" was taken up. But he was looking ahead, and worrying. "I hope to hell Paramount takes Sanctuary," he wrote Ben Wasson. "Dad left Mother solvent for only about 1 year. Then it is me." He finished the script for *Turn About* and sent it off to Hawks in Culver City.

There was time now for other things. As the eldest son, he received the massive old Bible John Wesley Thompson had given to William Clark Falkner. He read in the genealogical section and tried to trace the family back as far as he could. In the appropriate place he inscribed in purple ink the facts of his marriage and below that the birth and death dates of Alabama. He wrote his name in some of the books which his father had inscribed if not read: one-volume editions of Zola, Daudet, Maupassant, Balzac, Hugo, and Ibsen, Cabell's *The Silver Stallion*, and George Harris' *Sut Lovingood.* He intended to try a few short stories, but first he had another job. The final galleys of *Light in August* had been ready since July 21. He had to finish reading and correcting them if they were to make the scheduled October publication.

The job proved more time-consuming and exasperating then he could have expected. Whoever had done the editorial proofreading displayed little understanding of Faulkner's style and little sympathy with it. The blue-pencil changes and queries had the tone of an instructor impatient with the work of a student in freshman composition. In the first paragraph of Chapter 6, which began, "Memory believes before knowing remembers," the proofreader bracketed all but the first two lines and wrote, "Construction?" In blue pen Faulkner scribbled out the query and in a circle of his own wrote,

O. K.
damn it.

On galley 63 the proofreader boggled at a question used declaratively where Christmas said, "Well. Well. Well. What do you know about that." Below the circles where he had furiously tried to obliterate the question, Faulkner wrote,

O. K. as set,
goddam it.

On galley 67 the conscientious proofreader wondered if something was wrong with the verb in Calvin Burden's threat to his children, "I'll frail the tar out of you." He underlined it and wrote in the margin, "flail?" Like a man gone berserk in a Palmer penmanship exercise, Faulkner circled out the proffered alternative. Below it he scribbled,

O.K. as set
and written.
Jesus Christ.

On the whole, however, editor, typesetter, and proofreader had done a good job, and Faulkner made few corrections and almost no additions.

He sent the galleys back to New York and relaxed. "I was too busy and too mad all the time I was in California to write you," he wrote Wasson. "But now I am home again, eating watermelon on the back porch and watching it rain. I have just finished reading the galley of *Light in August.* I dont see anything wrong with it. I want it to stand as it is. This one is a novel: not an anecdote; that's why it seems topheavy, perhaps." Sam Marx had asked him about *Sanctuary.* "I told him I didn't think they could use it. It would make a good Mickey Mouse picture, though Popeye is the part for Mickey Mouse. The frog could play Clarence Snopes."

Now he had to start thinking about his return to Culver City, for he had agreed to return for the final script changes as soon as Hawks needed them. He had been home for over six weeks. When he did go back, Estelle would go with him. If he had been mad in California, he could start heating up again before his return, for the Selznick-Joyce Agency had sent him a statement requesting ten percent of the $250 weekly checks he had been receiving. "Do I owe it to them?" he asked Ben, "and is there any danger of them coming down here and taking a tithe of my pigs and chickens and cotton? Advise me at once." He was furious with Selznick. He had made a better deal for himself than his agent had: "I get $250.00 a week for staying in Oxford: he got that for only a six months' contract in California. I think I'll send him a bill today."

Hawks's summons came at the end of September. Though Faulkner disliked leaving home, he was glad of the continued income. He had only to look around him to see how fortunate he was, no matter how he might dislike the work and the locale. The September checks which the Ole Miss faculty received were the first regular payment in sixteen months. There had been two back checks during the summer, but it was a mystery how some of the teachers had survived, and it was said that more than one merchant had failed by extending credit to them and other hard-hit customers. Two hundred and fifty dollars a week was a spectacular salary for north Mississippi that fall of 1932.

By this time plans for the return to California had changed in one way. Estelle would not go back with him; she was pregnant and they could not risk the trip. Miss Maud would go instead. She had been keeping busy. With Auntee she went to the picture show faithfully every Saturday night, and the two would go driving in Miss Maud's little Chevrolet coupe. In the trunk would sit a small Negro boy whose job was to deal with engine or tire trouble. Other perils Auntee would deal with herself. According to Jack

Falkner, she always took certain precautions before they stopped at a gas station or country store. She would then assess the surroundings and, with grim pleasure, insert into an enormous .38-caliber revolver the number of cartridges she considered sufficient to deal with the dangers that might present themselves at that particular place. Faulkner knew the pleasure both women derived from these expeditions, but he thought it would do his mother good to get away from familiar surroundings for a while. Dean Falkner was back from spending the summer at a dude ranch in Tucson and was still restless. He liked the idea of going to California. With some wariness Miss Maud agreed, too. They would go west with the new head of the Falkner clan when he returned to Culver City.

First, however, Miss Maud had to be outfitted. Estelle took her to Memphis, where she was shocked at the prices. She followed her daughter-in-law's advice unquestioningly, but, as Faulkner later told his wife laughingly, she thought Estelle the most extravagant woman in the world. At the end of September they drove west. He found a larger place at 4021 La Salle Avenue, just three blocks north of Jackson. On Monday, October 3, he reported for work again at the studio.

Though gone, Faulkner had been far from forgotten, particularly by the studio manager, a gaunt worried man named M. E. Greenwood who had once worked as a faro dealer in Arizona. Now he accounted for each week's expenditures to the studio's executive offices in New York and requested the operating funds to be deposited to the Culver City accounts. Always convinced that writers were trying to put something over on him, Greenwood spent considerable time investigating possible frauds. He wrote to Marx: "Several times I reminded Mr. Thalberg that Faulkner was away from the studio and yet had drawn his salary. . . . A few days before Mr. Thalberg left I again reminded him and he said for you to advise me what the situation was." Again Marx put his reassurance in writing: "Howard Hawks approved his writing while out of town and there can be no doubt that Faulkner did plenty of work. . . . and there is no reason why he should not have been paid while out of town." Assigned now to Room 19 in "the Foreign Building," Faulkner went ahead with the changes Hawks needed.

Two weeks after his arrival, he had some business of his own to conduct. Paramount had decided to take up the option on *Sanctuary*, and Faulkner signed the contract on October 17. In due course Paramount would send its check for $6,750 to the American Play Company. Even after their commission, Faulkner would clear over $6,000 on the deal.

He took his mother and his brother sightseeing. There was a good deal to interest Dean, but Miss Maud did not care for southern California and her son found it difficult to get her outdoors at all. Fortunately, however, the work was going well enough for him to write Estelle that they planned to be home by the twenty-fifth. He saw Stallings from time to time and on one occasion went on a brief trip with Hawks and a friend who had a .410 over-and-under shotgun that Faulkner admired so much he wanted one like it. The friend was movie idol Clark Gable. In Hawks's car they drove one night into the Imperial Valley for some dove-hunting the next day. Hawks began to talk about books. Instead of freezing, as he usually did when people began to talk literature, Faulkner entered into the conversation. Though intelligent, Gable was not literary, and he remained silent. Finally he ventured a question.

"Mr. Faulkner," he said, "what do you think somebody should read if he wants to read the best modern books? Who would you say are the best living writers?"

After a moment Faulkner answered. "Ernest Hemingway, Willa Cather, Thomas Mann, John Dos Passos, and William Faulkner."

Gable took a moment to absorb that information. "Oh," he said, recovering, "do you write?"

"Yes, Mr. Gable," Faulkner replied. "What do you do?"

The off-payroll notice on William Faulkner, to take effect on Saturday, October 22, went into the MGM files. As he prepared to leave, Hawks suggested that he stay a bit longer and pick up some more of the easy money to be had in Hollywood. But the *Sanctuary* deal had gone through and now he was as anxious to return home as his mother was. Apparently Bill Hawks talked to him about it too, in his capacity as an agent. Faulkner said he would let them know if he changed his mind, and the three of them departed. They arrived home on schedule, where Faulkner promptly allotted some of the Hollywood money to have the old floors of Rowan Oak ripped out and replaced. Waiting for him at home were his author's copies of *Light in August*, and the reviews.

38

October, 1932-August, 1933

> This was upland country, lying in tilted slopes against the unbroken blue of the hills, but soon the road descended sheerly into a valley of good broad fields richly somnolent in the leveling afternoon. . . .
>
> Bayard stood for a while before his house. The white simplicity of it dreamed unbroken among the ancient sunshot trees.
>
> —*Sartoris* (6)

Each time Faulkner returned home from the West Coast it would take a while for him to reacclimate himself—to get Hollywood out of his system, as he once put it. This feeling may have intensified the reaction he said he felt toward *Light in August.* The rapture had been missing as he wrote, as with each book after *The Sound and the Fury,* but now, "I received a copy of the printed book," he said, "and I didn't even want to see what kind of jacket Smith had put on it. I seemed to have a vision of it and the other ones subsequent to The Sound and The Fury ranked in order upon a shelf while I looked at the titled backs of them with a flagging attention which was almost distaste, and upon which each succeeding title registered less and less, until at last Attention itself seemed to say, Thank God I shall never need to open any one of them again." If he was a different man from the one who had written *The Sound and the Fury,* he was more different still from the young novelist who had written his publisher three and a half years before that he would like very much to see reviews of *Sartoris.* He courteously told Smith, "the book looks fine," but he had no interest in seeing what the reviewers said about it. His publishers, trying to nurse the new firm of Harrison Smith and Robert Haas through the tail end of the Depression, read them with the closest attention.

Beginning in early October, the book was widely reviewed at considerable length. Faulkner might not be to the taste of many of these writers, but they approached the task with the feeling that he was a major figure and that assessment of his new work was a serious matter. On October 8, the day before publication, Henry Seidel Canby wrote in the *Saturday Review* that despite obscurity, turgidity, and sloppiness, "it is a novel of extraordinary force and insight, incredibly right in character studies, intensely vivid, rising sometimes to poetry, and filled with that spirit of compassion which saves those who look at life too closely from hardness and despair." Reviewers for the *Times* and the *Tribune* were even more laudatory. They might have approached the novel with trepidation and misread much of it, but they found they liked it more than they had expected.

On October 20, the Oxford *Eagle* ran a summary of review comments in which the paper's reporter called the new novel Faulkner's greatest work and noted that he was now "enjoying international fame for his early publications." The writer may have been drawing on George Marion O'-Donnell's enthusiastic review in the *Commercial Appeal* on October 9. The *Eagle* now had a stock biography which divulged the facts that "Faulkner, with an excellent mechanical turn, makes airplane models complete in every detail; he is an excellent artist. If ever his writing ability should fail him, he could make a living as a sign-painter." The reviews that appeared in New York just as Faulkner returned to Oxford conveyed less pleasure. Dorothy Van Doren found Faulkner to be repeating himself, writing about people whose actions take place "almost entirely in the viscera." If he ever disciplined himself properly, she wrote in *The Nation*, he might fulfill some of the large claims made for him. But before the end of the year critical opinion would swing in the opposite direction again. A sympathetic Mississippian, Herschel Brickell, wrote in *The North American Review* that *Light in August* was not only superior to *Sanctuary*, it was also "the most impressive of current fiction offerings." There was humor and tenderness as well as violence and horror—in short, the work of a genius.

At the moment the genius was thinking about a different kind of work. "Here I am at home again, thank God," he wrote Hal Smith. "It's fine that you are planning to come down soon. I will write you later and give you the word. I made enough jack in Hollywood to do a lot of repairs on the house, so all the floors will be out of it next month, and we will be living

Faulkner at his desk in the library at Rowan Oak.

with kinfolks. So you wouldn't have much fun then. I'll write you as soon as we open the house again and I have a keg ready to broach." As for the book of poems, "I chose the best ms and built a volume just like a novel." But if Smith wanted to, he could add anything that had appeared in *Contempo.* As for a title, Faulkner liked "Poems Miscellaneous" or "A Green Bough."

He had time now to relax for a while before he began work on the projected short stories he had mentioned to Ben. Young Malcolm Franklin had developed an interest in snakes. His stepfather was a very good amateur herpatologist. The two would go walking in the woods and bottom lands, and Faulkner would tell Mac what he could pick up and what he couldn't. He spent time on arranging new books in his growing library at Rowan Oak. He inscribed the copy of Constance Garnett's translation of *The Brothers Karamazov* which Random House had sent him. He wrote his name and the name of his home in each volume of the special limited edition of the Bible which Stallings had seen in Hollywood, a large handsome edition including the Apocrypha. Before the year was out, he had put fifty-one signed books on his shelves, more than for any year before or after.

It may have been at this time, as he unwound from his stay in Hollywood, that Faulkner worked on two short pieces—one a story and the other a sort of chronicle. On a piece of letter-size loose-leaf notebook paper, he neatly lettered a title page:

The Golden Book
of Jefferson & Yoknapatawpha County
in Mississippi
as compiled by
William Faulkner of Rowanoak

Rowanoak
MCMXXXII

Having thus suggested something of the medieval scholar, genealogist, and gentleman, Faulkner went on to write a 700-word biography of John Sartoris, born July 14, 1823, in South Carolina, and murdered in Jefferson after the war by Redlaw, his one-time partner turned rival. He added new lore to that which had already appeared in *Flags in the Dust* and *Sartoris*. It appears that he was doing this five-page chronicle for his own pleasure, unless he thought of it as raw material for fiction or as an appendix one day, possibly, to another work about the Sartoris family.

John Sartoris, great-grandson and ill-fated aviator, was the protagonist of the other work, entitled "With Caution and Dispatch," which may have been started even earlier in the year. There were resemblances to both "All the Dead Pilots" and "Turn About." This was natural enough after the work he did for Hawks and MGM. "Turn About" was still recent enough for something of that mood—a combination of comedy, melodrama, and tragedy—to get into this new story as well. Once again, harebrained John Sartoris was pitted against a commanding officer for the same girl. Flying from England to France, Sartoris suddenly precipitated action even wilder than the CMB torpedo attack in "Turn About." When his Camel nearly spun into the English Channel in a rain squall, he recovered as he was about to crash into the side of a Brazilian merchantman: "He was now travelling sideways down the after well-deck; two seamen were running madly toward a companionway in the rise of the poop." The story broke off after Sartoris had crash-landed on the deck.

On November 4 Ben Wasson sent "There Was a Queen" and "Black Music" to *Scribner's.* In less than a week Alf Dashiell had accepted the former at $300 for January publication and rejected the latter. The following month he would also reject "The Leg." By a fluke of timing, Louis

Cochran's long article appeared on a full page of the Memphis *Commercial Appeal* on November 6, presenting Faulkner as "now enjoying the Jack London relish of having editors, who once scorned his offerings, besiege him for them." It must have been about this time that he wrote Ben to ask about the money due him from the sale of *Sanctuary* to Paramount. Three weeks before, Morton Goldman, Ben's assistant, informed him that the check would come in a few days. "My address has been the Postoffice steps ever since," Faulkner wrote. He had used some of the California money to clear up old bills, and the renovation costs had apparently exceeded the estimate. It seems likely that he was also planning to add more land to his holdings. Though he had been sick for a week, he reported, Estelle was well, and they hoped to come up to New York for New Year's. But if the *Sanctuary* check did not come through soon, he would have to do something to bring in some cash.

Howard Hawks had told him to let him know when he needed money. "I got in a jam," Faulkner later said, "and did." The response was quick. "I have another offer from M.G.M. through Hawks," Faulkner wrote Ben, "a good offer, handled through Hawks' brother, who is also an agent. If I accept it, I will have to accept the brother too." He wanted Ben's help or advice about the Selznick-Joyce people, whom he expected to claim ten percent on the new job. "I want to get loose from them, and as long as it is Hawks who gets me the jack, I am going to let his brother handle any business that requires an agent out there. Let me hear from you." Hawks was as good as his word. Faulkner went back on the MGM payroll on November 28 at $600 a week. He would deal with Selznick-Joyce later.

On his MGM author's card he was charged to "War Story." This designation actually covered three sources for this potential film. The basic one was *War Birds: Diary of an Unknown Aviator*, which had been published in book form after its serial publication in *Liberty* magazine during the spring and fall of 1926. More than one screenwriter had tried to do a scenario based on John McGavock Grider's rather straightforward account of three American cadets who sail to Europe, train in England, and fight in France, where one of them is killed. Onto this story line Faulkner was to graft parts of "Ad Astra" and "All the Dead Pilots." By mid-December he was well into the script.

Shortly after he had gone back on the MGM payroll, he had received a proposition that might conceivably have tempted him had it come a few weeks earlier. Bennett Cerf had made arrangements with Robert Haas to do a limited edition of 550 copies of *The Sound and the Fury.* It was to be a special job by San Francisco's Grabhorn Press, a title which would adorn Random House's spring list and help enhance the firm's name during these difficult days of the slowly waning Depression. On December 8 Cerf offered Faulkner $500 for a ten- to twelve-page introduction and his signature on the copies. Eight days later Faulkner wrote thanking Cerf. "But I dont think five hundred is enough," he told him. "Why not wait until better times, when you can pay me a thousand or fifteen hundred? I imagine this sounds outrageous right at present. But maybe times will mend soon, and the book will wait." Cerf replied on the twenty-third that he hoped they could talk it over and work out an agreement when Faulkner and Estelle came into New York after Christmas. He sent along a gift copy of a special edition of Stephen Crane's *The Red Badge of Courage* so Faulkner could see what the Grabhorn Press could do.

Cerf waited and heard nothing. Hal Smith was having the same problem. On December 23, Smith too had sent a letter to Oxford, which had been paralyzed by snow and sleet. Being both friend and publisher, he could say what other Faulkner correspondents had doubtless wanted to say: "It has become as plain as the most incredible nose on an impossible face that you won't answer this or any other letter." But he sent Christmas greetings anyway. "Now if you should answer this," he went on, "and for Christ sake don't decide to do anything rash, you might add a line whether or not you will or won't add a twenty line introduction or preface to your volume of verse, which is going to be a most handsome affair, or Evelyn Harter never saw one." Cerf had to know if he could put *The Sound and the Fury* on the spring list. He sent a long day letter to Faulkner with one key sentence: WILL RAISE OUR OFFER TO SEVEN HUNDRED FIFTY DOLLARS AS TRIBUTE TO THE FAULKNER PRESTIGE. He waited again.

Faulkner answered in what must have been early January, 1933. "I have been busy as hell," he told Smith, "writing a movie script and taking care of the sick. Estelle and the children have been sick in rotation since the middle of November, and the day after Xmas Estelle succeeded in falling downstairs (no one would have been surprised if it had been me now, on Dec. 26) and she has been in bed ever since." There was no danger of a miscarriage and she was getting up now, but they would not make the trip they had planned. "We have decided to save the money and put heat in the house, anyway." His response to Cerf's wire was the same one he had made to the letter. He didn't need the money badly enough to settle for that figure and later they might both get more out of it. "Rotten weather here," he added, "as usual. However, I have a keg of good moonshine and four pounds of English tobacco, so what the hell, as the poet says." He thanked Cerf for *The Red Badge of Courage* and mentioned a set of galleys Viking had sent him of *God's Little Acre.* "I read it with a good deal of interest, but I still think the guy is pulling George Oppenheimer's leg. I believe that Alex. Woolcott [*sic*] and Lon Chaney's ghost wrote it."

Faulkner had completed the assignment of rights on "War Story" to MGM on December 15, and late that month or early in the new year he had mailed in his "1st dialogue script." On January 12, 1933, the MGM script department had the 143 mimeographed pages ready for distribution. Elliot White Springs had done a treatment of *War Birds* which introduced a British flier and a German who would shoot him down. The American diarist would down the German and marry the Briton's sister. Faulkner grafted bits of "Ad Astra" onto materials from the book and the treatment. He used many incidents and verbatim passages from "All the Dead Pilots." The script displayed a seemingly facile use of terms relating to scenes and camera shots, but the language was often stilted and marked by an awkward bravado. Clearly this was not his medium, but he was doing his best with it.

He had apparently cleared his desk of script work early enough to correct the proofs of *A Green Bough*, which had been pulled and stamped January 27, 1933. The setting copy he had sent to New York had included titles for each of the poems. Now he crossed out the titles and substituted roman numerals. He did little else and sent the proofs back to New York. The sequel to *The Marble Faun*, announced so confidently eight years before, had taken somewhat longer than expected, but at last it would appear. And six of the poems had been bought by *The New Republic*, where they would appear in three issues to be published in April and May, almost fourteen years after Faulkner's debut there with "L'Apres-Midi d'un Faune."

The studio continued to charge his time to "War Story" through February 19, when he was probably doing revisions, and would do so again for the last two weeks of March, when he was probably making further changes suggested by Hawks. Even if the script did not go before the cameras, Faulkner had something more than mimeographed pages to show for his work. "I have enough money now to finish my house," he wrote Ben Wasson on February 12. "Going to add another bedroom and bath, and put in heat and paint it." When they had met in Memphis the previous month, Wasson had offered to try for movie sales as well as magazine sales of his stories. Faulkner liked the idea, but to sell to Howard Hawks he had to go through Bill Hawks, and he didn't relish paying two agents while doing part of the selling himself. He knew, however, that he was no businessman. "I would like to have you protect me from myself," he told Ben, "but how to do it? I am under no written contract with anyone. This arrangement is like that of a field hand; either of us (me or M.G.M.) to call it off without notice, they to pay me by the week, and to pay a bonus on each original story."

On February 20 he began writing continuity and dialogue for a synopsis done by MGM writer Harry Behn of "Honor," one of Faulkner's own stories. He was dealing, of course, with the airman Monaghan again but in a very different milieu: the world of barnstorming aviators—specifically, a pilot, his wife, and their wing-walking partner who completed not only the act but the romantic triangle. As of March 6 the studio told him he would have to take a fifty-percent salary cut. He accepted it and continued with *Honor* until March 15, when he went back onto *War Birds* again. L. B. Mayer had okayed Faulkner's continuance on the payroll into mid-March. When that time was up, Sam Marx asked Mayer, Greenwood, and Hawks what to do. The word came back immediately from Hawks: he would like Faulkner kept on the payroll, and he would speak to Mr. Mayer about it. The material of *Honor* now bore a great deal more relevance to his daily life than any script so far, for on February 2, 1933, he had begun taking formal instruction in flying.

"When Faulkner came to me for lessons," Vernon Omlie later said, "he told me not to say anything about it. He said he wanted to get back his nerve and learn to fly all over again before anybody knew what he was doing." He was not able to manage it. But when reporters discovered that a reputed combat pilot was taking lessons, Faulkner had a double explanation. Not only was he trying to regain the nerve lost in two plane crashes, but "He says there have been so many radical changes in planes and flying since he was a Canadian 'leftenant' that he has to learn all over again." For some time, apparently, he had been content to ride along on short hops from the Memphis airport. But lately, with more aerial activity in Oxford as well as Memphis, his interest had quickened. Besides, he had enough money for flying and there was no manuscript on his desk. If he needed an example, there was that of his brother. A full two years earlier, said Johncy, he had been flying from an island in the middle of Moon Lake. His instructor was a preacher whose airplane bore no identifying numbers, just the legend "Jesus Saves." The lessons had ended abruptly when the preacher had flown away with the money John had paid in advance.

William Faulkner could not have chosen a better instructor than Captain Vernon C. Omlie. They had probably met at the Memphis airport in the late 1920's, and then in the fall of 1932 Omlie had started making weekend trips to Oxford. Flying from a landing strip in a little valley south of town, he taught Ole Miss students and offered sightseeing flights. He was a virile six-footer, a quiet kindly man with keen eyes set in a weathered face that gave him a faint resemblance to Gary Cooper. Born in North Dakota, he had started flying in 1916. After service on the Mexican border, he had been an instructor during the war. Then he had drifted into barnstorming. In 1921, he met Phoebe Fairgrave in Minneapolis. "A bit of a schoolgirl," ran one account, "weighing less than 55, she was 'haunting' the flying field, insisting that the management let her walk the wings of a plane. She finally persuaded Captain Omlie to let her get out on a wing, but he made her put on a harness and tied a rope to it, so he could pull her back into the cockpit if she slipped. They did this a number of times and finally organized an aerial circus." Big Vernon Omlie took the tiny woman with him, her hair cropped like a man's, her face heavily scarred. He taught her to fly. They toured the Midwest and then followed the Mississippi south. On February 18, 1922, they were married, and later that year they found themselves in Memphis. They had been playing county fairs and small towns but they had little to show for their work beyond their airplane, the parachutes stowed in it, and the flying clothes they wore. They decided to stay in Memphis, Phoebe Omlie later said, because "we were stranded and broke."

There they prospered. They started a flying school and their own company, Mid-South Airways. They made aerial maps and flew mail and supplies during the great flood of 1927. The first woman to receive a license, Phoebe won airplane derbies and set records—one of them for the women's parachute jump. Now Vernon drove a long white Cord, and every year they would go to the National Air Races at Cleveland, where they would see such friends as Jimmy Doolittle. If they went into the ballroom of the Hotel Peabody of an evening, the spotlight would swing away from the singer on the bandstand to follow Vernon Omlie to his table. Their Memphis apartment was filled with mementos of the life they had made: the photographs of fliers standing by their planes, the trophies they had won, the iron mouthpiece by which Phoebe had swung from the plane in the barnstorming days.

Omlie began Faulkner's instruction in a Waco F biplane. After the first session on February 2, they waited until February 21 to resume. But thereafter, for the next two months, they would fly together every week but one —sometimes just once a week, in one week four times. "I had quite a time with Bill," Omlie told another pilot and mutual friend. "He had trouble getting the feel of the controls. He had to learn to use the instruments, not the seat of his pants, but he still tried to do it the old way, trying to get the old feel back, but he couldn't." He was doing well enough by mid-March, however, to go on a cross-country flight with Omlie from Oxford to Memphis. They flew together, still in the Waco, on April 17, 18, and 19. By now Faulkner had nearly seventeen hours of dual instruction, substantially more than the average before a student went on his own. Then, on April 20, he soloed, going aloft for three-quarters of an hour. In due course his other two brothers would follow him. Jack would later describe the rapture of flight in terms Antoine de Saint-Exupéry might have used. Faulkner never described his feelings, but on this April day, nearly fourteen years after he had entered the RAF, he must have found considerable satisfaction in soloing —a feat he had often imagined and often described, but which he was now doing, most probably, for the first time. What kind of pilot was he? Vernon Omlie, the barnstormer, was celebrated for his emphasis on aerial safety. He apparently inculcated this in his pupil, who probably found this approach congenial. Though Faulkner had to learn how to recover from a stall and a spin, he did not care for aerobatics. His preference was for straight and level flight. After he received his license in mid-November, he flew Jack up to Memphis on several occasions. On those flights, Jack remembered, "he could have balanced a cup of water on his head and it wouldn't have spilled."

In Oxford it was not his flying or his books that had been making news, but his motion pictures. In March it was reported that Paramount and MGM were vying to see which could finish its Faulkner film first for a premiere showing in Oxford. At Paramount, *Sanctuary* had become *The Story of Temple Drake* and finally went into production with villainous-looking Jack La Rue playing Popeye to blond Miriam Hopkins' Temple. The part of Popeye had earlier been offered to George Raft, who had played numerous hardened killers but declined this role because it would mean "professional suicide." "Turn About," retitled *Today We Live*, was ready first, and its national premiere was scheduled for Oxford on April 12. The Memphis papers took ample note, and so did the Oxford *Eagle*.

In January the *Eagle* had been purchased by Curtis H. Mullen, who was assisted by his plump, bespectacled son, Phil. Accepting the inevitable comic-strip nickname "Moon," Phil used it for a column called "Moonbeams." He had a taste for literature not common among the editors of country weeklies, and for the next two decades he would comment at intervals on William Faulkner and his work. For Oxonians who formed opinions without knowing Faulkner or reading his fiction, Mullen's comments very likely were an influence. Over the years they would also gauge the slowly changing attitudes of Oxford toward him. In one of his first columns Mullen wrote, "To be a successful author of the modern school it takes a good memory of all the dirty stories told in your teens. . . . Tiffany Thayer takes sex, makes it humorous and interesting; Faulkner makes it disgusting." He wondered in a subsequent issue, "How can they make a moving picture out of Faulkner's *Sanctuary*?" A few weeks later, however, he told his readers that the author was being praised in the London *Times*, and remarked, "Few Oxford people realize the distinction of having as a native son, William Faulkner." Mullen was not a literary critic, he said, but he knew why he read and liked Faulkner. He had been thoroughly disgusted with *Sanctuary* but not bored. Faulkner's characters reminded him of Sax Rohmer's insidious Dr. Fu Manchu. Mullen had read *Light in August* and was eagerly looking forward to others. "Reading such books is like seeing a side show of wax figures and not being disappointed. I consider myself sane, normal and healthy and through Mr. Faulkner I can satisfy my curiosity as to the actions of those 'different people.' "

Mullen was in the audience, some of whom had come from as far as Memphis, on Wednesday evening, April 12, for the premiere. Sallie Murry watched while Bob Williams, as owner of the Lyric Theatre, made an address of welcome to her cousin. "No one," he said, smiling, "is any happier to have you here than I am." Faulkner thanked him and made a short talk in reply, "mentioning that writing a play and dialogue for the screen was somewhat different from writing a book. As a novelist he has absolute say as to what appears therein, while writing the play was subject to changes by the scenario authorities and the picture director." Among the capacity crowd in the theater was a reporter for the *Commercial Appeal.* He noted that "Faulkner brought his immediate family to the theatre, together with his 'hired-help,' whom he wanted to show, he said, 'that he worked sometimes.' " Like the New York and Los Angeles critics, the Memphian objected to the overly clipped British dialogue which Faulkner had given to Franchot Tone and Robert Young, but he had superlatives for almost everything else. Everyone, apparently, was happy about the film.

The premiere was one of three events which made April of 1933 an exceptional month for Faulkner. Unquestionably, the premiere must have given the least satisfaction of the three. On April 20 he had soloed in Vernon Omlie's Waco. On the same day, in New York, Harrison Smith and Robert Haas had published *A Green Bough.* Among the book's forty-four poems were works familiar to Faulkner fans, such as "The Lilacs," and others, such as "My Epitaph," which would become familiar later on. There was a wide variety, for he had included specimens of the ballad-style poems he had written in his teens and others as different as the poem about tourists that suggested E. E. Cummings. He had placed the longer poems first, following "The Lilacs" with "Laxly reclining, he watches the firelight going"—the poem in which the distraught lover hears his beloved play the piano and then watches her mount the stair. Poem II, originally called "Floyd Collins," had been called "The Cave" before he deleted the titles. There were more love poems than any other kind—short lyrics, such as "I see your face through the twilight of my mind," and passionate sonnets, some with pastoral imagery still, and intense verses couched in familiar poetic diction. It seemed an anthology, being not so much a gathering of new work as a collection of poems done at different times and in different styles which Faulkner still liked now, years later. Like Thomas Hardy, publishing early poems in his old age, Faulkner had earned a hearing for these poems not so much with his prior verse as with a series of novels which had shocked his readers with their violence and tragedy. As Hal Smith had promised, Evelyn Harter had done an attractive job of composition and Lynn Ward had provided a striking title-page illustration.

The few reviews that appeared could not have changed the poet's assessment that the work was second-rate. On April 28 Hal Smith wrote that the book had been "excellently reviewed, though I don't agree with all of your critics." He sent along two or three reviews. "I've often thought that I wrote the novels because I found I couldn't write the poetry," Faulkner would say later, "that maybe I wanted to be a poet, maybe I think of myself as a poet, and I failed at that, I couldn't write poetry, so I did the next best thing." He had asked Horace Liveright if he could print his verse, and he was pleased when Smith published the book he said he had put together as carefully as he would a novel. But with the exception of one brief effort, years later, he was through with verse. He would never publish another poem.

By the end of March, MGM was charging Faulkner's time against an idea he had suggested to Sam Marx called *Mythical Latin-American Kingdom Story.* As Marx later remembered the action, "a Christlike young man leads a revolt against tyranny." Retrospectively, the story showed "an uncanny resemblance to what many of us imagined Fidel Castro to be like, in those early days when he was just a shadowy figure of a rebel in a mountain lair." To create the Latin-American setting, Faulkner drew upon his imagination as he had done for "Carcassonne" and "Black Music," both of which took place in Rincon. Again he used this place-name, suggesting some connection, perhaps, between the "mythical kingdom" and Puerto Rico. One of the central characters may have had an analogue closer to home. A barnstorming flier, he bore the title of captain. His meanness was that of John Sartoris, but his flying prowess suggested Vernon Omlie. It was a very melodramatic script with dialogue alternately stilted and heroically rhetorical. Although Faulkner had suggested the idea, he may by now have lost interest in it. What emerged unmistakably from these pages was the sense that this was—as he had repeatedly said—a medium totally different from his own. He could use the technical terms with some facility now, but there was as much difference between his scriptwriting and his fiction as there was between his poetry and his fiction. It was a moneymaking job. It may not have cost any depletion of his creative reserves, just of his time and energy, but this was enough to engender anger and disgust. At the same time, he remained grateful to Hawks. He needed the work and he did it.

If the bond between Faulkner and MGM had not been quite the field-hand-and-master relationship Faulkner had described to Wasson, it has been a tenuous one as Hollywood arrangements went. Faulkner had been rehired partly because Hawks thought $600 a week was a good investment if only to have first call for film rights on Faulkner stories. Faulkner kept sending in his pages, and by late February Hawks expected that Faulkner would return to the coast within a month. He felt that the *War Birds* scenario could be made screenworthy "if Faulkner would come to the studio and work on it with Hawks's supervision and cooperation. . . ." But first Hawks had to finish the picture he was shooting. It may well have been that the unacceptability of *Mythical Latin-American Kingdom Story* signified the end of the unorthodox arrangement which had continued for nearly twenty weeks. Among those who knew that Faulkner was drawing a studio salary a thousand miles away in Mississippi, M. E. Greenwood could scarcely have been the only one who objected. Given that era in the history of the film industry, Hawks deserved credit for proposing it and Mayer for permitting it. But finally, Faulkner had to leave Oxford or go off salary.

The subsequent events passed into Hollywood lore, and though Faulkner denied some of the accounts, he helped to perpetuate them. He said he received a telegram from the studio asking where he was. Soon after he replied, a long-distance call ordered him to report to director Tod Browning, who was in New Orleans on location for a picture alternately entitled *Louisiana Lou* and *Bride of the Bayou.* Unlike Harry Rapf in both appearance and métier, Browning had directed Lon Chaney in such films as *The Freaks* and excelled generally when the protagonists were deformed and the action vicious. Favoring double-breasted bold-checked suits, he was a thin man who wore a brooding expression and a stiletto-tipped waxed mustache. Among Browning's credits was the original *Dracula*, a very different work from his present project.

Faulkner wanted to leave home less now than ever. Estelle had recovered from the fall at Christmas, but he was still seeing to it that she got plenty of bed rest. It had been at just about this time in the last pregnancy that the baby had come prematurely. Besides this, he had just soloed and he was preparing to buy an airplane. If he were to complete this deal, however, and another which he had in mind, he would need to stay on the studio payroll a bit longer. He had been directed to get on the first plane to New Orleans. He decided to follow his instructions to the letter.

"I could have got on a train in Oxford and been in New Orleans eight hours later," he said. "But I obeyed the studio and went to Memphis, where an airplane occasionally did go to New Orleans. Three days later one did." Once he got to New Orleans, Faulkner said, the continuity writer refused to let him see the story until he had shown the writer some dialogue. When he placed the problem before the director, he was told not to worry and to get a good night's sleep for an early start the next morning. For days thereafter they would travel a hundred miles in a motor launch each morning to reach the elaborately constructed set. It was composed of Cajun huts with false fronts whose backs opened on empty space above the waters of the bayou. Browning, Faulkner, and the others would arrive just in time to have lunch and make the return trip to New Orleans before dark. The story's climax came in the form of two telegrams. The first, Faulkner said, read, FAULKNER IS FIRED. MGM STUDIO. Browning assured Faulkner that he would call the studio immediately and obtain not only his reinstatement but an apology as well. The next telegram read, BROWNING IS FIRED. MGM STUDIO.

The truth was simpler and not nearly so entertaining. He was in New Orleans by April 26. His later account was apparently correct, however, about the lack of progress on the script. On May 5 Sam Marx wired Browning at the Hotel Roosevelt in New Orleans for a report on how Faulkner was doing and an estimate of the prospects for the screenplay. Browning replied immediately. PARTY REFERRED TO IN YOUR WIRE BRILLIANT CAPABLE MAN BUT HAD UNFORTUNATE START, he wired Marx. Besides this, his dialogue was unsatisfactory. Browning added something the studio already knew: HE WILL NOT GO TO CULVER CITY TO FINISH DIALOGUE UNTIL AFTER BIRTH OF CHILD DUE IN JUNE BUT WISHES TO WRITE AT HIS HOME IN OXFORD. Understandably, Browning was not in favor of this arrangement. It fell to Sam Marx to break the news with another telegram to the Hotel Roosevelt: OWING TO NECESSITY BROWNING SCRIPT BEING COMPLETED HERE AT STUDIO AND YOUR INABILITY TO RETURN HERE I BELIEVE IT BEST WE RELIEVE YOU OF YOUR ASSIGNMENT STOP MANY THANKS FOR ALL YOU HAVE DONE STOP STUDIO FEELS THIS SYSTEM OF WORKING IS NOT FEASIBLE CONSEQUENTLY WE WILL BE MOST HAPPY TO CONTINUE YOU ON STAFF HERE AT ANY TIME YOU ADVISE US YOU WILL COME TO CALIFORNIA STOP I HAVE ASKED HOWARD HAWKS TO WRITE YOU AND PLAN OUT SOME DEAL FOR THE FUTURE.

Faulkner was back in Oxford by May 9 at the latest, but he was not quite through with MGM yet. In spite of his dissatisfaction, Browning had needed some more material. Faulkner worked at home again for part of a week, sent his material to Browning in New Orleans, and finally went off the payroll as of May 13. But it would be nearly four months before the last detail of the *Louisiana Lou–Bride of the Bayou* saga fell into place.

Faulkner began flying again almost every week. By mid-June he was flying dual again with Vernon Omlie, but in a different airplane. This was a big, powerful Waco C cabin cruiser, equipped with a 210 h.p. Continental engine and capable of carrying four passengers. Selling for just under $6,000 new, it was a popular aircraft which had a good rate of climb. Its two big wings gave it stability which almost eliminated the possibility of stalling, and its flaps were meant to help make it possible to land on smaller-than-average fields. Faulkner enjoyed flying the trim red craft.

Though the Memphis papers were not now recording his activities, his name did appear in the New York *Daily Mirror.* Walter Winchell reported in his column that the Faulkners were "anticipating a blessed expense." What they expected, or hoped for, was a boy. They planned to name him Bill.

On June 20 he incurred another expense. From Mrs. Sallie Bailey Bryant he bought three lots bordering his property at Rowan Oak. He drew two checks to her, one for $1,800 and another for $700, the balance to be paid when he redeemed an $800 note signed the same day. He was probably entertaining thoughts of buying the Waco, but first he would add to his holdings in a way that both the Old Colonel and the Young Colonel would have approved. He was doing it now when he could, before the remainder of the $8,000 he had cleared at MGM this year was gone. Very likely the motive uppermost in his mind was not so much enlarging his holdings as safeguarding something increasingly precious and difficult to protect: his privacy. On Friday, June 23, Mrs. Bryant gave him a warranty deed.

That evening, the moon rose large and bright in the clear starry sky. The Faulkners decided to go for a ride in the soft moonlight. They drove northeast, through town and out to the College Hill Road, past the church where they were married. At last Faulkner turned and drove back toward town, but as he headed for home Estelle stopped him. "Billy," she said, "you'd better go right on to the hospital." He drove to Dr. Eugene Bramlett's long, low white hospital. About daybreak Estelle gave birth to a girl. The baby weighed scarcely more than five pounds, but she did not need the incubator which her father had presented to Dr. Bramlett two years before. When Faulkner came in to see his wife on Saturday morning, he found her disappointed over the baby's sex. He told her she mustn't feel that way. "There are too many Faulkner boys anyway," he said. They called their daughter Jill.

This time when Estelle came home from the hospital only one nurse accompanied her. Miss Bee moved into Rowan Oak to stay during the baby's early weeks. Jill was blue-eyed and fair, with blond hair. She might be small, but she was a robust eater, and Miss Bee was satisfied with her growing weight. She was joined later by a member of Miss Lida's household. Narcissus McEwen was a few inches over five feet and a substantial number of pounds over two hundred. By the time Miss Bee was ready to leave, easy, good-natured Mammy McEwen was ready to take over as Jill's nurse.

Faulkner had not been offering his wife empty consolation in Bramlett's hospital. He adored the baby. In one of her first pictures she was held, coated and bonneted, on her father's lap as he sat on the brick steps at the

With Jill on the steps of the front gallery, Rowan Oak.

left of the front gallery. Fatherhood had come late to him. He was now nearly thirty-six, and to some who saw him with his daughter—then and later—all the clichés about paternal love came to mind. At such moments she was more than the apple of his eye; she was what he would call his fictional child, Caddy Compson: "my heart's darling."

As much as his constant financial concerns allowed, he must have felt a kind of euphoria, or at least contentment. The young man whom some had called Count No 'Count had come a long way. He had married his childhood sweetheart. They had a little girl. Though his royalties were still modest, he was internationally known. Though he constantly felt a pinch for money, he had bought one of the county's oldest houses, and in a modestly baronial way he was refurbishing it and adding to his lands.

It may have been with something of this feeling of well-being that, though rarely a joiner, he put his name down on a membership list. It was a new organization called the Crusaders, and when it was chartered in Jackson that year Faulkner was listed as one of the executive directors. The object of the crusade was to legalize liquor and beer in Mississippi. The Twenty-first Amendment, repealing prohibition, was now being ratified by the states. But even if the amendment were ratified, the state law would remain on the books unless the pro-repeal forces were mobilized to defeat what some called an alliance between the Baptists, the bootleggers, and the county sheriffs. Looking back much later, Faulkner said he had joined the organization "one hot summer night over a bottle of gin." But he was disappointed and angry at the outcome, and he would continue to espouse the Crusaders' objectives in skirmishes to come.

It was time to look to his finances again, particularly with his new responsibility. Three days after Jill's birth he had written to Ben Wasson. "Well, bud," he said, "we've got us a gal baby named Jill. Born Saturday and both well." Then he turned to business. Wasson had been writing him about Cerf's idea for the Grabhorn Press–Random House edition of *The Sound and the Fury.* "All right," he answered. "Let me know about it, if he will use the colored ink. I like that. I will need time to lay it out again. How many different colors shall I be limited to? Just what does he want in the introduction? I'm ready to start right away." He was now willing to accept Cerf's last offer of $750, partly because other revenue probably had to be written off. "What about the Cape & Smith business?" he asked. "Is all that lost?" (It was.)

He ended the letter with current activities: "Working spasmodically at a novel." It was probably the novel he had mentioned to Stallings and Boyd in California, the one about the Snopeses. It may by now have borne the Balzacian title *The Peasants.* His fellow admirer of Balzac, Phil Stone, would have approved. Stone had told Emily Whitehurst that he thought *Light in August* was Bill's best book so far, but he looked forward to the Snopes saga. He was apparently convinced that it would be his friend's great work. The longer it took to appear, the more impatient he became. But Faulkner went on at his own pace, the 1934 publication date still vague and tentative.

There was another project which might further delay the completion of the Snopes book. Before Jill's arrival Faulkner had written Sam Marx asking for the right to do *Mythical Latin-American Kingdom Story* as a novel. Marx asked Hendrickson to draw up the papers. The script was not right for a motion picture, and if Faulkner turned the story into a novel they might then have a better basis for a scenario. In July Marx forwarded the papers to Faulkner, together with a request for assignment of the rights on "Honor," "Ad Astra," and "All the Dead Pilots." For once Faulkner proved himself a good businessman. He had written those stories before he went to work for MGM. Shouldn't there be some further payment if he were to assign rights? Marx and Hendrickson both granted his point, and the matter was dropped there. Faulkner had closed his letter with the comment, "I would like to know how Tod is coming with *Louisiana Lou.* I was getting pretty steamed up over it when I got the air. He's a fine fellow. Give him my best when you see him, and Howard Hawks too." When Marx replied on August 24, he supplied the final detail of the *Louisiana Lou* story—which Faulkner would rework in his retelling. "Regarding the production of 'Louisiana Lou,' there have been some changes made and I understand Tod will not direct it. So you see he got the air, too."

In mid-July Faulkner had received a check from Hal Smith along with a contract for his signature. The title of the new novel may not have been specified. Both were probably thinking of the Snopes book, but Faulkner could satisfy the terms of the contract with any novel that was acceptable to Smith. As he had done in his letter to Marx, Faulkner tried to safeguard his interests. He would not cash the check until he had Smith's response to his request that his royalties be increased to fifteen percent on the first printing and twenty percent on subsequent ones. He objected to Clause VIII of the contract, which gave the publisher the first option on his next novel. Faulkner did not mind giving this to Smith. However, "in this contract the option is not to you but to a company. Vide the J. Cape affair, excusing which I would not be needing two thousand dollars now, not having got a cent of the four thousand odd which their royalty statement showed for April of last year. That's why I dont like option clauses; though if you insist, etc." This was the kind of negotiation which should have been handled by Ben Wasson, but Faulkner had the habit of interposing himself between his agent and editors and publishers and making deals which would later prove disadvantageous. He did this sometimes because of personal relationships with people who bought his material and sometimes because he was anxious to make a sale more quickly than he thought his agent could. The effect was to create confusion, dilemmas, and, in a later instance, near catastrophe. He was aware that in some situations he behaved like a coon in a tree, but he would continue to persist in doing these things, to the helpless annoyance of future agents and to his own anguish.

Ben had apparently been doing his best to help Faulkner meet his new expenses. Two new bedrooms had been added upstairs, heat put in, and more paint and paper applied. Besides this, money had probably been earmarked for an airplane. And soon Maud Falkner would be almost completely dependent upon her son for support. Ben had recently told him about a book on the Mississippi River in which a potential publisher was interested, and *Vanity Fair* said they would like an article by Faulkner on that subject. But things had suddenly changed. "I think I would like to write a book like that, but I believe it would take some time; first, to write something as outside of my line as nonfiction; and second, to get done with what I have on hand now to start it. I am hot with a novel now, and until I get that underway, a short story now and then is about all I had better undertake. I'd like to talk about it with the guy later on. Maybe I could promise something definite, which I cant do now, as I am about to contract with Hal for the novel, setting it for the fall of 1934. If he doesn't farm the idea out in the meantime, we'll talk about it in the fall. We are going to christen Jill about October, and you are expected down then." In the letter he enclosed "another story."

In the last paragraph of the letter to Smith, Faulkner had turned to other matters. "We are all well. I have turned out three short stories since I quit the movies, so I have not forgot how to write during my sojourn downriver." It appears that one of these stories represented an attempt, like the projected novelization of *Mythical Latin-American Kingdom Story*, to salvage something more from the time of bondage. It was a story which wound up on Alf Dashiell's desk in August. Dashiell rejected it. "The main fault, it seems to me, is that the reader will not accept the chief element in the plot, namely that a guest would consider it his bounden duty to drink any liquor that might be sent to his room by his host and after all there is not much difference between pouring the liquor down the sink and pouring it down the throat of a servant." The story obviously was a rewritten version of *Manservant*, the first script Faulkner had worked on at MGM, itself a revised version of the story "Love" dating back at least to 1921. The work in Hollywood had in no way affected Faulkner's thrifty use of material.

In the previous month Dashiell had also rejected "Elly," which Faulkner may or may not have included in the three new stories he mentioned to Hal Smith. (This was a revision of "Selvage," written four and a half years before.) It is possible that the third was "Lo!," which did not sell immediately either. "Lo!" was another story in which Faulkner picked up and developed a character he had briefly introduced earlier. In "A Mountain Victory" protagonist Saucier Weddel had spoken of his father, Francis Weddel, a half-white Choctaw chief, builder of the mansion Contalmaison, who "drove to Washington once in his carriage to remonstrate with President Jackson about the Government's treatment of his people, sending on ahead a wagon of provender and gifts and also fresh horses for the carriage . . . ." Whereas "A Mountain Victory" was tragic, "Lo!" was comic, though it was not without some of the grisly humor that often marked Faulkner's Indian stories. Faulkner had changed Weddel from half-Choctaw to half-Chickasaw. The purpose of the tribal journey to Washington was also changed, or at least particularized. Weddel's nephew had murdered a white man who had cheated him. Now the chief had brought him to Washington for trial by the Great White Father himself. The humor in the story derived principally from the incongruous encampment of "the People" on the White House grounds and in the very corridors themselves, until the harried President not only exonerated the culprit but conferred lasting and illegal advantages upon the pleasant, courteous, and implacable Weddel and his tribe.

Writing in some discouragement to Wasson, Faulkner sent him another story which he did not identify. "I suppose 'Lo' is another dud," he wrote. "But maybe this one will sell. I'd hate to see it gutted, but I hope the Post will take it. Or maybe Cosmopolitan; they ought to pay well." By now, perhaps mid-August, he had either cooled off again on the novel or concluded that he had no choice but to put it aside. "Think I will try the

'Mississippi' article for Vanity Fair if its still open, or something for 'Esquire.' Just what did they want, if you remember?"

Faulkner had not published a story since "There Was a Queen" had appeared in the January issue of *Scribner's.* Now he went through his files looking for stories he could send out again. He sent out "Artist at Home" with very few changes. It was accepted by *Story* (III), to appear there in August. He reread "Beyond the Gate" and then began it all over again. At the end of the story he made it clear that the whole experience was probably a moment's fantasy in the Judge's brain. It was the kind of strategy Ambrose Bierce had used in his famous tour de force "An Occurrence at Owl Creek Bridge." He did not, however, surrender the story's philosophical-religious implications. Yet it was in this area that difficulties arose, even after the story, retitled "Beyond," had been bought by *Harper's* for $350. When it reached the proof stage Faulkner wrote Ben with some impatience about the editor's questions. "To me the answer seems obvious: The writer is trying to explain a story and some characters by writing it down; that's what a story is. If it doesn't come off to the reader, the only alternatives I know are, to delete that part which needs explanation, which as [editor Lee F.] Hartman says, seems to do nothing toward carrying forward with the story; or explain it by a footnote, like this: the agnostic progresses far enough into heaven to find one whom his intelligence, if not his logic, could accept as Christ, and who even offers him an actual sight and meeting with his dead son in exchange for the surrender of his logic, agnosticism. But he naturally and humanly prefers the sorrow with which he has lived so long that it not only does not hurt anymore, but is perhaps even a pleasure, to the uncertainty of change, even when it means that he may gain his son again." After this unusual explication, Faulkner went on to form. "That is what I intended to tell, and hoped that I had. I thought I had chosen the best method, touching the whole thing pretty lightly by careful deliberation in understatement. It is a tour de force in esoteria; it cant be anything else. I have mulled it over for two days now, without yet seeing just how I can operate on it and insert a gland. I'll hold the proof, and you get in touch with Hartman and if he can tell us just what he would like to have inserted, I'll invent some way to do it." Apparently no typescript or proof survives to reveal whether Faulkner performed the surgery. When the story appeared in the September issue of *Harper's*, the only discernible difference was that the last paragraph was somewhat longer than it had been in manuscript form, making it clear that the Judge, back in his home in Jefferson, was now composing his limbs in death, at the end of this "tour de force in esoteria." This taste, which Faulkner had displayed much earlier in such stories as "The Leg" and "Black Music," would appear very little from now on.

Meanwhile, plans had been going forward in New York and San Francisco for the new edition of *The Sound and the Fury.* Cerf had written to Ed Grabhorn explaining how the character of Benjy had troubled many readers throughout his difficult section. To solve this difficulty, "we have hit upon the idea of printing this first section in three colors, one color to represent the character's extreme youth, the second color to represent the adolescent period, and the third color to represent things that are happening at the present time. Faulkner himself is marking this section so that the printer will know exactly what color each paragraph must appear in. Personally, I think the three colors should be black, maroon, and either dark blue or dark green, but I want your opinion on this as soon as you can give it to me." Faulkner would supply the introduction in a couple of weeks and the color division even sooner.

But then six weeks passed and neither one had arrived. Cerf wrote to Faulkner without success and then turned to Ben Wasson, who also wrote him. Faulkner finished the introduction in mid-August and sent it to Wasson with a covering letter. "The enclosed explains itself. I have worked on it a good deal, like on a poem almost, and I think that it is all right now. See what Bennett thinks and let me know."

The introduction he enclosed had gone through at least three stages. The surviving page of his manuscript showed how uncomfortable he felt as he started: "Bennett Cerf told me he wants in this introduction, How I came to write The Sound and The Fury, what I think of it after 5 years, and an explanation of the first section, revealing, I think, what Benjy was trying to tell and why I let him tell it." Granting that there was, outside of fiction, "a logical economy of cause and effect" and "admitting for the moment my own theory that any introduction to any book, written by a fiction writer, is likely to be about 50% fiction itself, this is how I would answer all 3 of his queries." He began by supplying background on the unpromising start which he felt his first three novels constituted.

By the time he was ready to type out his manuscript, he had abandoned the reference to Bennett Cerf and preceded his description of his early labors with a 1,000-word essay on writing in the South. "Art is no part of Southern life," he wrote. Then he described how it was different in New York and

Chicago. The reason was simple: the latter two—representing the East and the Middle West—were young and vigorous, whereas the South was "old since dead . . . killed by the Civil War." The "new South" was not Southern at all but merely a land of immigrants trying to remake the South along Northern lines. "Yet this art, which has no place in Southern life, is almost the sum total of the Southern artist. It is his breath, blood, flesh, all." He went on from there to the most conscious scrutiny of Southern writing he had ever attempted.

"Because it is himself that the Southerner is writing about, not about his environment; who has, figuratively speaking, taken the artist in him in one hand and his milieu in the other and thrust the one into the other like a clawing and spitting cat into a croker sack. And he writes. We have never got and probably will never get, anywhere with music or the plastic forms. We need to talk, to tell, since oratory is our heritage. We seem to try in the single furious breathing (or writing) span of the individual to draw a savage indictment of the contemporary scene or to escape from it into a make-believe region of swords and magnolias and mockingbirds which perhaps never existed anywhere. Both of the courses are rooted in sentiment; perhaps the one who writes savagely and bitterly of the incest in clayfloored cabins are [*sic*] the most sentimental. Anyway, each course is a matter of violent partizanship, in which the writer unconsciously writes into every line and phrase his violent despairs and rages and frustrations or his violent prophesies [*sic*] of still more violent hopes. That cold intellect which can write with calm and complete detachment and gusto of its contemporary scene is not among us; I do not believe there lives the Southern writer who can say without lying that writing is any fun to him. Perhaps we do not want it to be."

Now he turned to his own career. "I seem to have tried both of the courses. I have tried to escape and I have tried to indict." In five more pages he described the way he had reached a turning point, how in *The Sound and the Fury* he "did both at one time." He related the planless, subjective, free-flowing, and wish-fulfilling way he had begun the work, the manner in which the Benjy section had grown, and how he had been compelled to write the following three sections to clarify it. He continued in this intensely personal vein to the end. "There is a story somewhere about an old Roman who kept at his bedside a Tyrrhenian vase which he loved and the rim of which he wore slowly away with kissing it. I had made myself a vase, but I suppose I knew all the time that I could not live forever inside of it, that perhaps to have it so that I too could lie in bed and look at it would be better; surely so when that day should come when not only the ecstasy of writing would be gone, but the reluctance and the something worth saying too. It's fine to think that you will leave something behind you when you die, but it's better to have made something you can die with. Much better the muddy bottom of a little doomed girl climbing a blooming pear tree in april to look in the window at the funeral." Below these last lines he typed in the legend "Oxford./19 August, 1933."

He was finished, but only with this version, for he would rework this matter and reduce it by half in an undated typescript, excising the essay on art in the South and employing a broader, more flamboyant style. "I wrote this book and learned to read. I had learned a little about writing from Soldiers' Pay—how to approach language, words: not with seriousness so much, as an essayist does, but with a kind of alert respect, as you approach dynamite; even with joy, as you approach women: perhaps with the same secretly unscrupulous intentions. But when I finished The Sound and The Fury I discovered that there is actually something to which the shabby term Art not only can, but must, be applied. I discovered then that I had gone through all that I had ever read, from Henry James through Henty to newspaper murders, without making any distinction or digesting any of it, as a moth or a goat might. After The Sound and The Fury and without heeding to open another book and in a series of delayed repercussions like summer thunder, I discovered the Flauberts and Dostoievskys and Conrads whose books I had read ten years ago. With The Sound and The Fury I learned to read and quit reading, since I have read nothing since." He went on to say that he seemed to have learned nothing since. The "anticipation and joy" which he had felt with *The Sound and the Fury* were gone. But now, as he looked back over the seven novels he had published, this one still moved him. He compressed the story of the old Roman and his vase into one sentence and then concluded, "So I, who never had a sister and was fated to lose my daughter in infancy, set out to make myself a beautiful and tragic little girl."

In the covering letter which Faulkner sent to Ben with the introduction, he ended on a happy note he did not often sound in his correspondence: "We are fine. Jill getting fatter and fatter. Estelle has never been so well."

On August 24 Ben sent the introduction to Cerf with the notation that he would ask Bill right away for the colors for the first section of the novel.

On the same day Faulkner sent Cerf a note of apology. He had mislaid his letter about the new edition and had just found it. "I will send you at once the color-marked copy. As I have only one copy of the book, please ask the printer to take good care of it and return it to me." Now he was as good as his word. Cerf received the book on Tuesday morning, August 29, the Benjy section marked for the three-color printing. He promptly sent Ben a $500 check. The remaining $250 would be paid when Faulkner signed the sheets for the new edition. Two weeks later, insured for $100, the book was on its way to Ed Grabhorn in San Francisco.

In his letter to Cerf, Faulkner had closed, "We are getting along fine. I hope to see you this fall." What he did not tell Cerf was how he intended to make the thousand-mile trip. He was planning to pilot his own plane. He had begun to fly with regularity, making up for what he had missed, living now in actuality some of the experience he had known before only in imagination.

39

June, 1933–February, 1934

Here still the blue, the headlands; here still he
Who did not waken and was not awaked.
The eagle sped its lonely course and tall;
Was gone. Yet still upon his lonely hill the lad
Winged on past changing headlands where was laked
The constant blue. . . .

—*A Green Bough* (40)

The engines are long since throttled back; the overcast sinks slowly upward with no semblance whatever of speed until suddenly you see the aircraft's shadow scudding the cottony hillocks; and now speed has returned again, aircraft and shadow now rushing toward one another as toward one mutual headlong destruction.

—"Impressions of Japan" (76)

Two days after Jill's birth, Faulkner was flying the big Waco again with Vernon Omlie. In late July and early August they switched to a Stinson. Then, on August 15, Faulkner made a two-hour solo flight in the Waco. His logbook now showed just under thirty-three hours of flying time. On September 5 he made a two-hour cross-country flight, and three days later he logged two more hours' solo. That same day he appeared in the newspaper again. On page 2 the Memphis *Press-Scimitar* ran a photograph of Estelle holding Jill. "If she doesn't go to sleep," the caption read, "little Jill Faulkner should get a good glimpse of the Memphis skyline, the winding river, and sundry points this afternoon, because her flying father, William

210 h.p. Waco C cabin cruiser, NC13413. Owner, William Faulkner.

Faulkner, famed Mississippi novelist, is going to take her bye-bye in an airplane."

Like her parents, Jill enjoyed flying. The only thing that worried Faulkner was the possibility of overloading when he took off with Narcissus McEwen aboard, but the Waco lived up to its performance specifications. After Faulkner logged a half-hour of night flying, they had dinner and spent the night with Arthur Halle and his wife. It had been a pleasant outing for all of them. On their return to Oxford the next morning they found that the *Press-Scimitar* photo had not gone unnoticed. Almost as soon as they walked in the door at Rowan Oak, the telephone rang. It was Eugene Bramlett, wanting to speak to Estelle. What kind of a mother was she? Didn't she know Jill could have burst her eardrums? Estelle listened patiently until Dr. Bramlett finished his bawling out. She checked Jill again and found that she still showed no ill effects. Nor did she in the months thereafter when they went to Memphis regularly once a week. They would take a suite at the Peabody, with one room for Jill and Narcissus and the other for themselves. They would visit the Halles and go to dinner with Aunt 'Bama and her husband Walter. And they would fly.

As September wore on and Faulkner gained more experience, he began taking more passengers aloft. On some days he would take Mac, now nine, and Johncy's two boys—ten-year-old Jimmy and five-year-old "Chooky." If the cabin Waco with the big NC13413 on the fuselage was not available, he would rent an old open-cockpit Waco. Strapping the three boys into the two front seats, he would climb into the pilot's cockpit behind and take off. Often Vernon Omlie would join them and the two men would alternate in flying the boys over the city and countryside. On one of these days *Press-Scimitar* reporter Null Adams photographed Faulkner and the three boys just after they had landed. There was no place at the Oxford airport where he could keep his plane, Faulkner told him, so it stayed in Memphis. "Flying is about the only fun I have. I'm too busy writing novels to come here often." He was now at work on one that was set in a Mississippi town, but he would not name it until he was finished. He had never heard of anybody making money writing novels, he said, but he hoped to avoid movie work in spite of the fact that he made $35,000 out of it. "If I ever need the money badly enough I'll do some more movie work. It's a fast way to make money but never again if I can get along without it."

He continued to take instructions from Vernon Omlie. On September 13 he logged two more hours, and *Press-Scimitar* photographer Charlie Schneider memorialized the occasion with a picture of the plane next to two men pitching hay. It was captioned "150-miles-an-hour Pays Salute to 2½ miles in Airport Scene." Two days later they made the 400-mile round trip to Jackson and back. The next day Faulkner spent nearly five hours in the air making another 400-mile round trip, this time from Memphis to Vicksburg and back. Before the day was over he and Omlie went to Batesville, Mississippi, landing at an American Airways emergency field where Faulkner took the plane up alone for a quarter of an hour. They stayed at Batesville overnight, returning to Memphis and then Oxford.

Some of this flying was done in the interests of Omlie's Mid-South Airways, and on some stops the veteran pilot may have made expense money by taking local citizens aloft on brief flights. When Faulkner bought the Waco he entered into an arrangement with Omlie. Vernon could use the plane from time to time as he taught Dean Falkner to fly. Faulkner would also pay for the lessons.

Dean was now twenty-six, and his older brother was concerned about him. He had graduated in engineering and then studied law. He had written a number of short stories and he had tried painting. He might do a series of oils and then, in a surge of dissatisfaction, destroy the canvases. If he had his share of the family's visual gift, he also shared the propensity for drinking. He was more outgoing than his brother and dated a number of girls. He had brought one to Rowan Oak, a smart brunette from Columbus named Ruth Ford who was working for her M.A. in philosophy at Ole Miss. Now he was keeping company with a pretty Mississippi State graduate, a blue-eyed blond named Louise Hale. Dean still loved sports. He was a crack shot and a par golfer. Sometimes when he and Louise drove to Memphis it would take them hours and hours to get there because Dean would stop constantly along the road to watch Negroes playing baseball. There were no signs of his settling down and giving his life a constructive direction. He was still the high-strung, hot-tempered boy who had prompted football coach Homer Hazel to say, "He plays so hard and hits so hard he'll get himself killed."

As Faulkner watched his brother approaching his late twenties without a clear vocation, his feelings were paternal as well as fraternal, and with the love there was anxiety. It was clear that mixed with Dean's talent was a streak of violence. This was the kind of personality and temperament Faulkner knew on another level: a pattern very like that of young John Sartoris, who soared aloft and then plummeted to his death, leaving his brother to grieve obsessively for him. But in this case Faulkner saw the promise of a solution. Dean was intelligent and well-coordinated. He would have a dependable aircraft to fly and one of the best men to teach him.

In the last week of September Faulkner and Omlie logged more time in the Waco. They went on a cross-country to Little Rock and Abilene. A week later Faulkner flew into Batesville and trouble. Making a normal approach, he came in for a landing. "I chose a part of the field which would lead me into trouble unless I stopped the airplane before rolling into it," he later explained. "After I was on the ground and had slowed to where I no longer had rudder and elevator control, I saw that I would not be able to stop before reaching an unmowed part of the field where the hay stood waist high.

"The airplane entered this grass traveling about 15 miles an hour, when I saw a soft spot of earth ahead. I decided not to try to put on the brakes because of the high grass, so I cut the switches. It struck the soft spot and nosed over on its back.

"I unfastened my belt and got out and examined the airplane. The propeller was bent and ribs in the top wing were broken." Faulkner walked away from the landing, but it would be three days before the plane could fly again. Vernon Omlie came down from Memphis and helped supervise the installation of a new propeller and ribs. After Faulkner took it up for a test flight, he and Omlie flew it back to Memphis. "I was not injured," Faulkner summed up, "though I perhaps deserved to be as the price of carelessness and disregard of advice."

But the mishap was no deterrent. "I am not superstitious. The airplane's number has two 13s in it, and we got it ready to fly again on Friday the 13th. I shall continue to fly, though not on my back on the ground, I think." The accident had, naturally, been duly reported in both the Memphis daily papers.

Hal Smith might well have felt some trepidation about these activities of one of the firm's best-known authors—one who had also been advanced royalties on an unnamed and undelivered novel. Smith wrote and asked about the novel. "I dont think the novel will be ready for spring," Faulkner replied in a letter nonchalantly dated "something October." There was actually more than one possibility. "I have been at the Snopes book, but I have another bee now, and a good title, I think: REQUIEM FOR A NUN. It will be about a nigger woman. It will be a little on the esoteric side, like AS I LAY DYING."

Smith had proposed a collection of short stories. "It has been almost 16 months since I have written anything original or even thought in such terms," Faulkner replied. "I dont know what I have in short stories. I will take a day off soon and go through them and see if we can get a book we wont be ashamed of. I'll let you know." Then he looked ahead. "I shall have to peg away at the novel slowly, since I am broke again, with two families to support now, since my father died, and so I shall have to write a short story every so often or go back to Hollywood, which I dont want to do. They are flirting with me again, but if I can make a nickle [*sic*] from time to time with short stories, I will give them the go-by."

Before the month was out they were able to discuss future plans when Smith came down for Jill's christening. Reverend McCready performed the ritual in St. Peter's Episcopal Church, with Jack Falkner and Sallie Murry Williams standing as the baby's godparents. There was a champagne supper party afterwards at Rowan Oak, with the guests from Memphis and New Orleans. Faulkner had gone to Memphis to buy the champagne as well as some things Mrs. Oldham wanted for a dinner party she gave in Hal Smith's honor. Smith stayed on for over a week and then departed for a short visit to New Orleans. The tentative plan was for him to come back to Rowan Oak for some hunting. When he returned, however, Faulkner was drinking, and after a few days Smith went on to New York.

It may have been now, as Faulkner recovered, that he completed and sent to New York a short story which approached some of the matter of "Evangeline" from a new vantage point. Using an omniscient narrator, he employed one of his favorite strategies as he began "Wash" with a 400-word segment in present time. Then he went into an extended flashback which continued to about the midpoint of the story, where he returned to present action and drove relentlessly on to the violent climax. A malaria-ridden poor white, Wash Jones has "looked after" the plantation of Colonel Sutpen while the Colonel has been away fighting in the Civil War. At its end, with his wife dead, his son killed, and his plantation depleted, Sutpen has returned to recoup what he can. Idolizing Sutpen, Jones has simply watched the sixty-year-old man's seduction of his fifteen-year-old granddaughter. He tells Sutpen, "I know that whatever you handle or tech, whether hit's a regiment of men or a ignorant gal or just a hound dog, that you will make it right." But two years later, when Milly bears Sutpen a daughter, Jones realizes Sutpen cares less for her than the mare which has just foaled. He cuts Sutpen down with a scythe. After killing Milly and the baby, he burns the shack that is their home. Then he goes out to his death swinging the scythe at the posse.

Faulkner invested this tale of seduction and retribution with symbolic significance. Its climax was built around the awful revelation that had blasted Jones: he had been totally deceived about Sutpen and all he represented. Preparing for the death and immolation of his pathetic line, Jones thinks, "*Better if his kind and mine too had never drawn the breath of life on this earth. Better that all who remain of us be blasted from the face of earth than that another Wash Jones should see his whole life shredded from him and shrivel away like a dried shuck thrown onto the fire.*" In "Wash" Faulkner had a tight story with great impact. He perhaps knew that he also had the imaginative point of entry into a rich, complex, even tangled combination of motives and events. In later life he would often say that the writer would look at people and wonder why they did the things they did, what lay behind the actions that formed and shaped their lives. During much of the next three years he would be musing over the forces and events which brought Colonel Sutpen and Wash Jones to that apocalyptic moment by the warped shack in the river bottom. On November 2 *Harper's* bought the story for $350.

On October 26 the *Press-Scimitar* had run a follow-up on Faulkner's aerial mishap. It showed how little daunted he had been. "Faulkner is planning to leave here in his plane Sunday night," it read, "with his brother and Vernon Omlie for New York." It was the morning of November 1 when they took off on the first leg of the journey to Murfreesboro, in central Tennessee. The next day they flew to Washington, and on November 3 they were in New York, Faulkner having flown a total of four hours on the trip. After they checked in at the Algonquin, he left Omlie and Dean to their own activities while he attended to business and some pleasure.

As usual, there were magazine editors who wanted to see him. There was also a change to be made. Ben Wasson was about to leave the American Play Company to join the Shulberg, Seldman Agency in Hollywood. Morton Goldman, his assistant, was planning to leave too to start a small agency of his own, handling perhaps a dozen writers. He asked Faulkner to come with him, and Faulkner agreed. There was talking to be done at Smith & Haas too, not only about the Snopes book but about the collection of short stories Smith had suggested for the new year. This was an opportunity for Faulkner to become better acquainted with Robert K. Haas. One of the founders of the Book-of-the-Month Club, he had earlier retired from business only to return to it when he invested in Smith's new firm. The two men were in many ways opposites. Whereas Smith was a very outgoing man who enjoyed the interpersonal end of publishing, Haas was composed and contemplative. He was of medium height, with gray hair, black eyebrows, and a thin aesthetic face. Though he was a member of the class of 1911 at Yale, his appearance made one visitor think of the way a Florentine nobleman should look. He wore impeccable conservative clothes which accorded with his quiet reserve. In spite of all these attributes, there was another side which he had demonstrated during the war. Then an infantry captain, he had gone out under heavy shellfire to rescue a man who lay paralyzed in both legs. For his heroism he had received the Distinguished Service Cross. At Smith & Haas, his colleagues relished his wry wit and admired the enormous vocabulary that made word games a constant pleasure for him. Faulkner liked Haas, and as time went on he came increasingly to rely upon his help and understanding.

Bennett Cerf wanted to talk to Faulkner about the limited edition of *The Sound and the Fury.* He had already asked Ed Grabhorn for specimen pages and a suggested binding, and now he wanted to go over some of the details. Gregarious and outgoing, Cerf gave a cocktail party at his apartment for Faulkner. Dorothy Parker, Frank Sullivan, Harold and Alice Guinzburg, and a number of Faulkner's other New York friends were there.

But the guest of honor was not. When he did arrive, much later, it was immediately clear that he was in no other way behind the rest of the guests. Cerf was serving powerful martinis. As they drank them, Sullivan recalled, Faulkner (never one to allow veracity to stand in the way of a good story or a friendly gesture) "announced he was commandeering Mrs. Parker and me to come to Oxford and stand godparents to a new Faulkner just arrived." The party continued on that happy note for a while, but as it wore on Faulkner's powers of resistance waned, and before long he was gone.

It was Vernon Omlie who flew the Waco out of New York on November 11 and set the course for Washington and then home. Apparently the better part of a month passed before Cerf heard anything from his guest. When he did, it was in the form of an apology. "I'm mighty sorry I made more or less of a fiasco of my part of the afternoon at your place. I was sick. It had started coming on soon after I got to New York, and I made the mistake of trying to carry on on liquor until I could get back home. That was the reason I was so near blotto, though it is no excuse. Anyway, that's why I was late and why I left soon."

In these years something was always going on at Rowan Oak. They would go to picture shows, and two weeks after Faulkner's return from New York he had felt well enough to take Estelle and Cho-Cho to Memphis to see his friend Marc Connelly's play *The Green Pastures*. Rowan Oak would often seem a house full of children. Young Jack Stone would come to see Mac, and sometimes Jimmy would join them to play Tarzan, swinging on the vines hanging from the cedar trees in front of the house. Or they could ride, for Faulkner had given Mac a fast little Texas quarter horse they called Dan Patch. Though he himself did not ride much, everyone knew when he did. Big Dan (who was considerably larger than Dan Patch) was a beautiful bay with a distinctive gait: he liked to rack, or single-foot, his legs moving in lateral pairs but not quite simultaneously, so that the tattoo of the four hooves could be heard blocks away. When Faulkner did not go to deer camp, he would take Mac and Jimmy and their friends out hunting on Thanksgiving Day in the woods nearby. It would be five o'clock before they would sit down to dinner, the table and sideboard covered with turkey, ham, possum, potatoes, turnips, jams, hot breads, and the other traditional fare. Johncy and his family would be there and so would Miss Maud, if only briefly. But Faulkner would not be at the table this year.

This year he was going to hunting camp—away from family, children, and his workroom, in the company, for a short time, of adult males only. Near the end of the third week of November he set out with the others for General Stone's lodge, below Batesville in the Tallahatchie bottom land thirty miles west of Oxford. At the Batesville train station the wagons were waiting to carry them and their gear to the lodge, where old Ad, the cook, and his helper, Curtis, had been established for nearly a week. There Faulkner was not to find the relaxation he sought. He was susceptible to sudden and prolonged bouts of hiccups which seemed to strike unpredictably and bore no relation whatever to sobriety. They would go on uninterrupted until he could neither eat, drink, nor sleep. Suggestions of folk remedies would come in to Rowan Oak—drinking water, breathing in a paper bag, standing on his head. He would always try them all. He might also resort to whiskey. Finally, after three or four days, they would disappear, leaving him totally exhausted and in an execrable humor. Now, in the midst of a comradely hunt, the hiccups struck. With the involuntary spasms regularly racking him, he could not go out for deer, and the rough accommodations of the lodge did little to make the affliction more bearable. Finally the others became concerned and took him into the town of Batesville, where the hiccups finally stopped. The hunt by now had been spoiled for him, but it would not be a total loss.

Back home at Rowan Oak he sat down at his desk in the west wing and began to write. "I am now working at a story which the POST should like," he told Morty Goldman in an undated letter. "I am sorry I didnt see you again. I got into my usual drinking gang and drank pretty hard for a time after reaching home, was taken sick, quit drinking, had hiccoughs for forty-eight hours, and as a result I am expecting to be notified that I have permanently ruined my stomach and must live from now on upon bread and milk. I hope not, but I still feel pretty bad, though I am working all right."

His uncomfortable experience had supplied him with material for the story and so had the members of the party, especially Uncle Ad, who had cooked for many Oxonians on hunts in the Delta. Suratt told the story. Lucius Provine tried to cure his hiccups—brought on with too much bear meat and whiskey in Major de Spain's hunting camp—by holding his breath, swallowing a buckshot, and drinking water while standing upright and hanging from a tree limb by his knees. An annoyance to the whole camp, he finally followed Suratt's suggestion that he go to John Basket, a whiskey-making Indian, for a remedy unknown to white men. Later he rushed back to camp in terror and attacked Suratt: the Indians had nearly burned him at the stake. Suratt finally solved the mystery. Old Ad had warned the Indians that a revenue agent was coming. It was Ad's revenge for an old wrong: twenty years earlier Provine and two other drunken whites had burned the celluloid collars Ad and his friends were wearing. For Ad, the item was irreplaceable: "Hit wuz blue, wid a red picture of de race betwixt de Natchez en de Robert E. Lee running around hit." Faulkner had tried for all the comic effects plus mystery and retribution. He had also drawn upon several strata of Yoknapatawpha County: the Indians, the blacks, the aristocracy and their friends, and poor whites in their good and bad aspects as exemplified in Suratt and Provine.

As soon as he finished the story he sent it directly to *The Saturday Evening Post.* "Get in touch with them," he told Goldman, "they keep on protesting how they love me; make them pay $1000.00 if you can. And for God's sake, get the money to me as soon as possible. Of course, if they dont want it, get what you can and where you can, and quick. Tax time is coming here, and I dont want to draw on Smith unless I have to."

He had very probably also gone into his files and extracted the unpublished story "Bench for Two." On the first page of it he very carefully worked out the sums involved in the computation of the burial insurance which figured in the story. Then he went on to rewrite it in eight manuscript pages. He retitled it "Pennsylvania Station" and sent it off to Goldman, who submitted it to Alf Dashiell on November 27. Four days later Dashiell wrote back to say that they had seen it in another version. It was very skillful but not especially interesting, and, in view of the number of stories they were already holding for publication, he would have to turn it down.

Goldman sent it out again as soon as it came back. He felt that Faulkner was desperate for outlets for his stories. The recurrent theme of the letters, it seemed to him, was Faulkner's straitened circumstances. He couldn't go to the post office, he once wrote, for fear of seeing people he owed. He was desperate for money and hoped for a windfall of some kind. One day when Goldman was lunching with editor Harry Burton of the *Post*, Burton set forth what he considered the basic formula for fiction in women's magazines. Goldman immediately sent it to Faulkner, who said he would try it, but no formula story followed. Though Goldman felt it was a privilege to represent Faulkner, he found him a difficult client. At New York parties like those in November, Faulkner would be approached by three different editors and agree to do something for each of them. It seemed to the agent that Faulkner lived with self-made confusion about sales of his work. It was devastating. When he made his own deals, he might accept $200 for a story which would have brought considerably more elsewhere. He might sell reprint rights for $25, and the check might never come. Goldman was also distressed about book contracts his client signed, as well as his condition at the time he signed them. Both the advance and the royalty rate would be too low in his judgment. He would ask Faulkner to let him negotiate the agreement, but Faulkner would go ahead and sign the contract Smith offered anyway. It was a frustrating situation.

Both these stories sold, however. The *Post* paid $900 for "A Bear Hunt" and *The American Mercury* took "Pennsylvania Station" at $200. "Needless to say," Faulkner wrote Goldman, "I shall be glad to have the checks, what with Xmas and tax time too close for comfort." He was thinking now not only about magazine sales but about the collection of short stories. He did not think Smith would want to include "A Bear Hunt" in the collection, but he had just sent him "a long unpublished story to include. . . ." That story may have been either one of two manuscripts, both of which had vexed histories.

Although Faulkner's struggles on the Rue Servandoni with *Elmer* had never produced a salable manuscript, he still had not given up. At some point he had reworked the material in fifty-seven typed pages entitled "A Portrait of Elmer." Into it he telescoped most of the action of *Elmer*, framing a series of flashbacks with a beginning and ending in present time. Sitting with Angelo in the Parisian twilight drinking beer at the Dôme, Elmer thinks about his previous European adventures and the meeting to come with Myrtle Monson and her mother. As he returns to his hotel in the Rue Servandoni, his bowels make an overpowering demand. While Myrtle and her mother await his arrival, he rushes to the bathroom. There, in a passage that suggests Leopold Bloom's outhouse scene in *Ulysses*, Elmer finds there is no paper in the fixture. With regret he takes from his pocket the only picture he has managed to paint in his short career now symbolically ended. Compared with *Elmer*, this version showed more finesse in the compression, flashbacks, and internal monologue. But Elmer still was neither very amusing nor sympathetic. And the ending did not have enough force to justify the bathroom scene—the kind of lapse of taste that bothered Phil Stone. "A Portrait of Elmer" would not be included in the book of short stories, but this was by no means the last time Morty Goldman would try, at Faulkner's request, to sell it.

The "long unpublished story" may also have been one that Faulkner referred to in two other undated letters written to Goldman in late 1933 or early 1934. "The CHRISTMAS TREE story which you mention was a continuation of that one by the same title which you now have," Faulkner wrote, "the same characters who got married at the dance, with the dice and the forged license, etc. I wrote it first years ago, and I have mislaid it. I rewrote it from memory, the first part, in the short story which you now have, and I had forgot the characters' names: hence the difference." It was not surprising that Faulkner should have forgotten elements of the story. At some point he had used the setting of his MGM treatment *The College Widow* for a synopsis entitled *Christmas Tree.* Set in "a small southern college city," its two scenes introduced Howard Maxwell and Mrs. Houston and her daughter, Doris. In a short-story version comprising fifteen manuscript pages, Faulkner changed the locale to the Delta and then followed the story of Howard and Doris through their marriage to a happier ending than that of *The College Widow.* Faulkner told Goldman that if an editor showed interest, he was willing to rewrite the rest from memory, and it would probably run to 20,000 words in all. "If you can interest someone and he wishes, I will send a kind of synopsis of the rest; I probably could take a word limit also. You might see what can be done, as I had rather not undertake it right now unless I knew it would sell at once." Faulkner's situation was all too familiar: "Let me know as soon as you sell anything. I am living on credit now and trying to write a novel at the same time." "Christmas Tree" was destined, however, for a more obscure fate than *Elmer*.

In his desperation, Faulkner was apparently offering all of his unsold work, no matter how dim the prospects might seem on the basis of past refusals. He even sent out "Love" again, bearing a label advising that all communications should be addressed to Morton Goldman. This story too would remain unpublished.

Not so "Wash." It would appear in *Harper's* magazine for February, 1934, the same month in which "A Bear Hunt" would come out in the *Post* and "Pennsylvania Station" in the *Mercury*. A small check came from *Story* for "Elly." After five years it would finally appear—also in the month of February. A browsing reader might well have thought that the author of four stories appearing in major magazines in one month must be affluent as well as popular. The truth was that these checks were barely enough to tide him over the holidays.

The week before Christmas he turned from short stories to the idea for the novel he had mentioned to Smith in his October letter, the idea "about a nigger woman" that would be "a little on the esoteric side, like AS I LAY DYING." At the top of a manuscript sheet he inscribed the title "Requiem for a Nun" and dated it "17 December 1933." He wrote a paragraph describing the jail and its surroundings in a way that suggested portions of *Sanctuary* and "That Evening Sun." He began the second paragraph with a man approaching the jail but discarded the sheet without identifying him. Then, inscribing a fresh sheet with the same title and date, he changed the setting to Gavin Stevens' nearby law office, where Stevens questioned a Negro man and his wife, the latter nursing an injured arm and a bandaged neck. When the man finally responded to Stevens' questions, he said that he did not want to prosecute anyone:

" 'But I aint going to have no woman nor man neither coming in my house with a nekkid razor trying to cut my wife's throat.'

" 'I know you are not,' Stevens said. 'That's why I sent for you: to do something about it.' "

There was an implication that the woman had been attacked by another woman named Eunice, but Faulkner failed to develop the situation further and abandoned this start after a page and a half. Then he apparently put the story aside for some future time.

One event near the end of 1933 probably pleased him more than the forthcoming February appearance of "Wash," "A Bear Hunt," "Pennsylvania Station," and "Elly." On December 14 he took off in the red Waco with George A. Wiggs aboard and flew for an hour and a half. When they landed there were more entries than usual to make on various forms. Department of Commerce Inspector Wiggs passed him. Under "Remarks" Faulkner wrote in his pilot's log, "Flight test, Pilot License." He was duly issued License No. 29788. When he took the Waco up again on December 30—now a licensed pilot as well as plane-owner—he simply made the prosaic practical notation, "Paid 20 gal gas $5.18."

He stepped up the pace of his flying activities as the new year began. He took the Waco aloft four times during the month of January, 1934, logging a total of six and a half hours of flying time. Jack, who had been flying with him from time to time, was now absent. His Veterans' Administration job had ended; reaccepted by the FBI, he had reported to Washington for a retraining course on January 2. But Faulkner did not lack for company. Vernon Omlie would be with him and by now Dean was often there. Faulkner had even interested Cho-Cho in flying. On weekends, when she was free from her studies at the Mississippi Synodical College in Holly Springs, she would go up to Memphis with her stepfather for instruction by Vernon Omlie.

Flying was a complete and necessary change from the work he did at his desk, where he was now polishing another story. Called "Mule in the Yard," it was comic and meant to sell quickly, hopefully to the *Post*. Set "in the old halcyon days when even the companies considered their southern branches and divisions the legitimate prey of all who dwelt beside them," the story grew out of I. O. Snopes's regular practice of arranging for mules and other stock to wander onto the railroad tracks so that he might sue for damages. Mrs. Mannie Hait is comfortably housed out of the railroad's settlement for the death of her husband while in Snopes's employ. When one of Snopes's mules kicks over hot ashes which burn up her house, she tells Snopes she will pay $10 for the mule—$140 less than it is worth: the wages Snopes never paid Hait because he died trying to earn them. When Snopes refuses, she manages to shoot the mule. He cannot sue her, for a court case would reveal his frauds against the railroad.

Mannie Hait is much like Maud Littlejohn of "Spotted Horses." She even curses the mule with the same phrase Mrs. Littlejohn uses on the horse. But unlike her, she succeeds in besting a Snopes. Technically the story was simple and straightforward, told in orderly chronology by an omniscient narrator. But it was far from conventional. There was much of the macabre in the grim humor arising out of the mangling of man and mule by freight trains. And though this story might be designed to sell quickly to a "slick" magazine, it was a further exploration of the ingenuity and rapacity of the Snopeses in their incursions into the life of Yoknapatawpha County.

During January, Hal Smith had been looking ahead and had written proposing to Faulkner a job that involved another writer's work and asking about Faulkner's own fiction. Faulkner was slow to respond, but on January 31 Smith received an undated letter which quickly disposed of the first subject: André Malraux's novel *Man's Fate*, the Goncourt Prize winner for 1933. "I dont read French easily enough to do justice to Malraux's book," Faulkner wrote, "and I doubt if I could write an introduction to anything, anyway. I'll look at the translation if you like, though." Then he turned to the other subject: "About the novel. I still think that SNOPES will take about two years of steady work. I could finish the other one in good time, if only the Snopes stuff would lie quiet, which it wont do. However, I will have my taxes and insurance paid and off my mind by March first. Then I intend to settle down to the novel and finish it. As it is now, and trying to not have to draw on you, I have written one short story each month, trying to sell to the Post." He went on to describe his financial situation in the most imperative terms he could. "As I explained to you before, I have my own taxes and my mother's, and the possibility that Estelle's people will call on me before Feb. 1, and also my mother's and Dean's support, and occasional demands from my other two brothers which I can never anticipate." And he still had the insurance and tax money to find in March.

"I seem right now to rush from pillar to post and return," he summed up. "Perhaps the best thing as regards the novel would be for me to draw from you to the full amount of our agreement and get all this off my mind and concentrate on the novel. If I did this, I believe I might promise it for late fall printing—provided I could stop worrying about what I would use for money next year, with royalties already spent. Anyway, I will settle upon the one which I can finish soonest, and I will try to give you a definite promise by March first."

Mulling over his choices, he concluded that the Snopes novel would take too long to complete. So he began the other one, working not as a writer inspired by an idea which had ripened to the point where he needed only to work it out on paper, but rather as a craftsman who was doggedly trying to combine materials he had on hand to shape them into some coherent form. He took the central situation of "Wash" and attempted to graft it onto the matter of "Evangeline." Calling the new work *A Dark House*, he substituted two characters named Chisholm and Burke for the "I" narrator and his friend Don of "Evangeline." He dispensed with the initial telegram and scene-setting but borrowed many lines word-for-word as Burke tried to tell the story of Sutpen and his children over Burke's persiflage. After the first segment, consisting entirely of dialogue between the two, he began a second segment as third-person narrator, introducing more material about Sutpen before the two men took up the story again as Burke told Chisholm about Wash Jones, who, he said, had shot Sutpen for fathering an illegitimate child on his daughter (rather than his granddaughter, as in "Wash"). The three-page manuscript fragment ended as Chisholm refilled the glasses and Burke prepared to delve deeper into the background of Sutpen's story.

On February 11, Faulkner dated a fresh sheet of his manuscript paper with the wide printed margins and began the story again. Now he moved closer to the original approach of "Evangeline," setting the scene in the first paragraph and writing so rapidly that he left out words as he went: "The room was hot because summer and it built to rent for $1.00 a day with meals and not for comfort and for people who would never return." He began the dialogue and went on for a page and a half to the point where Burke was about to launch into his tale. Then he stopped again. On a fresh page he wrote "A Dark House" at the top, rewrote his introductory scene-setting paragraph, began the dialogue again, and once more abandoned the effort, this time after completing only three quarters of the page. He was groping for another approach to the problem. Before the day was over he found it.

He had to move through at least two more steps. The first one was still another adaptation of earlier methods; the second was radically different. One undated sheet showed how he must have made the first attempt. Again he used the identical exchanges in the dialogue, but this time he grafted elements of *The Sound and the Fury* onto "Evangeline," for it was Quentin who began to tell Shreve about Wash and his relationship with Sutpen. Another manuscript sheet, untitled but dated "11 February 1934," demonstrated the radical solution. On this page there was no Shreve, and the first paragraph consisted principally of a letter to Quentin Compson from his father: "And now the blurred sharp mechanical *Jefferson Jan 12 1910 Miss* the *My dear son* in his father's long sloping hand *Miss Rosa Coldfield was buried yesterday. She had been in a coma for about a week and two days ago she died without regaining consciousness and without pain as they say and whatever they mean by that. . . .*" Mr. Compson went on with a series of reflections on death to which his son responded with a curiously divided consciousness made up of "the two separate people in me, the Quentin Compson preparing for Harvard in the South, the deep South dead since 1865 and peopled with old garrulous baffled ghosts . . . and the Quentin Compson who was still too young to deserve yet to be a ghost. . . ." Now there were two Quentins and no Shreve, but the hot hotel room had survived, transformed, at the start of the second paragraph, into a room in Miss Rosa's house: "Through the still hot weary dead afternoon of that dead summer the two of them sitting in what she still called the office because her father had called it that, the dim hot room with the blinds all closed and fastened because when she was a child someone had told her that light and moving air brought heat and that dark was always cooler so that when in the late p.m. the sun finally reached that side of the house and shone through the shutters the room would become latticed with yellow slashes full of motes that he would always think of as being flecks of old dead dried paint. . . .There was a wistaria vine on a frame before one window where now and then sparrows came in brown random clouds making a dry vivid dusty sound before going away. . . ." Now the descriptive matter had been functionally integrated into the story, helping to characterize not just the circumstances of the telling but something of Miss Rosa Coldfield, who would be revealed as Sutpen's sister-in-law, and something too of that long-dead time when the drama of Sutpen and his children had been acted out.

The problem of solving the mystery and understanding its larger meanings would still devolve ultimately upon Quentin, but the mystery would be shared and explored by other characters within the story. They would be less reticent and more articulate than Raby in "Evangeline" while still being intimately involved in the events themselves. Although this method would probably provide a more viable solution to the problems of *A Dark House* than the earlier approach, it would also make a complicated story even more complicated.

It must have been at about this point that Faulkner wrote Smith an undated letter reporting his progress. "I believe that I have a head start on the novel," he began. "I have put both the Snopes and the Nun one aside. The one I am writing now will be called DARK HOUSE or something of that nature. It is the more or less violent breakup of a household or family from 1860 to about 1910. It is not as heavy as it sounds. The story is an anecdote which occurred during and right after the civil war; the climax is another anecdote which happened about 1910 and which explains the story. Roughly, the theme is a man who outraged the land, and the land then turned and destroyed the man's family. Quentin Compson, of the Sound & Fury, tells it, or ties it together; he is the protagonist so that it is not complete apocrypha. I use him because it is just before he is to commit suicide because of his sister, and I use his bitterness which he has projected on the South in the form of hatred of it and its people to get more out of the story itself than a historical novel would be. To keep the hoop skirts and plug hats out, you might say." Faulkner was optimistic about the writing. "I think I can promise it for fall," he said.

After the good news came the bad. "Now hold your hat," he wrote. He needed $1,500: $600 for insurance due March 4 and the rest for income tax due March 15. "I have heard of writers who got themselves, or their publishers, into this fix, but I never thought I would do it too. But I am, and you are too. But anyway," he concluded, "I'm still sober and still writing. On the wagon since November now." This may, in fact, have been the beginning of a year's abstinence he imposed on himself when Jill was a very little girl. He wanted to show he could do it, he told Estelle. Apparently this new discipline helped with his writing. What was good for his vocation must also have been good for his avocation.

On January 4 a sketch of the author had appeared on the front page of the Oxford *Eagle*, one in a series entitled "Prominent Citizens of Oxford." Faulkner was twelfth in the series (which would run to sixty), having been preceded by the mayor, the university football coach, two physicians, and Joe Parks, among others. (His uncle would be thirty-fifth in the series.) The caption described Faulkner as EMINENT NOVELIST, POET AND SCENARIO WRITER, LICENSED AIRPLANE PILOT.

Though scarcely more voluble in flying groups than literary circles, Faulkner enjoyed the "hangar flying" that most private pilots like to engage in sitting around the small lounges that face out toward the runways. He would smoke and talk with Vernon Omlie and other Memphis fliers such as Bob Carpenter and Charlie Fast, who would occasionally fly down to Oxford. At the Memphis airport on January 29, returning from Batesville, Faulkner must have heard a good deal of conversation about a coming event. A new airport had been built in New Orleans on land laboriously reclaimed from Lake Pontchartrain. Named after Colonel A. L. Shushan, president of the Levee Board, it was to be dedicated Friday afternoon, February 9. The fliers would have little interest in the politicians' speeches, but they would flock to see the races and other aerial events. Even the Mardi gras theme had been planned to harmonize with the dedication. Floats illustrating "Conquest of the Air" would move down the noisy, jammed, bunting-draped streets bearing effigies ranging from Daedalus' failure to Lindbergh's triumph. For professionals the meet offered a promising opportunity to earn money in a sporadic and chancy profession. For the ordinary private pilots, here was a chance to see such celebrated airmen as Michel De Troyat, who was billed as the "European acrobatic champion," Milo Burcham, the "world champion upside down flier," and Captain W. Merle Nelson, who attached Roman candles to the lower wings of his "comet plane." A local hero would be there, racer James R. Wedell, along with pilots such as Harold Neuman and Roger Donrae, who had come from as far away as Kansas City and Milwaukee to compete. There would be parachute jumpers—not only well-known veterans such as Clem Sohn and

Ben Grew but a girl named Eris Daniels, whose working clothes included whipcord breeches and knee-length boots just like a man's.

The men must have talked about making up a group to go down, for Vernon and Phoebe Omlie always tried to attend such events. On February 9, however, when the Louisiana State University band played before the rows of assembled dignitaries and Colonel Shushan heard both himself and his airport eulogized, Faulkner was in Memphis again, where he took the Waco up for a twenty-minute flight. It was actually a poor day in New Orleans for the rain had begun to fall and continued throughout the ceremonies. Though Milo Burcham flew upside down as advertised, the committee decided the weather was too poor to draw a good crowd, even if it had been safe for the racers, stunt fliers, and jumpers. The two days' program of events was postponed. On the following Monday, February 12, the newspapers carried the information that the events would be held for three days beginning on Wednesday, the fourteenth. Most of the Mardi gras would be over, but the aviators and spectators could just stay on for a few more days.

Faulkner had been in New Orleans at Mardi gras nine years before, when he and Phil Stone had visited Elizabeth Anderson before his supposedly imminent departure for Europe. He may have thought back to the time, twenty-three years before, when he had gone to Memphis to see Louis Paulhan and Glenn Curtiss speed above the dirt track and wooden grandstand in flimsy planes with not a tenth of the power of those that would be roaring around the pylons of the race courses out beyond Shushan Airport and the waters of Lake Pontchartrain.

At home, in his workroom at Rowan Oak, the problems presented by *A Dark House* were still formidable despite the new approach he had worked out. It must have been a relief to put them aside. On February 14 he made the twenty-five-mile trip over to Batesville. There he met Vernon Omlie and they took off in the Waco. They had planned to fly to New Orleans that day but instead put down at Jackson. On the next day the red cabin cruiser touched down on the runway in New Orleans.

40

February-October, 1934

At the end of each lap would come the mounting and then fading snarl and snore of engines as the aeroplanes came up and zoomed and banked away, leaving once more the scuffle and murmur of feet on tile and the voice of the announcer reverberant and sonorous within the domed shell of glass and steel in a running commentary to which apparently none listened, as if the voice were merely some unavoidable and inexplicable phenomenon of nature like the sound of wind or of erosion. Then the band would begin to play again, though faint and almost trivial behind and below the voice, as if the voice actually were that natural phenomenon against which all manmade sounds and noises blew and vanished like leaves.

The rotunda, filled with dusk, was lighted now, with a soft sourceless wash of no earthly color or substance and which cast no shadow: spacious, suave, sonorous and monastic, wherein relief or mural-limning or bronze and chromium skilfully shadow-lurked presented the furious, still, and legendary tale of what man has come to call his conquering of the infinite and impervious air.

—*Pylon* (26, 37–38)

When Faulkner and Omlie arrived on February 15, people were still talking about the events of the day before. De Troyat had given his aerobatic exhibition and Clem Sohn had jumped from an altitude of 10,000 feet, falling for 8,000 feet before opening his parachute for a safe descent. Jack Monahan had not been so fortunate. A cross wind blew him against the seawall and knocked him out of the competition with injuries. That night real disaster struck. Merle Nelson took off for his aerobatic display, the devices on his wings firing to give the "comet plane" effect. Dangerously close to the ground he went into a loop at what seemed full throttle. He went over the top of the loop and began the downward swoop when something happened. He may have been blinded by one of the airport lights. Whatever it was, he did not pull out. The small craft plowed into the ground and burst into flame. One of Faulkner's friends, New Orleans *Item* reporter Hermann B. Deutsch, wrote up the fatal crash in detail. Faulkner would see other newspaper friends during this visit to New Orleans, and by accompanying Deutsch he saw more of the meet and met more of the fliers than would have been possible otherwise.

The star of Thursday's events was Jimmy Wedell, an airplane designer and builder as well as a racer. He was a young man who had first come to prominence at the National Air Races in Cleveland three years before. In the midst of a race there, the wing of his small low-wing monoplane had begun to flutter. Wedell tried desperately for altitude so he could jump, but then the wing steadied and he nursed the ship in for a precarious landing. He and his brother worked on it all night, and the next day he took it up again and won second place in the Thompson Trophy race. The following year they built three more planes which finished second, third, and fourth. Then, in September of 1933, Wedell broke Colonel Roscoe Turner's land plane record with a speed of 306.33 m.p.h. This represented the beginning of an extraordinary year in which he won the free-for-all races at every major national mees. By 1934 he often had to fly exhibitions because no one would race against him. The committee felt itself fortunate that he had flown in from nearby Patterson, Louisiana, to enter the meet.

Wedell was entered in the day's major event, a twenty-five-mile race, but other events provided even more spectacular thrills for the crowd. Roger Donrae had no trouble with his 550 cu. in. engine until the fifth lap when he rounded the home pylon. It stalled, coughed into life again, then cut out once more. Somehow Donrae managed to pull the plane up near the lake and gain enough altitude to bring it in for a dead-stick landing. A pilot in another race nearly went into the lake when his crankcase cracked as he rounded the second pylon. Losing compression steadily, he limped back two miles over water for a safe landing. Wedell's performance was less dramatic. He simply climbed into his airplane, warmed it up, taxied out, took off, and won his race.

Hermann Deutsch introduced Faulkner to Jimmy Wedell, who had no more idea than Phoebe or Vernon that one of Faulkner's characters had an almost identical name but a Chickasaw-Choctaw-French background. It was Wedell's world they were in, and he was the greater celebrity here. Nearing thirty, he was a friendly man with a long face. He had a large, almost bulbous nose, strong slightly protruding teeth, and ample ears. In boyhood he had lost the sight of one eye in a motorcycle accident. Since then, however, he had been uninjured in his quest for speed despite two or three near-escapes from death. Wedell was different from some of the barnstormers and tramp aviators at the meet. He was not interested so much in aerobatics and racing as in speed, he said. He wanted to get from one place to another as fast as possible, and developments in racing planes today could be applied to airline passenger aircraft tomorrow. Like Omlie, he offered charter flights and student instruction. If there was any measure of security in this risky industry, he must have had as much of it as most. Faulkner would remember him very clearly.

The bad weather continued intermittently, and so did the mishaps. On Friday, the sixteenth, Harold Neuman's 1,000 cu. in. engine failed just as he passed the home pylon. He missed the runway but brought the aircraft in to a crash-landing in a pool of water. When he tried to exit from the plane, he could not get out of the cockpit. He was quickly released, however, and then embraced by his wife, who had run to him from the grandstand, carrying their baby. Faulkner apparently witnessed this event with Deutsch, who had the good reporter's faculty for being where things happened. "If somebody in the Yale Bowl was going to be shot," Faulkner told him, "you'd be standing next to him."

Because of delays caused by the bad weather, Omlie could not stay to the end of the meet and returned home. Faulkner now went to stay with another newspaper friend, Roark Bradford, and his quick, outspoken wife, Mary Rose. Many of the old newspaper crowd would still wind up at Brad's place for drinks and talk at sunrise. It may have been at one of these sessions that the Bradfords invited Faulkner to move into a room in their apartment until he left for Oxford. Brad had changed little—still the raconteur and dialect artist. After a few drinks he might recite an encomium of the Confederates, climaxed by his calling his wife to a rigid and exaggerated posture of military attention as he asked, "What army do you belong to?" She would then give the standard reply: "The Army of Northern Virginia, sir, by God, sir, the greatest fighting force ever assembled!" Faulkner accepted their offer and moved his suitcase from the hotel, but, after a day or so, they did not see him.

By now men and machines were wearing out as the meet dragged on, though Jimmy Wedell seemed impervious as he set a world's record on Saturday of 266 m.p.h. over a 100-kilometer course. That same day Ben Grew went up for another parachute-jumping exhibition. A small man getting on in years, he was flown by a twenty-seven-year-old Ohioan named Charles N. Kenily in what Deutsch called a "stick-and-string airplane." According to the New Orleans *Times-Picayune*, he was a barnstormer who had "brought his plane here for any flying which he might be employed to do, without any official place on the race program." During his droning climb to altitude, his wife sat watching in the grandstand, holding their baby in her arms. At last they reached the jumping height. Buffeted by the slipstream, Grew slowly climbed out of the back cockpit and stepped onto the wing. At that moment the ring of his ripcord fouled on something projecting from the flimsy craft. The white silk of the chute popped out of the canvas pack and into the slipstream where it instantly became entangled with the rudder and tail elevator surface. The announcer giving the public-address commentary stopped in mid-sentence as Grew either jumped or was pulled off the wing. Perhaps not realizing that his lines were still fouled, he pulled the ripcord releasing his emergency chute. The plane's controls by now must have begun losing response, and Kenily turned and looked back to see what was wrong. Spectators saw him stand up in the cockpit looking at Grew. There was nothing he could do. The plane swiftly began to lose altitude with Grew dangling helplessly beneath it. Suddenly, as they dipped below a thousand feet, Kenily was seen to go over the side and drop from the aircraft. He plummeted into the lake a few instants before the plane smashed into the water a hundred yards from shore and submerged in a cloud of spray. One of the small boats that sped out to the debris recovered Grew's body, smashed by the impact. Kenily was never found.

While Deutsch wrote the story, Faulkner was with other friends. They probably included Guy and Helen Baird Lyman, who lived in New Orleans, where Lyman's business was prospering. Faulkner had had enough by now, however, and sometime after midnight on what must have been Sunday morning, the eighteenth, he went back to the Bradfords' apartment. He appeared "sober but brutally hung over and ravenously hungry." After consuming bacon, eggs, and coffee prepared for him by Mary Rose, Faulkner launched into "a disjointed, confused, nightmarish tale" of accepting a ride from two motorcyclists, a man and a woman who were aviators at the meet. He had gone out to Shushan with them, he said, with stops along the way for bootleg whiskey, after which had followed more drinking, flying, and carousing before he had returned to town. Later that day he took off in the Waco. He had flown only a half-hour or less on the fifteenth and sixteenth. Now he logged two hours and fifteen minutes before the Waco touched down at Batesville again. Unless he turned around and flew back in someone else's plane, he was not at Shushan on Monday morning when, in accordance with a note written before his last flight, the ashes of Captain Merle Nelson were scattered over the lake from a plane in the gray morning against the sky filled with scudding clouds. But Faulkner knew about it, about the ceremony which Deutsch called Nelson's "last gay gesture."

What Faulkner carried away with him was not the grandiose future of commercial aviation projected in the gaudy decorations of the new air terminal, but rather its opposite: the sense that the men he had seen, like the dead or curiously superannuated fliers of "All the Dead Pilots," were strange anachronisms. "They were ephemera and phenomena on the face of a contemporary scene," he recalled later. "That is, there was really no place for them in the culture, in the economy, yet they were there, at that time, and everyone knew that they wouldn't last very long, which they didn't. That time of those frantic little aeroplanes which dashed around the country and people wanted just enough money to live, to get to the next place to race again. Something frenetic and in a way almost immoral about it. That they were outside the range of God, not only of respectability, of love, but of God too. That they had escaped the compulsion of accepting a past and a future, that they were—they had no past. They were as ephemeral as the butterfly that's born this morning with no stomach and will be gone tomorrow." He was now presented with a spectacle very like that so powerfully impressed on his imagination during the war: fliers going up day after day, knowing that any one flight might be their last. There were no Fokkers or Pfalzes to shoot them down, but at the speeds they reached wings buckled and crankcases cracked, and that was enough. Now, however, another dimension intensified the stresses intolerably. The men's families were with them—women and children—who flew with them and occasionally watched them die.

The following Sunday and the Sunday after that he was back in Memphis flying again. At this time he and Estelle would drive up to Memphis in the new Chevrolet on Saturday and register at the Peabody. One Saturday evening they had dinner there with Aunt 'Bama and Walter McLean. When they finished, Billy asked Estelle what she wanted to do that evening. 'Bama and Walter were going to a dance at the country club but Estelle didn't want to go because she wasn't dressed properly. Besides, they couldn't stay out too late because Billy was going to fly the Waco in the morning. Finally she thought of something.

"I want to go and see Miss Reba and Mr. Binford at Miss Reba's place on Mulberry Street," she said.

Her husband sat and looked at her.

"I've never seen one of those places, Bill," she argued, "and I want to see one before I die."

He protested that it was no place to take a lady, but soon Aunt 'Bama joined in on Estelle's side.

"If I weren't dressed for the country club I'd want to go too, Billy," she said.

"It simply wouldn't be right," he replied, and lapsed into stony silence.

"Couldn't you just call and see if it would be all right?" Estelle asked him.

"No," he said shortly. With that they rose and left the table, bidding the McLeans goodnight. As they walked up to the elevator in the lobby he spoke again. "Are you sure you want to go?" he asked her.

"Yes, I am," she answered firmly.

"All right," he told her, "if you'll be very quiet and subdued, I'll take you." He turned and walked toward the desk.

"Bill," his wife hissed, "you won't call from the desk!"

"They won't know who I'm calling," he said, and went to the telephone.

"Bill, what did you say?" Estelle asked him when he returned.

"I said I was going to drop in for a short visit and bring my wife," he replied.

"And it's all right?"

"Yes."

They parked the car on Mulberry Street and quietly made their way up the steps of a big frame house. Faulkner rang the bell. It was opened by a Negro maid who ushered them into an unoccupied parlor full of tawdry gilt furniture. Then their hostess entered, alone, the original of Mr. Binford having gone to his reward long before.

The original of Miss Reba was a big woman, now about fifty, whose huge body was clothed in a dress which might have been elegant were it not stretched to tent-size to cover her bulk. She seemed blowsy too, in part because she was already tight though the hour was early and the house was quiet. There was a tankard of beer in her large hand.

She greeted Faulkner warmly and then spoke effusively to his wife. "I'm so glad you come along with Bill, dearie," she said and offered some beer. "I always drink beer this time of evening, then I switch to gin later. It makes the gin go so much farther."

As they settled into an exchange of small talk, Estelle's disappointment grew. There was no excitement, and she knew now that her husband had no intention of letting her see anything else or any other part of the house, and probably their hostess had the same idea. This was a moment of respectability and she doubtless wished it to be uninterrupted. It seemed to Estelle that the woman had no idea Bill was a writer. She guessed that she knew nothing of *Sanctuary* and would have protested it as an affront to the respectability of her establishment. After twenty minutes Estelle was ready to leave. The big woman saw them to the door, full of cordialities as they said good night. The next morning they were out at the airport on time, flying the Waco.

The fact that Faulkner continued to fly regularly during the late winter and early spring of 1934 did not mean there was any surcease from financial problems. There were expenses in Memphis now, as well as Oxford, for Faulkner had sent Dean there to live with Vernon Omlie during his training. Dean showed signs of becoming the best pilot of all four brothers, and he helped Vernon, but there were still bills to be paid. It was probably at this time that Faulkner wrote Morty Goldman. "Maybe this one will hit Cosmo. If so, please get the money as soon as possible. Ask them to please let us have it quick. I always need money bad, but this time I am desperate, as I had believed the Post would take the other surely." Though he did not name the enclosed story, it was probably "Mule in the Yard." He was immediately going to begin something else, though he did not yet know what. He had a plan for a series of pieces to be entitled *A Child's Garden of Motion Picture Scripts.* As he envisioned them, they would be "burlesques of the sure-fire movies and plays, or say a burlesque of how the movies would treat standard plays and classic plays and novels, written in a modified form of a movie script." At any rate, there would be something more soon. "And in God's name get me the money as fast as you can." By mid-March there were results. Goldman had sent "Mule in the Yard" to *Scribner's.* After Faulkner trimmed a thousand words, Dashiell bought it for $300 and scheduled it as the lead story for the August number.

Newspaper headlines in the late winter of that year gave the family news of Jack Falkner's whereabouts without always mentioning his name. He had barely arrived at Charlotte, North Carolina, for his new FBI assignment, when John Dillinger staged a spectacular escape from prison at Crown Point, Indiana. Convinced of a connection between the desperado and the much-publicized George Edward Brewer kidnapping in St. Paul two months earlier, the FBI transferred a number of agents to special squads in St. Paul. "There followed many months of relentless work by the FBI," Jack wrote later, "always interesting, sometimes uncomfortable, and not infrequently dangerous." Before the cases were closed he would go underground, living in disguise in a gangster's hideout, and he would engage in pitched battles fought with machine guns. Again Maud Falkner had something very real and concrete to worry about.

Her eldest son was getting a different kind of newspaper coverage at home. "*Oxford Magazine* is on the Press," announced the Oxford *Eagle* on March 29. Phil Mullen and his brother, Dale, were using the *Eagle* printshop when the printer was not making up the newspaper. One of those most interested was Phil Stone. His contribution, the *Eagle* reported, was to be "William Faulkner, the Man and His Work." There would also be poems by Dale Mullen and Emily Whitehurst and an article by Miss Ella Somerville on Stark Young, whose new novel, *So Red the Rose*, would appear in the summer. The first number of *The Oxford Magazine* came out on April 1.

If Faulkner read Phil Stone's foreword, it must have filled him with misgivings about the series to follow. Though Faulkner was the town's most widely known citizen, Stone wrote, "perhaps twenty years of personal association with him, closer than is true of anyone else in the world, give me a better opportunity to record of him many things that no one else knows. . . ." To one already resentful of any attempt to "ride on his coat-tails," it could not have been a promising beginning. Moreover, Stone was once more mixing praise and blame. Though he called his friend "one of the most outstanding of American prosewriters," one who might find a permanent place in American literature, he seemed not to recognize some of the strides Faulkner had made since Stone had introduced *The Marble Faun*, even going so far as to repeat some of those early judgments: the portrait he would write would be that "of a simple-hearted country boy leading the life of a country squire except for the vice of spoiling good white paper with little black marks." Stone gave with one hand and took away with the other. Faulkner was "one of the most noted exponents and appliers of modern technique in the art of the novel," a follower of Joyce. But though there was talent there of a high order, "I am equally sure that as yet he has shown no trace of genius and, I am sorry to say, I have grave doubts that he ever will be a genius. I even have disquieting fears that so far as concerns literary achievement he has gone as far as he will ever go." The articles which would appear on June 1 and November 1 would be unlikely to halt the gradual deterioration in the relationship between the two men. If Faulkner read them, the effect would have been the reverse. For years the two would continue to see each other, and Faulkner would give many tangible evidences of his regard for Stone and those early days, but it was a long process of alienation nonetheless. The pupil had outstripped the teacher, and though the teacher had loyally predicted his success, he could not always recognize it when it came, nor could he concede that his friend's aesthetic judgments could be superior, finally, to his own.

On April 10 Stone wrote to Hal Smith requesting permission to quote from Faulkner's books. Smith's reply six days later provided an insight into the publisher's thinking about his star author. Stone would be performing a valuable service, Smith said, for Faulkner was not an exhibitionist, and "extraordinarily little has been written about him. I don't mean about his books, because hardly any writer today gets a more copious press, but about the man himself. During his earlier books I think it is likely that the mystery with which he surrounded himself has been especially valuable. He has been the sort of writer about whom legends of all kinds collect. Perhaps it is now time to bring him out in the limelight, although I am sure he will always remain a strange figure in our literary history."

During that April of 1934 the subject of these letters made little progress toward his next contribution to American literary history. The Snopes book apparently did not move appreciably, and whatever he had been able to do with the history of Colonel Sutpen seems not to have pleased him particularly. He was completing what he would later call "an air story," entitled "This Kind of Courage." On April 26 Goldman was able to send it to Dashiell, who took a little over a week to reject it because of its strongly "mannered" style. It might sell, he thought, if it were done "much more simply." It was not strange that Faulkner was writing about fliers rather than a nineteenth-century planter-soldier and an early twentieth-century entrepreneur. He was still immersed in flying, logging time in both his plane and the open-cockpit Waco that Omlie used for instruction. By April he would set up as something of a barnstormer himself.

On Saturday and Sunday, March 31 and April 1, the merchants of Oxford sponsored an air circus. Dean Falkner was in charge. Vernon Omlie performed stunt flying each afternoon, and another Memphian, George Goff, thrilled the crowd with an exhibition of parachute jumping. The next day Faulkner was flying Vernon's Waco F off the same rough Oxford field. There was more flying in Memphis on the weekends, and in late April bright orange handbills were circulated:

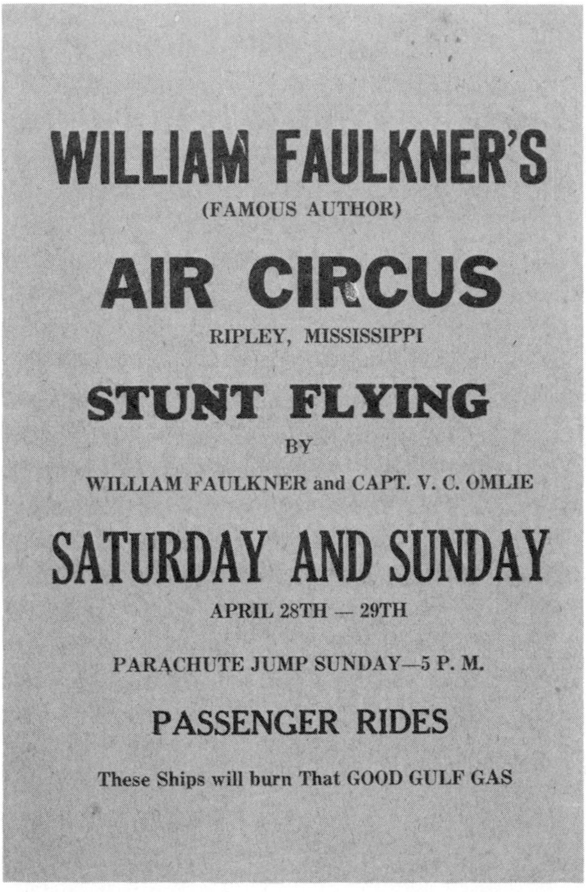

WILLIAM FAULKNER'S

(FAMOUS AUTHOR)

AIR CIRCUS

RIPLEY, MISSISSIPPI

STUNT FLYING

BY

WILLIAM FAULKNER and CAPT. V. C. OMLIE

SATURDAY AND SUNDAY

APRIL 28TH — 29TH

PARACHUTE JUMP SUNDAY—5 P. M.

PASSENGER RIDES

These Ships will burn That GOOD GULF GAS

William Faulkner's Air Circus.

Faulkner had been practicing. His pilot's log noted one hour of aerobatics in Vernon's Waco F on April 21, and a week later he flew his own plane from Memphis southeast to the Old Colonel's town and landed in a pasture near Highway 15 on the southeastern outskirts. Johncy and Miss Maud had flown up with him, and Vernon and Dean were there. So was Louise Hale. They were ready to give any venturesome residents of Tippah County their money's worth. He flew the two-cockpit Waco F for thirty-five minutes on Saturday and for the same length of time again on Sunday. He did not write "acrobatics" under "Remarks" as he had done for April 21, but it seems clear that he participated somehow in his air circus, perhaps by taking passengers for rides, perhaps by flying George Goff to jumping altitude. He remained in Ripley until Monday, taking the open plane aloft again for a brief flight before returning to Memphis in the cabin Waco.

One Oxonian who had made the trip to Ripley was Taylor McElroy, who had that week announced as a candidate for circuit judge of the 3rd Judicial District. When he came out to the field, Faulkner walked over and greeted him.

"Taylor," he said, "I want to help you. I see you've started your campaign. I got an airplane and I want to loan it to you. All you'll have to do is furnish the gasoline." Faulkner liked this country boy who had made good and who, as mayor of Oxford, had given Johncy the job of city engineer.

"Why, thank you, Bill," McElroy said. "I never thought of running that way." He was stalling for time. He did not know of anything that would defeat him more quickly than campaigning in his rural constituency with an airplane, but he did not want to appear ungrateful. "I'd like to think it over."

"Well," Faulkner said, "give me some of your literature."

McElroy gave him some handbills, and he and Omlie scattered them over Ripley. Though McElroy did not pursue the offer, the one-day aerial campaigning apparently did him no harm, for he carried Tippah County by two to one.

Again the press kept track of Faulkner's activities, one time noting that "He and his brother are planning to do a little Sunday afternoon barnstorming in Southern communities this summer, with a Negro pilot whom they call Black Eagle." After Narcissus McEwen had joined the Faulkner household as Jill's mammy, her brother George began to move into the family's orbit, too. It was nothing domestic that had attracted him, however. Faulkner assigned him jobs to do around Rowan Oak but also took him along when they went flying. He bought George a helmet and a pair of goggles, and the big man wore them, to the admiration of his friends, whether the day's activities were to be aerial or not. "Bill said he used to come to work in them," Johncy remembered, "just to remind Bill that they could go flying instead of doing whatever Bill had laid out for him to do that day." McEwen was more than just a passenger. Faulkner would prime the engine and George would go to the propeller. Even on cold mornings, when it would be hard to turn, George would grasp the blade, pull, and spin it through its arc. As he leaped back, the engine would usually catch and roar into life. "Bill always said George could throw it through, get in the cockpit and fly halfway to Memphis before it gave out."

During the winter and early spring of 1934 the book of short stories had been going through production. Smith and Faulkner had settled on fourteen stories, to be published under the title *Doctor Martino and Other Stories.* They ranged from "Honor," first published in July, 1930, to "Elly" and "Wash," which had just appeared in February. The only new ones were "The Leg" and "Black Music," which he had finally despaired of selling. In mid-April the reviews began to appear.

The first of the major notices gave a foretaste of the rest. Writing in the book section of the *Herald Tribune*, F. T. Marsh labeled the stories of *Doctor Martino* "generally slighter and more artificial" than those in *These 13*, but the book had "its fine passages, its pure Faulknerian touches," and was "very much worth reading." Later notices would tend to go to either extreme. The Boston *Transcript*'s anonymous reviewer found the volume bound together by "a single strand of horror"; to bring such a thing off, the writer had to show himself a virtuoso, and this Faulkner "most decidedly fails to do." Some of the warmest praise would come from abroad. The *Literary Supplement* of the London *Times* found that though the stories varied in merit, they all bore "the stamp of a remarkable mind and a very rare imaginative gift." Faulkner was "without doubt one of the most powerful, original and ingenious writers of fiction now at work." The stories had been scrutinized in Hollywood as well as the literary centers. Sam Marx had all of them synopsized for study in the MGM story department, but none, finally, seemed like picture material.

At home in Oxford, Moon Mullen noted that "Critics have loosed some scathing remarks the past few weeks about William Faulkner's latest book of stories." He quoted *Time*'s verdict that the stories were "merely potboilers." But he did not blame Faulkner. "As the Greek philosophers have so aptly put it, a guy's gotta eat." These negative views doubtless helped fix further in most local minds the image of Faulkner's work. When *Lazy River* had played at the Lyric Theatre in mid-March, some Oxonians had gone to see it under the impression that it was a Faulkner screenplay. Mullen had quoted one moviegoer's surprised assessment: "Bedogged if it wasn't good!"

Faulkner's position vis-à-vis other native authors was clearly demonstrated with the appearance in early August of the novel Ella Somerville had admiringly noted in *The Oxford Magazine.* Stark Young's *So Red the Rose* was a long family chronicle in which the lives of the McGehees of Montrose and their kinfolk, the Bedfords of Portobello, epitomized all that was best in the idealized "Old South" as it followed the trials of these members of the planter aristocracy through the ordeal of the war and its aftermath. Ellen Glasgow would speak for most Southerners when she called *So Red the Rose* "the best and most completely realized novel of the Deep South in the Civil War that has yet been written." Moon Mullen struck the same chord: "The beauty, the luxury, the romance of the Old South, it's all there. Ladies and gentlemen, in the superlative sense of those words, march across the pages." There it was. When most readers wanted the McGehees and the Bedfords if they were to read about their native region, Faulkner gave them the Compsons, the Bundrens, Popeye, Tommy, Gowan Stevens, Temple Drake, Joe Christmas, Joanna Burden, Lena Grove, and Lucas Burch. Why should they, few of them literary specialists, prefer Yoknapatawpha County to The Old Plantation? What they could not know, in the spring and summer of 1934, was that Faulkner was finally preparing for something more to their liking.

On May 10, 1934, Morton Goldman sent "Lo!" to Alfred Dashiell, who replied that it was "not a magazine piece." Again Dashiell made suggestions for revision, as he had for "This Kind of Courage." Faulkner did not feel he could take the time to stop and revise the story. There was a new one, quite different from both, on his mind. He was thinking about a story centering around two boys and their families in the latter part of the Civil War, as the tide began to run strongly against the Confederacy. If it seemed promising he could then do three or four more, running through the end of the war and into the early years of Reconstruction, when the survivors tried to wrest control of their land from its captors and reimpose something like the kind of conditions they preferred. Both boys would be twelve years old at the start. One was Bayard Sartoris, son of Colonel Sartoris and grandfather-to-be of the twins, Bayard and John. The other was Ringo. Bayard would tell the story retrospectively. Though Ringo was a Negro, this posed no problem, because, Faulkner would write in a later revision, "Ringo and I had been born in the same month and had both fed at the same breast and had slept together and eaten together for so long that Ringo called Granny 'Granny' just like I did, until maybe he wasn't a nigger anymore or maybe I wasn't a white boy anymore, the two of us neither, not even people any longer: the two supreme undefeated like two moths, two feathers riding above a hurricane." Faulkner would employ a familiar and useful strategy: he would be dealing with youthful experience presented in maturity. There would be opportunities for all kinds of nuances, and as for the subject matter, that would be rich enough too—a view of the war both particular and at times panoramic, and, on the personal level, rites of initiation of several kinds.

The atmosphere and many of the events Faulkner would use were ready to hand. The first story began in July of 1863. John Wesley Thompson Falkner had been fourteen then, and his memories had been reinforced by his years in the Sons of Confederate Veterans, by the hospitality and help he had given over the years to veterans and widows. By now the Sartoris family saga must have been almost as firmly established in Faulkner's mind as that of the Falkners. ("The Golden Book of Jefferson & Yoknapatawpha County" had certainly listed more items from the Sartoris annals than appeared in those of the Falkners.) As for the Negro family, they apparently came as quickly to mind as did Dilsey Gibson and her family. Faulkner took the first name of his childhood playmate, Joby Strother, and used it as the name of the grandfather of Ringo (born Marengo). The rest of the family appeared. In all, three of his family would bear the same first names as the Strother servant family in *Sartoris*, but Faulkner either had forgotten or did not care.

The setting was the Sartoris plantation, watched over in Colonel Sartoris' absence by a character who had not appeared before: Miss Rosa Millard. As John Sartoris' mother-in-law, she fulfilled the same function that his sister, Aunt Jenny Du Pre, had in *Sartoris.* Just as Aunt Jenny owed something to Auntee and Maud Butler Falkner, so Granny Millard may have been modeled in part on Lizzie Vance Falkner and Lelia Dean Butler. According to Falkner family lore, the climax of the story owed something to Lizzie Vance's supplying false information to Yankee Colonel DeWitt Thomas about Bedford Forrest's strength on that far-off day when he whipped the Yankees so soundly at Brice's Crossroads.

Here, however, it was the concealment which provided the climax. Bayard and Ringo fire a musket at a Yankee officer and kill his horse.

Fleeing to the house, they crouch beneath Granny Millard's chair, concealed by her skirts, as she lies to the Union officer to protect them. Underlying the story was another strategy of concealment which served to link it to the vignette out of which *The Sound and the Fury* had grown. In that story, the Compsons had tried to spare the children the knowledge of Damuddy's death, wake, and burial. Here, Granny Millard and the responsible servants tried to spare the two twelve-year-olds as much as possible of the war and the prospect ahead. Still believing that Bayard's father was away fighting the Yankees in Tennessee, they gradually learned—upon his return—of the imminent invasion. In the subsequent events they discovered the depredations of an occupying army. Comedy was provided by Granny Millard's continuing concern with discipline, as demonstrated at the end with the boys blowing bubbles from mouths washed out for swearing. Technically the story was straightforward. Chronology proceeded in a straight line. The vantage point of retrospect provided flexibility where it was needed, and in the one instance where Bayard had to relate something he could not possibly have seen, Faulkner simply had him tell it as seen by one of the servants, Louvinia.

By the time he finished, the story was something over 6,000 words. He titled it "Ambuscade" and sent it to Morty Goldman. His covering letter began with a reference to a story that was probably "A Bear Hunt": "I'll leave this to your judgment: The Post paid $900 for the other one, a sketch; maybe they will pay $1500 for this. If they will, I will promise to let them see three or four more as good or better than this one during the year. Tell them that with $1500 I can pay my N.R.A. income tax." Before he mailed it he scribbled a postscript: "Dont tell them though that I said to take what you can get for it." The *Post* indicated enough interest for him to begin the second story.

In the 8,000-word story "Retreat," the boys were nearing fourteen, and their initiation proceeded apace. Suspicious that Loosh, Ringo's uncle, will betray the hiding place of the family silver to the Union troops, Granny Millard has the chest dug up from the orchard and sets out through the Federal lines to find safekeeping for it somehow in occupied Memphis. When a Yankee patrol takes Tinney and Old Hundred, the two mules, the boys set out on a "borrowed" horse to trace them, knowing the mules will throw the Yankees. Later they help Colonel Sartoris capture a Yankee unit before the action ends at Sartoris when another detachment comes for the reburied silver. The Colonel escapes but the Yankees burn the house, leaving Bayard, Ringo, *and* Granny crying, "The bastuds! The bastuds!"

Through much of the story there was comedy as well as action, but by this time three generations—taught by the enemy—have become horse "borrowers": Bayard and Ringo, John Sartoris, and Granny Millard. And the picture has darkened, with the house a ruin and the silver gone. Having betrayed them, Loosh leaves Sartoris to seek freedom in the wake of the Northern armies.

Faulkner sent "Retreat" and his correspondence with the *Post* editors to Goldman. "What do you think of this?" he asked. "Let the Post keep this second story until I finish the third and send it to *you* before you talk price, because I think the third story will be the most novel (damn the word) of all. Then tell them they can have the two for four thousand and I will let them have the subsequent three for five thousand more. That will be ten thousand for the series of six, and I believe they have paid more than that for serieses [*sic*]." He would write the third one and send it soon.

He called the third story "Raid." Running to nearly 10,000 words, it was the longest and, as he had predicted, the most novel of the three. Here Granny and the boys set out to find Colonel Dick, the Union officer of "Ambuscade," to seek recompense for the silver and the mules. At another ravaged plantation Faulkner introduced another new character: Drusilla Hawk, a young kinswoman widowed by the war before she could become a bride. The best woman rider in the county, she dresses like a man and braves the Yankees like a man, wishing only to ride with John Sartoris' troop. If Faulkner knew the Old Colonel's *The Siege of Monterey*, its heroine might have provided a model. According to friends, however, there was one much closer, Tochie Oldham—as good as the boys and sometimes better at the games they played, pretty, high-spirited, and ill-fated. As Granny followed Colonel Dick's trail into Alabama, Faulkner wrote his biggest scene of the series, the vast hordes of Negro slaves following a Federal column only to be held back by cavalry while the infantry crosses a bridge promptly blown up after them. In spite of this Granny obtains from him an order directing Union forces to recompense her in kind.

At this point Faulkner made a subtle and necessary change in strategy. Wrongdoing—chiefly in the form of Bayard and Ringo's cursing—had been a source of comedy. At the end of "Retreat" Granny had not only used forbidden language but had also appropriated property not hers. This model of rectitude and enforcer of family standards was now to become—at first under the necessities of survival in wartime—herself a transgressor of these standards. Through a clerical error, her requisition is made out for

10 chests of silver and 110 mules. Faulkner derived comic effects from her collecting horses by dismounting Yankee patrols, arriving home at Sartoris with 122 mules and horses and an unnumbered group of Negroes. At the story's end she knelt by the road with the two boys to pray for forgiveness. As the boys had passed through initiation into a species of corruption, so had she.

The editors of the *Post* agreed to the idea of a series. This was what Faulkner needed: top magazine rates for more than one story. But suddenly there was a problem. "I have been stewing for about three weeks now on the Post stories," he told Morty Goldman in an undated letter. "I have been trying to cook up three more with a single thread of continuity, like the other three, with the scene during Reconstruction time. I cannot get started, I seem to have more material than I can compress. I have just now decided that the trouble is this:

"The Reconstruction stories do not come next. In order to write them, I shall have to postulate a background with the characters which they embrace. Therefore, there must be one or two stories still between the War–Silver–Mule business and the Reconstruction; I am just starting one which will be a direct continuation of the return home with the mules, which should be included in the series of three which are done; perhaps it will bring to an end that phase, and I can get into the Reconstruction ones which for some reason will not start themselves. Please pass this on to the Post; I will send in this fourth story as soon as possible."

But the fourth story would not come. Phil Stone was suffering from no such problem, however. The forthcoming appearance of the second number of *The Oxford Magazine* was heralded with the information that "it has been decided to issue definitely six more issues, for it will take those six issues to carry Phil Stone's biography of William Faulkner. Subscriptions are being taken on that basis." The second issue, it was announced, would also contain a contribution by the subject of the biography.

When the magazine appeared it contained no Faulkner work, but Phil Stone had supplied his first installment: "The Man: Background." Stone sketched in geography, economy, and "the 'Rise of the Redneck.' " Faulkner's grandfather and uncle were leaders in the Vardaman faction, he wrote. "It is this social and political upheaval that is the dominant theme of Faulkner's saga of the Snopes family . . . which work, if ever completed, may become his greatest book and possibly the grandest book of humor America yet has seen." He closed with an account of the careers of the Old

Colonel and his son. If Stone continued in the present vein, the series would develop into a valuable biographical sketch. At first he took a very offhand tone in his letter to Hal Smith on April 10. "This series will probably not be good enough for a book," he had written. A few lines later he had qualified the statement somewhat. "Of course, if you should later decide that the stuff can be arranged so as to make a book which would be worthwhile you and I can then discuss that." Now, moving further into his subject matter, Stone was seeing more than just vicarious pleasure in Faulkner's writing.

Faulkner continued flying at regular intervals, often in Memphis on the weekends, through May and into June. By now flying had become Dean's profession, as his brother had hoped, and he was often busy with passenger rides and flight lessons. Then on one late June day a shocking piece of news spread through the offices and hangars. Jimmy Wedell was dead. On Sunday afternoon, June 24, he had taken off with Frank Snearing from the field outside Patterson, Louisiana, where the Wedell-Williams Air Service was based. At three hundred feet Wedell leveled off to begin the lesson. Suddenly the plane dipped out of control and crashed. The men who pulled Wedell's body out of the wreckage could not be sure who was at the controls, and Snearing was too badly injured to tell them. The man who had survived the deadly competition of racing pilots had died teaching a beginner.

Two days later William Faulkner executed a three-page Last Will and Testament in Phil Stone's office. In four days he was going on a trip. He would travel partway by air, and he wanted his affairs in order. All his property and its income would go to Estelle for her lifetime or until she remarried. The principal was to be held intact for Jill. Miss Maud would have the income and manuscripts of *Soldiers' Pay* and *Sanctuary*. Appointed as Jill's Testamentary Guardians and Executors of the will were "my Brother, M. C. Falkner, and my friend, Phil Stone."

The flirtation from Hollywood had continued, and Faulkner had welcomed it. Graeme Lorimer, of the *Post*'s editorial staff, would not offer as much for the whole Bayard-Ringo series of stories as Faulkner wanted. He decided to accept Hawks's contract offer, which was the kind he preferred. Universal Studios would hire him for a short time at a salary of $1,000 a week. There was no set term of weeks with options and the rest of the legal hedges. He would work until the job was done or he was no longer needed. He was making no noticeable progress on *A Dark House* or the Snopes book. A short time away might help him. And the work could scarcely be more of an ordeal than *Louisiana Lou* had been. He might even find it as painless as *Today We Live.* Before he left Oxford on July 1, Phil Mullen asked him about the new assignment. Faulkner "said that he had no idea as to what story he was going to work on." Mullen added, "Neither have I but I'll risk a guess that it's not *The Little Minister.* . . ." The Memphis *Press-Scimitar* ran a photograph of him standing by the wing of a plane. He carried a hat, trench coat, and alligator briefcase. His face looked thin. He was gazing straight ahead, unsmiling—not grim, but resigned.

Checking into the Hollywood Roosevelt Hotel, he began work immediately after the usual conference in which Hawks explained what he wanted. He was to work on the adaptation of a novel by Blaise Cendrars entitled *Sutter's Gold.* A friend named Gloria Stuart lent him a book on Sutter and another on gold mining in California. As it turned out, this was not the only property he would be working on. By Saturday, July 7, he was able to write an encouraging letter home to Estelle: "I made a synopsis of the play, and yesterday Howard and I talked, and we decided that I shall spend another week here in order to get as much of the script on paper as possible, have a talk for final corrections, then come home and make what we hope will be the final draft. So unless something unforeseen comes up, I now plan to start home about next Monday."

In several ways it was shaping up as a pleasanter stay than the previous one. He was no longer a stranger, and besides Californians like Hawks he could turn to former Mississippian Hubert Starr. "Weather good and cool here, fine sleeping," he wrote. "Starr now lives down on the beach, in a canyon. I am moving down to stay with him today. It is a good place to hide out and work; he is alone now and I will have the house to myself all day long. I can put on bathing suit right in the house and walk 2 blocks to the beach."

The scenery, so unlike that of Culver City, seemed to remind him of his European trip. "I tried some very good ale at a German Hof-brau restaurant, a lady string band there, and the proprietor's daughter, about 3 or 4, like a Dresden doll, with a toy violin helping them. I enjoy it—heavy, good German food and sentimental Bavarian music under a vine trellis."

On another piece of hotel stationery he enclosed a drawing for Jill: a graceful and amusing fine-line ink caricature of himself. A pair of wings were carrying him from California to Rowan Oak. He was smoking a pipe and carrying a box of gifts for all the family, including the servants—

Mammy, Earl, and Pauline. Clutched in the same hand was a small sack marked with a dollar sign. The sketch was signed "Your friend and admirer, Pappy."

Estelle's letters were reassuring. The children were fine and she felt well, better than she had in a long time. This was what he needed, for he was already suffering the onset of loneliness. Besides, the job situation had changed. "Finished another synopsis today," he wrote, "and am waiting now to hear about making a movie of the recent play, Mary of Scotland. Will get to work on that right away, as it is the next job. Will let you know soon as I can when to expect me." He loved them, missed them, and blessed them.

On Friday, July 20, he typed an air-mail letter explaining what was happening. It also explained, in part, why Faulkner did not particularly relish working in Hollywood, even for one as generous as Hawks. "The situation is now this," he began. "I made a draft of 'Sutter's Gold,' then Hawks came in with the second story, the crisis affair of which I wrote you. I made a treatment of that, finished it, took it to Hawks (this was about Tuesday of last week) whereupon he told me of the plan about Mary of Scotland. We discussed it that afternoon while he was waiting to hear from the studio if they had permission to do it or not. No word came; Hawks drove me back to Santa Monica, told me he would send me word tomorrow (Wednesday). Dead silence until Friday, when I telephoned him myself (no phone here; you walk down to the beach to find one) and he said nothing about MARY at all, but that he was making corrections on SUTTER and would send that to me tomorrow (Saturday). Dead silence again until Tuesday. The corrections came, I tried to telephone Howard, could not get him, telephoned his brother, my agent, told him Howard had told me (as I wrote you) that I could get away about this coming weekend. He told me that Howard had talked to him, and that he was at the moment arranging to get my money for the second or [Margaret] Sullavan story, and that I would hear from him (Hawks 2) tomorrow, which would have been last Wednesday. I have not heard yet, though today I finished the final treatment of SUTTER, and have just telephoned Hawks' home, telling him so and that I will wait here for word. I will have to see him, get an o.k. on the script, keep after his agent brother and get my pay for this and for the second treatment."

The end was now in sight, however. "Right now I believe that I will be in Memphis at eleven o'clock Tuesday morning. Surely they can clean things up for me by then, and Monday I will get a few presents for us and ours and take the plane Monday night." He hoped to get a good camera at a reduced price through the studio. "Then we can keep a regular diary of the children and Rowanoak."

While enjoying the solitude provided by Starr's house, he had not been a recluse. He had dined with Marc Connelly and seen a good deal of Ben Wasson, who would drive to Santa Monica and go down to the beach with him. But now he was more than anxious to return home, and he began to recognize danger signals. "I am getting nervous and a little jumpy to get home," he wrote, "at the fingernail chewing stage. I wasted a whole week doing nothing at all; that's what frets me about this business." He added a postscript in pen: "Done a little on the novel from time to time."

Hawks gave Faulkner the okay he needed, and he boarded his American Airlines flight on schedule. One of the other passengers was also a resident of the Mid-South. "Of all the authors in the country," said Richard Halliburton, travel writer and author of *The Royal Road to Romance*, "I've wanted to meet Bill Faulkner most, not only because I liked his books, but because to me he's a home boy." They were apparently well met. "I liked him immensely," Halliburton told the reporters when the passengers debarked in Memphis on a scorchingly hot July 24. He was shortly to depart again for the West Indies. Faulkner wanted nothing more than to go home and stay home. He kissed Estelle and Jill and they got in the car and headed for Oxford.

Five hundred miles to the north, Jack Falkner was also ready for some relaxation. Two days before, he and his fellow agents had caught up once more with the elusive and deadly John Dillinger at the box office of the Biograph Theatre in Chicago. There was a blaze of gunfire, and much of the work of the special FBI squad was suddenly over.

At home again, William Faulkner did not even pilot a plane for the next seven weeks. He had too much to do at his desk. The most pressing job was finishing Hawks's script. He also had to deal with the series for the *Post.* Graeme Lorimer wanted to know where they stood; he had asked Morty Goldman, but Morty had not even been informed that his client was in California. In late July, Faulkner brought Goldman up to date. "I could not get enough out of them for the series," he wrote. "So at the end of June I went out to California and got lined up with a moom pitcher script. I am working on it now, and I cannot say just when I will finish it. Maybe in a month; if I do, I may write the other stories or I may go back to the novel;

it all depends on how much or badly I need money at the time. That is, I would like to keep the Post hot for a while longer, so if, when I finish the script, I need more cash I can write the other stories. But I would not like to promise to do so, since I have had to put off the novel too much already."

Having dealt with his agent and current magazine customer, he turned to his publisher. He still did not know when the novel would be ready. "I believe that the book is not quite ripe yet; that I have not gone my nine months, you might say," he told Smith. "I do have to put it aside and make a nickel every so often, but I think there must be more than that. I have a mass of stuff, but only one chapter that suits me; I am considering putting it aside and going back to REQUIEM FOR A NUN, which will be a short one, like AS I LAY DYING, while the present one will probably be longer than LIGHT IN AUGUST. I have a title for it which I like, by the way: ABSALOM, ABSALOM; the story is of a man who wanted a son through pride, and got too many of them and they destroyed him."

He invited Smith down on November 20 for a week's deer hunt. "I will be sober (I have not had a drink since you left) and I want to show you the South: cotton and niggers, etc., that I failed to show you before. We can spend three days in the woods, and three more days looking at the Mississippi delta, where the cotton grows; we can take the aeroplane and go to New Orleans. You can get your duck shooting this time, also."

Later in August, Faulkner gave his agent a progress report: "I have caught up with the movie now; I have a good story out of California I want to write. I may do that first; otherwise I will get another one in the series; you should have it within four weeks. You can tell the Post this, if you think best; say I am starting the fourth one and you will submit it as soon as you get it." He would do one or the other; he had to keep the checks coming in. There had been one acceptance which was fine as far as it went, but which gave little sustenance. "Lo!," which had not been right for *Scribner's*, was taken by *Story*. Editor Whit Burnett wrote Goldman that it seemed to be "one of those off-the-track Faulkners which just suits us." He wanted to buy it for the September or October number "at our (alas) usual rates." It would be anthologized as one of the best short stories of the year.

As Faulkner reviewed what he could remember of his negotiations with the *Post*, his resentment burst through: "as I recall the business, I wrote them that I was going ahead with a series before the question of price came up. When price came up, they offered promptly to send the stories back to us if we did not want to take what they would pay; my later correspondence consisted of manuscripts. So perhaps the thing for us to do now is to recopy their letter to us and say, if they dont like the way in which the stories are submitted, to send them back to us and get a refund of the money. As far as I am concerned, while I have to write trash, I dont care who buys it, as long as they pay the best price I can get; doubtless the Post feels the same way about it; anytime that I sacrifice a high price to a lower one it will not be to refrain from antagonizing the Post; it will be to write something better than a pulp series like this."

"Hot as hell here," he had told Goldman; "I have to work in front of a fan; I write with one hand and hold the paper down with the other." Drifting through the window of his workroom he could sometimes hear the sounds of Mac Franklin, Art Guyton, and several other boys as they worked at a more direct method of dealing with the late summer heat. They had rigged up a cable system on which a pulley carried hoppers of dirt from a hill to a gully about 300 yards from the house. "It was at the lower end of a vast system of eroded gulleys," Art Guyton remembered, "at the tail-end of Mr. Bill's pasture." With the dirt they built a dam which spanned the fifteen-foot ditch and finally rose eight feet high. It would now amplify the slight trickle from the spring with the water that flooded through the gulley system with each week's rains. "Over a period of perhaps two months this provided us with an adequate swimming hole. The water was a little putrid because it was almost entirely stagnant and partly because there were some washings from the pasture into the mud hole." Swimming without suits, the boys were sometimes unable to leave the water because of the appearance of visitors who happened to be girls. The owner of the pasture never appeared there, but he did meet them on the tennis court he had built. He and Art Guyton had quickly been established as the top-seeded players in their impromptu tournaments. He played with them on many afternoons after his mornings at the desk. At other times he would take a mallet from the new croquet set. For a while he and Art fell into the habit of playing chess each afternoon, beginning at two-thirty or three, when Faulkner would bring out two glasses, one with ice and lemonade for the boy and what looked like the same thing for himself. Faulkner had taught him to play, and it was several years before Art was able to take a game from his teacher. By September, however, Faulkner was able to resume flying, and the afternoons with him in various aircraft were even more memorable to the boys than tennis or croquet.

Faulkner was also seeing a good deal of a young fellow townsman. At twenty-seven, E. O. Champion was service manager for the Haney Chevrolet Company in Oxford. In February Faulkner had bought a new Chevrolet coupe for $750. Whenever he brought it to the garage for any work, he would always ask Champ to do it for him. A short, stocky, affable man, Champ was not only an auto mechanic but a self-taught aviation mechanic as well. As did Faulkner, he liked flying so much that he had his eye on an airplane before he had even soloed. He went to Little Rock and bought it, a three-seat, open-cockpit biplane called a Command-Aire. It was powered by an air-cooled 90 h.p. Curtiss engine, the OX5, which was not as powerful as the one normally built into the plane but which was especially popular with barnstormers for its reliability. The plane took off and landed at about fifty miles per hour and cruised between eighty-five and ninety. The wheels had no brakes, and there was a metal tail skid at the rear. Champ soloed in the Command-Aire and now often took Faulkner up with him. They flew together on Sunday mornings especially. When they went on cross-country flights, Champ would do the piloting and Faulkner the navigating. Ten years the senior, Faulkner often spoke in a cautionary tone. "Champ," he would say, "if you have any doubt about it, don't do it." He preached safety aloft and on the ground. They talked flying all the time, Champ always eager to listen. Faulkner told about flying Sopwith Camels in England, how they threw castor oil so badly that you could hardly see to land. He would watch pilots bust them up every day, he said. It was a comfortable and companionable relationship. Only once did Champ attempt to read his friend's work. He began *Sanctuary* but did not finish it. Characteristically, Faulkner was glad to have literary elements excluded from this relationship.

On September 9 Faulkner took the controls of Champ's Command-Aire for a half-hour. Two days later he went to Memphis to fly his own Waco for the first time since June. On such trips as this Mac, Art, Jimmy, and Chooky would ride to Memphis in Faulkner's 1933 Chevrolet sedan. Art would be allowed to drive, steering between the potholes on the loosely graveled roads at speeds between fifty and sixty miles an hour. "In the car on the way to and from Memphis one of the special avocations of the younger boys was to think up fantastic tales and tell them to Mr. Bill with the suggestion that he write the tales and perhaps share the royalties [with them].” As it turned out, there was more danger involved in these outings than just travel on Mississippi highways of the year 1934.

“Once while Chooky and I were riding the front cockpit of a two-seater plane and Mr. Bill was flying, we had left the airport several miles behind and had climbed to an altitude of about 1500 feet when the engine began to sputter. It would kick off and on, and we continued to lose altitude. Mr. Bill did an almost 90 degree bank and headed back toward the airport. With a little bit of kicking and sputtering we finally came over the edge of the field with an altitude of some 50 to 100 feet left, and upon landing the engine cut out completely. To Chooky and myself this was just another experience, and we didn’t think a thing about it until many years later. So far as Mr. Bill was concerned, he was outwardly absolutely and completely calm. Therefore we considered this to be just one of the everyday, ordinary features of flying.”

Something happened a little later that day, however, that no one regarded with calm. The government inspector had finished his examination of the cabin Waco and the mechanic began to replace parts removed for the inspection. As he started to fasten the thin aluminum panel where one of the wings met the fuselage, “he noted that one of the main nuts holding the wing onto the fuselage was missing. At that moment he let out a yell and everybody came to look. The final theory was that the wing had been holding on by the tiny aluminum strip which had hundreds of screws on each side, one line of screws on the wing and one line of screws on the fuselage.”

Faulkner was now able to resume his barnstorming. The *Eagle* reported that he would sponsor an air circus then at the Markette field, six miles south of town, the weekend of September 15–16. Vernon Omlie would be the chief pilot, and there would be three planes, “including Faulkner’s 150-mile an hour cabin ship, shown here for the first time. There will be passenger rides and stunt flying each day and a parachute jump on Sunday.” Faulkner was also at the field three weekends later when a giant trimotor Ford, with a corrugated metal fuselage, flew in for a three-day stay, the largest plane ever seen in Oxford. Three weeks after that, on October 30, Faulkner found more excitement aloft in the Command-Aire. Champ had gotten a job in Dyersburg, seventy-five miles northeast of Memphis, and Faulkner was to fly him there and then return to Oxford. They made the trip up without incident. The OX5 was considered an efficient eight-cylinder engine, but it did not supply sufficient power for the Command-Aire at best. Faulkner was flying due south at 7,000 feet over Holly Springs when the engine lost a pin from one of the overhead valves. It began to run roughly and lose power. There was nothing to do but try to nurse it home and hope. Faulkner brought it in on the remaining seven cylinders. Later, he and the Black Eagle repaired the engine.

A week later there was more trouble, this time in the cabin Waco. On November 6 Dean or Vernon flew it down from Memphis and Faulkner put in fifteen minutes at the controls. Later he made a short notation under "Remarks" in his log: "Accident Undercarriage Prop, Spar." Johncy had the greatest respect for his brother's abilities as a navigator, but he had reservations about his skill as a pilot. "Bill did learn this much about flying," he wrote; "he never had a crash he couldn't walk away from. He did pretty good flying OX5 stuff but every time he was out in his Waco by himself and went into some strange field he did something to it. Usually it never amounted to more than wiping off a wing tip or blowing a tire but he did it nearly every time." On the same day that he had the mishap in the Waco, Faulkner logged ninety minutes in the Command-Aire, but it was almost three weeks before he flew again.

He had been making progress meanwhile with the stories for the *Post*, galvanized by settlement of the money differences. "Ambuscade" appeared on September 29, "Retreat" on October 13, and "Raid" on November 3. During September he completed and mailed directly to the *Post* the fourth and fifth stories, which he called "The Unvanquished" and "Vendée."

In "The Unvanquished" Faulkner continued the expansion begun with the introduction of old Buck McCaslin in "Raid." For one of the new characters he went back to a time earlier than that of *Father Abraham*, interpolating Snopes material into the 10,000-word story. Ab Snopes, Flem's father, sells back to Federal quartermasters the mules Granny and Ringo have commandeered using orders forged on stolen Federal stationery. Ab stands to Colonel Sartoris much as Wash Jones had stood to Sutpen: "it was Father that told Ab to kind of look out for Granny while he was away; only he told me and Ringo to look out for Ab, too. . . ." By the time the Federals stop them, they have "handled" 246 animals, selling 105 of them back to the Yankees for a profit, together with other resales, of close to $7,000. Although Granny has used the profits to save the county's poor in the war's devastation, the extensive practice of fraud and forgery has subtly corrupted her—who punished cursing and abhorred lying. Her natural self-assurance has become pride and arrogance. As she makes accounting of her proceeds she tells God, "It is true that I kept some of it back, but I am the best judge of that because I, too, have dependants who may be orphans, too, at this moment, for all I know. And if this be sin in Your sight, I take this on my conscience too."

Arguing that John Sartoris will need a stake on his return, Ab Snopes persuades Granny to use her forged order to repossess four horses from marauders known as "Grumby's Independents." (An acquaintance of Faulkner's, John Cullen, thought later that Faulkner was drawing on local lore.) Faulkner's problem here was to make this action credible: that Granny would believe a bushwhacker would respect an unenforced Federal order. He tried to do this by emphasizing her desperate desire, hedging his bet by Bayard's and Ringo's certainty of disaster as they try to keep her from the attempt. Curiously enough, the *Post* accepted this improbability (and the ensuing murder) but balked at one in the fifth story, "Vendée."

Taking his title from the coastal department in western France where a fratricidal royalist revolt broke out in 1793, Faulkner devoted the 9,000-word story to the revenge. When Bayard and Ringo finally face Grumby, deserted by his accomplices, he flings away his pistol and runs. After Bayard shoots Grumby, he and Ringo stake his body to the door of the shack where he murdered Granny. Then they fix his severed right hand to the board marking her grave so "she can lay good and quiet." On October 1, Graeme Lorimer wrote to Goldman that they liked the story but doubted Grumby's motivation: that he would refuse to ambush his two young pursuers for fear of further rousing the countryside against him, and that his nerve would fail again at the final showdown after the long drawn-out pursuit. "We have no objection to the grimness of the ending," Lorimer wrote, "and we feel that this can be made into a fine story for the series, provided Mr. Faulkner will bring about the boys' vengeance on Grumby more swiftly and keep Grumby in character throughout."

Faulkner agreed to the suggested rewrite but he resented it. He was caught: he wanted to be independent, but he needed the money. One afternoon, months before, he had read one of the stories to Estelle, Art Guyton, and a few others as they sat on the gallery at Rowan Oak. They were "completely mesmerized." Now, however, Art had learned from Miss Estelle that the *Post* editors had objected to the form of the stories. She and Mr. Bill were both upset about it, it seemed to him. Lorimer's objections to "Vendée" were valid, but it must have seemed to Faulkner another demonstration of what happened when you wrote "trash" because you needed money. "Post mss. was altered to their wishes and returned," he wrote Goldman on October 18. He had done more than that. On October 4 he had sent them another story called "Drusilla" which filled in more material he felt the series needed: material on the war's end and the Reconstruction.

This 6,500-word story was closest in tone and effect to the first two stories. Again there was homicide, but the emphasis was on action with a touch of the comic rather than on murder and retribution. For some of the motive force of the action, Faulkner used characters from *Light in August.* They were Calvin Burden and his grandson, Calvin, come to Jefferson to vote the newly franchised Negroes. John Sartoris kills them with his derringer. For the comic counterpoint, Faulkner used another struggle: the forces of respectability compelling the marriage of Sartoris and Drusilla Hawk, who has fought with his partisan cavalry regiment and now helps to work his plantation on a strictly platonic and muscular basis. It was a happy-ending story, with the carpetbaggers defeated and the principals married—two people obviously right for each other though not overtly romantic. Faulkner may have gagged as he wrote the last lines, when men of the old regiment gave the rebel yell: " 'Yaaaaay, Drusilla!' they hollered. 'Yaaaaaay, John Sartoris! Yaaaaaaay!' "

It was more congenial work than the scriptwriting, at any rate, and Faulkner had at least blocked in more of the Sartoris saga. He had also developed a useful character in Uncle Buck McCaslin (who helped the boys track Grumby), and he had worked with another of a type always appealing to him: Drusilla, the masculinized woman—brave, hardy, and toughened by war and loss, but fundamentally still very feminine and capable of love for the right man.

Faulkner had sent Goldman an appeal from one of the "little magazines" which he did not name. He was trying to do business with the "slick magazines," but he was still sympathetic. "Enclosed is a letter," he wrote. "I have no photographs and am too busy to fool with this, but if you can dig up a picture and some [mss] for him, it is all right with me. I like to help all these earnest magazines, but I have too goddam many demands on me requiring and necessitating orthodox prostitution to have time to give it away save as it can be taken from me while I sleep, you might say. But fix him up if you can."

There was another thing Faulkner asked Goldman to do. "Did you get wire about air story, COURAGE? I am writing a novel out of it, so please return it." He was apparently very much in earnest, for he added a postscript: "Dont forget the story, THIS KIND OF COURAGE. Send it back to me." Of this novel in embryo he would later say, "I wrote that book because I'd got in trouble with *Absalom, Absalom!* and I had to get away from it for a while so I thought a good way to get away from it was to write another book. . . ." Of the pile of manuscript pages in which he was trying to work out the story of Sutpen, only one chapter satisfied him. He would switch for a while to something easier. He would do, in fact, what he had done in *Mosquitoes*: turn to something contemporary, to something at his fingertips, and for models he would use people he knew intimately.

41

September, 1934–March, 1935

> The rest of this is composite. It is what we (groundlings, dwellers in and backbone of a small town interchangeable with and duplicate of ten thousand little dead clottings of human life about the land) saw, refined and clarified by the expert, the man who had himself seen his own lonely and scudding shadow upon the face of the puny and remote earth.
>
> —"Death Drag" (197–198)

For nearly a decade barnstorming aviators had intrigued Faulkner. He had sketched a three-man team in "Death Drag," and in "Honor" he had treated a romantic triangle involving a pilot, his wife, and his wing-walker. The MGM script of *Flying the Mail* had presented aviators in only slightly less uncertain pursuits. In the last half-year he had done a little barnstorming himself. He was financially involved in flying but much more deeply involved emotionally. Two incidents in the month of September, 1934, had affected him particularly.

On the fifteenth he and Dean were getting the Waco gassed up at the Memphis Municipal Airport before flying to Oxford for the weekend air circus. When Faulkner and a friend, Charlie Hayes, went into Mrs. Caya's luncheonette, Hayes introduced him to a young student pilot. Faulkner later described the introduction:

" 'This is Mister So-and-So,' Hayes said: that's the way I hear names, being completely lacking in that presence of mind which catches names at once." But then it registered. The name was Grider, " 'Mac Grider's son, George,' Hayes said." Faulkner looked carefully now and saw what the boy looked like: "Like he might be on the sophomore boxing team; big in the shoulders but not especially big anywhere else, in an open shirt and a pair of summer pants, with a young face good between the eyes and a mouth and chin more delicate than you might expect." They exchanged a few words and Faulkner left. When Faulkner saw him at the airport on the following Wednesday, Grider waited for him to say hello, and then volunteered a bit of information. "I soloed yesterday morning," he said. Now he was going to ask Charlie Hayes to use his box camera for a picture beside the airplane.

"Listen," Hayes quietly said to Faulkner, "I want you to do something. Knock out something for the papers about this: Mac Grider's son. Twenty-two years old. Second year at Annapolis. Soloed in a week."

"In a week?" Faulkner said. "He actually soloed inside of seven days?"

"Yes. He stuck at it pretty close; he's got to be back at school on the twenty-eighth. So you knock out something. Something he won't be ashamed of."

Even if George Grider did not remind Faulkner of young John Sartoris, the tableau of the young man beside the plane must surely have recalled the opening of "All the Dead Pilots": the snapshots of the young men of 1918 beside their machines of wire and wood and canvas. Faulkner wrote the piece for the *Commercial Appeal*, describing their meetings and telling the story of Mac Grider and *War Birds.* George Grider's generation was unlike that of the swaggerers of 1914–1918, but Faulkner was touched by this generation, too. Grider could have posed in expensive helmet and goggles, or even a replica of his dead father's uniform. "But he didn't: he just stood there where the sun would fall on him good, in clothes he might have put on to mow the back yard, while his companion squinted into the camera, turning gadgets and such. " 'Hurry up,' he said. 'I'd hate to have my face freeze like this.' "

Two weeks after the first meeting with Grider an event took place which touched him much more deeply. Sunday afternoon, September 30, found Dean in Batesville after a weekend of barnstorming together with Vernon and a jumper named Navy Sowell. Louise Hale had gone with them to Batesville. The weekend's work was over, and now, they decided, was as good a time as any to get married. It was six in the evening when they reached the Courthouse Square. Louise was prepared to be frugal from the start, but Dean insisted that they buy a wedding ring and persuaded a jeweler to open his store. Then they crossed the street to the Courthouse, where they were married, with Vernon and the jumper for witnesses. Now aged twenty-seven and a licensed pilot, Dean would support his bride and himself by flying.

They settled into married life quickly. In keeping with the Falkner tradition, they had eloped. They meant to keep the marriage secret as Jack and Cecile had done, but they found that they couldn't. So at Miss Maud's, two days later, with Auntee and Bill there too, Dean slipped out and bought a cake and some ice cream. When Louise began to serve them they asked her what the occasion was. Then she and Dean told them they were married. Everyone seemed pleased, and not long afterwards Bill gave a dinner for them at which most of the members of both families were present. The couple moved to Memphis, where Dean worked for Vernon at Mid-South Airways. Housing was no problem. In 1932 Phoebe Omlie had taken her Monocoupe on a 25,000-mile speaking tour for Franklin D. Roosevelt. After the election she went to Washington as the first woman appointed to the Department of Commerce's Bureau of Aeronautics. Now she inspected airfields and other installations, returning home for occasional visits. Vernon was alone in the big apartment on Lamar Avenue and there was hardly enough for Exie Hardimon, the maid, to do. So Dean and Louise moved in.

Faulkner was with them often, still as paternal as when Dean was a bachelor. "Always try to have at least fifty dollars in the bank to meet emergencies," he would tell them, and they listened. By now Dean, who looked more like Miss Maud than his brother, was balding. But he did what he could to be like his brother. He had grown the same kind of mustache, and he had changed the spelling of his name to Faulkner. His elder brother gave him the cabin Waco when he went into partnership with Vernon in the Memphis Flying Service. (He was also going to give him a complete set of his books when he could get them together.) Faulkner apparently had other hopes, and perhaps plans, for Dean. Lately he had been doing some surveying at the Oxford airfield. Federal WPA money was now promised to equip the field for heavier traffic, and at some point Faulkner typed out a one-page, single-spaced description of the duties and powers of an airport commissioner. He went to Lee Gainey, the business manager at the university, to enlist its support. As the Oxford airport grew, so would the need for an air service company. Dean was gaining experience in all phases of private commercial aviation, and he must have seemed to his brother the ideal person to do in Oxford what Vernon was doing in Memphis. They could just enlarge their present operation, and with aviation growing there was no reason why, in time, they could not expand their operation to Batesville and some of the other nearby cities. Perhaps Dean would be settled at last.

Faulkner was immersed in aviation. It was logical that he should now write about it again, and at length, though the house was far from quiet. On October 27, following the Sewanee–Ole Miss football game, the Faulkners gave a dinner dance for Alice McSpadden, a young friend of Estelle's, and all the other Memphis debutantes of the season and their escorts. Faulkner played the host and then escaped. If Morty Goldman had responded promptly to Faulkner's request that he send back to him the air story called "This Kind of Courage," Faulkner could have had it on his desk a few days before the party. From the start, and unlike the way he had struggled with *Absalom, Absalom!*, he now wrote with the kind of speed and concentration he had achieved before only with *As I Lay Dying*. By November 11, the first chapter of *Pylon* was on Hal Smith's desk in New York. This indicated other things besides speed (or haste), however. He was engaged in a demanding kind of composition. He was writing in longhand as usual, keeping the story going in his head and on paper, but then halting, in mid-stride almost, to go back and type up segments from the first part for mailing. Sending out part of his unfinished novel was a most unusual procedure for the meticulous craftsman who would normally compose a manuscript, rewrite much of it, and then type the whole thing to be sure of internal consistency before he sent it to the publisher. He had sometimes typed as he went, but this—even though he could refer to his carbon of the first chapter if he had to—was not the same. Smith may have been anxious to set the book in type as quickly as possible to ensure an early publication date. If this was the case, Faulkner cannot have enjoyed the accompanying sense of rush. Yet he was probably relieved to give Smith a manuscript, even if it was neither the first nor the second that Smith expected next. If these were the conditions under which he was writing, he may have felt a kind of distaste for the procedure. After the feeling that he had not gone his nine months with *Absalom, Absalom!*, this may have seemed like spontaneous conception, gestation, and parturition.

In general, the typescript would follow the manuscript without major alterations. One exception, however, came on the first page, where Faulkner attempted to set forth both locale and something of theme immediately in an experimental way. He juxtaposed three separate unitary segments, each one scissored from an early page and pasted together on a new sheet. They were the dedicatory plaque of a new airport, the program of flying events for Dedication Day, and a brief but highly impressionistic vignette of Mardi gras. (He had written, "INRI goblin demon parrotmask, parakeet and pierroquet, mardi gras and mardi grille. . . .") Then he opened the action with one of the minor characters. As he moved from composition to the revision of this untitled first page, he cut these three segments and provided a more conventional beginning for his opening chapter. When it reached New York in typescript form, it also had a title.

The first chapter was called "Dedication of an Airport," and it prefigured several directions the novel would take. As with *As I Lay Dying*, present action would cover only a short span, but lives would come to a climax in it. The dedication of Shushan Airport would provide a frame for his view of barnstorming aviation and its people. Feinman Airport, of New Valois, Franciana, was closely modeled after Shushan in New Orleans, the runways on land reclaimed from Lake Rambaud very like those resting on the oyster shells and other refuse poured into the waters of Lake Pontchartrain. The program of the day's events was close to the original, though the dates were February 14–16, 1935, rather than 1934. Among the competitors were a noted Frenchman, Jules Despleins, Lieut. Frank Burnham in his "Rocket Plane," and Matt Ord, world speed record holder.

There would be other correspondences. Faulkner opened with a tough, stocky, grease-stained mechanic named Jiggs who looked and sounded a good deal like the airplane mechanic in *Mythical Latin-American Kingdom Story*. Like him, Jiggs had deserted a wife and two children. His pilot was "not tall, with blue eyes in a square thin profoundly sober face." Roger Shumann flew as well if not as safely as Vernon Omlie. Unlike him, he lived a hand-to-mouth existence flying races in an obsolete airplane. Faulkner introduced Laverne Shumann, "looking almost like a man in the greasy coverall, with the pale strong rough ragged hair actually darker where it was sunburned, a tanned heavy-jawed face in which the eyes looked like pieces of china." Laverne Shumann obviously owed a good deal to Phoebe Fairgrave Omlie, but Faulkner elaborated something more: a *ménage à trois* completed by their parachute jumper, a man "with a bleak handsome face whose features were regular, brutally courageous" in spite of a narrow mustache above a delicate mouth, and eyes smudged with dissipation. Like Clem Sohn at the Shushan meet, he opened a flour sack during his jump to leave a white trail punctuated by his opening parachute. Faulkner added a touch of the grotesque with Laverne's taunting her six-year-old son, Jack, with his uncertain paternity. This would be a very different fictional view of aviation from that of, say, Sinclair Lewis, in a work such as *The Trail of the Hawk* (1915), in which a Midwestern youth would help reveal "the romance of the machine."

Throughout the novel Faulkner's concern with the abnormal would be reiterated, even though the courage of these vagabonds might be supranormal. The other principal character was a nameless reporter assigned to cover this air spectacle as Hermann Deutsch had been assigned to that in 1934. Unlike Deutsch, however, he was grotesquely thin. Faulkner insisted on his cadaverous, even skeletal appearance. Like the fliers, he was removed from the mass of mankind. As their lives were abnormal and divorced from humanity, so were the craft from which they made their living: "the trim vicious fragile aeroplanes and the pilots leaning upon them in gargantuan irrelation as if the aeroplanes were a species of esoteric and fatal animals not trained or tamed but just for the instant inert." (7) Their sound and the sound of the band were like that of the announcer, "as if the voice actually were that natural phenomenon against which all manmade sounds and noises blew and vanished like leaves." (26) Even the light illuminating the boots Jiggs wants to buy is unnatural: "an unearthly daycolored substance" (7), which also falls on "the pipes shaped like golfclubs and the drinking tools shaped like boots. . . ." (8)

Just as Faulkner rejected the stereotyped romantic view of the fliers, so he disdained the Mardi gras festivities. They are noisy and tawdry, dissolute and corrupt. Faulkner was using more consciously impressionistic description than in any novel since *Mosquitoes.* He had used compound words before, like Joyce, Dos Passos, and Wolfe, but here were far more than ever before, a dozen in the first three paragraphs alone: "lightpoised," "greasestained," and "Slantshimmered," he wrote. He was writing at top speed, but this would not limit his attempts at special effects. For some of these, he would return to one of his early literary masters. A newspaper account of the dedication declared that the airport had been "Raised up and Created out of the Waste Land" on the lake bottom. Six pages later in the novel, the reporter's appearance was described as that of something which had slipped from a cupboard and escaped in garments snatched from "an etherised patient." Having virtually paraphrased "The Love Song of J. Alfred Prufrock" in one of his early poems, Faulkner was now borrowing from it again as well as from "The Waste Land." He would clearly acknowledge his source in a number of ways in the course of the novel. It would be the kind of "creative borrowing" Eliot himself had employed to enrich the texture and heighten the allusiveness of his work. In one instance Faulkner would go to the same source for a borrowing Eliot had made: a gilded barge floating down the Nile.

By the end of the first chapter the reporter, fascinated by Laverne, had attached himself to the barnstormers. Still broke, still owing the generous madam who had let them sleep in one of her rooms when it was not being used for business, the barnstormers would spend the night with the reporter. The action was set for Chapter Two, "An Evening in New Valois."

If, before Faulkner continued, he had wanted to read a detailed account of how he became a writer, he needed only to turn to *The Oxford Magazine* for November 1. Phil Stone began with an anecdote of Dr. Will Murry followed by descriptions of Sallie Murry Falkner and the career of Murry Falkner. He sketched Oxford's Civil War past and its unique charm. Faulkner loved it, said Stone, and it was exactly the right place for him as artist and man. Though there had been only himself with whom Faulkner could discuss his aspirations, this was a good thing: "you may be sure I kept his feet upon the ground," Stone told all who would read. "Nay, I stood upon his feet to keep them on the ground. Day after day for years . . . he had drilled into him the obvious truths that the world owed no man anything. . . ." Stone's closing apostrophe to Oxford, briefly quoting *Sartoris*, was both well-written and deeply felt. For an installment in a projected series of at least six, the piece had a rather final ring to it, and it turned out to be the last segment. The conditions of the year 1934 were not congenial to a literary journal published in a rural county seat of north Mississippi. *The Oxford Magazine* had made its last appearance.

On November 23 Hal Smith received "An Evening in New Valois." Faulkner had opened the chapter with a paragraph leading to the headline proclaiming the death by fire of Lieut. Frank Burnham in his "Rocket Plane." He moved now from the world of aviation to the world of journalism as the reporter tried to explain people like the Shumanns to Will Hagood, his editor: "They aint human, you see. No ties; no place where you were born and have to go back to it now and then. . . ." (46) Having become obsessed with Laverne, he sketches in what he knows of her background: "Shumann and the airplane landing at Iowa or Indiana or wherever it is, and her coming out of the schoolhouse without even arranging to have her books took home, and they went off maybe with a canopener and a blanket to sleep on under the wing of the airplane when it rained hard. . . ." (46)

The extent of the Shumanns' indebtedness to the Omlies would now be clearer for anyone who, like Faulkner, inhabited the worlds of both literature and aviation.

As the reporter left the newspaper building, Faulkner incorporated two of the principal concerns of the novel into one economical image: a stack of late newspapers in the elevator weighted down by a dollar watch. Both the fliers and the journalists were concerned with time—winning times in races, the times of various editions, and the times of events—the rootless aviators seemingly cut off from any past and uncertain of any future, the journalists nominally concerned in their daily work with the relationship of past causes to present effects. The reporting of events suggested the other concern: the nature of truth, most problematical in the difference between the newspaper-propagated folklore of the air and the reality gradually perceived by the reporter in the lives of these people.

Moving into the street, he merged momentarily with the motion if not the life of New Valois, revealed, beneath the bogus display and vivacity of the Mardi gras, as a Dead City like that in "The Waste Land." Some of Faulkner's images suggested the sinister scenes and somber grotesques of Aubrey Beardsley: "grimacing and antic mimes dwarfed chalkwhite and forlorn" (53) without, and within, "the paperplumage, the parrotmask, a mixed party, whiskey-and-ginreeking. . . ." (59)

The reporter went along to the headquarters, the entrance under "a suave canopy with its lettered frieze: Hotel Terrebone." (58) (Faulkner's New Orleans favorite was the Hotel Monteleone.) Within the hotel were men who had risen in the world of aviation, who now wore "Madison Avenue jackets, who perhaps once held transport ratings . . . and perhaps have now only the modest Q.B. wings which clip to the odorous lapel the temperate silk ribbon stencilled Judge or Official. . . ." (61) But the expensive hotel still suggested the world of the traveling salesman and bought flesh—something like the implications of the Hotel Metropole in "The Waste Land." Faulkner was now using monosyllables as well as compound words, and occasionally they were the old four-letter monosyllables for bodily organs and actions.

In many passages the emotions of disgust and anger boiled up. Faulkner's antimodernist sentiments, so clear in his description of the airport and its inhuman noises, was now further generalized. As the reporter appealed to his editor for help for the fliers, this anger also invested Faulkner's description of an especial *bête noire*, the telephone: "The metal stalk sweatclutched, the guttapercha bloom cupping his breathing back at him. . . ." (65) Some of the anger, disgust, and unease that permeated these passages may have come from an unresolved ambivalence. His antimodernism was clear: electric lights were bloodless grapes, automobiles (though he had owned several) were popping stinking abominations, and airplanes were "trim vicious fragile" (7) machines, delicate, unnatural, and deadly. At the same time, however, he had been a hero-worshiper since childhood, when his imagination was stirred by the very names of airmen. In his development as an artist and thinker, he had tended to place a higher and higher valuation on the best of the past and harmony with organic nature. At the same time, on a different level, he still admired people like Wedell and Omlie; he wanted to be able to do the things they did. In some of his works he had used ambivalence and ambiguity profitably. Now it was unresolved, and it was probably making the work more difficult.

The reporter's foredoomed appeal ended with his being fired by Hagood (who in a general way resembled Roark Bradford). Near the end of the chapter, Faulkner reemphasized the motif introduced near its beginning by means of another set of newspaper headlines, "that crosssection out of timespace as though of a lightray caught by a speed lens for a second's fraction between infinity and furious and trivial dust. . . ." (75)

On November 25, two days after Hal Smith had received the second chapter in New York, Faulkner had completed his 112-page manuscript in Oxford. The manuscript showed how he had been working fast, revising partially on these pages and relying on the typing stage for numerous later revisions. Nearly every page revealed canceled lines or even paragraphs. Over half the pages had at least an additional line or two in the wide left-hand margin, and twenty-five pages bore paste-ons salvaged from rejected sheets. Now, with a complete, coherent manuscript to work from, he could concentrate all of his energies on the revision and typing.

On November 30 the third chapter arrived in New York, precisely seven days after the second chapter. Faulkner began "Night in the Vieux Carré" with a motif he was to employ as often as Joyce had used some of the motifs in *Ulysses.* Grandlieu Street bore evidence (as did Eliot's Thames) of the evening's sour pleasures: "a light curbchannelled spindrift of tortured and draggled serpentine and trodden confetti pending the dawn's whitewings—spent tinseldung of Momus' Nilebarge clatterfalque." (77) When the reporter stopped for absinthe, he bought it from a character who had already appeared in *Mosquitoes* and "Once Aboard the Lugger."

It was Pete (surnamed elsewhere Ginotta), in the same family restaurant-speakeasy in the Quarter where the same "decent withered old lady" (his mother) doctored the raw alcohol to suit the trade. (84)

Faulkner swiftly darkened his narrative. Halting the action momentarily, he interpolated a seven-page flashback. It described the reporter's oft-married mother and suggested that the reporter was just as deracinated as the fliers from the continuity and substance of the conventional family matrix. The reporter's consumption of the "absinthe" provided one of the most harrowing passages of drunkenness Faulkner would ever compose. Struck, kicked, and cursed by the jumper, the reporter was finally locked inadvertently outside his own tawdry apartment. Though the title "Night in the Vieux Carré" carried superficially the suggestion of sultry languor, perhaps of romance, it was in truth just as different from this sort of sugar-coating as the actual lives of the fliers were from any "romance of the machine" or "Conquest of the Air."

After an interval of five days, the fourth chapter, "Tomorrow," arrived in New York on December 5. The reporter's good intentions would now produce one disaster after another. His hospitality had started the alcoholic Jiggs on a drinking bout. Out of bitterly won knowledge, Faulkner described the moment of choice: "He could have heard sounds, even voices, from the alley beneath the window if he had been listening. But he was not. All he heard now was that thunderous silence and solitude in which man's spirit crosses the eternal repetitive rubicon of his vice in the instant after the terror and before the triumph becomes dismay—the moral and spiritual waif shrieking his feeble I-am-I into the desert of chance and disaster. He raised the jug. . . ." (118–119)

Faulkner first showed the fliers working in their element with speed and economy to repair the obsolete engine on which Shumann's life and their own next meals depended. But now the catastrophes capped disasters. Jiggs left the engine unrepaired to go for a drink. Shumann—like Harold Neuman at the dedication of Shushan Airport—was brought down by engine failure. When the plane came to rest on its back, the fliers were like a jockey, trainer, and owner with a dead race horse. As with Jack Monahan at Shushan, the jumper was injured when a gust of wind slammed him into an obstacle. Now Faulkner used counterpoint. In one of Laverne's rare speeches, she revealed just how far she was from the aviatrix of the popular imagination. She wanted not a Monocoupe like Phoebe Omlie's, not records like Jacqueline Cochran's, not acclaim like Amelia Earhart's: "all I want is just a house, a room; a cabin will do, a coalshed where I can know that next Monday and the Monday after that and the Monday after that. . . ." (165)

Six days later on December 12 Smith received the fifth chapter of *Pylon*, sixty-nine pages long, entitled "And Tomorrow." A hundred pages earlier the reporter had thought broodingly to himself "how he had not expected to see her again because tomorrow and tomorrow do not count because that will be at the field, with air and earth full of snarling and they not even alive out there because they are not human." (62) Faulkner had picked up this phrase and reused it for the titles of the fourth and fifth chapters. After borrowing chiefly from Eliot, he had gone once again to the passage from *Macbeth* which had given him *The Sound and the Fury*. Here, even more than in the earlier novel, "all our yesterdays have lighted fools/the way to dusty death."

When Faulkner opened this chapter he amplified the counterpoint of Laverne's thoughts. Matt Ord's home exemplified the kind of life toward which Laverne aspired, a scene almost as conventionally domestic as the distorted view of aviators that would appear in the same slick magazines: "they all stood now . . . in the livingroom of Ord's new neat little flowercluttered house. . . . they could hear a dinnertable being set, and a woman's voice singing obviously to a small child." (168) The Ords had what the Omlies could easily have afforded, what Dean and Louise Faulkner aspired to. Like Omlie, and perhaps like Wedell, Ord was not only a premier pilot and designer, he was a totally honest and just man, radiating the kind of integrity and simplicity that comes from most good men but which characterizes particularly a certain kind of engineer, scientist, or physician. Sympathetic, wanting to help, Ord would not accept the reporter's and Shumann's note for the dangerous plane they wanted to buy.

Faulkner's sympathies were so completely engaged by the fliers that when the reporter talked about their exploiters—Feinman and the others profiting from the airport and the meet—the prose again suggested Dos Passos: "Suppose instead of them up there on those damn hard chairs today it had been a gang of men hired to go down into a mine say, not to do anything special down there but just to see if the mine would cave in on top of them, and five minutes before they went down the bigbellied guys that own the mine would tell them that everybody's pay had been cut two and a half percent. . . ." (169) Later, however, Feinman's anti-NRA utterances were close to Faulkner's own views: "We have had our crops regimented and our fisheries regimented and even our money in the bank regimented. . . . But do you mean to tell me that Washington can come in and regiment a man that's trying to make his living out of the air? Is there a crop reduction in the air too?" (223–224) Feinman's self-interest and sophistry were blatant, but Faulkner was here drawing upon antigovernment feelings just as strong as his antimodernism.

As he had earlier interpolated a flashback to sketch part of the reporter's background, now he used one almost exactly as long to describe Laverne's first parachute jump. It contained an element of the sensationalism of *Sanctuary.* In something like a farewell gesture, Laverne had climbed back into the cockpit and made love to Shumann as he flew the plane. Moments later, her blown skirts revealing her nakedness, she became a mythic image of desire—a Venus descending from the clouds—to the gaping crowd and the sadistic police officer waiting below. The reporter could still think of the aviators, "they aint human" (231), but with each incident Faulkner showed Laverne not only human but more the victim, and Shumann not only an aeronautical expert, but capable of self-sacrifice and a kind of nobility. At the end of the chapter his plane began to disintegrate in midair: "They said later about the apron that he used the last of his control before the fuselage broke to zoom out of the path of the two aeroplanes behind. . . ." (234) An instant later, Shumann met his death by water.

Within four days Faulkner was able to mail the last two chapters, and they reached New York on December 15. The title of the sixth chapter, "Lovesong of J. A. Prufrock," pointed to the reporter just as other Eliot images had done with Mr. Talliaferro in *Mosquitoes* eight years before. As Lent began and the Mardi gras refuse was removed from the city, a crew dredged for the body of Shumann. Like Charles Kenily's body, it would not be recovered. Faulkner showed the continuing, agonizing education of the reporter (called, among other names, "Lazarus") as he sat with other newspapermen, one of whom expressed his revulsion at the death and then said, "But what the hell? He aint our brother." (238)

As he moved toward the end of the chapter, Faulkner interpolated two more shorter flashbacks. One two-page segment that described Dr. Shumann as treating "mostly Swede farmers" (274) may have reminded some readers of Sinclair Lewis' Dr. Will Kennicott in *Main Street.* If the young Roger Shumann resembled Lewis' Carl Ericson in *The Trail of the Hawk*, here his precocity suggested Jimmy Wedell. Another two-page flashback reaffirmed Laverne's role as victim and linked her with Lena Grove. Raised by an older sister, she too had begun to slip out a back window at night, introduced to illicit love by the brother-in-law who would shortly betray her.

Faulkner ended the chapter with a passage envisioning the reporter's lonely future—the note on which Eliot had ended "The Love Song of J. Alfred Prufrock." Then in an extended passage he evoked the sense of "Preludes" and "The Waste Land" as well: "It would be there—the eternal smell of the coffee the sugar the hemp sweating slow iron plates above the forked deliberate brown water and lost lost lost all ultimate blue of latitude and horizon; the hot rain gutterfull plaiting the eaten heads of shrimp; the ten thousand inescapable mornings wherein ten thousand swinging air-plants stippleprop the soft scrofulous soaring of sweating brick and ten thousand pairs of splayed brown hired Leonorafeet tigerbarred by jaloused armistice with the invincible sun: the thin black coffee, the myriad fish stewed in a myriad oil—tomorrow and tomorrow and tomorrow; not only to hope, not even to wait: just to endure." (284)

Early in "The Scavengers," the last chapter, came a passage of dialogue which sounded as though it might have derived from "This Kind of Courage." After the fruitless wait for the recovery of Shumann's body, one of the reporters turned on his callous and cynical colleagues: "You dirty-mouthed bastards. Why dont you let the guy rest? Let them all rest. They were trying to do what they had to do, with what they had to do it with, the same as all of us only maybe a little better than us. At least without squealing and bellyaching." (290) Articulating what the reporter had learned, he had formulated the novel's final judgment. The fliers were not inhuman; they were, in fact, more truly human than those who scorned them.

As he brought the novel rapidly to a close, Faulkner continued to draw from both earlier work and the immediate past. As Merle Nelson's ashes were scattered over Lake Pontchartrain, so a memorial wreath for Roger Shumann was dropped above Lake Rambaud. The reporter, feeling signals of imminent collapse, spoke a line previously given to Temple Drake and Joe Christmas: "Something is going to happen to me." (300) Then, as Laverne and the jumper brought the child to his grandfather in Ohio, Faulkner described the old man's home: "a bungalow, a tight flimsy mass of stoops and porte-cochères and flat gables and bays not five years old and built in that colored mud-and-chickenwire tradition which California moving picture films have scattered across North America as if the celluloid carried germs." (304) As Laverne's early life had suggested Lena Grove's, so her son's childhood prospects recalled those of Joe Christmas and Caddy Compson's daughter, Quentin.

At the novel's end some of the ambiguity was still unresolved. Faulkner despised not only the brummagem show of the Mardi gras and the corruption of the city (Feinman was more subtle but no less immoral than Huey P. Long and Theodore G. Bilbo), but the kind of modernism represented by automobiles, telephones, motion pictures, and the whining, roaring airplanes. He was aghast at some of the people who lived by flying and by the bizarre, tragic shapes of their lives. At the same time, he had owned a plane himself, he still flew frequently, and his brother made his living from the air. If he had known tramp pilots and jumpers, he also knew sturdy men like Vernon Omlie. And he could not help being touched by the death of Jimmy Wedell. Though images and sentiments in the novel might pull in opposite directions, there was finally no doubt of his feeling—his admiration, sympathy, and compassion—for these people, who were "outside the range of God, not only of respectability, of love, but of God too . . . . as ephemeral as the butterfly. . . ."

Faulkner had to postpone the luxury of relaxation after writing. In an undated letter, he apologized to Morty Goldman for his silence. "I have worked forced draft on the novel and finished it yesterday," he wrote. "I will try to get around to rewriting DRUSILLA as soon as I finish typing." When that was done, he sent the revised story to Goldman. In the undated covering letter he wrote that the manuscript of *Pylon* was now in Smith's hands. "I think I will send a copy of it to Howard Hawks, in California. I have not done it yet, though I am writing him today. I will let you know what he says about it." Now he could rest for a bit. "I shall take a holiday until after Jan. 1, then I will be sending you some more stuff."

He was still thinking about *Pylon.* One aspect of the novel worried him. When he wrote Smith to be sure of its safe arrival, he raised the question: " 'New Valois' is a thinly disguised (that is, someone will read the story and believe it to be) New Orleans. The 'Feinman Airport' is the Shushan Airport of that place, named for a polititian [*sic*]. But there all actual resemblance stops. Shushan Airport has a lot of capital S's about it, and an air meet was held there. But the incidents in Pylon are all fiction and Feinman is fiction so far as I know; the only more or less deliberate copying of fact, or the nearest to it, is the character 'Matt Ord', who is Jimmy Weddell [*sic*]. That is, Jimmy Weddell held the land plane speed record at one time in a ship built by himself, Weddell-Williams Co [*sic*], near New Orleans." In spite of all this, Faulkner insisted on the originality of the work: "But as I said, the story and incidents and the characters as they perform in the story are all fictional. But someone may read it and see into it what I didn't. Someone may or may not see a chance for a suit. You might decide whether there would be grounds for a suit, whether a suit would help sell the book, or whether to alter the location, etc., so there would be no grounds."

On December 28 Smith reassured him. "Offhand I don't believe that you need be concerned," he wrote. He liked the novel. He thought it was "a book that will jolt some of the literary tumblebugs and crickets off their perches. I expect some folk won't like it, but that needn't worry you. There are things in it that need to be changed, but only here and there." He would come down to visit them about January 15 for a few days if that was all right. He would bring the manuscript and his suggestions with him.

Some literary specialists, as opposed to the tumblebugs Smith had in mind, would eagerly await the new novel. Faulkner's whole body of work was being scanned by enthusiasts. In the December issue of *The Colophon* Aubrey Starke published an article entitled "An American Comedy: An Introduction to a Bibliography of William Faulkner." As early as Faulkner's Boni & Liveright days one member of the firm, Ken Godfrey, had begun a bibliography and collected many items, but this was the first substantial published work of the kind. For Oxonians who would not see *The Colophon*, there was another index of their fellow townsman's growing prominence. A faculty committee selected the ten most outstanding alumni and faculty members in the school's history, listing Alfred Hume first and Stark Young second. When they decided upon a second series, William Faulkner was thirteenth in the new listing.

He had not logged any flying time since November 25, when he was working under forced draft to finish *Pylon* and get it to Smith before the end of the year. Now he could fly again. On the day after Christmas he was in Columbus, and before he cut the switches of the cabin Waco on his return to Oxford, he had gotten in fifty minutes of flying time. It is possible that he spent part of that day at nearby West Point with Champ. "We were hauling passengers out of a cow pasture," Champ remembered, "and the engine kept quitting." When they found they could not remedy the difficulty there, they decided to get the plane back to Oxford for repairs if they could. After three forced landings they finally made it back.

"All this goes with it if you want to fly," Faulkner told his friend, perhaps feeling some kinship with people like Roger Shumann. As for the time spent on repairs, "You work ten hours on the ground for every hour in the air."

After all the intensive work behind him, there was more ahead. He would not log any more flying time for four solid months. On January 9, 1935, the eighty-four galleys of *Pylon* were ready, and Smith lost no time in making the trip he had planned. It was not, however, as easy as he might have expected, for it coincided with unseasonable mid-January floods. "Mr. Faulkner met Mr. Smith in Memphis and found driving back to Oxford via Holly Springs no easy matter," ran one account. "The fourth road they tried was passable by motor and not merely navigable." Safely home, Faulkner began to read the galleys.

He had accepted minor syntactical changes and even some deletions on the typescript setting copy, but he had not responded to comments by Hal Smith such as "This sentence is cockeyed" and "Incomprehensible to me," or questions like "Can't we have a paragraph in the next four pages?". He revoked some changes made apparently without his consent. The reporter's vision of hotel rooms used by prostitutes had been changed to "one thousand rented sleepings." (58) Smith apparently convinced Faulkner that they could not print the word he had used for the genitals, but often instead of "sleepings" Faulkner substituted five dots for the deleted letters. Elsewhere he substituted dashes for three-dot ellipses. He cut modifying phrases and clauses and added material only when it clarified sequence or motive. He cut a passage which suggested the Percy Grimm section of *Light in August*, when the movements of pursuer and pursued seemed dictated by "the Player." The reporter had turned into a street "as though the grim Spectator himself had so ordained and arranged. . . ."

After they had finished with the galleys, Smith stayed on for a while at Rowan Oak where they had more time to talk than they did during Faulkner's hectic visits to New York. Among the presents Smith had brought was one of the firm's new books, a novel of aerial combat by RFC ace Victor Yeates. Faulkner would later tell a friend *Winged Victory* was "the best of the war books." They talked about the Hollywood story Faulkner had mentioned in one of his letters to Goldman. He had written it as soon as he had finished *Pylon*, apparently, and it was now in Goldman's hands. Called "Golden Land," and set in Beverly Hills, it was impregnated with distaste and revulsion. Almost every paragraph seemed imbued with the unhappiness he had felt while he was in California. The terrain, the climate, the architecture, the people, their behavior, and their dress—all displeased him. If Popeye and Percy Grimm were monsters, so were real-estate man Ira Ewing, his wife, and children. He has long ago brought his widowed mother from Nebraska. She dislikes California and longs to leave as much as Maud Falkner had on her brief trip to Hollywood in 1932. Her son will allow her anything she wants but the money to return to her Nebraska home. (Like Faulkner, Ewing briefly visits his mother each morning.) His wife is a spiteful virago, his son a feline homosexual. His daughter is a Hollywood extra on trial for a sex orgy. Both have been corrupted in childhood by too much money. The greatest corruption, however, is Ewing's own. On his orders an assistant has given the story of the scandal to a daily newspaper. In return, the story will get thirty percent of the front page, which will also carry Ewing's photograph in the courthouse. The newspaper will print a thousand extra copies and distribute them from an advertising mailing list provided by Ewing. Beside him, Miss Reba was a paragon of virtue.

In late December or early January, Faulkner wrote Morty Goldman to ask, "Have you sold the Drusilla story yet? I can use money right now to beat hell." Goldman was able to tell him shortly that he had. Renamed "Skirmish at Sartoris," it would appear in the April issue of *Scribner's* rather than in the *Post.* "I am glad the story sold somewhere," Faulkner wrote in reply on January 23. "Here is a suggestion I want to make in regard to GOLDEN LAND. Hal Smith has been down here with me for a week; he thinks, and I agree with him, that I should have some other outlet for stories with the goodpaying magazines besides the Post. As it is, I sell either to Scribners and Harpers for pittances, or to the Post." Smith had a connection at *Cosmopolitan*, and if Goldman would send him the story he would try it. "As you say, with its flavor of perversion, possibly the only magazine which will consider it and which will or can pay well, will be Cosmopolitan." Goldman would still receive his commission, but "I want to see if I can establish a wellpaying alternative to the Post. Possibly it will help me get a better price from them." This had a very practical bearing in the immediate future. "I am going to dope out another series for the Post and work on it right away."

Faulkner felt himself chronically in need of money, but now more than ever, it seemed. The planned special edition of *The Sound and the Fury* had fallen through, and he would not receive the extra $250 for signing the sheets. For one thing, it was almost tax time. For another, W. C. Bryant had received inquiries about Bailey's Woods and now told Faulkner that he had to know his intentions. "Think on it and act: will arrange payments that will be easy & a low rate of interest on them," the old man wrote. He had in mind $500 in cash and ten $100 notes payable annually at five percent interest. There was no question in Faulkner's mind. He wanted these woods where they had played as children. They would further protect Rowan Oak and his privacy. Then he and the boys could hunt squirrels with less risk of drawing fire from other hunters.

Hunting was much in his mind now in another connection, which would also cost money—not as much, but any bill was unwelcome, even when it represented a bargain. On January 30, 1935, the Secretary of State of the State of Mississippi had issued the Charter of Incorporation of the Okatoba Hunting and Fishing Club. Its three incorporators were William Faulkner, R. L. Sullivan, and Whitson Cook. Faulkner had typed up the articles of the charter, which included the information that the authorized capital stock would be $100. General Stone transferred to the club all hunting and fishing rights on his lands, several thousand acres in the heart of the deer country near Batesville at the eastern edge of the Delta. They meant to keep a man there the year round and provide him with a cabin, land, and a modest salary. Faulkner wrote a friend in the state game commission asking that the man be made a deputy game warden. "It is our intention to protect the game which is fast being exterminated in that section," he wrote, "and we want the help of your department to help us accomplish this aim." Faulkner would make several trips to Batesville on this business and in early spring he would compose a substantial set of bylaws for the other members' approval. If more time than money was involved in this activity, it was by far the more plentiful of the two commodities in the late winter and early spring of the year 1935.

On Smith's return to New York he had written his thank-you note and promised Faulkner a pipe he had asked for and a check. Faulkner wrote back to thank him, adding, "for at least twenty minutes after it comes I should be solvent." Goldman would send "Golden Land" to Smith as soon as he could get hold of it. As for the possible sales of *Pylon* to the movies, Faulkner would tell Goldman that Smith was to handle that. He planned to get in some more quail-shooting before the season ended on February 20, "then I will settle down to work proper. I hope to hell you can gouge somebody for a thousand for GOLDEN LAND. That will give me two months to work at the novel before I have to boil the pot again." Faulkner took note of Smith's thanks. "We are all well. All the ladies express bright pleasure and appreciation of the suave metropolitan breath which you brought into our snowbound and bucolic midst." Taking Smith up on an offer he had made, Faulkner concluded the undated letter with practical instructions: "When and if the notion occurs to you to try to send some liquor, send me a bottle of good brandy. Pack it in excelsior and put a fictitious return address on it and send it by express."

Pressed as he was, there were some sales he would not make. In a letter to Goldman on February 18 he turned down three. He enclosed a letter he had received from the Centaur Press. They had gotten hold of a copy of *Marionettes* and proposed a facsimile edition, hoping, apparently, for a preface from him. "NO. Absolutely NOT," he wrote Goldman. "There is no copywright [*sic*]; I made about six of the books by hand. I dont know if they can be stopped or not, but stop them if you can. Get Smith to help you if necessary. Let me hear." He had been willing to publish early poems in *A Green Bough*, but *Marionettes* was either too personal or too immature to appear now that he had his place in "the establishment of literature," as he would much later call it. A suggested book on the Mississippi River posed a different problem. "I dont believe I can do it. I am a novelist, you see: people first, where second. To do a book like that would mean a sort of holiday, extra curricular work, you might say. And when I take a holiday, I damned sure wont spend it writing." There had been still another request. "Vanity Fair I think it was wrote me for a lynching article. Tell them I never saw a lynching and so couldn't describe one." His regular customers were still interested in new work from him. "I have nothing in mind at present for Mercury," he had to tell Goldman, however. "I am trying to bugger up an air story for Cosmopolitan. You might tell them I will try to get something soon. I must either hang something on them or on the Post; it all depends on which one I can invent first." In this same letter he told Goldman about another writer's work. Johncy had taken up literature.

Against his will, Faulkner was drawn into this new career. Johncy had begun making up stories to tell his seven-year-old son Chooky. Later he tried them on magazines. "I was still writing these short stories and having no luck with them, so one day Mother pinned Bill down and made him promise to help me." Johncy found his brother sitting in his yard reading when he arrived with what he thought his two best stories. "I could tell as soon as I saw him that he had got into something he wished he hadn't, and wouldn't have for anyone else but Mother. He told me to leave the stories and then sat there looking straight ahead." When Miss Maud told Johncy to return, he found his brother as before. Bill told him that the *Post* would buy the stories. John began to talk excitedly.

"Be quiet now and let me talk," Bill said. "That's what you came down here for, ain't it?" When Johncy subsided Bill told him that he could sign his name to the stories, too, to ensure their publication, but that would do John's career no good. He should send them in as they were. "He stopped talking and sat there looking straight ahead again. I knew he was through and it was time for me to leave. I left."

When the *Post* refused the stories Faulkner was irate, Johncy remembered. He had considered himself an expert judge of the kind of thing the magazine would buy. He put Johncy in touch with Goldman. "He is working on another story," Faulkner wrote his agent. "He will follow your advice in regard to present one."

By late February or early March "Golden Land" had been sold to *The American Mercury*, where Laurence Stallings ran the new books department. Either Goldman had not been able to retrieve it for submission to *Cosmopolitan* or Smith's contact there had been ineffectual. But Faulkner told Goldman that Smith would have the sale of *Pylon* to the movies, and the two men had a very unsatisfactory conversation about their respective areas. Faulkner tried to explain the situation to Goldman: "Under my contracts with Smith, he had the handling of the novels with regard to the movies and the stage. I hope you will forgive me for not straightening this out with you before, and hence confusing or embarassing [*sic*] you." This was not the first time or the last that Faulkner's verbal agreements would cause difficulty. "The only understanding that Ben and I ever had," he went on, "was the verbal one that the American play [*sic*] would handle short stories and magazine stuff, and that all novels etc. would be handled by myself. I was going along under that same idea, though you and I never discussed it. But as I submitted COURAGE to you as a short story, you may have, under the rules governing author and agent, an equity in it. You will have to let me know about that." He wrote another paragraph of apology for his "negligence" before he turned to current marketing problems. "I will try to get the story for Cosmopolitan soon. I am at work on another novel now, but as soon as I can cook up a yarn I will put the novel aside and write it." A proud man who avoided direct apologies, Faulkner preferred a clear gesture to explicit words. The last line showed how upset he was: "I am sorry about the other business."

Now, with income tax payments staring him in the face in March, he turned to other short stories. One of them was probably a story he would finally call "That Will Be Fine." In several ways it resembled the stories of the Compson children. It was full of comic effects until the last few pages, when domestic farce became domestic tragedy—unbeknownst, however, to the narrator, a seven-year-old boy named Georgie. Come from Jefferson to spend Christmas with his grandparents in Mottstown, potentially a youthful extortioner like Virgil Beard in *Sartoris*, he serves his uncle Rodney as a lookout and message-bearer. Forger, thief, and lothario, Uncle Rodney fares better for a time than did Uncle Maury Bascomb in *The Sound and the Fury*. But his luck does not hold. Whereas Uncle Maury is beaten by Mr. Patterson, Uncle Rodney is shot by Mr. Pruitt.

The old-fashioned celebration of Christmas, with families traveling to neighboring towns, with gift-giving and fireworks, owed something to Christmases spent with the Colonel and Sallie Murry Falkner at The Big Place, and perhaps to holiday visits to Grandpa and Grandma Murry in Ripley as well. And there was clearly one particular model ready to hand—another lively scoundrel and disgrace to a respectable family: Henry Falkner, dead like Rodney (supposedly) at the hand of an irate husband. Faulkner obtained a number of effects from the young narrator. His deadpan not-quite-knowing account of the men's anger and women's tears at Rodney's escapades was amusing. There was a comic dramatic irony in the quarrels and whispered asides which Georgie missed and the reader grasped. There was another kind of irony at the end when Georgie assumed that the "side of beef" carried into the house on a shutter was "a Christmas present for Grandpa."

It must have been during this same March that Faulkner wrote another story which drew directly upon Oxford lore. In early September of 1934 Uncle Bob Chilton had been killed in an automobile accident. Ever since the death of his brother, Uncle Top—who had lived on South Street not far from the Falkners—had run their drugstore with the aid of old Ad Bush, whose ice cream was as celebrated as his hunting-camp cookery. Oxford children continued to patronize the store. When Uncle Bob had entered his sixties, keepers of Oxford's conscience had begun to notice a change. They said he had begun to drink and associate with some of the livelier young women of Oxford. Before long they noticed that he was making regular trips to Memphis with his Negro chauffeur. Soon, as one observer put it, "He really was a good time papa to the pretty gold-diggers up in Memphis . . . . Because he had traded his life and youth for money, perhaps he changed to hate money, realized his mistake, and crowded all the living and fun he could into the short time he had to live." He managed a good deal before the automobile accident ended it.

"Uncle Willy" was narrated by a nameless fourteen-year-old boy. A Jefferson native like Georgie, he displayed only sympathy, loyalty, and love for the older man with whom he was juxtaposed. To him, Uncle Willy was "the finest man I ever knew," and not just because of his ice cream and baseball prizes. In spite of "the good women in Jefferson," Uncle Willy "wound up his life getting fun out of being alive and he died doing the thing that was the most fun of all. . . ." For him the most fun was taking dope. An addict for forty years, he loses his needle to Reverend Schultz and Mrs. Merridew. Taken into informal protective custody as Darl was taken off to the asylum at Jackson "one day last summer," he returns from Memphis with the liquor habit, a Negro chauffeur, and a fat blatant Memphis whore as his bride. When she leaves him a bankrupt, he is forced to undergo the Keeley Cure.

At this point, Faulkner drew upon personal experience for a new turn in his story line. Selling his last resources, Uncle Willy buys another car, a tent, and an airplane. His chauffeur will fly the airplane and old Job (his former ice-cream maker) will do the chores. Uncle Willy reveals the plan to the narrator: "We would head west. When we ran out of the house money we would stop at a town and take up passengers and make enough to buy gasoline and food to get to the next town. . . ." When Job betrays the plan, Uncle Willy takes the plane up and crashes it; death on his own terms is preferable to life on others'.

As in "That Will Be Fine," Faulkner had again yoked comedy and violent death. There was also smugness, religiosity, and meddling, which he condemned as he had other vices in such stories as "Dry September." This was not the last time he would use a group of runaways fleeing the law to seek adventure in the big world beyond north Mississippi.

Not only was he writing new stories, he was digging into his files and revising old material. In a new version of "The Brooch" he kept Howard much the same, but now his domineering mother looked like Mrs. Compson, "with a face the color of tallow and dark eyes both pupil-less and iris-less beneath perfect white hair." Her daughter-in-law was still a victim, "a vivid daring girl whose later reputation was due more to folly and the caste handicap of the little Southern town than to badness. . . ." So was Howard, his tragedy set in motion years before he finally placed the pistol in his mouth. Faulkner added a passage unusual for him: he spent 200 words discussing the effect of a novel on one of his characters and interpreting the symbolism of the response. The book was W. H. Hudson's romantic *Green Mansions.* The character had read it in the same edition Faulkner owned and inscribed "Rowan Oak 1931."

For another story which probably dates from this time, Faulkner turned to one of his favorite characters: Suratt, the itinerant sewing-machine salesman. The nameless first-person narrator told the story as he heard Suratt tell it. Present besides the narrator were three others: his grandfather, Doc Peabody, and Roskus, who operated a fan and served the drinks in the disused law office during the long hot summer afternoon. Suratt told how his father (a tenant of old man Anselm Holland of "Smoke") tried to best the horse trader, Pat Stamper, and lost. Elements of "Fool About a Horse" suggested the Southwestern tall tale, as Lum Suratt encountered not only a fabulous trader but a Negro horse handler who was a "magician." If Faulkner had read treatises such as Dr. A. S. Alexander's *Horse Secrets*, they must have come in handy now. But Suratt was not content with anything so simple as the "bishoping" Dr. Alexander described. To make the animal lively he employed saltpeter, tar, and a number ten fishhook. Later, stung by Stamper with a pair of sickly mules, he is forced to trade them for a fat horse which, washed free of black dye by rain, proves to be the horse Suratt had traded to Stamper, the fishhook still embedded where it was, the animal considerably fattened through the use of a hand-pump valve inserted in its leg. The ten manuscript pages ended with Vynie Suratt—reminiscent of Mrs. Armstid and Addie Bundren—forced to retrieve her cream separator in yet another costly transaction with Stamper. The tale was narrated retrospectively for comedy by Suratt, who had been twelve at the time the events had occurred. Faulkner typed the story and sent if off to Morty Goldman with instructions that it should go to the *Post.*

Roskus had worked for the Compson family, and it seemed that "Grandfather" was probably Jason Lycurgus Compson, Jr. (who lived until 1900), and the retrospective narrator, his grandson, Quentin MacLachan Compson, III, born in 1890. This use of Quentin Compson may have reflected the fact that though short stories kept Faulkner from *Absalom,*

Absalom! he was still considering technical problems in this novel in which Quentin would also narrate. Quentin performed the same function in another story which appears to date from this time, a story with the same setting he had used for "A Bear Hunt." He was clearly hoping again for the big money from the *Post.*

For "Lion," Faulkner drew again upon General Stone's camp and the tales of men like Ike Roberts and Bob Harkins who had gone on the hunt for nearly forty years. The events Quentin had experienced at sixteen were not related for comedy, as in "A Bear Hunt." They depended not so much upon Major de Spain, Old Ad, and Ike McCaslin (the son of Uncle Buck's old age) as upon Boon Hogganbeck and two animals. These animals were almost mythic: Lion, a hunting dog "like the chiefs of Aztec and Polynesian tribes who were looked upon as being not men but both more and less than men"; and Old Ben, "an extra bear, the head bear, Uncle Ike McCaslin called him. . . ." Old Reel Foot—a bear maimed in one paw like Old Ben—had been hunted by General Stone, Ike Roberts, and Bob Harkins. Other hunters such as John Cullen remembered him as they did the great dog who stood thirty inches tall and had an enormous chest, and who hunted Old Reel Foot. Faulkner would later recall this model for Lion: "He was a tremendous big brute . . . must have weighed seventy-five or eighty pounds."

Although the narrative began with comic notes—Boon and Old Ad vying to entice Lion to sleep on their pallets—the story soon resolved itself into a concern with the hunt and its investiture with meanings beyond the deaths of Lion and Old Ben. With their deaths, Major de Spain ceased to hunt. And in the last scene Boon Hogganbeck hammered furiously at his jammed gun, his quarry not a huge bear but scampering squirrels. When Faulkner drew up the bylaws of the Okatoba Hunting and Fishing Club, he had written three paragraphs under "Privileges and Restrictions." A member might offer guest privileges, "but with the understanding that it is done with discretion and due regard to the amount and condition of the game available and to the other Members' equity in the Club." On February 2 he had written Hunter Kimball, of the State Game and Fish Commission, "It is our intention to protect the game which is fast being exterminated," and now this same concern had gotten into his fiction. But he knew that no matter what the efforts of the Commission in Jackson, of well-meaning sportsmen such as the club members, the forest and the game he had known in boyhood were swiftly vanishing. The hatred of modernization so clear in *Pylon* was less overt here, but these events were part of the same historical process which saw asphalt roads and runways spread over the land as forest and wildlife diminished.

By the time Faulkner was ready to send "Lion" to Goldman, his financial situation had worsened. "Here is another one," he wrote in an undated latter. "I dont know who to suggest to try it on, since I made such a bust about the Post with FOOL ABOUT A HORSE, and Cosmo with THE BROOCH. The post might take it, since they took one last year about the same hunting camp." Whereas he had earlier asked Goldman, in effect, to defer to Smith, his thoughts were now running in the opposite direction. Goldman had never felt that Faulkner's arrangements with Smith were equitable, and Faulkner had about come to the same conclusion. "I contracted with Smith and took an advance on the novel I am now working on," he explained. "However, I do believe I can make more money through someone else. That is, I am not exactly satisfied. This in absolute confidence, of course. I am coming East in the fall and get myself straightened out. So in the meantime, just let the matter ride as it is until you hear from me. You might listen to what you hear, but dont let any suggestion come from us. I would rather come up there, tell Smith what I intend to do, try to get an offer from someone else and then see if Smith wants to come up to it or not. But I cannot and will not go on like this. I believe I have got enough fair literature in me yet to deserve reasonable freedom from bourgeois material petty impediments and compulsion, without having to quit writing and go to the moving pictures every two years. The trouble about the movies is not so much the time I waste there but the time it takes me to recover and settle down again; I am 37 now and of course not as supple and impervious as I once was."

Goldman continued to try for magazine sales, and occasionally there was a reprint fee. *The Golden Book* had promised Faulkner $25 for reprinting "Smoke" in the April issue but he had not received the check and asked Goldman to look into it. In the same letter he thanked Goldman for a $250 offer for "That Will Be Fine" from *The American Mercury.* "But that wont help me enough," he told him. "I need a thousand. I will just have to knock out something for the Post. I wish to hell I could find some man who would gamble on my future on a note, no contract. Damn these fool laws about usury anyhow." Although he had mentioned a thousand dollars, what he really needed, he said, was ten thousand. "With that I could pay my debts and insurance for two years and really write. I mean, write. The man who said that the pinch of necessity, butchers and grocers bills and insurance hanging over his head, is good for an artist is a damned fool."

In his distracted state of mind he had neglected to tell Goldman what to do about the offer from *The American Mercury.* By the time he repaired this omission, things were even worse: "Good God yes, let them have the story and do anything they want with it, just so I get the money as soon as possible. I couldn't wire you because I have no money to pay telegram with. Haven't had one cent since last story sold, wherever that was, and now I have to get a blasted check like this that the bank here wont or cant cash." The check was for a reprint of "That Evening Sun." He still had not received the *Golden Book* check. "I am writing two stories a week now. I dont know how long I can keep it up. This makes six or seven. Did you receive one named MOONLIGHT?" It was good he could not know he would never sell "Moonlight," not even in this revised version. Soon, however, there would be sales, though none for thousand-dollar fees. The *Mercury* took "That Will Be Fine" for July and "Uncle Willy" for October. *Harper's* bought "Lion" for December publication. It is doubtful if the three sales totaled a thousand dollars.

On top of the problems of tradesmen's bills and insurance premiums, there were taxes due. He hoped for some kind of deferred payment, but the Bureau of Internal Revenue pressed him. He had tried to earn the money by writing short stories but he had not earned enough. He did not want to take out second mortgages, and if he went to Hollywood it would mean putting off *Absalom, Absalom!* yet another time. There was only one strategy of evasion open to him. He began drinking. Miss Maud reacted with more than her usual concern—he had been so good for so long. Her method of pouring the whiskey down the sink worked no better than it had before. She finally called Champ and asked him to come and see if he could do anything.

Champ sat down at his bedside. "You know, Bill," he said, "you can't drink if you want to fly."

Faulkner looked up at him, his face drawn and his eyes deeply circled. "If you say quit, I'll quit," he said.

He began to taper off, and the bout was aborted. Before long, he would be flying with Champion again, displaying the qualities the younger man admired: intense powers of concentration and quiet courage.

His recovery coincided with one event and made possible another: the appearance of the initial reviews of *Pylon* and the beginning of the final manuscript of *Absalom, Absalom!*.

42

March-November, 1935

"So maybe you will enter the literary profession as so many Southern gentlemen and gentlewomen too are doing now and maybe some day you will remember this and write about it. You will be married then I expect and perhaps your wife will want a new gown or a new chair for the house and you can write this and submit it to the magazines."

—*Absalom, Absalom!* (9–10)

On March 25, 1935, the publication day of *Pylon*, Hal Smith wrote Faulkner that the reviews had started coming in and that they were satisfactory. They tended to praise Faulkner's power but deplore his assault on the reader's sensibilities. The reviews in April would grow more critical. Writing in *The New Republic*, Malcolm Cowley called the book a legend of contemporary life but noted a "lack of proportion between stimulus and response, [an] air of unnecessary horror and violence." For Sean O'Faolain, in *The Spectator*, *Pylon* was Dantesque, "with all the compulsion and terror of a great talent driven to frenzy." Though Faulkner was one of the finest of contemporary American writers, he might never learn "that brutality is not strength, nor facetiousness wit, and that, if America holds nothing sacred, art still does."

The Oxford *Eagle* announced that copies of *Pylon* received at the Oxford lending library were "being eagerly sought." (The same issue reported that Dean Faulkner and Vernon Omlie had put on an air show at West Memphis on Sunday, March 24.) Moon Mullen declared, "I don't know what to write, only that it's Faulkner and that the book adds not an iota to his literary stature. . . . His descriptive passages are as long and as unintelligible as ever to me . . . yet as paragraph after paragraph is read, the reader begins to fall in step with the characters and rushes on to some illogical and inconceivable climax." Other Southern reviews were strongly critical. The novel seemed so undisciplined to John Crowe Ransom of the Nashville *Banner* that he concluded, "William Faulkner is spent."

Reviews were still coming in during May. In *Current History*, John Chamberlain remarked what seemed to him "deliberate obfuscations" and wondered if Faulkner knew anything about the people he was writing about. But in the June issue of *Esquire*, Ernest Hemingway wrote, "your correspondent has been reading and admiring *Pylon* by Mr. William Faulkner." It was just as well, however, that Faulkner did not generally read comments on his work. And anyway, he was—as he would say in explanation—"already busy with the next one by that time." He inscribed a copy of the novel to Myrtle Demarest on March 26 and a page of the manuscript to Miss Elma Meek on April 18, but he was through with the book now and looking ahead.

On March 30 he had taken a sheet of paper with printed margins and written at the top, in blue ink, the title "Absalom, Absalom!." He underlined it twice and dated the sheet in the upper left-hand corner. He had a stack of manuscript material to use as he began this new version, and he would cut up a number of these pages to provide paste-ons for the new manuscript—a familiar process for him. The pages testified to the varying strategies he had employed. Two false starts, for instance, were set in Cambridge, Massachusetts, as Shreve handed Quentin a letter from his father describing the last days of Miss Rosa Coldfield. This approach would at the outset have made the story doubly retrospective, looking back half a year to events in Jefferson that started Quentin on his probing of events fifty years earlier. Faulkner abandoned it. He had done little or nothing with the novel since he had put it down to write *Pylon* and turn out the series of short stories. Then, he later recalled, "when I took it up again I almost rewrote the whole thing. I think that what I put down were inchoate fragments that wouldn't coalesce and then when I took it up again, as I remember, I rewrote it."

He had his principal characters well in mind: Sutpen and Wash Jones, as well as Quentin Compson at this phase of his life. There were elements of local history and lore for him to draw on if he chose. As Sutpen was the county's largest landowner, master of one hundred square miles of virgin bottom land lying twelve miles from Jefferson, so—according to Johncy Falkner—had been Colonel Barr, who "owned nearly all the land from here to Burgess, about twelve miles to the west." The father of the Potts twins,

Amodeus and Theophilus, had owned ten miles up and down the Tallahatchie, it was said. Alexander Hamilton Pegues had owned five thousand acres in the northeastern part of the county; he had not fought in the war which destroyed his home, but, like Sutpen, he had tried to summon the energy of a young man to rebuild it afterwards. His brother, Colonel Thomas Pegues, was another big landowner whose house had supposedly been built by a French architect. (A New Yorker with a French name had actually drawn the plans.) In Faulkner's childhood there were still a number of big houses out in the country—gaunt antique ruins such as the old Shipp place, eleven miles due south of town, built by Dr. Felix Grundy Shipp after his arrival with sixty-five relatives, servants, and slaves in 1833. Now the house was open and abandoned, the deep track near it still visible where the stage coach once passed by. Another landowner, listed in the 1860 census, was one Wash Jones. (Another Wash Jones, a Negro, had shot himself out of unrequited love in 1891.) The family burying ground of one such house, southwest of Oxford, shows the names Jones and Bond. As for merchants, there were several Oxonians whose ancestors had prospered before the war. W. S. Neilson had come into the county from Tennessee on New Year's Day, 1836, and his store was still running. Others, like Faulkner's fictional Goodhue Coldfield, had not been so foresighted and fortunate. The lore of the war and The Lost Cause, of course, Faulkner had in his bones. (There were even legends such as that of a sunken steamboat with gold in it.) Moreover, he had been using this kind of lore recently in the Bayard-Ringo series for *The Saturday Evening Post*. Thinking years later about his earlier, unsuccessful attempts to write the story, Faulkner said, "I decided that I didn't know enough at that time maybe or my feeling toward it wasn't passionate enough or pure enough. . . ." Whatever the nature of that block or hindrance, the pages now began to pile up.

It was usually Faulkner's custom when he completed a story or novel to burn what he called his "working papers." One such sheet that he may have used at this time escaped destruction. It showed how he was continuing to work at the problem that had perplexed him from the start: not the events in the lives of Sutpen and his children, but how to relate and interpret them. Though he had now fixed on the principal characters who would perform this function in present time, he was still confronted by complexities. The immediate crux was, exactly what did Quentin (and some of the others) know, and how did they find it out? To help himself work this out he sketched a kind of flow chart of information. At the top was Charles Sutpen, identified briefly as the man who had come to Jefferson, married

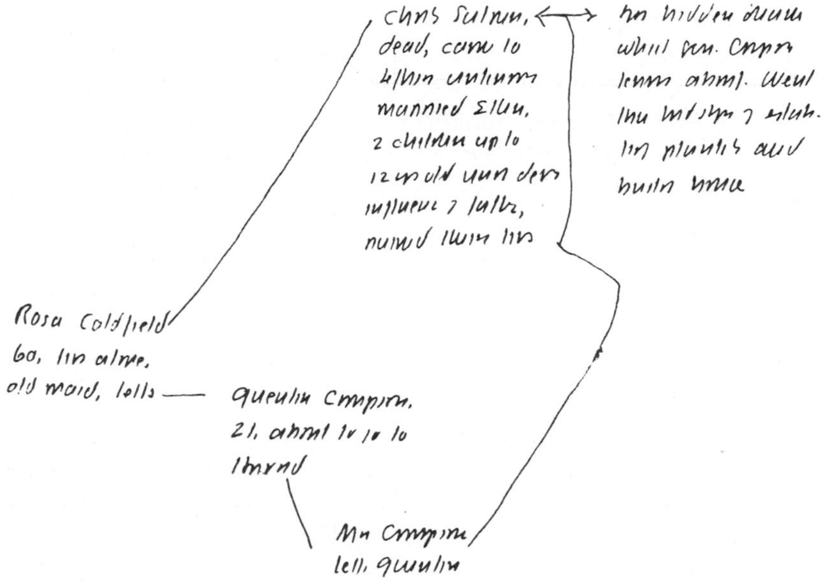

Notes for a novel called *Dark House* and then *Absalom, Absalom!*.

Ellen Coldfield, built a plantation, raised two children, and "ruined their lives." Faulkner drew a line from him down to Rosa Coldfield, at the left ("60, lives alone, old maid"), and then one from her down to Quentin Compson, in the center. He would learn some things about Sutpen from her. Another line linked Quentin to his father, who was a further source of information chiefly gleaned from his father, General Compson, a sometime confidant of Sutpen's. Faulkner had his major lines set up, but others would evolve, and the process of transmission would become more rather than less complex the further he worked his way into the novel.

Though he was dealing with events which had their beginnings early in the nineteenth century, he set their retelling in September, 1910, just before Quentin Compson went north to enroll at Harvard. (Characteristically, he did not check *The Sound and the Fury*, where Quentin first went to Cambridge in 1909.) From the beginning he signaled his method of supplying copious information about most of his principals, material that would be amplified and revised as the multiple narrators slowly pieced the story together. To unravel the enigma of Sutpen, he went back far before the time of "Wash," even before Sutpen's entry into north Mississippi as a young man in 1833. Now he revealed that there had been another son besides the one Sutpen had lost in the war. Writing with abbreviations that reduced *-ing* endings to a trailing line, he told how Quentin heard the story of Rosa Coldfield. Working intensively at her recital of her relationship with her sister Ellen and her sister's children, Faulkner made six attempts before he evolved a form that suited him. (Part of the fifth try would be saved for the next chapter.) Miss Rosa was a spinster obsessed with the image of a parvenu, a brigand, who had acquired virgin land under a cloud and then wrenched grounds and house from it by the efforts of naked slaves and a captive architect. Charles Sutpen had then married her sister Ellen for respectability. He had involved her theretofore irreproachable father in shady dealings, but his consummate offense was to regard her as he had Wash's granddaughter: not as a woman but as a breeder to give him a son.

For Rosa Coldfield, Sutpen's demonic figure was symbolic. He had been a military hero, but his all-pervading ego negated that. Like Wash Jones after his devastating insight, she asked, "Is it any wonder that Heaven saw fit to let us lose?" A year before, Faulkner had written Smith that Quentin would tie such accounts as Rosa's together and prevent them from being completely apocryphal. "I use him because it is just before he is to commit suicide because of his sister," he had told his publisher, "and I use his bitterness which he has projected on the South in the form of hatred of it and its people to get more out of the story itself than a historical novel would be." But now, as Faulkner rewrote the novel, Quentin too saw Sutpen in symbolic terms, or saw him as a man who, properly understood, might yield symbolic truth. Quentin's concern about the South was not just a projection of his concern over Caddy, though his conjectural incestuous feelings would make him hypersensitive to later events in the story and would dispose him to empathize with characters set in opposition to Sutpen.

As in *The Sound and the Fury* and *As I Lay Dying*, Faulkner was presenting differing views of a central character (as Conrad had done, for instance, with Axel Heyst in *Victory*). He was concerned with the nature of truth, as in *Pylon*. In *Sartoris* he had tried to express an aspect of the Southern character—brave, chivalric, foolish, and doomed. Over the previous eight years in *Father Abraham* and the Snopes stories he had treated the rise of the anti-Sartoris figure: Flem Snopes, a man bound by no scruples whatever. The Sartorises' class had come into Mississippi in the 1830's often as younger sons making their own way. But there was something of the new man about them. The latter stories in the Bayard-Ringo series had juxtaposed the two: men like John Sartoris and Ab Snopes. Now came Sutpen, as a midpoint between them. He had acquired his hundred square miles of Yoknapatawpha County in a manner not very different from the way Jason Lycurgus Compson gained his one square mile near Jefferson's center. But as Quentin's father said, Sutpen was "underbred." He might completely accept what he took to be the received code of the class to which he aspired, but it would be an imperfect acceptance. He would aim for the same display; he too would see the Negro as chattel. Yet for him there would be none of the gallantry, quixotic and foolish as it was, displayed by the Carolina Bayard Sartoris; there would be none of the learning and cultivation, colored by cynicism and dipsomania though it might be, which inhered in the mind and manner of Jason Lycurgus Compson, II.

As Faulkner worked at *Absalom, Absalom!* through the early spring in the west wing of Rowan Oak, many of his early concerns were fusing into a work of extraordinary power. There came a time in a writer's life, Faulkner would later say, when he was "hot," when he was young enough so that his creative energy was at a peak and experienced enough so that he had the craftsmanship to match it. He was writing now at a high pitch of intensity, giving Rosa Coldfield a rhetorical and poetic style that often veered toward hysteria. There was something of the frantic quality which marked segments of *Pylon*. From time to time he would employ again the device of compound words—"nothusband," "schoolprize" (7, 8)—but the texture was incomparably more dense. If the aviators seemed to be ephemeral, detached somehow from past and future, the reverse was true here. The roots of the present lay deep in the past, and narratives like Miss Rosa's would be the means of uncovering some of them.

For all of this quality, Faulkner would not neglect drama. The chapter endings would suggest the Bayard-Ringo series: dramatic and sometimes suspenseful, pointing toward action and revelations to come. He concluded the first with a "big" ending which piled one shocking detail on another. The scene was part of what Miss Rosa called a Sutpen "raree show," Sutpen fighting one of his slaves as the final climactic event. There to see him fight and gouge, stripped to the waist and wet with blood, was his small son, Henry. Then, after his wife's intrusion, came another image: two small faces looking down from the loft—his white and black daughters, Judith and Clytemnestra. Using the procedure he had followed during the composition of *Pylon*, Faulkner typed the chapter and, instead of waiting to complete the whole manuscript, sent it in to Hal Smith in New York.

He felt well enough physically and was sufficiently satisfied with the novel's progress to resume flying in April. He flew both Wacos from the Memphis airport early in the month for a total of three hours. The big plane now belonged legally to Dean, who had earned a transport license. His brother had sold it to him at a small figure with easy terms. Occasionally, now, there would be fishing trips, too, when Faulkner and Estelle would take Mac and Arthur Guyton along with them. But the novel was compellingly in his mind, and it was a full three weeks before he flew again.

He introduced the second chapter as he had the first one, with the heavy odor of wistaria. Then, as Quentin listened again, another narrator took up the tale, presenting his own subjective view of the truth. Quentin's father was nowhere near so personally involved as Rosa Coldfield, but there was no guarantee that his account was necessarily closer to objective truth than hers. More valuable than his ironic commentary was the information his father could pass on to Quentin, waiting with him in the veranda until it was time to accompany Rosa Coldfield out to the decrepit mansion still standing on Sutpen's Hundred. Faulkner was careful to provide a change of pace. For a dozen pages he told the reader what Quentin had heard; he did not present Mr. Compson as he spoke. And rather than a shrill feminine discourse, it was smoothly quiet and masculine, beginning in a leisurely way, using figures that were retrospective as a Currier and Ives print or smooth as a French Impressionist: "descendants of the same pigeons strutted and crooned or wheeled in short courses resembling soft fluid paint-smears on the soft summer sky."

Mr. Compson relayed to his son the story of Sutpen's early days in the county as he had it from General Compson: his gaining the land, his reappearance with the wild Negroes and the captive architect, and his building of the mansion, twelve miles from town and eight miles from any neighbor. Rosa Coldfield had obsessively described her reaction to Sutpen; Mr. Compson gave the town's as Sutpen began to cast about for a marriage that would provide respectability. In stories such as "A Rose for Emily" and "Death Drag," Faulkner had characterized events through the town's speculation about their nature and meaning. Now he was using this strategy to explore aspects of history as well.

A dozen pages into the chapter, Faulkner let Mr. Compson describe in his own voice the third phase of Sutpen's plan: his departure and return with rich furnishings for the great empty house, his facing down of a group of hostile townsmen. Sutpen's tragic flaw was becoming clearer through this narrative than it ever could through Rosa Coldfield's tale, distilled for forty-three years in neurotic hatred. Quentin's father spoke with the same *fin de siècle* air, the same world-weary cynicism of the veranda dialogues with his neurotic son in *The Sound and the Fury*. But he too was fascinated with Sutpen, and he could help reveal that tragic flaw; as Faulkner would later put it, Sutpen said, "I'm going to be the one that lives in the big house, I'm going to establish a dynasty, I don't care how, and he violated all the rules of decency and honor and pity and compassion. . . ."

As the section had a low-key beginning, so it had a low-key ending with what might have been an echo of *Mosquitoes.* Mr. Compson pictured Ellen Coldfield on the night of her ill-attended wedding as she and her husband moved through the hostile crowd toward the carriage for the journey to their dark and distant demesne. Consistent in his alternation of tone and mood of the two chapters, Faulkner opted for last lines of foreshadowing rather than drama: "Yes, she was weeping again now; it did, indeed, rain on that marriage." (58)

By now the season was changing. Uncle John had announced for county attorney and Ike Roberts was running again for sheriff and tax collector. With the end of the school year at Mississippi Synodical College, Cho-Cho would be home for the summer. The time for class photographs brought a glimpse of the past. Miss Robbie Eades came across a photo from 1908. Solemnly facing the camera in the back row was Billy Falkner. She sent the picture home with Malcolm Franklin. His stepfather put numbers on each of the figures, lettered in the names on the reverse, and sent the photo back.

Either the work was going so well that he could afford a good deal of time in Memphis, or he had run into problems that had to be mulled over before they could be solved. Thursday, April 25, he put in over an hour in his Waco and made his first recorded night landing. It seems likely that he wanted to be sure of his proficiency after the three-week layoff, for on Saturday and Sunday he and Vernon and Dean were to stage an air circus in Oxford. It would not be an ordinary one, for three other pilots, all of them well known in the Memphis area, would join them. "Capt. Omlie will bring Faulkner's Waco cabin, which is well known in Oxford," reported the *Eagle*, "and their recently acquired Command-Aire with its new famous Siemens-Halske engine made in Germany." They would thrill the crowd with formation flying, and then there would be aerobatics. As an added attraction, "Willie Jones, the only Negro wing walker and parachute jumper in the world, will make a jump from four thousand feet Sunday afternoon."

On Friday Faulkner practiced landings in the new Command-Aire for twenty minutes and later that day flew the plane to Oxford. On the first day of the air circus he took it up for a total of two hours, but he did not fly on the second day. He was represented aloft on that Sunday afternoon, however. After Willie Jones had performed his specialty, a miniature parachute was dropped. Suspended from it, as it drifted to the earth of Lafayette County, was a copy of *Pylon* autographed by the author.

He apparently kept the plane based in Oxford for two busy weeks. On the weekend of May 18 and 19 he flew the plane to Lexington, Tennessee, a hundred miles northeast of Memphis, for what was probably another aerial circus staged with Vernon and Dean. During the second half of the month his log looked almost as though he had been commuting between Oxford and Memphis. He spent considerable time with Dean and Louise at Vernon's place at 14 South McLean, often asking his brother to go off with him on flying trips. "I can't do that," the young husband would say. "I've got a wife, I've got to stay here."

Soon, however, the rush of activity stopped—not to resume for seven weeks. By this time Smith had returned the version of Chapter I he had received in April. Penciling in comments, he had written in one margin, "This is damned confusing" and then crossed out the page and the two that followed. When Faulkner typed a new version it differed from the manuscript in several places. He moved the opening action from 1910 to 1909, changing other references accordingly and tightening sentences for emphasis and logical sequence as he went. In typing Chapter II he sharpened his imagery and omitted details to obtain powerful understatement. By June 29 the chapter was in New York.

As he worked his way into the third chapter of his manuscript, he began with a comment from Quentin. With one other brief comment, it was the only word not spoken by his father. Mr. Compson supplied common knowledge augmented by what he knew from his father and mother. As he filled in more areas in the history of the house of Sutpen, he sketched in minor characters who sometimes resembled earlier Faulkner creations. Mr. Compson's developing portrait of Sutpen was basically consistent with that of Miss Rosa, though not so frantic. As befitted a classicist, he studded his narrative with allusions to mythological characters, to "Greek tragedy."

(62) As he presented this ancient chronicle of "singleminded unflagging effort" (72) to his son, Mr. Compson was acting not only as narrator but as the voice which spoke for the chorus: the townspeople of Jefferson who witnessed Sutpen's arrival, rise, and fall.

All the other major characters were seen in relation to Sutpen. His wife Ellen was acquiescent and—like the aviators of *Pylon*—ephemeral as a butterfly. Her mating and breeding cycle completed, she would soon vanish, looking a little like Mrs. Compson with "bafflement in the dark uncomprehending eyes. . . ." (86) Her two children were growing beyond her. Judith had passed through the stage that suggested Drusilla Hawk and Tochie Oldham: "the hoyden who could—and did—outrun and outclimb, and ride and fight both with and beside her brother. . . ." (67) This relationship, like that of "two cadets in a crack regiment" (80), was, "the town knew . . . closer than the traditional loyalty of brother and sister even. . . ." (79) Faulkner had treated this kind of closeness before, in "Adolescence" and in *Mosquitoes.* Later it would take on overtones suggesting the incestuous feelings Quentin declared in *The Sound and the Fury.* No longer a hoyden, Judith waited for maturity like Eula Varner, "parasitic and potent and serene. . . ." (67)

Through Mr. Compson's narrative Faulkner swiftly advanced his exposition: the arrival of Charles Bon, friend to Henry and potential suitor to Judith, and the coming of the war. He grafted Sutpen onto events in the history of the house of Sartoris: Sutpen rode north in '61 second in command to John Sartoris. Mr. Compson was not spinning a tale in perfect chronology, however; he jumped ahead to Goodhue Coldfield's self-immolation late in the war, to the service of Henry Sutpen and Charles Bon in the University Greys, to Rosa Coldfield's attempt to fulfill her sister's deathbed adjuration that she protect Judith, four years her senior. Mr. Compson had now advanced the tale almost to the point where "Wash" had begun: Wash Jones did for Judith and Ellen while the Colonel was away at the war.

As he related these events Mr. Compson used phrases suggesting the recurrent references to "the Player" near the end of *Light in August*, for there behind Sutpen "Fate, destiny, retribution, irony—the stage manager, call him what you will—was already striking the set. . . ." (72–73) Fate's stroke was announced at the chapter's end as Wash Jones hurriedly summoned Rosa Coldfield to Sutpen's Hundred. After Faulkner typed the chapter he penned a few words at the end in which Jones gave the reason for the summons: "Henry has done shot that durn French feller. Kilt him dead as a beef." He lost no time in putting it in the mail, and by July 22 it was on Hal Smith's desk.

On Saturday, July 20, he went to Memphis and flew with Champ. As he sat in the Mid-South offices with Vernon or stood at the counter of Mrs. Caya's store with Charlie Hayes, he could have worn, had he chosen, an emblem of a new distinction. In *Pylon* he had mentioned "the modest Q.B. wings" worn by veteran aviators. He was now a Quiet Birdman himself, admitted to the New York Hangar on July 1. He had the wings and the engraved metal plate bearing title, insignia, his number and signature, together with the testimony that he was "a certified goodfellow" and had "mounted alone into the realms beyond the reach of keewee and mo-dock. . . ." Veterans like Vernon Omlie might take an irreverent view. Seeing the insignia once on Faulkner's jacket, he said, "It means Bill is a queer bastard." Faulkner spoke quickly. "Wait a minute," he said, "it's Quiet Birdman." He would wear it often and proudly for the rest of his life.

They returned to Oxford in Champ's Command-Aire, but he would not fly again for two weeks, for he was facing an all-too-familiar problem. It was probably late July when he wrote to Morty Goldman, thanking him for some checks and a pipe. "The checks relieved the pressure somewhat," he said, "but, since none of the recent stories seem to be Post stuff, big check stuff, I can see another squall in the near future. On Sept. first I am going to need at least two thousand dollars." He was now toying with the idea of what would be—for him—a drastic and still temporary solution. "The only way I can think of to get it or part of it, apart from writing, is to try to sell some of my manuscript. It's all written in long hand; besides the short stories, I have SOUND & FURY, AS I LAY DYING, SANCTUARY, LIGHT IN AUGUST, PYLON. Will there be any market for it? Will you inquire around, without committing yourself, and see? I hate like hell to sell it, but if I dont get some money somehow soon, I will be in danger of having some one put me in bankruptcy and I will then lose my house and insurance and all. So just ask around and see what the reaction is."

Meanwhile he would see if he could bail himself out in the usual way without resorting to Hollywood. "I finished last week another chapter of the novel which I owe Smith, and now I shall try some more short stories, still with hopes of the Post; two for them would do the business. I am trying to get the novel done as soon as possible, so that when I come East I can make a better contract than I have. Keep this under your hat, of course."

The *Post* had not bought his recent offerings. Now he asked Goldman to send him "The Brooch" so he could rewrite it in accordance with Dashiell's suggestions. Goldman was to send "Fool About a Horse" to Dashiell. "Will rewrite that too if necessary," Faulkner added.

Dashiell bought both stories, and Faulkner managed to meet some of his obligations, including his yearly mortgage payment of $900 to Mrs. Sallie Bailey Bryant on July 29. But her husband had written Faulkner that it would take $500 to $1,000 for additional land that Faulkner wanted, land Bryant wished him to have. He would just have to write and sell more stories.

His desperation was indicated by one that he probably wrote during this summer or the preceding spring. He had apparently gone back to "Christmas Tree," which he had sent to Goldman more than a year before with the subsequent instruction that he would rewrite it to editorial specifications. Under the new title "Two Dollar Wife," he again recounted the bizarre courtship of Doris Houston and Howard Maxwell, renamed Maxwell Johns. Again there was the dance, the dice, and the wedding license as part of the stakes. Johns's antagonist was a Princeton student named Jornstadt who eventually lost not so much to Johns's skill as to the potency of his moonshine whiskey. The story was purchased by *College Life*, which apparently aimed at the same tastes catered to by *College Humor* and other magazines whose staples were cartoons, jokes, and undemanding fiction. The magazine was then advertising a $500 short-story contest, and it may have been this possibility that attracted Faulkner rather than the small sum this magazine was probably able to pay. He did not win the contest. When the story appeared in January of 1936 it was described as presenting "a pungent panorama of reckless youth. . . ." The tale of "madcap matrimony" was destined for thirty-five years of almost total obscurity. This probably suited Faulkner. One of the checks Goldman had sent him in July may well have been from *College Life*. It could scarcely have recompensed him for this potboiler he probably despised even as he wrote it.

By early August Jack Falkner was in the news again, "one of the crack investigators," according to a detective magazine, tracking the notorious Alvin Karpis. Bill's dangers and thrills were of a different kind. He managed to fly nine different occasions that month, usually with Dean or with Champion. Faulkner was doing most of his flying on weekends, and during August he took the controls on only three normal working days, for he was now immersed in Chapter IV of *Absalom, Absalom!*.

He began the chapter as omniscient narrator, returning to Mr. Compson and his son on their veranda and glancing briefly at Miss Rosa waiting in her dark house. Often Mr. Compson would describe events as he imagined them—combining fact and conjecture. But one item of evidence came at the end of the chapter: Charles Bon's three-page letter telling Judith Sutpen that they had waited long enough to marry. They had endured what Mr. Compson took to be a four-year probation, enjoined upon Bon by Henry, so that Bon might renounce the New Orleans octoroon married in a bogus ceremony and the son she had borne. Mr. Compson was gradually fleshing out the hypothesis he had advanced earlier. Now he argued that Sutpen had found evidence of the "marriage" in New Orleans, but that Henry had repudiated the evidence and his birthright because of his love for Bon. His interpretation would find a supersensitive listener in Quentin. The closeness of Henry and Judith was unsexual, Mr. Compson had insisted, like that of two cadets in a crack regiment (much more like that of Pat and Josh Robyn in *Mosquitoes* than Quentin's purported feelings toward his sister in *The Sound and the Fury*). The *real* closeness—though Bon, too, probably loved the adoring Judith after his own fashion—was between the boy and the man, the sophisticated outlander and the bucolic pupil. "Perhaps in his fatalism," Mr. Compson ruminated, "he loved Henry the better of the two, seeing perhaps in the sister merely the shadow, the woman vessel with which to consummate the love whose actual object was the youth—the cerebral Don Juan who, reversing the order, had learned to love what he had injured. . . ." (108)

Mr. Compson had advanced the narrative in the course of his speculations. He related the enlistment of the two, Bon's lieutenancy, Sutpen's command of the regiment, Ellen Sutpen's death, and the reappearance of the two boys at the war's end. Then, preparing to end the chapter, Faulkner decided that for maximum effect he would have to change the end of Chapter III. There Bon's murder came as a shock. He would delete that information and use it to end Chapter IV instead. This chapter would better prepare the reader for Bon's death, and—using only Wash's arrival to end Chapter III—he would prolong and heighten the suspense. Following the procedure he had set for this novel, Faulkner typed the chapter and put it in the mail to Smith, who had it by August 19.

It would be nearly two months before he would move ahead consistently on the manuscript again. He relaxed by flying on August 21, but then apparently gave that up—like the writing—and would log no more time until mid-September. He had been working rather steadily at this complex novel for four and a half months, and he must have been tired. And by now other concerns were growing acute. It was time for direct action. He bought a railroad ticket to New York. Boarding the train on September 23, he set out on the long-planned expedition to solve his financial problems by selling current work and by obtaining a better deal from Smith—or leaving him.

He checked into the Murray Hill Hotel at Park Avenue between 40th and 41st streets on Wednesday morning, September 25, and immediately set to work to sell the magazine rights to *Absalom, Absalom!*. On Friday he informed Estelle that the *Mercury* would not take it, "as it is too long. Goldman is now trying Scribner's and Harper. If that will not work, I have told Hal that I am coming down on him for money. He is non-committal; I dont know just what he will do about it. I will wait until I hear from the 2 magazines, then I will put it to the test."

He gave a full report. Some of the friends he had looked forward to seeing were in California: Corey Ford, Dorothy Parker, and others. He had seen only Bennett Cerf and his partner Donald Klopfer, who would tell him during his stay in New York that they wanted to publish his books and were willing to do so on his terms. He was considering all the possibilities. "I am saving H. Guinzburg until I have the round with Hal," he wrote. He had never forgotten Harold Guinzburg's liberal terms offered four years before in the hectic New York aftermath of *Sanctuary*. He also tried to assuage Estelle's worries: "My headache is gone now, and I feel better. I feet good and ready and 'hard-boiled' now enough to cope with Shylock himself."

He managed several social engagements along with the business. He saw Lenore Marshall. Hal Smith, of course, entertained him at his place, where Mrs. Sewell Haggard told him she liked his work.

"Why don't you write some more stories like those in the *Post*?" she asked.

His response was curt. "Third-rate Kipling," he said.

She later found that Smith shared the same opinion. The writing of the stories to order for the *Post* was a low point in Bill Faulkner's career, Smith thought.

Now he and Faulkner began to discuss his situation. On a sheet of Smith & Haas stationery Faulkner set down some figures. He owed about $500 to various Memphis stores and nearly $1,200 in Oxford, over half of it to the grocer. There were other obligations coming up—taxes, insurance,

$100 a month to Miss Maud and the same amount to Mrs. Oldham. If he were to spend the next three months on the novel, he would need about $3,400. *Scribner's* might pay a $1,000 advance for the serial rights to the novel, but then he decided that if they did take it they were more likely to offer $500. His memorandum, marked "10/2/35," went into his Smith & Haas file.

Three days later he reported the result to Estelle by letter. He had talked at length with Hal Smith and Bob Haas, as well as with Harold Ober, Haas's Scarsdale neighbor and steady horseshoe-pitching opponent. One of the best of New York literary agents, Ober represented other Smith & Haas authors and sometimes handled business for the firm on his trips to the West Coast. "I have settled the business," Faulkner wrote. "There are strings to it, of course, and I have agreed to go to to California for 8 weeks if Hal can get me a contract and so pay back the money which they loaned me. I took only the bare minimum, so it is not such a staggering sum. It will pay all bills, taxes, insurance, etc. and I included in it a sum for winter clothes for you and the children. We will shop carefully and pay cash, and it will do." Before he left for home he would find a plaid skirt and tam for Jill at Stern's. He had seen the Guinzburgs but only socially, it appeared. Smith must have argued that Faulkner should stay with him until he paid or earned back the advances he had received. *Absalom, Absalom!* was a Smith & Haas book, and the familiar option clause in the contract—of which Faulkner was so wary—may have committed him once again for still another book.

He told Estelle about their friends. "Sullivan is in Saratoga and everyone else is in Hollywood, where I have heard that Ben now actually has a job." Again he reassured her about himself. "I have seen 2 shows, dined out once, and I have a typewriter in my room and I am working on a story for Scribners. I drink in a very moderate way, two whiskeys before supper and no more, and I am actually enjoying drinks now, and everyone is amazed at my temperateness." He might check out of the Murray Hill to go up to Hal's place at Farmington, in Connecticut, but he would be home before long. He had an appointment with Graeme Lorimer at the *Post* offices on Thursday, October 10. After that, he would leave, at the end of the week.

When he came back from Connecticut he stayed at the Yale Club for two days as Bob Haas's guest. Then he transacted his magazine business and departed. He was back in Memphis on Sunday, October 13. On Monday he put in an hour's flying time in Vernon's open-cockpit Waco and the next day flew back to Oxford in the cabin plane. Dean was with him to fly it back to Memphis. One of his unpacking jobs was to put mementos of the New York visit on his bookshelves. From Harold Guinzburg he had Humphrey Cobb's *Paths of Glory*, a new novel about the tragic fate of a French regiment which was being compared with Erich Maria Remarque's *All Quiet on the Western Front.* The subject matter of one book was especially close to home: Robert M. Coates's *The Outlaw Years: The History of the Land Pirates of the Natchez Trace.* He was already a student of the battles and leaders of the Civil War; now he was fascinated by desperadoes such as Murrell and the Harpes, killers who had preyed upon travelers of the Trace. There were a number of other books. While he had been acquiring them there had been local news in the making.

Phil Stone was not in Oxford. To everyone's surprise, the confirmed bachelor was in New Orleans preparing to take a bride. After teaching school for five years, Emily Whitehurst had gone back home to Georgia and then enrolled in the Tulane School of Social Work. A month of classes had shown her that she didn't like it. Then Phil came down to visit her and proposed. She accepted, and on October 19 Stone married his adoring bride, sixteen years younger than he, in St. Paul's Episcopal Church in New Orleans. A month later the newlyweds would move into the old, six-columned home with General Stone and Miss Rosie.

If Phil had encouraged Emily in her writing and given her one of his literature tutorials, she had helped him in an equally significant way. He had gotten over his baldness syndrome. He could now allow his friends to see him without a hat. She was trying to bring him, a talker and observer rather than a doer, into the mainstream of life. For his part, Stone apparently felt that it would be only right now for Faulkner to help Emily in her writing career as he had helped Billy Faulkner. What she would not realize until later was that her husband no longer had that kind of energy to give. He was forty-two, and parenthood and professional distinction still lay ahead of him, but years later Emily Stone would discover what the psychic realities had been. "Phil Stone was burned out," she said. "His life was over when I married him, but I didn't know it."

For Faulkner there were echoes of the New York trip as he settled down to correcting proofs of "The Brooch" which had arrived from *Scribner's.* Morty Goldman had sent the fifty-seven-page typescript of "A Portrait of Elmer" to Bennett Cerf. Replying to Faulkner, Cerf regretted that it had come too late for a Christmas limited edition, even though he felt that at that length Faulkner was "squandering some of the finest material you ever had for a longer book as well as some of the best writing of yours I have ever seen." Cerf was more interested in other prospects, however, and he set them forth clearly: "I think we'd rather have you on our list than any other fiction writer living in America. I know that those are strong words, Bill, but I mean them. I was deadly in earnest too when I told you that you could write your own ticket with us. I don't want to say another word about this until everything is settled on your next book and you are ready to take the matter up, but when the time comes I'd like to feel that we are going to have first whack at discussing details with you because I know we'll make everything so attractive for you that you simply won't be able to turn us down." This would be, in effect, the end of "A Portrait of Elmer," but not the end of Cerf's other efforts.

Faulkner had not contented himself with putting new books on his shelves upon his return home on October 15. He inscribed that date on a fresh sheet of margin-ruled paper and started Chapter V of *Absalom, Absalom!*. Now the voice that spoke was Rosa's; the hearer, Quentin, sitting in her house. Her voice, italicized, would sustain the narrative up until the last page of the chapter, when the omniscient narrator would shift to Quentin's thoughts.

The narrative was taking on a more clearly contrapuntal quality. As the sixty-eight-year-old woman spoke, she assumed that others would have told Quentin certain things; some she elaborated, and some she contradicted, using certain refrains over and over. Though her speech was discursive, she resumed the story with Jones's summons to Sutpen's Hundred. And though she saw neither victim nor murderer, she watched Judith direct the building of her sweetheart's coffin. (She might have been Addie Bundren, "*giving them directions about making it . . . the slow, maddening rasp, rasp, rasp, of the saw, the flat deliberate hammer blows. . . .*" [151]) As she described the struggle to rebuild the plantation, there were vignettes suggesting the recent Bayard-Ringo series. Uncle Buck McCaslin screamed the rebel yell; stragglers prowled the land; Judith Sutpen, like Drusilla Hawk, was widowed before she was wed; and the taciturn Confederate Colonel returned to his desolate home: "*I stood there before the rotting portico and watched him ride up on that gaunt and jaded horse . . . he said 'Well, daughter' and stooped and touched his beard to Judith's forehead. . . .*" (159)

There were familiar effects. The chapter was almost all narrative flashback, and within it there was yet another coherent and extended one: Rosa's fourteen-year-old's fascination with her niece's love affair. But the most remarkable quality about the chapter was Rosa Coldfield's intensity. Her diction often had a Shakespearean ring: "*Do you mark how the wistaria, sun-impacted on this wall here, distills and penetrates this room . . .?*" (143) At times her frenzied reliving of the effect of Sutpen, the Demon, upon her sister and herself trembled on the verge of blank verse.

Consistent with Faulkner's narrative strategy, there were deficiencies to be remedied by others. And there were errors: the photograph Judith held, as she stood, newly bereft in her room, would prove not to be her own photograph given to Bon, as Rosa thought. There was no attempt to explain *why* Henry had shot Bon, only the unspoken assumption that such disaster might be expected from progeny of the demon. There was no explicit explanation for Rosa's departure from Sutpen's Hundred after agreeing to be the demon's bride, only the shuddering hint of something monstrous he had said. (In this chapter Sutpen's given name was not Charles but John.) At the end of the chapter, however, Faulkner again employed the suspenseful stop. Rosa interrupted Quentin's imagining of Henry's confession with the words, "There's something in that house." And it was not just Clytie, half-sister to Rosa's own niece and nephew. "No. Something living in it. Hidden in it. It has been out there for four years, living hidden in that house." (172) Faulkner had also achieved another effect: he had brought this narrative of the past into the immediate present with an ominous, portentous note.

Too absorbed in this inner life even to do much flying, he would still assume his social role periodically. In late October Dean and Louise had come down from Memphis for the weekend, Louise now four months pregnant. At times like this they might have a few people in. Louise would watch her brother-in-law as the conscientious host, actually trying to keep conversation flowing. "At what age were you happiest?" he might ask, or, trying an easier gambit, "Why do you smoke?" In desperation he once asked, "Who is your favorite movie star?" After one such unrewarding evening, he said, "Louise, I think I've proved the art of conversation is lost."

When just the family was there, the conversation would drift to flying. Johncy had soloed in March, earned his limited commercial license in May, and was now working toward a transport pilot's license. Dean was still giving instructions, flying charter jobs, and putting on shows. In July he had gone to Sikeston, Missouri, for the dedication of a new field, and often there would be a barnstorming weekend in some Tennessee town. He would be doing this soon again at home. "The Flying Faulkners," announced the *Eagle*, "both Bill and Dean, will stage another air show at Markette field next Saturday and Sunday, Nov 2 and 3." Both would perform stunt flying and provide passenger rides. And Willie Jones, still billed as "the only negro parachute jumper in the world," would perform again.

There was encouraging activity at the Oxford airport. It seemed certain to be granted WPA funds and labor for surveying, grading, hangars, and lights. Though Faulkner had been hoping for this, he was aware now that his brother was unsettled again, and that some sort of change was taking place inside him. Dean and Louise had enjoyed their time in Memphis with Vernon Omlie and their other flying friends, but it was beginning to pall, and now they had the coming baby to think of. They talked about what they should do. A professional pilot had to be away a lot, and it was an uncertain way to earn a living. "We must get out of this life," they told each other. For the present they would have to continue as they were, but they would start looking.

Faulkner helped his brother with the air show, though he flew for only a half-hour on Saturday in Champ's Command-Aire. Dean took passengers up in the cabin Waco. At the end of the show he prepared to fly it back to Memphis. The next weekend he and Navy Sowell, the parachute jumper, were going to put on a show in Pontotoc. Perhaps the two brothers could meet again then. Dean went back to Memphis; Bill, to Rowan Oak and *Absalom, Absalom!*.

He might not actually seat himself at his desk and pick up his pen until the morning, when he would rise shortly after first light. But at times like this, when he was hot on a novel, he would be working ofttimes even when he appeared to be just sitting on his front gallery and gazing out at one of the horses in the paddock. When he did begin Chapter VI, approaching the midpoint of his story, he introduced significant changes. From now on even more stress would be placed on interpretation, on getting at the meaning of Sutpen's life as well as the psychological mechanisms behind his actions. Quentin would fulfill this function. But here Faulkner had struck off in a new direction. As if to achieve something of a distancing effect, while yet retaining emotional intensity, he shifted to Quentin's Harvard dormitory and introduced a new character, his moon-faced bespectacled roommate, Shrevlin McCannon. (In a typical oversight, Faulkner neglected to use—or look up—the name he had given him in *The Sound and the Fury*: Shreve MacKenzie.) Not simply an aesthetic interlocutor, he would become coanalyst of these strange lives and destinies. He would take over the narrative from Quentin and carry it through to the end of the chapter. He would also help keep out the plug hats and hoop skirts. Shreve could ask the outsider's questions; he could play the skeptic. As Faulkner would later put it, "Well, the story was told by Quentin to Shreve. Shreve was the commentator that held the thing to something of reality. If Quentin had been let alone to tell it, it would have become completely unreal. It had to have a solvent to keep it real, keep it believable, creditable, otherwise it would have vanished into smoke and fury."

Faulkner was again manipulating his multiple narrators and other devices in a way that suggested Conrad. A letter from Mr. Compson to his son, mailed on January 10, 1910, brought word of Miss Rosa Coldfield's death. Shreve's questions about the old woman were like more general ones he asked: "*Tell about the South. What's it like there. What do they do there. Why do they live there. Why do they live at all. . . .*" (174) Quentin obviously distorted them in intent and sharpness. They touched one of his most sensitive nerves, and he was prepared to read into the story meanings which might provide equally large answers. Writing as omniscient narrator, Faulkner described Quentin's ride with Miss Rosa toward Sutpen's Hundred in the ominous darkness. Then he employed another version of his standard strategy: Shreve recapitulated the facts from the beginning of the account, querying Quentin about his own understanding of them.

As Shreve threw himself into the problem, his rhetoric became high-flown like Miss Rosa's, his diction Hellenized like Mr. Compson's. Occasionally he would piece out earlier information. Shreve tried to understand Miss Rosa's view of Sutpen: "if he hadn't been a demon his children wouldn't have needed protection from him and she wouldn't have had to go out there and be betrayed by the old meat and find instead of a widowed Agamemnon to her Cassandra an ancient stiff-jointed Pyramus to her eager though untried Thisbe who could approach her in this unbidden April's compounded demonry and suggest that they breed together for test and sample and if it was a boy they would marry. . . ." (177) Demon to Miss Rosa, Sutpen was to Shreve "*The ancient varicose and despairing Faustus*" who was ready to "*fling his final main now with the Creditor's hand already on his shoulder. . . .*" (182)

The narrative had now been carried beyond the time of "Wash." (After having Jones call his master "Mister John," Faulkner hit on his true name: Thomas.) Recollection advanced the story further: the raising of Bon's son,

Charles, by Judith and Clytie, and the death, in 1884, of the first two from smallpox. Familiar patterns had emerged in the interval. Charles Etienne Saint-Valery Bon, growing up almost white but one-sixteenth (it was assumed) Negro, recapitulated much of Joe Christmas' tragic alienation—marrying a charcoal-black woman, fighting almost masochistically, and courting death. Familiar images described his early life. With his mother, he stood at his father's cedar-grove grave in something that "must have resembled a garden scene by the Irish poet, Wilde . . . a woman created of by and for darkness whom the artist Beardsley might have dressed . . . followed by a bright gigantic negress carrying a silk cushion and leading by the hand the little boy whom Beardsley might not only have dressed but drawn. . . ." (193)

As the chapter moved to an end, Faulkner was internalizing it more and more within Quentin's consciousness. Shreve's words were revealed to the reader, but not his thoughts. Quentin's thoughts, revolving obsessively around events with a special meaning for him, became tinged with madness. He had gone from involvement to immersion: "*Yes. I have heard too much, I have been told too much; I have had to listen too much, too long* thinking *Yes, Shreve sounds almost exactly like father. . . .*" (207)

Faulkner was still withholding information to maintain suspense. Quentin and Luster had once been frightened, while trespassing, by Clytie and Jim Bond, the idiot mulatto product of Charles Etienne Saint-Valery Bon's self-lacerating marriage. Was there more than just their presence when Quentin reached Sutpen's Hundred with Miss Rosa that night? There was. " 'Wait then,' Shreve said. 'For God's sake wait.' " (216)

Faulkner had undertaken other writing apart from the novel and occasional short-story revision. One piece was a review of Jimmy Collins' *Test Pilot*. He gave the newspaperman-pilot credit for good anecdotes and professional ambition: "the book indicates that . . . he flew only to make money to support his family." But he regretted the last chapter, an obituary written by Collins himself and called "I Am Dead." (Collins had been killed on a test flight.) "I don't mean to make any commentary on twentieth-century publishing methods," wrote Faulkner, "the crass come-on schemes of modern day publishing, for whose benefit by an almost incredible fortuity Collins wrote the document, dared to it, I believe jokingly, by a friend. . . ." But it was this chapter which provided "the only figure or phrase in the book which suddenly arrests the mind with the fine shock of poetry: 'The cold but vibrant fuselage was the last thing to feel my warm and living flesh.' " Disappointed, Faulkner had hoped for a folklore of speed itself, "producing a literature innocent of either love or hate and of course of pity or terror, and which would be the story of the final disappearance of life from the earth. I would watch them, the little puny mortals, vanishing against a vast and timeless void filled with the sound of incredible engines, within which furious meteors moving in no medium hurtled nowhere, neither pausing nor flagging, forever destroying themselves and one another."

This apocalyptic vision did not keep him out of the air. After a two-week layoff, he flew Champ's Command-Aire again for a half-hour on Saturday, November 2. But he did not fly all that next week. He was busy with the book, perhaps already into Chapter VII. He would not even be able to get over to Pontotoc to help Dean put on the weekend air show. But Dean had 450 hours of flying time to his credit, three times as much as his brother, and Navy Sowell would be there to help him. He would be all right.

Louise had come down from Memphis with Dean and stayed with Miss Maud when he flew to Pontotoc on Saturday. Monday was Armistice Day, and they could spend a long weekend with their families. The first day of the show was perfectly ordinary—a few aerobatics and then the business of taking farmers up to see their places from the air. But then sometime after three o'clock on Sunday afternoon, rumors began to filter into Oxford about an airplane crash somewhere over near Thaxton, about ten miles west of Pontotoc. At Rowan Oak, Faulkner backed the Chevy around and drove to Miss Maud's little house on South Lamar. She and Louise got in the car and they drove east along Highway 6 toward Pontotoc. They passed Lafayette Springs, and as they crossed the county line and approached Thaxton they managed to hail a passing truck coming from that direction.

It was true. There had been a crash. Dean was dead.

Notes

The numbers at each left-hand margin indicate the pages and lines to which the citations following apply. Abbreviations for Faulkner works and the editions employed (those currently most reliable) are as follows:

AA — *Absalom, Absalom!.* New York, Random House, 1936; New York, Modern Library, 1951.
AGB — *A Green Bough.* New York, Harrison Smith and Robert Haas, 1933.
The Marble Faun and A Green Bough. New York, Random House, 1965.
ASI — *As I Lay Dying.* New York, Vintage, 1964; New York, Modern Library, 1967.
BW — *Big Woods.* New York, Random House, 1955.
CS — *Collected Stories of William Faulkner.* New York, Random House, 1950.
DRM — *Doctor Martino and Other Stories.* New York, Harrison Smith and Robert Haas, 1934.
EPP — *William Faulkner: Early Prose and Poetry,* ed. Carvel Collins. Boston, Little, Brown, 1962.
ESP — *Essays, Speeches & Public Letters by William Faulkner,* ed. James B. Meriwether. New York, Random House, 1965.
FAB — *A Fable.* New York, Random House, 1954 (fourth printing).
FIU — *Faulkner in the University,* eds. Frederick L. Gwynn and Joseph L. Blotner. Charlottesville, University of Virginia Press, 1959; New York, Vintage, 1965.
FR — *The Faulkner Reader.* New York, Random House, 1954; New York, Modern Library, 1959.
FWP — *Faulkner at West Point,* eds. Joseph L. Fant, III, and Robert Ashley. New York, Random House, 1964.
GDM — *Go Down, Moses and Other Stories.* New York, Random House, 1942.
Go Down, Moses. New York, Modern Library, 1955.
HAM — *The Hamlet.* New York, Random House, 1964 (third edition).
IID — *Intruder in the Dust.* New York, Random House, 1948; New York, Modern Library, 1955.
KG — *Knight's Gambit.* New York, Random House, 1949.
LIA — *Light in August.* New York, Harrison Smith and Robert Haas, 1932; New York, Random House, 1967.
MAN — *The Mansion.* New York, Random House, 1959; New York, Vintage, 1965.
MOS — *Mosquitoes.* New York, Boni & Liveright, 1927; New York, Liveright, 1955.
NOS — *William Faulkner: New Orleans Sketches,* ed. Carvel Collins. New York, Random House, 1968.
PF — *The Portable Faulkner,* ed. Malcolm Cowley. New York, Viking, 1946.
PYL — *Pylon.* New York, Harrison Smith and Robert Haas, 1935; New York, Random House, 1965.

NOTES

REQ — *Requiem for a Nun.* New York, Random House, 1951 (third printing).
REV — *The Reivers.* New York, Random House, 1962; New York, Vintage, 1966.
SAN — *Sanctuary.* New York, Random House, 1958; New York, Modern Library, 1958.
SAR — *Sartoris.* New York, Harcourt, Brace, 1929; New York, Random House, 1956.
S&F — *The Sound and the Fury.* New York, Jonathan Cape and Harrison Smith, 1929; New York, Random House, 1966; New York, Modern Library, 1966.
SP — *Soldiers' Pay.* New York, Boni & Liveright, 1926; New York, Liveright, 1954.
TMF — *The Marble Faun.* Boston, Four Seas, 1924.
The Marble Faun and A Green Bough. New York, Random House, 1965.
T13 — *These 13.* New York, Jonathan Cape and Harrison Smith, 1931.
TWN — *The Town.* New York, Vintage, 1961.
UNV — *The Unvanquished.* New York, Random House, 1938 or 1965.
WP — *The Wild Palms.* New York, Random House, 1939; New York, Vintage, 1964.
WT — *The Wishing Tree.* New York, Random House, 1964.

Abbreviations for other frequently cited works:

FCF — *The Faulkner-Cowley File: Letters and Memories. 1944–1962,* Malcolm Cowley. New York, Viking, 1966.
FOM — *The Falkners of Mississippi: A Memoir,* Murry C. Falkner. Baton Rouge, Louisiana State University Press, 1967.
LIG — *Lion in the Garden: Interviews with William Faulkner, 1926–1962,* eds. James B. Meriwether and Michael Millgate. New York, Random House, 1968.
MBB — *My Brother Bill: An Affectionate Reminiscence,* John Faulkner. New York, Trident, 1963.
MW — *"Man Working," 1919–1962: William Faulkner, A Catalogue of the William Faulkner Collections at the University of Virginia,* comp. Linton R. Massey. Charlottesville, Bibliographical Society of University of Virginia, 1968.
OTF — *Old Times in the Faulkner Country,* John B. Cullen, with Floyd C. Watkins. Chapel Hill, University of North Carolina Press, 1961.
SOS — *Son of Sorrow: The Life, Works and Influence of Colonel William C. Falkner, 1825–1889,* Donald Philip Duclos. Ann Arbor, Mich., University Microfilms, 1962.
WFL — *William Faulkner's Library: A Catalogue,* comp. Joseph Blotner. Charlottesville, University Press of Virginia, 1964.
WFO — *William Faulkner of Oxford,* eds. James W. Webb and A. Wigfall Green. Baton Rouge, Louisiana State University Press, 1965.

Abbreviations for frequently cited newspapers:

MCA — Memphis *Commercial Appeal.*
MPS — Memphis *Press-Scimitar.*
NOTP — New Orleans *Times-Picayune.*
NYHT — New York *Herald Tribune.*
NYT — New York *Times.*
OXE — Oxford *Eagle.*
RA — Ripley *Advertiser.*

Abbreviations for persons:

WF	William Faulkner	JB	Joseph Blotner
EF	Estelle Faulkner	BC	Bennett Cerf
JFS	Jill Faulkner Summers	SC	Saxe Commins
JMF	James M. Faulkner	MC	Malcolm Cowley
MCF	Murry C. Falkner (Jr.)	AE	Albert Erskine
SMW	Sallie Murry Williams	MG	Morton Goldman

NOTES

RKH	Robert K. Haas	HS	Harrison Smith
EJ	Else Jonsson	BW	Ben Wasson
DSK	Donald S. Klopfer	JW	Joan Williams
LRM	Linton R. Massey		
HO	Harold Ober		

Abbreviations for repositories:

ACLT Academic Center Library, University of Texas at Austin.

FCVA William Faulkner Collections, University of Virginia Library. Unless otherwise noted, letters from Faulkner to Anne Louise Davis, Morton Goldman, William Herndon, Horace Liveright, Harold Ober, Dorothy Olding, Harrison Smith, Ivan von Auw, Jr., Ben Wasson, and Joan Williams are in these collections, as well as letters from any of the above to Faulkner and to others. The collections also include all unpublished class conferences at the University of Virginia.

JFSA Jill Faulkner Summers Private Archive. This includes the Faulkner materials discovered at Rowan Oak in 1971 by Prof. James W. Webb; also Faulkner's report cards, pilot's log (all information on his flying in private aircraft comes from this source unless otherwise noted), passports, various letters, drawings, and the like, and the Greenfield Farm commissary ledger and studbook.

MCL Materials of the late Mrs. Walter B. McLean, courtesy Mrs. Norman N. Thompson.

MCUM Mississippi Collection, University of Mississippi.

NYPL New York Public Library, Astor, Lenox, and Tilden Foundations.

PUL Princeton University Library.

RH Random House. Unless otherwise noted, letters from Faulkner to Bennett Cerf, Saxe Commins, Albert Erskine, Robert Haas, Donald Klopfer, and Robert Linscott are from this source; also letters from any of the above to Faulkner and to others.

YUL Yale University Library.

Each citation of these sources in the Notes is made with the grateful thanks of the author to these people and institutions. Where no repository is listed for Faulkner's letters to persons not mentioned above, the recipients themselves are the sources, and their help is again acknowledged with grateful thanks.

Other abbreviations:

comp. compiled.

I interview, followed by the name of the person interviewed and the date. E.g., I: BC, 7 Oct. 1965.

recd. received.

repr. reprinted.

Most chapter epigraphs are from novels and are so identified. Chapter epigraphs from short stories reprinted in *Collected Stories* are not identified in the Notes. All epigraphs drawn from other sources are footnoted herein.

Faulkner's abbreviations, conventions of punctuation and capitalization, spellings, and misspellings are reprinted without change. Thus [*sic*] is not used except where confusion might otherwise arise.

All quotations from Faulkner's published and unpublished writings are made through the kind and gracious permission of Jill Faulkner Summers.

Each note refers to the sentence in the text ending on the line specified in the column at left. When two sentences end on the same line, the note will be introduced by the quotation of the last word from the relevant sentence. On pages bearing epigraphs, the line count will begin with the first line of the epigraph.

3

NOTES

Abbreviated bibliography (works with multiple references in notes to Volume One):

Anderson, Sherwood, "A Meeting South." *The Dial*, 78 (Apr. 1925). Repr. in Paul Rosenfeld, ed., *The Sherwood Anderson Reader*. Boston, 1947.

__________________, *Memoirs*. New York, 1942.

Basso, Hamilton, "William Faulkner: Man and Writer." *Saturday Review*, 45 July 1962).

Bettersworth, John K., *Mississippi: A History*. Austin, Tex., 1959.

Betts, Sarah Eva Furr, "Lee Maurice Russell and His Attempt to Democratize the University of Mississippi." (Unpubl. article, MCUM.)

Bondurant, Alexander L., "William C. Falkner, Novelist." *Publications of the Mississippi Historical Society*, III (1900).

Bowen, Frances Jean, "The New Orleans *Double Dealer*, 1921–1926." *The Louisiana Historical Quarterly*, XXXIX (Oct. 1956).

Brooks, Cleanth, *William Faulkner: The Yoknapatawpha Country*. New Haven, 1963.

Brown, Andrew, "The First Mississippi Partisan Rangers, C.S.A." *Civil War History*, I (Dec. 1955).

Brown, D. Alexander, *Grierson's Raid*. Urbana, Ill., 1954.

Brown, Maud Morrow, "The War Comes to College Hill." *The Journal of Mississippi History*, XVI (Jan. 1954).

Bross, Addison C., "*Soldiers' Pay* and the Work of Aubrey Beardsley." *The American Quarterly*, XIX (Spring 1967).

Buckley, G. T., "Is Oxford the Original of Jefferson in Faulkner's Novels?" *PMLA*, LXXVI (Sept. 1961).

Buttitta, Anthony, "A Memoir of Faulkner in the Early Days of His Fame." San Francisco *Sunday Chronicle*, (July 15, 1962).

______________,"William Faulkner: That Writin' Man of Oxford." *The Saturday Review of Literature*, XVIII (May 21, 1938).

Cantwell, Robert, "Faulkner's 'Popeye.' " *The Nation* (Feb. 15, 1958).

_______________, "The Faulkners: Recollections of a Gifted Family." Repr. in Frederick J. Hoffman and Olga Vickery, eds., *William Faulkner: Three Decades of Criticism*. New York, 1960.

Capers, Gerald M., Jr., *The Biography of a River Town: Memphis: Its Heroic Age*. Chapel Hill, N.C., 1939.

Chambers, Lenoir, *Stonewall Jackson*, I. New York, 1959.

"The Charm of Old New Orleans." *The Mentor*, 13 (Mar. 1925).

Clark, Emily, "A Week-end at Mr. Jefferson's University." *NYHT Books* (Nov. 8, 1931).

Cohen, Lester, "The Saint . . . and the Sinner." *Esquire*, LIV (Dec. 1960).

Coindreau, Maurice Edgar, "The Faulkner I Knew." *Shenandoah*, XVI (Winter 1965).

Collins, Carvel, "Faulkner and Anderson, Some Revisions." (Paper delivered at 82nd annual meeting of MLA, Chicago, Dec. 28, 1967.)

____________, "Faulkner's War Service and His Fiction." (Paper delivered at 81st annual meeting of MLA, New York, Dec. 28, 1966.)

____________, "The Interior Monologues of *The Sound and the Fury*." *Publications in the Humanities*, 6 (Dept. of Humanities, MIT, 1954).

____________, "The Pairing of *The Sound and the Fury* and *As I Lay Dying*." *Princeton University Library Chronicle*, XVIII (Spring 1957).

Coughlan, Robert, *The Private World of William Faulkner*. New York, 1954.

Dennis, Stephen N., *The Making of Sartoris: A Description and Discussion of the Manuscript and Composite Typescript of William Faulkner's Third Novel*. (Unpubl. Ph.D. thesis, Cornell U., 1969.)

Dos Passos, John, *The Best Times: An Informal Memoir*. New York, 1966.

NOTES

"A Dream of Service Come True," eds. Edmund Winston and Potter. Pontotoc *Sentinel*. Repr. in *The G.M.&.N. News* (Dec. 21, 1923). Repr. in *SOS*, pp. 43–5.

Emerson, O. B., *William Faulkner's Literary Reputation in America*. (Ph.D. dissertation, Vanderbilt U., 1962.)

Feibleman, James K., "Literary New Orleans Between World Wars." *The Southern Review*, I, N.S. (July 1965).

Garner, James Wilford, *Reconstruction in Mississippi*. New York, 1901.

Garrett, George P., Jr., "An Examination of the Poetry of William Faulkner." *The Princeton University Library Chronicle*, XVIII (Spring 1957).

Goldstein, Albert, "Discoveries of the Double Dealer." *Dixie, Times-Picayune States Roto Magazine*, 21 (Jan. 21, 1951).

Green, A. Wigfall, "William Faulkner at Home." *Sewanee Review*, XL (Summer 1932).

Harriman, Margaret Case, *The Vicious Circle*. New York, 1951.

Henry, Robert Selph, *"First with the Most" Forrest*. Indianapolis, 1944.

Hickerson, Thomas Felix, *The Falkner Feuds*. Chapel Hill, N.C., 1964.

Hoar, Victor, "Colonel William C. Falkner in the Civil War." *The Journal of Mississippi History*, XXVII (Feb. 1965).

Howe, Irving, *Sherwood Anderson*. New York, 1951.

Howorth, Lucy Somerville, "The Bill Faulkner I Knew." *The Delta Review*, 2 (July-Aug. 1965).

Hudson, Arthur Palmer, "When We Heard William Faulkner Was Dead." (Unpubl. essay.)

Inge, M. Thomas, "Donald Davidson on Faulkner: An Early Recognition." *The Georgia Review*, XX (Winter 1966).

Izsak, Emily K., "The Manuscript of *The Sound and the Fury*: The Revisions in the First Section." *Studies in Bibliography*, 20 (1967).

Kessel, Neil, and Walton, Henry, *Alcoholism*. Baltimore, 1965.

Kirwan, Albert D., *The Revolt of the Rednecks: Mississippi Politics, 1876–1925*. Louisville, Kty., 1951.

Knox, Robert Hilton, III, *William Faulkner's Absalom, Absalom!*. (Unpubl. Ph.D. dissertation, Harvard U., Apr. 1959.)

Langford, Gerald, *Faulkner's Revision of Absalom, Absalom!: A Collation of the Manuscript and the Published Book*. Austin, Tex., 1971.

Lemly, James Hutton, *The Gulf, Mobile, and Ohio*. Homewood, Ill., 1953.

The Letters of Sherwood Anderson, ed. Howard Mumford Jones, with Walter B. Rideout. Boston, 1953.

McHaney, Thomas L., "The Image of the Railroad in the Novels of William Faulkner, 1926–1942." (Unpubl. MA thesis, U. of N.C., 1962.)

Marx, Samuel, "Faulkner in Hollywood." Beverly Hills *Courier* (Oct. 1, 1965).

Massey, Linton, "Notes on the Unrevised Galleys of Faulkner's *Sanctuary*." *Studies in Bibliography*, 8 (1956).

Meriwether, James B., "Early Notices of Faulkner by Phil Stone and Louis Cochran." *Mississippi Quarterly*, XVII (Winter 1964).

———, "Faulkner, Lost and Found." *NYT Book Review* (Nov. 5, 1972).

———, *The Literary Career of William Faulkner*. Princeton, 1961.

———, "Notes on the Textual History of *The Sound and the Fury*." *Papers of the Bibliographical Society of America*, 56 (Third Quarter, 1962).

———, "Sartoris and Snopes: An Early Notice." *The Library Chronicle of the University of Texas*, VII (Summer 1962).

———, "Two Unknown Faulkner Short Stories." *RANAM, Recherches Anglaises et Américaines, Revue Annuelle*, IV (Strasbourg, 1971).

"Metro-Goldwyn-Mayer." *Fortune*, VI (Dec. 1932).

Millgate, Michael, *The Achievement of William Faulkner*. New York, 1966.

———, "Faulkner and the Air: The Background of *Pylon*." *The Michigan Quarterly Review*, III (Fall 1964).

———, "Faulkner in Toronto: A Further Note." *University of Toronto Quarterly*, XXXVII (Jan. 1968).

________________, "William Faulkner, Cadet." *University of Toronto Quarterly*, XXXV (Jan. 1966).

Miner, Ward L., *The World of William Faulkner*. New York, 1959.

Percy, William Alexander, *Lanterns on the Levee*. New York, 1941.

Price-Stephens, Gordon, "Faulkner and the Royal Air Force." *The Mississippi Quarterly*, XVII (Summer 1964).

Richardson, H. Edward, *William Faulkner: The Journey to Self-Discovery*. Columbia, Mo., 1969.

The Sherwood Anderson Reader, ed. Paul Rosenfeld. Boston, 1947.

Smith, Marshall J., "Faulkner of Mississippi." *The Bookman*, 74 (Dec. 1931).

Spratling, William, "Chronicle of a Friendship: William Faulkner in New Orleans." *The Texas Quarterly*, IX (Spring 1966).

Stallings, Laurence, "Faulkner in Hollywood." New York *Sun* (Sept. 3, 1932).

Stewart, George R., and Backus, Joseph M., "Each in Its Ordered Place." *American Literature,* XXIX (Jan. 1958).

Stone, Emily Whitehurst, "Faulkner Gets Started." *The Texas Quarterly*, VIII (Winter 1965).

________________, "How a Writer Finds His Material." *Harper's*, CCXXXI (Nov. 1965).

Stone, Phil, "William Faulkner: The Man and His Work." *The Oxford Magazine*, I (Apr., June, Nov., 1934). Repr. in James B. Meriwether, "Early Notices of Faulkner by Phil Stone and Louis Cochran." *Mississippi Quarterly*, XVII (Winter 1964).

Tinkle, Lon, "About Faulkner and Dallas." Dallas *Morning News* (July 15, 1962).

Toledano, Benjamin C., "Two-Sided, Not Two-Faced." *Liberator*, II (Spring 1963).

Wasson, Ben, "The Time Has Come," Greenville *Delta Democrat-Times* (July 15, 1962).

Webb, James W., "Rowan Oak, Faulkner's Golden Bough." *The University of Mississippi Studies in English*, 6 (1965).

William Faulkner: An Exhibition of Manuscripts, ed. James B. Meriwether. Austin, Tex., 1959.

Winston, Edmund, "Life of Colonel Falkner: A Glorious Word Picture of the Founder of the G.M.&N. by One Who Has Studied His Life." *G.M.&N. News*, V (Nov. 27, 1925).

Wobbe, James A., "How Faulkner Wrote Sonnet." New Orleans *Item* (Aug. 29, 1954).

Young, Stark, "The New Year's Craw." *The New Republic*, LXXXXIII (Jan. 12, 1938).

Page	*Line*	
3	8	Jun Takami, "Yesterday and Today," *Asahi* (Tokyo), 6 Aug. 1955, p. 3.
3	12	WF to JB.
3	17	WF to David Yalden-Thomson, 1961. I: Yalden-Thomson, 16 July 1963. Of the more than a dozen Falconers listed in the *Dictionary of National Biography,* one is given "Falkner" as an alternate spelling and most are of Scots ancestry. Both the Falkner entries in the *Dictionary* are of English ancestry.
3	19	WF to David Yalden-Thomson.
4	2	*FCF,* p. 110. So far as I have been able to determine, none of WF's surviving relatives can recall kilt, claymore, or Gaelic in connection with Dr. Murry.
4	6	WF to JB.
4	11	Alexander L. Bondurant, "William C. Falkner, Novelist," *Publications of the Mississippi Historical Society,* III (1900), p. 14.
4	19	SMW to JB, 29 July 1966.

NOTES

Page	*Line*	
4	21	When his son, Murry Jr., arrived in Europe during World War II, he was welcomed as returning to the land of his ancestors by cordial natives of both Ulster and Scotland. *FOM,* p. 172.
4	23	I: JMF, 18 Mar. 1965.
5	35	FCVA.
6	23	I: JMF, 18 Mar. 1965.
6	38	Unpubl. portion of class conference, U. of Va., 13 May 1957.
7	3	Unpubl. portion of class conference, U. of Va., 8 May 1957.
7	11	I: David Yalden-Thomson, 26 Apr. 1966.
7	15	*OXE,* 10 Dec. 1896.
7	19	*WFL,* p. 62.
7	25	WF sometimes used highly technical heraldic terminology, and used it with facility.
8	23	*MBB,* p. 138. In 1950, a Faulkner in Kentucky wrote John (William's brother) that he thought they were without doubt descendants of Francis Faulkner, of Anson County, N.C., who had fought during the period 1776–79 and attained the rank of sergeant. John Faulkner to Alabama F. McLean, 8 Dec. 1950.
9	2	J. W. T. Falkner and Alabama Falkner McLean, both children of the Old Colonel, declared that their family had come from Haywood County. I: JMF, 17 Mar. and 23 Nov., 1965.
9	5	According to Murry C. Falkner, WF's father. I: JMF, 17 Mar. 1965.
9	17	In the John Wesley Thompson Bible, William Clark Falkner's name is listed first, being followed by those of James and Frances. One family tradition has it that William was the second son. (I: JMF, 17 Mar. 1965.) The date of William Clark Falkner's birth has been another problem for biographers. In 1850 he married his second wife, a seventeen-year-old girl named Lizzie Vance. On November 13, 1852, she wrote her name, Lizzie H. Falkner, in the flyleaf of a large family Bible; in it she recorded several birth dates including her husband's: "6th July 1826." In the John Wesley Thompson Bible his birth date is recorded as "6 July 1825." Thompson served during Falkner's youth as his guardian, and one would think that he and his wife would have been closer to such facts than the seventeen-year-old bride, whose young husband may not have been averse to appearing only seven rather than eight years her senior. Another fact is the year of birth carved on William C. Falkner's cemetery monument: 1825. Donald Philip Duclos, in his University of Michigan Ph.D. dissertation *SOS,* notes that the Colonel's age as recorded in the census of 1860 also makes 1825 his year of birth (p. 22). Duclos' thoroughgoing work is the best single source of information on the Old Colonel, and I am much indebted to it.
9	24	I: JMF, 17 Mar. 1965. Presumably drawing upon the account of J. W. T. Falkner, Jr., Murry Falkner's younger brother, Duclos suggests that the move must have come at an earlier point and that the family stayed longer in Knox County, moving on when they apparently failed to prosper there.
9	33	Duclos writes, apparently

Page Line

upon information provided by J. W. T. Falkner, Jr., that two more sons were later born to Caroline Falkner. (*SOS,* p. 23.) None are listed in the John Wesley Thompson Bible or the Lizzie H. Falkner Bible.

9 35 "Mississippi" Duclos suggests 1842 as Falkner's departure date but recounts a version of J. W. T. Falkner, Jr., in which the date is 1837. (*SOS,* pp. 23, 28.) Other Falkner family lore supplies the 1839–1840 date. (I: JMF, 25 Nov. 1965.)

10 8 Bondurant, pp. 114–15. This version was followed by Edmund Winston in "Life of Colonel Falkner: A Glorious Word Picture of the Founder of the G.M.&N. by One Who Has Studied His Life," *G.M.&.N. News,* V (Nov. 27, 1925), pp. 5–9. The Gulf, Mobile & Northern Railroad eventually absorbed the Old Colonel's railroad.

10 16 Robert Coughlan, *The Private World of William Faulkner* (New York, 1954), p. 27.

10 17 I: JMF, 17 Mar. 1965.

10 26 Winston, p. 5.

11 6 In other versions he walks directly to Pontotoc rather than Ripley and the little girl is Holland Pearce, his first wife. In another act of prescience, he vows someday to construct a railroad over every mile of his long walk from Middleton to Pontotoc. For accounts of William C. Falkner's trip to Mississippi, see Bondurant, pp. 114–15; Winston, p. 5; Coughlan, pp. 27–8; and *SOS,* pp. 23–8. Without citing a source, Maud Morrow Brown writes that "it has been pointed out that the Vances did not come to Ripley until five years after the latest possible date for William's arrival." In "William C. Falkner, Man of Legends," *The Georgia Review,* X (Winter 1956), p. 422.

11 20 See John K. Bettersworth, *Mississippi: A History* (Austin, 1959), pp. 173–5; James H. Malone, *The Chickasaw Nation* (Louisville, 1922), pp. 317–22; and Ward L. Miner, *The World of William Faulkner* (New York, 1959), pp. 20–6.

11 27 Robert Walker, as quoted in Bettersworth, p. 175.

12 10 As repr. in *RA,* 1 May 1886.

12 11 With this and other data, Duclos argues convincingly that it was Thomas A. Word whom the boy sought and found rather than John Wesley Thompson. The records of Tippah County—scanty though they are for that period—show that the first murder case in the county (which then included both Pontotoc and Ripley, the county seat) was not tried until 1845. (*SOS,* pp. 28–32.) T. F. Hickerson quotes Andrew Brown, unofficial historian of Tippah County, as follows: "I have heard the Thompson-jail at Pontotoc story all my life, but it now appears as just another legend. Judge William Anderson told me that there is no record of Thompson's being in jail at Pontotoc charged with murder, and that the Circuit Court records there are complete enough to prove this. Personally, I think Falkner came straight to Ripley, and that J. W. Thompson was practicing law there at the time (1841)." (Thomas Felix Hickerson, *The Falkner Feuds* [Chapel Hill, N.C., 1964], p. 10.)

12 20 Reuben Davis, *Recollections*

NOTES

Page	Line	
		of Mississippi and Mississippians, p. 19, repr. in Bettersworth, p. 271, and Miner, p. 27.
13	5	John Wesley Thompson was the son of Nathan Thompson, who had been born in New Jersey and apparently moved south as a young man. His bride, Esther Black, was the daughter of Thomas Black, of Lincoln County, North Carolina. They had moved to Haywood County (whence Joseph Falkner would later head for Missouri) by the time John Wesley Thompson was born on April 28, 1809, the eleventh child among six boys and six girls. Justiania Dickinson Word had been born in Surry County, North Carolina, on October 21, 1815. By 1828 her father, a professional man, was working in Georgia. *A Topographical Analysis of the State of Georgia for the Year 1828 to be Continued Annually* bears the name of Thomas A. Word. By 1833, when they had moved to Clarkesville, Georgia (about eighty miles due south of Haywood County), she wrote a very fair hand and showed a nice talent for copying out verses if not, indeed, for writing some of her own. On October 11, 1833, John Wesley Thompson sent her some very elaborately lettered verse in a bold, sweeping hand:

> *My lips are mute, my eyes are dry;*
> *But in my breast and in my brain*
> *Awake the pangs that pass not by*
> *The thought that ne'er shall sleep again.*
> *My soul nor deigns nor dares complain,*
> *Though grief and passion there rebel;*
> *I only know we loved in vain*
> *I only feel farewell! farewell!*

In the Grand Jury indictment, Ezekiel McGravy spelled out the charges against the accused and three alleged accomplices: Elbridge G. Harris, Cuthbert Word, and William Hamilton. The foreman and eighteen other good men and true of Habersham County charged them with murder, specifically,

> that the said John W. Thompson, with a certain knife of the value of one dollar, which he, the said John W. Thompson, in his right hand then and there had and held the said Calvin J. Hanks in and upon the belly of him said Calvin J. Hanks then and there feloniously, willfully, and of his malice aforethought did strike and thrust, giving to the said Calvin J. Hanks then & there with the knife aforesaid in and upon the belly of him, the said Calvin J. Hanks one Mortal Wound of the breadth of two inches and depth of six inches. . . . [FCVA. See also Maud Morrow Brown, "William C. Falkner," p. 422.]

Little can be inferred from this indictment other than that this was a crime of frontier violence. Word was, of course, the maiden name of Justiania Thompson, and Cuthbert would later appear as a given name in the Falkner family. Had Cuth-

Page *Line*

bert Word come to Thompson's aid, or had the new in-law been drawn into a Word quarrel? We shall probably never know. One interesting possibility is that this real crime in Georgia gave rise to the story of the apocryphal one in Mississippi. See *FIU*, pp. 131, 212.

13 9 Five days after the murder, Thompson addressed a letter to Justiania, underscoring her name with elaborate flourishes. "In the midst of darkness light springs up," he wrote, and went on to assure her that "the virulent edge of tyranny and oppression" would be blunted. She should let her spirits rise by recollecting that "not even this thick gloom that gathers round your affection [*sic*] lover can sink the spirit that loved well to range the fields of light." With a Miltonic flourish he assured her that his spirit could "burst its chains and fetters and pass the walls that would confine it and climb the battlements of Heaven where justice, truth and mercy hold their omnipotent sway."

One month later, he dispatched to "Mrs. J. D[ickinson] Thompson, Home" five quatrains which he had called "Words on Withered Flowers." The poem concluded,

> *And when in age we shall appear,*
> *Declining, like those gems of latest bloom,*
> *May we, our little bark together steer*
> *Till we anchor, in* that haven of eternal noon.

In mid-October, in a hand not nearly so bold as previously, he wrote that there would probably be time now for only one more exchange of letters. He knew she wished to see him but wanted to spare her "the pangs consequent on meeting in this place." He knew her feelings:

> I am as profoundly assured of the kindness, tenderness and constancy of your every affection; and your devotedness of heart as though you were my constant attendant and yet I hope it will be our lot to prove the length and breadth of these affections; but even if we should not; how short the span!

The closing lines—asking that she burn any of his letters she did not want to keep—sounded like those of a man making his last farewell: "There are a few [letters] that will serve you as a frail memento of him who found but one on earth that he loved without alloy and you are she." As things turned out, John and Justiania Thompson were to have nearly forty years "to prove the length and breadth" of their affections. At the trial's end, when the jurors filed back after their deliberations, Curtis Ledford, the foreman, rendered their verdict: "We, the jury, find the prisoner John W. Thompson Not Guilty of murder. So say we all." And thus ended the case of State v. J. W. Thompson. FCVA.

13 22 FCVA.

14 11 Robert Cantwell, Introduction to Col. William C. Falkner's *The White Rose of Memphis* (New York, 1953), p. ix.

14 20 Bondurant, pp. 115–16.

NOTES

Page *Line*

15 7 *RA,* 17 Jan. 1846. For a detailed account, see *SOS,* pp. 36–47.

15 18 *RA* account (as repr. in Holly Springs *Guard,* 9 Jan. 1946) indicates that the 1,000 citizens gathered there on the morning of November 1 derived as much enjoyment from the spectacle as any crowd at Tyburn. Wearing his shroud, the condemned man was brought from his cell at 10:45 A.M. and placed in a cart. Hymn-singing, a sermon, and prayers went on until 1:30 P.M., when the minister and the sheriff descended from the cart and it was driven out from under McCannon. The murderer's amanuensis had been unable to attend to this spectacle with the concentration of many of his fellow townsmen.

Years later one of his best friends, Col. Matthew G. Galloway, recalled,

> On the morning of the fateful day, he deposited the pamphlets on the stand erected for the gallows and commenced selling them. The atrocity of the murder had drawn to the hanging an immense crowd. The demand was so great for the books at $1.00 apiece that every hour or two, Falkner had to go to his hotel to deposit his money. By night he was exhausted and worn out. He returned to Memphis the next day, paid Gurion (who had allowed him to publish the pamphlet on credit), and since has never wanted a dollar. [Jackson (Miss.) *Clarion,* 28 Nov. 1889.]

One version of these events has it that McCannon cooperated with Falkner on condition that the proceeds go to his wife and children.

15 21 Falkner had set down McCannon's claims that he had administered whippings to several citizens of Tuscumbia County, Alabama, when he had lived there. The exchange of violent editorials continued until Ford concluded it with a final rebuttal on January 31, 1846.

15 30 For contrasts between the 1st and 2nd Mississippi regiments, see Cantwell's Introduction to *The White Rose of Memphis,* pp. ix–xii. Falkner had enlisted as a private but was soon commissioned. (See Maud Morrow Brown, "William C. Falkner," pp. 423–4.) The roster of the regiment as it was mustered at Vicksburg on July 13, 1848, lists the names Private Thomas Falkner and Private Joseph Falkner. Neither name appears in either of the family Bibles, but it seems likely that they were related to William C. Falkner. (*RA,* 23 Apr. 1887.) James Word Falkner would later on hold the rank of lieutenant colonel, C.S.A. (*Historical Catalogue of the University of Mississippi, 1849–1909* [Nashville, Tenn., 1910], p. 104.)

16 4 W. C. Falkner, *The Siege of Monterey* (Cincinnati, 1851), Canto I, stanza xi.

16 12 I: JMF, 21 Mar. 1965.

16 29 When a witness named J. R. Moore examined Hindman's revolver, he discovered that the ammunition was the wrong size and that the hammer had merely driven the cartridges further into the chambers. This circumstance, together with the false report misrepresenting Falk-

Page *Line*

ner's speech to Hindman, gave rise to a theory: someone had set Hindman up for the murder. There was no tangible supporting evidence for this, but it may have helped convince Falkner that a malevolent enemy was working against him. On several occasions he would refer to one. See *SOS,* pp. 71–88.

16 30 Although most biographers have written that the case was postponed until 1851, the records make it clear that it must have taken place in 1849 or 1850 at the latest. See *SOS,* p. 77.

17 11 I: SMW, 19 Mar. 1965. See also *SOS,* p. 76.

17 14 In his preface to *The Siege of Monterey* (p. 5), he wrote:

> I have been persecuted and hunted down like a savage wild beast, and at every corner, instead of a friendship sweet, I find deadly foes, ready to take advantage when they find me unarmed. When that unfortunate rencounter occurred between myself and Mr. H., which resulted in his death, he, I believe, was instigated by a certain cowardly clan to take my life, and not from malice which he bore against me. I found a certain individual going around the streets trying to turn public feeling against me, and taking every undue advantage of my situation that he could.

An uneasy peace settled down which lasted through the year 1850, but when Thomas Hindman learned that Falkner had applied for a pension as compensation for the wounds he had suffered in Mexico, Hindman wrote at length to Jacob Thompson, his Congressional representative, denouncing Falkner's claims as a fraud. There would be others who would come forward with similar evidence, he wrote, except that "many honest and respectable persons would probably be deterred by the known character of Falkner for violence—His Bowie Knife & Pistols are constantly about his person." (Thomas C. Hindman, Sr., to Jacob Thompson, 9 Mar. 1850, in *Mexican War Pension Records,* as quoted in *SOS,* p. 58.) Thompson set an investigation of sorts in motion, and Falkner's pension was temporarily suspended.

17 25 *SOS,* pp. 85–8.

17 30 *Ibid.,* p. 80. One legend has it that Falkner concealed his pistol in the folds of his cape and fired through the cape. Andrew Brown to T. F. Hickerson, 1 Nov. 1963, University of North Carolina (Chapel Hill) Library. Cf. the account in *UNV* of Colonel Sartoris' custom of wearing his derringer clamped to his wrist and concealed by his coat sleeve.

17 34 The enemy he had forgiven, a certain "Mr. P. of Ripley," had been "canvassing the streets, trying as before to excite the community against me," wrote Falkner in the preface to *The Siege of Monterey* (pp. 6–7), "and I was credibly informed that he even electioneered with the venire after they were summoned to try me." The deputy clerk of the court who recorded some of the proceedings was Richard J. Thurmond, would later figure impor-

NOTES

Page	Line	
		tantly in Falkner's career.
18	1	Cantwell, Introduction to, *White Rose of Memphis,* pp. xiv–xv.
18	5	It may have been because he felt threatened that he left for New York before the end of March. Thomas Hindman had been told that Falkner planned to stop in Washington to seek reinstatement of the Mexican War disability pension. On April 1, Hindman wrote to the Secretary of the Interior, asking that the suspension of the pension remain in force. This time his attack failed, however, for when Falkner returned to Ripley in mid-May the pension had been reinstated in March, 1861, with the onset of the Civil War.
18	10	Maud Morrow Brown, "William C. Falkner," p. 425. In his first canto, Falkner described the nearly 4,000-line work as a story of "love, war, blood-lust and glory." He stuck to eight-line stanzas throughout the poem, and the last of them he did entirely in ottava rima. This was not the only borrowing from Lord Byron. He apparently had an eye on both *Don Juan* and *Childe Harold's Pilgrimage* as he wrote. The Maid of Saragoza of the second work may well have given him the idea for the love story of Bibo and Isabel, two young Mexicans, which balances the epic description of the siege of Monterrey. His preface showed that he was ready to follow up immediately on any success *The Siege of Monterey* might enjoy. "I have written the history of the bloody battle of Buena Vista, in poetry, which will be published soon," he informed the reader, but it never appeared.
18	19	Canto I, stanza xxxi.
18	27	The most interesting features of *The Spanish Heroine* were autobiographical: a young man leaving home and mother to go out into the world, receiving balm for his discouragement from a sympathetic young girl, having unwanted gunplay forced upon him, and eventually marrying his love.
18	33	Judge J. W. T. Falkner, Jr., as cited in *SOS,* p. 87
19	2	Falkner was still, apparently, a voracious reader, a close student of the Bible and Shakespeare, and though he had never had the opportunity for the study of Latin and Greek, he made a careful study of the master pieces of these great literatures in translation, gaining in this way a fair knowledge and appreciation of Homer and Virgil, and other classical authors. [Bondurant, p. 116.]
19	8	Bondurant, pp. 117, 123.
19	10	*RA,* 1 May 1889.
19	12	C. J. Frederick to *MCA,* repr. in *RA,* 30 Apr. 1881. Also repr. in *SOS,* pp. 84–5.
19	22	*Ibid.* Nearly twenty-five years later, Falkner put the protagonist of *The White Rose of Memphis* in nearly identical jeopardy. But his hero approached the duel with the resolve that he would not fire at all at his man, who was his friend as well as his opponent. Cantwell suggests that this and other circumstances of the duel in *The White Rose of Memphis* are autobiographical, from the arrangements made by a "Colonel Callo-

Page	Line	
		way" to the hero's mistaken arrest, imprisonment, and illness which prevent the duel. He also writes that in his old age, Col. Galloway affirmed the truth of these fictional events. See Cantwell's introduction, pp. xx–xxi.
19	27	Falkner executed the same kind of documents as did Thompson in these transactions. One of Thompson's handwritten bills of sale reads,

> Received of John W. Thompson $200.00 in full payment for a Negro woman named Sarah supposed to be about fifty years of age which said Negro woman I warrant to be sound in mind and body and a slave for life. I also warrant and defend this title to said slave unto the said John W. Thompson his heirs free from the lawful claims of any and all persons whatever. In witness whereof I hereto set my hand and seal this the 27th day of July, 1849.
>
> A. Biggs

Three years later he had bought "Emily, a mulatto girl slave" for $600. Thompson transacted three more such items of business in the months immediately before the projected duels: on January 7, 1857, he bought an eleven-year-old boy called Casi for $600, and on March 15 he paid $1,250 for "a Negro boy Sam age about 38 years. . . ." In the third transaction, $1,350 changed hands. The slave sold was "my boy Wash." The date was March 21 and the seller was W. C. Falkner. Perhaps he was feeling the pinch of the depression of that year, but, if the duel was indeed set for April 1, Falkner may have provided ready cash for his wife against the possibility of his death.

Thompson did not neglect his religious duties for his financial ones. On October 24 he bought a handsome new book entitled *The Works of Flavius Josephus, the Learned and Authentic Jewish Historian. To Which are Added Three Dissertations, Concerning Jesus Christ, John The Baptist, James the Just, God's Command to Abraham, Etc.* Thompson may have had a taste for the Scriptures and exegetical writings, but his main purpose was fulfillment of his Christian duty. In his bold, flowing hand he wrote, "John W. T. Falkner's Book . . . bo't . . . by John W. Thompson for his adoptive son." *WFL*, p. 88.

Page	Line	
21	1	See Andrew Brown, "The First Mississippi Partisan Rangers, C.S.A.," *Civil War History*, I (Dec. 1955), p. 373; also Maud Morrow Brown, "William C. Falkner," p. 428.
21	9	On May 3, they were at Corinth with nearly a dozen other units like themselves. Falkner's brother James was a first lieutenant in another Ripley unit called the Liberty Guards, and Falkner's friend Robert J. Hill headed another group of his townsmen who called themselves the W. C. Falkner Rifles. (See *SOS*, pp. 123–7.) WF wrote to MC, "My great-grandfather, whose name I bear, was a considerable figure in his time and provincial milieu. He was

NOTES

Page	Line	Note
		prototype of John Sartoris: raised, organised, paid the expenses of and commanded the 2nd Mississippi Infantry, 1861–1862, etc." (*FCF,* p. 66.)
21	14	The regiment was described in one dispatch as "in the most perfect drill. . . ." The newspaper correspondent reported that Falkner "though exceedingly strict with his men, is universally popular." Memphis *Appeal,* 26 July 1861.
21	16	*Ibid.*
21	33	See Lenoir Chambers, *Stonewall Jackson,* I (New York, 1959), pp. 356–92.
21	36	R. F. Nichols, ed., *Battles and Leaders of the Civil War,* I (New York, 1884–88), pp. 232–4.
22	9	Chambers, pp. 373, 377, 471.
22	19	Dunbar H. Rowland, "Military History of Mississippi," *Mississippi Official and Statistical Record* (Jackson, 1906), p. 430.
22	23	*Southern Historical Society Papers,* XIX, pp. 90 ff.
22	31	Memphis *Appeal,* 7 Aug. 1861; see *SOS,* pp. 131–4.
23	7	Dispatch in *The Mississippian,* repr. in Bondurant, p. 117.
23	8	Dunbar H. Rowland, *History of Mississippi: The Heart of the South,* II, p. 45, cited in Victor Hoar, "Colonel William C. Falkner in the Civil War," *The Journal of Mississippi History,* XXVII (Feb. 1965), p. 47.
23	15	Augustus L. P. Varian, *Old Ord's War Journal,* ed. by Andrew Brown, unpubl., Dept. of Archives and History, Jackson, Miss. This entry by Varian, a sergeant in Company B of the 2nd Mississippi, is dated July 21, the day of the battle. Since Johnston was well occupied during the day and called into conference by Jefferson Davis at 11 P.M. to discuss pursuit of McDowell's fleeing army, one wonders how he would have had time to dictate such a report and how Sgt. Varian would have learned of it so quickly. See Chambers, I, p. 388.
23	19	Bondurant, p. 117.
23	20	*SOS,* p. 133.
23	30	Falkner's specialty was the "spiral movement," in which the regiment, formed in columns of four, "was 'wound up' like the mainspring of a watch or the coil of a serpent, until the head of the column reached the centre and the whole command stood completely coiled around." (Dr. Dwight T. Witherspoon, "Unique Army Formation," repr. in *SOS,* pp. 135–6.) Falkner's favorite use of the maneuver came at Sunday morning services, when the thousand men of the regiment—in dress uniforms with fixed bayonets—would march out following the regimental band Falkner had organized and assiduously drilled. But few men of the 2nd seem to have enjoyed it. The chaplain felt it made the services too stiff and formal and finally persuaded the Colonel to abandon it.
23	37	They would enjoy the visit, he thought, for there were frequent parties and entertainments. A young woman who recorded some of them in her diary also recalled Falkner's hat, an old one "used during the Mexican War, with two bullet holes in the brim." (Enemies at home in Ripley declared that the holes were in the back.) Diary of Catherine Thomas Mer-

Page	*Line*	
		kell, cited in Maud Morrow Brown, "William C. Falkner," p. 429.
24	1	Bondurant, p. 118.
24	3	*SOS,* p. 137.
24	6	He was thinking, too, of the next election of officers, for on January 3, 1862, he wrote to Gen. S. L. Cooper. He was personally acquainted with Pres. Jefferson Davis, he said, who "is well aware of the fact that an officer who manages volunteers according to that discipline which is absolutely necessary to make them effective is not likely to stand much chance for re-election, when opposed by some one who promises to let each man do as he pleases. This being the case with myself; I would most respectfully ask the President for a commission in the Provisional Army." Old Records Section, Adjutant General's Office (National Archives, Washington), repr. in *SOS,* p. 139.
24	7	On his way to rejoin his regiment in April, Falkner made a side-trip to Richmond, where he gave his Congressman, J. W. Clapp, three letters recommending him for promotion to brigadier general. He asked that Clapp forward them to Davis with his own recommendation. One read, "Col. Falkner is brave, energetic, and temperate, and I consider him otherwise well qualified for this position." Dated 22 March 1862, it was signed by Thomas C. Hindman, Jr. Apparently, the feud was indeed over. Old Records Section, Falkner File, repr. in *SOS,* p. 143. See also Hoar, pp. 49–50.
24	15	Maud Morrow Brown, "William C. Faulkner," p. 429.
24	18	See Andrew Brown, as quoted in Hickerson, p. xi.
24	26	As quoted in Bondurant, p. 119; see also *SOS,* p. 145.
25	20	Old Records Section, Falkner File, Falkner to Hon. Thelan, 7 Feb. 1863. Repr. in *SOS,* p. 167.
25	22	"It is very mortifying for an officer of Spirit to be forced into retirement," Falkner wrote Davis, "while the clash of arms is resounding on all sides. I was cast aside simply because I done my whole duty, and I appeal to you . . . not to suffer a faithful officer to be discarded when he has been tried and not found wanting." Old Records Section, Falkner File, Falkner to Jefferson Davis, 16 May 1863, repr. in *SOS,* p. 149.
25	24	Now that the conscription law was passed, these new partisan units had a certain attraction, particularly "in such border regions as North Mississippi and West Tennessee, which after the summer of 1862 were overrun by both the Union and Confederate armies but controlled by neither. To add to the confused situation, the Secretary of War did not issue regulations under which rangers were to be paid for captured munitions until the spring of 1863. In Mississippi, the ironic result was that the rangers, many of whom had enlisted because of the prospect of what might be called legitimate plunder, gained little or no profit from their activities." Andrew Brown, "First Mississippi Partisan Rangers," pp. 371–2.
26	2	See Andrew Brown, "First Mississippi Partisan Rangers," p. 375, and *SOS,* p. 153.
26	6	Old Records Section, Falkner

NOTES

Page	Line	
		File, letter to Hon. Thelan, 7 Feb. 1863, repr. in *SOS*, p. 167.
26	10	See Andrew Brown, "First Mississippi Partisan Rangers," p. 372.
26	12	"75 Years Ago," *MCA*, 11 Aug. 1937.
26	16	See Andrew Brown, "First Mississippi Partisan Rangers," p. 377. Some suggested that Falkner staged the daring attack in pursuit of the fame that would lead to the general's stars that obsessed him.
26	23	*War of the Rebellion: A Compilation of the Union and Confederate Armies*, 1, XVII, 1, p. 42. See also *SOS*, pp. 157–62.
26	27	A dispatch of September 6 from Ripley reported that "Yesterday, a confederate company of Cavalry, under W. L. Dons ambushed a party of 100 Yankees near Chewala, and killed and wounded 40 of them. Col. Falkner, of the 2nd Mississippi Regiment, continued doing good work." (Repr. in *MCA*, 11 Aug. 1937.) Falkner reported that on the nineteenth the regiment had been attacked by Federal skirmishers, whereupon he had charged a thousand of the enemy, who fled, "and I am happy to say that with few exceptions my men behaved very well." (*War of the Rebellion*, 1, XVII, 1, p. 138.) On September 30 he had two major generals—Earl Van Dorn and Sterling Price—home for Sunday dinner in Ripley to decide where their forces would link up. (Samuel A. Agnew, *Diary*, Oct. 1, 1862, quoted in *SOS*, p. 162.) Two days later, Falkner was ordered to destroy track on the Mobile & Ohio Railroad. This he did successfully, thus helping to save the retreating Van Dorn. (Repr. in *MCA*, 6 Sept. 1937.)
26	34	On November 22, a force of 400 Federals nearly caught him thirteen miles south of Ripley. But again he showed he was on home ground: "Falkner with about 100 men escaped by dint of the hardest running, going in direction of Holly Springs." The Federal officer in charge noted with some satisfaction, "I consider Col. Falkner's regiment now broken beyond any hope of reorganization, and a great source of petty annoyances to our forces entirely removed." *War of the Rebellion*, 1, XVII, 1, p. 490, quoted in *SOS*, pp. 163–4.
27	7	Minutes of the annual meeting of the Congregation of College Church, 5 Jan. 1863, repr. in Maud Morrow Brown, "The War Comes to College Hill," *The Journal of Mississippi History*, XVI (Jan. 1954), p. 25.
27	16	Old Records Section, Falkner File, Falkner to Hon. Thelan, 7 Feb. 1863, repr. in *SOS*, p. 166. Gen. Johnston had replied, "I wrote to Gen. Cooper, such a recommendation as I thought due to a Col. equal to the *best* in the Army of Northern Virginia." When Falkner did receive authorization to reconstitute his regiment, the satisfaction was soured by the fact that he reported to Brig. Gen. James R. Chalmers. "I cannot help feeling that great injustice has been done me," he complained to Congressman Clapp. "The sting of mortification is not owing to the fact that I am to be commanded

Page *Line*

by Gen. C. He is a brave man and efficient officer, but is my junior in age and not my seignor [*sic*] in service. . . . He has been brig gen 12 months while I have been neglected and ignored by the govt. . . ."Andrew Brown, "First Mississippi Partisan Rangers," p. 383.

27 38 See D. Alexander Brown, *Grierson*'s *Raid* (Urbana, Ill., 1954). Andrew Brown wrote:

> It appears that Falkner's failure was as a brigade commander rather than as a Colonel of Partisan Rangers. He made no report on the affair, and Chalmers' report was confined to a terse statement of losses. But whether or not he was at fault, the defeat crushed Falkner militarily so completely that he never recovered. Soon afterward he reported sick, and except for short periods, was never again in active charge of the regiment. ["First Mississippi Partisan Rangers," p. 38.]

28 4 "April" *MCA,* 22 Apr. 1938.

28 6 When the 9th Illinois Cavalry burned New Albany, twenty miles south of Ripley, on the fourteenth, 200 of Falkner's Rangers were sent in pursuit along with another, separate detachment of 400 more men. Col. William Boyle led the larger group hard and fast after the raiders. Then he left word he would wait so they could join forces in the pursuit. Falkner never appeared, and Boyle received word that "Colonel Falkner could not for some reason proceed beyond Ripley." The enemy's lead now increased, and, with the possibility of numerical superiority gone, Boyle called off the pursuit. He later reported, "It is believed that with the cooperation of Colonel Falkner the expedition would have resulted most successfully." (See Andrew Brown, "First Mississippi Partisan Rangers," pp. 385–6.) Although there appears to be some question whether Falkner actually was with the detachment of his Rangers on that mission, he received a full measure of blame for its performance.

28 10 *Confederate Military Records in Possession of the War Department,* Papers of Confederate Notables (National Archives, Washington, D.C.) James R. Chalmers Papers, Falkner to Chalmers, 20 July 1863, repr. in *SOS,* pp. 175–6, 437–8. Also Andrew Brown, "First Mississippi Partisan Rangers," p. 386.

28 20 Andrew Brown, "First Mississippi Partisan Rangers," pp. 387–8.

28 23 Old Records Section, Falkner File, letter of resignation and certificate of Dr. W. D. Carter. See *SOS,* pp. 177–8. In the postwar oratory to come, Falkner's career would sometimes be romantically inflated. How did it actually measure up? In one assessment, it was

> the career of a colonel who started brilliantly but was unable to live up to his early promise. As a recruiter he had few equals in the Confederate service, but except at First Manassas he never attained distinction as a combat officer. Probably the best explanation is that he was a

NOTES

Page	Line	
		man whose reach always exceeded his grasp; his self-assurance and almost Napoleonic ambition led him into undertakings that he lacked the means to carry to fruition. In spite of his pride, his hypersensitiveness, and his somewhat arrogant manner, he was idolized by many of his soldiers, but with the notable exception of Joe Johnston in Virginia he apparently never was in the confidence of his superior officers. [Andrew Brown, "First Mississippi Partisan Rangers," pp. 388–9.]
28	36	See Robert Selph Henry, *"First with the Most" Forrest* (Indianapolis, 1944), p. 210. There were some similarities in Falkner's and Forrest's backgrounds. Called by one of his superiors "the greatest soldier the war produced," Forrest was pronounced by another "the greatest soldier of his time." Henry, quoting Gens. Dabney H. Maury and Joseph E. Johnston, p. 21. See also pp. 13–14.
29	3	Re-formed, it would remain in Forrest's command for the rest of the war, though it would sometimes still be referred to as "Colonel Falkner's 1st Mississippi Cavalry." See D. Alexander Brown, pp. 165–6; Andrew Brown, "First Mississippi Partisan Rangers," pp. 392–3, and Andrew Brown, "Sol Street, Confederate Partisan Leader," *The Journal of Mississippi History,* XXI (July 1959), pp. 170–1.
29	32	Henry, p. 304.
29	35	*War of the Rebellion,* 1, XXXIX, p. 171, repr. in Henry, p. 297.

Page	Line	
30	2	*Ibid.,* Ser. No. 78, p. 123, repr. in Henry, p. 307.
30	10	Andrew Brown, "First Mississippi Partisan Rangers," p. 396.
30	25	See Henry, pp. 328–44, and Andrew Brown, "First Mississippi Partisan Rangers," p. 397.
30	35	According to the rest of the story he thereupon attacked that very night, and thus "Forrest had taken advantage of the opportunity offered him by Nate Falkner and his mule." Judge John W. T. Falkner, Jr., and John W. T. Falkner, III, as reported in *SOS,* pp. 179–80.
31	5	As quoted in Henry, p. 338.
31	12	The Oxford post commandant made an official report of what had happened:

> On the morning of the 22nd . . . Maj. Gen. A. J. Smith . . . occupied the town with a large force of white and black troops . . . burning 34 stores and business houses, courthouse, Masonic Hall, 2 fine large hotels, besides carpenter, blacksmith, and other shops; also 5 fine dwelling houses, among the latter that of Hon. Jacob Thompson. General Smith in person superintended the burning. He refused to allow the citizens to remove anything of value from their burning dwellings. General Smith's conduct, also his staff and men, was brutal in the extreme, they having been made mad with whiskey for the occasion. The soldiers were licensed for any crime, such as robbery, rapine, theft, and arson.

Page	Line	
		[*War of the Rebellion,* I, XXIX, p. 400, Ser. No. 77.]
31	18	As one writer summed up, "The burning of Oxford resulted from cumulative hatred and frustration caused by the alleged Fort Pillow massacre and the failure of the Federal expeditions to eliminate the abhorrent Forrest. . . . It was probable, moreover, that hatred of Jacob Thompson acted as an additional motive. The people of Oxford and vicinity had from an early period of the war exhibited deep hatred of Yankees. That fact may also have supplied motivation for the burning of Oxford." Howard T. Dimick, "Motives for the Burning of Oxford, Mississippi," *The Journal of Mississippi History,* VIII (July 1946), p. 120.
31	21	Thomas Jordan and J. P. Pryor, *The Campaigns of Lieutenant General N. B. Forrest and of Forrest*'s *Cavalry,* pp. 550–1, as quoted in Henry, p. 341.
31	26	*War of the Rebellion,* Ser. No. 104, pp. 1289–90.
31	32	By February 7, 1863, his property had been confiscated and his family had been driven away—if his report to Mr. Thelan was accurate. Very little of his other assets can have remained, and there is no legend in the Falkner family of buried silver. A year later things were much worse. The whole countryside had a ravaged look. Tippah County was "rough, hopeless, God-forsaken" as it unfolded before the eyes of one of A. J. Smith's brigade commanders. "Its hills were steep, its mud was deep, its houses and farms were poor, its streams torrents of bottomless muddy water. . . ." Col. George E. Waring, Jr., *Whip and Spur,* pp. 109–10, quoted in Henry, p. 223.
32	2	This strategically located city was more than a base of Federal operations; the "significant role of Memphis in the war was its position as the depot for most of the contraband trade between North and South." (Gerald M. Capers, Jr., *The Biography of a River Town: Memphis: Its Heroic Age* [Chapel Hill, N.C., 1939], p. 152.) The Confederates needed medical supplies and munitions of all kinds, whereas the Federal government hoped to procure as much cotton as possible for shipment to the waiting mills abroad to prevent European intervention.
32	9	*SOS,* pp. 180–1.
32	16	Maud Morrow Brown, "William C. Falkner," p. 433. In an undated lengthy and expert critique of this article, Andrew Brown wrote T. F. Hickerson, "There is no doubt about Falkner and [R. J.] Thurmond being engaged in blockade-running. . . ." University of North Carolina (Chapel Hill) Library.
33	22	Of the 78,000 Mississippians who fought in the Confederate army, more than a third were killed or died of wounds or disease. In 1866, one-fifth of the state revenues was reportedly appropriated to supply artificial limbs to those maimed in the war. (James Wilford Garner, *Reconstruction in Mississippi* [New York, 1901], pp. 122–3.) Of all the smartly uniformed young University Greys who had marched off in '61, only 24

NOTES

Page Line

were still members of the unit at the end. A total of 35 men had been enrolled during the war. Thirty-eight were dead of wounds or disease or were missing. The figure on the company roll for "losses from all causes"—including transfer, discharge, and resignation, as well as battle losses—was 111. *(OXE,* 18 Dec. 1919.)

33 24 See Garner, p. 122.

34 2 W. S. Nielson was one citizen of Oxford who was faced with the problem of starting his business up again—finding the capital and credit to stock his department store and survive while he rebuilt a profitable trade. One of his sons recalled his first step. "I can well remember seeing him and my oldest brother go into the garden on a dark night and by the light of a lantern dig up gold which he had buried in the early days of the war. This was the reason we weathered the war, a thing very few Southern businesses did." Like Nielson in Oxford, W. C. Falkner in Ripley managed to provide for his family and still have considerable resources left over. *OXE,* 29 Oct. 1936.

34 13 Coughlan, p. 36.

34 16 See Bondurant, p. 123.

34 19 His imagination untrammeled as ever, Falkner presented in the fifth scene "The Battle of Manassas. Thrilling scenes on the bloody field." *RA,* 1 Mar. 1883.

34 38 The world of politics was turned upside down for men like Falkner. By the fall of 1867, the registration rolls of the state showed 46,636 white voters and 60,167 colored voters. When the general election of 1869 was held, the Jackson *Clarion* estimated that 15,000 white voters were disfranchised, 1,000 of them in Tippah County. Garner, p. 246.

35 16 Judge J. W. T. Falkner, Jr., as quoted in *SOS,* p. 24.

35 22 Most had been devastated. In a typical example, 30 of the 100 miles of the Memphis & Tennessee Railroad, running from Memphis to Grenada, were serviceable. Garner, pp. 142–4.

35 26 Garner, pp. 288–9.

35 35 In 1856, John Wesley Thompson and Dr. John Young Murry (J. W. T. Falkner's future father-in-law) were among twenty-two men who incorporated the Ripley Railroad Company. Although further plans were made, nothing more was done. Andrew Brown, quoted in Hickerson, p. 30.

36 2 *SOS,* pp. 197–8. On June 3, 1872, a quarter-million-dollar bond issue was floated to pay for rails and rolling stock. On the same day, the Colonel executed an agreement with the road whereby he paid $500 for first-class tickets over the entire line for himself, Mrs. Falkner, all his children (including the unborn), their spouses, and their children—for a period of fifty years. Brown, in Hickerson, p. 30. See also *SOS,* p. 198.

36 7 Perrin Lowrey, Sr., to JB, 12 May 1966.

36 11 The legislative act had stipulated standard-gauge, which meant fifty-six-pound rail. The narrow-gauge Ripley Railroad had been built with thirty-six-pound rail—sufficient, perhaps, for Tippah County freight and passenger traffic but not for the letter of the law. Moreover, though the line extended for more

Page	Line	
		than twenty-five miles, only twenty-one of them were within the state of Mississippi. See Jackson *Clarion,* 20 Mar. 1873, and Garner, p. 288.
36	13	The New York company was later replaced by Richard T. Wilson, who was acting for a combine connected to the expanding Pennsylvania Railroad. Working for or negotiating with Richard T. Wilson or his Southern Security Company was the former secretary of the Ripley Railroad Company, Mr. R. J. Thurmond. Within a few years he would have some very interesting results to show. See Brown in Hickerson, pp. 30–1; *SOS,* pp. 194–205; and Thomas L. McHaney, "The Image of the Railroad in the Novels of William Faulkner, 1926–1942," unpubl. M.A. thesis, U. of N.C., 1962, pp. 42–3.
36	16	"fellow" Sallie F. Burns to JMF, 21 Nov. 1964. Courtesy JMF.
36	22	On July 15, 1870, Lizzie gave birth to twins. One of them, Raleigh W. Falkner, died the next day. His sister, Mary J. Falkner, survived him by twelve days.
36	31	Remembered by his novelist great-grandson as being a kind of Scots patriarch, Dr. Murry was a physician and businessman who had other interests as well. He was a devout Methodist and Democrat, attending Sunday School conventions of the former and political conventions of the latter, and holding high offices in both. Sallie Murry's mother was a Holcombe whose great-grandfather, Philip, fought in the Revolution as a private in a regiment of South Carolina militia. Courtesy Elizabeth Weir McPherson and Dorothy Oldham.
37	1	On January 16, 1875, Sallie Murry Falkner gave birth to a son who died the same day, but the other two children were strong and growing.
37	8	In February, 1878, Thurmond replaced R. T. Wilson as trustee of the railroad. One-third of the bonds had been bought by two fellow townsmen, C. L. Harris and Chesley Hines. Little was revealed about the details of the transactions between Thurmond, Wilson, and the combine, but an air of legerdemain hung over the whole business for years thereafter. See Brown in Hickerson, p. 31, *SOS,* p. 202, and McHaney, "Image of the Railroad," p. 43.
37	11	The choice for arbitrator was J. J. Guyton, a former partner of both the major stockholders, according to rumor, in that conjectural firm which trafficked in contraband in Memphis. But Falkner felt he still had the advantage, for, after all, his adjutant in the old regiment had been this same J. J. Guyton. See *SOS,* p. 204.
37	27	I: EF, 11 Sept. 1962. JMF fixes the death at the University of Virginia in 1872. (See also J. W. T. Falkner, III, in *SOS,* pp. 345–6.) There is no record of Henry Falkner at the University of Virginia, and Alabama Leroy insisted that her brother was a complete gentleman who died of a ruptured appendix. Two facts are verifiable: William Henry Falkner died on January 5, 1878, and his body lies in a plain marble vault in the family plot in the Ripley

NOTES

Page	Line	
		cemetery. Engraved on that expanse of dull, weathered stone in mute reticence is the single word "Henry."
37	31	See *Dictionary of American Biography,* XVIII (New York, 1928–58), p. 78.
38	6	That he knew a good deal of law was evident from his satiric courtroom scenes. Quotations and allusions by his characters indicated the range of his other reading. He knew the *Iliad* through Pope, apparently, and also Pope's major essays in verse. There were other allusions to Dickens, Milton, Swift, and Defoe. The most numerous references were to Shakespeare, and a strong and unsurprising taste for Byron was indicated. There were other references to Twain, Cervantes, and Scott. See H. Edward Richardson, *William Falkner: The Journey to Self-Discovery* (Columbia, Mo., 1969), pp. 11–14.
38	18	Harry and Lottie Wallingford and their friend Eddie make the long trip to Memphis by foot after the death of Mrs. Wallingford. They are assaulted by Ben Bowles but they are also helped by kind persons, and once in Memphis, Harry and Lottie are taken in by a lawyer who is a relative. There is also a kindly father-surrogate who provides for Eddie until he is trained as a physician. Due to the machinations of Bowles and his mistress and the complicity of others, Harry is turned against Eddie and challenges him to a duel. Eddie accepts, knowing that he will never fire at his friend. Eddie's illness and false imprisonment prevent the duel.
38	21	Van Wyck Brooks, *The Times of Melville and Whitman* (New York, 1947), p. 335.
38	24	Although Falkner handled Negro dialect well, his dialogue tended often to be stagy and stilted, his narration and exposition wooden and verbose. It was the kind of writing found in many romances of the time, couched in the kind of style burlesqued by Nathanael West in *A Cool Million.* Falkner employed outlandish Dickensian grotesques and comic passages indebted to the frontier humorists. He used letters to help him convey information, moved from past to present, and shifted point of view from omniscient narrator to I-narrator (who was also omniscient) whenever it suited him. He made use of the devices of coincidence, withheld information, and mystery. Sometimes he ended his chapters abruptly and amateurishly; at other times he skillfully gained suspense in shifting from one sequence to the next. And throughout there was a strong narrative drive that even the contemporary reader is likely to feel.
38	37	Criticism has on the whole been kind to *The White Rose of Memphis.* A friend of the author wrote in her review that it was "a beautiful story, charmingly told, and haloed with an atmosphere of purity and sweetness." *(RA,* 7 Jan. 1882.) Twentieth-century observers have seen radically different things in the novel. One has posited a latent level of psychological aberrations and incest motifs which prefigures similar interests in the work of the Colonel's great-grandson. (See *SOS,* pp. 231–

Page	Line	
		3.) To its strongest adherent, the "baroque situations of the novel took on an imaginative strangeness, a kind of grandeur, linking them to the great works of fiction." And though its greatness was there only intermittently or potentially, *The White Rose of Memphis* was "a wonderful novel." (Cantwell, Introduction, pp. xxv–xxvi.)
39	6	*RA,* 10 Dec. 1881. In 1909, twenty years after the author's death, the publisher's preface to a thirty-fifth edition from new plates would record sales of his novel to that time at 160,000 copies. (Cantwell, Introduction, p. xxvi.) The success of the novel was the occasion of some extremely flattering publicity for Falkner which helped to magnify his public stature in north Mississippi and the surrounding area. *RA* reprinted letters from the Memphis *Appeal* which described his generosity, elaborated upon his wartime career, and enlarged upon his material success. (*RA,* 16 Apr. 1881.) A letter from C. J. Frederick, Falkner's law partner, called Falkner an acute judge of men. He was also unaffected: "Among strangers he is as bashful as a girl of sixteen, but among old and familiar friends he is lively, vivacious and most interesting, possessing a charming disposition and fascinating manner." (Memphis *Appeal,* 15 Apr. 1881, repr. in *RA,* 30 Apr. 1881.)
39	18	Winston, p. 7.
39	25	In the first person, Falkner introduces Mr. Barnard, a near-centenarian, who narrates the sad tale of his young friend Olivia Delroy. The fruit of a secret marriage between Kate Delroy and a vanished Englishman, Olivia is orphaned an hour after her birth. She is raised by the Falkland family virtually as a sister to their son, Oscar. But the two fall in love, a love shadowed only by Olivia's grief at her supposed illegitimate birth. Mysterious hostile forces at work and a false accusation of murder move the plot along. Falkner also uses satire of the legal process for comic relief. Though Oscar is acquitted, Olivia falls into melancholy at her own plight. She goes to England and finds her father, leaving Oscar behind to moon (like Benjy in *S&F*) over one of her little satin shoes, which he carries about in his bosom. William C. Falkner, *The Little Brick Church* (New York, 1882).
40	4	Ripley *Sentinel,* 26 Oct. 1882.
40	10	The travelers sailed on June 2, 1883, to visit England, France, Germany, Belgium, Holland, Switzerland, and Italy. Falkner's letters from famous sights and cities became a standard feature of the *Sentinel.* There were enough letters so that they continued to appear for five months after the announcement of the travelers' return in the issue of October 6.
41	13	Apparently almost everyone approved, not only then, when the rococo was smart and the Victorian was synonymous with elegance, but even fifty years later. One writer looking back to the time when this marvelous creation emerged as the carpenters and painters and plumbers cleared away, said, "When finished it was a work

NOTES

Page	Line	
		of art, with its gables, balconies, iron stairway, and artistic interior decorating." *MCA,* 7 Mar. 1937.
41	19	Col. J. L. Power in *RA,* 2 May 1885.
42	19	Under the original charter, the state had donated property to the railroad. When the company failed, many homesteaders had occupied and improved most of the land in compliance with subsequent laws. Ultimately, Mississippi Sen. Edward C. Walthall amended a bill so as to give the previously granted Federal lands to the railroad *except* for those occupied by homesteaders who had fully complied with the law. Construction would cost more because of added land purchases and more circuitous routes, but the construction would go on. James Hutton Lemly, *The Gulf, Mobile and Ohio* (Homewood, Ill., 1953), pp. 286–7.
43	6	J. W. T. Falkner, Jr., in *SOS,* pp. 299–301. In another version, "Mr. Thurmond went to Col. Falkner with a 'give or take' proposition. Col. Falkner, however, had anticipated it, and arranged for a $75,000 loan from a Memphis commission house." Winston, p. 9.
43	10	Falkner had told the eager and enthusiastic citizens that he could run the railroad there if they provided land for rights of way and terminals and $10,000. The first two items were no problem, but they were able to raise only $5,000. Two committeemen were appointed to go to Ripley. One began "timorously" to explain the difficulties they had encountered: "The Colonel meanwhile sat with folded arms steadily and inscrutably regarding the spokesman. When the climax was reached with the unmaterialized five thousand and the speaker's voice had almost lasped into a whisper, [and] the Colonel's eyes were blazing and boring through him, then suddenly he relaxed, gazed dreamily into a shadowed corner of the room and finally bending across the little table between himself and his visitors, he said, 'By G—, I'll do it. I always liked Pontotoc, and you are going to get the railroad.' " Then he went on to tell them about his youthful hardships, his resting on the tavern steps in Pontotoc, and the appearance of the little girl who later became his wife. "A Dream of Service Come True," Pontotoc *Sentinel,* probably by Edmund Winston and a co-editor named Potter; repr. in *The G.M.&N. News,* 21 Dec. 1923, and in *SOS,* pp. 43–5.
43	16	Some thought the leasing would provide better conditions for the convicts and encouragement to enterprise as well as profit, but one commentator wondered "how a system so barbarous could have been tolerated in any Christian community. It was evidently the product of human rapacity grafted upon the conditions that a defunct slavery had left behind it." J. H. Jones, "Penitentiary Reform in Mississippi," *Publications of the Mississippi Historical Society,* VI, pp. 111–28, as quoted in Lemly, p. 290.
43	18	Eight miles southeast of Ripley, Falkner went out of his way to oblige the sons of a departed friend, Gen. M. P.

Page	*Line*	
		Lowrey, who had founded a small college there. For $3,000, Col. Falkner put a jog in the line and Blue Mountain College was on the Gulf & Ship Island Railroad. Mrs. Perrin Lowrey, Sr., to JB, 11 May 1966.
43	25	"deal" *OXE,* 5 May 1887.
43	25	"extensively" On his way back from a business trip to the Gulf Coast, Falkner had stopped off to visit Jefferson Davis and his family at Beauvoir. *RA,* 19 Feb. 1887.
43	28	*RA,* 2 July 1887.
43	32	The Jackson *State Ledger* quoted an indictment of the convict leasing system which had appeared in the Nashville *Banner.* Repr. in *RA,* 23 July 1887.
44	2	See Stewart H. Holbrook, *The Story of American Railroads* (New York, 1947), p. 145. See also Albert D. Kirwan, *The Revolt of the Rednecks: Mississippi Politics, 1876–1925* (Louisville, 1951), p. 55.
44	5	Actually, wrote Kirwan, "compared to the treatment accorded these convicts . . . slavery was a mild and humane institution." P. 168.
44	24	It was, of course, no Penn Central system, for the "right of way had been chosen in an attempt to keep as many farmer shippers happy as possible and in an effort to keep expenses at a minimum. The Colonel once boasted that it was the cheapest railroad ever built, and later users have been inclined to agree with him. Instead of running as straight as possible, the road tried to stay on top of the ridges of the region in an effort to avoid the problems and expenses of bridging streams or bottom lands. In the light of later experience, it appears remarkable that this line was built at all. . . ." Lemly, p. 289.
44	31	Robert Cantwell, "The Falkners: Recollections of a Gifted Family," repr. in Frederick J. Hoffman and Olga Vickery, eds., *William Faulkner: Three Decades of Criticism* (New York, 1960), p. 55.
44	35	*RA,* 27 Oct. 1888.
44	36	Perrin Lowrey, Sr., to JB, 12 May 1966.
44	38	*RA,* 1 Dec. 1888.
45	2	*RA,* 22 Nov. 1888.
45	3	A business acquaintance from Pontotoc recalled the last time he saw Falkner, "seated just within the doorway of his home in Ripley, a silent, motionless figure gazing abstractedly in the direction of the two thin bands of steel that marked the line of his railroad, passing a short distance from his residence." "A Dream of Service Come True," as repr. in *SOS,* p. 445.
45	11	Although many farmers trusted Falkner as a man, there were increasingly obvious reasons why many Mississippians might not trust the Gulf & Ship Island Railroad. It had been hit by two damaging scandals. The first, in 1887, involved a cover-up of indebtedness to the state. (See Kirwan, pp. 54–7.) Things were made worse upon the breaking of the second scandal on May 1, 1889, when Gen. Wirt Adams, postmaster of Jackson and one of the directors of the railroad, died on a city street in a duel precipitated by a political argument. (Lemly, p. 288.)
45	28	According to one business as-

NOTES

Page	Line	
		sociate, Falkner told Baldwin "the road had great prospective advantage by building through a country so nicely timbered . . . a belt of what they called gumtree some thirty or forty miles, then into a pine belt. . . ." Heman Clark, as quoted in *SOS,* p. 312. Cf. "The Bear" and "Delta Autumn."
45	34	*The Southern Sentinel,* 6 June 1889.
46	2	Winston, p. 9.
46	3	"day" Cantwell, Introduction, *White Rose of Memphis,* p. xxiv.
46	5	*OXE,* 29 Aug. 1889.
46	12	The sculptor was C. Y. Rogers, who lived in Grand Junction, Tennessee, twenty miles west of Middleton on the road to Memphis. He made a model of plaster or wax which was sent to Italy. Mrs. Beulah May Price in *SOS,* pp. 338–9.
46	20	*SOS,* p. 319. This material was supplied to Duclos by Andrew Brown, who was connected to both principals in the feud in that Thurmond was his paternal uncle and Pink Smith, Falkner's zealous friend and advocate, was his maternal uncle. Brown writes that he began investigating the murder with a bias toward Falkner but soon began to see that "Both men had a point." (*SOS,* p. 332.) In "Testimonials re: The Falkner Feuds" (n.d., n.p.), Hickerson quotes Brown's reaction to "The Falkner Feuds" in a letter dated 17 April 1964. Brown wrote in part: "I am somewhat handicapped in judging it because, as you well know, I am so close to it that it is difficult at times to see the woods for the trees, and also I am very strongly on the Thurmond side in the Falkner-Thurmond business, just as you are." Hickerson also states that J. W. T. Falkner was fined for committing assault and battery upon Joe Brown, Andrew Brown's father, in the aftermath of Col. Falkner's death. (See Hickerson, p. 19 and *passim*; also *SOS,* p. 328.)
46	22	Four years younger, Thurmond had been born in northwestern North Carolina, and had moved with his family to Grand Junction, Tennessee, then to Ripley. He made his living from the law for a time as circuit clerk of the county. His participation in the war seems to have been desultory and uncertain, though it was sufficient to earn him the largely honorific title of "Captain." (See Hickerson, pp. 5–6, 9.) One remote relative wrote that "even the children knew he 'hid out' throughout the war years . . . ." (Sallie F. Burns to SMW, 23 Jan. 1964.)
46	27	"man" Hickerson, p. 5.
46	27	Andrew Brown in *SOS,* p. 322. By the late Eighties, Thurmond was supposedly worth half a million dollars, more than twice as much as Falkner. Some of it had come from the railroad and some from a Northern streetcar deal, but much of it from moneylending and real estate. Falkner despised this kind of business and apparently berated Thurmond for exploiting the poor and weak. And, of course, he detested and probably hated him for opposing the extension of the railroad. *SOS,* p. 320.
46	28	On November 1, 1886, Falkner had been fined $11 for

Page	Line	
		"swearing and cussing." Three cases further down on that day's docket was Thurmond's name—with the identical offense and fine. *SOS,* p. 321.
46	34	S. S. Finger, quoted by Andrew Brown in Hickerson, p. 7.
46	37	Col. Falkner was willing to try. He went to Thurmond and told him he thought there had been enough trouble and that they should patch it up. Thurmond's matter-of-fact answer was, "The only way you can be friends with me is to never speak to me again." (Andrew Brown in *SOS,* p. 323.) The Colonel's grandson felt, years later, that his abuse left Thurmond no recourse but to kill him if he wanted to stay in Ripley. (J. W. T. Falkner, Jr., in *SOS,* p. 324.) The Colonel's great-grandson guessed that "the old man probably drove him to desperation—insulted him, spread stories about him, laughed at him." (Cantwell, "The Falkners," p. 56.)
47	6	One newspaper later reported that the Colonel was tipsy—a report emphatically denied by another. It seems not unlikely that the Colonel may have been invited to have a drink to celebrate his victory and that he may have accepted. Whether or not he had, his conversation with Rucker was not one of celebration or braggadocio; they talked instead about the sawing of some lumber. Dispatch to Memphis *Avalanche,* 5 Nov. 1889, repr. in New Albany *Gazette,* 5 Nov. 1964; Memphis *Appeal,* 8 Nov. 1889.
47	11	"pavement" This is a combination of accounts by the Memphis *Appeal,* 8 Nov. 1889, and by J. W. T. Falkner, Jr., as quoted in *SOS,* p. 325. Andrew Brown's reconstruction is that Falkner, tipsy and accompanied by followers, stopped in front of Thurmond's office when he saw Thurmond sitting at his desk before an open window. According to Brown, Falkner mounted the steps of the porch, said something to Thurmond, and moved his hand toward his hip pocket as though perhaps drawing a gun, whereupon Thurmond picked up his pistol from his desk and fired. This account is at variance with those reported in the Ripley, Memphis, and Jackson papers.
47	12	Memphis *Appeal,* 8 Nov. 1889; Jackson *Clarion-Ledger,* 14 Nov. 1889. Mr. Will Ticer, not an eyewitness but at the time of the shooting a twenty-year-old neighbor of Dick Thurmond on Quality Ridge, wrote, "Thurmond came out of his office, walked to where they were, reached around the man to whom Falkner was talking and shot Bill Falkner—a plain case of murder." Will Ticer to JB, 5 Nov. 1967.
47	28	Lizzie Falkner had left for Memphis with her daughter Effie to live there permanently. (*The Southern Sentinel,* 31 Oct. 1889.) It appears there was some expectation, before Falkner ran for the legislature, that the whole family might move to Memphis. Falkner often stayed there at the Peabody or the Gayoso Hotel, of which he was a stockholder. It was apparently no secret that he and Lizzie did not get on

NOTES

Page	Line	
		well. (I: SMW, 17 Nov. 1966.)
47	32	Hickerson, p. 19.
47	36	Falkner had once helped Stephens, and he took the case just to get rid of Brown and Harris and go back to bed. (Maud Morrow Brown, "William C. Falkner," pp. 436–7.) "That was the worst thing I ever did," he later said ruefully. "I should have been on the other side, prosecuting, not defending." (I: JMF, 24 Nov. 1965.) Lizzie Falkner had managed on another line to get as far as New Albany, but once there she found there was no train scheduled till morning. Another handcar was found, and she was pumped north to Ripley over the same route Brown and Harris had traversed. (*RA*, 23 Oct. 1889.)
48	2	*RA*, 23 Oct. 1889.
48	20	*RA*, 15 Nov. 1889.
48	26	Years after, his great-grandson said, "People at Ripley talk of him as if he were still alive, up in the hills some place, and might come in at any time. . . ." Cantwell, "The Faulkners," p. 56.
48	29	*The Southern Sentinel*, 4 Feb. 1890.
48	33	*SOS*, p. 335.
48	37	I: SMW, 19 Mar. 1965. Bramlett Roberts also recalls hearing the same story. I: 21 Nov. 1965.
50	4	*The Southern Sentinel*, 26 Feb. 1891. Brown in Hickerson reports that Thurmond had four lawyers receiving a total of $8,500. P. 4.
50	6	Quoted in *Biographical and Historical Memories of Mississippi*, pp. 713–14.
50	8	*SOS*, p. 330.
50	26	*SAR*, p. 375.
52	7	One year she turned her energies to drama, directing *Enoch Arden* for the Oxford amateur drama club. (*OXE*, 31 Oct. 1889.) There were also festive occasions such as the party on New Year's Eve, 1888, where sixteen-year-old Holland Falkner came dressed as "Night" (a friend was "Morning") and her brother Murry—two years older and now a student and Sigma Alpha Epsilon brother at the University of Mississippi—came as "Cowboy." boy." (*OXE*, 3 Jan. 1889.)
52	9	At the office things were going well enough by the summer of 1889 for the partners to take in Sallie Murry's brother, John Young Murry, Jr., as a member of the firm. By September their expansion took another form, as construction was begun on a two-story brick building on the northeast corner of the Courthouse Square, which would house a store on the first floor and the law offices of the firm on the second.
52	13	William Anderson, "Comments on William Falkner and the Falkner Family," *The Southern Sentinel*, 19 July 1962.
53	3	Ned had also brought with him from Ripley his ample store of memories and tales. He had stood in the Courthouse Square that day in Ripley a quarter of a century before when the flames roared skyward. "There sho was a fire in Ripley that day," he would say, "and what them yankees did was mighty mean." William Anderson, *The Southern Sentinel*, 19 July 1962.
53	11	*MBB*, p. 11.
53	15	*OXE*, 18 Sept. 1890.
54	24	I: JMF, 17 Mar. 1965. All the rest of this account, except

Page Line

where otherwise specified, is from an interview with John Henry Anderson of Pontotoc, 19 Nov. 1966. Anderson was one of the schoolboys on the Square that day. One disparity between the two accounts is that the family version has Sallie Murry Falkner arriving on the handcar with her husband, whereas Mr. Anderson recalls that she arrived the following day, presumably on the first train in the morning.

54 37 I: JMF, as above.

55 15 I: JMF, 15 Nov. 1966.

55 16 J. W. T. Falkner was an organization Democrat. In these years when the spread of Populist sympathy and the growth of the Farmers' Alliance threatened the regular state Democratic organization which had been forged by L. Q. C. Lamar, J. Z. George, and others with the breaking of Radical Republican rule in 1876, Falkner and his partner Howry remained faithful to the organization.

55 21 *OXE,* 29 June and 3 Aug., 1893.

55 24 In May, Gov. Stone appointed J.W.T. Falkner delegate for his district to the interstate immigration convention to be held in Augusta, Georgia. In October, he was one of nineteen dignitaries invited to sit on the platform during the lecture of Gen. J. B. Gordon, Commander of the United Confederate Veterans, when he spoke "for two hours with magical eloquence [upon] Lee's surrender and . . . the closing scenes at Appomattox Court House." Later that month he was an honorary pallbearer when the remains of Lucius Quintus Cincinnatus Lamar—U.S. Senator, Secretary of the Interior, Supreme Court Justice, and architect of Democratic resurgence in Mississippi—were interred in the Oxford Cemetery. *OXE,* 17 May, 11 Oct., 18 Oct., and 25 Oct., 1894.

55 27 FCVA. On April 2, 1896, *OXE* reported that "through the efforts of Assistant Attorney General C. B. Howry, his former law partner, Sen. John W. T. Falkner . . . has been appointed and commissioned a special attorney for the U. S. to aid in the defense of Indian Depredation claims against the United States."

55 36 *OXE,* 16 Aug. 1894.

56 2 *OXE,* 11 Oct. 1894.

56 14 In 1891, Keeley had organized a company to administer this cure to sufferers in various parts of the country. By 1895, there were 359 chapters of the Keeley League claiming 30,000 members; "all of the men members were cured patients but in the women's auxiliary leagues many of the members were temperance workers." *Dictionary of American Biography,* X, p. 280.

57 8 *OXE,* 24 May 1894, 17 Jan. 1895.

57 10 The Butlers had been among Oxford's first settlers and at one time had owned the city's principal hotel (built by Jacob Thompson)—Charlie Butler's mother being forced from the building with only the clothes she wore when the Yankees burned it. Lelia Dean Swift was an ardent, "hard-shell" Baptist who was said by her family to be a cousin of the founder of the Swift meat-packing company. They lived on 11th Street, near the home of L. Q. C. Lamar, who once patted

NOTES

Page	Line	
		little Maud Butler on the head. Holland Falkner, Maud Butler, and the Lamar girls played together through their growing years. *MBB,* pp. 123, 13. I: Dorothy Oldham, 18 Nov. 1966.
57	14	*OXE,* 5 Apr. and 11 Oct., 1888.
57	18	I: EF, 26 July 1966.
57	20	*MBB,* p. 124.
58	1	*Ibid.*
58	4	I: EF, 26 July 1966.
58	12	*MBB,* p. 220.
58	19	*Ibid.,* p. 124.
58	21	*OXE,* 4 June 1896.
58	28	*OXE,* 1 and 29 Oct., 1896.
58	31	Sallie F. Burns to JMF, 21 Nov. 1964. Courtesy JMF.
58	33	It was actually a Saturday on which the marriage took place. The *OXE* reporter noted that "The young couple took their relatives and friends somewhat by surprise, but their congratulations and good wishes were nonetheless sincere for their future happiness and prosperity." 12 Nov. 1896.
61	8	*ESP.*
61	11	U.S. Census, 1890.
62	10	*OXE,* 9 Sept. 1897.
62	17	*OXE,* 7 Oct. 1897.
62	19	*MBB,* p. 10.
62	25	I: SMW, 19 Aug. 1964.
63	4	*OXE,* 21 Apr., 9 June, and 14 July, 1898.
63	7	*OXE,* 3 Feb. 1898.
63	8	*OXE,* 21 July 1898.
63	11	"Falkners" *OXE,* 10 Feb. 1898.
63	14	SMW to JB, 5 Sept. 1967.
63	18	*OXE,* 24 Feb. 1898.
63	23	*OXE,* 24 Aug. 1898.
63	32	*OXE,* 10 Feb. 1898.
63	36	Courtesy JMF.
64	2	*OXE,* 15 Dec. 1898.
64	8	*OXE,* 21 July 1898.
64	26	*MBB,* p. 21.
64	32	*OXE,* 26 Oct. 1899.
65	2	*OXE,* 9 Feb. and 9 Mar., 1899.
65	4	*OXE,* 11 May 1899.
65	8	*OXE,* 18 Jan. 1899.
65	12	FCVA.
65	22	*OXE,* 22 Feb. and 15 Mar., 1900.
65	26	*The Southern Sentinel,* 4 July and 14 Mar., 1909.
65	30	*The Southern Sentinel,* 24 Jan. 1901. Two weeks later, R. J. Thurmond departed with his daughter and son-in-law to reside in North Carolina. *The Southern Sentinel,* 14 Feb. 1901.
65	36	*OXE,* 20 June 1901.
66	7	WF to Mrs. Walter McLean, 9 Sept. 1925.
66	12	*OXE,* 26 Sept. 1901.
66	17	*OXE,* 3 Oct. 1901.
66	19	*OXE,* 17 Oct. 1901.
66	21	*The Southern Sentinel,* 17 Oct. 1901.
66	26	Cantwell, "The Faulkners," pp. 61–2.
66	27	*OXE,* 12 Dec. 1901.
66	32	*OXE,* 10 July, 7 and 28 Aug., 1902.
66	36	J. W. T. Falkner's reports as the Colonel's executor showed that each year the heirs (his stepmother, his three half-sisters, and himself) received a steady income from the railroad. In 1898, they received over $20,000, including rentals, railroad earnings, and royalties from *The White Rose of Memphis.* FCVA.
67	7	Winston, p. 9.
67	11	*OXE,* 25 Mar., 17 Apr., 9 May, and 24 July, 1902.
67	18	*OXE,* 11 Sept. 1902. It is possible that Sallie Murry Falkner may have been urging her husband to sell the railroad for her own reasons, to "get Dad away from Ripley, where there still were Thurmond partisans," according to John Faulkner. *MBB,* p. 14.
67	32	John Faulkner wrote that his father had tried unsuccess-

Page	Line	
		fully to borrow money to buy the railroad. *MBB,* p. 14.
68	4	*WFL,* pp. 25, 38, 39. I: EF, 9 Dec. 1964.
68	17	Lemly, p. 289.
68	27	*OXE,* 2 Oct. 1902.
70	10	*FOM,* p. 4.
70	11	*MBB,* p. 12.
70	28	*OXE,* 3 Jan. 1902.
70	31	U.S. Census, 1900.
72	38	Mrs. Minnie Holt Smith in "Oxford, Mississippi," unpubl. article, as quoted in Miner, p. 22.
73	6	I: JMF, 24 Nov. 1965.
73	27	U.S. Census, 1900.
73	39	Roswell W. Rogers, "Treeless Country," *OXE,* 8 Apr. 1915.
74	19	See "Mississippi–Lafayette County," *Cor. Home and Farm,* repr. in *OXE,* 29 Aug. 1895.
74	30	A. Wigfall Green, "William Faulkner at Home," *Sewanee Review* (Summer 1932), p. 296.
75	22	*MBB,* p. 14. The "Johnny Brown house" still stands on the west side of 11th Street between Buchanan and Lincoln.
76	17	Tom S. Hines, Jr., in *WFO,* p. 115.
76	25	*MBB,* p. 48.
77	7	*FOM,* pp. 13–14.
77	14	"Callie" *Ibid.*
77	16	Earl Wortham in *WFO,* p. 167.
78	7	*FOM,* p. 13.
78	23	See Phil Stone, "William Faulkner: The Man and his Work," *The Oxford Magazine,* I (Apr., June, Nov., 1934), repr. by James B. Meriwether in "Early Notices of Faulkner by Phil Stone and Louis Cochran," *Mississippi Quarterly,* XVII (Winter 1964), p. 158.
79	7	*FOM,* p. 8.
79	19	*Ibid.,* pp. 9–10.
79	28	*OXE,* 23 Oct. 1902.
79	32	*OXE,* 13 Nov. 1902.
79	34	*OXE,* 20 Nov. 1902.
80	5	*FOM,* p. 10.
80	15	*OXE,* 6 Feb. 1902.
81	1	*OXE,* 8 Jan. 1903.
81	8	*OXE,* 23 July and 10 Oct., 1903.
81	13	*OXE,* 26 Mar. 1903.
81	29	I: SMW, 15 Nov. 1967.
81	36	Sarah Eva Furr Betts, in unpubl. article entitled "Lee Maurice Russell and His Attempt to Democratize the University of Mississippi." MCUM.
82	18	*OXE,* 16 Apr. 1903.
82	28	*OXE,* 13 Aug. 1903.
82	33	*MBB,* p. 15.
82	37	Murry C. Falkner in *WFO,* p. 11.
83	6	"road" Earl Wortham in *WFO,* p. 167.
83	12	*OXE,* 5 Nov. 1903.
83	38	The Houston connection was by marriage and it was brief. "Governor of Tennessee, 1820," wrote William Carlos Williams, "he married Eliza Allen of a prominent family of Sumner County, of that state. After three months she left him. None knows the reason, both remained silent. He wrote, 'Eliza stands acquitted by me.' " "Descent" in Williams, *In the American Grain (1925)* (New York, 1956), p. 212.
84	15	As quoted in Kirwan, p. 10.
84	18	John Lynch, as quoted in Kirwan, p. 10.
84	21	*OXE,* 20 Aug. 1891.
85	10	I: EF, 9 Dec. 1964; Dorothy Oldham, 20 Nov. 1966.
85	38	I: EF, 9 Dec. 1964.
86	11	I: EF, 16 Aug. 1963.
87	34	SMW to JB, 16 Aug. 1967; I: SMW, 19 Mar. 1965. John Falkner wrote, "the four of us were together like we were one family. And Auntee treated us as such. No one could have been better to us

NOTES

Page	Line	
		than she was. She spoiled us. And of course we loved her and Bill would fight you about her. She was the Miss Jenny, the Granny Millard, all the women in *The Unvanquished* that Bill wrote about." *MBB,* p. 70.
87	37	I: SMW, 19 Aug. 1964.
88	3	*OXE,* 17 Nov. 1904.
88	13	*OXE,* 21 Jan. 1904.
88	15	*OXE,* 23 Feb. and 14 Dec., 1905.
88	18	*OXE,* 22 Nov. 1906.
88	21	*OXE,* 1 Feb. 1906.
88	22	*FIU,* p. 285.
88	24	*OXE,* 25 Jan. 1906.
88	25	*FIU,* p. 285.
89	6	*FOM,* p. 25.
89	10	*OXE,* 11 Aug. 1904.
89	14	*OXE,* 17 Aug. 1905.
89	17	*OXE*, 24 Oct. 1907.
89	23	*MBB,* p. 91.
89	25	*FOM,* p. 25.
89	39	I: EF, 18 Aug. 1967.
90	4	*OXE,* 24 Mar. 1904.
90	5	*OXE,* 10 Aug. 1905.
90	8	*OXE,* 11 Feb. 1904.
90	18	*FOM,* p. 12.
90	30	I: EF, 12 Feb. 1965.
90	34	*OXE,* 23 Mar. and 20 Apr., 1905.
90	35	*OXE,* 10 and 17 Aug., 1905.
91	5	*OXE,* 24 Aug. 1905.
91	8	*OXE,* 30 July 1903.
91	22	*OXE,* 31 Aug. 1905.
91	25	*OXE,* 9 Mar. 1905.
91	35	I: MCF, 31 Mar. and 1 Apr., 1965; SMW, 23 Nov. 1965.
92	15	*MBB,* pp. 23–4.
92	23	*FOM,* p. 10.
93	3	*Ibid.,* p. 18.
93	7	*WFL,* p. 58.
93	9	*FOM,* p. 17.
93	11	I: Felix Linder, M.D., and Dewey Linder, D.D.S., 24 Mar. 1965.
93	26	Stuart Noble in Kirwan, p. 137.
94	15	*OTF,* pp. 79–80.
94	18	I: Ralph Muckenfuss, M.D., 9 Apr. 1967.
94	21	I: Maggie Brown, 20 Nov. 1966.
94	25	*WFL,* p. 27.
94	29	Robbie Eades in *WFO,* p. 23.
95	7	James Baldwin, *School Reading by Grades: First Year* (New York, 1897), pp. 5, 128.
95	9	I: Felix Linder, M.D., and Dewey Linder, D.D.S., 24 Mar. 1965.
95	15	*OXE,* 19 Oct. 1905.
95	19	*OXE,* 15 May 1906.
96	4	I: JMF, 21 Mar. 1965.
96	8	I: SMW, 19 Mar. 1965.
96	16	I: Ralph Muckenfuss, M.D., 9 Apr. 1967.
96	20	I: SMW, 17 Jan. 1967.
96	30	Rose Rowland in *WFO,* p. 25.
96	35	*OXE,* 18 Jan. 1906.
97	1	*OXE,* 12 July 1888; 28 Mar. and 16 May, 1901; 15 Mar. 1906.
97	3	*OXE,* 26 June 1902, 7 May 1903.
97	21	Fred Emerson Brooks, *Pickett's Charge and Other Poems* (Boston, 1903), pp. 14–15.
97	23	*OXE,* 9 Feb. 1905.
97	29	Cantwell, "The Faulkners," p. 58. The appeal of this topic faded little, if at all, during the years of WF's youth. Eight years later, on July 3, 1913, *OXE* carried an account of the Battle of Gettysburg with particular emphasis upon Pickett's charge.
97	34	I: Ralph Muckenfuss, M.D., 9 Apr. 1967.
98	13	*OXE,* 17 May 1906.
98	16	I: SMW, 14 Nov. 1966.
98	20	*OXE,* 1 Nov. 1906.
98	26	I: SMW, 17 Jan. 1967.
99	6	*FOM,* p. 47.
99	10	*Ibid.,* p. 48.
99	16	*OXE,* 15 Mar. 1905.
100	4	*FOM,* pp. 46–7.
100	25	WF to JB.
101	2	*FOM,* p. 15.
101	10	*OXE,* 16 Mar. 1905.
101	12	*OXE,* 10 Apr. 1906.
101	24	*OXE,* 26 May 1886.
101	32	*OXE,* 9 Nov. and 19 Oct.,

Page	Line	
		1905. Scottish names occur often in WF's fiction. Some readers will recall Mrs. Littlejohn in *HAM.* Other names in *OXE* familiar to WF readers include Mrs. Burch (29 Apr. 1909), Lycurgus Ross (12 June 1912), Mr. Lonnie Quick (26 July 1917), and Mr. and Mrs. De Spain (18 Apr. 1918).
101	38	*OXE,* 5 and 12 Apr., 1906. Some readers may see here an original for Ernest V. Trueblood, WF's amanuensis in "Afternoon of a Cow."
102	4	J. A. Mitchell, *Amos Judd* (New York, 1901).
102	6	*FOM,* p. 17.
102	23	*OXE,* 13 Sept. 1906.
102	34	*MBB,* p. 15.
103	5	*FOM,* p. 7.
103	14	*FIU,* p. 249.
103	24	I: MCF, 31 Mar. 1965.
103	30	*Ibid.*
104	12	I: Myrtle Demarest, 30 Dec. 1966.
104	38	*FOM,* pp. 18–19.
105	5	Coughlan, pp. 33–4.
105	11	*FOM,* p. 6.
105	20	I: SMW, 17 Jan. 1967.
105	24	*OXE,* 3 and 17 Jan., 1907.
106	3	I: SMW, 17 Jan. 1967.
106	6	Compare with Eula Snopes's epitaph: "A Virtuous Wife Is a Crown to Her Husband/ Her Children Rise and Call Her Blessed." *TWN,* p. 355.
106	22	*OXE,* 14 Mar. and 9 May, 1907.
106	25	*OXE,* 21 Feb. 1907.
106	26	I: SMW, 17 Jan. 1967.
106	35	*OXE,* 14 Mar. 1907.
107	18	*OXE,* 2 May 1907.
107	25	*OXE,* 6 July 1903.
107	37	*MBB,* pp. 47, 68.
108	4	*OXE,* 6 June 1907.
108	7	I: SMW, 19 Aug. 1964.
108	14	*Ibid.*
108	19	*MBB,* p. 47.
108	25	I: EF, 19 Feb. 1965.
108	31	*MBB,* p. 47.
109	1	*Ibid.,* pp. 72–3. Cf. Sam Fathers and the beginning of the story "A Justice."
109	6	*MBB,* p. 72.
110	4	I: EF, 19 Feb. 1965.
110	13	See Waldemar Kaempffert, "Comets and Their Mystery," *Cosmopolitan,* XLIV (Nov. 1907), p. 3.
110	16	I: EF, 19 Feb. 1965.
110	21	*OTF,* p. 4.
110	29	*FOM,* p. 17.
111	1	I: Ralph Muckenfuss, M.D., 9 Apr. 1967.
111	10	I: MCF, 31 Mar. 1965.
111	15	*OXE,* 28 May 1908.
111	28	I: JMF, 27 Nov. 1965.
111	36	Coughlan, p. 33.
112	6	I: JMF, 27 Nov. 1965.
112	32	*MBB,* pp. 54–9.
113	5	*FOM,* p. 27.
113	22	Lafayette County *Press,* 9 Sept. 1908. See also "A Heinous Offense," *OXE,* 10 Sept. 1908.
114	5	*OXE,* 11 Jan. 1900.
114	23	*OTF,* pp. 97–8. Cullen and Watkins suggest parallels between the Patton case and elements of *LIA* and *SAN.*
115	25	*NYT,* 9 Jan. 1906.
116	7	*OXE,* 1, 15, and 22 Oct., 1908.
116	13	*OXE,* 18 Oct. 1906.
116	16	*OXE,* 31 Oct. and 19 Dec., 1907.
116	28	I: Dorothy Oldham, 14 Nov. 1966.
116	36	*OXE,* 16 July 1908.
117	7	*OXE,* 15 Oct. 1908.
117	9	*OXE,* 22 Oct. 1908.
117	21	Cf. the duties of Lucius Priest in *REV,* p. 4.
117	26	*FCF,* p. 67.
118	3	Tom Lea, *The King Ranch,* II (Boston, 1957), pp. 486–7. For this reference I am indebted to Prof. Philip Durham.
118	7	*OXE,* 25 Aug. 1887.
118	31	*FIU,* pp. 29–30. Although WF guesses here that he was ten at the time of the incident, a more likely dating in the light of other circumstances

Page	*Line*	
		is sometime during 1909. The stableman Buster Callicoat was the model for the character Boon Hogganbeck, who appears in *GDM, REV,* and elsewhere. According to Negro blacksmith Earl Wortham, who shod horses for WF, the so-called "spotted horses" were very common in Mississippi. "They had them right here in Oxford," he said, "and Water Valley . . . lots of different places." When asked if he remembered the auctions of such mustangs, he replied, "Say, do I remember? Oh, yes sir. I bought one." I: n.d., by James Webb. Courtesy Prof. Webb.
119	6	John Cofer to JB, 10 Aug. 1965.
119	9	*OXE,* 5 Aug. 1909.
119	28	*MBB,* pp. 15–16; Bramlett Roberts in *WFO,* p. 151. Residents of Oxford suggest that aspects of Ike McCaslin in "The Bear" are based on attributes of Mr. Ike Roberts.
119	30	*OXE,* 11 Feb. 1909.
119	36	Annie Grace Parks to JB, 7 Nov. 1967.
120	31	I: Ralph Muckenfuss, M.D., 9 Apr. 1967. It may have been about this time that, according to one report, Billy Falkner handprinted a newspaper which reported the doings of South Street and sold for one cent a copy.
121	17	*MBB,* pp. 108–10.
122	25	*FOM,* pp. 12–17; *MBB,* pp. 110–16. I have here relied mainly on Murry Falkner's account because he was two years older and it appears that John Faulkner may have introduced into his account recollections of subsequent ascensions at county fairs.
122	32	I: EF, 19 Feb. 1965; *OXE,* 28 Oct. 1909.
122	37	Unpubl. portion of class conference, U. of Va., 5 June 1957.
123	3	I: EF, 19 Feb. 1965.
123	16	*OXE,* 5 Aug. 1909.
123	18	I: Dorothy Commins, 20 Aug. 1965.
123	23	Coughlan, p. 33.
123	29	I: Dorothy Commins, 20 Aug. 1965.
124	16	See Jean Stein, "William Faulkner: An Interview," *The Paris Review,* 4 (Spring 1956), pp. 28–52, repr. in *LIG,* pp. 237–56. See p. 250.
124	24	*OTF,* p. 4; *MBB,* p. 56.
124	34	*OXE,* 18 May 1909.
124	35	*FOM,* p. 7.
125	10	I: Dorothy Commins, 20 Aug. 1965. WF recounted these conversations years later to Mrs. Commins, the wife of his RH editor.
125	22	*OXE,* 29 Mar. 1909.
125	23	*OXE,* 16 Nov. 1909.
125	27	*OXE,* 11 Nov. 1909.
125	31	*OXE,* 3 June 1909.
126	5	*OXE,* 16 Nov. 1919.
126	16	*OXE,* 14 Oct. 1909.
126	19	Earl Wortham in *WFO,* p. 167.
127	4	*OXE,* 8 Apr. 1909.
127	10	*OXE,* 16 July 1908.
127	22	*OXE,* 13 Jan. 1910.
128	4	*MBB,* pp. 78–80, 121–2.
128	7	Coughlan, p. 34.
128	11	*OXE,* 27 Jan. 1910.
128	18	"The Approaching Plunge of the Earth Through the Tail of Halley's Comet," *Current Literature,* XLVIII (May 1910), pp. 511–14.
129	7	I: EF, 9 Dec. 1964; MCF, 31 Mar. 1965.
129	29	Jackson *Weekly Clarion-Ledger,* 30 July 1903, as quoted in George C. Osborn, "A Country Editor Finds Himself: James K. Vardaman Champions Reform," *The Journal of Mississippi History,* VIII (Jan. 1946), p. 85.
129	36	Heber Ladner, "James Kimble Vardaman, Governor of

Page	Line	
		Mississippi, 1904–1908," *The Journal of Mississippi History,* II (Oct. 1940), p. 185.
130	11	William F. Holmes, "James K. Vardaman and Prison Reform in Mississippi," *The Journal of Mississippi History,* XXVII (Aug. 1965), p. 248.
130	24	Jackson *Weekly Clarion-Ledger,* 17 and 26 Mar., 1910, as quoted in Kirwan, p. 197; see also pp. 191–210.
130	31	*OXE,* 2 Feb. 1910.
131	7	*OXE,* 17 Mar. 1910.
131	25	William Alexander Percy, *Lanterns on the Levee* (New York, 1941), pp. 143–4.
131	29	*OXE,* 21 July 1910.
132	16	Jackson *Daily News,* 4 Dec. 1910; Jackson *Issue,* 30 Apr. 1910, as repr. in Kirwan, pp. 209, 207; Kirwan, pp. 209–10.
132	21	*OXE,* 20 Oct. 1910.
132	29	*OXE,* 21 July 1910.
133	17	*FOM,* pp. 66–77.
133	31	*OXE,* 13 Oct. 1910.
133	39	*OXE,* 24 Nov. 1910.
134	15	*FOM,* pp. 67–8.
134	20	*OXE,* 12 May 1910.
134	35	*OXE,* 20 Jan. 1910. Cf. Ab Snopes in *HAM.*
135	15	*FOM,* pp. 79–80.
136	5	*Ibid.,* pp. 53–61; *MBB,* pp. 97–100.
136	17	*FOM,* pp. 81–3.
136	22	*OXE,* 15 Sept. 1910.
137	6	*OXE,* 2 June 1910. Cf. *AA,* p. 122.
137	36	See Miner, pp. 28–31.
138	7	*OXE,* 27 Jan. 1910.
138	17	See E. O. Hawkins, Jr., "Jane Cook and Cecilia Farmer," *The Mississippi Quarterly,* XVIII (Fall 1965), pp. 248–51, for the use of this legend in *UNV* and *IID.*
139	3	I: EF, 30 Aug. 1967.
139	12	Miner, p. 50; Cantwell, "The Faulkners," p. 58; Bettersworth, p. 289.
139	18	*OXE,* 25 May 1911.
139	36	See *The American Monthly Review of Reviews,* XLII (Oct. 1910), p. 408. Cf. *ESP,* p. 38.
140	2	I: Ralph Muckenfuss, M.D., 9 Apr. 1967.
140	34	*MBB,* pp. 85, 122.
141	16	*Ibid.,* p. 27.
142	12	I: EF, 9 Dec. 1964.
142	23	*Ibid.*
143	4	I: Robert Farley, 3 Apr. 1965.
143	14	I: EF, 9 Dec. 1964.
143	20	*OXE,* 12 Jan. 1911.
143	22	*OXE,* 15 June 1911.
143	31	*OXE,* 12 Jan. 1911.
143	34	I: SMW, 14 Nov. 1966.
144	3	*OXE,* 16 May 1911.
144	9	*OXE,* 6 July 1911.
144	11	*OXE,* 10 June 1911.
144	13	*OXE,* 3 Aug. 1911.
145	1	Jackson *Clarion-Ledger,* 7 July 1910, and Vicksburg *Herald,* 5 July 1910, repr. in Kirwan, pp. 220–1.
145	10	Vicksburg *Herald,* 27 June 1911, quoting Pontotoc *Advance,* repr. in Kirwan, p. 227.
145	17	As quoted in Jackson *Clarion-Ledger,* 10 Aug. 1911, repr. in Kirwan, p. 230.
145	18	*OXE,* 3 Aug. 1911.
145	19	*OXE,* 14 Sept. 1911.
145	21	*OXE,* 31 Aug. 1911, 8 Jan. 1912.
145	24	*OXE,* 1 June and 28 July, 1911.
145	35	*OXE,* 2 July 1885.
146	4	*MBB,* pp. 70–1.
146	17	I: Myrtle Demarest, 30 Dec. 1966.
146	21	I: MCF, 31 Mar. 1965.
146	33	*OXE,* 12 Oct. 1911.
147	1	*FOM,* pp. 19–20.
147	13	*MBB,* p. 220.
147	37	*Ibid.,* pp. 92–4.
148	4	*FOM,* p. 79.
148	12	*MBB,* p. 127.
148	22	John Markette in *WFO,* p. 29.
148	36	I: SMW, 17 Nov. 1966.
149	7	*OXE,* 18 Jan. 1912.
149	24	Lee M. Russell File, Mississippi State Dept. of Archives (Jackson, Miss.), as quoted in Betts, pp. 5–6.
149	32	*OXE,* 8 Feb. 1912.

NOTES

Page	Line	
150	2	Betts, p. 7.
150	13	*MBB,* p. 126.
150	21	*Ibid.; OXE,* 5 Dec. 1912.
150	24	*OXE,* 7 Mar. 1912.
150	29	*OXE,* 23 May 1912.
150	36	*FOM,* p. 11.
151	10	*Ibid.*
151	15	*OXE,* 22 Jan. 1912.
151	17	*OXE,* 2 May 1912.
151	24	I: EF, 29 Mar. 1967.
151	25	I: Mrs. Ashford Little, 21 Jan. 1967.
152	5	*OXE,* 5 Nov. 1912.
152	9	*OXE,* 5 Dec. 1912.
152	20	I: EF, 29 Apr. 1968.
152	22	I: SMW, 17 Nov. 1965. An account of the U.D.C. celebration of the birth of Robert E. Lee noted that " 'The Bonnie Blue Flag,' sung by the Intermediate grade, had just reached its Zenith of appreciation when little Sallie Murry Wilkins marched to the front in full war-time costume and sang heartily and sweetly 'The Homespun Dress,' which brought forth much patriotic applause from the large audience." *OXE,* 29 Feb. 1912.
152	38	I: MCF, 2 Dec. 1965.
153	4	I: JMF, 14 and 19 Nov., 1966.
153	27	I: Earl Wortham, 10 Sept. 1964, by James Webb. Courtesy Prof. Webb.
153	32	I: SMW, 23 Nov. 1965.
154	3	"traveled" J. W. T. Falkner wrote in part: "I confess that the very cheapness and simplicity of the split log drag did not appeal to me at all and like the balance of the fools condemned it because I did not understand it or how a merely dragging two logs fastened together could convert the horrible roads we had in this county into a respectable highway for travel. Now I know it will do it, and anyone can be convinced if you will take the trouble to ride or drive from here to the Iron Bridge on the Tallahatchie River. . . . I was told when getting ready to take the trip through the country before leaving Oxford for Memphis . . . 'Oh, if you can make it to the Iron Bridge you are all right. The rest of the route has good roads.' With fear and trembling we tackled the route with grim determination to win and we did. To our utter astonishment, however, we found the road was nearly perfect to the Iron Bridge and in less than an hour we rolled up to it and in less than two we were in Tyro." (*OXE,* 27 June 1912.) The straight-line distance from Oxford to Tyro is about eighteen miles.
154	5	*OXE,* 18 May 1912.
154	10	Ripley *Sentinel,* repr. in *OXE,* 15 Aug. 1912.
154	12	*OXE,* 31 Oct. 1912.
154	23	I: JMF, 14 Nov. 1966.
155	3	I: Ralph Muckenfuss, M.D., 9 Apr. 1967.
155	11	*Ibid.*
155	19	I: Myrtle Demarest, 30 Dec. 1966.
155	34	I: MCF, 31 Mar. 1965; Ralph Muckenfuss, M.D., 9 Apr. 1967; Myrtle Demarest, 30 Dec. 1966.
157	3	*MBB,* p. 71.
157	15	*OXE,* 9 Jan. 1913.
158	7	I: MCF, 31 Mar. 1965.
158	23	*OXE,* 5 June 1913.
158	34	*OXE,* 11 Dec. 1913.
159	5	*OXE,* 7 Aug. 1913.
159	21	I: EF, 17 Aug. 1963.
159	23	*OXE,* 11 Sept. 1913.
159	35	*OXE,* 14 Aug. 1913.
160	3	*OXE,* 4 Dec. 1913.
160	6	*OXE,* 13 Nov. 1913.
160	14	*FOM,* p. 17.
160	22	I: EF, 17 Aug. 1963.
160	36	I: Ella Somerville, 22 Mar. 1965.
160	38	*OXE,* 22 Jan. 1914.

Page	*Line*	
161	2	*OXE,* 5 Mar. 1914.
161	7	*OXE,* 4 June 1914.
161	9	*OXE,* 11 June 1914.
161	20	Phil Stone, "I Know William Faulkner," *OXE,* 16 Nov. 1950, repr. 23 Feb. 1967.
161	27	I: Ella Somerville, 22 Mar. 1965.
162	4	Coughlan, pp. 38–9.
162	27	I am indebted here especially to Robert Coughlan; I: 30 Dec. 1964.
163	13	I: Emily Stone, 30 Nov. 1965.
164	2	Emily Whitehurst Stone, "Faulkner Gets Started," *The Texas Quarterly,* VIII (Winter 1965), p. 145.
164	11	See Phil Stone, "William Faulkner," p. 162.
164	16	"rally" *OXE,* 3 Sept. 1914.
164	18	*OXE,* 14 and 22 Oct., 1914.
164	30	Phil Stone, "I Know William Faulkner."
165	24	I: Ralph Muckenfuss, M.D., 9 Apr. 1967.
165	32	I am indebted to Mrs. Frederick Van B. Demarest for her kindness in allowing me to see the sketches.
165	38	WF to JB.
166	18	*OXE,* 30 Sept. 1915.
166	33	*MBB,* pp. 128–9. Cf. Possum McDaniel and Labove, the football player-schoolteacher in *HAM.*
167	1	*OXE,* 30 Sept. 1915.
167	12	*OXE,* 21 Oct. 1915.
168	8	*NOS.*
168	17	*ESP.*
170	7	Phil Stone, "William Faulkner," pp. 162–3.
170	9	Stark Young, "The New Year's Craw," *The New Republic,* LXXXXIII (Jan. 12, 1938), p. 283.
170	13	Emily Stone, "Faulkner Gets Started," p. 143.
170	19	*FOM,* p. 18.
171	2	"Verse Old and Nascent: A Pilgrimage," *EPP,* p. 116.
171	38	Emily Stone, "Faulkner Gets Started," p. 145; I: Emily Stone, 27 Mar. 1965.
172	18	Percy, *Lanterns on the Levee,* p. 148.
172	34	*OXE,* 16 July 1914.
173	9	*OXE,* 25 Feb. 1915.
173	15	I: Ralph Muckenfuss, M.D., 9 Apr. 1967.
173	17	*OXE,* 29 July 1915.
173	21	*OXE,* 5 Aug. 1915.
173	24	*OXE,* 12 Aug. 1915.
173	29	*OXE,* 16 Jan. and 16 Sept., 1915.
174	5	I: SMW, 26 Nov. 1965.
174	16	I: JMF, 24 Nov. 1965.
174	24	I: SMW, 14 Nov. 1966; *OXE,* 15 July 1915.
174	32	I: SMW, 23 Nov. 1965.
174	35	I: EF, 9 Dec. 1964.
175	9	"her" I: Mary Victoria Weinmann, 2 Feb. 1965.
176	10	I: EF, 9 Dec. 1964.
176	14	See *MBB,* p. 92, and "Mississippi," *ESP,* p. 24. John Cullen writes that WF hunted with Gen. Stone's camp when he was a boy and "killed a deer when he was only fifteen or sixteen years old." (*OTF,* p. 13.) However, John Faulkner writes that his brother did not hunt from the time he killed the dog "until he was grown and went on the deer hunt below Batesville." (*MBB,* p. 92.) Phil Stone's recollections also seem to indicate that WF began deer-hunting no earlier than about 1915.
176	30	Emily Whitehurst Stone, "How a Writer Finds His Material," *Harper's,* CCXXXI (Nov. 1965), pp. 160–1.
177	14	*OTF,* pp. 27–8.
177	23	*MBB,* p. 92.
178	19	I: Robert Farley, 3 Apr. 1965.
178	23	I: MCF, 31 Mar. 1965.
178	30	See Richardson, *William Faulkner,* p. 34.
179	4	WF to JB.
179	15	*MBB,* p. 130; *FCF,* p. 67.
179	19	I: MCF, 31 Mar. 1965.
179	21	I: EF, 29 Aug. 1964.

NOTES

Page	Line	
179	30	Marshall J. Smith, "Faulkner of Mississippi," *The Bookman,* 74 (Dec. 1931), p. 416.
180	14	*MBB,* pp. 132–3.
180	34	*Ibid.,* pp. 130–3.
181	3	*FOM,* p. 87.
181	6	*OXE,* 2 Mar. 1916.
181	9	I: MCF, 31 Mar. 1965.
181	16	*FR,* p. viii.
181	18	*OXE,* 22 June 1916.
181	34	*OXE,* 27 Apr. 1916.
181	37	*OXE,* 19 Oct. 1916.
182	8	*OXE,* 21 Nov. 1916.
182	38	I: Robert Farley, 3 Apr. 1965.
183	34	Ben Wasson, "The Time Has Come," Greenville *Delta Democrat-Times,* 15 July 1962.
184	1	*FIU,* p. 4.
184	21	"Verse Old and Nascent: A Pilgrimage," *EPP,* pp. 129–31. The analysis which follows in the text must necessarily move by inference and in a highly tentative way. WF said that it was during this period, from age seventeen to nineteen, that he composed the poems which appeared in *AGB* in 1933. (See *FIU,* p. 4.) And it appears likely that some of those poems, probably much revised, did indeed have their inception in this early period. The principal collections of WF's poetry are in the following: ACLT, FCVA, JFSA, and MCL. The largest, ACLT, comprises poems in holograph, ribbon, and carbon-copy form. Salvaged from the ashes of Phil Stone's home, many of the sheets are intact, but many others are singed fragments. FCVA includes chiefly ribbon copies of poems. JFSA includes a few holograph drafts. The MCL poems are typed on eleven sheets of legal-size bond paper. Some of these poems, like some in the other three groups, were published in *AGB* in 1933, whereas the rest remained unpublished. I am much indebted to Mrs. Norman Thompson for her kindness in allowing me to see them. It will take a great deal of comparative study to date these poems authoritatively. Those in MCL seem to me the earliest, probably dating at least from the summer of 1921 or earlier, though some of the pages in FCVA may date from the same time. The MCL poems are generally more imitative and suggest, I think, a young poet feeling his way as he tries a number of different forms, styles, and subjects. The difficulties of dating these materials are increased by WF's apparent habit of going through his poems from time to time and selecting various ones to make collections for friends or relatives, as with Mrs. Walter B. McLean (Aunt 'Bama), or perhaps with a view to submitting them to publishers or editors. Thus, poems written and revised at different times would appear together bearing some uniform characteristics.
184	24	His handwriting would undergo a curious and quite radical metamorphosis during the next ten years—as his personality and outward appearance gave signs of changing and as his métier would change from verse to prose. In the first stage his handwriting was large, attractive, and quite as legible as a copybook script though more individualistic. (This style aids, of course, in dating some of his verse as early work.) Next it began to be modified, still large and quite definitely not

Page	Line	
		printing but handwriting with connected letters—absolutely clear and legible, strongly vertical now and beginning to be angular, the bottoms of the *g*'s and *f*'s being simply straight lines but the tops of the *f*'s and *l*'s having clear loops. The exquisite lettering which he did in copying out original compositions such as *Marionettes* in about 1920 is probably a kind of intermediate stage. The letters were clearly printed now, thin-lined and rather vertical and angular, the chief idiosyncrasy being the regular reversal of the *s*'s. In the next stage he composed fiction, verse, and letters in printed characters—neat, quite small, very precise and thin-lined. Then later, particularly if the writing appeared to be hurried, it would seem to resolve itself almost entirely into vertical strokes of differing length, sometimes virtually illegible to others and by the next day, WF said, illegible to him too.
184	35	Sir Edmund Gosse and Thomas James Wise, eds., *The Complete Works of Algernon Charles Swinburne,* VII (London, 1926), p. 272.
185	1	ACLT. Another fragment uses Swinburne's phrase "lisp of leaves" from the same chorus. See poem V, *AGB,* p. 22, for further influence.
185	7	Some of Swinburne's long lines, as in "Hymn to Proserpine," seemed to find an echo in "Hymn," an unpublished four-stanza poem which begins, *Where shall we seek thee, O Beauty? aloft in the morning* *Where the hooves of the centaur ring like brass on the hill,* *Gold as flame where the flame of the young year runs* *Through copse and brake, swelling as music swells?* [*MCL*]
185	11	The third stanza of WF's unpublished poem ran, *When dawning warns of changes* *The promised morn estranges* *The mouth that mouthward ranges* *And love his throne descends;* *A lady and her lover* *Whose breast her own did cover* *Find, now his reign is over,* *No lovers are, nor friends.* [*MCL*]
185	18	ACLT. One *carpe diem* ballad of three seven-line stanzas uses the refrain "Heigh ho lads, for it's going to rain." At the end, WF penned a note: "Mrs. Oldham, of Oxford, who has musical talent, is composing music for this one." MCL.
185	23	A. E. Housman, *A Shropshire Lad,* IX (New York, 1924), p. 14.
185	28	This became poem XV, *AGB,* p. 35. In an interesting use of English materials, WF took the story of Dick Whittington and, in a tone Housman might have used, showed him rejecting his chances all for the love of a maid.
186	8	MCL.
186	9	Three of them became poems XI, XII, and XIII of *AGB.* For other Housman influences, see also VI and VII. Another unpublished poem also suggested Housman in

NOTES

Page	Line	
		tone, theme, and diction. In the seventeen quatrains of "Eunice," the poet painted the protagonist as a happy young girl and then, her lover dead, as a graceful, grieving woman whose feelings were counterpointed by those of the "lad and lass" in love in their turn. In the last third of the poem, the imagery used to describe Eunice begins to suggest one of T. S. Eliot's lone ladies. There are signs in *AGB* of the taste for Keats and Shakespeare which WF said took over when his passion for Housman had run its course. The last two of the five stanzas that made up poem X in that volume strongly suggested Keats, and one phrase, "A terrific figure on an urn," pointed to one of the great odes. Poem XXI commemorated the legendary Roland, employing archaic diction that might, like the subject, have been congenial to John Keats too. The six stanzas of poem XVI were spoken by a figure in "feathered cap and doublet" whose Elizabethan English elaborated on a metaphor very like that in the famous "All the world's a stage" passage from *As You Like It,* II, 7. But these were only a few verses, taken together, compared with the large number which testified to the influence of the other two poets.
187	30	I: J. R. Cofield, 17 Nov. 1965.
188	6	Housman, poem LXII, p. 93.
188	31	*OXE,* 1 Dec. 1916.
189	15	*FOM,* p. 88.
189	25	*OXE,* 5 Apr. 1917. Insurance rates were still relatively high in spite of the efforts of James K. Vardaman during his term as governor to bring them down. The Young Colonel had suffered loss by fire on more than one previous occasion. *OXE,* 10 Dec. 1904, had reported the repair of a recently burnt storehouse he owned. The same issue contained the following item: "The incendiaries John Foster, Herbert Kelly, and George Bowles were given a habeas corpus trial before Chancellor George Wilson last Wednesday." Cf. "Barn Burning."
190	9	*OXE,* 24 May 1917. Cf. Lee Goodwin's death in *SAN.*
190	33	I: BW, 28 Mar. 1965.
190	38	I: JMF, 24 Nov. 1965.
191	7	I: Emily Stone, 27 Mar. 1965.
191	11	Rose Rowland in *WFO,* p. 25.
191	16	*OXE,* 19 July 1917.
192	7	*"Desert"* *WFL,* p. 92.
192	8	*WFL,* p. 70.
192	14	I: MCF, 31 Mar. 1965.
192	17	*OXE,* 27 Sept. 1917.
192	22	*OXE,* 18 Oct. 1917.
192	33	*OXE,* 7 Feb. 1918.
193	6	I: EF, 22 Aug. and 9 Dec., 1964.
193	9	*Ole Miss,* 1918.
193	18	*The Mississippian,* 17 Apr. 1918; *OXE,* 25 Apr. 1918.
193	28	I: EF, 9 Sept. 1965, 29 May 1967.
194	38	I: EF, 22 Aug. 1964, 9 Sept. 1965, 29 Apr. 1968.
195	6	It was almost a copy of the one to be seen (in the same upper left-hand corner) looking down on the lovers who adorned covers of George Jean Nathan and H. L. Mencken's magazine, *The Smart Set.*
195	26	JFSA.
195	30	*MBB,* p. 133.
196	10	I: Mrs. Arthur Halle, 17 Mar. 1965.
196	17	*OXE,* 1 Feb. 1918.
196	26	I: EF, 9 Sept. 1965. John Faulkner attributed WF's rejection to his lack of two

Page	Line	
		years of college. (*MBB,* p. 134.) Army Air Service records in the National Archives contain no evidence of an attempt by WF to enlist in the U.S. Army for pilot training in the spring of 1918. Neither do these records supply a precise statement of all the requirements for acceptance. However, a document issued by the Office of the Chief Signal Officer on September 18, 1917, and entitled "The Present Practices of Accepting and Training Aviators" stated that the candidates "may be light in weight and youthful in appearance." The only specific requirement in the document was that the candidate "must be at least nineteen years old and preferably not over thirty." (Elmer Parker to JB, 20 Nov. 1967.)
196	33	I: Dorothy Conkling, 16 Mar. 1965.
197	3	I: Robert Coughlan, 24 Feb. 1967.
197	6	"action" I: EF, 22 Aug. 1967.
201	18	*EPP,* p. 64.
202	12	Edwin Rogers Embree, ed., *Life at Yale* (New Haven, 1912), pp. 14–23; "Yale's Two Hundredth Anniversary," *The World's Work,* XXXIII (Nov. 1916), pp. 7–8.
203	2	George Wilson Pierson, *Yale College: An Educational History, 1871–1937,* I (New Haven, 1952), pp. 445, 467–74.
202	4	I: Emily Stone, 30 Nov. 1965.
203	9	Carvel Collins, "Faulkner's War Service and His Fiction," talk delivered at the eighty-first annual meeting of the Modern Language Association of America, New York, 28 Dec. 1966. Prof. Collins did not give the date of the letter. But since WF went to work as a ledger clerk at "an armament company in Connecticut" on April 10 (*EPP,* p. 4), it seems likely that the Thursday on which he arrived was April 4, 1918. If Phil Stone was accurate when he later said that WF arrived in April, 1918, this would seem to establish April 4 definitely as his arrival date. (Phil Stone to Glenn Carey, as quoted by Gordon Price-Stephens in "Faulkner and the Royal Air Force," *The Mississippi Quarterly,* XVII [Summer 1964], p. 126.)
203	11	I: Emily Stone, 30 Nov. 1965.
203	19	*Ibid.*
203	31	Phil Stone to Robert Coughlan. I: Coughlan, 24 Feb. 1967.
203	34	Collins, "Faulkner's War Service."
204	4	Price-Stephens, "Faulkner and the Royal Air Force," p. 126.
204	6	*EPP,* p. 4.
204	8	*OXE,* 11 Apr. 1918.
204	14	*The Daily Mississippian,* 18 Apr. 1918.
204	23	I: EF, 18 Apr. 1968.
204	29	*MBB,* p. 134.
204	38	I: Mrs. James Hudson, 21 Nov. 1965.
205	4	*OXE,* 25 Apr. 1918.
205	10	*MBB,* p. 134.
205	13	*The Mississippian,* 24 Apr. 1918; *OXE,* 25 Apr. 1918.
205	16	*The Mississippian,* 1 May 1918; *OXE,* 30 May 1918. Cf. Quentin Compson *(S&F)* receiving, in Cambridge, an invitation to Caddy's wedding. WF did not, however, receive an invitation to Estelle Oldham's wedding. I: EF, 27 Oct. 1965.
205	21	Phil Stone to the editor, *OXE,* 21 Feb. 1935.
205	29	Carvel Collins, "War and Peace and Mr. Faulkner," *NYT Book Review,* 1 Aug. 1954, p. 13.
205	37	Collins, "Faulkner's War Service." Prof. Collins sug-

NOTES

Page	Line	
		gested that WF drew upon these men for characters in his story "Ad Astra." During this time, according to Collins, he also heard a story from a friend of poet Robert Hillyer's which he used in *FAB.*
206	3	I: Emily Stone, 27 Mar. and 30 Nov., 1965.
206	5	Michael Millgate, "William Faulkner, Cadet," *University of Toronto Quarterly,* XXXV (Jan. 1966), p. 117.
206	9	I: Emily Stone, 27 Mar. and 30 Nov., 1965.
206	13	Millgate, "William Faulkner, Cadet," p. 129.
206	29	I: Emily Stone, 27 Mar. and 30 Nov., 1965; Mrs. Stone to JB, 10 Feb. 1968.
206	33	Collins, "Faulkner's War Service."
207	3	Phil Stone later told his wife that he had wanted to serve in the field artillery, but he had been drafted and assigned to the Judge Advocate General's Corps and stationed at Yale with the rank of major. Because he wanted active service, he entered into the plan with WF to pass themselves off as Englishmen or Canadians. He said that after they had been provisionally accepted and had returned to Oxford in mid-June, it was necessary to forge additional documents. To notarize some of them, he said, they broke into the First National Bank at night and stole the seal of Eddie Avent, the cashier. When they returned to New York in early July, these documents stood the scrutiny of the recruiting officers but not, in Stone's case, that of the military police who checked his papers as he attempted to entrain in New York for Halifax. His forged draft card was marked "F," he said, which was proper for an American in the Judge Advocate General's Corps, but for a friendly alien—which he was supposed to be—"E" would have been the proper designation. According to Stone, the examining officer knew he was lying but was sympathetic. Instead of arresting him, he simply gave him back his papers. Stone then wired his father, who told him to see Col. Daniel I. Sultan, an Oxonian stationed at the War College in Washington. Sultan helped him avoid the trouble he seemed headed for as a result of forgery, being absent with leave, and attempting to enlist in a foreign army while still, presumably, being part of an American military unit. I have not been able to find any record of Stone's service or affiliation with such a unit. *OXE* for June 20, 1918, noted Stone's visit to his parents. *OXE* for August 1 reported that he "left a few days ago for the recruiting station in New York City where he expects to join the field artillery." I have been unable to find subsequent items about the results of that intention. As noted in the text, WF had left from Oxford for Toronto on July 8. I: Emily Stone, 27 Mar. and 30 Nov., 1965; Mrs. Stone to JB, 10 Feb. 1968.
207	7	Millgate, "William Faulkner, Cadet," p. 129.
207	17	John Faulkner wrote that his brother was nearly turned down by the British as well as the Americans. "He wasn't tall enough," he wrote. "Bill got mad and told them he was going to fly for someone and he guessed if they didn't need

Page	Line	
		him the Germans would take him. They needed flyers too. He asked them the way to the German embassy and the RFC man said, 'Wait, hold on a minute.' Bill waited and the man went inside an office and pretty soon he came back and told Bill they could use him." *MBB,* pp. 134–5.
207	29	*FOM,* p. 91.
207	30	*MBB,* p. 136.
207	31	*OXE,* 22 Aug. 1918.
208	12	*OXE,* 6 June 1918.
208	16	I: MCF, 31 Mar. 1965.
209	3	*OXE,* 27 June 1918.
209	9	*MBB,* p. 137.
209	29	I: Emily Stone, 30 Nov. 1965.
209	38	Malcolm Cowley, "American Writers and the First World War," lecture at U. of Va., 1 Nov. 1967.
210	3	John Dos Passos, *The Best Times: An Informal Memoir* (New York, 1966), p. 46.
210	14	James MConnell, "Flying for France," *The World's Work,* XXXIII (Nov. 1916), p. 53, (Mar. 1917), p. 508.
210	22	*FOM,* p. 89.
210	30	McConnell, p. 509.
210	35	Michael Millgate, "Faulkner in Toronto: A Further Note," *University of Toronto Quarterly,* XXXVII (Jan. 1968), p. 198.
211	23	RAF Certificate of the Service of William Faulkner. JFSA.
211	26	Millgate, "William Faulkner, Cadet," p. 118.
211	30	Millgate, "Faulkner in Toronto," p. 198. I am much indebted to these detailed and thorough studies by Prof. Millgate, as I am to Gordon Price-Stephens' helpful "Faulkner and the Royal Air Force."
211	38	RAF Certificate of Service. JFSA.
212	14	As quoted in Millgate, "Faulkner in Toronto," p. 199. Prof. Millgate also gives the names of other Cadet Wing personnel, such as Cadet Hogabom, suggesting them as originals for character names in "A Justice," *FAB,* and other WF works.
212	19	*MBB,* p. 137.
212	25	This contrast between the story of the revenge on the sergeant in WF's version as recalled by his brother and the recollection of another cadet suggests caution in the acceptance of some of the accounts WF gave, both at the time and later, about his RAF experience. See Millgate, "Faulkner in Toronto," p. 199.
212	38	*Air Force Album.* JFSA.
213	1	Collins, "Faulkner's War Service."
213	10	Millgate, "Faulkner in Toronto," p. 198.
213	15	Collins, "Faulkner's War Service."
213	16	Millgate, "William Faulkner, Cadet," p. 120.
213	27	Letter dated "Friday," prob. 6 Sept. JFSA.
213	39	*MBB,* p. 137.
214	12	*FOM,* pp. 91–6.
214	17	RAF Certificate of Service. JFSA.
215	7	Millgate, "William Faulkner, Cadet," pp. 118–23.
215	11	Millgate, "Faulkner in Toronto," pp. 198–9.
215	29	*Ibid.*
216	12	FCVA.
219	11	JFSA.
219	14	Millgate, "William Faulkner, Cadet," p. 123.
220	23	JFSA. Carvel Collins has suggested that it was during this time that WF's first poem appeared, in a Canadian publication.
221	21	Millgate, "William Faulkner, Cadet," pp. 118–21, 128.
221	22	Collins, "Faulkner's War Service."

NOTES

Page	Line	
222	6	*OXE,* 19 Dec. 1918; *FOM,* pp. 99–102.
222	9	*MBB,* p. 137.
222	17	Millgate, "William Faulkner, Cadet," p. 119.
222	19	Collins, "Faulkner's War Service."
222	25	Millgate, "William Faulkner, Cadet," pp. 122, 130.
223	10	*Ibid.,* pp. 129–30.
224	3	Collins, "Faulkner's War Service."
224	10	Courtesy JMF.
224	17	Millgate, "William Faulkner, Cadet," p. 121.
224	23	*Ibid.,* p. 130.
224	26	Millgate, "Faulkner in Toronto," p. 198.
225	3	*FOM,* pp. 90–1.
225	8	*MBB,* pp. 138–9.
225	10	I: Malcolm Franklin, 26 Sept. 1966.
225	14	Phil Stone to Robert Coughlan, 1953; I: Coughlan, 17 Nov. 1965.
226	4	See contributors' column, *Forum,* LXXXIII (Apr. 1930), p. lvi.
226	13	Millgate, "William Faulkner, Cadet," p. 125; "Faulkner in Toronto," p. 198.
226	37	JFSA.
227	29	Cadet Faulkner's roommates and classmates said he might have gone for a joy ride, but, for formal flight instruction, to a man those consulted denied the possibility. One of the officers demobilizing RAF personnel at Canadian bases at this same time emphatically declared that WF could not have done any flying after the Armistice. (Frank H. Ellis, quoted in Kenneth Lewis Webe, "Aviation in the Fiction of William Faulkner," unpubl. M.A.. thesis, Ohio State U., 1964, pp. 4–5, as cited in Millgate, "Faulkner in Toronto," p. 198.) Insofar as negative evidence goes, the RAF Certificate of the Service of WF supports this view.
228	15	JFSA.
228	28	*Ibid.* He had sketched the RAF wings there too. They also appeared in his copy of a book containing portions of *The Canterbury Tales* published by Macmillan in 1918. (See *WFL,* p. 62.) Neither I nor members of the Faulkner family have been able to determine the proper form of the word I have transcribed as "Australies."
229	11	WF to JB. In *War Birds: Diary of an Unknown Aviator* (New York, 1926), John McGavock Grider recounted a similar story said to have occurred in France in 1918. In 1933, WF did a 143-page film script based on this book for MGM.
229	16	WF to JB.
229	17	In *Winged Victory* (London, 1934), WF's favorite novel of aerial combat in World War I, Victor Yeates wrote, "Camels . . . were by far the most difficult of service machines to handle. Many pilots killed themselves by crashing in a right hand spin when they were learning to fly them." P. 25.
229	33	JFSA.
230	12	*Ibid.*
231	18	According to Carvel Collins, WF used his trip home from Canada in *SP.* "Faulkner's War Service."
232	11	*MBB,* pp. 138–9.
232	21	*OXE,* 19 Dec. 1918.
232	35	JFSA.
232	37	I: Robert Coughlan, 30 Dec. 1964.
233	2	I: Robert Farley, 3 Apr. 1965.
233	5	T. Ashby Woodson, M.D., to JB, 2 Feb. 1967.
233	10	I: MCF, 31 Mar. 1965.
233	11	*MBB,* p. 139.
233	17	*Ibid.,* p. 140.

Page	Line	
233	20	JFSA.
233	21	FCVA.
233	29	*OXE,* 2, 16, and 30 Jan., 1919.
233	31	*OXE,* 2 Jan. 1919.
233	39	*General Catalogue of the University of Mississippi* (Apr. 1919).
235	7	Emily Stone, "How a Writer Finds His Material," p. 160.
235	36	I: Dorothy Conkling, 16 Mar. 1965; *MPS,* 18 July 1929. Phil Stone said the name was actually Renaud, but the newspapers always used Reno, and usually Devaux rather than DeVaux. Dot Wilcox believed Reno abandoned his plans for the priesthood because of a girl rather than dice.
236	8	I: Emily Stone, 27 Mar. 1965.
236	11	I: BW, 29 Nov. 1965.
237	28	I: Dorothy Conkling, 16 Mar. 1965.
238	13	*Ibid.*
238	25	I: Dorothy Oldham, 17 Nov. 1967.
238	31	JFSA.
238	37	*OXE,* 13 Feb. 1919.
239	6	*Ibid.*
239	13	Adjutant Inspector's Dept., U.S. Marine Corps to Murry C. Falkner, 15 Apr. 1919. Courtesy JMF.
239	16	*FOM,* pp. 102–3.
239	20	*Ibid.*
239	23	*OXE,* 18 and 20 Mar., 1919.
239	26	*MBB,* p. 139.
239	35	Murry C. Falkner to Commandant, U.S. Marine Corps, 15 Apr. 1919. Courtesy JMF.
240	34	*TMF,* p. 12.
241	5	George P. Garrett, Jr., "An Examination of the Poetry of William Faulkner," *The Princeton University Library Chronicle,* XVIII (Spring 1957), p. 129.
241	12	*TMF,* p. 37.
241	22	*Ibid.*
241	26	*Ibid.*
241	32	See Garrett, pp. 126–7.
242	16	JFSA.
242	25	Phil Stone, Preface, *TMF,* p. 8.
243	3	*OXE,* 5 June 1919.
243	21	I: MCF, 31 Mar. 1965.
243	30	*MBB,* pp. 140–1.
243	34	*OXE,* 17 July 1919.
243	38	Kirwan, p. 294.
244	6	*OXE,* 17 Apr., 8 and 22 May, 1919.
244	12	Kirwan, p. 294.
244	13	*OXE,* 17 July 1919.
244	24	*MBB,* p. 221.
244	32	*OXE,* 4 Sept. 1919.
246	2	JFSA.
246	19	Phil Stone to the editor, *Saturday Review,* XLII (June 27, 1959), p. 23.
246	21	Courtesy Mrs. Jon Mallard.
247	3	Phil Stone to the editor, as above; I: Emily Stone, 27 Mar. 1965.
247	12	Courtesy Mrs. Donelson Lake.
247	21	What looks to be the earliest of five different versions was written on the other side of a sheet bearing the tentative beginnings of the poem about the pilot together with part of a pen-and-ink sketch of a leafless tree. JFSA.
247	29	I: EF, 17 Nov. 1966; *OXE,* 2 Oct. 1919.
248	2	JFSA.
249	15	*EPP,* p. 64.
249	22	*Ibid.,* pp. 62–3.
250	2	*OXE,* 9 Oct. 1919.
250	4	*The Mississippian,* 24 Sept. 1919.
250	11	*Bulletin of the University of Mississippi,* General Catalog Issue (1965), pp. 50–1.
250	14	I: Ralph Muckenfuss, M.D., 9 Apr. 1967.
250	19	*Ibid.*
250	21	I: BW, 29 Nov. 1965.
250	22	*WFO,* p. 37.
250	26	I: Ella Somerville, 18 Nov. 1966.
250	33	I: A. P. Hudson, 5 Oct. 1969.
250	34	*MBB,* p. 142.
251	3	I: JMF, 21 Mar. 1965.
251	20	Louis Cochran, "William

NOTES

Page	Line	
		Faulkner, Literary Tyro of Mississippi," *MCA,* 6 Nov. 1932, repr. in Meriwether, "Early Notices of Faulkner," p. 143. Hubert S. Lipscomb writes, "Faulkner had his own ideas in the interpretation of Shakespeare and frequently engaged in lively arguments with Dr. Bishop." These discussions presumably took place in private. Lipscomb to JB, 21 Sept. 1965.
251	25	I: JMF, 15 Nov. 1966.
251	32	I: Robert Coughlan, 24 Feb. 1967.
251	38	Louis Cochran in *WFO,* p. 102.
252	2	See Cochran, "William Faulkner," p. 143.
252	17	Louis Cochran in WFO, pp. 102–3.
252	20	*The Mississippian,* 10 Oct. 1919.
252	27	*The Mississippian,* 13 and 29 Oct., 19 Nov., 1919.
253	6	*EPP,* p. 41. As with two works to follow, "Landing in Luck" and "Sapphics," his name was spelled without the *u* when it appeared under the title "Cathay." This is probably due to an editorial change or error rather than to a reversion on WF's part to the earlier spelling. At this time WF and Phil Stone were interested in Ezra Pound and the imagists as well as T. S. Eliot. The title of the poem suggests *Cathay,* Pound's translation of the Chinese poet Rihaku, published in 1915. I: Emily Stone, 27 Mar. 1965.
253	15	*OXE* published "Landing in Luck" on November 27. The story appeared, as had those of BW and others, under the boxed heading "Weekly Short Story." Below that was the line "Edited by Professor Erwin." Although WF was not a member of this class, in which each student was assigned frequent themes, a fraternity brother recalled that either WF or Prof. Erwin read the story aloud. I: David Callahan, 25 Mar. 1965.
254	10	*EPP,* pp. 51–2. Richard P. Adams writes that Swinburne's "Sapphics" is "practically plagiarized in Faulkner's poem of the same name . . . ." ("The Apprenticeship of William Faulkner," *Tulane Studies in English,* XII [1962], p. 120.) WF's poem repr. in *OXE,* 27 Nov. 1919.
254	14	*The Mississippian,* 10 Dec. 1919.
254	19	I: Jeffrey Hamm, 16 Nov. 1966.
254	27	*The Mississippian,* 6 Nov. 1919.
254	36	I: SMW, 23 Nov. 1965.
255	8	I: Lowry Simmons, 15 Nov. 1966; SMW to JB, 18 Jan. 1968.
255	16	Wasson.
255	23	SMW to JB, 18 Jan. 1968.
256	4	I: Jeffrey Hamm, 23 Mar. 1965, 16 Nov. 1966; Lowry Simmons, 15 Nov. 1966.
257	4	I: David Callahan, 25 Mar. 1965.
257	6	I: Rufus Creekmore, 25 Mar. 1965.
257	15	I: MCF, 31 Mar. 1965.
257	33	SMW to JB, 18 Jan. 1968.
257	35	*OXE,* 1 Jan. 1920.
258	4	*OXE,* 25 Dec. 1919.
258	15	*MBB,* p. 128.
258	25	I: JMF, 15 Nov. 1967.
258	38	*FOM,* p. 69.
259	14	*OXE,* 8 Jan. 1920.
260	8	*OXE,* 15 Jan. 1920; I: SMW, 14 Nov. 1967.
260	24	I: Myrtle Demarest, 30 Dec. 1966; *MBB,* p. 128.
260	31	*MBB,* p. 73.
262	24	JFSA. The speaker's use of the soldiers' slang word "Blighty" for England sets the scene. To some readers

Page	Line	
		the women with their scarves may suggest lines from T. S. Eliot's "The Love Song of J. Alfred Prufrock."
262	28	See *EPP,* p. 11.
263	16	*Ibid.,* p. 54.
263	36	*Ibid.,* pp. 55–6.
264	10	Louis Cochran to Dr. Sykes Hartin, 3 May 1965. Courtesy Mr. Cochran.
264	31	Transcript of WF. Courtesy U. of Miss., kindness Prof. James W. Webb.
265	7	One of WF's books was an edition of Wilde's *Salome: A Tragedy in One Act,* illustrated by Aubrey Beardsley and published in 1912. WF inscribed his name in it but without the date. In 1933, he acquired a one-volume edition of Wilde's works. See *WFL,* p. 77. See also Addison C. Bross, "*Soldiers' Pay* and the Work of Aubrey Beardsley," *The American Quarterly,* XIX (Spring 1967), pp. 3–23.
265	30	*EPP,* p. 57.
266	17	*The Mississippian,* 23 Nov. 1923; Louis Cochran to JB, 25 Mar. 1967.
266	36	I: Ella Somerville, 18 Nov. 1966.
267	14	*EPP,* p. 58.
267	25	The parodist's use of "Bologna" rather than "Bogona," as in WF's version, suggests that he had taken the trouble to go to Verlaine himself or had seen WF's poem when it had come in to *The Mississippian.*
268	8	*EPP,* p. 60.
268	17	*Ibid.,* p. 59.
270	20	A poem in an adjoining column might have contained something either of imitation or of parody. Entitled "Nocturne," it worked with the idea of voices calling in the street at dusk, at night, and toward dawn. Its seriousness was undercut by the attribution "From the Memoirs of Prof. Fiddle, D.D." No matter what the nature of WF's achievement in verse, the poems in *The Mississippian* had grown more varied and lively since his first appearance in its columns.
270	34	F. was William Haralson. He did not actually know WF and thought of him, he later said, as an introvert and somewhat of a recluse. "He did not need any defense," Haralson wrote. "As I recall, what Louis Jiggitts wrote was intended to be entertaining and amusing. That is the same reason why I replied to what he wrote." Haralson to JB, 17 Feb. 1968.
271	6	*EPP,* p. 64.
271	21	WF found this idea amusing enough to use it as the basis for a *jeu d'esprit* he would write in 1937 and entitle "Afternoon of a Cow" and in *HAM.*
271	30	*EPP,* p. 70.
271	36	*Ole Miss,* 1919–20, XXIV, p. 105.
272	9	*Ibid.,* p. 145.
272	11	*Ibid.,* p. 155.
273	15	*Ibid.,* p. 157.
274	6	*Ibid.,* pp. 106–7.
274	12	*OXE,* 3 June 1920.
274	14	I: Dorothy Oldham, 21 Mar. 1965, 14 Nov. 1966.
274	27	Louis Cochran to JB, 22 Jan. 1968.
275	10	Courtesy Mrs. Calvin S. Brown; I: 23 Mar. 1965.
276	20	*OXE,* 27 May 1920.
277	9	*Ibid.*
277	14	I: Branham Hume, 23 Nov. 1965.
277	19	Arthur Palmer Hudson, "When We Heard William Faulkner Was Dead," unpubl. essay.
277	35	MCF to JB, 18 Jan. 1968; I: 2 Dec. 1965.

NOTES

Page	Line	
278	5	*OXE*, 13 May 1920.
278	17	I: Dorothy Oldham, 14 Nov. 1967.
278	24	I: Robert Farley, 3 Apr. 1965.
278	27	Rev. J. Allan Christian to JB, 22 Sept. and 11 Oct., 1965.
278	35	I: Robert Farley, 3 Apr. 1965.
278	38	I: MCF, 31 Mar. 1965.
279	7	Hubert Lipscomb to JB, 21 Sept. 1965.
279	15	Calvin S. Brown, Jr., in *WFO*, p. 46.
280	7	*Ibid.*
281	23	Calvin S. Brown, Jr., "Faulkner's Manhunts: Fact into Fiction," *The Georgia Review*, XX (Winter 1966), pp. 388–95.
281	26	*Ibid.*
281	37	ACLT.
282	5	*OXE*, 8 July 1920.
282	10	*OXE*, 12 Aug. 1920. In October the new census showed a population of 2,150, and there was rejoicing that Oxford was still a city. In December, however, Gov. Russell intimated that the report had been "padded." The town's population, his office maintained, was only 1,807. *OXE*, 21 Oct. and 30 Dec., 1920.
282	16	*OXE*, 2 Sept. 1920.
282	18	*OXE*, 23 Sept. 1920.
282	26	I: Dorothy Oldham, 25 Nov. 1965.
283	7	Coughlan, p. 43.
283	8	I: Lowry Simmons, 19 Nov. 1966.
283	17	Lucy Somerville Howorth, "The Bill Faulkner I Knew," *The Delta Review*, 2 (July–Aug. 1965), p. 38.
283	20	*EPP*, pp. 18–19.
283	22	I: BW, 28 Mar. 1965.
283	29	Howorth, p. 39.
283	34	Philip Davidson to JB, 27 Sept. 1965.
284	7	There were discussions of the best-known western modes such as that of the commedia dell'arte and the Punch and Judy show, with photographic illustrations such as the frontispiece, in which a dryad and two fauns danced in arrested motion, the thin strings rising from their delicate limbs to the invisible puppeteer above. Helen Haiman Joseph, *A Book of Marionettes* (New York, 1920).
284	30	Howorth, p. 39.
285	5	Sen. A. B. Schauber, *Board Minutes*, 1912–32, pp. 183–4, in Betts, p. 8.
285	13	Betts, p. 9.
285	17	*The Mississippian*, 14 Jan. 1920.
285	27	"year" *The Mississippian*, 3 Nov. 1920.
285	38	Betts, pp. 9–11.
286	10	I: Lowry Simmons, 19 Nov. 1966.
286	19	Betts, p. 11; *The Mississippian*, 10 Nov. 1920.
286	22	Betts, p. 10.
286	32	I: Lowry Simmons, 19 Nov. 1966.
286	35	*OXE*, 4 Nov. 1920.
287	2	Betts, p. 11.
287	6	I: Lowry Simmons, 19 Nov. 1966.
287	10	I: Jeffrey Hamm, 16 Nov. 1966; David Callahan, 25 Mar. 1966; Wade Creekmore, 26 Mar. 1965. *MBB*, p. 144. T. Ashby Woodson, M.D., to JB, 17 July 1967. Charles S. Wood, M.D., to JB, 9 Mar. 1968.
287	17	WF's transcript. See also John Pilkington, Jr., "William Faulkner and the University," *The Ole Miss Alumni Review*, 15 (Fall 1962), pp. 2–5.
287	25	*OXE*, 9 Feb. 1921.
287	33	I: Jeffrey Hamm, 22 Mar. 1965; Wade Creekmore, 26 Mar. 1965; David Callahan, 25 Mar. 1965; Lowry Simmons, 19 Nov. 1966. *The Mississippian*, 17 Nov. 1920.
287	37	*OXE*, 2 Dec. 1920.

Page	Line	
287	38	*The Mississippian,* 1 Dec. 1920.
288	4	Betts, p. 11.
288	26	William Alexander Percy, *In April Once* (New Haven, 1920).
289	1	*EPP,* pp. 71–3.
289	8	*Ibid.,* p. 110.
289	27	JFSA.
291	7	*ESP.*
291	18	*OTF,* pp. 29–30.
292	3	WF told MC "he was about to go to Cuba as an interpreter (he didn't know Spanish) when Stark Young told him that he ought to try living in NY and promised to get him a job at Lord & Taylor's bookstore." (*FCF,* p. 108.) In "Mississippi" WF wrote: "His official capacity was that of interpreter, since he had a little French and the defuncting company had European connections. But no interpreting was ever done since the entourage did not go to Europe but moved instead into a single floor of a Memphis hotel where all . . . had the privilege of signing chits for food and theatre tickets and even the bootleg whiskey . . . ." (P. 22.)
292	16	I: Mrs. James Hudson, 21 Nov. 1965; Myrtle Demarest, 30 Dec. 1966.
293	5	I: Dorothy Conkling, 16 Mar. 1965.
293	13	Florrie F. Levy to JB, 24 June 1967.
293	35	I: Robert Farley, 3 Apr. 1965.
294	13	Phillip E. Mullen, Osceola (Ark.) *Times,* 22 Dec. 1966.
294	35	I: Emily Stone, 27 Mar. 1965.
294	39	I: Robert Coughlan, 24 Feb. 1967.
295	3	I: Emily Stone, 27 Mar. 1965.
295	6	"her" I: Malcolm Franklin, 26 Sept. 1966.
295	10	I: Emily Stone, 27 Mar. 1965.
295	34	ACLT. See James B. Meriwether, *The Literary Career of William Faulkner* (Princeton, 1961), pp. 8–9, 55.
296	2	William Van O'Connor, *The Tangled Fire of William Faulkner* (Minneapolis, 1954), p. 17.
296	5	*WFL,* p. 77.
297	5	Bross, p. 5. Beardsley treated subjects that must have been especially appealing to WF. He had done a vignette for Mallarmé's "L'Après-midi d'un Faune," with, besides the fauns and satyrs, no less than nine various Pierrots. And for Volume II of *The Yellow Book* he had done a series called "Comedy-Ballet of Marionettes," I, II, and III. See *The Early Work of Aubrey Beardsley* and *The Later Work of Aubrey Beardsley* (New York, 1967), *passim.*
298	3	ACLT. The Grey Figure and the Lilac Figure enter, converse in free verse, and then withdraw as Marietta enters the garden. Slipping out of her sketchy gown, she steps into the pool. She does this at every full moon, and the Shade of Pierrot, "born in Paris town," comes to watch her. It is May, and the invisible chorus tells him that they have "moon madness." The drawing facing p. 13 showed a stylized version of Pierrot's costume. Now the Shade of Pierrot courts Marietta, and a drawing facing p. 21 showed them in silhouette. Five pages further, the two Figures watched the Shade of Pierrot, gesturing, his hand on his heart, to Marietta, pirouetting before him. After Marietta leaves, the Shade of Pierrot addresses mad, exultant words to his mother, the moon.

NOTES

Page	Line	

The Spirit of Autumn enters the garden playing a violin. A garden nymph, pining for her love, sings a short, sad little lyric. On p. 32 WF had drawn the two Figures gazing at the silhouetted figure of the Spirit of Autumn, a peacock near him. It is September, and the two Figures speak of the coming of winter and the mortality of all things.

Marietta reappears in a flame-colored gown. As she stares into the pool, one of the Figures wonders if the shade of Pierrot has deserted her. Why, he asks, do they fly to do his bidding, "we who know him for the white sensual animal that he is?" Here in another drawing, opposite p. 40, Marietta reclined beside the pool, the two Figures and the Spirit of Autumn watching her. The two Figures praise her beauty in language that suggests the Song of Solomon. Realizing that she will grow old, Marietta speaks of the future: "I shall walk in the gravel paths of my formal garden. When I walk, the green motion of my gown will be repeated by the jade on my finger nails. . . ." This passage may suggest not only Amy Lowell's "Patterns" but also some of the imagery Pound employed in his translations of Chinese poems. An illustration facing p. 47 showed Marietta sitting on the garden wall, a peacock on either side like book ends, facing her. "I shall sit on a grey wall," she says, "and I shall swing my painted legs." As she ages, the peacocks will eat the jewels from her feet and the jewels from her hair. Her golden eyelids will attract them and their cold feet will mark her body. The tailpiece was a drawing in which Marietta lay nude on a bier between two tall, jointed candles, the Shade of Pierrot standing there, his hands raised in shock and his stricken face reflected in the oval mirror behind the bier.

Page	Line	
299	9	Howorth, p. 39.
299	11	"members" Philip Davidson to JB, 27 Sept. 1965.
299	13	*The Mississippian,* 12 Jan. 1921.
299	23	*Ibid.*
299	27	*WFL,* p. 85.
300	13	William Stanley Braithwaite, ed., *Anthology of Magazine Verse for 1920 and Year Book of American Poetry* (Boston, 1920), pp. ix–xii. JFSA.
301	10	*EPP,* pp. 74–6.
301	14	"year" *LIG,* p. 17.
301	19	I: Emily Stone, 27 Mar. 1965.
301	23	Coughlan, p. 54.
301	31	*OXE,* 24 Mar. 1921.
301	33	*OXE,* 7 Apr. 1921.
302	2	Capers, p. 234.
302	4	"done" I: Ralph Muckenfuss, M.D., 9 Apr. 1967.
302	6	I: William Boozer and Albert Capley, 12 Nov. 1966.
302	9	I: Shelby Foote, 12 Nov. 1966.
302	20	William D. Miller, "Rural Values and Urban Progress: Memphis, 1900–1917," paper delivered at the 32nd annual meeting of the Southern Historical Association, Memphis, Tenn., 12 Nov. 1966.
302	29	*MCA,* 12 Dec. 1908, as quoted in Miller.
302	38	Miller, *passim.*
303	8	Gerald Capers to JB, excerpt from paper on rural lag in Southern cities, delivered at the 32nd annual meeting of the Southern Historical Association, Memphis, Tenn., 12 Nov. 1966.

Page	Line	
303	38	Miller, *passim*; I: William Boozer and Albert Capley, 12 Nov. 1966.
305	24	*FOM,* pp. 107–11; I: MCF, 31 Mar. 1965.
305	28	I: BW, 28 Mar. 1965.
305	30	*The Mississippian,* 9 Mar. 1921.
305	34	*The Mississippian,* 21 Mar. 1921.
305	37	*OXE,* 7 Apr. 1921.
305	39	*OXE,* 23 June 1921.
306	1	I: Branham Hume, 23 Nov. 1965.
306	2	*General Catalogue of the University of Mississippi,* 1921.
306	3	*OXE,* 5 May 1921.
306	4	*OXE,* 2 June 1921.
306	14	*EPP,* p. 77.
306	22	*FOM,* p. 125.
306	28	Russell Pigford, M.D., to Dorothy Oldham, 22 June 1965. Courtesy Miss Oldham.
306	31	I: BW, 28 Mar. 1965.
306	33	*OXE,* 12 May and 11 Aug., 1921.
306	34	*OXE,* 2 June 1921.
307	4	*MBB,* p. 142.
307	7	I: Branham Hume, 23 Nov. 1965; MCF, 2 Dec. 1965. See also Phillip E. Mullen, *OXE,* 16 Nov. 1950; *MBB,* p. 142; *OTF,* p. 11.
307	18	JFSA. There are draft versions of some of the poems in *Vision of Spring* in ACLT.

308 13 Sinister notes suggested Beardsley's dark gardens and shadowy figures:

> *Columbine leans above the taper flame:*
> *Columbine flings a rose.*
> *She flings a severed hand at Pierrot's feet.*

The imagery is impressionistic and fantastic. Pierrot plays,

> *And lets the notes fall slowly through his fingers*
> *Like drops of blood, crimson and sharp:*
> *He shatters a crimson rose of sound on a carpet of upturned faces.*

Page	Line	
308	33	An early draft had been typed on the other side of a sheet on which he had typed one of the Swinburnian poems written in couplets and long verse paragraphs. It too was little changed in *Vision in Spring.* ACLT.
309	8	A considerably different version of this section, badly charred, is signed by WF and dated July, 1920. ACLT.
310	11	The first, third, and fifth stanzas are spoken by Youth, the second and fourth by the lover. Another version of the poem, only slightly different from this one, bears the following line under the title: "to V. de G. F." Victoria de Graffenreid Franklin celebrated her second birthday on February 8, 1921. It would not have been uncharacteristic of WF to dedicate a poem to a child who would be able to read it only several years later. FCVA.

311 6 When WF published the poem twelve years later, he totally altered the meaning and effect of the lines:

> *At the turn she stops, and trembles there,*
> *Nor watches him as he steadily mounts the stair.*
> [*AGB,* p. 15.]

Page	Line	
311	24	When another version appeared in *AGB,* it was sixty lines shorter than that version in *Vision in Spring.* WF used only the first, second, and last stanzas. Euridyce was gone and so, for that matter, was Orpheus. *AGB,* p. 42.
311	28	When WF printed "Philosophy" as poem V of *AGB,* he

NOTES

Page	Line	
		rewrote only two lines and altered only a few words. There "thickets" was erroneously printed as "tickets." P. 22.
312	8	Coughlan, p. 44.
312	16	See *EPP*, pp. 82–3.
312	29	Only in the A.E.F. drawing did he spell his name with a *u*.
313	4	I: MCF, 31 Mar. 1965.
313	15	I: J. D. Thames, 29 Nov. 1965.
313	16	Edith B. Douds to JB, 7 Feb. 1968.
313	24	*OXE*, 16 June 1921.
313	28	*OXE*, 23 June 1921.
313	29	*OXE*, 30 June 1921.
313	32	*OXE*, 15 Sept. 1921.
313	37	*OXE*, 11 Aug. 1921.
314	2	I: Emily Stone, 30 Nov. 1965.
314	7	*OXE*, 25 Aug. 1921.
314	23	*OXE*, 21 July and 11 Aug., 1921.
314	30	I: Emily Stone, 30 Nov. 1965.
314	37	WF to JB.
315	8	Maud Morrow Brown in *WFO*, p. 38.
315	10	Young, "New Year's Craw," p. 283.
315	14	Stark Young, *The Pavilion: Of People and Times Remembered, of Stories and Places* (New York, 1951), p. 59.
315	21	Young, "New Year's Craw."
315	22	*OXE*, 30 Nov. 1950. In neither *The Pavilion* nor his letter to *OXE* does Young date this offer. In "New Year's Craw," written in 1938, Young says that it happened in the summer of 1920. On the basis of available evidence, it seems likely that the discrepancy comes from a slip of memory as Young wrote about these events seventeen, not eighteen years later. For a view of WF in Young's fiction, see Hubert Alexander, Jr., "William Faulkner: The Young Poet in Stark Young's *The Torches Flare*," *American Literature*, 43 (Jan. 1972), pp. 647–8. In this 1928 novel set in Oxford, Eugene Oliver is peripheral but clearly resembles WF in appearance and family.
315	31	*OXE*, 13 Oct. and 10 Nov., 1921.
315	37	Coughlan, p. 56.
316	4	*FCF*, p. 46.
316	5	I: Emily Stone, 30 Nov. 1965.
316	8	Marshall J. Smith in *LIG*, p. 14.
317	22	*Ibid.*
318	2	Young, "New Year's Craw," p. 283. The two men's memories also were at variance on the size of Young's quarters. Carvel Collins quotes from a letter in which Young mentions introducing WF to Elizabeth Prall "in whose house I had a room, the room Bill shared for a time." *EPP*, p. 20.
318	5	Coughlan, p. 56.
318	14	I: Elizabeth Anderson, 29 Jan. 1965; Walter Rideout to JB, 13 Jan. 1968.
318	32	I: Elizabeth Anderson, 29 Jan. 1965.
318	37	I: Emily Stone, 30 Nov. 1965.
318	38	*FCF*, p. 108.
319	17	"The Lure of Greenwich Village," *The Literary Digest*, 65 (May 8, 1920), p. 46; Corinne Lowe, "The Village in a City," *Ladies' Home Journal* (Mar. 1920), p. 28.
319	26	Lowe, p. 28. In his copies of James Branch Cabell's *Figures of Earth* and *Jurgen*, WF wrote his name and the address "35 Van Dam [*sic*] St., New York City." (See *WFL*, p. 20.) Mrs. Anderson described his room as being on Vandam Street. The first volume was of the third printing of April 1921; the second, the eleventh printing, of 1923. The second volume obviously would have had to have been purchased during one of his

Page	*Line*	
		subsequent stays in New York. In his syndicated column for October 15, 1953, Earl Wilson stated that during the 1920's WF lived on Hudson and Varick streets.
320	2	ACLT.
320	6	FCVA.
320	11	*The Metropolitan Museum of Art; Catalogue of the Collection of Casts* (New York, 1910), p. 121. This poem was published as XVII in *AGB,* p. 39.
320	20	FCVA.
320	31	Phil Stone in Meriwether, "Early Notices of Faulkner," p. 141.
320	34	See Carl R. Dolmetsch, *The Smart Set: A History and an Anthology* (New York, 1966), pp. 37–8.
321	7	Willard Huntington Wright, *The Creative Will* (New York, 1915), p. 33.
321	13	*EPP,* p. 74.
322	14	Wright, pp. 24–7, 44, 145–6, 195, 205, 207, 218, 221–2, 259, 226.
322	16	James B. Meriwether writes, "According to Faulkner (interview March 12, 1958), it was written around 1919 or 1920 or 1921 and is 'about the first short story I ever wrote.'" (*The Literary Career,* p. 87.) The style suggests that the story came after "Landing in Luck." (FCVA.)
322	28	Cf. stories set in Jefferson and also the character of Temple Drake in *SAN.* Another unpublished story is also entitled "Moonlight." The second one, also in FCVA, runs to thirteen pages. It appears to be of a later date and was handled at one time for WF by MG, his agent from 1932 to 1938. This version has much in common with the first, though it is much less hard in tone.
323	13	"Love" also exists in the form of a seemingly complete manuscript and two manuscript fragments, all later than the typescript version. FCVA.
323	30	Herbert Cahoon to JB, 22 July 1968. WF was a guest at Percy's Delta home at least once, when he played tennis there (though not well). I: Alfred Kazin, 18 Aug. 1972.
324	25	For a list of plays that WF may have seen, see James E. Kibler, Jr., "William Faulkner and the Provincetown Drama, 1920–1922," *The Mississippi Quarterly,* XXII (Summer 1969), pp. 226–36.
325	4	Mrs. John Joice to JB, 20 Oct. 1965.
325	7	MCF to JB, 18 Jan. 1968.
325	20	*OXE,* 7 Apr. 1921.
325	22	Clipping datelined "University, Miss. Dec. 2." JFSA.
325	23	I: Robert Coughlan, 24 Feb. 1967.
325	27	I: Emily Stone, 30 Nov. 1965.
325	35	Marshall Smith in *LIG,* p. 14.
325	36	I: Elizabeth Anderson, 29 Jan. 1965.
326	5	I: Elizabeth Anderson by Walter B. Rideout, quoted in Michael Millgate, *The Achievement of William Faulkner* (New York, 1966), p. 9.
326	16	I: Emily Stone, 27 Mar. 1965.
326	18	Phil Stone to Louis Cochran, 28 Dec. 1931, in Meriwether, "Early Notices of Faulkner," p. 139.
327	6	*AGB,* p. 55.
327	12	Clipping datelined "University, Miss. Dec. 2." JFSA.
327	13	*The Mississippian,* 9 Dec. 1921.
327	18	*The Mississippian,* 16 Dec. 1921.
327	21	I: Jeffrey Hamm, 16 Nov. 1966.
328	10	T. A. Bickerstaff to Charles East, 10 Mar. 1965. Courtesy

Page	*Line*	
		Messrs. Bickerstaff and East.
328	14	I: Branham Hume, 23 Nov. 1965.
328	20	"carefully" Edith B. Douds to JB, 7 Feb. 1968.
329	15	I: Albert Goldstein, 2 Feb. 1965; Frances Jean Bowen, "The New Orleans *Double Dealer,* 1921–1926," *The Louisiana Historical Quarterly,* XXXIX (Oct. 1956), pp. 443–4.
329	20	Julius Friend in *The Golden Goose,* Ser. 3, No. 1, pp. 12–13.
329	24	Benjamin C. Toledano, "Two-Sided, Not Two-Faced," *Liberator,* II (Spring 1963), pp. 17–18.
329	33	Albert Goldstein, "Discoveries of the Double Dealer," *Dixie, Times-Picayune States Roto Magazine,* 21 Jan. 1951, p. 6.
330	3	Toledano, pp. 17–18.
330	28	James K. Feibleman, "Literary New Orleans Between World Wars," *The Southern Review,* I, N.S. (July 1965), pp. 705–6.
330	32	Edna St. Vincent Millay, *Aria da Capo: A Play in One Act* (New York, 1921).
330	37	Elizabeth Atkins, *Edna St. Vincent Millay and Her Times* (Chicago, 1936), p, 78.
331	16	As quoted in Norman A. Brittin, *Edna St. Vincent Millay* (New York, 1967), pp. 44, 96–102.
331	26	*EPP,* pp. 84–5.
332	12	*Ibid.*, pp. 86–9. The author of the remark WF attributed to "a Frenchman, probably," was in all likelihood George Moore. See *TMF,* p. 7.
332	30	*EPP,* pp. 90–2.
333	33	*Ibid.*, pp. 93–7.
334	13	The early background material in "Adolescence" suggests the basic situation of the Bundren family in *ASI.* Juliet's mother was a schoolteacher crudely courted by farmer Joe Bunden. She dies worn out by childbearing. Her children's names and their diversity suggest the Snopeses. After Juliet came Cyril, then Jeff Davis Bunden, who is elected to the state legislature but hanged as a horse thief in Texas. Bud eventually becomes a college Latin teacher. FCVA.
334	27	Hubert Lipscomb to JB, 21 Sept. 1965.
335	4	*OXE,* 9 Feb. 1922.
335	5	*OXE,* 4 May 1922.
335	8	*OXE,* 9 Mar. 1922.
335	17	SMW to JB, 21 Sept. 1970.
335	22	I: JMF, 19 Jan. 1967.
335	34	*FOM,* p. 111.
335	38	I: JMF, 19 Jan. 1967.
336	6	Last Will and Testament of John Wesley Thompson Falkner, Oxford, Miss., Mar. 23, 1912, the Chancery Court, Oxford, Miss.
336	10	*OXE,* 12 Jan. 1922.
336	15	Edith B. Douds in *WFO,* pp. 50–1.
336	17	I: Branham Hume, 23 Nov. 1965.
336	22	*OXE,* 10 and 16 Feb., 1922.
336	30	Edith B. Douds in *WFO,* p. 50.
336	38	*Ibid.*
337	4	I: Emily Stone, 27 Mar. 1965.
337	7	"tennis" I: BW, 29 Nov. 1965.
337	11	Edith B. Douds in *WFO,* p. 53.
337	14	*OXE,* 9 Feb. 1922.
337	18	*OXE,* 27 Apr. 1922.
337	25	*EPP,* p. 98.
337	31	*Ole Miss,* XXVI, 1922, p. 226.
337	34	*The Double Dealer,* III (June 1922), p. 337, repr. in *EPP,* pp. 99–100.
337	36	I: Emily Stone, 27 Mar. 1965.
338	1	Emily Stone, "Faulkner Gets Started," p. 148. In the May issue, *The Double Dealer* had published a brief sketch entitled "A Divine Gesture." The author was identified in the

Page	Line	
		notes as "Ernest M. Hemingway, a young writer who lives in Paris and enjoys the favor of Ezra Pound." In the June issue, the space not occupied by the six quatrains of "Portrait" was given over to the single one of "Ultimately," by Ernest M. Hemingway.
338	7	*FOM,* pp. 111–12.
338	12	Clifton B. Webb in *WFO,* pp. 125–6.
338	17	"rapidly" Ben Gray Lumpkin in *WFO,* pp. 55–6.
338	20	T. Ashby Woodson, M.D., to JB, 17 Mar. 1966.
338	22	Philip Davidson to JB, 27 Sept. 1965.
338	36	Ben Gray Lumpkin in *WFO,* p. 56.
339	8	Mary Betsy Waddle in *WFO,* p. 140.
339	10	George Healy, Jr., in *WFO,* p. 58.
339	16	*FOM,* p. 113.
339	28	I: Robert Farley, 3 Apr. 1965.
339	32	Howorth, p. 39.
339	37	*FOM,* pp. 114–15.
340	1	*OXE,* 5 Jan. and 22 June, 1922.
340	11	*MBB,* pp. 145–6.
340	15	WF to Mrs. W. E. Stone, IV, 5 Sept. 1922. Courtesy W. E. Stone, V.
340	25	Kirwan, pp. 281, 284, 292–3, 298–300.
340	29	*OXE,* 26 July 1922.
340	31	*FOM,* p. 114.
340	34	*OXE,* 27 July and 17 Aug., 1922. Hubert D. Stephens was the son of Judge Zacharias M. Stephens, chief defense counsel for Richard J. Thurmond in his trial for the murder of Col. William C. Falkner.
341	4	Kirwan, pp. 301–2.
341	6	*OXE,* 7 Sept. 1922.
341	23	*MBB,* pp. 158–9. John Faulkner's account of the horse sale, which he describes as the germ of the story "Spotted Horses," constitutes the retelling, by a noted anecdotist, of an account given him by two other noted anecdotists. How much of the story is fact may remain undiscoverable.
341	29	I: Judge Taylor McElroy, 17 Nov. 1967.
342	1	I: JMF, 21 Mar. 1965.
342	8	I: MCF, 31 Mar. 1965.
342	20	I: Sam White, 10 Feb. 1964, by James Webb. Courtesy Prof. Webb.
342	32	*OXE,* 7 Dec. 1922.
342	36	*OXE,* 14 Dec. 1922.
343	3	*OXE,* 21 Dec. 1922.
343	7	*Ibid.*
343	12	Kirwan, p. 299.
344	18	*EPP,* pp. 101–3.
344	19	*OXE,* 11 Jan. and 22 Feb., 1923.
344	21	*The Mississippian,* 2 Mar. and 13 Apr., 1923.
345	4	*FR,* p. viii.
345	10	I: MCF, 2 Dec. 1965.
345	14	*OXE,* 4 Jan. and 22 Feb., 1923.
345	34	*FOM,* p. 118.
345	38	I: George Healy, Jr., 3 and 4 Feb., 1965.
346	6	I: Mary Victoria Weinmann, 2 Feb. 1965.
346	18	*OXE,* 8 Mar. 1923.
346	23	Calvin Brown, Jr., in *WFO,* p. 46.
346	34	*OXE,* 19 Apr. 1923.
347	5	*OXE,* 3 May 1923.
347	11	*WFL,* p. 127.
347	15	FCVA.
347	23	*MBB,* p. 146.
347	26	*OXE,* 18 Oct. 1923.
347	31	Rev. J. Allan Christian to JB, 22 Sept. and 11 Oct., 1965.
347	38	*MBB,* p. 147.
348	6	I: J. B. Roach, 23 Nov. 1965.
348	11	I: Eugene Bramlett, M.D., 18 Nov. 1967.
348	15	Calvin Brown, Jr., in *WFO,* p. 47.
348	27	I: C. C. Hathorn, 18 Nov. 1967.
348	37	I: Hassell Smith, 18 Nov. 1966.

NOTES

Page	Line	
349	6	I: Sollie Crane, 25 Mar. 1965.
349	8	I: Chester McLarty, M.D., 21 Mar. 1965.
349	11	I: Robert Farley, 3 Apr. 1965.
349	15	*The Mississippian,* 2 and 9 Nov., 1923.
349	20	*WFL,* p. 15.
349	28	John Ralph Markette, "Railroad Days," in *WFO,* p. 29.
350	13	FCVA.
350	20	I: J. D. Thames, 29 Nov. 1965.
350	23	*OXE,* 19 July 1923.
351	4	Carvel Collins suggests that the names of WF and Bell may have been borrowed without their consent by members of the staff of *The Mississippian.* (*EPP,* p. 24.) There is nothing in the texts of the Blue Bird ads that can clearly be identified as bearing the marks of WF's style. However, throughout his life he showed a taste for hoaxes of this kind, and it is not unlikely that "Bell, Falkner, Jiggitts, Unlimited Underwriters" did actually work together on this short-lived project. Cordiality apparently existed between WF and Jiggitts, who visited WF at his home in the 1930's. (I: EF, 8 Feb. 1966.) John Faulkner attributes full responsibility to his brother: "The next year Bill started his Bluebird Insurance Company. . . ." (*MBB,* p. 144.) So does Prof. A. P. Hudson, who later ran the counter-hoax described below. (Hudson to JB, 8 Apr. 1965.)
351	11	See *MBB,* pp. 144–5.
351	31	The officers of The Blue Bird Insurance Co. repudiated the testimonials printed over their names. "It is a gross injustice," ran the denial, "to say that President Falkner has permanently retired in the Post Office. He merely takes temporary naps—during business hours." *The Mississippian,* 25 Jan. 1924.
351	36	His financial condition was sound enough, however, to permit him to lend his brother John the sum of $103.35. John Faulkner wrote that he and his older brother were sometimes mistaken for each other, and that once WF was dunned for a payment John owed on a sewing machine. Answering in his brother's name, WF had promised to make the payment the following week. *MBB,* pp. 251–2. Cf. V. K. Ratliff and Mink Snopes in *HAM.*
352	3	*OXE,* 6 Mar. 1924.
352	8	*The Mississippian,* 3 Apr. 1924.
352	11	*WFL,* p. 93.
352	14	Coughlan, p. 48.
352	16	*WFL,* p. 77.
352	18	I: MCF, 31 Mar. 1965.
352	22	*FIU,* p. 20.
352	33	*Ibid.,* p. 24.
354	2	I: Dorothy Conkling, 17 Nov. 1965.
354	10	*MCA,* 21 Apr. 1924.
354	17	*OXE,* 13 Mar. 1924.
354	19	*OXE,* 1 May 1924.
354	21	*OXE,* 17 July and 28 Aug., 1924.
354	29	*OXE,* 8 and 15 May, 1924. I have been unable to find any account in *The Mississippian* or *OXE* of the results of either the semifinal or final round of the tournament.
354	36	I: MCF, 31 Mar. 1965.
355	30	Hudson. This would become poem XVIII, *AGB,* p. 40.
356	10	ACLT.
356	24	*Ibid.,* FCVA.
356	30	T. A. Bickerstaff to Charles East, 10 Mar. 1965. Courtesy Messrs. Bickerstaff and East.
357	9	I: Robert Farley, 3 Apr. 1965.
357	11	I: Branham Hume, 23 Nov. 1965.

Page	Line	
357	14	I: A. P. Hudson, 4 Apr. 1965.
357	17	T. Ashby Woodson, M.D., to JB, 17 Mar. 1966.
358	10	I: Robert Farley, 3 Apr. 1965. As far as Rotary in Oxford was concerned, WF was anticipating a bit. The club would be organized in November. I: William Reed, 14 Nov. 1966.
358	26	FCVA.
358	32	*Ibid.*
359	8	*Ibid.*
359	16	Wayne Sneed to the editor, Jackson *Daily News,* 16 July 1962.
359	23	W. H. Hutchinson to JB, 17 Nov. 1965.
359	38	*OXE,* 28 Aug. 1924.
360	9	I: A. P. Hudson, 4 Apr. 1965.
360	12	I: MCF, 31 Mar. 1965.
361	6	Emily Stone, "Faulkner Gets Started," p. 147.
361	17	*Ibid.,* p. 145.
361	28	FCVA.
361	36	*OXE,* 24 July 1924.
361	38	*OXE,* 8 and 22 May, 1924.
362	17	FCVA. This letter was first made available to me through the kindness of the Harvard University Library, before it was published in full in *The New Yorker* (Nov. 21, 1970), p. 50.
363	22	FCVA.
364	19	*Ibid.* Curiously enough, Jimmy Jones was listed as one of the aggrieved patrons in both paras. 1 and 2.
364	21	Coughlan, p. 58.
364	34	I: Branham Hume, 23 Nov. 1965.
364	36	*MBB,* pp. 142–3.
364	38	I: MCF, 31 Mar. 1965.
365	16	I: George Healy, Jr., 3 and 4 Feb., 1965; Healy, "Writer's Reports," *Dixie, Times-Picayune States Roto Magazine,* 4 July 1954; Healy in *WFO,* pp. 57–8.
365	23	*FOM,* pp. 112–14.
365	25	I: Dorothy Oldham, 21 Mar. 1965.
365	31	*FOM,* p. 114.
366	2	*MCA,* 14 Dec. 1950.
366	10	FCVA.
366	15	*NOS,* pp. xi–xii.
366	21	John Faulkner writes, "Anyhow, the preacher collected all the stories he could about Bill's drinking and told them from his pulpit. He said Bill was unfit to be a scout leader and that the troop should be taken away from him." *MBB,* p. 152.
366	30	I: BW, 28 Mar. 1965.
367	6	*Ibid.*
367	32	Sherwood Anderson, "New Orleans, *The Double Dealer,* and the Modern Movement in America," *The Double Dealer,* III (Mar. 1922), pp. 119, 124–6.
368	10	*FIU,* p. 231.
368	11	I: Elizabeth Anderson, 29 Jan. 1965; BW, 28 Mar. 1965.
368	29	*FIU,* p. 230. In answering the next question put to him, WF said that his reason for making the trip "was to get a ship." (P. 231.) When he and Stone would come to New Orleans together in early January, 1925, Anderson would not be there, having left for a two-month lecture tour. Anderson later spoke of first meeting WF in the winter, when he was wearing an overcoat. This would suggest early March, when he returned from the tour. (Sherwood Anderson, *Memoirs* [New York, 1942], p. 473.) However, it seems more logical that their first meeting must have taken place earlier and that in writing of these events nearly twenty years later—and at a time when he had gone through a long and increasingly painful period of mental anguish and self-doubt—Anderson telescoped the two meetings, or forgot

Page	Line	
		the first one, or chose not to mention it. (See Irving Howe on Anderson's "paramnesia" concerning *Winesburg, Ohio*'s critical reception, *Sherwood Anderson* [New York, 1951], p. 112.) The possibility that he chose not to mention it or perhaps even suppressed the memory of the meeting is supported by circumstances surrounding the writing of "A Meeting South," the story that argues most convincingly for the date of the first meeting between the two men as sometime early in November or possibly even prior to that. On November 12, 1924, Otto K. Liveright, Anderson's literary agent, acknowledged receipt of the manuscript of "A Meeting South." (Walter Rideout, as described in Millgate, *The Achievement,* p. 16.) The central character, a slight, lame young Southerner who is a poet and who drinks heavily, seems unmistakably modeled on the persona WF often assumed in New Orleans. Apart from the physical appearance, mannerisms, and statements of "David" in the story, he was unequivocally identified as WF by EF, Phil Stone, and BW. Clinching the case for the meeting which produced "A Meeting South" is, I think, Prof. James K. Feibleman's testimony that Sherwood Anderson talked to him about the evening of that meeting and that he recalls WF's mentioning it, too. (I: 1 Feb. 1965. See also Feibleman, p. 710.)
368	36	Dos Passos, p. 141.
369	3	Waldo Frank, as quoted in Howe, p. 123.
369	5	WF, "A Note on Sherwood Anderson," *ESP,* p. 4.
369	9	Roger Sergel in Howe, p. 241.
369	12	*FIU,* p. 260.
369	22	Hamilton Basso, "William Faulkner: Man and Writer," *Saturday Review,* 45 (July 28, 1962), p. 11.
369	32	I: Mrs. Julius Friend, 3 Feb. 1965; Marc Antony, 1 and 3 Feb., 1965.
370	8	Sherwood Anderson, "One Puzzled Concerning Himself," *The Double Dealer,* VII (Jan.–Feb., 1927), p. 100.
371	13	I: Keith Temple, 5 Feb. 1965; Flo Field, 3 Feb. 1965; Marc Antony, 1 Feb. 1965; Mr. and Mrs. Carl Carmer, 23 Aug. 1965; Harold Levy, 5 Feb. 1965. See also *New Orleans City Guide,* Federal Writers' Project (Boston, 1938), pp. 217–19.
371	25	Howard Mumford Jones, ed., with Walter B. Rideout, *The Letters of Sherwood Anderson* (Boston, 1953), pp. 141–2.
371	34	I: EF, 18 Feb. 1965.
371	38	Sherwood Anderson, "A Meeting South," *The Dial,* 78 (Apr. 1925), pp. 269–79, repr. in Paul Rosenfeld, ed., *The Sherwood Anderson Reader* (Boston, 1947), pp. 274–84.
372	21	I: George Healy, Jr., 3 and 4 Feb., 1965.
373	1	ACLT. In response to an inquiry if they could use some of the facts in the biographical sketch to promote sales of the book, Stone wrote that they didn't really understand the problem but that WF had said they were free to use any facts, "real or imaginary," that they cared to.
373	11	ACLT.
373	22	*Ibid.,* FCVA. On October 29, Stone's secretary typed out a clean copy of another poem. Like a Housman poem, "The Gallows" juxtaposed the subject's awful fate to his mother's love and hopes in his in-

Page	*Line*	
		fancy. At the same time, it endowed the nameless victim with attributes which suggested those of Christ, if only slightly. It would appear in *AGB* as poem XIV, pp. 34–5.
374	4	FCVA, ACLT.
374	6	*OXE,* 30 Oct. 1924.
374	12	I: Emily Stone, 30 Nov. 1965.
374	37	ACLT.
375	15	*Ibid.*
375	29	*Ibid.* The Armistice Day poem became poem XXX in *AGB,* p. 53.
376	3	ACLT. "Pregnancy" became poem XXIX in *AGB,* p. 52.
376	7	ACLT.
376	12	*OXE,* 4 Dec. 1924.
376	30	I: EF, 9 Sept. 1965.
377	4	*Ibid.*
377	16	ACLT.
377	24	FCVA.
377	32	*Ibid.* As poem XXXVII of *AGB,* it would show "Lilith" in place of "Cleopatra."
378	6	FCVA. There would be few changes when it appeared on p. 59 of *AGB* as poem XXXVI; "the surging wind" would become "the stallion, Wind," and a space would clearly separate octave and sestet.
378	25	JFSA.
378	31	*FOM,* p. 118.
379	20	*TMF,* pp. 6–8.
379	27	I: Robert Farley, 3 Apr. 1965.
379	30	I: J. D. Thames, 29 Nov. 1965. Prof. Leon Edel has suggested a number of correspondences between the personalities, concerns, and works of Hawthorne and WF. I: 30 Mar. 1966.
379	32	I: Branham Hume, 23 Nov. 1965.
380	3	ACLT.
380	8	See *The Delta Review,* 2 (July–Aug., 1965), p. 35.
380	15	All poems in this sequence courtesy Mrs. Frederick Van B. Demarest.
380	33	The last four poems in the sheaf were all dated 1924: "The Gallows," October 29; "Pregnancy," November 10; "November 11th," November 21; and "To Elise," December 10, rather than the earlier dating of December 5 on the previous version. This dating of two typed copies of "To Elise" five days apart points up the fact that such dating proves only that a particular copy was made on a particular day. While it might conceivably be the first typed version done from a newly composed holograph draft, there is no way of knowing this unless such substantiating evidence is present, which is rarely the case among the materials I have been able to examine.
381	9	"Indian Summer" would lose its title as poem XXXV of *AGB,* p. 58.
381	14	"Wild Geese" would become poem XXVIII of *AGB,* p. 51.
381	27	This became poem VIII of *AGB,* p. 27.
382	7	"March" would become poem XLII of *AGB,* p. 65. WF had dated one version of this poem "15 December 25." Courtesy Henry W. and Albert A. Berg Collection, NYPL.
385	17	FCVA.
388	19	*New Orleans City Guide,* pp. 6–39, 210–19; "The Charm of Old New Orleans," *The Mentor,* 13 (Mar. 1925), pp. 28–46; John Smith Kendall, "New Orleans," *The American Review of Reviews,* LXXIV (Dec. 1926), pp. 613–23; George Marvin, "The Mistress of the Mississippi," *Outlook,* 139 (Apr. 15, 1925), pp. 568–71; Kenneth L. Roberts, "The Charm City," *The Saturday Evening Post,* 199 (Jan. 8, 1927), pp. 20–1, 137–

NOTES

Page	Line	
		42; Bettersworth, pp. 45–120.
388	26	*NOS,* p. xviii.
388	29	I: Emily Stone, 30 Nov. 1965.
389	2	*OXE,* 22 Jan. 1925.
389	7	I: Elizabeth Anderson, 29 Jan. 1965.
389	9	I: Harold Levy, 5 Feb. 1965.
389	10	I: Louis Andrews Fischer, 2 Feb. 1965.
389	17	Carvel Collins, "Faulkner and Anderson, Some Revisions," paper delivered at the annual meeting of the Modern Language Association, Chicago, 28 Dec. 1967.
389	24	ACLT.
390	11	Frances Jean Bowen, pp. 443–56; Friend, pp. 16–17; Goldstein, pp. 6–7; Toledano, pp. 17–18.
390	20	*The Double Dealer,* VII (Jan.–Feb., 1925), p. iii.
390	32	*Ibid.,* pp. 83–5; repr. in *EPP,* pp. 109–12.
391	4	*Ibid.,* p. 85; repr. in *EPP,* p. 113.
391	8	*Ibid.,* pp. 102–7; repr. in *NOS* as specified below.
391	16	In an untitled short story typescript (FCVA), there are two central characters named Frankie and Johnny. The "Frankie and Johnny" section of "New Orleans" is an almost word-for-word excerpt from pp. 8 and 9 of the twenty-three page typescript. In the story WF described the parents of Frankie (Frances)—an unlucky prize-fighter (now dead) and his wife, apparently driven to loose living. The story ended with Frankie pregnant but not alarmed, meditating rather on her own condition: "she felt as impersonal as the earth itself: she was a strip of fecund seeded ground lying under the moon and wind and stars of the four seasons . . . ." In "The Kid Learns" WF would reverse the process, taking these two characters and expanding their story (with a different ending) rather than compressing it. This relationship suggests that some of the other sections of "New Orleans" may also have been taken from presumably rejected short stories. WF may have been cleaning out his files, using what he could of material which in earlier forms had not proved acceptable.
391	26	*NOS,* pp. 3–11.
391	35	*Ibid.,* pp. 11–13.
392	2	*Ibid.,* pp. 13–14.
392	28	Henry W. and Albert A. Berg Collection, NYPL.
392	37	Feibleman, pp. 706–7.
393	1	Sherwood Anderson, *Dark Laughter* (New York, 1925), p. 76.
393	6	Basso, p. 11.
393	11	I: Mr. and Mrs. Carl Carmer, 23 Aug. 1965.
393	37	*NOS,* p. xxvi.
394	18	I: Mr. and Mrs. Carl Carmer, 23 Aug. 1965.
394	22	*Ibid.*
394	26	"The Charm of Old New Orleans," p. 41.
394	31	I: Harold Levy, 5 Feb. 1965; Flo Field, 3 Feb. 1965; James Feibleman, 1 Feb. 1965.
395	5	John Faulkner writes that Bradford, as feature editor of the paper, bought the sketches from WF for $10 each. (*MBB,* p. 154.) George Healy, Jr., who joined the paper over a year and a half later, recalls that Phil Stone told him the sum was $5. (*WFO,* p. 59.) William Spratling reported that WF was paid $15 for each of the stories. (I: 30 Jan. 1965.) Prof. Collins set the figure at probably "the going rate of between fifteen and twenty-five dollars for a half-page of the Sunday feature section." (*NOS,* p. xix.) In

Page *Line*

one set of typescripts, each of the first four sketches that appeared in *NOTP* is included under the general title "Sinbad in New Orleans." On one of the sheets, WF listed his address as 624 Orleans Alley, New Orleans. Because it appears that he did not move to that address until March, these typescripts may date from that time or later and represent an attempt to gather the sketches together for publication in book form. On the other hand, WF may simply have added his name and address to the sheet after he moved, the title being a tentative one superseded by "Mirrors of Chartres Street." The sketches are entitled "Chartres Street" (published as "Mirrors of Chartres Street"), "Damon and Pythias Unlimited," "Home," and "Royal Street" (published as "Jealousy"). (Henry W. and Albert A. Berg Collection, NYPL.)

395 20 *NOS,* pp. 15–18. Collins suggests that the title may have been chosen for ironic contrast with the "Mirrors of Downing Street" feature and with "Mirrors of Washington," which *NOTP* ran. (P. xxvii.) Some of the sketches to follow used "Mirrors of Chartres Street" as a subtitle.

395 31 Morovitz shared a curious mannerism with the beggar of the first story: the habit of addressing a hearer as "fellow." This usage (and the race track setting) might have owed something to Anderson. *NOS,* pp. 19–27.

396 11 *NOS,* pp. 28–33.

396 25 *Ibid.,* pp. 34–40.

396 38 According to Walter Rideout, this book was probably owned by Elizabeth, not Sherwood Anderson. I: James Meriwether, 22 Jan. 1968.

397 9 FCVA. WF had used this death-in-life motif in "The Lilacs." His use of the phrase "The greening corridors" suggests that this poem may have been meant for the projected second volume of verse, to be entitled *The Greening Bough,* which had been mentioned in the "Notes on Contributors" in the Jan.–Feb. issue of *The Double Dealer.* Another version, dated at New Orleans "9 February 1925," is entitled "Endurance." Henry W. and Albert A. Berg Collection, NYPL.

397 16 *NYT,* 17 Feb. 1925.

397 23 JFSA.

397 31 I: Emily Stone, 30 Nov. 1965.

397 32 *NOS,* p. xxxi; Collins, "Faulkner and Anderson."

398 2 I: Branham Hume, 23 Nov. 1965; *The Mississippian,* 23 Jan. 1925.

398 6 George Healy, Jr., in *WFO,* p. 59.

398 25 *The Scream,* I (May 1925), pp. 11, 14, 15. An unsigned drawing on p. 12 of the Freshman Issue of *The Scream,* 1925–26, Vol. II, shows a two-seater biplane seen from above, possibly the work of WF or John Faulkner. MCUM.

398 31 *MCA,* 10 Mar. 1925.

398 37 James B. Meriwether, ed., *William Faulkner: An Exhibition of Manuscripts* (Austin, 1959), p. 6. Another version of this poem was dated in ink "1 March 25." (Henry W. and Albert A. Berg Collection, NYPL.) Poem XXVII of *AGB* would end with an almost identical stanza. (P. 50.)

399 10 One sheaf of ten poems—

NOTES

Page	Line	
		typed with black ribbon on legal-size white paper without watermark—looks to be a collection such as might be made for a book manuscript. The only dated poem in this group is "To Elise," which bears the line "5 December, 1924." FCVA.
399	37	ACLT. The bottom of this sheet was burned, so the last six lines are taken from the typed copy in FCVA, where the poem bears the title "A Child Looks from His Window." It would appear thus in *Contempo,* II (May 25, 1932), p. 3.
400	11	Phil Stone in Meriwether, "Early Notices of Faulkner," p. 138.
400	16	I: Ross Brown, 19 Nov. 1966.
400	17	*OXE,* 5 Mar. 1925.
400	19	*Letters of Sherwood Anderson,* pp. 135–6.
400	21	*FIU,* p. 231.
400	24	Collins, "Faulkner and Anderson"; I: Elizabeth Anderson, 29 Jan. 1965.
400	30	"nubbin" Sherwood Anderson, *Memoirs,* p. 473. Though Anderson had apparently blocked out the memory of the earlier meeting, his memory for the details of this one seems accurate. The weather would have suggested a trench coat. The temperature fell during the first week of March, 1925. The coldest day that week was the third, with a low of thirty-six degrees. Late October and early November of 1924, when their first meeting seems to have taken place, were warm.
400	31	*FIU,* p. 21.
400	35	I: Elizabeth Anderson, 29 Jan. 1965.
401	4	Sherwood Anderson, *Memoirs,* p. 473.
402	13	I: William Spratling, 28 Jan. 1965; Spratling, "Chronicle of a Friendship: William Faulkner in New Orleans," *The Texas Quarterly,* IX (Spring 1966), p. 35. For a slightly altered version, see *File on Spratling: An Autobiography* (Boston, 1967).
402	18	*FIU,* p. 21.
402	28	Feibleman, p. 709.
403	28	"A Note on Sherwood Anderson" in *ESP,* pp. 4–8. WF here wrote that the letter he described was his reply to Anderson's first letter. However, Anderson's letter makes it appear that WF began the exchange. *Letters of Sherwood Anderson,* pp. 162–4.
404	13	Courtesy Newberry Library, Chicago, Ill.
404	30	*Letters of Sherwood Anderson,* pp. 162–4. The Flu Balsam story seems obviously to be a version of the "dream" WF recalled Anderson's telling him.
405	12	Courtesy Newberry Library, Chicago, Ill.
405	17	WF was still writing verse that linked love and death. One poem, which began "Knew I love once?" was dated in ink "25 March 25." It would become poem XXXIII of *AGB,* p. 56. Another, somewhat longer, began "Green is the water, green. . . ." It suggested death by water after the manner of Eliot but carried a much stronger erotic suggestion. Dated in ink "2 April 25" and entitled "Drowning," it would become poem XIX of *AGB,* p. 41. Henry W. and Albert A. Berg Collection, NYPL.
405	23	ACLT.
405	32	I: Emily Stone, 30 Nov. 1965.
405	34	I: James Feibleman, 1 Feb. 1965.
406	1	*ESP,* p. 7.

Page	Line	
406	7	Sherwood Anderson in *We Moderns: Gotham Book Mart, 1920–1940* (New York, 1940), p. 29.
406	10	I: William Spratling, 28 Jan. 1965; Spratling, "Chronicle of a Friendship," p. 35.
406	28	Henry W. and Albert A. Berg Collection, NYPL. The second sheet bears another address: "1136-2nd St."
408	13	FCVA.
408	20	Collins, "Faulkner and Anderson."
408	31	*SP,* p. 5; *AGB,* p. 53.
409	5	*SP,* p. 7; *AGB,* p. 8.
409	12	*SP,* p. 23.
409	19	Collins, "Faulkner's War Service"; Spratling, "Chronicle of a Friendship," p. 36; I: Spratling, 29 Jan. 1965.
409	28	I: EF, 23 Feb. 1965.
409	35	See Bross, pp. 3–23.
410	9	Collins, "Faulkner and Anderson."
410	18	ACLT. See Anderson, "A Meeting South," in *Sherwood Anderson Reader,* pp. 274–84.
410	30	I: Mrs. Julius Friend, 3 Feb. 1965; Margery Gumbel, 28 Dec. 1965; Lucille Antony, 1 Feb. 1965.
410	34	I: Margery Gumbel, 28 Dec. 1965; Anita Loos, 22 Apr. 1965.
411	35	I: Anita Loos, 22 Apr. 1965, 18 Jan. 1966.
412	1	I: Bruce Manning, 4 June 1965.
412	6	*Sherwood Anderson Reader,* pp. 380–90.
412	17	*NOS,* pp. 41–5.
413	8	JFSA.
413	29	*NOS,* pp. 46–54. For a prefiguring of Lena Grove of *LIA,* see the bottom of p. 47.
413	34	*ESP,* p. 21.
414	7	*NOS,* pp. 55–60.
414	16	*EPP,* p. 92.
414	29	Henry W. and Albert A. Berg Collection, NYPL. Pursuing the girl, the man fell from a log into a stream. The sense of the imminence of death was somehow reinforced by the touch of a female body in the water. It was the girl, who fled again as the man clambered out to follow her. The combination of water, girl, and danger suggests Little Sister Death of *Mayday,* "The Kid Learns," and *S&F.*
414	36	I: Keith Temple, 5 Feb. 1965.
415	14	*EPP,* pp. 8–9.
415	21	See Lon Tinkle, "About Faulkner and Dallas," Dallas *Morning News,* 15 July 1962.
416	8	"Sherwood Anderson," Dallas *Morning News,* 26 Apr. 1925; repr. in *NOS,* pp. 132–9.
416	32	*ESP,* pp. 4–6.
417	8	*Letters of Sherwood Anderson,* p. 148.
417	17	I: William Spratling, 28 Jan. 1965.
417	27	I: Samuel Gilmore, 3 Feb. 1965.
417	28	I: William Spratling, 28 Jan. 1965.
417	35	I: Mr. and Mrs. Marc Antony, 1 Feb. 1965.
418	1	*NOS,* pp. xxiv–xxv.
418	9	Basso, p. 11.
418	15	*NOS,* pp. xxiv–xxv.
418	20	I: William Spratling, 30 Jan. 1965.
418	38	I: Spratling, Gilmore, and Mr. and Mrs. Antony, as above.
419	14	Basso, p. 12. One night at dinner, WF told friends that he had spent the whole day with the Gates Flying Circus and had even done some wing-walking. Coughlan, p. 64.
419	18	I: Helen B. Lyman and James Lyman, 19 June 1965.
419	27	I: William Spratling, 28 Jan. 1965.
419	29	I: Mr. and Mrs. Marc Antony, 3 Feb. 1965.
419	30	I: James Meriwether, 24 Jan. 1968.

NOTES

Page	Line	
419	38	*The Double Dealer,* V (Jan. 1924), p. iv.
420	26	I: Margery Gumbel, 28 Dec. 1965.
421	20	I: Harold Levy, 5 Feb. 1965; James A. Wobbe, "How Faulkner Wrote Sonnet," New Orleans *Item,* 29 Aug. 1954.
421	28	*The Double Dealer,* VII (Apr. 1925), p. 148, repr. in *EPP,* p. 119.
422	19	*The Double Dealer,* VII (Apr. 1925), pp. 129–31, repr. in *EPP,* pp. 114–18.
422	22	*Letters of Sherwood Anderson,* p. 144; Howe, p. 182.
422	27	The April issue of *The Double Dealer* also contained "The Tragedy of James Joyce," a dialogue between Benjamin Gilbert and Paul Rosser, and a generally unfavorable review by Julius Weis Friend of *Those Barren Leaves* by Aldous Huxley, whose influence would appear in WF's second novel and whose work WF by now was probably reading.
423	11	Collins, "Faulkner and Anderson."
423	32	FCVA.
424	6	See *SP,* pp. 78, 68, 67.
424	30	*NOS,* pp. 61–5. The only other work of this time to feature "The Rosary" prominently was F. Scott Fitzgerald's *The Great Gatsby,* which was widely reviewed during April and May of 1925. The novel and the story contained the same sinister incongruity: a religious song, guns, and death.
424	36	*NOTP,* 10 May 1925, repr. in *NOS,* pp. 66–9.
425	28	Henry W. and Albert A. Berg Collection, NYPL.
425	35	*NOS,* pp. 70–5.
426	29	*NOTP,* 24 May 1925, repr. in *NOS,* pp. 76–85.
427	6	Repr. in *NOS,* pp. 86–91. Collins has identified "Little Sister Death" as part of St. Francis' "Canticle of Creatures" and noted her reappearance in the unpublished tale *Mayday* and in the Quentin section of *S&F.* Hijacking would figure in *SAN* and *LIA. NOS,* p. xxx.
427	13	I: Mrs. Louis Andrews Fischer, 2 Feb. 1965; Flo Field, 3 Feb. 1965; Hermann Deutsch, 2 Feb. 1965.
427	20	I: Keith Temple, 5 Feb. 1965.
427	34	*FIU,* p. 21. For a semifictional account, see *EPP,* pp. 28–9.
427	36	I: Robert Coughlan, 24 Feb. 1967. Cf. *Once Aboard the Lugger,* below.
427	37	I: George Healy, Jr., 4 Feb. 1965.
428	1	I: MCF, 31 Mar. 1965.
428	4	I: William Spratling, 28 Jan. 1965.
428	9	For more on Slim, see *NOS,* p. xxv. *Once Aboard the Lugger* and *MOS* both made use of rumrunners named Pete and Joe. Pete and his mother would reappear in *PYL.*
428	27	I: Margery Gumbel, 28 Dec. 1965.
428	34	FCVA.
428	37	I: Robert Farley, 3 Apr. 1965.
429	1	Borrowing from Marine lore which Jack Falkner surely knew, WF gave one soldier the legendary cry of the Marine sergeant in Belleau Wood: "Come on, you bastards! Do you want to live forever?" (P. 179.)
429	9	The line from "Fantoches" is on p. 134, those from "Winged Victory" on p. 227. Margaret Powers' lines recalling Swinburne's "In the Orchard" appear on p. 181. See Adams, p. 120.
429	28	See *SP,* pp. 192, 152, 206, 261–3, 269. WF was also experimenting with character types: Cf. Cecily and Temple

Page	Line	
		Drake, her weak father and Horace Benbow, in *SAN.*
430	8	"finished" Collins, "Faulkner and Anderson."
430	9	FCVA.
430	14	*Letters of Sherwood Anderson,* pp. 139–40, 156.
430	20	*FIU,* p. 22.
430	23	I: Elizabeth Anderson, 29 Jan. 1965.
430	29	I: EF, 18 Feb. 1965.
431	20	Undated newspaper clipping, prob. 24 May 1925.
431	24	I: James Meriwether, 6 Mar. 1968.
432	5	*ESP.*
432	20	Hudson.
433	24	I: Mrs. Walter Lewis, Mrs. William Stone, IV, 30 Mar. 1965.
434	26	*Mississippi: A Guide to the Magnolia State,* W.P.A. Writers' Project (New York, 1938), pp. 286–90.
435	22	I: Mrs. William Stone, IV, Ann Farnsworth, Mrs. Thomas Leatherbury, 30 Mar. 1965; Chester McLarty, M.D., 21 Mar. 1965.
435	29	William Stone, V, in *WFO,* p. 79; I: Mrs. William Stone, IV, 30 Mar. 1965.
436	15	William Stone, V, to JB, 7 Sept. 1970.
436	29	I: Ann Farnsworth, 30 Mar. 1965.
437	5	*Ibid.*
437	21	William Stone, V, to JB, 7 Sept. 1970.
437	30	I: Samuel Gilmore, 3 Feb. 1965.
438	13	I: Ann Farnsworth, 30 Mar. 1965.
438	21	I: Helen B. Lyman, 19 June 1965.
439	3	*The Double Dealer,* VII (June 1925), pp. 185–7. WF's using the date August, 1925, beneath the dedication of "The Lilacs" as the poem was put into the June issue of the magazine suggests that he may have been commemorating something. One wonders if A. . . . . and H. . . . . might have been the British officers who encouraged him in New Haven to try for the RAF. It is also possible, of course, that the June issue may have come out late, in August, since publication of the magazine had become erratic. The poem is reprinted as I, *AGB,* pp. 7–11.
439	7	I: Helen B. Lyman, 19 June 1965.
439	11	*OXE,* 2 July 1925.
439	14	I: Ann Farnsworth, 30 Mar. 1965.
439	19	Edith B. Douds in *WFO,* p. 51.
439	27	I: Ella Somerville, 18 Nov. 1965.
439	32	I: Branham Hume, 23 Nov. 1965.
440	7	Hudson.
440	12	I: A. P. Hudson, 4 Apr. 1965.
440	17	I: Emily Stone, 27 Mar. 1965.
440	36	I: Mrs. Arthur Halle, 17 Mar. 1965.
441	7	WF to Mrs. Walter McLean, undated, prob. early Sept. 1925. MCL.
441	16	I: Mrs. Norman Thompson, 15 Mar. 1965.
441	27	I: Dorothy Conkling, 16 Mar. 1965. In another version of this story, Phil Stone told his nephew that Miss Maud had sewn a twenty-dollar gold piece into the lining of his coat. William Stone, V, in *WFO,* p. 83.
441	30	Spratling, "Chronicle of a Friendship," p. 36.
441	33	I: William Spratling, 29 Jan. 1965.
441	34	I: J. Auzine, 1 Feb. 1965.
442	5	Spratling, "Chronicle of a Friendship," p. 36.
443	12	FCVA.
444	4	Spratling, "Chronicle of a Friendship," p. 36.
444	5	"officers" I: William Spratling, 29 Jan. 1965.

NOTES

Page	Line	
444	8	JFSA.
444	12	Spratling, "Chronicle of a Friendship," p. 37.
444	15	*NOTP,* 13 Dec. 1953.
444	28	*Elmer,* p. 3. FCVA.
445	11	*NOTP,* 26 July 1925, repr. in *NOS,* pp. 92–103.
445	17	*NOS,* p. 93. Store owner Will Gibson suggests Will Varner, and attributes of Ek foreshadow those of Suratt, later V. K. Ratliff, in *HAM.* Cf. "The Liar" and the episode of the spotted horses in *HAM.*
445	31	Repr. in *NOS,* pp. 104–7.
445	38	I: William Spratling, 30 Jan. 1965.
446	19	Henry W. and Albert A. Berg Collection, NYPL.
446	28	*NOS,* p. xxiv.
447	25	Spratling, "Chronicle of a Friendship," pp. 37–8; I: 28 Jan. 1965.
447	26	I: BW, 28 Mar. 1965.
447	32	Spratling, "Chronicle of a Friendship," p. 38.
447	36	I: William Spratling, 28 Jan. 1965. There are a number of discrepancies between WF's accounts of the Italian part of the trip as he recorded them in post cards and letters and in those of Spratling as he put them down forty years later. In his letter to his mother from Paris dated "Thursday 13 1924 [*sic*]," WF mentioned being in Stresa before going to Sommariva. Later in the same letter he wrote, "I met Bill again at Stresa Tuesday, and we got a train for Montreux." These are the only two instances in which he mentions Spratling in the Italian phase of the trip. In every other instance he writes as though alone, from the Rapallo post card to the letter mentioned above. Spratling writes, "Our itinerary was vague, based mostly on points north and east, Vicenza, Pavia, and so on, places where I wanted to make pencil drawings. . . . A few days of this and we took our separate routes, to meet later in Paris." (P. 38. JFSA.) Their wanderings together could have been only brief, more likely immediately after Spratling's release in Genoa than at their first or second meeting in Stresa.
448	1	Describing the shoreline and sea at Rapallo, WF would write of "a pearl-and-amythest [*sic*] lambence. . . ." *Elmer,* p. 100. FCVA.
448	5	Michael Reck, *Ezra Pound: A Close-Up* (New York, 1967), pp. 48–51.
448	11	Phil Stone in Meriwether, "Early Notices of Faulkner," p. 141.
448	13	Reck, pp. 48–51.
448	17	I: William Spratling, 28 Jan. 1965.
448	21	JFSA.
448	32	*Ibid.*
448	36	WF to Mrs. Walter McLean, 9 Sept. 1925. MCL.
449	4	WF to Mrs. Murry Falkner, 7 Aug. 1925. JFSA.
449	9	WF to Mrs. Murry Falkner, "Thursday 13 1924 [*sic*]." JFSA.
449	20	WF to Mrs. Walter McLean, 7 Aug. 1925. MCL.
449	30	*Ibid.*
450	5	WF to Mrs. Murry Falkner, "Thursday 13 1924 [*sic*]." JFSA. The identity of the princess on the Alp presents something of a problem since the last Doge of Venice abdicated in 1797 and the *Almanach De Gotha* (1939) fails to list a member of the Russian royal family who might conceivably have been the lady's father-in-law.
450	23	*Ibid.*
450	33	Sherwood Anderson to Phil

Page	Line	
		Stone, 17 Aug. 1925, *Letters of Sherwood Anderson,* pp. 145–6.
451	28	JFSA.
451	32	I: William Spratling, 30 Jan. 1965.
451	38	WF to Mrs. Murry Falkner, 25 Aug. 1925. JFSA. The two works the paper would publish in September were clearly short stories, and it seems highly unlikely that WF would have called them "articles."
452	11	I: William Odiorne, 7 June 1965.
452	22	*Ibid.;* William Spratling, 30 Jan. 1965.
452	25	*FIU,* p. 58.
453	20	JFSA. In his correspondence WF followed a practice he would carry over into his fiction: the omission of apostrophes in contractions such as "don't" and "won't" in which, he apparently felt, the meaning was perfectly clear. He had also begun to omit the period occasionally from abbreviations such as "Mrs."
453	35	JFSA.
454	13	*Ibid.*
455	2	*Ibid.*
455	26	FCVA. Elmer's family suggests the Bundrens in *ASI.* Charlotte Rittenmeyer in *WP* represents a further development of Jo-Addie's type, and Harry Wilbourne is almost as passive with her as Elmer is with Jo-Addie.
455	35	FCVA.
456	20	WF to Mrs. Murry Falkner, 30 Aug. 1925. JFSA.
456	35	JFSA. He began with a reference to an airplane crash. "The Captain's 'washout' was funny, but it will teach him a lesson. That is, when its got a gasoline engine in it you've got to watch it all the time. He learned his cheaper than I did, at that."
457	23	*NOS,* pp. 108–20. WF's bootlegger shared with Gatsby a taste for gaudy shirts and rubies. Other lines suggested Sherwood Anderson: "he seems to enjoy my company, and some day I hope to get a story out of him. . . ." The kind of crime WF described happened a good deal closer to home than New Haven. Memphis gangster "Popeye" Pumphrey said of a rival gang: "At one time they engaged in working the 'sheriff racket,' which consisted of hijacking small town booze runners who believed that the men were officers. They flew liquor across the Mexican border...." *MCA,* 25 June 1929.
458	29	*NOS,* pp. 121–31. There were attitudes familiar in the work of the Polish expatriate, and specific facts or incidents suggested counterparts in three novels, one novella, and one short story. The story's opening description of the *Diana* and her men suggested the *Patna,* of *Lord Jim,* with her outcast white officers and silent lascar crew. To a lesser extent, it suggested the *Nanshan* of *Typhoon.* The extreme Englishness of the mate, Mr. Freddie Ayers, may suggest that of Major Ayers in *MOS.* The young officer, Leggatt, in "The Secret Sharer" had also killed a crewman, though in different circumstances. The scene in which the officers chase their Chinese "quarry," the assistant engineer crying "Gorn aw'y!," is an early use of the comic hunt motif to be seen in later works such as the story "Was."
459	6	WF to Mrs. Murry Falkner, postmarked 6 Sept. 1925. JFSA.
459	12	*FIU,* pp. 55–6.

NOTES

Page	Line	
459	16	See end of *SAN,* p. 380.
459	26	Elmer loved—and was humiliated by—a cruel and beautiful boy of godlike beauty. Except for the hostility, the relation vaguely resembled that of Tadzio and Jaschiu in Thomas Mann's *Death in Venice.* The 130 pages of typescript comprise four chapters of Book One, two of Book Two, and two of Book Three. There are nineteen unnumbered pages and several pages which are only slightly different versions of pages in the units mentioned above. FCVA.
459	36	*Elmer,* p. 44. WF said "the writer don't have to know Freud to have written things which anyone who does know Freud can divine and reduce to symbols." (*FIU,* p. 147.) "Everybody talked about Freud when I lived in New Orleans," he said, "but I have never read him." (Jean Stein in *LIG,* p. 251.)
460	10	*Elmer,* p. 66.
460	25	WF to Mrs. Murry Falkner, 6 Sept. 1925. JFSA.
461	9	*Ibid.*
462	18	WF to Mrs. Murry Falkner, 10 Sept. 1925. JFSA.
463	6	In his letter to his mother dated 13 September 1925, he said that he had received a letter from Aunt 'Bama "last Wednesday," which would have been September 9. In his reply to Aunt 'Bama he told her he had received her letter "today." He made no mention in the letter of having received any money from her.
463	24	JFSA.
464	7	William Hoffmann to JB, 1 and 25 Oct., 1965.
464	22	WF to Mrs. Murry Falkner, 13 Sept. 1925. JFSA.
466	11	WF would describe such a concert (even to Massenet and Berlioz) in the last paragraph of *SAN,* fusing it with material which seems to have come from the sketch about the girl, the Luxembourg Gardens, and death.
466	26	WF to Mrs. Murry Falkner, postmarked 22 Sept. 1925, 9:30 (A.M.), prob. written Sept. 21. (JFSA.) The comment in this letter about Cézanne was clearly an adaptation of a line in the first paragraph of "Out of Nazareth." (*NOS,* p. 46.)
466	29	*The Mississippian,* 18 Sept. 1925.
467	14	Ludwig Lewisohn, ed., *A Modern Book of Criticism* (New York, 1919), p. iv. Lewisohn hoped the book would help by showing the liberal critics that "their battle" was long since won in France, that a philosophical basis for the new criticism had been provided in Germany, and that the "chief creative minds" of England and Ireland "are fighting with them." (P. iv.) In "The Criticism of Contemporaries," Jules Lemaître recalled his indignation at critics who condemned works of Hugo and Flaubert for lack of good sense and good taste while missing their lyric radiance and plastic perfection. "But," Lemaître observed, "one must love a thing to understand it well and thoroughly." WF underlined this sentence in blue ink. In the margin he wrote, "True, true, true. To have said: One must understand a thing to love it—how cold, cold. But to love and forgive—well, at sight, is better than comprehension. A dry thing at best." (P. 16.) Under the title "Experience and Creation," Wilhelm Dil-

Page Line

they declared, "*Goethe is that seer of life who revealed to all the poets and philosophers who came after him the art of interpreting human life simply upon the basis of its own reality. . . .*" (P. 52.) He continued, "the content of a poetic work, which raises a concrete event to true significance, has its foundation in the personal experience of the poet and the circle of ideas in which he lives." (P. 53.) The foundations of poetic activity rested mainly on experience, insight into it, and the "widening and deepening of experience through ideas." (P. 53.)

In the book's end papers, WF wrote "vide Wm. Dilthey" and filled the rest of the page with comment. "Bunk," he began. "It takes a German to accept an arbitrary and usually false premise and arrive with unimpeachable logic at a conclusion not only unsound but impracticable. Goethe, for instance. Quite correct here, for Goethe deliberately made himself a poet, and so is unique in all history. Shakespeare: after money and position, at least trying to write plays—taking the first thing that came to hand, which was the stage[,] becomes a poet by accident. Shelley trying to fancy himself an atheist and a democrat, Keats trying to seduce Fanny Brawne with words, Verlaine washing his emotional dirty linen, Swinburne like a bird in the top of a tree—all became poets by accident. What did they care about establishing any correlation between the important facts of hunger and sex and death and any sort of spiritual world? Bunk. A real poet hasn't got time to do that. Particularly as the German critics are sure to do it for him, overriding him with the bland courtesy of undertakers that appear before the corpse is even dead. Stick to your music, ye logical dull men. Let the French who are aware of the utter unimportance of ideas make criticism." He ended with a date and place: "2? September 1925/Normandy." (JFSA.)

Page	Line	
468	8	WF to Mrs. Murry Falkner, 3 Oct. 1925. JFSA.
468	19	JFSA.
469	20	WF to Mrs. Murry Falkner, 3 Oct. 1925. JFSA.
469	28	JFSA.
470	2	WF to Mrs. Murry Falkner, 3 Oct. 1925. JFSA. On September 25, *The Mississippian* had noted the resignation of the campus postmaster, Sonny Bell, who "succeeded Mr. William Faulkner, who resigned last year to enter the field of literature."
470	22	*Modern Book of Criticism*, p. 74. JFSA.
470	37	*Ibid.*, p. 79.
471	19	*Ibid.*, pp. 82, 84.
471	26	*Ibid.*, p. 178.
471	31	*FIU*, p. 103.
472	11	WF to Mrs. Murry Falkner, 3 Oct. 1925. JFSA.
472	32	JFSA.
473	2	*Ibid.*
473	28	*Ibid.*
474	12	FCVA.
474	21	FCVA.
475	34	WF to Mrs. Murry Falkner, 7 Oct. 1925. JFSA.
476	19	WF to Mrs. Murry Falkner, postmarked 9 Oct. 1925. JFSA. The dogs of Tunbridge Wells suggest the pets of Miss Reba Rivers in *SAN*, "small, woolly, worm-like dogs. . . ." P. 170.
476	35	WF to Mrs. Murry Falk-

NOTES

Page	Line	
		ner, 9 Oct. 1925. FCVA.
477	14	WF to Mrs. Murry Falkner, 15 Oct. 1925. FCVA.
477	23	See Ernest Hemingway to Carlos Baker, in Baker, *Hemingway: The Writer as Artist* (New York, 1956), pp. 75–6.
477	33	FCVA.
477	37	Anita Loos, *A Girl Like I* (New York, 1966), pp. 255–6.
478	4	Manuel Komroff to JB, 22 Sept. 1965.
478	7	WF to Horace Liveright, Oct. 1927. FCVA.
478	13	*FCF,* p. 109.
478	20	WF would use the name Everbe Corinthia again thirty-five years later, in *REV.*
478	36	*CS,* pp. 823–42.
479	10	*Elmer,* p. 85. FCVA. WF described Myrtle's "humanness" and said that "Henry James would have called it vulgarity. . . ." In spite of this, WF's treatment of the American heiress and fortune hunters in Europe could have owed something to such works as *Portrait of a Lady, The Golden Bowl,* and *The Wings of the Dove.* The name Wohleden may have been suggested by Katrina Carter's maternal line, the Wohllebens.
479	21	*Ibid.,* p. 102.
479	23	*Ibid.,* p. 104.
479	25	*Ibid.,* p. 105.
479	30	WF to James Meriwether, 12 Mar. 1958, in Meriwether, *The Literary Career,* p. 81.
480	28	*AGB,* poem IV, pp. 20–1. Cf. E. E. Cummings' poem XXVII, "Memorabilia," collected in *Is 5* (1926), repr. in *E. E. Cummings, Poems: 1923–1954* (New York, 1954), p. 183.
481	1	*William Faulkner: An Exhibition of Manuscripts,* p. 6. Emily Stone recalls that "Ernest V. Simms" told

Page	Line	
		Mencken that WF was studying at the Baptist Seminary in Paris. I: 30 Nov. 1965.
481	3	I: Emily Stone, 27 Mar. and 30 Nov., 1965.
481	4	Phil Stone to Four Seas Co., 10 Aug. 1925. FCVA.
481	8	Four Seas Co. to Phil Stone, 14 Aug. 1925. FCVA.
481	10	FCVA.
481	13	R. S. Tower to Murry Falkner, 19 Oct. 1925.
481	16	Murry Falkner to General Accounting Office, 26 Oct. 1925. FCVA.
481	22	J. R. McCarl to Murry Falkner, 9 Nov. 1925. FCVA.
481	31	I: Harold Levy, 5 Feb. 1965.
481	32	I: William Odiorne, 7 June 1965.
483	7	*OXE,* 17 and 25 Nov., 1925.
483	13	JFSA.
483	29	*Ibid.*
488	1	Lester Cohen, "The Saint . . . and the Sinner," *Esquire,* LIV (Dec. 1960), p. 78.
488	9	I: Manuel Komroff, 22 Jan. 1965; Komroff to JB, 22 Sept. 1965. Mr. Komroff recalled that WF had a manuscript under his arm and a letter of introduction from Sherwood Anderson. Anderson later told Komroff that he had thought Komroff would understand WF better than Liveright and would therefore give the manuscript into sympathetic hands. But *SP* had been accepted by this time and *MOS* would not be accepted until late 1926. Replying to an inquiry by Komroff, WF wrote on July 27, 1949, "I dont remember that letter. I knew Anderson in New Orleans. When I left him there, I went to Europe, so I dont think he could have given me a letter to someone in New York." (FCVA.) Komroff seems likely to have been remembering the letter

Page	Line	
		which accompanied or preceded WF's mailing of the manuscript of *SP.* The manuscript to which he referred might conceivably have been *Elmer.*
488	16	I: MCF, 31 Mar. 1965.
488	22	*MBB,* p. 155. John Faulkner also reported that his brother had traveled steerage—a fiction paralleling his assertion that he worked his way across on a tramp steamer.
488	27	*OXE,* 30 July 1925.
488	28	*OXE,* 8 Oct. 1925.
488	30	*OXE,* 22 Oct. 1925.
488	36	I: Dorothy Oldham and Ella Somerville, 18 Nov. 1967.
489	5	*Ibid.*
489	13	*WFL,* pp. 34, 40, 44.
489	16	JFSA.
489	39	C. M. Smith in *WFO,* pp. 63–4; I: 25 Nov. 1965.
490	2	*MBB,* p. 155.
490	17	*CS,* pp. 877–94.
490	34	*Ibid.,* pp. 843–76. If "Mistral" had something of WF's and Spratling's Italian travels about it, the dialogue suggested the banter of Jake Barnes and Bill Gorton in *The Sun Also Rises.* The brief appearance of a fiddler and a piper recalled WF's earlier stories.
491	1	JFSA.
491	7	*Ibid.*
491	24	FCVA. See Meriwether, *The Literary Career,* p. 81. Della's description suggests Dilsey in the fourth section of *S&F.* BW used *The Devil Beats His Wife* for the novel he published in 1929.
491	32	ACLT.
491	35	*OXE,* 20 Jan. 1926.
492	4	*MCA,* 12 Feb. 1926.
492	10	*MBB,* p. 141. John Faulkner dates the hole-in-one about 1919, but an *Item* interview places it in 1926. See *LIG,* p. 4.
492	13	*MCA,* 8 Aug. 1925.
492	16	*MCA,* 13 Nov. 1925.
492	21	I: Dorothy Conkling, 16 Mar. 1965; Malcolm Franklin, 26 Sept. 1966.
492	32	Although Pumphrey declared he had married in the spring of 1930, his mother told a reporter that he was afraid of girls. When he was in a hospital at age twenty-three, recovering from a broken leg, his mother arrived to find him in tears. He indicated a nurse and whispered, "Mother, that girl said she was going to bathe me." *MCA,* 25 June 1929.
492	37	The place and dating here are highly tentative. The source is Carvel Collins' "A Note on 'Sanctuary,'" *The Harvard Advocate,* CXXXV (Nov. 1951), p. 16. Collins does not list the place but gives the time as "One evening in the mid-nineteen-twenties." He does not name Pumphrey but writes that the actual gangster killed himself eight months after the publication of *SAN.* The novel appeared February 9, 1931, and Pumphrey shot himself October 28, 1931. (See Robert Cantwell, "Faulkner's 'Popeye,'" *The Nation* [Feb. 15, 1958], pp. 140–1, 148.) Wigfall Green also wrote that Popeye was "undoubtedly Popeye Pumphrey, a Memphis racketeer who recently attempted suicide." (A. Wigfall Green, p. 304.)
493	4	I: Dorothy Oldham, 21 Mar. 1965.
493	7	"The Big Shot" appears to survive only in a thirty-seven-page typescript. The use of the formula story with surprise ending recalls WF's apprenticeship, but the stylistic dexterity (in spite of numerous flourishes) suggests a

Page	*Line*	
		later date than the *NOTP* sketches. The first recorded magazine submission of the story appears to have been January, 1930, but it may have gone out earlier. See Meriwether, *The Literary Career,* p. 170.
493	23	FCVA.
493	35	"Dal" is a shortening of Martin's first name, the whole of which is not disclosed. Dallas, in Lafayette County, is close to what seems to be the equivalent of Frenchman's Bend in Yoknapatawpha County. Just as there are other resemblances between Martin and Flem Snopes (*HAM*), so there are others between the landowner and Thomas Sutpen (*AA*)—in addition to the obvious one between Martin and Sutpen.
494	16	*MPS,* 18 July 1929.
494	18	In "Dull Tale," a thirty-three-page typescript, WF emphasized the character of the socialite Dr. Gavin Blount, president of the Nonconnah Guards, who was again corrupted by Dal Martin. After Martin financed an art gallery named for Blount's grandfather (killed serving with Nathan Bedford Forrest), Blount felt compelled to issue to Martin's daughter the sought-after invitation to the Nonconnah Guards Ball. Plagued by conscience, Blount later committed suicide. JFSA.
494	27	I: JMF, 21 Mar. 1965.
494	31	I: Robert Coughlan, 24 Feb. 1967.
494	33	I: SMW, 15 Nov. 1967.
495	1	I: Emily Stone, 27 Mar. 1965.
495	9	I: Mr. and Mrs. Marc Antony, 1 and 3 Feb., 1965.
495	18	Wobbe, p. 18.
495	20	I: Caroline Durieux, 5 Feb. 1965.
495	27	I: Flo Field, 3 Nov. 1965.
495	38	I: Mr. and Mrs. Marc Antony, 3 Feb. 1965.
496	3	Basso, p. 12.
496	6	I: Louis Andrews Fischer, 2 Feb. 1965.
496	13	Frances Bowen Durrett, "The New Orleans Double Dealer," in William E. Walker and Robert L. Welker, eds., *Reality and Myth: Essays in American Literature in Memory of Richard Croom Beatty* (Nashville, Tenn., 1964), p. 213.
496	16	George Healy, Jr., in *WFO,* pp. 59–60.
496	37	Courtesy Miss Anita Loos. See *FIU,* p. 193, for WF's adaptation of an aphorism of Miss Loos's creation, Lorelei Lee.
497	5	*Letters of Sherwood Anderson,* pp. 151–2.
497	13	WF to Manuel Komroff, 27 July 1949. FCVA.
497	21	*Letters of Sherwood Anderson,* p. 155.
497	30	Walter Rideout in Millgate, *The Achievement,* p. 19.
497	35	I: Elizabeth Anderson, 29 Jan. 1965.
498	1	*Letters of Sherwood Anderson,* p. 129.
498	7	I: William Spratling, 29 Jan. 1965.
498	38	Sherwood Anderson, *Memoirs,* p. 474.
499	10	*ESP,* p. 5.
499	13	James Schevill, *Sherwood Anderson: His Life and Work* (Denver, 1951), pp. 5–6.
499	18	WF to JB.
499	22	*ESP,* p. 5.
499	25	Collins, "Faulkner and Anderson."
499	37	I: BW, 28 Mar. 1965.
499	38	I: James Feibleman, 1 Feb. 1965.
500	6	Robert A. Jeliffe, ed., *Faulkner at Nagano* (Tokyo, 1956), repr. in *LIG,* p. 120.

Page	Line	
500	18	Unpubl. portion of class conference, U. of Va., 15 May 1957.
500	26	Sherwood Anderson, *Memoirs,* pp. 333, 339–40.
500	27	*FIU,* p. 281; *ESP,* p. 10.
500	33	*ESP,* pp. 10, 5, 6.
501	2	Sherwood Anderson, *Memoirs,* p. 477.
501	4	I: Elizabeth Anderson, 29 Jan. 1965.
501	23	*Letters of Sherwood Anderson,* pp. 145, 152.
501	27	*DRM,* p. 276, repr. in *CS,* pp. 799–821.
501	38	*CS,* pp. 807, 805, 809–10. The narrator's last gesture toward his old life is a letter to the New York *Times* dated "New Orleans, La./April 10 . . . ." A port named Rincon is located near the northwest tip of Puerto Rico. Another Rincon appears in Joseph Conrad's *Nostromo.*
502	14	"Carcassonne," in *T13,* repr. in *CS,* pp. 895, 899.
502	19	FCVA.
502	23	*FIU,* p. 22.
502	26	There were a number of interesting correspondences. The protagonist, of whom WF wrote, "the galloping horse filled his mind again with soundless thunder," suggested the obsessed Gail Hightower of *LIA.* One phrase in the poet's stream of consciousness—"*where fell where I was King of Kings but the woman with the woman with the dog's eyes to knock my bones together and together*"—suggested the passage from *Agamemnon* in which the murdered king speaks of Clytemnestra's refusal to close his dead eyes, the passage which gave WF the title of *ASI.* (WF to JB.) Another passage about "bones knocking together to the spent motion of falling tides in the caverns and the grottoes of the sea" suggests both the end of Eliot's "The Love Song of J. Alfred Prufrock" and the "Death by Water" section of "The Waste Land." The dream horse's destination, "the barn where sleep was stabled," may bring to mind Sherwood Anderson's linking of his dream horse and sleep. The protagonist's wish "to perform something bold and tragical and austere" may recall WF's plea, at the end of "Verse Old and Nascent," for someone to write "something beautiful and passionate and sad." The place of the story, Rincon, may, like Naples in "Divorce in Naples," be Genoa adapted for present purposes.
503	7	Dating obviously presents a problem here, and composition may have taken place one or two years from the date tentatively assigned. (JFSA.) WF appears to have taken the title, curiously enough, and perhaps with ironic intent, from an English school song: *We're good at games like rugger* *And snooker and lacrosse,* *And once aboard the lugger* *We are never at a loss.*
503	11	WF to Frederick Gwynn; Gwynn to JB, in conversation, Spring 1957.
503	22	I: BW, 28 Mar. 1965.
503	25	*The Record,* XLVI, Sigma Alpha Epsilon (Mar. 1926), p. 245.
503	31	FCVA.
504	1	*Ibid.*
504	7	*OXE,* 28 May 1926.
504	8	"Theatre" *OXE,* 17 Mar. 1926.
504	9	*OXE,* 28 Apr. 1926.
504	12	*OXE,* 12 May 1926.

NOTES

Page	Line	
504	13	*OXE,* 17 Mar. 1926.
505	4	Thomas D. Clark in *WFO,* pp. 69–71.
505	14	*NYT Book Review,* 11 Apr. 1926. I am indebted here to Prof. O. B. Emerson's extremely helpful doctoral dissertation, *William Faulkner's Literary Reputation in America,* Vanderbilt U., 1962.
505	18	*Letters of Sherwood Anderson,* p. 155.
505	20	"veterans" *The Literary Review,* 3 Apr. 1926.
505	22	*The Saturday Review of Literature,* 24 Apr. 1926.
505	24	Springfield *Republican,* 4 Apr. 1926; *Independent,* 17 Apr. 1926.
505	26	*NYHT Books,* 6 June 1926.
505	28	*The New Republic,* 23 June 1926.
505	31	*The International Book Review,* 26 July 1926.
505	36	*The Literary Digest,* as quoted on dust jacket of *MOS.*
506	2	*NOTP,* 11 Apr. 1926.
506	7	Nashville *Tennessean,* 11 Apr. 1926. See O. B. Emerson, "Prophet Next Door," in *Reality and Myth,* pp. 237–74; also M. Thomas Inge, "Donald Davidson on Faulkner: An Early Recognition," *The Georgia Review,* XX (Winter 1966), pp. 454–62. The *MOS* dust jacket quoted a number of laudatory reviews. Among them was a statement in the St. Louis *Globe-Democrat* that "the book is likely to become a classic." The Baltimore *Sun* reviewer wrote, "this seems to me to be one of the books that will be worth reading a few years from now. . . ." A home voice, that of the New Orleans *Item,* called the book *"the best written novel about the war."*
506	12	I: Louise Meadow, 27 Nov. 1965.
506	16	*OXE,* 9 June 1926.
506	20	*OXE,* 28 July 1926.
506	21	*OXE,* 7 July 1926.
506	30	William Stone, V, in *WFO,* pp. 77–8.
508	9	*ESP.*
508	24	I: Ann Farnsworth, 30 Mar. 1965.
509	7	I: Helen B. Lyman and James Lyman, 19 and 20 June, 1965.
509	13	"The History of *The Southern Lumberman,*" *The Southern Lumberman,* 193 (Dec. 15, 1956), pp. 110–15.
510	25	I: Helen B. Lyman and James Lyman, 19 and 20 June, 1965.
510	29	I: Ann Farnsworth, 30 Mar. 1965.
511	2	I: Helen B. Lyman, 20 June 1965. See *NOS,* p. 29, and *EPP,* p. 18. See also Carvel Collins, "The Interior Monologues of *The Sound and the Fury,*" *Publications in the Humanities,* 6 (Dept. of Humanities, Massachusetts Institute of Technology, 1954), pp. 29–56, repr. in *Studies in The Sound and the Fury,* comp. by James B. Meriwether (Columbus, O., 1970), pp. 59–79.
511	11	See Meriwether, "Notes on the Textual History of *The Sound and the Fury,*" *Papers of the Bibliographical Society of America,* 56 (Third Quarter, 1962), p. 295.
511	22	I: Helen B. Lyman, 20 June 1965.
511	27	I: Betty Carmer, 23 Aug. 1965.
512	2	I: Ann Farnsworth, 30 Mar. 1965.
512	10	I: Helen B. Lyman, 19 June 1965.
513	11	I: Myrtle Stone and Mrs. Thomas Leatherbury, 30 Mar. 1965.
513	16	William Stone, V, in *WFO,* p. 80.

Page *Line*

513 22 FCVA.

514 25 See Frederick L. Gwynn, "Faulkner's Prufrock—And Other Observations," *The Journal of English and German Philology,* LII (Jan. 1953), pp. 63–70. In describing New Orleans as a courtesan "weary too of ardent ways," WF was using again a phrase from his poem "Estelle" (ACLT), borrowed originally from Stephen Dedalus' "Villanelle of the Temptress" in James Joyce's *Portrait of the Artist as a Young Man.*

514 34 Henry W. and Albert A. Berg Collection, NYPL.

515 9 Talliaferro is an old name which is pronounced "Tolliver" in certain areas of the South and often carries a certain social cachet.

515 37 I: William Spratling, 30 Jan. 1965.

516 5 It may not be entirely fanciful to suggest a triad of names: Baird-bird-Robyn. WF distributed more than a few private references through the book.

517 10 "I don't mind the heat," Fairchild tells Gordon. "I like it, in fact. Like an old racehorse, you know." (P. 49.) In August, 1924, Anderson wrote from New Orleans to his brother Karl, "It is hot, but like an old horse I feel better, in the heat." (*Letters of Sherwood Anderson,* p. 128.)

517 22 Under the title "La Lune ne Grade Aucune Rancune," WF typed out the poem (*AGB,* XXXII) repr. herein on p. 327. Below the last line WF typed:

> rote for saM G81m9re b%
> wY99iam 7 mqan 3ill#a@
> 7 ;ean
> bY wiLL*am f@Ulkn8R
> 7 ha'e to9k lE$$on$ o% 5he 5ype@ritt(r "ut 7 keelp ?onfu9ing it rrkh dam W8th my !lute 7 me%n fl@rt 7 %ean FULTE. [FCVA, repr. in Meriwether, *The Literary Career,* Fig. 4.]

This version of the poem was never given to Gilmore and he heard of it only in a roundabout way. (I: Gilmore, 3 Feb. 1965.) I am not aware of any connection between Mark Frost and poet Robert Frost.

518 28 Collins writes that aspects of Pete and his brother, Joe, may have been suggested by a New Orleans bootlegger called "Slim." *NOS,* p. xxv.

518 36 See *NOS,* pp. xxiv–xxv.

519 5 I: William Spratling, 30 Jan. 1965; Samuel Gilmore, 3 Feb. 1965.

519 16 WF had drawn on his travel memories for more than Lake Maggiore. Writing of the *Nausikaa,* he thought of the *West Ivis* and the *Republic,* using the word "stateroom" then crossing it out to substitute "cabin," replacing "seawater" with "lake water." All of which suggests that though he spent time boating on Lake Pontchartrain with Anderson and others, he still had to draw imaginatively on his own longer voyage.

519 17 In her domination of David and the difference between their social backgrounds, Pat also suggests Charlotte Rittenmeyer with Harry Wilbourne in *WP.*

520 2 FCVA. Linton Massey informs me that bell imagery similar to that in WF's letter to Helen Baird appears in Donn Byrne's *Messer Marco*

NOTES

Page	Line	
		Polo (1921). The ultimate source may perhaps be found in Edmond Rostand's *Cyrano de Bergerac.*
520	19	Maurier's marriage for respectability anticipates that of Thomas Sutpen in *AA*. The two joyless faces suggest those of Eula and Flem Snopes in *HAM.*
522	16	See "Carcassonne" in *CS,* p. 897; *MOS,* p. 162; *NOS,* pp. 39–41.
522	39	*ESP,* p. 8.
523	5	FCVA.
523	8	*OXE,* I Sept. 1926.
523	11	*OXE,* 16 July 1926.
523	14	I: Myrtle Stone and Mrs. Thomas Leatherbury, 30 Mar. 1965.
523	26	WF changed several of the time segments, with "Seven Thirty" becoming "Seven O'-Clock" and "Eight Thirty" becoming "Eight O'Clock." He transposed the order of several sections. Perhaps anticipating this likelihood, he had numbered the first 153 pages by typewriter, erasing and renumbering after adding new segments of five and then ten pages. From p. 154 to the end of the book, he numbered the pages in ink. FCVA.
523	28	I: Robert Farley, 3 Apr. 1965.
523	30	I: BW, 29 Nov. 1965.
523	34	I: Sallie Elliott, 24 Mar. 1965.
523	37	Edith B. Douds in *WFO,* p. 52.
524	7	I: EF, 18 and 29 Apr., 1968.
524	18	Repr. in *NOS,* pp. xxxiii–xxxiv. Collins writes that WF gave the interview in the autumn of 1926. Since he had arrived on a Sunday and planned to return to Oxford on Monday, to come back to New Orleans at the end of September, it seems possible that he returned to New Orleans on September 19 and

Page	Line	
		planned to travel to Oxford on the twenty-seventh and then back to New Orleans on, perhaps, Friday, October 1.
524	30	*Letters of Sherwood Anderson,* pp. 161–2.
524	38	I: William Spratling, 29 Jan. 1965.
525	6	I: Mr. and Mrs. Marc Antony, 1 Feb. 1965.
526	16	Spratling, "Chronicle of a Friendship," p. 36; I: 30 Jan. 1965.
525	25	I: Flo Field, 5 Feb. 1965.
526	2	I: Mr. and Mrs. Marc Antony, 1 Feb. 1965.
526	23	I: Margery Gumbel, 28 Dec. 1965.
526	34	For the dating, see James B. Meriwether, "Sartoris and Snopes: An Early Notice," *The Library Chronicle of the University of Texas,* VII (Summer 1962), pp. 36–9.
527	2	Jean Stein in *LIG,* p. 255.
527	5	*Letters of Sherwood Anderson,* p. 129; see "Father Abraham: A Lincoln Fragment," in *Sherwood Anderson Reader,* pp. 530–602.
528	2	Arents Collections, NYPL.
529	11	Phil Stone said that Admiral Dewey Snopes, like Wallstreet Panic Snopes, was a name which he created. As reported by H. Edward Richardson, Stone claimed a considerable part in the elaboration of the Snopes saga: "Faulkner often found it necessary to return to Stone's office in order to check his lore." See H. E. Richardson, "The Ways That Faulkner Walked," *The Arizona Quarterly,* 21 (Summer 1965), p. 138.
531	9	Arents Collections, NYPL.
531	23	*OXE,* 18 Aug. 1926.
531	26	*SAR,* p. 43.
532	19	Beinecke Library, YUL.
532	33	WF pronounced Bayard "Baird" and accented the

Page *Line*

first syllable of Sartoris. This uncommon name was to be found in the town of Sardis, twenty-three miles northwest of Oxford. (See Cleanth Brooks, *William Faulkner: The Yoknapatawpha Country* [New Haven, 1963], p. 383.) In 1874 U.S. Grant's daughter had been married in the White House to a young Englishman named Algernon Sartoris.

533 38 FCVA. I am indebted to Prof. Douglas Day for his kindness in allowing me to study his collation and analysis of the manuscript and typescript of *Flags in the Dust* and *SAR*.

534 6 See Richard T. Dillon, "Some Sources for Faulkner's Version of the First Air War," *American Literature,* 44 (Jan. 1973), pp. 629–37.

534 9 FCVA. WF apparently added the new material in two parts, for five pages bore the numbers 01 through 05. Two more, following p. 02, bore the numbers 002 and 003. In *The Making of Sartoris: A Description and Discussion of the Manuscript and Composite Typescript of William Faulkner's Third Novel* (unpubl. Ph.D. thesis, Cornell, 1969), Stephen N. Dennis suggests that pp. 01–05 may have begun as a short story and that the expansion of one paragraph on p. 02 by the addition of pp. 002–003 may represent a transitional stage between the story and its development into the novel. (Pp. 52–5.) I am much indebted to Prof. Dennis for his kindness in allowing me to study this thoroughgoing work.

534 36 I: Flo Field, 3 Feb. 1965.

535 29 *Sherwood Anderson & Other Famous Creoles: A Gallery of Contemporary New Orleans,* Drawn by Wm. Spratling & Arranged by Wm. Faulkner, Published by Pelican Bookshop Press in Royal Street New Orleans MCMXXVI. Repr. in facsimile in *The Texas Quarterly,* IX (Spring 1966), pp. 41–96.

535 30 Millgate, *The Achievement,* p. 19.

536 3 Spratling, "Chronicle of a Friendship," p. 36.

536 8 *ESP,* pp. 10, 6.

536 12 I: William Spratling, 30 Jan. 1965.

536 14 *OXE,* 29 Dec. 1926.

536 19 I: MCF, 31 Mar. 1965.

536 24 *Ibid.*

536 29 I: C. M. Smith, 25 Nov. 1965.

537 2 I: JMF, 17 Mar. 1965.

537 11 I: Emily Stone, 30 Nov. 1965.

537 20 I: Robert Coughlan, 29 Dec. 1966.

537 29 Emily Stone, "Faulkner Gets Started," p. 143.

537 38 I: Emily Stone, 27 Mar. 1965.

538 2 I: MCF, 31 Mar. 1965.

538 7 I: Robert Coughlan, 24 Feb. 1966.

538 11 The story Caspey tells of his exploits in the army may owe something to that book which WF and Jack enjoyed so much, *The Military Wildcat.*

538 32 As quoted in Meriwether, "Sartoris and Snopes," pp. 36–7.

539 9 I: Margery Gumbel, 28 Dec. 1965.

539 21 I: EF, 8 Aug. 1963; 18 and 29 Apr., 1968.

539 31 After thanking Liveright for "the Napoleon," WF added, "The world certainly owes Lytton Strachey a debt for making history readable." Apparently WF felt that Ludwig had been influenced by inconoclastic works such as Strachey's *Eminent Vic-*

Page	Line	
		torians (1918) and *Queen Victoria* (1921).
539	38	I: BW, 28 Mar. 1965.
540	24	FCVA. In terms of the printed text, these four excisions came at the bottom of p. 44, before "Twelve O'Clock" on p. 156, before "Eleven O'-Clock" on p. 177, and after ". . . the comic aspect of it" on p. 185.
541	3	*White Beeches* was eventually submitted to Scribner's after WF typed it. When it was returned, EF angrily burned it, nearly setting her mother's roof afire as the incinerated pages floated out of the chimney. WF was furious with her for burning the manuscript after one rejection. I: EF, 18 Mar. 1965.
541	9	*Who's Who in America, 1928–1929,* p. 741.
541	23	FCVA.
541	31	Arthur Guyton, M.D., to JB, 5 Oct. 1967.
541	35	I: Victoria Fielden, 27 Oct. 1964.
542	9	*WT,* pp. 74, 76.
542	28	*Ibid.*, pp. 82, 79, 6, 12. The children also meet a ninety-two-year-old man named Egbert. Only one year younger than Will Falls, he is like him a candy-loving veteran of the Civil War. WF later dropped the hyphen in the book's title.
542	31	Robbie Eades in *WFO,* p. 23.
543	17	Undated letter. Courtesy Harvard University Library.
543	26	Courtesy Harvard University Library.
543	38	I: Dorothy Conkling, 16 Mar. 1965.
544	13	JFSA.
544	22	Dennis, p. 131.
545	5	FCVA. Cf. the imaginary horse in "Carcassonne" and Jewel Bundren and his spotted horse in *ASI.*
545	12	I: Judge Taylor McElroy, 18 Nov. 1967.
545	15	*OXE,* 2 May 1929.
545	17	Buck Collins was a big, fair-haired man who weighed over 200 pounds. After he came into town from Beat Two, he was elected tax assessor and in 1929 kept a grocery on the Square. WF was a good customer who often talked with Collins. Collins would mix his salve himself from powder, a tube of a jellied substance, and other ingredients. When a patient came in to be treated, Collins would take him to the back of the store and scrape the growth with a dull knife until it was raw. Then he would pack it with the dryish, gunpowder-black salve. Thirty days later, the patient would return and Collins would remove the scab. (I: Boyce Collins, 27 Nov. 1965.) The growth was gone, one patient said, "but I had a hole right through my nose, too." (I: J. C. Goforth, 27 Nov. 1965.)
545	19	I: Dean Mallard, 16 Mar. 1965.
545	24	I: James Adams, 26 Mar. 1965. G. T. Buckley argues for Ripley, New Albany, Pontotoc, Holly Springs, and Batesville as partial models for Jefferson in "Is Oxford the Original of Jefferson in Faulkner's Novels?" *PMLA,* LXXVI (Sept. 1961), pp. 447–54. A convincing argument for Oxford is found in Calvin S. Brown, Jr., "Faulkner's Geography and Topography," *PMLA* (Dec. 1962), pp. 652–9. For the change from "Oxford" to "Jefferson," see Dennis, p. 34.
546	34	I: Bern Keating, 29 Nov. 1965. Horace Benbow also resembles J. Alfred Prufrock when he listens to his own words, "hearing them linger

Page	Line	
		with a dying fall. . . ." P. 176.
547	10	Thomas D. Clark in *WFO*, p. 72.
547	29	Information on the flood comes from *NYT* of the day cited.
547	30	The first printing of *MOS* totaled 3,047. A second in September added 500. Of the 2,500 copies of *SP*, all but 307 had been sold, so a second printing of 1,000 was made in April, 1927, but nearly all of it would be remaindered. FCVA.
548	29	New York *Evening Post*, 11 June 1927.
548	37	New York *World*, 12 June 1927.
549	2	Miss Hellman still felt as she had when she recommended the manuscript for publication: it was full of "the kind of swift and lusty writing that comes from a healthy, fresh pen." *NYHT*, 19 June 1927.
549	6	Boston *Transcript*, 2 July 1927.
549	10	Nashville *Tennessean*, 3 July 1927.
549	14	*NOTP*, 3 July 1927. A hostile review appeared in the Springfield *Republican* on July 17. To another reviewer the novel was urbane but demonstrated that Americans simply could not write satire as Huxley, Douglas, and Firbank could. *The New Republic*, XLI (July 20, 1927), p. 236.
549	22	I: Helen B. Lyman, 19 June 1965.
549	25	I: Ann Farnsworth, 30 Mar. 1965.
549	31	JFSA.
550	8	*ESP*.
551	9	"Books," Chicago *Tribune*, 6 July 1927. See Dr. Hans Bungert, "William Faulkner on *Moby-Dick:* An Early Letter," *Studi Americani*, 9 (Rome, 1964), pp. 371–5.
551	22	*OXE*, 2 and 30 June, 1927.
551	26	*OXE*, 7 July 1927.
551	32	*OXE*, 28 July 1927.
552	14	Both WF letters are undated. Liveright's reply to the first one is dated 23 July 1927, to the second, 1 Aug. 1927.
552	35	Jean Stein in *LIG*, p. 239.
553	9	Louis Cochran in *WFO*, p. 224.
553	36	Horace Liveright to WF, 1 Aug. 1927.
554	3	See *MOS*, p. 225. WF also echoed a favorite poem, "The Phoenix and the Turtle," in two allusions later deleted. See Dennis, pp. 106, 108.
554	12	FCVA.
554	22	I: Dorothy Oldham, 17 Nov. 1967.
554	32	I: Helen B. Lyman, 19 June 1965.
555	9	I: Thomas Kell, 30 Mar. 1965. Millgate writes in *The Achievement* that WF spent "much of his time" in Pascagoula in 1926, 1927, and 1928. (P. 23.) In some instances where there appears to be no precise corroborating evidence, I have assigned specific events to the time periods that seem most likely.
555	17	I: Carl Carmer, 23 Aug. 1965.
556	4	I: Thomas Kell, 30 Mar. 1965. The sum owed Stone, Kell thought, was $725.
556	33	This echo of Keats's "Ode on a Grecian Urn" would be followed by others.
557	6	Among the relocated sections were the garden scene between Narcissa and Aunt Jenny, Bayard's adventure with the wild horse, and Horace Benbow's return to Jefferson. (Dennis, pp. 80–1.) Although the FCVA typescript represents a later stage or combination of stages than that discussed in the text above, the changes it shows are probably similar. P. 242

Page	Line	
		became that number finally only after previously having been, in succession, pp. 131, 139, 227, 167, 137, and 246. This same metamorphosis had occurred in the following seven pages too, the passage in which Horace returned from the war to be met by Narcissa. Finally WF assembled a 513-page sequence which suited him. Then, without bothering to renumber them, he added pp. 490–583 from yet another sequence.
557	14	WF to Mrs. Walter McLean, "Wednesday." (MCL.) It is possible that the book referred to may have been *MOS,* which was completed on September 1, 1926, also a Wednesday.
557	33	WF dated the letter "sunday–october" and wrote in it that the book "goes forward to you by mail Monday." Liveright, replying on October 20, 1927, a Thursday, recapitulated what WF had written with the phrase "and you say you're posting it to me on Monday. . . ." The previous Monday was October 17. Dennis distinguishes pages from *SAR* in FCVA which represent a second typescript of *Flags in the Dust* and suggests that it was this one which WF sent to Liveright rather than the one whose last page is dated September 29, 1927. (P. 70.) Since it seems unlikely, however, that WF could have done a new typescript between September 29 and October 17, he may have retyped sections of the work rather than the whole.
558	10	*OXE,* 7 July 1927.
558	11	*OXE,* 4 and 25 Aug., 1927.
558	21	*OXE,* 15 Sept. 1927.
559	6	*OXE,* 22 Dec. 1927. Cf. Appendix to *S&F,* p. 420.
559	27	*MBB,* pp. 157–8.
560	18	Horace Liveright to WF, 25 Nov. 1927.
560	24	Courtesy Beinecke Library, YUL.
561	24	*MBB,* p. 156. One surviving WF sending schedule lists stories submitted to magazines between January 23, 1930, and January 9, 1932. (FCVA, repr. in Meriwether, *The Literary Career,* pp. 167–80.) Although John Faulkner supplies no dates for the stories and schedule he describes, it seems likely that some would have fallen in 1928 and 1929, particularly since WF had, according to his brother, been devoting much of his energy to short stories after his return from Europe and had been submitting his work to popular magazines for years.
561	26	*OXE,* 22 Dec. 1927.
561	29	*FOM,* pp. 120–1.
562	5	J. W. Harmon in *WFO,* pp. 93–4. Mr. Harmon dates this incident 1928 or 1929.
562	30	WF to Horace Liveright, undated; Liveright's reply dated 27 Feb. 1928.
563	10	Dated "Thursday." MCL.
563	18	WF also thanked Liveright for his copy of a limited edition of Isadora Duncan's *My Life* printed for the firm's authors and other friends. He had never seen a more beautiful book; "even Shakespeare himself could hardly have done that volume justice."
563	27	I: BW, 28 Mar. 1965.
563	33	*OXE,* 19 Feb. 1920.
563	37	*OXE,* 2 Feb. 1928.
564	2	*OXE,* 16 Feb. 1928.
564	8	I: EF, 7 Aug. 1963.
564	18	I: EF, 29 Apr. 1968.
564	31	*ESP,* pp. 34–5.
564	35	Hugh N. Clayton, "The Brass Horn Turns to Gold,"

Page *Line*

unpubl. note. Courtesy Prof. James W. Webb.

565 1 *SAN* (ML ed.), p. v.

565 11 Edith B. Douds to JB, 7 Feb. 1968; *OXE,* 21 June 1928; I: Ella Somerville, 22 Mar. 1965.

565 18 Courtesy Beinecke Library, YUL.

566 2 FCVA. See Norman Holmes Pearson, "Faulkner's Three 'Evening Suns,'" *Yale University Library Gazette* (Oct. 29, 1954), pp. 61–70. I am not trying to prove that "That Evening Sun" (or "A Justice" in the discussion to follow) in its present form predates *S&F* but to suggest rather that it is the kind of story of the experiences of the Compson children which WF said *S&F* developed from. I have no sending schedule, agent's record, or conclusive manuscript evidence which would permit accurate dating of the inception and writing of this story. WF offered it to *Scribner's* in October, 1930, and sold it three weeks later to *The American Mercury,* where it appeared as "That Evening Sun Go Down" in March, 1931. Revised, it appeared as "That Evening Sun" in *T13,* published September 21, 1931. The handwriting of "Never Done No Weeping When You Wanted to Laugh" appears very similar to, if not identical with, that in the manuscript of *S&F.* In "A Justice," which first appeared in *T13,* WF also used Quentin Compson as narrator of a story in which Candace and Jason appear. In neither story does their brother, Benjamin, appear, and the servants who are mentioned in the three versions of the story noted above—T.P. and Frony—are a generation older than Luster, who appears more often in *S&F* than any other save his grandmother, Dilsey. In an unpublished paper entitled "Three American Novels: A Genetic Approach," Leon Howard argues that WF experimented with the use of the "immature observer" as narrator first in the story that became "That Evening Sun" and afterwards in *S&F,* "for it hardly seems possible that, after writing *The Sound and the Fury,* he could have abolished Benjy from his place among the Compson children or have allowed Quentin to tell a story at the posthumous age of twenty-four."

566 15 *OTF,* pp. 72–3. When it came to the decline of the Compson family, WF had only to look at his own. His grandfather had once practiced law with Judge Charles Bowen Howry, protégé of Lucius Quintus Cincinnatus Lamar; now his uncle was a henchman of Theodore "The Man" Bilbo. Mrs. Compson somewhat resembled "Miss Rosie" Stone, who suffered from hypochondria and who, according to her son Phil, was "always hoping for the worst." I: Emily Stone, 30 Nov. 1965.

566 23 *MBB,* pp. 72–3.

566 36 *CS,* p. 360.

566 38 FCVA.

566 39 Unpubl. portion of class conference, U. of Va., 15 Apr. 1957.

567 7 *LIG,* p. 146.

567 19 Draft No. 2 of unpubl. introduction to *S&F,* pp. 5–6, for special RH edition to be manufactured by Grabhorn Press, planned in the summer of 1933 but never completed. JFSA.

NOTES

Page	Line	
567	24	*LIG,* p. 146.
567	38	*NOS,* p. 55.
568	3	*LIG,* p. 146. See also Meriwether, "Notes on the Textual History of *The Sound and the Fury,*" pp. 285–316. Cf. Winnie Verloc and her handicapped brother, Stevie, in Joseph Conrad's *The Secret Agent.*
568	28	Draft No. 2, pp. 6–7. (See note for 567/19 above.) JFSA.
569	1	Draft No. 3, p. 4. (See note for 567/19 above.) RH. Repr. in James B. Meriwether, "Faulkner, Lost and Found," *NYT Book Review* (Nov. 5, 1972), pp. 6–7.
569	5	From Maurice Coindreau's introduction to his French translation of *S&F,* repr. in translation in *The Mississippi Quarterly,* XIX (Summer 1966), p. 109. Most accounts WF gave of the genesis of the novel were substantially the same as those quoted here. See *FIU,* pp. 6, 31–2. Cf. the Compsons at Damuddy's death—Quentin, eleven; Caddy, seven; Jason, five; Maury, three—and the Falkners at Damuddy's death—Billy, not quite ten; Sallie Murry, eight; Jack, eight; Johncy, not quite six.
569	33	FCVA. In one of many manuscript changes, WF substituted Luster, T.P.'s nephew, as Benjy's nurse.
570	8	A number of guides attempt to establish the objective facts of the Compsons' lives, e.g.: George R. Stewart and Joseph M. Backus, "Each In Its Ordered Place," *American Literature,* XXIX (Jan. 1958), pp. 440–56, and Edmond Volpe, *A Reader's Guide to William Faulkner* (New York, 1964), pp. 353–77. When he was reminded that, in the Old Testament, Benjamin was held hostage for Joseph, WF remarked, "Yes, that's why I used the names interchangeably." *FIU,* p. 18.
570	15	Meriwether, "Faulkner, Lost and Found," p. 7.
570	18	Beinecke Library, YUL.
570	22	In 1960, BW told Prof. James B. Meriwether that *Flags in the Dust* was rejected by eleven publishers. (Dennis, p. 76.) He told me in 1965 that there had been eighteen rejections. (I: BW, 28 Mar. 1965.)
570	29	Meriwether, "Faulkner, Lost and Found," p. 7. WF confused the dates involved, as he would often do thereafter. He said of *Flags in the Dust* that he "continued to shop it about for three years" before he closed the door and began to write for himself. Liveright wrote his letter of rejection on November 25, 1927, and it was in reply to Liveright's letter of February 27, 1928, that WF wrote of the new novel he hoped to finish within eight weeks.
570	39	Meriwether, "Faulkner, Lost and Found," p. 7.
571	5	Meriwether quotes this passage from Maurice Coindreau's introduction to his translation, *Le bruit et la fureur* (Paris, 1938), p. 14. See "Notes on the Textual History of *The Sound and the Fury,*" p. 288, where he also writes that Coindreau reported that WF had described the time of the book's composition as one "when personal problems had placed him under a severe strain."
571	20	Draft No. 2, pp. 7–8. (See note for 567/19 above.) JFSA.
571	24	FCVA.
571	27	*LIG,* p. 147. After the original p. 2, he inserted p. 2b. He did four separate p. 4's, deciding

Page	Line	
		to move three of them to other points later in the story. One of them he used as p. 8 before he finally placed it as p. 9. On p. 2b, at the top line, he began using the device of italics to indicate the shift from one time-level to another. By p. 3 he had changed Benjy's nurse from T.P. to Luster. And on p. 9, which had earlier been p. 8 and p. 4, he portrayed action before the name-changing, when Benjy still bore his baptismal name of Maury. This was an afterthought, however, as WF had written Maury above a canceled Benjy. And, curiously enough, before that he had written out, then canceled, a form of one of his favorite names: Davy. (See Emily K. Izsak's "The Manuscript of *The Sound and the Fury:* The Revisions in the First Section," *Studies in Bibliography,* 20 (1967), pp. 189–202). On May 27, 1958, Frederick Gwynn and I called WF's attention to the assertion in Stewart and Backus, pp. 440–1, that WF here "set booby traps" for the reader. WF responded immediately and forcefully: "To that I'll say that it's absolutely untrue. A detective story writer deals with provable facts after a fact. The writer of a book like this is involved with truth which cannot be proved but must only be believed." When he was shown the map of the Compson household and estate provided in the article, he said that the branch and the ditch were "in general where they should be" but that the house and golf course were "almost completely reversed."
573	3	Courtesy Lenore Marshall. WF later changed these dates but used the "fine sound" and Benjy's pasture on p. 217 of the novel. Here too he appropriated material. The sequence in which Quentin leans from a train window and surprises an old Negro man with the cry "Christmas gift!" had come from an experience of Phil Stone's on a trip from New Haven to Oxford. I: Emily Stone, 30 Nov. 1965.
573	18	FCVA. I am indebted to Emily K. Izsak for allowing me to read her unpublished essay, "Revisions in the Second Section of the Manuscript of *The Sound and the Fury.*"
573	34	Shortly before his suicide, Quentin would recall his father's words to him: ". . . we must just stay awake and see evil done for a little while . . . ." This is a paraphrase of part of the third quatrain of Housman's "Be Still, My Soul," from *A Shropshire Lad.*
574	4	FCVA.
574	6	As Pat planned to follow Josh to college, so Caddy had done in grade school: "we had to let her go to the next year, so she could be with him." (P. 326.)
574	12	I: BW, 28 Mar. 1965.
575	13	*CS,* p. 898. For some of the literary echoes in Quentin's section, see Collins, "The Interior Monologues," pp. 59–79.
575	33	WF dated his copy of *Ulysses* "1924." *WFL,* p. 77.
576	1	See *FIU,* p. 18.
576	9	*LIG,* p. 147.
576	16	FCVA. On only four pages had WF used his wide left-hand margin to insert new material. On almost every page there were the notations

Page	Line	
		at various points in the left-hand margin—28, 50, 19, 32, 17, 31—indicating that he was keeping track of length as he wrote, apparently counting usually in about sixty-line segments and then starting over. It is possible that the even sequential nature of the Quentin section of the manuscript is owing to its being a revision and fair copy of one or more earlier ones. However, I am not aware of any external evidence of an earlier manuscript. (See Meriwether, "Notes on the Textual History of *The Sound and the Fury,*" pp. 290–1.) In addition, when using large blocks of earlier manuscript in later manuscript versions, WF seems often to have cut passages from the earlier pages and pasted them onto the new manuscript version.
577	8	Draft No. 2, p. 9. (See note for 567/19 above.) JFSA.
577	12	*LIG,* p. 147.
577	20	For Christian analogues see Carvel Collins, "The Pairing of *The Sound and the Fury* and *As I Lay Dying,*" *Princeton University Library Chronicle,* XVIII (Spring 1957), pp. 114–23.
577	33	With the fourth section of the novel, he began a new counting system. In the left-hand margin of each page but the last two were numbers running from one to five. Each represented ten manuscript lines. Thus he was counting in blocks of sixty lines, as he had done in the third section, but much more regularly and accurately. There would be many meticulous revisions, but with the completion of this fourth section—three of its pages slightly spattered near the margins with the cream house paint—the manuscript as a unit was finished. FCVA.
578	12	FCVA. In "Hemingway and Fitzgerald in *The Sound and the Fury,*" *Papers on Language & Literature,* Vol. 2, No. 3 (Southern Illinois Univ., 1966), John M. Howell suggests certain debts to *The Sun Also Rises* and *The Great Gatsby.* (Pp. 234–42.) Indebtedness to Fitzgerald might be seen also in the manuscript where WF assigned a full name to Deacon, the Negro factotum among the Harvard undergraduates: James J. Hill Listenbee. (Hill, of course, was one of Gatsby's models.) WF later substituted the name Nelson A. Miles and then dispensed with any proper names for Deacon. In "Faulkner's Raskolnikov," *Modern Fiction Studies,* IV (Summer 1958), pp. 169–72, Frederick L. Gwynn noted parallels between Quentin Compson and the protagonist of Dostoevsky's *Crime and Punishment.* Later Gwynn noted "a Negro slave named Roskus, a father who's a run-down reader of the classics, a mother named Caroline, another father who is a Scotsman who fought with a claymore at Culloden Moor but ran away to North Carolina, whose son fights in a battle against Tarleton's army in South Carolina" in James Boyd's novel *Drums,* of 1925. (Gwynn to JB, 26 Oct. 1960.) Much of this information first appeared in the appendix WF wrote for MC's *The Portable Faulkner* (New York, 1946), pp. 737–56. By that time, WF knew Boyd personally.
578	36	Preface to ML ed. of *SAN,* 1932, p. vi. Here again WF

Page *Line*

stated incorrectly the length of time (two years) which *Flags in the Dust* had then remained rejected.

578 39 Maurice Coindreau, "Preface to 'The Sound and the Fury,'" transl. by George M. Reeves, *The Mississippi Quarterly,* XIX (Summer 1966), p. 109.

579 3 *SAN* (ML ed.), Introduction, p. vi.

579 7 *OXE,* 21 June 1928.

579 9 Gwynn, "Faulkner's Raskolnikov," pp. 169–70.

579 28 Thomas D. Clark in *WFO,* pp. 73–4.

580 2 Meriwether, "Notes on the Textual History of *The Sound and the Fury,*" p. 289.

580 7 I: Shelby Foote, 20 Nov. 1965.

580 11 I: EF, 18 Apr. 1968.

580 20 *Publishers Weekly,* 113 (June 9, 1928), p. 2387; 109 (Feb. 20, 1926), p. 591.

581 15 I: BW, 28 Mar. 1965.

581 17 Dennis, p. 68.

582 23 I: BW, 28 Mar. 1965.

583 12 *Ibid.*; MG, 23 Apr. 1965.

583 29 I: Eric J. Devine, 15 Aug. 1965; Mr. and Mrs. Carl Carmer, 23 Aug. 1965.

584 9 Beinecke Library, YUL.

584 22 FCVA. Again I am indebted to Profs. Douglas Day and Stephen N. Dennis. The analysis of BW's deletions is tentative because they were made upon the setting copy of *SAR,* which is not known to have survived. (See Dennis, p. 95.) Two cuts from *SAR* would reappear set in type on unrevised gals. 21 and 6 of *SAN*: Horace Benbow's disgust at carrying home shrimp from the railroad station every Friday for Belle, and the unexpected meeting of Horace and Narcissa in the Benbow house one noon. (See Dennis, p. 112.) Similarly, passages in *SAR* which are not in the existing carbon typescript probably represent additions to the missing setting copy.

585 12 Phil Stone to Bess Condon, dated about December, 1928, by Emerson in *William Faulkner's Literary Reputation,* p. 649.

585 21 I: Manuel Komroff, 22 Jan. 1965.

585 30 Spratling, "Chronicle of a Friendship," pp. 38–9.

585 37 I: BC, 20 Sept. 1967.

586 12 Spratling, "Chronicle of a Friendship," p. 39. Whether or not WF chatted with Liveright, it appears that he did go to the firm's offices where he saw Louis Kronenberger. In describing the encounter thirty-seven years later, Kronenberger wrote that it was decided "to ask him to put [*Flags in the Dust*] aside and accept an advance on a new book. I was delegated to broach the offer, and I remember we talked about it in a sort of summerhouse at the office where I used to read manuscripts in hot weather. Or, rather, I talked about it, with increasing embarrassment as Faulkner said nothing. Nor did he, any more than O'Neill, speak when I had finished. He simply sat on. I had, of course, given him upsetting news; but he sat on and on, while I made an effort at small talk or a pretense of reading a manuscript; sat on for what seemed hours, to get up at last, say very courteously 'good-bye' and leave." Kronenberger, "Gambler in Publishing: Horace Liveright," *The Atlantic Monthly,* 215 (Jan. 1965), pp. 94–104.

586 21 MCL.

NOTES

Page	Line	
586	28	WF to BW, prob. July 1929.
587	6	Meriwether, "Faulkner, Lost and Found," p. 7.
587	10	I: BW, 28 Mar. 1965.
587	18	I: Owen Crump, 9 June 1966.
587	25	I: Carl Carmer, 23 Aug. 1965.
587	36	Basso, p. 12.
588	18	I: Eric J. Devine, 15 Aug. 1965.
588	31	Leon Scales to JB, 23 June 1965. It seems likely that it was during this period that WF stayed at 35 Vandam Street, the address he inscribed in a 1923 printing of James Branch Cabell's *Jurgen. WFL,* p. 20.
588	35	Unpubl. portion of class conference, U. of Va., 6 May 1957. One of his earliest revisions had been to substitute Luster for T.P. on the first page.
589	13	FCVA. See Izsak, "The Manuscript of *The Sound and the Fury,*" pp. 189–202.
589	15	*S&F,* p. 5. In the manuscript, it had been Mr. Compson who had hit and kicked T.P. when he had gotten drunk on the champagne for Caddy's wedding reception. In revision, WF assigned these actions to Quentin.
590	1	Unpubl. portion of class conference, U. of Va., 5 June 1957.
590	15	The three flat-iron passages occur on pp. 105, 111, and 125. I am indebted to Prof. Leon Howard for calling these changes to my attention. One change between typescript and book was toward less rather than more clarity: "two six-pound flat-irons weigh more than one tailor's goose." (P. 111.) In the typescript, the clerk told Quentin that an eight- or ten-pound flat-iron was called "a tailor's goose." This was deleted at some subsequent stage.
590	26	FCVA.
590	28	I: BW, 28 Mar. 1965. Meriwether, "Notes on the Textual History of *The Sound and the Fury,*" p. 289.
591	17	Leon Scales to JB, 23 June 1965.
592	12	*Ibid.*
592	19	I: Flo Field, 4 Feb. 1965.
595	21	I: Owen Crump, 9 June 1966.
595	25	Alfred Dashiell to WF, 3 Nov. 1928. Scribner Archive, courtesy PUL. It seems reasonable to assume that WF was making similar submissions, with similar results, to other magazines such as *Forum, Cosmopolitan, Harper*'s, and *The American Mercury.*
596	5	*Ibid.* It is not possible to say definitely which version of "Moonlight" WF submitted. He apparently worked over "Bench for Two" very carefully. He would subsequently rewrite it as "Two on a Bench," and in somewhat expanded form it would be published as "Pennsylvania Station" in *The American Mercury,* XXXI (Feb. 1934). The first two pages of the manuscript were written on "Howard Bond," which he had also used for the manuscript of the Benjy section of *S&F.* FCVA.
596	26	"Once Aboard the Lugger," *Contempo,* I (Feb. 1, 1932), pp. 1, 4.
597	9	JFSA.
597	22	Scribner Archive, PUL.
597	33	I: Owen Crump, 9 June 1966; BW, 28 Mar. 1965. It does not seem likely that the sum WF said he had received—between $200 and $500, Crump thought—could have been an advance on *S&F,* since no decision had yet been made about publication. Neither could it have been a fee for a

Page *Line*

story, and it would be more than two months before he did sign a contract for the new book. One possibility is that HS, who was just about to leave Harcourt, Brace to open his own publishing house, may have advanced the money as a loan. According to Vincent Sheean, HS knew that WF "was broke" and, before he left Harcourt to found his own firm, gave WF $100. I: Sheean, 16 Aug. 1965.

598 27 The dating of WF's departure must, like the times of his other activities during this stay in New York, be tentative. In copy no. 40 (of 1,000) of an edition of Art Young's *On My Way* done especially for "the authors and other friends of Horace Liveright," WF inscribed his name, his Oxford address, and the date "12 Dec. 1928." *(WFL,* p. 59.) Owen Crump himself left New York before the end of December, 1928. His recollection that WF stayed with him for a period of six to eight weeks suggests that the Sunday on which he left was the ninth of December rather than the second.

599 15 *OXE,* 29 Nov. 1928.

599 21 *OXE,* 27 Dec. 1928.

600 2 *Ibid.*

600 15 WF to Alfred Dashiell, undated; Dashiell to WF, 22 Dec. 1928. Scribner Archive, PUL.

600 33 FCVA.

601 15 In an undated letter, WF wrote Dashiell that he had submitted a story in December which he feared had been lost, and that he was now sending the carbon. Dashiell's reply on February 23, 1929, identifies it as "Selvage." Scribner Archive, PUL.

601 17 *OXE,* 17 Jan. 1929.

601 23 *OXE,* 3 Jan. 1929.

601 33 *OXE,* 14 Feb. 1929.

602 6 W. M. Reed, "Mr. Mack Remembers 'Bill,'" *OXE,* 12 July 1962.

602 10 *OXE,* 21 Feb. 1929.

602 27 Courtesy Harcourt Brace Jovanovich.

602 33 *Ibid.*

603 6 I: BW, 28 Mar. 1965.

603 11 I: Mrs. Sewell Haggard, 17 Apr. 1965.

603 13 I: Eric J. Devine, 15 Aug. 1965. In an earlier interview, BW said that HS had sent him to Harcourt, Brace to inquire about the novel and that he had brought the rejected typescript back to HS himself. (Meriwether, "Notes on the Textual History of *The Sound and the Fury,*" p. 292.) Vincent Sheean recalled that though Alfred Harcourt was not lavish with money, he was an amiable man who let his authors go elsewhere if they felt they should go. (I: 16 Aug. 1965.)

603 23 Courtesy American Play Co.

604 9 Alfred Dashiell to WF, 23 Feb. 1929. Scribner Archive, PUL.

604 13 I: EF, 15 May 1968.

604 27 FCVA.

604 29 WF to Alfred Dashiell, undated, Scribner Archive, PUL.

604 31 WF to Alfred Harcourt, undated, courtesy Harcourt Brace Jovanovich.

604 34 FCVA.

605 9 *FIU,* pp. 90–1. *SAN* (ML ed.), Introduction, p. vi.

605 34 I: Ann Farnsworth, 30 Mar. 1965.

606 27 In *Who's Who,* WF's name had been followed by that of the Hon. Albert Bacon Fall, Secretary of the Interior under Harding and one of those most deeply implicated in the

NOTES

Page	Line	
		Teapot Dome oil scandal.
607	35	St. Louis *Post-Dispatch,* 7 Sept. 1924; *MCA,* 18 and 19 Dec., 1932; Boyce House, *Cub Reporter* (n.p., 1947), pp. 92–7.
608	6	*MCA,* 25 June 1929, 23 July 1930. Pumphrey had acquired his nickname in childhood. When he became excited in a losing game of marbles his brother said, "Look at his eyes pop." When *SAN* appeared, some Oxonians thought that the model was not Pumphrey but a man named Laughter, from Hernando.
608	16	*MCA,* 3 Dec. 1919.
608	18	*OXE,* 24 Mar. 1921.
608	20	*OXE,* 1 Dec. 1921.
608	23	*OXE,* 17 Sept. 1925.
608	26	*OXE,* 21 July and 11 Aug., 1926.
608	28	*OXE,* 3 Nov. 1927.
608	32	*OXE,* 18 Apr. 1929.
609	12	W. H. Hutchinson to JB, 1 Nov. 1965.
609	36	FCVA.
610	6	By the time Ch. II was ready for final typing, the middle half of p. 6 was a manuscript segment cut from some other sheet and pasted onto the manuscript page. The same was true in varying degrees of all but two of the remaining nine manuscript pages of the chapter. P. 10 comprised three separate paste-ins, and the only lines written on p. 10 were the two blocks of three, each of which provided continuity. And he had tried p. 10 as p. 8 before he had once again made it 10.
610	10	He tried p. 18 in twenty-one other places before finally fixing it there. Ch. IV became Ch. III, then IV again, and then III. It remained Ch. III when he typed it, but before he bound it with the other typed chapters, he changed it to IV again.
610	21	Marginal numbers on some pages showed that he was counting words again, as he had done sometimes with *S&F.*
610	29	FCVA.
611	7	WF's letter recd. 13 Apr. 1929. Courtesy Harcourt Brace Jovanovich.
611	13	*Outlook,* 20 Feb. 1929.
611	15	*NYHT Books,* 24 Feb. 1929.
611	18	*NYT,* 3 Mar. 1929.
611	31	WF's prose was dynamic and complex, wrote Davidson. Thematically, there were occasional touches of humor, but "there is really nothing but tragedy." There were probably larger meanings too: "I cannot help suspecting some allegorical meaning is in 'Sartoris.' " Nashville *Tennessean,* 14 Apr. 1929, repr. in Inge, pp. 454–62.
612	3	I: James Adams, 26 Mar. 1965.
612	12	I: Robert Coughlan, 25 Feb. 1967.
612	27	Emily Stone, "Faulkner Gets Started," p. 144.
613	7	I: BW, 28 Mar. 1965.
613	18	John Reed Holley in *WFO,* p. 86.
613	19	I: Mrs. Almond Coleman, 10 Oct. 1965.
613	22	I: Malcolm Franklin, 26 Nov. 1966.
613	23	I: EF, 7 Aug. 1963.
613	25	*OXE,* 18 Apr. 1929.
613	26	*OXE,* 9 May 1929.
613	28	*OXE,* 28 Feb. and 30 May, 1929.
613	38	Courtesy American Play Co.
614	10	He pierced the pages with fine wire and glued muslin on the spine. Then he attached thin cardboard covers to the muslin, covered the spine with a vellum-like paper, and glued another kind of paper over the covers. He chose a mot-

Page	Line	
		tled pattern that was brown with subdued hues of purple, blue, beige, and gold. He had bound *SP* the same way. FCVA.
614	30	*SAN*, unrevised gal. 6. FCVA. The Horace-Narcissa relationship was, like that of Caddy and Quentin, another variation on a theme.
615	8	Unrevised gal. 5. FCVA.
616	23	Unrevised gal. 101.
617	1	Unrevised gal. 103.
617	9	JFSA.
617	20	I: EF, 23 Feb. 1965.
618	2	I: Lenore Marshall, 10 Nov. 1964.
618	7	I: Evelyn H. Glick, 16 Nov. 1964.
618	10	I: Louise Bonino, 11 Nov. 1964.
618	14	*SAN* (ML ed.), Introduction, p. vi.
618	32	*FOM*, p. 125.
619	3	I: EF, 7 Aug. 1963, 22 July 1965.
619	7	I: Dorothy Oldham, 17 Jan. 1967; SMW to JB, 22 Mar. 1971.
619	9	I: SMW, 14 Nov. 1967.
619	33	I: EF, 7 Aug. 1963; Dorothy Oldham, 17 Jan. 1967.
620	10	I: EF, 29 Apr. 1968.
623	11	I: EF, 9 Sept. 1965.
624	1	*OXE*, 10 Dec. 1936.
624	5	I: EF, 7 Aug. 1963, 17 Sept. 1965.
624	9	I: SMW, 14 Nov. 1967.
624	11	I: Mrs. Almond Coleman, 10 Oct. 1965.
624	22	I: EF, 26 Apr. 1967.
624	32	*Ibid.*; Malcolm Franklin, 26 Sept. 1966.
625	8	I: Myrtle Stone, Mrs. Thomas Leatherbury, and Ann Farnsworth, 30 Mar. 1965.
625	26	I: EF, 7 Aug. 1963; 28 Apr. and 9 Sept., 1965.
625	34	I: Myrtle Stone and Mrs. Thomas Leatherbury, 30 Mar. 1965.
626	4	I: Mrs. Martin Shepherd, 31 Mar. 1965.
626	16	I: Thomas Kell, 30 Mar. 1965.
626	19	WF to BW, prob. early or mid-July, 1929.
627	9	Millgate prints all of this letter but the paragraph quoted immediately above: *The Achievement*, pp. 93–4.
627	10	BW to JB, 12 Apr. 1966.
627	19	WF to BW, prob. mid- or late July, 1929. Courtesy Shelby Foote.
627	22	I: BW, 29 Nov. 1965.
628	10	FCVA.
628	15	Evelyn Scott, *On William Faulkner's "The Sound and the Fury"* (New York, 1929), pp. 6, 5.
628	21	Undated. WF suggested Phil Stone and Ella Somerville, Drs. Bishop, Bondurant, and Calvin Brown, and the university library. He listed Aunt 'Bama in Memphis and Odiorne in Paris, and three book reviewers: John McClure, John McGinnis, who had commissioned his Sherwood Anderson essay, and Donald Davidson.
628	27	Arthur Hawkins to JB, 9 July 1965.
628	34	Scribner Archive, PUL.
629	10	FCVA.
629	17	I: Victoria Fielden, 27 Oct. 1964.
629	28	I: EF, 29 Apr. 1968.
629	33	I: EF, 26 Apr. 1967, 29 Apr. 1968.
630	1	I: Samuel Gilmore, 3 Feb. 1965.
630	15	I: Mrs. Martin Shepherd, 31 Mar. 1965.
630	22	I: EF, 7 Aug. 1963.
630	25	*MBB*, p. 161.
630	29	I: Mr. and Mrs. Howard Duvall, Jr., 17 Nov. 1966.
630	34	One of the two brothers was probably WF's grade-school classmate, Donald Furr.
630	38	Thomas D. Clark in *WFO*, p. 71.
631	10	I: EF, 23 Feb. 1965.

NOTES

Page	Line	
631	12	I: Malcolm Franklin, 26 Sept. 1966.
631	17	I: Robert Couglan, 24 Feb. 1967.
631	30	I: EF, 7 Aug. 1963, 29 Apr. 1968.
631	34	*MBB,* p. 245.
632	3	*OTF,* p. 71.
632	20	FCVA.
632	24	Scribner Archive, PUL.
632	26	Many readers, Hansen thought, would find WF as incoherent as Joyce. Writing in *Outlook* on October 16, 1929, F. L. Robbins referred to WF as Joyce's "most able and consistent American disciple."
632	36	Boston *Evening Transcript,* 23 Oct. 1929.
632	38	*NYT,* 10 Nov. 1929.
633	2	*The Saturday Review of Literature,* VI (Dec. 28, 1929), p. 601. In January, *The Missippian* would summarize the favorable reaction to the novel in literary magazines. (Undated clipping, JFSA.) They would still be appearing in the following June, when Julia K. Wetherill Baker would write in *NOTP* that *S&F* was "one of the finest works in the tragic mood yet to appear in America." (29 June 1930.)
633	9	*Publishers Weekly,* 117 (Mar. 1, 1930), p. 1083.
633	11	Meriwether, "Notes on the Textual History of *The Sound and the Fury,*" p. 299.
633	22	WF to Mrs. Walter McLean, undated. MCL.
633	34	FCVA.
634	7	*SAN* (ML ed.), Introduction, p. vii.
634	8	See Laurence Stallings, "Faulkner in Hollywood," New York *Sun,* 3 Sept. 1932. WF mentioned no wheelbarrow, telling Stallings that he would crawl back to a comfortable spot in the coal bunker and write in pencil in a notebook.
634	16	I: EF, 23 Feb. 1965.
634	34	Meriwether, "Faulkner, Lost and Found," p. 7.
635	2	SC to Perry Miller, 19 Nov. 1956; SC Collection, PUL, courtesy Mrs. Saxe Commins. SC, WF's editor, had asked WF for the source at the request of Prof. Miller. WF later volunteered it to JB. (See Collins, "The Pairing of *The Sound and the Fury* and *As I Lay Dying,*" p. 123.) The title was now more apt than when he had used it for the two shorter versions of the central action of *Father Abraham.* The second version to use that title was seventeen pages long, five shorter than the first one. It also represented a major stylistic change. There were no quotation marks, for it consisted entirely of dialogue—heavy with dialect—and unrelieved by so much as a single "he said." The setting was still the porch of Varner's store, and V. K. Suratt still tried to find out from Flem Snopes how much he had made from the auction of the spotted horses. Through Suratt's questions and comments, together with I. O. Snopes's defense and admiration of his cousin Flem, the whole story of the auction was told. (JFSA.)
635	13	FCVA.
635	16	Millgate, *The Achievement,* p. 111.
635	23	Phrases describing Jewel Bundren locked in a struggle with his spotted pony were virtually identical with others describing Buck struggling with one of the ponies.
635	25	"Vardaman" as the given name of the Bundrens'

Page	Line	
		youngest child (whom some critics have called an idiot) was not satire directed at the Vardamanites—and not even humor, as in the cases of names such as Admiral Dewey Snopes and Montgomery Ward Snopes—but rather another means of characterizing these hill people, as with their dialect. At this time such a family would be likely to name a child after Sen. Vardaman, just as other families would later name sons after Pres. Franklin D. Roosevelt.
635	37	*FIU,* p. 87. The first flashback in *Elmer* had a scene suggesting the one of Darl's burning Gillespie's barn. (FCVA.) The flood of 1927 was recent enough for WF to draw on it freely, as he would in great detail nine years later in *WP.* For floods, burials, and families possibly analogous to those in the novel, see *OTF,* pp. 84–8.
636	28	FCVA.
637	5	See Millgate, *The Achievement,* p. 107.
637	23	FCVA. The deleted passages would have preceded the opening paragraph of Dewey Dell's interior monologue on p. 25 of the book.
637	32	*LIG,* p. 255.
638	3	Gibson's store and its rural environs in "The Liar" seem an early study of what would become Varner's store in Frenchman's Bend. Some of the names had literal antecedents. The activities of Lonnie Quick were reported in *OXE,* 29 June 1911 and 26 July 1917. J. B. Bundren's campaign for supervisor in Beat Four was reported in *OXE,* 2 Feb. 1910.
638	10	This was one manuscript which may have been typed all at once rather than in sections as it was composed. At the start of each of Tull's six monologues, the same process of correction appeared. In the manuscript, WF used the caption "Tull." Later, perhaps in the first revision, he crossed it out and substituted "Vernon Tull." Finally, perhaps on another revision, he canceled that alternative and settled on "Tull."
639	7	I: JMF, 15 Nov. 1966.
639	16	Roscoe B. Fleming, "William Faulkner: A Major American Novelist," unpubl. essay. FCVA.
639	19	I: EF, 20 Feb. 1965.
639	36	Medford Evans, "Oxford, Mississippi," *The Southwestern Review,* XV (Autumn 1929), pp. 46–63.
640	2	I: BW, 28 Mar. 1965.
641	4	FCVA. The deleted passage would have come immediately after the word "football" on p. 203.
641	7	Armstid thinks the Bundrens are "crazy" (p. 182); to others they are simply incomprehensible.
641	27	Caroline Compson had said of Jason, "he was to be my joy and my salvation." (P. 127.) Addie Bundren says of Jewel, "He is my cross and he will be my salvation." (P. 160.)
641	33	FCVA.
642	2	Setting copy, *ASI.* ACLT. The name of the drugstore clerk may have been another of the private references WF sometimes enjoyed. One of his post office assistants had been "Skeet" Kincannon.
642	6	FCVA.
642	8	*SAN* (ML ed.), Introduction, p. vii.
642	10	FCVA.
642	29	I: BW, 28 Mar. 1965.
642	35	Walter Allen, "Literary Letter from London," *NYT*

NOTES

Page	Line	
		Book Review, 15 Nov. 1964; see also Richard Hughes, "Faulkner and Bennett," *Encounter,* XXI (Sept. 1963), pp. 59–61.
643	6	Jean Stein to JB, 24 Sept. 1969.
643	25	FCVA. It seems likely that WF did not write down the names of all the magazines at the beginning.
644	15	FCVA. The story was published in a special RH edition in 1931. Although there were some revisions, the printed version was substantially the same as the manuscript version. Cf. *WP* for another woman who deserted her husband and children to follow her lover to a western camp, only to find death in her sacrificial pursuit of love.
645	3	The cigarette-smoking thug was "full of dope," a man in "city clothes, with a face like a shaved wax doll, and eyes with a still way of looking and a voice with a still way of talking." He was a stealthy "smallish man," an expert with pistol and silencer, who exuded a sickening air of evil. (*KG,* pp. 16, 23.) The printed versions of the story in *Harper's,* CLXIV (Apr. 1932), and in *KG* are very close to the manuscript version.
645	16	None of the plain white letter-size pages was numbered, as if to make shifting easier when a page bore an independent segment, as more than one did. FCVA.
646	5	In manuscript and typescript, the action was divided by five Roman numerals deleted in the printed story. There the paragraph before the last was substantially rewritten. ("Fox Hunt," *CS,* pp. 590, 607.) WF may have derived some of the lore from James Boyd—a Master of Foxhounds—whom he had met in Charlottesville in 1931.
646	18	FCVA.
646	35	JFSA.
647	1	Cf. Miss Minnie Cooper and Mrs. Minnie Porter, WF's sixth-grade teacher for a few weeks in Sept., 1909, until she suffered a nervous breakdown. A photograph of Mrs. Porter when she subsequently taught at the Lafayette County Agricultural High School shows short gray hair, round spectacles, dark-circled eyes, a mouth tilted upward to the right, and a cheek creased as though in a permanent tic. *OXE,* 23 July 1925.
647	36	*IID,* p. 148.
648	8	"Thrift" would appear on September 6, in the same issue with F. Scott Fitzgerald's "A Woman with a Past."
648	17	Tinkle; Meriwether, *The Literary Career,* pp. 173–4.
649	10	*CS,* pp. 428, 421. The story's eleven manuscript pages showed a good deal of shifting and changing. FCVA.
649	16	FCVA. For details of acceptances see Meriwether, *The Literary Career,* pp. 167–80.
649	34	*CS,* p. 551.
650	19	*Ibid.,* p. 144. The girl Hawkshaw married was Susan Reed. Like Corinthia Bowman in "Selvage," she suffered under a repressive parental figure and reacted with promiscuity. She also suggested Miss Quentin Compson: "she never drew any lines: schoolboys, married men, anybody—would get her a report card every month and she would fill it out herself and take it home for Mrs. Murchett [her guardian] to sign." Hawkshaw's dead fiancée bore a name which had appeared

Page	Line	
		previously in "The Liar" and the *ASI* manuscript: Starnes.
652	29	James W. Webb, "Rowan Oak, Faulkner's Golden Bough," *The University of Mississippi Studies in English,* 6 (1965), pp. 39–47; *OXE,* 10 Dec. 1936; *MBB,* p. 162. I: EF, 29 May 1967; Dorothy Oldham, 18 Nov. 1966.
653	2	I: EF, 29 May 1967.
653	9	Deed of Trust, Sallie Bryant to WF, 12 Apr. 1930; W. I. Stone to W. C. Bryant, 12 Apr. 1930. JFSA.
653	14	J. W. T. Falkner to W. P. Anderson, 12 May 1930; W. I. Stone to WF, 13 May 1930; W. C. Bryant to WF, 13 May 1930; J. W. T. Falkner to WF, 19 May 1930. JFSA.
653	24	*The Mississippian,* 18 Apr. 1930, reprinting George Moreland's *MCA* column commenting on a *North American Review* article by Herschel Brickell. Earlier, a librarians' journal had noted WF's conversational brilliance and spontaneous inventiveness before closing with the information, "He doesn't like cities—his hatred of New York is particularly poisonous after a few days' visit." *Wilson Bulletin,* 4 (Feb. 1930), p. 252.
654	6	The most important change in "Drouth" was to reverse sections one and two, so that the story began not with the sketch of Minnie Cooper's background but with the rumor which would precipitate the lynching. (FCVA.) *OXE,* 14 Aug. 1930, reported, "Record-breaking Drought Enters Eighty-Seventh Day and Still No Rain in Sight." Sheriff Ike Roberts, Master of Hounds of the Tyro-College Hill Foxhunters Association, was forced to call off the chase at the annual meet because of the drought.
654	23	Scribner Archive, PUL.
655	3	"Beyond the Gate" appears to exist in typescript only; pp. 4, 1, 21. (FCVA.) *CS,* pp. 789, 792.
655	25	For the reader who cares, the Geneva Peace Conference ended in August of 1927. BW apparently supplied little material to the *Mercury.*
656	20	FCVA.
656	33	JFSA.
656	35	The quatrain WF cited was placed seventeenth in Fitzgerald's first edition of his translation of *The Rubáiyát of Omar Khayyám,* eighteenth in the third, fourth, and fifth editions. (FCVA.) "Lizards in Jamshyd's Courtyard" appeared in *The Saturday Evening Post,* CCIV (Feb. 27, 1932), pp. 12, 13, 52, 57.
657	20	I: EF, 4 Aug. 1963.
657	24	I: Victoria Fielden, 27 Oct. 1964; Malcolm Franklin, 26 Sept. 1966.
657	34	I: EF, 23 Feb. 1965.
658	12	*MBB,* pp. 162–3.
658	17	I: MCF, 31 Mar. 1965.
658	25	JFSA.
660	29	I: EF, 9 Sept. 1965, 19 June 1968.
661	1	Sir James George Frazer, *The New Golden Bough* (abridged), ed. by Theodore H. Gaster (New York, 1961), pp. 307, 312, 347, 155. See Webb, p. 43.
661	23	Gordon Price-Stephens, "The British Reception of William Faulkner, 1929–1962," *The Mississippi Quarterly,* XVIII (Summer 1965), pp. 122–3; Heinrich Straumann, "The Early Reputation of Faulkner's Work in Europe: A Tentative Appraisal," *English Studies Today,* 4th

Page	Line	
		Ser. (Rome, 1966), p. 446.
661	29	*OXE,* 19 June 1930.
661	35	I: W. M. Reed, 20 Nov. 1965; Branham Hume, 23 Nov. 1965.
662	5	*OXE,* 19 June 1930.
662	10	I: SMW, 15 Nov. 1967.
662	22	I: JMF, 21 Mar. 1965. *OXE,* 3 July 1930, noted that Mr. and Mrs. William Faulkner had moved into the old Bailey home.
662	25	*OXE,* 10 July 1930.
662	32	I: Robert Penn Warren, 19 Jan. 1966.
663	1	Thomas D. Clark in *WFO,* p. 75.
663	28	*CS,* pp. 330, 338.
663	31	FCVA. In the typescript, WF expanded several passages, notably those about Issetibbeha and his wife and Moketubbe's mother. He also divided the story with Arabic numerals. The details about the New England captain's drunkenness and the slaver's being a Unitarian were added after the typescript stage.
664	4	*FIU,* p. 39.
664	17	I: EF, 19 June 1968.
664	34	JFSA. Of eight surviving manuscript pages, four bore paste-ons of various sizes from some earlier manuscript version, but most of the material was newly written. When WF had finished the typing, the story ran to fifty-eight pages. It was now closer to the form he had used in *Father Abraham* than in the versions which he had written under the title "As I Lay Dying." The story now began as the men on the porch of Varner's store observed the approach of the spotted horses. WF then continued with the action, saving the material on Eula Varner and her marriage to Flem Snopes for an interpolation much later in the story. As he typed, WF had counterpointed the gullibility of the men who will be cheated at the auction with the skepticism of Mrs. Littlejohn, who observes the proceedings as she goes about her chores. One effective addition was a whole section which followed Mrs. Armstid home to care as best she could for her children—hungry and ill-clothed—before riding back to Frenchman's Bend to look after their injured father. The story ended with the men on the porch discussing the pursuit of the horses. The last word was given to Admiral Dewey Snopes, asking his father Eck for their remaining though uncaught horse. FCVA.
665	4	*OXE,* 4 Sept. 1930.
666	21	*OXE,* 28 Aug., 4, 11, and 18 Sept., 1930; J. W. Harmon and J. Byron Gathright in *WFO,* pp. 90–1; I: Mrs. J. Byron Gathright, 27 Nov. 1965.
666	37	*OXE,* 25 Sept. 1930; Sherwood Anderson, "They Come Bearing Gifts," *The American Mercury,* XXI (Oct. 1930), p. 129. On the last page of the article (p. 137), Anderson wrote, "Neither of them ever brought me to read a word they had written. I never saw anything they had written until it was published."
667	7	WF to Edith Greenburg, undated. Courtesy Miss Greenburg.
667	10	FCVA.
667	23	*ASI* lacked the intensity and power of its predecessor, wrote Mrs. Baker, but it was further proof that WF was one of the best American novelists. (*NOTP,* 26 Oct. 1930.) On October 19, 1930,

Page *Line*

the anonymous *NYT* reviewer had granted that the quality of WF's mind was of a high order but reacted against characters presented "in fluid Joycean terms" and felt compelled "to put this book in a high place in an inferior category."

667 29 *The Nation,* 131 (Nov. 5, 1930), p. 500; Basil Davenport said WF knew, as few poets did, that the inarticulate also have thoughts that lie too deep for tears. WF cut the knot by presenting what they *could* say in realistic form; what they could not, in a rich and subtle prose. "The compromise cannot be called entirely successful, but the facing of the problem is another evidence of Mr. Faulkner's self-reliant experimentalism." *The Saturay Review of Literature,* VII (Nov. 22, 1930), p. 362.

667 33 For sales figures, see Walker Gilmer, *Horace Liveright: Publisher of the Twenties* (New York, 1970), p. 256.

667 36 WF inscribed a copy of *ASI* to Myrtle Ramey [Demarest] on Nov. 13, 1930, at Oxford.

667 38 I: EF, 13 Aug. 1963.

668 6 *WFL, passim.*

668 7 W. M. Reed in *WFO,* p. 184.

668 11 *OXE,* 16 Oct. 1930.

668 13 I: Emily Stone, 27 Mar. and 30 Nov., 1965.

668 29 Emily Stone in *WFO,* pp. 96–8.

669 3 I: Emily Stone, 27 Mar. 1965.

669 26 The manuscript showed evidence of considerable revision, and eight of the fourteen pages bore paste-ons from an earlier draft. WF continued to revise between manuscript and typescript, cutting a whole section and reworking Jubal's speech to differentiate it from that of the mountaineers. FCVA.

Page *Line*

670 14 Arthur Guyton, M.D., to JB, 5 Oct. 1967.

670 25 John Reed Holley in *WFO,* p. 87.

671 10 H. L. Mencken Papers, Manuscript Division, NYPL. When WF returned the story with a short covering note, Mencken cut another reference to Nancy's swelling belly, made additional paragraph divisions, and inserted Roman numerals dividing it into five sections. When WF would later collect the story, he would retain a few of Mencken's minor editorial changes, but would restore the cuts he made. I am indebted to Leo M. J. Manglaviti for allowing me an early reading of his essay entitled "Faulkner's 'That Evening Sun' and Mencken's 'Best Editorial Judgment,'" *American Literature,* XLIII (Jan. 1972), pp. 649–54.

672 3 JFSA.

672 12 FCVA.

672 22 How much WF worked over this story is indicated by two other manuscripts. One, a single page entitled "A Dull Tale," is all about Dal Martin's daughter. A complete version of eleven pages (close to the typescript from which the version submitted to the *Post* presumably came) bears four tentative titles: "Resurgence," "Two Men," "[indecipherable] Armageddon," and "Episode." JFSA.

672 27 A report entitled "A Deplorable Affair" appeared in *OXE,* 13 Jan. 1910: "On Saturday morning about 8 o'clock, Mr. Henry Tabor and Mr. Pete Callicoatt met in the public road about 5 miles south of town and Mr. Cal-

NOTES

Page	Line	
		licoatt was killed by Mr. Tabor, receiving several gunshot wounds, dying several hours later. The two men were neighbors, and since they had a difficulty about 2 years ago both had been placed under peace bonds but trouble was expected between them." John Cullen suggests that these events may have provided the basis for the circumstances of Mink Snopes's murder of Jack Houston in *HAM.* (See *OTF,* pp. 106–7.) This portion of *HAM* clearly grew out of "The Hound."
673	5	Linton Massey, "Notes on the Unrevised Galleys of Faulkner's *Sanctuary,*" *Studies in Bibliography,* 8 (1956), pp. 195–208. I am much indebted to this valuable study.
673	19	*LIG,* p. 123.
673	24	*SAN* (ML ed.), Introduction, p. vii. WF usually quoted HS as objecting, "I've had the plates made." This normally would have come as a final step before the actual printing. The version WF told might have been meant to improve the story for an audience of laymen.
673	31	*SAN* (ML ed.), Introduction, p. vii.
673	36	The first fourteen galleys were newly typed, composed of new matter plus revised and rewritten old matter. ACLT.
674	6	*OXE,* 27 Mar. 1930.
674	7	*OXE,* 22 May 1930.
674	10	*MCA,* 1 Jan. and 7 June, 1930.
674	13	*MCA,* 24 and 25 June, 1929; 15 Aug. 1930; Cantwell, "Faulkner's 'Popeye,'" p. 148. Eight months after *SAN* was published, Pumphrey shot himself after a doctor had told him that a brain disease (supposedly venereal) would kill him in a few months. *MCA,* 29 Oct. 1931.
674	20	I: EF, 1 Dec. 1966.
674	31	*MCA,* 8 Aug. 1945.
674	37	WF added Mr. Binford's first name in *MAN.* John Cullen describes a house such as Miss Reba's and a girl he likens to Temple Drake. The original of the jailed Negro murderer he identifies as one Dave Bowdry. *OTF,* pp. 80–3.
675	7	Massey.
675	8	Prof. Gerald Langford argues that WF actually lessened the novel's effectiveness by reducing the complexity of Horace Benbow's character and the extent of his role and by flattening the verbal texture of descriptive and expository passages. Langford, *Faulkner's Revision of Sanctuary: A Collation of the Unrevised Galleys and the Published Book* (Austin, Tex., 1972), pp. 3–33.
676	3	WF tried to make everything as clear as possible. Pinned to an editor's correction slip dated December 5 was a notation that there were to be no apostrophes with the contractions "don't" and "can't" when new matter was set. There were numerous corrections on the galleys which he had allowed to stand, usually aimed at greater clarity—for instance, specifying the name of a speaker rather than using "he" or "she." ACLT.
676	6	Unpubl. portion of class conference, U. of Va., 15 Apr. 1957. On that occasion WF said that he got a job passing coal in a power plant to pay his share of the costs. It appears that he was here postdating the job he held earlier in the year. It seems more likely that his share of the costs, whatever it was, would

Page	Line	
		have been deducted from his royalties on sales. WF had retained the jailed Negro murderer in the revised version. He had heard the story, he said, from Roark Bradford. "I waited two years for him to use it but he never did." Marshall J. Smith, p. 414.
676	20	*SAN* (ML ed.), Introduction, p. viii. Much later he looked back at both revision and preface. "I rewrote the book and did the best I could with it to make it an honest book. And I was still ashamed of that first attempt because that was the only time I ever betrayed, well, call it the Muse, you might say. . . . but I did the best I could with the material as it was and so I'm not ashamed of the book now." Unpubl. portion of class conferences, U. of Va., 25 Feb. and 27 Apr., 1957. See Millgate, *The Achievement,* pp. 113, 123, for further discussion of the aesthetics of WF's revisions. See Cleanth Brooks, pp. 389–91, for exploration of the discrepancies in the novel, and pp. 387–9 for a useful chronology of events.
676	26	FCVA.
676	37	*CS,* p. 186.
677	6	In the typescript, WF substituted "England" for "Toronto." Warren became "Captain Warren," and later a member not of the RAF but of its more glamorous predecessor, the Royal Flying Corps. FCVA.
678	25	I: EF, 9 Sept. 1965.
678	32	*OXE,* 1, 22, and 29 Jan., 19 Feb., 1931.
678	36	I: Emily Stone, 27 Mar. 1965.
679	6	I: W. M. Reed, 19 Nov. 1966.
679	14	Sinclair Lewis, "The American Fear of Literature" (pamphlet published by Harcourt, Brace).
679	18	WF to HS, undated, prob. late Jan. 1932. RH.
679	28	WF made these entries on a sheet he later used in making a carbon copy of "The Brooch." He did not list the titles of the stories, but the other data indicate the titles. FCVA.
679	38	Scribner Archive, PUL.
680	10	FCVA.
681	23	I: EF, 27 Oct. 1965.
682	2	MCL.
682	5	See John Ralph Markette in *WFO,* p. 27.
682	17	MCL. WF later recorded the date of Alabama's death in the John Wesley Thompson Bible as 16 January 1931. Courtesy JMF.
682	23	I: SMW, 19 Aug. 1964.
682	33	I: EF, 27 Oct. 1965.
683	12	*Ibid.*; Myrtle Demarest, 30 Dec. 1966; Lenore Marshall, 10 Nov. 1964; BW, 28 Mar. 1965; Manuel Komroff, 22 Jan. 1965. Komroff to JB, 22 Sept. 1965.
683	14	*OXE,* 23 Sept. 1937.
683	20	I am unable to find any evidence of the wreck or injury.
683	31	Scribner Archive, PUL.
684	9	Howard's mother had kept house for him in Charlottesville for all four college years. WF had called her Mrs. Weddel in the manuscript but then crossed out that name used earlier in "Mountain Victory." She was like Miss Emily, wooed by a dashing outsider. FCVA.
684	21	Alfred Dashiell to WF, 20 Feb. 1931. Scribner Archive, PUL.
684	23	WF to Alfred Dashiell, 25 Feb. 1931. Scribner Archive, PUL. See Meriwether, *The Literary Career,* pp. 170–3.
684	35	New York *World,* 10 Feb. 1931.

NOTES

Page	Line	
684	38	New York *Sun,* 13 Feb. 1931.
685	4	*NYT Book Review,* 15 Feb. 1931.
685	13	FCVA.
685	19	*The Bookman,* LXXIII (Apr. 1931), p. 188.
685	23	*The Nation,* CXXXII (Apr. 15, 1931), p. 422.
685	29	*The Saturday Review of Literature,* VII (May 21, 1931), p. 673.
685	37	*Publishers Weekly,* CXX (Oct. 3, 1931), p. 188.
686	3	Typed copies of reviews identified only by reviewer. Courtesy Mrs. Jon Mallard.
686	5	Woollcott warned that the reader had to beware: "There are plenty of intelligent and sensible people whom the book would make really ill. For compared with 'Sanctuary,' the later Emile Zola's most earnest quests into the squalor of life seem like merry sunlit pages out of 'Little Women.' " Writing on the postwar novel in *The Bookman,* Gorham Munson thought he could foresee in WF's rise the waning of Ernest Hemingway's vogue. Munson objected to WF's characters and subject matter almost as much as Canby had, but WF was better at atmosphere than Fitzgerald and superior in power to Hemingway. Munson, "Our Post-War Novel," *The Bookman,* LXXIV (Oct. 1931), pp. 142–3.
686	17	*NOTP,* 26 Oct. 1931.
686	23	Memphis *Evening Appeal,* 26 Mar. 1931.
686	29	I: EF, 29 Apr. 1968.
687	8	I: SMW, 26 Nov. 1965.
687	10	I: C. M. Smith, 25 Nov. 1965.
687	19	Coughlan, pp. 77–8.
687	23	*MBB,* pp. 170–1.
687	29	I: Robert Coughlan, 24 Feb. 1967.
687	35	FCVA.
687	36	*Ibid.*
688	3	In the *Mercury,* Nancy's lover had been changed from Jesus to Jubah. The idea for the change was not WF's but editor H. L. Mencken's. Mencken was afraid that the name Jesus would suggest a Mexican rather than a Negro. (SC to Norman Holmes Pearson, 24 Jan. 1955; courtesy Beinecke Library, YUL.) When WF reprinted the story, he changed Jubah back to Jesus.
688	16	Of the fourteen manuscript pages, four had sizable paste-ons and two more bore marginal inserts. WF had obviously worked over the story with care, doing at least two manuscript versions before he reached the typing and revision stage. His setting of Cranston's Wells, Mississippi, was a summer resort much like the one his family had patronized at Lafayette Springs. FCVA.
688	25	*CS,* p. 627.
689	10	This manuscript showed the same kind of work as that of "Doctor Martino." Again, WF had apparently done at least two handwritten drafts before he had sat down at the typewriter. (FCVA.) The situation of the tubercular lover standing in the elements outside the beloved's house and then later dying suggests another triangle: that of Michael Furey and Gretta and Gabriel Conroy in James Joyce's "The Dead."
689	18	Courtesy American Play Co.
689	25	*MBB,* p. 163.
689	31	JFSA.
689	38	FCVA.
690	18	*CS,* p. 511.
690	23	In one beginning of the manuscript WF wrote, "In 1918 I was photographic officer of a

Page	Line	
		B.E. squadron." After eight lines he abandoned that opening. The one he finally chose began retrospectively. In the manuscript the narrator had a cork leg; when the story was printed, WF would make it a mechanical leg. In one way Sartoris was the same: "a tall lad with pale eyes in a face that could be either merry or surly, and quite humorless." He was also a half-literate man with a vocabulary of scarcely 200 words and a talent for violence that left him nearly toothless before the end of the story. Again WF had worked carefully. The paste-ons and inserts—together with the false start—showed how he had tried to shape the story. FCVA.
690	36	*CS,* p. 512.
691	3	It is possible that WF submitted this story to *Woman's Home Companion* rather than *Collier's.* The subject matter seems, however, to argue for *Collier's.* FCVA.
691	12	WF described the auction and the stampede of the horses at length. He increased Mrs. Littlejohn's role as outraged yet taciturn commentator. And he took Bundren and Mitchell off the porch of Varner's store in the last scene. *Scribner's,* LXXXIX (June 1931), pp. 585–97.
691	18	Scribner Archive, PUL. Queried about "Spotted Horses," WF answered, "I have written a dozen versions of it. I would have to see them all to unravel them myself. . . ." (Unpubl. portion of class conference, U. of Va., 7 Mar. 1957.) There was a response from ordinary readers to this story as well. One wrote to call to the author's attention certain discrepancies as to time in his fiction. He replied, "As you say, I am availing myself of my prerogative of using these people when and where I see fit. So far, I have not bothered much about chronology, which, if I am ever collected, I shall have to do." He added that "Spotted Horses" took place about 1900, when Suratt was about twenty-five. In *SAR* he was forty-five. (Undated letter, WF to Mr. Thompson. FCVA.)
692	3	"Beyond the Talking," *The New Republic,* LXVII (May 20, 1931), pp. 23–4; repr. in *ESP,* pp. 186–8.
692	7	WF to Horace Liveright, 18 Feb. 1927.
692	15	Courtesy American Play Co.
692	26	WF to Mrs. Murry Falkner, 7 Oct. 1925. JFSA.
692	29	One fragmentary four-page manuscript of "Victory" on Mulberry Bond paper displayed a clear calligraphy like that of *S&F.* Five pages in a heavier blue ink on Fidelity Onion Skin were done in quicker, harder-to-read, probably later writing. The two typescripts were quite similar to each other, the earlier fifty-one pages long and the later fifty-seven pages long. FCVA.
692	39	The typescripts began with the protagonist's shipwright grandfather in the leisurely fashion of a novel. WF drew on his Toronto experience for battalion inspection and upon his imagination for a trench raid: "It was short and sharp, for surprise was theirs." Transitions also suggested the early manner: "Time passed on like a pilgrim too deeply immersed in habit and weariness to pause for rest

NOTES

Page	Line	
		. . . ." The manuscript fragments probably came *after* the typescript. WF may have used the new manuscript material as a kind of framework, fitting into it what he could salvage from the earlier typescripts. He shortened the story considerably. Instead of describing Gray's heroism in a long narrative section of romantic battle writing, he reduced it to a paragraph by referring to the military dispatches which described it. FCVA.
693	11	Scribner Archive, PUL.
693	13	In a follow-up letter, WF told BW, "I may get up there in the fall. I hope so. I need a change. I'm stale. Written out." *Harper's* purchased "The Hound" on May 8, 1931, and "A Fox Hunt" on April 21. (Courtesy *Harper's*.) For each sale, BW received one-fourth of the American Play Company's 10 percent agent's commission. (Henry W. and Albert A. Berg Collection, NYPL.)
693	33	Kyle Crichton to WF, 23 July 1931. Scribner Archive, PUL.
694	30	*LIG,* pp. 5–15.
696	4	J. R. Cofield in *WFO,* p. 109.
699	4	JFSA.
699	26	The Scribner Archive does not contain WF's letter to Crichton explaining that he must try for the big prices first; this can be inferred clearly from Crichton to WF, 28 July and 6 Aug., 1931. Scribner Archive, PUL.
699	31	FCVA.
700	3	*CS,* p. 157.
700	13	I: Judge Taylor McElroy, 23 Mar. 1965.
700	24	Turl and Tom-Tom's sobering fall into a ravine suggested WF's mishap on the long-ago possum hunt.
700	25	No manuscript or typescript of "Centaur in Brass" has come to light to reveal the story's form when it reached *Scribner's.*
700	35	Scribner Archive, PUL.
700	36	FCVA.
700	38	Kyle Crichton to WF, 6 Aug. 1931. Scribner Archive, PUL.
701	23	*LIA,* p. 466. The elder Hightower's death in a henhouse may suggest, in a kind of double entendre, the ignominious death of the dashing Van Dorn at the hands of an outraged husband. Some readers, recalling WF's early fondness for the novels of Henryk Sienkiewicz and the tribute WF paid him in his foreword to *FR,* may see some connection between Sienkiewicz's cavalrymen and WF's. The ironic note comes through more strongly in the work of other writers such as Günter Grass: "O insane cavalry! Picking blueberries on horseback. Bearing lances with red and white penants. . . . Picture-book charges. . . . Oh, so brilliantly galloping! Always waiting for the sunset. Both foreground and background must be right before the cavalry can attack. . . ." Grass, *The Tin Drum,* trans. by Ralph Mannheim (New York, 1964), p. 251.
701	33	FCVA. Manuscript materials for the novel that became *LIA* also exist at ACLT. The process of composition was complex—not so much so as with *SAN,* but much more so, for instance, than with *ASI.* Consequently, the following conjectures about composition must be highly tentative.
702	2	WF wrote a two-and-a-half-page scene in which Hightower told his wife in some detail the story of his grand-

Page *Line*

father's death in the henhouse. The scene was set on a train—presumably the ride which took Hightower and his bride to his new church in Jefferson. There was the suggestion of a cleavage between the minister and his prim yet sympathetic wife. There was also the hint of a quizzical reception by the townspeople. ACLT. See *LIA,* p. 215.

702 16 I: EF, 23 Feb. 1965.

702 19 FCVA.

702 28 *FIU,* p. 74.

702 33 *LIA,* p. 465. On another occasion WF elaborated further on the title's meaning: "in August in Mississippi there's a few days somewhere about the middle of the month when suddenly there's a foretaste of fall, it's cool, there's a lambence, a luminous quality to the light, as though it came not from just today but from back in the old classic times. It might have fauns and satyrs and the gods. . . ." (*FIU,* p. 199.) WF apparently did not share this information with his publishers. Writing for the firm of Smith & Haas on June 29, 1934, Louise Bonino informed Gyldendal, WF's Norwegian publisher, that the meaning of the title was to be found on p. 251: "That was in September. Just after Christmas she told him that she was pregnant." Miss Bonino went on to add that the title "refers to the fact that Lena's child would be born in August, and that losing her heaviness, she would again become light."

703 5 ACLT.

703 19 Meriwether, "Faulkner, Lost and Found," p. 7.

703 33 WF had called the town Mottson in *S&F* and *ASI,* but from now on he would use Mottstown. He was naturally making use of Lafayette County lore. G. Hightower had been president of Mississippi A&M for years before he had gone on to head a farmers' group, and Burch, Bunch, and Burden were to be encountered as often as Bundren in the annals of the county. See *OXE,* 7 Dec. 1922, 19 June 1930.

704 24 ACLT; *LIA,* p. 245.

704 33 FCVA. Of the 187 pages of the final manuscript, seventy-nine would bear passages cut from a previous page and pasted onto the final one. There might be only one or as many as four. They might constitute a few lines or most of the page, being connected to each other by a few lines of new material. In a few instances, the paste-ons would occupy the whole page. They would be found in almost all sections of the final manuscript, and the material in them would come from all the major segments of the narrative. Some sequences of pages would have been tried in as many as six different locations before finding their final order in the completed manuscript.

704 36 FCVA.

704 38 Courtesy *Harper's.*

705 9 *NYT Book Review,* 27 Sept. 1931.

705 12 *NYHT Books,* 27 Sept. 1931.

705 15 FCVA.

705 31 Charlottesville *Daily Progress,* 22 Oct. 1931; *NYHT Books,* 8 Nov. 1931.

706 2 James Southall Wilson to WF, 15 Sept. 1931.

706 11 WF to Wilson, 24 Sept. 1931.

706 13 Wilson to WF, 2 Oct. 1931.

706 15 WF to Wilson, 5 Oct. 1931; Alderman Library, U. of Va.

NOTES

Page	Line	
706	17	Lewis Mattison to JB, 14 May 1967; "Literary Notes," Jonathan Cape and Harrison Smith, undated.
707	24	Charlottesville *Daily Progress,* 19 Oct. 1931.
708	10	*The Bookman,* LXXIV (Sept. 1931), pp. 17–24.
708	18	Scribner Archive, PUL. WF had probably helped make this sale by revising to answer the earlier criticism that Ginsfarb was too close to caricature. He had done this very simply without altering appearance, character, or action. Ginsfarb spoke, the narrator said, "in the diction of Weber and Fields in vaudeville, making his *wh*'s into *v*'s and his *th*'s into *d*'s." *CS,* p. 187.
708	20	FCVA.
708	24	JFSA.
709	7	WF to EF, 22 Oct. 1931. JFSA.
709	27	*Ibid.*
709	35	Lewis Mattison to JB, 14 May 1967.
710	10	WF to EF, 22 Oct. 1931. JFSA.
710	18	Emily Clark, "A Week-end at Mr. Jefferson's University," *NYHT Books* (Nov. 8, 1931), p. 1.
710	23	I: Paul Green, 16 Oct. 1968.
710	35	Charlottesville *Daily Progress,* 23 Oct. 1931.
710	36	Allen Tate to Mrs. Robert Tunstall, 31 Oct. 1931. Alderman Library, U. of Va.
710	37	*Letters of Sherwood Anderson,* p. 250.
711	5	Miss Glasgow discoursed upon compassion—to her the most essential element of a great literature. Taking a line very like WF's in his review of *The Road Back,* she cited that novel, Arnold Zweig's *The Case of Sergeant Grischa,* and Thomas Mann's *The Magic Mountain* as works informed by the pity and compassion learned in defeat. *The Saturday Review of Literature,* VIII (Nov. 7, 1931), p. 266; Emily Clark.
711	9	I: Dayton Kohler, 31 Dec. 1964.
711	17	Emily Clark.
711	30	*Letters of Sherwood Anderson,* pp. 250–1, 254.
712	2	Emily Clark.
712	15	I: Julia Wilson, 9 Mar. 1965.
713	2	I: Dayton Kohler, 31 Dec. 1964.
713	23	Emily Clark.
713	30	I: Dayton Kohler, 31 Dec. 1964.
713	34	I: Paul Green, 3 Aug. 1966.
713	36	*Letters of Sherwood Anderson,* p. 253.
714	2	Emily Clark.
714	5	Charlottesville *Daily Progress,* 26 Oct. 1931.
714	7	Lewis Mattison to JB, 14 May 1967.
714	13	*College Topics* (U. of Va.), 4 Nov. 1931.
714	14	*LIG,* p. 16.
714	19	Emily Clark.
714	30	*Letters of Sherwood Anderson,* pp. 252–3.
714	33	Paul Green noted that Josephine Pinckney, of the South Carolina Pinckneys, was foremost of those who had hurried over to gush at WF in the rotunda of the Farmington Country Club the instant before he became ill. I: 2 Nov. 1968.
714	36	*Letters of Sherwood Anderson,* p. 253.
715	10	Lewis Mattison to JB, 14 May 1967.
715	24	Emily Clark.
716	9	In the interview, published November 2, WF was quoted as saying he had just returned from Chapel Hill, North Carolina, with Paul Green. (*LIG,* pp. 16–18.) According to Green, however, they went to New York City, not to

Page	Line	
		Chapel Hill, at the conclusion of the conference. (I: 11 July 1968.) When WF mentioned Green, the reporter may have misunderstood or misinterpreted the rest. Or, WF may simply have offered the first excuse that entered his mind upon seeing the young man who had come to take him up on an appointment WF did not expect to materialize.
716	20	I: Paul Green, 11 July 1968; Milton Abernethy, 23 Apr. 1965.
716	34	FCVA. Seven of his short stories would have appeared in national magazines by the end of 1931, two more in special volumes. Two of his stories would be anthologized that year: "Thrift" in *O. Henry Memorial Award Prize Stories of 1931* and "That Evening Sun Go Down" in *Best Short Stories of 1931.*
717	34	I: EF, 17 Oct. 1967.
718	3	Neil Kessel and Henry Walton, *Alcoholism* (Baltimore, 1965), p. 71.
718	8	I: Louis Andrews Fischer, 3 Feb. 1965. More than one observer noted, however, that WF could consume quantities of alcohol out of all proportion to his size. A better understanding of conditions like his will doubtless come with increased knowledge of the biochemical processes involved.
719	5	Meriwether, "Faulkner, Lost and Found," p. 7.
719	9	Sherwood Anderson, *Memoirs,* p. 353.
719	19	*MBB,* pp. 148–9.
719	29	See Robert N. Linscott, "Faulkner Without Fanfare," *Esquire,* LX (July 1963), pp. 36, 38.
719	30	I: Peter De Vries, 16 Oct. 1970.
720	27	See Kessel and Walton, pp. 33–9.
721	24	*Ibid.* A further word on after-effects: pneumonia is a common aftermath of drinking bouts. Delirium tremens, which usually occurs within seventy-two hours of the cessation of drinking, can be produced by trauma, surgery, or sleep deprivation. The mortality rate is as high as 15 percent. Insomnia is characteristic of alcoholics. Some get very little sleep and become progressively more jittery as a result.
721	33	A working definition of an alcoholic is that he is one who has lost control of the drinking pattern to the extent that it interferes with his interpersonal relationships, family, or socioeconomic situation, or involves him with the law. (I: Harry Hyer, M.D., 13 Aug. 1968.) If WF can be said to have suffered from alcoholism, it was a kind of periodic and volitional alcoholism. As he aged, the incidence of extended drinking bouts decreased.
722	13	I: Paul Green, 11 July 1968. The memories of Messrs. Green and Abernethy are understandably imprecise on some of the dates, times, and other elements in what was to prove a particularly hectic series of events. Part of the following account is therefore constructed by inference.
722	35	*WFL,* p. 43.
722	37	I: BC, 20 Sept. 1967.
723	1	FCVA.
723	6	I: Paul Green, 11 July 1968; Milton Abernethy, 23 Apr. 1965.
723	24	I: Milton Abernethy, 23 Apr. 1965. Harry Hansen's New York *World-Telegram* column for 5 Nov. 1931, "Book Marks for Today," gives the Union Square Hotel as the

NOTES

Page	*Line*	
		place where WF stopped at this time. Abernethy's recollection is that it was the Hotel Algonquin, where WF definitely did stay later in his visit. Anthony Buttitta records the Algonquin as the hotel at which WF stayed on this first arrival in New York in 1931. Buttitta, "William Faulkner: That Writin' Man of Oxford," *The Saturday Review of Literature,* XVIII (May 21, 1938), p. 7.
724	22	I: Milton Abernethy, 23 Apr. 1965.
725	5	I: A. P. Hudson, 4 Apr. 1965.
725	7	I: Milton Abernethy, 23 Apr. 1965.
725	21	Anthony J. Buttitta, "A Memoir of Faulkner in the Early Days of His Fame," San Francisco *Sunday Chronicle,* 15 July 1962.
726	2	I: Mrs. William Couch, 10 Sept. 1968.
726	14	Phillips Russell to JB, 15 July 1968.
726	34	Undated newspaper clipping, New York *World-Telegram,* prob. 5 Nov. 1931.
726	36	Undated letter, WF to BW, prob. 19 Jan. 1932.
727	4	*NYT Book Review,* 8 Nov. 1931.
727	10	I: Milton Abernethy, 23 Apr. 1965.
727	23	JFSA.
727	38	I: Baxter Elliott, Sr., n.d., by James Webb. Courtesy Prof. Webb.
728	22	WF to HS, undated, recd. 20 July 1933.
728	24	WF to RKH, undated, recd. 10 June 1940. FCVA. The publisher WF referred to was probably Harold Guinzburg.
729	13	Robert Ballou to JB, 22 Oct. 1964.
729	16	I: David Yalden-Thomson, 16 July 1963.
729	21	I: BW, 29 Nov. 1965.

Page	*Line*	
729	22	Coughlan, p. 106; I: 24 Feb. 1967.
729	28	Tallulah Bankhead, *Tallulah: My Autobiography* (New York, 1952), pp. 189–92.
729	33	Coughlan, p. 106.
730	12	Maurice Edgar Coindreau, "The Faulkner I Knew," *Shenandoah,* XVI (Winter 1965), p. 27; I: 24 June 1965. A French translation of *SAN* was already under way.
730	21	I: Louise Bonino, 11 Nov. 1964.
731	5	I: Mrs. Sewell Haggard, 17 and 23 Apr., 1965.
731	23	I: Dorothy Parker, 17 Apr. 1965.
732	2	I: George Oppenheimer, 16 Apr. 1965.
733	32	I: Robert Lovett, 16 Aug. 1965.
734	1	Millgate, *The Achievement,* p. 33.
734	2	BW, 28 Mar. and 29 Nov., 1965.
735	8	Frank Sullivan to JB, 7 Mar. 1966.
735	18	Corey Ford to JB, 11 Feb. 1966.
735	24	*CS,* p. 475.
736	21	*Ibid.,* p. 509.
736	26	*The Saturday Evening Post,* CCIV (Mar. 5, 1932).
736	27	I: Robert Lovett, 16 Aug. 1965.
737	19	JFSA.
737	38	I: EF, 9 July 1968.
738	30	*NYHT,* 14 Nov. 1931, repr. in *LIG,* pp. 19–22. Nearly ten years before, *OXE* and many another Southern newspaper had printed accounts of segregation in the North with captions such as "Negroes Dying in Northern Cities by the Hundreds" and then gone on to describe the ravages of cold and malnutrition.
739	6	I: Eric J. Devine, 15 Aug. 1965.
739	13	*WFL,* pp. 81, 24.
739	31	I: Paul Green, 3 Aug. 1966;

Page	Line	
		Green, *Plough and Furrow* (London, 1963), pp. 43–4.
740	7	I: George Oppenheimer, 16 Apr. 1965.
740	19	Lillian Hellman, "Dashiell Hammett: A Memoir," *The New York Review of Books,* 8 (Nov. 25, 1965), p. 20. See also Carvel Collins, "Nathanael West's *The Day of the Locust* and *Sanctuary,*" *Faulkner Studies,* II (Summer 1953), p. 23.
740	36	Hammett had won his first promotion for catching a man who had stolen a ferris wheel. Later he had worked on cases involving such notorious figures as gambler Nicky Arnstein and actor Fatty Arbuckle. As a Motor Ambulance Corps sergeant in France he had contracted penumonia, which had spelled the end of his Pinkerton career. Hellman, pp. 18–21. Stanley J. Kunitz and Howard Haycraft, *Twentieth Century Authors* (New York, 1942), pp. 607–8.
741	33	Hellman, pp. 18, 21; I: 17 Jan. 1966.
743	27	I: Lillian Hellman, 17 Jan. 1966; BC, 20 Sept. 1967; BW, 24 Mar. 1965. Alfred Knopf to JB, 7 Aug. 1968. See Sara Mayfield, *The Constant Circle: H. L. Mencken and His Friends* (New York, 1968), p. 202.
743	33	I: Mrs. Sewell Haggard, 17 Apr. 1965; BW, 28 Mar. 1965.
744	5	*SAN* (ML ed.), Introduction, pp. vii, viii. Recalling the novel and that introduction twenty-five years later, he said, "I was still ashamed of it when I wrote that preface, I still didn't like the book, and I still am sorry that I wrote the first version of it. And that was the reason for the preface." (Unpubl. portion of class conference, U. of Va., 27 Apr. 1957.) For resemblances between this introduction and Ernest Hemingway's introduction to *The Torrents of Spring,* see Thomas L. McHaney, *William Faulkner's The Wild Palms: A Textual and Critical Study* (Ann Arbor, Mich., 1969), p. 247.
744	8	BC to BW, 25 Nov. 1931.
744	9	BW to BC, 8 Dec. 1931.
744	15	BW to BC, 25 Nov. 1931; WF to BW, undated, prob. 19 Jan. 1932.
744	24	I: Manuel Komroff, 22 Jan. 1965.
745	2	Repr. in *LIG,* pp. 23–4.
745	4	I: BW, 28 Mar. 1965.
745	7	Meriwether, "Early Notices of Faulkner," p. 161.
745	9	I: Eric J. Devine, 15 Aug. 1965.
745	12	I: Lenore Marshall, 10 Nov. 1964.
745	13	*NYT Book Review,* 29 Nov. 1931.
745	32	I: Lenore Marshall, 10 Nov. 1964; see also Marshall, "The Power of Words," *Saturday Review,* XLV (July 28, 1962), p. 17.
745	34	I: EF, 3 July 1968.
746	10	MPS, 31 Nov. 1931, repr. in *LIG,* pp. 25–7.
746	15	WF to James Southall Wilson, postmarked New York, N.Y., 6 P.M., 30 Nov. 1931, Alderman Library, U. of Va.
746	35	JFSA. I: EF, 3 July 1968; 19 Feb. 1965.
747	5	Frank Case, *Tales of a Wayward Inn* (New York, 1938), pp. 18, 60–8.
747	13	Margaret Case Harriman, *Blessed Are the Debonaire* (New York, 1956), pp. 41–2.
747	24	Margaret Case Harriman, *The Vicious Circle* (New York, 1951), pp. 59–60.
747	29	I: EF, 19 Feb. 1965.
747	34	John Dos Passos to JB, 7 Oct. 1969.

NOTES

Page	Line	
747	38	Harriman, *The Vicious Circle,* p. 112.
748	4	Unidentified clipping. JFSA.
748	5	*Idyll in the Desert:* "Of this edition four hundred copies were printed in the week of December 7 nineteen hundred and thirty-one by The Harbor Press, New York . . . Signed by the Author William Faulkner at Random House."
749	1	I: EF, 3 July 1968; BW, 28 Mar. 1965.
749	2	*WFL,* pp. 14, 16.
749	9	I: EF, 29 May 1967.
749	18	Courtesy MGM.
750	10	*OXE,* 6 Oct. 1932.
750	12	*OXE,* 8 Dec. 1932.
750	16	*OXE,* 4 Dec. 1931.
750	21	*OXE,* 31 Dec. 1931.
751	1	WF to Alfred Dashiell, 16 Dec. 13.
751	3	Dashiell to WF, 19 Dec. 1931. Scribner Archive, PUL.
752	26	I: Louis Cochran, 4 June 1965; Cochran and Phil Stone in *WFO,* pp. 103–6, 215–29.
752	30	Marshall J. Smith, pp. 411–17.
753	1	WF to BW, undated, prob. 19 Jan. 1932.
753	6	Frank Sullivan to JB, 7 Mar. 1966. I: EF, 27 Oct. 1965; BW, 28 Mar. 1965.
753	19	WF to HS, undated.
754	6	See Buttitta, "William Faulkner," pp. 6–8, and "A Memoir of Faulkner." EF remembered that her husband did not play phonograph records while he was writing, but that the only ones he would listen to were those of Gershwin compositions and a few classical recordings she owned. (I: 19 Feb. 1965.) WF apparently pulled Buttitta's leg at times during his visit, and this seems to have been one of those occasions. When Buttitta published an account more than six years later, he wrote, "Another interest that is giving Bill a satisfaction he had never known before is his four-year old boy Joe. The youngster means a great deal to him." (Buttitta, "William Faulkner," p. 8.) At this time WF's daughter Jill was four.
754	19	Buttitta, "A Memoir of Faulkner." In this account the geography of Yoknapatawpha County is radically condensed and several of the details are erroneous—a result, perhaps, of Buttitta's trying to recall them over thirty years later.
754	22	*Ibid.* The two longest poems were "Vision in Spring" and "April" ("Somewhere a slender voiceless breeze will go"). Besides "Spring" and "My Epitaph," the others included "Twilight," "I Will Not Weep for Youth," "Knew I Love Once," "To a Virgin," and "Winter Is Gone." The tenth poem, "A Child Looks from His Window," would ultimately appear in a later issue. *Contempo,* I (Feb. 1, 1932) and II (May 25, 1932).
754	30	Duschnes replied on BC's letter.
755	1	HS to BC, 8 Jan. 1932.
755	28	HS to WF, 15 Jan. 1932.
756	3	Undated, prob. mid-Jan. 1932.
757	3	WF to BW, undated, prob. 19 Jan. 1932.
757	28	WF to HS, undated, prob. 19 Jan. 1932.
757	29	HS to Casanova Book Shop, 21 Jan. 1932. Writing WF on 3 Feb. 1932, HS told him he would receive $150 royalty. This may have been from "Turn About," which would appear in the *Post* on March 5.
757	38	*Contempo,* I (Feb. 1, 1932), p. 3.

Page	Line	
758	3	Carl Petersen to JB, 15 Nov. 1967.
758	17	WF had sent "Turn About" to BW on January 9. BW's wire is referred to in WF's undated reply, which was received in BW's office on January 26, 1932. WF had closed with the kind of reminder that would usually follow a visit to New York: *"Dont forget the pipe."* Returning home after each trip, he would discover that he had left behind a pipe, gloves, or even a jacket. Friends would usually retrieve and return them.
758	20	Henry Nash Smith in *LIG,* p. 32.
758	28	Levees on the Tallahatchie had begun to give way before the flood WF mentioned as early as January 3. Although it stopped rising by January 11, permitting refugees to return, the Red Cross was still aiding refugees in Mississippi as late as January 30.
758	35	WF to HS, undated.
758	38	Courtesy *Harper's.*
760	15	Smith's interview was published in the Dallas *Morning News,* 14 Feb. 1932. His visit actually took place between mid- and late January. I: James Meriwether, 30 Dec. 1970. Interview repr. in *LIG,* pp. 28–32. See also Tinkle.
760	17	Phil Stone in *WFO,* p. 225.
760	22	I: JFS, 9 July 1968.
761	2	WF to BW, undated.
761	27	FCVA.
761	33	But this area was naturally not the exclusive province of women. Hightower and Byron Bunch discussed it, the one-time professional theologian asking the amateur, "are you going to undertake to say just how far evil extends into the appearance of evil? just where between doing and appearing evil stops?" P. 289.
762	17	Among characters reappearing in this novel was Maxey, of "Hair," whose barbershop was the scene of "Dry September," where McLendon had appeared. A Eustace Grimm, perhaps related to Christmas' murderer, Percy Grimm, had connived with Flem Snopes in "Lizards in Jamshyd's Courtyard."
762	23	*LIA* ms., p. 4. FCVA.
762	24	*Ibid.,* p. 155.
762	27	The legibility was decreasing, and abbreviations such as "AM" and "thot" (for "thought") were appearing frequently. Untypically, he made notes to himself at the top of some pages. On what finally became p. 108 he wrote, "Escape of Christmas into the country. First night." Two pages later, on what in the end became Ch. 13, he wrote, "The week of the hunt for Christmas, from the fire to his disappearance at the cotton house." P. 14. FCVA.
763	5	*OXE,* 13 Mar. 1919. J. T. Buckley writes that Calvin Burden, Joanna Burden's grandfather, may have been suggested by Nelson G. Gill, a Midwesterner who came to Mississippi after the Civil War and founded the Gill School for Negroes at Holly Springs. Buckley, pp. 447–54.
763	13	*OXE,* 24 Oct. 1907.
763	19	*FIU,* p. 72.
763	20	*LIA,* ms. p. 78. FCVA.
763	28	*Ibid.,* ms. p. 88.
764	11	It might be argued that Grimm was thinking about "the Player," but this does not seem consistent with either his psychology or the syntax of the passages.
764	23	It appears from the manuscript that WF must have had clearly in mind the sequence

NOTES

Page	Line	
		of events up through Ch. 6, the first of the six chapters describing Christmas' life through flashbacks. The final manuscript was put together of paste-ons from an earlier version. As he began to rework the material he had one unpleasant surprise: a page was missing. He wrote to *Contempo*: "I have lost a page from the novel mss. Page No 12. For God's sake see if I left it in the office. It is a complicated chapter and I cant reconstruct it. Send it right away if you find it." Buttitta and Abernethy wired him back that they couldn't find it. He went ahead, presumably rewriting from memory and inventing where he had to. (Buttitta, "A Memoir of Faulkner.") With Ch. 7, in which McEachern whips the eight-year-old boy, WF began to experiment with chapter order. He had tried this chapter as 8, 9, 10, and 11 (the last twice) before fixing it as Ch. 7. He did the same thing with the next six chapters (which took the story one chapter beyond Joanna Burden's death), trying one of them in four different places before the final one and trying all of them in at least three different places. Thereafter he moved only Ch. 19, which had been 17. (FCVA.)
765	9	John Riddell, "Popeye the Pooh," *Vanity Fair,* 38 (Mar. 1932), pp. 49, 66. The piece was published later that year by Charles Scribner's Sons with other Ford burlesques in *In the Worst Possible Taste,* with Miguel Covarrubias' illustrations. WF was portrayed in a checked romper suit standing in a corncrib, a toy shovel in one hand and a toy pail containing an ear of corn in the other. It may have given him some pleasure to be a subject for the artist who had provided the model for *Sherwood Anderson & Other Famous Creoles* not seven years before.
765	14	WF to BW, undated.
765	15	On p. 168 he had hit another short sequence where he had cut and added and repaged twice, but apart from that it went smoothly. He had made some minor alterations. Grimm's Store, in Mottstown, became Dollar's Store. Byron Bunch's term of service with the lumber mill was changed in pen from six years to seven. FCVA. ACLT.
765	22	I: JW, 15 Nov. 1964.
765	36	WF to BW, undated.
766	5	BC to HS, 9 Apr. 1932.
766	13	WF to BW, undated. It is possible that this magazine submission could have been "A Portrait of Elmer" or "With Caution and Dispatch," though it seems more likely that WF tried to sell them at a later date.
766	15	*Salmagundi,* Casanova Press, Milwaukee, 1932; 525 numbered copies.
766	21	In a little over a month, WF's second $50 check from the venture would be arriving. (ACLT.) Casanova Press had experienced no difficulty about permissions with Hemingway. When he gave his consent for the reprinting of his poem "Ultimately," he also asked Paul Romaine to wish WF the best of luck. Hemingway thought WF was going well and said that he sounded like a "good skate." (Parke-Bernet Sale No. 2350, May 4, 1965, Collections of Manuscripts, Ernest Thompson Seton, et. al., p. 24.)

Page	Line	
766	25	WF to HS, recd. in HS's office 20 July 1933.
766	28	*Publishers Weekly,* 121 (Mar. 19, 1932), p. 1396; (Apr. 30), p. 1887; (May 7), p. 1952.
766	33	Samuel Marx to JB, 21 Mar. 1966.
767	5	Coindreau, "The Faulkner I Knew," pp. 27–8.
767	11	Edwin Seaver, "A Chamber of Horrors," New York *Sun,* 13 Feb. 1931.
767	19	Samuel Marx to JB, 21 Mar. 1966.
767	26	Courtesy MGM.
767	29	WF to BW, undated.
767	35	Unpubl. portion of class conference, U. of Va., 15 Apr. 1957.
768	16	Coughlan, p. 86; I: 24 Feb. 1967.
768	20	Jean Stein to JB, 8 Feb. 1969.
768	23	*WFL,* p. 35.
771	24	"Metro-Goldwyn-Mayer," *Fortune,* VI (Dec. 1932), pp. 63, 51; Eileen Creelman, "Picture Plays and Players," unidentified newspaper clipping. FCVA.
772	19	Samuel Marx to JB, 21 Mar. 1966; Marx, "Faulkner in Hollywood," Beverly Hills *Courier,* 1 Oct. 1965.
772	25	"Metro-Goldwyn-Mayer," p. 63; *NYT,* 25 Dec. 1932.
773	4	Marx; Samuel Marx to JB, 21 Mar. 1966.
773	11	Samuel Marx to F. L. Hendrickson, 10 May 1932.
773	12	Kate Corbaley to M. E. Greenwood and others, 11 May 1932. Courtesy MGM.
773	20	Marx.
773	23	*NYT,* 25 Dec. 1932.
773	27	Samuel Marx to F. L. Hendrickson, 19 May 1932. Courtesy MGM.
773	29	Stallings.
774	3	Though the MGM "Author's Record" charged WF's time for three weeks to *Manservant,* he also worked on two other extended treatments during that period. Courtesy MGM. Marx.
774	19	Kate Corbaley to WF, 1932. Courtesy MGM. It is possible that the script represented another attempt to find a picture for John Gilbert, a star of silent films. (Samuel Marx to JB, 21 Mar. 1966.) Even though WF was trying to follow scenario format by dividing the material into many scenes, he was still using stage terminology, as when he wrote, "Enter Das." (JFSA.)
774	24	JFSA.
774	26	Courtesy MGM.
775	3	JFSA.
775	14	Courtesy MGM.
775	24	*Ibid.* There were echoes here of the hostility of John Sartoris for his squadron commander, Captain Spoomer, and of Sartoris' end as recounted in *SAR.* This last fight, above the clouds, suggested a William Butler Yeats poem which was a favorite of WF's, "An Irish Airman Foresees His Death." There were suggestions too of another book which WF had probably found useful in earlier treatments of aerial combat on the Western front: *War Birds: Diary of an Unknown Aviator.* See p. 792.
776	8	JFSA.
776	29	Stallings.
777	3	I: Jacob Zeitlin, 9 June 1965.
777	23	Stallings. See *WFL,* p. 87.
777	36	Stallings.
778	12	Courtesy MGM. A character type in this scenario would also appear in others such as *Latin-American Kingdom Story* and *God Is My Co-Pilot*: the man who had deserted his wife and daughter.
778	19	*Turn to the Right* was "about a couple of crooks who hide away in farm country and go

NOTES

Page	*Line*	
		straight under the benign influence of their trusting neighbors and highly honest locale. It was so full of sweetness it possibly turned WF's stomach, he probably read it and returned it with a report he could do nothing to help it reach the screen. No one ever did, in fact." Samuel Marx to JB, 21 Mar. 1966.
778	22	Courtesy MGM.
778	26	Undated letters, WF to BW, prob. Oct. 1932.
778	31	Courtesy American Play Co. The purchase of *SAN* had been urged by Paramount executive Meritt Hubbard, who had been an editor at *The Saturday Evening Post.* Hubbard later said that he had encouraged WF in the writing of the book and had promised that Paramount would buy it. Carol Brandt to JB, 17 July 1972.
779	1	I: William Hawks, 15 June 1965.
779	37	I: Howard Hawks, 3 and 10 June, 1965. See also Bob Thomas, "Faulkner Likes Film Writing," New York *World-Telegram & Sun,* 17 June 1955.
780	4	WF to BW, undated, prob. Oct. 1932.
780	9	I: Howard Hawks, 3 June 1965.
780	11	Courtesy MGM.
780	21	I: Frank Gruber, 12 June 1965.
780	34	I: Howard Hawks, 10 June 1965.
781	5	I: Robert Buckner, 8 June 1966.
781	8	Stallings.
781	27	I: Howard Hawks, 10 June 1965.
781	37	I: SMW, 23 Nov. 1965.
781	38	I: EF, 9 Dec. 1964.
782	7	I: Dorothy Oldham, 17 Jan. 1967.
782	26	I: EF, 17 Oct. 1967.
782	27	WF to JB.
782	35	I: SMW, 23 Nov. 1965.
783	12	*OXE,* 11 Aug. 1932; I: JMF, 24 Nov. 1965.
783	15	*FOM,* pp. 200–1.
783	25	Last Will and Testament of Murry C. Falkner (Sr.), Chancery Court, Oxford, Miss.
783	27	JFSA.
783	32	WF to BW, undated, recd. in BW's office 25 Sept. 1932.
783	34	An early mimeographed draft of "Turn About" (not the official studio first draft) bears the date 24 Aug. 1932. Courtesy MGM.
784	2	I: JMF, 18 Mar. 1965. Courtesy JMF.
784	5	*WFL, passim.*
784	6	WF to BW, undated, recd. 25 Sept. 1932.
784	33	ACLT. At the passage recounting the offer of reward money by Joanna Burden's New Hampshire nephew, the proofreader-editor reminded the author that he had told the reader that Joanna Burden's only brother had died in Jefferson at the age of twenty. Was this passage correct? "Correct," answered the author tersely. "A town rumor. He is a 3rd cousin. The town called him nephew: not Faulkner." *LIA,* p. 278.
785	1	ACLT. When the galleys were received in New York, someone decorously crossed out the curses.
785	6	WF to BW, undated, prob. late Sept. 1932.
785	9	WF to BW, undated, recd. 25 Sept. 1932. WF also told Stallings about the watermelon and the rain. He disliked the constant sun of California. "Beautiful cloudy weather here," he wrote. Stallings.
785	13	I: EF, 17 Oct. 1967.
785	21	WF to BW, undated, prob. late Sept.

Page	Line	
785	29	*OXE,* 6 Oct. 1932.
785	34	I: EF, 8 Aug. 1963.
786	5	*FOM,* pp. 133–4.
786	11	I: Louise Meadow, 27 Nov. 1965.
786	15	I: EF, 8 Aug. 1963.
786	18	Samuel Marx to M. R. Craig, 6 Oct. 1932. Courtesy MGM.
786	32	M. E. Greenwood to Samuel Marx and Marx to Greenwood, 11 Oct. 1932. Courtesy MGM.
786	38	Courtesy American Play Co.
787	3	I: EF, 8 Aug. 1963.
787	5	EF to HS, undated, prob. mid-Oct. 1932. JFSA.
787	8	I: JMF, 24 Nov. 1965.
787	21	I: Howard Hawks, 3 June 1965.
787	23	Courtesy MGM.
787	29	Roark Bradford, "The Private World of William Faulkner," *'48: The Magazine of the Year,* 2 (May 1948), p. 93.
787	31	I: EF, 9 Sept. 1965.
787	32	WF to HS, undated, prob. late Oct. 1932.
788	19	Meriwether, "Faulkner, Lost and Found," p. 7. Many years later, HS said that he had sent a sketch of the proposed cover for *LIA* and that WF had approved it. If so, WF perhaps meant that he was not interested in the finished job.
788	24	WF to HS, prob. late Oct. 1932.
789	11	*The Saturday Review of Literature,* IX (Oct. 8, 1932), p. 153. J. Donald Adams discovered justice and compassion in WF's work for the first time. The pattern of the novel was "streaked with red" but it was still "an astonishing performance," which showed WF to be "a stylist of striking strength and beauty" who had finally demonstrated that he could "lift his eyes above the dung-hill." *NYT Book Review,* 9 Oct. 1932.
789	28	*The Nation,* CXXXV (Oct. 26, 1932), p. 402.
789	33	*The North American Review,* CCXXXIV (Dec. 1932), p. 571.
790	6	WF to HS, undated, prob. late Oct. 1932.
790	11	I: Malcolm Franklin, 26 Nov. 1966.
790	17	*WFL,* pp. 81, 87.
791	18	John Sartoris' mother was a Spoade—kin, perhaps, to Quentin Compson's fellow student at Harvard. Rather than chronicling next the life of his brother, the "Carolina Bayard," WF now described, at much less length, the life of Bayard, the son of Col. John Sartoris, whose marriage to a girl named Vervay (?) of "Rosmerholm," Yoknapatawpha County, produced two sons: John, who was killed in aerial combat in France, and his brother Bayard, who did not live long enough to see his son Benbow. At that point the manuscript, now rain-stained, mouse-chewed, and more illegible than not, breaks off. FCVA.
791	33	WF told James Meriwether that the story dated "from about the time of 'Turn About.'" HO's records showed that the story was submitted to him "early in 1940." (Meriwether, *The Literary Career,* pp. 87–9.) As AE was preparing a table of contents for a projected volume of collected stories, he asked that HO send him any WF stories he had on hand. On February 25, 1948, HO sent "With Caution and Dispatch" and three other stories. (HO to RKH, 25 Feb. 1948.) "With Caution and Dispatch" is one of WF's less

NOTES

Page	Line	
		successful stories. It seems likely that he began it when he said he did, bringing it only much later to the point at which he was willing to have it offered for sale. WF's autograph corrections on the typescript are made in a hand resembling that of the late 1940's. In the story Sartoris makes a forced landing near "a night-flying coast defense squadron," which suggests the Lovett influence at work in "Turn About." The huge Brazilian flag on the ship's side which suddenly looms above Sartoris suggests, of course, the huge Argentine flag which suddenly looms above Claude, Ronnie, and Bogard in the CMB. Sartoris taunts his sweetheart's escort about his decorations with the same line which he had used about Spoomer's in "All the Dead Pilots": "D.S.T. Distinguished Series of Thighs." In what may be a vaguely autobiographical memory, WF introduced an American sergeant who had once lived in Memphis while working as "a dick on the Frisco RR," a line which ran through New Albany a few blocks from the house where WF was born. There are two surviving typescripts of varying lengths. (FCVA.)
791	35	BW to Alfred Dashiell, 4 Nov. 1932.
791	36	Dashiell to BW, 10 Nov. 1932.
791	37	BW to Dashiell, 15 Dec. 1932; Dashiell to BW, 23 Dec. 1932. Scribner Archive, PUL.
792	4	Repr. in *WFO,* pp. 216–24.
792	14	WF to BW, undated, prob. Nov. 1932.
792	15	I: Howard Hawks, 3 and 10 June, 1965.
792	23	WF to BW, undated, prob. Nov. 1932.
792	25	Courtesy MGM.
792	35	*Ibid.* In February, 1927, it had been revealed that the diary was that of John McGavock Grider, a Memphian who joined the Royal Flying Corps, trained in England, and died in France. The diary had come into the possession of his friend and fellow American, Maj. Elliot White Springs, who had enlivened Grider's account with descriptions of wartime parties and love affairs and then sold it to *Liberty,* to George H. Doran Co., and to MGM. He had turned over a substantial part of the profits to the Grider family in 1927. *MCA,* 13 Feb. and 1 July, 1927; Clayton Knight to JB, 24 Feb. 1968; *War Birds: Diary of an Unknown Aviator* (New York, 1926).
793	14	*WFL,* p. 25. "Mountain Victory" had meanwhile appeared in *The Saturday Evening Post,* CCV (Dec. 3, 1932).
793	17	*OXE,* 22 Dec. 1932.
794	20	John Sartoris became the diarist, who engaged in the same running battle with Capt. Spoomer over Antoinette which had been central to the short story. Again Bayard saw his brother die, his killer turning out to be the wounded baron exhibited in the French café by Monaghan in "Ad Astra." But in the script Bayard Sartoris brought both Antoinette and the German home to John's dismayed widow, Caroline, to help her raise John Sartoris' posthumous son and namesake. The film was to close with the fourteen-year-old boy's coming into knowledge and acceptance of the extraordinary past of the

Page	Line	
		strange ménage in his home. (Courtesy MGM.) Howard Hawks kindly gave JB access to another version, a 100-page finished film script entitled *A Ghost Story,* the rights to which are owned by Mr. Hawks.
794	25	ACLT.
794	31	Poems VII, XXVIII, XXX, and XXXVII of *AGB* appeared on April 12, 1933, XXXIV on April 19, and VI on May 3.
794	35	Courtesy MGM.
795	18	*Ibid.*
795	20	Samuel Marx to Howard Hawks, L. B. Mayer, and M. E. Greenwood, 20 Mar. 1933.
795	21	Howard Hawks to Samuel Marx, 20 Mar. 1933. Courtesy MGM.
795	27	Memphis *Evening Appeal,* 27 Mar. 1933.
795	32	Undated clipping, prob. 10 Apr. 1933.
796	3	*MCA,* 8 Nov. 1950.
796	8	*OXE,* 6 Oct. 1932.
796	31	*MPS,* 6 Aug. 1936.
796	39	I: Louise Meadow, 27 Nov. 1965.
797	8	I: E. O. Champion, 22 Mar. 1965.
797	27	I: MCF, 31 Mar. 1965.
797	37	Undated clipping. JFSA.
798	1	*OXE,* 9 and 23 Feb., 1933.
798	12	*OXE,* 9 Mar. 1933.
798	13	*OXE,* 23 Mar. 1933.
798	23	*OXE,* 6 Apr. 1933.
798	32	*OXE,* 13 Apr. 1933.
799	1	*MCA,* 13 Apr. 1933.
799	19	*AGB,* poems I, XLIV, XII, XIII, IV, III, XXII, XLI, and XXIV.
799	26	James Meriwether to JB, 24 Jan. 1968.
799	28	Writing in *The Saturday Review of Literature* on April 29, William Rose Benét called it the work of a "gifted amateur." As a poet, "He does not truly know his way about. He almost seems to be precocious, peculiarly enough, rather than accomplished." (IX, p. 565.) The next day Eda Lou Walton wrote in *NYHT Books* that if WF had not chosen fiction, he probably would have ranked as "one of the better of the minor poets of this period." It would be twenty-five years before a sympathetic critic would write that his poetry demonstrated "an attempt to achieve, within the limitations which he demanded for verse, new variations on the oldest themes." (Garrett, p. 134.)
799	34	*FIU,* p. 4. The one poem which actually did appear after the publication of *AGB* was poem VI of that volume, coming out in *The New Republic* on May 3, the last of a group of six from the book which had been bought by the magazine before book publication. Poem XXXVII repr. in *The New Republic,* 22 Nov. 1954.
800	7	Marx.
800	15	Courtesy MGM.
800	32	M. E. Greenwood to Samuel Marx, 17 Feb. 1933. Marx to WF, 21 Feb. 1933. Greenwood to Marx, 3 Mar. 1933. Courtesy MGM.
801	9	*LIG,* pp. 241–3.
801	15	"Metro-Goldwyn-Mayer," pp. 58, 116.
801	19	I: EF, 27 Oct. 1965.
802	2	*LIG,* pp. 241–3.
802	22	Courtesy MGM. Between April 12 and 20, WF had been flying almost every day. He did not fly between April 20 and May 9. On April 26, Kate Corbaley wrote him from MGM for his assignment of rights on *Louisiana Lou.* (Courtesy MGM.) On April 26, a New Orleans bookseller wrote an indignant

NOTES

Page	*Line*	
		letter of protest to HS over WF's refusal to autograph copies of his books. In a mollifying letter on April 28, HS explained that WF did not like to autograph books "and when he was in New York a year ago or more I believe that he told a man of some distinction that he had made it a rule not to give his autograph unless he personally knew the person who had asked for it."
802	27	Samuel Marx to WF, 13 May and 24 Aug., 1933. Courtesy MGM.
803	1	Undated clipping. MCL.
803	3	I: EF, 27 Oct. 1965.
803	14	JFSA.
803	27	I: EF, 27 Oct. 1965; JFS, 16 Aug. 1968.
803	35	*Ibid.*
805	25	Tom S. Hines, Jr., in *WFO,* p. 114.
806	1	WF to BW, 27 June 1933.
806	6	I: Emily Stone, 27 Mar. and 30 Nov., 1965.
806	17	Courtesy MGM.
806	24	WF to Samuel Marx, 19 July 1933. Courtesy Indiana University Library.
806	28	Samuel Marx to WF, 24 Aug. 1933. Even though *Mythical Latin-American Kingdom Story* was found to be unsatisfactory as a film possibility, the MGM script department went ahead with the mimeographing of the 110-page scenario on August 26, 1933. Courtesy MGM.
807	5	WF to HS, recd. 20 July 1933.
807	32	WF to BW, undated, prob. mid- or late July 1933.
808	6	Alfred Dashiell to BW, 25 Aug. 1933. Scribner Archive, PUL.
808	24	Weddel seems based on Greenwood Lefore, who interested WF. A half-Choctaw chieftain and the builder of Malmaison, he once traveled to Washington to appeal to Pres. Jackson for protection against a dishonest Indian agent. (See *Mississippi: A Guide to the Magnolia State,* pp. 403–4, and *FIU,* p. 44.) "Lo!" was reprinted in *CS,* pp. 381–403. The discrepancy between the two accounts could of course be attributed to the differences between the truth and the version of it the son would give years after his famous father's death.
808	36	In a letter to BW on July 31, 1933, Dashiell rejected a WF story which he did not name but which clearly seems to have been "Elly," which BW had sent him on July 21. Dashiell felt that the story was a bit dated and that its sexual theme verged "too closely upon the pathological." Scribner Archive, PUL. *CS,* pp. 207–24.
809	2	WF to BW, undated, poss. mid-Aug. 1933.
809	13	Courtesy *Harper's.* WF retold the story on nine manuscript pages, but he tightened it by cutting some of the early material in which the Judge and the Swiss moutain guide became aware that they had crossed into the Hereafter. He also provided a frame for the story which helped to give it symmetry.
809	34	WF to BW, undated.
810	17	BC to Ed Grabhorn, 28 June 1933.
812	8	JFSA.
812	32	Meriwether, "Faulkner, Lost and Found," p. 7.
812	36	WF to BW, undated.
812	38	Courtesy American Play Co.
814	14	*ESP.*
815	17	I: EF, 2 Mar. 1965.
815	18	I: Mrs. Arthur Halle, 17 Mar. 1965.
816	7	I: JMF, 21 Mar. 1965.
816	17	Undated. MCL.

Page	*Line*	
817	3	Barbara Izard and Clara Hieronymus, *Requiem for a Nun: Offstage and On* (Nashville, 1970), p. 30.
817	8	I: Louise Meadow, 26 Nov. 1965.
817	12	I: JMF, 27 Nov. 1965.
817	16	I: EF, 3 July 1968.
817	22	*MBB,* p. 167; I: MCF, 31 Mar. 1965.
818	8	*MPS,* 26 and 11 Oct., 1933.
818	9	*MCA,* 11 Oct. 1933. Vernon Omlie's calm notation under *Remarks* in WF's log was simple: "Mishap—Prop."
818	28	Courtesy RH.
818	39	EF to JB, 17 Sept. 1968.
819	36	Courtesy *Harper's.*
820	12	I: BW, 28 Mar. 1965.
820	21	I: MG, 23 Apr. 1965.
820	23	I: JFS, 6 Aug. 1968.
820	31	I: Mrs. Robert Haas, 29 Dec. 1964.
820	35	BC to Ed Grabhorn, 15 Sept. 1933.
821	8	Frank Sullivan to JB, 7 Mar. 1966.
821	17	WF to BC, undated. BC's reply dated 12 Dec. 1933.
821	21	*OXE,* 23 Nov. 1933.
821	24	I: JMF, 15 Nov. 1966.
821	36	I: Malcolm Franklin, 26 Sept. 1966.
822	6	*MBB,* pp. 156–8.
822	19	I: EF, 17 Feb. 1967; JFS, 12 Aug. 1968.
822	28	WF asked MG to send "Black Music," which would be included in the new book of stories, to *Minotaure,* in Paris. "I doubt if they will pay at all, but I had a very nice letter asking for something, and as I like BLACK MUSIC and I dont believe anyone in America will want it, please send it to them."
822	31	To introduce Suratt and provide background material, WF began with the first-person narrator who had, presumably, told such stories as "A Rose for Emily." After a 1,300-word introductory section, he vanished and Suratt took over.
823	6	*CS,* p. 79.
823	10	*OTF,* p. 111.
823	16	Undated, prob. Dec. 1933.
823	24	Scribner Archive, PUL.
824	8	I: MG, 23 Apr. 1965.
824	16	Undated, prob. Dec. 1933. WF closed with a short paragraph: "I will take this opportunity to wish you a Merry Xmas too, and when or if you hear from Ben, tell him to write to me, goddam him."
824	37	At some time WF had made one-page manuscript starts on versions of *Elmer* entitled "Growing Pains" and "Myrtle and Elmer." He also typed four pages entitled "Portrait of Elmer Hodge." A tone poem like that at the end of *SAN* helped bring "A Portrait of Elmer" to a close: "And now the hour, the moment, has come. Within the Garden, beyond the dusk and the slow gateward throng, the hidden bugle begins. Out of the secret dusk the grave brazen notes come, overtaking the people, passing the caped policemen at the gates, and about the city dying beneath the waxing and bloodless moon evening has found itself. Yet still within the formal twilight of the trees the bugle sounds, measured, arrogant, and sad." (FCVA.) According to dealer Philip C. Duschnes, the typescript of "A Portrait of Elmer" MG offered him was done "in the early 1930's." (Duschnes to LRM, 9 June 1960.) It seems likely that WF did little or no revision on the story when it was offered in the middle 1930's. It may well have been in this form before the com-

NOTES

Page	Line	
		position of *SAN*, and a middle-aged spinster teacher in the story shows characteristics which suggest an early study of Joanna Burden. Elmer's flight from his home in a railroad boxcar suggests Joe Christmas' wanderings. Elmer's experiences in a wintry Michigan lumber camp might almost anticipate the situation of Harry Wilbourne and Charlotte Rittenmeyer in the Colorado mining camp in *WP*. I am grateful to Mrs. Emily Iszak for allowing me to read her unpublished study of *Elmer*.
825	15	JFSA.
825	24	For further details, see James B. Meriwether, "Two Unknown Faulkner Short Stories," *RANAM, Recherches Anglaises et Américaines, Revue Annuelle*, IV (Strasbourg, 1971), pp. 23–30.
825	29	JFSA.
826	20	*Ibid.*
826	26	Undated newspaper clipping. JFSA.
826	36	*FOM*, p. 124.
827	3	Undated newspaper clipping. JFSA.
827	27	There were other resemblances between the two stories in the images describing the animals. Four years before WF wrote the story, *OXE* for 2 Jan. 1930 reported that two Negroes, Barney Weeks and Vanna Ford, living between Holly Springs and Waterford, bought a white mule for $5 and tied it to the Illinois Central railroad track. The engineer blew his whistle, but he could see that the mule was tied. He was unable to avoid killing it, and the Negroes were jailed for trial. The reader may remember the question posed in the Old Colonel's time, as to what residents were going to do when the railroad came through, and also the answer: "gwine ter sue it." See also *OTF*, p. 104.
830	9	JFSA.
831	4	I: EF, 3 July 1968.
831	13	Judge John Falkner would be thirty-fifth in the series. *OXE* for 25 Jan. 1934 had described "One of the outstanding social events of the season" when EF—assisted by Mrs. Oldham, Mrs. Holland Wilkins, and Mrs. Murry Faulkner—gave a tea honoring her houseguest, Mrs. Hugh Hairston of Columbus.
831	19	I: E. O. Champion, 22 Mar. 1965.
832	2	Michael Millgate, "Faulkner and the Air: The Background of *Pylon*," *The Michigan Quarterly Review*, III (Fall 1964), pp. 271–7. I am much indebted to this valuable essay. I: Hermann Deutsch, 2 Feb. 1965.
832	31	*MBB*, p. 273. In his logbook for February 14, WF had written "Memphis" in the *From* column and "New Orleans" in the *To* column. He crossed out "New Orleans" and wrote above it "Jackson," entering no explanation under *Remarks*.
834	1	Millgate, "Faulkner and the Air."
834	8	*NYT*, 15 Feb. 1934.
834	12	I: Hermann Deutsch, 2 Feb. 1965.
834	27	*NYT*, 25 June 1934.
835	14	*Ibid.*; I: Hermann Deutsch, 2 Feb. 1965.
835	23	*NYT*, 17 Feb. 1934; Millgate, "Faulkner and the Air," p. 273.
835	26	I: Hermann Deutsch, 2 Feb. 1965.
835	30	*MBB*, pp. 273–4.
836	2	I: Carl Carmer, 23 Aug. 1965.
836	11	As quoted in Millgate,

Page	Line	
		"Faulkner and the Air," p. 273.
836	30	I: Hermann Deutsch, 2 Feb. 1965.
836	35	*Ibid.; MBB,* p. 274.
837	4	Richard Bradford to JB, 9 Aug. 1969.
837	29	*FIU,* p. 36.
839	20	I: EF, 2 Mar. 1965.
839	26	*MBB,* p. 176. In early March, Dashiell phoned a qualified acceptance of "Mule in the Yard" to MG, elaborating in a letter on March 6. Dashiell hoped for the pace of "Spotted Horses" and thought WF could achieve it by cutting some of the "philosphical passages." On March 12, MG was able to send the 6,000-word story back to Dashiell, "cut at least 1000 words and pointed-up." Scribner Archive, PUL.
840	15	*FOM,* p. 124.
840	26	Phillip E. Mullen, Osceola (Ark.) *Times,* 22 Dec. 1966.
841	9	*The Oxford Magazine,* pp. 13–14, repr. in Meriwether, "Early Notices of Faulkner," pp. 149–150.
841	35	WF to MG, undated, prob. mid-Oct. 1934.
841	38	Reading "This Kind of Courage," Dashiell regretted "a style which is so definitely mannered." Scribner Archive, PUL.
842	9	*OXE,* 29 Mar. 1934.
843	13	Though G. T. Buckley writes that he met WF on April 23 after he had flown into Ripley, there is no pilot's log entry for that date. If he was there in addition to his visit of the following weekend, he and his mother and brother may have gone to Memphis and flown down in the cabin Waco with Omlie. If Omlie had done all the piloting, WF of course would not have recorded any time in his log. Buckley, p. 450.
843	16	*OXE,* 26 Apr. 1934.
843	32	I: Judge Taylor McElroy, 23 Mar. 1965.
843	36	Undated newspaper clipping. JFSA.
844	11	*MBB,* pp. 169–70.
844	17	The other stories included "Fox Hunt," "The Hound," "Death Drag," "There Was a Queen," "Smoke," "Turn About," "Beyond," and "Mountain Victory."
844	23	*NYHT Books,* 17 Apr. 1934.
844	27	Boston *Transcript,* 30 June 1934.
844	31	The *Times* reviewer made an acute observation about resemblances in this volume to works of Kipling, suggesting a similarity between "Turn About" and "Sea Constables." WF would later say of his CMB sailors that they were pure Kipling; he just took them off the elephants. I: Mrs. Sewell Haggard, 29 Dec. 1965.
844	34	Courtesy MGM.
844	39	*OXE,* 3 May 1934. Like more than one of his fellow citizens, Mullen displayed an ambivalence toward WF's work. Because of his profession, Mullen revealed it clearly.
845	15	*NHYT Books,* 22 July 1934.
845	18	*OXE,* 6 Sept. 1934.
845	30	Scribner Archive, PUL.
846	7	*UNV,* pp. 7–8.
846	37	I: JMF, 14 Nov. 1966; EF, 17 Feb. 1965.
847	18	"Ambuscade," *The Saturday Evening Post,* 207 (Sept. 29, 1934), pp. 12–13, 80–1.
847	27	Undated, prob. Spring 1934.
848	6	*The Saturday Evening Post,* 207 (Oct. 13, 1934), pp. 16–17, 82, 84–5, 89.
848	14	Undated.
848	26	I: BW, 28 Mar. 1965; Emily Stone, 30 Nov. 1965.
848	38	*The Saturday Evening Post,*

NOTES

Page	Line	
		207 (Nov. 3, 1934), pp. 18–19 ff.
849	23	Undated. When "Ambuscade" appeared in the issue for September 29, it would be followed by an editorial note which read, "This is the first of a series of stories by Mr. Faulkner in which these same two boys will appear." The next two would appear in the magazine on October 13 and November 3, with phrases such as "sons-of-bitches" carefully shortened to "sons" for the family audience, though the editors did allow "bastuds" to stand. P. 81.
849	30	*OXE,* 17 May 1934.
850	1	Stone related what was known locally of Col. Falkner's career (reproducing Gen. Johnston's letter of commendation). He conscientiously used Edmund Winston's article on the Old Colonel and helped propagate legend as well as fact. Meriwether, "Early Notices of Faulkner," pp. 152–3.
850	22	*NYT,* 25 June 1934.
850	25	*OXE,* 5 July 1934.
850	30	JFSA.
850	34	Edmund Grainger to JB, 23 Mar. 1966.
851	5	*OXE,* 5 July 1934.
851	9	Undated clipping. JFSA.
852	3	JFSA. SMW had always called her grandfather "Pappy," as common a term in children's usage as "Papa," and one WF obviously preferred.
852	11	WF to EF, 12 July 1934. JFSA.
853	12	JFSA. WF may have done some of this work on one and a half ms. pages bearing the title *Dark House.* The fragment begins, "A plantation in the South in 1858. Col. Sutpen, his daughter Judith, his son Henry." Without any indication of narrative strategy (or explanation of the fact that Sutpen is a colonel three years before the outbreak of war), the synopsis chronologically develops the action up to the point at which Henry Sutpen, having learned of Charles Bon's mulatto wife and son, has threatened to kill Bon if he persists in his courtship of Judith Sutpen. Then it breaks off in mid-sentence. A similar but untitled sketch of the same length begins, "A plantation in the South in 1860." If WF did write these pages at this time, they may represent an effort to get the complicated sequence of events straight. The fact that WF was in Hollywood suggests still another possibility: these paragraphs read much like a synopsis or outline for a scenario. And if WF did not now think of the film prospects for Sutpen's story, he would later. JFSA.
853	21	*MCA,* 25 July 1934.
854	4	Morty was to use his own judgment, but if they insisted on a deadline for the other stories, he was not to accept it. "If they will leave the matter open for a few months longer, I will let you know as soon as I can whether or not I can write the other three, and when." He closed with a social note: "I saw Ben. He looks fine and seems to be happy as a cockroach." WF to MG, 29 July 1934.
854	21	WF to HS, dated "Thursday," poss. 2 Aug. 1934.
854	28	WF to MG, undated.
854	33	Whit Burnett to MG, 17 July 1934. Courtesy PUL.
854	34	Edward J. O'Brien, ed., *The Best Short Stories of 1935 and the Yearbook of the American Short Story* (Boston, 1935).

Page	*Line*	
		Though "Lo!" appeared in *Story* for November, 1934, it was for some reason placed by O'Brien among the next year's prize stories.
855	9	WF to MG, undated.
855	38	Arthur Guyton, M.D., to JB, 5 Oct. 1967.
856	26	I: E. O. Champion, 23 Mar. 1965.
857	24	Arthur Guyton, M.D., to JB, 5 Oct. 1967.
857	30	*OXE* 13 Sept. 1934.
857	33	*OXE,* 27 Sept. 1934.
858	6	E. O. Champion, 22 Mar. 1965.
858	17	*MBB,* p. 168.
859	5	"The Unvanquished" would appear in the *Post* on November 14, 1936 (Vol. 209, pp. 12–13, 121–2 ff.). Repr., with revisions, as "Riposte in Tertio" in *UNV,* where the above quotation appears on pp. 167–8.
859	10	Cullen said his father told him similar stories. See *OTF,* pp. 66–7.
859	22	"Vendée" did not appear in the *Post* until December 5, 1936 (Vol. 209, pp. 16–17, 86–7 ff.); *UNV,* p. 211.
859	30	"As a rule," wrote Graeme Lorimer, recalling his father's editorial policies as well as his own, "we bought Faulkner stories if we could understand them—and sometimes even if we couldn't. It was *Post* policy to buy or reject, but only in exceptional circumstances did we make suggestions for revision to an established author." This was one of those exceptional circumstances. Lorimer to JB, 14 Mar. 1966.
859	32	I: MG, 23 Apr. 1965.
859	37	Arthur Guyton, M.D., to JB, 5 Oct. 1967.
860	21	Under the title "Skirmish at Sartoris," the story was published in *Scribner's,* XCVII (Apr. 1935), pp. 193–200; *UNV,* p. 242.
861	4	WF to MG, prob. 18 Oct. 1934.
861	7	*FIU,* p. 36.
863	28	"Faulkner Writes Air Saga as Mac Grider's Naval Son Solos After Week at Stick," *MCA,* 13 Sept. 1934. Grider graduated from Annapolis in 1936 and served in submarines in World War II. *MCA,* 30 June 1939.
863	34	*OXE,* 4 Oct. 1934.
864	19	I: Louise Meadow, 26 Nov. 1965, 16 Nov. 1966.
864	28	I: Louise Meadow, 27 Nov. 1965.
864	33	JFSA.
864	34	Mrs. Paul Pope, Jr., to JB, 28 June 1967.
865	9	*MCA,* 18 Sept. 1934; I: EF, 30 June 1965.
865	12	A final page of the surviving typescript, much like the last page of *PYL,* indicates that "This Kind of Courage" was a thirty-page short story. In length and subject matter it would have resembled "Death Drag" and "Honor." JFSA.
865	16	In an undated letter, to which HS replied on December 28, 1934, WF listed all the chapter titles. Someone in HS's office added the dates when each arrived.
866	5	JFSA. For another, probably earlier version of p. 1, titled "Thursday," see Meriwether, *The Literary Career,* Fig. 13.
866	20	Millgate, "Faulkner and the Air," p. 272.
866	24	There were other echoes of earlier work in the novel's first chapter. Col. H. I. Feinman, chairman of the Sewage Board and builder of the airport, is a wealthy Jew. The ubiquitous Mardi gras colors are purple and gold. Cf. "Wealthy Jew" in "New Orleans," *NOS,* p. 3.

NOTES

Page *Line*

868 4 See Millgate, *The Achievement,* pp. 138–49; Olga Vickery, *The Novels of William Faulkner: A Critical Interpretation* (Baton Rouge, 1964), pp. 145–55; and Donald T. Torchiana, "Faulkner's *Pylon* and the Structure of Modernity," *Modern Fiction Studies,* I (Summer 1952), pp. 20–3.

868 24 Meriwether, "Early Notices of Faulkner," pp. 162–3.

869 28 The wings identified members of The Quiet Birdmen, an organization of pilots formed after World War I. Although there was apparently some concern originally with charitable works, the organization seems by this time to have become purely a social one.

870 16 For a time Bradford was Sunday editor of *NOTP.* George Healy remembers him as "an outdoor type [who] enjoyed golf and sailing, was partially bald and very gentle." He also wore horn-rimmed glasses occasionally. Healy adds, "I suspect that Will Hagood is a composite rather than a single person." George Healy, Jr., to JB, 27 Sept. 1968.

870 28 JFSA.

872 2 This chapter gave an opportunity to show some of the lore he had absorbed in the hangar at the Memphis airport. Shumann's engine had run hot during the race he had won. He proposed to remove the engine head and apply a micrometer to the valves and valve stems to see which had expanded and stuck in the engine's normal firing cycle. After grinding the parts, they would apply the micrometer again to determine the proper measurement, replace the parts, replace the head, and clean and replace the engine's supercharger. When this was not done, the engine heated up again, lost power, and forced Shumann to come in for a power-off, dead-stick crash-landing.

872 13 In an echo, perhaps, of E. E. Cummings' poem "I sing of Olaf, glad and big," Jiggs had cried, "there is some crap I will not eat. . . ." P. 110.

872 36 The echoes of Eliot persisted in the reporter's description of a story for the Sunday feature section: "It's about how the loves of Antony and Cleopatra had been prophesied all the time in Egyptian architecture only they never knew what it meant . . . ." (P. 204.) WF had by now repeated the "Nilebarge clatterfalque" image, bringing to mind not only Eliot's use of Cleopatra's barge in "The Waste Land," but her death as well. As Eliot had counterpoised these great lovers of antiquity with modern ones, so WF may have been doing the same thing, though his lovers were more dramatic than Eliot's stenographer and her carbuncular clerk. Millgate notes the similarity between Feinman and the callous financiers of Dos Passos' play *Airways, Inc.* (See Millgate, *The Achievement,* p. 145.)

873 21 Some witnesses of the deaths of jumper Ben Grew and pilot Charles Kenily thought that Kenily may have tried to free Grew's shrouds from the plane, a gesture consonant with the one WF gives to Shumann. (See Millgate, "Faulkner and the Air," p. 273.) It has been suggested

Page	Line	
		that the sadistic police officer resembles Percy Grimm. A later analogue is Butch Lovemaiden in *REV.*
873	31	WF sketched the breakup of the group as Jiggs prepared to leave—beaten, hungover, grotesque, and (in a curious echo, perhaps, of *TMF*) "the comedy cartoon centaur," but human enough to sell his prized boots for farewell gifts. Often WF referred to Hollywood for comparisons, as when the reporter had mentioned Laverne's "Harlow-colored hair." (P. 44.) Now, in possibly a more direct recollection, the reporter received a post card from his honeymooning mother at the Hotel Vista del Mar, Santa Monica, California. (P. 270.)
874	16	In novels such as *LIA,* the flashbacks had been much longer. The shortness of these flashbacks may have been due not only to the proportions demanded by the space occupied by present-time events but also because WF's imagination and interest were not so powerfully engaged in this work.
875	3	Dr. Shumann accepts the child—not wholly sure he is Roger's—with the understanding that Laverne (pregnant now with Holmes's child) will make no attempt to see him during the lives of himself and his wife. A furious "shabby wildhaired old man," Dr. Shumann is as convinced of Laverne's bitchery and abomination as ever Doc Hines was of that of Milly and the dietitian. (P. 312.) Mrs. Shumann will try to give the child the love her husband cannot give, as Mrs. Hines tried to do. But the cycle is starting again. Six-year-old Jack Shumann will be as much a victim as six-year-old Joe Christmas was.
875	18	*FIU,* p. 36. As Hermann Deutsch had written a colorful and romantic account of the dropping of Nelson's ashes, so the reporter had described the dropping of the wreath by a fellow competitor of Shumann's. The description of his aircraft might almost have fitted the Command-Aire, underpowered with the OX5 engine, which E. O. Champion and WF regularly flew.
875	28	In the first letter, he asked the help of MG and BW in locating the books Gloria Stuart had lent him. "Damn it," he added, "she should not have trusted me with a book you can't buy in the drug store."
876	7	WF had opened the undated letter with thanks to HS for a flask which had arrived. "I couldn't find one in Memphis that would hold enough to make it worth carrying with me," he explained, "or with a cup large enough to drink from."
876	19	*The Colophon,* 19 (Dec. 1934), pp. 1–12.
876	27	*OXE,* 13 Dec. 1934.
877	3	I: E. O. Champion, 22 Mar. 1965.
877	7	ACLT.
877	11	Unidentified newspaper clipping. JFSA.
877	27	WF's last correction gave the final newspaper headline the same type size as the others; typescript setting copy. FCVA. Gal. proofs 14, 53, 54. ACLT.
878	16	Reminiscent of Fitzgerald's Jay Gatsby, Ewing at the age of fourteen has fled, "on the brakebeam of a westbound freight, the little lost Ne-

NOTES

Page	*Line*	
		braska town" of his birth. The "old strong harsh Campbellite blood" has been corrupted in him, and now "it was his trembling and jerking hands that he watched as he shook the two [aspirin] tablets onto the glass shelf and set the tumbler into the rack and unstoppered the gin bottle and braced his knuckles against the wall in order to pour into the tumbler." *CS,* p. 702.
878	38	Grabhorn Press, still in straitened circumstances, had never supplied the promised dummy of the novel. On February 4, 1935, DSK wrote Jane Grabhorn asking for the return of WF's marked-up copy of the novel.
879	3	W. C. Bryant to WF, 12 Feb. 1935. Bryant was not only generous and considerate, he was a fan of WF's. He wrote, " 'Raid' kept my thoughts on Robert Peel, Manager of Polk Plantation, whose farm hands in 1866 took up a march of religious fervor to 'Cross the Jordan & Go over into Canaan.' They got as far as Yocona River & some crossed, tho Peel retrieved most of them." JFSA.
879	24	WF to Hunter Kimball, 2 Feb. 1935. JFSA.
881	13	*MBB,* pp. 205–6, 171–2.
881	15	WF to MG, 18 Feb. 1935.
882	2	WF to MG, 9 Mar. 1935.
882	28	*CS,* p. 286.
882	34	*OXE,* 13 Sept. 1934.
883	5	*OTF,* pp. 111–13.
883	19	*CS,* pp. 225, 228.
883	26	*Ibid.*, p. 241. This motif was, of course, not new. Twain had used a young white boy and a Negro in flight from the law in *Huckleberry Finn.* Secretary, the chauffeur, wore a cap and goggles when he flew, just as WF's fellow airman George MacEwen, "the Black Eagle," did. And if Secretary owed something to George, so did old Job to Uncle Ned—a terrible sneak, JFS would later remember, who would tell on her with an unbearably sanctimonious air.
883	33	WF's anti-NRA feelings emerged again when Uncle Willy learned he could not take flying lessons without a doctor's permit: "damn if these Republicans and Democrats and XYZ's ain't going to have it soon where a man can't even flush the toilet in his own bathroom." P. 241.
883	38	*Scribner's,* XCIX (Jan. 1936), p. 7. *CS,* pp. 648–9.
884	8	*WFL,* p. 68.
884	30	FCVA. "Fool About a Horse," *Scribner's,* C (Aug. 1936), p. 82.
884	37	*S&F,* pp. 408–12.
885	15	"Lion," *Harper's,* 172 (Dec. 1935), pp. 68–9.
885	19	*OTF,* pp. 27–37.
885	20	*FIU,* p. 59.
885	34	JFSA.
887	16	According to Hiram Haydn, WF received a $2,000 advance on *Absalom, Absalom!* from HS on February 5. Robert Hilton Knox, III, *William Faulkner's Absalom, Absalom!,* unpubl. Harvard Ph.D. dissertation (Apr. 1959), p. 5.
887	34	I: E. O. Champion, 23 Mar. 1965.
888	14	*The New Republic,* 82 (Apr. 10, 1935), p. 254.
888	18	*The Spectator,* 154 (Apr. 19, 1935), p. 688. On March 21, Harold Strauss had written in *NYT* that the novel had "the explosive power and time-stopping intensity of the old Faulkner. . . ." On the same day Mark Van Doren had strong misgivings in *NYHT*

Page *Line*

as to "whether Mr. Faulkner can afford to keep on publishing such novels . . . he has never written a better one than this; but there is danger in that very fact, for he is so able at his job of outraging our emotions that we may end by having none for him." This would be tragic, for "he has one of the greatest natural gifts to be found anywhere in America at the moment." Nine days later in the New York *Post,* Herschel Brickell called *PYL* "one of Mr. Faulkner's best executed pieces."

888 22 *OXE,* 28 Mar. 1935.

889 1 *OXE,* 4 Apr. 1935.

889 3 Nashville *Banner,* 24 Mar. 1935. Ransom later paired Stark Young and WF—charm on the one hand and power on the other. Even though Ransom's heart seemed to be with Young, he conceded that WF was "the most exciting figure in our contemporary literature just now; he is original, and he has not been classified. It is my impression that his critics as yet have hardly got beyond the exclamatory stage. It is still being discovered that he is a powerful new genius, with a bias toward horror and the morbid." (*The Virginia Quarterly Review,* XI [Apr. 1935], p. 197.) Walking with Robert Penn Warren on the Louisiana State University campus, Ransom talked about the book and its author: "William Faulkner is Greek," he said. (I: Robert Penn Warren, 19 Jan. 1966.) Ralph McGill seemed closer to the Southern consensus when he wrote in the Atlanta *Constitution* that though the novel constituted a great story, he was getting tired of WF's unfamiliar and unimportant subjects. (7 Apr. 1935.)

889 6 *Current History,* 42 (May 1935), p. xvi.

889 8 Ernest Hemingway, "On Being Shot Again: A Gulf Stream Letter," repr. in William Whyte, ed., *By-Line: Ernest Hemingway* (New York, 1967), p. 200.

889 11 Unpubl. portion of class conference, U. of Va., 6 May 1957.

889 20 ACLT.

889 26 JFSA. At the very bottom of one of these sheets, however, as if it were an afterthought or a reminder, WF wrote the line that would finally open the story for him: "Through the long still hot weary dead afternon, that dead summer they sat in what she called the office. . . ." One of the openings set in Cambridge WF would eventually use for the beginning of Ch. VI.

889 31 *FIU,* p. 76. This suggests, of course, that earlier dated manuscripts of novels may have been preceded by works as extensive and as prior to the final manuscript as these fragments were to this final manuscript of the long delayed *ABS.*

889 38 *MBB,* p. 48.

890 2 I: Emily Stone, 27 Mar. 1965.

890 5 Elizabeth Kerr, *Yoknapatawpha: Faulkner's "Little Postage Stamp of Native Soil"* (New York, 1969), pp. 55, 246–7.

890 14 Knox, pp. 33, 37

890 19 *OXE,* 17 Sept. 1891.

890 23 I: EF, 28 Sept. 1962.

890 27 *FIU,* p. 76.

890 30 Linton R. Massey, ed., *"Man Working," 1919–1962: William Faulkner: A Catalogue of the William Faulkner Col-*

NOTES

Page	Line	
		lections at the University of Virginia (Charlottesville, 1968), p. vii.
891	7	JFSA.
892	12	ACLT. See Gerald Langford, *Falkner's Revision of Absalom, Absalom!: A Collation of the Manuscript and the Published Book* (Austin, Tex., 1971).
894	3	He flew in the cabin Waco on April 2, 3, and 4, taking the open-cockpit Waco aloft as well on the first two days.
894	5	*MPS,* 11 Nov. 1935.
894	7	Arthur Guyton, M.D., to JB, 5 Oct. 1967.
894	25	*ABS,* p. 31.
895	9	*FIU,* p. 35.
895	17	Near the end of *MOS,* WF had interpolated a short history of Mrs. Maurier's husband, a parvenu like Sutpen who had sought respectability with a proper marriage. They had issued from the church to face a speculative and faintly derisive crowd, "her beautiful secret face beside that cold, violent man . . . ." P. 326.
895	21	*OXE,* 28 Mar., 4 and 18 Apr., 1935.
895	26	I: Malcolm Franklin, 26 Sept. 1966.
896	3	*OXE,* 25 Apr. 1935.
896	10	*Ibid.*
896	14	He flew for two hours on Sunday and then four hours and twelve minutes more on the next day before cutting the switches back at the airport in Memphis.
896	16	He took that plane on twenty flights during May.
896	19	I: Louise Meadow, 26 Nov. 1965.
896	27	FCVA.
896	28	See Langford, *Faulkner's Revision of Absalom, Absalom!,* p. 22.
896	35	The new minor characters included the aunt who raised Rosa Coldfield after her mother's death and subsequently departed one night by a back window (like Lena Grove and Laverne Shumann) to marry a mule trader (as Zilphia Gant's mother had done), the mule trader subsequently running afoul of Union troops as Granny Millard (though not Ab Snopes) had done.
898	2	FCVA. WF continued to strive tenaciously for the effects he wanted. It took him four drafts to describe as he wished Rosa Coldfield's about-face when she decided to accept Sutpen's marriage proposal. See p. 67.
898	9	Clayton Knight to JB, 8 Feb. and 25 Mar., 1966.
898	13	JFSA.
898	16	I: Malcolm Franklin, 26 Sept. 1966; Leland Hayward, 21 Jan. 1966. Murry Falkner to JB, 23 July 1966. One qualification was that a prospective member have 200 flying hours and be a man one would like to spend the evening with.
898	20	On July 18 WF had written to MG asking him to obtain a pipe for him at Dunhill's. If his $10 credit there would not cover it, MG was to pay the difference out of his check from *College Humor* if it had come in. (WF presumably meant the check for "Christmas Tree.") Arents Collections, NYPL.
899	7	Dashiell scheduled "The Brooch" for publication in January, 1936, and "Fool About a Horse" for the following August.
899	9	W. C. Bryant to WF, 3 July 1935. JFSA.
899	28	Meriwether, "Two Unknown Faulkner Short Stories," pp. 20–3.

Page	Line	
899	35	*OXE,* 8 Aug. 1935.
899	37	They would navigate by the section lines which appear every two miles in Mississippi, composed often of fences or a growth of trees. On cross-country flights they would stay at an angle of ten degrees to the lines. I: E. O. Champion, 23 Mar. 1965.
900	4	It was a humorous glance at Miss Rosa as eccentric and frugal spinster, the same kind of impulse which had provided, near the end of the previous chapter, Mr. Compson's 200-word comic vignette describing "what a Southern lady is. . . ." P. 86.
900	32	See Langford, *Faulkner's Revision of Absalom, Absalom!,* p. 23.
901	2	On Sunday, September 15, WF and Champ went up in the Command-Aire again, as they did the following Sunday. On Monday, the twenty-third, WF flew the cabin Waco to Memphis, Dean probably accompanying him after having brought the plane down for his use.
901	7	WF to EF, 27 Sept. 1935. JFSA.
901	20	BC to WF, 7 Nov. 1935.
901	25	WF to EF, 27 Sept. 1935. JFSA.
901	34	I: Mrs. Sewell Haggard, 17 Apr. 1965.
902	6	RH.
902	18	JFSA.
902	23	WF to MG, 4 Dec. 1935.
902	33	WF to EF, 5 Oct. 1935. JFSA.
902	36	WF to RKH, dated "Sunday," prob. 12 Sept. 1948.
903	10	He inscribed the day's date—October 15—in Horatio Colony's *Free Forester: A Novel of Pioneer Kentucky.* HS had given him one of Smith & Haas's new titles, Fletcher Pratt's *Ordeal by Fire: An Informal History of the Civil War.* Lenore Marshall had inscribed a copy of her book of poems, *Only the Fear. WFL, passim.*
903	17	*OXE,* 19 Oct. 1935; I: Emily Stone, 17 Mar. 1965.
903	27	I: Robert Coughlan, 29 Dec. 1966.
903	32	I: Emily Stone, 30 Nov. 1965.
903	35	Scribner Archive, PUL.
904	11	BC to WF, 7 Nov. 1935.
904	19	ACLT.
905	6	She described herself in pentameter: "warped chrysalis of what blind perfect seed: for who shall say what gnarled forgotten root might not bloom yet with some globed concentrate . . . ?" P. 144.
905	23	In this chapter, WF did four versions of Clytie's blocking Rosa from going up the stairs to Judith on the day of Bon's death. Five other passages were canceled and rewritten. See Langford, *Faulkner's Revision of Absalom, Absalom!,* pp. 29–32.
905	25	During the latter part of October, he managed only one and a half hours of flying, on Sunday, October 20.
905	27	*OXE,* 31 Oct. 1935.
905	32	I: Louise Meadow, 26 Nov. 1965.
905	36	Olivia Browne, "The Flying Faulkners," *MCA,* 8 Nov. 1950.
905	38	Courtesy Mrs. Jon Mallard.
906	5	*OXE,* 31 Oct. 1935.
906	8	*OXE,* 7 Nov. 1935.
906	16	I: Louise Meadow, 27 Nov. 1965.
906	21	*OXE,* 14 Nov. 1935.
907	9	*FIU,* p. 75.
907	20	The buggy ride "That evening . . . in the moonless September dust . . . heavy with sixty days of dust" (p. 175) suggested the atmosphere of "Dry September."
908	12	There were other echoes: Sut-

Page	Line	
		pen's coffin, like Red's in *SAN*, had rolled and fallen from its place. The spinster Judith, imperiously commanding Judge Benbow and others, was much like Miss Emily Grierson. One passage looked ahead to *GDM*: Judge Benbow speculated with shock and incredulity upon the possible parentage of Charles Etienne Saint-Valery Bon: "the child might be Clytie's, got by its father on the body of his own daughter." P. 201.
908	25	When WF revised, he shifted from Shreve's narrative to Quentin's point of view. He also broke up a number of long sentences, especially in Mr. Compson's narrative at the chapter's end. See Langford, *Faulkner's Revision of Absalom, Absalom!*, pp. 34–5.
909	8	*The American Mercury*, XXXVI (Nov. 1935), pp. 370–2; repr. in *ESP*, pp. 189, 190, 192.
909	12	As noted earlier, his progress with the manuscript—except for October 15 and the starting and finishing dates—can only be inferred.
909	15	*OXE*, 14 Nov. 1935.
909	28	I: Louise Meadow, 19 Mar. 1965.